THE BUILDINGS OF ENGLAND

FOUNDING EDITOR: NIKOLAUS PEVSNER

LONDON I:
THE CITY OF LONDON

SIMON BRADLEY AND NIKOLAUS PEVSNER

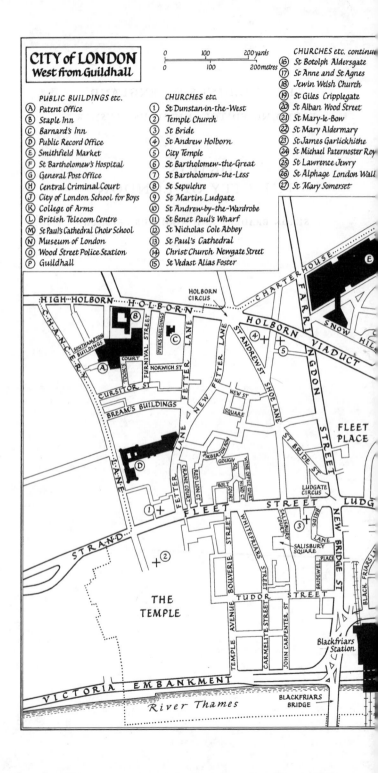

CITY of LONDON
West from Guildhall

0   100   200 yards
0   100   200 metres

PUBLIC BUILDINGS etc.
- Ⓐ Patent Office
- Ⓑ Staple Inn
- Ⓒ Barnard's Inn
- Ⓓ Public Record Office
- Ⓔ Smithfield Market
- Ⓕ St Bartholomew's Hospital
- Ⓖ General Post Office
- Ⓗ Central Criminal Court
- Ⓙ City of London School for Boys
- Ⓚ College of Arms
- Ⓛ British Telecom Centre
- Ⓜ St Paul's Cathedral Choir School
- Ⓝ Museum of London
- Ⓞ Wood Street Police Station
- Ⓟ Guildhall

CHURCHES etc.
- ① St Dunstan-in-the-West
- ② Temple Church
- ③ St Bride
- ④ St Andrew Holborn
- ⑤ City Temple
- ⑥ St Bartholomew-the-Great
- ⑦ St Bartholomew-the-Less
- ⑧ St Sepulchre
- ⑨ St Martin Ludgate
- ⑩ St Andrew-by-the-Wardrobe
- ⑪ St Benet Paul's Wharf
- ⑫ St Nicholas Cole Abbey
- ⑬ St Paul's Cathedral
- ⑭ Christ Church Newgate Street
- ⑮ St Vedast Alias Foster

CHURCHES etc. continued
- ⑯ St Botolph Aldersgate
- ⑰ St Anne and St Agnes
- ⑱ Jewin Welsh Church
- ⑲ St Giles Cripplegate
- ⑳ St Alban Wood Street
- ㉑ St Mary-le-Bow
- ㉒ St Mary Aldermary
- ㉓ St James Garlickhithe
- ㉔ St Michael Paternoster Roy
- ㉕ St Lawrence Jewry
- ㉖ St Alphage London Wall
- ㉗ St Mary Somerset

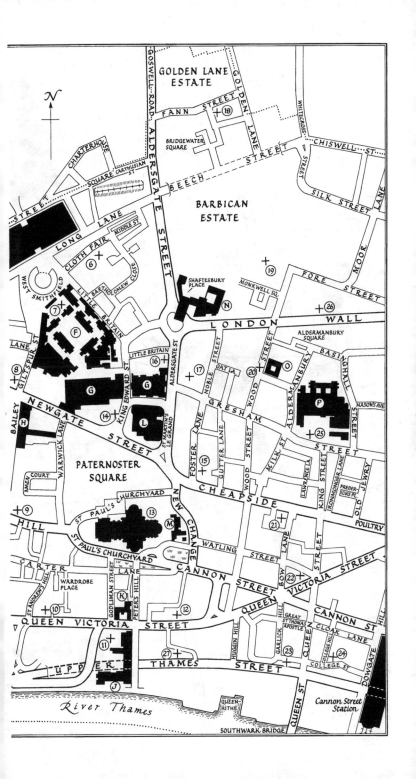

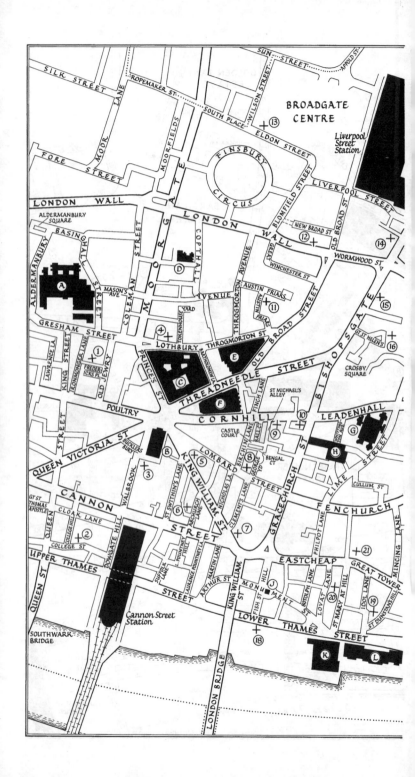

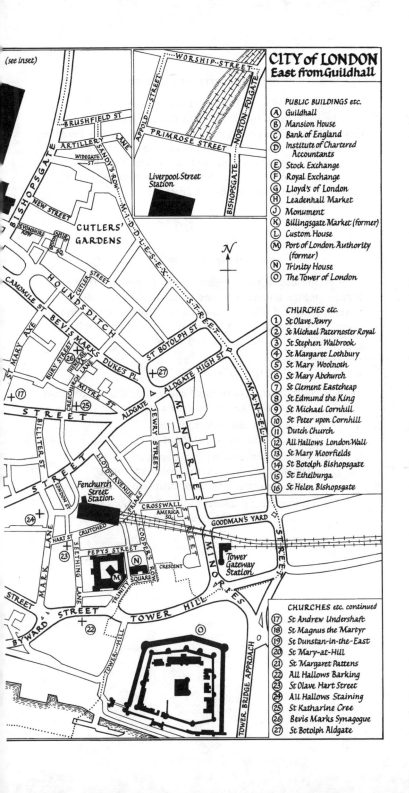

(see inset)

CITY of LONDON
East from Guildhall

PUBLIC BUILDINGS etc.
- Ⓐ Guildhall
- Ⓑ Mansion House
- Ⓒ Bank of England
- Ⓓ Institute of Chartered Accountants
- Ⓔ Stock Exchange
- Ⓕ Royal Exchange
- Ⓖ Lloyd's of London
- Ⓗ Leadenhall Market
- Ⓙ Monument
- Ⓚ Billingsgate Market (former)
- Ⓛ Custom House
- Ⓜ Port of London Authority (former)
- Ⓝ Trinity House
- Ⓞ The Tower of London

CHURCHES etc.
1. St Olave Jewry
2. St Michael Paternoster Royal
3. St Stephen Walbrook
4. St Margaret Lothbury
5. St Mary Woolnoth
6. St Mary Abchurch
7. St Clement Eastcheap
8. St Edmund the King
9. St Michael Cornhill
10. St Peter upon Cornhill
11. Dutch Church
12. All Hallows London Wall
13. St Mary Moorfields
14. St Botolph Bishopsgate
15. St Ethelburga
16. St Helen Bishopsgate

CHURCHES etc. continued
17. St Andrew Undershaft
18. St Magnus the Martyr
19. St Dunstan-in-the-East
20. St Mary-at-Hill
21. St Margaret Pattens
22. All Hallows Barking
23. St Olave Hart Street
24. All Hallows Staining
25. St Katharine Cree
26. Bevis Marks Synagogue
27. St Botolph Aldgate

PEVSNER ARCHITECTURAL GUIDES

The Buildings of England series was created and
largely written by Sir Nikolaus Pevsner (1901–1983).
First editions of the county volumes were published by Penguin
Books between 1951 and 1974. The continuing
programme of revisions and new volumes has been
supported by research financed through
the Buildings Books Trust since 1994

THE BUILDINGS BOOKS TRUST

was established in 1994, registered charity number 1042101.
It promotes the appreciation and understanding of architecture
by supporting and financing the research needed to sustain new
and revised volumes of The Buildings of England, Ireland,
Scotland and Wales.

The Trust gratefully acknowledges:

grants to cover the costs of research and writing this volume from
THE CORPORATION OF LONDON

a research grant from
THE BRITISH ACADEMY

assistance with photographs from
THE ROYAL COMMISSION ON HISTORICAL
MOUNUMENTS OF ENGLAND

a grant to cover the costs of text illustrations from
KINNEY AND GREEN

London

I

THE CITY OF LONDON

BY

SIMON BRADLEY

AND

NIKOLAUS PEVSNER

THE BUILDINGS OF ENGLAND

YALE UNIVERSITY PRESS
NEW HAVEN AND LONDON

YALE UNIVERSITY PRESS
NEW HAVEN AND LONDON
302 Temple Street, New Haven CT 06511
23 Pond Street, London NW3 2PN
www.yale.edu/yup
www.yaleup.co.uk
www.pevsner.co.uk
for
THE BUILDINGS BOOKS TRUST

Published by Penguin Books 1997
Reprinted with corrections 1998, and with further corrections 1999
First published by Yale University Press 2002
2 4 6 8 10 9 7 5 3 1

ISBN 0 300 09624 0

Printed in China
through World Print
Set in Monotype Plantin

The Corporation of London and the City of London have grown up together. Together they represent both the City's history and its future.

As the local government for the City, the Corporation is older than Parliament and its modern role as an effective, world-class local authority is built upon centuries of experience. But today the Corporation is also a prime promoter of the City as the world's leading international financial and business centre, and it must be skilled in identifying – and meeting – the requirements for twenty-first-century success.

An essential part of this is the provision of a leading-edge business and residential environment of the highest quality. The Corporation is concerned to raise awareness of the City's unique heritage and potential and is itself aware of its own significant responsibility as a planning authority. Sponsorship of this new title – a timely, highly expert and detailed commentary on the City's unmatched architectural heritage – is part of this strategy. No other financial centre in the world can compare with the City of London where ancient street patterns host the dynamic glass and steel structures which mark the end of the twentieth century. We hope this volume will excite and enlighten those who delve into it.

Judith Mayhew
Chairman
Corporation of London Policy and Resources Committee

CONTENTS

LIST OF TEXT FIGURES AND MAPS

PHOTOGRAPHIC ACKNOWLEDGEMENTS

We are grateful to the following for permission to reproduce photographs:

Bank of England, by permission of the Governor and Company: 82
Conway Library, Courtauld Institute of Art, London: 21 (© F. H. Crossley, M. H. Ridgway), 29, 30, 34, 86, 87, 88, 89, 107, 119
Corporation of London: 19
Crown Copyright. Historic Royal Palaces: 10, 15, 24
English Heritage Photo Library: 138, 139, 141
Peter Jenkins, Inskip and Jenkins: 154
A. F. Kersting: 3, 9, 28, 33, 52, 78, 79, 116
Lloyds TSB Group Archives: 126
London Metropolitan Archives: 110
Museum of London: 7, 8
Museum of London Archaeology Service: 6
Mercers' Company: 23
National Westminster Group Archives: 99, 122
Ove Arup and Partners (Photo Harry Sowden): 144
Perfecta Publications: 39
RCHME Crown copyright: 1, 2, 4, 11, 12, 13, 14, 16, 17, 18, 20, 22, 25, 26, 27, 31, 32, 35, 36, 37, 40, 41, 42, 43, 44, 45, 46, 47, 48, 49, 50, 51, 53, 54, 55, 56, 57, 58, 59, 60, 61, 62, 63, 64, 65, 66, 67, 68, 69, 70, 71, 72, 73, 74, 75, 76, 77, 80, 81, 83, 84, 85, 90, 91, 92, 94, 95, 96, 97, 98, 100, 101, 102, 103, 104, 105, 106, 108, 109, 111, 112, 113, 114, 115, 117, 118, 120, 121, 123, 124, 125, 127, 128, 129, 130, 131, 132, 133, 134, 135, 136, 137, 140, 142, 143, 145, 146, 147, 148, 149, 150, 151, 152, 153, 156, 157
Skidmore Owings and Merrill (Photo James H. Morris/Axiom): 155
Warburg Institute: 38

The photographs are indexed in the indexes of artists, and streets and buildings and references to them are given by numbers in the margin of the text.

ABBREVIATIONS AND
LIST OF CITY ARCHITECTS

Area Authorities
MBW Metropolitan Board of Works (1855–88)
LCC   London County Council (1888–1965)
GLC   Greater London Council (1965–86)

Other Abbreviations
RCHME Royal Commission on Historical Monuments of
      England
RIBA   Royal Institute of British Architects

CITY SURVEYORS AND ARCHITECTS

After Betty M. Masters, 'The City Surveyor, the City Engineer, and
the City Architect and Planning Officer', *Guildhall Miscellany*, April
1973

Clerk of the City's Works, later Architect and Surveyor, 1478–1891

1478–9	Edward Stone	1676–91	Thomas Aylward
1479–?	John Coke	1691–2	John Noyes
?–1518	Roger Wright	1692–3	James Fell
1563?–79	Thomas Wheler	1693–1711	John Olley
1579–81	William Rawlyns	1711–24	Isaac Olley
1581–6	Hugh Mantle	1724–34	George Smith
1586–93	Richard Pegrym	1734–68	George Dance the
1593–9	Thomas Bowes		Elder
1599–1609	William Fowler	1768–1816	George Dance the
1609–25?	Simon Marshall		Younger
1625?–46	William Dun(ne)	1816–43	William
1646–58,	John Cock(e)		Mountague
1661		1843–63	James Bunstone
1661–2	James Hayton		Bunning
1662–76	Nicholas	1864–87	Horace Jones
	Duncombe	1887–91	Alexander Peebles

City Surveyor from 1891

1891–1905	Andrew Murray	1975–84	R. W. P. Luff
1905–31	Sydney Perks	1984–5	J. E. Maithieson
1931–44	F. C. J. Reed		(acting)
1945–54	George Halliday	1985–	E. T. Harthill
1955–74	R. S. Walker		

Surveyor, later Engineer and Surveyor, to the Commissioners of Sewers, later City Engineer

1746–68	George Dance the Elder	1905–14	Frank Sumner
		1914–37	E. E. Finch
1766–90	George Wyatt	1938–64	F. J. Forty
1790–1814	Nathaniel Wright	1964–74	Harold King
1815–32	Samuel Acton	1974–81	G. W. Pickin
1832–46	Richard Kelsey	1981–9	L. W. E. Groome
1846–94	William Haywood	1989–95	C. Snowden
1894–1905	D. J. Ross	1995–	R. F. V. Aylott

Planning Officer, later City Architect and Planning Officer

1947–61	H. A. Mealand	1979–86	Stuart Murphy
1961–79	E. G. Chandler	1987–	Peter Rees

FOREWORD

The City of London was first surveyed by the Buildings of England *in Sir Nikolaus Pevsner's* London 1: the Cities of London and Westminster *(1957). A revised edition was published in 1962, and a further revision (by Bridget Cherry) in 1973. The present volume is the third instalment of the overhaul and expansion of the London volumes, following* London 2: South *(1983) and* London 3: North West *(1991). Separate volumes on* London 4: North *and* London 5: East and Docklands *are in preparation. A further volume will be devoted to the parts of Westminster covered by the old* London 1. *The division of* London 1 *into two volumes necessarily means that neither new volume can by itself give the whole story of the architectural development of London; but the special character and unique architectural inheritance of the City are properly addressed here for the first time.*

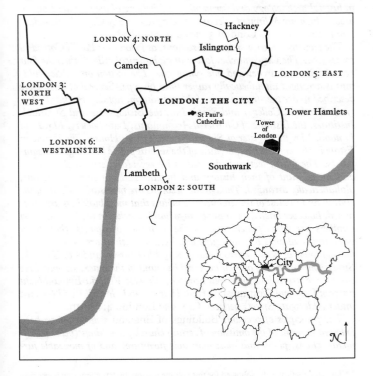

The City within Greater London

The first edition described a City in which the process of reconstruction after the Blitz had barely begun. None of the bombed City churches had been restored, and recent buildings were still very few. Many street entries recorded only scattered archaeological discoveries. About an eighth of the text consisted of descriptions of plate, notably that of the City's Livery Companies. Later editions found many more new buildings to survey, but left the format unaltered. The present edition reflects the revaluation since the 1950s of the City's Victorian and pre-war buildings, many more of which are described and assessed. It also takes account of the vast amount of new architecture of the 1980s and 90s, and of the revolution in archaeological understanding of medieval and (especially) Roman London that the building boom facilitated. Space has also been found for fuller historical accounts of the streets and of important buildings which no longer exist. In most cases these are described in introductory paragraphs to the gazetteer entries. The area covered is that defined by boundary revisions in 1994, which tidied up the ancient, straggling outline between the City and its neighbouring boroughs to suit present-day topography. The exception is that the Tower of London and its immediate precinct, administratively part of the Borough of Tower Hamlets, are included with the City.

The general introduction gives an account of the growth and development of the City, from prehistoric times to the present. The chapters are organized chronologically, with subdivisions mostly according to building type. The post-war period has been split into two chapters, in recognition of the quantity and importance of the more recent buildings. For the geology, industrial archaeology and vernacular architecture of the Greater London area, which are of limited relevance to the present-day City, the introduction to London 2 or London 3 should be consulted.

The gazetteer is arranged in five sections, as follows. St Paul's Cathedral comes first. The City churches follow in alphabetical order*, then the four non-Anglican churches and one synagogue. The section on public buildings is arranged alphabetically rather than by type. Several of them were described under the street entries of the old edition, notably Barnard's Inn (now Gresham College) and Staple Inn, the Bishopsgate and St Bride's Institutes, the Institute of Chartered Accountants, Law Society, Lloyd's of London, Lloyd's Register of Shipping, and Trinity House. The Barbican Estate is also entered here, because of the several public buildings it encompasses. The fourth section is devoted to Livery Halls, with a short introductory account of their history and functions. Then come the streets, alphabetically arranged. Though the accounts are necessarily selective, the quality and interest of the architecture means that most buildings are mentioned, however briefly. Premises change hands quickly in the City, so street numbers are given preference over the names of occupants, though for important buildings both are supplied. Perambulations are provided only for two areas of dense, narrow alleys, N of Fleet Street, and S of Cornhill. Streets without entries of their own will be found in the index. In only three cases have streets had to be split between volumes: Victoria Embankment between City and Westminster; High Holborn and Goswell Road (entered under Aldersgate Street) between City and London 4: North.

The principles of previous Buildings of England volumes have been followed in terms of the omission of certain church furnishings (bells, hatchments, chests, plate, and most moveable furniture) and of moveable fur-

---

* The alphabetical order followed for this volume is letter-by-letter ignoring lower case words such as the, and, by etc.

nishings in secular buildings. Description of an interior does not imply that the building is open to the public. Where a pair of dates is given for a building, the first is generally that for the acceptance of the design, the second for its completion. For modern buildings the names of job architects of schemes by large firms are given when these are known. Brackets are used for interiors that were not inspected.

The description is of the City early in 1997, though some interiors visited early on (research began in 1994) may have been altered by the time of writing. Buildings threatened with demolition are pointed out in some cases, though readers should bear in mind that the City is quicker to rebuild than anywhere else in Britain. As ever, information from readers on errors and omissions is always welcome.

PREFACE TO THE 1998 REPRINT

Various minor alterations have been made to the text, reflecting new information and corrections kindly sent in by readers. In early 1998 the process of rebuilding the City is once more in full swing, a list of demolitions from which follows; it will be seen how rapidly the commercial architecture of the 1950–60s in particular is being replaced.

Bishopsgate, No. 158 (Wadmore & Baker, 1885–6); King William Street, Nos. 47–51 (R. Angell, 1913); Aldersgate Street, Alder House (G. & T.S. Vickery, 1922–5); Queen Victoria Street, Bank of London and South America (Victor Heal, 1950–7); Wood Street, former Nestlé (T.P. Bennett & Son, 1957–8); and Nos. 90–91 (Gunton & Gunton, 1957); Holborn Viaduct, Williams National House (Ronald Ward & Partners, 1961–3); Basinghall Street, Woolgate House (C. Lovett Gill & Partners, 1963–8); Lombard Street, National Westminster Bank (Mewès & Davis, 1963–9).

PREFACE TO THE 1999 REPRINT

This second reprint incorporates some thirty small corrections sent in by sharp-eyed readers, which arrived too late for the first corrected edition.

ACKNOWLEDGEMENTS

A great debt has been inherited from the old London 1 *volume in its three successive incarnations. Above all I was fortunate to have Sir Nikolaus Pevsner's text as a starting point. Much of his writing remains in the present volume. In the new and amended sections I hope to have caught something of his tone. Acknowledgements are also due Bridget Cherry and Ralph Merrifield, Sir Nikolaus's collaborators on the 1973 edition. Initial research for the first edition was carried out in 1950–3 by Mrs K. Michaelson. Sir Nikolaus also drew on the Lists of historic buildings and other information compiled for the then Ministry of Housing and Local Government, by Mrs Bradshaw and J. H. Farrar. Mr H. S. Goodhart-Rendel made available his notes on Victorian church restorations, and Sir Thomas Kendrick his on Victorian glass. Jon Manchip White wrote the Roman entries for the first edition, and Professor W. F. Grimes revised them for the second. Proofs were read by H. L. Howgego of the Guildhall Library, H. Clifford Smith, the Rev. Canon Atkins, Margaret Whinney and Ian Nairn. George McHardy, R. H. Harrison and Nicholas Taylor, amongst many others, provided much assistance on points of detail. Corrections and additions submitted by readers of the earlier editions proved very useful when the revisions came around.*

For the present volume my first debt is to fellow members of the Buildings of England *staff: to Elizabeth Williamson, whose judicious editing refined and rendered down many long drafts without impairing their flavour; to Stephany Ungless, for her scrupulous attention to the texts in proof; to Alison McKittrick, for her no less scrupulous assistance in locating and preparing illustrations; and to Bridget Cherry, for much expert help and guidance. John Newman, advisory editor, made many helpful suggestions on the C17 and C18 sections. Georgie Widdrington designed the book, Antonio Colaco the cover and Lesley Straw the inset. Judith Wardman was the indexer. Secretarial assistance was ably supplied by Caroline Reed, Sabrina Needham and Susan Machin. The drawn plans are the work of Alan Fagan, the maps of Reginald and Marjorie Piggott. Many of the photographs were specially taken by Derek Kendall of the RCHME (which was most generous where photographs were concerned).*

The book has benefited enormously from two specialist contributions. Dominic Perring of AOC Archaeology updated the late Ralph Merrifield's introductory chapter and gazetteer entries on Roman London (1973), in line with the enormous growth in knowledge of the subject since then. John Schofield of the Museum of London Archaeology Service revised the chapters on the Middle Ages and the C16, and described numerous archaeological discoveries of the period for the gazetteer. In addition, the Mansion House entry is by Sally Jeffery, architectural historian to the Corporation of London, who suggested numerous improvements to the accounts of other Corporation buildings. Malcolm Tucker's entries on Thames crossings in London 2: South *form the basis of the present accounts, while parts of the descriptions of Holborn, High Holborn and Chiswell Street were supplied by Bridget Cherry. In addition the account of St Paul's incorporates some of the late Priscilla Metcalf's revisions for the entry in* The Cathedrals of England and Wales, *1985.*

The work of revision would not have been possible without the generous financial support of the Corporation of London, under Michael Cassidy, until very recently Chairman of the Policy and Resources Committee; this was supplemented by a half-year grant from the British Academy and a grant towards the cost of illustrations from Kinney and Green. I am also most grateful to many of the Corporation's own staff for help and guidance: to Ralph Hyde, Jeremy Smith, John Fisher and others at the Guildhall Library; to all at the Corporation of London Record Office; to Peter Rees, Kate Williamson, Stuart O'Callaghan and others at the Planning Department; and to Roy Thomas at the Environmental Health Department, who made available for inspection its rich collections of material on the C19 *and early* C20. *Peter Guillery of the* RCHME *took a close interest in the progress of the book. Olwen Myhill of the Centre for Metropolitan Studies supplied valuable bibliographical details. I am also indebted to the library staff of the Courtauld Institute, Institute of Historical Research, Society of Antiquaries, National Monuments Record, Camden Local History Library, and the Council for the Care of Churches.*

*Others who read and commented on drafts of the text include Bob Crayford, Robert Potter, Martin Stancliffe, Philip Ward-Jackson and Jo Wisdom on St Paul's; Paul Jeffery (*PJ*), Donald Findlay (*DF*) and Teresa Sladen (*TS*) on churches; John Keyworth on the Bank of England; Ann Saunders on the Royal Exchange; and Geoffrey Parnell and Jeremy Ashbee on the Tower of London. Laurie Kinney supplied much information on problematic buildings, and generously made available the City premises of his firm, Kinney & Green. To Geoffrey Fisher (*GF*) and Adam White (*AW*) thanks are due for much information and help concerning church monuments. The following authors kindly allowed access to proofs of works in progress: Anthony Geraghty (*AG*), on Wren's City Church Office; Peter Jefferson-Smith, on Edward I'Anson; Paul Jeffery, on Wren's churches; Lynn Quiney, on the Law Society; and Caroline Swash (*CS*), on post-war stained glass. I am also grateful to the authors of several unpublished theses which have been consulted: Danny Abramson, on the* C18 *and* C19 *Bank of England (Ph.D., Harvard, 1993); Nicholas Brawer on East India House (M.A., 1996); Georgina Russell on Decorated tracery (M.A., 1973); Robert Scourfield on Livery Halls up to 1666 (M.A.), and Caroline J. Simon on the elder Somers Clarke (M.A., 1982); the last four all at the University of London.*

Much invaluable information came from the London Division of English Heritage under Andrew Saint, both from their unpublished records and from conversations and correspondence with Chris Miele, Susie Barson, Elain Harwood and Roger Bowdler. Catherine Steeves of the Survey of London assisted with buildings on the City's boundary with Clerkenwell. Further information was provided by the archivists and custodians of the City's institutions. I am particularly grateful to Andrew Griffin at St Bartholomew's Hospital, Ian Murray at the Inner Temple, Lesley Whitelaw at the Middle Temple, David Young at Christ's Hospital, Claire Ketley at the Stock Exchange, and John Watts at the Royal Exchange. For the Livery Halls I am much indebted to the following: Dai Walters and Major Charles O'Leary (Apothecaries), Claud Blair (Armourers and Braziers), J. Tomkins (Bakers), Ian Lester (Carpenters),

*David Wickham (Clothworkers), R.J. Perrin (Coopers), K.S.G. Hinde
(Cutlers), Penelope Fussell (Drapers), Meryl Beamont (Fishmongers),
Andrew Gillett (Founders), David Beasley (Goldsmiths), Elliott Viney
(Grocers), John Cope (Haberdashers), Anthony Douglass Mathews
(Innholders), Susan Andres (Ironmongers), Ursula Carlyle and Anne
Sutton (Mercers), J.A. Bayford (Merchant Taylors), Hillier B.A. Wise
(Painter-Stainers), Maj.-Gen. J. St J. Grey (Pewterers), Robin Myers
(Stationers), and Brian Coghlan (Vintners). Many of the above also
answered queries concerning their companies' other City properties.*

  *Steven Brindle, Sir Howard Colvin, Ian Dungavell, the late Charlotte
Haslam (Landmark Trust), Professor Michael Port and C. Douglas
Woodward (City Heritage Society) kindly answered written correspondence.
The architects Jeff Adams (Rolfe Judd), Martin Haxworth, Donald
Insall, J. Sampson Lloyd, Robin Booth (Fitzroy Robinson), G.E. West
and Sir William Whitfield supplied information concerning their firms'
work, and Stuart Lipton and Geoffrey Wilson gave generously of their
time to answer queries on Broadgate and Cutlers' Gardens.*

  *Thanks are also due for assistance and information to Tabitha Barber,
Martin Biddle, Tye Blackshaw, Charles Brooking, Lida Lopes Cardoso,
Janice Carpenter, the Rev. Oswald Clarke, Thomas Cocke, Nicola
Coldstream, Sue Cox, David Crellin, Dan Cruickshank, Jo Darke,
Ptolemy Dean, the Rev. Richard Hayes, David Honour, Frank Kelsall,
David Kynaston, Caroline Lightburn, Norman Niblo, Elizabeth Norman,
Maggie Peek, Richard Pollard, John Robinson, Matthew Saunders,
Keith Scholey, Paul Sutherland, Robert Thorne and Peter Wood. I am
also grateful for corrections and amendments sent in since 1973 by Ashley
Barker, Joanna Bird, Vanessa Brand, Geoff Brandwood, Dennis Corble,
Peter Cormack, Peter Eyres, R.N. Hadcock, S. Hickin, Christopher
Monkhouse, J.R. Piggott, Michael Shearer and Roger White. Last
but not least I thank those, too numerous to mention, who showed me the
interiors of the City's endlessly fascinating buildings.*

INTRODUCTION

THE CITY OF LONDON

The City of London is the oldest part of the capital, and one of the most rewarding architecturally. To most people its name is synonymous with high finance, and many of the grandest and most flamboyant of the buildings lining its well-kept streets do indeed house bankers, brokers and the like. Though a high proportion of its architecture is post-war, careful design and rich materials generally preclude the effect of a bleak modernist monoculture, especially where buildings of the booming 1980s and 1990s are concerned. Victorian and early c20 commercial buildings survive in great numbers too, though a high proportion have been internally reconstructed. But one cannot walk far without being reminded of a time when the City was a place of residence as well as of work. Churches, houses 2 and livery halls are intermingled with the architecture of commerce, and here and there stretches of the medieval City wall may still be seen. Off the main streets lie little enclaves of alleys and courts, still 4 wholly domestic in scale and largely domestic in appearance.

Panorama of City of London.
Engraving by Samuel and Nathaniel Buck, 1749

Even when older buildings are nowhere to be seen, the irregularity of the medieval streets (often outlandishly named) serves as a reminder of the City's ancient origins. Long, broad highways and numerous cut-throughs made by the Victorians cross and recross the ancient network. The same street plan also creates endlessly surprising juxtapositions and vistas, in which the silhouettes of St Paul's and the City churches collide with the extraordinarily varied outlines of the post-war towers. On Saturdays and Sundays the pedestrian can enjoy this rich mixture untroubled by crowds of workers or heavy traffic (though weekdays are best for church visiting). But even in the busiest streets one is rarely far from a little-visited close or quiet churchyard.

This distinctive mixture requires some explanation. The starting-point is the Roman settlement, whose wall and gates were taken over when King Alfred restored the City in the C9. The present rambling street layout dates in its bare outlines from that time. In the C11 the SE part of the City was taken for the Conqueror's Tower of London, which has lain outside the jurisdiction of the City ever since (though included in the present volume). By the C12 the City had more than made up this loss by adopting land outside its walls, especially at the NE and across the valley of the Fleet River on the W. These boundaries remained unaltered after the C16, when building began to spread rapidly W, towards Westminster, and into the present East End. Even after the Great Fire, in which some two-thirds of the City was destroyed, the opportunity to reform the government of the metropolis was passed up. Nor was the disappearance of the residential population in the C19 and C20 enough to change matters, and even today the Aldermen who form the City's governing body are elected according to the system of territorial Wards established in early medieval days.

The poetic half-fiction of an autonomous, quasi-medieval commune is reflected in the public and religious buildings of the City. Elections and ceremonial functions are held at the C15 Guildhall, the greatest medieval civic building in England. Once a year a new Lord Mayor, who is also the chief magistrate, is installed in the great Palladian Mansion House, facing the famous crossing by the Bank of England and the Royal Exchange. The population is still served by numerous churches, sometimes no more than a few yards apart; and though only a minority still has parochial status, none of the surviving forty or so has been deconsecrated. Only slightly less numerous are the grand Livery Halls of the various City Guilds, membership of which is still required to become a full Citizen, though few members still practise their nominal trades.

This architectural palimpsest is best appreciated in the centre of the City, especially in the streets around the Royal Exchange. Further afield the story is somewhat different, as large areas are devoted to specialized functions with their own strongly defined architectural character. Some of these have declined or disappeared in the C20, most notably that along the waterfront, where large office blocks of the 1970s and later stand in place of the teeming warehouses that once served the City's material trade. However, new precincts were also established during the reconstruction of the 1950s and 60s, of which the most remarkable lie side by side NW of St Paul's: the residential and cultural citadel that is the Barbican Estate, and the new street called London Wall, an attempt to create a new urban model based on planned office buildings strung out along a road and linked by elevated walkways. Walking w from here, one encounters Smithfield meat market, with its great Victorian buildings, and facing it from the s the enclave of St Bartholomew's Hospital. Continuing sw, across the valley of the old Fleet River, a series of large and small premises remain from the printing and newspaper industry that flourished in and around Fleet Street until the 1980s. At the w end of Fleet Street, running down to the Thames, lies the leafy labyrinth of the Inner and Middle Temple. Other buildings connected with the legal world stretch N along Chancery Lane and Fetter Lane.

The E part of the City, more obviously commercial, is varied by such nuances as the concentration of shipping and insurance firms in the se quadrant, and the tailing-off of the E and NE fringes into the inner East End, with narrow streets and rougher architecture. In the far NE lies the Broadgate Centre, by far and away the best office precinct in London, built on old railway land in the later 1980s.

150, 152

All these districts are squeezed into an area of just over one square mile: a smaller extent than Hampstead Heath, and one only slightly larger than Kensington Gardens and Hyde Park combined. A brisk walk of twenty minutes or less will take one from the Temple to the Tower, while ten minutes or so will suffice to cross the City from the river to the its northern boundary. Users of this book will of course prefer to explore the Square Mile at a more leisurely pace.

THE ROMAN CITY OF LONDON

BY RALPH MERRIFIELD AND DOMINIC PERRING

The architectural history of London begins with the founding of the first ROMAN TOWN some time after the invasion of Britain by the armies of Claudius in A.D. 43. The only Roman structure of consequence to survive into recent times was the city wall, and our knowledge of the Roman settlement is based almost entirely on archaeological investigation. This began haphazardly in the c17, although early antiquaries were more interested in artefacts and inscriptions than in the generally unspectacular remains of the city's streets and buildings. Hundreds of more thorough excavations have taken place in recent years, as basements and foundations of new buildings have dug ever deeper into the buried strata. Whilst there is relatively little to see, Roman London is therefore one of the most thoroughly studied of all ancient cities.

No settlement of any significance existed on the site before A.D. 43, although there are indications of casual occupation of the region from after the end of the last Ice Age, c. 13,000 B.C. The initial sites were temporary hunting camps strewn with rubbish from the manufacture of flint tools and the butchery of animals. The first settled farming communities of the New Stone Age (Neolithic) did not appear until about 4,500–3,500 B.C. The earliest finds from the

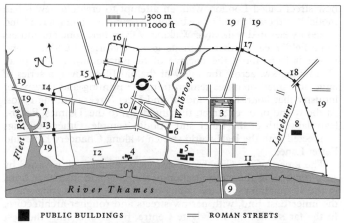

Legend:

■	PUBLIC BUILDINGS	=	ROAD STREETS
—	C3 TOWN AND WATERFRONT	⌐	PRESENT DAY WATERFRONT
⊥	LATE C4 BASTIONS ON TOWN WALL		

1	Fort (*c.*A.D. 100)	11	Hypocaust
2	Amphitheatre (*c.*A.D. 70–80)	12	Public buildings,
3	Second forum (*c.*A.D. 85–140)		possibly temples
4	Huggin Hill public baths (*c.*A.D. 70–90)	13	Ludgate
5	'Governor's Palace'	14	Newgate
6	Temple of Mithras (*c.*A.D. 240)	15	Aldersgate
7	Temple	16	Cripplegate
8	Basilica (late C4)	17	Bishopsgate
9	Bridge	18	Aldgate
10	Public baths	19	Cemeteries

Roman City of London

City are flint implements of this period, but these were not associated with permanent habitations.

The Thames grew in importance as a trade route in the Bronze Age, especially after *c.* 1,500 B.C. Large defended enclosures of this period are known at Carshalton and near Heathrow, and a network of wooden trackways crossed the peat bogs flanking the Thames in Southwark and Docklands. Many Bronze Age swords and weapons have been recovered from the bed of the Thames, especially between Battersea and Brentford. They were probably thrown into the river in funerary rites or other ceremonies. In the Iron Age some hill-forts were built in what are now the suburbs of London, and several farmsteads and small hamlets are also known. Sporadic finds of late Bronze Age and early Iron Age pottery have been made on sites in the City, and a later Iron Age burial found at the Tower. Otherwise the City remained largely uninhabited: there are no prehistoric houses and enclosures, and insects and seeds extracted from pre-Roman stream beds witness an arcadian environment, innocent of extensive farming or human settlement.

Conquest and Foundation

Caesar left an extensive account of his two forays into Britain in 55 and 54 B.C., from which it can be deduced that he passed close to the site of London, although no archaeological trace of either expedition has been found. By the time of the Claudian conquest, the dominant chieftains of SE Britain had established rival strongholds at St Albans (*Verulamium*), Colchester (*Camulodunum*), and Silchester (*Calleva Atrebatum*). The Thames lay close to the boundary between these incipient states, and was a comparative backwater. Accounts of the Claudian conquest of Britain stress the strategic importance of the Thames crossing in the early military campaigns, and one or more army camps would have been built to protect it. These have not yet been found, but were likely to have been placed initially on the S side of the river.

Recent archaeological work in the City indicates that London itself was probably founded *c.* A.D. 50, some 5–10 years after the conquest, although a slightly earlier date cannot yet be entirely discounted. The site would have been immediately attractive to a Roman administration concerned with establishing lines of communication and supply, especially once the initial campaign had secured the SE part of the Province and the army was pushing deep into the British interior. The Thames was much broader then than now, and the tidal reach extended much less further upstream from London Bridge. At high tide much of present-day Lambeth would have been underwater. There were eyots on the S bank, on the line of Borough High Street in Southwark, which provided valuable access through the marshes to the main channel of the river. These were already the site of a small Iron Age hamlet. Opposite these islands, the Thames cut directly against two low hills, and this was the place where the main Roman crossing of the river was engineered. The hills were well-drained and plentifully watered by fresh natural springs and small streams. St Paul's Cathedral surmounts the W hill, which was defined by two rivers: the Fleet to the W, now set in a drain beneath Farringdon Street and New Bridge Street, and Walbrook to the E. The Walbrook rose in marshy ground N of Moorgate and flowed into the Thames W of Cannon Street Station. This river valley has been much levelled out over the last 2,000 years, but is still evident where Cannon Street dips down at the junction with Walbrook. The hill E of the Walbrook had its highest point near Leadenhall Market. It was separated from Tower Hill to the E by the Lorteburn, a small stream now entirely lost, which rose near Fenchurch Street Station and flowed into the Thames at Custom House.

When the Roman road network was laid out it inevitably centred on the river crossing. This vital strategic point could also be reached from the Continent by ships sailing up the Thames, so that from the beginning London became what it has been ever since – a great centre for communication by land and water. A key factor behind the subsequent success of London was its position as the furthest inland location with both a tidal port and access to Watling Street, the busiest military way leading through London to Verulamium and the NW. Since goods could be carried by water at a fraction of the cost of carrying them by land, the port of London thrived for as long as the needs of military supply sustained such commerce.

The site of the crossing, about 160 ft (50 metres) downstream of the present London Bridge, can be fixed from the evidence of approach roads found on both sides. It is still not known, however, if a bridge was built or a ferry preferred. Since the river was in many respects the more important approach, and a fixed bridge would have disrupted traffic, a ferry may initially have been the more attractive option. The lack of a permanent bridge would explain why some of the earliest Roman quays lay above the river crossing, rather than below it. It is possible that temporary bridges formed from boats lashed together – like that shown on Trajan's column in Rome – were used to facilitate traffic during particular military campaigns.

The Early Roman City

There are many different interpretations of the earliest status of London, but it was perhaps most likely to have been a supply base, i.e. neither a civilian foundation nor a fort. If so, the decision to build London was probably made *c.* A.D. 50 by the Governor Ostorius Scapula, at the same time as it was decided to plant a veteran colony at Colchester. Although Londinium was given a Celtic name it had a wholly Roman character. The first settlement was set out to the N of London Bridge, over the E of London's two hills. A waterfront revetment found in 1996 at the junction of Lower Thames Street and Fish Street Hill has been dated from its tree-rings as early as A.D. 52. A grid of lightly cambered gravel streets was laid out around two main arterial roads. The main E–W road has been observed underlying the E end of Lombard Street and the W end of Fenchurch Street. It was laid out parallel with the river as the cross-street of a planned nucleus – very like the *via principalis* of a fort. The principal N–S road came up Fish Street Hill to form a T-junction with this street where Gracechurch Street now meets Fenchurch Street. N of this junction was a gravelled area, London's first great open space and public forum. Nearby, facing on to the main E–W street, were buildings with mud-brick walls set over concrete footings. These are likely to have been administrative buildings and storehouses built for the Provincial administration. In one of them was a large store of grain imported from the eastern Mediterranean, perhaps a consignment destined for the army campaigning at this time in Wales, burnt when the building was razed in the revolt of A.D. 60. The main area of settlement lay S of these buildings, and included another E–W road under Cannon Street and the W end of Eastcheap. From Eastcheap the land dropped fairly sharply to the river-bank, which lay a short distance N of Upper and Lower Thames Street. Everything to the S of this line was reclaimed from the Thames in more recent stages of London's growth.

The earliest Londoners of note would have been the merchants and agents contracted to supply the Imperial forces, and the officials seconded from those forces to regulate them. When Boudicca (Boadicea), Queen of the Iceni, rebelled against the Romans in A.D. 60, we know that London, in the words of Tacitus, 'was not dignified by the title of a *colonia* [like Colchester], but abounded with dealers and was a celebrated centre for supplies'. Many of the rather flimsy buildings hurriedly thrown up to house these first inhabitants have now been found. They had earth floors and walls of wattle and daub. Several were so cheaply built that they needed extensive repair every few years, but some interiors were given a more 'civilized' appearance by means of painted wall plaster and cement floors.

Soon after its foundation, London attracted suburbs along the three busy main roads into town. The road s through Southwark to Canterbury and the coast was the site of an important settlement (*see London 2: South*). The w road provided access to both Silchester and St Albans (*Verulamium*), after forking r. at Marble Arch. This bridged the Walbrook w of the Mansion House, and was found by Wren in the construction of his tower of St Mary-le-Bow s of Cheapside. Its further progression is marked by Newgate Street and Holborn. The suburb along this road had spread as far w as Christ Church, Newgate Street, within a few years of London's foundation. A smaller E suburb developed beside the road to Colchester, now beneath Aldgate. These suburbs all displayed the same principal characteristics. Shops, workshops, smithies and taverns were housed in rectangular timber buildings set gable-end-on to the main street, evidently competing for a considerable volume of passing trade. 'Strip' buildings of this type have been recognized in most of the civilian sites that sprang up outside Roman forts and at posting stations throughout Rome's northern Provinces. A few circular buildings of British type were also found in these suburbs, usually serving as stores and outhouses behind the 'strip' buildings. Quarry pits dug to extract clay and gravel for building works and occasional pottery kilns were also hidden behind the houses and shops. Some land here was also used for burial grounds, which according to Roman custom could not be placed within the town precinct. Several small nucleated cemeteries of early date have been found in peripheral areas (*see* Central Criminal Court, p. 291). Some open plots on the very edge of town were defined by V-shaped ditches of a type generally associated with military sites. These plots may also have been enclosed by fences and it is likely that they were stock-enclosures.

London had grown with remarkable speed to become the largest town in Britain before Boudicca and her rebels descended on it with fire and sword and razed it to the ground. Those inhabitants who had not fled were cruelly massacred. The burnt daub of their early dwellings has often been seen as an orange-red layer in the lower levels of excavations throughout both the town centre and the suburbs. Little if anything survived the torch. London's suburbs and industrial quarters were slow to revive and the population was much reduced, although in other respects London made a rapid recovery from disaster. In A.D. 63 a substantial timber quay was built on the waterfront just E of London Bridge, and this was most likely to have been a public initiative. London was now the administrative centre of the Procurator, the high official responsible directly to the Emperor for the financial and economic affairs of the Province and for the administration of Imperial estates and monopolies. According to Tacitus it was the Procurator, C. Julius Alpinus Classicianus, who complained to Nero of the excesses of the Governor, Suetonius Paulinus, in punishing the Iceni for their revolt under Boudicca. Classicianus died in office a few years after; his imposing inscribed funerary monument has been found, reused as building material in a much later bastion of the City wall on Tower Hill (a replica may be seen next to a surviving stretch of the Roman town wall on Tower Hill: *see* p. 611).

Revival after c. A.D. 70

London's main revival came only after A.D. 70. The fall of Nero and his eventual replacement by the Emperor Vespasian ushered in a period of renewed expansion in Britain, and a series of campaigning Governors pushed forward the limits of the Province. This period of growth was marked in London by a vigorous public building programme. One of the first and most important new buildings was the FORUM built between A.D. 71 and 85, the site of which straddles the modern Gracechurch Street. Its two central courtyards were London's main public meeting places and ceremonial parade grounds. Like most of Roman London's public buildings, the forum had walls of concreted ragstone blocks, separated at intervals by courses of red tile. The main entrance was through the s range, at the junction of Gracechurch Street and Lombard Street. This wing had a double range of rooms, the outer rooms perhaps housing shops opening on to the street to the s. The E and W wings initially contained a single range of rooms only, but in subsequent reconstruction an inner portico was added. The main range of the building, the basilica, formed the N side of the inner courtyard. This range was both a court of justice and a town hall where the council and magistrates – and perhaps also the Provincial authorities including the Governor – met to perform their civic duties. It contained a central nave with a raised floor, separated by piers from side aisles of unequal width. A raised tribunal for the magistrates may have been placed at the E end. The very presence of this building suggests that London enjoyed some form of local self-government, but we do not know the constitution or status of the town at this time. W of the forum, between Gracechurch Street and George Yard, stood a broadly contemporary brick-walled building within an enclosed precinct, believed to have been a small Classical temple. A plausible reconstruction shows the temple to have been approached by a low flight of steps, with two substantial columns flanking the doorway to a small cella.

Work on the construction of a new, enlarged FORUM started only a few years later, c. A.D. 85. The main ranges of the new complex were constructed around the earlier one, which remained standing during the early phases of construction. This ambitious new project suffered frequent delays and was not finished until c. A.D. 140. When complete it was nearly four times the size of its predecessor, and was the largest such Roman complex N of the Alps. As previously, the forum was entered from the s and the main basilica lay beyond two courtyards. The new basilica measured 172 ft (52½ metres) from N to s and 547 ft (167 metres) from E to W: longer than Wren's St Paul's. Its remains have been traced from St Michael's Alley, W, to Whittington Avenue, E, chiefly in excavations of 1881–3, the 1930s, and 1987. The walls, of ragstone with brick bonding courses, descend nearly 30 ft (10 metres) below modern street level. Arcades of brick piers (*see* p. 311) divided the central nave from aisles to N and s, and an apse was set at the E end.

To the s of the forum stood an unusual aisled building with mud-brick walls with external buttresses. Partitions divided the narrow aisles into small chambers. Other rooms were later added along the sides, in one of which a latrine was found. Aisled buildings are rare in Romano-British towns, although not uncommon in

c. A.D. 71–85

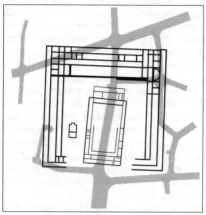

c. A.D. 85

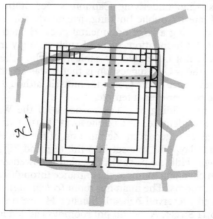

c. A.D. 140

Forum.
Development of the first and second buildings. Plans

rural contexts, and there is speculation that this may have been an assembly hall for a town guild. The building was redesigned early in the C2, when one room was decorated with a painted architectural fantasy with a robed woman standing with arms aloft in the foreground: one of the earlier British examples of this popular Roman style.

The forum was not the only major public building project of the late C1 and early C2. In this period a series of massive timber EMBANKMENTS was constructed over the Thames foreshore, and these established waterfront terraces where a variety of public buildings was erected. The most extensive quays, built c. A.D. 70–80, consisted of massive oak baulks stacked horizontally to form a revetment. They were held in place by equally large timber tie-backs and infilled by dumps of rubbish and earth. Timber structures built on the waterfront at the same time were probably used as shops and warehouses. One such long open-work structure stood on the foreshore in front of the embankment a short distance downriver from the main Thames crossing (between Fish Street Hill and Botolph Lane), reached by timber gangways. This was London's main dock and landing stage, and the river bed here was littered with rubbish from the breaking up of imported cargoes. A rectangular timber structure found on the foreshore adjacent to Fish Street Hill may have been part of a bridge pier erected c. A.D. 85–90.

By A.D. 100 rows of masonry transit sheds and shops had been erected behind the quays on this terrace, on either side of the main river crossing. These had raised timber floors and open fronts closed by timber shutters. The waterfront was further extended at various stages in the C2 and early C3 to secure space for new quayside constructions. By the end of this process the N bank of the Thames had advanced some 500 ft (c. 150 metres) over the pre-Roman foreshore, including the full width of the strip now occupied by Upper and Lower Thames Street.

Further upstream, on the E angle of the confluence of Walbrook and Thames – i.e. underlying Cannon Street Station – stood a monumental late C1 public building, irregularly laid out around a courtyard containing a large ornamental pool. Heated rooms were also included. Its foundations were of such strongly made cement that they could not be shifted by explosives when the station was being built in 1864. One suggestion is that it was an official palace, possibly the residence of the Governor himself, although it may have been a public bath or even a temple.

A waterfront building of c. A.D. 70–90, W of the Walbrook, can more securely be identified as a public BATH HOUSE. It stood where natural springs emerged from the junction of the gravel and impervious London clay, and was set into the terraced hillside on both sides of Huggin Hill (see p. 522). The plan followed the usual progression from changing rooms at the entrance through a suite of cold, warm and hot rooms. The main hot room (*caldarium*), uncovered in 1987, has been preserved beneath Senator House on the S side of Queen Victoria Street. A second hot room was added later to the N, and a heated suite to the E, before the baths were demolished about the mid C2. The hillside to the N and W had been extensively terraced, and foundations and building debris, including imported marbles, suggest that other public buildings stood nearby. These

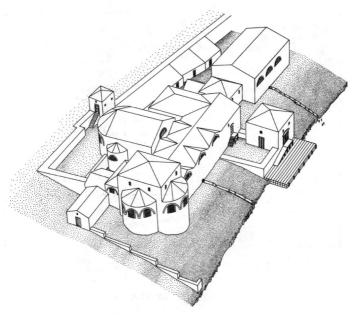

Huggin Hill baths. Reconstruction

possibly included a temple precinct on the slopes of Ludgate Hill s of St Paul's (*see* p. 507).

In a sparsely occupied area NW of the town, a fairly large stone FORT was built late in the C1 or early in the C2 (*see* p. 572), perhaps to replace an earlier but as yet undiscovered fort on the same site. It occupied an area slightly under 12 acres (5 ha.): less than a quarter of the size of the great legionary fortresses, but bigger than most auxiliary forts. Like most forts of this period it was rectangular with rounded corners, laid out on a playing-card-shaped plan, and had the usual internal turrets and external V-shaped ditch. It was probably intended as a barracks for troops serving under the Procurator and Governor, or otherwise on attachment to London. Parts of stone-walled buildings that may have been C2 barrack blocks were excavated in 1962 in Wood Street, near St Alban's church. Tombstones and inscriptions show that many such soldiers were stationed at London throughout the Roman period, where they played a key role in arranging the financial and administrative affairs of army and Province. Memorial stones to soldiers from three different Roman legions have been found in London, of which the Second Augusta is the best represented. The fleet (*Classis Britannica*) may also have had a London base, perhaps in Southwark.

To the E of the fort, beneath Guildhall Yard, recent archaeological work has uncovered traces of the Roman AMPHITHEATRE. This was built *c.* 70–80 A.D. in a natural hollow formed by the shallow valley of a tributary to the Walbrook. The earth banks of this oval stadium were originally retained by timber walls, but those enclosing the arena were replaced in stone and tile *c.* 120 A.D., when the amphi-theatre was comprehensively remodelled. Even after this rebuilding,

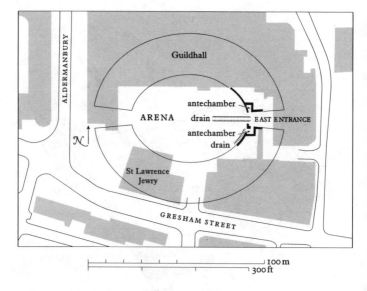

Amphitheatre. Plan

most of the structure was still of wooden construction, including the tiers of seats. These may have accommodated about 8,000 spectators, who would have been entertained by animal-baiting as well as gladiatorial contests. The E entrance to this later arena is (in 1997) being prepared for public display (*see* p. 305).

These various public buildings adorned a populous and industrious city, the largest and richest in the Province. The streets were closely lined with shops and houses, behind which lay such industrial premises as bake-houses, glass-works, potteries, tanneries and water-mills. The Walbrook valley was particularly favoured for industrial use, exploiting the ready supply of running water, while the bakeries clustered alongside the principal roads to either side of the forum. Rows of small self-contained 'bed-sitting' rooms were also found in commercial parts of the early C2 town, as behind the forum or in the main suburbs. These probably provided rented accommodation for the growing urban workforce.

Most HOUSES of this period were single-storey timber-framed constructions with wattle-and-daub partitions, weatherboarded external walls, and roofs probably of thatch. They can be reconstructed from the evidence of surviving studs, wall-plates and braces. An important group of such timbers, reused as piles beneath constructions associated with alterations to the so-called Governor's Palace, were found during excavations at Cannon Street Station. Reception rooms of modest pretension – probably dining rooms, with cement floors and walls simply painted – were found behind some of the commercial 'strip' buildings. The more expensive houses, which in the C1 and C2 preferred the S-facing slopes overlooking the Thames (as in the area of Cannon Street, *see* p. 441), had walls of unfired mud bricks, usually with whitewashed exteriors. Only at the better houses did these rest on stone footings, and the concreted brick and masonry walls used in public buildings were also rare in town-houses before the mid C2. Superior houses were also more likely to have had roofs of red or yellow tile. In the very best, sophisticated black and white mosaic and marble inlay (*opus sectile*) floors were used in the main reception rooms, which were decorated with wall-paintings following contemporary Italian fashion. Glazed windows were rare even in such houses, and underfloor (hypocaust) heating was not used in domestic contexts until the second half of the C2.

The late C2 and C3: stagnation and revival

In the 120s London was devastated by a great fire every bit as damaging as that of 1666. The cause and history of this disaster are unknown, but precious little of the town escaped destruction. The bright red debris from clay walls fired and destroyed in this 'Hadrianic' fire of London is a common feature on most archaeological sites in the City. Rebuilding was swift, and the post-fire houses show some improvement over their predecessors, notably the greater use of masonry construction. The earliest domestic bath-suites also date from the mid C2. However, the second half of the C2 witnessed a massive contraction, especially in the suburbs, and many areas previously densely packed with houses were converted to gardens. The poor survival of later Roman levels, a consequence of post-Roman disturbance, has made it difficult to study these changes properly, but London's pre-eminence within Britain was being challenged by alternative administrative centres, such as York, whilst the volume of military demand and traffic was considerably reduced with the end of the great military campaigns and the establishment of secure provincial frontiers. Many public facilities seem to have been neglected in this period, and the public baths at Huggin Hill were disused by the end of the C2. One of the few additions to the town was an octagonal building overlooking the Fleet River just outside Newgate (*see* p. 573). This is most likely to have been a temple of the Romano-Celtic type widely preferred in Gaul and Britain.

After several decades of contraction, accompanied in some parts of the Province by problems of disorder and decay, the arrival of a new Imperial dynasty intent on the restoration of civil order and public confidence seems once again to have revived London's fortunes. Several major public building projects of the early C3 seem likely to have been initiated during the late C2 power struggle between the Emperor Septimius Severus and Clodius Albinus, a Governor of Britain and rival for the Imperial purple. Some works may be attributable to Clodius Albinus, but Severus also took a particular interest in British affairs after his reconquest of the Province in A.D. 197. Expropriations from the defeated followers of Albinus may perhaps have defrayed the costs of renewal and contributed to an economic revival.

By far the most impressive of these early C3 public works was the construction of the masonry TOWN WALL. London's limits were previously defined by a bank and ditch, which enclosed a smaller area. Part of a town ditch of this earlier phase, redundant by the mid C2, was found at the Baltic Exchange in 1995 (*see* p. 592). The pattern of streets and burials shows that during the C1 and early C2 the

The town wall at Tower Hill, by F. W. Fairholt, 1852

town had seen a series of planned enlargements, and the new wall of *c.* A.D. 200 was built to enclose a slightly larger area than that occupied by the city during its period of greatest extent in the early C2. With immense labour, this mighty wall was raised on the landward side of the city, extending for more than two miles from the Tower to Blackfriars, and enclosing an area of just under 330 acres (133 ha.). This acreage is larger than that of any other Roman town in Britain, and is exceeded by only four towns in Gaul. The construction of the town wall was in many respects a public refutation of the previous period of contraction, and it defined an ambitiously large area, several corners of which were never actually occupied during the Roman era.

The wall started in the SE corner of the Tower of London (*see* p. 367). From the Wardrobe Tower it runs approximately N across Tower Hill to Aldgate (*see* p. 416), then turns NW to Bishopsgate. Here it swings W and continues to St Giles Cripplegate (*see* p. 543), with a distinct deflection to the N at the point where it meets the NE corner of the earlier fort N of Aldermanbury. In this section the N and W walls of the fort were reused, reinforced by the addition of an inner wall. Between Aldermanbury and the rectangular corner S of St Giles Cripplegate (*see* p. 545), and between this NW corner of the fort and its SW corner in Noble Street, the Roman wall is therefore of a different character, consisting of a double wall without the courses of bonding tiles found elsewhere. At the SW corner of the fort in Noble Street, opposite Oat Lane (*see* p. 572), the wall turns W across St Martin's le Grand to the former G.P.O. N of Newgate Street (*see* p. 297). Here it swings abruptly S, and makes its way beside the Old Bailey (*see* p. 292) across Ludgate Hill. The wall probably continued S from Ludgate to meet the river near Blackfriars Station, though there is a possibility that the circuit was not completed here until slightly later. This was undoubtedly the case for the riverfront, which was originally left open along its full length.

The wreck of a barge carrying a cargo of Kentish ragstone was found sunk in the mouth of the Fleet River, by Blackfriars Bridge, in 1962 (*see* p. 566). Its character and date are consistent with the view that it had been bringing building material for the construction of the wall, probably from quarries near Maidstone. About 1,300 similar barge loads would have been required to complete the wall. Foundations were of puddled clay and flints, or occasionally clay and ragstone. At ground level on the outside was a plinth of large chamfered blocks of red Kentish sandstone, at the corresponding level inside a triple facing-course of tiles. Above, both faces were of squared ragstone laid in regular courses, with a core of ragstone rubble set in hard white lime mortar. At intervals of five or six courses, a double or triple course of bonding tiles was laid right through the wall. At these points there was usually an offset on the inner face to reduce the thickness of the wall, which was 7–10 ft (2–3 metres) thick immediately above the plinth. The greatest height of surviving wall recorded is 14 ft (4 metres) above the plinth. The tile course at this point is likely to have supported a parapet protected by a crenellated breastwork. Some of the round-topped coping stones from the breastwork have been found reused in later contexts. Culverts were built where the wall crossed streams; and a metre-wide arched opening for one of the principal tributaries of the Walbrook was protected by a rail of five iron bars. Outside, at a distance of 9–17 ft (2¾–5¼ metres) from the plinth, lay a V-shaped ditch, between 10–16½ ft wide and 4–6½ ft deep (3–5 metres and 1¼–2 metres). The earth from this and the foundation trench was piled in a bank against the inner face of the wall to make a rampart about 6 ft 6 ins. (2 metres) high, tailing off some 13 ft (4 metres) from the wall.

The wall was punctuated at intervals by gateways, allowing the passage of Roman roads that are mostly still followed by modern highways. The road to Colchester via Old Ford passed through Aldgate; Ermine Street, the road to Lincoln and York, through Bishopsgate; the road to Silchester and the w, through Newgate; and a road along the Strand, ultimately joining the Silchester road, through Ludgate. These main gates are all likely to have been built as free-standing structures before the construction of the wall. Newgate, the best known, had a double carriageway flanked by two square towers. Aldersgate was a later insertion, probably replacing an earlier postern. Other postern gates are likely to have been located at Moorgate and Tower Hill. Small towers on the inside of the wall perhaps housed stairways to the parapet walk.

Other early c3 building projects included new timber quays along much of the riverfront, and London's port seems greatly to have revived in this period. Part of an impressive arcaded building of this period set behind the waterfront, found in excavations at Queen Street, may possibly have served as a state warehousing facility. Large blocks of architectural stonework, datable on stylistic grounds to the late c2 or early c3, were found reused in a c4 addition to the sw angle of the town wall. They came from two dismantled constructions which suggest that a TEMPLE PRECINCT had been built or restored in this area. One was a monumental arch of Lincolnshire limestone, at least 26 ft (8 metres) high, which had formed part of a ceremonial gateway. Figures of classical gods flanked the arch, and its frieze was filled with busts and other items perhaps representing the days of the week. The other, a decorative limestone screen 19 ft (6¼ metres) long and sculpted with pairs of gods in recessed niches, probably stood within a temple forecourt. Both structures were attractively and competently carved.

Cemeteries lay alongside the main roads into town and in the surrounding extra-mural areas. The W cemetery covered much of the area between Smithfield and the Old Bailey, the N cemetery extended from Finsbury Circus in the W to Spitalfields in the E, and the E cemetery covered a large area S of Aldgate High Street. It is estimated that the E cemetery contained well over 100,000 graves. Some of the more important monuments and tombstones lay close to the main streets, but lesser roads gave access to numerous grave fields defined by boundary ditches. In the early phases cremation was the favoured burial rite but inhumation was increasingly preferred, and some later burials were laid in lead coffins or packed in chalk. Offerings of food, jewellery and clothing were frequently placed in the graves.

The Late Roman City

Several of London's other public buildings fell into disuse comparatively early on. The most notable is the forum, which was largely demolished *c*. A.D. 300. Workshops were built over certain other redundant public buildings, such as the Huggin Hill baths and 'Governor's Palace'. All this reflects the general decline of civic life in the later Empire, under which the affairs of London were increasingly likely to have been conducted from increasingly opulent private houses rather than in public fora.

From the late C2 onwards, many such LONDON HOUSES were stone-built, or half-timbered over stone foundations. They often contained one or two rooms with hypocaust heating and others with mosaic pavements. Such houses have been found throughout the walled area, though sites close to natural supplies of water were preferred. They were concentrated along the Walbrook valley, as evidenced by the houses found beneath the Bank of England (*see* p. 280). Others stood near springs on the banks of the Thames as at the Coal Exchange in Lower Thames Street (*see* p. 549). A few houses, perhaps suburban villas, were also found at the more attractive sites outside the town walls. These are evidenced by the tessellated pavements found near St Andrew Holborn and beneath St Bride Fleet Street (now in the Museum of London). Commercial and industrial premises were less common than previously, and consequently the cheaper timber and clay forms of construction were less in evidence, although earth-walled houses were still being built in the C3 and C4.

Social changes are also reflected in the increased popularity of oriental cults, which placed emphasis on an ascent to personal salvation through induction into private rites and mysteries. An inscription from London attests the refurbishment of a temple of Isis in the mid C3. One of London's most celebrated Roman discoveries, the TEMPLE OF MITHRAS, was probably built in the 240s, and continued in existence well into the c4. It stood behind a private house on the E bank of the Walbrook (*see* p. 584). This stream in earlier times had revetted banks, but being only 13–16 ft (4–5 metres) wide it can only have allowed passage to the smallest boats. Its banks were much frequented before London's late c2 decline, and a rich variety of votive offerings and domestic refuse has been recovered from the infilled stream channels. (Much earlier in the Roman period, the Walbrook had been the recipient of more macabre votive offerings of human skulls, deriving perhaps from Celtic ritual practice.)

The mid c3 was a sluggish period. Some of the most interesting finds of this period are the collections of coin forger's debris (broken coin moulds) recovered from sites associated with the town wall. These allowed an illegal (but probably officially sanctioned) production of coin to address the lack of Imperial supplies reaching the Province. The most significant late c3 work was the extension of the city wall along the Thames riverfront. This construction consisted of a tile-coursed stone wall about 7 ft (2 metres) wide set over a chalk raft resting on timber piles. Marshier ground at the w end, at the confluence of the Thames and Fleet, was even then left undefended, and the circuit was not finally completed until somewhat later. The line of this riverside wall generally falls beneath the s carriageway of the present Upper and Lower Thames Street. Nothing is known of the gateways and posterns that would have permitted access through it to the river crossing and waterfront. There can be no doubt, however, that the entrance into London across the bridge would have been marked by a magnificent gateway. Most of the quays along the Thames saw no further extension and addition after the mid c3, and dockside activity may then have been restricted to two or three official sites where watergates were provided through the city wall. The pattern of river erosion suggests that for a period in the c3 the Thames was no longer tidal at London, and this may have contributed to a decline in trade. Military supply was in any case now concentrated on coastal rather than inland routes, and the importance of the E coast route direct to York and Hadrian's wall limited the need to trade through London.

London saw a revival, at least as an administrative centre, in the closing years of the c3. In A.D. 286 Britain came under the control of the usurper Carausius, who established a mint in London. His successor, Allectus, was responsible for the erection of a massive public building over previously open ground overlooking the river in the sw corner of the city. The piles used in its construction have been tree-ring dated to A.D. 293–4. Nothing is known of its external appearance, but the 27 ft (8½ metre) wide foundations of reused ashlar were clearly capable of supporting an imposing superstructure. This was perhaps an extension to the temple complex believed to have stood in the area, or may have been a palace built following the example of Constantius's palace at Trier. The brief episode of this 'British empire' ended with the re-conquest of the Province by Constantius in A.D. 296, and by the mid c4 this public building had been demolished and the cleared site occupied by timber-framed houses or workshops.

Excavations in 1992 uncovered the remains of another large late Roman public building, a basilica with walls up to 13 ft (4 metres) thick, which had been constructed over an earlier road on top of Tower Hill some time after A.D. 350. Although only a small fragment has so far been revealed, tentative reconstructions of its plan suggest that it was amongst the largest buildings in Roman London, perhaps over 300 ft (100 metres) long. A central nave, aligned E–W, was apparently flanked by double aisles formed of columns or piers set over footings which measured up to 6 ft 6 ins. (2½ metres) across. Sadly little of the superstructure had survived later robbing, and little is known of its external appearance. The date and character of the building are not inconsistent with its identification as London's first great cathedral. Other evidence of Christianity is scanty: a small lead alloy bowl with the chi-ro emblem has been found near Throgmorton Street, while a bishop from London is known to have attended the Council of Arles in 314.

Other public works in later Roman London were restricted to the city defences. In the second half of the C4, D-shaped bastions were added to the outer face of the town wall at approximately 180 foot (55 metre) intervals. Built over chalk footings and incorporating much reused earlier masonry, these structures are found only along the E half of the circuit, between the Walbrook and the Tower. A new flat-bottomed city ditch was also dug in this period. Excavations within the Tower of London have exposed part of a large wall that may have formed part of a defensive salient built here in the late C4 (*see* p. 367). This is the latest known public construction of Roman date from Roman London. Some finds from late Roman burials also witness a continued military presence in the capital, particularly a type of decorative bronze buckle used in late C4 and C5 military dress.

It is not yet possible to chart the course of London's decline accurately over the closing years of the C4. The latest historical reference to London as a functioning Roman city was made in the context of the expeditions led by Theodosius to restore order to the Province after barbarian incursions in A.D. 367–9. By this time London had gained the honorific title of Augusta, but it is likely to have been a city in decline. By *c.* A.D. 400 many houses had been abandoned, although some sites were still occupied into the early C5. Very little of Roman London appears to have long survived the withdrawal of the Roman administration *c.* A.D. 410, and there is no evidence to suggest the presence of an urban community beyond the mid C5. Although some medieval streets were relaid to Roman alignments, it is unlikely that any roads remained in continuous use through the earliest medieval period, during most of which the largely empty city is perhaps more likely to have been dominated by fields than abandoned to wilderness. The only element of Roman London to have survived as a significant feature into the post-Roman period was the encircling wall.

Many of the Roman finds mentioned above may be seen in the Museum of London. Displays cover the Mithraeum and its sculpture, the temple precinct by the Thames, and the building timbers found at Cannon Street. Collections of other artefacts are arranged to illustrate such themes as religion and trade. They provide a context for the display of some mosaic pavements, including those from Bucklersbury and Milk Street (*see* pp. 585 and 557): amongst the best of more than thirty mosaic floors lifted from sites in London

since the C17. There are also many funerary monuments, although 7
the restored monument of Classicianus from Tower Hill is at the
British Museum. Other important artefacts there include the mosaic 5
found at Leadenhall Street which shows Bacchus riding a tiger (*see*
p. 529). Smaller displays of finds from the City are at the Bank of
England Museum (*see* p. 280) and at the Tower Hill Pageant (*see* Tower
Hill), where finds from recent waterfront excavations are on show.

THE SAXON AND MEDIEVAL CITY
OF LONDON

Growth of the City, 457–c.1500

In 457, the Anglo-Saxon Chronicle reports that the Britons of Kent
fled to London from the Saxon invaders. All is dark until 604, when
St Paul's Cathedral was founded by Mellitus at the request of King
Ethelbert of Kent. The policy of the Augustinian mission was to re-
establish continuity with the Roman settlement (cf. Canterbury
Cathedral, within the Roman walls); but while C7 coins of Londinium
have been found it is unclear to what extent the Roman city proper
was still inhabited. Bede famously described early C8 London
(Lundenwic) as the capital of the East Saxons and 'the market
(*emporium*) of many peoples coming by land and sea'; but it was
realized in the 1980s, from plotting chance finds of the previous century or so, that he referred not to the Roman city but rather to the
area immediately to the w, along the Strand around Aldwych.
Excavations since have found lanes, traces of timber buildings, pits
etc. to indicate a large (but not necessarily permanently occupied)
settlement between Westminster and the Roman city, from the river
northwards at least as far as the Roman road beneath Holborn and
Oxford Street. In the C9 London was raided several times and the
city occupied by the Danes. In 886 Alfred, after his defeat of the
Danes, restored the walled city and made it habitable (*Londinium
restauravit et habitabilem fecit*). At this time it seems that the site of
Lundenwic was abandoned. In 982 London was again sacked, but
London Bridge had been rebuilt by 1000, and *Aetheredeshyth* (later
Queenhithe) and Billingsgate established or re-established as impor-
tant landing-points on the river for goods and people.

Whatever may be the reasons, there is hardly anything of ANGLO-
SAXON ART AND ARCHITECTURE in London. Standing remains
are confined to part of the w end of All Hallows Barking. The foundations point to an aisleless church of *c.* 70 ft by 24 ft (21 metres by
7 metres) with ample use of Roman brick; an arch and portion of a
quoin at the NW corner still survive. They are difficult to date, but
current opinion (supported by excavated examples at other church
sites) is that the fragments are C11, and not C7–C8 as previously
thought. The C11 is also the date of fragments of two Saxon crosses
at All Hallows Barking and the splendid gravestone in Viking style 8
found in St Paul's Churchyard and now at the Museum of London.

Other features of Anglo-Saxon London may be reconstructed
from chronicles, street names and excavations. The courses of many
main streets were determined by the gates in the Roman town wall.

Other, lesser streets were laid out in a modified grid, much of which is now overlain by later roads such as Queen Victoria Street. That street formation was under way there in the 890s is suggested by two charters of 889 and 898–9 concerning a tenement called *Hwaetmundes Stan*, on the site of the Roman baths at Huggin Hill. The telling point is that only the later charter mentions streets bounding the property. The name indicates a stone-built structure, perhaps an enclosure for goods. The street called Aldermanbury is derived from the name of an ancient royal or civic building, based on the E gate of the Roman fort, which seems to be the last relic of the palace of the Saxon Kings up to the time of Edward the Confessor's move to Westminster. The nearby church of St Alban Wood Street perhaps originated as the palace chapel. In the C12 Guildhall was established a short distance SE of Aldermanbury, and the aldermen moved there.

The importance of London to the NORMANS is indicated in the three castles with which they secured it. The greatest still stands as the royal White Tower with its chapel, one of the most poignant pieces of evidence of the Early Norman spirit. The other pair, Baynard's Castle and Montfitchet Tower, which lay at the w end of the City near St Paul's, were demolished in the late C13. The principal royal palace remained at Westminster, at a respectful distance from the jealously independent citizenry. Otherwise the City is poor in Norman remains. Nothing survives from the rebuilding of St Paul's Cathedral between c. 1087 and the late C12, and standing monuments are limited to the crypt of St Mary-le-Bow (the only parish church with recognizably Norman work), and the E parts of the Augustinian church of St Bartholomew-the-Great, founded in 1123 (*see* Religious Buildings, below).

What did medieval London look like? Archaeological excavations especially of the last twenty-five years have filled in the picture enormously. The City wall was still the physical boundary on the landward side. Its two-mile length was based on its Roman predecessor, except for two expansions at the ends where it met the river. The first was in the E, where the Tower broke through the City wall in the mid C13 in one of its periods of concentric expansion. The other, in the w, followed the settling of the Blackfriars at their second site in 1275. This was made possible by re-routing the City wall s of Ludgate to run further w, along the E bank of the Fleet, so that it gave them, and the City, more intramural space. The wall retained six Roman gates, all known from as early as the C11: Aldgate, Bishopsgate, Aldersgate, Cripplegate, Newgate, and Ludgate. Moorgate is a C15 addition, and there was a medieval postern at the Tower, N of the moat. The Roman riverside wall had been left to crumble, so London could spread directly into the river, adding about 15 per cent to its physical area during the medieval period, and this mostly in the C12 to C14. The more significant excavations in this area are detailed in the entry on Upper Thames Street. After the C14 the timber revetments which bounded hundreds of private riverside properties (and some public landing-places) were often replaced by stone walls, which did not need frequent repair. This put an end to the reclamation process itself, and indeed after the Black Death in 1348 there was probably little need for further expansion.

Outside the wall, suburbs grew up in the Fleet Street–Strand area,

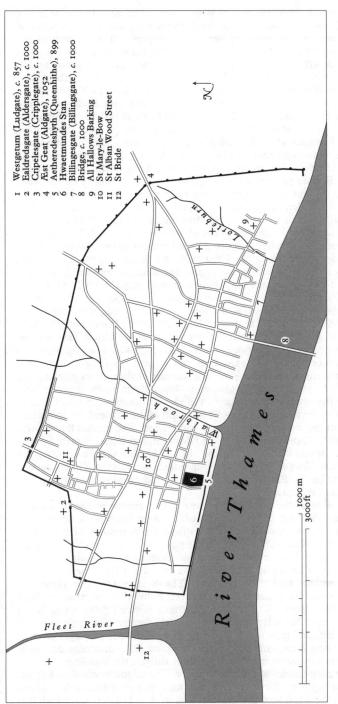

1   Westgetum (Ludgate), c. 857
2   Ealdredsgate (Aldersgate), c. 1000
3   Cripelesgate (Cripplegate), c. 1000
4   Æst Geat (Aldgate), 1052
5   Aetheredeshyth (Queenhithe), 899
6   Hwaetmundes Stan
7   Billingesgate (Billingsgate), c. 1000
8   Bridge, c. 1000
9   All Hallows Barking
10 St Mary-le-Bow
11 St Alban Wood Street
12 St Bride

City of London, c. 1050

of which Fitzstephen, who wrote about 1174, already speaks as of a *suburbio frequente continuante* between London and the *palatium regium* and mentions its *horti spatiosi et speciosi*. These 'spacious and beautiful gardens' belonged no doubt to big mansions, and of these more will be said later. The present City boundary, set apparently by the early C12, reflects this extramural growth, and perhaps also embodies earlier territorial jurisdictions. It goes to Temple Bar, a great deal further W than the Roman wall and Ludgate. It also extends beyond the walls to the N and E, where ribbon developments along most of the other main highways outside the gates (Aldersgate, Bishopsgate and Aldgate) are known by the early C11. Otherwise the main suburban development was across London Bridge, in Southwark. The bridge appears to have been on the same line as its C1 Roman predecessor, though the line was probably cut between the C4 and 1000, when it seems the bridge was back in business. One wooden bridge was destroyed in 1091, the next in 1136. The bridge which stood till long after the end of the Middle Ages was designed by the chaplain *Peter of Colechurch*, and built in 1176–1209. Its nineteen arches supported, besides the roadway, a central chapel and a gatehouse at the Southwark end. Buildings, probably shops, began to encroach on it almost immediately and remained until mid-C18 repairs; the main structure was replaced only in 1831.

Streets within the walls were narrow, in certain areas chiefly pathways between the walls of religious precincts and private mansions. Bury Street, for example, divided Holy Trinity Priory from the 'Inn' or mansion of the Abbot of Bury St Edmunds. Widest was the principal street of Cheapside (or Westcheap), half-way along which an Eleanor Cross was raised shortly after 1290 (fragments at the Museum of London) – the last but one of the crosses marking the funeral progress of the Queen to Westminster. Cheapside also had, for the needs of the markets, the earliest London conduit, traces of which were found in 1995. It was built in the C13 and brought water from the Tyburn, that is from Paddington. The market flowed over into the adjoining streets, and Milk Street, Bread Street, Poultry etc., remind us of it. On the site of the Mansion House was the Stocks Market for flesh and fish, established in 1282. Other markets were held at Eastcheap, Billingsgate, Leadenhall and Smithfield, the latter two still active.

Most of the goods for these markets arrived at the hithes and wharves along the river, from which steep lanes went up into the City. Street and church names here are reminders of this trade. St James Garlickhithe records the place where spices were unloaded. St Michael Paternoster Royal has nothing to do with kings, but refers to La Reole near Bordeaux and the places where the wine merchants had their quarters. The Steelyard of the Hanseatic League, now beneath Cannon Street railway station where its high viaduct crosses Upper Thames Street, covered three acres, all on reclaimed land. It was the largest establishment of a single group of traders, and grew out of a landing-place with royal privileges given to German merchants before the Conquest. Like merchant depots in other towns, such as the English in Bruges, the buildings followed the native styles of the host country. The league received its English privileges in the C13, and although it was expelled by Queen Elizabeth I, it kept the legal possession of its London site, which was sold only in 1853. Trade of a different kind was carried on in Lombard Street, the haunt of Italian bankers from the C14, and the nucleus of the future financial district.

The main tributaries of the Thames were also used by ships, as shown by the name Old Seacoal Lane off Farringdon Street, which follows the course of the Fleet River. Gradually however these small tributaries degenerated into sewers. The Walbrook was already partly covered in 1300 and had disappeared completely by the C16. For the Fleet River the corresponding dates are as late as 1737–64.

Religious Buildings 1066–c.1550

The greatest religious monument of the old City, ST PAUL'S CATHEDRAL, was wholly rebuilt between c. 1087 and the late C12. Though recased by Jones, the Norman nave stood into the 1670s, and we know much of its appearance from Hollar's engravings. It was twelve bays long, and had above the arcade a large gallery with one large unsubdivided opening for each bay of the arcade (as at St Etienne at Caen) and a clerestory with wall-passage. The two w towers stood outside the aisles. Of the Augustinian priory of St Bartholomew-the-Great, founded 1123, the C12 choir survives. The three-storey elevations of the choir interior, without vertical divisions, 11 have a somewhat eclectic appearance, due in part to protracted construction up to c. 1160. Thus the main arcade arches are still unmoulded, but in each arch of the gallery are four lesser arches which probably represent a later insertion.

Most of the other medieval MONASTIC HOUSES of the London area lay in the country outside the City, as would indeed be expected: at Westminster (Benedictine, c. 1050), Southwark (Augustinian, c. 1106), Bermondsey (Cluniac, 1082), East Smithfield (St Mary Spital, Cistercian, 1349), and so on. But in London, like in a few other towns, such as Canterbury, several houses were to be found inside the walls. These mostly indicate early foundations, i.e. before the early C13, when there was still space for laying out the standard monastic plan, although often on cramped sites. Thus within the walls were the Augustinian priory of Holy Trinity, Aldgate, founded 1108 and surviving in one standing fragment in Leadenhall Street, and the Benedictine nunnery of St Helen Bishopsgate, founded c. 1200–15 in connection with an older parish church, and surviving alongside it. There was also the important mid-C11 collegiate establishment at St Martin's le Grand. From the C13 they were joined by the friaries, whose policy was to choose urban sites, often next to markets. The house of the Franciscans (Greyfriars, established in 1225) was N of Newgate Street, that of the Dominicans (Blackfriars) S of Ludgate Hill (1276, relocated from the first house at Shoe Lane, 1221, just outside the walls). Those of the Austin Friars (1253) and Crutched Friars (1298) were where the streets so named survive. The houses of the Clares or Minoresses, founded 1293, were in the Minories immediately outside Aldgate on the E, that of the Carmelites (Whitefriars), founded c. 1253, w of Ludgate off Fleet Street.

Then there were charitable religious foundations such as Rahere's St Bartholomew's Hospital, founded in connection with the priory, or (outside the City) Queen Matilda's mid-C12 St Katharine by the

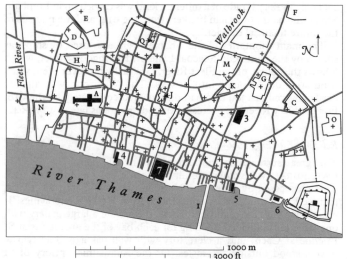

```
                                              ┌─────────┐ 1000 m
                                              └─────────┘ 3000 ft
```

I	London Bridge	5	Billingsgate (main range)
2	Guildhall	6	Custom House
3	Leadenhall	7	Steelyard
4	Queenhithe (main range)		(of the Hanseatic League)

GREATER CHURCHES, MONASTERIES AND HOSPITALS

A	St Paul's Cathedral precinct, 604	J	Hospital of St Thomas of Acon, 1227–8
B	St Martin's le Grand, c. 1056	K	Hospital of St Anthony, 1243
	(collegiate church of)	L	Priory of St Mary Bethelehem
C	Holy Trinity Priory, Aldgate		(Bedlam Hospital),1247
	(Augustinian), 1108	M	Austin Friars, 1253
D	St Bartholomew's Hospital, 1123	N	Blackfriars
E	St Bartholomew's Priory		(Dominican), 1275 (relocation)
	(Augustinian), 1123	O	Holy Trinity Abbey, Minories
F	Hospital of St Mary, 1197		(Order of St Clare), 1298
G	St Helen's Priory	P	Crutched Friars
	(Benedictine), c. 1200–15		(Order of the Holy Cross), 1298
H	Greyfriars (Franciscan), 1225	Q	Elsing Spital, 1331

City of London c. 1500

Tower. For hospitals, of course, sites outside the walls were better. The leper hospitals of St Giles-in-the-Fields and St James (the later St James's Palace), w of the City, date back to 1101 and the CII respectively. The City had Bethlehem Hospital for the insane, founded after 1247 at first outside Bishopsgate, and (just outside the boundary) the Hospital of St Mary Spital further along Bishopsgate, founded in 1197. Within the walls lay the hospitals of St Thomas of Acon in Cheapside (1227–8), St Anthony of Vienne, Threadneedle Street (1243), and Elsing Spital, a hospital for the blind founded in 1331 with secular priests but quickly turned over to the Augustinians; the shattered church tower survives on London Wall (*see* St Alphage). The Fraternity of the Papey in Camomile Street, established for poor priests in 1442, took over the former parish church of St Augustine. The two military orders had their London houses also outside the walls, the Templars at the Temple (*c.* 1160 on that site; *see* below), and the Order of St John just N of the City at Clerkenwell (*c.* 1100).

The Temple Church marks the entry of the GOTHIC STYLE into

London. The earliest pointed arches in London are those of the crossing of St Bartholomew-the-Great, which are datable *c.* 1145–60. The Temple Church was consecrated in 1185. It is a round church in deference to the form of the church above the Holy Sepulchre. The form was favoured by the military orders and occurred about 1140 at St John in Clerkenwell. But the forms used in the Temple Church are essentially Gothic, a Gothic undoubtedly familiar with France and probably also with Canterbury where rebuilding of the choir had begun in 1175; quatrefoil Purbeck piers with shaft-rings and capitals enriched by stiff-leaf foliage, pointed arches, and slim vaulting shafts standing on the capitals of the piers. Only in the blank triforium do the interlaced round arches of the English Norman style make an appearance.

12,
p.
267

Next in date in the Gothic conquest of London come Southwark Cathedral, begun shortly after 1212, and then the very special case of the choir added to the Temple rotonda (consecrated 1240). This is a hall-choir, that is a room in which the aisles are of the same height as the nave. The piers are extremely slender and a unity of space is thus achieved which is very different from the classic French Gothic separation of streams of space from each other. The retrochoir of Winchester had preceded the Temple in this scheme, and it also occurs in the retrochoirs of Southwark and Salisbury at about the same time. It must be regarded as an English speciality, and at the Temple its linear thinness of forms and its airiness will be found aesthetically entirely successful. The windows of the Temple choir are still all lancet-shaped, the standard form of Early English Gothic.

13

In France plate tracery appeared as early as about 1170, and bar tracery was invented at Rheims shortly after 1211. Plate tracery can be seen in London at St Bartholomew-the-Great's nave, *c.* 1230. Bar tracery arrived the moment the whole or nearly the whole High Gothic of Rheims was assimilated, in the rebuilding of Westminster Abbey, begun in 1245. This innovation, as far as London was concerned, was also to be found in the retrochoir of St Paul's (the 'New Work'), which was begun in the 1250s. It was, however, preceded by the rebuilding or remodelling of the chancel proper *c.* 1221–41. For many details of the C13 work at St Paul's we have to rely on Hollar's engravings, though the S E corner of the undercroft below the choir survives beneath a manhole immediately E of the present cathedral, and many pieces of carved stone are retained from the medieval building. Hollar shows St Paul's to have been more English than the Abbey, especially in the shape of the piers with sixteen instead of four shafts. The tierceron vaults of St Paul's had no ridge-ribs, so perhaps they were not dependent on Westminster. An advanced French source is indicated in one motif, the E wall with its rose-window with pierced spandrels standing on a tier of lancets. What can be recognized of details in Hollar's engraving seems in the chancel as well as in the retrochoir to be late rather than mid C13. The building appears to have been more or less finished in 1283, but the paving was laid down only in 1312. In the end St Paul's was 585 ft (178 metres) long and, with the spire heightened in the C14, 489 ft (149 metres) high.

p.
156

The cathedral was no doubt a work of major importance in the sequence of later C13 events. It is too easily forgotten. We are even less well informed on the group of London churches which, though built with less splendour, were probably of yet higher significance, the CHURCHES OF THE FRIARS. The Blackfriars' Church, begun probably in 1279, was about 220 ft (67 metres) long, the Greyfriars' church of 1306 300 ft (91 metres) long, the Whitefriars and Austin Friars (both mid-late C14) respectively about 260 ft and 265 ft (79 and 81 metres). They followed the standard plan for friars' churches, having plain oblong naves with aisles and clerestory, then two solid walls across with a tower over the middle of the space between them, and then the chancel with or without aisles. All this was of the greatest spatial uniformity, unsubtle but forceful, and effective rather by scale than by detail. The nave of the Austin Friars survived in use as the Dutch Protestant church until 1940. Of the others, traces remain of the Blackfriars in and around Carter Lane, and a crypt from Whitefriars is preserved in Whitefriars Street. There is also part of the Minoresses' cloister remaining in a C19 building in Haydon Street, off Minories; as a female mendicant order they did not need a great preaching church, however.

Now for the PARISH CHURCHES of medieval London. Very few of the 110 or so known survived the Great Fire, and many of these were subsequently rebuilt. The story of their development can however be filled in from archaeology, documentation and topographical

All Hallows London Wall.
Engraving by R. West and W. H. Toms, 1730

views. The first churches appear to have begun as the private chapels of manors and larger tenements. Twenty-seven such churches are datable before 1100: a figure that is almost certainly too low, since archaeological investigations have repeatedly demonstrated that most churches antedate the first written record of their existence. In some cases a pre-Conquest origin is suggested by church dedications, though their reliability as a guide has been contested. The four churches (three surviving) dedicated to the Saxon St Botolph are examples. Only in the C11 and C12 were these churches made parochial. New foundations of the same period made up the full late medieval complement. Some chapels acquired parochial status as late as the C15 (St Katharine Cree, St Stephen Coleman).

The Saxon work at All Hallows Barking has already been described. Of Norman work there is almost nothing (St Bartholomew-the-Great was of course a priory). Lanfranc's C11 crypt of St Mary-le-Bow is a special case, probably connected to the Canterbury workshop. Gothic parish churches begin with the ambiguous (and very exceptional) case of St Helen Bishopsgate, a nunnery church to which a parish nave was added. The two naves and chancels lie side by side. The church has C12 and C13 parts, but is to the eye mostly mid C14 and of about 1475, when Sir John Crosby was its benefactor. St Ethelburga nearby, badly damaged by a terrorist bomb in 1993, is a little older, around 1400; very small, with only one aisle, and only one-sixth the area of St Sepulchre outside the City's w wall. Of the C15 are St Olave Hart Street, the tower, porch and much of the nave of St Sepulchre, and the aisles of All Hallows Barking (damaged in the Second World War but remade in C15 style, replacing arcades of two medieval periods). Early C16 is the rebuilding of St Peter ad Vincula, the church within the Tower. As elsewhere in England, the Reformation found parish church building in full flood: churches rebuilt on the eve of the Reformation and beyond include St Andrew Undershaft (1520–32), St Giles Cripplegate (c. 1545–50), and also St Katharine Cree (tower, c.1504). Masonry of this and older periods has been observed at several churches to be encased in Wren's external renderings, for instance the N aisle of c. 1500 surviving to full height at St Mary-at-Hill (revealed when damaged by fire, 1988).

Like most English parish churches, these buildings were commonly the product of centuries of growth and enlargement. The complexity of this process is known from excavations. The kernel was generally a single-celled Saxon or Saxo-Norman church or chapel (St Bride, St Benet Sherehog, Poultry). The first stage of growth might be represented by an apse (St Bride, St Pancras Soper Lane, Queen Street). The fabric generally included much reused Roman brick, as at All Hallows Barking, though at least one church, St Andrew Holborn, is described as built of timber (c. 959).

The addition of N and S aisles to the nave began at some churches around 1230. The C13 also saw chapels added towards the E ends of some churches, especially attached to the chancel. Undercrofts from below such chapels survive at St Bride (c. 1300) and All Hallows Barking (C14). Later in the Middle Ages chapels were more commonly formed by parclose screens within the aisles. The standard late medieval form of nave and two aisles only appears around 1400, and is confined to the larger churches. A clerestory is generally present, and there is usually no structural division between nave and chancel. A tower appears near the w end as a matter of course from the C14 (St Giles Cripplegate, All Hallows Staining). These were intended primarily as belfries, a function served in other cases by turrets (St Ethelburga, C15–C16) or in exceptional cases by detached bell-towers (St Bride, C12). Quite a number of w towers survive, some recased by Wren when he rebuilt the churches after the Fire.

p. 244
16, p. 223

17

p. 211

Pre-Fire views reveal that the commonest form was a square crenellated top with corner turret, as at All Hallows Staining; the type
is familiar from all over the Thames Valley. These crenellations
first appear in the mid C15, both on the tower and the church
proper. Grander churches had tall corner pinnacles (St Sepulchre,
old St Michael Cornhill, with angle buttresses) or a spire (St Laurence
Pountney, St Dunstan-in-the-East). St Mary-le-Bow was exceptional in having a C15 stone lantern on flying buttresses, like that
surviving at St Nicholas, Newcastle upon Tyne. One peculiarity of
many London churches was that the main entry was usually through
the tower rather than through a separate porch (St Andrew
Undershaft, St Katharine Cree). The grand porches familiar from
great town churches elsewhere are represented only by a mid-C15
three-storey example at St Sepulchre.

By the C15 ragstone had long overtaken reused Roman work as
the preferred material, used sometimes as rubble (St Ethelburga),
sometimes in good, large, even courses (St Andrew Undershaft).
Reigate stone, being more easily carved, was used for dressings; in
the C14 also it was employed with flintwork in alternating bands, as
may be seen at St Helen Bishopsgate and St Bartholomew-the-
Great. Plain ashlar is rare, though sections of C16 work were
preserved in Wren's rebuildings of St Mary Aldermary and St Mary-
at-Hill.

Gothic details may briefly be described. Church windows are of
little interest; mostly there is no tracery at all, just stepped lancet
lights under a depressed arch (All Hallows, St Andrew Undershaft,
St Peter ad Vincula). Where tracery is introduced it has simple
panelling motifs. Piers vary in shape, but exhibit no outstanding
19 originality. They may be quatrefoil (St Olave, Guildhall E crypt), or
of four shafts with four diagonal hollows (St Andrew Undershaft, St
Peter ad Vincula, Guildhall), or of the same section with triple shafts
17 in the four hollows (St Giles), or with the wave-mouldings doubled
(St Helen). There are much-restored sedilia in the C14 Lady Chapel
of St Bartholomew-the-Great, which also has a very pretty oriel of
c. 1517 from which the Prior could overlook the choir. Roofs are
much renewed and generally of little distinction.

FUNERAL MONUMENTS make a modest show in comparison to
the splendours of Westminster Abbey. Many were in Old St Paul's
and the friars' churches and were destroyed with them. The pages of
Stow give a melancholy idea of their number and magnificence. The
20 earliest surviving monument is the only one of the famous Knights
which escaped war damage at the Temple Church. It is of c. 1225.
About a generation younger is the effigy of a bishop in the same
church, his head characteristically framed by a trefoiled gabled arch.
In the late Middle Ages the canopied tomb became a standard type.
The early C15 commemorative monument to Rahere in his foundation of St Bartholomew-the-Great has a canopied tomb-chest
with effigy and two attendant bedesmen. The grandest surviving
21 tomb is that to John Holand, Duke of Exeter (†1447), now at St
Peter ad Vincula, originally part of a chantry chapel at St Katharine
by the Tower. It has alabaster effigies of the Duke and his two wives
beneath an unusually elaborate canopy. The fullest sequence is at
22 St Helen, notably the late C14 recumbent effigies of John de
Oteswich and wife, and the tomb-chest with alabaster effigies of Sir

John Crosby (†1476) of Crosby Hall and his lady. A common, less ambitious late medieval type in and around London is the wall monument in the form of a tomb-chest with shallow-headed canopy, where brasses, often placed vertically at the back, are substituted for effigies. Some of these tombs functioned also as Easter Sepulchres. Many are entirely of Purbeck marble, the material in which the brasses were set: two unusually fine examples are the tombs of Alderman Croke (†1477) at All Hallows Barking, and of Hugh Pemberton (†1500) at St Helen. A variant of this type is the tomb at St Helen to Johane Alfrey (†1525), which follows a distinctive London design whose earliest known appearance is at St Mary, Lambeth, 1507. The Alfrey tomb uniquely both served as an Easter Sepulchre and incorporated a squint below. A wholly Gothic version of the formula persisted into the later C16 (Ann Packington †1563, St Botolph Aldersgate). A much more sophisticated relic of the final phase of Gothic sculpture is the figure of the dead Christ at Mercers' Hall, probably carved *c.* 1520–30 by a Flemish artist as part of a mourning tableau.

MEDIEVAL CHURCH FURNISHINGS are scanty. The best collections of BRASSES are at All Hallows Barking, notably the Flemish Evyngar brass (†1533), and at St Olave Hart Street. St Bartholomew-the-Great and St Peter ad Vincula have simple C15 fonts; St Andrew Undershaft has modest heraldic stained glass of *c.* 1530. No screens survive, but St Helen has a few C15 stalls, relics of the nunnery. Painting is represented by four fine late C15 Flemish panels at All Hallows Barking, from the vanished Royal Lady Chapel associated with the church. There is also an excellent (if damaged) painted Crucifixion with Saints of *c.* 1400 at the Byward Tower, Tower of London.

Secular buildings 1066–c.1550

Largest of the standing monuments is the CITY WALL itself, which is medieval in the sections remaining above present ground level. Some kind of repair was doubtless instituted by Alfred, and Norman accounts describe the wall as requiring battering rams and siege engines for assault. The first documented work is in the early C13, when the bastions on the w were added; the last major campaign was in 1476–7, between Aldgate and Aldersgate. Only in Tudor times did buildings encroach and the outer ditch fill up. By comparison with York, or even with Oxford, the remains are fragmentary; the most impressive sections are at the E, on Tower Hill and behind Coopers' Row, and N of the modern street called London Wall, where may be seen several of the bastions and part of the diapered brick parapet of 1476–7. The older work, of stone, characteristically displays the scattered reuse of the Roman tile courses. Of the gates, there remain visible only the C13–C14 foundations of the Tower postern already mentioned, laid out on Tower Hill.

For the highest military grandeur one must of course turn to the Tower. The White Tower belongs to the class of hall keeps, unknown in France, though possibly Norman or Frankish in origin, and not frequent in England. They are bigger but in proportion less high than the more usual tower keeps. The White Tower is the second largest in England, after Colchester. It has four storeys, with

10 angle turrets and an apsidal extension for the chapel in the E wall near its S end. The storeys are subdivided into three apartments each; yet the apartments are large. The upper storey has a gallery or wall passage all round, one of the earliest in English architecture. Investigations in 1996 indicated that the first roof was lower and of steeper pitch, so that the gallery must originally have been open to the air. The White Tower is built of Roman building material (of which there would have been a large amount littering the C11 City) and some Caen stone, the finest stone used in medieval London architecture. Later secular buildings, like churches, used ragstone, with internal work of chalk and flint.

15 The late C12 saw a great expansion of the Tower of London, but only in the C13 was it converted from a Norman to a truly High Gothic fortress. The new type of fortification, brought home by the Crusaders who had seen it applied in Byzantium and the castles in Syria and the Holy Land, was that of the curtain wall with bastions instead of a keep. It was applied as early as 1196 by Richard Coeur-de-Lion at Château Gaillard in Normandy. He also began to apply it at the Tower. But the consistent construction of first one and then two concentric curtain walls within a moat took place under Henry III and Edward I. Dover and Framlingham are amongst the other earliest English examples of the new system. The apartments were finished to a high standard to provide Henry III with a royal palace in the towers along the river. Henry's great hall has entirely disappeared; it lay immediately behind these towers and communicated with them. A feature of Edward I's work was the extremely early use of brick, imported from Flanders, though before the C16 it was used only rarely. The repairs to the City walls in 1476–7 mentioned above are one example, the cellar of Crosby Hall (*see* below) is another.

14, p. 356

Civic buildings, that is to say buildings raised by the citizens, attained to such grandeur more slowly. In the early Middle Ages there was still no administrative unity within the walls. Land in London was distributed on the same manorial system as in the countryside. Traces of these divisions remain in the City's Wards. With the development of trade the need grew for more efficient administration of the City, and in the troubles of the C12 and early C13 London obtained that independence which had become the privilege of towns in Italy, France and the Empire. The charters which established these liberties were granted from *c.* 1130 onwards. The privilege of a mayor, aldermen, and an independent court of justice dates from *c.* 1192. The constitution was modelled on that of Rouen. By the 1190s London's GUILDHALL had stood on the present site for at least seventy years. As rebuilt by *John Croxton* in 1411–*c.* 1430, this still rivals the town halls of Italian and Flemish cities, in spite of C18 alterations and the Second World War. The chief difference is that its situation, hemmed in by other buildings, limited the elaboration of the façade to a narrow porch facing Guildhall Yard. The Guildhall consists of a broad undercroft, of which the plainer W part was retained from the previous Guildhall of *c.* 1270, and a Great Hall 151 ft (46 metres) long: the same length as the Salone dei Cinquecento in the Palazzo Vecchio in Florence, and only slightly smaller than the King's new hall at Westminster. Six statues ornamented the Guildhall porch (four were found in a Welsh garden in 1972, and are now in the Museum of London). This self-

19 p. 301

confidently civic C15 architecture was also apparent in an adjoining chapel and library, in the market (with chapel and school) at Leadenhall (1440, excavated 1985–6), and in the C15 City gates known through later plans and engravings. The bridge gate (1426), with City arms and statues on its outside face, should not be forgotten. Other less spectacular public enterprises included at least five public bath-houses of good repute, known by the early C15, and a public lavatory built by Queen Matilda 'for the common use of the citizens', recorded as being altered in 1237.

Much patronage came from wealthy private individuals. In a chivalrous tribute to such great merchants, Edward III and his court dressed as mayor and aldermen when jousting at Smithfield in 1359. The greatest single patron of architecture was Richard Whittington, Lord Mayor in the early C15. In his lifetime he rebuilt St Michael Paternoster, built and furnished a library at Greyfriars, and added a ward to St Thomas's Hospital in Southwark; after his death in 1423, his executors gave money for the completion of the Guildhall complex and founded almshouses in College Hill and a giant tide-flushed public lavatory off Upper Thames Street.

The most common public or semi-public buildings by the late Middle Ages were however the HALLS OF THE LIVERY COMPANIES. The beginnings of the City's numerous guilds or livery companies as friendly societies go back to the C12; incorporation dates (mostly later than their actual establishment) start in 1272 with the Saddlers. Up to the end of the C14 ten to twelve more were incorporated, including the powerful Merchant Taylors (Edward III was a member), the Goldsmiths (who were at the same time bankers), the Grocers (that is wholesalers), the Drapers, and the Mercers. The Goldsmiths had the first known hall (1339). By c. 1475 there were twenty-seven, mostly founded or acquired in the C15. These premises were generally based on a courtyard house, usually bequeathed to the company by a rich member. The standard medieval hall-and-solar plan was well adapted to communal ceremony and to private business, so houses could remain long in company use without substantial alteration. Common additions were an armoury, further parlours, and sometimes a chapel; luckier companies had gardens for members' recreation, of which the best remaining is that behind the Drapers' Hall. Physical remains are scanty: the halls' concentration around Cheapside and along the River laid them open to the Great Fire (forty-four of fifty-one burnt), and the only visible medieval fabric is at Merchant Taylors' Hall: a mid-C14 vaulted undercroft, the C15 Great Kitchen, and a vaulted 'buffet' or recess of c. 1500 at the dais end of the Livery Hall, the shell of which is C14. But the courtyard plan is still apparent elsewhere, e.g. at the C17 Skinners' and Tallow Chandlers' Halls, which perpetuate also the usual medieval provision of lettable tenements along the main street front. p. 404

Much more survives of guilds of one special type, those of the lawyers. Their INNS OF COURT and INNS OF CHANCERY, as they increased in power, built up a belt of collegiate premises to the W of the City boundaries. By the late C14 they had leased the Temple from the Order of St John and established the Inns of the Inner, Middle, and Outer Temple there. To the E was the smaller Serjeants' Inn, to the N Clifford's Inn, and (just outside the City) Clement's Inn

and Lincoln's Inn. Yet a little further N came Barnard's Inn, Staple
Inn, and (again outside the City) Gray's Inn. Only the Temple,
Gray's Inn and Lincoln's Inn survive as Inns of Court proper. Their
collegiate plan is familiar from Oxford and Cambridge: gatehouse,
hall, chapel, and blocks of chambers around courts and gardens.
The best medieval remains are at Lincoln's Inn Old Hall (1489–92)
and gatehouse (1518; *see London 4: North*). The Inns of Chancery
ceased to function as legal institutions in the C19. Several have
entirely gone (Furnival's, Thavies'), and the survivors have found
other uses. The only medieval work under either head in the City is
the two C14 vaulted chambers at the Inner Temple Hall and the
18 toy-like hall of Barnard's Inn of *c.* 1400.

This little hall was doubtless typical of those of the many large
PRIVATE MANSIONS OF MEDIEVAL LONDON. These are increasingly coming to light through a combination of studies of archaeology, engravings and documentary records. Like the livery halls
they had a gatehouse or passage to the street, an inner courtyard,
and a hall. All we possess, and that not *in situ*, is the exceptionally
grand Crosby Hall, a stone-built London merchant's hall of
c. 1460–70, of proud size and excellent workmanship with a large
bay-window at the dais end and a fine open timber roof. This stood
off Bishopsgate; it was taken down in 1908 and re-erected in
Chelsea (*see London 3: North West*). The Drapers' Hall is heir to the
mansion of Thomas Cromwell, Earl of Essex, a stone-built mansion
by *James Nedeham* of the Royal works (1532); the present building
perpetuates its courtyard plan. There are also street names such as
Suffolk Lane, referring to the de la Poles, Dukes of Suffolk, and
Warwick Square, which was based on the courtyard of Warwick the
Kingmaker's mansion. A notable suburb of larger houses lay along
Fleet Street and the Strand towards Westminster, held by abbots
and priors who came to the royal court. This development started
as soon as the court crystallized at Westminster in the early C13,
with the first probably being that of the Chancellor in Chancery
Lane.

The early medieval population cannot be estimated with any
probability. In 1380, for a poll tax return, it appears to have been
c. 20,000. There were still plenty of gardens and open spaces, but
land for public use could only be found outside the walls, notably
beyond Moorgate. As London grew in wealth and population, more
and more space was taken up by the HOUSES of tradesmen and by
shops and markets. The precincts and the mansions remained, but
except for a gateway or gatehouse they tended to disappear behind
rows of houses. From excavations and the study of documents
(which survive in numbers from about 1250) it is clear that most
ordinary London houses were at first entirely timber-framed, with
low stone walls appearing from about 1200. From about 1100
entirely stone-built houses also appeared, in the streets off Cheapside
and near the waterfront. By 1212, after a number of serious fires,
London had building regulations which governed party walls, roofs
and drains, so that in succeeding centuries the standard of construction in the capital probably equalled that of other European cities.
Archaeological excavation has uncovered many fragments of these
smaller houses, but only one or two scraps of vaulted undercrofts
remain to be inspected, e.g. at Nos. 68–72 Queen Victoria Street

and No. 20 St Swithin's Lane. In matters of detail, more is known
about houses from about 1580, which will figure later.

THE CITY FROM THE EARLY
SIXTEENTH CENTURY TO THE GREAT FIRE

From Henry VIII to James I, 1508–1625

The GROWTH OF LONDON from the C16 onwards was extraordinary. Its importance to the life of the nation spared the capital
the stagnation that overtook many English provincial cities in the
C15. Thereafter its growth continued, mainly because of the centrali-
zation in London of the nation's political and economic life: simply
put, the legal and governmental business that brought people to
Westminster also brought custom to the shops and warehouses of
the City. In no other European country were these processes and
functions so potently combined. The extraordinary expansion that
resulted meant that England was one of the most urbanized countries in Europe by 1650, despite the small size of its provincial cities.
By 1700 London was the largest city in western Europe.

This growth can be measured most directly by population figures.
Though not all of the increase was accommodated within the walls
of the City, the C16 did see the population density rise dramatically.
By 1605 it is estimated that there were 225,000 people, of whom
75,000 lived in the City, 115,000 in the Liberties (which included
such precincts as St Martin's le Grand, Blackfriars, Duke's Place
Aldgate, and also the areas between the gates and the outer bars),
and 35,000 in the out-parishes. The City population in *c.* 1530 has
been estimated as only 35,000, so even within the square mile more
than twice as many people had to be housed within two generations.

New building outside the bars grew so quickly that the Government
was seriously alarmed and tried to check the growth of London. The
City concurred in this, having no interest in bringing those newly-
built-up areas under its sway. Acts were brought out forbidding the
building of any new houses with less than 4 acres of ground. The
first is of 1580. Others followed in 1583, 1593, 1605, and so on. The
area to which these restrictions applied varied from 2m.(3¼ km) to
the absurd figure of 7 m. (11¼ km) around London – that is, as far as
Chiswick and Tottenham. The Acts were too clumsy and naïve to
be obeyed, but they discouraged decent building and encouraged
surreptitious, quick, and shoddy work – and of course as much sub-
dividing inside the City as possible.

The natural direction of growth was along the river. To the E,
Blackwall and Ratcliffe, with Deptford, became important settle-
ments as a result of the growth of the navy in the C16. Land around
Wapping was embanked and built up. Further N lay Stepney, an
immense parish composed of several hamlets isolated in marshland.
In Elizabethan times the parts nearer the City were built up: the
origin of the East End in the sense in which we use the term. Stow
wrote that, in his youth, Petticoat Lane (the modern Middlesex
Street) had hedges and fields on both sides, whereas now there was
'a continual building of garden houses and small cottages', and

Whitechapel High Street was 'pestered with cottages and alleys'. To
the w, the main street remained the Strand leading to Westminster,
lined by the late c16 with small houses on both sides, with streets
and lanes stretching down to the foreshore between the great mansions facing the river. In the c17 large houses were also built along
Holborn, the route w from the City towards St Giles, and by c. 1600
houses had also crept N towards St Giles, up St Martin's Lane.

Another consequence of this growth was to encourage the movement of certain activities outside the City. The long-established
cockpits and brothels of the South Bank were joined in Elizabethan
times by the new theatres, although the first were opened in
Shoreditch, N of the City (1576 and 1577). In the City were Richard
Burbage's theatre in Blackfriars and another theatre in the Whitefriars
(rebuilt 1629); but after the Restoration the theatres moved to the
West End. The dense settlement of the City also prompted much of
the remaining industrial activity to move outside (mostly to the E),
where land was cheap and trade unrestricted by the City guilds. The
Netherlandish sculptors who transformed the manufacture of funerary monuments in the later c16 (see below) had their workshops in
Southwark, since foreign workmen were not allowed to do business
in the City proper.

So much for the growth of London outside the bars. Such expansion apart, the most drastic change wrought on c16 London was of
course Henry VIII's DISSOLUTION OF THE MONASTERIES and
the confiscation of their properties. These were granted or sold to
Henry's most trusted courtiers. Holy Trinity Priory went to Lord
Audley, Blackfriars to Lord Cobham, and the Marquess of Winchester
built himself a house on part of the precinct of the Austin Friars
(hence Great Winchester Street). Outside the City, the Charterhouse
passed to Lord North, the leper hospital of St Giles to Lord Dudley.
Soranzo, Venetian Ambassador to England, who wrote home in
1551 of the mixture on the banks of the river in London, referred
to 'many large palaces making a very fine show, but ... disfigured
by the ruins of a multitude of churches and monasteries'. This is
indeed what must have been most conspicuous during those years of
transition. The great houses of the abbots and many of those of the
bishops were also forfeit, including most of the sequence along Fleet
Street and the Strand.

Where monasteries were not taken over as mansions, they were
broken up or subdivided for the use of those too poor to own houses.
Plans of the precinct of Holy Trinity Priory, preserved in the
Hatfield papers, indicate that it rapidly degenerated into a warren of
houses and tenements. The N aisle of St Bartholomew-the-Great
retains similar makeshift enclosures from later in the c16. The
best-preserved street layout of the period is Middle Street and its
neighbouring passages and alleys, laid out from c. 1590 by Lord Rich
on the former land of St Bartholomew's Priory. Accommodation
was also found by the gradual infilling of many gardens and back
yards. The ditch immediately outside the City walls was encroached
upon along most of its length as early as c. 1500, though the Civil
War prompted some clearance in 1642–3.

The choir of St Bartholomew survived because it was taken over
as a PARISH CHURCH. Other monastic churches so adopted and
surviving in whole or part were St Helen Bishopsgate and St Alphage

London Wall. New parishes were established within other ex-monastic precincts at the old Minoresses' church (Holy Trinity Minories, 1539) and at Blackfriars (St Ann, rebuilt 1598). A few parish churches disappeared or were merged: St Mary Axe was demolished in 1561, and the parishes of St Audoen and St Nicholas Shambles united into the new one based on Christ Church, the old Greyfriars' chancel. The appearance of many of the churches in the mid C16 is captured on the so-called copperplate map, a pictorial representation of London on which major buildings are shown. One later foundation, St James Duke's Place (built on the site of the chapter house of Holy Trinity Priory, 1622) formed part of the wave of repairs and rebuilding in the 1620s–30s (*see* below).

The HOSPITALS attached to the religious orders fared less well, being dissolved in most cases in 1538–47 (St Thomas of Acon, St Augustine Papey, Elsing Spital). The hospital of St Anthony of Vienne in Threadneedle Street had ceased by 1565. Others survived: St Bartholomew's Hospital was refounded in 1544 (its oldest surviving buildings, apart from the church of St Bartholomew-the-Less, are C18), and the hospital of St Mary Bethlehem in Bishopsgate was not suppressed but granted to the City. In 1553 the buildings of Henry VIII's Bridewell Palace were set up as a combination of hospital, workhouse and prison. By 1600 London had five hospitals to deal with the sick, impotent and vagrants together. The C16 also saw several more almshouses established, though none survives within the City.

The other great watershed of the C16 was the arrival in England of the RENAISSANCE STYLE. Though the City was linked to all Europe by trade and travel, the first conduit of the new manner into England was the court of Henry VIII. At first the prevailing influences were Italian or French. Of this false dawn the City possesses major monuments by two of the Italian artists enticed to England to work for the King. The most important of these men was the Florentine sculptor *Pietro Torrigiani*, author of the monuments to Henry VII and his Queen and to the Lady Margaret at Westminster Abbey. He is represented in the City by the monument of Dr Yonge (†1516) from the 29 former Rolls Chapel, now at the Public Record Office. Like the Royal tombs, it is a work of exquisite beauty, with none of the angularity and restless tension of Gothic sculpture. The second artist is *Benedetto da Rovezzano*, who in 1524–9 made for Cardinal Wolsey the stern but nobly proportioned black marble sarcophagus at St 28 Paul's, now part of Nelson's tomb. Otherwise the new style was avidly but unreflectively assimilated as a decorative fashion, of which the lost 'mantell of wainscot with antyke' installed in the royal apartments at the Tower in the early 1530s was doubtless typical. The hall of Barnard's Inn preserves two overmantels with Renaissance details, probably of the mid C16. The greatest monument of the early English Renaissance lay outside the City: it was Old Somerset House on the Strand, a sophisticated essay in the Franco-Italian manner (1547–50). But the conscious revival of disciplined architectural forms derived from Roman antiquity had to wait for the advent of Inigo Jones.

In default of new churches or royal palaces, the Renaissance manner found its most robust expression in the new SECULAR ESTABLISHMENTS of the C16. The period saw a considerable expansion in foreign trade, demonstrated by a range of trade-related buildings. The Custom House, rebuilt in 1559, is shown as a turreted building in a pre-Fire engraving. It was soon eclipsed as a symbol of the Elizabethan City by the Royal Exchange in Cornhill (1566–70), the joint enterprise of Sir Thomas Gresham and the City. Gresham had been the Queen's agent at Antwerp and had been much impressed by the Exchange (*Beurse*) of 1531 there. Antwerp was suffering commercially from the Dutch Wars of Religion; London should take advantage of this chance and capture some of the Flemish trade. So Gresham pleaded for an Exchange for London, which became the Royal Exchange when the Queen solemnly opened it in 1568. Modelled on the Antwerp building, it was designed by *Hendryck van Paesschen* of that city; the timber came from Gresham's manor of Battisford in Suffolk, but the stone came at least partly from Flanders. The complex comprised a quadrangle of Doric arcades with shops and storage compartments above, and a tower. The arcades and shops inspired imitations in the West End, notably the New Exchange s of the Strand (1603–10).

Special architecture for the great new trading companies does not at first seem to have been necessary. The Muscovy Company, the Turkey Company, the Levant Company adapted ordinary houses. The East India Company, the most famous of all, which was founded in 1600, carried on in the house of Sir Thomas Smythe, its first Governor, until 1621, then rented Crosby Hall until 1638, then went back to the new Governor's house (Sir Christopher Clitherow's) in Leadenhall Street. From 1648 they used an adjoining private house, Craven House. Only in 1726 did they acquire a big new building.

Gresham's own mansion, further down Bishopsgate, became the first home of Gresham College, established as a kind of embryonic university under his will (†1579). In this he was following a trend towards lay education begun by Colet, who had founded St Paul's School on a site E of the Cathedral in 1510. It was joined by the Mercers' School in Cheapside (re-founded 1541), Christ's Hospital, created from the premises of the Grey Friars in 1552, and Merchant Taylors' School in Suffolk Lane (1561). In 1611 Charterhouse School was set up in the old monastic buildings, just N of the City.

Gresham College shared with the first Royal Exchange the motif of Doric arcades around an inner *cortile*. That Gresham's understanding of the Renaissance style was in advance of most of his con-
31 temporaries is suggested also by his tomb at St Helen Bishopsgate. Fashioned after a Roman sarcophagus, it is of outstandingly fine workmanship, fluted up the sides and with thick strapwork cartouches. Elsewhere, the new fashion was used more nearly as deco-
25 ration pure and simple. At the Middle Temple Hall (1562–c.72, probably by *John Lewis*) the details of the double hammerbeam roof, itself a Gothic form, are translated into classical entablatures, finials and columns. The plain brick and stone exterior of the Hall also preserves the Gothic proportions. The little hall of Staple Inn (1581) is similar, though now mostly post-war reconstruction. But the most characteristic decorative feature of the date was the strapwork fashion. It invaded England from the Netherlands around the mid C16, and in so far as their names are known its most successful practitioners are usually Flemish or Dutch. The City's greatest piece of wood-carving in the style is the screen of the Middle Temple Hall,

of the early 1570s. Its lower stage is made up of a well-observed Doric order. Elizabethan schemes of SECULAR DECORATION are represented otherwise by three much-decayed murals at Carpenters' Hall, which also preserves some late C16 carvings. Where panelling survives, as at the Inner Temple Gateway, it is not of special interest.

OVERMANTELS of the Jacobean period may be seen *ex situ* at The Cock (No. 22), Fleet Street, and at the former Court House by St Andrew Holborn, the latter example especially magnificent. The combination of strapwork with classical columns is repeated in the CHURCH MONUMENTS of the later C16. Of these by far the most and the best are again in Westminster Abbey, but the City has some exceptionally good tombs from the 1560s and 1570s, including a group of three attributed by Adam White to the *Cure* workshop. The Pickering monument at St Helen (†c. 1574) is an early example of the free-standing type with a canopy of columns, which here number six. The others represent another common type of the late C16 to early C17, in which kneeling effigies in niches confront one another: the Alington monument (†1561) at the Public Record Office (formerly Rolls Chapel), and the Blount monument at St Peter ad Vincula (†1564, extended after 1592) in the Tower. Of this group the last has the finest effigies, of the usual alabaster. Single recumbent figures are represented by the Throkmorton monument at St Katharine Cree (†1570) attributed to the *Cure* workshop, and the Plowden monument at the Temple Church (†1584). The former has an unusual trabeated frame, the latter the more common round-headed niche, with obelisks. Obelisks appear also on the Spenser monument at St Helen (†1609, attributed to *Nicholas Johnson*), which combines recumbent and kneeling figures.

The wall-mounted monuments which appear from the mid C16 generally have small kneeling figures (Sir Andrew Judd †1558, St Helen; Sir Thomas Offley †1582, St Andrew Undershaft). Two curious exceptions may be mentioned: the Legh monument at St Dunstan-in-the-West (†1563), which has little caryatids, and the Smalpace monument at St Bartholomew-the-Great (†1558 and †1588, attributed to *Giles de Witt*), which combines small busts with an incised slate panel. Of monuments from the early C17 that of John Stow (†1605) at St Andrew Undershaft is a good instance of the frontal seated figure, here represented writing at a desk. It may also be by *Johnson*. Such monuments show the steady penetration of classical motifs into polite visual culture. Another conspicuous example was Ludgate, rebuilt by *William Kerwin* in 1586 with a pilastered frontispiece and statues in niches, some of which survive at St Dunstan-in-the-West.

TUDOR AND JACOBEAN HOUSES were necessarily slower to adopt the new fashions. The City in the C16 and C17 was still the home of great men, but it would be a mistake to think of them as exclusively urban creatures. As early as the mid C14 the great City figure Sir John de Pulteney had both a City mansion, off Suffolk Lane, and a great country house at Penshurst in Kent. Of those who lived in the City in 1595, 121 also possessed country seats, although not all of these men were merchants. About half of them lived in wards on the fringes of the City: twenty-five to twenty-eight in the Ward of Farringdon Without, that is W of Ludgate, twelve in the Ward of Bishopsgate, eleven in that of Cripplegate, nine in

Portsoken, eight in Aldgate. But of the great houses of the C16 and early C17 there remains only a brick wall from the house of Jasper Fisher ('Fisher's Folly'), built 1567–79, hidden behind C19 buildings in Devonshire Row, off Bishopsgate. Fisher was a Clerk in Chancery: a reminder that not all City-derived fortunes came from trade. The use of brick is also significant, for it was to bring classical proportions and detail within the reach of owners and tenants who could never have aspired to a mansion of stone.

Lesser houses were still generally timber-framed in the late C16. Their forms can be reconstructed from lease-plans (for example the work of Ralph Treswell in 1610–12), deeds, illustrations, and archaeological excavation. They followed a range of house-types, from old (but now cramped) courtyard houses to dwellings only one room in plan but up to six storeys high on main street frontages. This increase in height is evidence in itself of the premium on accommodation caused by the bewildering growth of London. The earliest
24 surviving dwelling is the Queen's House at the Tower, built 1540 and later: a straightforward gabled affair enlivened by double-curved diagonal struts. The inner faces of some towers there also incorporate C16 timber framing (Byward Tower, St Thomas's Tower). Houses facing the main highways made more use of the jetty, as at the much-restored group on the High Holborn front of Staple Inn, built 1586 and later. They have two overhangs and half-octagonal oriels, with shops on the ground floor and access to the upper chambers from the courtyard behind. The gatehouse made over the old w front of St Bartholomew-the-Great in 1595 is also timber-framed. Of these two only Staple Inn has (modest) carved decoration, though in the case of other houses built at around the same time and since demolished (e.g. at the sw corner of Chancery Lane) it reached extraordinary levels of exuberant grotesquerie. Large areas of external plasterwork might be enlivened by pargeting, of which examples in Golden Lane and Little Moorfields lasted long enough to be
26 recorded. For interior plasterwork one must go to the Inner Temple Gateway (1610–11), which has an intricate pattern made up of the familiar raised bands. Above the jettied oriels of its street front is a balustraded gallery, a common feature of houses of this period on main thoroughfares. The galleries may have been intended as viewing platforms. The formula of an elaborate oriel with gallery above appeared more lavishly at the gateway to Sir Paul Pindar's house in Bishopsgate (c. 1624), the front of which is preserved at the Victoria and Albert Museum. But within a decade *Inigo Jones* was busy laying out Covent Garden, N of the Strand, to a regular classical design of stone and brick. With such innovations the story of London's architecture enters a new chapter.

From Charles I to the Great Fire, 1625–66

INIGO JONES rose to prominence at the court of James I; his first London building, the Queen's House at Greenwich, was started in 1616, his Banqueting House in Whitehall three years later. Only in the 1630s, however, did he set his stamp on the City, with the remodelling of the w end of Old St Paul's. Its most dramatic feature was a giant Corinthian portico completed in 1639, wherein Jones expressed his lucid architectural personality more satisfactorily than in his refacing of the Romanesque nave. This singling-out of one significant motif and its realization according to one governing system of proportion is of course based on the theory and practice of the Italian Renaissance. Jones knew the works of Palladio at first hand, and could draw also on his published works and on those of other theorists such as Serlio. The pages of Serlio in particular contained much that had already been naturalized in England; but never before had the philosophy of design behind the detailed forms been put into practice. Jones was primarily the architect to an increasingly narrow circle of courtiers, but he did make several other architectural sorties into the City. How far his style was compatible with the City's own evolving traditions will appear in due course.

CHURCH ARCHITECTURE underwent a revival in the 1620s and 1630s, during which decades repairs or partial rebuilding are recorded at more than half of the City churches. No doubt much of this merely made up for years of neglect; but at St Katharine Cree all but the tower was rebuilt in 1628–31. The result is instructive in its mixture of Gothic and classical forms. The arcades are Corinthian, with round coffered arches, but they support flattened rib-vaults of plaster. Externally the church appears approximately Perp, but with curious stepped three-light windows, and an E window derived from the C13 retrochoir of Old St Paul's: a sign that the living, evolving tradition of Gothic was dead. The immediate juxtaposition of Gothic and classical parts is also found at Lincoln's Inn Chapel, c. 1619–23, and in much C17 work at Cambridge and (especially) Oxford. The completed tower of St Mary Aldermary in 1626–9 and the rebuilt St Alban Wood Street in 1633–4 (demolished) were at least partially Gothic, though the evidence is complicated by further rebuilding after the Great Fire; the brick tower of St Bartholomew-the-Great, 1628, also has simple Gothic motifs. Most tantalizing of all, St Michael-le-Querne was entirely rebuilt in 1638–40, on a new site at the W end of Cheapside, with *Jones* as a consultant to the parish. His advice appears to have been less than welcome, though whether questions of taste or of politics lay behind the conflict is unclear, for the church was destroyed without a trace in 1666. When churches were again rebuilt and embellished towards the end of the Interregnum, the results were modest and the few ornamental features (notably the œil-de-bœuf window) wholly in the artisan style: the tower of All Hallows Barking (1658–9), and the little vestry at St Olave Hart Street (1661–2, with a charmingly naïve plaster ceiling). One speciality of C17 City churchyards was the *memento mori*. There are stone gateways adorned with cadavers or skulls at St Katharine Cree (1631) and St Olave Hart Street (1658), and 'Resurrection stones' carved with scenes of the Last Judgement at St Andrew Holborn and St Mary-at-Hill.

CHURCH FURNISHINGS of the date are naturally confined to the area that escaped the Great Fire. STAINED GLASS of c. 1630 with foliage patterns may be seen at St Katherine Cree. There is also much secular heraldic work of the late C16 and C17 at Middle Temple Hall. The only remaining PULPIT is at St Helen, a very good example of strapwork decoration. It probably dates from a campaign of embellishment of the early 1630s, although the forms show little advance from the no less fine pulpit of 1613 at All Hallows Barking (destroyed). More advanced in style is the beautiful inner s doorcase at St Helen, probably also of the 1630s. FONTS are represented by three pieces, all of 1630–2. That at St Katharine Cree still has strapwork ornament in the Jacobean manner. At St Helen and St Andrew Undershaft the form of a faceted bowl on a baluster appears, a type multiplied in the churches refurnished after the Great Fire.

The font at St Andrew was made by *Nicholas Stone*, whose involvement in the London building world is assessed below. But it is as a carver of FUNERARY MONUMENTS that he is most significant. These owed much to Dutch fashions, for Stone spent the years 1606–13 working for Hendrik de Keyser, Amsterdam's Master Mason, whose daughter he married. The survival of Stone's notebooks means that we are unusually well-informed about his activities, which coincided with a new originality of types and conceits, very different from the relative stability of late C16 compositions. Partly this was due to the greater tolerance of religious imagery: the Chamberlayne monument at St Bartholomew-the-Great (†1617), attributed to *Maximilian Colt*, already has angels holding back curtains to show the kneeling effigy. *Stone*'s grandest monuments in London are at Westminster Abbey, but the City has his most famous sculpted portrait: the standing shrouded figure of Dr John Donne at St Paul's, made 1631–2. His monument to Sir Julius Caesar (†1636) at St Helen Bishopsgate is a black marble sarcophagus with the conceit of a document carved in parchment-coloured marble instead of an effigy. Lesser tablets by the artist also adopt black and white marble instead of alabaster, of which the Hutton monument at St Dunstan-in-the-West, made 1640, adopts the increasingly popular formula of pedimented tablet with columns. His sculpture in the round is represented by the statue of Queen Elizabeth in the Guildhall Art Gallery collection, made *c.* 1622 for the Royal Exchange.

Stone's architectural frames tend to be purer than the usual London masons' work of the early C17 referred to above. Their favourite coarse, eclectic classical ornament appears at the monument to Elizabeth Freshwater (†1617) at St Bartholomew-the-Great. A greater restraint appears at the monument to Sir Hugh Hamersley (†1636) at St Andrew Undershaft, which has columns and pediments closer to Stone's preferred forms. It has attendant figures of soldiers, a device that recurs at the atmospheric Bond monument (†1643) at St Helen. The kneeling effigies seen at the Freshwater and Hamersley monuments were increasingly supplanted by the device of a bust in a niche, on which a greater degree of portraiture might be attempted. Circular niches came first (Cuthbert Fetherstone †1615, St Dunstan-in-the-West); oval niches supplanted them (Lady Richardson †1639, St Botolph Aldersgate; James Rivers †1641, St Bartholomew-the-Great). The bronze bust of Sir Peter le Maire at St Margaret Lothbury, 1631 (not displayed in 1996), is attributed to *Hubert Le Sueur*, the favourite sculptor of Charles I's court, though it is uncertain if this was ever intended to form part of a monument. The only signed monument of the period, *Henry Boughton*'s tablet to Anthony Abdy (†1640) at St Andrew Undershaft, is not of special interest.

Turning to SECULAR BUILDINGS, the case of Goldsmiths' Hall offers a happier instance of *Jones*'s collaboration with the City than St Michael-le-Querne. The hall was rebuilt in 1635–8 by *Nicholas Stone* under Jones's direction, as a quoined, two-storey palace with

a central courtyard: a work structurally sound enough to survive
the Great Fire. Stone had previously worked with Jones at the
Banqueting House, at which he was master mason. Jones also built
a little oval anatomy theatre at the Barber-Surgeons' Hall (1636–7,
demolished). The division of responsibility between Jones and Stone
at Goldsmiths' Hall depends in part on how far the canon of Jonesian
buildings may be stretched to include less pure, more Mannerist
details and devices. The front of old Thanet House in Aldersgate

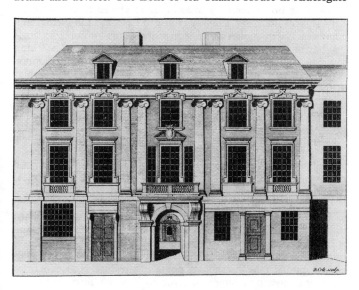

Aldersgate Street, Thanet House (later Shaftesbury House).
Engraving by B. Cole, *c.* 1750

Street (*c.* 1641, demolished), with its pilasters and intermittent
entablature, raises similar difficulties. It also serves as a reminder
that the outer fringes of much of the City were still in favour with the
aristocracy in the mid C17.

Such buildings represented an advance in proportion and purity
of vocabulary on the classical style as the artificers of the City understood it. Only drawings and prints remain of such works of theirs as
the service block and porch at Leathersellers' Hall (1623 and 1632,
attributed by Summerson to the carpenters *Clark* and *Anthony
Lynnett* respectively). Favourite motifs which appeared there included
banded columns, open segmental pediments and eared aedicules
framed by half-pilasters. The style, dubbed 'Artisan Mannerism' by
Summerson, derived from Serlio and from such later C16 authors as
du Cerceau and Wendel Dietterlin. It may still be seen in the s doorcase at St Helen, nearby, which may also be by *Lynnett*; dated 1633. 33

The ordinary HOUSES that made up the bulk of the City were
rarely favoured with such ornate treatment. However, the spread of
building in brick did allow a number of new formulas for their street
fronts. It was encouraged by a royal Proclamation of 1605, never
properly enforced, which forbade the use of timber for house fronts

(further Proclamations from 1615 attempted with mixed success to regulate floor heights and to ban horizontal windows). Symmetrical brick fronts surmounted with a shaped pedimented gable date from about 1610. Two long-lost examples in Holborn, one based on a surviving drawing by *Jones*, are known from John Smythson's drawings of 1619. The next significant development came in the 1630s and involved the visual unification of several houses by means of a giant pilaster order. The first terrace to follow this pattern was built by the City bricklayer *Peter Mills* in Great Queen Street, w of the City, shortly after 1637. Lindsey House in Lincoln's Inn Fields, built a few years later, applies a purified version of the formula to a single five-bay house. It may have been by *Nicholas Stone* or by *Jones* himself, who was certainly interested in promoting a classicized London vernacular. To that end he gave the capital the greatest single display of the giant order (though of pilaster-strips merely) in the arcaded 'piazzas' of Covent Garden, which was also the first of London's squares. He also designed some astylar houses for Lord Maltravers's property in Lothbury and Tokenhouse Yard (*c.* 1638), though these may not have been built. Such a self-denying formula was less appealing to the City than the giant order, which could more easily assimilate a show of fashionable brick ornament. There was a good example in Great St Helen's, dated 1646, and many more doubtless perished in the Great Fire.

On the whole, however, the City was already too densely built up to allow new developments on a scale to match the West End. When the Goldsmiths' Company laid out New Street Square on their land N of Fleet Street in the 1650s, its centre was filled with houses rather than left open. Nor do the few houses that remain from this period approach the threshold of polite architecture. Houses of brick are represented by a single survivor on Tower Green, within the Tower of London. It has three simple straight gables and brick bands, and has been dated to the 1630s. A compromise between brick and timber is represented by Nos. 41–42 Cloth Fair, a very substantial C17 merchant's house built possibly as early as *c.* 1614. Its brick front is interrupted by twin pedimented wooden bays and crowned by weatherboarded gables. A similar formula appears on a smaller scale at Nos. 46–47 Aldgate High Street, where the fronts are of rendered timber. They may post-date the Great Fire, for it is clear that timber-framed or at least timber-fronted houses were built in the later C17 despite the provisions of the Rebuilding Act of 1667 (*see* p. 68 below). No. 74 Long Lane is a small late C17 house where a later owner has attempted to disguise the timber-framing with mathematical tiles. The large timber-fronted houses at Nos. 2–3 Middle Temple Lane (Temple) were built as late as 1693–4.

REBUILDING THE CITY AFTER
THE GREAT FIRE

The Great Fire of 1666 is the watershed in the history of C17 London. It marks the beginning of the AGE OF WREN, for *Sir Christopher Wren* (1632–1723) was to dominate the architecture of

London into the next century. His multifarious attainments had already won him the post of Professor of Astronomy at Gresham College, in 1657. His uncle Matthew Wren was Bishop of Ely and a leading figure in the Restoration Church. This connection had already secured for Wren the task of rebuilding Pembroke College chapel, Cambridge, and even before the Great Fire his mind was busy with further schemes to modernize Old St Paul's. He could hardly have guessed then at the opportunities lying ahead.

The Fire destroyed 13,200 houses and laid waste 436 acres, including some five-sixths of the City within the walls. The burnt area went from the Temple and Fetter Lane in the w, up to Aldersgate and Cripplegate in the N, and E as far as Leadenhall Market and Tower Hill. Speculative PLANS for rebuilding in a more modern,

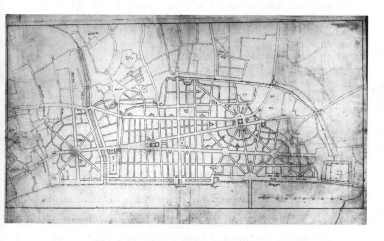

Wren's plan for rebuilding the City, 1666

more commodious, and more dignified way appeared at once. Of these *Wren*'s is familiar. It shows the influence of his stay in Paris in 1665. The dominance of French models had already been demonstrated at St James's Park, the first piece of axial and formal planning in London, laid out by Charles II in 1660–2. The principal motif of Wren's plan was the *rond-point* with radiating avenues. Wren proposed five of these, the main one having a new Royal Exchange in its centre close to the site of the old, another (only a half *rond-point*, just like Henri IV's projected Place de France) radiating from the N bridgehead of London Bridge. The largest however was to be the centre of a new West End, in Fleet Street at about the N end of Bouverie Street. A monumental quay was to run from the Tower to the Temple: a feature subsequently enacted but never fully realized. As it turned out, the only feature of the plan to be carried out was the canalization of the Fleet Ditch (1670–4).

The grand quay appeared also in the plans by *John Evelyn*, which followed the same Parisian plans as Wren's except that the *rond-points* were ruthlessly imposed on a grid of square and oblong blocks and that apart from *rond-points* there were squares from the centres of whose sides streets radiated. A degree of rigid uniformity not reached by any of the others characterized the cellular plan put forward by *Richard Newcourt*, in which the City consisted entirely of a chequerboard of units composed of L-shaped blocks of houses at the four corners of a square with a church in the middle. *Valentine Knight* proposed an uneven net of streets running mostly E–W, with a new canal cut through from Billingsgate to the N part of the Fleet River. Plans made by *Peter Mills* and by *Robert Hooke* do not survive.

However, to execute any of these ambitious plans it would have been necessary to pool and then redistribute all private property in the City. The procedure was therefore rejected as far too complicated in the circumstances. The nation was at war, the homeless were clamouring for their houses, and shopkeepers and merchants for the premises from which they could trade and earn money. So in the end the plan of the rebuilt City followed the old. The wall remained, and the City gates were repaired or rebuilt (Moorgate and Temple Bar both completed 1672). Inside the City there was a fair amount of street widening, but the only new streets were Queen Street and King Street, made as a straight connection between Guildhall and the Thames. All the rest were rebuilt on their old sites.

A class of building less prominent in the rebuilt City was the great house, for one effect of the Fire was to accelerate the movement of polite society towards the West End, closer to Westminster and to areas of undeveloped land in St James's, Soho and Piccadilly. In the decades after the Fire those magnates whose houses had escaped the flames tended to move westward, the sites of their mansions being redeveloped for ordinary houses. The Earl of Devonshire, heir to 'Fisher's Folly' off Bishopsgate, sold up in 1675; Bridgewater House burned down in 1687 and was not rebuilt. Devonshire Square and Bridgewater Square were laid out on their sites. The expansion of London on a large scale was necessary in any case, for the population continued to grow. There were 375,000 Londoners in 1650, 490,000 in 1700, by which time London was the largest city in Western Europe – an increase all the more remarkable when one considers that 100,000 had died of the Plague in 1665–6.

The bulk of the new buildings were ordinary HOUSES, and here the REBUILDING ACT OF 1667 did achieve a lasting improvement in the fabric of London. To prevent the recurrence of fire, the new houses were to be faced in brick. Moreover, the houses were classified according to size, and regulated according to the width of the street on to which they faced. External woodwork was confined to doorcases, window-frames and cornices. The regulations extended inside to the specifications of the timber frame and the minimum thickness of the brick walls. Brick was already the fashionable material of mid-C17 London, and to some extent the Act merely codified the best existing practice; but its stipulations were obeyed much more widely than the ineffectual regulations of the early C17. It created a common vocabulary of flat, narrow, even fronts with regular upright windows, which lasted with refinements until the early C19. Enforcement was the responsibility of *Robert Hooke, Peter Mills* and *John Oliver*, with *Edward Jerman*, who together undertook a survey of the burnt area on behalf of the City. *Wren, Hugh May* and *Roger Pratt* represented the Crown. The progress of rebuilding can be followed from the City surveyors' records and from Ogilby and

Morgan's maps of 1676 and 1681–2. By the end of 1673 most of the City's houses had been rebuilt, the busiest years being 1668–9. Such rapidity was only possible by opening the City to builders and craftsmen from outside its own guilds, in whose decline the Fire marked a further stage. In the process many plots were thrown together, for a mere 8,000 houses took the place of the 13,200 destroyed. The population figures for the City after the Fire reflected this consolidation: almost 200,000 in the early 1660s, but only some 140,000 by 1700, by which time it probably accounted for just over a quarter of the populace of London.

Of the four sizes of house specified by the Act, the largest is the least important for our purposes. We have seen that the aristocracy no longer favoured the City, so the occupants of these great houses were mostly the grander merchants, of the kind who might aspire to the Mayoralty and a knighthood. The houses tended to stand some way back from the street facing a courtyard, in the manner of the medieval houses they often replaced, and this means that the present street plan preserves traces of their presence: Frederick's Place is one example, the close off the E side of Walbrook another. Exceptions are not unknown: the house of Sir William Turner in Cheapside, built 1668 and demolished c. 1930, had an ornate four-storey street front, of carved stone rather than the usual brick. But of these great houses the only survivor is the former Deanery off St Paul's 63 Churchyard, built in 1672 by *Edward Woodroffe* and *John Oliver*, perhaps with *Wren*'s assistance. It has a symmetrical brick front with large windows and a hipped roof. Timber is confined externally to the cornice and doorcase. There is also the Master's House at the Temple, a post-war replica of the original quoined and pedimented building of 1667. It has three storeys, one short of the maximum for great houses under the Act.

The second sort of house, also limited to four storeys, was to front 'high and principal streets', though only six streets were so identified. The general appearance of the greater house of ordinary type can still be seen at the Temple, where fires in the 1670s and 1680s 65 destroyed most of the older houses spared in 1666. They have horizontal brick bands dividing the storeys, sash-boxes set almost flush, and in some cases the original wooden dentil- or modillion-cornices. The sashes are generally later insertions replacing cross-windows with casements, an example of which remains on the timber-framed No. 3 Middle Temple Lane. Doorways range from simple arched openings with a stone key block to pedimented doorcases of rubbed and moulded brick, on the grandest houses also with applied columns (No. 5 King's Bench Walk).

Many of these chambers were built by that dubious entrepreneur *Dr Nicholas Barbon*, an M.D. of Leiden in Holland, and a shrewd and unscrupulous provider of houses. He was also busy off the Strand, building houses on the gardens of Buckingham House, and from 1674 laying out Essex Street and Devereux Street immediately E of the Temple. In the City he was responsible for Devonshire Square and for houses in Mincing Lane. Barbon's houses, being contracted for on a large scale, were much more uniform in appearance than the ordinary high streets of the City, which were rebuilt by thousands of different owners at their own speed without troubling to match the houses to either side.

More numerous survivors may be seen of the third type, limited to three storeys, which lined the ordinary streets and closes of the City. Even so, very few remain from the original thousands. The well-preserved groups in Neville's Court and Bartlett's Buildings, off Fetter Lane, were war casualties. Others, in Gresham Street, Russia Court off Milk Street, and Racquet Court off Fleet Street, were demolished as recently as the 1970s. The survivors remain in groups of two or three at most. Occasionally their builders can be identified. Nos. 1–3 Amen Court were built in 1671–3 by *Edward Woodroffe* for the canons of St Paul's. *Barbon* built Nos. 5 and 6 Crane Court, N of Fleet Street, in *c.* 1670, and No. 21 College Hill in *c.* 1688: the latter characteristic of the later C17 in being squeezed on to spare land behind the street front. The fourth, smallest type is represented by the much-altered shops at Nos. 124–126 Cheapside, dated 1687, which are little more than two rooms set above one another.

These regular brick frontages concealed an interesting variety of PLANS. The houses of the Temple were of a type familiar also from the Oxford and Cambridge colleges, with pairs of chambers arranged symmetrically about a central staircase placed either at the front or at the rear. A block of chambers of *c.* 1663 at Clifford's Inn, demolished in the 1930s, shows that this type was well-established before the Great Fire. It was of three storeys with a hipped roof and tall chimneystacks. The Amen Court houses also have a central staircase, with one room to either side and another in a rear extension. No. 17 Gough Square (Dr Johnson's House), off Fleet Street, built *c.* 1700, has a central staircase with one room on either side and a windowless back wall: a typically pragmatic response to an awkward site, characteristic of the expedients employed on the many crowded, irregular plots of the City. Other houses of moderate size adopt the plan favoured in many London houses from *c.* 1650 to *c.* 1680, in which the staircase is placed centrally between the front room and the back room. The type is best seen at No. 47 Aldgate High Street (the Hoop and Grapes), one of the pair of timber-framed houses already referred to. Here the staircase is lit from a lightwell alongside. The central staircase also appears at two pubs in Fleet Street, although without the lightwell: The Old Bell at No. 96, probably 1669, and The Tipperary at No. 66, 1667–8. Only in the 1680s did the staircase move to the rear of the house, where it could be lit from the side. Smaller houses, with only one room per floor, placed the staircase in one corner and boxed it in. The rear part of the Cheshire Cheese, No. 145 Fleet Street, betrays its origins as two such houses joined together. A specialized type that has entirely disappeared is the greater galleried inn, which clustered off such streets as Bishopsgate and St Martin's le Grand. The last survivor, in Catherine Wheel Alley off Bishopsgate, went in the early C20. The late C17 George Inn, off Borough High Street in Southwark, shows what they were like (*see London 2: South*).

INTERIORS survive less well. The greatest group is at the Temple, where many of the chambers retain bolection-moulded panelling and partitions. A few original overmantels also remain. Elsewhere the best-preserved feature is usually the staircase. The two at St Paul's Deanery are typical. Both have heavy closed strings and square newels. The greater has spiral balusters on spherical bases, the lesser, simple turned balusters. Of the former type No. 22 College Hill also has a good example. In other houses the staircase has been replaced in whole or part, so that often only the plainer upper sections remain. Very little plasterwork survives, notably at No. 5 Crane Court, off Fleet Street, and also at the Sir John Cass School, where a ceiling of 1669 from a great merchant's house in Botolph Lane is preserved. Both have a big circular or oval wreath in the tradition of Jones or Webb, a type also seen at Innholders' Hall. The school also has from the Botolph Lane mansion a remarkable series of panels painted with oriental scenes by *Robert Robinson*, 72 1696.

The PUBLIC BUILDINGS of the City were also rapidly rebuilt in most cases. Some stone buildings proved capable of repair, notably the Guildhall itself. It was re-roofed in 1667–71, probably by *Peter Mills*, and the porch rebuilt by *Edward Pierce*. The shells of Grocers' Hall and Merchant Taylors' Hall were also repaired, although the latter was rebuilt in the C19. *Wren*'s most important secular works lie outside central London. He did design the new Custom House (1669–71), a pilastered brick structure with a pedimented centre and projecting wings, in a manner suggestive of such mid-C17 Dutch architects as Jacob van Campen. It lasted only until 1718. Other secular buildings in the City that can be associated with Wren include the cloister block at the Temple (1680–1, rebuilt in near-replica), the Chapter House in St Paul's Churchyard (1712–14, undocumented), and the columnar Monument to the Great Fire in Fish Street Hill 66 (1671–6). The latter seems to have been a collaboration between *Wren* and *Hooke*. *Hooke*'s other public buildings in the City were all demolished in the C19. The Royal College of Physicians in Warwick Lane (1672–8) was a consequential building in the manner of a French *hôtel*, with a domed octagonal entrance block housing the theatre and the main range behind. Its pilasters, carved stone garlands and round windows reflected Hooke's informed knowledge of Continental architecture, as did his Bethlehem Hospital on the site of the present Finsbury Circus (1675–6), a grand composition of pavilion blocks of pronouncedly Dutch flavour. During the 1670s he also rebuilt Bridewell Hospital, much of Christ's Hospital (with *Peter Mills* and *John Oliver*), and the Merchant Taylors' School in Suffolk Lane. A less well-known figure is *Roger North*, a bencher and architectural amateur, whose Middle Temple Gateway (1683–4) was long attributed to *Wren*. It is a straightforward exercise with a pediment and pilasters on a rusticated base.

Other prominent architects typically rose from the ranks of the City crafts. The figure of *Edward Jerman* stands out, though his death in 1668 prevented the completion of much work in hand. Jerman held the post of City Carpenter between 1633 and 1657, until 1650 jointly with his father Anthony, Past Master of the Carpenters' Company. We have encountered him already as one of the surveyors appointed by the City after the Great Fire. His chief design was the new Royal Exchange (1667–71), the thin tower of which was the first new steeple to break the skyline of the resurgent City. Its plan derived closely from the old, but with the addition of an entrance loggia derived from Covent Garden, and such rich and impure devices as twin segmental pediments raised on giant half-columns, and round-headed tracery on the tower.

A similar richness is characteristic of the buildings of the CITY
LIVERY COMPANIES, most of which were completed by the late
1670s, though brick was commonly used instead of stone. In no
instance does it appear that the Companies employed an architect
from outside the City. *Jerman* provided designs for the Drapers,
Fishmongers, Haberdashers, Mercers, Wax Chandlers and Weavers,
and repaired the halls of the Barber-Surgeons and Goldsmiths.
Vintners' Hall and the refurbishment of Merchant Taylors' Hall may
also be his. Of these buildings the former Fishmongers' Hall stood
out for its assimilation of the astylar manner used in the 1650s
by Peter Mills, notably at Thorpe Hall, Northamptonshire, and
developed after the Restoration by Roger Pratt and Hugh May.
Carpenters' Hall, just outside the burnt area, was rebuilt in 1664–71
by the carpenters *John Wildgos* and *William Pope*, with a giant order
and central pediment. The rest were typically richer and showier. Of
68 *Jerman*'s work only Vintners' Hall survives, if it is his, cocooned
within later alterations and refacings that have concealed the original
U-shaped plan; there is also a reused ceiling at the present
Goldsmiths' Hall and a fragment of his Drapers' Hall. Fishmongers'
67 Hall was finished by the carpenter *Thomas Lock*, whose Apothecaries'
69 Hall survives, while *John Oliver* finished the Mercers' Hall, and
designed the well-preserved Skinners' Hall on his own account. Its
main front has the unusual feature of chequered brickwork. Of the
C17 halls the least altered inside and out was Brewers' Hall, by
Thomas Whiting, a future Master of the Bricklayers' Company,
which was destroyed in 1940. Its large-windowed brick front and
arcade with blocked tympana were imitated with variations by
Capt. *John Caine*, another bricklayer, at his Tallow Chandlers' Hall.
Both halls characteristically followed the medieval plan, with the
main building facing a courtyard reached by a passage from the
street. These entrances were usually marked by elaborate carved
stone frontispieces. The greatest of these, by *John Oliver* for Mercers'
Hall, survives at Swanage, Dorset, reconstructed as part of the
Victorian Town Hall. The E doorcase at Merchant Taylors' Hall,
though almost certainly of 1844, gives a good idea of the appearance
of the rest. A surviving exception to this pattern is Stationers' Hall,
which faces a small alley. Behind it, overlooking a small garden, is a
simple C17 warehouse: the oldest survivor of this building type in the
City, and an uncommon feature for a livery hall, most of which had
no role in material trade. Other halls, especially the smaller ones,
appear to have been built under the direction of a committee of the
livery rather than an architect. The Painter-Stainers' and Innholders'
Halls, both partly surviving, were probably built by this method,
which the Bakers' Company still preferred to use for their new hall
in 1720: further evidence, if it were needed, of the City's conservatism in architectural matters. The interiors of the Livery Halls are
discussed on p. 374.

Two surviving buildings remain to be mentioned, each in its way
typical of the vigorous display of the City artisans in the mid C17.
The first is the former Whittington's College at No. 22 College Hill,
a mysterious mason's structure with twin stone gateways, open pediments stuffed with carving, and wreathed circular windows above.
64 The other is the College of Arms, by the bricklayer *Maurice Emmett
Jun.* and the herald *Francis Sandford* (1671–88, altered). With its

badged pilasters on pedestals, this might have been designed forty years earlier, though the interiors have woodwork of a standard to match contemporary churches and Livery Halls. The later C17 work at the Tower should also not be forgotten. Much work was carried out in 1670–86 to bring the fortifications up to date, though the great bastions envisaged by *Sir Bernard de Gomme* in the 1660s came to nothing. The Grand Storehouse of 1688–91 has gone, but the New Armories of 1663–4 remain to show the standards reached by London bricklayers on the eve of the Great Fire. It has the transitional feature of half-hipped gables.

The City Churches and St Paul's Cathedral

St Paul's apart, the CITY CHURCHES are Wren's principal contribution to the appearance of London. To this day they are the outstanding accents of the City, and some of them individually its highest architectural attainments. Of the 107 parish churches in the City existing in 1666, 85 were burnt. Of these, 34 were not rebuilt, though their sites were often used as burial grounds, which have sometimes survived as open spaces. All the rest, that is 51 churches, were rebuilt, as was St Andrew Holborn, outside the burnt area but in a poor structural condition. Of these churches only 24 remain, plus six towers.

How the churches were built has been the subject of much debate. Funds came from a tax on coal enacted in 1670, that is they were state, not parish funds. A third of the money was allocated to the churches, a third to St Paul's, and the remaining third to pay for street improvements. The tax was renewed in 1686 and 1700 to allow the churches and St Paul's to be completed. The churches were entrusted to a Commission, which swiftly appointed Wren 'to direct and order the dimensions, formes and Modells of the said Churches'. He was joined by *Hooke* and by *Edward Woodroffe*. Woodroffe died in 1675 and was replaced by *John Oliver*, though neither seems to have played a part in the work of design. The case of Hooke is altogether different. We have already seen him working together with Wren, at the Monument, and it is clear from his secular buildings that he was amongst the most capable architects of the day. Drawings in his hand strongly suggest that he and not Wren was the author of several of the churches, notably St Benet Paul's 45 Wharf and St Edmund the King.

Furthermore, several churches were begun by impatient parishes without waiting for directions from the Commissioners, and these cannot be attributed either to Wren or to Hooke. The naves of St Michael Cornhill and St Sepulchre are the surviving examples, both of them churches where a large part of the medieval fabric had survived and could be reused. The continuing shortage of money meant that Wren was himself reluctant to demolish sound medieval fabric, and many of the churches are, in their lower stages at least, structurally medieval: a circumstance usually betrayed by irregular angles in the plan. St Anne and St Agnes and St Andrew Holborn have recased w towers, St Michael Cornhill and St Mary-at-Hill later replacements of medieval towers repaired after the Fire. Furthermore, attribution of the later spires is complicated by the employment of *Nicholas Hawksmoor* and *William Dickinson*, who worked in

Wren's office respectively after 1693 and 1695. It would be unwise to treat a church as an architectural orphan simply because there is no documentary evidence tying it to Wren, for there can be no doubt that he remained in overall control. But it may be better to regard several as collaborative, even somewhat contingent exercises rather than as manifestations of a single architectural genius.

Wren had few guides as to what a Protestant church should look like. The practice of the Restoration Church required a dignified emphasis on the E end, from which altars had been removed during the Revolutionary period; indeed, a dozen of the new churches had chancels, though they were mostly very shallow. But it was also expected that due prominence be given to the pulpit and desk, from which the Word was preached and the congregation led through the liturgy. In his very last years Wren set out his own understanding of the problem in a well-known memorandum: the principal requirement is 'that all who are present can both hear and see'; for Romanists it may be enough 'if they hear the Murmur of the Mass, and see the elevation of the Host', but English churches 'are to be fitted for Auditories'. The last requirement, and the need to accommodate the swollen congregations of amalgamated parishes, explains the extensive use of galleries, which were already being installed in the City in the 1620s. It also explains why Wren felt free to experiment with centrally planned churches, which had been the paramount problem of church design in the Italian Renaissance. Modifications of it were still eminently topical in Italy and France in Wren's day. But these considerations in no way explain the unique variety of plans which Wren devised in the course of his work for the City churches. It is this variety that makes their study so rewarding, and we may not be wrong in discovering in it also something of the scientist's delight in experimenting. How many types of useful parish church can be developed? What use can be made of types worked out in other countries and in other ages? Such thoughts must have exercised Wren's mind as he produced design after design, from 1670 to 1686. In some cases a direct derivation from an antique prototype is documented or can be inferred. At the same time this variety can also be looked at as a national, not an individual phenomenon. It is inconceivable that a French architect of the Age of Louis XIV or indeed an Italian or a German Baroque architect would have gone so far in changing from one principle to another in plans as well as elevations. From this point of view also Wren's plans deserve close study. An effort is here made to arrange them systematically, whether they survive or not; a † means that the church (or its relevant part) has disappeared.

The smallest and most common type is represented by a single unaisled interior without distinctive spatial features. The walls were often markedly irregular, due to the retention of the medieval plan. The tower was placed usually in the NW or SW corner (St Michael Paternoster Royal); sometimes it projected in whole or part (St Mary Somerset †). This asymmetry seems to have been due as much to Wren's preferences as to the medieval arrangement. St Olave Jewry (†) was exceptional in the regularity of its plan, for Wren gave it a central W tower and unique tapering coffin-shaped sides: the latter a clever response to a site that was curtailed on one side. St Edmund the King, probably by *Hooke*, also had a tower placed

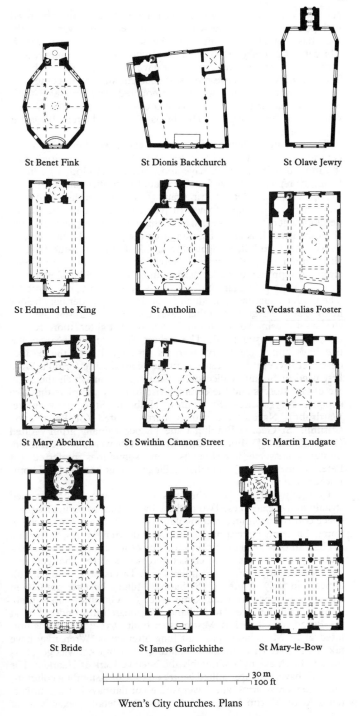

St Benet Fink

St Dionis Backchurch

St Olave Jewry

St Edmund the King

St Antholin

St Vedast alias Foster

St Mary Abchurch

St Swithin Cannon Street

St Martin Ludgate

St Bride

St James Garlickhithe

St Mary-le-Bow

30 m
100 ft

Wren's City churches. Plans

centrally on the entrance front. The ceilings were commonly coved, with penetrations from the windows. A more complex variant of this type has a single aisle, often on the same side as the tower (St
53 Margaret Lothbury, St Clement Eastcheap). The main space in such churches represents the former nave and other aisle combined. The walls invariably have ranges of pilasters, turning to columns in the aisle, where a gallery was accommodated (St Margaret Pattens, St Benet). St Lawrence Jewry is also of this type, as is St Vedast,
42 where the church patched up by the parish had to be rebuilt again in 1695–1701.

The remaining churches fall into two categories, longitudinal and central, with many transitions between them. The longitudinal is the most usual plan, with nave and aisles in the Gothic tradition. Columns replace piers, and groined vaults or tunnel-vaults of plaster the open roofs and load-bearing vaults of English Gothic, with king-post trusses concealed above. In part this represents the further development of the type seen at St Katharine Cree, stripped of residual Gothicisms. It is indeed striking that the parochial rebuildings at St Michael Cornhill, St Sepulchre and St Dunstan-in-the-East (†) all adopted simple Tuscan or Doric arcades. Many of Wren's churches represent a similar perpetuation of the medieval plan type
49 (St Augustine †, St Mary Aldermanbury †, St Peter upon Cornhill). The Gothic churches of St Alban (†) and St Mary Aldermary belong in the same category. In other cases he worked without the constraint of reusing so much old fabric, and a tighter, more regular design was the usual result. The earliest, St Bride, Fleet Street, has five bays and a clerestory: features associated with the basilica described by Vitruvius. Later churches adopted the formula Wren first used at St James Piccadilly, Westminster, in which the aisles are of two storeys and the columns rise from square piers that also support the galleries (St Andrew Holborn, St Andrew-by-the-Wardrobe). Naves were usually barrel-vaulted (St Peter upon Cornhill, St George Botolph Lane †), occasionally groin-vaulted (Christ Church †). For the aisles groin-vaults were more common, though transverse barrel-vaults were sometimes preferred (St Peter upon Cornhill), and flat ceilings not unknown (St Dionis Backchurch †).

Centrally planned City churches are far fewer, being confined strictly to five examples. Two of these had domes spanning a square space contrived within a rectangular plan. At St Mary Abchurch the dome is a hemisphere springing from low down the walls. St Swithin (†) had an octagonal domical vault. The other three follow the venerable type of the inscribed cross or cross-in-square. The type goes back to the Early Christian centuries (e.g. Tarrasa in Catalonia, C6), appears in Italy in the C9 (S. Satiro, Milan), became popular in Milan and Venice with the Renaissance (S. Giovanni Crisostomo, Venice), and then went to Holland. It appeared in London first at the Broadway Chapel in Westminster, built 1635–42, and was imitated at St Matthias Poplar not long afterwards. Wren may have taken the pattern from these buildings or from knowledge of its recent Dutch exemplars, notably the Nieuwe Kerk at Haarlem. His versions have a square vaulted centre on four free-standing columns, four equal cross-arms, and lower vaulted or flat bays in the four cor-
48 ners. At St Martin Ludgate (1677–86) the detail is exactly as at

Haarlem: groin-vaulted centre, tunnel-vaulted arms, flat-ceilinged corner bays. At St Anne and St Agnes (1677–87) the corner bays have saucer-domes. St Mary-at-Hill (1670–4) had a central lantern, since rebuilt. But from the European point of view the most characteristic problem of church design in the C17 is neither the longitudinal nor the central plan, but the combination of the two. In Italy and France, and later in Germany, the symbol of this typically Baroque tendency is the oval. Wren in his most interesting plans is a European in this sense. He does not often make use of the oval, but combinations of longitudinal with central elements fascinated him as much as they did Bernini or Le Vau or Balthasar Neumann. Examples can again be divided into two groups: central plans elongated, and longitudinal plans centralized.

First central plans elongated. St Mildred Bread Street (†) was a plain parallelogram and had a saucer-dome above the centre and short barrel-vaulted bays to the E and W. St Antholin (†) had an elongated octagon of columns and an oval dome set within an irregular space that tapered towards the W. St Benet Fink (†) was an elongated decagon with an elongated hexagonal centre on columns and an oval dome with a lantern. Then longitudinal plans centralized. These are usually associated with lesser entrances in the N or S walls of the church, which in most cases appear to have passed out of use at an early date. St James Garlickhithe is of five bays with a coved ceiling. The aisles are narrow, the arcade has giant columns and a straight entablature. But for the wider middle bay the entablature turns to the outer walls, thus forming a central transept rising to the height of the nave ceiling. Similarly at St Mary Aldermanbury (†) the nave had five bays and a barrel-vault, but the middle bay was groined where it was intersected by a barrel-vaulted transept. St Magnus appears to have been similar originally. The type is a descendant, but not a copy, of de Keyser's Westerkerk in Amsterdam. A different line of descent can be traced for St Mary-le-Bow, which has the exceptional feature of three wide bays of different widths and piers with applied half-columns: features the *Parentalia* tells us were derived from the Basilica of Maxentius in Rome.

St Stephen Walbrook, begun in 1672, is the most complex case and one which can be regarded as a trying-out of some elements for St Paul's. It is longitudinal but has a large dome with lantern lighting. The dome is intersected by the nave and chancel axis as well as a transeptal cross-axis. But the dome is much wider than the width of the arms and stands within a square of twelve columns. To gain the bottom circle of the dome eight arches are built up, four over nave, chancel and transept ends, and four at the diagonals. The outer corner bays moreover are treated as at St Mary-at-Hill. But for a full analysis of this truly Baroque conception, pp. 261–2 must be consulted. 47, p. 261

The EXTERIOR ARCHITECTURE of the churches was also highly varied. In most cases the churches were partly hidden by the surrounding houses, or faced narrow alleys where architectural display would have been inappropriate. But even the smallest and plainest churches had at least one show front. At St Lawrence Jewry, St Dionis (†) and St Michael Wood Street (†) the E front was developed into a grand pedimented composition with pilasters or half-columns. The exposed E end of St Matthew Friday Street (†) was

given a row of five identical round-headed windows. The E end of
St Olave Jewry (†) had a big Venetian window. At St Peter upon
Cornhill it is elaborated into two storeys. In other cases the sides
were developed into symmetrical compositions with even windows
and doorcases at each end (St Andrew Holborn, St Bride). St Anne
and St Agnes has the rare feature of a strong central emphasis on
each side, made by the gable over the central window. Round-
headed windows were the most common type, though segment-
43 headed windows were also used (St Martin, St Andrew Holborn).
Larger windows have mullions and transoms, especially those at the
42 E and W (St Stephen, St Vedast). Surrounds ranged from simple
frames to ornate hoods on brackets (St Nicholas Cole Abbey,
St Magnus). Circular windows were used for clerestories or set over
doors. St Michael Queenhithe (†) had a continuous sequence of
them above the round-arched windows of the three main fronts.
Oval windows also appear (St Stephen Walbrook, St Antholin †).
Doorcases are usually fairly plain, rising to pedimented surrounds of
2 rusticated stone (St Antholin †) or columns (St Margaret Lothbury),
46 and at St Mary-le-Bow to an elaborate composition with columns
and cherubs in a niche, taken from Mansart. Other typical features
include quoins and the adornment of the parapet with urns and
pineapples (Christ Church †, St Edmund). Wren appears to have
taken much of his vocabulary from Jones's refacing of Old St Paul's,
particularly from the windows of the nave aisles and clerestory, and
from the simple treatment of the towers.

Brick was used sometimes in default of stone for lesser elevations
(St Mary-le-Bow), sometimes for a whole church (St Clement
Eastcheap, Andrew-by-the-Wardrobe). The brick was often rendered
then or later, and St Andrew-by-the-Wardrobe was so noted by
Hatton in 1708. Only rarely was brick used for effects unobtainable
45 from stone, notably at St Benet Paul's Wharf, attributed to *Hooke*,
which has chequerworked brick, alternating evenly with stone on
the striped quoins. These walls were not of solid brick but of brick
facing to a rubble core, which allowed the economical reuse of the
old stone: a method also used *inter alia* at the College of Arms.

Some of the grandest effects were obtained when the tower was
united with the nave by scrolls or curved screen walls to make a
43 formal composition, as at St Martin and St Edmund; and this brings
us to the TOWERS and SPIRES generally. Jones's St Paul Covent
Garden had only an apologetic belfry, but the City parishes were
proud of their steeples and of the bells they housed, and in the event

Wren's City church towers and spires, drawn by G. Cobb.
Top row: St Clement Eastcheap; St Andrew Holborn;
St Mary Somerset; All Hallows Bread Street; St Mary Aldermary;
St Michael Cornhill
Second row: St Mary Aldermanbury; St Lawrence Jewry; St Benet Fink;
St Mary Magdalen; St Peter upon Cornhill; St Mary Abchurch
Third row: St Augustine Watling Street; St Nicholas Cole Abbey;
St Edmund the King; St Margaret Pattens;
St Antholin Watling Street; St Michael Paternoster Royal
Bottom row: St Stephen Walbrook; St Mary-le-Bow;
St Bride; St Michael Crooked Lane; Christ Church Newgate Street;
St Magnus the Martyr

30 m
100 ft

every new church had a proper tower. They are more varied and unpredictable even than the church plans, and it has been remarked more than once how carefully they were distributed so that similar designs nowhere stood too close together. Just to describe the different types of balustrade used would take a long paragraph. The
p.
25 steeples were certainly the feature most admired by the visitor to London. 'Londra è il paese dei bei campanili', wrote Count Algarotti in 1753. He knew only one steeple in Italy worthy of comparison. Yet it appears that Wren may have come to the idea of a forest of tall steeples only by stages. Of the great steeples only St Mary-le-Bow was conceived and executed in the first wave of church building, up to 1680. St Bride and St Magnus have similarly broad, pilastered towers, which suggests that stone spires were intended for them from the start. At other churches a steeple was erected as an afterthought, and at St Edmund a small cupola of the 1670s was actually removed in the early C18 to make way for the present leaded spire. It may be that Wren did not expect money from the Coal Tax to continue to roll in for so long. Whatever the reason, the business of adding spires to existing towers kept his office busy well into the 1710s, and there is no reason to suppose that the plainer towers would not have been given steeples too if the Coal Tax had not expired in 1717.

The simplest type is therefore the plain square tower with parapet or balustrade (St Clement Eastcheap, St Andrew-by-the-Wardrobe). The next stage was the addition of pinnacles or obelisks at the corners (St Andrew Holborn, St Olave Jewry, also the eight-pinnacled St Mary Somerset). Four of the five Gothic towers, St Alban Wood Street, St Christopher-le-Stocks (†), St Michael Cornhill and St Mary Aldermary, were also of this type. In other cases a modest leaded turret was provided (St Anne and St Agnes, St Mary Aldermanbury †). Jones's W towers at Old St Paul's were doubtless an influential precedent for this type. At St Lawrence, the cupola was elaborated with architectural elements into something more like a true spire. Another more elaborate treatment was to set the lantern on a dome
45 or broad base: at St Benet Paul's Wharf and St Benet Fink (†) the lantern was of lead, at St Mary Magdalen Old Fish Street (†) of stone. Greater height was achieved when a spirelet or leaded obelisk replaced the lantern. St Peter upon Cornhill has a spirelet on a
2 rounded dome, St Mary Abchurch and St Margaret Lothbury an obelisk on a square ogival dome. At St Martin the dome is a bell-shaped octagon. St Augustine Watling Street has a broadly similar profile, but a much more complicated vocabulary of small superimposed stages. Greater height might also be achieved by drawing the cupola upwards into a trumpet shape (St Nicholas Cole Abbey, St Edmund); still greater height by following the Gothic precedent of an elongated octagonal spire (St Margaret Pattens, St Swithin †, St Antholin †).

The largest and most complex spires were generally of stone. Three closely related designs at St Michael Paternoster Royal, St
41 James Garlickhithe and St Stephen Walbrook have recessed two-stage structures with playful detail and small columns. The first has an octagonal core, the others a square one. Each of the others is *sui generis*. St Mary-le-Bow modulates from a circular colonnaded stage through a ring of unique stone arches or bows to a modified becolumned octagon and terminal obelisk. Christ Church made

similar use of columns, but applied them to a square core. St Michael
Crooked Lane (†) had a circular leaded core, garnished with volutes
rather than columns. At St Bride the spire is developed entirely from
one octagonal motif, repeated in four diminishing stages below the
usual obelisk, with much piercing of the lower three. The most
Baroque of all is St Vedast, with its Borrominesque contrast between   42
a first concave-sided stage and a second convex-sided stage of the
spire. St Magnus has a tall octagonal cupola of stone, modelled on
the tower of the Jesuit church at Antwerp.

The one Gothic spire in this category is St Dunstan-in-the-East,   44
where a needle-spire is carried on four steep flying buttresses thrown
up diagonally from the corner pinnacles, much as in the Gothic
steeple of old St Mary-le-Bow and St Nicholas Newcastle. The use
of the GOTHIC STYLE for several of the churches is indeed the most
convincing proof of Wren's belief in variety rather than uniformity.
In a memorandum of 1713 on Westminster Abbey he does admit
that the classical is the 'better style', but he suggests that the Gothic
examples amongst his 'Parochial Churches of London. . . appear not
ungraceful but ornamental'. It is the very opposite of the attitude to
architecture and decoration at the Court of Louis XIV. The boldest
of Wren's other efforts in the Gothic style is the interior of St Mary   49
Aldermary. This is a problematic building in terms of patronage
(it was paid for by a private benefaction) and the survival of pre-Fire
work in the walls and tower, but there can be no doubt that the
delightful fan-vaults and Gothic saucer-domes are by Wren or his
office.

The towers themselves are usually square in plan and straight-
sided. Exceptions are the oblong tower of St Augustine and the tower
of St Olave Jewry, with its battered lower stages. Lower stages have
round-headed or circular windows similar to those that light the
church, but for the bell-stage straight-headed openings are sometimes preferred (St Margaret Pattens, St Augustine). At St Benet
Fink (†) the opening is oval, while St Peter upon Cornhill has
triple openings on each side instead. All Hallows Bread Street (†)
had similar triple openings, but they were a later addition, set above
the bell-chamber and open to the air. Sometimes the bell-stage is
tied to the cornice by a pediment (St Nicholas Cole Abbey, St Benet
Gracechurch †) or by ornamented keystones (St Mary Somerset,
St Martin Ludgate). The three great towers of St Bride, St Mary-le-
Bow and St Magnus in addition have paired pilasters flanking the
bell-stage.

Questions of authorship for the spires are different again from
those of the church proper, especially where the later designs are
concerned. Wren was so busy at St Paul's, Greenwich and Hampton
Court that delegation must have been almost irresistible. The
increasingly Baroque flavour of many of the steeples is not in itself
enough to dismiss them from the canon of Wren's works, for his
towers at Greenwich and on the W end of St Paul's show a similar   38
development. But many of the spires make inventive use of certain
motifs familiar from the later work of *Hawksmoor*, notably masks
instead of cherubs' heads, Baroque volutes, and obelisks of more
classical profile, and it may be that several of the designs are wholly
or partly from his pen. He worked in the office only between 1695
and 1701, but a drawing exists in his hand for the steeple of St

Edmund, built 1706–7. The explanation may be that he continued informally to work for the office, or that drawings were used some years after they were made. The latter may be the likelier explanation, particularly as the office more than once erected on one tower a steeple originally designed for another. There is evidence for this in an album of drawings in the Guildhall collection, datable *c.* 1700, one of which shows the tower of St Michael Paternoster Royal with the steeple eventually built at St James Garlickhithe.* These steeples may be associated with Hawksmoor, as may that at St Stephen Walbrook, the third of the trio of inset stone steeples. He may also have had a hand in the spires of St Vedast and St Augustine and the tower of St Andrew Holborn, with its strange openings and finials. At St Michael Cornhill there is documentary evidence for his involvement, though only for the uppermost stage of 1718–22. The rest of the tower, in a less vigorous Neo-Gothic, was probably by *William Dickinson*, who remained in the City church office; he has also been associated with the completion of the tower of St Mary Aldermary in 1701–4.

3   The only task of rebuilding comparable in scale and duration to the City churches was that of ST PAUL'S, declared complete only in 1711. Not much need be said here about the history and the style of the cathedral. For a more detailed appreciation pp. 159–68 can be turned to. Already when Wren was consulted early in 1666 to give his views on the further repair of Old St Paul's he pleaded for replacing the crossing tower by a dome. The dome was the great Renaissance innovation in church architecture. Wren had seen recent examples in Paris, which he had visited in 1665, and knew engravings of Bramante's projected dome for St Peter's and of the dome designed by Michelangelo for the same church, which was finally completed in 1590. It was Wren's dream to give the skyline of London a dome equal to the finest of Rome and Paris; and when after the Fire

37   he submitted his Great Model to indicate how he wished to see St Paul's rebuilt, it was a centrally planned Greek cross that he proposed, on the lines of the designs for St Peter's, crowned by a dome and with a mighty pedimented giant portico. Details, especially the concave quadrants between the arms of the cross, are of French derivation (Lepautre). However, as it had happened in Rome, so in London: the clergy objected to the central plan, and Wren's next design, the one which received the Royal Warrant in 1675, was indeed of surprisingly traditional design, all aisled, with a long nave, choir and transepts, very much like an English Norman Cathedral such as Ely. Wren altered almost everything in execution (indeed, his ideas had almost certainly changed even before the Warrant was signed), but he did keep to the general plan. The climax of the building is the dome, which, on the example of the C14 octagon at Ely, is given a diameter the size of nave and aisles together. The com-

39   bination of longitudinal and central elements in the domed space is managed with great ingenuity, on lines similar to those worked out a little before for St Stephen Walbrook. The nave and chancel are vaulted with saucer-domes, and the clerestory windows cut into the vaults with penetrations forming three-dimensional arches at the line of intersection, an ingenious and Baroque form. Baroque also are, as

* *See* Paul Jeffery, *Architectural History* 35 (1992).

has already been said, the details of the W towers built in 1705–8,   38
and it is particularly characteristic of Wren's faith in variety that
he contrasted the restlessness of the W towers with the reposeful,
harmonious profile of the dome. The dome of St Paul's is indeed
closer to the High Renaissance of Bramante than to Michelangelo's
more elongated and dynamic shape. Yet where Bramante had an
even colonnade all round his drum, Wren uses a rhythm of alter-
nation between groups of columns and blocked bays with niches.

For its full effect St Paul's needs its FURNISHINGS. Wren had at
his disposal masons, stone-carvers, wood-carvers and smiths of outstanding ability, many of whom had honed their skills on the parish
churches before beginning work at the cathedral. Several of the chief
masons were accomplished carvers, including *Edward Pierce, Jasper
Latham* and *William Kempster*. Pierce incidentally also gave us the   40
best likeness of Wren, the bust at the Ashmolean, Oxford. The other
main carvers in stone or wood were *Grinling Gibbons, Jonathan Maine*   52
and *Caius Gabriel Cibber*. The plasterwork was by *Henry Doogood*
and *Chrysostom Wilkins*, and the magnificent ironwork by *Tijou*.   51

In the PARISH CHURCHES there is plenty of work of the same
quality, though of course not quite on the same scale. The Coal Tax
paid for the furnishings at only two parishes, St Andrew-by-the-
Wardrobe and St Mary Somerset. Elsewhere they were the responsibility of the parishes. In a few cases they are older than the churches
housing them, having been ordered for the temporary 'tabernacles'
that did duty for many parishes waiting for their new church. When
the new church was handed over, vestries often commissioned furnishings modelled on those in other churches which they had seen
and admired. Churches which had survived the Fire frequently procured similar fittings. The results have a remarkable consistency of
style and quality. Their importance greatly transcends the capital,
for they influenced at first or second hand the whole Restoration
church. The best complete ensemble was at St Mary-at-Hill, where
the high pews and galleries were supplemented by good work of
1848–9. Badly damaged by fire in 1988, it awaits restoration in 1996.
Much of the woodwork in other churches was lost in the Second
World War, although it has been augmented by pieces saved from
churches demolished in the C19 and before.

The greatest ornament is reserved for the REREDOSES. All have
panels with the Decalogue, Creed and Lord's Prayer, usually framed
by columns or pilasters and surmounted by a pediment or pediments and urns in various combinations and proportions. They are
often larger that Wren anticipated, sometimes so much so that they
block the E window. Evidence from St Mary-at-Hill and St Magnus
(a two-storey reredos) suggests that they may have been enlarged
and extended into the C18 in some cases. At churches with projecting chancels, such as St James Garlickhithe and St Margaret Pattens,
the reredos tends to be more modest. Besides the architectural
elements there is usually rich carving of foliage, garlands and cherubs'
heads. Only at St Mary Abchurch can the carving be attributed to   54
Gibbons, who is associated by an indestructible popular myth with
any good late C17 wood-carving in England, but who worked for
Court, Government and Nobility far more than for the City. *Wren*
himself designed a new reredos for the Temple Church (1682–3),
which nicely illustrates how congregations in older churches tried to

keep up with the new fashions. Sculpture was occasionally incorporated: St Michael Paternoster Royal preserves two excellent
sculpted stone figures of Moses and Aaron, from the former All
Hallows the Great, while fine Baroque angels of gilt wood perch on
the reredos of St Magnus.

Against the reredos stood the COMMUNION TABLE, the legs or
supports of which were sometimes elaborated: as standing angels at
60 St Benet Paul's Wharf, with cherubs at St Clement Eastcheap,
perching doves at St James Garlickhithe. St Stephen Walbrook has
an elliptical table, following the outline of the COMMUNION RAILS.
At St Stephen these have balusters of the usual spiral form, with
foliage carving on the posts and rail. Variant baluster types include
the open double-helix (St Margaret Lothbury), shafts tapering from
a central ring (St Edmund), and miniature Doric piers (St Peter upon
Cornhill). At St Olave Hart Street the base rests on little carved
lions. In the early C18 wrought iron was preferred: at St Andrew
Undershaft (by *Tijou*, 1704), St Magnus and St Sepulchre. St
Edmund, St Martin and St Mary Abchurch also have C17 or early
C18 railed enclosures around their fonts.

PULPITS are all of one hexagonal type with fielded panels on each
face, but are given variety through the different shapes employed
(square, oval, round-headed) and through different patterns of
carved foliage and cherubs' heads. That at All Hallows Barking has
pedimented sides. Where the stairs survive, the balustrade generally
matches the communion rails (St Clement, St Edmund). The great
testers or sounding-boards survive less well, but there are excellent
55 examples with standing cherubs and other adornments at St Clement,
St Margaret Lothbury and St Stephen Walbrook. At St Mary
Abchurch the pulpit retains both its tester and its lofty original staircase, for pulpits of this period originally comprised only the highest
part of a 'three-decker' ensemble. St Paul's has a lectern of 1720, in
the traditional form of an eagle of brass. DOORCASES are often very
fine indeed. The series at St Martin and St Mary Abchurch are
amongst the best. All the churches were wainscotted, though this
was plain by comparison.

58   FONTS were an opportunity for the masons to display their skills,
and the names of their makers are often recorded. The usual pattern
is an octagonal shaft and bowl ornamented with foliage and cherubs'
heads. That at St Margaret Lothbury has four reliefs of Biblical
scenes on the bowl. St Paul's has, in the N transept, a gigantic elliptical
font of grey marble, designed by *John James* and made in 1726–7.
FONT COVERS were made to match, although these are not always
displayed. The usual type has a low decorated base and an ogee top.
At St Stephen Walbrook and St Edmund the base is unusually tall
and the top is adorned with little figures. St Mary Abchurch has a
four-sided top with figures that is raised and lowered on a spiral
shaft. St Nicholas Cole Abbey, St Clement Eastcheap and St Peter
upon Cornhill have covers with eight open ribs, the latter two enclosing a carved dove. The cover at All Hallows Barking has an extra-
57 ordinary wooden sculpture of cherubs, flowers and ears of wheat. It
is attributed to *Gibbons*. Also in the Gibbons style, though not
original to the City, is the excellent carving of King David at St
Botolph Aldgate.

In exceptional cases a SCREEN was provided, airy examples of

which remain at St Peter and St Margaret Lothbury. Such a promi- 53
nent feature was too 'High' for most parishes, although the nominal
boundary of the chancel was sometimes marked by little carved
figures of the lion and unicorn on the pew ends (St Anne and St
Agnes, St Mary Abchurch). The lion and unicorn also appear on the 54
ROYAL ARMS, of which most churches possess a set. Those at St
Benet Paul's Wharf and St Margaret Pattens are amongst the finest. 59
Sometimes they were modelled in plaster, although none of these
remains. SEATS were mostly cut down and reordered in the C19, but
some high pews remain at St Mary Abchurch, and several churches
keep the tall churchwardens' pews at the far W. At St Margaret
Pattens they have canopies. GALLERIES remain at St Benet Paul's
Wharf and St Margaret Pattens, with WEST GALLERIES at many
more churches. Many of the latter supported organs, which in the 56
late C17 were mostly supplied by *Renatus Harris* or *Bernard Smith*
('*Father Smith*'). Though the instruments have generally been much
rebuilt, the remaining cases abound in fine wood carving. Those at
St Katharine Cree, St Mary Woolnoth and St Peter upon Cornhill
are by *Smith*, those at St Andrew Undershaft, St Clement and St
Sepulchre by *Harris*.

A peculiarity of the City churches is the SWORD REST, which was
used by the Lord Mayor on his state visits. The earliest example, of
wood, is at St Helen (1665), and St Mary Aldermary and the Vintners'
Hall preserve wooden examples dated 1682 and 1705 respectively.
But the usual material was wrought iron, used either in attachments
to a single shaft (pole type) or as an upright symmetrical frame (frame
type). The earliest dated example is at St Magnus (1708), though 61
there are references from at least 1680. The design did not much
alter throughout the C18, from which particularly good sequences
may be seen at All Hallows Barking and St Olave Hart Street.
Another use of metalwork was for the delightfully varied weathervanes of the steeples: a key for St Peter upon Cornhill, a gridiron for
St Lawrence, a dragon of copper for St Mary-le-Bow, and so on.
Other church metalwork includes railings, of which there are good
early C18 examples at St Dunstan-in-the-East and the churchyard of
St Peter Cheap, off Cheapside. The greatest sequence, of cast iron,
surrounds St Paul's.

PAINTING was used sparingly in most churches, though there is
evidence that painted curtains etc. were once common at the E end.
Figures of Moses and Aaron were sometimes incorporated in the
reredos, of which examples remain *in situ* at St Stephen Walbrook and
St Magnus, *ex situ* at St Anne and St Agnes, St Margaret Lothbury
and St Michael Cornhill. The most spectacular decoration is at
St Mary Abchurch, where *William Snow* painted the dome in *c.* 1708
with seated Virtues and a heavenly choir. The greatest scheme of the
early C18 was however the decoration in *grisaille* of the dome of
St Paul's by *Thornhill*, 1716–20. STAINED GLASS was not unknown,
but the only large window, in St Andrew Undershaft, was destroyed
by a terrorist bomb in 1992. It had five upright figures of monarchs,
of *c.* 1690–1700. A good deal of heraldic glass was lost from the
churches in the Second World War, though an *ex situ* panel remains
at St Magnus. There is also a panel of *c.* 1664 showing Henry VIII at
St Bartholomew's Hospital, and minor C17 heraldic glass at several
of the Livery Halls.

CHURCH MONUMENTS of the later C17 and early C18 survive in large numbers, though many perished in the Blitz. Large compositions are rare, however. The reason is not hard to see. The wealthy preferred to be regarded as belonging to their country (or suburban) estates, where they were often Lords of the Manor. So they wanted to be buried away from London. Hence the great wealth of sumptuous monuments in the home counties. Whole types of monument of great importance from the national point of view cannot be seen in the City, notably that with life-size figures in contemporary costume standing in niches, common from the last decades of the C17. There is however the Martin monument in St Paul's crypt (†1680). It has two kneeling figures against a columned reredos. There is only one each of the standing effigy type (Sir Andrew Riccard †1672, St Olave Hart Street) and the semi-reclining effigy type (Sir John Hiccocks †1726, Temple churchyard), neither in good condition.

Wall monuments of relatively modest dimensions make up the remainder. There are busts at St Olave Hart Street (Mrs Pepys †1669, by *Bushnell*, and one other), St Sepulchre (Edward Arris †1676 and wife), and St Stephen Walbrook (Sir Percival Gilbourne †1694). The Tillotson monument (†1694) at St Lawrence Jewry, attributed to *Gibbons*, has a portrait relief and attendant cherubs; *Francis Bird*'s monument in St Paul's crypt to Jane Wren (†1702) a disappointing relief of St Cecilia. The pedimented and columned tablet remained popular, though black and white marble fell out of fashion. The columns sometimes took spiral form (Sherwood monument †1690–1703, St Mary Abchurch). At the Pyne monument (†1677) at St Peter ad Vincula they are fashioned as cannon barrels. Larger tablets were adorned with urns and with cherubs, cherubs' heads and drapery (Rachel Chambrelan †1687, St Helen; Thomas Davall †1700, St Mary-at-Hill). Other architectural forms include the standing column (All Hallows Barking, †1696 and †1699 or later) and the obelisk (Cottle monument, St Benet, probably early C18). The most enjoyable are often of the cartouche type, which dispense with architectural forms in favour of shields, scrolls and drapery, with cherubs' heads and skulls the usual ornament. All Hallows London Wall (†1684) and St Bartholomew-the-Great (†1685 and 1704 and later) have good examples. The type remained popular well into the C18: *see* the Gale monument, St Peter upon Cornhill (†1739 and †1741). Signed or documented pieces are uncommon, but include works by *Thomas Cartwright Sen.* (St Andrew Undershaft), *William Kidwell* (St Mary-at-Hill), *John Settle* and *Thomas Stayner* (all at St Dunstan-in-the-West), and *William Stanton* (St Andrew Holborn and Temple Church). Many of these artists also worked as master masons.

The greatest concentration of SCULPTURE was at St Paul's, notably *Francis Bird*'s sequence of reliefs and skyline statuary made in 1706–23. The reliefs on the transepts were by *Gibbons* and *Caius Gabriel Cibber*, the latter also responsible for the relief on the base of the Monument. The greatest free-standing monument was *Bird*'s Queen Anne immediately in front of St Paul's, surrounded by four allegorical figures (1709–12, replaced by a C19 replica). The first statue in the City raised as a public monument was the equestrian figure of Charles II, erected in 1675 in the Stocks Market, but removed in the C18 for the Mansion House. Statues of monarchs were also a feature of the Royal Exchange, where they were set in

niches above the arcades, as at the C16 building. *John Bushnell*'s
swaggering figures of Charles I and Charles II (1671) survive at the
Central Criminal Court. Also kept there is a contemporary figure of
Sir Thomas Gresham, designed by *Bushnell* but carved by *Edward
Pierce*. *Pierce* also carved the fine bust of Thomas Evans at Painter-
Stainers' Hall (1688) and the figure of Sir William Walworth at 70
Fishmongers' Hall, *c.* 1685. Trinity House has a lead sculpture of
Capt. Maples by *Jasper Latham*, 1683. *Quellin*'s statue of Sir John
Cutler at Grocers' Hall, also of 1683, was destroyed in the fire there
in 1965. Less markedly Baroque is *Nicholas Young*'s bust of Gideon
de Laune at Apothecaries' Hall, 1671. *John Young Jun.*'s triumphal
pediment from the former Grand Storehouse at the Tower, carved
in 1691, also warrants mention.

THE CITY FROM 1700 TO 1840

The City remained overwhelmingly residential well into the C19,
although its proportion of the burgeoning population of London
continued to decline. Bankers and barristers no less than shopkeepers
were happy to live above their places of work into late Georgian
times. But the relationship of the City with the rest of London
steadily changed, notably as the fashionable West End became ever
larger and more populous. The very topography of the City was
baffling to outsiders, accustomed to the street grids and squares of
most of the rest of London. A foreign visitor in 1815 found the City
still a place of 'little, narrow, crooked streets, forming a labyrinth,
out of which it is not easy to extricate yourself when you have once
entered it'. By that time the City was regarded more than ever as a
distinctive enclave with its own traditions, its own social networks
and Whiggish or radical politics, and its own preoccupations with
commerce and finance. Even the hours of rising and dining were
different.

These peculiarities tempered the effect on the City of the main
stylistic changes in C18 and early C19 architecture. There was no
court or aristocracy to direct the course of taste, and many of the
City's leading figures maintained a robust independence from such
fashions. Hogarth's *Marriage à la Mode* (1744) plays satirically with
the contrast between the nobleman's pretentious Palladian mansion
and the City merchant's cross-windowed counting-house. The high
Palladian style of Campbell, Burlington and Kent indeed made little
headway in the City, though the softer Rococo fashion which succeeded it is slightly more in evidence. The City was not averse to
richness and grandeur, but did not always fully understand the styles
it adopted. The eclectic interiors of *George Dance the Elder*'s Mansion
House (1739–52), of which more below, demonstrate this uncer-
tainty in abundance.

After about 1760 the story is more complicated. New streets were
laid out, and new bridges built. Above all, in 1768 the City appointed
George Dance the Younger as its Clerk of Works, in succession to his
father. The elder Dance, appointed in 1735, had transformed what
was a largely administrative post into something like that of official

architect to the City. He was the son of the mason Giles Dance, and
had himself begun his career in that trade: a story typical of the emerging architectural profession in the C18. The choice of the younger
Dance to follow his father was in practice anything but a vote for
continuity, however. The young architect had learnt his art during
six years in Italy, where he had befriended Piranesi, and must have
mingled with the Rome scholars of the Paris Academy. On his return,
he restored the City to the forefront of English architecture with a
succession of extraordinarily innovative Neoclassical public buildings. He also showed great powers of invention in town planning,
which was pursued by the Corporation with some vigour from the
1760s.

Of the younger Dance's contemporaries the most important were
Sir Robert Taylor, Surveyor to the Bank of England 1765–88, and his
successor *Sir John Soane*, 1788–1833, although neither had as large a
City practice. Left to themselves, City institutions (Livery Companies
especially) often preferred architects, such as the *Jupp* dynasty, who
had risen from the building world nearest to hand. Consequently
many celebrated names in C18 British architecture never designed a
building in the City proper. Absences include Burlington and Kent,
as already indicated, and from later generations Chambers, 'Athenian'
Stuart, Wyatt and Nash.

The years after 1815 saw an acceleration of public works and
street improvements, in the City no less than in the West End. The
dominant figure of this period was *Sir Robert Smirke*. He received the
lion's share of the great public commissions, many of them awarded
by the Government rather than the Corporation. The period also
saw the further development of specialized premises for commerce
and trade, so that by 1840 the City contained a bewildering richness
of building types, new alongside old.

RELIGIOUS ARCHITECTURE was still a matter of active endeavour for the City's crowded congregations. Work continued into the
1710s on the spires of the churches and on St Paul's, as we have seen.
50 New buildings start with the synagogue in Bevis Marks (1699–1701),
plain outside in the manner of a large Nonconformist chapel, but of
great dignity and beauty inside and in its fittings. The other surviving religious buildings of the period are all rebuildings of parish
churches that had escaped the Great Fire, or were inadequately
repaired after it. The little Holy Trinity Minories, built in 1706 by an
unknown architect and destroyed in 1940, belonged to the same
tradition of vernacular City classicism as the synagogue. Next in
78 sequence was *Hawksmoor*'s St Mary Woolnoth, 1716–27, the only
church in the City paid for under the Fifty Churches Act of 1711,
after the rules were bent to allow rebuilding of existing structures.
Even amongst Hawksmoor's churches, the ingenuity of its centralizing plan and the dramatic and capricious exterior are outstanding.
This was far too personal a style to find ready imitators. The next
rebuildings, of St Botolph Bishopsgate (1725–8, by *James Gould*)
81 and St Botolph Aldgate (1741–4, by *George Dance the Elder*), reverted
instead to the Wren tradition as carried on in Westminster in the
1710s and 1720s by James Gibbs, the most influential church architect of the early C18. They are of brick with quoins and stone spires
or steeples. In plan St Botolph Bishopsgate is a simple barrel-vaulted
basilica, while the flanks of St Botolph Aldgate show traces of an

imperfectly developed cross-axis. St Katharine Coleman, of 1739–40 by *James Horne* (demolished), was also Gibbsian in detail, though very impoverished.

Dance the Younger's first building was All Hallows London Wall 79 (1765–7). In its exquisite and exceptionally thoughtful interior the twin Neoclassical concerns with antique sources and logical simplification are harmonized. Its vault, apse and lunettes served the builder-architect *Nathaniel Wright* as the model for his reconstruction of St Botolph Aldersgate in 1789–91, though with the addition of aisles. *William Hillyer*'s earlier rebuilding of the nave of St Alphage (1775–7) was a more conservative pedimented box, the medieval tower being retained. The next rebuildings were *Jesse Gibson*'s St Peter-le-Poer (1788–92, dem. 1874), one of a sprinkling of circular classical churches in late C18 England, and *S. P. Cockerell*'s St Martin Outwich (1796–8, dem. 1908), with a markedly French front of grooved stone. None of these churches had much in the way of a steeple.

Gothic arrived with *Dance the Younger*'s rebuilding of the octagonal vaulted nave of St Bartholomew-the-Less in 1789–91. This was a very stark affair, made more archaeologically correct in *Thomas* 95 *Hardwick*'s rebuilding in the 1820s. Archaeological ambition also marked *David Laing*'s rebuilding of the nave of St Dunstan-in-the-East in 1817–21, which had an aisled plaster-vaulted interior, the details reasonably correct Perp; only the shell survives, however. The last flourish of the centralized plan was *John Shaw Sen.*'s St Dunstan-in-the-West (1830–3), an inventive design with an octago- 94, nal nave with iron-framed roof and an octagonal lantern steeple. p. This was the final instance in which a medieval City church was 215 replaced by a new building, though short-lived new churches were provided in three poor districts: NW of Bishopsgate (All Saints Skinner Street, by *Michael Meredith*, 1828–30, Gothic); N of Fleet Street (Holy Trinity Gough Square, by *John Shaw Jun.*, 1837, Neo-Norman); and W of Moorfields (St Bartholomew Moor Lane, a classical church by *C. R. Cockerell*, 1849–50). There was also the Neo-Norman St Thomas in the Liberty of the Rolls, by *C. Davy* and *J. Johnson*, 1842 (dem. 1886), on the site of Bream's Buildings.

The most numerous buildings remaining from the C18 are the ordinary HOUSES of the citizens. The final development of the greater post-Fire house may be seen in the City at the grand red brick mansion of *c.* 1700 in Chiswell Street, known as the Whitbread Partners' House, and at the pair of 1703 at Nos. 1 and 2 Laurence Pountney 73 Hill. The doorcase and cornice of the latter are virtuoso displays of carving, without peer in the City. But Acts of 1707 and 1709, aimed at reducing the risk of fire, banned timber cornices and required *inter alia* that window-frames be recessed into the brickwork. The Acts were not strictly enforced, so the flush sash-box can be found well into the C18; but the use of elaborate carved woodwork declined thereafter except for the doorcase. In exceptional cases this might be of carved stone, as at No. 57 Mansell Street, 1725. Here a Doric 74 broken-pedimented doorcase embraces the window immediately above, forming part of an all-over composition that represents a late flourish of vernacular Baroque in London. A more common early C18 doorcase type, with pilasters and a frieze with an upswept centre, may be seen at No. 42 Crutched Friars, of about the same date. That at No. 4 Philpot Lane has a segmental pediment instead. Other fashions of the early C18 were the use of narrow half-bays at one end or both ends of the façade (Nos. 69–70 Long Lane; No. 5 Charterhouse Square) and the decoration of the ends of the house by giant pilasters of rubbed brick (Nos. 14–15 Took's Court, *c.* 1720). The houses in Took's Court have segment-headed windows, another early C18 motif also seen at No. 4 Essex Court in the Temple and at Nos. 3–5 Wardrobe Place. The latter form part of a good contemporary row in a quiet and intensely atmospheric setting. Nos. 24 and 25 Widegate Street have tiled attics with the long windows known as weaver's windows, associated with the silk trade in nearby Spitalfields. Slightly later, perhaps of *c.* 1730, are Nos. 27 and 28 Queen Street, a stately pair with pedimented Ionic doorcases reached up steep flights of steps. No. 4 College Hill, of about the same date, has a good moulded brick cornice. Its conservative features include the use of red brick and (if it is original) the pedimented carved doorcase: more evidence, perhaps, of a delay in transmission of West End fashions to the City.

The grandest remaining mid-C18 houses are Nos. 12 and 13 Devonshire Square, built probably in the 1740s. The Ionic columns of their doorcases are set against rusticated stonework. They are unusual amongst City houses in having front areas, as was the norm in the new developments of the West End and elsewhere. The reason is that in the City most houses necessarily reused old plots and frontage lines, whereas newly laid-out streets were able to exploit the system of 'made ground' in which the roadway was raised up by earth excavated from the house sites proper.

Houses of the later C18 are generally of less interest, rarity value apart. A late example of the type of mansion set back from the street may be seen in White Lion Court, N of Cornhill, said to be of 1767. *Robert Adam* and his brothers were responsible for a modest speculative development of merchants' houses in Frederick's Place in the 1770s: a side-show by comparison with their great Adelphi scheme in the West End, and one which in the end was completed by the builder-architect *Samuel Dowbiggin*. Several of the houses have pedimented doorcases with columns or pilasters. The smaller Nos. 5–7 New Street, probably of the 1780s, have doorcases of similar type. Lesser houses survive in number in the alleys off the S side of Cornhill, where fires in 1748 and 1765 did much damage. To counter such conflagrations, a new Building Act in 1774 further restricted the use of exposed timberwork. This encouraged the recession of the doorcase within the door void, as at the late C18 Nos. 43–46 Chiswell Street. The doorway of No. 22 Charterhouse Square, by *J. W. Long* (1786–8), has *Coade* stone dressings of the type familiar from Bedford Square.

One striking feature of houses on the City's high streets was their great height in relation to their width, which remained that of the narrow medieval plots. No. 33 Fleet Street and the very tall No. 48 Cornhill are the best surviving examples, both of two bays and five storeys. Tall houses were encouraged by the 1774 Act, which abandoned the provisions introduced in 1667 relating the maximum permitted height to street width.

The chief interest of the INTERIORS is usually the staircase, which became increasingly refined and elaborate as the C18 progressed. At

No. 1 Laurence Pountney Hill the staircase has an open string, the square newel is dispensed with, the spiral balusters are slimmer than the late C17 norm, and the rail sweeps up at its upper end. The next development was the use of a column for the newel, as in the reconstructed staircase of *c.* 1730 at the Police Station in Old Jewry. It exhibits fluted balusters alongside the familiar spiral pattern, and makes early use of mahogany. The ends of the treads are enriched. Good, broad staircases of similar type remain at Nos. 12 and 13 Devonshire Square, also arranged around an open well. Lesser houses had staircases of a more economical dog-leg plan, as at No. 4 College Hill. Iron balustrades are unknown or have not survived, though the Whitbread Partners' House in Chiswell Street has a staircase of *c.* 1756 with a Chinese Chippendale balustrade. Stairhalls are generally panelled at least to dado level, and often to full height. Panelling remained in favour for other rooms well into the mid C18, of which Nos. 12 and 13 Devonshire Square have a good ensemble.

While destruction without record of so many greater houses and interiors in the City makes comparisons with the West End difficult, it does seem that the City was less fashion-conscious in its houses than the West End. This may explain the absence of the iron-balustraded stone staircases popular for greater houses there from the second quarter of the C18. Nor is there much rich mid-C18 plasterwork in City houses, the only notable example to survive being the Rococo work of *c.* 1740 at No. 2 Suffolk Lane, a substantial post-Fire merchant's house. The Rococo manner also appears in the fireplace of the reception room added to the Whitbread Partners' House in Chiswell Street. A few other house interiors preserve good mid-C18 doorcases, notably No. 21 College Hill and No. 9 Idol Lane, the latter of *c.* 1770. No. 4 Frederick's Place deserves mention for *Dowbiggin*'s oval staircase and for the survival of alterations by *Soane* of 1806–9.

An account of the INSTITUTIONAL BUILDINGS of the C18 may begin with the LIVERY HALLS. The most imposing example from the first half of the C18 was *Thomas Holden*'s Gibbsian Ironmongers' Hall in Fenchurch Street (1748–50, demolished *c.* 1917). A traditional courtyard plan was perpetuated behind its rich pedimented front. Interiors remain from the reigns of the first two Georges at Skinners' Hall (by *Dance the Elder*, 1737) and at Stationers' Hall (a strongly Rococo room by *William Robinson*, 1757). The livery halls also demonstrate the revolution in interior decoration associated with the Adams better than any surviving private house. Best preserved is the tiny and entirely charming Watermen's Hall, an early work by *William Blackburn* (1778–80), with its oval-ceilinged Court 84 Room. The front, of stone, introduces quirky iconographical peculiarities, a feature also seen at the front range of Skinners' Hall, by 83 *William Jupp Sen.*, 1778–9. This is much grander, being five bays wide with an applied portico. An applied portico was also used at Drapers' Hall, largely rebuilt by *John Gorham* in 1773–8, with markedly Adamesque interiors. It was demolished in the C19. *Samuel Wyatt*'s Trinity House (1793–6), which accommodates similar functions to a livery hall, is more original in the plan and elevation, as p. one would expect from the architect; the fine interiors are post-war 372 reconstructions. *Robert Mylne*'s refacing of Stationers' Hall in 1800–1, 85 also of Portland stone, is sparer and flatter. All of the above elevations, where they survive, make use of *Coade* stone for ornament, that at Skinners' Hall and Trinity House modelled by *John Bacon the Elder*.

The largest complex of philanthropic buildings in the City is at St Bartholomew's Hospital. The rebuilding of ancient hospitals and the founding of new ones was indeed the most important charitable enterprise in C18 London. The gatehouse, by *Edward Strong Jun.*, 71 1702, is a markedly Baroque performance, with angle pilasters and sculpture by *Bird*. Just within lies the hospital's great quadrangle, 75, designed without fee by *Gibbs* in 1728–30. Three blocks remain of 76 the original four, refaced in the C19 but originally of Bath stone, its first use in London. It is also the most significant example in the City of the Palladian revival of the early C18. The style first appeared in the City at *Colen Campbell*'s astylar Rolls House off Chancery Lane (1717–24, demolished), part of the legal quarter between the City and West End. In general, however, this learned and sophisticated plainness seems at first not to have been much appreciated by the City's worthies. Of other City hospitals and almshouses all that remains is the gatehouse block of the Bridewell Hospital in New Bridge Street, by *James Lewis* (1802–8), with a straightforward applied Tuscan portico.

PUBLIC BUILDINGS were opportunities for the Corporation to display its wealth and prestige. The greatest surviving building of the C18 City straddles the division between public and private architec- p. ture: it is the MANSION HOUSE, by *Dance the Elder*, erected in 317 1739–52, after a competition, as the official residence of the Lord Mayor. At the same time it served as his court house and as the centre of polite City society. In style it is typical of the way the City tempered aristocratic fashions from the West End with its own prefer- ence for the sound and solid. The manner is Palladian, rather heavily handled, especially in the awkward original skyline with its two giant attics. The unique plan, since slightly altered, provided a triumphal sequence of rooms and spaces intended for frequent entertainment. It led from within the portico through vestibules and an open court at *piano nobile* level to the great Egyptian Hall behind, derived from Vitruvius via Lord Burlington. The interiors combine Palladian 77 architectural forms, extravagant Rococo ornament, and such curi- ously old-fashioned features as the timber instead of stone open- well staircases.

The other centre of the City's government was the GUILDHALL, the subject of much attention by *Dance the Younger* in the later C18. All that remains is the porch or frontispiece which he added in 1788–9 (*see* fig., p. 300). Its contempt for orthodox proportions and eclectic admixture of Indian and Gothic motifs illustrates Dance's healthy appetite for novelty. In iconographic terms it seems to refer to the City's antiquity and to the sources of its trading wealth. Dance had earlier given the Guildhall a new Common Council Chamber (1777–8, destroyed 1908), an audacious exploration of the potential of pendentives to create the type of top-lit interior later taken up by Soane.

Altogether the most remarkable of Dance's buildings for the Corporation was NEWGATE GAOL (1769–78), the most consistent and terrifying display of rusticated stone in English architecture. In this is was highly characteristic of the preoccupation with an expressive *architecture parlante* which Dance shared with his friend Piranesi, his pupil Sir John Soane, and the leading French Neoclassicists. The architecture was more sophisticated than the plan, which was of the courtyard type superseded in the early C19 by more elaborate radial layouts that allowed greater surveillance and segregation. The gaol and its adjacent and contemporary Sessions House survived, nonetheless, until 1902. Dance's less well-known Compter or prison in Giltspur Street, 1787–91, lasted only until 1855.

Other public buildings owed their existence to trade and commerce. The new Custom House, by *Thomas Ripley* (1718–25, burnt 1814), a Government commission, was a pedestrian reprise of Wren's design. The Excise Office in Old Broad Street, by *William Robinson* of the Board of Customs (1769–75, dem. 1854), was a Palladian exercise rather in the manner of Chambers, though of a lower order of inspiration. The Corporation was responsible for a number of markets and exchanges, all utilitarian in character. The Stocks Market, displaced by the Mansion House, was rehoused further w in buildings by *Dance the Elder* (1737) in Farringdon Street, made by covering over the Fleet. He also built the Corn Exchange in Mark Lane (1747–50). It was joined in 1770 by the first Coal Exchange, by an unknown architect, in Lower Thames Street nearby. All were demolished in the C19.

Great COMMERCIAL BUILDINGS were often more demonstrative. They begin with the semi-public premises of the great trading companies, a building type with no equivalent in the West End. South Sea House in Threadneedle Street was a heavy, rather plain block by *James Gould*, 1724–5 (demolished 1902). Its counterpart was the East India Company's offices in Leadenhall Street, built 1726–9 by *Theodore Jacobsen*, and rebuilt in 1796–9 by *Henry Holland* and *Richard Jupp*. In this latter form it was one of the great monuments of the City, as befitted the place from which British India was administered, with a grandiose hexastyle Ionic portico adorned and surmounted by sculpture by the elder and younger *Bacon*.

The BANK OF ENGLAND belongs in the same corporate, semi-public category as the trading company headquarters. Its first purpose-built premises went up in 1732–4. Jacobsen had competed unsuccessfully for their design, the commission going instead to *George Sampson*. Its situation in Threadneedle Street further consolidated the financial centre of the City, which depended on face-to-face contact and easy circulation within the relatively small area centred on the Royal Exchange. Sampson's confident Palladian design had a pedimented front block with an Ionic order on a rusticated basement, with two enclosed courts behind. Such splendid display advertised how essential to the nation the deficit finance managed by the Bank had become since its foundation in 1694. The oldest work to survive at the present Bank is the reconstructed Court Room and Committee Room of 1767–8 by *Sir Robert Taylor*. Taylor began his 82 career as a sculptor, in which capacity he carved the pediment figures at the Mansion House, but soon showed that architecture was his true *métier*. His twin colonnaded wings, grand top-lit banking halls and rotunda at the Bank lasted only until the early C19, when they were rebuilt by *Sir John Soane*. Soane's remodelling of the Bank had begun in 1788 and was not completed until 1827. Of his work there remains externally most of the great grooved screen wall, demarcated by his favourite Tivoli order of Corinthian columns. Inside, some paraphrases of his ingeniously vaulted banking halls were made in the inter-war rebuilding, from one of which a more accurate version of the Bank Stock Office was made for the Bank Museum in 1986–8. More details of the present and past premises may be found in the gazetteer entry.

PRIVATE BANKS did not emulate the Bank of England's formula of enclosed, top-lit banking halls. Instead, they operated from ordinary houses, with a side entrance into the front room or 'shop', used as the banking hall, and a rear parlour used for private interviews. In this respect they were no different from ordinary merchants' houses, such as the surviving No. 11 Ironmonger Lane (1768), where the front room was intended as a counting-house from the start. Purpose-built banks with living accommodation above appear sporadically from the mid C18. The two chief examples, both demolished, were *Taylor*'s Asgill's Bank (1757) and *Dance the Younger*'s Martin's Bank (1793–5), both in Lombard Street. Each had a stone-faced ground floor with round-arched windows, the former with an applied Doric order. *Soane* used an all-round-arched stone front at his Praed's Bank, No. 189 Fleet Street (1801, largely demolished). The earliest survivor is *Charles Parker*'s Hoare's Bank, 1829–30, Fleet Street, an exceptionally restrained seven-bay composition of Bath stone. Though considerably larger, it shared with its predecessors the ground-floor division into two rooms (the 'shop' exceptionally well-preserved) and the devotion of the upper floors to private living accommodation.

Insurance companies were next to aspire to grand premises, though at first not averse to taking them over ready-made. The Royal Exchange Assurance occupied offices within that building as early as 1720. The Sun Fire operated from *Taylor*'s Bank Buildings, a set of grand houses erected in front of the Bank of England in 1764–6 (demolished). The first company to build ambitious headquarters for itself appears to have been the Amicable Assurance in Serjeant's Inn (1793, destroyed 1941), to designs in the idiom of Chambers by *Ezekiel Delight*.

Other examples of COMMERCIAL ARCHITECTURE owed much to the great increase in purely financial business that followed the French invasion of the Netherlands in 1794 and the subsequent flight of capital from Amsterdam. The foundations were thus laid of London's pre-eminence as the financial centre of Europe as well as its most prosperous trading port. The best-known is the Stock Exchange (1801–2, dem.), built by *James Peacock* in Capel Court, off Bartholomew Lane. Stock had previously been traded in a coffee-house in Threadneedle Street, and at the Bank itself. The Exchange had a sophisticated frontage with a curved Doric porch below a big lunette. Inside was a galleried trading room. *John Walters*' Auction Mart, where property sales were held, was built in 1808–9 just N of the Stock Exchange, with an oddly-proportioned Palladian front to Bartholomew Lane (dem. 1865). The Sale Rooms in Mincing Lane, a Grecian structure by *Joseph Woods*, 1811–12, were for the auction of cargoes such as tea and India rubber. The future of City finance increasingly lay with such specialized Exchanges rather than with the all-purpose Royal Exchange or with the old coffee houses.

WAREHOUSES also grew larger and more ambitious as the C18 progressed. Around 1700 London overtook Amsterdam as the chief

European port for *entrepôt* (re-exported) trade. Since international trade was restricted to the 'Legal Quays' of the City, demand for warehouse space was intense, extending even to areas some way from the foreshore. It was increased by the institution in 1793 of the bonded warehouse system, under which duty needed to be paid only when stock was released: a further encouragement to *entrepôt* trade. Demand diminished only with the abolition of the City quays' monopoly on international trade in the 1800s, leading to the establishment of new enclosed docks downstream. The greatest surviving warehouses in the City were built for the East India Company off Cutler Street between 1769 and *c.* 1820, though much of the complex was demolished in the late 1970s. There remains *Richard Jupp*'s Old Bengal Warehouse (1769–71), markedly formal, though above the stone-dressed ground floor all of sober unadorned brick. Of later ranges, those of the later 1790s were designed by *Henry Holland*, 90 although he merely carried on in Jupp's manner. Similar groups of tall, secure brick warehouses were built in the later C18 off Crutched Friars and Seething Lane. Lesser C18 warehouses are represented by the plain S range at Apothecaries' Hall (1780–6, designed by *Richard Norris*); the partly residential W wing, of the same build, makes an effort at the conventions of polite architecture. Of other early industrial buildings the only survivors of note are at Whitbread's brewery in Chiswell Street, notably the great Porter Tun Room (1774): a reminder that brewing was amongst the first London industries to go over to large-scale, highly capitalized production. More typical of small-scale trade are the house and crane-shed of *c.* 1800 at No. 20 St Swithin's Lane, used by wine merchants after 1805.

The 1760s are notable as the beginning of what might be called the City's AGE OF IMPROVEMENT. Early stirrings of civic feeling had given the City the power to charge a rate for street lighting in 1736, extended in 1766 to cleaning and paving, in emulation of the Westminster Paving Act (1762). In the 1760s also projecting street signs were replaced by consecutive house numbers. A related concern to ease circulation inspired a number of improvements to the street plan in the 1760s. These really began with the overhaul of old London Bridge in 1758–62. *Dance the Elder* and *Sir Robert Taylor* removed the houses and rebuilt several of the spans. The approach was also widened, with a pedestrian passage made through the tower of St Magnus. Then in 1760–9 *Robert Mylne*'s noble Blackfriars Bridge was erected, and the remaining part of the Fleet Ditch, S of Fleet Street, was covered over to form the approach road, New Bridge Street. Thus London acquired a third river crossing, situated between London Bridge and the new Westminster Bridge of 1738–49.

The next obstacle to fall was the City wall, which was still maintained in the early C18 (the medieval Bishopsgate was indeed rebuilt as late as 1733–4). All but one of the gates in the wall were torn down in 1760–1; the last, Newgate, in 1776–7. With the gates gone the wall itself was no longer useful, and large sections were demolished in the later C18. Where standing remains survive, it is generally because they were incorporated into other structures built up against them.

Part of the land thus released in the E was used for *Dance the Younger*'s residential development for Sir Benjamin Hammett off the Minories, 1768–74. The main parts were called Circus (now almost erased), Crescent and America Square, and the devices of a crescent and a circus appeared here for the first time in London, albeit on a diminutive scale. The source is probably the slightly earlier work of the elder and younger John Wood at Bath. The fronts of some houses in Crescent remain, supplemented by replicas. They have Doric doorcases with innovative details, but are otherwise unremarkable. The other houses have gone, and the ensemble can no longer be appreciated as such. The line of the wall was breached in several places elsewhere, either by short new streets or by the extension of existing ones (a process that continued into the C20); but nowhere else was the opportunity for innovative replanning seized.

Dance's other great planning enterprise involved Moorfields, the last great area of open land left in the City and its immediate fringes, laid out as a public garden as far back as 1605–13. Finsbury Square, N of the City, was built up on this land in 1778–91, the streets immediately s planned *c.* 1793, and Finsbury Circus planned in 1802. The last, on an oval rather than a circular plan, was laid out as late as 1815, by Dance's successor *William Mountague*. The two main enclosures were ambitiously treated. The houses on the w side of Finsbury Square, given by Sir John Summerson to *James Peacock*, were organized into an elaborate symmetrical pilastered composition with emphasis on the ends in the Neoclassical manner. The rest were plainer, as were the houses of Finsbury Circus. The latter were of four storeys, with round-headed windows on the first two floors. The end houses of each quadrant were set slightly forward. Such consistency and grandeur in ordinary houses were rare in the City, with its mosaic of leases and landowners, and it is sad to record that all the houses of square and circus have been destroyed. There remain only the converted carcases of some early C19 houses in South Place, w of Eldon Street. Other schemes planned by Dance which have entirely vanished include Skinner Street, built 1802–3 but overbuilt by Holborn Viaduct later in the C19, and (probably) Jewin Crescent, 1805, on part of the site of the Barbican Estate. His schemes for the Bridge House Committee, being on the South Bank, lie outside the scope of this book.

The second great period of IMPROVEMENTS began towards the end of the Napoleonic Wars. It depended not on the exploitation of open land but rather on the cutting of new streets through the existing fabric. The first improvements concerned bridges. The City acquired a third river crossing with the construction of the elder *Rennie*'s Southwark Bridge (1814–19), which exploited the existing alignment of King Street and Queen Street. Then in 1823–31 London Bridge itself was rebuilt slightly upstream, also to Rennie's designs, with an elevated approach carried on a viaduct across the line of Upper and Lower Thames Street. The new alignment was continued by the new King William Street (1829–35), which cut N and NW to the crossing by the Mansion House. In the later 1830s the route was continued N of Prince's Street, itself straightened in 1798–1805, up to the site of the old Moorgate, to form the s part of the present street of that name. These grand gestures recall the improvements carried out by John Nash in the West End, and Nash's stucco architecture served as the model for *Sir Robert Smirke*'s façades along the new streets. A few of these remain on the w side of Moorgate.

The decades from 1810 to 1840 were also distinguished for ambi-

tious PUBLIC BUILDINGS, in the City no less than in the West End.
The prevailing styles were the sober Greek Revival associated with
Sir Robert Smirke and William Wilkins, and a richer manner which
carried on from late C18 Neoclassicism, associated with John Nash.
First in chronological sequence is the Custom House, built by *David
Laing* in 1812–17 but reconstructed after structural failure by *Smirke*,
1825–8, in a more Grecian manner. Its grand elliptical-roofed Long
Room is testimony to Smirke's audacious exploitation of cast-iron 91
construction. The architect's paramount effort in the Grecian manner
in the City was the General Post Office in St Martin's le Grand, but
this was demolished in 1912. Smirke was also much occupied at the
Inner Temple, where he worked in both Gothic and astylar classical
idioms. Much of this work was destroyed in the Second World War,
but several of his houses and blocks of chambers survive in King's
Bench Walk. A Grecian building at once grander and more refined
than Smirke's Temple buildings is the Law Society in Chancery
Lane, of 1829 and later, by Smirke's pupil *Lewis Vulliamy*. The new 92
Corn Exchange in Mark Lane, of 1827–8 by *A. B. Clayton* and *George
Smith*, was in much less pure Grecian manner, with a skyline similar
to Soane's adventures with the style at the Bank. The earliest Neo-
Gothic secular building to survive in the City is the crude gatehouse
of Clifford's Inn of the early 1830s, attributed to *Decimus Burton*; but
on the whole the City has very little to show for the pervasive neo-
medievalism of the time.

George Smith was also busy at several EDUCATIONAL BUILDINGS,
of which one survives: the former Mercers' School in College Hill, a
little stuccoed palazzo built in 1829–32. His chief work was the very
large St Paul's School, twenty-one bays long, built immediately E of
the Cathedral in 1823–4 (dem.). The private libraries and institutes
which flourished in Britain at about this time were represented by
William Brooks's London Institution (1815–19, dem.), the portico of
which formed the central accent of the N side of Finsbury Square.
John Shaw Sen.'s Great Hall at Christ's Hospital (1825–9, dem.) was
the largest Neo-Gothic building yet seen in the City, and *J. B.
Bunning*'s City of London School off Milk Street (1835–7, dem.)
was also Gothic. Typical of the much smaller Ward or parish schools
of the period is the St Bride and Bridewell Schools in Bride Lane,
1840, a neat little building like a Nonconformist chapel.

The CITY LIVERY COMPANIES joined in the general enthusiasm
for civic grandeur, of which their Halls now constitute the best-
preserved survivors. The brick-fronted Armourers' and Braziers'
Hall and stuccoed Dyers' Hall (both 1839–41) are modest but satisfying buildings, respectively by *J. H. Good* and *Charles Dyer*. The
Fishmongers' Hall (1831–5), the masterpiece of *Henry Roberts*, 96,
demonstrates the pervading influence of his master Smirke in its use p.
of concrete and cast iron and its refined Grecian elevations, tempered 386
within by a rich eclecticism. Its counterpart is *Philip Hardwick*'s
Goldsmiths' Hall (1829–35), in a richer classical manner. Both are of 97,
Portland stone on plinths of granite, a material previously confined p.
in London to kerbstones and quays, but which began to be applied 390
to more architecturally ambitious forms at about this time. The
Fishmongers' staircase hall also has columns of polished granite rather
than the usual scagliola. Both the Goldsmiths' and Fishmongers'
staircases start in one flight and break into two, which return in two

flights to a landing over the foot of the stair. This favourite type of the early C19 is also found at *Hardwick*'s City of London Club in Old Broad Street (1833–4), the only remaining counterpart in the City to the great clubs of the West End. *Hardwick* was also busy at St Bartholomew's Hospital, designing several simple, refined buildings in the 1840s.

The surviving monuments of EARLY C19 RELIGIOUS ARCHITECTURE have already been described. Some mention is also needed here of the grand non-Anglican buildings put up at this time, none of which remains. The best examples were all built as part of the Moorfields development. *William Jay*'s Albion Chapel in Moorfields (1815–16) and *William Brooks*'s Unitarian Chapel in South Place (1824) were assertive pedimented classical structures. Both were surpassed by *John Newman*'s Roman Catholic church of St Mary Moorfields (1817–20) nearby, also Grecian, but still more ambitious in scale. Parts of the spectacularly lit interior survive in its late Victorian successor in Eldon Street.

The ordinary STREET ARCHITECTURE of the City during the period was more than ever built with commercial as well as residential uses in mind, at least on the main streets. The great exception was Dance's Moorfields development, mentioned above, which shows that there was a continuing demand for substantial, entirely residential houses amongst the City's élite. By contrast, *Soane*'s Bank Buildings in Prince's Street, 1801–10 (dem.), a speculative development of five houses undertaken for the Bank of England, were arranged internally to suit commercial uses on the ground floor, with living accommodation above. Their elevations had incised pilasters and weird Grecian doorcases, organized into a palatial composition: an extreme example of the dissatisfaction with the self-effacing fronts of most C18 houses that overtook house-builders in the early C19. The tendency can be observed even in quite minor houses: for example, the front of Nos. 4–5 Middle Street, *c.* 1820, is divided by a recessed round-headed panel. The full range of such novelties is best studied in the line engravings of Tallis's *Street Views* (1838–40 and 1847), where they appear slotted in between the older houses. The survivors were often built as pubs. The former Sugar Loaf, No. 65 Cannon Street, *c.* 1825, has Grecian stone aedicules against the usual stock brick. The Magpie in New Street has the tripartite windows popular *c.* 1830. The Hand and Shears in Middle Street (1830) has segment-headed reveals to the windows. It shares with the Rising Sun in Carter Lane (*c.* 1840) the motif of Ionic columns. Professional architects sometimes turned a penny on such jobs: the Lord Raglan at No. 61 St Martin's le Grand preserves part of *L. N. Cottingham*'s refronting of 1830.

The best SHOPFRONT of the period in the City is the symmetrical Grecian composition applied to No. 43 Eastcheap some time in the 1830s. Good, representative late C18 shopfronts may be seen at No. 9 Laurence Pountney Lane, No. 145 Fleet Street and in the Temple at No. 4 Middle Temple Lane. There were once hundreds more: a guidebook of 1803 described two main shopping 'routes', one traversing the City via Leadenhall Street, Cornhill, Cheapside, St Paul's Churchyard, Ludgate and Fleet Street; the other, intersecting, running from Bishopsgate and Threadneedle Street to Cheapside, then along Newgate Street, Snow Hill and Holborn. The fashionable covered shopping arcades of the West End were, however, not taken up in the City. The nearest equivalent was perhaps the short, symmetrically composed shopping street called St Bride's Avenue, laid out by *J. B. Papworth* on the s side of Fleet Street in 1825–30 and now entirely demolished.

So far little has been said of SCULPTURE. The middle part of the C18 is scanty, with nothing to compare with the great tableaux of Westminster Abbey. The architectural sculpture by *Sir Robert Taylor* for the Mansion House has already been mentioned; his other work included the figure in the Bank of England pediment of the 'Old Lady of Threadneedle Street' (preserved at the present Bank). But the leading contemporary sculptors were of Continental origin. From Antwerp in 1720 came *Michael Rysbrack*, who left a fine relief of Pegasus at the Inner Temple (1737–9), and minor Palladian monuments at St Margaret Pattens (1740) and St Michael Paternoster Royal (†1750, with bust). *Louis François Roubiliac* arrived from Lyons in 1732. The City has a small monument of his at St Botolph Aldersgate (†1750, with portrait relief), the lively standing lead sculpture of Sir John Cass (1751), at the Sir John Cass School, and a bust of Shakespeare at the Barbican Centre (1760). Two earlier arrivals from Antwerp (*c.* 1717), *Laurent Delvaux* and *Peter Scheemakers*, are represented respectively by standing figures of George I at the Public Record Office, and of Capt. Sandes at Trinity House, a lead figure of 1746. The most talented English-born sculptor of this period was *Sir Henry Cheere*, who carved the figure of William III at the Bank of England (1734), and a grand fireplace at Goldsmiths' Hall (1735). The architect-designed church monuments that are such a feature of the C18 elsewhere are as far as is known not represented, though architectural compositions of obelisks, sarcophagi etc. were increasingly popular. The anonymous monument to Sir Richard Hoare (†1754) at St Dunstan-in-the-West is the largest example.

The later C18 and early C19 are much richer, due to the sequences of multiple figure groups at Guildhall and St Paul's. At Guildhall they begin with *J. F. Moore*'s disappointing Alderman Beckford (1770–2, the central figure modelled on an earlier version at Ironmongers' Hall), and continue with the elder *Bacon*'s Pitt the elder (1782, the highlight of the sequence), *James Smith*'s Nelson (1806–10) and *Bubb*'s Pitt the younger (1806–13).

By then production of patriotic MONUMENTS FOR ST PAUL'S was in full swing, and these constitute by far the greatest repository of sculpture of the period in England: nineteen multiple figure groups; over a dozen lesser monuments set high up, carved in varying degrees of relief; and the beginnings of a regiment of standing statues which proliferated into the mid C19. The enterprise of populating the cathedral began with the statues of four national benefactors, placed on pedestals against the piers of the dome: John Howard, the prison reformer, and Dr Johnson, both 1791–5 by the elder *Bacon*; Sir   88 William Jones, the oriental scholar, 1799 by the same; and Reynolds by *Flaxman*, 1803–13. The busiest decades were from the 1800s to the 1820s. It is characteristic that in the case of *Banks* one must go to the Abbey for works before 1800, to St Paul's for later works. There   86 too are some of the best works of *Flaxman* and *Rossi*, and (from a younger generation) of *Sir Richard Westmacott*, *Chantrey* and the   87,89 younger *Bacon*. They are mingled with works by such lesser artists as

Hopper, Kendrick and *Charles* and *Samuel Manning*. Their most significant innovation in iconography is the shift from Roman to modern dress. The influence of the Parthenon frieze is detectable here and there, most strikingly in several reliefs by *Chantrey. Banks* carved in addition two circular reliefs for the Bank of England, *c.* 1799, where is preserved also a superlative overmantel by *Westmacott, c.* 1790.

The one notable name missing from this roll is that of *Nollekens*, whose portrait busts may however be seen at St Margaret Lothbury (Anne Simpson, 1795), at the Bank of England, and at several of the Livery Halls. Of other portrait busts in churches, that of Milton at St Giles Cripplegate (1793), by the elder *Bacon*, is notable. Bacon also carved monuments at St Edmund the King (1786) and St Katharine Cree (1794), with allegorical female figures in relief. Fishmongers' Hall has an example of his collaborations with the *Coade* works, an allegorical group in the round (1791). Continental sculpture of the early C19 includes major pieces by *Thorvaldsen* and *Rudolph Schadow* at Drapers' Hall, though neither was commissioned for the building.

PAINTING, that is wall and ceiling painting, is not nearly so well represented. At St Andrew Undershaft there survives part of a scriptural scheme by *Robert Brown*, probably of 1725–6. Painted altarpieces of scriptural subjects were occasionally introduced to churches: at old St Mary Magdalen, *c.* 1720, also by *Brown*, now at St Martin Ludgate; at St James Garlickhithe, by *Andrew Geddes*, 1815. The E end of All Hallows London Wall was designed to accommodate a painting by *Nathaniel Dance-Holland*, after Pietro da Cortona. The most important secular scheme is by Thornhill's son-in-law, *William Hogarth*: the two great canvases at St Bartholomew's Hospital (1735–7), where they line the staircase up to the Great Hall. Few other secular institutions had anything comparable, although the late C18 easel paintings by *Benjamin West* at Stationers' Hall and *Gainsborough Dupont* at Trinity House are large enough to dominate the spaces in which they hang. Trinity House also had a painted ceiling by *J. F. Rigaud*, an unusual feature for the late C18, a plausible replica of which was made in the post-war restoration.

A variation on painted altarpieces for churches was STAINED GLASS. One outstanding window, a night-piece of the Agony in the Garden (1788), remains at St Botolph Aldersgate. Its artist *James Pearson* is represented also by a heraldic panel at Middle Temple Hall, one of several places where the tradition of armorial glass was kept up. The Law Society preserves a good sequence from the old Serjeants' Inn in Chancery Lane. St Andrew-by-the-Wardrobe has a window of *c.* 1712–16 by *Joshua Price*, introduced in the post-war restoration.

CHURCH FURNISHINGS of the C18 and early C19 are naturally much less numerous than those of the late C17. New churches such as St Mary Woolnoth and the three St Botolphs retain most of their original fittings. Highlights include the magnificent baldacchino and bulging pulpit at St Mary Woolnoth and the fanciful pulpit at St Botolph Aldersgate, which is supported on a dwarf palm tree. Many churches acquired organs only in the C18 or early C19, and most of the great organ-builders are represented: the *Jordans* (St Magnus the Martyr, 1712), *Thomas Griffin* (St Helen, 1742–4, St Margaret Pattens, 1749), *John Byfield* (St Botolph Aldgate, 1744),

G. P. England (St Stephen Walbrook, 1765), *Samuel Green* (St Botolph Aldersgate, 1791). Though the instruments often do not survive, the superb cases almost always do. Exceptional individual fittings include the finest of all the carved pelicans that adorn the City churches, carved as late as 1775 by *Joseph Glazeley* for St Michael Cornhill, and 80 *Robert Mylne*'s superb circular pulpit for St Paul's of 1803, long in store.

THE VICTORIAN CITY FROM 1840 TO 1900

Depopulation and Modernization

The Victorian era saw the City transformed, from a residential area with specialist commercial and financial functions, to a financial and commercial enclave with a dwindling residue of inhabitants. The population in 1841 was 123,000, a modest decline from 128,000 in 1801. Thereafter the decline was rapid: 107,000 in 1861, 51,000 in 1881, 27,000 in 1901. The population of London (LCC area) meanwhile grew from 959,000 in 1801 to 4,425,000 in 1901.

The depopulation was brought about by several complementary processes. Firstly, the City was less and less a smart place to live. In 1845 an observer wrote that its middle classes all 'move either towards the west, or emigrate to the suburbs – the one for fashion, the other for economy and fresh air'. Secondly, from the 1840s large areas were levelled for railways and new roads: a process at its peak in the 1860s–70s, which was also when the population fell most rapidly. The railways and roads in turn made it easier to live outside the City but travel in for work. The population was sped on its way by the ever-rising value of land and rents. The architect Edward I'Anson remarked in 1872 that the wealthy citizen might support a suburban villa or West End mansion merely from the rent of the drawing-room floor of his ancestral City home.

The transformation was especially marked in the financial centre, where hundreds of small firms sought space as near as possible to the Royal Exchange and Bank of England. The advent of the electric telegraph in the 1840s encouraged an enormous turnover in bills, stocks and shares, most of which were nonetheless still traded face to face. Old houses were rebuilt in large numbers, their sites commonly combined to form bigger and bigger commercial buildings (it has been calculated that four-fifths of City buildings standing in 1855 were rebuilt by 1901). The City the Victorians made supported a much greater density of workers than it ever had of residents. Already in the 1850s an estimated 200,000 workers walked in to the City every day. The great crossing by the Bank was for long the busiest in Britain, while in 1897 even the lesser junction of Cheapside and Newgate Street was passed by an average of twenty-three vehicles a minute during working hours. By this time the City was the undisputed financial capital of the world.

As the population declined, many buildings lost their *raison d'être* and were demolished. The most conspicuous casualties were the parish churches. Earlier losses were due to specific improvements: St Christopher-le-Stocks in 1782–4, for the Bank of England; St

Michael Crooked Lane in 1831, for the London Bridge approaches; St Bartholomew Exchange and St Benet Fink in 1840–4 for the new Royal Exchange. Under the Union of Benefices Act (1860), however, the Church was empowered to demolish redundant churches and sell the sites to finance church extension in the suburbs. From the late 1860s the demolition of City churches became routine, many of Wren's masterpieces being amongst them. Those in the financial centre were especially vulnerable. Protests saved individual churches (St Stephen Walbrook was threatened more than once, incredible to relate), but could not halt the process. Their site values calibrate the demand for City land as the Victorian economy boomed: an estimated average of £2,000 in 1833; £24,000 for St Benet Gracechurch in 1868; £47,000 for St Dionis Backchurch in 1878. Here and there the tower alone was kept: at St Mary Somerset (dem. 1869) and All Hallows Staining (dem. 1870) as landmarks, at St Olave Jewry (dem. 1892) as part of a rectory. Only after c. 1905 did the process slacken, by which time twenty churches had gone. It is incidentally to these demolitions that we owe the fittings in many remaining churches, some transferred on demolition, others brought back in restoration after the Second World War.

Less well-known is the decimation of the Livery Companies, enrolments in many of which declined drastically. Sixteen were wound up between 1833 and the 1880s, and several more Guilds sold their halls. Charitable bodies which abandoned the City for more spacious suburban or country sites included almshouses (e.g. Judd's Almshouses (Skinners' Company) in Great St Helen's, closed c. 1892), and many schools (St Paul's in 1884, Christ's Hospital in 1902). Temple Bar was dismantled in 1878 for road widening, though the stones were re-erected in Hertfordshire. The coming of the railways made obsolete the great galleried coaching inns of the City, all of which had gone by 1911. The fate of Dance's Newgate Gaol and Giltspur Street Compter has already been noted. Contemporary accounts of the Victorian City are full of laments for the loss of such familiar landmarks.

The RAILWAYS were the greatest single manifestation of the new age. First to arrive was the London and Blackwall Railway, whose Fenchurch Street terminus was opened in 1841, on the eastern edge of the City. All was quiet until the convulsions of the 1860s, when all at once several companies sought a terminus in the City proper. On the S side of the City the rush owed much to the deadly rivalry of two companies, the South Eastern and the London, Chatham & Dover, previously accommodated at stations on the South Bank. The London, Chatham & Dover bridged the river to a small terminus at Blackfriars in 1864 (expanded 1883–6), and built a second terminus on Holborn Viaduct, N of Ludgate Hill, in 1874. The South Eastern responded with a bridge to a terminus at Cannon Street, opened 1866. Into the N part of the City came the North London Railway, to a terminus at the top of (Old) Broad Street (1864–5). It was joined in 1873–5 by the Great Eastern Railway, which extended from its Shoreditch station to a new terminus at Liverpool Street alongside. Besides these termini there were large goods depots, the biggest lying alongside Broad Street and between Mansell Street and Minories, the latter reached by a spur from the Fenchurch Street approach.

The buildings of these RAILWAY TERMINI were on the whole

less impressive than those further W, both in their train sheds and main buildings. Nor have the C19 structures lasted well. Only Liverpool Street preserves anything like its original appearance, and even here *Edward Wilson*'s original train shed of 1873–5 was 111 extended in 1985–91. It is transeptal, in the manner pioneered in the 1850s at Paddington, but with Gothic detailing. In 1985–91 also the rather mean Gothic terminus building was demolished or rebuilt in replica, although *Charles & C. E. Barry*'s imposingly Neo-Chambord Great Eastern Hotel (1880–4 and later) survives almost unaltered. At Fenchurch Street *George Berkeley*'s amiably amateurish front of 1853–4 remains, but all behind is C20 rebuilding. Of the others, *W. Baker*'s Broad Street (1866), French Second Empire with a train shed of parallel ridge-and-furrow pattern, was demolished in 1985. The contemporary Cannon Street, by *J. Hawkshaw* and *J. W. Barry*, had a magnificent arched roof between tall turrets (the latter alone surviving), and an Italianate station hotel by *E. M. Barry* (demolished). At Blackfriars and Holborn the train sheds were insignificant, though the latter had a terminus hotel in the French pavilion-roofed fashion by *Lewis Isaacs* (1874–6, demolished).

UNDERGROUND RAILWAYS began to link all the London termini during the 1860s. The first, the Metropolitan Railway, was opened between Paddington and Farringdon in 1863. It was extended S and E into the City in 1865, to Moorgate, and on to Liverpool Street and Aldgate in 1876. Connections with Liverpool Street and the Blackfriars-Holborn Viaduct line allowed through running. Its counterpart on the S side was the Metropolitan District Railway (the present District Line), opened between South Kensington and Westminster Bridge in 1868 and extended in 1870–1 through Blackfriars to the misleadingly named Mansion House station on Queen Victoria Street. In 1884 a further extension via Cannon Street and Tower Hill joined it with the Metropolitan, creating the modern Circle Line.

The second generation of underground lines, which lay much deeper, depended for their construction on various forms of tunnelling shield rather than the more disruptive 'cut and cover' methods of the pioneers. The first of the new type was a short-lived cable-operated route opened between Tower Hill and Bermondsey in 1870. Later lines were electrically operated. The City and South London Railway (the present Northern Line) was opened between Stockwell and King William Street in 1890, then extended via a new alignment to Bank and Moorgate in 1900. At Bank, it connected with the self-contained route from Waterloo, opened in 1898, and with the E–W Central London Railway (Central Line), also opened in 1900, and extended to Liverpool Street in 1912.

There is little to show for the underground lines architecturally, as might be expected. The Metropolitan's parsimonious French terminus in Liverpool Street survives, by *Edward Wilson*, 1876. Aldgate station preserves an arched roof and cutting walls of the same date. The head office of the City and South London at No. 141 Moorgate is a good gabled Free Style building by *T. Phillips Figgis*, 1900. Elsewhere the stations of the deep tube lines were mostly incorporated within speculative office blocks, as at *Delissa Joseph*'s Nos. 31–33 High Holborn, 1900.

The first generation of underground lines was able to exploit the

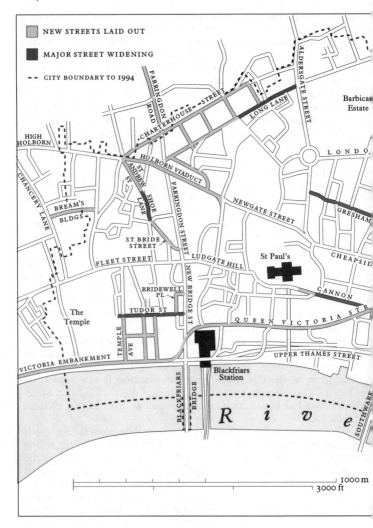

routes of the great STREET IMPROVEMENTS of the mid C19 (*see* map). The Corporation kept up the momentum of the 1820s and 1830s with Gresham Street, made in 1845 by widening and amalgamating lesser lanes, and with the w extension of Cannon Street, laid out in 1847–54 to improve the route between St Paul's Churchyard and King William Street. Then in 1855 the Metropolitan Management Act created the first central authorities with administrative powers throughout London, one of which was the Metropolitan Board of Works. Two powerful bodies were now dedicated to improving the City, and work went on apace.

The MBW was responsible for a great new route that linked the West End with the heart of the City by the Bank. The road entered the City in the shape of the Victoria Embankment, planned in 1860

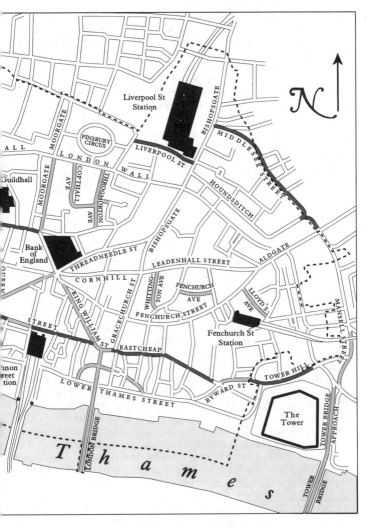

Major street improvements, 1820–1900

and constructed in 1864–70 from the w up to Blackfriars Bridge, which the Corporation obligingly rebuilt. The route continued as Queen Victoria Street (made 1867–71), which ran e and then NE to a junction with Poultry in front of the Mansion House. Beneath the new route lay sewers, water and gas mains, and for much of the way also the Metropolitan District Railway.

The Corporation tackled the route into the City from the NW. From a new junction at Holborn Circus, the great Holborn Viaduct was built eastward, over the Fleet valley, to the w end of Newgate Street. Its substructure incorporated the usual services, plus vaults for rent. Two lesser routes were built from Holborn Circus. Charterhouse Street runs NE along the N side of the new Smithfield Market (itself planned over a huge basement served by the Metropolitan

Railway). To the SE runs St Andrew Street, the widened Shoe Lane, and St Bride Street, to the new Ludgate Circus made at the crossroads of Fleet Street, Ludgate Hill, New Bridge Street and Farringdon Street. In 1882–4 the E extension of the Metropolitan District Railway prompted the widening and straightening of the Eastcheap-Great Tower Street, with a new street called Byward Street cut through to Trinity Square. Land enclosed by the Victoria Embankment was laid out by the Corporation in the 1880s and 90s as a grid of new streets (Carmelite Street, John Carpenter Street, Tudor Street): the only area of the City planned on this pattern. The 1890s saw parts of Middlesex Street widened to improve circulation around the NE fringe, by Spitalfields Market, while Mansell Street was extended to cope with traffic from the new Tower Bridge: projects overseen by the London County Council, set up in 1888 with powers over all London outside the City.

The Architecture of the Victorian City

The most conspicuous feature of the Victorian age was of course the enormous PROLIFERATION OF ARCHITECTURAL STYLES. Some derived from the Middle Ages or the Renaissance at home and abroad. Others strove to synthesize a new idiom appropriate to the age of steam, iron and commerce. Few City streets cannot show an example of at least one of these trends, or of the multifarious hybrids between them. The *lingua franca* of the 1840s and 50s, now rarely surviving, was still the Italianate manner introduced at Barry's West End clubs *c.* 1830, realized in stone on grand buildings, in stucco or stucco and brick on lesser ones. It was challenged by other historically derived styles: a few instances of the native Jacobean, Gothic and Tudor Gothic from the mid 1830s; a much richer, thicker Venetian Cinquecento with columns in the 1850s, especially for banks; French Renaissance for most building types from about 1860. Other architects developed a fancy mix-and-match eclecticism, for which a variety of English Baroque and French sources were ransacked. The style first appeared in the City at *Tite*'s Royal Exchange (1841–4), for which *see* below. By the 1860s the Italianate style is often hard to separate from the rich admixture of French, Italian and medieval motifs. More frankly medieval was what might be called Ruskinian Gothic, of Italian and especially Venetian character, which appeared in the mid 1850s and reached a peak in the following decade, used for every commercial type from banks to warehouses.

Late Victorian styles begin shortly after 1870 with the Queen Anne manner, a return to small-scale, domestic Old English and Northern Renaissance forms in red brick and terracotta, often combined with white plaster or rendering. Several leitmotifs of the style first appeared at *Norman Shaw*'s New Zealand Chambers in Leadenhall Street (1871–3, destroyed), although its domestic associations made it more popular in the West End. City buildings did however reflect the movement away from bold accents to modest details such as little superimposed pilasters and the like, especially after 1880. Such buildings are often difficult to classify in terms of style, but as a general rule early Renaissance is preferred to medieval, and North European to Italian. More ambitious and rich buildings sometimes followed the innovations of *John Belcher* and *Beresford Pite*'s Institute of

Chartered Accountants, designed 1888 and built 1890–3: dense-textured Neo-Baroque architectural forms, with small-scale sculpture closely integrated. This is one of the few Victorian buildings in the City with interiors worthy of its ornate façades, for grand elevations in the City all too often concealed mere warrens of small offices. In the 1890s also the free forms of the Arts-and-Crafts manner begin to appear alongside the established styles.

Hand in hand with this stylistic profusion went an unprecedented expansion in the range of BUILDING MATERIALS, brought to London first by canal, then by rail. Hard red and blue Midland brick, red sandstone, coloured granite, and every variety of manufactured terracotta and faience appeared in the Victorian streetscape alongside the familiar London stock brick, stucco, and such long-established imports as Portland and Bath stone. More revolutionary than any of these in its effects on architecture was structural ironwork, especially when used as an exposed glazed framework, rather than concealed in foundations or roof in the early C19 manner. The train sheds of the railway termini described above were its greatest manifestation, preceded chronologically by several important public buildings of about 1850 (*see* below). Even in more conventional buildings iron made possible a much higher proportion of window to wall, although the material was rarely exposed except in the form of window frames and slim iron colonnettes. Certainly there was nothing comparable to the exposed-iron-framed office buildings of Glasgow and Liverpool, for which absence fire-insurance regulations seem to have been responsible.

Public Buildings

Public buildings of the Victorian City begin with the ROYAL EXCHANGE of 1841–4, built after a fire destroyed the old Exchange. *Tite*'s new building was innovative in its bare-faced eclecticism, and in its realignment with a great portico facing the crossing by the Mansion House. The plan was more conservative, however (it p. 329 retained a courtyard and bell-tower), and its use of materials was generally unadventurous.

Other public buildings fell to the architects of the Corporation and the Office of Works. The most remarkable by far was the lamented Coal Exchange in Lower Thames Street, by the Corporation's architect *J. B. Bunning* (1847–9, dem. 1962), Italianate externally but all iron and glass within, with a domed hall encircled by richly ornamental galleries. One can still see something like it, on a smaller scale, in the iron-framed Round Room added in 1864–6 to *Pennethorne*'s Public Record Office, the greatest single undertaking by the Office of Works in the Victorian City (1851–96). Stern, mini- 98 mal Gothic elevations conceal its advanced iron-framed fireproof construction externally. Pennethorne was also responsible for the audacious iron-framed library of the Patent Office (1866–7), rebuilt in similar, larger form to designs by *Sir John Taylor* in 1899–1902. Taylor's elevations are poor and parsimonious, a fault shared with the former West Range of the General Post Office in St Martin's le Grand, of 1869–73 by *James Williams* (demolished).

Bunning's successor as City Architect was *Sir Horace Jones*, an able but less innovative personality, most of whose works for the

Corporation remain. They include the three great MARKETS of Smithfield (1866–7), Billingsgate (1874–8) and Leadenhall (1880–1). The former two (both since altered) are low, spacious structures, loosely Franco-Italianate externally, with thermally efficient but visually undramatic roofs of timber and glass on iron supports. Later extensions at Smithfield, of less interest architecturally, extended the complex W up to Farringdon Road. Leadenhall Market, fitted ingeniously into the old street pattern, is more adventurous both stylistically and in its exploitation of cast-iron ornament. Jones's great twelve-sided Council Chamber at Guildhall (1883–4, destroyed 1940) was also iron-framed, but with conventionally Gothic cladding. His library at Guildhall survives, a capacious but uninspired exercise in the English Perpendicular (1870–2).

New or enlarged EXCHANGES were required as trade and commerce expanded. The Stock Exchange, owned by a private consortium, was rebuilt in 1853–4, by *Thomas Allason Jun.*, with a glazed dome and tunnel-vaults framed in timber rather than iron. In 1882–7 *J. J. Cole* added a marble-lined extension with another glazed dome. The external elevations were of less interest, and the whole complex was demolished in the 1960s. Less successful was *Edward Moxhay*'s Hall of Commerce in Threadneedle Street, sophisticated classical premises built in 1842–4 in the false hope of attracting business from the Stock Exchange and the burnt Royal Exchange (demolished). The Royal Exchange did begin to lose business in the later C19, to such new enterprises as *John Gordon*'s Wool Exchange in Basinghall Street (1873–4) and the Metal Exchange in Whittington Avenue (1882), both demolished. There remains the Baltic Exchange in St Mary Axe, of 1900–3 by *T. H. Smith & W. Wimble*, though its future is uncertain after damage by a terrorist bomb in 1992. It had backward-looking classical elevations, with a spacious trading floor lit by glazed domes and half-domes.

The City is surprisingly rich in Victorian EDUCATIONAL and INSTITUTIONAL BUILDINGS. Small-scale mid-Victorian schools remain in the churchyards of St Botolph Bishopsgate (1861) and St Sepulchre (1874–5). *Penrose*'s old St Paul's Choir School in Carter Lane, also 1874–5, displays the Italian *sgraffito* decoration introduced to London at the Victoria and Albert Museum in the 1860s. The former City of London School on Victoria Embankment, by *Davis & Emmanuel* (1880–2), rich French Renaissance, is planned rather like the compact multi-storey Board Schools that proliferated in the rest of London from the early 1870s. Nearby stand *Blomfield*'s Sion College (1880–7), red brick Gothic, and (in John Carpenter Street) *Jones*'s former Guildhall School of Music, 1885–7, in a C17 French manner. The old Birkbeck College in Bream's Buildings, 1883–5 by *Fowler & Hill*, was demolished *c.* 1960. The significant innovation of the early 1890s was the foundation of three institutes for adult education, financed by amalgamated parochial charities. The former Cripplegate Institute in Golden Lane (by *Sidney R. J. Smith* and *F. Hammond*) and the St Bride's Institute off Fleet Street (by *R. C. Murray*) are conventional red brick buildings. The third of the trio is the wholly exceptional Bishopsgate Institute, by *C. Harrison Townsend*, an advanced Art-Nouveau-flavoured terracotta design. The eastern fringe of the City was also served by the Sir John Cass Foundation, with a technical institute in Jewry Street (1898–1901) and a school in

Duke's Place (1908), both by *A. W. Cooksey*, the first Free Style, the latter already Neo-Wren. The one outstanding hospital building is the library and museum block at St Bartholomew's, an extraordinarily pure Italianate palazzo by *I'Anson*, 1877–9.

Several HALLS OF THE LIVERY COMPANIES were rebuilt in Victorian times, notwithstanding the contemporary decline of other Guilds. The best interiors are at *Herbert Williams*'s palatial Drapers' 110 Hall (1866–70), though the street front there was rebuilt in 1898–9 by *T. G. Jackson* and *Charles Reilly Sen.*, to a rather weak red brick design. The *ne plus ultra* of the becolumned High Victorian Venetian manner is *W. W. Pocock*'s Carpenters' Hall (1876–80), though the interiors were a wartime casualty. The Cutlers' Hall, by *T. Tayler Smith* (1886–7), is a mild Neo-Jacobean building. Less wealthy Guilds rebuilt their premises to maximize rental income, with only a small suite for the Livery. The only survivor of this type is *George Aitchison Jun.*'s former Founders' Hall at No. 13 St Swithin's Lane, 1877–8, externally indistinguishable from ordinary offices.

The richest late Victorian buildings in the City, both difficult to classify, are the Institute of Chartered Accountants and Lloyd's Register of Shipping. The Accountants' building, 1888–93 by *John Belcher* and *Beresford Pite*, has already been mentioned for its revolutionary reconfiguration of late Mannerist Italian forms and for its 113 seamless integration of sculpture (by *Thornycroft* and others). *Collcutt*'s Lloyd's Register (1899–1901) achieves a similar fusion of architecture and sculpture (mostly by *Frampton*) inside and out, with unusually rich painted decoration within.

The street improvements initiated by the Metropolitan Board of Works and the LCC did not bring much new public architecture from those bodies in their train. Two former FIRE STATIONS remain, both Tudor Gothic: one for the MBW at Nos. 162–164 Bishopsgate, by *George Vulliamy* (1884–5), the other by the *LCC Architects' Department* at No. 7 Carmelite Street, 1896–7.

The LCC Architects were also busy at the TEMPLE, where they restored the Inner Temple Gateway in 1900–6, under *W. E. Riley*. The rear wing added at that time has the Voyseyish character of the Council's best contemporary work. Most Victorian architecture at the Temple was due to the rebuilding of older chambers. The favourite manner was Tudor of the Gothic or Elizabethan variety, with some classical interludes. The exceptions include *H. R. Abraham*'s Middle Temple Library of 1858–61 and *Sydney Smirke*'s Inner Temple Hall of 1866–70, unabashedly Gothic buildings both destroyed in the Second World War, *E. M. Barry*'s Temple Gardens block (1878–9), fantastically elaborate French Renaissance, and 100 *T. G. Jackson*'s Nos. 2–3 Hare Court (1893–4), a rare instance at the Temple of the Queen Anne manner.

Still greater changes took place at the TOWER, which was refortified against a hungry populace in the 1840s, but treated more as a national monument thereafter. Its medieval parts were restored, first by *Salvin* (1852–69), then with much less understanding by *(Sir) John Taylor* of the Office of Works. Of new buildings the largest is the naïvely Gothic Waterloo Barracks (1845 by Major *L. A. Hall*), the most interesting *Salvin*'s former Engine House of 1863, plain brick Gothic reminiscent of Philip Webb, which stands on Tower Hill nearby.

Commercial Architecture

BANKS come top of any list of commercial building types in terms of prestige, expense and number. Nonetheless, they were remarkably slow to build grand premises for themselves. Until the 1850s they were mostly private concerns, operating from modified houses in the manner already described. Those in the West End tended to serve personal customers, while those in the City facilitated business and trade and acted as agents for country banks. Joint-stock banks were allowed within London in 1833, but did not establish themselves in the City without a struggle. The first was the London and Westminster Bank, which built highly individual premises in Lothbury to a design by *Cockerell* and *Tite*, 1837–9 (demolished). It had an astylar channelled stone façade with statuary on the end piers, and a central entrance to a domed double-height banking hall: all features designed to impress the customer with the newcomer's financial staying power. Then in the 1850s the joint-stock banks were at last admitted to the Bankers' Clearing House, then in Abchurch Lane, where cheques and orders were exchanged. A wave of imposing new buildings followed, of which two remain: the City Bank at No. 5 Threadneedle Street, by Messrs *Moseley* (1855–6), and *George Aitchison Sen.*'s more sober Union Bank at No. 14 Fleet Street, 1856–7. Each is Italianate, with a large-windowed rusticated ground floor and a strong top cornice. Upper floors were typically used partly for rent, partly for a boardroom, and partly for lodgings for the staff.

Surviving banks of the 1860s begin with *E. N. Clifton*'s dignified palazzo for the National Bank at Nos. 13–17 Old Broad Street, 1861. Next comes *Gibson*'s mighty and entirely untypical National
99 Provincial Bank at No. 15 Bishopsgate (1864–5 and later), a single-storey, top-lit building bedecked with giant columns inside and out. A trend characteristic of the 1860s was the elaboration of the palazzo formula to new heights of richness and debasement; the most extreme example was *C. O. Parnell*'s Westminster Bank in Lombard Street (1860–1 and 1875, demolished). Other banks used applied columns in the Cinquecento manner associated with Venice and in particular with Sansovino. *F. W. Porter*'s Union Bank branch, No. 95 Chancery Lane (1865), has them in superimposed screens. The formula remained popular into the late C19, as at *J. Macvicar Anderson*'s Commercial Bank of Scotland, Nos. 60–62 Lombard Street (1889–90). Its columns follow the fashion for polished granite that held sway between *c.* 1860 and *c.* 1900. The Fleet Street branch of the Bank of England, by *Sir Arthur Blomfield* (1886–8), mixes granite columns with square belvedere towers. At *Scott & Cawthorn*'s Hill & Sons Bank at Nos. 64–66 West Smithfield, 1885, the palazzo formula dissolves into late Victorian looseness.

Relatively few banks broke away from Italian Renaissance conventions. *Waterhouse*'s Clydesdale Bank in Lombard Street (1866, demolished) was a forbidding exercise in the architect's early Gothic manner. *William Burnet*'s Imperial Ottoman Bank at No. 26 Throgmorton Street (1871), one of the first generation of foreign banks to set up in the City, is round-arched Quattrocento. *T. Chatfeild Clarke*'s Royal Bank of Scotland (Nos. 3–5 Bishopsgate, 1877), of Bath stone, has a giant order and applied arcade linking banking hall and first floor. *Collcutt*'s City Bank on Ludgate Hill (1890–1) is in his round-arched, striped brick and terracotta manner. The most colourful late Victorian bank has gone: *Knightley*'s Birkbeck Bank in High Holborn (1895–6), a lurid exercise in coloured terracotta with a domed and galleried banking hall. The contemporary Union Bank of Australia at Nos. 71–73 Cornhill (1896), by *Goymour Cuthbert*, is quieter and more sophisticated, the main accent being provided by sculpted caryatids.

The MERCHANT BANKS and PRIVATE BANKS of the City furnish some interesting exceptions to this parade of grandeur. Such famous banks as Barings and Rothschilds emerged gradually from the ranks of trading 'houses' shortly after the turn of the century, and remained dominated by family members. There was therefore no need to dazzle the depositor or shareholder with columns and marble. Barings' headquarters in Bishopsgate, in origin a large mansion set back from the street, was given an unabashedly domestic brick front by *Norman Shaw* in 1881 (demolished *c.* 1973). Some examples remain of lesser merchant banks, notably a very domestic pair by *E. A. Gruning*: Huth's at No. 11 Tokenhouse Yard (1869–71), and Frühling & Goschen's at No. 12 Austin Friars (1881–2). Though little known, the former is a very early example of red brick used with terracotta decoration. By contrast, Hambros' premises at No. 123 Old Broad Street (by *Edward Ellis*, 1864–6) are indistinguishable from ordinary Gothic office chambers of the date.

Private banks are less important, since they declined rapidly once exposed to competition from the joint-stock banks. Sometimes they were bought up and rebuilt by joint-stock banks (No. 19 Fleet Street, the former Gosling's, by *A. C. Blomfield*, 1898–9). Others amalgamated for protection: *H. Cowell Boyes*'s Prescott, Dimsdale, Tugwell & Cave's at No. 50 Cornhill (1891–2) is one example, loosely late C17 domestic in manner. It also has, disused, a very well-preserved banking hall: a feature that has elsewhere survived poorly, if at all. As a rule one is lucky to find much more than the original columns, though *Macvicar Anderson*'s British Linen Bank, Threadneedle Street (1902–3) retains a colourful ceiling of *Burmantofts* terracotta. At several early banks the original hall was remodelled within two generations: that at the former City Bank in Threadneedle Street, for example, is the creation of *T. B. Whinney*, 1909.

INSURANCE OFFICES are more widely distributed throughout the City, with many near the legal quarter in Fleet Street and Chancery Lane as well as in the main financial district. Functionally their requirements resembled those of the banks, namely a large hall for public business with suites of offices above. Externally, however, much greater stylistic latitude was thought appropriate. Examples survive from as early as the 1830s: *Hopper*'s Atlas Assurance in Cheapside (1834–6 and later), still as much late classical as Italianate, and *John Shaw Jun.*'s Law Life Assurance at No. 187 Fleet Street (1834, extended), very early Neo-Jacobean. *Sancton Wood*'s Queen's Assurance in Gresham Street (Nos. 42–44, 1850–2) is an excellent demonstration of the dissolution of the Italianate manner into ornamental display. The close-set shouldered arches of its ground floor appear to derive from *C. R. Cockerell*'s Sun Life Assurance in Bartholomew Lane, built in 1842 and needlessly destroyed in 1970. Other mid-C19 survivors are *Shaw Jun.*'s London & Provincial, 1853–5, and *Bartleet*'s hopelessly uncouth Promoter, 1860, respectively at No. 21 and No. 29 Fleet Street, *J. W. Penfold*'s Neo-Jacobean Law Union at No. 126 Chancery Lane (1857), and *Bellamy*'s urbanely Palladian Law Fire Office, a few doors up at No. 114 (1857–9). The last retains a fine spacious staircase, an unusual feature in a commercial building. *Waterhouse*'s hard red Gothic manner appeared at the Prudential in Holborn in 1879, though the oldest part was rebuilt between the wars in the manner of the larger late C19 extensions. *T. Chatfeild Clarke*'s London & Lancashire Life at Nos. 66–67 Cornhill (1880–1), ornate early French Renaissance, is more typical of the late Victorian preferences for the delicate and pretty. Lost buildings of note are the elder *Belcher*'s Royal Exchange Assurance, Lombard Street (1857), which initiated the Victorian rebuilding of that street, its much showier successor in the same street (1863–6), *Robert Kerr*'s National Provident in Gracechurch Street (1863), an early exercise in the mansarded Louis XIV manner, and *Deane & Woodward*'s Crown Life, New Bridge Street (1858), the first explicitly Ruskinian building in the City, rapidly swept away by the railway to Holborn Viaduct.

One other group of buildings can compare with banks and insurance offices: the DISCOUNT HOUSES, built for the joint-stock companies set up after 1858 to manage short-term credit. The business required centrally located premises with a grand front hall like a bank's. The National Discount at Nos. 33–35 Cornhill, built 1857–8 by the brothers *Francis*, is an early instance of the mixture of French and Cinquecento motifs. It was also one of the few Victorian City buildings for which a competition was held. The elder *Somers Clarke* adopted a wholly unexpected Venetian Gothic manner at his General Credit in Lothbury (No. 7), 1866: perhaps the finest building of its period in the City, at once learned and convincingly of its time. The Union Discount in Cornhill (Nos. 39–41), of 1889–90 by *Macvicar Anderson*, has the architect's conservative superimposed columns and a fine terracotta-ceilinged front hall.

Next comes the ordinary COMMERCIAL ARCHITECTURE of the City, the offices and the warehouses, in all their richness and variety. Their architects are in many cases little-known. Though the number of practising architects increased enormously during the period, tenders in *The Builder* suggest that the lion's share of work (warehouses in particular) went to relatively few offices, including the very prolific *Herbert Ford* and such partnerships as *Tillott & Chamberlain* and *Tress & Innes*. Such firms were themselves based mostly in the City: 177 of some 650 architects listed in the *Post Office London Directory* for 1863 have E.C. addresses, that is in the City and the area immediately N.

The first purpose-built SPECULATIVE OFFICES are said to have been those in Clement's Lane designed *c.* 1823 by *Annesley Voysey* (dem.). Their plan and appearance are obscure; did they use iron uprights and lightweight internal walls for internal flexibility, in the manner of many Victorian office chambers? The oldest survivor of these is *I'Anson*'s No. 22 Finch Lane, 1845–6, the rear part of a great Italianate terrace of offices called Royal Exchange Buildings (1842–4, dem.). It has exceptionally large windows, daylight being a precious resource in such buildings. Many of most interesting offices of the 1850s–70s are those which try to reconcile architectural decorum with this need to admit as much daylight as possible. One way forward was offered by the increased use of structural iron in the outer walls. *Aitchison Sen.*'s Union Bank in Fleet Street (1856–7), otherwise conventionally proportioned, uses it for example to frame the large windows of the banking hall. Office blocks could get away with less decorous façades than banks. *I'Anson*'s Fenchurch Street Chambers, *c.* 1857 (dem.), had huge cross-windows separated by iron colonnettes set against stone piers, but the façade was stylistically nondescript. A more elegant solution was to fashion the windows as a series of superimposed round-headed arcades, a device facilitated by the medieval Italian fashion. The finest remaining example is *Aitchison Jun.*'s Nos. 59–61 Mark Lane, of 1864 for the City of 103 London Real Property Company. Here the iron framing is concealed behind the exquisitely Ruskinian stone front. It also had an iron staircase (since destroyed), although stone staircases were more common as a means of giving consequence to shared interiors. Other instances of this attractive medieval round-arched manner include *Fred Jameson*'s polychromatic No. 103 Cannon Street, 1866, and *I'Anson*'s No. 65 Cornhill, 1870. *Edward Ellis*'s hulking Nos. 19–21 Billiter Street (1865) is much coarser, but of similar ancestry. Pointed arches were also adopted, as at *T. Chatfeild Clarke*'s No. 25 Throgmorton Street, 1869–70, and *Ford & Hesketh*'s Library Chambers in Basinghall Street, 1877–8.

Behind such assured façades there often lay an elaborate arrangement of lightwells and set-backs, contrived to admit light without infringing neighbouring 'ancient lights'. An important innovation in this matter was *I'Anson*'s use of white-glazed brick at the rear of his Royal Exchange Buildings. In many cases more ingenuity was lavished on the lightwells, set-backs and basement bulkheads of Victorian offices than on their elevations. St Michael's Buildings off Cornhill, by *E.A.B. Crockett*, 1873 (demolished), was a typical example. In gloomy closes and side-streets polite architectural formulae were sometimes given up almost completely. Dyers' Buildings off Holborn, 1871–8 by *John Wimble*, is a compellingly grim example.

More common and more long-lived than the explicit medievalism of the 1860s was a rich, debased Italo-French manner with passages of medieval carving. One can observe the progress of this miscegenation in the SE part of Chancery Lane, rebuilt for road widening *c.* 1855–65. No. 125 of 1855–6 and Nos. 119–120 of 1860 are still Italianate, but Nos. 123–124 of 1858–9 and No. 115 of 1863 can only be described in terms of a mixture of stylistic ingredients. The most imposing example of this high eclecticism to survive is Nos. 39–40 Lombard Street, 1866–8 by the brothers *Francis*, for the City Offices 101 Company. It also illustrates the advent of ever-larger office blocks, encouraged by the ready capital that such joint-stock undertakings could muster, and by the City's own consciousness of the value of the land on which it stood. There would have been more such giant blocks had not the business of assembling large properties from separate leases been so slow and costly.

A similar showy eclecticism was much in evidence in the NEW STREETS laid out from the mid 1860s onwards. The land on either side of these streets was parcelled up and sold off by the authorities with a minimum of control over what the new buildings should look like. Even the quadrants of Ludgate Circus, three of which survive, are to wholly different designs. Indeed, the hope was commonly

St Michael's Buildings, off Cornhill. Elevation and plan

expressed that, left to themselves, architects would produce a varied
and dignified ensemble in differing styles and materials, in the manner of historic European cities. The most common style is a sort of
Franco-Italian, derived at first or second hand from the palazzo, but
with such motifs as segment-headed windows, two- or three-light
windows with mullions fashioned as square pilasters, the horizontal
linking of the aedicules, and (frequently) a roofline enlivened by
dormers or a mansard. Sometimes called the 'Holborn Viaduct

manner', it survives best on the N side of Newgate Street. The style
lingered here and there into the 1890s, e.g. at No. 46 St Mary Axe
(1894). Grandest of the new streets architecturally was Queen Victoria
Street. Highlights included *John Walter II*'s premises for *The Times*,
1868–74, the greatest of Victorian newspaper offices in the City
(dem. 1962), and the exceptionally rich group on the N side at the E
end, demolished in 1994 for the new No. 1 Poultry, of which *J. & J.
Belcher*'s Mappin & Webb building was a spectacular French-inflected
Gothic block, reminiscent of William Burges. Notable survivors
include *I'Anson*'s British and Foreign Bible Society at No. 146
(1867–9), Italianate with incised medieval decoration, *F. J. Ward*'s
Albert Buildings at Nos. 39–53 (1871), towering French Gothic, and
Whichcord's National Safe Deposit at No. 1 (1873–5), relatively sober
Italian Renaissance. Besides such wholly new streets, much rebuild-
ing resulted from the widening of older routes, and these too are good
hunting-grounds for later Victorian commercial architecture. Ludgate
Hill and Eastcheap have stretches of the 1880s, Fleet Street of the
1890s, all standing on the S side.

The laissez-faire architecture of the new streets is in marked contrast with certain private developments. At Throgmorton Avenue,
built from 1875 for the Carpenters' and Drapers' Companies under
the supervision of *Charles Reilly Sen.* and *W. W. Pocock*, the buildings
have generally similar classical façades of stone, with strong horizontals and small-scale detail. Lloyd's Avenue, built up after 1899
under the surveillance of *Collcutt* and *B. Emmanuel*, is also composed
of classical stone buildings, though the façades are more varied and
demonstrative. Carlisle Avenue, E of Jewry Street, was built up after
1894 entirely by *Delissa Joseph*, though all buildings have gone.

Joseph was one of several City architects who adopted the late
Victorian fashion for TERRACOTTA, as at his Nos. 18–19 Eldon
Street, *c.* 1893 (since painted). Some earlier uses of terracotta and
faience have already been noted. The fancy, playful red-brick-and-
terracotta manner of Mayfair and Chelsea found little favour in the
City, though *Runtz*'s Nos. 54–55 Cornhill (1893) is a good minor
example of the style. The use of stone was no barrier to prettiness or
elaboration, however: *Aston Webb & Ingress Bell*'s No. 23 Austin
Friars (1888) and Metropolitan Life Assurance at Nos. 13–15 Moorgate
(1890–3) are amongst the most original buildings of the date, the
first free Romanesque, the second late Flamboyant Gothic.

Other offices of the 1890s appropriate motifs from the Free Style
or Art Nouveau associated with such architects as Voysey, Lethaby
and Mackintosh. The style flourished into the 1900s, and indeed
should be regarded as an Edwardian style as much as a late Victorian
one. Lethaby is the presiding influence at *Charles Reilly Sen.*'s No. 28
Austin Friars, 1894, while the very sophisticated No. 133 Fleet
Street, of 1904–6 by an unknown architect, owes something to
Harrison Townsend. Other practitioners were *George Vickery* (e.g.
Nos. 58–59 West Smithfield, 1906) and *Paul Hoffman*, the best of
whose City buildings is Nos. 7–10 Old Bailey, 1908–10. *Voysey* him-
self is represented by restored office interiors at Cable House, New
Broad Street, of 1906–10.

So far little has been said of the WAREHOUSES and INDUSTRIAL
PREMISES of the City. Massive clearances of these were made by
bombing N and S of St Paul's, and by post-war redevelopment along

the river and elsewhere. As a result two important types are now almost extinct: the bonded warehouses of the foreshore, and the monster textile warehouses around Wood Street and St Paul's Churchyard. Nevertheless, enough warehouses remain for the main lines of their development to be traceable. Industrial buildings proper are much scarcer, and only a handful warrant mention here. As in other Victorian cities, City warehouses were often remarkably ornate, especially where the building was also used for the display of goods. Indeed, one cannot easily distinguish the more ornate warehouses from offices of the more modest, brick-built variety. The great sequence

pp. 442–3 of Italianate brick and stucco premises of the early 1850s in Cannon Street and Queen Street served both functions, while *John Young & Son*'s draper's warehouse at No. 12 Little Britain, 1858–9, anticipates the round-arched medieval offices of the 1860s. Young & Son developed a pleasingly logical formula at No. 23 and No. 31 Eastcheap, both round-arched neo-medieval warehouses of the early 1860s: the ground floor and first floor, where goods were displayed, are ornamented, but the upper floors, used for storage, are kept plain. From *c.* 1875 an extensively glazed first floor is often used for such display warehouses; *Ford & Hesketh*'s Nos. 115–117 Newgate Street, 1879, is a good example.

Gothic was most in fashion for warehouses in the 1860s and 70s. The pioneer appears to have been the elder *Somers Clarke*'s staggering Printing and Publishing Co. in West Smithfield (1860), a flush-walled mass with Flemish polychrome details and crow-stepped gables; but this fell victim to the new Charterhouse Street a decade later. The masterpiece of polychromatic Gothic self-advertisement in the
104 City is *R. L. Roumieu*'s bristling vinegar warehouse at Nos. 33–35 Eastcheap, 1868. Gothic warehouses elsewhere are more restrained, though often no less naïve; Nos. 6–8 Bow Lane, by *T. K. Green*, 1871, is a good example. One influential formula for narrow fronts, introduced at *Burges*'s No. 46 Upper Thames Street, 1866 (dem.), was to combine twin pointed bays under a single Gothic relieving arch and gable. Dirty Dick's pub at Nos. 202–204 Bishopsgate, 1870, perpetuates the type. Messrs Collinson & Lock's warehouse in St Bride Street, an early work by *Collcutt* (1872–3), also has a gable and a Gothic relieving arch, but here it frames a shallow canted bay, derived perhaps from Shaw's New Zealand Chambers.

Other specialized late Victorian warehouses or trading premises of note include *Knightley*'s Nos. 30–32 Fleet Street (1883), for the map-makers Messrs Philip, and *M. E. Collins*'s pretty coconut warehouse at Nos. 18–20 Creechurch Lane (1891–2): the latter a good example of the use of ornament for advertisement. The purpose-built cold store arrived in the 1890s, when several were built in or near Charterhouse Street to take advantage of Smithfield Market. They have large, mostly blind fronts, variously dressed up. The best is *A. H. Mackmurdo*'s Nos. 109–113 Charterhouse Street, early Neo-Wren of 1900. Still larger is Nos. 5–13 St Paul's Churchyard (Messrs Pawson & Leaf), by *Herbert Ford*, 1895–8. It combined living facilities for staff with four storeys of general warehousing, behind a Northern Renaissance exterior of stone, indistinguishable from office chambers of the same date. The printing industry premises of Tudor Street and Carmelite Street derive their special character from their red brick and terracotta details and their broad rectangular sites, which exploited the newly laid-out street grid. In most cases they appear to have combined the functions of warehouse and factory. Apart from these, the only industrial buildings of interest to survive are at Whitbread's brewery in Chiswell Street, notably the brewery depot of 1867, converted into flats in 1995.

The application of fashionable styles to warehouses and industrial premises ran in parallel with the continuing development of more sober, utilitarian premises. Warehouses with simple load-bearing walls of brick continued to be built until the 1860s. The best surviving examples are Peek Bros. at No. 31 Lovat Lane (1852), the pilastered railway warehouse at No. 44 Crutched Friars (1855–6), and *Herbert Williams*'s big wool warehouse for Messrs Cooper at No. 21 New Street (1863–8). The ghosts of two more, both originally dramatized with large pediments, linger on through imaginative conversion of their lower storeys after wartime bomb damage. Both were designed by builder-contractors. *James Ponsford*'s former City Mills building, 1850, became the Mermaid Theatre in 1959 (*see* Queen Victoria Street). *George Myers*'s former tea warehouse on Tower Hill, 1864, survives only in its massively rusticated lower stages. Its vaulted interiors display characteristic fireproof construction, with cast-iron columns supporting transverse girders from which span air-brick arches: a system taken over from the pioneering early C19 mills of the industrial North.

The increasing use of such structural ironwork encouraged a new treatment of the façade, in which brick was restricted to broad piers between iron-framed bays accommodating windows or loading doors. An early example, glazed unusually extensively, was the Bradbury Greatorex warehouse in Aldermanbury, 1845, by an unknown architect. No. 48 Upper Thames Street (Brook's Wharf), 1874, is more typical of the later Victorian type with windows set in shallow recessed bays between broad pilaster-piers. Where more light was needed, thin iron colonnettes made possible wide, flat- or segment-headed windows, seen at *J. H. Stevens*'s ungainly No. 2 Crane Court, off Fleet Street (1863), and Nos. 33–43 Charterhouse Square (1876–8), partly by *Coutts Stone*.

Residential Buildings and Pubs

New DOMESTIC ARCHITECTURE was scarce. *Ewan Christian* built a good terrace of canons' houses in the Norman Shaw manner at Amen Court (1878–80). Working-class housing is represented by a gallery-access tenement block by *Sir Horace Jones* of 1874, just N of Charterhouse Street: the survivor of several such buildings by Jones for the Corporation, the first undertaken in early as 1862 in Farringdon Road, N of the City (demolished). The largest enclave within the City was in Middlesex Street, built in 1883–5 and replaced in the 1960s. What may be the last merchant's house built in the City is Nos. 6–7 St Mary-at-Hill, a tough brick Gothic building by 102 *Ernest George & Thomas Vaughan*, 1873.

The transient population was catered for by several new HOTELS, which were much more a feature of the Victorian City than is often realized. A late example of the coffee-house-cum-tavern is the former Rainbow at No. 15 Fleet Street, of 1859–60 by *Rawlinson Parkinson*. This venerable type was overtaken by the great railway hotels, described above. *Evans Cronk*'s former Spiers & Pond's Hotel in Holborn Viaduct, Nos. 1–10, 1874, is in the French fashion of the 1870s. Contemporary hotels in Salisbury Square, New Bridge Street, Aldersgate Street and Fleet Street have not survived.

The City is still plentifully supplied with PUBS. They are mostly small, with few great gin palaces. The Brewers' Italianate manner of the mid C19 may be seen at such pubs as the Red Lion in Eldon Street, *c.* 1860. Later pubs sometimes had large dining rooms on upper floors to exploit the huge captive lunchtime market, as at the Fleece Tavern at No. 6 Queen Street, 1878. Buildings by specialist practices proliferate from *c.* 1880. Good later examples include *Hooker & Hemmings*'s former King & Keys, 1884, and *Saville & Martin*'s Punch Tavern, 1894–7, at No. 142 and Nos. 98–100 Fleet Street respectively. The most enjoyable late Victorian pub exteriors in the City are *M. E. Collins*'s jaunty The Ship at No. 3 Hart Street, 1887, and the Fox and Anchor at No. 114 Charterhouse Street, on the City fringes, of 1898 by *W. J. Neatby* of *Doulton*'s, with a cheery faience front. The best pub interior is at the Black Friar in Queen Victoria Street (No. 174), transformed by *H. Fuller Clark* and others after *c.* 1905 into a glowing vision of Arts-and-Crafts cosiness. The well-known duo of *Treadwell & Martin* have left no pubs in the City, but part of their Buchanan's Distillery remains at No. 80 Fetter Lane (1902), a characteristically inventive gabled front.

Religious Architecture

New RELIGIOUS ARCHITECTURE was mostly the preserve of non-Anglican faiths. The French Protestants had a Gothic church in St Martin's le Grand, 1842–3, the Greek Orthodox a Neo-Byzantine church in London Wall, 1850, both by *T. O. Owen*, both demolished in the 1880s. The Great Synagogue in Duke's Place, rebuilt in 1852 by *John Wallen*, was destroyed in the Second World War. The largest Nonconformist chapel is *Lockwood & Mawson*'s City Temple in Holborn Viaduct, 1873–4, Italian Renaissance, with a tower to one side rather in the Wren manner. Hardly less assertive was *Tarring*'s Congregational Memorial Hall in Farringdon Street, a Gothic pile of 1872–5, demolished *c.* 1970. *George Sherrin*'s Roman Catholic St Mary Moorfields, 1899–1903, is modest by comparison, the front with the character of street architecture.

Victorian CHURCH RESTORATION in the City is of unusual interest. Medieval churches were re-medievalized in the approved manner, most notably the literal-minded but scholarly campaign of 1841–3 at the Temple Church by *James Savage*, *Sydney Smirke* and *Decimus Burton*. The many classical churches presented different problems to restorers. Until the early 1850s they were treated with remarkable respect: at St Mary-at-Hill (*James Savage*, 1848–9) and St Stephen Walbrook (*John Turner*, 1849–50), the carver *W. Gibbs Rogers* was employed on woodwork very close in spirit to the age of Wren. The City's ecclesiastical heritage is also deliberately evoked at *John Davies*'s rectory in Martin Lane (1851–3), with its steeple-like bell-tower and clock projecting in the C17 manner.

Sir George Gilbert Scott broke this consensus with his transformation of St Michael Cornhill, 1857–60. His new porch is rich Italo-French Gothic, his interior Lombardic, with inserted tracery, polychrome decoration (mostly removed), and a new marble reredos. The church also has the best Victorian stained glass in the City, a powerful sequence by *Clayton & Bell*. Other drastic schemes followed, 106 all at churches destroyed or burnt out in the Second World War: by *Scott* at St Alban Wood Street, 1858–9; by *Woodthorpe* at St Mary Aldermanbury, 1863, and St Swithin, 1869; by *Teulon* at St Andrew Holborn, 1869–72 (though Teulon's Gothic rectory and court house remain there). From *c.* 1870 a gentler approach prevailed, and even so fierce a spirit as *Butterfield* kept most of the fittings in his campaigns at St Clement Eastcheap (1872) and St Mary Woolnoth (1875–6). *Pearson* is represented only by a porch at All Hallows Barking, from work of 1884–95, and by a few fittings at St Helen Bishopsgate (1892–3).

Other architects busy on City church restorations include *Sir Arthur Blomfield* and (especially) *Ewan Christian*, the architect to the Ecclesiastical Commissioners. They and their late Victorian contemporaries routinely removed all galleries but that at the w, cut down pews, and formed a raised chancel with stalls, but tended not to replace C17–C18 fittings with new ones. St Stephen Walbrook suffered more badly than most, its pews being replaced with benches by *Alexander Peebles* in 1886–7. Generally new work was confined to stained glass (much of it in itself unusually good) and stencilled or painted decoration, the latter since removed without exception. The most appealing scheme is *Bentley*'s embellishment of St Botolph Aldgate (1888–95), which he transformed with white-painted balustraded galleries and a graceful plaster angel frieze. A similar Aesthetic influence pervades *Sir William Blake Richmond*'s late Victorian mosaics in the choir and aisles of St Paul's, of 1892–1904. Their confident Byzantinizing style contrasts with the weaker, more pictorial mosaics designed in the 1860s for the space under the dome, though they are if anything even more alien to the setting.

Sculpture and Decoration

Victorian SCULPTURE appears in great strength at St Paul's. *Marochetti*'s Melbourne monument (†1848 and 1853) is an early instance of the revival of polychromy. Its greatest manifestation is *Alfred Stevens*'s magnificently architectural Wellington monument, 107 the greatest of all Victorian church monuments, begun in 1857 but completed only in 1912. In the 1860s recumbent effigies took over from standing statues as the preferred form for other figures. Most of the leading Victorian sculptors are represented by these figures or by the lesser monuments that proliferated in the crypt. They include several excellent pieces by the 'New Sculptors' *Alfred Gilbert*, *Hamo* 119 *Thornycroft* and *George Frampton*, and one bust by *Rodin*, the artists' single greatest inspiration. There are also important sequences of standing figures by various sculptors at the Central Criminal Court (British monarchs, made 1863–70 for the Palace of Westminster), and at the Mansion House (figures from English literature, commissioned 1853–61). The best collection amongst the Livery Companies is at Goldsmiths' Hall, including four figures of the Seasons by *Nixon*, 1844.

PUBLIC SCULPTURE also proliferated in the period. Not all can be mentioned here. *Chantrey*'s equestrian figure of Wellington was erected in 1844 in Cornhill, in front of the Royal Exchange. Behind that building stands more Victorian and early C20 sculpture, including a fountain with *Dalou*'s figure of a nursing mother, 1879. The obligatory figure of Prince Albert, an uninspired equestrian affair by *Charles Bacon*, 1874, may be found at Holborn Circus. His Queen is commemorated by *C. B. Birch*'s figure at the S end of New Bridge Street (1896). Birch also did the griffin on the monument in Fleet Street that replaced old Temple Bar (1880). More self-effacing is the peculiar plaque-lined loggia commemorating civilian heroism, conceived in 1887 by *G. F. Watts* and erected in the churchyard of St Botolph Aldersgate, by then converted to a public garden ('Postman's Park').

ARCHITECTURAL SCULPTURE is plentiful. The Victorian preference for historical and exotic costume appears at *Richard Westmacott the Younger*'s pediment at the Royal Exchange. The City's history is also commemorated by statues of historical figures on the late 1860s blocks flanking Holborn Viaduct, the parapets of the viaduct proper being adorned with big bronze allegories. Decorative carving of commercial buildings with heads and foliage and so on is also common. Specialist artists or workshops such as *F. G. Anstey*, *Gilbert Seale* and *Daymond & Son* did much of the work. More ambitious reliefs may be seen e.g. at the General Credit in Lothbury (by *Redfern*, 1866) and at No. 15 Bishopsgate (by *Hancock*, 1864–5, with figures by Messrs *Colley* on the parapet). For late Victorian work the best buildings to study are the Institute of Chartered Accountants and Lloyd's Register of Shipping, as already noted. *Benjamin Creswick*'s spontaneous terracotta figure frieze at Cutlers' Hall, 1886, also rewards close scrutiny.

PAINTED DECORATION was much less popular. The only schemes that need be mentioned here are the paintings by *Brangwyn* and *Moira* at Lloyd's Register, and the sequence of historical canvases at the Royal Exchange, by *Lord Leighton* and others, 1895–1922. By *Brangwyn* also is the fine sequence at Skinners' Hall, mostly of 1902–9.

THE CITY FROM 1900 TO 1940

The Edwardian City was the financial capital of the Empire, as Westminster was its political capital, and in this role it prospered as never before. Its involvement with manufacturing and with general material trade continued to diminish, the City serving instead as the place from which trade was financed and directed. The change should not be exaggerated, for large quarters of the City remained primarily industrial in character, but their buildings will concern us less here. Most businesses were still fairly small – the average workforce before 1914 was less than ten – but the number of very large firms rose steeply, especially after the First World War. That war slowed down but did not interrupt the process of rebuilding, which quickly recovered in the 1920s. That decade was the golden age of commercial architecture in the City, with palatial new banks and company headquarters in Portland stone by such architects as *Lutyens, Baker, Cooper, Sir Aston Webb, Burnet & Tait* and *Mewès & Davis*: the respected senior figures and firms of the day. The sequence stops abruptly in the early 1930s, as the Depression began to bite. The daytime population continued rising nevertheless, and at rush hour and in the lunch hour the streets were busier than ever before. The figures are: 1911, 364,000; 1921, 437,000; 1935, an estimated 500,000, that is, almost 740 persons an acre (for comparison, the estimated total for 1995 is only 250,000). Planning during the period was dominated by street widening schemes to cope with this growth and with the influx of motor vehicles that accompanied it.

Before describing the course of C20 architecture, a summary is called for of the underlying changes in construction and technology. Electric light became widespread in the late C19, the first recorded example in the City being *J. A. Chatwin*'s Lloyds Bank, Lombard Street, 1887 (dem.). The preoccupation with natural light was thus relaxed, and deeper plans with smaller lightwells became possible. In the 1890s the introduction of passenger lifts encouraged an increase in building height, reined in only by the Building Act of 1894. This fixed the maximum cornice height at 80 ft ($24\frac{1}{3}$ metres), with two further storeys permitted in set-backs. In the 1900s fully framed buildings of reinforced concrete and steel became common, which in turn encouraged the inexorable movement towards larger buildings. These innovations, it should be added, merely caught up with American or Continental practice, and for all its wealth and power the City remained more traditional in its architectural expectations than the booming cities across the Atlantic.

The best place to study the shift in scale from the Victorian to the Edwardian era is in and around Finsbury Circus, where the cessation of numerous house leases in the 1890s allowed the construction of new office blocks on a scale not seen before in the City. The oldest survivor is Salisbury House, 1899–1901, by *Davis & Emmanuel*, whose Finsbury Pavement House in nearby Moorgate (dem.), completed 1900, was one of the first London offices to have lifts in the lobby. Both Salisbury House and the adjacent and more vigorous London Wall Buildings, by *Gordon & Gunton*, 1901–2, adopt the giant order, in line with the general movement towards strong accents and away from late Victorian small-scale prettiness. At *Belcher & Joass*'s Electra House, Moorgate (1900–3), the full artillery of domes and decorative sculpture is deployed, to bombastic effect. The use of blocked columns and other Neo-Baroque devices is associated also with *Norman Shaw*, whose only surviving work in the City is also his last, the comparatively subdued No. 8 Lloyd's Avenue (1907–8). Later in the 1900s the extravagantly busy skylines in favour around 1900 gave way in many quarters to something altogether cleaner-lined, of which *Sir Ernest George & Yeates*'s Royal Exchange Buildings, Cornhill (1906–10) is a good example.

The first PUBLIC BUILDING in the City in the mature Edwardian Baroque manner was *Mountford*'s domed Central Criminal Court, 1900–7. It stood on the site of Dance's celebrated Newgate Gaol, and is itself an excellent example of the interest in graduated, expressive rustication that the Gaol inspired amongst Edwardian architects. *Sir Edwin Cooper*'s Port of London Authority (1912–22) is still ₁₂₁ bolder in its massing and in its rhetorical use of sculpture in the

round. Both buildings were the result of important competitions.
Official architecture, which is to say Government buildings, is disappointingly tame by comparison. Its chief monument is *Sir Henry
Tanner*'s King Edward Buildings at the G.P.O. (1907–11), in style
not much advanced from his earlier North Block there (1889–95).

King Edward Buildings is however of interest for its REINFORCED-
CONCRETE FRAMING (*Hennebique* system), which appears unadorned
on the wholly utilitarian rear wing. Early examples elsewhere in the
City have been destroyed in most cases (e.g. No. 35 New Broad
Street, by *F. W. Marks*, 1907–8, *Kahn* system), although others may
survive unremarked. Restrictions on its use were not completely
relaxed until 1915. STEEL FRAMING infiltrated the building world
more gradually, as a superior substitute for structural iron. The first
entirely steel-framed building in London is Mewès & Davis's Ritz
Hotel, Piccadilly (1903–6). More liberal building laws passed in
1909 encouraged its further use, after which it rapidly became the
norm. The most striking manifestations in the City are discussed
below.

One aspect of building technology of particular interest to the
smoky City was the use of dirt-resistant glazed terracotta or faience
(the unglazed variety passing out of fashion in the 1900s). All-white,
light-reflecting façades in narrow streets appear from the late 1900s
(Asia House, Lime Street, 1912–13 by *Fair & Myer*). Coloured
faience, of the kind associated with Halsey Ricardo, was a shorter-
lived fashion, rarely seen after 1910 (e.g. Bolton House, Cullum
Street, 1907 by *Aiselby*).

In COMMERCIAL ARCHITECTURE up to *c.* 1920 the lead was taken
by the insurance companies. Such buildings as *Dunn & Watson*'s
Scottish Provident Institution, Nos. 1–6 Lombard Street (1905–8);
Gordon & Gunton's Royal Insurance Buildings, Nos. 24–28 Lombard
Street (1910); *J. McMullen Brooks*'s Norwich Union Insurance,
Nos. 49–50 Fleet Street (1911); and *J. Macvicar Anderson*'s Phoenix
Fire Assurance, Nos. 3–5 King William Street (begun 1915, with a
very fine hall) are larger and more ambitious than most of the banks
of the day. The one monster amongst these has been demolished:
Edmeston & Gabriel's heavy London and South Western, 1909–12,
on the N corner of Gracechurch Street and Fenchurch Street. A
lesser insurance headquarters, the Edinburgh Life at Nos. 2–4
Birchin Lane (by *Dunn & Watson*, 1910), is a good example of the
Neo-Palladian fashion that came in at the beginning of the 1910s; its
most notable exemplar in the City is the former Gresham College in
Gresham Street, by *Dendy Watney* and *Sydney Perks* (1911–13). All
these buildings are or were classical structures of Portland stone or
other limestones, with columns or pilasters raised on a basement
storey. Speculative office blocks were more likely to dispense with
the order. In the details, a tendency towards squared-off ornament
sometimes appears: a movement associated in its early, avant-garde
phase with *Charles Holden* (the radically plain Law Society extension,
1902–4), and *J. J. Joass* of *Belcher & Joass* (No. 88 Fleet Street, 1900–2,
and the demolished Winchester House extension, Great Winchester
Street, 1901–5). In buildings of the 1910s and 1920s it often takes on
a somewhat French flavour.

After 1920 BANKS led the field. The Bank of England was itself
reconstructed by *Sir Herbert Baker* 1921–39, within Soane's perimeter

wall, itself altered in several places. Baker's tower of axially planned p.
offices, arranged around a cavernous garden courtyard, was almost as 277
unlike contemporary banks as Soane's building was in its time. Around
it are clustered the headquarters and major branches of the main clearing banks, many of which had grown enormously by merger and
acquisition at the end of the 1910s. They were built to impress inside
and out, with vast banking halls (mostly surviving) and richly appointed
suites of offices for the senior staff, in various traditional styles, with
much use of mahogany and fibrous plaster. The 'front of house' architects responsible for the conception and elevations are given here; the
structure and detailed planning were often worked up by less well-
known partnerships. *Mewès & Davis* began the sequence with the
London, County & Westminster Bank headquarters in Lothbury,
1921–32, and a slightly smaller branch at Nos. 51–53 Threadneedle 122
Street (1922–31), the latter in an urbane Italian Renaissance manner
that derived from the American firm Mead, McKim & White.
Lutyens's Midland Bank, Poultry, 1924–39, is more rich and inventive in its marshalling of Italian Cinquecento elements. *Cooper*'s
adjacent National Provincial, 1929–32, is tamer but still impressive,
with a rather old-fashioned sculpted group on top. The most austere
of the series is *Sir John Burnet*'s Lloyds at Nos. 15–22 Cornhill, 126
1927–30, with noble, straightforward Corinthian elevations. *Baker*'s
group of Glyn, Mills & Co. and Martin's Bank at Nos. 67–70
Lombard Street, 1930–2, appropriates the domestic Neo-Georgian
brick idiom preferred by merchant banks, of which *Victor Heal*'s
Lazard's at Nos. 10–11 Old Broad Street (1925) is the chief survivor.

Of other lesser banks, *Vickery & Joass*'s former Commonwealth
Bank of Australia, No. 8 Old Jewry (1930–1) stands out for its
convincing simplification of the giant order; *Lutyens*'s Midland
Bank, Nos. 139–144 Leadenhall Street (1929–31) for its playful
turreted skyline. Amongst foreign banks one curiosity is the use of
the revived Adam style in favour across the Atlantic (No. 147
Leadenhall Street (Grace & Co.), 1926–7, by *J. W. O'Connor* of New
York; Royal Bank of Canada, No. 6 Lothbury, 1932, by *S. G.
Davenport* of Montreal).

The architects of the great clearing banks were much in demand
for other HEADQUARTERS BUILDINGS of the 1920s and early 1930s,
notably for insurance companies, shipping firms and great industrial
concerns. The finest is perhaps *Lutyens*'s Britannic House in Finsbury 123
Circus (1921–5), with impeccably calculated fronts on three sides.
The main elevations are remarkable for placing the order high up,
marking the position of the board rooms: a nice illustration of the
loosening of spatial hierarchies that followed the introduction of lifts.
Cooper built Lloyd's (1925–8) and the adjacent Royal Mail House
(1928–30) in Leadenhall Street, of which Lloyd's fine frontispiece
survives as part of the present building. There is also his former
Spillers, No. 40 St Mary Axe (1922–4). *Mewès & Davis*'s Hudson's
Bay House, Nos. 52–68 Bishopsgate (1926–8) is Palladian in detail,
if not in proportion. Unilever House in New Bridge Street, by *Burnet,
Tait & Partners* and *J. Lomax Simpson* (1930–2), is much more radi-
cally simplified, though the vocabulary is still predominantly classical. Notable headquarters for insurance firms include the Ocean
Accident, No. 36 Moorgate (1928) by *Sir Aston Webb & Son*, and the
Commercial Union, No. 24 Cornhill, by *Maurice Webb* (1929), both

playful in composition and vocabulary, in a manner quite distinct from Lutyens. *W. Curtis Green*'s London Life Association, Nos. 81–82 King William Street (1925–7) and Scottish Widows, Nos. 28–30 Cornhill (1934–5), are more sober, in the American Beaux-Arts manner.

Though most of the buildings so far mentioned are steel-framed, their façades do little to advertise the fact, beyond the occasional deployment of bronze spandrel panels instead of stone bands at the floor divisions. For a more explicit advertisement of the frame, mercantile or speculative offices are a better source. Two early examples stand out: *F. W. Troup*'s faience-faced headquarters and warehouse for Spicer Brothers in New Bridge Street (1913–17), in which the grid-like façade is still disciplined by classical proportions overall, and the wonderful Holland House in Bury Street, 1914–16 by the Dutch architect *H. P. Berlage*, also faience-faced, but with close-set chamfered uprights without period precedent. *Richardson & Gill*'s stone-faced Moorgate Hall, 1915–16, was in a similar reductive classical manner to Troup's, though less insistent on the frame within; its demolition in the 1980s was a serious loss.

The greatest contemporary impact, however, was made by *Burnet & Tait*'s Adelaide House (1921–5), aided by its unprecedented height and conspicuous position on the London Bridge Approach. Its façades derive more closely from American prototypes, particularly of the Chicago school, with an admixture of fashionable Egyptian motifs. The Chicago formula of repeated storeys unified by close-set uprights was made much of by *L. Sylvester Sullivan*, at his Courtaulds' warehouse in St Martin's le Grand (1924–5) and elsewhere. Speculative offices of the 1920s were quick to adopt cast-metal spandrels and window surrounds, stonework sometimes being reduced to a thin strip framing the front, especially on narrow fronts (e.g. No. 46 Moorgate, by *T. P. Bennett* & *J. D. Hossack*, 1925).

The use of metal infill to a stone frame found a ready reception in the NEWSPAPER OFFICES in and around Fleet Street. *Percy Tubbs, Son & Duncan*'s former *Glasgow Herald* building, 1927 (Nos. 56–57) is a good, ornate example of the narrow front type. More substantial buildings combined offices with printing works, of which the most advanced in its time, though rather utilitarian in elevation, was Northcliffe House in Tudor Street, 1925–7 by *Ellis & Clarke*. The best cases of architecture as advertisement are in Fleet Street: the *Daily Telegraph* at Nos. 135–141, by *Elcock & Sutcliffe* and *Thomas Tait*, 1928–31, a colourful Egyptianizing pile, and *Sir Owen Williams*'s celebrated *Daily Express* building, 1930–3, at Nos. 120–129. The latter has a brilliantly engineered concrete frame and pioneering streamlined curtain-walled elevations of black glass. The interior, by *Robert Atkinson*, shows Art Deco at its most luxurious and fantastic.

The streamlined fashion, with its easily assimilated devices of rounded corners and continuous window bands, made rapid progress after *c.* 1930. It was used in the City for smart flats (at Florin Court, Charterhouse Square, by *Guy Morgan*, 1936), and for further newspaper offices (Harmsworth House, Tudor Street, by *Tubbs, Duncan & Osburn*, 1937–9). It also caught on for speculative offices, most strikingly at the giant, black-and-cream-striped Ibex House, Minories, by *Fuller, Hall & Foulsham*, 1935–7. The more committed wing of the Modern Movement appears in the City only at No. 115 Cannon

Street, a shopfront by *Walter Gropius* and *Maxwell Fry*, 1936, distinguishable by nuances of vocabulary from such smart shopfitters'
work as Messrs Fox, at No. 118 London Wall just off Moorgate. In less 131
up-to-date buildings the 1930s see a stripped, simplified manner take
over. There is a representative stone-faced group at the E end of Cannon
Street, S side. Even *Lutyens* reined himself in, as his headquarters for
Reuters and the Press Association in Fleet Street shows (1934–8).

INSTITUTIONAL BUILDINGS are of less interest, and only two
warrant mention here: *Sydney Tatchell*'s Ironmongers' Hall, 1922–5,
for its extraordinary Neo-Jacobean interiors, and *M. E. & O. H.
Collins*'s quirky Chartered Insurance Institute, 1932–4, one of several
traditionally detailed but inventive City buildings by the partnership.

Of SCULPTURE one might mention the memorial group to Lord
Kitchener in St Paul's, by *Sir William Reid Dick*, 1925. There is much
excellent architectural sculpture up to *c.* 1930, by such artists as *Reid* 128
Dick and *H. W. Palliser*. Free-standing public sculpture is entirely a
matter of First World War Memorials. The most moving of these is
not a work of sculpture, however: it is *Lutyens*'s temple-like Mercantile 124
Marine Memorial in Trinity Square, 1926–8.

REPLANNING AND RECONSTRUCTION:
1945–*c.* 1975

In 1945 large areas of the City lay waste. Air raids had accounted for
a great swathe of property E of St Paul's, stretching from Upper 3
Thames Street to the S edge of Camberwell. Other districts badly
affected lay immediately N of St Paul's, S of Holborn, and in the SE
part of the City along Great Tower Street. The damage had lasting
effects on the economic make-up of the City, especially in the central part, which was deserted by the bombed-out publishing and
clothing firms in favour of the West End. The post-war City was
therefore more than ever dominated by finance and office-based
commerce. The newspaper industry was the exception: it held on to
its traditional fastness in and around Fleet Street until the late 1980s.
The City's historic buildings also suffered heavily from bombing:
twenty-three of the forty-nine churches and twenty-five of the thirty-
six livery halls were badly damaged or destroyed, and large parts of
the Temple were levelled.

What form the rebuilt City should take was keenly debated, for a
much greater role for TOWN PLANNING was anticipated in post-war
reconstruction. As early as 1942, the impatient Modernists of the
MARS Group had published a speculative general plan for central
London, in which the City streets were remade on a modified grid.
From the opposite corner came the Royal Academy Planning
Committee's Beaux-Arts-inflected proposals for central London,
dominated by grand axes and *rond-points*. While nothing so drastic
was implemented, the progress of post-war reconstruction can be
understood in terms of such polarities between Modernism and tradition. Significantly, both plans also assumed that the City would be
replanned in conjunction with London as a whole, although the City
occasionally proved less tractable.

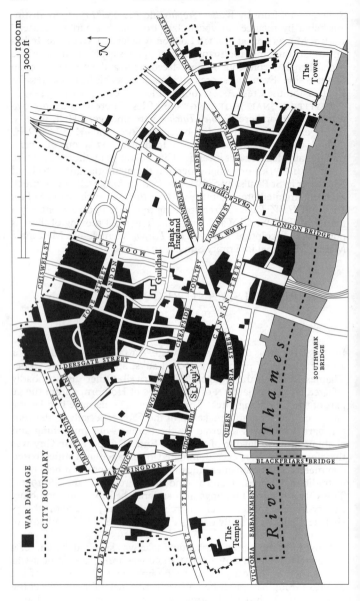

Areas of
Second World War
bomb damage

The City's own intentions were set out in the report *Reconstruction in the City of London* (1944), largely by its Engineer, *F. J. Forty*. The most notable proposal was a grandiose ring route approximately following the old City wall line, with roundabouts at major intersections. Forty's architectural proposals were conservative: a sequence of 'cornice line' blocks to the old maximum height of 80 ft (24 metres), plus 30 ft (9 metres) in set-backs. This formula seemed stuffy and unimaginative to the men of the LCC. Furthermore, its high densities took no account of the policy of decentralization set out in *J. H. Forshaw* and *Sir Patrick Abercrombie*'s *County of London Plan* (1943). The Corporation responded with a new plan, by *Charles Holden* and *W. G.* (later *Lord*) *Holford* (submitted 1947; published as *The City of London: a record of destruction and survival*, 1951). It too proposed a ring road, but lifted part of it up on stilts. The chief restriction on building density changed from cornice height to plot ratio, that is the proportion of floor space to site area. This was fixed at 5:1, rising to $5\frac{1}{2}$:1 by the Bank: a measure that anticipated a Modernist architecture of slabs and towers, arranged with picturesque asymmetry around traffic-free gardens and courts.

Though the LCC's planners were given authority over the City in 1947, their efforts were initially concentrated elsewhere. Left to itself, the Corporation dropped most of the more radical planning measures. The ring road was lowered, and in the event only the s part was fully realized (1963–80). This involved the transformation of both Upper and Lower Thames Street into a main E–W road, partially realigned, and with an extension of Victoria Embankment from the w. The new road effectively marked the end of the City as a conduit of river-borne trade. Otherwise only one entirely new major road was built, and not on the line proposed: the new London Wall or 'Route XI' (*see* below). It was not until the later 1950s that radical planning ideas returned to favour, as will appear.

The ARCHITECTURE of the post-war period may now be considered. The Corporation was empowered in 1948 to acquire land by compulsory purchase, for resale to developers on long leases. Post-war building restrictions favoured housing and industry, so little was built in the City before *c.* 1950. The first new buildings to appear demonstrated that commercial clients had yet to be won over to the Modern Movement, at that date still associated with the nascent Welfare State. Its acceptance from the mid 1950s onwards owed much to the ready assimilation of Modernism into the commercial mainstream in the USA. Thereafter American architecture remained the single most important source of new styles and planning concepts for the City (and for British commercial architecture generally), though these were usually interpreted by English commercial practices rather than copied directly.

The first OFFICE BLOCKS were mostly built under the so-called Lessor Scheme, in return for a fixed-term lease to the government. They were stone- or brick-clad, generally very large, and unimaginatively detailed (though often wearing better than their curtain-walled successors). The usual style was a denatured Neo-Georgian, here with touches of pre-war streamlining (Atlantic House, Holborn Viaduct, by *T. P. Bennett & Son*, 1951), there rigidly formal (*Gunton & Gunton*'s St Swithin's House, St Swithin's Lane, 1949–53). The largest, *Victor Heal*'s New Change Buildings, Cheapside, combines 133 formal and informal elements, not wholly successfully; it was completed as late as 1960. The classicism of such buildings affronted progressive-minded critics: Pevsner called it 'a style of timidity, of playing safe, of introducing just enough of the C20 to avoid being ridiculous and keeping just enough of giant columns and the other paraphernalia of Empire to stake the claim of remaining a great nation' (1957). Nonetheless, designs of traditional ancestry went up well into the later 1950s. When specially commissioned, these sometimes achieved real, if unexpected, distinction. *Richardson*'s Bracken

153 House (for the *Financial Times*), Cannon Street, 1955–9, is an intelligent recapitulation of his stripped-classical 1920s manner, in fine dusky red brick. Best of the stone-faced Neo-Georgian buildings is *Antony Lloyd*'s suave National Provident Institution, Gracechurch Street (1957–9); the grandest, *Terence Heysham*'s prodigious Lloyd's, Lime Street (1950–7).

Stone facing was also taken up for such explicitly Modernist buildings as *Brian O'Rorke*'s former General Steam Navigation, Lower Thames Street (1956–9, threatened), a subtle free-standing composition of interlocking rectangles. More characteristic of wider 1950s fashions, however, are those (mostly speculative) blocks which adhered to the cornice line but adopted more colourful and decorative materials. A good early example is *Ronald Ward & Partners*' slate-faced Compter House, Wood Street (1953–6). The best work in this friendly vein was done by *Trehearne & Norman, Preston & Partners*. The firm's first post-war effort, St Bridget's House, off Tudor Street (1950–1, with later extensions), has been reclad, but the very pretty Clements House, Gresham Street (1954–7) survives,

134 its explicitly displayed stone-clad frame with mosaic- and crazy-paving-like infill. The firm's Gateway House (Wiggins Teape), Cannon Street (1953–6), of brick, has a set-back glazed top storey for boardrooms, a favourite feature of the 1950s–60s (compare *Fitzroy Robinson & Partners*' Aldermary House, Queen Street, 1959–63). Gateway House and Clements House were also provided with airy double-height entrance halls (altered at the former), another feature that became popular at about this time.

Much less individual elevations were used for the first building to break decisively with the cornice line formula: Bucklersbury House, Queen Victoria Street (*Owen Campbell-Jones & Sons*, 1953–8). It followed one of the rare interventions in the City planning process by the LCC, dismayed at an old-fashioned street-hugging design initially proposed for the site. Despite being set back some way from the street, the executed building achieved greater volume by carrying up the main slab to fourteen storeys. Three six-storey wings project, with space beneath for car parking – the last increasingly valuable as City bomb-sites gave way to rebuilding. The plan placed a premium on natural light, which easily penetrates the shallow floors; the usual internal plan was a spine corridor with offices to r. and l. The cladding was a neutral combination of Portland ashlar and pastel floor-bands: a much-imitated compromise between London tradition and the asperities of advanced Modernism. The tower-and-podium formula arrived with Fountain House, Fenchurch Street (*W. H. Rogers* and *Sir Howard Robertson*, 1954–8), where the podium still clings to the street line. A more compelling juxtaposition of parts marks *Howard, Fairbairn & Partners*' St Clare House, Minories (1956–7). Both towers

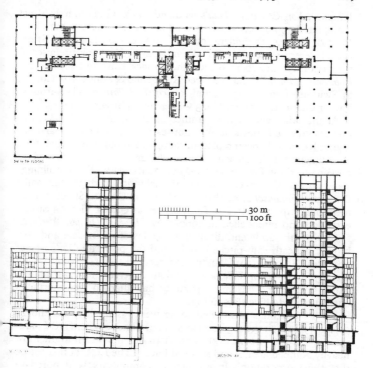

Queen Victoria Street, Bucklersbury House.
Typical floor plan, third to seventh floor, and sections

employ curtain-walling, a material increasingly favoured from the mid 1950s, used indiscriminately with concrete- and steel-framing alike.

The architecture of BANKS showed a slower progression from faltering traditionalism to the embrace of new materials and free composition. Some banks clung to Portland stone designs commissioned years before: *A. T. Scott & V. Helbing*'s Barclays Bank, Lombard Street (1959–64, dem.) derived from a commission from Scott's erstwhile partner *Baker* (†1946); Coutts Bank, part of *Whinney, Son & Austen Hall*'s Nos. 10–15 Lombard Street (completed 1961), from a design made in 1938. The C18–C19 tradition of ground-floor columns or pilasters to mark the banking hall was revived by *Victor Heal*, notably at his Bank Buildings, Prince's Street (1949–62). A more up-to-date equivalent for banking halls favoured from the late 1950s was coloured stone: black marble at *Trehearne & Norman, Preston & Partners*' Yorkshire Bank, Cheapside (1958–9), serpentine marble at *Biscoe & Stanton*'s OCB Corporation (former National Bank of China), No. 111 Cannon Street (1961–2).

The later 1950s also saw banks adopt compositions with office towers, though the pioneers were both demolished in 1995: *Ley, Colbeck & Partners*' Goodenough House (Barclays), Old Broad Street (1955–60), an ungainly Portland-faced slab-and-podium affair, and

Whinney, Son & Austen Hall's Midland Bank, Gracechurch Street (completed 1961). BANKING HALLS are of less interest, but *Brett, Boyd & Bosanquet*'s golden-domed Coutts & Co., Lombard Street (1961) deserves mention. But the most arresting bank premises of the period are merchant banks, and so lack banking halls: *Fitzroy Robinson & Partners*' marble-faced Rothschild & Sons (New Court), St Swithin's Lane (1963–5), and *R. Seifert & Partners*' glass-fronted former Guinness Mahon, No. 3 Gracechurch Street (1964–8).

At the other end of the commercial spectrum lie INDUSTRIAL BUILDINGS. Thames-side warehouses put up after the war have themselves mostly been replaced, though material trade (wine, furs, etc.) lingered in its ancient riverside haunts into the 1970s. More remains to show for the NEWSPAPER INDUSTRY. Three buildings stand out, all of them combining editorial offices with printing halls:
153 the former *Financial Times* (Bracken House) in Cannon Street, already mentioned; the former *The Times* offices in Queen Victoria Street, extended and remodelled in 1960–5 by *Llewelyn Davies, Weeks & Partners*, with subtle and distinctive façades of green slate and grey mosaic beneath split-pitched roofs; and the powerful *Daily Mirror* premises, Holborn (1957–60, future uncertain 1997). The last was of interest for *Sir Owen Williams*'s ingenious concrete frame, on a much wider grid in the basement printing hall than in the enormous curtain-walled office slab on top.

All the buildings mentioned so far were essentially independent designs, in which the requirements of developer or client were paramount. For WHOLESALE REPLANNING one must turn to the most heavily bombed area, N and NE of St Paul's. The LCC at first feared that the Corporation's investment in compulsory land purchase might be squandered in piecemeal private developments. In the event, however, the Corporation proved more than amenable to large-scale replanning. Four new precincts resulted, all of them of exceptional interest and ambition.

The City was eager to stay the inexorable decline of its resident population, so two of the zones were devoted to HOUSING. The first, the Golden Lane Estate, occupied the N part of the bombed area (transferred to the City 1994). The young partnership of *Chamberlin, Powell & Bon* won the competition to design it (1952) – the most important such competition since that for Churchill Gardens, Westminster (1946). The estate belongs in character with that development and with other such early traffic-free post-war schemes as *Tecton*'s Spa Green, Finsbury, and Hallfield, Paddington (*see London 4: North* and *London 3: North West* respectively). The plan has slabs
p.   arranged around a separate central tower on a controlling grid.
508 Accommodation is dense (200 persons per acre was specified for inner London in the 1943 plan). Buildings are carefully detailed and well-serviced, so that the 'hard' landscaping is not oppressive, and colour is used with unabashed boldness. An oversailing concrete canopy to the tower and a frankly late-Corbusian shallow-arched
138 canopy on the last block to be completed (1962) betray the restiveness of younger architects with the straightforward vocabulary and shallow decorative finishes of the day – a trend barely apparent in commercial architecture of that date.

This quest for a more massive, monumentally expressive architecture distinguishes the second of the four replanned precincts, the

same architects' Barbican Estate, immediately s (first plans 1956). p. 282
The traffic-free mixture of slabs and towers (here three in number)
was carried on from Golden Lane, with two differences: the integration of several public buildings for education and the arts (*see* p. 136
below), and the decision to set pedestrian circulation on a two-storey
podium. As executed from the early 1960s onwards, the buildings
took the expressive potential of concrete to a theatrical extreme. The
estate's combination of tower blocks, pedestrian decks and aggressively urban materials, often disastrous in working-class housing
elsewhere, found acceptance due to the quality of design, construction and maintenance, as well as to the comfortable circumstances of
its mostly professional occupants.

The raised deck also featured in the area immediately s, the third
area of major replanning and the pre-eminent monument to the
post-war concern with TRAFFIC CIRCULATION. At its heart was a
new E–W through road coded Route XI, and later named London
Wall (plan published 1955). This was turned to advantage as the
spine of a giant office development, planned on the Corbusian principle of vertical separation (pedestrians above traffic). Buildings
were of two types, both deliberately anonymous in style: six curtain-
walled and steel- or concrete-framed tower blocks, regularly spaced
and designed to a uniform module (though designed by private architects), and lower slabs in a mixture of curtain-walling and stone 137, p. 541
facing. Their commercial success set the seal on the City's embrace
of this brand of Modernism, reflecting its global transformation into
the architecture of big business. Lots of shops and pubs were provided at podium level in anticipation of the rebirth of pedestrian life
on the upper level. The ensemble can still be appreciated, though its
windswept upper level will appeal to few, and the balance of the
buildings was upset by replacements from the late 1980s.

The perceived success of London Wall, and the planners' continuing preoccupation with traffic circulation, led in 1959 to the momen-
tous decision to extend vertical segregation throughout the entire
City. It was anticipated that the walkways (called 'ped-ways') could
be gradually constructed within new buildings, and linked by
bridges as adjacent sites were also rebuilt. As more and more of the
City was renewed, pedestrians would gradually move to the upper
level. In some areas the walkways were to follow separate alignments, with new public squares and shopping spaces within the larger
new developments (the example of Venice was greatly favoured at
the time). It was hoped that this new elevated public realm would
have all the intricate and picturesque appeal of the old. The City
could thus achieve efficient traffic circulation without the expense of
much compulsory purchase: a pragmatic response to its high land
values. The exact routes were secret, but a plan of 1965 shows some
30 m. altogether. From this it is clear that complete rebuilding of
vast areas was envisaged. Only churches, livery halls and other
historic buildings would remain, stranded, at street level.

Most large buildings designed in the 1960s and early 1970s therefore make provision for the walkway. This usually required the waste-
ful duplication of reception areas, that on the ground floor being
merely an interim. In many cases the walkway has been enclosed
for office space, for the policy was abandoned in the mid 1970s,
and rarely achieved anything like a useful network outside its first

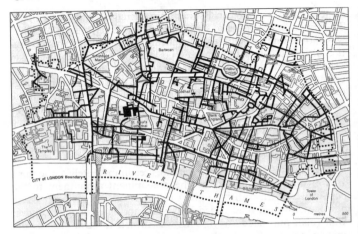

As proposed in 1963

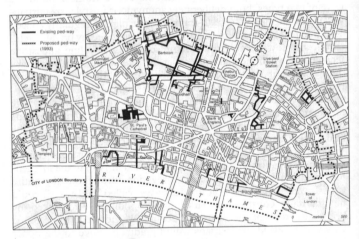

As existed in 1992.
Ped-way network

strongholds. Apart from London Wall, only on Upper and Lower Thames Street and at the S end of Bishopsgate can one walk for any distance at the upper level. But traces of the scheme may be seen on the first or second floors of office blocks all over the City. *Mewès & Davis*'s National Westminster Bank, Lombard Street (1963–9) even has a glazed-in ped-way section over a porte-cochère for drive-in banking: an extreme instance of dedication to the demands of the motor vehicle.

The informal aesthetic associated with the ped-way is best seen at Paternoster Square, the final area of large-scale replanning N of St Paul's. It was conceived as a giant pedestrian plaza raised over a car park, with steps up from St Paul's Churchyard. The buildings, all by *Trehearne & Norman, Preston & Partners* (built 1962–7), were designed on a controlling grid as a mixture of slabs of low and medium height, with one slim tower. They have the dull, dark palette that succeeded the 1950s fashion for pastels and small-scale decorative patterns, with much stone facing in deference to the cathedral. Even so, the precinct never found general acceptance, and after protracted discussion the whole is due in 1997 for complete rebuilding at the old ground level. The same fate has already overtaken its contemporary equivalent s of St Paul's, where falling ground allowed the provision of two floors of parking below the level of the churchyard.

A few more PLANNED PRECINCTS deserve mention. The smaller Tower Place development, w of Tower Hill (*A. Beckles Willson*, 1962–6) again mixes low slabs and one modest tower. Their raw concrete is unappealing, though the whole is generally well-proportioned. Like Paternoster Square, it illustrates the difficulties of reconciling the upper circulation level with historic buildings, for the Tower itself must be reached down awkward steps from podium end: a reminder of how much less flexible the walkway system is than common streets and pavements on land as hilly as the City's. Other developments to incorporate a plaza at the upper level include the *Corporation of London Architect's Department*'s Middlesex Street Estate (1965–75), a harsh concrete quadrilateral around a raised central court and slim tower: more typical of 1960s public housing than the Barbican Estate. A loosely similar commercial composition is *R. Seifert & Partners*' and *F. Norman James*'s Drapers' Gardens, Throgmorton Avenue (1962–7), which also has a tower, central court and grand stairway from street level.

This brings us to the question of TOWERS generally. Scepticism that the London clay could support tall buildings was refuted by the technique of bored piles cast *in situ*, developed in the 1950s by *A. W. Skempton*. The first commercial towers, dating from the end of the 1950s, have already been mentioned. The 1960s saw multiplication of the forthright rectilinear envelopes influenced by Mies van der Rohe's American prototypes. The straightforward towers of London Wall belong in this category, although their curtain-walling is inferior to the bespoke towers built for large companies. Since the latter were air-conditioned within sealed windows, greater control was possible over their everyday external appearance. Tallest (by 1 ft) is Britannic Tower, Ropemaker Street (formerly B.P.), by *F. Milton Cashmore* and *Niall D. Nelson*, 1964–7 (alterations proposed 1996). Its graduated concrete framing appeared externally sheathed in stainless steel. Closer to the Miesian model is the impeccably finished Commercial Union Assurance tower, Leadenhall Street (*Gollins, Melvin, Ward &* 142 *Partners*, 1963–9, reclad 1992–3), a steel-framed cantilever from a concrete core, planned with a contrasting tower half as high for the P&O. The success of the pair owes much to the street-level plaza between them, though the blocks were also linked to the ped-way. The Kleinwort Benson tower in Fenchurch Street (1963–8), by *CLRP Architects* and *Wallace F. Smith*, also finished to a high standard, fits less well into the streetscape.

The tower could also be shaped or modelled, following the precedent of Ponti and Nervi's Pirelli tower in Milan (1955–8). Such towers begin in the City with the little Kempson House, Camomile Street (1959–61), an elongated hexagon by *C. Lovett Gill & Partners*, completed just before Portland House and the strongly modelled Millbank Tower, both in Westminster. Perhaps the most persuasive is *Seifert*'s convex-sided tower at Drapers' Gardens, already mentioned. Its projecting grey-mosaic-clad sills have aged well, and its solid top storey is a more satisfactory termination than other shaped towers (e.g. the practice's International Press Centre, Shoe Lane, 1968–75). Its cantilevered construction was also more audacious than the regular framing used for earlier City towers. But the most spectacular are the three fierce residential towers of the Barbican Estate, which are dramatized by exposed open framing with massive curved balconies interpenetrating. Nothing so explicitly Brutalist was thought proper for a commercial tower, though pre-cast concrete was used (rather unimaginatively) for the Barclays Bank tower, Gracechurch Street (*CLRP Architects*, 1968–72), a chamfered square in plan. The seven-sided tower above the Stock Exchange, by *Llewelyn Davies, Weeks, Forestier-Walker & Bor*, 1964–72, is more carefully modelled, though the result is not wholly successful. Its chamfered pre-cast concrete mullions recall the profile and texture (though not the materials) of the Smithsons' *Economist* group in St James's Street, Westminster (1960–4). The choice of the self-consciously difficult Brutalist aesthetic for the Exchange was surprising, for the manner was never popular in the City. One other example warrants mention:

143 the extension of the Institute of Chartered Accountants, by *William Whitfield*, 1964–70. The new part appears as a compact, strongly modelled mass, its various elements structurally distinct. Junctions between the new and old work were handled with unusual sensitivity for the date, including replication of part of the C19 design.

It is customary to blame the loss of the steepled City skyline on these post-war towers, though in practice only the tallest spires showed above the great broad blocks that were already the norm by the mid C20. More serious is the loss of coherence caused by the failure to group tall buildings properly. From the old financial heart, E of the Bank, they surge up in a mass that communicates a sense of

1 excitement worthy of the area. The tallest of all, *Seifert*'s NatWest Tower, Old Broad Street (1970–81), makes a very effective centre-piece to the group, though the details are rather lacklustre for a commissioned building. The Barbican's towers also serve in some measure to define the N edge of the City. But one can only greet with relief the prospect of demolition of the taller towers and slabs built further W.

CLADDING MATERIALS are of particular importance in the City, since the uniform floors of most office blocks can rarely be modelled expressively. The later 1960s saw all-over treatments increasingly preferred over the contrasted materials in favour from the mid 1950s. The taste for rougher textures encouraged the use of the cavity-filled Portland stone known as roach, popularized at the Economist Building and in work outside the City by such firms as Powell & Moya (*see* e.g. *Gotch & Partners*' octagonal tower, Cheapside, 1971). More widely popular, because more suggestive of luxury and wealth, was polished stone of various types. Its introduction in the later 1950s for bank fronts has already been noted. The next step was to use it as an all-over facing, for which its dirt-resistant qualities made it ideal. The first instance in the City is the ungainly Clydesdale Bank, Lombard Street, by *Maurice H. Bebb* and *Notman & Lodge*,

1963–4. But its heyday came only in the 1970s, when numerous exotic varieties increasingly supplanted concrete and mosaic as the favourite cladding, Portland stone being then in eclipse. An influential (American-derived) prototype was *Yorke, Rosenberg & Mardall*'s flush-fronted former Scandinavian Bank, Nos. 36–38 Leadenhall Street, 1970–3, which has thin, even floor strings and uprights clad in yellow-brown stone and large windows between. The treatment was repeated with variations at the firm's Dashwood House, a square eighteen-storey tower in Old Broad Street (1972–6), and imitated e.g. at *Elsom, Pack & Roberts*'s contemporary pair of office blocks in Cannon Street (Nos. 110–114). Polished stone was also used for more strongly modelled façades, such as the former Manufacturers Hanover Trust, Prince's Street (1970–2), which has strong interlocking horizontals and verticals clad in Blaubrun granite. Its architects *Fitzroy Robinson & Partners* became the favourite City firm of the 1970s and 80s. Their best work of the 1970s is the Banque National de Paris, King William Street (1974–8), at which the classical echoes are even stronger. 145

Another imperishable cladding material in favour from the later 1960s was metal: stainless steel at *Raymond J. Cecil & Partners*' Bowring House, Great Tower Street (1970–2); bronze-anodized aluminium at two buildings of 1970–5 by *Sheppard Robson & Partners* in Lime Street – the last particularly attractive and well-proportioned. The 1970s also introduced plastic or glass fibre derivatives, which promised to be easily worked and dirt-resistant. The most notable is *Whinney, Son & Austen Hall*'s Crédit Lyonnais, Queen Victoria 144 Street (1973–7), a pioneering exercise in glass-fibre-reinforced cement. It makes good use of a difficult triangular site. The angling and chamfering of its pre-fabricated members carries on a fashion that arrived in the later 1960s, represented by several buildings by *R. Seifert & Partners* with massive angled piers (e.g. Faryners House, Monument Street, 1969–71), and expressed more thoughtfully at *Casson, Conder & Partners*' W.H. Smith, New Fetter Lane (1972–6). The mirror-glass fashion arrives with *Halpern & Partners*' gaudy PWS Group, Minories (1971–5). Red or brown brick also came back into favour for offices at around this time (e.g. *Fitzroy*'s Nos. 24–30 West Smithfield 1971–4). The best, *Saunders Boston*'s riverside blocks of 1972–5 off Upper Thames Street, have already been demolished.

Post-war PUBLIC BUILDINGS have already been touched on. The Stock Exchange typifies the difficulty of reconciling a distinctive composition with the demands of the ped-way scheme. More satisfactory results were achieved when architects were less constrained. The *Ministry of Works*' architects built some good TELEPHONE EXCHANGES from the mid 1950s onwards, the best, in Farringdon Street (1956–60), an imposing composition of stone-faced and glazed slabs. Later exchanges (e.g. Baynard House, Queen Victoria Street, 1972–9) favour unappealing pre-cast concrete panels. Otherwise, buildings by government architects are represented only by a meagre 1950s effort at the Patent Office. The LCC and its successor, the Greater London Council, always rare intruders into the City's architectural world, are responsible for the former School of Navigation (now London Guildhall University), Minories (1966–70), an aggregate-faced L-shaped block.

The Corporation of London preferred to commission private architects, as at the Barbican and Golden Lane Estates, rather than build up a large architectural department of its own. The result was a stylistic pluralism, quite unlike the house styles evolved by the LCC. It first appeared in 1951, the year of the Festival of Britain, in St Paul's Churchyard. The *Corporation of London Architect's Department* erected a pretty information kiosk in the Swedish-inflected Modern manner then in favour, but the City turned to *Sir Albert Richardson* to lay out a new garden nearby, complete with moulded stone parapets and classical trimmings. For the Guildhall itself, the Corporation retained the services of *Sir Giles Gilbert Scott*, who had drawn up plans to rebuild the auxiliary offices in the 1930s. The resulting offices N of Guildhall, built 1955–8 in a distressingly old-fashioned 1930s idiom, suggest this loyalty was misplaced. Later work by *Richard Gilbert Scott*, 1966–75 (W offices and library, and courtrooms to the N), expanded Guildhall Yard from the narrow approach Croxton and Dance both knew. The new buildings, of fine concrete and stone, use distinctive, if mannered forms, partly in deference to the C15 Guildhall. A new art gallery on the E side by *R. Gilbert Scott* and *D. Y. Davies Associates*, due for completion in 1997, will conform to their precedent.

Less prestigious building types include multi-storey car parks, of which six were planned in 1956 and completed 1961–70. Three survive, that in Minories (by *E. G. Chandler*, the City architect) an unapologetically Brutalist affair. The Poultry Market at Smithfield (1962–3 by *T. P. Bennett & Son*, replacing a burnt Victorian structure) has an audacious clear-span concrete dome. By contrast, two important 1960s commissions went to the traditionalist firm of *McMorran & Whitby*: the Police Station in Wood Street, 1962–6 and the Central Criminal Court extension, 1966–72. Both are stone-faced, with shallow-arched windows, sparely adorned with classical details and reminiscences: designs that seemed outlandishly old-fashioned when new, but which can now be appreciated as amongst the more original City buildings of the time.

The largest concentration of new public buildings lay within the Barbican Estate, for which *Chamberlin, Powell & Bon* were also the architects. The City of London School for Girls was completed first, in 1969, just as the first residential buildings were occupied (the arts and educational buildings of the Estate may indeed be regarded partly as unusually lavish integrated services for residents). The Guildhall School of Music and Drama followed, in 1977. The schools share the tough aesthetic and compact planning of the residential parts, from which they are distinguished by different patterns of framing and fenestration, and by greater use of brick. Last to be completed, in 1982, was the Barbican Centre. Here the planning is less successful, partly due to revisions which squeezed more functions in; nor do the concrete and white-tiled elevations readily communicate the various internal functions. The much-criticized circulation areas are the weakest feature, though the innovative theatre interior, with its oversailing balconies, must be accounted a success. But the complex demonstrates a remarkable commitment by the Corporation to the cultural life of the City and of London in general: like the South Bank complex before it, it has helped shift the centre of gravity away from the West End. It also restores a theatrical presence to the City after an absence of centuries, in which it was preceded by the Mermaid Theatre off Queen Victoria Street: an inventive conversion by *Devereux & Davies*, 1957–9, of the lower shell of a warehouse of 1850 (since swallowed up in dull late 1970s offices).

Of other EDUCATIONAL BUILDINGS, the thoughtfully planned and friendly St Paul's Cathedral Choir School, by *Leo de Syllas* of the *Architects' Co-Partnership* (1962–7), enlivens the E end of St Paul's Churchyard. The construction of the Museum of London (1968–76, by *Powell & Moya*) completed the London Wall scheme, the final tower of which rises from the superstructure. It also fulfilled a long-standing need by bringing together the mutually complimentary historical collections of the Corporation and the London Museum. The building's ingenious planning does its best to overcome the awkward site, though the result falls short of the architects' best work.

TRANSPORT BUILDINGS, which is to say railway termini, followed the depressing tendency of the 1960s and 70s to replace the main building with anonymous office blocks (Blackfriars and Cannon Street; also Holborn Viaduct, replacing the terminus hotel destroyed in the war). The Fleet Line (later Jubilee Line) was planned in the late 1960s to run through the City, but fell short. Certain buildings of the 1970s were built to accommodate its stations, of which *Arup Associates'* No. 80 Cannon Street (1972–6) combines stalky steel legs with an ingenious system of external lattice framing. HOSPITALS, important architectural expressions of the Welfare State elsewhere in Britain, are represented only by minor extensions at St Bartholomew's.

The dilemma of how to integrate old and new work was faced most acutely by architects of POST-WAR RESTORATION SCHEMES, for which it is necessary to skip back a few decades. Only in exceptional cases were badly damaged commercial buildings repaired (e.g. *Hopper*'s former Atlas Assurance, Cheapside). More attention was devoted to the LIVERY HALLS, most of which had suffered damage. Their restorers had to contend with the strictures of air-raid compensation, which fell short of the full cost of reinstatement. It is unfortunate also that the 1950s and 60s were a low point in traditional craftsmanship. Nevertheless, the Fishmongers and Stationers managed to re-create their lost interiors with some success. The Goldsmiths curiously plumped instead for a mixture of Neo-Louis XV (drawing room, by *F. Billerey*, 1951) and a simplified wood-panelled modern manner. The more severe damage at Merchant Taylors' Hall resulted in some uneasily traditional (though excellently crafted) interiors by *Sir Albert Richardson*, completed 1959. The Carpenters contrived an entirely new building within the old shell – a great novelty for the 1950s, before the 'façade-job' was so named. Its Banqueting Hall uses exotic inlaid woods to create luxurious surroundings without reliance on traditional forms. But the best combination of restored and new work is not at a livery hall but Trinity House, where *Richardson* re-created Samuel Wyatt's interiors with remarkable success in 1952–3, and added a pretty new wing in subtle relationship to the old.

Other livery halls had to be entirely rebuilt. Acutely tradition-conscious, the companies nearly all went for more or less Neo-Georgian designs: another instance of the C20 City's preference for traditional private or intimate spaces, already seen in the nostalgic

Ironmongers' Hall and in the Neo-Wren boardrooms of the inter-war period. While the desire to evoke past glories is understandable, the wells of Neo-Georgian inspiration were undeniably drying up by the 1950s. Yet it has to be admitted also that Modernist architects were slow to demonstrate the potential of the style for prestigious interiors, given good finishes and the right materials. Art Deco had managed this between the wars, but its posthumous twitches in the City do not carry conviction (see the hall in *Sir Giles Gilbert Scott*'s Guildhall offices, intended for livery companies without premises of their own).

The resulting buildings are externally at best mild and pretty (Pewterers, by *D. E. Nye & Partners*, 1959–61), at worst nerveless (Brewers, by *Sir Hubert Worthington*, 1958–60) or stuffy (Mercers, by *Noel Clifton*, 1954–8). It does not help that several incorporated large volumes of office space for rent, eroding the distinctiveness of the building type (Mercers; also *H. Austen Hall*'s Clothworkers' Hall, 1955–8). The interiors vary widely in quality. The Mercers' and (especially) *Kenneth Peacock*'s Leathersellers' Halls (1949–*c*.1959) are extremely good; the halls of less wealthy companies can be painful indeed. It is to be hoped that some of them will follow the Haberdashers, who demolished their dull 1950s hall and offices in 1996, and intend to build new premises in West Smithfield.

One hall of this first wave was in a Modernist idiom: the Bakers', by *Trehearne & Norman, Preston & Partners*, 1961–3 (altered). It has a broad podium for the livery and a square tower of offices on top. The dramatically articulated Salters' Hall, by *Sir Basil Spence*, 1968–76, reverses this arrangement, the Company being accommodated on top of the offices. Its interior is another example of the use of fine woodwork to achieve decorative effects without period trimmings. The Plaisterers' Hall (*John Davies*, 1970–3), also planned in two parts, puts the Company in a giant basement below and behind a discrete office tower. The twist is that the livery suite is bizarrely arrayed in Adamesque plasterwork: a *reductio ad absurdum* of the split between business-like public image and traditional private spaces.

At the LEGAL INNS, the demand was for new chambers to replace those lost, and for these a comfortingly traditional style was favoured. The Inns of Chancery, by this date of course legal bodies in name only, were either rebuilt in replica (Staple Inn, by *Sir Edward Maufe*, 1954–5) or in a weak, loose Neo-Georgian (Serjeants' Inn, by *Devereux & Davies* and *Sir Hubert Worthington*, 1951–8). *Maufe* and *Worthington* were also busy in the 1950s at the Middle Temple and Inner Temple respectively, the latter having been particularly badly damaged. Here and there lost buildings were re-created: the two architects collaborated on a new Master's House based on the old, and Maufe gave the Middle Temple something close to Wren's lost cloister block. Other parts were rebuilt differently. Maufe's Middle Temple Library and Queen Elizabeth Building are pretty and like-able; but the safety-first architecture of the remainder is terribly dull in large quantities, especially in Worthington's new Inner Temple.

The most important single restoration project at the Temple, however, was the Temple Church itself, the destroyed aisles and vaults of which *Walter H. Godfrey* re-created with scrupulous care in 1947–57. This leads us to CHURCH RESTORATION generally. Many parish churches were no less badly damaged, though their shells mostly remained. The Church hierarchy by now accepted their importance as monuments, so only five were wholly written off: the Wren churches of St Stephen Coleman, St Mildred Bread Street, St Swithin Cannon Street and St Mary Aldermanbury (the latter re-erected in the USA), and the little Holy Trinity Minories. Of St Alban and St Augustine only the towers were kept, the latter incorporated into the new St Paul's Cathedral Choir School. The burnt-out shells of Christ Church Newgate Street and St Dunstan-in-the-East were more fortunate, the steeples being restored and the nave walls used to enclose new public gardens. That at St Dunstan, made 1967–71, is particularly well-planned and attractive. At Christ Church, however, the scandalous demolition of the E wall for road widening in 1974 spoils the effect. The site of St Mary Aldermanbury also became a public garden.

Two churches were entirely new. The destroyed Dutch Church was rebuilt by *Arthur Bailey* (1950–4) as a pleasant, somewhat tame stone-faced structure, uninfluenced by the revolution in planning associated with the Liturgical Movement. It was raised up above a lower hall for secular uses: a plan also followed at the modest Jewin Welsh Church, Fann Street (1956–61 by *Caröe & Partners*).

Eleven more severely damaged Anglican parish churches were fully restored. Some benefited from the system of Guild Churches, which aimed to promote or explore particular aspects of the mission of the Church. Even so there is nothing to parallel the innovative reconstructions of bomb-damaged churches in contemporary Germany, a difference which says much about differing national attitudes to the recent past. Only at the medieval All Hallows Barking, restored by *Lord Mottistone* of *Seely & Paget* (completed 1958), was anything drastically new attempted; and even here the concrete-vaulted nave is traditionally detailed, though in a quirky, independent-minded way. Of the Wren churches, the most altered was St Michael Paternoster Royal (by *Elidir Davies*, 1966–8), where the nave was shortened to allow offices to be inserted. *Marshall Sisson*'s reconstruction of St Andrew-by-the Wardrobe in 1959–61 adopted another solution, putting offices in closed-off aisles beneath the re-created galleries.

The rest are generally faithful to the pre-war architectural details, with the odd exception of St Giles Cripplegate, restored as the parish church of the Barbican Estate by *Godfrey Allen* (completed 1960). Its curious late C18 E end was replaced with one to a medieval pattern, on the strength of evidence located in the wall: an echo of the usual techniques of Victorian church restoration. The other medieval casualty, St Olave Hart Street, responded well to straightforward restoration (by *E. B. Glanfield*, 1951–4). Of the Wren period churches, *Cecil Brown*'s restoration of St Lawrence Jewry as the Corporation's church (1954–7) and *Stephen Dykes Bower*'s collegiate replanning of St Vedast (1953–63) deserve the palm. At the former, new carved fittings in a traditional idiom were provided; at the latter, the architect incorporated Wren-period church fittings saved from C19 demolitions. Dykes Bower's characterful rectory alongside is also worth seeking out. A less successful essay in the collegiate fashion is *Godfrey Allen*'s restoration of St Bride (1955–7), where the galleries were omitted and the aisles screened off to create a space that is too long and narrow. *Seely & Paget*'s restoration of St Andrew Holborn, completed 1961, reinstated the galleries and thereby also the old proportions. Wren's shell was re-created at St Mary-le-Bow and St Nicholas Cole Abbey (respectively by *Laurence King*, 1956–64, and *Arthur Bailey*, 1961–2), but furnished in each case in a manner wavering indecisively between period imitation and something more decidedly contemporary.

The post-war period also saw enormous advances made in church archaeology, both at sites of churches destroyed in the bombing or in the Great Fire, and in buildings under restoration. The displays in the crypts of All Hallows Barking and (especially) St Bride add immeasurably to the visitor's understanding of the evolution of the parish church plan in London.

CHURCH FURNISHINGS of the period are for the most part tactfully traditional, even when, as at St Lawrence, they do not replicate their predecessors. The most memorable installation is not in a parish church, but at St Paul's: the exultantly Baroque baldacchino by *Dykes Bower*, completed 1958, replacing the destroyed Victorian reredos. Otherwise the most inventive work was done in STAINED GLASS, both in restored churches and in others which had lost windows to the bombs. Nowhere else in England can one see such a concentration of good work of the period. St Paul's has windows by *Brian Thomas*, introduced as part of the refurnishing of the E end, though the artist's best work is to be seen in St Vedast and St Andrew Holborn. Comparably strong, intricate designs are achieved at *Carl Edwards*'s E windows at the Temple Church, though their inspiration is early medieval rather than Renaissance. *Max Nauta*'s excellent window at the Dutch Church also stands out. Less powerful colours, clearer, thinner lines and a preference for areas of clear glass characterize the work of the artists who carried on the pictorial pre-war style: *Christopher Webb* (St Lawrence Jewry), *Lawrence Lee* (St Magnus, 1949–53, and St Mary Aldermary, 1952), *Gerald Smith* (St Sepulchre, 1946 etc.), *M. C. Farrar Bell* (St Botolph Aldersgate, 1955–8) and *Hugh Easton* (St Peter upon Cornhill, 1951–60). A more modern school combined strong colours with much bolder leading: an approach vastly more compelling artistically, though undeniably at odds with architecture of the Wren period in particular. Highlights are *John Hayward*'s sequences at St Mary-le-Bow and St Michael Paternoster Royal (1964 and 1968), and *Keith New*'s work at St Nicholas Cole Abbey and All Hallows Barking (1962 and 1964).

Little work of note has been installed since the post-war restoration schemes were completed, so the story can swiftly be brought up to the present. The favourite addition has been figurative sculpture, notably by *Josephina de Vasconcellos* (St Paul's and St Bartholomew-the-Great, 1957 and *c.* 1990), and *John Robinson* (All Hallows Barking, 1970). The best monument is *Epstein*'s bust of Stafford Cripps at St Paul's, 1953. St Paul's also has good examples of the post-war revival of letter-cutting, notably those by *David Kindersley*. Abstract and semi-abstract sculpture is represented by two late works in Travertine by *Henry Moore*: a Mother and Child at St Paul's, 1983, and a circular altar at St Stephen Walbrook: the latter the centrepiece of a drastic and fiercely contested re-ordering of that church (1978–87, by *Robert Potter*). *Quinlan Terry*'s no less controversial re-ordering of St Helen Bishopsgate (1993–5, after damage from terrorist bombs) has not produced any new fittings of note. St Ethelburga was partly destroyed in the second of these explosions (1993); the details of its restoration have yet to be decided.

THE FINANCIAL CAPITAL
c. 1975–96

The mid 1970s mark something of a breathing-space in the City's post-war development. The market for commercial office space, always subject to booms and slumps, had been distorted by Governmental restrictions imposed in 1964. Removal of these restrictions in 1970 prompted a surge of new building, only for the economic slump of the middle of the decade to spoil the office market. In consequence the City has few large offices of the late 1970s.

The date to bear in mind for COMMERCIAL ARCHITECTURE AFTER 1980 is 1986, when the 'Big Bang' saw the regulation of trading in stocks and shares relaxed, allowing dealing from screens rather than face-to-face. At the same time banks were permitted to undertake trading on their own behalf, in line with American practice. Foreign banks were already rushing into London, the number with offices there rising from 135 in 1969 to 470 by 1984. The result was a surge in demand for wide, unobstructed dealing floors, usually accommodated in a new type of broad, deep and relatively low 'groundscraper' building, of which many also included an atrium. The demand is reflected in planning permissions for office floor space, which tripled in area between 1985 and 1986, and nearly doubled again between 1986 and 1987, to some 12,700,000 square ft (1,180,000 square metres). It has been estimated that half the office volume of the City was rebuilt between 1985 and 1993: a figure that can only be compared with the rebuilding after the Great Fire.

The dominance of electronic trading also meant that a location near the Bank and Stock Exchange was no longer necessary, encouraging relocation to new sites on the City fringes. From the City's point of view, there was also a danger that banks and exchanges would move further, to the large, modern and cheap buildings being erected in the Docklands. The important dates are 1981, when the London Docklands Development Corporation was set up, and 1985, when the first proposals for a great office complex at Canary Wharf were published. The abolition of the GLC in 1986 removed the only body that might have adjudicated between the City and its new rival. The hope of the Reichmann Brothers, chief developers of Canary Wharf, was that the financial centre of gravity would shift irreversibly away from the City to the new complex. In the event sufficient new buildings were provided in the City to prevent this. Many used railway land, either by 'air rights' structures contrived over the platforms of the termini (at Fenchurch Street by *Fitzroy*'s, 1983–7; at Cannon Street by *BDP*, 1987–91), or following the abandonment of old stations and routes (Broad Street and Holborn Viaduct, for which *see* below). These schemes are a reminder of the density of transport routes into the City, something the Docklands sorely lacked. Many more new sites were procured by demolition, often of quite recent buildings; indeed, well over a quarter of post-war City buildings mentioned in the last edition of *London 1* (1973) are no more.

The ATRIUM OFFICE BLOCK is the characteristic product of this boom. Sometimes unjustly derided as a cliché, it has in fact been responsible for an enormous increase in the variety and interest of the office as a building type. Once more the source is America, which has a long tradition (rarely taken up in the City) of public access to and through the foyers of large commercial buildings. Besides its connotations of prestige and its improvement of the working environment in general, the atrium usually also functions as a means of controlling internal air quality and circulation. One of its preconditions was therefore the widespread adoption of air conditioning from the later 1960s, which made possible a shift away from the shallow plans of the first post-war building wave. The deep, tall, open floors that took their place appear as early as 1971–6 at *Fitzroy*'s Aldgate House, Aldgate High Street. The atrium was introduced to the City at *Fitzroy Robinson & Partners*' Institute of London Underwriters, Leadenhall Street (1972–8), where it is concealed behind even façades. Its theatrical potential as a grand street entrance was first realized in *Fitzroy*'s Lloyds Chambers, Mansell Street (1980–3), though this is less successful than the firm's extravagant former Standard Chartered Bank, Bishopsgate (1980–5, since altered). Here it appears as a tall, broad indoor garden, glazed to the street, within a polished-stone-clad framework that develops the manner of the practice's Banque Nationale de Paris (*see* above). At the Royal Bank of Canada, Queen Victoria Street, by *Sidney Kaye Firmin Partnership* with *Crang & Boake* (1983–8), the atrium passes through the whole building on a series of levels, appearing externally as big glazed entrances in the manner of a shopping mall. At the British Telecom Centre (by the *Department of the Environment* (*British Telecom Services Division*), 1980–5), the atrium appears as narrow glazed sections between rather uninspired stone-faced ranges facing the street; at *Covell Matthews Wheatley Partnership*'s Samuel Montagu, Lower Thames Street, 1983–5, it is top-lit and entirely concealed within an envelope of blue mirror glass. The last three contain lifts of the 'wall-climber' type.

All these atrium blocks are eclipsed by the City's two chief essays in the high-tech manner. At *Richard Rogers Partnership*'s Lloyd's of
146 London (1978–86), the enormously tall atrium is but one feature in an audacious and entirely original reconfiguration of the functions and services of a modern office building, doubly exceptional for the City in being so intensely personal a design (*see* p. 313 for illustration). It is a performance which no degree of familiarity can make stale. The other, austere and restrained by comparison, is *Arup Associates*' No. 1 Finsbury Avenue, Broadgate (1982–4). This can claim to have been the first fully-fledged atrium block to be completed in the City, though the space (infilled in 1996–7) is concealed within the even, skeletal façades.

No. 1 also demonstrated the potential of 'fast-track' construction, with all-steel framing (floors included), dry internal finishes, and high-specification prefabricated cladding. These American-derived techniques were pioneered at a modest building by *Renton Howard Wood Levin Partnership* in Cutler Street (Cutlers' Court, designed 1981): an outlier of the giant Cutlers' Gardens scheme (*R. Seifert &*

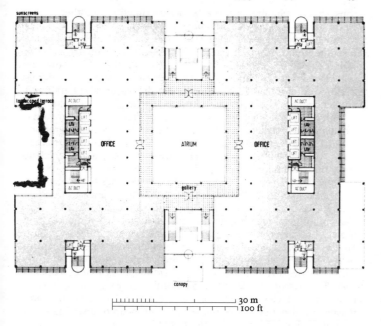

No. 1 Finsbury Avenue. Plan, level 1

Partners, 1978–82). This turned the East India Company's great p.
warehouses into a civilized traffic-free precinct, at the cost of demo- 476
lition of half of the buildings and the reduction of most of the others
to retained façades. It also shows the developer, Greycoat Estates, 90
assimilating American ideas of hard-landscaped public spaces.

The City's single greatest exercise in these fast-track methods is
the Broadgate Centre, the later stages of which were built 1985–91 150,
(though one block, Broadwalk House, is concrete-framed). It was p.
planned by Rosehaugh Stanhope, heirs to the developers of Cutlers' 435
Gardens, in conjunction with British Rail, whose Liverpool Street
station was remodelled and extended with great panache as part of
the scheme. The site of the former Broad Street station provided the
rest of the land. With its well-planned and highly individual public
spaces, lavish free-standing sculpture (*see below*), grand water-
features and subtle planting, this is by far the most attractive and
impressive piece of post-war planning in the City. The blocks of
the s part, by *Arup Associates*, have solid external stone screens and
atriums interrupting the façade at the entrances. The eclectic architecture of the n phase, by the American firm *Skidmore, Owings &
Merrill*, is less satisfactory. The best block is Exchange House, which 152
makes very effective use of external steel framing: a method also
used, though to very different effect, at two of *SOM*'s blocks at the
same developer's Fleet Place (1990–2). Here the public spaces are 155
less successful, due to the awkwardly long and narrow site: the former Holborn Viaduct station, released by the re-routing of the old
London, Chatham & Dover Railway underground.

English high-tech and American steel framing both represent

conscious developments of the Modernist functional aesthetic. Such recent buildings as *Sir Denys Lasdun*'s triple-skinned island block called
156 Milton Gate, Chiswell Street (1987–91) and the minimal front of
157 Insignia House, Mansell Street (*Elana Keats & Associates* and *John Winter & Associates* with *Jonathan Ellis-Miller*, 1990–1) show the continued vitality in the hands of English architects of another Modernist tradition, that of the all-glass front. But the majority of City buildings since the early 1980s have returned to the past for inspiration.

This POSTMODERNIST philosophy of design appeared early on in a blatantly non-structural display of columns at *Boyd Auger*'s refronting of Clifford's Inn, facing Fetter Lane (1983). A similar archness marks the pilastered No. 70 Fleet Street (1983–6) and the relentlessly bizarre infill in the City Village scheme, Lovat Lane (1981–4), both by the *Thomas Saunders Partnership*. Buildings of more enduring appeal include *J. Sampson Lloyd*'s gabled and jettied Founders'
147 Hall (1984–6), which pays homage to the C17 architecture of Cloth Fair in a playful way that transcends the usual neo-vernacular formulae that came in with the 1970s. The same architect's Pellipar House, Cloak Lane (1987–91) and redevelopment of the old Mercers' School site, Fetter Lane (1988–92), are witty and well-crafted fronts with inventive arrays of superimposed columns. *Richard Dickinson* of
148 *Rolfe Judd Group Practice*'s No. 68 Cornhill (1981–4), a stone-faced façade full of clever quotations and echoes of past architectural masters, is also a tactful response to the problem of inserting a new front in a sequence of older buildings of high quality.

More typical of the Postmodernism that became the commercial norm in the later 1980s is the bold, simplified manner of *Terry*
149 *Farrell*. His No. 36 Queen Street (1982–6) and No. 69 Fenchurch Street (1986–7) introduced several much-imitated devices for commercial fronts: the tripartite division of the façade, roughly proportioned to imply a base, giant order and cornice; the cutting-back of the front at the entrance to expose a turret or glazed bow; strongly contrasted colours; and big, simplified key-blocks. An important influence on the architect was the pioneering Postmodernist work of the American architect Michael Graves: a debt which appears most strongly at *Farrell*'s huge Alban Gate, London Wall (1988–92), which began the replacement of the 1960s buildings there. Another favourite source was the Viennese Secession, evoked in Farrell's Queen Street building and taken up in much recent work by *Fitzroy*'s (No. 55 Bishopsgate, 1988–91). The influential use of colour and of schematized, historically resonant forms is also characteristic of the work of the late *James Stirling*, who was enlisted for Lord Palumbo's No. 1 Poultry (to be completed 1997): a design made in 1986–8, but delayed by attempts to save the important High Victorian buildings on the site. The development represents an unwelcome return to the wholesale erasure of the City's older fabric (though less drastic than *Mies van der Rohe*'s designs for a tower block and public square on the site, made 1962–8).

American influences appear also in the recent work of two large commercial firms well represented in the City. *RHWL Partnership*'s No. 1 America Square, 1988–91, is an 'air rights' block with a flavour of 1930s New York. *GMW Partnership*'s Minster Court, Mincing
151 Lane, 1987–91, is a flagrantly populist pile of peaks and gables made up of three shallow-arcaded blocks; their Barclays Bank, Lombard

Street, 1986–94, culminates in round-topped silvery towers. These three buildings have the usual deep plans, but stand out more because of their impact on the skyline: a characteristic shared by the American firm *Kohn Pederson Fox Associates*' well-planned redevelopment of the former *Telegraph* site in Fleet Street, for Goldman Sachs (1988–91). The work of *SOM* has already been mentioned; a third large American practice, *Swanke Hayden Connell*, is represented by a brash block on London Wall (Nos. 55–60, 1988–92).

Such spectacles apart, the infiltration of historically derived forms into commercial architecture also developed a tendency towards blockish, chunky stone-clad forms apparent from the later 1970s. *Chapman Taylor Partners*' Friary Court (Touche Ross), Crutched Friars (1981–5, with a spectacular water feature in the American manner), is a good, if late, example of the type. *RHWL Partnership*'s jazzy recladding of the 1950s blocks in Tudor Street for KPMG (1984–6) sees Egyptianizing touches creep in. Elsewhere, the simplified high-relief manner has been used in attempts to harmonize with neighbouring older buildings, generally by the device of echoing something of their proportions. Good examples include *Kenzie Lovell Partnership*'s River Plate House, Finsbury Circus (1986–90) and *Fitzroy*'s No. 1 Threadneedle Street (1987–91). Recent efforts have approached historical pastiche, as at *Fitzroy*'s No. 120 Old Broad Street (1989–93), in the manner of Mewès & Davis, or *Whinney Mackay-Lewis Partnership*'s bombastic, beporticoed Vintners' Place, an atrium block on Upper Thames Street (1990–3).

The bulk of post-war PUBLIC ART in the City is of recent vintage, so can be discussed here. Large-scale public SCULPTURE is so much a feature of the present-day City that it is a surprise to learn how little from the C20 dates from before 1969. In that year bold abstract pieces by *Antanas Brazdys* and *Allen David* (a fountain) were installed near Guildhall, respectively in Basinghall Street and Aldermanbury. So many pieces have been erected since then that only a few can be mentioned here. More figurative traditions are represented by works by *Elizabeth Frink*, *Bainbridge Copnall*, *Georg Ehrlich* and *Michael Ayrton* in and around St Paul's Churchyard (1973–5), with another small figure by *Ayrton* at St Botolph Aldersgate (1973). Naturalistic sculpture includes *John Robinson*'s hammer-thrower at Tower Hill, and *James Butler*'s statues for the Corporation of John Wilkes (1988) and J.H. Greathead (1993), respectively in Fetter Lane and Cornhill. The surprisingly modest amount of public art at the Barbican Centre has recently been augmented with new works by *Matthew Spender* and others, as part of *Pentagram*'s improvements there. But the greatest patrons of sculpture have been Rosehaugh Stanhope, at their Broadgate and Fleet Place developments (1985–91 and 1990–2). The concentrations of gigantic and genuinely challenging works there, inspired by the public spaces of such American cities as Seattle, as yet have no parallel in an English city. British artists represented include *Stephen Cox*, *Bruce McLean* and *Barry Flanagan*; foreign artists, *George Segal*, *Jacques Lipchitz*, *Richard Serra* and *Fernando Botero*. Other privately commissioned works deserving of mention are *Michael Sandle*'s St George and the Dragon (1988) off Tudor Street, *Eduardo Paolozzi*'s self-portrait at Bracton House, High Holborn (1987) and *Althea Wynne*'s three horses at Minster Court, Mincing Lane (1989–90).

Works of art integrated with buildings are rarer. Architectural sculpture was carried on into the 1950s on such traditional buildings as St Swithin's House, St Swithin's Lane (figures by *Siegfried Charoux*) and New Change Buildings, Cheapside (work by *Wheeler* and others), but fell out of fashion with the advance of Modernism. Of 1960s work, *Henry Moore*'s sundial in front of *The Times* in Queen Victoria Street and works by various artists inside B.P.'s Britannic Tower in Ropemaker Street were removed when those buildings were sold. Works remaining *in situ* include *D. Annam*'s ceramic murals at the Farringdon Street Telephone Exchange (1960) and *John Hutton*'s engraved glass screens at Bucklersbury House, Queen Victoria Street (*c.* 1958). Another screen by *Hutton* (1979) is at Butchers' Hall; other notable works at the Livery Halls include *John Piper*'s tapestries at Grocers' Hall (1968) and stained-glass windows at Bakers' Hall (1969). The Guildhall School of Music (Barbican) has a delicate, understated stained-glass frieze by *Celia Frank, c.* 1977. More recently, stained-glass artists have found favour with developers of commercial buildings: *Brian Clarke* at *RHWL*'s No. 100 New Bridge Street (1990–2, an outlier of the Fleet Place scheme) and No. 1 America Square; *Goddard & Gibbs Studios* at BKB House, King William Street (1986–9 by *Ronald Ward & Partners*).

No mention so far has been made of peacetime demolitions, or of the backlash against further rebuilding which they provoked. The rate of destruction of (especially) Victorian and Edwardian buildings from the 1960s onwards was indeed alarming. In that decade Lombard Street lost the important banks by *Waterhouse* and *Parnell*, and the Coal Exchange fell victim to the widening of Lower Thames Street. The destruction continued into the early 1970s with the group at the SE corner of Bishopsgate, including *Norman Shaw*'s Baring Bros. Many other buildings which have survived were also threatened at this time, including Liverpool Street station and the City of London Club. Besides such landmarks, the City's close-knit streets and alleys were also being rapidly redeveloped, often for large buildings of extraordinary drabness (*see* e.g. *C. Edmund Wilford & Sons*' Fleetbank House, Salisbury Square, 1971–5).

The new mood was reflected in the important *Save The City* report, published in 1976 by the Society for the Protection of Ancient Buildings, Georgian Group, Victorian Society and Civic Trust. By that date much more of the old City had been safeguarded, either by Listing (ninety-eight C19 and C20 buildings in 1972 alone), or by the designation of Conservation Areas (the first eight in 1971; more in 1974 and later). The characteristic minor architecture of such streets as Bow Lane was thus safeguarded, and the ped-way scheme effectively extinguished as a comprehensive system.

The return to more vernacular forms for HOUSING, of great importance nationally in the 1970s, appears in the City only at *Trehearne & Norman, Preston & Partners*' spacious but architecturally disappointing Guinness Trust Estate, Mansell Street (1977–81), and at *Hubbard Ford & Partners*' private Queensbridge House, Upper Thames Street (1972–5), both clad in the inevitable brown brick. However, the City lacked much scope for the kind of community-based or nostalgic 'heritage' projects popular elsewhere (the conversion of Whitbread's Brewery in Chiswell Street by *Wolff Olins* and *Roderick Gradidge*, 1977–9, is one exception).

The growing numbers of protected buildings were often updated by the drastic practice of RECONSTRUCTION WITHIN RETAINED FAÇADES. This expedient was pioneered by *Fitzroy Robinson & Partners* at Nos. 13–15 Moorgate in 1966, but was not widely adopted until the early 1980s. One intriguing harbinger is *Sheppard Robson & Partners'* Nos. 150–152 Fenchurch Street, completed 1976, where a narrow retained front of the 1860s is deliberately incorporated like a giant applied panel. *Fitzroy's* Union plc at Nos. 39–42 Cornhill (1975–9) inventively combines two late Victorian properties (by *Macvicar Anderson* and *Tabberer*). The favourable reception given to such early schemes faltered once it was clear that the 'façade-job' had become the standard response of developers and owners to buildings they were not allowed to demolish. However, the better schemes preserve or re-create at least the entrance spaces of the buildings (*see* e.g. the former British and Foreign Bible Society, Queen Victoria Street, or the former Phoenix Fire Assurance in King William Street, respectively by *T. P. Bennett & Son*, 1987–9, and *Fitzroy Robinson*, 1983–7). The success or failure of such schemes depends also on the appropriateness of any new side or rear elevations (especially common where several properties are amalgamated), and on the detailing of any added storeys. *Fitzroy's* reconstruction of the Royal Exchange (1986–91) manages to squeeze in an extra storey towards the courtyard which respects the discipline of the super-imposed orders, while not appearing too obtrusive externally. Of other schemes with added storeys, *Whinney Mackay-Lewis Partnership's* overhaul of Basildon House, Moorgate (1988–92) manages unusually well; but a heavy and uninteresting slated or leaded mansard is more common. The tail emphatically wags the dog at the former Cripplegate Institute, Golden Lane, heightened and enormously extended in 1987–92 (*Ergon Design Group*). Even this is preferable to the deplor-able practice of demolition and rebuilding in replica, of which No. 1 St Paul's Churchyard is the largest example (by *John Gill Associates*, 1985–7, impersonating a warehouse by *Herbert Ford*, *c*. 1896). Perhaps the best single scheme of internal reconstruction is *Inskip & Jenkins's* 154 refurbishment of Lutyens's Britannic House, Finsbury Circus (1987–9). The elevations and circulation spaces were treated with scrupulous respect, but a bold and well-detailed new atrium was inserted instead of the original twin lightwells. No less successful is *Michael Hopkins's* development of Bracken House (1988–91), Cannon 153, Street. Here the new work appears unapologetically between p. *Richardson's* retained fronts as a green-glazed, steel-framed mass 445 containing new offices and a concealed atrium.

In conclusion, some predictions about the FUTURE OF THE CITY'S ARCHITECTURE may be offered, at least as far as types and uses are concerned. The demand for broad floor-plates continues, with several very large schemes under construction or in prospect (e.g. Bull Wharf, Upper Thames Street, and on the former Garrard House site, Gresham Street). Smaller tenants can be accommodated in old or refurbished properties, of which the City has no shortage, and this flexibility must be accounted an advantage.

A very recent development is the revival of proposals for very tall buildings, encouraged by the abolition of plot ratios for exceptional cases in 1993. The end of the 1980s saw the return of new buildings tall enough to make an impact on the skyline, as has already been

noted, though they did not vie in height with the wave of tall buildings of the 1960s.* The latest schemes owe much to competition
between the City and other financial centres, notably with Docklands,
where the central tower of Canary Wharf rises to 824 ft (251 metres),
half as high again as the NatWest Tower, and with Frankfurt, where
Norman Foster's Commerzbank reaches some 926 ft (282 metres).
In these circumstances height threatens to become an end in itself, as
at *Foster*'s gigantic new tower 1076 ft (328 metres) high, proposed for
the Baltic Exchange site in St Mary Axe in 1996. This looks unlikely
to proceed at the time of writing, although the proposed remodelling
and heightening of Britannic Tower, Ropemaker Street, may yet go
ahead; the choice of the Catalan architect *Santiago Calatrava* is
symptomatic of the very recent tendency to enlist prestigious 'big
names' for sensitive projects. The present skyline should certainly
not be regarded as immutable.

The spread of Conservation Areas (34 per cent of the City in
1997) and of Listing generally means that new buildings are increasingly likely to be built at the expense of large post-war offices. However, changes in information technology are continuing to reduce the
minimum viable floor height, which at air-conditioned properties of
1970s vintage is already sufficient to justify refurbishment on the old
frame – the negative image of the familiar façade-job (e.g. *Sheppard
Robson*'s work at the Whitbread Site, Chiswell Street, 1996).

As to older buildings, no alternative to the practice of rebuilding
and amalgamation behind retained façades can easily be foreseen if
they are to produce high commercial returns. The long-empty group
of banks and insurance offices between Old Broad Street and
Threadneedle Street is the most conspicuous example. Particular
problems are presented by specialized buildings no longer required
for their original purpose. By the time this book appears, Sion College
and the Public Record Office will have joined this category. It is
therefore pleasing to record the Corporation's commitment to the
future of Smithfield and Leadenhall Markets (both restored or
under restoration), the recent refurbishment of the Custom House,
and the decision of Lloyd's Register of Shipping to retain its premises,
with a new extension by the *Richard Rogers Partnership*. The rejection
of the Templeman Report (1994), which proposed the closure of all
but a dozen of the remaining City churches, is no less gratifying.

Another encouraging development is the growing number of smaller
buildings being converted to flats, even in such former redoubts of
high finance as Cornhill: a much more sympathetic fate than the
drastic demands of modernization for office use. New residential
buildings are also under construction in the City again, though so far
the results are undistinguished (Bridgewater Square and Little Britain).
The everyday environment for both residents and workers has been
enormously improved by the diversion of traffic away from most of

---

* Tall buildings in post-war London began with the Shell Centre on the South Bank,
completed 1962, at 338 ft (103 metres). The important landmarks thereafter are, in
order of height and with date of completion: Millbank Tower, Westminster, 1963, 382 ft
(116½ metres); Commercial Union, City, 1969, 387 ft (118 metres); Britannic Tower,
City, 1967, 395 ft (120 metres); Hilton Hotel, Westminster, 1963, 405 ft (123½ metres);
Euston Centre, Euston Road, c. 1968, 408 ft (124⅓ metres); Barbican flats, City, late
1960s, 412 ft (125½ metres); Post Office Tower, Marylebone, 1965, 579 ft (177½ metres);
NatWest Tower, City, 1981, 600 ft (183 metres); Canary Wharf Tower, Docklands,
1991, 824 ft (251 metres).

the centre, a measure introduced to protect the City after two destructive terrorist bombs in 1992 and 1993. 1,300 new residents were brought within the City by the boundary changes of 1994, raising the total to an estimated 7,155 in 1995. The main alterations were to add to the City the w side of Mansell Street, the remainder of the Broadgate Centre and Golden Lane Estate, and the E side of Chancery Lane. These changes, combined with the widespread late C20 movement back to living in city centres, means that the City will enter the next millennium with a rising resident population for the first time in nearly two centuries.

FURTHER READING

The literature concerned with London is vast, and a high proportion of it relates in some way to the City. *The Bibliography of Printed Works on London History to 1939*, edited by Heather Creaton (1994), lists nearly 22,000 items on the capital. Other bibliographies include *London* (1996, vol. 189 in the *World Bibliographical Series*) by the same compiler, a shorter guide with longer citations, including some post-war items. A bibliography specifically for the City was compiled by Raymond Smith for the National Book League in 1951. The fullest collection of material relating to the City is at the Guildhall Library. The best all-purpose reference book on London is the *Encyclopaedia of London*, edited by B. Weinreb and C. Hibbert (2nd ed. 1992). Of single-volume histories, C. Hibbert's *London, the Biography of a City* (1986) and Roy Porter's *London, a Social History* (1994) stand out. S. E. Rasmussen, *London, the Unique City* (revised edition, 1967), is still the best introduction to the topography and development up to the C20.

On the Prehistoric and Roman periods the most recent studies are by Gustav Milne (English Heritage, 1995) and Dominic Perring (1991), both called *Roman London*. Peter Marsden, *Roman London* (1980), and Ralph Merrifield, *London, City of the Romans* (1983), also remain valuable. All these books in turn contain detailed bibliographies. H. Chapman et al., *The London Wall Walk* (1985), and C. Jones, *Roman Mosaics* (1986), are well-illustrated introductions, both produced for the Museum of London. *Interpreting Roman London* (1996), edited by Joanna Bird, Mark Hassall and Harvey Sheldon, contains several relevant essays. The Council for British Archaeology has produced detailed surveys of areas and themes, of which the recent *The Upper Walbrook Valley* (C. Moloney, 1990), *The Development of Roman London West of the Walbrook* (D. Perring and S. Roskams, 1990), and *Public Buildings in the South-West Quarter of Roman London* (1993) are relevant. Other studies include Peter Marsden, *The Roman Forum Site in London* (1987), and Gustav Milne, *The Port of Roman London* (1985) and *From Roman Basilica to Medieval Market* (1992). The chief journals for the Roman and medieval period are the *Transactions of the London and Middlesex Archaeological Society* and the *London Archaeologist*. Field reports from 1973 onwards, when an archaeological unit devoted to the City was first established, are kept at the Museum of London.

The standard history of Saxon and early medieval London is C.N.L. Brooke and G. Keir, *London 800–1216* (1975), which also takes account of post-war archaeological discoveries. Many of these are described in more detail by their excavator W.F. Grimes, in his *The Excavation of Roman and Medieval London* (1968). There is no recent archaeological account; an *Archive Guide* with site-by-site bibliography is in preparation by the Museum of London. The early period is covered by Alan Vince, *Saxon London* (1990) and by Martin Biddle in the introduction to M.D. Lobel (ed.), *The British Atlas of Historic Towns*, vol. 3, *The City of London* (1989). A series of monographs on seven of the largest monasteries and hospitals in and around the City is in preparation by the Museum of London. Secular properties are surveyed by John Schofield in *Medieval London Houses* (1995), with a gazetteer of sites, and *The London Surveys of Ralph Treswell* (in London Topographical Society, 1987), which makes available an important collection of house plans of *c.* 1600. The same author's *The Building of London* (1984, 2nd ed. 1993) is a succinct account of sacred and secular buildings between the Conquest and Great Fire, while his article in *Transactions of the London and Middlesex Archaeological Society* 47 (1996) summarizes what is known of the medieval parish churches. The *British Archaeological Association Conference Transactions* for 1984 (1990) contains several important articles, notably those on late medieval church monuments (Bridget Cherry), the Temple Church (C.M.L. Gardam) and Old St Paul's (Richard Gem). John Stow's *Survey of London* (1603) is available in several editions, the best that by C.L. Kingsford (1908, reprinted 1971). Mirielle Galinou (ed.), *London's Pride, The Glorious History of London's Parks and Gardens* (1990), touches on an overlooked aspect of the City's history. Eilert Ekwall, *Street Names of the City of London* (1955) also deserves mention. Monographs on particular sites and buildings include G. Home's *Old London Bridge* (1930) and C. Barron's *The Medieval Guildhall of London* (1974). A separate bibliography of the Tower is given on p. 357. The most ambitious exercise in medieval urban history so far published, albeit only in microfiche, is D.J. Keene and V. Harding, *Historical Gazetteer of London before the Great Fire*, 1, *Cheapside* (1987); further studies, of the Walbrook and Aldgate areas, may be consulted at the Centre for Metropolitan History.

Essential topographical tools for the post-medieval period are Bernard Adams, *London Illustrated, 1604–1851*, and the five volumes of historic map facsimiles produced by the *London Topographical Society*, 1982–92. Other maps are catalogued by J. Howgego, *Printed Maps of London c. 1553–1850* (2nd ed. 1978) and R. Hyde, *Printed Maps of Victorian London 1851–1910* (1975). Of historical and architectural studies, N.G. Brett James, *The Growth of Stuart London* (1935), puts the City in its contemporary urban context. The London Topographical Society has published the surveys made in the post-Fire rebuilding (1962–7), a process of which T.F. Reddaway, *The Rebuilding of London after the Great Fire* (1940), remains the standard account. D. Knoop and G.P. Jones, *The London Mason in the Seventeenth Century* (1935), is also valuable. The literature on Wren includes works by Margaret Whinney (1971) and Kerry Downes (1982); other items are listed after the account of St Paul's (*see* p. 183). An unrivalled account of the design and construction of the

C17 City churches is Paul Jeffery, *The Parish Churches of Sir Christopher Wren* (1996). Gerald Cobb, *City of London Churches* (3rd ed. 1989), remains the best overall survey of the churches and their fittings, including the medieval period. G. Godwin and J. Britton, *The Churches of London* (2 vols., 1838) has an entry for every City church.

For the late C17 to the early C19 the essential work is Sir John Summerson's peerless *Georgian London* (1945, latest revision 1988). For the urban fabric there is *Good and Proper Materials, the Fabric of London since the Great Fire*, ed. Ann Saunders (1989, London Topographical Society). C. C. Knowles and P. H. Pitt, *The History of Building Regulations in London 1189–1972* (1972), deserves mention in this connection. Georgian houses are described in D. Cruickshank and P. Wyld, *London, the Art of Georgian Building* (1975). D. Cruickshank and N. Burton, *Life in the Georgian City* (1990), has many valuable insights concerning the day-to-day use of buildings. Contemporary topographical accounts include Edward Hatton, *A New View of London* (1708), and Strype's revision of Stow's *Survey* (1720). James Elmes's profusely illustrated *Metropolitan Improvements* (1827) and *London in the Nineteenth Century* (1829), and John Tallis, *London Street Views* (1838–47), are available in modern facsimile. John Britton *et al.*, *Illustrations of the Public Buildings of London* (3 vols., 1825–38), contains good measured drawings.

There is no single overview of the Victorian period. C. Welch, *A Modern History of the City of London* (1896), is a diverting and well-illustrated yearly chronicle. The best historical account is David Kynaston, *The City of London* (2 vols., 1994–5), which concentrates on the City's financial growth between 1815 and 1914 (a third volume covering the period to the mid C20 is in preparation). K. Young and P. Garside, *Metropolitan London, Politics and Urban Change 1837–1981*, explains the evolving relationship of the City with the rest of London. Francis Sheppard, *London 1808–1870, the Infernal Wen* (1971), is also useful. The best architectural accounts, though partial, are by Sir John Summerson, reprinted in his collected essays *The Unromantic Castle* (1990), on the Victorian rebuilding of the City (1840–70) and the London building world of the 1860s. Gavin Stamp and Colin Amery, *Victorian Buildings of London 1837–1887* (1980), includes many examples from the City. The impact of the railways is covered in T. C. Barker and Michael Robbins, *A History of London Transport* (2 vols., 1963–74); H. P. White, *A Regional History of the Railways of Great Britain*, vol. 3, *Greater London* (2nd ed. 1971), and A. A. Jackson, *London's Termini* (2nd ed. 1983).

For the C20, the Corporation's *Reconstruction in the City of London* (1944) has excellent maps of the City just before the Second World War, while Charles Holden and W. G. Holford, *The City of London, a Record of Destruction and Survival* (1951) combines later plans for post-war reconstruction with a perceptive account of the City's history and character. Lionel Esher, *A Broken Wave, the Rebuilding of England 1940–1980* (1981), gives a concise overview of the outcome. The extraordinary story of the elevated walkway project is told by M. Hebbert in the *Journal of the American Planning Association*, 59 (1993). The important report *Save the City* (1976) argues against wholesale redevelopment in favour of preserving the City's traditional character and buildings. For present planning policy there is the *City of London Unitary Development Plan* (latest ed. 1994).

General surveys of buildings and monuments include the RCHME's volume (1929), the fourth of five volumes covering London, although this excludes anything later than 1714. Details of the many Listed buildings are given in the Department of National Heritage's *Lists of Buildings of Historic and Architectural Interest*. On demolished buildings there is *From Splendour to Banality, the Rebuilding of the City of London 1945–1983* (SAVE Britain's Heritage 1983), a collection of photographs 'before and after', and H. Hobhouse, *Lost London* (1971), which gives a longer view of architectural change.

The many buildings of national importance in the City are covered by general architectural histories, of which Sir John Summerson, *Architecture in Britain 1530–1830* (revised 1991), *Victorian Architecture* by R. Dixon and S. Muthesius (1978) and *Edwardian Architecture* by A. Service (1977) are the best starting-points. For individual architects H. M. Colvin, *Biographical Dictionary of English Architects 1600–1840* (3rd ed. 1995), the *Directory of British Architects 1834–1900* (British Architectural Library, 1993) and A. S. Gray, *Edwardian Architecture, A Biographical Dictionary* (1985), should be consulted. A. Service, *The Architects of London* (1979), is a series of pithy essays on leading figures up to the late C20. For individual buildings contemporary periodicals are usually the best source: the *Illustrated London News*, *The Builder* and *Building News* (later *Architect and Building News*) for the C19; the *Architectural Review*, *Architects' Journal* and the *London Architect* for the C20. For sculptors there is Rupert Gunnis, *Dictionary of British Sculptors 1660–1851* (3rd ed. forthcoming); for the C16 and early C17 a dictionary is in preparation by Adam White.

For particular building types, J. Booker, *Temples of Mammon, the Architecture of Banking* (1990), and M. Girouard, *Victorian Pubs* (1975), are the standard works. W. A. D. Englefield and P. J. A. Lubbock, *The Halls of the Livery Companies of the City of London* (1981), is illustrated with numerous early C20 drawings. Richard Saxon, *The Atrium Comes of Age* (1994), discusses several examples in the City. Monographs on architects of particular significance for the City include Dorothy Stroud, *George Dance* (1971), G. E. Cherry and L. Penny, *Holford, A Study in Architecture, Planning and Civic Design* (1986), and Andrew Saint, *Richard Norman Shaw* (1976).

Studies of particular sites, properties and institutions are numerous, many of them excellent. F. J. Froom, *A Site in Poultry* (1950), is a pioneering historical study of a small City plot. Of other works, Penelope Hunting, *Cutlers' Gardens* (1984), and A. Forshaw and T. Bergstrom, *Smithfield Past and Present* (2nd ed. 1990), stand out. Susie Barson and Andrew Saint, *A Farewell to Fleet Street* (1988), is the essential guide to the growth and premises of the printing industry. The *Survey of London* covers the parishes of All Hallows Barking (vol. 9, 1924) and St Helen Bishopsgate (vols. 12 and 15, 1929 and 1934), although these are much less comprehensive than later volumes in the series. Most City churches have detailed published histories. Two notable recent examples are by Paul Jeffery, *The Parish Church of St Vedast-alias-Foster* (2nd ed. 1994), and *The Parish Church of St Mary-at-Hill* (1996), both for the Ecclesiological Society. Of the Livery Halls, Jean Imray, *The Mercers' Hall* (London

Topographical Society, 1991), and Priscilla Metcalf, *The Halls of the Fishmongers' Company* (1984), give admirable accounts of the succession of buildings on the site. A volume on the Royal Exchange, edited by Ann Saunders, is under preparation for the London Topographical Society. Many other works are noted in the relevant gazetteer entries. Peter Jackson, *Walks in Old London* (1993), brings together comparative historic views of numerous City streets.

Finally one should list guides and surveys suitable for immediate reference. Church guides include Sir John Betjeman, *The City of London Churches* (2nd ed., 1993), Elizabeth and Wayland Young, *London's Churches* (1986), and B. F. L. Clarke, *Parish Churches of London* (1966). Traces of the lost churches and their parishes are recorded in Gordon Huelin, *Vanished Churches of the City of London* (1996). Elain Harwood and Andrew Saint, *London* (English Heritage, 1991), and Ian Nairn, *Nairn's London* (1966, revised 1988), include lively accounts of selected City buildings. Ann Saunders, *Art and Architecture of London* (1984), covers the whole capital rather more comprehensively. Eric Robinson, *Illustrated Geological Walks, London* (2 vols., 1984–5), surveys the City's buildings from the unusual angle of their exotic and multifarious cladding stones. For the last ten years or so there is Samantha Hardingham, *London, A Guide to Recent Architecture* (2nd ed. 1994).

CITY OF LONDON

ST PAUL'S CATHEDRAL

OLD ST PAUL'S AND ITS PREDECESSORS

The medieval cathedral in its completed form was one of the largest and finest in England. It is far better known than any other building destroyed in the Great Fire, thanks principally to Hollar's illustrations to Dugdale's *History of St Paul's Cathedral* (1658).

It was 585 ft (178 metres) long, that is, longer even than Winchester, and (to the top of the spire) 489 ft (149 metres) high. The C11–C12 nave was 100 ft (30½ metres) wide and internally no less high; the C13 choir only slightly narrower. Chapter house and cloister were important C14 additions. The neglect into which the cathedral fell after the Reformation was remedied in 1633–42, when *Inigo Jones* classicized the exterior of the nave and transepts and added a great W portico. Further remodelling was under discussion when the Great Fire consumed the cathedral in 1666.

Nothing definite is known of the cathedral of the Roman City. Restitutus of London was one of three British bishops at the Council of Arles, 314. The site of his church is unknown; it cannot have been the great basilica recently discovered on Tower Hill, which was built in the late C4 (*see* Introduction, p. 41). The building of the first cathedral on the present prominent site is attributed to Mellitus, Bishop of London, in 604. Its form, and that of its Anglo-Saxon successors, is obscure. The ROMANESQUE CHURCH was an ambitious enterprise, begun by Bishop Maurice after a fire destroyed its predecessor in 1087. Work continued under his successor Bishop Richard (1108–27), who is said to have completed 'a large part'; William of Malmesbury, writing *c.* 1120–5, refers to its size (*capacitas*) and magnificent decoration, but also to the financial difficulties of completing it. There was damage from another fire in 1133, and building funds were still being sought in 1175. The nave was twelve bays long, the same number as Winchester, which may have been its inspiration. It was impressive in size but conservative in form, with a three-storey elevation on the pattern of St Etienne, Caen, in Normandy: massive, regular, composite piers with three stepped shafts to each face, those on the nave side reaching to the roof; a large gallery with undivided arches; and a clerestory, probably altered for the later rib-vault. The w end seems originally to have been without towers. The transepts were aisleless, each with an E apse, and with an entrance to an eastern crypt. This housed relics of St Erkenwald, which were transferred to 'a more honourable place' in 1140. Fragments discovered in Wren's crypt in 1996, of Marquise stone with small quantities of Upper Greensand and Caen, may have come from the transepts or the C12 crypt. They have stylistic affinities with late C11 to early C12 work in Normandy and at Anselm's choir at Canterbury. Hollar's views

Old St Paul's Cathedral, interior of choir.
Engraving by Wenceslaus Hollar, 1658

show that this church was later vaulted, probably in the early C13. A timber steeple over the crossing tower was completed in 1222, according to Stow. A further consecration in 1241 suggests C13 alterations to the choir.

The Romanesque E end was superseded by the GOTHIC 'NEW WORK', another long endeavour, started in the 1250s and not ready for furnishing until the early C14 (paved 1312). This was London's greatest ecclesiastical building enterprise of the later C13. It consisted of twelve bays in all: seven new bays added to the remodelled or rebuilt Romanesque choir, with a new crypt below to replace St Faith's church on the site. The wider fifth bay from the crossing (on the site of the Romanesque apse) housed the shrine of St Erkenwald, chief focus and inspiration for the new E end. Like Westminster Abbey (begun 1245), the New Work combined English and French traditions, although the two buildings were very different. The most remarkable feature, known from views by Hollar and others, was the E wall with pinnacled buttresses flanking a vast area of glazing: a row of tall lancets below a rose window with glazed spandrels, inspired by the N transept of Notre-Dame, Paris. The inventive tracery elsewhere drew on other progressive French Rayonnant Gothic developments of the later C13, for example the pointed trefoils and the relationship of lancets and foiled circles in the aisle windows (cf. also St Etheldreda, Holborn, c. 1284, *London 4: North*). But in other respects St Paul's adopted English rather than French traditions: a straight E end, as used c. 1260 for the Angel Choir at Lincoln, instead of the French chevet adopted at Westminster; piers with clustered shafts; and a tierceron vault probably with a ridge rib (not shown by Hollar, but suggested by a surviving boss).

Few changes were made to the church proper thereafter. The SPIRE was the most vulnerable feature: renewed in 1315 (the first of the C14 great needle-spires); burnt by lightning and rebuilt 1444–62; struck again in 1561 and not rebuilt. The S transept façade was rebuilt 1387–8. The usual chapels were founded within, the latest, to St Paul, in 1521.

By the early C16 a great complex of auxiliary buildings had grown up around the cathedral, girdled by a high wall erected between the early C12 and mid C14. Many were secularized or destroyed at the Reformation, and are consequently less well known. Hollar's illustration preserves the appearance of the CHAPTER HOUSE and two-storey CLOISTER, in progress c. 1332, W of the S transept. The mason in charge was *William de Ramsey*. The chapter house was exceptional for two reasons: its unique position within the cloister garth, and its early intermingling of Perp motifs with the repertoire of Decorated Gothic: blank panel tracery in the spandrels of the undercroft, descending mullions, straightened-out reticulated tracery, etc. The work was closely contemporary with the earliest Perp work at Gloucester, the S transept (1331–7). The vocabulary of both designs probably derives from St Stephen's Chapel in the Palace of Westminster. The chapter house was level with the upper cloister storey. It resembled those at York and Southwell (Notts) in the omission of a central pier. Further W, lying S of the W front, was the parish church of St Gregory, known by 1010. It was separated from the W front proper by a stone tower, from the C15 called the

Lollards' Tower. N of the W front was the bishop's residence, E of which lay the Pardon Churchyard, surrounded by a cloister in which were mid-C15 paintings of the Dance of Death. In its centre was the Chapel of St Thomas Becket and St Anne, by tradition a mid-C12 foundation by Becket's father Gilbert. To the N lay the College of Minor Canons, rebuilt here in 1408. To the E, beyond the N transept, stood Paul's Cross (*see* Cathedral Precincts). The Jesus bell-tower, a detached campanile such as Westminster Abbey and several cathedrals also possessed, stood in the NE part of the precinct. Three colleges on the S side housed priests for the main chapels.

Efforts to restore the cathedral began in 1620, when a Royal Commission was appointed to consider necessary measures. Nothing was done until 1631, when a new Commission was called together under Bishop Laud. Work started in 1633, with *Inigo Jones* in charge, and stopped when the Civil War began in 1642. The transformation he wrought has no parallel in the history of England's cathedrals, though classical remodellings of great medieval churches were fairly frequent on the Continent. He refaced the W, N, and S walls of the nave and transepts in rusticated Portland stone, modernizing the Romanesque details with new heavy cornices, classical windows, and pilasters instead of buttresses. The angles between aisles and clerestory were masked by volutes of the Italian kind. The choir, on the other hand, was restored externally without the Gothic details being changed, so the flanks never made a coherent composition. The W end was a different matter. This had a giant Corinthian portico, given by the King and built 1635–9. Jones probably based his design on Palladio's reconstruction of the portico of the Temple of Venus and Rome. It was eight columns wide, with close-set square angle columns making ten in all. A balustrade with statuary surmounted the cornice, and modest square towers with lanterns flanked the whole. Fragments of the columns were discovered in the foundations of Wren's SW tower in 1996, from which their height has been calculated at 40 ft (12 metres), their diameter at 4 ft: dimensions rather smaller than previously thought. Even so, the portico must have looked truly magnificent to anyone walking up Ludgate Hill. John Evelyn called it 'comparable with any in Europe' and Roger Pratt one of the two 'only remarkable buildings in England' – the other being the Banqueting House.

SURVIVING REMAINS of Old St Paul's may be summarized briefly. The fragments of Jones's portico join the extensive collection of moulded stones discovered over the years, now housed in the S triforium. The outer walls of the present crypt are indeed made of stone from Old St Paul's, as their varied shapes show. Only two, in the SW part, have mouldings showing outwards: both similar voussoirs of *c.* 1130. S of the nave, in a narrow strip of garden, remains of the C14 chapter house (buttress foundations etc.) are still visible. The SE corner of the crypt (the old St Faith's Chapel) is preserved beneath a manhole beyond the present SE corner – a reminder that the pre-Fire church extended further E. This was excavated and conserved by *F. C. Penrose* in 1878. Its mouldings are consistent with a date in the 1250s.

THE EVOLUTION OF WREN'S DESIGN

The cathedral suffered grievous damage after 1642, and after the Restoration yet another repair commission was appointed. *Wren*'s burgeoning architectural ambitions and family connections with senior churchmen recommended him for the task of repair, and it was to this body that he presented his first report and design, on 1 May 1666. He suggested continuing Jones's project by recasing the nave interior 'after a good Roman manner', under a new vault. But his principal suggestion was to replace the crossing tower by a dome, which would have been the first dome built in England. Wren was convinced of its necessity to mark the cathedral's superiority, on the pattern of St Peter's and of the great new domed churches of Paris, which he had visited in 1665. It was to have been as wide as nave and aisles together, with big L-shaped piers of masonry closing all the aisles where they met the crossing. The dome was uncommonly steep in outline and consisted of two separate domes within, the inner of masonry and open in the middle, the outer of timber. The nave was covered with saucer-domes, with penetrations from the clerestory windows. Several of these features find echoes in the present cathedral. Estimates for the work were ordered on 27 August. But on 2 September the Fire broke out, and raged until 7 September.

There was some confusion after the Fire as to what to do with the burnt cathedral carcase, and in particular whether its nave and portico might be repaired. Only in 1668 was a warrant issued to raze what remained of the E parts; and it needed the collapse of a pier in the nave, in which services continued until 1673, for the decision to be reached to rebuild the whole. Wren presented several designs before the final one was agreed. The first, completed in early 1669, met with the approval of the King. Men of greater architectural experience were less convinced: Sir Roger Pratt called the design 'wholly different from that of all the cathedrals of the whole Worlde'. It was indeed strange, if ingenious. It consisted of a domed W end, and then an odd choir with arcades open to the outside and not into the church, but with galleries above them opening into the choir. The arcades were no doubt meant to be a replacement of Paul's Walk in the old nave, where the perambulating citizens carried on their business. A fragmentary model of this choir remains in the Trophy Room at St Paul's (*see* p. 182).

The increase in the Coal Tax in 1670 encouraged Wren to conceive a much grander building, which can be regarded as his ideal cathedral church: the GREEK CROSS DESIGN, 1671–2, and its later variant, the so-called GREAT MODEL. The latter, the greatest of 37 English architectural models, is also in the Trophy Room. Made of wood by *William Cleere* in 1673–4, it measures nearly 20 ft (6 metres) long. It is centrally planned, but with a W addition in front of which rises a portico still more splendid than Jones's, with a pediment and columns that would have risen 55 ft (16½ metres) high. An oval W anteroom connects the portico with the church, which is crowned by a large dome on a drum, majestic enough to dominate the skyline as the medieval spire had done. It rests on eight equal arches, from which open four cross-arms of equal length, with sub-centres on the diagonals. The cross-arms are connected externally by sweeping concave quadrants, the one element of surprise in a design which otherwise evidently derives from the various early C16 proposals for St Peter's in Rome and on projected and recently erected domed churches in Paris. The quarter-circles are indeed also a French motif: they occur e.g. in one of the fantastic palace plans of Antoine Le Pautre, published in 1652. Wren probably also knew John Webb's drawing for an ideal church on a Greek cross plan with convex curves between the arms. But the germ of the plan may have been more mundane – the need to avoid a block of houses on the N side of the churchyard, not pulled down until 1710.

However, this domed structure was too contrary to English precedent to find favour with the clergy, then preoccupied with the revival of dignified performances of cathedral worship. So Wren had to abandon it, in favour of a new design at once more in accordance with tradition and much less satisfactory aesthetically. It had a portico and W towers similar to Jones's (and was perhaps to have included some fabric from them), and a plan very much like an English Norman cathedral: a long nave and transepts, and a long choir with an apsed end. All that Wren tried to keep otherwise was his large domed central space, and even that he made more palatable by raising on the top a crazily elongated spire. This plan received the Royal Warrant in May 1675, and is therefore known as the Warrant Design.

Fortunately, it was allowed that Wren would have 'the liberty, in the prosecution of his work, to make some variations, rather ornamental than essential, as from time to time he should see proper' (*Parentalia*). He certainly took advantage of this licence, and was liberal in calling ornamental what he considered essential. Indeed, it is likely that Wren had no sooner completed the Warrant Design than he began to re-think it for the better. The design was drastically reworked, the first phase (the 'Penultimate' design identified by Summerson) a brief staging-post on the way to the present cathedral. The aisle walls were carried up as high as the clerestory, and in the end the dome, transept fronts and W front were also very different. All these later designs took shape as drawings only, which the *Parentalia* explains were less prone to unsought criticism than the Great Model had been.

THE PRESENT CATHEDRAL

On 21 June 1675 the first stone was laid at the E end. There is no sign of any second thoughts thereafter, as Kerry Downes points out: evidence that the outlines of the present plan were already fixed in Wren's mind by then. He abandoned the medieval alignment, preferring a newly excavated axis more SE–NE. Vaughan Hart observes out that Wren's alignment follows that of the sunrise of Easter 1675, and that Wren had resigned as Savilian Professor of Astronomy at Oxford only two years before. Rather than build in stages, he laid foundations for every part as quickly as possible: another safeguard against parsimonious meddling or partial completion. The principal dates marking the progress of the fabric are as follows: transept ends begun in 1677, nave foundations in 1681, first storey of choir and transept walls completed 1685, foundations of the W front dug in 1686. The pediments of the two transepts date from 1698. But the designs for the w towers and the dome, as carried out, are later than 1702. By then the choir was at last completed. Furnished in 1694–7, it was consecrated in the latter year. The chapel for Morning Prayer (St Dunstan's Chapel), NW, was opened in 1699. The w towers were built in 1705–8. The dome was finished in 1708 and the whole building declared complete by Parliament in 1711. The chief material was of course Portland stone, from the quarries already opened up by Inigo Jones. Expenditure for the period 1675–1712 has been calculated at £722,779.

Wren had been thirty-four at the time of the Fire; he was seventy-nine in 1711. In the last years he had much trouble with his Commission, which accused him of deliberately delaying completion. He had perhaps really no longer been always watchful enough with the workmen. But it was mostly a matter of political machinations, similar to those that effected his dismissal as Surveyor-General in 1718. Still, he lived to see his cathedral complete, which is more than was granted to Bramante or Michelangelo.

The fabric's subsequent history is reassuringly uneventful. Cathedral Surveyors after Wren included in the C18 *John James* and *Henry Flitcroft*, then *Robert Mylne* (1766–1811). C19 Surveyors were *S. P. Cockerell, C. R. Cockerell* and then *F. C. Penrose* (1852–97), who oversaw the embellishment of choir and crossing. In the C20, the younger *Somers Clarke* fitted up the SW chapel, 1901–6, *Sir Mervyn Macartney* reinforced the crossing piers, 1925–30, and *Godfrey Allen* dealt with damage from the Second World War. This came chiefly from two direct hits, on the choir in 1940 and on the N transept in 1941. Cleansing the exterior stonework of its crust of soot was instituted in 1964, giving new views of the fine and excellently preserved C17 carving (though the discoloration of the lower stage proved ineradicable). Since 1974 the Victorian mosaic on the choir vaults has also been cleaned. A further programme of restoration was instituted in 1993.

EXTERIOR

St Paul's Cathedral is 510 ft (155½ metres) long (460 ft (140 metres) 3 internally), and to the top of the lantern 365 ft (111 metres) high. The outer walls are 111 ft (34 metres) high, the nave inside 91 ft (27¾ metres) high. As building proceeded from E to W, so we will describe it. It has already been said that the first alteration made by Wren between Warrant Design and execution concerned the disposition of the outer walls. This was to affect the appearance of the whole building. The Warrant Design had a nave with clerestory and lower aisles like a medieval English cathedral. In the execution Wren carried up the outer aisle wall to nave height, as a screen wall – that is, he erected an outer two-storey elevation, the upper section of which was wholly a make-believe. In this Wren established himself at once as a man of the Baroque and not of the Renaissance. The high outer walls add dignity to the whole structure and act as a broad unbroken podium for the all-dominating dome. Additionally, they help to buttress the thrust of the main vault. When one looks down from the dome behind these walls, a row of flying buttresses also appears on each side. Wren did not mind using this medieval method of counteracting the thrust of the vaults, as long as it was not normally evident to the eye.

His wall unit then for the whole building is two-storeyed. The wall is rusticated and there are coupled pilasters on both floors, Composite over Corinthian. The lower storey has a round-headed window in an eared frame with scrolled keystone, and garlands and cherubs' heads above. The upper storey has a blank window with a niche in an aedicule with Composite columns and a pediment. Below the blank window in the base of the aedicule a real window appears, lighting the roof space over the aisle vaults and invisible from the aisles below. The whole is raised on a basement with segment-headed windows to the crypt. As an enrichment garlands are introduced beneath the lower cornice, and intermittently beneath the upper cornice at the E end, the transept fronts, and the NW and SW chapels. A balustrade finished the unit, in 1717–19. Wren would have preferred a solid parapet, but his Commission insisted. He was cross about it and said: 'Ladies think nothing well without an edging.' Stylistically the origin of the unit as a whole is the Banqueting House and Inigo Jones's and John Webb's Palladianism altogether. The unit is repeated all along the building with four modifications. The first is that at the E end the upper storey of the apse has columns instead of pilasters and instead of a balustrade an attic flanked by volutes. The second concerns the TRANSEPTS. Here, first of all, in the four re-entrant angles between aisles and transepts are square additions containing vestries and a staircase. They also help to buttress the dome. Secondly, the fronts of the transepts have in the middle semicircular porches composed of six columns, a motif Wren may have derived from the façade of Pietro da Cortona's S. Maria della Pace in Rome (1656–9). Above the porch is a window with more decoration than used otherwise and then, instead of the balustrade, a pediment and five statues. The doorways into the transepts have the odd motif of framing quarter-columns, more familiar from the work of such less erudite architects as Peter Mills than from the court style.

Towards the W end, with more radical changes from the Warrant Design, there are also more irregularities in the exterior. They reflect the fact that Wren had decided to precede his nave by a single bay larger than the nave bays proper, flanked by two-storey structures in line with the W towers. These house chapels opening off the aisles and above them the library, S, and Trophy Room, N. The large W bay is reminiscent of the Great Model, the whole W end generally of the W transept of Ely Cathedral. The projections serve also to equalize the apparent length of nave and choir, at three bays each. Each begins on the ground floor to the N and S with one of the usual windows, flanked by narrower bays with niches. Above appear the windows of the upper rooms. W of this section is a non-symmetrical bay with one small arched window in a coffered niche. This bay ought to be read as the base of the W towers which stand on it.

The WEST FAÇADE continues the system of the W nave bay for the bays below the W towers. But in the middle is a two-storeyed portico of coupled columns (drawings datable to the 1690s show Wren toying with the idea of a giant order). In this portico again

Wren's affinity with the Continental Baroque is obvious. On the ground floor there are six pairs of columns, on the first floor only four, i.e. the outer pairs below merge with the bays belonging to the towers, in line with the coupled pilasters of the w wall (the unit motif). The four central pairs carry the free-standing columns of the first-floor balcony. The lower columns are 40 ft (12 metres) high, the same height as Jones's, which they resemble also in such details as the cabled fluting: a self-conscious gesture of homage by Wren. Above is a pediment with a relief of the Conversion of St Paul and again statuary (for these *see* p. 164).

The WEST TOWERS are the broadest, most substantial and most 38 Baroque of all Wren's spires. Above the sturdy clock stage they turn round, with pairs of columns carrying straight entablatures projecting in the diagonals, and convex sections with pairs of matching columns between them. Three further stages with urns and complex volutes lead up to an octagonal lantern and an ogee cap with gilt pineapple finial. The stone structure is mostly open, so the whole is much more intricate than this description can convey. The design may have been fixed as late as 1703–4, for official engravings published 1701–3 still show the bland versions of Bramante's Tempietto drawn in 1675. But Wren was probably just keeping his evolving intentions for them close to his chest.

Finally the DOME (on its structure, *see* Interior below). It is in the 3 most telling contrast to the w front – though not well seen from there – achieving a final repose far more convincing than St Peter's, where the *slancio* upward never ceases. Wren, just as he relished variety in his City churches, could consciously develop this contrast between Baroque dynamics and an ultimate end in peace and harmony. The base of the drum below the colonnade is left entirely plain. The drum with its peristyle is a direct descendent of Bramante's unexecuted design for St Peter's, illustrated by Serlio. It is only when we look carefully that in one way at least Wren even here betrays his faith in the style of a different century. Bramante intended an even colonnade all round his drum. Wren's is not even. In eight places the columns do not stand free, but pieces of wall reach out towards them and appear adorned with niches, between them. The reason is structural and also practical (they house staircases), the effect Baroque – though mildly so by comparison with the towers. The infill is of tawny Ketton stone, which keeps the Portland stone columns visually discrete. Above the peristyle is a balustrade, and then the drum rises yet higher, carrying on the diameter of the wall behind the colonnade. This attic has near-square windows. Above this at last follows the dome. It is of an elongated section, but so much less so than e.g. St Peter's that from almost any viewpoint it seems a perfect hemisphere. Bramante's intended dome for St Peter's was indeed hemispherical. What makes Wren's dome also look more at rest than the dome carried out at St Peter's, probably to Michelangelo's design, is the absence of lucarnes and the extreme shallowness of the ribs. The ribs of the dome of St Peter's lead the eye upward all the time. At St Paul's the crowning lantern is a glorious and indeed decidedly Baroque design with pairs of coupled columns projecting on the four sides, an upper stage with a little dome, and a ball with cross – all no more than a final weight on the dome, heavy enough and not too heavy. The ball is in fact 6 ft (nearly 2 metres) in diameter. Ball and cross were faithfully re-done in 1821–2, by *C. R. Cockerell*.

The other notable C19 project was *Penrose*'s reconstruction of the W steps, after 1872. He made them descend evenly on all three sides of the first flight, following early drawings by Wren, who changed his mind and built a single sweeping flight instead. The C19 steps rise towards the centre, in the ancient Greek manner. The stone is Guernsey diorite. Flanking LAMP STANDARDS by *Lutyens*, 1933.

The ARCHITECTURAL SCULPTURE of the exterior, though commonly overlooked, is the greatest such ensemble of the English Baroque. The W PEDIMENT of the Conversion of St Paul (1706) is by *Francis Bird*, a fine composition of several mostly mounted figures. It catches something of the drama of Bernini's famous equestrian statue of Constantine in the Vatican, which Bird must have seen. He was paid £620. Also by Bird, though somewhat tamer, seven RELIEFS of scenes from the life of St Paul around the W door (mostly 1711–14). From l. to r., continuing around the W door recess, they are: the Stoning of Stephen, the Conversion of the Gaoler of Philippi, Paul before Felix or Festus, Paul preaching at Berea (the largest and most Raphaelesque composition, over the gigantic central door), Paul before Agrippa, Paul bitten by the viper, and Paul's sight restored. Two more below the upper cornice: Festus and the Jews, r.; Conversion of a Roman, l. By Bird too the STATUES on the W pediment, at the base of the towers (four seated Evangelists), and on the transepts (1720–3). Some of the latter have been replaced by C20 replicas (e.g. by *Henry Poole*, between the wars): an acceptable substitution as part of the effect Wren intended. Compare Wren's First Tract: 'No sort of Pinnacle is worthy enough to appear in the air, but Statue'. The ultimate source is probably Palladio's *Quattro Libri*.* The reliefs in the transept pediments (1698) are by *Grinling Gibbons* (N, the royal arms) and *Caius Cibber* (S, with phoenix rising from the flames).

Other carving, on a much smaller scale, can be read only in closer views. The outer W doorcases have unusual overdoors with cherubs emerging from foliage at each end. The more familiar cherubs' heads appear over the low doorways at the far W on the N and S sides, the latter (the DEAN'S DOOR, carved by *William Kempster*) particularly fine. The superbly rich and fluent stone carvings below the windows were made by *Gibbons*, *Edward Pierce*, *Jonathan Maine*, and others. This wealth of carving probably grew from Wren's memory of such Parisian buildings as the Great Court of the Louvre and the Hôtel de Sully. The carvings mix the familiar vocabulary of swags, drapery, flowers and cherubs' heads with more obviously emblematic books, torches, pelicans, doves etc. They follow matching sequences on the N and S sides, though with detailed differences in execution.

The less delicate carving higher up was carried out by the principal masons engaged on the cathedral. The first were *Joshua*

*Bob Crayford points to evidence that Wren originally intended smaller, paired figures, and a ring of urns above the peristyle.

Marshall (†1678) and *Thomas Strong* (†1681). The former's con-
tracts passed to *Edward Pierce*, *Jasper Latham* and *Thomas Wise
Sen.*, the latter's to his brother *Edward Strong Sen.* In addition,
later masons were *Thomas Wise Jun.* and *Thomas Hill*, later still
John Thompson (W front), *Samuel Fulkes* (W front and NW tower),
Ephraim Beauchamp, *Nathaniel Rawlins*, *Christopher Kempster*,
William Kempster (SW tower), and *Edward Strong Jun.* (lantern).
The master carpenters were *John Longland*, *Israel Knowles*, and
later *Richard Jennings*; the master bricklayers *Thomas Warren*, then
John Bridges followed by *Robert Billinghurst*; the master plumbers
Matthew Roberts, then *Joseph Roberts*.

INTERIOR

On entering the cathedral, the first impression is one of ordered
   spaciousness and somewhat cool perfection. The colour of the
   stone is beautiful, and the exquisite quality of the carving is at
   once felt. It was executed by the same masons and carvers who
   worked on the exterior, though here softer freestones were used as
   well as Portland, notably from Caen and from Beer in Devon.
   The plasterwork, by *Henry Doogood* (†1707) and then *Chrysostom
   Wilkins*, contributes less towards the overall effect.
A reminder of the plan is called for. First, the large W bay with its
   apsed chapels l. and r., acting as a kind of forebuilding, reminiscent
   of Ely or Lincoln. Then the nave of three bays with aisles, a
   domed space as wide as nave and aisles together, with supporting
   bays on all four sides and beyond them one-bay transepts with
   aisles, and a three-bay eastern arm with aisles, plus apse: basically,
   to say it once more, a design like a Norman cathedral, and particularly Ely, with its forebuilding and wide crossing. (On the
   spaces under the W towers, *see* below.)
The NAVE has arcades set out with great single pilasters towards the
   nave and lower coupled pilasters to the arcade arches – piers not
   unlike those of the Val-de-Grâce, which Wren had seen in Paris.
   The difference is that the arches interrupt the main entablature,
   eliminating the architrave and frieze except above the pilasters.
   Wren derived this unorthodox feature from the Basilica of
   Maxentius (Temple of Peace) in Rome, as given by Serlio (cf. St
   Mary-le-Bow). The cornice proper breaks out in line with the
   pilasters, which are continued upwards by short flat piers in the
   blank zone between arcade and clerestory. The cornice supports a
   narrow balcony with a fine wrought-iron railing, which projects
   with the projections of the entablature. From the upper piers
   spring the transverse arches of the nave vault. The bays between
   the arches are saucer-domed, and as there are also large clerestory
   windows (invisible from outside because of the aisle screen wall),
   there are penetrations in the form of three-dimensional arches
   curving forward until they touch the domes. These domes, Wren
   said, derived from engravings of Hagia Sophia at Constantinople,
   though he would also have seen them at the Val-de-Grâce.
The AISLES also have saucer-domes, and windows placed in
   coffered niches. The ambiguity between niche and window as well
   as the more noticeable ambiguity between W–E vault and transverse penetrations are once again a sign of the C17, the Baroque

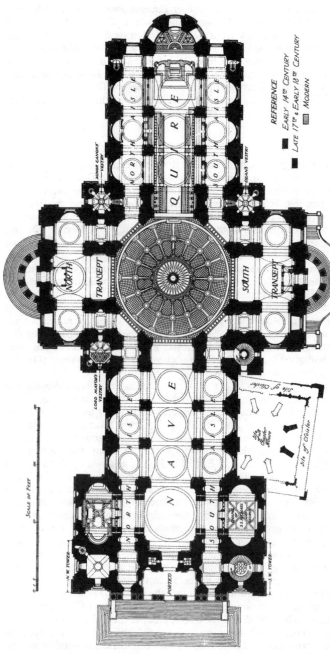

St Paul's Cathedral. Plan

century. Over the larger w bay is a larger dome, and the arch on each side into the aisle is here set out with coupled columns. Another arch with a pair of coupled columns on each side leads into the oval side chapels. They have richly decorated groin vaults and diagonally coffered apses.

Between the nave and the domed crossing a piece of solid wall had to be inserted, here as well as at the inner ends of transepts and choir, to provide a massive enough support for the dome. These pieces of solid wall are tunnel-vaulted and coffered and help to create a feeling of suspense before the whole width and height of the domed space are revealed. The DOME rests on eight arches of even height but uneven width, and to obtain these Wren had to invent some structural intricacies which are aesthetically not wholly successful. The domed space has a diameter equal to nave and aisles together. That means that nave aisles, transept aisles, and choir aisles meet within the domed space, as at Ely's octagon. Wren has treated the corners as niches. But as the aisle openings are low compared with the giant arches he needed to carry his dome, he gave these niches their own, segmental arches, repeated the niche motif above, that is at clerestory level, by means of a kind of box or balcony, and then gave these niches arches of the height and width which he required for his dome. The segmental below the semicircular arch is a distracting motif. *Cibber* carved the keystones.

The drum is visible from inside with its windows separated by pilasters, with a C19 statue in every fourth bay in line with the crossing piers. Its walls slope markedly inwards to the dome above, which is the innermost of three domes. It is of brick and has a circular opening at its top, through which one looks into what seems a second dome: an effect much favoured by the Baroque architects of Italy and France. But the second dome is not a true dome at all, but a brick cone which carries the weight of the lantern. It has circular openings which give on to the volume enclosed by the outer dome, the lead-covered dome which makes the skyline of London. This third dome is built of timbers resting on the brick cone and the stone drum. A light-well just short of its summit, invisible from below, admits daylight into the space between the inner and the pierced middle dome. Nor does the ingenuity stop there, for the thrust is further contained by *Tijou*'s great iron chains, notably that encircling the base of the dome within the walls. Those who object to the screen walls over the aisles as a structural fiction may well object to the concealed brick cone also: Pevsner considered it an ungraceful expedient, 'a scientist's solution rather than a born architect's'. But Wren's conception of architecture recognized no such distinctions.

Four square projections in the angles between nave and transepts and choir and transepts (visible outside and on the plan) contain the octagonal vestry of the Lord Mayor (NW), and the circular vestries of the Minor Canons (NE) and the Dean (SE); the SW projection houses the STAIRCASE. Every visitor who is able should take the time to go up the dome from here. One climbs first a shallow, spacious newel staircase, to where passages lead out on to the Whispering Gallery around the base of the drum. Looking down, the height already seems immense, yet one is barely half-way to the crown of the inner dome. Its paintings may best be inspected from here (*see* Furnishings p. 172 below). Close to, however, it is the sheer, inward-sloping ashlar around the lower drum, some 15 ft (4½ metres) high, which most impresses. From the Whispering Gallery, narrower newel staircases within the blocked bays of the peristyle ascend to a broad balustraded walkway around the lantern of the main dome (called the Stone Gallery). C20 iron staircases and walkways fitted between the outer shell and the brick cone continue from here up to the balcony around the base of the lantern (called the Golden Gallery). Its railings are dated 1832, i.e. later than Cockerell's reconstruction of cross and ball. The final ascent, to the tiny (and weatherproof) chamber just below the summit, is alas now closed to the public.

The ROOF STRUCTURE of the rest of St Paul's is a straightforward affair of kingpost oak trusses, with each tie-beam a single timber, except for the scarf-jointed W members. It employs screw-headed bolts, an innovation of the post-Fire decades.

Finally, the space under the SW tower houses the GEOMETRICAL or DEAN'S STAIRCASE (mason and carver *W. Kempster*), an elegant and audacious piece of engineering in stone, spiralling around the wide open well. Inigo Jones had introduced the device at the Queen's House at Greenwich, but on a smaller scale. A short, solid flight curves from the entrance from the church down to ground level. Looking back here, one sees that the wall below the first landing has unusually rich and licentious stone carving, crowned by glorious ironwork by *Tijou*. The whole serves as a frontispiece to the disused entrance from the S churchyard, placed for the convenience of the Deanery in Dean's Court (*see* Streets: St Paul's Churchyard). Tijou's balustrade proper, and the stone tread ends, are much plainer. Two complete revolutions climb to the LIBRARY above the SW chapel. This tall and amazingly well-preserved chamber is lined with original bookcases and fine panelling and woodwork carved by *Jonathan Maine*, 1709, with rich console-brackets beneath the timber gallery. Excellent carving too on the stone uprights over the gallery. (Similar carving in the TROPHY ROOM, NW, which never received its intended joinery.) Further up the SW tower, a CLOCK by *Smith* of Derby, 1893, replaces the early C18 instrument.

For the Chapel of St Michael and St George (former Consistory Court) beneath the library, and Chapel of St Dunstan (former Morning Prayer Chapel) beneath the Trophy Room, *see* Furnishings pp. 171 and 170 below.

FURNISHINGS

As completed in the early C18, St Paul's was supplied with no more furnishings than were needed for the performance of cathedral service in the choir. Of this self-contained enclave the stalls, screens, organ, and lectern remain. Their exquisite metalwork and woodwork are amongst the finest done at the time anywhere in Europe. In addition, the NW chamber was fitted up as a chapel for morning prayer, the SW chamber as the Consistory Court, besides the library and Trophy Room described above. The font stood in the nave, which was otherwise unencumbered. It was (and is) enlivened by Wren's superb black-and-white marble PAVEMENT, mostly laid diagonally, with under the dome a great concentric design centred on an exquisite compass-like sunburst. This is best appreciated from the Whispering Gallery, though the present loose chairs usually hide part.

The church remained without monuments other than those in the crypt until after 1790. Then it was decided to commission four statues of national benefactors for the corners under the dome, out of public funds (see CROSSING, below). The conception of St Paul's as a kind of semi-secular Pantheon is highly characteristic of the Enlightenment. It was also coloured by what had happened at Westminster Abbey, where monuments often to obscure personages had accumulated haphazardly through the C18. Unforeseen in 1790 were the Revolutionary and Napoleonic Wars, which threw up legions of naval and military heroes for commemoration (Parliament voted some £40,000 for the purpose between 1802 and 1812 alone). A committee of Royal Academicians, set up in 1794, approved the designs, for which large figure groups were at first preferred. Dissatisfaction with the results led to a new committee in 1802, dominated by connoisseurs such as Sir George Beaumont, Charles Townley and (later) Thomas Hope, with powers to alter a sculptor's conception, or award one man's design to another.

The results are remarkably unified in style, usually to the detriment of the individuality of both sculptors and subjects (Mrs Esdaile called them the Peninsular School). Where personality is more conspicuous, it will be emphasized in due course. The highest tally is *Sir Richard Westmacott*'s eight (of some thirty-six commissions); the best work is by *Flaxman* and *Chantrey*; much work also by *Rossi*, *Banks* and *Bacon Jun*. The large standing monuments gave a new lease of life to the multiple figure group, otherwise out of favour in the late C18. They are allegorical and mostly rather frigid, with varying degrees of realism in dress and in incident. The small-scale reliefs on the plinths often have more immediate appeal. So many were commissioned that after 1816 only standing statues could be added, along with further reliefs set high up on the walls. Victorian proconsuls and other empire-builders were honoured with more standing statues and with reliefs in the apses of the nave and transepts. Greater Victorian monuments are mostly in the nave N aisle; several displaced older pieces are in the crypt.

Numerous though the monuments are, it is the DECORATIVE SCHEME that the visitor notices first: not Thornhill's painting of the dome shortly after its erection, but the Victorian mosaics. They were instituted in 1864, after much debate, with the spandrels of the crossing, and extended throughout the choir in 1892–1904 by *Sir William Blake Richmond* (see CROSSING and CHOIR, below). Their hieratic patterns and shimmering glow of gold and colour are utterly alien to anything Wren or his contemporaries might have envisaged; but how cold the interior would be without them.

The furnishings are here described in topographical order from the NW entrance: N aisle, nave, S aisle, crossing, S transept from the W, N transept from the W, choir, choir aisles, crypt, other parts of the building.

CHAPEL OF ALL SOULS, N of the NW entrance (i.e. beneath the NW tower): KITCHENER MEMORIAL, designed by *Detmar Blow* and *Sir Mervyn Macartney*. Recumbent marble effigy with St George and St Michael and a large Pietà, all by *Sir W. Reid Dick*, 1922–5: a theatrical assemblage, depending on the fall of light from the W window. Tentative Expressionist touches in the pose of Christ. Iron SCREEN by *Bainbridge Reynolds*.

NORTH AISLE. CHAPEL OF ST DUNSTAN. Between the columns spiky iron railings (by *T. Robinson*) and then an exquisitely designed and carved wooden SCREEN, with fine Corinthian columns and a centre with two square Corinthian pillars with columns in front, lithe open pediment, vases, and garlanded coat of arms. With the other fittings, made by *Roger Davies* and *Hugh Webb*; carved by *Maine*, 1698. Apsed ends, with stalls at the W; no reredos, since originally for the service of Morning Prayer only. MOSAICS by *Salviati* from the early 1870s, when the E end was raised. – MONUMENT to John Howell †1888. Florid relief of Christ's head crowned with thorns, signed *Robert Cauer*, 1867. – AISLE proper. MONUMENTS. First bay. Lord Leighton, by *Sir Thomas Brock*, 1902. Leonine recumbent bronze effigy, high up on a marble sarcophagus. Below, seated allegorical bronze figures of Painting and Sculpture. Sculpture holds Leighton's 'Sluggard'. – Behind, 57th/77th Regiment Crimean War Memorial, by *Marochetti*. Reliefs of mounted figures. – Further l., bronze relief of Archbishop Temple at prayer, by *Pomeroy*, 1905. – Second bay. General Gordon †1885, by *Boehm*. Bronze effigy on a black marble sarcophagus, rather dull, but with a pretty relief behind of the General teaching little African boys. – Reliefs behind, l. to r.: by *J. Forsyth*, to the Afghan campaign (1879–80), marble, with operatic biblical scene; by *Boehm*, to Gen. Sir Herbert Stewart †1885, tripartite, bronze, with central portrait; by *Marochetti* to Gen. Torrens †1855, with Crimean battle scene. – On the pier between second and third bays, Earl Roberts †1914, dignified marble bust by *John Tweed* in rich Michelangelesque bronze and marble surround. – Third bay. William and Frederick Viscounts Melbourne †1848 and 1853, by *Marochetti*. Black doorway with inscribed false doors; two ample-bodied marble angels l. and r. Somewhat fevered in mood.

NAVE. Two large bronze CANDELABRA, 1897–8 by *Henry Pegram* (W end). On the stems representations of the Creation, with different days (birds, beasts etc.) at different levels. Three-sided base with reliefs of the Temptation, Labouring in the Wilderness, and the Crucifixion. – MONUMENT to Wellington, *Alfred Stevens*'s *magnum opus*, under the far E arch of the N aisle. A noble conception richly realized, without vulgarity, bathos or excessive earnestness. Begun in 1857; completed only in 1912, thirty-seven years after Stevens's death (the crowning statue executed by *Tweed*). The vocabulary comes from the Cinquecento and especially from Michelangelo, the composition from such tombs as that of Queen Elizabeth in Westminster Abbey, that is a 'four-poster' with big middle arch. Columns set in front of the four main ones to E and W as well as N and S, making twelve in all. The decoration of the column-shafts all-over acanthus, like fish-scales. Dramatically contrasted tones: white marble, dark bronze. Frieze of bronze, with cherubs' heads.

Bronze panels on the pedestal too, listing Wellington's victories. Sarcophagus with bronze effigy under the arch. Two large allegorical bronze groups sit on the ends (Valour and Cowardice, 107 Truth and Falsehood). Upper columns behind them, with enriched shafts. Equestrian statue on top, one arm extended in cold command. One small but familiar feature, because copied in many materials all over England: the little lions sitting upright on the railing, originally designed by Stevens (after that at the foot of the Bargello staircase in Florence) for railings by the entrance lodges at the British Museum, removed from there 1896 (*see* also the Law Society). Until 1893 the unfinished work stood in the s w chapel. – IRON BALCONIES over the main entablature partly by *Tijou*, i.e. of Wren's time (nave w end); extended E through the whole church by the younger *Somers Clarke*, *c.* 1900. – GRILLES in the floor, like coal-hole covers of pierced brass. Installed 1878–81, in connection with heating in the crypt.

SOUTH AISLE. CHAPEL OF ST MICHAEL AND ST GEORGE, by the s w entrance. Built as the Consistory Court, but adapted as a chapel by the younger *Somers Clarke*, 1901–6. SCREENS and RAILINGS as in the chapel opposite, and also by *Maine* and *Robinson*, but later: 1706. WOODWORK inside partly original (master joiner *Sir Charles Hopson*), partly C20 work by *Henry Poole* (thrones, reredos), incorporating carved work removed from *Gibbons*'s choir stalls in the C19. By *Poole* also the angels and St George atop the reredos. The angels in particular show how Edwardian sculptors appropriated the Baroque idiom just as well as Edwardian architects. The central group of St Michael and angels by *Edwin Russell*, 1970. The saint appears to float out of the niche. – w of the chapel, MEMORIALS to the Coldstream Guards, Crimean (N, by *Marochetti*, 1856) and Boer Wars (s, by *W. Goscombe John*, 1904), both mediocre.

SOUTH AISLE. MONUMENTS. First bay. Capt. Richard Rundle Burges, by *Thomas Banks*, 1797–1802. The youthful hero is nearly naked. A hovering Victory hands him a sword across an impossibly phallic cannon. More surely handled plinth relief, with naval figures after the Antique. Without its pedestal, and not in its original position. – Around the niche, three Biblical reliefs by *Woodington*, 1862, representing War. Very academic. Moved from the s w chapel, where they made a setting for the Wellington Monument. – Second bay. Bishop Middleton of Calcutta. By *J. G. Lough*, 1832. With eyes upraised, he blesses with a grand solemn gesture a kneeling Indian youth and maiden. His lawn sleeves are enormous. – In the niche behind, gelid reliefs by *W. Calder Marshall*, 1863, representing Peace. From the s w chapel. – PAINTING on the pier between second and third bays, *Holman Hunt*'s Light of the World, signed and dated 1851–1900, i.e. much later than the version in Keble College, Oxford. To be moved. – Third bay. Capt. Westcott, 1802–5 by *Banks*. Diagonal composition: Westcott swoons and is held by an anguished angel, who appears to be falling over too. On the plinth fine Father Nile with many swarming little children, after the Antique. Flanking, naval battle scenes, in lower relief. Also *ex situ* and without its pedestal. Reliefs behind with battle scenes: by *Noble*, r., to Capt. Lyons †1855, with portrait; by *Marochetti*, l., to Granville Gower Loch

†1853. In the centre another Biblical scene from the SW chapel by *Calder Marshall*, 1863.

CROSSING. In the four diagonals four marble STATUES of benefactors of the English people (*see* p. 169 above). They are: Sir William Jones (SW), who has been called 'the first European to open the treasures of Oriental learning, the poetry and wisdom of our Indian Empire', by the elder *Bacon*, 1799; John Howard (SE) by the same, 1791–5; Dr Johnson (NE) by the same, 1791–6; Sir Joshua Reynolds (NW) by *Flaxman*, 1803–13. Flaxman's Reynolds, dull for this sculptor, stands in modern dress by a broken column with a relief of Michelangelo. By contrast, Bacon has dressed Johnson and Howard as Roman heroes. Neither seems comfortable with his bare chest and bare legs (Margaret Whinney compares Johnson to a tired pugilist). Howard holds a key and his plan for the improvement of gaols, with loosened chains at his feet. Jones is a little more Rococo in attitude and draperies. Fine reliefs against the pedestals of Howard and Jones, the former, of prison relief, especially delicate. – PULPIT designed by *Lord Mottistone*, 1964, very large, in the Wren style. For its predecessors, *see* p. 182 below. – LECTERN. Of brass, by *Jacob Sutton*, bought in 1720 for £241. A splendidly naturalistic spread-eagle. Pedestal of square baluster form, the feet fashioned as little lions. – RAILINGS. Those over the arches of the diagonals are late C17, by *Robinson* and *Thomas Colburne*. (– WOODWORK in the vestries by *Cleere*, carved by *Pierce*, 1685 (NW), in the others carved by *Maine*, 1696.)

DECORATION. Wren had the interior painted to resemble white marble, with blue and gold used sparingly at the E end – all stripped away by *Penrose*, 1872–5. For the DOME he envisaged mosaic decoration by Italian artists, but its embellishment was instead entrusted by the Commission to *Sir James Thornhill* (1716–20). He painted eight monochrome scenes of the life of St Paul, in round-headed *trompe l'œil* niches enlivened by gilding. He also painted coffering on the outer dome, where it appears through the oculus: a Baroque effect that never fails to delight, though the illusionistic architecture below is generally less convincing. The compositions it frames owe much to the Raphael cartoons. They are: St Paul's Conversion, the Punishment of Elymas, the Cure at Lystra, the Conversion of the Gaoler, St Paul preaching at Athens, the Ephesians burning books, St Paul before Agrippa, and the Shipwreck at Malta. Further scenes painted by *Thornhill* around the Whispering Gallery in 1719–21 have disappeared. – SCULPTURE in the drum of the dome. Neo-Baroque figures of Fathers of the Church, designed by *Kempe* and made in 1892–4 by *Farmer & Brindley* (sculptor *Winnington*). – MOSAICS. In the eight spandrels of the crossing, four Prophets (E) designed by *Alfred Stevens*, the Four Evangelists (E) designed by *Watts*. Commissioned in 1864–5 but not completed until *c.*1891. Stevens's Isaiah and Watts's St John are as designed, the others slightly modified by *W.E.F. Britten*. *Salviati & Co*. of Venice did the work, with their usual literal Renaissance pictorialism. – In the diagonal apses, scenes by *Richmond*, *c.*1900, more Byzantine in style: Crucifixion as Tree of Life, NE; Resurrection, SE; Entombment, SW; Ascension, NW. For the rest, *see* choir, below.

SOUTH TRANSEPT. Almost entirely an affair of MONUMENTS. W AISLE. The first of the standing statues encountered are Admiral Lyons by *Noble*, 1862, and Dr Babington by *Behnes*, 1837, worthy but unremarkable; the latter's body modelled by *M. L. Watson*. – One relief high up: Gen. Sir Isaac Brock †1812 by *Westmacott*, c.1815. Fallen General with soldier and Canadian Indian, strongly modelled. – Gen. Sir R. Abercromby, by *Westmacott*, 1802–5. Large, vivacious group on an oval plinth, much more Baroque and realistic than his later groups here. The mortally wounded General is lowered from his prancing horse by a soldier; both figures in contemporary dress. Fallen enemy underfoot; two big frontal sphinxes l. and r. – Gen. Sir John Moore, by *Bacon Jun.*, 1810–15 (s wall). Much gentler than the Abercromby monument. A demi-nude man and an angel lower the General into his grave. The main vertical accent a putto with a big flag. – To the r. of this, statue of Sir Astley Cooper †1842 by *E. H. Baily*. – Against the w crossing pier, facing s, statue of Capt. Sir William Hoste by *Thomas Campbell*, 1834. – Transept NAVE. Nelson by *Flaxman*, 1808–18, w wall. On a big circular pedestal a statue so convinc- 86 ingly a portrait (though *sans* eye-patch) that it makes most of the others around look dummies. The meaning is also unusually lucid: Britannia urges his example on two sailor boys, l., composed and carved with tender life; a lion crouches as if mourning, r. Pedestal with stern sea gods in relief. – Opposite, Marquis Cornwallis by *Rossi*, 1811. Wooden-looking figures compared with Flaxman's. Seated Britannia and India; an Indian maiden looks up to Cornwallis on his circular plinth. His ceremonial robes compromise between the Antique favoured by Bacon and Banks and the modern dress preferred e.g. by Flaxman. – Above Nelson, relief to Capt. Hardinge †1808 by *Charles Manning*, mourners by a bier. – Above Cornwallis, relief to Capt. Miller, 1801–5 by *Flaxman*, figures holding a portrait medallion, in lower relief than most. – Statues w and e of the doorcase: Gen. Gillespie, looking up in a romantic way, by *Chantrey*, 1816; Generals Pakenham and Gibbs by *Westmacott*, 1816–23, an informal group of two friends. – Further w, high up, Boer War Colonial Troops Memorial, 1905, by *Princess Louise*, Queen Victoria's daughter. Memorable bronze angel with mighty wings. Further e, Turner, the painter, †1851, by *MacDowell*.

EAST AISLE. Against the s wall, Lord Collingwood, 1813–17 by 89 *Westmacott*. He lies on the prow of a ship-cum-bier, Fame gesturing behind him, Father Thames in front with clambering putti. More putti in medallions on the prow, mostly shown in boats ('the Progress of Navigation'): a strange but charming disjunction of scale and mood. – Against the e wall, Admiral Earl Howe, by *Flaxman*, 1803–11. Standing figure with Britannia seated behind, on a prow with nicely stark Neoclassical detail. Two female figures, l., mourning lion, r.: reminiscent of his Nelson monument, but infused with far less life. – Relief to Col. H. Cadogan by *Chantrey*, 1814, w wall. A fine piece, radically stylized. The Colonel, in high relief, falls back into comrades' arms; the charge continues, l., with overlapping figures in the Parthenon frieze manner. – Relief to Gen. Ross by *Josephus Kendrick*, 1823, e wall. Allegorical mourners and bust; formulaic. – Below, bronze tablet to Capt. Scott and others, by *S. Nicholson Babb*, 1915, with poignant relief of the doomed expedition. – STATUES: w wall, Sir H. Lawrence by *Lough*, 1862, poor; E wall, Gen. Sir J. Jones †1843, by *Behnes*, very stern; against the pier, facing S, Gen. Lord Heathfield by *Rossi*, 1823–5, livelier than most of the single statues. – INNER PORCH. An impressive piece of carving, made up in the C19 from parts of Wren's choir screen and organ gallery, removed in 1861 (*see* below). Noble fluted Corinthian columns, two square and two round on each side, the inner pair free-standing and of marble. Gorgeous frieze of paired cherubs' heads; garlands and swags between the capitals, carved by *Gibbons*. Cupboards or closets in the sides, with doors with delicate iron grilles. Corresponding parts in the N transept were destroyed in the Second World War.

NORTH TRANSEPT. In the W AISLE, against the E wall, mild terra-cotta STATUE of Virgin and Child by *Josephina de Vasconcellos*, 1957. The wrong material for St Paul's, and to be moved to the crypt – MONUMENTS. Reliefs high up: Gen. Hoghton †1811 by *Chantrey* (W), similar to his Cadogan monument, but with a winged Victory; Col. Myers (E), by *Josephus Kendrick*, 1817, Hercules and Minerva shake hands in front of his bust: 'of complete bathos' (Gunnis). – Below, W wall, C.R. Cockerell, the architect, †1863. Crowded, with portrait superimposed on his favourite Ionic column. Designed by *F. P. Cockerell*, executed by *Thomas Woolner*. – In the N bay, W wall, Gen. Sir T. Picton by *Sebastian Gahagan*, 1816. Bust on pedestal, with rigid standing allegories of Valour (a Roman soldier), Genius and Victory. – Flanking reliefs: West Middlesex Regiment monument, r., by *Forsyth*, 1877, starchy; East Middlesex Regiment (Crimea), l., by *Noble*, 1856, strangely haunting, with mourning soldiers receding to infinity. – FONT. 1726–7 by *Francis Bird*, to designs by *John James*, made 1717. A vast oval bowl of grey veined marble, with gadrooned stem, bowl and lid. A piece of the lid lifts out for use. It cost £350. Base and railings *c.* 1960. – Transept NAVE. MONUMENTS. Capt. Faulknor (W), 1797–1803 by *Rossi*. Britannia looks down as the Captain, in antique dress, falls from rocks into the arms of Neptune. Victory holds up a wreath. Big dolphin below. Foolish. – Gen. Dundas (E), 1798–1805, by *Bacon Jun.*, executing a commission of his father's. The composition builds up well from l. to r. Britannia crowns his bust, on a pedestal with a good relief of a battle scene. Flanking, quizzical lion and girl and boy. Mechanical draperies. – Above, two reliefs: Generals Craufurd and Mackinnon †1812 (W), also by *Bacon Jun.*, a tomb with attendants; Generals Mackenzie and Langworth, inscribed '*C. Manning* invt., *S. Manning* fect.', 1810, similar but less delicate. – Against the N wall, Gen. A. Hay †1814 by *Hopper*. He sinks back on a naked athlete, ignored by another soldier, l. (replacement head). – Generals Gore and Skerrett, designed by *W. Tallimache* and carved by *Chantrey*, 1825. Britannia mourns at a tomb, comforted by Immortality. Characteristic of Chantrey's demure melancholy, though the heads are below his usual standard. – E AISLE. Middlesex Regiment Chapel (NE). PAINTING. Virgin with St Luke and a donor, school of *Titian*, *c.* 1550. MONUMENTS. Reliefs to Lord Meath †1929, by *Hermon Cawthra*, Sir Charles Napier by *G. G.*

Adams, 1860. – Against the crossing pier, RELIEF high up to Gen. Bowes †1812 (w), by *Chantrey*. Another of his Parthenon- 87 flavoured compositions: a vigorous battle scene crowding the frame, with the General falling into a comrade's arms. Acutely stylized, but without allegory. Skilful transition from sculpture in the round to low relief. – Relief to Gen. Le Marchant (E), †1812 by *Rossi* (designed by *J. Smith*). Tomb-and-mourners type. – Below, monuments to Sir Arthur Sullivan (w) by *Goscombe John*, bronze tablet with angel and portrait medallion, and to Sir J. Stainer (E) by *H. Pegram*, both 1903.

CHOIR. The original furnishings date from 1695–7, but the general impression now is very different from that in Wren's day. The altar then stood in the E apse, with a low wrought-iron screen enclosing the sanctuary. The stalls went W as far as the middle of the first E bay of the crossing, returning against the choir screen and organ gallery, on which the organ was placed centrally: an arrangement which offered only a low, narrowed vista into the choir. Now the organ is split up (*see* below), and a low rail keeps the choir space open to the eye – perhaps more so than one would like.

At the entrances to the N and S choir aisles wrought-iron SCREENS by *Tijou*. Each is divided into three by openwork Corinthian pilasters. The panels between also predominantly of vertical pieces, but at the top scrolls and curly leaves unfurl. His former sanctuary screens are now in the E bays of the choir arcades (*see* below). – Across the choir, a low COMMUNION RAIL, with brass rail and wrought-iron foliage and busts below, much inferior to the other work. – The ORGAN is by *Smith*, 1694–c. 1704. The giant CASE, designed by *Wren*, is a piece of miraculous carving, with angels and cherubs carved by *Gibbons* on three levels, as well as the usual garlands etc. It can still be enjoyed in its present arrangement, as halved (by *Penrose*, 1872) between the N and S side of the first bay of stalls. The arrangement is summarized by Michael Gillingham as follows: The present N case is the old E front, with a facsimile *chaire* case before it; the present S case is the old W front, with the old E front *chaire* case before it (for the original organ gallery and screen, *see* S transept inner porch, above). Instrument by *Willis*, 1872, rebuilt by *N. Mander*, 1973–7. – The CHOIR STALLS were made by *Hopson*, assisted by 52 *Hugh Webb*, *Roger Davies* and *John Smallwell*, and carved by *Gibbons* under Wren's supervision. Of German oak with limewood carving, equally admirable seen from the front or the back (in the aisles). Here incidentally – as in the organ case, the doorcases and other places – smaller iron grilles are used to fill in openings, and these deserve study too. Each bay of the stalls at the back has a tripartite composition, with coupled Corinthian columns to emphasize the centres and exquisite flower wreaths and garlands at capital level. Above the enriched cornice a balustrade with square balusters. Doorcases with straight entablatures to various small rooms within the thickness of the stalls. The fronts are gayer, with openwork cupolas enriched by cherubs' heads and volutes, columns with ornamental shafts to mark the principal seats, and a top cresting of feathery curls. The BISHOP'S THRONE (S range) has a canopy on columns carved with a brocade effect;

open lantern with mitre and cherubs. Only slightly less grand is the LORD MAYOR'S STALL, set centrally in the same range. Facing, N, the BISHOP'S DOMESTIC STALL and DEAN'S STALL; the latter, formerly part of the organ screen, with acanthus canopy with two singing putti, the back of the stall carved with an open Bible, crossed swords, flowers etc. – SCREENS. The former sanctuary screens by *Tijou* are now in the E bays of the choir arcades. Much scrollier in design than the aisle screens. Broader iron screens in the next bay to the W incorporate Tijou's GATES, formerly at the W choir entrance. On the double central gates little medallions of Saints. The matching W gate on each side and the gilt-pilastered uprights are by *Bodley & Garner*, 1890.

BALDACCHINO at the E end by *S. E. Dykes Bower* and *Godfrey Allen*, 1949–58. The idea was suggested by a footnote in *Parentalia*, and by a contemporary drawing then believed to represent Wren's intention for a baldacchino for St Paul's (Kerry Downes however identifies this as Hawksmoor's design for an unexecuted equestrian monument to William III). In any case, the baldacchino makes a fine effect, in keeping with the Baroque qualities of Wren's building. Of oak, with three Corinthian columns at each corner, two fluted and one twisted. Broader than it is deep, so the dome on top with its oval piercings is oval on plan. The plan and the open segmental pediment owe something to Stevens's Wellington Monument. It is one of the virtues of the present baldacchino that light from the E, blocked by Bodley & Garner for more than half a century, penetrates Wren's choir as intended. The baldacchino replaces *Bodley & Garner's* marble reredos of 1886–8, damaged in the Second World War. Pieces of its sculpture remain at the E ends of the S aisle (Virgin and Child) and N aisle (Crucifixion). Modelled by *Guillemin*; carved by *W. Brindley* (assistant *C. J. Allen*). In the S aisle also the 1690s COMMUNION TABLE, made by *John Smallwell*, hardly larger than that for a parish church. Even with its reredos, designed by *John James* and carved by *Bird*, 1725, the E end looks under-furnished in old views (though it was of course visible only from within the choir). By the high altar, two standard CANDLESTICKS with rich Renaissance arabesque, cast from a pair at St Bavon, Ghent, said to have been made by *Benedetto da Rovezzano* for Wolsey's tomb (*see* Crypt, p. 180 below). Behind the altar, the AMERICAN MEMORIAL CHAPEL, again by *Dykes Bower* and *Allen*, with stalls and panelling round the apse, carved in lush Wren style by *George Haslop*. – STAINED GLASS in the E window by *Brian Thomas*, *c.* 1958. Scenes from the Life and Passion of Christ. Blue and golden yellow. – CHANDELIERS of glass, *c.* 1958, not looking at home.

The MOSAICS throughout the choir and aisles are by *Richmond*. He was appointed in 1891, partly on the recommendation of Bodley, who was in charge of the overall decoration. Close study of the Byzantine mosaics at Ravenna and Monreale resulted in designs more stylized, hieratic, and closer to Eastern techniques than the earlier work in the crossing; closer, too, to Burges's Early Christian proposals twenty years before. Messrs *Powell* supplied the large tesserae, set at angles in the Byzantine way, to catch and reflect light. Eclectic compositions, veering from highly stylized pattern-making (e.g. in the domes) to academic figure-modelling

(Adam and Eve), with Art Nouveau excursions here and there, the general effect of great confidence. Wren's architecture, coloured and gilded to match, blends in better than one would expect. Dates are 1892–6 (choir), 1896–1904 (aisles). Saucer-domes in the choir, E to W, show the Creation of the birds, fishes (all blues and greens, with mighty spouting whales), and beasts. Twelve androgynous angels in the pendentives, arms extended. Flanking the clerestory windows big figures of prophets, Sibyls and Old Testament figures. In the panels above the railing, not easily seen, Adam, N, and Eve, S, and stylized beasts, birds, plants etc. The arcade spandrels show angels of the Passion (E bay), with in the bays further W the Creation of the firmament and the Annunciation (N side) and the Expulsion from Eden (S side). Further E and in the apse, Old Testament scenes and Virtues in the lower zones, Christ in Glory flanked by Recording Angels in the half-dome of the apse. The aisles, more easily inspected close to, mostly have formal compositions of angels, with at the E end Apollo, N, and Demeter, S.

MONUMENTS. S AISLE, W to E. John Donne, Dean of St Paul's and poet, by *Nicholas Stone*, 1631–2. Standing upright in his shroud on an urn, like a spectre. It started a macabre fashion for similar effigies (e.g. Sir John Astley's, at All Saints, Maidstone, Kent). Stone appears to have conceived it as a recumbent figure, but for lack of room placed it upright on the separately carved urn. The epitaph was Donne's composition. Completion of the effigy was subcontracted to *Humphrey Moyer*, the original surround to *Robert Flower*. Restored and set up here *c.* 1818, following Hollar's engraving from before the Great Fire. – Bishop Blomfield, routine marble figure on a sarcophagus, by *George Richmond*, 1868. – Bishop Creighton. Bronze statue, one hand raised in blessing; by *Sir Hamo Thornycroft*, 1905. A fine piece, more Rodinesque than usual for the artist. – N AISLE. SCULPTURE. Mother and Child, by *Henry Moore*, 1983. Of Travertine, successfully modelled in the round, but without the appealing texture of the artist's early carved works. – Low wooden VESTRIES in the two W bays, the first made from a C19 organ console, the second (central bay) by *Macartney*, *c.* 1925.

CRYPT

The crypt extends under the whole church. It is low, with extremely massive piers and groin- or tunnel-vaults of rendered brick. The main piers support those of the upper church, with the largest masses at the crossing. Rows of small, square piers support the floors of the main vessels, with heavier piers beneath the dome. Within these, an octagonal space with a ring of eight Tuscan columns marks the very centre. Much of the aisles and transepts are closed to the public, and other parts have recently been converted for new uses: the N transept for a museum in 1981, the nave S aisle for a shop in 1994; a refreshment room was formed at the W end in 1997. So there is little feel of unity to the whole. But it was never a highly finished space.

Entrances are in the transept E aisles. Over each a carved cartouche with skulls: a reminder that the parishioners of old St

Faith's church retained burial rights beneath. Other early inter-
ments included those, like Wren and his family, with a special
claim on the building. A few architects and artists followed in the
later C18 and early C19, mostly with plain slabs. Only later in the
C19 were new monuments set up in great numbers. Most are
modest wall-mounted tablets with busts or portrait reliefs mostly
in bronze or marble, not all worth individual mention. Conveniently clustered according to profession, they make a rich hunting ground for explorers of the by-ways of Victorian public life.
Nelson and Wellington alone have each a mighty sarcophagus,
conspicuously placed on the main axis. Other large C19 monuments are refugees from the cathedral proper. Additions are still
made, the largest recent pieces (Falklands and Gulf War
Memorials) lettered slabs. Lastly, the crossing aisles house
pathetic remnants of C16–C17 effigies from monuments in Old St
Paul's.

FURNISHINGS. Description is from E to W. At the E end, the
CHAPEL OF THE ORDER OF THE BRITISH EMPIRE, designed
by *Lord Mottistone* (of *Seely & Paget*), 1959–60. Mostly traditional
fittings, less swaggering and more genteel than Dykes Bower's
work upstairs: iron RAILS with dark grisaille glass panels by *Brian
Thomas*; silvered FURNITURE and FONT in a sort of Vogue-
Regency manner. Vile polished grey marble tiles around the
perimeter, like lino. – STAINED GLASS also by *Brian Thomas*, the
manner similar to his upper windows. – Further W, oak SCREEN
of 1993–4, designed by *Martin Stancliffe*, with carved openwork
panels by *Tony Webb* and *Hannah Hartwell*, rustic C17 style.

SOUTH AISLE, E to W. The outer wall first, then the piers.* Against
the E wall, Mary Wren †1712, elaborate undulating cartouche;
better than average. – Edmund Wiseman †1704, oval plaque with
sumptuous surround; clumsy broken pediment. Attributed to
William Woodman Sen. (GF). – In the recess, r., Jane Wren, Sir
Christopher's only daughter, †1702, by *Francis Bird*. Relief of
St Cecilia at the organ, with angels. Delicate, but undeniably
naïve. – Randolph Caldecott, the illustrator, by *Alfred Gilbert*,
1887–95: beautiful painted aluminium figure of a boy, with strange
head-dress, holding a medallion. Pedimented niche with tall
bronze baluster-columns. – William Holder †1697 and his wife
Susannah, Wren's sister, by *Gibbons*. Broad tablet with double
inscription. – S wall. In the first recess, black marble slab to Wren
himself (†1723); on the W wall above, big inscription panel
(designed by *Mylne*, 1807), reproducing the famous: 'Si monu-
mentum requiris, circumspice'. – Godfrey Allen †1986, bronze
bust by *David McFall*, 1959, a humane portrait of old age. –
James Barry. Wall-mounted bust of *Coade* stone, 1819; the first
artist's monument in this corner to ignore Wren's non-figurative
example. Other early burials (Turner, Dance the Younger, Fuseli,
West, Reynolds etc.) have plain slabs; later ones ledgers of brass or
brass inlay. These include: Holman Hunt †1910, by *Eric Gill*;
Millais and Lord Leighton, both †1896, both designed by *Norman
Shaw*; further W and most splendid, Alma-Tadema †1912. –

*In the locked-off area to the SE, cartouche to Sir Simon Baskerville by *Nicholas Stone*,
1642.

Sudan Special Correspondents, 1888, a vulgar brass like a magazine frontispiece. Designed by *Herbert Johnson*, engraved by *Gawthorp*. – In the next recess, against the s wall, *Chantrey*'s monument to Bishop Heber †1826, shamefully dismantled. He kneels in prayer. Drapery and expression both excellent. Alongside, relief of him baptizing. – Sir Edwin Landseer, by *Woolner*, 1882, with reliefs of the artist and of his 'Chief Mourner'. – In front, an inscribed granite ledger to Rennie, †1821, eloquently plain. – Earl of Lytton, bronze relief by *Gilbert*, 1892–1902. A tight, close composition, cultivatedly enigmatic in the fin-de-siècle way. Miniature portrait on a casket, wreathed in smoke from a guttering lamp held by a child. Two female mourning faces above. Set up after the bankrupt artist's exile; the surround designed by *Lutyens*. – First pier, E face. Sir Aston Webb †1930, by *William McMillan*; Van Dyck (†1641), C17 style with bust by *H. Poole*, 1928; George Richmond †1896, red marble with delicate bronze roundel by *Sir W. Blake Richmond*. – s face. Mostly war correspondents from the 1900s. The palm goes to Sir William Russell †1907, a bronze bust by *Sir Bertram Mackennal*. – w face. Rev. Henry Venn, by *Noble*, 1875, a good bust with kindly expression. – N face. Unworthy tablet to Lutyens by *W. Curtis Green*, 1946. – George Frampton. Smiling sculpted bronze child holding a miniature of his Peter Pan. By *Ernest Gillick*, 1930. – Sir Alfred Gilbert, with oval relief of Eros by *Gilbert Ledward*, 1936. – Hamo Thornycroft, glum bronze portrait by *C. L. Hartwell*, 1932. – Second pier. E face. Dr Billing † 1898, with unusual painted ceramic portrait. – Benjamin Webb, the Ecclesiologist, †1885, by *Armstead*. Demi-figure in niche. Not Gothic, which is proscribed within the cathedral walls. – s face. Sir J. Goss †1880, designed by *Belcher*, with pretty relief of choirboys by *Sir H. Thornycroft*, 1886. – W.C.F. Webber †1881, by *Woodington*.

NORTH AISLE. At the E end, John Martin †1680, publisher, and wife. The largest late C17 monument remaining in the City. Reredos back, with columns and inscribed drapery. Two figures in contemporary dress kneel facing each other, reading from books resting against a pyramid of more books. On the base two babies watched over by cherubs' heads. The composition seems deliberately to update a familiar Jacobean formula. Attributed to *Edward Pierce* (GF). – s wall, E to w. Canon Liddon †1890, recumbent effigy by *Kempe*. – Frank Holl, the portraitist: lively bust by *Boehm*, 1889; big black marble surround by *Alfred Gilbert*, 1893. – George Clement Martin, by *H. Pegram*, 1917. – First pier. s face. Sir William Orchardson, coloured marble, with small bronzes of Napoleon and the 'Farmer's Daughter', after his paintings. By *W. Reynolds-Stephens*, 1913. – w face. Sir Albert Richardson †1966, designed by *Marshall Sisson* and carved by *D. McFall*. – N face. John Singer Sargent †1925, Crucifixion designed by *Sargent*. Large bronze figures in relief, with attendants contorted to gather Christ's blood. A version of that designed in 1903, for the Boston Public Library; the mood still latest C19 Symbolism.

NORTH–SOUTH PASSAGE, w of the screen. N SIDE, facing E, Sir Stafford Cripps by *Jacob Epstein*, 1953, a very expressive bronze bust with hands. – s SIDE, also facing E, Ivor Novello by *John Skelton*, 1973, a highlight amongst the post-war carved portraits. –

In the S AISLE bay, clockwise from the N entrance: Col. MacDougall †1862, mediocre bust by *G. G. Adams*; J. Wasdale †1807, unassuming urn signed *R. Blore*; Richard Bourke, Earl of Mayo †1872, with bust; Bishop Jackson, marble recumbent effigy, quite stylized, by *Woolner*, 1887; Thomas Bennet †1706, big pilastered marble tablet; Sir John Macdonald †1891, with bust; Sir Henry Parkes, bust by *Brock*, 1887; Capt. Thompson, again by *Adams*, 1860. – Also the ledger of Robert Mylne, the architect, †1811.

Further W, beyond C17 RAILINGS that mark the W boundary of the former Chapel of St Faith, Wellington †1852, on the central axis between the great E piers of the crossing. A free-standing Cornish porphyry sarcophagus by *Penrose*, 1858, impressively severe. Plinth of grey granite, with lions' heads. It must have been conceived in response to Napoleon's tomb at the Invalides (installed 1840). The burden of narrative and representation lies of course with Stevens's monument in the nave above. By *Penrose* the MOSAIC FLOOR, 1860s–70s, extending W into the crossing. But the setting is unsatisfactory, neither wholeheartedly enriched nor plain and as found. – Uniform inscribed TABLETS to C20 soldiers (1979). – In the passage into the crossing, N side, Sir Samuel Browne, with marble relief of a sepoy by *Forsyth*, 1903.

CROSSING. E of the rotonda, a N–S CROSS-PASSAGE with mostly late Victorian military pieces. N side, W wall: Col. Sir William Wyllie †1909, large portrait relief. – Major Fred. Jackson †1938, with nice bronze relief of a polar scene by *A. Southwick*. – Gen. Sir John Inglis, designed by *W. H. Seth-Smith*, with bronze reliefs by *Derwent Wood*, 1896, one of the siege of Lucknow. – Sir Charles McGregor, bust on enriched plinth, by *S. Albano* of Florence, 1889. – S side, W wall. Falklands War Memorial by *David Kindersley*, 1985. The artist's chaste lettering may be seen on several other, smaller tablets in the crypt. – Under the dome, Nelson †1805. The splendid black marble sarcophagus, of generously curved outline but otherwise unornamented, was made by *Benedetto da Rovezzano* in 1524–9 for the tomb Cardinal Wolsey falsely anticipated at Windsor. C19 pedestal of granite and black and white marble, probably by *Mylne*, 1806–7. On top Nelson's coronet on a cushion. – BAYS AROUND THE ROTONDA, clockwise from the E. First bay (main axis). Florence Nightingale by *A. G. Walker*, 1916. Red marble and alabaster, the portrait relief rather too gentle for its redoubtable subject. – Second bay. Capt. Sir J. Hawley †1885, with marble bust; porphyry slab to Earl Beatty, the last interment in St Paul's, by *Lutyens*, 1938. – Admiral Lord Beresford †1919, with good relief by *Tweed*. – Admiral Sir Fred. Richards †1912, blurry portrait by *Pomeroy*. – Fourth bay. Field Marshal Lord Napier of Magdala. Wall-tablet by *Woodington*, 1891; ghastly grey marble ledger in front. – Fifth bay, i.e. the passage from the rotonda to the nave. Two early C19 monuments from the upper church: Capt. G. Duff, by *Bacon Jun.*, 1805, S, the usual mourners by a tomb; Capt. J. Cooke, N, of the elevated relief type, a female mourner pestered by macrocephalic cherubs, atrociously bad, yet by *Westmacott*, c. 1807–10. – Sixth bay. T. E. Lawrence †1935, bronze bust by *Eric Kennington*. – Gallipoli Memorial, designed by *Richard Kindersley* with bronze

relief by *Mary Beattie Scott*, 1995. – Eighth bay. Lord Freyberg
†1963, with small but powerful bronze portrait by *Oscar Nemon*.
SOUTH CROSSING AISLE. Mostly large monuments from upstairs
or fragmentary effigies from Old St Paul's. From the E: Dean
Milman, 1876 by *F. J. Williamson*. Effigy on a sarcophagus, with
troubled expression. – Gen. W. Napier, statue by *G. G. Adams*,
1860. – Sir Thomas Heneage †1594 and wife, upper halves of
recumbent effigies. – Admiral Lord Rodney, by *Rossi*, 1810–15.
Rodney stands on a square pedestal in modern dress. A
Neoclassical demi-nude winged Victory commends him to the
Muse of History. Somewhat chilly figures. – Admiral Malcolm, by
E. H. Baily, 1842, standing statue. Flanked by *Cibber*'s two big
urns on circular Roman altars, much weathered, from the S
churchyard wall (replaced by copies there). – Gen. Charles
Napier, statue by *G. G. Adams*, 1856. A prodigious profile. – Sir
John Wolley †1595 and wife, damaged seated figures. – Upper half
of the recumbent effigy of William Hewit †1599.
NORTH CROSSING AISLE. Nicely fitted up in 1981 as a museum
and treasury for the display of plate from churches of the Diocese.
Skeletal steel GATES by *Alan Evans*. The display cases by *Higgins,
Ney & Partners* are good work, spare and clean. – MONUMENTS.
Tablet to Sir Philip Sidney, with sensitive portrait; by *Lida Lopes
Cardozo* and *David Kindersley*, 1986. – Nicholas Bacon †1579,
upper half of a recumbent effigy, head on a half-rolled-up mat. –
Recumbent effigy of Sir William Cokain †1629, more complete.
NORTH–SOUTH CROSS-PASSAGE W of the rotonda. N side, E wall:
George Washington, bronze bust on pedestal, most unexpected:
by *Oroway Partridge*, given 1921. – R. J. Seddon, by *Frampton*,
1909. Marble portrait relief and allegorical figures of Justice and
Administration. Bronze surround, of uncanonical architectural
forms. – Sir Bartle Frere, a fancy combination of slab and wall-
tablet, 1888. – W. B. Dalley †1888, by *Boehm*. – W. M.
Hughes †1952, bronze relief, a near-caricature. – Sir George Grey,
with bust by *Onslow Ford*, 1901, in coloured marble surround. –
S side, E wall. W. E. Henley, the poet, †1903, an excellent free
bronze head by *Rodin*. – W wall. Pilot Officer Fiske †1940,
unabashedly Neo-Georgian, designed by *Richardson*. – William
Huggins †1910, and wife †1915, by *H. Pegram*. – Edward
Vansittart †1892, a good piece with marble portrait relief and
figure of an angel, by *Frampton*.
NAVE. S wall. Charles Reade, by *G. M. Curtice*, 1886. – Sir Walter
Besant, bronze with relief of bust by *Frampton*, 1902, framed by
slender Art Nouveau trees. – Further W, statue of Lord St Vincent
by *Baily*, 1823–6, a pensive figure. One of the Committee of
Taste's last two commissions, with Lord Duncan (*see* below). –
N wall. George Nottage †1885. Marble tablet with portrait. In
front, a fine incised bronze slab by *Hart, Son, Peard & Co*, with his
likeness in Mayor's robes. – Sir G. Williams by *Frampton*, 1908,
bust with two excellent seated allegorical figures, more interesting
than the portrait. – Further W, statue of Henry Hallam by *Theed*,
1862. In academic robes, holding pen and books. – Against the W
piers, N side, Captains Mosse and Riou, by *Rossi*, 1805. Two
demi-nude allegorical figures holding portrait medallions. Rather
inert; inferior lettering. – S side, Gen. Sir W. Ponsonby, designed

by *Theed* and carved by *Baily*, 1816–20; large group. The half-naked hero sinks from his fallen horse. Victory bends to offer a wreath. Unintentionally comic, not least because of the General's Regency whiskers. – W END. Two C17 marble COLUMNS, from the former organ gallery. – STATUES: N side, Admiral Duncan by *Westmacott*, 1823–6, S side, Hon. M. Elphinstone by *Noble*, 1863, robed. (In the Nave S aisle, not normally accessible, Thomas Newton †1807, nice relief by *Westmacott*.)*

LIBRARY, TROPHY ROOM AND TRIFORIUM

For the library *see* Interior, p. 168 above. The corresponding Trophy Room, above the NW chapel, is part of the museum of St Paul's. This contains *Wren*'s models for St Paul's, the First Model and the Great Model. On the First Model *see* p. 159; on the Great Model *see* pp. 159–60. A new display illustrative of St Paul's history, to designs by *Gordon Bowyer*, was completed in 1996. – PULPITS. In the triforium passage outside the trophy room, two C19 pulpits, overtaken by changing fashions. The earlier of 1803, by *Mylne*. A beautiful circular piece on a tall pedestal with big lion's paws. In need of restoration. Its successor by *Penrose*, 1860, in coloured marbles in the Italian medieval tradition, lies dismantled. – SCULPTURE. Several busts, including Sydney Smith by *Richard Westmacott Jun.*, 1835 (library), and George Cruickshank by *J. Adams Acton*, 1881 (S triforium, removed from the crypt). – Also a large collection of moulded stones from Old St Paul's (*see* Old St Paul's and its Predecessors, p. 158 above).

CATHEDRAL PRECINCTS

The early C18 RAILINGS round the cathedral partially remain (supporting wall lowered 1879; some resiting C19–C20). They are very early examples of cast-iron work, disliked by Wren, who wanted wrought iron. Made 1710–14 by *Richard Jones* at Lamberhurst, Kent (the Weald was the contemporary centre of iron smelting).

Before the W front a MONUMENT to Queen Anne, 1886, an indifferent copy (by *Richard Belt* and *L.A. Malempré*) of the important original group by *Francis Bird*, 1709–12, now at St Mary's Place, Holmhurst, Sussex. The four attendant figures are England, Ireland, France and America. The churchyard in front has attractive paving and polished Shap granite bollards, laid out by *Penrose* in the 1880s.

On the NE in the leafy churchyard, PAUL'S CROSS, a tall Doric column with an elaborated Baroque base. Designed by *Sir Reginald Blomfield*, 1910, the figure by *Mackennal*. It commemorates the famous wooden preaching cross, or combined roofed pulpit and cross, known in 1241, rebuilt in 1448 and 1595 and torn down in 1643. Just inside the NW gateway, a concrete circle marks a medieval well, discovered in 1970. Within the railings further W, STATUE of John Wesley, unveiled 1989: a replica of the late C19

---

* Wellington's funeral carriage of 1852, long on display here, is now at Stratfield Saye, Hampshire.

work by *J. Adams Acton*. Also some wasted early C18 figures from the parapet. In the s churchyard by the nave a bronzed resin FIGURE of Becket by *Bainbridge Copnall*, 1973, shown as if violently fallen back (restored after storm damage, 1987). The low pedimented cell E of the s transept is the entrance to the burial chamber for the parish of St Gregory, by *John James*, 1715–16. For remains of old St Paul's here, *see* above, p. 158.

Early ROMAN BURIALS and four large pottery kilns were discovered in the churchyard in 1672, and many more burials have turned up since. They are associated with suburban sprawl alongside the Roman road beneath Newgate Street (q.v.). Two important VIKING GRAVE-SLABS were found on the s side of the church-yard in the C19. The finer, an C11 piece with a relief of a fantastic beast in Ringerike style, is now at the Museum of London. 8

For the Chapter House, N, and former Deanery, s, *see* Streets: St Paul's Churchyard. For the canons' houses, w, *see* Streets: Amen Court.

FURTHER READING

The starting point for Old St Paul's is Dugdale's *History of St Paul's Cathedral* (1658). G.H. Cook, *Old St Paul's Cathedral*, 1955, should be read together with articles by Richard Gem, J.P. McAleer and R.K. Morris in *B.A.A. Conference Transactions 1984* (1990). Wren's St Paul's is discussed in the literature on the architect, beginning with the *Parentalia* by Stephen Wren (1750). The *Wren Society*'s volumes (1924–43) include the building accounts and many draw-ings. Jane Lang, *Rebuilding St Paul's* (1956), is a lively, impression-istic account. W.R. Matthews and W.H. Atkins, *History of St Paul's* (1957) is also valuable. Recent studies are by Kerry Downes, *Sir Christopher Wren: the design of St Paul's Cathedral* (1988), and Vaughan Hart, *St Paul's Cathedral* (1995). On the post-war repairs *see R.I.B.A. Journal*, December 1948. Peter Burman, *St Paul's Cathedral* (New Bell's Cathedral Guides, 1987) covers monuments and decoration. On the C19 embellishments *see* J. Mordaunt Crook in *Antiquaries' Journal* 60 (1980) and John Physick, *The Wellington Monument* (1970).

CHURCHES

ALL HALLOWS BARKING
Great Tower Street

First mentioned 1086 as a daughter church of Barking Abbey, Essex. All Hallows is the only London church with standing fabric of Anglo-Saxon vintage (*see* below and Introduction p. 43), revealed by the same severe bomb damage that made necessary the drastic post-war reconstruction by *Lord Mottistone* of *Seely & Paget* (N aisle opened 1949; re-dedication 1957). Other survivals are apparent from outside: C15 aisle walls and NW wall, mid-C17 W tower, and NW porch from *Pearson*'s late C19 restoration.

The C15 aisles have three-light windows with pointed lights under depressed arches. Above rises a new Perp clerestory and E wall of brick. The latter's gable and lacy parapet are based on the Great Hall at Hampton Court. On the gable a relief carved by *Cecil Thomas* of the lamp of the Toc H organization, founded by All Hallows' former rector 'Tubby' Clayton. W tower, also of brick and at an angle to the rest of the church, of 1658–9: a rare period (*Samuel Twine*, bricklayer). Very humble and plain, with the simplest string-courses and round-headed openings. Over the W door the typical artisan's device of a little *œil-de-bœuf* window in a rectangular panel. The stone cornice and spiritedly Baroque copper-clad spire, added in 1958, give the tower a posthumous late-Wren flavour, and make it an important landmark in views from E and W. A square ogee-topped cupola crowned the tower until 1940. Early C18 views suggest the C17 parapet was crenellated. *Aitchison* made unexecuted designs in 1863 for a new French Gothic W end with a sturdy SW tower and spire (drawings in City of London Record Office). Two-storey Perp NW porch and vestry of stone, hard-edged, added by *Pearson* during restoration of 1884–95 to face the newly-made Byward Street (carver *Nathaniel Hitch*). Together with the W wall of the C15 N aisle, the steeple, and the plain post-war SW vestry, it gives the church a very picturesque W aspect. A new parish centre by *John Phillips*, partly underground, is planned for the SE corner of the churchyard (1996).

The nave INTERIOR was courageously reconstructed by *Lord Mottistone* to a new design, with a cross-ribbed free Perp vault of fine grey concrete. Odd Carolean–Baroque-detailed beams like gallery fronts span the intervals between the limestone-faced piers, saving it from starkness. The church had received aisles *c.* 1230–40. Until 1940 two W bays survived, with circular piers and double-chamfered arches. Some fragments remain, assembled in the undercroft. The clerestory and E parts of the former arcades were C15, the date also of the rood stair and loft doors in the surviving N wall. Part of the tiled medieval floor is exposed nearby. In the C14 the chancel was rebuilt and possibly extended, and a SE chapel added; its CRYPT survived the rebuilding of the S aisle and may be inspected (now the Chapel of St Francis). Stone tunnel-vault with single-chamfered transverse arches, an unusual motif. Blocked windows in the S wall. Here is displayed a Byzantine RELIEF of two peacocks with a foliage border, of high quality. NW of the crypt, two C17 or C18 burial vaults.

REMAINS OF THE SAXON CHURCH. Destruction by bombing of most of All Hallows' nave in the Second World War exposed standing Anglo-Saxon fabric at the W end. Initially this was dated to the C7–C8, i.e. not long after All Hallows' mother house at Barking Abbey, Essex (founded c. 660–70); but an C11 date is now preferred, from comparisons with several other excavated City churches. The remains consist of a NW quoin of Roman bricks, visible from a first-floor vestry, and a section of wall at the SW, pierced by an arch. By the C16 this opened into a SW tower, as shown in Wyngaerde's view of c. 1540 (could this have been heightened from a two-storey *porticus* or side chamber?) Its voussoirs are also of Roman brick, used here in a single order (cf. Brixworth, Northants). More Roman brick in the jambs, mixed with squared rubble. In the crypt remains have also been found of an E wall of early date, which suggests a length of some 70 ft (21 metres) for the Saxon church. Remains of a second wall some 30 ft (9 metres) further E probably date from a C13 extension.

The lengthy main UNDERCROFT, excavated by Mottistone, is entered beneath the tower. In it are displayed the remains of two TESSELLATED PAVEMENTS from a C3 or early C4 Roman house. One remains *in situ* between the tower's Saxon foundations. The other has been relaid in modern times as part of the crypt floor. – Also displayed here, fragments of three SAXON CROSSES found after the bombing. The first is the head with a cross in a circle and an inscription. Experts date it c. 1000. The name 'Werhenworth' appears on the second, sculptured cross, which is the most important Saxon survival of its date in London (c. 1030–60). Remains of figures indicate a standing Christ (as at Ruthwell in Dumfries and Galloway and Bewcastle, Cumberland), a man with tied legs, and two men side by side. There are also addorsed beasts and interlacings. The third fragment is in the early C11 Ringerike style, but almost certainly carved locally. On the back is part of a stylized lion (cf. the St Paul's grave slab in the Museum of London). – At the E end, a medieval ALTAR TABLE of stone from Chastiau Pelerin, the Crusaders' castle at Atlit below Mount Carmel, in Israel.

OTHER FITTINGS are a mixture of original, new and second-hand pieces. – PULPIT from St Swithin Cannon Street, c. 1682. Panels with thick garlands and heavy segmental pediments. Enormous tester like a flat bracket fungus, by *Lord Mottistone*. – FONT COVER. 1682, attributed uncontestedly to *Grinling Gibbons*; one of the finest 57 of the period, exquisitely carved in the round with cherubs, leaves, flowers, wheat-ears, fir-cones etc., wholly unlike the usual late C17 architectural formulae. It stands with its plain post-war FONT in a baptistery made in the SW vestry. – ORGAN. By *Harrison & Harrison*, 1957. The white-painted case copies that of Renatus Harris's instrument, destroyed in 1940. – ROYAL ARMS. Late C17; larger than usual. – Carved COMMUNION TABLE and brass COMMUNION RAILS, after late C17 and C18 fittings destroyed in the war. – C16

COMMUNION TABLE (N chapel). – Wrought-iron SWORD RESTS of 1727, 1755 and 1760. All larger and richer than average, that of 1755 extraordinarily so. – The post-war LECTERN incorporates wrought-iron rails of *c.* 1705 and a carved panel from the former Jacobean pulpit. – PAINTINGS. Main altarpiece, Last Supper by *Brian Thomas, c.* 1957. – N chapel altarpiece with four late C15 Flemish panels of good quality. From the Royal Lady Chapel N of the church, founded by Richard I and made collegiate in the C15. It may have been a separate building, or else have been subsumed into the present church in the C15 rebuilding. – ALMS BOX of brass on a fluted pedestal, dated 1787. From Christ's Hospital. – SCULPTURE. Small wooden figures of St James of Compostela (C15, nave), St Roche (*c.* 1520, nave), and St Anthony of Egypt (C16, rood stair door). Two works by *John Robinson,* 1970: a bronze group called Mother Love, SW corner; bust of Christ, baptistery. – STAINED GLASS. Heraldic glass by *Farrar Bell & Sons,* 1948–58. – Baptistery windows by *Keith New,* excellent work of 1964. – CURIOSA. Several large model ships suspended in the S aisle.

MONUMENTS. Alderman John Croke †1477, an important piece. Tomb-chest below canopy with two straight-sided depressed arches towards the front and a straight cresting. Fan-vault with pendants beneath. The Purbeck carving is less standardized than average for the date. Two brasses of kneeling groups remain on the back. The tomb serves as a receptacle for the TOC H LAMP, a delicate Arts-and-Crafts gilt piece by *Alec Smithers,* 1923. – Jerome Benali †1583–4, kneeling figure in pilastered frame. – Francis Covell †1621 and wife †1643–4. Figures only, reset. – Giles Lytcott †1696, wife, son and son's wife. Monument in the form of a column, flanked by putti. – Also in the form of a column, and also with a few putti, the Winder Monument (†1699 and †1717). – Toc H Memorials: two tomb-chests with recumbent bronze figures by *Cecil Thomas,* of the Hon. Alfred Forster, 1926, and the Rev. Clayton, 1972. – BRASSES in the chancel and N chapel, the fullest series in the City. In 1643 some had 'superstitious' texts defaced. William Tonge †1389, shield and circular inscription only. – John Bacon †1437 and wife, 2 ft figures with interlaced scrolls (N chapel). – Alderman John Croke, *see* above. – Thomas Gilbert †1483, tablet only. – Resurrection with soldiers, arched late C15 panel, from a late C15 canopied altar tomb destroyed in 1940, probably used as an Easter Sepulchre. – John Rusche †1498, 3 ft figure. – Christopher Rawson †1518 and two wives, 19 in. figures. – Andrew Evyngar †1533. An important Flemish panel, 33 in. long, with husband and wife, children behind and Pietà above (a similar brass formerly at St Mary at the Quay, Ipswich, is in the museum collections of Ipswich Borough Council). – William Thynne †1546 and wife, 30 in. figures – William Armar †1560, brass plate with kneeling figures. – Roger James †1591, 3 ft figure.

ALL HALLOWS LONDON WALL

1765–7, *George Dance the Younger*'s first building. It replaced a medieval church first recorded *c.* 1130 on the same site up against the City wall. The N wall of Dance's church indeed rests on the wall's Roman foundations, the semicircular vestry on those of one of the bastions.* Simple exterior but exquisite interior, an important inspiration to Dance's pupil, Soane. Brick, narrow, made more imposing by being raised up on a crypt. Placed so that the s side, with three semicircular windows high up, flanks London Wall, the projecting apse remains visible, and the w front faces a small churchyard. The ashlar-faced w tower projects beyond the body of the church. Steps up to a Tuscan doorway with frieze and pediment. Plain round-arched bell-stage with corner piers. Circular domed cupola above, more delicate, with the entablature broken out over a ring of Corinthian columns. The St Paul's-pattern cross and ball were added by *Blomfield*, 1898.

The interior shows a restraint in number and thickness of motifs 79 unprecedented in England and doubly remarkable if one considers that Dance was twenty-four when he designed the church. No aisles, just the nave and a diagonally coffered apse. Fluted Ionic columns placed against the outer walls carry the semicircular tunnel-vault of the nave. Minimal entablature, no more than an enriched Antique frieze. The vault itself has no projecting transverse arches, just even, shallow coffering, so that the display of carrying is further reduced. The only lighting is from the three semicircular windows piercing the tunnel-vault between the columns. The decoration of the apse derives from the Temple of Venus and Rome (DF). While Dance's later buildings were sparing in their use of Antique motifs, we can recognize here the Neoclassical desire to follow the Ancients more faithfully. But it is the restraint of the detail, the emphasis on purity of spatial expression, and such features as the radical elision of the architrave that most clearly point forward to Soane. Sir John Summerson's theory that this elision betrays the influence of Laugier's Rationalist theories has been challenged by Giles Worsley, who points out that Soane's lectures identify the source in Dance's direct observation of Roman buildings.

The FURNISHINGS were altered in 1890–1, first by *Carpenter & Ingelow*, then by *Blomfield*, and again in 1960–2 by *David Nye*, who restored the church after war damage. Until 1994 the church served as the headquarters and library of the Council for the Care of Churches. – REREDOS. Large oil painting of Acts IX by *Sir Nathaniel Dance-Holland*, after Pietro da Cortona; presented by the younger Dance, the artist's brother. Fine original frame. – W GALLERY on Tuscan columns. – Simple PULPIT, reached from the vestry via a pedimented doorway in the N wall. The pulpit stands mid-way between apse and gallery. – FONT. Late C17 bowl from St Mary Magdalen Old Fish Street, on a baluster of 1902. – FONT COVER by *David Nye*; also the ALTAR, SCREENS etc. – STALLS by *Nye*, reusing *Blomfield*'s, in turn cut down from *Dance*'s pews which rose to dado level. – ROYAL ARMS probably *c.*1700, repainted. – RAILINGS of iron, reusing *Goodall*'s communion rails of 1766. – ORGAN by *Noel Mander*, 1962, in a case of *c.*1880 by *Hill*, from the Manor House, Highbury. – CHANDELIER by *Lukyn Betts*, 1766 (companion being made 1995–6: DF). – SWORD REST of iron, 1753. From All Hallows Staining. – MONUMENTS. Edmond Hammond

*Curious late C18 Gothick trimmings, added to make the vestry an ornamental feature to gardens formerly lying N, were demolished in 1905.

†1642, with strapwork. Attributed to *John & Matthias Christmas*
62 (GF).– Joan Bence †1684, cartouche attributed to *Jasper Latham*
(GF). – Joseph Patience, architect, †1797. By *Thomas Patience*. Bust
on a plinth with circular relief, set on a sarcophagus.

At the E, PARISH HALL of brick (altered), by *H. I. Newton*, 1902, on
the site of Dance's rectory. It sheltered poorer workers who arrived
on statutory cheap early morning trains, as they waited for their
workplaces to open. To the w of the w end, a stretch of the medieval
CITY WALL is incorporated in the churchyard wall: *see* London Wall,
p. 540.

ALL HALLOWS STAINING
Mark Lane

Pulled down in 1870 except for the humble and much-restored
medieval w tower, now standing between the Clothworkers' Hall
(q.v.) and the N wall of Minster Court (*see* Mincing Lane). The
church is recorded by the late C12. The tower's lowest stage may be
of this date, though the earliest firmly datable feature is the early C14
cinquefoiled two-light w window. Of the same period the blocked E
and s arches, best seen from inside. The NW stair turret, late C14 or
C15, seems formerly to have extended to a vanished top stage
(shown on the C16 copperplate map. *See* Introduction p. 59). The
church was a nondescript mixture of medieval work and repairs of
1674–5. The tower was saved on the initiative of the Clothworkers'
Company and restored in 1873.

In 1872–3 two bays of a C12 CRYPT, from the former Lambe's
Chapel in Monkwell Street near Cripplegate, were added below the
ground to the E. That chapel was established in the late C16 by
William Lambe of the Clothworkers' Company in the buildings of a
former hermitage called St James-in-the-Wall. This was first
recorded in 1189, but the crypt's details suggest a date *c.* 1140: low
column-responds with lobed volute capitals, moulded ribs with
zigzag or spiral ornament.

CHRIST CHURCH NEWGATE STREET

The tower and part of the bombed shell of *Wren*'s church remain, on
the site of the chancel of the Franciscan (Greyfriars) church, established 1225 and rebuilt from 1306. It was the second largest church
of medieval London at 300 ft (91 metres) by 89 ft (27 metres). The
former nave is marked by an avenue of trees to the w. The old
chancel was made parochial in 1547, superseding the nearby
churches of St Nicholas Shambles and St Audoen or Ewin, in connection with the foundation of Christ's Hospital to the N (dem.
1902; *see* Newgate Street). *Wren* rebuilt the church in 1677–87,
shortening it at the w (masons *John Shorthose* and *Richard Crooke*).

The tower stands forward of the w wall. It is one of the most splendid
in London. Above the first cornice, the bell-stage has louvres divided
by pilasters, crowned by segmental pediments and a balustrade.

Everything above was added 1703–4 (mason *Edward Strong Jun.*). Recessed next stage, also square, ending in an even free-standing colonnade. Twelve big urns on top, from *Lord Mottistone*'s restoration of the shell in 1960, replacing (albeit in concrete) those removed in 1814. Rising out of them a dainty square pierced spire with vase and ball finial. The solution can be called a square version of St Mary-le-Bow. Neo-Georgian brick offices attached at the SW, by *Seely & Paget Partnership*, 1981, imitate a vestry of 1760 formerly on this site.

In front lie fragments of stone pineapples etc. from the old walls, partly demolished for road widening at the E end in 1974. Wren's reuse of the lower stages of the medieval walls and the foundations of the pier bases was revealed here in 1976. His W and E walls had the unusual feature of buttresses in line with the aisle colonnades, as if he did not fully trust these old foundations. The N wall and part of the S remain, with quoins and round-headed windows. Nave and aisles, the former groin-vaulted on Composite columns, the latter flat-ceilinged, disappeared in the Second World War. The magnificent plasterwork (by *Doogood*) went with them. The interior was notable otherwise for its exceptional breadth and for its steeply-raked galleries to accommodate the boys of Christ's Hospital. A GARDEN made in 1989 fills the truncated shell. Pergolas mark the positions of the piers.

ST ALBAN WOOD STREET
(Tower only)

Wren's correct Perpendicular Gothic tower stands in the middle of the roadway. Restored 1964; in 1984–5 converted into a house by *Frederick Burn, Smith & Partners*. It stood within the NW corner of the church, built 1682–5, the bomb-damaged shell demolished 1955. The tower dates from 1682–7 (first two stages) and 1687–8 (remainder). The mason of both phases was *Samuel Fulkes*. It has flat angle buttresses and another buttress in the centre of each side. They die back into the tower above the level of the belfry aperture imposts. On the N and W sides the central buttresses rise from grotesque mask-corbels. They mark the height of the lost church. Two windows on each side on each tier, bell-openings of two lights, and small cusped circular apertures. The weak pinnacles were renewed in 1878, in a different stone.

St Alban's is documented as early as *c.* 1085, but excavation in 1962 revealed remains probably of an even earlier church. This had a W tower, rectangular nave and square-ended chancel, the latter parts butt-jointed but of similar construction and probably conceived as a whole. While not inconsistent with an CII date, they may have been the remains of the late C8 chapel of King Offa, identified as the ancestor of St Alban by the chronicler Matthew Paris. To this were added N and S chapels, later extended into aisles. Later still a NE chapel was built. The outer walls were reconstructed in the C17, but attribution of their forms is difficult, for the burnt-out medieval shell which Wren restored had itself been rebuilt in 1633–4 (master mason *Edmund Kinsman*, carpenter *Matthew Banckes Sen.*). According to Strype, Inigo Jones was one of a party which surveyed the old church; but no connection with the rebuilding is proven, though Kinsman did much work for Jones elsewhere. The aisle windows had the odd tracery of the C17, but the piers inside were of the accepted four-shafts-four-hollows variety. Wren gave the church star-shaped plaster lierne-vaults. Apse added by *Scott*, who restored the church in 1858–9.

ST ALPHAGE LONDON WALL

The shells of the C14 crossing tower and N transept, gutted by bombing, are visible from the pedestrian walk on the N side of London Wall. They are the remains of the priory church of Elsing Spital, founded 1331 as a hospital for the blind staffed by secular priests, and taken over by Augustinian Canons in 1340. Walls mostly of flint with some rubble. Two tall plain arches to W and N. Similar but lower arch in the N transept W wall. The E crossing arch is also lower, of three orders with quarter-round mouldings, framing a seg-ment-headed doorway with a cusped niche on the inside. This may have screened the canons' chapel to its E from the hospital space, which was possibly in the 'nave' itself. The rest, demolished in 1923, comprised work of 1775–7 by *William Hillyer*, with a pedimented E front to the old line of Aldermanbury, and a lesser front on to London Wall, N (Gothicized by *Henry Ling*, 1914).

The old parish church proper, abandoned at the Reformation in favour of the vacated priory, was built on the line of the CITY WALL to the N (cf. All Hallows London Wall), where scanty remains are still visible (*see* London Wall, p. 543).

ST ANDREW HOLBORN
Holborn Viaduct

King Edgar's renewal of the Charter of Westminster Abbey, *c.* 959, mentions a St Andrew's Church of timber here. The mid-C15 fabric of its successor stood outside the area burned by the Great Fire, but became ruinous and was rebuilt 1684–6 by *Wren*, the largest of his City churches (*Edward Pierce* and *William Stanton*, masons, *John Longland*, carpenter, *Robert Dyer*, plasterer). Accounts published in *Wren Soc.* Vol. X contain references confirming Wren's authorship. Gutted in 1941 and rebuilt by *Seely & Paget* (reopened 1961).

Wren preserved the C15 tower, but refaced it in 1703–4, retaining the angle buttresses and pointed lower windows. Hollow-chamfered pointed arches survive within it, on W, N and S. At the same time the top stage with its bulbous pinnacles with vases was added, each crowned until the Second World War with a weathervane. The large upper windows are remarkable. A shallow open segmental pediment on pilasters with fluted capitals is placed within a round-headed frame: a deliberate discord. In the tympanum is an oval opening. The cornice above has pairs of deep brackets at each end, instead of Wren's usual even modillions or dentils. In all this the hand of *Hawksmoor* may be suspected. On the W front, facing a garden made in 1970, STATUES of schoolchildren from the former Parish School in Hatton Garden, built 1696.

The church itself is evenly treated to suit its island site. Stone-faced, aisled and balustraded, of seven bays. Round-headed windows, set over segmental ones in the central five bays, over pedimented doorways in the end bays. Low NW and SW vestibules, like those at St Clement Danes, Westminster (1680–2), where Wren also kept the medieval tower. The NE and SE bays house vestries. The C20 restorers faithfully re-created the lofty barrel-vaulted interior, with its groin-vaults over the aisles on Corinthian columns rising from the gallery fronts. Two-storeyed Venetian window in the shallow chancel. All these features appear at Wren's St James Piccadilly (1676–82), save only that St James's aisles have transverse barrel-vaults. The circular skylight over the chancel was probably first made in alterations by *J. H. Good*, 1818. The excessive gilding dates from 1975. St Andrew is now the headquarters church of the Royal College of Organists.

FURNISHINGS. Nothing remains from *Teulon*'s restoration of 1869–72. The replacement font, pulpit and organ come from the Foundling Hospital (*see London 4: North*). – FONT. Presented to the Hospital in 1804. Slender stone baluster with small basin. – PULPIT. Mid C19, on an absurdly short Corinthian column. The body is characteristically Victorian in that it reverts to an earlier type of arched panels. – ORGAN by *Noel Mander*, 1990, within the modest Kentian CASE given by Handel in 1750, perhaps designed by the Hospital's architect *Theodore Jacobsen* (lower parts re-created to the C18 design by *Julian Harrap*, 1990). – REREDOS, after the pre-war piece, and other fittings by *Seely & Paget*. – CHANDELIERS of 1977. – STAINED GLASS. E window, Last Supper and Ascension, by *Brian Thomas*, 1961, red and green to match the painting of the plaster-work. – More glass by *Thomas* in the NW CHAPEL, reached from beneath the tower. Here, ALTAR RAILS and part of the REREDOS from St Luke's Old Street, *c.* 1733. – MONUMENTS. Captain Thomas Coram, the founder of the Foundling Hospital, †1751. A mere plain chest. Above it a standing weeping putto and wall-mounted heads, from the former Manningham monument (†1722). – William Mellish †1690 and wife †1702, NW chapel. Black and white marble tablet carved with stiff swags of fruit and cherub heads, by *William Stanton*. Brought in 1993 from the redundant St Leonard, Ragnall, Notts. – SCULPTURE. Stone slab of the Last Judgement, C17, on the N wall facing the former churchyard. Said to come from the former burying ground of the workhouse in Shoe Lane. Small figures; innumerable bodies climbing out of their graves. Christ above as in an Ascension. – GATE PIERS. Made *c.* 1870, with steps down from Holborn Viaduct. Good wrought-iron GATES, apparently post-war.

RECTORY, COURT HOUSE and VESTRY CLERK'S OFFICE to the s, built around a courtyard in 1868–71 by *Teulon*. They replaced buildings lost to the new St Andrew Street. Plain stock brick Gothic with stone dressings, all on a modest scale and looking singularly humble against Wren's church. The circular stair-tower with its conical spire marks the staircase to the Court House, distinguished by its big three-light traceried windows. Interiors with typical tough

Teulon forms: Gothic fireplaces, Rectory staircase (E) with timber screen, etc. (Court Room with hammerbeam roof with affinities to Teulon's church designs. Restored by *David Gazeley*, 1994, in polychromatic High Victorian Gothic style. Here a grandiose early C17 fireplace and overmantel from the previous Court House. Stuart arms in the centre, carved figures of Saints in flanking niches, with, below them, small reliefs from scripture. Terms flank the fireplace proper.) Also by *Teulon* the endearing little LODGE, with a big central chimneystack, at the courtyard entrance.

ST ANDREW UNDERSHAFT
Leadenhall Street and St Mary Axe

A regular aisled Perp building with a shallow chancel, entered through a tower set to one side at the SW: all features typical of the medieval City church in its final development. The name comes from the shaft of the maypole, set up opposite every year until 1517 and destroyed as an 'Idoll' in 1547 (Stow). The church is first mentioned in the early C12. C15 SW tower with NW stair turret. Upper stage of 1695, altered 1883 by *T. Chatfeild Clarke* who added the spiky pinnacles and turret. Restored S doorway, square-headed, of two orders with wave mouldings and panelling above, C15 or C16 (original panelled DOOR, with ironwork). All the rest was rebuilt 1520–32, at the expense first of Lord Mayor Sir Stephen Jennings (†1524), then of William Fitzwilliams. This part is of good, even squared ragstone with a plinth, best seen on the N side. Rendered E parts and S wall, the latter hidden by buildings on Leadenhall Street. Grander and loftier inside than the exterior suggests, though plain and somewhat dry in the details. Nave and aisles of six bays, the chancel unmarked by any structural division. Arcades with depressed arches on slim piers of the familiar four-shaft-four-hollow section, with capitals only to the shafts. Four-light aisle windows and three-light clerestory windows. Tracery only in the large, restored E and W windows, of five lights, mullioned and transomed. The S arcade stands free of the tower, so that the interior is wholly regular and the clerestory uninterrupted. A blocked light in the tower's E face, towards the S aisle, indicates that this was an external wall before the aisle was added. Blocked doorway in the N aisle wall to the former rood stair, which is housed in an external turret. Nave roof with main ribs on small curved braces and little corbels; faithfully renewed 1949–50 reusing C16 bosses. N aisle roof, C16. Moulded ribs form squares, each subdivided into four further squares. Square bosses of angels with shields. NE VESTRIES: late C17, E, with stone-built W addition by *Clarke*, 1883.

FITTINGS are of a mixture of periods (restorations 1704; 1875–6 by *E. Christian* and *A. Blomfield*, who made the low-walled chancel; Blomfield's brother was rector here). (In store in 1997: two SWORD RESTS, C18, one from All Hallows Staining, Mark Lane, dated 1722; BENCHES, late C18, with painted figures of St Andrew). – FONT. By *Nicholas Stone*, 1631. Simple octagonal bowl of white marble on a black marble baluster stem. The derivation of the post-Fire type from such designs is clear. FONT COVER, C17, but later than the font. – FONT RAILS with twisted balusters, perhaps made from 1630s communion rails. – PULPIT. Late C17, above average, with unusual circular marquetry panels. On it brass CANDLESTICKS with figures of St Andrew. – DOORCASES to N and S, pedimented with engaged columns, probably of 1704. On the N one a domestic-looking late C18 CLOCK by *E. Pistor*, from the former W gallery. – Carved Gothic REREDOS of 1830. – Wrought iron COMMUNION RAIL by *Tijou*, 1704. – ORGAN. By *Renatus Harris*, 1695–6 (altered 1749–50, 1858, etc.). Excellent CASE with two seated angels on the convex-curved top. Blomfield crammed it into the S arcade, lopping off the finials (two carved mitres reset on the side). – PAINTINGS. In the spandrels of the arcade, scenes in grisaille from the Life of Christ. By *Robert Brown*, probably of 1725–6. Brown's figures of the Apostles between the clerestory windows have gone. – STAINED GLASS. The important C17 W window was alas largely destroyed by the terrorist bomb of 1992. In its five lights were figures of monarchs between Edward VI and William III; the latter suggesting a date *c.* 1690–1700. According to Dennis Corble, however, it was given by Sir Christopher Clitherow (†1642) and the last figure was a later addition. The tracery lights survive in the restored window (1996), which has shields instead of figures. – E window. Noble Crucifixion and Ascension by *Heaton, Butler & Bayne*, 1875–6. – Aisles. Heraldic glass in the heads of *c.* 1530 commemorates donors to the rebuilding. It is the City's oldest intact group of stained glass. – MONUMENTS. In the N aisle older monuments, including several Lord Mayors. Brass to Nicholas Leveson †1539, wife and children. Groups of kneeling figures. – Sir Thomas Offley †1582 (chancel). Kneeling figures facing one another across a prayer desk, in an enriched frame with columns. Attributed to *Cornelius Cure* (GF). – Simon Burton †1593. Brass plate in stone frame. – John Stow †1605, author of the *Survey of London*. An early example of a full-length upright figure, but shown stiffly seated at a table and writing in the Elizabethan scholarly tradition. Flanked by square pillars with ribbonwork etc. Perhaps by *Nicholas Johnson*. – Alice Byng †1616, with little kneeling figure. – Sir Hugh Hamersley †1636. Large and impressive wall-monument with kneeling figures under curtains. Two soldiers representing the Honourable Artillery Company stand outside the flanking columns. Female figures recline on half-pediments above. Said to be by *Thomas Madden* (AW). – Anthony Abdy †1640, signed *Henry Boughton* (W end). – Sir Christopher Clitherow and family †1642–62, with rustic cornucopia. – W. Innes †1795, with portrait relief. – S aisle. Margery Turner †1607. – Edward Warner †1628, with columns, attributed to *Stone* (AW). – Many good cartouches. The best are: J. Jeffreys †1688, attributed to *Thomas Cartwright Sen.* (GF). – Charles Thorold †1691, convex, signed by *T. Cartwright Sen.* – Peter Vansittart †1705, big and wonderfully rich, with well-carved skulls, garlands and cherubs' heads, high up. Attributed to *Thomas Cartwright Jun.* (GF). – Others apparently also by the *Cartwrights* (e.g. H. Sykes †1710). – Two more C17 monuments are hidden by the organ.

ST ANDREW-BY-THE-WARDROBE
Queen Victoria Street

Known from *c.* 1170. The Wardrobe was the stores department of the Crown (including arms and clothing), transferred from the Tower to a site nearby in the mid C14, and destroyed in 1666. The church was rebuilt in 1685–94 by *Wren*, gutted in 1940, and restored by *Marshall Sisson* in 1959–61. Wren's craftsmen were *Nicholas Young*, mason, *Thomas Horn*, bricklayer, *John Longland*, carpenter, and *Henry Doogood*, plasterer.

The church presides dramatically over the street behind a terraced churchyard. Very plain red brick, much patched, with quoins (but Hatton (1708) found it 'finished or rendered over in imitation of stone'). Round-headed windows above, segmental-headed below. The sw tower projects beyond the body of the church. It is square, of four stages, with a straight top. On the uppermost angles plain piers instead of quoins; weathervane from St Michael Bassishaw, 1712. Removed in 1959–61 were embellishments to bell-stage and parapet by *Thomas Garner*, *c.* 1875, and all but the pediment of an ornamental s portal of 1902. This entrance was moved *c.* 1824 from the adjacent bay to the E. Garner's balustrade on the tower survives, replacing Wren's parapet, which had circular piercings. The churchyard wall with urns and wrought-iron gates was made in 1901 as a memorial to Professor Banister Fletcher, probably by his son *Sir Banister*. Crucifix by *Walter Tapper*.

The interior is aisled, with five regular arcaded bays on piers instead of the usual columns. Tunnel-vaulted nave divided into bays with circular plaster wreaths, groin-vaulted aisles. In the restoration the plasterwork, piers and gallery fronts were re-created, but the aisles have been divided off on the ground floor by solid panelling, and are used as chapel, vestries and offices. The Redundant Churches Fund and Ancient Monuments Society had offices within the church until 1991.

FURNISHINGS. The parish was a poor one, and, exceptionally, the C17 fittings were financed by the Coal Dues. All were destroyed in 1940 except a sword rest and two monuments. The replacements have been steadily assembled from various sources. – PULPIT (with stem and stairs of 1966), FONT and FONT COVER all by *Edward Pierce*, made for St Matthew Friday Street. – New REREDOS designed by *Arthur Ayres*, different from its predecessor but incorporating some old work. – ROYAL ARMS of *c.* 1685, over the tower doorway, from St Olave Jewry. – CHAMBER ORGAN in w gallery, made by *Snetzler* for Teddesley Hall, Shropshire, 1769. – SANCTUARY CHAIR of 1687. – SCULPTURE. Two small wooden figures: St Anne, North Italian of *c.* 1500, holding a small group of Virgin and Child; St Andrew, *c.* 1600. – In the w gallery, memorial RELIEFS to Shakespeare and Dowland, designed by *Peter Foster*, carved by *Paul A. Cooper*, *c.* 1990. – SWORD REST, early C18. – Brass CHANDELIERS, early C18. – STAINED GLASS. w window: Conversion of St Paul, an early work by *Joshua Price*, *c.* 1712–16, after a painting by *Sebastiano Ricci*; made for Bulstrode Park, Buckinghamshire. Painted in enamel stains, the style with strange reminiscences of Giulio Romano. – s aisle windows by *Carl Edwards*, 1968. – MONU-

MENT. Rev. Saunders †1836, by *Samuel Manning* (W gallery).
Obelisk with relief of angels bearing him upwards.

ST ANNE AND ST AGNES
Gresham Street

Known by the early C12, as St Agnes. In medieval times both names
were used, though at first not together, and the present dedication is
unique. Rebuilt after the fire in brick by *Wren* who is named in the
accounts as supplying the design, though *Hooke* has also been
suggested as designer and certainly made several visits to the site.
Built 1677–87, the bulk of work done by 1681. The bricklayer was
John Fitch; other craftsmen *Robert Walters* and *William Hammond*,
masons, *John Hayward*, carpenter, *John Sherwood*, plasterer, and
Thomas Dobbins, plumber. The parish employed the joiners
Cheltenham (a parishioner), *Fuller* and *Page* for the fittings. Restored
by *Braddock & Martin Smith* in 1963–8 after war damage, and now
used by the Lutherans. Before the war it was visible only through a
narrow gap in the buildings of Gresham Street, but land S and E
of its churchyard has been cleared and a garden made with low
serpentine walls (1971–2).

Not a big church, so its attraction is of a homely sort. The centralized
plan is immediately apparent from the E, S and N elevations with
their central shaped and pedimented gables, each with a big round-
headed window rising above the cornice of the bays to each side.
Rusticated brick surrounds to these windows and the similar, smaller
flanking ones, and brick quoins also at the angles. The warm red
Berkshire brick of the E and S fronts dates from the restoration, when
the walls were rebuilt from sill level. The church had been stuccoed
in 1820–1 by *Charles Tyrell*, and the N side is stuccoed still. (Other
restorations in 1763–4, 1781–2 by *James Peacock*, 1800, 1838–9 by
W. M. Brookes, 1849–50 by *John Wallen*, and 1887–8 by *Ewan
Christian*.) The tower, also stuccoed, is plain and small, placed centrally at the W. It looks too small for the church, the consequence of
reusing the lower stages and NW stair-turret of the C14 tower (see
the door with two-centred arch facing the internal lobby N of the
tower). Simple square lantern on a truncated weatherboarded
pyramid (contracted for in 1680). It looks more like an artisan's
design than something from the Wren office. Contemporary
weathervane made by *Robert Bird*, in the shape of an A, for Anne
and Agnes. The SW vestibule, rebuilt since the war, originally
housed the staircase to a vanished W gallery. The NW vestry is
probably that built by *John Bird*, 1706 (Colvin).

The wainscotted interior is of the cross-in-square plan type, like St
Martin Ludgate and St Mary-at-Hill, and raises the same problems
of derivation as those churches (*see* Introduction p. 76). Here it has
a groin-vaulted central square on four Corinthian columns of wood,
four vaulted Greek-cross arms, and small lower corner cells with
circular panels. The walls are not quite parallel, but the divergence is
not obvious. In the corners of each cell winged cherubs' heads. The
architraves of these cells rest on corbel-capitals of free design. In the
post-war restoration the slim plaster ribs of Wren's central cross-vault

were omitted, and Ewan Christian's decorative scheme entirely erased. This plainness is becoming to its present Lutheran use.

FITTINGS were mostly salvaged from elsewhere. Chief original survival is the REREDOS. By *Cheltenham*, a refined tripartite design with fluted Corinthian pilasters and a scrolly broken pediment. The garlanded urn on top replaced the C17 royal arms some time in the C18. Flanking it, large PAINTINGS of Moses and Aaron, *c.* 1700, from St Michael Wood Street. – COMMUNION RAILS. Post-war. – PULPIT. Incorporating panels salvaged from that at St Augustine Watling Street, by *Maine*, 1687. – FONT. Post-war, marble, of C17 baluster design. The original is at St Vedast. Bell-shaped COVER from St Mildred Bread Street (by *Cleere*, 1682). – S DOORCASE. With engaged Corinthian columns and broken segmental pediment of Wren period, from Dunster Castle, Somerset. Splendid carved gilt angel on top, from the organ case of St Mildred Bread Street (1744). – ORGAN. 1991, by *R. J. Winn*, using older parts; in an ugly CASE from Southery Methodist church, Norfolk. – SCULPTURE. From St Mildred the tiny carved figure of Time dated 1682–3 over the vestry door, and the Lion and Unicorn on the E columns. – ROYAL ARMS. Carved, Stuart, from St Mary Whitechapel. – SANCTUARY CHAIRS. Late C17 style, but probably Victorian. – LECTERN in the form of a standing angel, *c.* 1900. From All Saints, Bermondsey. – CROWN and two MITRES in the middle of the N wall, from an early C19 organ case. – Two restored BUSTS below the central S window, moved here in 1844 from a monument to Sir James Drax †1662 and his son Henry †1682, erected at the site of St John Zachary, Gresham Street. Attributed to *Pierce* (GF).

ST AUGUSTINE WATLING STREET

For the surviving tower of Wren's church, *see* St Paul's Cathedral Choir School, in which it is now incorporated.

ST BARTHOLOMEW-THE-GREAT
West Smithfield

The most important C12 monument in London, though only a fragment remains of the church founded in 1123. Rahere, a prebendary of St Paul's and later an Augustinian canon, established St Bartholomew as an Augustinian priory with a hospital adjoining (cf. the Augustinian St Thomas's Hospital, Southwark, founded *c.* 1106 in connection with the rebuilt St Mary Overie). The hospital survived the Reformation (see p. 331). The canons' church was about 280 ft (85 metres) long to the E wall of the choir; but, except for a fragment of the W front, the C13 nave from the easternmost bay to the W was pulled down *c.* 1543 when the parish took over the C12 choir and crossing from the new owner, Sir Richard Rich. As well as the choir, crossing and W front fragment, the Lady Chapel, added E of the choir *c.* 1330, also survives. In 1404–9 a Papal indulgence records work including the rebuilding of the cloister (partly surviving); other Perp features probably come from the same campaign. The present exterior, however, is largely post-Reformation, both c16–c17 and by *Aston Webb* in 1886–98. Earlier restoration by *Hayter Lewis* and *William Slater*, 1864, largely internal, is less apparent. Little trace of previous restorations, by *T. Hardwick*, 1790–1 and 1808, and *John Blyth*, 1830s. The c16 and c17 changes began in earnest after the brief monastic revival under Mary I, when St Bartholomew became a Dominican house (1555–8): the parish rebuilt the N gallery as a schoolhouse in the later c16 and added the SW tower in 1628. Much of the rest of the fabric fell into decay or was converted to other uses as the surroundings were more densely developed: a plan in Wilkinson's *Londinia Illustrata* (1821) shows the church hemmed in by buildings along Cloth Fair (N) and around Bartholomew Close (S), the S transept in ruins, and houses made within the Lady Chapel and N transept. All this explains the dearth of medieval fabric. c16 and c17 work was retained by Aston Webb, who owed his employment to the fact that his brother, E.A. Webb, was churchwarden.* Though not an architect one associates with church restoration, he responded thoughtfully to the task: his own sharp, wiry free Gothic in flint and Portland stone for the W front and new transepts; more archaeological insertions in the medieval context (Lady Chapel and interiors). The latter are carefully distinguished, perhaps in response to pressure from the Society for the Protection of Ancient Buildings. It is an intelligent, honest solution, but not always an immediately appealing one. Progress was slow, since much adjacent property had to be bought up and cleared. The finishing touches kept Webb busy here until 1928. Only slight restorations since.

The GATEWAY opens into the forecourt or churchyard from West Smithfield. The two half-timbered upper storeys with braces were built as a house for Sir Philip Scudamore, 1595, and much restored in 1916 by *Webb* with picturesque gable and shallow oriels. The gateway proper incorporates the restored c13 W doorway to the S nave aisle. Of four orders, with dogtooth but always without shafts, as the plinth reveals. Probably of *c.* 1230, like the rest of the nave. To its r. a blank arch, suggesting the whole lower front was arcaded. Iron gates by *Blyth*, 1856 (lower part); carvings of St Bartholomew (above) and a Crucifixion, by *W.S. Frith*, 1917, the latter a war memorial to Webb's son. To the r. a red brick house, a reconstruction of 1950–2 by *Seely & Paget* and *L.B. Smith* of the pre-war gatehouse extension of *c.* 1700 (earlier restoration 1932).

Exterior

The footpath to the church follows the line of the demolished nave along the S aisle. On its r., part of the c13 S aisle wall. The W FRONT is really *Webb*'s attempt to make the best of a bad job (1893). He added the two-storeyed S PORCH at the SW angle of the remaining fabric, and refaced with shallow, weak arcading the patched-up brick wall thrown across the E end of the nave in the 1540s. All is in flint and Portland stone with much chequerwork. On the porch triangular-headed panelling and a sinuous niche canopy, rising through the gable merlon to end as a foliate cross. Immediately behind appears

---

* E.A. Webb's *Records of St Bartholomew Smithfield* (1921) is the best account of the church and precinct.

the embattled brick TOWER of 1628, built over the far E bay of the S
nave aisle. It replaced a parochial steeple of uncertain date on the N
side. Its plan is rectangular, broader (N–S) than it is deep. Debased
three-light tracery under rounded heads in the lower openings.
Pretty little square timber lantern on top.

The rest of the exterior must be seen from Cloth Fair, N, accessible
across the raised churchyard. First the easternmost and only surviving bay of the NAVE, exposed by demolitions in 1914. The clerestory
has a renewed two-light plate-traceried window of c. 1230, with a
plain circle above two lights. The aisle has gone, so one sees below
only the outlines of the C13 aisle vault, superimposed on the C12
arcade and gallery. From this it is clear that the first bay of the nave
belonged with the C12 crossing, but was modified to match
the C13 work. Next to this bay Webb's N TRANSEPT, with a porch
and a big octagonal turret set asymmetrically. Three tall lancets,
much pattern-making in stone and flint. Beyond this lies the choir.
The ground floor is from the restoration of 1864. The N GALLERY
preserves a rare and instructive example of the *ad hoc* adaptation of
great monastic churches after the Reformation. Brick facing of
c. 1600 shows where the schoolroom was made within. Two- and
three-light Tudor windows, square-headed, with four-centred
arches. Small hipped roof to each bay, partly concealed by the parapet. The early C17 schoolmaster's house, E, is two storeys higher,
with a brick stair-turret and half-hipped roof. The school moved out
only in 1889. The C14 Perp clerestory appears above, beneath a
brick parapet. Two-light tracery, restored in 1864.

At the E end, Webb's apse clerestory, with twin panelled octagonal
turrets, and below and beyond it the low four-bay LADY CHAPEL.
A will of 1336 calls this 'newly constructed'. Excavations in 1988
revealed two phases of construction, perhaps closely following each
other, which suggest that the chapel was already under way before
the C12 E end was demolished. Rich inserted a floor in 1544 to make
the chapel into a house. Of this date probably the tiny single W light
on the N side. When *Webb* restored the chapel in 1895–8 it had been
heightened in brick and had latterly functioned as a fringe factory.
A good deal of C14 banded flintwork remains. Webb's are the blind
E wall, the S wall apart from sections around the lower buttresses,
and most of the even three-light windows. His tracery is firmly Perp,
not flowing. A stone and flint-faced extension to the church offices
by *Anthony New*, 1989, fills part of the sunken court around the
chapel (N side). The S side is visible from Bartholomew Close,
reached by an alley E of the E wall. Immediately W of the Lady
Chapel here lie C16 brick foundations, from the demolished lodging
of Prior Bolton. Projecting from the next bay to the W, the lower
walls of the C12 Chapel of St Stephen, otherwise demolished in
1849. Curiously shaped, with apses on the S and E, and *Webb*'s
VESTRY of 1914 on top.

Interior

The church represents the four-bay choir of the priory church with
the gloomy crossing, transepts, and the first bay of the nave. The
choir of 1123 etc., not long, has an apsed E end with an ambulatory
(restored), originally with three radiating chapels, the outer pair

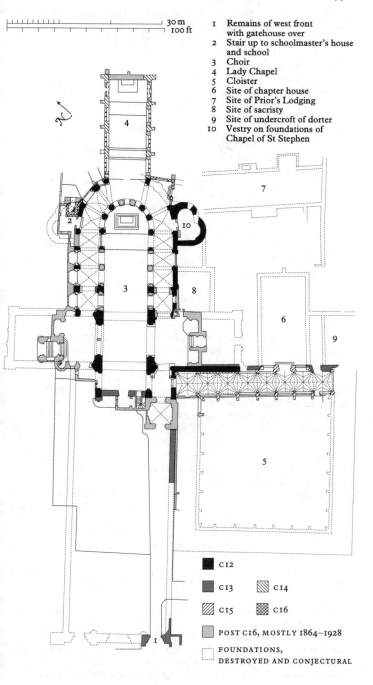

30 m
100 ft

1 Remains of west front
   with gatehouse over
2 Stair up to schoolmaster's house
   and school
3 Choir
4 Lady Chapel
5 Cloister
6 Site of chapter house
7 Site of Prior's Lodging
8 Site of sacristy
9 Site of undercroft of dorter
10 Vestry on foundations of
   Chapel of St Stephen

■ C12

■ C13   ▨ C14

▨ C15   ▨ C16

▨ POST C16, MOSTLY 1864–1928

□ FOUNDATIONS,
  DESTROYED AND CONJECTURAL

St Bartholomew-the-Great. Plan

double-apsed (cf. Norwich, begun 1096). The remains of the SE chapel have already been described; the NE chapel is destroyed; the E chapel replaced by the C14 Lady Chapel. Excavations beneath the last in 1911 revealed a section of straight walling indicating that the C12 chapel was longer than those to either side.

11   The CHOIR, four bays long, has massive cylindrical piers with many-scalloped capitals and unmoulded arches with a finely moulded running extrados with billet decoration. Four slender sub-arches in the gallery openings, with one relieving arch also with billet decoration. The clerestory, C14, retains the C12 wall passage. The C12 internal elevation may derive from Reading Abbey (founded 1121), which likewise lacked any vertical division of the bays, though the two lower storeys of near-equal height and the rather old-fashioned groin-vaulted ambulatory with plain cross-ribs recall the late C11 Chapel of St John in the White Tower.* The first campaign ended probably c. 1133, when disruption to the priory's government is recorded. A set-back on the broad compound pier immediately E of the crossing may mark the position of a temporary party wall. This would give a date of c. 1145–60 for the following campaign under Prior Thomas, which built the longer W choir bay, crossing, transepts and E bay of the nave. It is likely that the lesser arches were inserted into the gallery at the same time, perhaps to strengthen it, since the main imposts make no provision for any such arcade.

The E end, much altered in the C14 and later, was restored to the Norman plan in 1864 (the stilted arches and two central columns) and 1886 (gallery and clerestory). In the gallery, *Webb* carried on the blank arches of the first bay from the W, but with two sub-arches instead of three. Hatched tympana and the use of Bath stone further distinguish the new work. The C12 E end had been altered in two stages: first in the early C14, when the two central piers were removed and the ambulatory modified for the new Lady Chapel; then c. 1405, when a new square E end was made further W, curtail-ing the first bay of the apse slightly. Its alignment is marked by the truncated E sub-arch of the gallery bay. Here a restored Perp shaft, perhaps from the jamb of an E clerestory window, has been incor-porated into Webb's graceful chancel arch. Of 1864 the two central piers, and the piers and half-piers of the two W bays.

The abrupt end of the extrados moulding on the crossing piers probably corresponds to the E end of the canons' stalls, which would have extended under the crossing. The C12 appearance may be reconstructed further from remains of red, black, and yellow paint of that date discovered in the C19 on the arcade voussoirs, and from the corbel-courses across E and W crossing arches, which indi-cate a flat wooden roof some 47 ft (14 metres) high: lower than *Webb*'s present kingpost roof of 1885–6, incorporating medieval tie-beams.

A very pretty addition is the oriel window on the S side of the gallery. The date is probably shortly before 1517, when recent expenditure by Prior Bolton is mentioned. It served as a kind of ORATORY accessible from his lodgings to the S. It has a three-light opening in the front and single-light canted sides, all glazed. Bolton's rebus appears in the central quatrefoiled panel below. A doorway

* *See* Lawrence Hoey, *Journal of the Society of Architectural Historians* 48 (1989).

also with Bolton's rebus in the spandrels survives in the SE corner of the AMBULATORY (the present Chapel of the Knights Bachelor), in a section of plastered early C16 brick walling. The ambulatory and aisles mostly retain the plain C12 responds. On the S side, a blocked two-centred C14 doorway in the first bay from the W gave access to a sacristy, destroyed by fire in 1830. The aisle and ambulatory vault is largely concrete of 1893, apart from two C12 bays in the NE corner, just N of two pointed C14 arches by the Lady Chapel entrance. In the second of these bays a restored late C14 three-light window. The plain C12 arch in the next bay was the entrance to the demolished NE chapel, foundations of which were uncovered in 1988 (corresponding arch on the S). Further W on this side, three deep recesses with late C14 moulded arches, mostly renewed in 1864. They formerly opened into the parochial Chapel of All Saints, built *c.* 1395 as an E extension of the N transept and demolished *c.* 1542.

The CROSSING has full shafts on the N and S arches, corbels on the E and W, and arches of two orders. These parts were probably built in the mid C12, so the stilted N and S arches here may well be the earliest major pointed arches in London. In the spandrels round-headed blind arches and sunk lozenges. W and N arches rebuilt probably *c.* 1405 to correct settlement, hence the polygonal caps to the shafts. If there was a crossing tower, as is likely, it may have been taken down at this time, since a new bell-tower (perhaps an isolated structure) is mentioned as part of the C15 work. Early C15 strainer screen of two depressed pointed arches on the N side, much damaged in the C18–C19 when a smithy occupied the transept. C12 foundations of a S screen were uncovered in 1864.

The TRANSEPTS are *Webb*'s, to an uncomfortably truncated plan. The N transept has a blind gallery and a screen of tracery behind the lancets, the S transept (the present baptistery) twin lancets carried further down. The medieval transepts were some 40 ft (12 metres) deep. The arches into the chancel aisles and into the S nave aisle remain, incorporated into Webb's fabric. On the S side also a C12 gallery arch over the nave aisle arch, with three restored sub-arches.

The NAVE was originally ten bays long. The surviving bay lay immediately E of the pulpitum, part of which probably remains within the W wall. As is clear also from the exterior, the surviving bay is C12, the design similar to the straight parts of the chancel, but modified *c.* 1230 when Gothic aisles were carried up to the crossing. Of this date the wall-shafts in the S aisle bay under the tower, with foliage and bell-shaped capitals, and on each side the plate-traceried clerestory window of *c.* 1230, blocked on the S side by the tower. Excavated fragments show that the Gothic nave had Purbeck-shafted piers. There is no evidence of vaulting of its central vessel. Each of the blocked gallery openings is pierced with a C15 doorway, the N one containing steps up to the level of the crown of the lost C13 aisle vault.

Finally the LADY CHAPEL. Webb's E wall has blind niches of C13 pattern. Of the C14 the N and S windows close to the E wall, the S window being SEDILIA as well. Detached shafts to the inside to form the seats, and a similar arrangement on the N. Webb's window jambs are distinguishable by their octagonal shafts. His open wooden roof is arcaded above the trusses. CRYPT underneath the E part, reached through the new church offices via the NE ambulatory. Entry is through a four-centred doorway, early C16, with carved vines and grapes in the spandrels. The segmental barrel-vault and chamfered transverse ribs were largely reconstructed in 1895.

Furnishings

Except for monuments the church is poor in furnishings. Fine wrought-iron SCREEN to the Lady Chapel, 1897, designed by *Webb* and made by *Starkie, Gardner & Co.*, with foliage cresting and candlesticks on top. By the same the screens in the N crossing arches, 1893. – HIGH ALTAR by *Seely & Paget*, 1950, with openwork Tudor-Gothic uprights, weird and effective. A vast early C17 painted reredos on canvas, representing in false perspective an elaborate classical structure crowned by obelisks, was destroyed in 1828. – LECTERN by *Webb*, four-sided with little figures, made from old roof timbers. (A pulpit of stone, also by *Webb*, was removed in 1930.) – STALLS, SCREEN, ORGAN CASE and W GALLERY, 1886–93, of oak, Gothic and unexceptional. Grouped under the crossing. On the lower organ case sickly paintings of monks by *F. E. Beresford*. – FONT of *c.* 1405, the only medieval one in the City proper. Plain, massive octagonal basin and pedestal. – BENCHES. Two pieces of *c.* 1700 with ornate open backs, apparently of foreign workmanship. – DOOR into the cloister, *c.* 1600. – SCULPTURE. The Risen Christ, by *Josephina de Vasconcellos*, *c.* 1990, strikingly juxtaposed with a C13 stone COFFIN (N aisle). – ALTAR PIECE in the Lady Chapel, after Murillo. MONUMENTS. Choir. Rahere †1144. In the NE position preferred for founders' monuments. Made when the E end was remodelled *c.* 1405. The design is very similar to Sir Bernard de Brocas's tomb in Westminster Abbey (†1395) and Gower's monument in Southwark Cathedral (†1408). Tomb-chest under canopy with recumbent effigy of Reigate stone in Augustinian habit. At the feet two small kneeling bedesmen and a larger angel holding a shield. Canopy with three cusped arches crowned by tall concave-sided crocketed gables set against blank panelling. Cresting at the top. Some *Coade* stone repairs of 1815 (by *William Croggan*). The back wall is pierced in three little arches to the ambulatory. Arcading up to the C15 E wall line was destroyed in 1864. – Percival Smalpace †1558 and wife †1588, an odd composition with pilasters and two frontal busts like passport photographs separated by a mullion. Slate panel below with incised figures of the pair's naked corpses. Attributed to *Giles de Witt* (GF). – Sir Robert Chamberlayne †1615. Kneeling figure under a convex architectural canopy with two well-carved standing angels holding two curtains open. Style of *Colt* (GF). Other versions at Jesus College, Oxford, and elsewhere. – Two grand cartouches with cherubs' heads: John Kellond †1685, attributed to *Edward Pierce* (GF); Jonathan Whiting †1704 and wife †1727, by *Theophilus Allen*.– N aisle. Francis Anthony †1623, with charmingly naïve incised columns with rose-garlands. – S aisle. Sir Walter Mildmay †1589, Chancellor of the Exchequer and Founder of Emmanuel College, Cambridge, and wife. Big standing wall-monument of rich alabaster and coloured marble, with flanking columns but no effigy. – Anthony Lowe †1641, tablet with ornamented frame. – James Rivers †1641, '. . . Who when ambytyon, Tyrany &

Pride/Conquer'd the Age, conquer'd hymself & Dy'd'. Frontal bust, book in hand. Attributed to *William Wright* (AW). – Edward Cooke †1652. Similar. Attributed to *Thomas Burman* (GF). – John Millett † 1660, still with ribbon-work. – S transept. Elizabeth Freshwater † 1617, a remarkable piece, though small. Kneeling figure under a pedimented arch. The scrolly volutes and half-pilasters resemble the style which appears on a larger scale at St Helen Bishopsgate in 1633. – N transept. Thomas Roycroft, printer, †1677, with columns, the apron carved in the form of spines of books. – City of London Yeomanry War Memorial, 1926 by *Webb*, with carved angels. – Lady Chapel. Rev. Sir Borradaile Savory †1906. Mid-C17 style with Edwardian Baroque touches. Surely *Webb*'s design.

Monastic Remains

From the SW porch, the main entrance leads via the tower into the tile-roofed CLOISTER. The E side remains, in origin *c.* 1160 (see the N doorway facing into the cloister), but rebuilt *c.* 1405. Of this date the three N bays, restored in 1905 after use as a stable, with some stonework reused in the tierceron vault. The remainder is mostly by *Webb*, 1923–8, replacing vaulting which collapsed in 1834. Flowing reticulated tracery distinguishes these bays. C15 entrance arches into the former CHAPTER HOUSE (sixth bay). It was rectangular, measuring some 53 ft (16 metres) by 28 ft (8½ metres). Surviving fragments suggest a date also *c.* 1160. The W wall, uncovered in 1912, had three arched C15 openings fitted into the older fabric. Further S, behind the C15 fabric and partly obscured by it, remains of an early C13 round-arched doorway, with trefoiled cusping in the tympanum and a segment-arched doorway below. The dorter to the S, with a fine vaulted undercroft, lasted until 1870. The S and W sides of the cloister garth are enclosed by 1950s ward blocks of St Bartholomew's Hospital (*see* Little Britain).

ST BARTHOLOMEW-THE-LESS
St Bartholomew's Hospital

The church of St Bartholomew's Hospital stands just inside the main gate on West Smithfield. Its C15 SW tower and W vestry survive from one of the several former hospital chapels, here made parochial in 1546–7 as part of the re-foundation. The rest is an interesting octagonal brick church of 1823–5 by *Thomas Hardwick*, perpetuating work by *George Dance the Younger*, 1789–91 (altered in 1862–3 by *P. C. Hardwick*).

Very plain and humble tower with SW stair-turret and parapet of brick. Renewed W doorway, with two-light window above, also renewed. Could its odd plain tracery be C17? Inside the tower, heavy moulded arches with hollows and thick triple shafts. At half-height unusual banding, the mouldings continued around the walls. W and N walls of the vestry rebuilt in brick, with a restored Perp W window over a doorway blocked by *T. Hardwick*, indicated by surviving sections of rubble walling. Buttresses on the N side of the church were added possibly *c.* 1842, when *Philip Hardwick* rebuilt the hospital's screen wall just beyond.

The raised floor of the interior is the first surprise. It may date
95 from *Dance*'s work. *Thomas Hardwick*'s rebuilding owed much to
Dance, who introduced an octagonal Gothic vault fitted into a
square by triangular chapels open to the centre. Pointed lunette windows high up pierce a swooping star-shaped plaster rib-vault. Its
construction is of iron, after Dance's timbers rotted. Dance put
windows only in the lunettes, a device consistent with his fondness
for dramatic lighting effects (cf. his similarly polygonal Gothic
church at Micheldever, Hants, 1808). To *P. C. Hardwick* are due the
projecting sanctuary with half-octagonal end and the geometrical
tracery of the lunettes. The effect of the ensemble remains pre-
archaeological (see especially the intersecting tracery), and has its
modest charm. Restored by *Lord Mottistone* of *Seely & Paget* after
war damage, 1950–1.

FITTINGS. PULPIT of alabaster, designed by *P.C. Hardwick*,
1864. – Gothic PEWS with linenfold carving. They look *c.* 1825. –
STAINED GLASS. E window by *Hugh Easton,* 1950. – CARVINGS. On
the vestry wall, four C15 carvings of angels with shields, apparently
reset. The best-preserved pair hold the royal arms. – PAINTINGS.
In the vestry: Crucifixion by *Cigoli, c.* 1600. – St Bartholomew,
C17, Spanish or Italian. – MONUMENTS. Brass in the vestry to
William Markeby †1439 and wife, with small figures. – Canopied
tomb, *c.* 1500, with shallow arch and quatrefoil frieze, not rich. Mid-
C18 alterations. – Serjeant Balthrope †1591. Kneeling figure in
niche. – Tablet to Mary Darker †1773, with little relief, and more
ambitious tablet with putti by an urn to John Darker †1784; both by
J. Bingley.

ST BENET PAUL'S WHARF
(ST BENET WELSH CHURCH)
Queen Victoria Street

45 First mentioned in 1111. The present building of 1678–84, almost
certainly *Hooke*'s design, since he made drawings both of the executed design and of a preliminary version (AG). His craftsmen were
Thomas and *Edward Strong Sen.*, masons; *Israel Knowles*, carpenter;
William Cleere, joiner; *Doogood & Grove,* plasterers; *Matthew Roberts,*
plumber. One of the most lovable of the post-Fire church exteriors,
delightfully Dutch. Small, of red and blue brick chequerwork, with
stone quoins of even size alternating with brick. Modillion cornice.
Hipped roof, with, over the N aisle, three equal projections, also
hipped. To the N and S round-headed windows with stone-carved
garlands above. In the preliminary design a low attic stage is shown
above these garlands. To the E a group of three, the middle one
blank because blocked by the reredos inside, and then one more
blank window representing the N aisle. Stone-carved garlands here
too.

The tower is at the NW end of the nave but set back S of the N
aisle, a picturesque arrangement due to the reuse of the medieval
tower foundations and lower core. Stubby lead spire on an octagonal
lantern above a lead dome with lucarnes. The Blackfriars Underpass
scheme of the 1970s has left St Benet isolated and battered by noise

from the raised flyover called White Lion Hill (w). In its original setting, at the sw corner of Benet's Hill and the old alignment of Upper Thames Street, the s and e sides were most exposed, not the n and w ones as at present. A churchyard on the n was truncated c. 1870 for Queen Victoria Street, and a little nw vestry of 1692 demolished and replaced by one made in the sw entrance lobby, with a new entrance made under the tower. St Benet became the Welsh church in 1879.

The interior is of homely and intimate irregularity, unusual in its full entablature and flat, not coved, ceiling. Corinthian columns to the n aisle, which retains its gallery. Smaller gallery on the w, s of the tower. By means of the columns and pilasters the square shape of the main space is stressed. The N GALLERY was formerly used by members of Doctors' Commons in Queen Victoria Street, and is still used by the College of Arms there (q.v.). Modest restorations in 1891 by *Herbert Knight* and c. 1950 by *Godfrey Allen*, who removed a tiled Victorian floor. Fire damage to the NE corner, 1971, was made good by *J. R. Stammers*.

The C17 FURNISHINGS are largely intact. Magnificent COM-MUNION TABLE, possibly Flemish, with sumptuous figures as legs, 60 a little seated figure of Charity on the stretcher, garlands etc. Among several fittings given by Sir Leoline (Llywelyn) Jenkins in 1686. – COMMUNION RAIL with twisted balusters. – STALLS and PEWS with original parts. – LECTERN attached to the stalls. – Simple REREDOS without columns or pilasters but with a big segmental pediment flanked by pairs of urns.– PULPIT rather simple, with later stairs and stem. Its TESTER hangs under the tower. – Fine DOORCASE to the tower lobby. In its broken pediment magnificently carved ROYAL ARMS. – Carved and painted armorial CARTOUCHES on the n gallery front. – ORGAN, w gallery. By *Hill, Norman & Beard*, 1973, based on a predecessor by *J. C. Bishop*, 1832. – WALL PANELLING. – Two SANCTUARY CHAIRS. – Modest iron SWORD REST. – Octagonal FONT. The stem ends in a capital. The bowl also octagonal, with four cherubs' heads. Contemporary COVER. – POOR BOX on four twisted balusters matching the communion rails. – MONUMENTS. Sir Robert Wyseman †1684 with good portrait bust in medallion. Attributed to *Gibbons* and (the bust) to *Arnold Quellin* (GF). – Mark Cottle †1681 and wife. Black and white marble obelisk with draped canopy, sphere and shield. Probably early C18. – Dr Bryce †1688 and Gregory King (Rouge Dragon Pursuivant) †1712, cartouches. – A C19 inscription records the burial here of Inigo Jones. His monument, designed by *John Webb*, perished in the Great Fire.

ST BOTOLPH ALDERSGATE

First mentioned in the early C12. A view of 1739 shows an aisled building of C15 character, the n wall altered after fire damage in 1666. The present church is C18 and C19, though when the vaults were emptied in 1892–4, the n and s walls were found to stand on medieval foundations. The medieval pier bases indicated that the old nave was 7 ft (2 metres) narrower. N and e walls were rebuilt in 1754, then the rest of the church in 1789–91 by *Nathaniel Wright*.

The E end was rebuilt further back to widen Aldersgate Street, possibly by the Parish Surveyor *J. W. Griffith* (Colvin), under a faculty of 1829 (DF).

The E wall is of channelled stucco (painted dark green), with a Venetian window between coupled Ionic columns on a plinth, and pediment above. Flanked by two-storey entrance recesses. Wright's front was of brick, without columns but otherwise similar. The rest is very modest externally. Stock brick with arched windows and a small W tower, also on medieval foundations and out of alignment with the nave. On it a square dome and starved wooden bellcote. A spindly chimney sticks up to its NE. Buildings abutting the N and W fronts were demolished in the C19.

The interior is a surprise: well-preserved late C18, of extreme elegance. Coffered E and W apses, concealed outside behind flat fronts, with galleries, vestries etc. in the angles. Square pillars to N and S carry a fine Greek frieze that continues round the E apse and across the W gallery. Corinthian columns supporting a full entablature (also continuing around the apses) are set above these piers, with the gallery fronts between them. All is painted, with much marbling and wood-graining in dark colours. Coved ceiling with very big plaster rosettes (still with C19 gas sunburners), lit by four interpenetrating lunettes on each side. Apses, lunettes, the reduction of the lower entablature to its frieze and the tight conception of the whole design are all reminiscent of Dance's All Hallows London Wall. Convex-fronted W gallery on Ionic columns. From a top-lit W lobby curved twin staircases rise to the galleries. Those on either side of the organ were for schoolchildren, who were taught in the adjoining upper rooms.

FITTINGS are a mixture of C18 pieces and good replacements from the restoration by *J. Blyth*, 1873–4 (later work by *Ewan Christian*, 1892–4). – Fine simple PULPIT of *c.* 1788, smoothly inlaid, set on a palm tree. Its tester (also on a palm tree) was removed by Blyth. – Mahogany COMMUNION TABLE of 1787. (In the E vestibule another table, dated 1639.) – COMMUNION RAILS of mahogany and gilded iron, *c.* 1788. – Iron MACE REST of 1788. – Good PEWS of 1874, free classical. – Large FONT of coloured marble, given 1878. Contemporary FONT COVER in rich Victorian-cum-Wren style, designed and given by *Seddon*, who was baptized here. – ORGAN on the W gallery. By *Samuel Green*, 1791, in a five-towered case with Adamesque ornament (instrument rebuilt by *Henry Speechley*, 1867). – STAINED GLASS. A full sequence. E window, Agony in the Garden, 1788 by *James Pearson* from designs by *Nathaniel Clarkson*. Dark sepia painted glass, the style like Correggio. Indeed set like a painting in a round-headed frame with curtains of plaster; grisaille panels with figures inset below and either side. Pearson's lesser flanking windows were lost in the Second World War. The replacements are poor, in a clashing style. – N aisle, four windows of the Life of Christ by *Ward & Hughes*, 1886, in a very painterly style. – S aisle by *M. C. Farrar Bell*, 1955–8, four historical scenes in a story-book manner. – N gallery, three windows by *Ward & Hughes*, 1890; one of 1939 (W) by *A. K. Nicholson* (CS), bold, if old-fashioned. – S gallery, three windows made by *Lavers & Barraud* to designs of *Stephen Salter*, 1865. They came from St

Matthew Spring Gardens, Westminster (dem.), in 1885, with one new window (Resurrection) to match (TS).

MONUMENTS. A good collection, mostly from the previous church. – Ann Packington †1563, a late example of a Gothic altar tomb. Quatrefoils etc. on the chest, and an enriched crested canopy with flattened arch. Against the back wall kneeling figures incised in the manner of a brass. The matrices indicate a Trinity and three groups of kneeling figures. – Christopher Tamworth †1624 and wife †1637, with cherub, skull and hourglass. – John Coston and family, dates to 1637. Tablet with three shrouded skulls. Attributed to *Humphrey Moyer* (GF). – Elizabeth Ashton †1662 and Lady Richardson †1639, both wall-monuments with frontal busts in niches, the latter attributed to *William Wright* of Charing Cross (GF). – Sir John Micklethwaite †1682 and Richard Chiswell †1711, cartouches. Attributed respectively to *Gibbons* and *William Woodman Sen.* (GF). – Elizabeth Smith †1750, by *Roubiliac*. Simple tablet, portrait medallion above. – Zachariah Foxall †1758 by *John Annis*, with putti holding a medallion; obelisk behind. – Catherine Meade, by *R. Cooke*, 1793, with mourner in relief. – Rev. William Webber, portrait relief by *Forsyth*, 1881.

The CHURCHYARD (Postman's Park) is entered from Aldersgate Street through good early C19 railings with a Gothic drinking fountain of 1870 attached. It was laid out as a park in 1880–90, together with the adjacent burial grounds of Christ Church Newgate Street and St Leonard Foster Lane. W of the church is a Japanesey LOGGIA, conceived in 1887 by the painter *G. F. Watts* as a memorial to civilian lives lost in acts of heroism and erected in 1899. As Watts wrote to *The Times* in 1887, 'the national prosperity of a nation is not an abiding possession, the deeds of the people are'. Timber, with a pitched tiled roof and on the rear wall fifty-three artistically lettered glazed plaques composed mostly by Watts or his widow, at once moving and unintentionally quaint. The latest is dated 1930. Central niche with a tiny wooden STATUETTE of Watts in robes by *T. H. Wren*, added *c.* 1907. In the garden also lots of fine trees, a fountain, and a bronze SCULPTURE of a minotaur by *Michael Ayrton*, erected 1973.

ST BOTOLPH ALDGATE

First mentioned 1125, but the dedication indicates a Saxon origin. Excavations inside the crypt at the S end in 1990 indeed revealed burials suggesting a C10–C11 foundation. Stow records a rebuilding in the early C16 by the patron, Holy Trinity Priory. The present church is by *Dance the Elder*, 1741–4. It is aligned N–S, so that it faces down Minories. Brick S (ritual W) tower, flanked by domed side entrances as at Wren's St Clement Danes. The rise of the tower is nicely separated from the façade proper by a pediment finishing the latter. Obelisk spire, with a clock stage. The short and broad church body gives it a sit-up-and-beg look. Side windows enriched by Gibbs surrounds, and in the middle of the W, E and the N (altar) sides, one Venetian window each. Drawings by Dance at the Soane Museum show external double staircases here (DF; date of removal

uncertain). Below this on the W and E sides another tripartite opening, with round arches and rusticated inner jambs to the crypt door,
a strangely unorthodox feature. On the E side discreet brick offices of
1987 by *John Phillips*.

The interior retains galleries on three sides resting on the
pedestals of Tuscan columns that rise to the roof. But the general
impression has been considerably changed by the redecoration
undertaken 1888–95 by *Bentley*. Due to him is the remarkably original
81 ceiling in a kind of free Arts and Crafts Gothic – admittedly a style
entirely out of keeping with Dance's. In the coving are lithe standing
figures of angels in high relief holding shields; bands of square boss-
like leaves. Bentley also lowered the galleries by some 18 in. and gave
them white-painted balustraded fronts which do much to lighten
the interior. He retained the flat C18 E (ritual) end rather than add
an external chancel for the choir. In this and in the retention of
galleries Bentley was deliberately respectful to C18 convention.
Redecorated 1965–6 by *J. S. Comper* after a fire.

FONT. Circular, with nice domed cover. Some of the C18 font rails
have been incorporated in a SCREEN. – ORGAN CASE probably by
John Byfield, 1744, W gallery; ORGAN with pipework attributed to
Harris, from an instrument given by Thomas Whiting, 1676 (restored
by *N. Mander*, 1966). – REREDOS. Original, with Corinthian
columns. On the panels, batik hangings by *Thetis Blacker*, 1982. –
PULPIT. Simple, inlaid, *c.* 1745. The Sacred Heart and other details
suggest it may not have been made for an Anglican church. – COM-
MUNION RAIL, C18, of wrought iron. COMMUNION TABLE. Late
C17 with twisted legs, reconstructed. – SWORD REST, C18, heavy. –
STAINED GLASS. E window by *Charles Clutterbuck*, *c.* 1850, after
Rubens's Deposition. – Other windows by *Goddard & Gibbs*,
1969–72. The NE (ritual) chapel has engraved glass screens by *David
Peace* and *Sally Scott*, 1988. – SCULPTURE. Sumptuous late C17
panel with King David surrounded by musical instruments. *Gibbons*
style. From St Mary Whitechapel. – MONUMENTS. The best are in
the baptistery (created under the tower during the restoration of
1965–6 by *R. Tatchell*). Thomas Lord Darcy put to death by Henry
VIII, and others; tablet with emaciated recumbent effigy between
Corinthian columns, *c.* 1560–70. – Robert Dow †1612 with bust in
niche, made 1622–3 by *Christopher Kingsfield* (repaired 1675). – Bust
of Sir John Cass by *Eric Winter*, 1966, after the full-length figure by
Roubiliac in the Sir John Cass School (q.v.). – In the churchyard,
abstract SCULPTURE: Sanctuary by *Naomi Blake*, 1985.

ST BOTOLPH BISHOPSGATE

First mentioned in the late C12, but almost certainly a late Saxon
foundation like its City namesakes. Rebuilt in 1725–8 to a design by
James Gould, by a consortium of masons: Gould's son-in-law *George
Dance the Elder*, his father *Giles Dance*, *John Townshend* and *Thomas
Dunn*. A stately, solid, stone-faced E front faces Bishopsgate. The
church is properly oriented, so that the altar is behind the street
front beneath the tower, flanked by entrance lobbies. The centre has
coupled Doric pilasters, a frieze, and a pediment. Above this rises
the square tower: first a channelled stage with markedly Baroque

corner piers or pilasters carved with cherubs' heads, then a pilastered bell-stage more in the Wren manner, crowned by a circular cupola with ogee cap and urn. Quoins mark the corners. Sides and w end of red brick with windows in two tiers, the upper tier round-headed with keystones carved with cherubs' heads, and linked by a moulding at impost level. The steeple with its stone frontispiece derives from Wren; the free-standing site and the uniform treatment of the church body recall the later and cheaper of the 'Fifty Churches', e.g. the nearly contemporary St Luke Old Street (*London 4: North*). The parish had sought unsuccessfully to rebuild its church from the fund. Italianate s doorcase facing the churchyard added in restoration by *Bentley*, 1890–2 (DF) (earlier work by *A. T. Carter*, 1878). w window of Venetian form, a somewhat ungainly alteration of 1755. The church was restored after war damage by *N. F. Cachemaille-Day*, 1947–8, and again by *Kevin Stephenson* after bomb damage sustained in 1992–3.

The usual entrance is through the s door. The galleried interior has a barrel vault on giant Corinthian columns. Restrained plasterwork with motifs of mitres, crowns, cherubs' heads and bibles. The entrance lobbies flanking the tower have very domestic-looking gallery staircases with paired balusters and enriched strings. The interior was altered by *Michael Meredith* in 1821, and from that time dates the dome above the centre of the nave, with lantern lighting in a glazed drum, its unadorned forms and small panes from the outside startlingly like a fashionable architectural device of the mid 1990s. The chancel was remodelled by *Carter*, and again by *Bentley*; the NE chapel by *Joseph Hill*, 1929. In the chancel, large framed MOSAICS of the Life of Christ, 1892. – Original PULPIT, hexagonal and inlaid. The stair looks later. – COMMUNION TABLE of C17 type with twisted legs and lions' feet. – LECTERN, with little cherubs, by *Bentley*, sensitively done. – STALLS also by *Bentley*. – PEWS look like *Carter*'s work from 1878, in an enriched classical style not unsympathetic to the context. – FONT. 1720s. – ORGAN of 1764 by *John Byfield*, divided either side of the w window in 1893 (instrument rebuilt 1949). – Iron SWORD REST with arms of 1835. – STAINED GLASS. E window a Crucifixion, Renaissance style, designed by *F. W. Moody*, made by *Powell & Sons*, 1869. A w window of 1876 by the same artists was replaced after war damage by a window by *Hugh Easton*, in turn removed after bomb damage in 1993. – MONUMENTS. Plain tablet on the gallery stairs (NE) to Sir Paul Pindar †1650, whose early C17 house was in Bishopsgate nearby. Its façade is now at the Victoria and Albert Museum. – On the chancel arch, John Tutchin †1658, a skeleton holding up an inscribed cloth, attributed to *Edward Pierce* (GF); Andrew Willaw †1700, enriched cartouche. – Rev. William Rogers †1896, with portrait relief, designed by *Bentley*. – Mosaic WAR MEMORIAL by *William Glasby*, c. 1920, still in the Burne-Jones manner.

The large open space to the s is the old CHURCHYARD, one of the first to be made into a garden (1863). It extends nearly up to the old line of the City wall. The paved path across it passes under wrought-iron lanterns of the overthrow type. They look early C19. FOUNTAIN of 1972; Gothic memorial CROSS to Lord Kitchener, 1916.

The PARISH HALL w of the church was built as an infants' school in 1861 in nice harmony with the style of the church (which was an unusual thing at the time). It is a simple pedimented block in red brick with stone dressings, with paired Doric columns within a rusticated arch at the entrance. On this front two STATUES of charity children, a boy and a girl, of *Coade* stone, put up in 1821 on the former building in Peter Street. Round-headed windows face the church, the central one of tripartite quasi-Venetian form. On the other side an ornamented chimney stack. Converted to a Hall in 1905. Between 1952 and 1994 it doubled as the Fanmakers' Hall, after further adaptation by *White Allom* (inside, panelling of 1726, from a demolished house in Northants). – By its entrance the TOMB of Sir William Rawlins †1838: a sarcophagus on lions' feet on an elaborate table, enclosed with railings freakishly mixing Neoclassical urns and torches with death's heads, heraldry and crucifix finials.

ST BRIDE
off Fleet Street

1671–8 by *Wren*, on medieval crypts excavated after the Second World War. The church has the tallest of all Wren's spires, built in 1701–3. It stands 226 ft (69 metres) high, said to have been cut down from 236 ft (72 metres) in 1764. The church was gutted in 1940 and restored by *Godfrey Allen* in 1955–7. The outer walls remain, with round-headed aisle windows (circular in the end bays), and oval clerestory windows. E end with tripartite window under an open pediment, the arch above the centre light concentric with the main window arch. C18 views show the main aisle windows were similarly mullioned. The church body is of five bays with slightly projecting chancel. Pedimented NW doorcase. The craftsmen were *Joshua Marshall* and *Samuel Fulkes*, masons; *Benjamin Leach*, bricklayer; *John Longland*, carpenter; *John Grove*, plasterer.

Big impressive stone tower, slightly projecting, rather flatly articulated on the W face. Pedimented W doorcase with columns. The bell-stage has broad segmental pediments on pilasters, an unexceptional device but one not used elsewhere amongst Wren's towers. Columns at the corners, the corners above them recessed. Eight urns on the parapet. Four carved masks on each suggest *Hawksmoor* had a hand in their design (PJ). The spire is of five octagonal stages, telescoped and of diminishing height, a logical and original solution, but not as satisfying to look at as other major Wren steeples. Its resemblance to that on the dome of the Warrant design for St Paul's (1675) was noted by Gerald Cobb. That the design was made before 1700 is also suggested by the diminishing stages (albeit apparently square), sketched on top of the existing tower in Morgan's panorama of 1682. The first three tiers are arcaded, with corner pilasters. Engaged columns on the fourth stage, originally crowned by eight little urns. Obelisk above. The spire's mason was *Fulkes*. It has been much repaired: in 1764, 1803, and 1901–2.

The interior was remodelled by *Allen*. It has rather ungainly giant Tuscan double columns (renewed), standing N–S. They carry arches, above which rises a barrel-vault with penetrations from the clerestory windows. The aisle bays are groin-vaulted. All this follows Wren's design, including the ashlar-faced walls – an unusual feature. Margaret Whinney remarked on the similarity of the roof and (destroyed) galleries to Perrault's reconstruction of Vitruvius's Basilica at Fano, likewise of five bays. This was published in 1673, too late for St Bride. Did Wren discuss it with Perrault in Paris in 1665? The galleries seem to have been an afterthought, since the Vestry settled the design only in 1675. They used to cut clumsily across the columns of the aisles, an unsatisfactory arrangement which probably explains why Wren came to prefer double-height aisles, as at his St James Piccadilly, where the columns rise from the level of the gallery fronts. Allen replaced the galleries with stalls aligned E–W, screening the aisles. They have Wrenish carving. At their W ends big STATUES of saints by *David McFall*. – Free-standing REREDOS by *Allen*, after Wren's at the Chapel Royal, Hampton Court. STAINED GLASS in its central opening and illusionistic PAINTING around it by *Glyn Jones*, a juxtaposition so unsympathetic that it is a surprise to learn it was designed as an ensemble. The E end had been much altered: by *John Deykes*, 1822–3, *Champneys*, 1885–6 and 1892–3, and *H. M. Fletcher*, c.1935; restoration also in 1863 and by *Arding, Bond & Buzzard*, 1875. – Other fittings also in Wren's style. – ROYAL ARMS carved by *Kenneth Gardner*. – FONT COVER with a model of a bell-shaped turret, after an early drawing for the tower. – SCULPTURE. By the font, two charity children from the former St Bride and Bridewell Schools (*see* Bride Lane), probably of 1711; terracotta head by *Marjorie Meggitt*, c.1985. – The S doorway leads to a Neo-Georgian RECTORY by *J. R. Stammers*, 1958.

ROMAN AND MEDIEVAL REMAINS. A staircase at the NW gives access to the CRYPTS, excavated by Professor Grimes in 1952–3. This constituted the first complete archaeological investigation in England of a parish church plan. It was followed up in 1992–3, and the accompanying display updated.

The red and yellow tessellated floors of two rooms of a late Roman suburban villa terraced into the hillside overlooking the

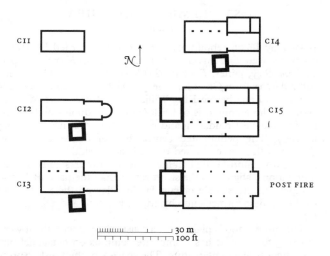

St Bride. Plans showing its development

River Fleet are displayed *in situ*, concealed from direct inspection by substantial medieval foundations, but visible in periscopic views via mirrors. The excavations also revealed two phases of Saxon work. The first, a modest masonry structure of the C6, cannot be firmly identified as a church, though the early Christianization of the Roman burial site may be posited (attested perhaps by the holy spring called Bridewell, which gave its name to Bridewell Palace to the s). The second was an apsed early to mid-C11 church, given an enlarged square E end late in the C12. The Norman church also had a campanile half-way down Wren's s aisle, not bonded in. A narrow N aisle was added in the early C13. A Lady Chapel was added to its E not long afterwards, adjoining the chancel on the N side. It was externally slightly wider than the N aisle, so a short W return wall joined them.

On display are some 30 ft (9 metres) of the chapel's N wall, and a three-bay rib-vaulted CRYPT inserted *c.* 1300. The N wall has chequered masonry of squared chalk and ragstone. At the W, remains of a former N entrance, blocked *c.* 1400 when the N aisle was widened. The crypt preserves traces of a N doorway into the church-yard and a splayed light-shaft in the E wall, made into a door in the 1950s. The change in coursing some two feet above the floor level marks the older foundations of the Lady Chapel proper. Chapel and crypt were thus originally self-sufficient, separately entered, and with their own Guild priest and services.

Wren reused the medieval foundations where possible, i.e. beneath the outer walls and beneath two s arcade piers, which rest on the N wall of the campanile. Sleeper walls for the arcades were built up with medieval material. Another VAULT built by Wren was found, tunnel-vaulted and running all along the s aisle, and another of 1750 with piers. There were also two bone-holes. In one of them the skulls and bones were arranged ornamentally in squares.

ST CLEMENT EASTCHEAP
Clement's Lane

1683–7 by *Wren*, rebuilding a church first recorded by 1106. His craftsmen were *Edward Strong Sen.*, mason; *Israel Knowles*, carpenter; *William Grey*, joiner; *Doogood & Grove*, plasterers. The confusing suffix derives from Great Eastcheap, which extended to the s end of Clement's Lane before King William Street was built. Wren's un-assuming little church is of brick with stone quoins and dressings, its down-at-heel rendering and painted stucco at last under repair in 1997. The pedimented central bay of the W front projects slightly, with a large blocked round-headed window over a door in a concave round-headed frame. The SW tower stands on reused foundations, aligned to the street rather than the nave. Balustraded parapet, but no steeple or cupola. An alley on the N side leads E to the modest former churchyard, with a tree and railings of C18 type.

The interior too is plain, with a s aisle aligned with the tower and tapering to the E. It has Composite columns on octagonal plinths carrying a straight entablature. The space E of the s aisle represents an extension made after the Great Fire (PJ). Otherwise it is safe to assume that the nave occupies the space of the medieval nave and N aisle. The order continues around its walls in the form of pilasters, Wren's usual way of giving unity to a single-aisled space. They support groined arches piercing the coving. Above the aisle a clerestory of three lunettes. The N windows are blocked apart from three segment-headed upper lights, and since the S windows are also blocked the interior is dark. The ceiling was largely renewed in 1925 by *G. E. Nield*, to a simplified pattern. Only the central enriched elliptical panel is original. Alterations by *Butterfield*, 1872 and 1889, modified since mostly by *Sir Ninian Comper*, 1932–4. – The chief interest of the interior lies in its original WOODWORK, for which the parish paid *Thomas Poultney* for joinery and *Jonathan Maine* for carving. Butterfield and Comper have not left quite enough to save it from feeling underfurnished. – REREDOS in three pedimented parts with big engaged Corinthian columns and half-pilasters and flaming urns above. Reassembled and embellished by *Comper*, with gold-ground painted figures by *W. Butchart* in an unsuitably genteel Quattrocento manner, the frame painted blue and gilded to match. – The SEATING was rearranged by Butterfield. Old woodwork reused in the stalls includes parts of the former S gallery front. – COMMUNION RAIL with turned and carved balusters. – Noble ORGAN CASE (1696, by *Renatus Harris*). Placed by Butterfield in the aisle, but perched over the W doorcase in 1936. – Excellent big PULPIT, hexagonal with oval panel. Giant tester surmounted by festooned 55 segmental pediments in the centre of each side and cherubs dancing on the angles. The balusters of the stair match the communion rails. – Four fine pilastered DOORCASES: three at the W; the best, to the NE vestry, otherwise similar but with a big broken segmental pediment. In the vestry an excellent contemporary OVERMANTEL with swags and festoons surrounding a fielded panel. – Carved in the panelling of the S aisle, a large GRAFFITO dated 1703. – ROYAL ARMS, Stuart, painted, S aisle. – BREAD SHELVES, now not normally displayed. – COMMUNION TABLE with coarsely carved cherubs as supporters. – FONT. Octagonal on an enriched baluster stem, of marble, by *Maine*. The pretty wooden cover (not normally on display) matches that at St Peter upon Cornhill (q.v.). – Iron SWORD REST, with painted mace and sword, probably C18. – From *Butterfield*'s work a few survivals, such as the polychromatic FLOOR TILES and good STAINED GLASS in the N clerestory. – No monuments of note.

ST DUNSTAN-IN-THE-EAST
St Dunstan's Hill

The Gothic shell and steeple, set prominently half-way up the Hill, survived the bombs of 1941. The steeple is *Wren*'s, built in 1695–1701 (*Ephraim Beauchamp* mason). The rest by *David Laing*, 1817–21. This replaced the fire-damaged shell, patched up in 1668–71 without the aid of the Rebuilding Commissioners, following a private benefaction. An excellent GARDEN with a fountain, made 1967–71 by the *Corporation of London Architect's Department*, now occupies Laing's shell and the surrounding churchyard. The C17 and C19 churches were both large, but smaller than the substantial medieval collegiate foundation here, probably of *c*.1100. C12 and C13 carved stonework of high quality discovered in Harp Lane in 1974 may have come from this building. Before the Fire it had a leaded spire, and a s aisle rebuilt in 1381. *Henry Yevele* supervised the foundations, but there is no evidence that he designed the aisle.

44   Wren's new steeple must be among the 'some few examples' of Gothic churches in the E of the City he laid claim to in a letter to the Dean of Westminster in 1713. Payments were also made to *Hawksmoor*, who may have assisted with the design (PJ). *William Dickinson* supervised the work. The style was doubtless chosen to match the reused Gothic exterior, though as reconstructed this had Tuscan arcades inside. Soaring needle-spire, pierced below, carried on four steep flying buttresses – the principle of St Mary-le-Bow before the Fire, and also of St Nicholas, Newcastle, and Edinburgh Cathedral, both C15, but here carried up in a single visual sweep. The buttresses die into the spire in a strange stepped sequence. Lucarnes between. Big octagonal spire-like pinnacles on the angles of the square tower-top and a lesser intermediate pinnacle to each of the battlemented parapets. *Sir Herbert Baker & Scott* reconstructed the spire in 1953. The tower has three main stages of increasing height, with diagonal buttresses turning octagonal on the top. Typically post-medieval are the broad horizontal divisions made by the stringcourses between the stages. Tracery in the windows and belfry openings with lights cusped at the bottom as well as the top. Two-centred s and w doorways with crocketed hood-moulds starting oddly from incurved volutes. These crockets are in detail also by no means Gothic. Of the Wren period too the iron railings here, mixing Gothic and classical motifs (*James Ray*, smith). The tower was restored 1970–2 by *Seely & Paget Partnership* for use as a rectory, but now serves as offices.

Of Laing's church only the N and s walls, lower E wall and the shell of the NE porch remain. The tracery was restored *c.*1970. According to Eastlake in 1872, the true designer was Laing's pupil *William Tite*, though the rebuilding accounts nowhere mention him. The huge expenditure of £36,000 is still palpable in the solid Portland walling with deep concave reveals, a more substantial treatment than the Commissioners could afford for their contemporary Gothic churches. Costly too the excellent cast-iron Gothic railings, E. Much detailing copied from greater medieval churches in a manner characteristic of the day: see e.g. the pinnacle reset in the N churchyard (mason and carver *Thomas Piper*), after Winchester Cathedral nave. Laing's nave had an impressive lierne vault of plaster.

ST DUNSTAN-IN-THE-WEST
Fleet Street

94   A Gothic octagon with a s tower, built 1830–3 by *John Shaw Sen.*, completed after his death in 1832 by his son, also *John*. The last of the medieval City churches to be rebuilt, and, for reasons of street widening, on a site N of the previous church (first mentioned *c.*1170). Shaw's church looks so much at home in the street that its

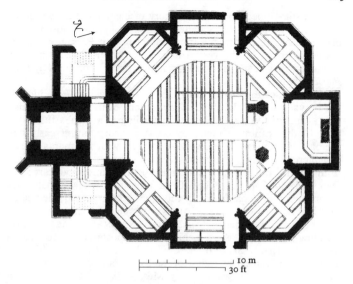

St Dunstan-in-the-West. Plan

unlikeness to most contemporary Anglican churches is easily over-looked. But the centralized plan (a consequence of the restricted site) went out of fashion *c.* 1800, and the combination of con-spicuous tower and concealed brick walls recalls Wren rather than the Commissioners' churches on their usual island sites.

Tower of Ketton stone, topped with a tall, delicate octagonal lantern designed on the pattern of All Saints Pavement at York, that is with long unglazed Perp openings and a lacy pinnacled parapet. Big pinnacles and chamfered corners make the transition from four to eight sides. The tower makes a fine, picturesque group with the CLOCK to its r. and then the statue of Queen Elizabeth. The clock was made by *Thomas Harris* in 1671 (for £35), saved in 1828 by Lord Hertford, and brought back to the church in 1935 from St Dunstan's, his villa in Regent's Park. On a black and gold bracket, but now without its C17 carved surround. Above this in a wooden Ionic aedicule two figures of men l. and r. of a feigned door, belabouring two bells – the arrangement familiar from Italian clocks, e.g. in the Piazza S. Marco in Venice and at Padua. The STATUE of Queen Elizabeth was made probably in 1586 (modern inscription) by *William Kerwin*, for the Ludgate, demolished in 1760. The AEDICULE with its decorated pilasters and open segmental pedi-ment is also from Ludgate, of *c.* 1667, but still very impure in its forms. Also from Ludgate, decayed STATUES of King Lud and his sons, kept in the vestry porch. Outside the church the NORTHCLIFFE MEMORIAL of 1930, obelisk designed by *Lutyens* with bust by *Kathleen Scott*.

The octagonal space inside is treated on principles not of, say, English chapter houses but of classical centrally planned churches. The four main axes have pointed plaster tunnel-vaults with trans-verse ribs, the four diagonal recesses also with rib-vaults. The main vault is star-ribbed above a clerestory of eight identical windows. The structure is of iron. Chancel on the N, i.e. the church is not oriented. Another entrance from Clifford's Inn Passage in the W vessel, balanced by the vestry doorway on the E. The SE and SW recesses, which originally housed galleries, have decorations by *F. H. Fowler*, 1881.

FITTINGS of the 1830s, designed by *Shaw Sen.* or *Jun.*, include the PEWS, made by *W. & L. Cubitt* (shorn of their poppy-heads), FONT, and PULPIT with linenfold panelling. – ALTAR SURROUND with Gothic canopies made by *Swaby*; incorporating early C16 Flemish Flamboyant woodwork. – STALLS with fragments of late C17 pierced carving. – ICONOSTASIS, in the NE chapel. Brought from Antim Monastery, Bucharest, in 1966. Of limewood, carved by *Petre & Mihai Babic*, c. 1860, with paintings in a wholly Renaissance idiom by *Petre Alexandrescu*. In the other recesses, altars dedicated to other Eastern churches. – ORGAN by *Joseph Robson*, 1834, in a case probably designed by *Shaw Jun.* – STAINED GLASS. Walton Window by *Kempe*, 1895, behind the iconostasis.* – (Ritual) E window by *Gerald Smith* of *A. K. Nicholson Studios*, 1950. Tracery lights from *Willement*'s window of the 1830s, otherwise destroyed in 1944. – SE and SW windows by Messrs *Taylor*, 1881–2. – Iron SWORD REST, frame type, 1745.

MONUMENTS in the chapels. Nothing very spectacular, but varied, and rewarding close attention. Clockwise from the entrance: brass to Henry Dacres †1530 and wife, kneeling figures, reset. – William Morecroft †1657, jowly frontal bust, characterful but somewhat gauche. In niche with looped curtains, altered above the cornice. Attributed to *Joshua Marshall* (AW). – Edward Marshall, the master mason, †1675, and wife, tablet with weeping cherubs, c. 1678 by the *Marshall* workshop (AW). Edward Marshall had rebuilt much of the old church in 1661–2. – Gerard Legh †1563, small tablet of good quality, flanked by male and female caryatids suggestive of French influence. – Cuthbert Fetherstone †1615, frontal bust in gristly circular niche. – Sir Richard Hutton, by *Nicholas Stone*, 1640. Small Michelangelesque tablet in black and white stone. – Richard Peirson †1718 and others, high up, reset in a Gothic frame. – Elizabeth Moore †1668, attributed to *Joshua Marshall* (AW). – Hobson Judkin †1812 'the honest solicitor', circular tablet with tiny skulls: 'Go reader and imitate Hobson Judkin'. – Concealed behind the iconostasis: Elizabeth North †1612, the usual kneeling figure, with dainty strapwork decoration; Thomas Valence †1601, with enriched frame. – Thomas White, founder of Sion College, early C17 style; designed by *Blomfield*, 1877. – Kneeling male figure, late C16. – Margaret Talbot †1620, slate incised with kneeling figure in perspective-box architectural setting; alabaster frame. – Albert Faber †1684, signed by *John Settle*. – Damaris Turner †1703, big cartouche. – Sir Richard Hoare, by *Thomas Stayner*, 1723. Tablet with scrolly surround and no effigy; two putti on top. – Sir Richard Hoare †1754, much larger. Sarcophagus with carved fluting. On it a putto with portrait medallion. – Edward James Auriol, drowned in the Rhône in 1847. Bust of white marble in a niche, lying on a pillow as if asleep; hand on heart. Very naturalistic; young features; hardly of English work-

---

* Augustus Hare, *Walks in London* (1901), gives it to *Bacon*.

manship. – Over the entrance from the porch, John Shaw †1832; circular tablet with angels, a naïve but pleasing Romantic composition, doubtless designed by *Shaw Jun*.

ST EDMUND THE KING
Lombard Street

First mentioned by 1157–80. The present church of 1670–4 is almost certainly by *Hooke*. The evidence is a drawing of the w front in his hand, initialled by Wren and inscribed 'With his M(ajes)ties' Approbation' (*Wren Soc*. IX, pl. 15). It differs from the present church in having carved garlands along the side pieces and on top a balustrade and little low turret, later replaced. The craftsmen were *Abraham Storey*, mason; *Maurice Emmett Jun.*, bricklayer; *George Clisby* and *Henry Wilkinson*, carpenters; *Thomas Whiting*, joiner; *Daniel Morrice* and *John Sherwood*, plasterers. It lies N–S and the s front is developed boldly into a ritual w end. According to the *Parentalia* this alignment was due to the high value of land in the street; but the medieval predecessor also lay N–S. Three-bay façade with quoins. Arched windows with key blocks carved with cherubs' heads, under straight hoods on brackets. Strangely gauche mullioned windows to l. and r. below. Quoined slightly projecting middle bay, carrying a small pediment. Above this rises the tower and spire. The outer bays send up to the tower concave pieces in the Italian façade tradition. At their outer ends and on the tower parapet urns and pineapples. Behind this parapet an octagonal leaded lantern and a slightly concave-sided short spire, completed as late as 1706–7 (mason *W. Kempster*, carpenter *Richard Jennings*, plumber *Joseph Roberts*). It was stripped *c*. 1900 of twelve flaming urns in two tiers. A drawing for this steeple exists in the hand of *Hawksmoor*. So here, it seems, is a 'Wren' church designed by two other architects, albeit under his supervision. Projecting CLOCK on the tower, *c*. 1810. The best view of the spire is from George Yard, adjoining part of the former churchyard, NE. N and E walls, originally of brick with a wooden cornice, were refaced excessively trimly by *Caröe & Passmore* 1929–32, when the Yard was opened out. Of this date also the churchyard RAILINGS.

Entrance is made via a circular domed lobby beneath the tower. The interior is spatially without interest (rearranged by *Butterfield*, 1864 and 1881). No subdivision, just an oblong with a flat ceiling on the usual coving. Nave ceiling crudely replaced after bomb damage in 1917, with a mechanically detailed plaster frame to the big central panel and an ugly little central skylight, first made in 1725. Round-headed recesses around the walls, pierced with windows on ritual s and E. Small projecting chancel with pendentives and semicircular ceiling, which replaced a tall timber lantern-cum-clerestory some time after the mid C18. On the ceiling now a ruined PAINTING, probably from Butterfield's work. Excellent WOODWORK (*Thomas Creecher*, joiner). PANELLING of the walls, complete except for a NE recess, apparently contrived by Butterfield as an organ chamber. – Flanking the chancel two fine Corinthian DOORCASES with broken pediments, palm fronds, and flaming urns added after 1707 (carver *Henry Swarbrick*). – Matching urns on the REREDOS were formerly on the s door. Otherwise flat and simple with a segmental pediment on half-pilasters, but with plenty of good foliage carving. On it PAINTINGS of Aaron and Moses by *Etty*, 1833. – COMMUNION TABLE with big scrolly legs. – COMMUNION RAILS with balusters of unusual form, tapering symmetrically from a carved central ring. – CHURCHWARDENS' PEWS with carved fronts. – Other SEATING with reused panelling. – LECTERN. The same. – PULPIT. Of the usual type, but specially good quality. No tester, but STAIRS with balusters matching the communion rails. – Nicely carved ORGAN CASES, one of 1701–2, the other a replica of 1880. One is set over the entrance, the other near the pulpit. – Six mysterious carved POSTS or piers on the wall of the tower. – FONT. Marble with acanthus decoration and within a good, solid rail with twisted balusters on a semi-elliptical plan (the COVER, with small figures of apostles, is not normally displayed). – ROYAL ARMS. Late C17. From St Dionis Backchurch Fenchurch Street (dem.). – SWORD REST. 1753. – STAINED GLASS. E window, Christ in Glory. Designed by *Charles Hardgrave* (exhibited 1886), and made by *James Powell & Sons*. (Destroyed, a late 1860s window, made in Munich for St Paul's, rejected, and brought here *c.* 1905). – Flanking windows by Messrs *Taylor*, 1886. – Royal Fusiliers Memorial window by *Percy Bacon*, *c.* 1922. – MONUMENTS. Dr J. Milles, President of the Society of Antiquaries. Standing figure of Hope by an obelisk, leaning on an urn and pointing upwards. By the elder *Bacon*, 1786. – E. Ironside †1753. Substantial sarcophagus and obelisk in coloured marble. – Susan Horne †1835, by *Baily*.

ST ETHELBURGA
Bishopsgate

In 1993 a terrorist bomb destroyed the W end and most of the N wall of St Ethelburga: the greatest loss to the City's churches since the Blitz. Only 55 ft (17 metres) long, it was a unique survivor of the smaller medieval City churches, mostly lost in 1666. Its atmosphere was, unforgettably, that of a sleepy village church. The unique dedication to this C7 saint suggests great antiquity, but the first mention is only in 1250. A carved base of *c.* 1200, found reused in the walls, may be from the first church, which was wholly rebuilt in the late C14. No tower, though the entrance bay, W of the aisle, was separated from the nave by an arch like a tower arch. Its S respond remains, with S wall and arcade, E wall, and the lower E part of the N wall. The four-bay S arcade has piers with four shafts and four hollows, and two-centred double-hollow-chamfered arches. Two late C14 PISCINAE, one each in chancel and aisle. Late C15 five-light E window, renewed probably in *R. J. Withers*'s restoration, 1861–2. In the S aisle four plain pointed windows.

Opinion on the future of these remains has been divided. *Blee Ettwein Bridges*' competition-winning scheme, rejected in 1996, proposed for them a giant glazed enclosure like a reliquary, intended as a memorial to victims of terrorism, with offices to the E. A rival scheme for complete reconstruction was proposed by *Rothermel Thomas* and *Richard Griffiths* (structural advisers *Alan Baxter & Associates*). In 1997 it was announced that the church will be reconstructed as a Centre for Peace and Reconciliation, to be designed by the firm of *Purcell Miller Tritton*. Their greatest challenge will be to re-create convincingly the funny little Bishopsgate front, which sat impudently between towering c20 offices. It was of ragstone like the rest, with a late c14 doorway and a broad three-light late c15 window, off-centre. Its brick upper parts and plain parapet replaced a crow-stepped gable probably in 1835 (by *William Grellier*); the square timber bell-turret dated from rebuilding in 1775, replacing a short c15–c16 spire. A weathercock dated 1671 survived the blast. Before 1932, the front was rendered and very picturesquely half-hidden by timber-framed shops, dated 1570 and 1613.

FITTINGS. A surprising amount was salvaged. Of the pretty furnishings by *Comper*, 1912, the PARCLOSE SCREEN survives. – FONT. Gothic, c18 or c19. – Fine FONT COVER from St Swithin Cannon Street, by *Kedge*, 1687. – WALL PAINTING. Crucifixion by *Hans Feibusch*, 1962, over the altar. – PAINTING. Christ healing; Flemish, early c16; attributed to *Peter Coeke van Aelst*. Only fragments remained of the STAINED GLASS: by *Kempe* (E window, 1878), *L. Walker* (1928–30, four windows showing the adventures of Henry Hudson), and *Hugh Easton*, 1936; also some good c17 heraldic glass.

ST GILES CRIPPLEGATE
Barbican

A large church mostly of *c.* 1545–50, i.e. at the end of the medieval church-building tradition. Much restored in the late c19 and again by *Godfrey Allen* after severe bomb damage (reopened 1960). It now serves as the centrepiece of the Barbican Estate's main open space. Overshadowed by massive concrete forms and paved right up to the walls, it looks in its situation by the lake almost as if dismantled and brought from elsewhere; but it also anchors the late c20 environment in the wider urban context – in part by marking the true ground level, something visitors to the Estate may find elusive – and in an older history.

The church is recorded as having been built by Aelmund the priest *c.* 1102–15. According to Stow, the former vicarage stood on the site of an earlier church further W, but this may only have been a wayside shrine (by tradition the church marks the resting place of the body of King Edmund Martyr outside Cripplegate in 1010). The addition of guild chapels to the church on the present site in the c14 culminated in its complete rebuilding in 1390. The c16 rebuilding, following a fire of 1545, is thought to have reused the c14 plan, which tapers markedly from W to E with the tower slightly off axis. Substantial late c14 work survives in the chancel walls, better visible since cleaning in 1994. c14 work also remains in the base of the tower, which has angle buttresses to the outer corners, a big NW stair-turret and two-light windows. Brick top stage with panelled parapet and stubby pinnacles, added by *John Bridges* in 1682–4. Its two-light tracery differs from that of the restored lower apertures, but its forms are also late c19 and not 1680s Gothic. The pretty open cupola is a post-war restoration. Otherwise, the church was refaced in ragstone by *F. Hammond* (S side 1884–5, redone after the fire damage in 1897; N side 1903–5).

17   Inside, the nave and aisles are of seven bays with a partly project-ing chancel, the ritual chancel extending also to the two bays furthest E. The stone piers have a moulding of four shafts connected by deep hollows with thin filleted diagonal shafts. The hollows con-tinue around the arch. Aisle windows of three lights with simple panel tracery, on the N simpler than on the S. Fine shafts up to the roof between depressed-arched windows. The carving of corbels, stops etc. is renewed. The E end was much altered in the C18, and the chancel arch dates only from 1858–9 (galleries removed 1862). The Perp E window is post-war, based on late C14 traces discovered during restoration (replacing a large *œil-de-bœuf* window of 1704 with glass of 1791 by *Pearson*). A two-light N chancel window was opened up at the same time; the answering S window remains blocked. The post-war roof is arch-braced. Traces survive of the ROOD-LOFT DOORWAY (S wall), battered double SEDILIA with near-equilateral arches (restored with salvaged Roman tiles), and PISCINA in a square-headed surround. They look late C14.

Few FITTINGS survived the war and the church has been re-furnished, partly with items from elsewhere. The big new W GALLERY by *Cecil Brown* has tall Composite columns. On it an ORGAN CASE, from St Luke Old Street, of 1733 by *Jordan & Bridge*; rebuilt in 1970 by *Noel Mander*, with casework of 1684 from St Andrew Holborn (behind). – FONT with elegant stem and bowl with acanthus leaves, and domed COVER, with pilasters and garlands, both from St Luke Old Street. – SWORD REST. C20. – STAINED GLASS. E window, Crucifixion by *A. K. Nicholson Studios*, 1957. – Armorial W window by *John Lawson* (*Faithcraft Studios*), 1968. – SCULPTURE. Four busts of *c.* 1900 (Milton and Defoe by *Frampton*; also Cromwell and Bunyan), on loan from the Cripplegate Institute. – Bronze statue of Milton (who is buried here) by *Horace Montford*, 1904. It formerly stood N of the church, facing the old line of Fore Street (its battered pedestal, designed by *E.A. Rickards*, stands outside, minus Montford's reliefs). – MONUMENTS. Thomas Busby †1575, damaged bust from a once large monument. – John Speed †1629. Bust, damaged in the war, restored 1971 in a replica of part of the old surround. Attributed to *John & Matthias Christmas* (AW). – Elizabeth de Vallingin †1772 (part), with circular plaque of a female mourner, pyramid and urn. – Thomas Stagg †1772, tablet abruptly inscribed: 'that is all'. – Bust of John Milton, by the elder *Bacon*, given by Samuel Whitbread in 1793. The pedestal has a little carving of the serpent and apple. – Bust of Sir William Staines †1807, by *Charles Manning*, from a large monument destroyed by bombing.

Around the church is a brick-paved area planted with trees, partly on the site of the pre-war churchyard. The late C19 GAS LAMPS, scattered about like saplings, were brought here from Tower Bridge. Some early C19 tombstones of rounded-coffin type, with other slabs reused as seats. The huge monolith of the Stanier vault (S side) is worth looking at. A church hall is accommodated below ground level E of the chancel.

For the old Cripplegate and the remains of the City wall exposed S of the church, *see* London Wall, pp. 544–5.

ST HELEN BISHOPSGATE
Great St Helen's

An unexpected relic hidden behind the massive office buildings of Bishopsgate, facing a little churchyard with two tall trees. It is the fragment of a Benedictine nunnery, with the nuns' church completely preserved. The nunnery was established *c.* 1200–15 by William, son of William the Goldsmith, in connection with an existing parish church (known possibly before 1010, certainly by *c.* 1140). Hence the odd arrangement of the present church, with twin naves of almost equal width, i.e. the nave of the former nuns' church (now N aisle) built against and parallel to the nave of the parish church, with its s transept with C14 E chapels. Most of the reliable external features date from *c.* 1475. The next date is *c.* 1632–3, when the exterior was embellished and the interior refurnished. Minor later restorations 1807–9 (*Robert Chapman*), between 1831 and 1845 (*Tite*); major work in 1865–8 (*J. F. Wadmore*), 1874–5 (*E. B. I'Anson*), and 1892–3 (*Pearson*). St Helen was damaged by the terrorist bombs of 1992 and 1993, and was restored and drastically reordered by *Quinlan Terry*, 1993–5, who swept away most of Pearson's work.

EXTERIOR. Walls are of random rubble, of which some C12 fabric remains in the parish nave s wall, perhaps also in its E wall. Of the C13 the whole w and N walls of the church, most of the E wall, and the s transept. The w front is exceedingly pretty, with two low- 16 pitched embattled gables, and in lieu of a tower a timber bell-turret with square dome and open lantern between. This was first made 1568–9, but the present structure looks *c.* 1700 (repairs were mentioned in 1696; see however its casing, inside). w windows of *c.* 1475, with the usual depressed arches. No tracery, and – unusually – no cusping. The N and s halves of the building do not quite match here: the l. window only has a (C19) transom and a C16 doorway below; the r. doorway is early C14. The placing of the middle buttress indicates the slightly greater width of the nuns' church.

On the s side some visible C13 features: two non-matching lancets in the transept w wall (one blocked), and remains of three more in the s transept wall. One of those in the w wall has been partly destroyed by *Terry*'s ornate eared doorcase, dated 1995. A first-floor piscina on the transept w wall, s end, remains from a vanished two-storey appendage built *c.* 1400; traces of squints have also been found. Much brick patching to this wall, perhaps from 1807–9; more in the main s wall. This was heightened in the late C15, with three-light windows. Traces also of a blocked two-light window of *c.* 1400, E. Further w a pedimented stone doorway dated 1633, amongst 33 the earliest examples of a rather Mannerist mid-C17 style which flourished in the City and the counties NE of London and is connected with the architect-bricklayer Peter Mills. Frame with ears, half-pilasters outside it, and other weird angular forms; doors to match (cf. the contemporary sw door). Summerson suggested as the designer the carpenter *Anthony Lynnett*, who was busy at the time at the Leathersellers' Hall to the N (q.v.). Two chapels were added to the s transept some time before 1374, in line with the main E wall. They have Dec windows, largely of 1874–5. C14 parapets of banded stone and flint. In the main E windows, tracery of 1865–8

(S, Perp) and 1993–5 (N, curvilinear Dec, replacing geometrical work of 1865–8).

More C13 remains in the N wall of the nuns' church, visible from a narrow passage behind the buildings of St Helen's Place: one lancet at the W end, remains of three more beyond. The present windows here are C15, of varying heights to be clear of the former conventual buildings. Beneath the sills at the W end runs the weathering course of the former cloister, remains of which were uncovered and destroyed in 1922. The other buildings opened off it in the usual way. The E range lasted until 1799, latterly as the Leathersellers' Hall. Though greatly altered, it retained the vaulted crypts of the C13 dorter and chapter house. All that remains is a stub of the former W sacristy wall, with blind arches and a vault springer beyond. Further E a plain double-chamfered C13 doorway into the choir, and three squints.

INTERIOR. Until the restoration of 1993–5, the nave and S transept floors were several steps lower, with steps up to the two separate chancels: mostly the work of *Pearson*, who lowered the nave and fitted up the S chancel with screens and stalls. The precise medieval arrangement is unclear, although the transept was undoubtedly much lower than now. *Terry* remade the floor at one indiscriminately high level throughout. Walls are rendered and painted cream, except in the SE chapels. The inspiration seems to be the scrubbed, light-filled church interiors of C17 Holland, as painted by artists such as Saenredam. The remodelled interior is intended to allow flexible use for the church's current preaching-based services, which it undoubtedly suits better than Pearson's compartmented High Church arrangement. But few church interiors were less suited to such root-and-branch treatment. The restoration shows no sense of a creative dialogue between past and present, for all its Neo-Georgian trimmings. The loss to the viewer's perception of the unique early history of the church is also grave. The effect of the uniform floor level on the S transept is particularly unhappy, as a glance at its truncated central pier will show. The even sea of stone flags also laps absurdly close to those of the standing monuments which remain at the previous floor level.

The arcade between the two churches has, towards the W, four fine slim bays which allow access between the N aisle (former nuns' nave) and parish nave. The piers have four attached shafts with capitals, and double-wave mouldings in the diagonals without capitals. They date from *c.* 1475, paid for in part by Sir John Crosby's bequest. Between the two chancels are two arches opened up at different periods: the W arch early C14, the broad and low E arch *c.* 1420. A late C15 moulded doorway in the N wall leads to a narrow staircase in the thickness of the wall, probably the night stair from the dorter. Twin arches of *c.* 1475 open to the S transept and chapels. The pier between the chapels, of *c.* 1375, has four sturdy shafts and small diagonal hollows. The Gothic S window of the transept is early C17 (can it be *c.* 1633?). Ogee-headed NICHES on the chapel E walls, late C14, much renewed, in three vertical pairs. Two PISCINAE of the same date below, with square heads and shelves, now at floor level. The ROOFS throughout contain original material. They are of low pitch and tie-beam construction. All but that of the SE chapels were partially ceiled in 1993–5. The wagon-

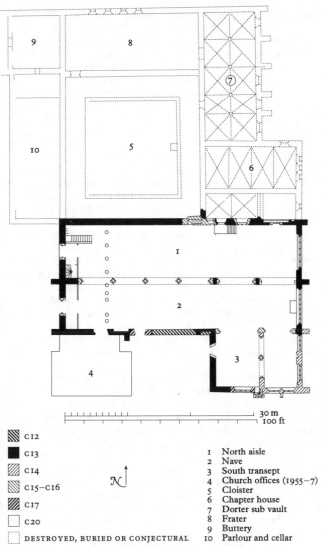

St Helen Bishopsgate. Plan

Legend:

- CI2
- CI3
- CI4
- CI5–CI6
- CI7
- C20
- DESTROYED, BURIED OR CONJECTURAL

N↑

1 North aisle
2 Nave
3 South transept
4 Church offices (1955–7)
5 Cloister
6 Chapter house
7 Dorter sub vault
8 Frater
9 Buttery
10 Parlour and cellar

30 m
100 ft

roofed s transept has a pretty c19 timber clerestory with Gothic windows.

OTHER FITTINGS. Much reordered in 1993–5, with movable seating arranged to face the PULPIT on the s wall. This is a glorious piece of carpentry, richly decorated with architectural forms, and with a large tester with bay-leaf frieze. It may be of *c.* 1633. c18 alterations to the back-board. – DOORCASES. An outstandingly good c17 example against the parish nave s wall. It is probably that paid for in the early 1630s, though it is more advanced in style than the contemporary fittings. The style derives from Inigo Jones and Nicholas

Stone and leads to the late C17 style favoured in the City. The use of fluted columns is the most telling feature. Swan-necked pediment, with standing lions flanking a tall attic block. Its inscription ('the gate of Heaven') is emphasized by the doorway motif in the cresting and in the *trompe l'œil* panels of the DOORS: a nice conceit. A second doorway in the S transept, a made-up piece, was moved from the W end in 1993–5. It has strapwork pilasters still of Jacobean type. Broken segmental curly-ended pediment, with re-clining angels and a shield, formerly part of a reredos (*see Survey of London* Vol. 9, 1924). The different styles of all this joinery may reflect different dates, or the patronage of different livery and trading companies in a single campaign of embellishment. – COMMUNION TABLE. Early C18. Twisted legs, inlaid top. From St Martin Outwich. – SCREEN. Across the S transept, the former 1890s chancel screen, delicate late Gothic, by *Pearson*. – REREDOS by *Pearson* (cut down), triptych with gilt and polychrome relief of the Resurrection. – CHOIR STALLS. Thirteen C15 stalls from the nuns' choir, with grotesque arm-rests; no misericords. Supplemented by C19 fittings. – W GALLERY by *Terry*, extending across both naves. Neo-Georgian, with Doric columns. Sections of *Pearson*'s parclose screens reused in the lobbies below. On the gallery a mahogany ORGAN CASE by *Thomas Griffin*, 1742–4, with three towers and serpentine flats (instrument rebuilt by *Goetze & Gwynn*, 1995).– Alongside, pretty rusticated timber CASING of the W bell-turret, with pilasters. – POOR BOX, late C18, on a bearded caryatid probably of *c.* 1632. – FONT. 1632. Of baluster type, black and red marble. Contemporary COVER with ogee top. – BAPTISTERY by *Terry*. Hexagonal, for baptism by immersion, sunk into the parish nave floor. – EASTER SEPULCHRE in the N wall of the nuns' choir, doubling as the monument of Johane Alfrey †1525. Square-headed, crested recess with four-centred splayed and panelled arch: a design used for other early C16 London tombs (e.g. at Lambeth and Hackney). Not well preserved. Its special feature is below: instead of the usual quatrefoiled chest, an arcade of cusped pointed lights, open behind as a squint for the nuns to look into the church from the sacristy. – SCULPTURE. Excellent small seated female figure, *c.* 1600 (S transept). Alabaster; style of *Colt*? – TILES. Medieval and C19 tiles are preserved at the old floor level around the SE chapels, in a boarded-over trench. – SWORD RESTS (nuns' church). Two, one wrought iron of the frame type, C18. The other is a great rarity. It is of wood and bears the remarkably early date 1665. Two elegantly twisted columns carry an entablature with a coat of arms above flanked by two angels. – STAINED GLASS. Shakespeare window, nuns' nave, 1884. – C15–C17 fragments in adjoining windows. – Clear glazing replaces the destroyed E windows (1866–7, by *Powell*, N, and *Heaton & Butler*, S).

MONUMENTS. St Helen has the best pre-Fire collection of any London parish church, augmented in 1875 by several from the demolished St Martin Outwich, Bishopsgate (marked M). First the BRASSES (to be reset in the SE chapels). John Leventhorp †1510, in armour. – Civilian and wife, *c.* 1470. – Nicholas Wotton †1482,M rector of St Martin Outwich; small figure. – Another priest, *c.* 1500.M – Thomas Wylliams †1495 and wife, in civilian dress. – Robert Rochester †1510, in armour. – Lady in stiff cloak, *c.* 1535. – Other monuments. The mighty tomb of Francis Bancroft †1727, 9 ft (nearly 3 metres) square, 'like a house', was alas removed in 1892. Listed topographically: nuns' choir: Johane Alfrey (†1525), *see* Easter Sepulchre, above. Free-standing in front of it, Sir Thomas Gresham, the creator of the Royal Exchange, †1579, a remarkable tomb-chest in the manner of an antique sarcophagus. No effigy on the black marble slab. Fluted sides with excellently understood classical details above and below the fluting, and big coats of arms. More restrained even than his Exchange's relatively pure Northern Renaissance, it speaks eloquently of the informed personal taste of a well-travelled merchant prince. – By it, under the first arch between nuns' church and parish church, Sir William Pickering †*c.*1574, much more typical of Elizabethan exuberance. Recumbent effigy under six-poster, an early appearance of the type. Coffered arches, transverse lesser arches with guilloche; achievement on top like a locket. Attributed to the *Cure* workshop (AW). Inscription on a separate tablet, parish choir N wall. Contemporary iron RAILINGS with knobs on twisted finials. – E wall: Sir Andrew Judd, merchant, †1558. Tiny, with kneelers. The inscription tells of his travels 'To Russia and Muscova/To Spayne Gynny without fable'. – N wall, from the E: William and Esther Finch, †1672 and †1673, grand tablet with columns and oval wreath. Attributed to *W. Stanton* (GF). – Peter Gaussen †1788, obelisk with relief of cherubs and a woman holding a portrait relief; much agitated drapery, not well done. – William Bond †1576 and family, of the usual type, with kneelers. Attributed to *Gerard Johnson Sen.* (GF). – Martin Bond †1643, military relief in a frame with columns, seated pensively inside a tent with assistant figures on guard: a monument with much atmosphere. Bond appears as in youth, when he commanded the trained bands raised against the Armada. Other figures poignantly in Civil War dress. Attributed to *Thomas Stanton* (GF); freely copied from Sir Charles Montagu's monument (†1625), Barking, Essex. – Valentine Moortoft †1641. Pedimented tablet with black marble columns, a common type. Attributed to *Nicholas Stone* (AW). – Elizabeth Thompson †1828. Stereotyped mourners in relief. – Lady Lawrence †1682. Urn on a chest, incomplete. Attributed to *Bushnell* (GF). – Hugh Pemberton †1500,[M] stately Purbeck tomb-chest with canopy, straight-topped and crested. Three cusped depressed arches on the front, one each on the W and E sides, each with a crocketed blank ogee gable. Little niches on the diagonals of the canopy piers. Chest with the usual quatrefoils with shields. Brasses partly remain against the back wall. – Alderman Robinson †1599 (W gallery). Two pha-lanxes of kneelers between columns. – Free-standing beneath the second arch from the W, *William Kerwin*, the City Mason, †1594. Miniature railed tomb- chest without effigy. Inscribed figures on the sides. In the inscription he says of himself: 'Aedibus attalibus Londinum decoravi'. What buildings were these?

Parish nave, from W: Sir John Spencer, Lord Mayor, †1609 and wife (s wall). Standing wall-monument, with on the tomb-chest two tall flanking black obelisks, a kneeling figure, and two recumbent figures. Against the wall two shallow coffered arches and fine ribbonwork framing the inscriptions. Big achievement on top (cf. such monuments in Westminster Abbey as that of the Countess of Hertford, 1598). Attributed to *Nicholas Johnson* (AW). – Richard Staper †1608[M] (s wall). The kneeling figures are more ambitiously treated in perspective than usual. – Between parish chancel and s transept Sir John Crosby †1476 and wife. Crosby Hall was close to Great St Helen's. Purbeck tomb-chest with quatrefoil panels separated by double buttresses. Excellently carved alabaster effigies, he in armour, she with a head-dress fashioned as a smooth block. s

22 transept: John de Oteswich and wife, late c14M. Alabaster effigies with narrow parallel folds in the draperies. The chest is modern. – Sir Julius Caesar (Adelmare), a judge in the Court of Admiralty, †1636, by *Stone* (paid £110). Plain tomb-chest, black marble top, and in lieu of the effigy the rare conceit of a flat parchment document with seal, carved in white marble as if it were lying on the black slab. It bears in self-consciously archaic black letter a testimony that Sir Julius was ready at any time to pay the debt of nature. Moved to the nuns' choir in 1875; moved back and repaired after severe damage sustained in 1992. – Rachel Chambrelan †1687. Elaborate upright tablet with standing cherubs. Attributed to *Gibbons*. – W. Bernard †1746, a large and clumsy architectural construction.

In the CHURCHYARD, altar tomb to Joseph Lem †1686: the master bricklayer? The Neo-Georgian brick RECTORY, s side, replaced *Pearson*'s vestry here in 1966–8. Free-standing CHURCH OFFICE at the NW, by *Kenneth Lindy, J. Hill & Partners*, 1955–7, likewise Neo-Georgian, with a copper mansard.

ST JAMES GARLICKHITHE
Garlick Hill

First mentioned *c.* 1170; made collegiate in 1481. The size of the pre-Fire church is reflected in the scale of *Wren*'s replacement of 1676–82. The mason was *Christopher Kempster*, bricklayer *Thomas Warren*, carpenter *Israel Knowles*, plasterers *Doogood & Grove*, joiner *William Cleere*. The tower, finished 1685, projects at the w. w doorway arched, with a cherub's-head keystone, and demi-columns overlapping pilasters carrying a pediment. Square tower with round-headed openings (ashlar-faced in 1944; later repairs by *D. Lockhart-Smith* and *Alexander Gale*, 1954–63). Then a pierced parapet with delicate uprights fashioned like hourglasses, and bulgy corner vases.

41 Recessed, a delightful spire added in 1713–17 to a design possibly of *c.* 1700 in which Hawksmoor may have had a hand (*see* Introduction p. 82). It belongs with those at St Stephen Walbrook and St Michael Paternoster Royal, all three carried out by *Edward Strong Jun.*, mason, and *Richard Jennings*, carpenter. First stage square with diagonally projecting coupled colonnettes standing in front of pilasters. Each pair carries a projecting entablature, with more vases and a flattened angle scroll on top. Above, a tiny square stage, then a tinier concave stage with a finial. The CLOCK on the tower, dated 1682, is a replica of 1988 of one destroyed in the Blitz. RAILINGS in front given by the Vintners' Company, *c.* 1965.

The w front itself has paired close-set arched windows flanking the tower, with the returned clerestory walls rising above and segmental half-pediments with volutes joining them to the tower: an unusual composition. Lesser doorways beneath the windows. Plainer s and N fronts, of brick, the key blocks of the windows uncarved. Each has five arched windows, the middle one considerably higher. These middle windows acquired their circular shape and cast-iron tracery probably in 1866 (other restorations 1815, 1838, 1854, 1883–5). Traces of Wren's original round-headed mullioned window may be seen on the N side, above a blocked square-headed doorway. The s front was originally built against, with a light-well to the central window, but widening along Upper Thames Street in 1973 has exposed it. The stucco and blind window outlines here were added *c.* 1981 by *Michael Biscoe*. The centre of the s front was reconstructed again (by *Biscoe & Stanton*) after a freakish accident in 1991, when a crane fell on to it from across the street.

The interior explains the tall windows of the N and s walls. It is an ingenious minor version of one of the ideas of St Stephen Walbrook – a combination of longitudinal and central planning, but with the dome left out. Nave of five bays, very high, with flat ceiling on broad coving with penetration from segment-headed clerestory windows (central panels painted with clouds *c.* 1992). The coving rises on a straight entablature carried by the tall Ionic columns of the nave. The narrow aisles are lower and flat-ceilinged. Projecting chancel between pilasters, with windows on N and s. It is narrower than the nave; the proportions such that the chancel is one-third of the total width and the aisles one-sixth each. The middle bay of the nave is wider than the rest, and the entablature is not carried through but returned to the outer walls so as to form central transepts in line with the blocked N doorway outside.

Post-war restoration has erased Victorian traces (e.g. of *Champneys*' redecoration, 1886), and the church is now an orderly showcase for the unusually fine ensemble of Wren period WOODWORK (parochial joiners *Fuller* and *Robert Layton*; carver *W. Newman*). Rich COMMUNION TABLE by *Fuller*, with scrolled legs and doves perching on the feet. – COMMUNION RAILS with twisted balusters. – Big, exceedingly finely carved PULPIT from St Michael Queenhithe, with big flat-topped tester and elegant staircase with twisted balusters. – REREDOS. Tripartite, with two Corinthian columns between pilasters and a straight entablature. A pediment was removed in 1815 to accommodate the PAINTING of the Ascension by *Andrew Geddes*, whose brother was the curate here: splendidly Rubenesque in colouring, but somewhat weakly drawn. – STALLS with back screens from St Michael Queenhithe. – CHURCHWARDENS' PEWS, W, carved by *Newman*. On them HAT STANDS of iron. – WAINSCOT, painted dark blue *c.* 1992. No grand doorcases; instead, Corinthian pilasters flank doorways to E and (in the vestibule) to W. – Octagonal FONT by *Kempster*, a common type. The plain ogee cover is no longer displayed. – Two iron SWORD RESTS, each with carved LION and UNICORN supporters (one set from St Michael Queenhithe, perhaps of 1681). – ROYAL ARMS. Large piece in s transept, from St Michael; smaller one belonging to St James's, early C19, on the N wall. – WEST GALLERY of *c.* 1714 on openwork iron stanchions with Corinthian capitals. On it an ORGAN by *Knopple*, called 'lately erected' in 1719. Trumpeting cherubs with palm branches on the case, which has four towers rather than the usual three. On the summit the scallop shell of St James. – Generous double STAIRCASE from the vestibule, with swept ends and twisted balusters. – BUST of Thomas Cranmer by *Mary Quinn*, 1989, on the screen of the stalls. – CHANDELIER of glass, remade after the 1991 accident to original designs of 1967 by *Arnold Montrose*. Based on an C18 example at Emmanuel College, Cambridge. – MONUMENT. Peter Jones †1694, with cherubs holding back drapery. Apparently by *Thomas Cartwright Sen.*, a version of his Thorold monument at St Andrew Undershaft (GF).

ST KATHARINE CREE
Leadenhall Street

The most important church in London between Jones and Wren – a building of 1628–31, a rare period for churches. Creechurch means Christchurch, and Christchurch refers to the priory of Holy Trinity within the precincts of which St Katharine stood (*see* Leadenhall Street). It may have begun as a cemetery chapel, but became fully parochial in 1414. The new church was under the patronage of Bishop Laud and was consecrated by him. Only the SW tower of *c*. 1504 goes back to the Middle Ages. Doorcase and circular cupola with columns of 1776. E of the tower the C17 S side faces Leadenhall Street. Squared ragstone, the reused foundations of the previous S wall visible. Odd three-light cinquefoiled windows to aisle and clerestory, straight-headed, with the centre light a little higher than the others. Aisle windows eared, with eared aprons. A similar window at St Mary, Goudhurst, Kent, where the London mason *Edmund Kinsman* was busy in 1638, makes him a possible designer (Colvin). The present straight parapet, C18, replaced segmental pediments above the centre and end aisle windows, as well as wavy cresting on the clerestory, tower, and E and W walls. A fragment of the latter survives against the tower, facing Creechurch Lane (W). Thinly pedimented large W window (blocked 1686), above a doorway without Gothic reminiscences. On the S aisle wall a delicate SUNDIAL of 1706.

35   Inside, Gothic returns in full strength in the E window. Above five plain lights is set a sixteen-light rose inscribed in a square with pierced spandrels: a French device, imitated at Old St Paul's retrochoir (begun 1256), which may be the model here. The interior is of six bays, truncated by the skewed W wall. Corinthian columns carry arches without intervening entablature, a remarkable departure from Perp traditions at the time (cf. the wholly Gothic arcades of Lincoln's Inn Chapel, *c*. 1619–23). The arch soffits are coffered. Above the clerestory a flat, spidery rib-vault (of plaster) with ridgeribs and one pair of transverse tiercerons. The two chancel bays are treated more ornately than the rest. Big bosses like badges, mostly with arms of the City companies. The vault responds rise from corbels roughly like Ionic capitals. The aisles are rib-vaulted as well.

Reminiscences of the church's narrower C15 predecessor may be seen in the narrowness of the NW aisle bays (C15 walling here) and in the surviving respond of the old S arcade (W tower wall). The latter betrays the C17 raising of the floor, indicated by excavations in 1928 to have lain previously 5 ft (1½ metres) below. Victorian restoration in 1878–9 by *R. P. Notley*; post-war repairs by *Marshall Sisson*, 1956–62, reconstructing the vaults and S aisle. Formerly home to the Industrial Christian Fellowship, housed in flimsy offices in the aisles; since 1997 home to the City Churches Development Group.

FURNISHINGS. FONT. Octagonal, marble, doubtless of c. 1631, still with strapwork etc. Contemporary ogee-domed COVER. – REREDOS. Modest, with Corinthian pilasters; probably of 1728. – COMMUNION TABLE. Finely carved, c. 1780. – PULPIT. Elegant work of 1732, the tester much inlaid. – LECTERN. Made up of C17 parts. – ORGAN. 1686 by *Father Smith*. Beautifully carved CASE with three towers and cherubs on pedimented flats between. – DOORCASE to NW vestry, dated 1693. – Two iron SWORD RESTS, with arms of 1787 and 1820. – ROYAL ARMS. C17. – STAINED GLASS. In the E window rose, foliage etc. of 1630, repaired by *Pearson*, 1777. Lower lights of 1878. – N aisle: Transfiguration, by *Kempe*, c. 1890. – S aisle: Christ walking on the waters, by *M. C. Farrar Bell*, 1963. – MONUMENTS. Sir Nicholas Throkmorton †1570. Oblong; recumbent figure between Tuscan columns with heavy entablature. Elaborate strapwork cartouche at the back. Attributed to the *Cure* workshop (GF). – Bartholomew Ellnor †1636, with robed mourners. Attributed to *Humphrey Moyer* (GF). – Richard Spencer †1667, with black marble columns. Attributed to *Thomas Cartwright Sen.* (GF). – Samuel Thorp by the elder *Bacon*, 1794. Standing woman bent over an urn. – Ralph Clay †1815, by *Sherwood* of Derby. – Some good early C18 cartouches, e.g. Sir W. de Bouverie †1717.

In the churchyard (entry from Mitre Street), a Portland stone DOORCASE dated 1631, formerly facing Leadenhall Street E of the church. Ionic half-pilasters; in the pediment a cadaver. Built by William Avenon, Goldsmith. It frames a fountain of 1965, when the churchyard was laid out as a garden by *D. W. Insall & Associates*.

ST LAWRENCE JEWRY
Gresham Street

1671–80 by *Wren*, on the site of a church recorded by c. 1190. Restored by *Cecil Brown* in 1954–7 after it was gutted in 1940. It stands proudly and conspicuously between Gresham Street and the extended Guildhall Yard. Wren's craftsmen were *Edward Pierce*, mason, *Thomas Newman*, bricklayer, *John Longland*, carpenter, *Thomas Mead*, plasterer. It cost £11,870, an unusually high sum. The whole church is stone-faced as befits its isolated site, less common in the C17 than now.

Facing King Street, the newly made processional route to Guildhall, Wren provided a spectacular E front. Four attached Corinthian columns on a podium carry a pediment set against a big attic storey. The flanking bays have Corinthian pilasters at the corners and eloquent arched niches in round-headed surrounds. Similar niche in the centre bay, with large arched windows in the bays to either side. The impost mouldings run across the front between the columns and all five bays have rich carved festoons above. The side towards Gresham Street is also treated as a façade: five arched windows in the centre, flanked by straight-headed entrances with circular windows above, the bays unevenly spaced. In the attic small segment-headed windows.

The W tower has tall obelisk pinnacles and a balustraded parapet. The bell-chamber below has on each face a round-headed opening in a shallow square-headed recess. The restored spire, of glass fibre, faithfully reproduces the four pedimented faces and octagonal spirelet of its leaded predecessor. Weathervane of 1732 in the form of the saint's gridiron. Quoined w front, far more modest than the E, with irregular windows N of the tower, where the vicarage is now accommodated. The plainer treatment here and on the rubble-faced N front is explained by their original setting facing narrow lanes. The w front is not square with the N and s sides, as is betrayed by the spire, which is a true square in plan. The visual effect on the tower seen from the w resembles that of distortion in a camera lens.

The interior is particularly spacious but was never of exceptional architectural interest. It has a wide nave six bays long, with a N aisle (the present Commonwealth Chapel) that stops one bay short of the E end: the result of the Corporation having taken the old NE bay to widen Guildhall Yard after the Fire (PJ). The N gallery here was removed by *Blomfield*, 1866–7. Corinthian pilasters to the nave, with four columns marking the aisle. Clerestory on the N and s sides, supplemented by a single circular light piercing the coving above the altar. Wren made the E wall of uneven thickness so the inside could be square with the N and s walls, as the differing depth of the window jambs shows. The ceiling is evenly divided by enriched ribs, faithfully following the old form.

Brown restored St Lawrence as a Guild church to provide a setting for Guildhall ceremonies, hence the unusual degree of pomp and circumstance in the new fittings. They were all to his design, which gives a welcome feeling of unity, in contrast to the bittiness of some restored City church interiors. The old church was noted for its glorious woodwork (by *Pierce* and *Kedge*), and the dark oak and ornate forms of the new PULPIT, REREDOS, N SCREEN etc. were intended as a C20 equivalent. In style they are traditional rather than explicitly Neo-Wren or modern, with devices unknown to C17 City joiners, such as the winged angels on the screen. – ROYAL ARMS and CHANDELIERS, also by *Brown*. – ORGAN. Older instrument adapted by *Noel Mander*, 1957, in a near-copy of *Harris*'s late C17 case with its later additions. – ALTARPIECE of St Lawrence, by *Brown*. – STAINED GLASS by *Christopher Webb*, dated 1959–60. A complete sequence of windows with historical figures in an academic fancy-dress style with lots of plain glass: unobtrusive, but less successful than the new fittings. – Ironwork SCREENS to the N aisle, the central one given in 1974, flanked by later additions made by *REME Workshops*. – Simple FONT of *c*. 1620, from Holy Trinity Minories. – Good PEWS from Holy Trinity Marylebone, probably from the restoration there by the elder *Somers Clarke*, 1876. – MONUMENT. John Tillotson, Archbishop of Canterbury, †1694, with a portrait relief above weeping cherubs, much restored. Attributed to *Gibbons*. – PAINTING. Martyrdom of St Lawrence, C16 Italian, in the entrance lobby. – Off here to the N, a narrow CHAPEL in a former stair-lobby. It perpetuates that made here in 1943, also designed by *Brown* with glass by *Webb*. A vestry further N was until 1940 exquisitely fitted up with carved panelling and ornate plasterwork, all by the artists of the church, with a painted ceiling by *Isaac Fuller II*: a very great loss.

ST MAGNUS THE MARTYR
Lower Thames Street

Begun by the parish in 1668 (mason *George Dowdeswell*); completed by *Wren*, *c.* 1671–84 (cupola added 1703–6); the body of the church much altered in the 1760s and later. Wren's craftsmen were *John Thompson*, mason; *Matthew Banckes Sen.* and *Thomas Lock*, carpenters; *William Cleere*, joiner; *Doogood & Grove*, plasterers. The Westminster Charter, a C12 document spuriously dated to 1067, mentions a church here, but an early C12 foundation is more likely. The church lies well below King William Street and the London Bridge approach, its w front almost touching the foot of that huge square cliff Adelaide House. Curiously enough, the conjunction of the vigorous and imaginatively detailed steeple with the tree close to it and the sheer wall of the C20 building is entirely successful.

The tower is big, massive and square, with paired pilasters on the top stage and a pretty pierced parapet. Above rises a large and solid octagonal lantern of stone, arcaded and pilastered. On it a lead-covered dome with little lucarnes and a concave obelisk spire, the whole 185 ft (56 metres) high (cf. the Jesuit church, Antwerp, 1614–24, of which Wren's office had a drawing). *Samuel Fulkes* was mason, *Abraham Jordan*, carpenter, *Joseph Roberts*, plumber. The model for it was made as early as 1684. – CLOCK projecting from the w tower wall, by *Langley Bradley*; dated 1709 on the face, 1700 on a benefaction board inside. Its present plain pediment made by 1807, replacing ornamental statuary.

The rest has a problematic history. When Wren took over the job, the parish had already raised part of the N front. Responsibility for the present N wall, of seven bays, cannot now be apportioned, though it has Wren's familiar cherub's-head keystones and straight hoods on brackets. Before the 1760s it was of nine bays, embracing the tower at the w. A broad three-bay pediment emphasized the centre, where the front breaks forward. In the middle bay here is a blocked doorway below a circular window, straight architrave and carved garland. But between 1762 and 1768 the two w bays were demolished for a pedestrian route through the tower, allowing the roadway on to old London Bridge to be widened. The tower's lowest storey thus became an external porch. Its N and S entrances are in concave-arched niches, apparently C17, with paired pilasters etc. added to the w pier to match Wren's applied temple front on the w face. The architect was possibly *Dance the Elder*, who made designs for the widened road. The N aisle pediment and tall flanking parapet were removed probably in 1782, when *J. Tricker* made the other windows round. So the upper parts now look a bit raw. Scrolly brackets reset against the tower, over the aisles, mark the parapet's original level. The S wall was rebuilt in 1803 by *Samuel Robinson*, who omitted key-blocks from the round-headed windows. Rendering here and on the E front of *c.* 1980, by *Laurence King & Partners*; until the later C20 both were built against in whole or part. Low SW RECTORY (former Sexton's House), of brick and stone with tripartite windows. Perhaps by *Robert Smirke*, who built the previous rectory on King William Street, 1833–5. The bay next to the church has a round-headed window in a splayed frame, typical of *c.* 1850: an addition?

The original form of the interior is even more problematic, since no entirely reliable illustration survives from before 1760. In that year a fire caused the upper parts to be reconstructed by *Peter Biggs*, the work completed according to Godwin's *Churches of London* (1839) before the passage beneath the tower forced further alterations. Aisles and chancel fit into a near-rectangle, the S aisle tapering to the E. Slender Ionic columns with cabled fluting rise from octagonal pedestals. The aisles have flat ceilings, the tunnel-vaulted nave deep transverse penetrations from oval clerestory windows, out of alignment with the aisle windows. The clerestory is difficult to date. Preliminary drawings by Wren show two treatments: one like the present arrangement but with segment-headed lights instead of oval ones; the other, apparently a preliminary version, with a flat ceiling resting on upright walls with rectangular windows. The oval lights are therefore almost certainly a later introduction.

A related mystery concerns the spacing of the columns. Wren's preliminary version shows seven columns, aligned with the bay divisions of the N wall. But the plan of St Magnus in Ogilby and Morgan's map (1676–9), usually a reliable guide, has columns irregularly spaced to form a double bay in line with the blocked N door. This implies the presence of an internal transept of some kind (cf. St James Garlickhithe, q.v.). The arrangement of the bays was altered in the 1760s when the first bay W of the tower was taken to make a lobby under the organ, and again during *Martin Travers*'s restoration of 1924–5, when an extra pair of columns was inserted in the double bay. So now there are six not quite regular bays in all, including the organ bay. The present clerestory pays no regard to any cross-axis, or to the spacing of the aisle bays generally. This is consistent with a date in the 1760s, by which time the N entrance had fallen out of use. Why, then, was the double intercolumniation perpetuated, when the clerestory entablature is continuous? Nor is a date in the 1760s entirely plausible for the clerestory; its sober plasterwork, intermittently fluted and coffered, looks half a century later. Might it not date from 1814, when *The Beauties of England and Wales* tells us that the church was 'beautified'? It is certainly a long way from anything Wren might have employed.

The especially sumptuous WOODWORK, though altered, is still one of the richest remaining ensembles in the City (joiners *William Grey* and one *Massey*). *Travers*'s additions of 1924 and later are interesting examples of the extreme High Church taste for the Continental Baroque. – Towering two-storey REREDOS, divided into five by Corinthian columns. Carved pelican over the centre, with PAINTINGS of Moses and Aaron on each side. The upper stage was reconstructed by *Travers*; photographs indicate the reredos was partly reassembled *c.* 1890. Surrounded by carving in the central roundel is a painted Glory, doubtless that mentioned in 1708, repainted perhaps in 1814. Carved urns with wriggling flames. To either side sit fine Baroque carved angels, not mentioned in 1708, but recorded by 1810. Crucifixion group on top by *Travers*. – SIDE REREDOSES: SE, C17, made up of *Massey*'s former doorcase in the N wall; NE altar by *Travers*, with reused C17 woodwork framing a PAINTING of the Virgin and Child after Van Dyck. – COMMUNION TABLE, C17,

modest, SE. – Magnificent W GALLERY with a projecting centre, 56
reached from the W lobby by matching dog-leg staircases with finely
twisted balusters. Its date is probably 1712, which would match the
ORGAN by *Abraham Jordan Sen. & Jun.*, the first 'swell-organ', it is
said (instrument since rebuilt. DF). It has a boxy case, the top
treated as a big interrupted pediment, richly carved below with trophies of musical instruments. On the parapet four iron COLUMNS as
standards for lights, with Queen Anne's monograph. Repairs of 1886
recorded on the gallery front may have been by *I'Anson*; there was
work by *E.B. I'Anson* in 1893 (Colvin). – Corinthian SCREEN and
DOORCASE by *Massey*, 1677, set against the W lobby wall. – Lobby
SCREEN with nice octagonal glazing, doubtless of *c.* 1760, with C17
carved work reset below. – CHURCHWARDENS' PEWS at the W end.
– PULPIT by *Grey*, with rectangular panels. The massive TESTER
has inverted segmental arches, with carved garlands between vases
sweeping along the top.

Iron COMMUNION RAILS with repoussé ornament, probably of
c. 1705. – FONT. Octagonal gadrooned bowl given in 1683, on a later
stem of Greek-cross plan. Ogee-shaped COVER with four pedimented faces. – BENEFACTORS' BOARD by the font, late C17, with
carved garlands. On it a PAINTING of the Baptist by *Alfred Stevens*,
after Murillo. – Iron SWORD REST of 1708. – BENCHES in Bavarian 61
Rococo style, and SCULPTURE of St Magnus, both by *Travers*. –
AUMBRY. Late C16 Flemish, with diminutive carved caryatids. –
STAINED GLASS. N aisle, armorial windows by *A. L. Wilkinson*,
1953–60. – S aisle by *Lawrence Lee*, 1949–53, still in the genteel
manner of his master Travers (CS). – NW window with armorial glass
dated 1671, from the former Plumbers' Hall off Cannon Street
(demolished 1863). – MONUMENTS. A good collection especially of
the C18 and early C19. – Thomas Collet †1704. Sculpted cherubs
hold aside curtains. – Robert Dickins †1705, draped cartouche with
cherubs' heads. Attributed to *Thomas Cartwright Jun.* (GF). – Sir
James Sanderson †1798. Grand sarcophagus and trophy on an
obelisk. – Miles Stringer †1799, with columns, obelisk and urn, and
tiny sculpted figures in the frieze; by *Simpson* of London Bridge. –
Thomas Preston †1826, by *Reeves & Son* of Bath. Urn and weeping
tree, like a bookplate in high relief. – Miles Coverdale memorial,
Gothic, by *George Sharp* of Gloucester, 1837.

ROMAN REMAINS. Beneath the tower is a sorry-looking fragment of
dried and blackened timber, one of many massive oak baulks used in
the construction of the early Roman embankment (*see* Upper
Thames Street). It was found on the other side of Lower Thames
Street in 1931. The tower itself marks the point where the later
Roman riverside wall was likely to have been breached by a monumental gateway leading from the bridge into the city. W of the tower
also some VOUSSOIRS from the C12 London Bridge, found in 1921
during excavations for Adelaide House.

ST MARGARET LOTHBURY

First mentioned *c.* 1185; rebuilt *c.* 1441 and again by *Wren* 1683–92
(tower completed 1698–1700). Wren's craftsmen were *Samuel*

Fulkes, mason, *John Longland*, carpenter, *William Cleere*, joiner, *Henry Doogood*, plasterer, and *Matthew Roberts*, plumber; on the tower, *Samuel Fulkes*, mason, *John Longland*, carpenter, *William Knight*, plumber. In plan an irregular oblong with the tower rising in the SW corner. Restoration work in 1978 (by *Gerald Dalby* of *D. W. Insall & Associates*) revealed medieval foundations to the N and E walls. They indicated that the C12 church was extended E in the C15, on a large foundation arch across a tributary of the Walbrook.

2   Stone-faced S front towards Lothbury. Unusually grand S doorcase in the tower, with pediment on free-standing columns. The tower bay is balanced at the E by the vestry windows. Three windows between, arched, with ears, the parapet above them pierced with balustraded sections. The tower is square and plain and crowned by an uncommonly pretty lead spire, an obelisk on a square-domed base. Paul Jeffery attributes its design to *Hooke*. The E front, visible from a narrow passage, has Wren's favourite composition of three large round-headed windows, the central one larger, the lesser ones to each side with lower sills and circular windows over. All are now blocked. On the N the church faces the little St Margaret's Court. Vestry and parish room here added 1908–10 by *H. C. Ingram*, son of the rector A. J. Ingram.

The interior has a nave with a S aisle which runs between the E face of the tower to the W face of the vestry (gallery removed 1881). The plan suggests retention of the old foundations, including the S entrance through the tower, characteristic of medieval London (*see* Introduction p. 52). Corinthian columns to the aisle, matching pilasters to the other walls. Coved ceiling, intersected by groining from the round clerestory windows. Modest circular panels in the central section. The E wall is markedly skewed. – Exceptionally fine FURNISHINGS, including many from demolished churches installed 1890–8 by *Walter Tapper*, who was then in *Bodley & Garner's* office. – FONT from St Olave Jewry (q.v.). Baluster stem and round bowl with cherubs' heads and between them reliefs of Adam and Eve, Noah's Ark, Baptism of Christ, and Baptism of the Eunuch – of great finesse. Gibbons's font at St James Piccadilly is carved with the same scenes, but there is no evidence he worked here. – SCREENS.

53   Chancel screen from All Hallows the Great (dem. 1894). It was made in 1683–4 and carved by *Woodruffe* and *Thornton*. By tradition the gift of a German merchant called Theodore Jacobsen; but recent research shows that it was a parochial commission.* It is one of two surviving Wren screens in City churches (the other, at St Peter upon Cornhill (q.v.), is similarly composed but less delicate and ornate). It runs right across the church and has four divisions on each side of the middle entrance. They are separated by tapering twisted openwork balusters. The pilasters of the entrance are also pierced. They carry a wide open segmental pediment filled with the royal arms. Below the pediment a big eagle with spread wings forming the arch. The effect of the piercing is exquisite but undeniably top-heavy. – Pretty S aisle screen, made 1891 to designs by the rector's brother *W. Rowlands Ingram*. The base is the reused COMMUNION RAIL of St Olave Jewry. The upper stage has slender close-set balusters alternately of wood and wrought iron. – COMMUNION RAIL also

---

* *See* Paul Jeffery, 'The great screen of All Hallows the Great', *T.A.M.S.* 37 (1993).

with two-strand openwork twisted balusters, and acanthus carving along the top. – COMMUNION TABLES. Two, with twisted legs, that in the S aisle from St Olave Jewry. – REREDOS. Sumptuous piece with Corinthian columns carrying two segmental pediments with urns. Openwork foliage volutes at the sides. The blank panel above it marks where a mediocre and intrusive relief of the Ascension (by *W. R. & H. C. Ingram*, 1910) has been plastered over. – Flanking the reredos, in the former NE and SE windows, big PAINTINGS of Moses and Aaron, *c.* 1700 (from St Christopher-le-Stocks). – REREDOS in the S aisle, simple, with broken segmental pediment, twin pilasters, and hanging garlands; incongruously painted 1908 with an Annunciation by *Sister Catherine Weeks*. From St Olave Jewry. – PULPIT. Splendidly carved, the flowers, fruit etc. partly openwork. The very large and grand TESTER is from All Hallows the Great, given to that church by Theodore Jacobsen. On it dancing cherubs, an eagle etc. – W GALLERY. C18, surprisingly simple, with Doric columns. On it, modest ORGAN, 1801 by *G. P. England* (restored by *Bishop & Son*, 1983–4). – READING DESK and other miscellaneous pieces incorporating woodwork of the Wren period. In the NW vestry, PANELLING from demolished churches. – Two SWORD RESTS, C18, of iron. – Two CANDELABRA from All Hallows the Great, brass, dated 1704 and 1760, in the chancel. The rest copies of 1962. – STAINED GLASS. Post-war armorial windows, some by *Goddard & Gibbs*, 1969.

MONUMENTS. In the S aisle Ephraim Skinner †1678, Sir Nathaniel Herne †1679, similar tablets with columns and broken pediments, both from St Olave Jewry. Attributed to *Thomas Cartwright Sen.* (GF). – Also in the S aisle, two fine BUSTS: Alderman Boydell (of the 'Shakespeare Gallery'), designed by *Banks* in 1791 and carved by *F. W. Smith*, 1820, for St Olave Jewry; Ann Simpson by *Nollekens*, 1795; her plain sarcophagus-tablet nearby also signed by him. – Rev. Watts Wilkinson †1840 by *Wyon*, with severe full-length figure in high relief. – Many other large but plain tablets. – A large bronze bust of Sir Peter le Maire attributed to *Le Sueur*, 1631, from St Christopher-le-Stocks, is no longer displayed.

ST MARGARET PATTENS
Eastcheap

First recorded in the C12, and rebuilt as late as 1538 after the old building collapsed. Stow thought the name derived from nearby pattenmakers, but it may commemorate one Ranulf Patin, canon of St Paul's and a parish landowner. The present church by *Wren*, 1684–7. His craftsmen were *Samuel Fulkes*, mason, *Thomas Woodstock*, carpenter, *William Cleere*, joiner, and *Doogood & Grove*, plasterers. Since 1954 it has been a Guild Church.

WEST front to Rood Lane, of stone, tripartite, with a large round-headed central window above a doorcase, flanked by two lesser and lower ones with circular windows above. The S front, of brick with early C19 rendering, has a mixture of circular and round-headed windows. The NW tower has square-headed bell louvres and one of the most remarkable of the late spires (of 1698–1702): polygonal and lead-covered, as if it were medieval, but with equally needle-shaped corner pinnacles at the foot of the square tower top. Balustrade between these pinnacles. The group of five needles is very effective, though a little harsh; more so since the spire lost the little urns which originally crowned the second of its three stages of apertures. The mason was *Fulkes*, with *Abraham Jordan*, carpenter, *Matthew Roberts*, plumber, and *Jonathan Maine*, carver. Paul Jeffery suggests it may be by *Hawksmoor*; he points out payments by the parish to 'Sir Christopher Wren's clerk'.

The interior is a plain rectangle with a N aisle and small projecting chancel, lit by circular clerestory windows cut through the coving. Corinthian pilasters around the walls turn into full columns across the aisle (now the Lady Chapel). A N gallery and a W gallery are separated by the tower. The N gallery, reached by a pretty staircase with twisted balusters, runs awkwardly across the columns one-third of the way up. It was converted into conference rooms in 1955–6 during restoration by *A. W. Moore & Son* (earlier renovation by *R. P. Day*, 1892). Much original WOODWORK survived reseating in 1879–80: twin canopied CHURCHWARDENS' PEWS (W), one dated 1686, for the parishes of St Margaret and St Gabriel Fenchurch, once not uncommon in the City churches, but surviving only here; BEADLE'S PEW, NE corner; low CHANCEL SCREEN with reused carved work; REREDOS with Corinthian columns and a broken segmental pediment, narrow to fit the chancel but of excellent quality (gilded 1886); COMMUNION RAILS with twisted balusters; lesser REREDOS in the N aisle, made from a former doorcase; simple hexagonal PULPIT, testerless, with an iron hourglass stand. – Two sets of Stuart ROYAL ARMS; that above the entrance exceptionally fine. – C17 HAT-PEGS, N aisle. – W SCREEN below the gallery, 1791. – WAINSCOTTING in the lobby, 1834. – ALTARPIECE. Christ at Gethsemane, attributed to *Carlo Maratta*. – In the N aisle a *Della Robbia* TONDO, installed by a late C19 neo-Jacobite rector, J. L. Fish. – ORGAN. 1749 by *Thomas Griffin* (much rebuilt), in a fine three-towered contemporary CASE with carved trophies of musical instruments. – Two iron SWORD RESTS, the larger dated 1723. – FONT. Octagonal, carved with cherubs' heads and foliage on the bowl in the usual manner. The cover is no longer displayed. – The C19 copper CROSS and BALL on the S wall, copied from those at St Paul's, were formerly on the spire.

MONUMENTS. Sir Peter Vandeput and family, cartouche erected 1686. Attributed to *Jasper Latham* (GF). – Susannah Batson †1727; a charming small piece with cherubs' heads. Attributed to *Robert Hartshorne* (GF). Both are convex and applied to columns. – Sir Peter Delmé †1728, by *Rysbrack* (erected 1740), a big hanging architectural monument with reclining cherubs on a pediment and terminal scrolls with female heads, the forms fashionably Kentian. – John Birch †1815, large with weeping cherubs and urn by *Charles Regnart* (W gallery). – Mary Ann Graves †1843, bad relief of seated figure, by *John Ely Hinchliff*.

ST MARTIN LUDGATE
Ludgate Hill

On a site adjacent to the former Lud Gate, and first mentioned *c.* 1138. Geoffrey of Monmouth's fantastic claim that Cadwallader founded the church in 677 may yet be evidence for a pre-Conquest foundation. The present church of 1677–86 is by *Wren*, or perhaps *Hooke*, whose diary records 31 visits before and during construction. It cost £5,378 (*Nicholas Young*, mason; *Allan Garway* and *Thomas Horn*, bricklayers; *Henry Blowes, Robert Day, Matthew Banckes Sen.*, carpenters; *Doogood & Grove*, plasterers; *William Draper*, joiner; *William Emmett*, carver; *John Talbot* and *Peter Read*, plumbers). St Martin suffered the least air-raid damage of any City church and is generally in an excellent state of preservation.

The pre-Fire church stood clear of the City wall, with a tower up against it pierced by an arch. Wren's church lies further w and incorporates part of the Roman town wall in its w wall. As at St Edmund the King, the alignment is N–S, and the S front is here treated 43 similarly as a three-bay stone-faced composition with central tower slightly projecting. Three tall windows (here segment-headed), all with the usual straight hoods. Doorway below the middle window. Volutes above the side windows curve up to the tower. Smaller volutes ease the transition between the square tower and a short octagonal stone stage. From this rises a charming Dutch- or Scandinavian-looking lead spire, with an octagonal bell-shaped dome, iron balcony, and then an open-arched stage supporting the tall leaded spirelet: a nice foil to St Paul's when one looks up Ludgate Hill. The modest brick N front, facing the courtyard of the Stationers' Hall, has a projecting central bay with a blocked entrance.

What appears to be a ritual w end proves inside to be the façade to a S narthex with a gallery above, allowing the church proper to be correctly oriented, besides insulating it from street noise. The double stairs to l. and r. date probably from *Ewan Christian*'s generally restrained restoration, 1892–5 (earlier restoration by *Edward Cresy*, 1824. DF). Previously a single flight rose immediately within the door. The plan is otherwise similar to St Anne and St Agnes, though taller in its proportions: square, with a smaller central 48 square on four Composite columns and a rich, deep cornice. The central square is groin-vaulted. Tunnel-vaulting to the main axes. Pilasters mark off the remaining lower corner sections, which are covered with flat ceilings. All this is divided from the narthex by three arches on broad pillars. The arches are coffered but otherwise unmoulded.

FITTINGS. Within the S arches a GALLERY, which has a superb panelled substructure with three pedimented DOORCASES of the richest design (joiner *William Grey*, carver *William Emmett*). Ionic half-columns to the central doorcase, which has within the pediment carved cherubs holding a wreath and crown. Plainer Corinthian doorcases, flanking, not *in situ*: probably from the former outer lobby. Above, reset fronts from the old gallery, which projected further. More good woodwork in the other fittings (joiners *Athew, Draper* and *Poulden*; carvers *Cooper* and *W. Newman*). w GALLERY.

Set well back from the crossing piers. The stairs have twisted
balusters. – REREDOS rather flat, with pilasters only. Raised centre
with segmental arch and pediment. – PULPIT with oval panels, of
the usual Wren type, but with stairs with exceedingly slender twisted
balusters (i.e. probably later). – COMMUNION RAILS, three-sided,
with twisted balusters. – COMMUNION TABLE with thick twisted
legs. – CHAIR for two churchwardens, typical of its date (1690) and
with cane seat and back. – Miscellaneous other contemporary woodwork, e.g. in the PEWS and STALLS, some of it from St Mary
Magdalen Old Fish Street. – FONT. 1673, from the 'tabernacle' (*see*
Introduction p. 83). Bulgy baluster and fluted bowl with palin-
dromic Greek inscription. Behind it a C17 carved marble pelican. –
FONT RAILS. 1703. – ORGAN of 1847, by *Theodore Bates* of Ludgate
Hill. – ROYAL ARMS. Early Victorian; perhaps a C17 piece repainted.
– CHANDELIER. Very large, of brass. The central one brought from
St Vincent's Cathedral, West Indies, *c.* 1777. – SWORD REST. C18,
much restored. From St Mary Magdalen. – PAINTING. Large picture
of the Ascension by *Robert Brown*, 1720, brought in 1890 from St
Mary Magdalen. Also some Old Master copies of *c.* 1900. –
STAINED GLASS. By *Powell*, late C19. – MONUMENT. Little brass of
Thomas Beri, 1586 (N wall). From St Mary Magdalen. An identical
brass is at Walton-on-the-Hill, Lancs. – Not normally displayed are
carved BREAD SHELVES from St Mary Magdalen and the ogival
FONT COVER.

ST MARY ABCHURCH
Abchurch Lane

First mentioned in the late C12 and probably named after a benefactor such as Abbe or Abbo. A vaulted chamber below the churchyard, said to be of the C14, was revealed after bombing in the
Second World War. It must have formed the undercroft of a lost
chantry chapel. The present church is by *Wren* and dates from
1681–6. It cost £4,974. *Christopher Kempster* was mason, *John Bridges*
and *John Evans* bricklayers, *Thomas Woodstock* carpenter, *Doogood &
Grove* plasterers and *Thomas Dobbins* plumber. Red brick with stone
dressings; almost as homely as St Benet Paul's Wharf. Three bays
each to S and E, with round-headed windows with circular lights
over, flanking a large segment-headed window (the E one blocked).
Hipped roof. To the S an open space, the former churchyard, prettily
paved to a pattern by *E. I'Anson* in 1877. NW tower with quoins,
carrying on a square ogee-domed base a small pierced lantern and
then the sweetest lead obelisk-spire (slightly altered 1884). The
church room was added to the N in 1914–15 by *W. Campbell-Jones*, in
connection with his Gresham Club in Abchurch Lane (q.v.).

The interior is a surprise, for although the area is small, Wren
made it look very spacious indeed by giving it one big dome on eight
arches. There are no aisles; all that he did was to groin the corners so
as to lead on to the base of the dome, which has a hemispherical
profile continued below the cornice in pendentives on Corinthian
pilaster-capitals. At the SW the dome rests on a pilaster and a full
column, which carry it across a gallery. Font enclosure below. The
PAINTING of the dome is unparalleled by any other Wren church. It

was done in 1708 or shortly after by *William Snow*, for £170. It represents the Name of God in Hebrew surrounded by rays, clouds and heavenly choir in colour above, divided by a painted cornice from architectural motifs with seated figures of Virtues in monochrome around the four oval windows. The most recent of many restorations were in 1946–53 by *W. Hoyle* and *E.W. Tristram* after severe bomb damage, and in 1994–5 by *Tom Organ* and *John Burbidge*. The rest of the church was restored by *Godfrey Allen*, 1945–57.

FURNISHINGS. Huge REREDOS by *Grinling Gibbons* himself, 54 1686. Two original requests for payment for the 'olter pees' were found in 1946. Reassembled 1948–53 after it was blown into two thousand pieces in 1940. Tripartite, the centre with coupled Corinthian columns, carrying sections of a segmental pediment. Behind and above, an attic with four vases and a raised, concave-sided centre crowned with a Garter monogram: a device not found elsewhere. Limewood pelican, garlands etc. exquisitely carved. – COMMUNION TABLE, made in 1675 by *Almandy Howart* for the temporary 'tabernacle' (*see* Introduction p. 83) and unusually small. – Late C19 COMMUNION RAILS. – Other woodwork by joiners *William Grey* and *Thomas Creecher*, carver *William Emmett*. The most intact set surviving, for Victorian alterations (by *I'Anson*, 1878–9) were modest, and little has come from elsewhere. – PULPIT. 1685 by *Grey*, thickly carved, with large tester with upswept sides and garlanded urns on a square Ionic pillar. Still at its original height, with intact wine-glass stem and stairs complete with twisted balusters and big curved platform. – FONT of marble by *William Kempster*, 1686, a fluted octagon on a slender stem. Wooden FONT COVER by *Emmett*, square and strongly architectural, with statuettes of the Four Evangelists under curvy pediments. It is raised by a spiral wooden screw like a narwhal's tusk. – FONT RAILS with twisted balusters and enriched square piers. – PANELLING to the walls. – W GALLERY with oval and circular panels and cherubs' heads. Late C17 GRAFFITI inside. – ROYAL ARMS by *Emmett* on the gallery front. – Richly carved DOORCASES by *Emmett*, that to the S especially fine, with segmental pediment on Composite pilasters, garland frieze with a central shell, urns and cherubs. That facing it on the N a little plainer, with a gilded copper pelican (by *Robert Bird*) which was the weathervane until 1764. – Some of *Creecher*'s original PEWS, N and S, with openwork panels of carved foliage, very tall so that one sits high up inside. Also two churchwardens' pews (W). – LION and UNICORN on the front pew. – SWORD RESTS. Two, of iron, with arms of 1812 and 1814, but probably older. – Unusual CANDELABRA on the pews, made 1957 using mahogany columns from Lockinge House, Berks. – ORGAN CASE of 1717, from All Hallows Bread Street, replacing that lost in 1940. Flanking screens by *Lord Mottistone*. Instrument by *Mander*, 1954. – POOR BOXES. Two, square on square pillars, made 1694 by *Creecher*.

MONUMENTS. Sherwood family †1690–1703, with twisted columns and lots of cherubs. Attributed to *William Woodman Sen.* (GF). – Sir Patience Ward †1696. Good tablet with mourning putti, and, at the top, between urns, an allegorical figure (Patience?) on a tall concave-sided pedestal. Attributed to *Thomas Cartwright Sen.* (GF). – Benjamin Eaton †1730 and wife †1741, by *Sanders Oliver*. –

Matthew Perchard †1777, also by *Oliver*. – Martha Perchard †1787, with carved female mourners or virtues. – Some good floor slabs, exposed by the removal of I'Anson's raised floor in 1954.

ST MARY ALDERMANBURY
See Streets p. 413

ST MARY ALDERMARY
Queen Victoria Street

First mentioned *c.* 1080, but almost certainly much older: Aldermary is thought to mean the elder Mary, i.e. the oldest City church so dedicated. The present church is the chief surviving monument of the C17 Gothic revival in the City, and – with Warwick – the most important late C17 Gothic church in England. It is also the most mysterious of the City churches.* Rebuilding began in 1510 following a bequest by Sir Henry Keeble, and the body was probably finished shortly after 1528, when another bequest was made for roofing the nave. Further work in 1626–9 completed the tower, after a further bequest requiring it to follow the 'ancient pattern. . . [of] the foundation of it laid 120 years since'. After the Great Fire, the church was, unusually, rebuilt with money from yet another bequest. There is no evidence for the tradition that its benefactor Henry Rogers specified that the new church should copy the old: his will stipulated only that the money go to a City church, and it was his niece Anne Rogers who selected St Mary. The choice of style appears to have derived rather from the reuse of substantial medieval remains.

First the body of the church, which is an aisled and clerestoried rectangle with Perp windows throughout. The rebuilding was carried out in 1679–82, supervised by the *Wren* office (*Edward Strong Sen.*, mason; *John Longland*, carpenter; *Thomas Creecher*, joiner; *Henry Doogood*, plasterer; *Jonathan Maine*, carver). It was surveyed by *John Oliver*, but not necessarily designed by him, for such work formed part of his routine duties. Indeed, Wren's authorship is as likely here as at any other undocumented City church. However, the appearance of the exterior is due largely to refacing in stone by *Charles Innes* of *Tress & Innes* in 1876–7, after the making of Queen Victoria Street exposed the S and E sides. Innes exaggerated the Perp details of buttresses, etc., and added the doorcase, quatrefoil parapet (partly surviving), octagonal corner buttress and NE vestry wall.

It is with the windows that the difficulties begin. The aisle windows may follow in detail those of their C16 predecessors. Reused Caen stone, still visible in the S window reveals in the C19, suggested that the medieval walls were retained in the C17; but, when the ashlared N wall to Watling Street was exposed in the 1830s, traces of exterior buttresses were found surviving only to sill level, and out of alignment with the blind windows inside (opened up in 1840 by *Tress*). These windows were themselves aligned with the arcades and with the S aisle windows. So either the church begun in 1510 was much less regular than was then usual, or the spacing of

---

* *See* H. M. Colvin, *Architectural History* 24 (1981).

the bays was altered at the C17 rebuilding, reusing only the lower medieval walls and resetting some window mouldings for economy. This interpretation guarantees that the window outlines conform to the pre-Fire ones, even if they may be in new positions, although Wren's big E and W windows, no less correctly Perp, were apparently made without reused stone. S. Lockwood's study of the church draws attention to the cast-iron trusses inserted in the aisle roof space by *Samuel Ainger* in 1825. Ainger was awarded the Society of Arts' Gold Medal for his work.

The big SW tower was not reconstructed until 1701–4, with Coal Tax money (*John Clarke*, mason). Repairs of 1674–5 suggest it had survived the Fire well, but subsequent refacing makes it difficult to distinguish any earlier work. The lowest stage at least looks authentically Perp, with its four-light window and panel tracery. The big bulky polygonal buttresses, too, should probably be accepted as an original feature. Gerald Cobb noted their similarity to those of the C15 drawing for the campanile of King's College, Cambridge. They have paired panels grouped in five tiers of three (two on the lowest stage), moulded rings on the shafts at the angles, and smaller shafts at the angles of the big polygonal pinnacles. These – a characteristic feature in the City skyline from many points – are attributed by Sir Howard Colvin to *William Dickinson* on the strength of his drawing for a central tower at Westminster Abbey, which has similarly bottle-shaped pinnacles. (Kerry Downes gives the tower to *Hawksmoor*, though it was Dickinson who had charge of the City churches office by 1701.)

Much of the interior seems at first straightforward Perp: six bays, slim piers with the familiar four-shafts-four-hollows section, four-centred arches, three-light Perp aisle and clerestory windows under four-centred arches. But the piers stand on reused medieval rubble (proved during rebuilding in 1935), so they must have been Wren's work. The walls may be similarly deceptive.

Above the arcades, however, all is clearly C17. Wren's ceilings are plaster fan-vaults, in the nave as well as the aisles. They rest on vaulting shafts, in their turn starting from entirely Wrenish cartouches in the spandrels. They display the arms of Henry Rogers and of the patron, Archbishop Sancroft of Canterbury. Fan-vaults for a whole parish church is something unheard of, though not for major monastic churches such as Sherborne or Bath. Such fan vaults did not of course have the oversized central roundels, which are sunk like shallow saucer-domes. But supposing Wren was imitating a vault of 1629 and not of *c.* 1520? Fan-vaults, most commonly non-structural, were still in use in the early C17: a similar example is at the 1630s Convocation House in Oxford which, as Kerry Downes points out, Wren would have known. Still, the value of Wren's work lies not in the extent to which it copies accurately, but in its very originality, the freedom with which he treated precedent, and the fun which he evidently had in playing with Gothic forms (see the enriched panelled barrel-vault made over the short projecting chancel, with its skewed E wall).

FITTINGS. Carved Gothic STALLS, PEWS, W SCREEN etc. of *c.* 1876, with PANELLING of 1886: a near-complete ensemble of good quality but uninspired design. – Carved wooden REREDOS of 1914, designed by *J. Douglass Mathews & Son*. – COMMUNION

TABLE. *c*. 1700, of oak, with white marble top. – The late C17
PULPIT survives: of the usual type, with cherubs' heads, on a base of
1876. Made by *William Grey*, probably carved by *Jonathan Maine*. –
FONT. Fluted bowl on baluster, dated 1682. Enclosed in RAILS with
twisted balusters, probably reused communion rails. – SWORD
REST. A rare example of oak, 1682, tall, with superbly carved flow-
ers, fruit etc. and the royal arms on top. – DOORCASE, a sumptuous
piece with Corinthian pilasters and broken pediment, from St
Antholin Watling Street (dem.). – POOR BOX on a flat twisted stem.
– Brass LECTERN. Eagle type, unusually elaborate, *c*. 1876. – ORGAN
last rebuilt in 1908 (*Norman & Beard*), with pretty stencilled pipes. –
PAINTING. Transfiguration, in the blind window in the N aisle.
Probably by *Clayton & Bell*, *c*. 1876. – STAINED GLASS. E window,
Crucifixion, by *Lawrence Lee*, 1952. – W window, risen Christ, by
John Crawford, 1952. – Other windows by *Lee*, *c*. 1955. All unattrac-
tively pale. Lee followed the outlines of designs by the late *Martin
Travers* (CS). – MONUMENTS. John Searle †1714, above average.
Time and Death suspend drapery held open by cherubs. By *William
Woodman Sen.*, the drawing now in the V and A Museum (GF). –
René Baudouin †1728. Big gristly cartouche with pediment and
weeping cherubs. Signed by *Joseph Pasco* (GF). – In the chancel,
tablet with wreathed urn, signed by the younger *Bacon* but otherwise
uninscribed. – MEMORIAL. Relief of St Antholin Watling Street,
1880 by *C. H. Mabey*, from the former site.

ST MARY-LE-BOW
Cheapside

By *Wren*, 1670–80, with an C11 crypt from the medieval church.
The tower stands out some distance to the N because Wren found
here a Roman gravel roadway, which made an admirable new
foundation. Behind it is a vestibule, and only S of that the church,
built on an enlarged site 1670–5 (mason *Thomas Cartwright
Sen.*, bricklayer *Anthony Tanner*, carpenter *Matthew Banckes Sen.*,
plasterers *John Grove Sen. & Jun.*). The vestibule is continued to the
E by the rector's lodging. Of the church only the modest outer walls
of brick with stone dressings survived the war. The interior was
rebuilt by *Laurence King*, 1956–64, reproducing Wren's design
(Victorian restorations by *J. L. Pedley*, 1867, and *Blomfield*, 1879).
The W side is a three-bay façade with a big pediment connected
with the aisle fronts by small curved pieces. Central doorway with
segmental pediment on carved brackets. Large arched central
window, smaller lower arched side windows each with a circular
window above, and an oval window in the pediment. As restored,
they have gratingly inappropriate metal mullions. Corresponding E
front. The S front has a projecting centre with another doorway and
a circular window above; the other windows are arched.
  But the glory of the church is its steeple, the proudest of all Wren's
steeples, and at 224 ft (68 metres) second in height only to St Bride
(q.v.). It was raised in 1678–80, the first true steeple made after the
Fire, and cost £7,388 as against £8,033 for the rest of the church.
The square tower is especially broad and high. Entrances from the
street and churchyard by big doorways each lying back in a rusti-

cated niche, with little angels on top flanking an oval window: motifs taken from J. Hardouin Mansart's Hôtel de Conti, as Viktor Fürst pointed out. Each doorway has Tuscan columns and a heavy triglyph frieze, like those of Wren's Trinity College Library, Cambridge (1676). The room under the tower has a vault with a circular opening in the centre. It is a triumph of the skill of the tower's masons, *Thomas Cartwright Sen.* and *John Thompson*, that it withstood the fire inside the steeple and the crashing down of the bells in 1941. The iron balcony facing Cheapside is said to be a reminiscence of the temporary grandstands (called 'silds' after low market structures of the C12–C14 here), from which tournaments were viewed. The bell-stage above has coupled Ionic pilasters. Above this is a balustrade with openwork angle pilasters in the form of volutes moving up to the top. Between them the spire rises, with a conical core but a splendid architectural dress. First a rotonda of free-standing Corinthian columns. If the steeple has a fault, it is their excessive slenderness; but their order follows the proper vertical sequence. On them a second balustrade, then again volutes moving up to the graceful top stage, which is of a Greek-cross type with further projections in the re-entrant angles. It carries twelve Composite colonnettes (renewed in granite by *George Gwilt Jun.*, 1818–20), to correspond to the twelve columns below. Obelisk to finish; on it a very large copper WEATHERVANE, a dragon, made by *Robert Bird* in 1679 from the wooden model of *Edward Pierce*.

Below the church lies an exceptionally important CRYPT. It dates from *c.* 1077–87, when the church was rebuilt by Lanfranc of Canterbury as the London headquarters of his Archiepiscopal fee. There are certain affinities with contemporary crypts at Canterbury Cathedral, St Augustine's Abbey, Canterbury, and Rochester. If one accepts a date after the fire of 1087 for the crypt, then a further connection between the Canterbury workshop and the rebuilding of that date at Old St Paul's may be implied. It may be the vaults here, and not the flying buttresses on the pre-Fire steeple of 1512 at the SW, which gave the church its suffix *de arcubus* (of the arches or bows). About sixty per cent of the material survives, compromised by Wren's repairs and post-war insertions. It consisted originally of a nave and two aisles, separated by heavy unmoulded piers with Roman brick reused in the outer order of voussoirs. The S aisle has been fitted up as a chapel, entered from the churchyard via a W extension built in connection with the medieval SW tower. The nave and N aisle are reached from the vestibule beyond the tower. Converted to a restaurant in 1989, so little feeling of antiquity remains. The nave, now partitioned at the W, was originally subdivided into three parallel vessels by columns with single-scallop capitals, some of which survive. Each bay was groin-vaulted. Thus there were altogether twelve vaulting bays in the nave, and four larger ones in each aisle. Only the N aisle retains C11 vaulting. Blocked round-headed windows in the aisles and larger recesses in the E wall indicate the crypt originally stood above ground, perhaps as the lower part of a two-storey chapel in the Carolingian tradition.* The upper part of an C11 newel staircase found in 1959 in

---

* See Richard Gem's reconstruction of the crypt, in *B.A.A. Conference Transactions 1984* (1990).

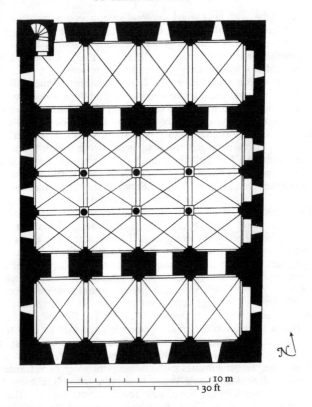

St Mary-le-Bow. Plan of the crypt

the NW corner may have led to the upper level. It probably also served a tower on the N which collapsed in 1271, when damage to property here is recorded. On the newel behind, two star-shaped GRAFFITI in C11 style. Two PIER BASES of early C13 pattern, found in 1955 and displayed in the vestibule, are the only evidence for a rebuilding of that date. Their form suggests the use of Purbeck shafting, unusual in a parish church.

The church itself has an almost square nave of three wide arches on piers with attached Corinthian demi-columns. The ghost of a cross-axis appears in the greater width of the central bay, in line with a long-blocked S doorway. The *Parentalia* identifies this arrangement of bays and columns as derived from the Basilica of Maxentius in Rome. More demi-columns support dosserets and an ornamental feature over the E window. The piers carry the transverse arches of an elliptical tunnel-vault, pierced by segment-headed clerestory windows. The narrow aisles have transverse tunnel-vaults. Keystones are carved with the heads of those involved with King's restorations.

The new FURNISHINGS, designed by *King*, are mostly of oak, some explicitly Neo-Georgian, others plainer but still traditionally

detailed. Two PULPITS; BISHOP'S THRONE behind the altar, with
REREDOS made by *Faithcraft Studios* (CRUCIFIX on it by *Simon
Robinson*, 1994); SACRAMENT HOUSE in the S aisle; ORGAN CASE
at the W end, made by *Dove Bros.* – Hanging ROOD designed by
John Hayward, carved by *Otto Irsara* of Oberammergau. – Good
STAINED GLASS also by *Hayward*, 1964, but with colours and forms   136
too hot and strong for the gilt and pastel gentilities around it. The
NE window shows the bombed City churches. – Wrought-iron aisle
SCREENS made by *Grundy Arnatt*. – RELIEF of St George and the
Dragon by *Ragnhild Butenschøn*, 1966, N chapel. – BUST of Admiral
Philip by *C. L. Hartwell*, 1932, formerly on St Mildred Bread Street.
– SCULPTURE, Virgin and Child by *Karin Jonzen*, 1969, vestibule. –
At the entrance to the S crypt, etched glass SCREEN by *Hayward*, 1960.

ST MARY-AT-HILL

First mentioned in the late C12. The town house of the abbots of
Waltham adjoined it. The present church is a mixture of periods
outside and in, preserving the plan and much of the fabric of *Wren*'s
rebuilding of 1670–4 (*Joshua Marshall*, mason; *Thomas Lock*,
carpenter; *John Grove*, plasterer). Wren reused the medieval W end
(in turn rebuilt 1787–8 by *George Gwilt Sen.*) and the N and S walls,
which he heightened. In 1694–5 *Wren* or his office had added a
lantern to the previous W tower. His E end, facing the street called
St Mary-at-Hill, has a mullioned and transomed Venetian window
(blocked 1767) and an open broken pediment. In it a semicircular
window, made during alterations by *James Savage*, 1826–7, and
blocked in 1848. Carved festoons above the side windows were
chiselled off before the 1830s. Another festoon probably stretched
below the central window. The fabric of Wren's N wall, facing the little paved churchyard, was revealed to be substantially medieval by
investigations in 1984 and again in 1990–1, following a serious fire in
1988. Rebuilding of the aisles is recorded *c.* 1487–1504, which tallies
with the N wall's ashlared Kentish rag (partly exposed) and traces
there of segmental-arched pointed windows, retained and modified
by Wren. *Savage* put in the present iron-framed round-headed
windows in 1826–7. *Gwilt*'s W tower and flanking bays to Lovat Lane
are of plain yellow brick (bricklayer *John Harrison*, mason *Thomas
Piper*). Domestic-looking fanlights to the doors; crenellated parapet.
The S wall may be inspected from the narrow Church Passage
(called Priest's Alley in the C15). Beneath the rendering this is also
chiefly medieval. It also had Perp windows until 1826–7. Densely
built-up surroundings prevent these disparate parts from being
easily visible together, so that St Mary presents a completely
different character whether approached from the W or E.

The plan is one of the most interesting among remaining Wren
churches. It derives directly or indirectly from the Byzantine
quincunx plan, i.e. it possesses a square domed centre resting on
four free-standing columns. The plan may have been suggested by
the form of the old church, which had transepts formed within the
space of the aisles. Cross-arms of even (or nearly even) length and
lower flat-ceilinged sub-centres in the four corners (cf. St Anne and

St Agnes, and St Martin Ludgate). Until alteration in the 1820s the cross-axis served doorways on the N and S, traces of which are hidden by the wainscot. The columns are a curious variant of the Corinthian order, described by Hatton (1708) as 'the workman's own invention', but in fact taken from Serlio (PJ). Vaults and ceilings were renewed in 1826–7 by *Savage*. His also are the pilasters on the N and S walls. The 1820s plasterwork juxtaposes delicate repetitive patterns with passages in a fleshier Neo-Wren style (e.g. the pendentives). The shallow dome is coffered. Its C17 plasterwork was plain, the lantern very much larger. *Savage* returned in 1848–9 to add the dome's central cupola and the windows piercing the chancel vault. The roof and ceiling, burnt in 1988, have been excellently restored on a new laminated timber structure by *The Conservation Practice*, 1990–2.

Most of the notable WOODWORK remains in store in 1997. Its full restoration is an urgent priority. It is partly late C17 (joiner *William Cleere*), admirably altered and added to by *W. Gibbs Rogers* in 1848–9. His work can hardly be distinguished from that of the C17 joiners, a feat which few would expect from an Early Victorian craftsman. Until the fire of 1988, the ensemble survived intact but for tinkering to enlarge the chancel in 1881. In situ in 1997: *Rogers's* W SCREEN and the lower part of the W GALLERY right across the W arm and W sub-centres, minus *Rogers's* carving. Probable dates for the gallery are 1692–3 (centre), extended in 1787 to just beyond the columns, in 1849 to the N and S walls. – STAIRCASE up to it from the NW lobby to a DOORCASE bearing the date 1672. – C17 COMMUNION TABLE, smaller than usual. – Two SANCTUARY CHAIRS given 1845, C17 style and incorporating C17 work according to the RCHME. – FONT. With reeded octagonal bowl. – STAINED GLASS. Only narrow decorative borders survive from *Willement's* scheme of *c.* 1850. The rest was removed in 1967–9 during redecoration by *Seely & Paget*. – CANDELABRA. Six modern pieces in C17 style. – MONUMENTS. John Harvey †1700, cartouche signed *William Kidwell*. – Thomas Davall and his wife Anna †1700. Big, with urns and arms. Attributed to *Francis Bird* (GF). – Henrietta Vickars †1713, draped cartouche with cherubs' heads. – Rev. W.J. Rodber †1843, with bust by *Nixon*. – Some other pieces from St George Botolph Lane (dem.). – In the NW vestibule: Isaac Milner †1713, with columns and weeping cherubs, by *Edward Stanton*. – William Smyth and family †1723–52, urn on obelisk. Attributed to *Sir Robert Taylor* (GF). – Also in the lobby, SCULPTURE. Relief of the General Resurrection, *c.* 1600, damaged (cf. St Andrew Holborn; also St Giles-in-the-Fields, Holborn, Camden). Formerly at the Billingsgate Ward Schools in St Mary-at-Hill; doubtless originally over the churchyard entrance.

In store: REREDOS with Corinthian columns to the raised centre, good carving and nice open finials on top. Grander than that described by Hatton (1708), so probably extended later in the C18. – Fine PULPIT with stairs and tester, perhaps a C17 fitting embellished by *Rogers*, 1849, perhaps wholly new then. He signs the backboard. – Also by *Rogers* the carved LION and UNICORN, and ROYAL ARMS from the W gallery. – ORGAN by *William Hill & Son*, 1849. – COMMUNION RAIL, C17, with twisted balusters. – C17 ROYAL ARMS, from St George Botolph Lane. – BOX PEWS and CHURCHWAR-

DENS' PEWS, the only complete set from a Wren church. – Ogee-domed FONT COVER. – Six SWORD RESTS of wrought iron, specially elaborate. Two came from St George. Dated between 1770 and 1854, but most are probably older.

Projecting from the SE corner of the church, a pedimented CLOCK on a rich bracket. S of this corner a carved C17 DOORWAY with pediment, decorated with skull and crossbones made for a former entrance into the N transept, superseded when the W end was rebuilt. It leads beneath a two-storeyed C17 vestry to Church Passage. Adjoining the vestry, *Savage*'s gaunt brick RECTORY of 1834 has clumsily irregular fenestration suggestive of later alterations.

ST MARY SOMERSET
Upper Thames Street

The tower only of *Wren*'s church, in a brave little garden on the N side where the traffic thunders into the tunnel under Peter's Hill. Known from *c.* 1150–70 and named possibly from one Ralph de Sumery. Rebuilt on a smaller, regularized site, 1685–94 (mason *Christopher Kempster*, bricklayer *John Evans*), one of the last group begun after the Fire. The rest of the church, a simple aisleless rectangle with round-headed windows, was demolished in 1869, but an Act of Parliament saved the SW tower, which projected to make a feature on the E corner with the lost Old Fish Street Hill. Segment-headed doorways and alternating circular and round-headed openings above, then eight wildly Baroque pinnacles (restored 1956), flanked with little scrolls and crowned alternately with square fluted vases and panelled obelisks. These taller obelisk-pinnacles stand not at the corners in the Gothic manner, but centrally on each face. Magically varied silhouettes result.

ST MARY WOOLNOTH
Corner of Lombard Street and King William Street

1716–27 by *Nicholas Hawksmoor*, replacing a fire-damaged medieval church partly rebuilt in 1670–5. That work was apparently directed by *Sir Robert Vyner*, not Wren; called 'Modern Gothick' by Hatton in 1708.[*] First recorded 1191; Woolnoth probably commemorates an C11 founder named Wulfnoth. Hawksmoor's was one of the so-called Fifty New Churches, strictly intended to serve new areas of London. *John James* assisted with the drawings, but the results are plainly Hawksmoor's own. Here he created the most original church exterior in the City of London, very different from his big, isolated churches elsewhere – a difference due in part to the demands of a cramped site. At £16,542 it cost more even than St Mary-le-Bow (chief mason *Thomas Dunn*; carpenters *William Seagar*, *John Meard*, *Thomas Denning* and *James Grove*; plasterer *Chrysostom Wilkins*).

[*]*See* David Cast, *J.S.A.H.* 43 (1984).

The W façade has a projecting centre with banded rustication and cylindrical Tuscan columns at the angles also banded with the same rustication – a very ingenious and wholly successful motif. Semicircular steps (added in *Butterfield*'s restoration of 1875–6), up to a round-headed doorway in a rusticated niche. The semicircular window above lights the ringing chamber. The tower rising above this is in plan much broader than it is deep (cf. Hawksmoor's Christ Church, Spitalfields). First a broad base with three completely unmoulded square windows. The principal storey above is treated in three bays with attached Composite columns so as to give the impression of two W towers that have merged. Indeed the top of the façade is split into two square turrets. The effect is of powerful forces firmly held in check. The lower part of the façade has curious affinities with Vanbrugh's Seaton Delaval (Northumbs), begun 1718, i.e. designed at about the same moment as St Mary. Hawksmoor and Vanbrugh had already collaborated for years, at Castle Howard (North Yorks) and Blenheim (Oxfordshire), but in the second decade worked independently from one other. Low doorways flanking the tower are for external access to the galleries, as stipulated by the Fifty Church Commissioners. Good iron RAILINGS of *c.* 1900, extended l. and r. *c.* 1992 when curved screen walls housing entrances to the Underground were removed. Crypt and plinth of the church were used most ingeniously in 1897–1900 as a booking hall for the Underground, requiring the insertion of steel girders beneath floor and walls (engineers *Sir Benjamin Baker, Basil Mott and David Hay*).

78   The N elevation has three very large round-headed frames, heavily rusticated. Inside the frames blank niches framed by columns set diagonally. They carry a straight entablature curving boldly back into the wall – a motif as personal as any in the Italian Baroque or at Baalbek. Blockish sills on big brackets intensify the feeling of great depth. Surprisingly delicate central balustrade above the corbel-cornice, marking the width of the clerestory behind it. The absence of windows insulated the interior from the noise of Lombard Street. The remarkable and quite unexpected difference between this and the fenestrated five-bay S elevation is to be explained by the fact that, before the construction of King William Street, the S wall could be seen only in steep foreshortening, from a narrow and therefore quieter alley. The lower part is now masked by the single-storey former Underground station by *Sidney R. J. Smith*, 1897–8. This has a Hawksmoorish rusticated centrepiece, let down by mediocre flanking figures in low relief. Through the arch, l., one of Hawksmoor's bays may be inspected to full height: rusticated lowest aperture like those on the N, then a tall round-headed recess with a blind rusticated opening below a round-headed window high up (in this bay only also blind). Also hidden from the outside is Hawksmoor's little low SE VESTRY with its Venetian window.

The interior (altered by *Butterfield*) is much more monumental than the exterior would make one expect: completely centralized, with a square high space carried by four groups of three giant Corinthian angle columns. Above the straight entablature the clerestory has big semicircular windows. Kerry Downes notes its derivation from an earlier design by Hawksmoor, based on the Egyptian Hall as described by Vitruvius, with evenly spaced columns and rectangular clerestory lights. Square ambulatory, formerly with galleries reached by doors in the w angles. Redecorated in sober white and cream, 1996.

The WOODWORK is as original as its setting, though not necessarily to Hawksmoor's designs. GALLERY FRONTS, set back against the walls by *Butterfield*, with big openwork brackets, on odd outward-tapering PIERS (actually the former square columns cut in half). Made by *John Meard*, carved by *Thomas Darby* and *Gervase Smith*. – The W ORGAN GALLERY survives. ORGAN CASE dated 1681, instrument attributed to *Father Smith*, adapted 1727 by *Gerard Smith*. Second organ in the N aisle by *Hill*, 1913. – BALDACCHINO with beefy twisted columns and a richly ornamented canopy, much grander than the compositions in relief of reredoses in Wren's churches. Made by *Meard*, carved by *Gabriel Appleby*. Butterfield's raising of the chancel has jammed it up into Hawksmoor's elliptical chancel arch. – Polychromatic PAVING by *Butterfield*, of graduated richness from plainish central aisle to coloured marble chancel. – COMMUNION TABLE with marble top, 1720s. – PULPIT of mightily bulging shape, made by *Darby* and *Smith* and inlaid by *Appleby*. The TESTER, on tall square columns, echoes the shape of Hawksmoor's ceiling. – LECTERN, PEWS and STALLS with reused woodwork. – COMMUNION RAILS of wrought iron (*John Robins*, smith). – ROYAL ARMS of 1968. – HELM, GAUNTLETS, etc., of Sir Martin Bowes, *c.* 1550, in a case by the altar. – MONUMENT. W. A. Gunn †1806, in the gallery. Woman seated by an urn.

ST MICHAEL CORNHILL

A lively mixture: classical body of 1669–72, Gothic tower of 1715–22, and porch and other alterations of 1857–60 and later. After the Fire, the church except for the tower was rebuilt on parochial initiative. The rector consulted 'skilful workmen' in 1669, and a model or design was shown at the vestry in that year (*Wren Soc.* XIX). So there is no reason to suppose Wren's office was responsible for the design. The craftsmen were *Nicholas Young*, mason; *Anthony Tanner*, bricklayer; *Thomas Gammon* and one *Miller*, carpenters; *William Cleere*, joiner; *John Grove*, plasterer. The speedy completion suggests the reuse of much medieval work. In 1715–22, the old tower of 1421 was finally taken down and rebuilt in the Gothic style with big angle turrets and pinnacles. A lost drawing of tower and spire before 1421, preserved in a late C16 copy, shows octagonal buttresses suspiciously like those of the present tower: did its lower stages survive to influence the form of the C18 work?* There were two phases of work. The first, to 1717, reached the shallow machicolated cornice. Designer probably *William Dickinson*, who was in charge of winding down Wren's City Church Office; mason *Samuel Fulkes*. The much richer bell-stage and tall pinnacles above were built in 1718–22 by *Hawksmoor* for the Commissioners for the Fifty New Churches. They have panelled buttresses and masks alternately young and old (mason *Edward Strong Jun.*, carver *Joseph Wade*). The

---

*For what may be earlier designs by *Hawksmoor* for a new tower, *see* Paul Jeffery, *Architectural History* 36 (1993).

pinnacles echo the forms of the C15 spire. The break in building was because the City Church money ran out, and a new Act was needed to divert funds from the New Churches' coffers.

Then in 1857–60 St Michael became the first City church to be thoroughly remodelled to High Victorian taste, at the hands of *Sir George Gilbert Scott* (with the parish architects *W.A. Mason,* then *Herbert Williams*). According to his *Recollections* (1879), Scott 'attempted by the use of a sort of early Basilican style, to give a tone to the existing classic architecture'. But the elaborate porch to Cornhill is Gothic, taking its cue from the tower, though in a rich and defiantly inharmonious Continental manner. Tympanum sculpture by *J. Birnie Philip*, Michael Disputing with Satan about the Body of Moses. The style recalls such medieval Italian artists as the Pisani or Lorenzo Maitani. WAR MEMORIAL by the door: small bronze group by *Richard Goulden*, 1920. St Michael drives away War. Scott added Lombardic tracery and ornate surrounds to the windows, best seen from the former churchyard to the s with its two trees. The round-headed aisle windows are Scott's restoration of the C17 design; they had been made circular by *George Wyatt*, 1790. Also Lombardic is Scott's little vaulted cloister between the churchyard and St Michael's Alley, where it is dated 1868. The E side of the churchyard is made by the tall RECTORY and VESTRY of 1913–14 by *Charles Reilly Sen.*, crudely done in brick.

The entrance is from Cornhill. The C17 interior is simple, with aisles of four bays and slightly projecting chancel, and groined vaults on tall Tuscan columns carrying arches. Egg-and-dart carving to the capitals. The N aisle is windowless. In the aisle vaults circular skylights, of uncertain date. *Scott's* transformation remains immediately obvious despite well-meaning post-war attempts to tone it down. 'The great ugly stable-like circles of the clerestory become roses under his plastic hand', wrote the *Ecclesiologist*. These survive only in the tower bay, the rest having been made plain *c.* 1952. Angel corbels below the cross-ribs carved in timber by *Birnie Philip*, with other stone-carving. Scott's polychrome wall decoration was replaced in 1960 by genteel blue, gold and white.

FURNISHINGS. Scott made a clean sweep of these. His replacements are of exceptional interest and quality. – REREDOS by *Scott,* Italianate, of Derbyshire alabaster with Cosmati-type marble inlay. It incorporates C17 PAINTINGS of Moses and Aaron by *Streeter*.* – COMMUNION TABLE. Late C17. – COMMUNION RAILS from Scott's campaign, with fine sinuous wrought-iron foliage. – Fine PULPIT, on a stocky marble column, and eagle LECTERN, carved by *W. Gibbs Rogers*, 1859. – PEWS also by *Rogers*, 1859–60, loosely medievalizing, with highly individual carvings (e.g., SW, a scapegoat after Holman Hunt's painting of 1856). – FONT. Octagonal gadrooned bowl of 1672 on a stem of 1860. – ORGAN. Much rebuilt; on it four cherubs' heads from the case of the *Renatus Harris* organ of 1683–4. – SWORD REST. C18. – SCULPTURE. Large wooden 80 figure of a pelican and its brood (W end). Ferocious-looking, like a pterodactyl. Carved by *Joseph Glazeley* for the former altarpiece, 1775. – Bronze head of Christ by *J.-B. Clésinger*, 1868, a salon piece

*The C17 reredos and communion rails survive at St Lawrence, Great Waldingfield, Suffolk (K.E. Campbell, *London Topographical Record* 27 (1995)).

(s aisle). – STAINED GLASS. An important early scheme designed for Scott by *Clayton & Bell*, 1858, and probably made by *Heaton & Butler*. The excellence of the ensemble in design and colouring may still be seen in the big E oculus (Christ in Glory). The s aisle   106 windows (Life of Christ) were cruelly deprived of their decorative backgrounds in 1952. The w window (Crucifixion) is part of the same scheme. – DECORATION. Stencilling in the surround of the E window is all that remains of Scott's decorative scheme, executed by *George Trollope & Son*. Here also four roundels with sculpted heads of Evangelists.

MONUMENTS. A good selection of mostly medium-sized pieces: John Vernon †1615 (remade after the Great Fire), demi-figure elegantly gesticulating. Attributed to *William Woodman Sen.* (GF). – Several substantial late C17 tablets, including: Sir William Cowper †1664 and wife †1676; Sir Edward Cowper †1685 (large and unimaginative, with twisted columns); John Huitson †1689. Attributed respectively to *Jasper Latham, Thomas Cartwright Sen.,* and *Edward Pierce* (GF). – Platt monument, 1802, with cherub, by *Richard Westmacott Sen.* – Mrs Asperne †1806, concave drapery with cherubs' heads: of *Coade* stone.

The vestry has reset PANELLING from its late C17 predecessor. Fine carved OVERMANTEL here, the delicate swags etc. suggesting a date c. 1700.

ST MICHAEL PATERNOSTER ROYAL
College Street

First mentioned c. 1100. Named from the rosary (paternoster) makers, who worked nearby, and from La Reole, a tenement known from the mid C13, named after a town in Gascony and popular with merchants from that province. Dick Whittington, whose house was next door, rebuilt the church in 1409 and in his will founded a college attached to it, in College Hill (q.v.). The present church by *Wren*, 1685–94 (*Edward Strong Sen.*, mason; *William Cleere*, joiner; *Thomas Denning*, carpenter; *Henry Doogood*, plasterer). In plan a plain oblong with SW tower, the W front slightly out of true. This and the S front are stone-faced and balustraded, with arched windows with winged cherub's-head keystones. The S entrance is through a segment-headed doorway adjoining the tower. N and E fronts partly of brick, the E vestry a post-war replacement of a C17 structure. Until the war the raised centre of the parapet above it had a triangular pediment.

The tower is plain but crisply finished, with matching arched windows and a pierced parapet. In 1713–17 the beautiful steeple was added (mason *Edward Strong Jun.*, carpenter *Richard Jennings*), one of the group of three also comprising St Stephen Walbrook and St James Garlickhithe, designed possibly as early as c. 1700, perhaps by *Hawksmoor* (see Introduction p. 82). It is as light and graceful as its fellows. First a recessed open octagon with eight columns set in front of the angles, each with its own little projecting piece of entablature surmounted with a square urn, then a smaller open octagonal stage with urns, and a little circular solid stage on top. Blast damage in 1944 imperilled the church, and many furnishings were lost, but in

1966–8 it became the final City church to be restored, by *Elidir Davies*, for the Missions to Seamen. (Earlier restorations by *James Elmes*, 1820, a thorough job by *Butterfield*, 1866, and by *Ewan Christian*, 1894.)

Inside, the Mission's offices occupy the tower space, the former W vestibule and the first W bay, truncating the reconstructed church interior. This makes a spare and cool setting for the surviving fittings and the new stained glass. The new ceiling is shorter by one bay but follows Wren's simple coved pattern. – Original REREDOS, tripartite with four engaged Corinthian columns and some good carving. Two flaming urns above, the pediment removed probably in 1820. – Flanking stone SCULPTURES of Moses and Aaron, from All Hallows the Great (dem. 1894). They have a fine Baroque swagger, far above the quality of the average (and more common) painted figures. Aaron formerly held a censer, but his hands were lost in the Blitz and have been restored in a gesture of blessing. Moses formerly held a rod pointing to the Decalogue. Was the use of sculpture at All Hallows inspired by that at James II's short-lived Whitehall Chapel (1686)? – PULPIT, original, of the usual type and with good carving. Shallow TESTER, made up of the upper part of the cornice only. – Chunky FONT given 1865, with coloured marble columns and inserts in the style of *Butterfield*, and probably designed by him. C17 COVER of two stages, big but plain. – ORGAN CASE. Post-war replica of *Jordan*'s case from All Hallows the Great, 1749, incorporating some fragments from it. Instrument by *N. Mander*. On the organ gallery, good ROYAL ARMS of William III, original. – COMMUNION RAILS with some reused carved work. – LECTERN. Of wood, also incorporating carved work. The attached figure of Charity trampling Avarice, 1992, replaces a C17 piece from the W gallery of All Hallows the Great, refixed here but later stolen. – Also from All Hallows the very large brass CHANDELIER, with three diminishing tiers each of twelve arms. – STAINED GLASS. E windows by *John Hayward*, 1968. Big dramatically posed figures with strong diagonals and bold colours. The SW window showing Dick Whittington also by *Hayward*. Other windows are plain with irregularly-patterned leading. – SWORD RESTS. Two, of iron, one very large, both probably C18 but remade. Also a HAT RACK of iron. – MONUMENTS. Jacob Jacobsen †1680, enriched cartouche, from All Hallows. Attributed to *Jasper Latham* (GF). Thomas Coulson †1713, convex with pilasters and pediment. Attributed to *Robert Hartshorne* (GF). – Sir Samuel Pennant †1750, by *Rysbrack*. Tablet with Palladian details, and bust above.

ST NICHOLAS COLE ABBEY
(COLE ABBEY PRESBYTERIAN CHURCH)
Queen Victoria Street

A *Wren* church of 1672–8, conspicuously exposed on the N side, higher up and at a slight angle to the street. Used since 1982 by the Free Church of Scotland. First recorded *c.* 1130; the name is a corruption of Cold Harbour, a shelter for travellers. Wren's craftsmen were *Thomas Wise Sen.*, mason, *Henry Blowes*, carpenter,

William Cleere, joiner, and *John Sherwood* and *Edward Martin*, plasterers. Medieval work has been traced in the S and W walls. The rebuilt church seems to be wider than its predecessor, however, perhaps to accommodate parishioners from St Nicholas Olave, with which the parish was united after the Great Fire (PJ). Reordered 1874, partly restored 1928–31, and burnt out in 1941. Reconstruction was by *Arthur Bailey*, 1961–2. The upper part of the NW tower was rebuilt, the hexagonal leaded spire remade taller than before, but retaining the trumpet shape and delicate iron balcony near the top. On the summit a weathervane of a ship from St Michael Queenhithe (formerly in Upper Thames Street).

The body of the church is a balustraded stone box with quoins. It has Wren's favourite arched windows under straight hoods on brackets. Wren built it with main fronts to Fish Street (the present Distaff Lane), N, and Old Fish Street Hill, E. Three similar but slightly larger windows here. W wall, originally facing a narrow alley, of rubble and brick. The four E windows on the S side were opened up *c.* 1874.

The interior, light and somewhat cold, is a completely straightforward rectangle with a flat, uncoved ceiling and Corinthian pilasters. Wren's swags of plaster over the E windows have been re-created, as have small pendants at the junction of the ceiling beams, first made in 1884. A few original fittings were saved (*Richard Kedge*, joiner). They have been bleached to match new panelling, seating etc. in the Wren style. – FONT COVER. By *Kedge*, very handsome, with foliage carving and openwork scrolls supporting a crown. The FONT is a modern copy, without the black marble stem of the old piece. – PULPIT. Late C17 too, not large, with rectangular panels and the usual festoons, swags and cherubs' heads; without its tester and on a modern base. – COMMUNION RAIL. With twisted balusters; late C17, surviving in part only. – ROYAL ARMS (W gallery). Large, C17, formerly on the reredos. – WOODWORK from the reredos is reset on the S doorcase; other pieces in the W gallery (two gilded cherubs), etc. – SWORD REST of 1747. Wrought iron, frame type. — CHANDELIER. Of brass, with 24 branches in two tiers; mid C18. – ORGAN by *Noel Mander*, 1962. – CARVING. A medieval carved stone head found during restoration is preserved behind panelling by the S door. – STAINED GLASS. E windows by *Keith New*, 1962. Dark and rich in colour and painterly in style, showing the influence of Chagall. The theme is the Extension of the Church. – No monuments, but in the NW vestry shattered ledger-slabs laid crazy-paving-wise. Here also a STATUE of St Nicholas, gilt metal, from the overthrow of the gateway to Queen Victoria Street, made *c.* 1874; its walls, gates and stairs remain there.

ST OLAVE HART STREET

A modest church, and, since the bombing of St Ethelburga in 1993, the smallest of the City's intact medieval churches. St Olave also has most interesting work of the late Commonwealth and the years of Anglican Restoration just before the Great Fire. The church occupies the corner of Hart Street and Seething Lane. Walled churchyard to the S, remarkably secluded and atmospheric, with headstones and a big central lime tree alongside the sw tower. A church is first recorded here in the late C12. The dedication suggests the presence of Scandinavian traders in the area. The present building preserves some fabric in the w end from *c.* 1270, including a crypt. The aisles and tower date from mid-C15 rebuilding, for which money was left by Richard and Robert Cely, skinners. Ragstone walls, with much original masonry visible especially at the e. The aisles run through to the e front, i.e. there is no structurally separate chancel. Restored e window, curvilinear Dec, owing more to mid-C19 taste than fidelity to context. Due either to repairs by *Scott*, 1863, or restoration by *Blomfield*, 1871 (other repairs in 1823 by *J. B. Gardiner*, 1853, and 1891–2 by *E. Christian*). The restored e windows of the aisles are C15 (N), early C16 (S). Aisle and clerestory windows of early C16 type with three pointed lights under a depressed arch. The best exterior view of the rest is from the churchyard. Entrance from Seething Lane is through a renewed GATEWAY typical of its date of 1658: round-arched doorway in a big eared frame, big segmental pediment carved with skulls and bones, and skulls either side, bristling with iron spikes along the top. From a design by Hendrik de Keyser (Roger Bowdler). The clerestory was rebuilt in the restoration by *E. B. Glanfield*, 1951–4, after the church was gutted in 1941. Also his the heavy parapets and the regrettable low stone porch by the tower, with weak Gothic detail. The tower has a sw stair-turret but is otherwise unbuttressed. Brick upper stages of 1732, by *John Widdows*. Each face has a round-arched belfry opening with stone impost and key blocks and a big circular opening above. The octagonal wooden lantern is a larger version of the pre-war one. Attached at the se, a humble gabled brick VESTRY of 1661–2, i.e. contemporary with the gateway, though, lacking a model for imitation, it reverts to more vernacular forms: square w windows, tiny œil-de-bœuf s lights. A plaque on the s aisle wall marks the position of a former doorway to the gallery for the Navy Office in Seething Lane, contemporary with the vestry but removed in 1853.

The usual entrance is from Hart Street. The floor level is well below the street. Interior of three bays, in plan a near square of 54 ft (16½ metres) except that the e wall tapers to the s. Glanfield's restoration successfully retained an atmosphere both intimate and antique, aided by a number of surviving fittings. Of the C13 the w nave wall, behind the organ, and an adjacent section of wall to the N, w of the C15 N aisle. Beneath the nave here a two-bay C13 CRYPT, its w part in line with these walls. It is cross-vaulted, with single-chamfered ribs. A blocked lancet in its w wall shows it was formerly partly above ground. It housed a well, probably pre-dating the church's extension over it from the e.* Aisles of late C13 type, partly renewed 1951–4, with two-centred moulded arches on quatrefoil piers of Purbeck marble. Capitals have been made octagonal in the C15 fashion. The bays are regularly spaced but do not coincide with the line of the e wall, to which the arcades are joined by short spur walls. The N tower arch extends just w of the nave wall, indicating that a further w extension of the nave was intended. This would have given a plan of more orthodox proportions had the N aisle also been so extended. The roof is *Glanfield*'s, a renewal of one said to

---

* John Schofield suggests it may come from a C13 house.

have been of 1632 but more plausibly described by the RCHME as C15. Vestry doorway (SE), C15, with quatrefoils in the spandrels and a well-preserved original DOOR.

OTHER FITTINGS. PULPIT. Hexagonal with carved swags and cherubs' heads, *c.* 1685, from Wren's St Benet Gracechurch (dem.). – COMMUNION RAIL, late C17, with twisted balusters and deep embellished top rail. It rests on crouching lions. – REREDOS by *Glanfield*, of oak. – ORGAN likewise post-war, of oak. By *John Compton Organ Co.* – FONT. Post-war. – SWORD RESTS. Four, of wrought iron, two from All Hallows Staining (dem. 1870). The dates are 1715, 1736, 1741, 1781. – STAINED GLASS. E windows, prettified figures of Christ and Saints by *Arthur Buss* (of *Goddard & Gibbs*), 1954. Aisle windows also by *Buss*. Over the S porch a heraldic window by *John Hayward*, 1970. – MONUMENTS. A rich collection especially of the C16–C17, augmented from All Hallows Staining and St Katharine Coleman (dem. 1926), but depleted by wartime losses. The most notable are original to St Olave. – BRASSES: to Lord Mayor Sir Richard Haddon †1524, with kneeling figures of two wives and five children (S aisle); to Thomas Morley †1566, a palimpsest, the inscription in its Gothic frame worth reading; also several C17 brasses. – Sir John Radclif †1568, fragment of recumbent figure. – Lady Radclif †1585, kneeling figure only, mounted on the chancel wall. – Peter Cappone, Florentine merchant, †1582, with battered kneeling figure in pedimented aedicule. From All Hallows Staining. – Sir James Deane †1608, above the vestry door. A grand tripartite piece with kneeling figures of Sir James and his three wives. Corinthian columns between. At the top, achievements surrounded by strapwork. – Bayninge brothers †1610 and †1616, N of the altar, with kneeling figures at prayer. It swerves round the corner of the impost. Attributed to *Christopher Kingsfield* (GF). – Above, Mrs Pepys †1669, by *John Bushnell*, with good frontal bust in an oval niche, the surround partly destroyed in the war. Margaret Whinney described her expression 'as if admonishing her wayward husband'. She indeed looks towards the former Navy Office gallery, where he sat. – Sir Andrew Riccard †1672, swaggering standing figure in Roman dress, erected by the Levant Company of which he was chairman. Attributed to *Bushnell* (GF). – Elizabeth Gore †1698, with routine bust. – Matthew Humberstone †1694, cartouche with carved heads. – Sir William Ogborne, Master Carpenter to the Board of Ordnance, †1734, cartouche. He was much employed at the Tower. – Memorial tablet to Samuel Pepys designed by *Blomfield*, 1884, with portrait roundel.

VESTRY. A remarkable interior of great charm, of 1661–2. Plaster ceiling with central angel holding book and palm, surrounded by an 36 oval bay-leaf wreath. In the spandrels cherubs' heads. The style is rustic by comparison with Wren's craftsmen's efforts in the next decade. Walls have plain PANELLING with a pilastered fireplace. Above it a grisaille painted OVERMANTEL, restored *c.* 1980. The subject appears to be profane: The Three Graces. It has been attributed to *De Witte*.

In Hart Street adjoining (w) is a substantial gabled RECTORY by *Glanfield*, 1954, vestigially Gothic in Portland ashlar. Carving of St Olave by the Norwegian artist *Carl Schou*.

ST OLAVE JEWRY
Ironmonger Lane

By *Wren*, 1671–9; demolished 1892 apart from the projecting W tower, W wall and part of the NW wall, which were converted into a rectory for St Margaret Lothbury. Excavations in 1985–6 uncovered, in the SW corner, foundations of a small C9–C11 predecessor, of roughly coursed ragstone and reused Roman brick. It had a nave and a W appendage, probably a tower. During removal of human remains in 1888–9, Wren's reuse of later medieval foundations was noted, including in the tower two responds of a C14 E arch and one of a C15 N arch, presumably connected with aisles documented in 1435–65. The tower overlooks a secluded railed garden made from the churchyard, the site until 1666 also of the little St Martin Pomary. Wren's mason was *John Shorthose*.

The tower has a Doric doorcase with segmental pediment, plain parapet, and tall obelisk corner pinnacles. In profile it is gently battered, the only one of Wren's towers so treated. The clock face is dated 1824, but its pedimented stone surround is Wren's. Nice ship weathervane, from St Mildred Poultry (dem.). In 1892 oval windows replaced half-pediments on the flanking W walls, and extra windows were cut in the N and S sides of the tower. The C19 E addition was replaced in turn in 1986–7 by the American architects *Swanke Hayden Connell*. The new brick round-arched walls resemble those of Wren's church, but stop short of Old Jewry. Wren's church had a coffin-shaped plan tapering out and then in towards Old Jewry, partly determined by the line of St Olave's Court on the S. The Old Jewry front was remarkably Palladian, pedimented, with quoins and a Venetian window with columns and full entablature. The obvious influence is Jones's Queen's Chapel, Westminster.

ST PETER UPON CORNHILL

Prominently sited on what is by a few feet the highest ground in the City. By tradition very ancient (Stow records a claim to C2 foundation); but it probably originated in Saxon colonization of the old forum, the courtyard of which may have served as its churchyard. The first definite mention is as late as *c.* 1127. By the mid C15 it had a stone-built school, repaired in brick by the executors of Sir John Crosby (†1475) of Crosby Hall (*see* Great St Helen's). The church was substantially repaired *c.* 1630, and the parish made unsuccessful attempts to patch it up after the Great Fire.

The present structure, however, is of 1677–84, by *Wren*, probably assisted by *Hooke*. A drawing in Hooke's hand for St Clement Danes, Westminster, includes a version of St Peter's tower (AG). The craftsmen were *Joshua Marshall* and *Abraham Storey*, masons; *Thomas Warren*, bricklayer; *William Cleere*, joiner; *Thomas Woodstock*, carpenter; *Edward Freeman* and *Richard Howes*, carvers; *Doogood & Grove*, plasterers. It cost £5,647. The pre-Fire site was truncated by ten feet at the E to widen Gracechurch Street. St Peter is still surrounded by buildings on most sides, like many City churches before the C20, while its proximity to St Michael Cornhill reminds one of the former density of churches within the walls. From Cornhill may be seen only a porch with inset Ionic columns and part of the upper wall, rising at an angle above C19 shops. Windows with sunk carved spandrels appear above. That on the r. is circular with imposts unusually returned round the bottom. The best view of the spire is from the churchyard to the s, which lost its plane trees in 1995. Here the steeple shows most happily: the plain brick tower ends in three close-set round-headed openings, above which a neat leaded dome supports a little lantern and an obelisk spire of copper. Original weathervane in the shape of St Peter's key. Below ground the tower rests on a reused vault, dated to the C14 or C15 (RCHME). The walls of the church are stuccoed, with three round-arched windows. The E view from Gracechurch Street, one of Wren's 'show fronts', is grander: ground floor of five uniform arched windows separated by pilasters, the central three bays slightly broken forward to support the upper floor of one arched and two circular windows, topped by a broken pediment. The upper floor is connected with the wider lower floor by curved pieces in the Italian façade tradition.

The interior (restored 1872 by *J.D. Wyatt*) is of five bays. The nave is tunnel-vaulted, the aisles with transverse tunnel-vaults pierced by cross-arches from pier to wall. The pillars have attached Corinthian pilasters towards the nave, with shorter Doric pilasters rising to the springing of the arcade arches. The pillars are distorted slightly and skilfully in section to hide the irregular plan. Excavations in 1990 confirmed that Wren had reused the medieval pier foundations, probably mid C15. Kerry Downes suggests that Wren's roof was made unusually shallow to reduce the load on these old foundations; and this may also explain the unusual lack of clerestory lighting. With the old WOODWORK (joiners *Thomas Poultney* and *Thomas Athew*) and stained glass this makes the interior darkly atmospheric. REREDOS. Unusually low, to avoid obstructing the windows, with simple Ionic pilasters, not specially ornate. – CHAN-CEL SCREEN right across nave and aisles. Introduced by the rector at the rebuilding, William Beveridge, who was greatly concerned with the sanctity of Communion. One of only two screens provided in Wren's churches; as the earlier of the pair it apparently served as the model for the other, now in St Margaret Lothbury (q.v.). The sections are divided by very slim shafts with pendants between. The centre curves up and is flanked by broad fluted Corinthian pilasters, with a carved lion and unicorn on either side of the central royal arms: an elegant, unacademic composition. Lesser pediments to the aisle entrances. – FONT. Marble, octagonal, with leaves growing up the lower stem; given 1681. Contemporary COVER with a carved dove enclosed in eight brackets with cherubs' heads (cf. St Clement Eastcheap). – PULPIT. Splendid big wooden piece with large tester. – The large W GALLERY and ORGAN CASE (by *Smith*, 1681–2) are also original. ORGAN by *William Hill*, in consultation with the Rev. H.J. Gauntlett, 1840 (rebuilt 1959), incorporating parts from Smith's instrument. – STAIRCASE to the gallery in the tower, of two flights. – DOORS and DOORCASES. Four, at w; of fine workmanship, with Corinthian pilasters and broken pediments. – COMMUNION RAILS with square Doric pillars for balusters, similar to the shafts of the screen. Altered 1872. – COMMUNION TABLE. Top on Doric pillars, of the same style and date as the communion rails. Enlarged

1872. – BREAD SHELVES (W wall). – SANCTUARY CHAIRS, two, late C17. – CHURCHWARDENS' PEWS, backs only, at the far W. – POOR BOX of wood. – Relics of the 1872 restoration include the brass LECTERN, polychromatic TILES, and GAS JETS (W end). Victorian benches were unfortunately removed *c.* 1990. – STAINED GLASS. Coarse E windows by *C. A. Gibbs*, 1872. Obtrusive windows on martial themes in the aisles by *Hugh Easton*, 1951–60. One window by *A. K. Nicholson Studios*, 1950, s aisle. – MONUMENTS. J. and I. Gale †1739 and †1741, big, with cherubs' heads and winged skulls. – Woodmason children, 1782, with cherubs' heads, said to be designed by *Bartolozzi* and carved by *Ryley*. The children had perished in a fire. – Richard Gibbs †1864, with portrait bust probably by *Weekes*. – A few C17–C18 tablets, none special. – Wrought-iron GATE to the churchyard with figure of St Peter, said to be of 1853 but looking C18. Churchyard landscaped 1997.

CHAPEL OF ST PETER AD VINCULA
see TOWER OF LONDON

ST SEPULCHRE
Holborn Viaduct

First mentioned in 1137, when it was given to the Priory of St Bartholomew. The dedication supplanted an earlier one to St Edmund, apparently because the church stood outside the NW City gate, like the Holy Sepulchre in Jerusalem. Grandly rebuilt in the mid C15 by Sir Hugh Popham, Chancellor of Normandy, who added the surviving s porch. The present church is essentially a restoration of 1667–71 of the burnt-out C15 shell. C17 Gothic windows were made round-headed in 1789–90, then mostly made Perp again by *A. Billing*, 1879–80. His also are the s aisle buttresses, but he left the bald C18 parapet alone. C17 SUNDIAL here. The big round-headed main E window also survives, between the restored windows of the aisles. It may be of *c.* 1670 or *c.* 1790. To the C15 belongs the big proud W tower, heavily restored by *W. P. Griffith* in 1873–5. He Gothicized the window tracery and replaced the already large pinnacles (remade 1712–14, probably by *Dickinson*) with others still more oversized. The tower is embraced by the aisles. Popham's three-storey s porch was also refaced by Griffith, without feeling. His is the oriel over the door, where until 1790 there was a statue of Popham in a niche. The wrought-iron GATE looks *c.* 1700. The fine two-bay panelled and cusped lierne-vault survives, as does a ribbed and pointed barrel-vault to the former first-floor priest's chamber.

The roomy, loose interior, largest of the post-Fire City churches, exactly follows the outlines of the large C15 building. Seven bays, with no division between nave and chancel. Groin-vaulted aisles and a flat nave ceiling, on arcades of Doric columns standing on tall octagonal plinths. Tiny figures of angels at the springing of the vaults. No evidence connects this rebuilding with Wren (cf. the prompt, parish-led rebuildings at St Michael Cornhill and St

Dunstan-in-the-East, both also with Doric or Tuscan arcades). The likeliest designer is *Joshua Marshall*, mason to the rebuilding (carpenter *Hodgkins*, plasterer *Blount*). Deeply coffered nave ceiling, made 1834 by one *Clark*, originally pierced by octagonal skylights. Clark also introduced the clumsy dentil cornice of the aisles. The three C15 tower arches may rest on old foundations, since they are not aligned with the outer walls. *Billing* restored the arches and also removed the galleries and pews. Round-headed windows of 1790 survive in the CHAPEL OF ST STEPHEN (now Musicians' Chapel), off the N aisle. Otherwise this contains more C15 traces than any other part of the interior: two niches l. and r. of the E window, a TOMB RECESS in the N wall with lozenge-panelled and cusped coving, and a PISCINA. Two more PISCINAE in S and N aisles (the latter best-preserved, with shelf and two arches). Near the chapel also a rood-loft doorway (N wall).

OTHER FURNISHINGS. FONT. Marble, baluster stem and fluted bowl with cherubs' heads, probably of 1670. Ogee-shaped COVER of the same date. – Second FONT COVER from Christ Church Newgate Street, also ogee-shaped, very grand, with four urns at the base and an angel on top. – Matching PULPIT and LECTERN, by *Pratt* of Bond Street, 1854, in the Wren style and extremely convincing. Since lowered, but still facing one another across the nave, early C19-fashion. – REREDOS. Tripartite with segmental pediment on Corinthian columns. It looks *c.* 1670. Hatton in 1708, however, reported a piece with Ionic entablature and two marble (marbled?) columns. – Late C17 ORGAN CASE, altered, but still magnificent. Five towers of pipes with segmental pediments between and angels on top. Parts of the gallery fronts remain below. The much-rebuilt ORGAN has parts from an instrument of 1675–6 by *Renatus Harris*. Formerly in the w gallery, removed to the N chapel in 1879, to the N aisle in reordering by *Sir Charles Nicholson*, 1932. – CHURCHWARDENS' PEWS, w end, with some C17 woodwork. – COMMUNION RAIL. Wrought iron; early C18. – SWORD REST. Also wrought iron; early C18. – ROYAL ARMS. Of 1714–1800, or else an earlier set repainted. – BENEFACTION BOARDS of *c.* 1700, with carved cherubs' heads (w vestry). – TILES, medieval, from Christ Church (N aisle at W). – STAINED GLASS. N chapel. Two good windows to Melba and John Ireland, by *Brian Thomas*, 1962–5. – Other windows by *A. K. Nicholson* (St Stephen Harding window, N aisle, 1932); *Gerald Smith* (A. K. Nicholson memorial window, 1938; Musicians' window, 1946; E windows, 1949–52); *Francis Skeat* (S aisle, 1968). In the N aisle a window of 1896, from the demolished Cordwainers' Hall. – MONUMENTS. Edward Arris †1676 and wife, with two frontal busts in circular niches. – Amongst the late C17 cartouches, those to Thomas Sawyer and family †1672–93 and Sir Thomas Davies †1679 are notable, the latter attributed to *Jasper Latham* (GF). – John Yates †1807, with urn and weeping figure.

DRINKING FOUNTAIN. Set into the churchyard wall at the SE, the central part of the first fountain erected by the Metropolitan Drinking Fountain Association, 1859. An elaborate Neo-Norman surround was dismantled in 1867, when the old churchyard was truncated for Holborn Viaduct. – By the porch, TOMB of Edward Chandler †1780, with both carved and *Coade* stone ornament.

WATCH-HOUSE. Facing Giltspur Street on the N side of the church. Of stone, bow-fronted, joined to the church by a single-storey vestry with Venetian window. A replica of 1962 by *Seely & Paget* of a structure of 1791, destroyed in the Second World War; according to Dorothy Stroud by *Dance the Younger*. On its wall a BUST of Charles Lamb by *W. Reynolds-Stephens*, 1935, from Christ Church. The watch-house was built to guard the churchyard from bodysnatchers. Good wrought-iron GATES alongside. They look late C18.

ST SEPULCHRE'S SCHOOL (former). Facing Snow Hill Court NW of the church, by a garden made from part of the churchyard, reached through *Griffith*'s splendid Gothic cast-iron railings. Built 1874–5, perhaps also to Griffith's design (contractor *William Pigsley*). Low, stuccoed, only just Gothic.

ST STEPHEN WALBROOK

First mentioned probably *c.* 1096, as part of the founder's gift to Colchester Abbey. It lay first on the W side of the street called Walbrook, but was rebuilt in 1429–39 on the E side. John Harvey gives the C15 architect as *Thomas Mapilton*. This pre-Fire church is recorded as having two lesser chapels and a cloister by the late C15. Its successor is by *Wren*, 1672–80. Masons were *Thomas Strong Sen.* and *Christopher Kempster*; carpenter *John Longland*; plasterers *Doogood & Grove*; plumber *Thomas Aldworth*; and joiner *Roger Davies*. It cost £7,652. Though on a smaller site than before the Fire, it is still amongst Wren's largest churches. It is also the one for which there is strongest documentary evidence of his close involvement: the parish paid him 20 guineas for his 'greate care & extraordinary pains taken in ye contriving ye designe of ye church & assisting in ye rebuilding ye same'. It is the most majestic of his parish churches, and in at least one essential point a try-out for St Paul's, where many of the craftsmen also worked.

The exterior was in Wren's time even more hemmed in than now, with houses built up against the N side of the NW tower and the whole S side. The N side originally faced the Stocks Market (the site now occupied by the Mansion House). Wren at one stage intended to accommodate the market in colonnades attached to the church, but the plan was abandoned. The present exterior with its rough masonry and brickwork hardly hints at the grandiose interior: on the contrary, the outside is of little interest from near by. Simple bracket-cornice to N and E walls, not carried round the other fronts. The central bays rise up through this cornice, originally flanked with carved scrolls, surviving on N and E. The copper-clad dome with its lantern and cupola is visible from some angles. From a distance the church is dominated by a spire added to the tower in 1713–15, which cost a further £1,838 (*Edward Strong Jun.*, mason, *Richard Jennings*, carpenter). Square urns on the tower balustrade date from the same time. The design is related to the contemporary steeples at St James Garlickhithe and St Michael Paternoster Royal, all three perhaps by *Hawksmoor*. Like them the design may date from as early as *c.* 1700 (*see* Introduction p. 82). It is among the most playful City church spires, far recessed behind the balustrade and with a main stage which is square with three columns set ahead of the square at each angle. The entablature is carried forward to follow these little bastions. The same motif is repeated, smaller and without columns, above, and then follows a tiny lantern. The tower seems additional to the building as it was originally conceived, as a glance at the plan immediately shows. Ogilby and Morgan's map (1676) shows the church without it. The lower stages accommodate a vestry. Ashlar facing has replaced much original rough masonry since the war.

The main entrance is s of the tower, up twelve steps inside a lobby. The doorway to the street has above it an oval window and thick garlands. The staircase leads into an exedra or w apse of the nave – the first unexpected motif. From this vantage-point the church appears at first longitudinal and of classical composition, ending, one can see, round the E altar, with just such another bay as that in which one is standing. A number of slender Corinthian columns accompany that procession on the l. and r. They are all of the same height – that is, the church is of the hall-church type. It consists, we can read at once, in this w part, of a nave with oblong groin-vaulted bays, aisles with square flat-ceilinged bays, and narrow outer aisles. But almost at once it becomes clear that the church is in fact not simply longitudinal, but leads to a splendidly dominating dome with a lantern to let in light from above. It is this ambiguity

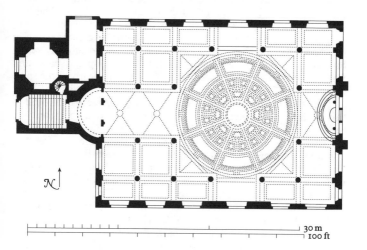

St Stephen Walbrook. Plan

between two interpretations of the space within what is really no more than a perfectly plain parallelogram that connects St Stephen with the international Baroque, in spite of Wren's English insistence on the cool and isolated columns and on classical decoration. The spatial ambiguity does indeed go much further, for, once the dome is reached, one sees that the church can also be understood in quite a different way – as a central building with a dome on eight arches of which four arches form the introduction to cross-arms of equal height and, it seems at the first moment, equal length. The transepts are actually a little shorter than the chancel. They come to an end very soon against the walls of the outer parallelogram.* And the nave consists of course of two bays, not of one. But the interaction of cross and dome – two central motifs – is all the same as potent a spatial effect as the interaction of longitudinal and central. That Wren wanted this double meaning is clear for instance from the way in which the chancel has the same groined vaulting as the nave, but the transepts are barrel-vaulted. The next complication concerns the fact that the dome rises over a square space. That in itself is nothing unusual, and in Italy and France pendentives would have been used as a connecting motif. But Wren wished his dome to stand not on solid piers but on slender columns. So instead of one pier in each corner he has three columns, spaced so as to make each corner clear as a corner. It is in point of fact only at the level of the entablature that the whole ingenuity of all this comes to life. The columns carry a straight entablature, and this traces for us first the length of the nave on the l. and r. (and in the E parts of course of the chancel), then turns and marks the corners of the central span, and then turns again to run to the l. and r. of the transepts against the N and S walls. This motif of the corners of a central space with straight entablatures and flat-ceilinged corner-pieces can – an additional interpretation – also be seen as a grander version of St Martin Ludgate. And now what happens above the entablature? Here again a motif of Baroque ambiguity is used to reach the circular base of the dome. The four arches of nave, chancel and transepts Wren had available without difficulty, but he needed four more of the same height and width in the diagonals, and to obtain these he threw arches diagonally across his corners. So below the arch the result is a triangular space, and Wren covered it with a half-groin-vault. All this is clearly in the spirit of St Paul's.

The other architectural features of the interior seem incidental to this brilliant ensemble. Kerry Downes has noted the similarity of the entablature to a drawing by Webb for the King's Cabinet at Greenwich, 1666. It has the same shallow architrave and frieze of continuous leaves, so Wren is likely to have been borrowing here. On the N and S walls it rests not on pilasters but on flat capitals with free motifs of cherubs, shells, and the arms of the Grocers' Company, who gave money for the rebuilding. The rich plasterwork on the main ribs of the vault, the spandrels, and above all on the coffered dome is especially enjoyable. The E window is arched with a transom. The two mullions are carried up above the transom as a smaller concentric arch. In the other windows there is a large variety of forms, round-headed and segment-headed, semicircular, circular, and around the outer walls repeated ovals.

So (largely) Pevsner described the interior in 1957. War damage to the dome and elsewhere had been made good in 1948–52, by *Gilbert Meadon* of the firm of *Duncan Cameron*, followed by *Godfrey Allen*. The interior has since been transformed again, in a controversial restoration conceived by Lord Palumbo and carried out in 1978–87 by *Robert Potter* of *Brandt Potter & Partners* (engineers *Ove Arup & Partners*). Its centrepiece is an irregularly rounded altar to a design

---

* Remains of a N doorway may be seen on the outer wall, giving a functional justification for the cross-axis. It was blocked as early as 1685.

commissioned by Lord Palumbo for the church from *Henry Moore* and carved from rough Travertine in 1972. In assessing the changes three things should be made clear. Firstly, subsidence caused by the Walbrook beneath had reduced the structure to a parlous state, and it has undoubtedly been saved from collapse by Lord Palumbo's generosity. Secondly, the repairs to the fabric have been carried out with great ingenuity and tact. A reinforced concrete ring has been inserted around the top of the walls, crossing the E window through the transom. Above this, a steel girdle now runs around the clerestory, visible only where it crosses the nave between the first and second W bay. The floor had to be remade in concrete and steel and is now evenly paved in polished buff stone. Thirdly, what was actually swept away was not of the Wren period but largely the result of refurnishings of the late C19 and C20. St Stephen was widely regarded from the beginning as Wren's masterpiece amongst the City churches, and repairs in 1791, 1803–4 (by *James Peacock*) and 1814 were generally respectful, culminating in 1849–50 in a restoration by *John Turner* who was required by the vestry to restore the church to 'the state in which it was left by Sir Christopher Wren'. But the vestry later thought it could go one better, and *Alexander Peebles* remodelled the interior in 1886–7. Apart from that which survives at the W there were no galleries to remove, but the church still had its high pews that rose to the level of the bases of the columns. Objections were raised by the Grocers' Company, patrons of the living and donors of most of the original fittings; but the plan was put to arbitration and, sad to relate, was largely approved by a committee of senior architects under *F. C. Penrose*. So the pews were replaced by movable seating on a new floor of mosaic, although in a compensatory gesture the octagonal pedestals of the columns were made square, in the (possibly mistaken) belief that this was the original form. This mosaic floor and the contemporary glass have now gone, as have *Keith New*'s E windows of 1961, and the new plain glazing at least is more in the spirit of Wren's day.

On the other hand – as visitors who have read this far will already have discovered – there is no doubt that the reordering around the new altar and its stepped plinth goes against the grain of the interior by emphasizing its centralizing tendencies at the expense of its longitudinal ones. The altar also obstructs one's natural desire to walk E along the central aisle and experience the unfolding nuances of Wren's interior. A central altar furthermore does violence to the origin of all Wren's churches as settings for the liturgy of the Restoration church, with its revival of the E position for the altar. And all this remains the case whether or not one admires the altar, its surrounding beechwood SEATING (by *Andrew Varah*), and the cool redecoration of the interior for themselves.

OTHER FURNISHINGS. Plenty of excellent woodwork of the Wren period survives, stained near-black (joiners *Stephen Colledge* and *Thomas Creecher*, carvers *William Newman* and *Jonathan Maine*). – REREDOS. Tripartite with Corinthian columns and rich carving below the cornice and again below the dado. By *Creecher*, assisted by *Newman* and *Maine*. The frieze closely resembles that on the church's own entablature. Between the columns, PAINTINGS of Moses and Aaron, late C17, probably those which *William Davies* was paid for in 1679. Segmental pediment of *c.*1850, carved by *W.*

Gibbs Rogers after a drawing for the original by *Creecher*. (The original pediment had been removed to make way for an altarpiece of the burial of St Stephen by *Benjamin West*, painted in 1776 and not now shown.) – Small COMMUNION TABLE and COMMUNION RAILS. Both of unusual semi-elliptical form, calculated no doubt to suit the domed interior. The table has scrolly brackets for legs and ball feet. The rails have an enriched top and the usual twisted balusters. Both also by *Creecher*, *Newman* and *Maine*. The altar steps and chequered black and white paving also survive in their original form. – W LOBBY with pedimented doorcase on Corinthian three-quarter columns, below a glorious ORGAN GALLERY. ORGAN CASE above by *England*, 1765. Trumpeting angels on the towers, with cherubs between. Instrument of 1888, much rebuilt. – On the gallery good carved ROYAL ARMS, Stuart. – PULPIT and TESTER. By the same team as the reredos. Modelled according to the accounts on that at St Lawrence Jewry (destroyed). Hexagonal, much enriched, with inlaid panels. The staircase has strong twisted balusters of late C17 type, but the work looks later. A square Ionic column supports the tester on which putti dance. Its sides have inverted segmental mouldings. The low ogee-dome is a reinstatement of 1987. – PANELLING on the walls with the Grocers' arms. – The former front of the N chancel STALLS, now by the font. A pretty design with circular openings and cherubs' heads in the spandrels. In the Wren manner, but inscribed as by *Thomas Colley*, 1887. – DOORCASE to the E lobby, pedimented. – FONT of stone, made 1679 by *Thomas Strong*, with cherubs' heads and festoons. Its wooden COVER carved by *Newman*. Octagonal, unusually tall, with carved panels between twisted colonnettes below, little urns, and around the domed top seven small figures of virtues and one C20 one of Christ – SWORD REST of wrought iron, dated 1710, from St Ethelburga. – CHANDELIERS of brass by *Potter*, c. 1985, late C17 style. – PAINTING. Adoration of the Magi, not big, attributed to *Cigoli*, over the NW vestry door. – In the vestibule, a MOSAIC panel of St Stephen, from the floor laid in 1887–8. – MONUMENTS. On the columns flanking the altar, two convex examples: John Lilburne †1678 (S), with cherubs, small figures of man and wife in contemporary dress, and on top others of death and a maiden; Robert Marriott †1689 (N), with twisted columns. Attributed respectively to *Jasper Latham* and *James Hardy* (GF). Many tablets above the wall panelling. – Percival Gilbourne †1694, with bust and urns; attributed to *John Nost* (GF). – Sir Samuel Moyer †1716, with cherubs holding up inscribed drapery, attributed to *William Woodman Sen.* (GF). – Deschamps family, 1776 by *S. Oliver*, a pretty piece. – Rev. and Mrs Wilson, 1784 by *J.F. Moore*, also pretty, more ornate. – George Street †1786, draped urn. – Thomas Stonestreet, founder of the Phoenix Assurance, 1803 by the younger *Bacon*, with a ship's rigging and a hand-operated fire-engine in delicate relief. – George Croly †1860, Italianate, with bust. – John Dunstable, the C15 composer, monument in early Renaissance style with coloured mosaic, by *Powell*, 1904. – Vanbrugh is buried here, but has no monument.

ST VEDAST ALIAS FOSTER
Foster Lane

Probably a post-Conquest foundation, since the dedication – known elsewhere in England only at Tathwell, Lincs. – is to a Frankish saint. The present church is by *Wren* of 1695–1701. It is the second post-Fire church here, replacing one restored on parochial initiative from burnt ruins after 1669 and completed by the Rebuilding Commissioners in 1672. Wren was probably not consulted over this design, which was aisled with a central W tower. His new church has instead a SW tower forming a feature towards Cheapside, and combines in one space the former nave and N aisle leaving a single S aisle (cf. e.g. St Clement Eastcheap). Craftsmen were *Edward Strong Sen.*, mason; *John Longland* and *Philip Rogerson*, carpenters; *John Smallwell*, joiner; *Matthew Roberts*, plasterer. Cleaning of the S wall in 1992–3 revealed that medieval fabric had survived both rebuildings: ten feet of dressed ragstone rubble, with part of the jamb of a blocked doorway, possibly reset. The wall to the E may also be medieval but has lost its facing. Old rubble was also reused in the tower. The W front is oddly gauche, though no more so than, say, Wren's Greenwich Observatory: plain parapet with round-headed windows flanking an excessively large three-light transomed window. A similar window on the E front was made round-headed in the 1850s. Segmental heads to the W doorway and belfry openings.

The main appeal is the spire added 1709–12 at a cost of £2,958, the most Baroque of all the City church steeples – in the sense of the style of Borromini. Above the Doric frieze of the tower, first a stage with closely-grouped diagonal pilasters of free Composite type and concave wall between, then a more recessed stage with convex wall between plain pilasters, and then the panelled obelisk spire with corner scrolls. The lower stages have big rectangular openings in each face. The light and shade effects of this arrangement are delightful. They cannot be described. The mason was *Edward Strong Jun.*, bricklayer *Matthew Fortnam*, carpenter *Richard Jennings*. (Rebuilt in 1837 by *Samuel Angell*, but not altered.) Was Wren the author? *William Dickinson* supervised the work, but there is no parallel for it in his other designs. Paul Jeffery argues rather that it is by *Hawksmoor*, perhaps designed some years earlier. While no documents tie Hawksmoor to the work, its simplified forms, the concave and convex games and the obelisk termination are indeed features one associates with him; furthermore, Wren's usual urns and vases are absent.

The quiet interior was reconstructed in 1953–63 by *S. E. Dykes Bower* after war damage. The coved ceiling and Tuscan S aisle arcade with cherub's-head keystones were re-created, but the aisle is now screened off except at the E. The walls are not parallel, at the E markedly so. FURNISHINGS. None of the original furnishings escaped the war (or *Ewan Christian*'s reordering of 1885–6), and the present set are from different sources, mostly Wren period. New woodwork is dark-stained to match. – FONT, octagonal with square base, by *Thomas Hill*, and FONT COVER with ogee-domed top, by *Cheltenham* and *Page*, both from St Anne and St Agnes. – REREDOS. Modest, with Corinthian pilasters and segmental pediment, smaller than its predecessor. From St Christopher-le-Stocks; recovered from

St Mary Magdalen, Great Bursted, Essex. – COMMUNION RAIL. From the same source. – PULPIT. From All Hallows Bread Street. Richly carved, especially in the elaborate allegories and symbols up the angle-posts, with some modern work. – PEWS. New, and convincingly arranged college-chapel-fashion. PAVING of chequered marble, also new, adding to the collegiate atmosphere. – Excellent big ORGAN CASE by *Harris & Byfield*, 1731, made for St Bartholomew Exchange. Three towers, separated by serpentine flats. Instrument by *N. Mander*, 1955. – LECTERN by *Dykes Bower*. – ROYAL ARMS from St Matthew Friday Street (N wall). – SCULPTURE. Carving of Dove and Glory, with eight cherubs' heads, by *Edward Strong Sen.*, 1697. Formerly over the E window; now on the E tower wall, inside the aisle. – STAINED GLASS. Three E windows illustrating the life of St Vedast, by *Brian Thomas*, 1961. The close-patterned style, reminiscent of the C17, suits the restored Wren interior impeccably. – S aisle E window with panels salvaged from windows fitted by 1857, early work by *Clayton & Bell*. – AUMBRY in S aisle by *Bernard Merry*, 1992. – COMMUNION TABLE in S aisle, reconstructed late C17, from St Matthew Friday Street. – SWORD REST. From St Anne and St Agnes, plain and tall, of iron pole type. Probably of 1680. – MONUMENTS. William Fuller †1659, with scrolls. – William Hall †1680, convex cartouche. Attributed to *Jasper Latham* (GF). – John Davenport †1683, broken pediment on pilasters. – From St Matthew Friday Street: Sir Edward Clark †1703, with twisted columns and very rich emblematic carving; Rev. George Avery Hatch †1837, with bust by *Samuel Nixon*.

The associated buildings to the N make an engaging group. No. 4 Foster Lane is *Dykes Bower*'s RECTORY, completed 1960. Brick with stone dressings in shallow relief under a pediment, a pattern-making design evocative of Continental Neoclassicism. On the first floor, a large and highly-coloured MURAL of Jacob's dream, by *Hans Feibusch*, 1959. A passage between rectory and church leads to a charming paved courtyard with a wall-fountain, faced opposite by the little red brick CHURCH HALL, built 1691 as the school-house of St Leonard Foster Lane. Five cross-windows and modillion cornice, then a tiled roof and cupola with diagonal pilasters added in restoration by *Dykes Bower*. He also re-created the tiny two-storeyed wooden S cloister, with an open loggia below a sashed gallery linking hall and rectory. The loggia extends also along the front of the rectory making an L-shape. Around its walls are displayed part of a ROMAN PAVEMENT found in 1886 on the site of St Matthew Friday Street, a RELIEF of a head by *Epstein*, and two cherubs from a lost monument.

TEMPLE CHURCH

The Temple Church of St Mary is not a parish church; it is like Westminster Abbey a Royal Peculiar. It serves both Middle and Inner Temple. Built in two phases: nave and porch in *c.* 1160–85, chancel in *c.* 1220–40. C19 restorations in 1825–30 by *Sir Robert Smirke*, 1841–3 by *Sydney Smirke* in collaboration with *Decimus Burton*, following the dismissal of *James Savage*, and 1862 by *St Aubyn* (consultant *Sir George Gilbert Scott*). They refaced much of the church in Bath stone, and generally left their marks everywhere. In addition in 1941 the church was severely damaged and had to be thoroughly restored, by *Walter H. Godfrey* in collaboration with *Carden & Godfrey*, 1947–57. All Purbeck marble members were replaced, and the church was completely refaced internally.

The NAVE was consecrated in 1185 by Patriarch Heraclius of Jerusalem, a fact recorded in an inscription destroyed in alterations of 1695; but it was already in some sort of use in 1161. It dates from the Transitional phase between Norman and Gothic. The PORTAL is round-headed and of three orders of columns with intermediate colonnettes, extremely richly decorated, with lozenge, reel, and ribbed leaf motifs: all characteristic late Norman devices. The capitals are partly waterleaf, partly of the trumpet-like scallop variety, partly of other leaf formations. The design is related to that of Dunstable Priory, Beds., and to a sculpted fragment surviving from the Westminster Abbey Infirmary, probably all by one London craftsman. Restoration in 1842 and again by *Caröe* in 1912 renewed much, including the whole innermost order, and comparison with original voussoirs now in the V and A Museum indicates that some minor alterations were made.* The PORCH in front of the portal is rib-vaulted with Gothic detail, and has a pointed archway. In the C12 it apparently led on to a cloister to the s, a fact disguised by the addition of gables to all three sides in 1862 by *St Aubyn*, who removed a C17 block of chambers on top.

The nave itself is circular, as was the Templars' tradition, maintained in homage to the Sepulchre of Christ. Most of the medieval circular churches known in England are connected either with the Templars (here; the first Templars' church, Holborn; etc.) or the

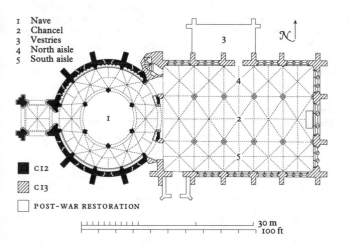

Temple Church. Plan

---

* On the C19 restorations in general *see* J. Mordaunt Crook in *Architectural History*, 1965, and C. M. L. Gardam in *B. A. A. Conference Transactions 1984* (1990). On the portal in particular *see* George Zarnecki in *Essays Presented to Hans Wentzel* (1975).

Hospitallers (e.g. St John Clerkenwell, *see London 4: North*).*
Crenellations on top of the drum of the Temple Church nave
probably re-create an original feature thought appropriate to a
military order. Wholly reliable restored features include the stringcourse and corbel table; on the s side these are *Robert Smirke*'s work,
following an unaltered section of the exterior exposed when he
demolished the Chapel of St Anne (*see* below). The restored
buttresses are massier than the originals. The high ambulatory
parapet is post-war. It re-creates one added in 1695 and removed
in 1862, when *St Aubyn* restored the N side. Original C12 work
may be seen on the exterior only in several of the capitals to the
nook-shafts of the windows and in the small wheel window over the
porch.

12   The circular nave is 59 ft (18 metres) across internally. Six
grouped piers form a broad, rib-vaulted ambulatory with a triforium
above and a clerestory above that, with slim, round-headed
windows. The main piers are of Purbeck marble, the first known
architectural use of this material in London. They consist of two
strong and two slenderer shafts, arranged quatrefoil-wise and with a
big shaft-ring. The (recarved) capitals are mostly waterleaf. Above a
continuous bench around the ambulatory wall runs blank pointed
arcading, with billet motif in the arches and heads in all the
spandrels. Heads renewed by *Robert Smirke*, responds largely by
Savage. The ambulatory windows are slim and round-headed. The
triforium is essentially blind arcading of intersected arches with
Purbeck colonnettes, and open only in two small oblong doors or
windows for each bay of the arcade below. Intersected arches are a
Norman motif, but this motif apart, the fact to be realized about the
Temple Church is that it is one of the earliest Gothically conceived
and executed buildings in England. If one forgets the circular shape
for a moment and thinks of it as a normal design of nave and aisles,
it will at once be seen that it is much more consistently Gothic than
the Cistercian buildings of England of *c.* 1150–75 (except for Roche
Abbey, Yorkshire). At the same time it may well be earlier than the
Canterbury choir of William of Sens (begun 1175). It has excellently
detailed pointed arcade arches, vaulting-shafts starting immediately
on the capitals of the piers, and provision for stone vaulting with
wall-arches or dosserets (the sexpartite wooden vault is a post-war
re-creation of *Smirke*'s design). All this is perfectly up to date from
the French point of view. The replacement of a gallery by a triforium
is indeed so much ahead of its time that it will not fit into any system
of development based on the Île-de-France alone.

     The chancel of this church was no doubt aisleless (as e.g. at Little
Maplestead). Foundations of a straight wall about half-way down
the present chancel were found during the post-war restoration.
Whether that tells in favour of an E end without an apse cannot yet
be said. Equally surprising was the discovery after the war of an
UNDERCROFT below the W half of the present S chancel aisle. It has
a bench along the walls, and short columns on the bench as if for

---

* The others are: Bristol; Dover; Aslackby, Lincs.; Temple Bruerne, Lincs.; Garway,
Herefs. (Templars); St Giles, Hereford; Little Maplestead, Essex (Hospitallers).
Cambridge and Northampton have circular parish churches dedicated to St Sepulchre.
Only the last three mentioned survive above ground, along with a ruinous circular
chapel at Ludlow Castle, Shropshire.

vaulting. The one capital still *in situ* looks *c.* 1170. No Purbeck marble is used. The undercroft has a PISCINA and an AUMBRY, and a staircase led into it from the chancel. If, as usual, the Temple Church was built from the E, then a date *c.* 1170 for an addition of this kind to the chancel is not surprising. But what was it used for? Another CRYPT, from the former Chapel of St Anne, lies SE of the round nave. This is early C13 work, with short strong shafts for vaulting. *Smirke* demolished its superstructure in 1826–7.

About 1220 a new enlarged CHANCEL was begun. Henry III 13 attended its consecration in 1240. Though wholly refaced, the exterior is faithful to the C13 except in a few details (e.g. hoodmoulds and stops of the 1820s–40s, lancet openings in the E gables of the 1840s). The low porch was added in 1953. The chancel was designed on the hall principle, on the pattern of the Winchester retrochoir and exactly contemporary with the Salisbury retrochoir, that is with aisles of the same height as the nave. In its proportions, however, it has none of the excessive slimness of Winchester and Salisbury. It is in fact one of the most perfectly and classically proportioned buildings of the C13 in England, airy, yet sturdy, generous in all its spacing, but disciplined and sharply pulled together. The measurements are: height to vault 36 ft 3 in. (11 metres), to pier capitals 20 ft 10½ in. (6⅓ metres). The aisles are narrower than the central vessel. Tall Purbeck piers of the classic French Gothic section (cf. Salisbury, begun 1220): circular core with attached shafts in the main axes. Moulded capitals. Quadripartite rib-vaults with elegantly moulded ribs. The transverse arches are as thin as the ribs. Stiff-leaf bosses in the vaults. Tall lancet windows in stepped groups of three. To the interior they are shafted with detached Purbeck shafts. Only the E windows have in addition headstops, flat dish-like bosses of stiff-leaf foliage, and, in the centre group, two blank elongated quatrefoils above the lower windows. A similar quatrefoil in the middle spandrel of the DOUBLE PISCINA. The two arches here are trefoiled. At the W end of the chancel, in the bays between the nave ambulatory and the chancel aisles, elaborate (renewed) vertical stiff-leaf bands lead up to head corbels. Behind the reredos and along the aisles remains of the blank arcading. A curious feature is the penitential cell, housed in a NW turret with a squint into the chancel.

REREDOS. Made in 1682–3 by *William Rounthwaite* under the supervision of *Wren*, who refitted the interior. *William Emmett* was paid £45 for carving it. Removed by *Smirke* in 1840 and exhibited until 1953 at the Bowes Museum, Barnard Castle, Co. Durham. Centre with Corinthian columns carrying a big segmental pediment. Two Corinthian columns which supported the organ loft of 1680–2, between the chancel and the nave, remain in the Bowes Museum. – FONT. 1842, Norman style. – ORGAN by *Harrison & Harrison*, given 1954. CASE designed by *Emil Godfrey*, 1966, loosely based on the C17 one by *Smith*. In a large chamber built out from the N wall. – Other fittings (PULPIT etc.) in a loosely Neo-Wren style, the seating arranged collegiate-fashion. – STAINED GLASS. The three E triplets in the chancel have glass by *Carl Edwards*, 1957–8, among the best post-war glass in London, intricate and delicate. Historical scenes in roundels of C13 type alternate vertically with heraldic subjects. – In the S aisle windows fragments from *Willement*'s E window of 1842.

Willement also decorated the vault with polychromatic roundels and foliate scrolls: an important and influential scheme, based according to the artist's plausible claim on traces of the original decoration (TS). – In the nave, good windows by *Ward & Hughes* in C13 style, 1853 and later (TS). – Some of Willement's excellent encaustic TILES have been relaid in the nave triforium. – BRASS of Edward Littleton, 1664, with vainglorious display of arms.

MONUMENTS. Of the famous series of C13 Purbeck marble
20 effigies of knights only one survived the war intact, the so-called Robert de Ros (†1227). The others were seriously damaged, but have been restored and re-dedicated. All had been heavily restored already, notably in the early 1840s by *Edward Richardson,* whose efforts were much criticized. They include William Marshall Earl of Pembroke †1219, his sons William (†1231) and Gilbert (†1241), and Geoffrey de Mandeville †1144. The others are unidentified. They represent not Templars proper but the order's most illustrious supporters. – s aisle of chancel: effigy of a bishop (Sylvester of Carlisle †1255?), also of Purbeck marble. Well carved, typically mid-C13 drapery, blessing hand, in the other the crook with stiff-leaf decoration, head within a gable on projecting brackets. Two small figures of angels in the spandrels. – Between chancel and nave: Edmund Plowden †1584, Treasurer of the Middle Temple, recumbent effigy below thin coffered arch; very small obelisks l. and r.; against the back wall big strapwork cartouche. – Richard Martin †1615, Recorder of London. He kneels before a desk holding an open book, also below a coffered arch. – Mrs Esdaile attributed it to *William Cure II.* – Minor late C17–early C18 monuments: Sir John Williams †1669, attributed to *William Stanton* (GF); George Wylde †1679, signed *William Stanton;* Sir John Witham †1689, signed by *Thomas Cartwright Sen.* (– In the staircase to the triforium, an early C19 BUST.)

In the raised CHURCHYARD, N, the mouldering monument of John Hiccocks †1726, with reclining figure in contemporary dress. Also the plain stone coffin lid of Oliver Goldsmith †1774. Nearer the Church several eroded medieval TOMB-SLABS.

ST MARY MOORFIELDS (R.C.)
Eldon Street

1899–1903 by *George Sherrin.* Portland-faced façade, so much like street architecture that it is easily overlooked amongst its commercial neighbours (Sherrin also did Eldon House next door). Arched portal in a kind of free Flemish style of *c.* 1600, with sculpted Virgin and Child by *Daymond & Son* above and in character. The upper storeys house the presbytery. Steps down to the interior, aligned N–S. The simple nave is dimly lit from lunettes pierced through the barrel-vault. Four bays, with marble columns to a ritual s aisle and pilasters around the other walls. Details are really Quattrocento (carving of panelling and fittings by *Daymond*). Six columns around the apse come from the church's Grecian predecessor in Moorfields (hence the present name). Demolished in 1900, it was for much of the C19 the grandest Roman Catholic church in London: 1817–20

by *John Newman*, the E end designed by *G. B. Comelli* with columns framing a spectacular panoramic fresco of the Crucifixion by *A. M. Aglio*. A smaller version remained in the present church until 1964.*
– HIGH ALTAR by *Comelli*. – FONT. *c.* 1820. – PAINTINGS. Uncompleted figure frieze by *G. A. Pownall*, 1925–6.

CITY TEMPLE (CONGREGATIONAL)
Holborn Viaduct

Little more than the street front survives from the building of 1873–4. By *Lockwood & Mawson*, best known for Bradford Town Hall and other Yorkshire buildings. Of Bath stone, the centre recessed behind a two-storeyed portico, the bay to the r. continued upwards as a square tower topped by an enriched stone lantern with a cupola. (No answering tower was ever intended to the l.) The juxtaposition of portico and tower evokes St Paul's as if in challenge, and the paired columns of the turret also derive from Wren. But the eclectic admixture of motifs of the Venetian Renaissance etc. strikes the true High Victorian note, reminiscent of the grand civic Neo-Renaissance of the North rather than the Anglocentric 'Wrenaissance' of the next generation.

The Temple was built at the great cost of £35,000 for its charismatic minister Joseph Parker, who was determined not to forsake the increasingly depopulated City. The congregation traces its origins back to 1640. Its previous (but not original) home was in Poultry. On completion, it was second in size only to Spurgeon's Tabernacle in Southwark amongst the Nonconformist chapels of London. Schoolrooms, offices and the minister's house were in a large basement, reached from Shoe Lane: an example of the later C19 trend towards multi-functional Nonconformist buildings. But after bombing in 1941 all was rebuilt differently inside and out by *Lord Mottistone* of *Seely & Paget*, 1955–8. The result is a curious hybrid: the body of the church has a concrete frame, its verticals exposed and copper-clad, with stone panels between. The end bays of the old building are retained, like book ends. The cupola was given a more Wren-like profile and a squat attic was added to the far l. bay.

Inside, the vast principal hall has a deep gallery as in a theatre or cinema. The style teeters uneasily between traditional and 'contemporary', with strange Wedgwood-blue decorative bands on the walls and around the apse etiolated columns of cedar, framing a round window by *Hugh Easton*. The C19 interior was clerestoried and galleried all round, with a colossal central pulpit of inlaid marble. Instead of a clerestory, a floor of offices now sits above the auditorium. The new lower hall is reached from Shoe Lane. Alterations in 1971 by *Seely & Paget Partnership* created new offices etc. from part of the main hall. In the vestibule BUSTS of Parker by *C. B. Birch*, 1883, and of the Rev. Weatherhead († 1960) by *K. Wojnarowski*.

---

* *See* Ralph Hyde in *Country Life*, 182, 1988.

DUTCH CHURCH
Austin Friars

The church of the Austin Friars was founded in 1253 by Henry III's Constable Humphrey de Bohun and rebuilt after 1354. At the Dissolution only its long, lean and spacious preaching nave was kept, given in 1550 to the Dutch Protestants. It was heavily restored in 1863–5 by *E. I'Anson* and *William Lightly* after fire damage, and destroyed in 1940 by a direct hit. One of its pier bases (four shafts, four hollows) is reset on the plinth of its smaller replacement, by *Arthur Bailey*, 1950–4. Bailey built offices on the E part of the old site (completed 1957). Together they make a pleasantly boxy group in Portland stone.

The church is symmetrically composed to the street, with a tall four-light window between low wings on a low rustic base. The entrance lies l. of this, carrying a thin, elegant lantern with a spirelet. On it a jaunty weathercock by *John Skeaping*. Carving by *Esmond Burton*. The entrance leads into a kind of raised transept, with steps down to a lower hall. The church interior is aisleless with a shallow coffered tunnel-vault and ashlared walls with fluted pilaster-strips. Tall two-light windows to N and S. Organ stair surmounted by a spindly tubular metal frame. – STAINED GLASS. Best in colour and design is *Max Nauta*'s large W window; other windows by *Hugh Easton* (NE), *William Wilson* (N transept), *D. Kok* (S, of *c.* 1962). More glass by Nauta in the lobby. – Large TAPESTRY, Tree of Life, by *Hans van Norden*. – Big brass CHANDELIERS of traditional type.

JEWIN WELSH CHURCH (PRESBYTERIAN)
Fann Street

By *Caröe & Partners*, 1956–61, replacing a bomb-damaged chapel of 1878–9 by *Charles Bell*. The name commemorates the chapel before that, in the old Jewin Crescent on the Barbican site. Solid brick rectangle with square SW tower and pitched copper-clad roof. On the tower a pyramidal copper roof with a big square urn finial. Half-heartedly Gothic W window with triangular head and tracery in diagonal lines. (Interior with the traditional U-shaped gallery and central pulpit before the organ. Pointed concrete arches support the roof. STAINED GLASS by *Carl Edwards* in W window and clerestory.)

SPANISH AND PORTUGUESE SYNAGOGUE
Off Bevis Marks, s side

The oldest surviving English synagogue, still very largely as built in 1699–1701. It succeeded the first synagogue of the Jewish resettlement, in nearby Creechurch Lane (1656, enlarged 1674). Jews were still forbidden from building in a high street, hence the position in a court, facing Heneage Lane on the E; yet by tradition royal favour was shown when Princess Anne (later Queen) gave one of the main beams. Another tradition is that its Quaker builder, the carpenter *Joseph Avis*, returned to the Congregation the difference between the cost and his higher estimate. The design may be his, or may follow a model supplied in 1694 by another carpenter, *Henry Ramsey*. It is an undemonstrative brick rectangle with windows in two tiers, round- or elliptical-headed. Even the plinth is of brick. The nice big lamp on iron brackets over the entrance looks late C18. NE vestry, C19, of no architectural ambition.

Inside, a flat ceiling with small rosettes, and a three-sided gallery 50 on twelve wooden Tuscan columns: that is, like the body of a contemporary established church or a superior Nonconformist chapel. The general arrangements also owe much to the Great Synagogue at Amsterdam (1675). The galleries have lattice fronts. At the corners square piers instead of columns. The FURNISHINGS resemble slightly plainer versions of those of Wren's churches. – Two-storeyed ECHAL or Ark with Corinthian columns, marbled and grained. It houses the Torah scrolls. The design is very similar to a tripartite reredos, but with big Baroque scrolls on the upper stage. On it the Decalogue in Hebrew, painted by one *Cordoueiro*. – Silver SANCTUARY LAMP, given 1876. – RAILS in front with twisted balusters, on the pattern of communion rails, but taller. Similar rails surround the elaborate BIMAH, the platform from which the Torah and Benediction are read. The stairs up to it, with straight balusters, were added *c.* 1730. – Ten hefty brass CANDLESTICKS (for the Ten Commandments), on Bimah and Ark rails. – Dominating the central space, seven gorgeous BRASS CHANDELIERS hung low, representing the seven days of the week. One came from Amsterdam. – BENCHES, open-backed, very domestic-looking, with distinctive flat openwork uprights. They face inwards, according to the Sephardic rite. Hinged seats allow the storage of prayer books and shawls. Some plainer benches from the Creechurch Lane Synagogue. – More domesticity in the PRESIDENT'S CHAIR (*c.*1750) and CIRCUMCISION CHAIR (*c.* 1790, Sheraton style). – Canopied CHOIR STALL, *c.* 1830 (N wall).

Other treasures are kept in the S vestry, which is part of an office development by *Peter Black & Partners*, 1978–81, facing Heneage Lane. Four excellent MANTLES of *c.* 1600, C17, and early C18; C17 and C18 PLATE (Scroll Mounts, Bells, etc.); and a PAINTING of the Tablets of the Law by *Aaron Chavez*, 1675. This came from the Ark at Creechurch Lane, but was rejected for the new Synagogue because its figures of Moses and Aaron contravened the Second Commandment.

PUBLIC BUILDINGS

ALDGATE UNDERGROUND STATION
Aldgate High Street

By *C. W. Clark*, 1925–6, in his white faience style, familiar from other Metropolitan Line stations. Two-storeyed, with central canopied entrance between shops. Within, arched iron roof and arcaded brick retaining walls, from the first station of 1876.

BANK OF ENGLAND
Threadneedle Street

The masterpiece of *Sir John Soane*, 1788–1827, drastically reconstructed and heightened by *Sir Herbert Baker*, 1921–39. Baker's stack of offices rises above Soane's reworked perimeter wall. Soane in his turn had extended and partly rebuilt the premises by *George Sampson*, 1732–4 and later, and *Sir Robert Taylor*, 1765–88. Baker's interiors include recapitulations of Soane's famous top-lit halls, and a reconstruction of Taylor's Court Room. Public access is normally limited to the Museum, made 1986–8, partly as a re-creation of Soane's Bank Stock Office.

THE BANK'S DEVELOPMENT

From Sampson to Cockerell, 1732–1850

The Bank began in 1694 at Mercers' Hall, but moved within months to Grocers' Hall (qq.v.). In 1724 it bought as its own premises the mansion of its first Governor, Sir John Houblon, in Threadneedle Street. *George Sampson's* new building here, 1732–4 (additions 1745–51), marked the arrival in the City of the Palladian style. The front block had Ionic columns on a rusticated ground floor, with two secure, formal courts in line behind it, slightly off-centre. The Seven Years War greatly increased the Bank's business, for which *Sir Robert Taylor* added single-storey wings up to Bartholomew Lane, E (1765–70), and Prince's Street, W (1767–74 and 1780–7). They had matching windowless walls ornamented with niches and paired columns. Taylor thus kept the Bank secure, and concealed the irregular alignments of some interiors. Within, the E block had four aisled top-lit banking halls, arranged around a great domed rotonda derived from the Pantheon. The W block had in the centre the former churchyard of St Christopher-le-Stocks (dem. 1782–4). This was not a Wren church proper: the shell was patched up after the Great Fire, but was largely rebuilt by *Dickinson*, 1711–14. The N side of *Taylor*'s block was formed by the Court Room and Committee Room of 1767–8 (*see* below), the s side by further banking halls.

Soane took over on the eve of the French wars, which again saw business increase enormously (300 clerks employed in 1792, 900 in 1813). His work was threefold: the expansion N to Lothbury, 1795–1807, forming the present irregular quadrilateral; the reconstruction of Taylor's fast-decaying E banking halls on fireproof principles (1792–1823); and the rebuilding of the s wall to match his own to the N (1823–7). The basic elements – blind screen walls, secure internal courts, and top-lit banking halls – were inherited from his predecessors. In every case, however, Soane transfigured them into something sparer and stranger. The screen wall became a sheer, grooved cliff of Portland stone, interrupted by columns and pilasters at the corners and at the entrances (some false). Correspondence was haphazard between the alignments which this screen wall suggested and the true internal arrangement. The exceptions included the great Lothbury Court, N, with steps up to screens of columns flanking a grand entrance derived from the Arch of Constantine: one of several theatrical interludes which also served to manage the numerous axial intersections within.

The banking halls were Soane's most famous contribution. Each had a broad side-lit dome on pendentives resting on clean, spare arches, with groin- or transverse barrel-vaulted side bays with lunettes. The narrow barrel-vaulted aisles were windowless. The basic configuration depended more on his predecessors than is commonly realized. A similar dome had appeared at *Taylor*'s Reduced Annuities Office, begun 1782 and finished by Soane, while its evolution owed much to discussions with Soane's master Dance the Younger, who had used shallow pendentives in his domed Council Chamber at Guildhall, 1777–8 (q.v.).* None but Soane, however, could have refined the formula so scrupulously. He worked out five subtly differing permutations in the reconstruction of Taylor's four banking halls, S E, and the new Consols Office, immediately N (1792–1823). The Bank Museum gives an idea of what they looked like (*see* Interiors below). Soane adopted hollow-pot vaults for light, fireproof construction – their first employment in an English public building – and used repetitive cast ornament and *Coade* stone statuary for economy. Other interiors were lit from the formal courtyards, or from lesser courts formed from left-over pockets of space. Besides the usual functions of a bank, this strange labyrinthine citadel served also as a barracks, banknote printing house, and (until 1838) as a stock exchange. It had no true predecessors, and was to have no imitators. Taylor's remaining banking halls, SW, were rebuilt by *C. R. Cockerell* (1834–5, and again 1848–50). The Chartist panic prompted him in 1848 to make a balustraded firing platform around the parapet.

Reconstruction 1916–42

The First World War entailed another enormous increase of business, and the Court of Directors decided on rebuilding in 1916.

* *See* Sir John Summerson in *Architectural History* 27 (1984).

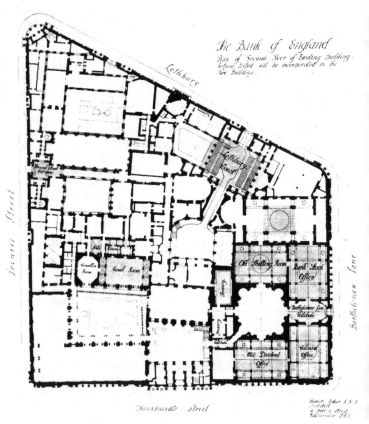

The Bank of England
Plan of Ground Floor of Existing Building.
Portions shaded will be incorporated in the
New Building.

Plan before Baker's reconstruction of the 1920s and 30s.

The space needed was to be found by raising a multi-storey block within the retained perimeter wall, and it was hoped that other interiors could also be salvaged. Initial favourite for the task was the Bank's Surveyor *F. W. Troup*, who made designs in 1920. *Baker* arrived on the scene through his friendship with Cecil Lubbock, Deputy Governor, and by 1922 he had elbowed Troup out. Work began in 1923 and was finished in 1939 (interiors 1942). The engineers, *Oscar Faber*, pioneered the use of welded steel framing (contractor *Holloway Bros.*). Plans to retain the most important interiors proved impracticable, though the new top-lit banking halls of the perimeter are more faithful to Soane's models than is commonly realized. Even so, Pevsner's judgement (1957) still stands, that the rebuilding was the worst individual loss suffered by London's architecture in the C20. Baker did reconstruct Taylor's Court Room and Committee Room, though he could not resist tinkering with them. A further irritant is the self-congratulatory account of the Bank in Baker's autobiography (1942); for the distinction between

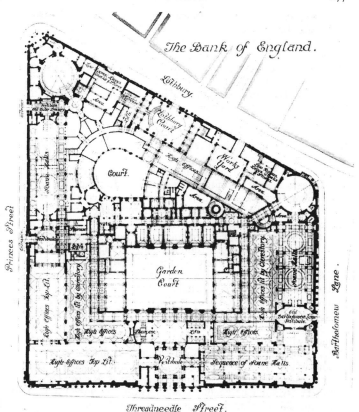

Plan of Baker's proposed reconstruction.
Bank of England

his architectural personality and Soane's is a matter not of taste,
but of the gulf between talented professionalism and imaginative
genius.

EXTERIOR

Baker's great pile dominates most of the more distant views. The
most successful part is the Threadneedle Street front, the only place
where a coherent (if domineering) relationship is achieved with
Soane's perimeter wall. Here a vast portico of coupled columns
comes forward in line with the projecting colonnade of the main
entrance. Against the rusticated base of the portico, above the
lower balustrade, are set six giant figures by *Sir Charles Wheeler*, who
carved the exterior sculpture and designed the bronze doors (Baker's
decorative programme inside and out derives unconvincingly from
the suppositious origins of banking in ancient Greece). Towards
Lothbury two more such pedimented porticoes, less wide, with

more good figures; towards Prince's Street one semicircular central projection. Baker's vocabulary generally appears not as a considered response to particular circumstances, in the way of Soane's restless endeavours, but as a kit of parts to be deployed complacently and regardless of context. The recurrent motif everywhere is a singling out of odd principal windows by rather weak aedicules, or by a favourite Baker form with segmental head and foot. Both are entirely out of sympathy with Soane's style – as is the gruesome hipped pantiled roof.

The PERIMETER WALLS repay closer scrutiny. They differ from Soane's design in two main respects: the replacement of his weird skyline attics and acroteria, mostly by *Cockerell*'s uniform balustrade, and the remodelling of the N wall by *Baker* to suit the new interior. To Soane is due the Corinthian order, with its deeply undercut bases and capitals with the characteristic rosette of the Temple of Vesta at Tivoli, and also the long stretches of immaculately laid Portland stone, with uniform grooved rustication.

The S FRONT, 1823–7, is a regular and grandly formal composition. Paired columns at the rounded corners. Eight columns stand forward in the centre (where Sampson's front was) with Soane's replacement for Taylor's wings on either side. Each of these has six recessed columns between matching three-bay pilastered sections with blind square-headed openings. The narrow bays flanking these openings originally had smaller blind niches, square above oblong, which Baker blocked. Soane's two-storey effect survives within the portico, where the lower openings are round-headed. Above, where Wheeler's figures now stand, Soane had put a full attic storey.

The W FRONT is at 440 ft (135 metres) the longest of the four fronts. The dates are 1823–5, S part, and 1802–5, N part. The join is marked by two recessed columns about two-fifths of the way N. Two matching paired columns appear further N; but the front, which can only be seen obliquely, is not symmetrical. The best view is from close to, where the lines of the rustication stretch ahead almost to vanishing point: walling as implacable in its way as that of Dance's Newgate Gaol (*see* Central Criminal Court).

TIVOLI CORNER, NW, 1804–7, was one of the most celebrated features of Soane's Bank. The columns remain: four set in a quadrant, with four more in pairs breaking forward at each end. Urns on the quadrant were added by *Cockerell* to match their neighbours. Behind the cornice rose an elaborate attic, removed by *Baker* in 1936 when he opened out the space within the columns as a pedestrian passage. Instead there is a flattened copper-roofed rotonda, crowned by *Wheeler*'s gilded statue of Ariel. Tivoli Corner was one of the features Baker had promised to preserve, and his slipperiness was denounced in a pamphlet by Arthur Bolton of the Soane Museum. Yet the passage is also one of Baker's most successful interventions, strikingly top-lit by a simple oculus in the shallowest stone dome.

The N FRONT is Baker's rebuilding of Soane's work of 1792–5, E, and 1802–5, W. The present centrepiece with its pairs of recessed columns reproduces the former entrance to Lothbury Court, E, which Soane duplicated when he added the W part. In the W niche a statue of Soane by *Reid Dick*, 1937.

The E FRONT is of 1795–1805 in its N quarter, of 1823–5 in the rest. The inset columns in the centre are a purely compositional device, for the entrance lies immediately s: a relic of Taylor's shorter front, in which the entrance formed the central feature.

INTERIORS

The only public access is to the MUSEUM from Bartholomew Lane, E, via Baker's domed, double-apsed approximation to Taylor's former entrance vestibule. The main space is a persuasive re-construction of Soane's BANK STOCK OFFICE (1792–3) by *Higgins Gardner*, 1986–8. It uses the shell of one of the aisled halls which Baker paraphrased from those of Soane. The Bank Stock Office is identified by Summerson as the first interior in which Soane's empirical, radically simplified style found mature expression. The central space has the characteristic flattened pendentive-dome and side-lit lantern, with simple iron brackets supporting the cupola. The outer bays have groin-vaults. Grooved pilaster-strips instead of an order, a band of Greek fret instead of a cornice. Inscribed lines and rosettes on other surfaces emphasize their planes and volumes. The yellow-glazed lunettes and the arrangement of desks etc. are based on Gandy's contemporary perspectives. The statue of William III by *Sir Henry Cheere*, 1734, comes from Sampson's Bank.

New display rooms at the N end lead through to *Soane*'s DIAGONAL VESTIBULE (1815), remade here by Baker using the original Ionic corner columns and plaques. Flat fluted pendentive-dome with a central oculus, opening on to a similar oculus slightly above: a miniature example of Soane's quizzically perverse double-skinned effect. To the r., a triangular half-vestibule of matching design shifts the axis to the diagonal. (The original context was further w, at the angled junction of corridors between the Rotonda and Front Courtyard.) Baker's ROTONDA, a plain cylinder with an oversized lantern, opens off the cross-axis of the vestibule. Paired Ionic columns in the lantern. Around the walls, caryatids from the dome of Soane's Consols Office, which Baker had reused in his version of the domes to the s (the second dome, still intact, lights the museum office mezzanine, over the smaller galleries). Busts of the younger Pitt and Charles James Fox, by *Nollekens*, 1808.

Otherwise the best approximation to Soane's BANKING HALLS lies in the E part of the s front. Here Baker reproduced the Old Dividend Office almost exactly, but sabotaged the proportions by adding at either end a version of the domed centre bay of the Old Colonial Office (both originally 1818–23). The central dome has paired caryatids and in the pendentives circular plaster reliefs and caducei (the emblem of Mercury), also reused. Differences from the Bank Stock Office formula include main arches that are round, not segmental, and the transverse barrel-vaulting of the lesser bays, with incised diagonal coffering. The outer domes have little (reused) Ionic columns up in their lanterns. Baker treated the corresponding halls on the w side more freely, with a mannered Soanian dome four times repeated, but based the halls on the N part of the w side on Soane's Old Shutting Room (1795–6), a close variant of the Bank Stock Office.

The sequence of halls is punctuated by Baker's own ENTRANCE HALL, s, and w VESTIBULE, each with monolithic black-marble columns and a very shallow stone dome. Ahead of the Entrance

Hall, a double-height hall with broad gallery, off which rises, l., Baker's favourite set-piece: an open-well STAIRCASE, climbing from three storeys below ground to five (of seven) above it. In the ground-floor circulation spaces fine mosaics after the Roman manner by *Boris Anrep*. The quality of the C20 work is extremely high throughout: fine Hopton Wood stone facing; plasterwork by *Joseph Armitage*; bronze balustrade designed by *Wheeler*. On the third floor, over the galleried hall, is a near-exact version of *Soane*'s Prince's Street vestibule (1804–5). It has heavy Greek Doric columns and barrel-vaulted passages to the square central space, which is spanned by a flat fluted dome on grooved pendentives.

The GARDEN COURT, larger than its predecessor, is a grandiose failure: too short N–S in relation to its width, and too high and hemmed-in altogether. Arcaded loggias cross the ends. In the garden a War Memorial by *Richard Goulden*, 1921. On the N side, singled out by Corinthian columns, are *Taylor*'s Court Room and Committee Room of 1767–8, reconstructed on the first floor on axis with the main entrance. The very large COURT ROOM is managed 82 with triple arcades at each end (cf. Taylor's dining room at Trewithen, Cornwall, 1764). They rest on paired Corinthian columns. Three close-set Venetian windows, their upper panels glazed, with Corinthian columns as mullions. The urns above the mullions are Baker's. The fine sage-green colour scheme is post-war (by *John Fowler*). The ceiling has an octagonal central panel with a sunken roundel and much refined Neoclassical ornament, without the interpolated roundels and rosettes of the Adams' contemporary work. Baker simplified the plasterwork of the walls, but retained the late C19 medallions of monarchs' heads. Three fireplaces, the central one banished by Baker but reinstated by *Sir Albert Richardson*, 1952. W of the Court Room, as at the old Bank, *Taylor*'s COMMITTEE ROOM, a generous elongated octagon also with a Venetian window. Good fireplace with half-columns. The heavy pedimented doorcase is Baker's. In the ANTEROOM, N, a fireplace with exquisite overmantel relief of Apollo and the Muses, by *Sir Richard Westmacott* c. 1790; from the former Queensberry House, Westminster. Ground-floor OFFICES for the Governor and Deputy Governor, immediately below, with excellent fireplaces, cabinets etc. by *Taylor*, reset. In the DEPUTY GOVERNOR'S ROOM a fireplace from Nuthall Temple, Notts (c. 1757, dem. 1929).

Finally *Baker*'s garbled version of Soane's LOTHBURY COURT, N (originally 1798–9), again too high in its proportions. The triumphal entrance arch and flanking screens are the features imitated (reused columns and urns, and between the columns *Thomas Banks*'s circular reliefs of Night and Day). Against the outer wall, above the columns, *Taylor*'s carved figure of Britannia (the 'Old Lady of Threadneedle Street'), c. 1745, from the pedimented range facing the old front courtyard, and *Coade* statues of the Four Continents (1801).

ROMAN REMAINS. Excavations for Baker's building in 1933–4 exposed two late C2 or early C3 ROMAN MOSAIC PAVEMENTS. The larger and finer was relaid at the foot of Baker's staircase. Its central roundel is missing. The other pavement, also much restored, is in the Museum, with other Roman finds. (The centrepiece of a third pavement, found here in 1805, is at the British Museum.) All came from richly decorated town houses on the banks of the Walbrook.

BARBICAN

There is nothing quite like the Barbican Estate in all British architecture. It combines two favourite concepts of radical post-war planning: the traffic-free housing precinct linked by elevated walkways, and the giant multi-functional 'megastructure', to use the jargon of the time. They are expressed in cyclopean reinforced concrete forms, massive far beyond utility (and indeed the flats were never meant to be cheap), all to designs by one single, private practice: *Chamberlin, Powell & Bon*. Such boldness was made possible by the wasteland left N of Gresham Street by the Blitz, which allowed one to walk for over half a mile without passing a single standing structure, and by the City's readiness to finance the costly new housing, schools and buildings for the arts, which did not falter in the quarter-century from conception to completion (1956–81).

The germ of a residential scheme N of the new road called London Wall appeared in the joint LCC–City rebuilding plan of late 1955 (*see* London Wall and Introduction p. 130). The Corporation's concern to stem the depopulation of the City, which had previously issued in *Chamberlin, Powell & Bon*'s Golden Lane Estate immediately N (q.v.), led it meanwhile to commission a scheme from the same architects for the present area, also submitted in 1955. Its dense chequerboard of low blocks and small courtyards was superseded in 1956 by a larger plan for the whole area between the commercial part of London Wall and the Golden Lane Estate. Within this plan the broad outlines of the present vast and powerful 35-acre (14 hectare) development were already visible. Like Golden Lane, it mixed towers and slabs arranged on a grid, excluded traffic, and integrated amenities and services for the residents. A revised plan presented in 1959 was linked with the walkways along London Wall. Population density was 200 per acre, the standard figure for Inner London in the 1943 Plan (*see* Introduction p. 127). Provision was also made for the City of London School for Girls and the Guildhall School of Music, which had outgrown their C19 premises in John Carpenter Street (q.v.). The forms of the architecture were still relatively lightweight at this stage. In 1960 the structural engineers *Ove Arup & Partners* began clearing the site and straightening the railway alignment to Moorgate beneath. Work on the buildings began in 1963. By this date, the present, more monumental system dependent on the raw mass of *in situ* reinforced concrete had been adopted. Elain Harwood suggests that the change of style had its roots in the engineers' adoption of deep beams spanning between wide-spaced cross-walls, which the architects then exploited as a feature beneath the external balconies.

The Completed Development

The changed aesthetic is exemplified by the reworking of the three TOWER BLOCKS, their unmistakable silhouettes prominent in long views. They stand S of the covered-in line of Beech Street, from a rectangle to a more interesting r.-angled triangle plan, each differently aligned. At 412 ft (125½ metres) they were the highest residential buildings in Europe, one of forty-three, two of forty-four storeys above the podium. They have wild and wilful top features and jagged balconies passing between the inner and outer uprights of the external framing. Parapets are electrically heated to prevent the build-up of ice. Three flats per floor, arranged around a triangular lift lobby. Living rooms occupy the outer corners.

The rest of the plan may briefly be described, though its special features are best appreciated from the second-floor podium between and beneath the blocks. Flats are mostly in long terraces of up to eleven storeys, forming large courts or piazzas. With the towers, they contain 2,113 flats, housing a maximum of 6,500 people. Their 140

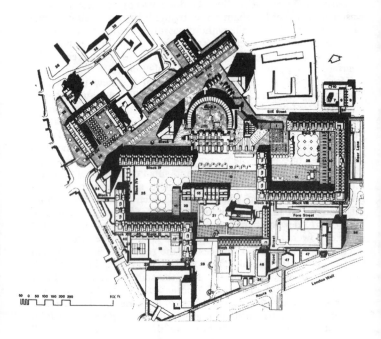

Barbican Estate. Plan

different plans vary greatly in arrangement and size, more so than the usually family-centred public housing of the date. All have pre-fabricated kitchens, with *Garchey* waste disposal systems to separate wet waste from dry. Completion was between 1968 and 1973. Intended for rent, most have been sold since 1981. At the SE they are arranged around and partly over a lake and water garden. On the S side of the main lake is a paved piazza between the Girls' School, W, and the church of St Giles Cripplegate, E (q.v.). An arm of the lake doubles back beneath the school to run S of this piazza, where it lies like a moat in front of a preserved stretch of City wall (*see* London Wall). On the N side of the lake, facing a broad terrace and divided by the cross-slab, lie the Guildhall School, E, and Arts Centre, W. The latter has on its N side a formal crescent of flats, called Frobisher Crescent. At the far NE a public-service block. Space is intensely and often ingeniously used: for example, the N lakeside terrace is made over the boxed-in route of the Underground railway, and the roof of one lower sw block doubles as a playground for the Girls' School. 2,500 parking spaces are provided, mostly below ground level. A dual carriage-way planned in 1959 to run N–S in a concrete box across the middle was fortunately abandoned.

Circulation is on the podium, left open but sheltered by the cantilevered upper storeys of the terraces for much of its length. Rising ground means the N part is a storey higher. The two levels intersect rather confusingly around the Barbican Centre. The surrounding walkways may be followed as far as Goswell Road (N), Guildhall (S), and Moorgate (E). The urban explorer should therefore cast off his or her instinct to cling to ground level as soon as possible. Steps lead down to the lakeside terraces, in which play is made with levels stepping up and down in the fountains and cascades of the lake, all disciplined by the grid plan. Gardens around the lake are reserved for residents, as in Georgian town squares. The exception lies to the sw, accessible from London Wall. Here, the massive forms of the flats are poignantly juxtaposed with the medieval remains of the City wall and the curtain-walled early 1960s buildings.

Now for the details of the ARCHITECTURE. The main material is concrete with dark-grey Penlee granite facing, bush- or pick-hammered, used in tough masculine forms on a mighty scale. Podium blocks are of contrasting load-bearing engineering brick, dull red in colour. Matching tiles pave the podium on top. Its 12 acres are enclosed by massive, deep balconies with rounded lower edges, echoed on a smaller scale in the tower block balconies. Upper flats on the long blocks have straight balconies. Much of the deck is interrupted by the entrance staircases to these blocks, each serving two flats per floor, set between giant cylindrical columns. These columns are exposed to full height where the podium is omitted, at the sw and marching across the lake. Otherwise the dominant motif is the semicircular curve, employed inverted in the sills of the podium windows, and echoed in white-painted canopies to the top flats. These have glazed ends lighting double-height interiors – clear derivations from the post-war work of Le Corbusier, whose all-encompassing planning and architecture of extreme mass are prevailing influences. More rounded forms in the cascade spout and circular islands in the lake, the fountains on its edge, and the various big vents and stair-towers scattered about the podium. The concrete is offset by varnished hardwood window frames, and at Frobisher Crescent by slatted external screens. Blue-green handrails and blue-green and dark-red panelling etc. recall the architects' bold palette at Golden Lane, without compromising the general solemnity.

It must be allowed that none of this is for the faint-hearted. Though the asymmetrical planning and absence of one all-commanding viewpoint recalls the picturesque ambience of some post-war New Towns, that adjective inadequately describes the experience of perambulating these huge spaces. The aesthetic is rather that of the Sublime. It is apparent in the stunning height of the tower blocks seen from below and in the tremendous unbroken length of several lower blocks (Ben Jonson House, NE, measures some 600 ft or 183 metres), no less than in the thrillingly vertiginous crossing of the lake on a gangway slung between the tall columns of the cross-slab. From here one can overlook the rushing water of the cascades as if from a bridge across some mountain gorge.

Man-made Sublime is not everyone's domestic ideal, it is true; but that a Barbican address has remained in demand surely owes as much to this backdrop of grandeur as to its location, well-serviced security and convenience for lovers of culture.

The part N of Beech Street lacks a central 'lung' and is in consequence less satisfactory. It is not helped by the intrusion between the slabs of the N side of *Frank Scarlett*'s MURRAY HOUSE, completed 1958, a stone-faced and curtain-walled office block on Beech Street, begun before the N area was incorporated in the plan. On the S side appear the towers; between them, at an angle, the convex wall of Frobisher Crescent and one of the lower slabs. The lack of alignment is because the N part follows the grid of the Golden Lane Estate instead. SCULPTURE at the NE corner by *Charlotte Mayer*, 1990, a spiral of polished steel rods. Further W, a FOUNTAIN with little bronze dolphins, by *John Ravera*. At the corner of Beech Street and Whitecross Street, at ground level, a tall shaft for an ELECTRICITY SUBSTATION, completed 1969. At the NW corner by Aldersgate Street rises a sixteen-storey tower for the YMCA (completed 1971), more economically designed and closer to municipal Brutalism of the 1960s, with free-standing fire-stairs on the S. It balances the tower of the Golden Lane Estate, NE. A hotel and sports centre intended further N and E were not built. Castellar metaphors creep in here and there around the perimeter, e.g. the mannered gatehouse-like brick staircase block with slit windows on Aldersgate Street, or the low crenellated wall of the private gardens of Andrewes House facing Fore Street, off London Wall.

Public Buildings

These are differently treated from the residential blocks and from each other. First to be completed, in 1966, was MILTON COURT, the free-standing public services block at the NE. A fire station (with prominent practice tower), coroners' court, and the City weights and measures office are housed in a calculatedly awkward design in plain, sheer concrete. Pilotis support two storeys of maisonettes on top. A bridge across Silk Street joins the rest of the complex.

CITY OF LONDON SCHOOL FOR GIRLS, 1962–9. The main block faces the lake on the S. Its distinguishing feature is a series of exterior concrete girders resting on broad red brick piers. A SW wing containing gym, sports ground and prep school passes under a residential block. Within the SW angle, where the main block bridges one arm of the lake's moat-like extension, a self-effacing single-storey addition by *Trevor Dannatt & Partners*, 1990–1.

GUILDHALL SCHOOL OF MUSIC AND DRAMA, opened 1977. The core is a theatre and concert hall, each designed for both teaching and performance. They are screened on two sides by three storeys of small practice studios, projecting over an open colonnade towards the lake. Each studio is separately expressed as a red brick box with angled corner windows. Barrel-vaulted canopies over the library interrupt the roofline, matching those of the surrounding blocks. Generous but plain circulation spaces. In the larger windows, abstract STAINED GLASS frieze by *Celia Frank* (CS).

140　　Finally the BARBICAN CENTRE, 1968–82. The brief was to accommodate the Royal Shakespeare Company, London Symphony

Orchestra, a library and an art gallery, expanded after work began (1971) to squeeze in conference facilities and a lesser studio theatre. The upper parts are expressed towards the lake, slotted in between repeated giant uprights of plain concrete and softened by lush hanging foliage. First on the r. a projecting white-tiled three-storeyed section housing restaurants and cafés, then an inset rounded glazed staircase. The business end beyond has recessed glazing to the foyer, over which cantilevers a concrete balcony, with the library in a white-tiled box on its underside and white-tiled windowless boxes housing the cells of the art gallery above. The theatre is betrayed externally only by its concrete fly-towers, r. High up, a giant polygonal conservatory wraps around it. The theatre's auditorium and the concert hall (the Barbican Hall) are accommodated mostly underground, with offices, facilities for conferences etc. above and around them. The raised terrace of Frobisher Crescent is formed on the hall's roof.

Such ingenious compactness, alas, was not achieved without loss of clarity. The trouble begins at the street approach, at the corner of Silk Street and Whitecross Street, which appears little better than a giant loading-bay: an extreme case of the Barbican's forbidding appearance from outside, in just the wrong place. Inside, the freely flowing spaces of the foyer, though impressive in scale, are notoriously confusing, especially to the first-time visitor. Levels, landings and staircases are multiplied, with no immediately apparent correspondence with the venues they serve, and the floor slopes alarmingly downwards by the stalls of the Barbican Hall. A profusion of bars, desks and kiosks interrupts the space, already crowded by vast square piers. Alterations by *Pentagram*, 1993–5, have improved the signage but multiplied the confusion by their (otherwise welcome) wheelchair bridge across the theatre end. On negotiating this maze, one enters the main interiors with more of a feeling of relief than of a climax.

The BARBICAN HALL is a pleasant space, with seating for 2,000 in three radial tiers, and pale fluted wood panelling breaking out into organ pipes around the stage. The ceiling's great concrete cross-beams are exposed, but warmly coloured seating fabric and directed lighting soften the general effect. Curved wooden balcony fronts added 1994. The THEATRE is more innovative. Audacious oversailing galleries give clear views and minimize the distance of even the uppermost of the 1,200 seats from the thrust stage. Complex access foyers to either side take the place of aisles. The ART GALLERY is on two floors. The main, upper level has small galleries opening off a central passage, better suited to instructive or small-scale displays than grand works of art. The passage overlooks a void open to the noisy foyer far below, mostly filled by a staircase which, like the gallery's grand external approach up steps at the w end, has not found a proper use. A separate lower gallery, made within the curve of Frobisher Crescent, links the ends of the foyer around the space of the hall. Worst-served of the other facilities are the cinema and studio theatre buried in the basement; best-served is a little cinema on the top level, reached by a glazed walkway marvellously threaded along one wall of the conservatory.

WORKS OF ART. Of note in the foyer, a suspended iridescent Perspex SCULPTURE by *Michel Santry*, and two busts: *Roubiliac's*

Shakespeare (1760) and *Epstein*'s Vaughan Williams. By the lake, SCULPTURE of horses' heads by *Enzo Plazzotta*, 1969. More pieces came with *Pentagram*'s renovations: a big suspended gilded figure group by *Matthew Spender* by the entrance from the bridge, and an upswept glazed canopy to the road entrance, designed by *Diane Radford* and *Lindsey Bell* (its gilded Muses by *Bernard Sindall* removed 1997). On the hall's exterior towards the foyer an all-over pointillist MURAL by *Polly Hope*, too soft and pretty for the context.

A Note on the Area before 1945

The main visible relic is the City wall, already mentioned. The name Barbican records a separate, outlying fortification, demolished in 1267 after the Barons' Wars, according to Stow. In his time the area was being built up. In the street formerly called Barbican (the W part of the present Beech Street) lay such large mansions as Thomas Wriothesley's early C16 Garter House. The part of Beech Street E of Golden Lane, made in 1786–8, belongs with *Dance the Younger*'s replanning of the Finsbury and Moorgate areas. Here also was the first Jewish cemetery known in England, mentioned in 1177: hence Jewin Street, with on its N side Jewin Crescent, built in 1805, possibly also by *Dance*, roughly where the present Frobisher Crescent stands. The district filled up later in the C19 with warehouses and factories, a fire-prone mixture: London's largest conflagration since the Great Fire was here (1897), in which four acres of buildings were damaged or destroyed.

BARNARD'S INN
(GRESHAM COLLEGE)
Off Holborn to the s

An improbable and delightful survival from the former Inn of Chancery: the toy-like C15 hall, with little C18 and C19 buildings clustered around it. The Inn is recorded shortly after 1422 as the house of Henry V's Chancellor John Macworth, Dean of Lincoln. By 1435 it was leased by Lionel Barnard, and used by students of law. In 1888 the Inn's trustees bought the freehold, only to sell it on to the Mercers' Company in 1892, for their school (closed 1959). In 1991–2 the site was redeveloped for the Mercers by *Green Lloyd Architects*. Older buildings were restored for the use of Gresham College, and some of *T. & H. Chatfeild Clarke*'s school buildings (1893–4) were reconstructed.

Entrance is through Nos. 20–23 Holborn. Ahead, hemmed in, 18 appears the trim and tiny HALL, probably early C15 (the Inn was called 'new built' in 1439). It measures 37 ft by 22 ft 6 in (roughly 11 metres by 7 metres). One remarkable feature: the original octagonal lantern or louvre, with trefoil-headed openings and ogee top. Much of the roof is also original. It has arched braces to two hollow-chamfered tie-beams, with kingposts with curved struts to the collar above. Stock brick walls conceal the original ragstone. Simple square s porch, added some time before 1929. Above, an almost unbroken row of square-headed windows (renewed), interrupted by piers marking the wall-posts of the roof. Coved cornice of *c.* 1660. Doric pilasters formerly marked the bay divisions. Early C16 linen-fold panelling inside, probably from rebuilding recorded in 1510, but with added bands of Renaissance busts and scrolls on the two overmantels which cannot be earlier than *c.* 1530. Armorial stained glass, 1545 and later. Exposed in the cellar, a section of chalk-and-tile walling, probably antedating the C15 hall.

Attached to the hall's E wall is a two-storey stock brick house, dated 1770 on the archway into the central courtyard (formerly the Inn's garden). Balustrade on top, added when a storey was removed some time after 1894 (perhaps in 1909–10, when the range to Holborn was rebuilt). Pretty single-storey LODGE, N, possibly of the same date. SW of the hall, the Inn's former LIBRARY: no more than two bays with large round-arched windows in shallow reveals, dated 1805. Overmantel with foliage carving, apparently C18, re-set. In the SW corner, parts of the *Chatfeild Clarke*'s school, loosely Jacobean red brick and Ancaster stone, with matching storeys inserted in the reconstruction. More bits on the E side, re-set. Between them, part of *Green Lloyd*'s development on the S part of the old Inn site (*see* Fetter Lane).

GRESHAM COLLEGE has led a peripatetic existence. Founded under Sir Thomas Gresham's will (1579) as a kind of university for London, it began in his mansion off Bishopsgate, under the management of the Corporation and the Mercers' Company. Professors lectured in seven subjects, including geometry and astronomy: posts filled at different times respectively by Hooke and the young Wren. In 1710 the College took rooms in the Royal Exchange, and moved when that burned to new premises in Gresham Street (by *George Smith*, 1842–3, rebuilt 1911–13, q.v.). The City University took over the former curriculum in 1966, but the College was independently reconstituted in 1984.

BILLINGSGATE MARKET (FORMER)
Lower Thames Street

By *Sir Horace Jones*, 1874–8, converted to offices by the *Richard Rogers Partnership*, 1985–9. The ancient market is mentioned in Ethelred's *Institutes of London*, *c.* 1000. Stow thought the name commemorated a Saxon proprietor called Beling or Biling; the 'gate' was in the former riverside wall (*see* Introduction p. 41). Foreshore extensions on either side had turned the Saxon quay into a useful inlet by the C13. The first representation of a market building is an arcaded structure shown on a drawing of 1598. Its much-repaired post-Fire successor was replaced by *Dance the Younger*, 1799–1800. By this date it specialized in fish. The remaining dock was filled in for a new, rapidly outgrown covered market by *Bunning*, 1848–52. This was Italianate, with a central tower. Its arcades between office pavilions and its basement shellfish market reappear in Jones's building.

Jones's market cost £271,407. It is of yellow brick, Portland-dressed, in style markedly French. Arcaded ground floor between three-bay end pavilions towards street and river. Upper windows with rounded top corners, a typically weak early to mid-Victorian motif. Three-bay central pediment, with Britannia seated on the apex. Frenchy roofs with romping dolphins on the pavilions, which were meant to house pubs (cf. Smithfield Market). Jones eschewed iron and glass for the market hall in favour of wood and brick, which were less prone to overheating (cf. Smithfield again). Structural ironwork is used where appropriate, e.g. in the central double colonnade running N–S, supporting a gallery from which cured fish was sold, and E and W colonnades, rising to lattice roof girders. These support glass louvres in wide-span mansards, one per side, and slatted and boarded dormers above. Shops and warehouses lined E and W walls. Shellfish were sold in a double-height vaulted basement below.

Use as a fish market ceased in 1982, three decades after the last deliveries by water. *Rogers*'s conversion turned the market hall into a giant dealing floor, the wings into offices. The minimal new insertions are immediately recognizable. A lower gallery is fitted beneath the central colonnade, with E–W extensions at each end communicating between the wings' upper storeys. Glazed screens and roofs make a sealed environment within the C19 structure. In 1996 still awaiting a tenant.

BISHOPSGATE INSTITUTE
Bishopsgate

By *C. Harrison Townsend*, 1892–4, amongst the most original buildings of the date in London. One of three educational foundations founded out of moribund City charities after 1890. The others were the St Bride's Institute (q.v.) and the Cripplegate Institute (*see* Golden Lane).

117 The chief interest is the narrow front, of buff terracotta (*Gibbs & Canning*'s), with broad arched entrance, and a frieze of flat stylized leafy trees above, modelled by *William Aumonier*: an early and influential exploration of the material by an Arts-and-Crafts architect. The big arch and other details point however to America, especially to Richardson (Townsend's special study) and even Sullivan. Above, a large mullioned and transomed window between polygonal angle turrets with sturdy, oddly detailed spires. A steep slated hipped roof rises in two stages.

The plan is long and irregular, with necessarily more economical fronts on to Brushfield Street, N, and Fort Street, E. The former especially has the asymmetry Townsend developed to startling effect at e.g. his later Whitechapel Gallery (*see London 5: East and Docklands*). Plain but well-preserved interiors: clerestoried hall, boardroom over the entrance, and rear library with glazed dome. The latter's novelty was its provision for open public access to the bookshelves. In 1994 No. 14 Brushfield Street, a C18 house, was incorporated (by *Lloyd Leroy*). A new recital hall is to be constructed over the E part.

BLACKFRIARS BRIDGE

Of 1860–9 by *Joseph Cubitt* and *H. Carr*. Five wrought-iron arches faced with cast iron, on granite piers, but founded on caissons. The decoration involved arcaded cast-iron parapets and enormous attached columns in red granite with leafy Portland stone capitals, kept when the bridge was widened on the W in 1907–10. They support little half-octagonal refuges. The columns evoke the paired Doric columns on the piers of *Robert Mylne*'s predecessor of 1760–9. This had nine slightly elliptical arches in Portland stone. Scouring of the footings necessitated its replacement.

BLACKFRIARS STATION
Queen Victoria Street

A miserable job. The London, Chatham & Dover Railway spanned the Thames from London Bridge station to a small terminus on Ludgate Hill in 1864 (Act 1860). In 1884–6 the construction of a parallel bridge to the E allowed its replacement by a new terminus further S (the present site). The lines to the W continue N to join the former Metropolitan Railway at Farringdon, N of the City, so the station was never a fully-fledged terminus. But it deserved better than *R. Seifert & Partners*' mute L-shaped office slab of 1971–7, replacing a weak two-storey Italianate terminus of red brick of 1883–6 (engineers *H. M. Brunel, W. Mills* and *J. Wolfe Barry*). Re-set on the new concourse, stone blocks from its pilastered entrances, inscribed with fifty-four multifarious destinations, Bromley next to Bremen. Other circulation spaces are cramped and shapeless. Utilitarian 1960s train shed. Part of the C14 or C15 river wall was found beneath the N end in 1985. Remodelling by *Alsop & Störmer* is proposed, to accommodate more through traffic (1996).

BLACKFRIARS RAILWAY BRIDGES. Piers only remain from the original bridge of 1862–4, by *Joseph Cubitt* and *F. T. Turner*. One of the strangest sights in London, marching across the river, carrying nothing nowhere. Treated ornamentally, as four-shafted Romanesque columns. They range with the piers of the contemporary Blackfriars Bridge, W (*see* previous entry). Lattice girder spans of up to 185 ft (56½ metres) were removed in 1985. The abutments contain stone reused from the C18 Westminster Bridge. On the S abutment magnificent cast-iron pylons bearing the insignia of the L.C.D.R. The 1880s bridge, E (ST PAUL'S RAILWAY BRIDGE), by *Wolfe Barry* and *H. M. Brunel*, has five wrought-iron arches.

BRITISH TELECOM CENTRE
Newgate Street

Of 1980–5 by the *Department of the Environment* (*British Telecom Services Division*), project architect *Gordon Jones*. The Portland-clad load-bearing walls have rounded corners and close-set tiers of horizontal windows between vertically recessed strips. They make three separate buildings, linked by bridges under a large but awkwardly shaped atrium, glazed in parallel barrel-vaults and served by wall-climber lifts: all novelties when the building was designed. To Newgate Street this appears as a glazed wall, at odds with the forbiddingly solid elevations. On the site of the former G.P.O. West Range (*see* General Post Office).

CANNON STREET STATION

Built 1865–6 on a grand scale for the South Eastern Railway (Act 1861), in response to the London, Chatham & Dover Railway's incursion on to Ludgate Hill (*see* Blackfriars Station). Engineers *J. Hawkshaw* and *J. W. Barry*. From this first building survive the substructure with its splendid arcaded flanking walls of stock brick (reconstructed), and the monumental towers by the river (restored 1986). The latter have square leaded domes and spires as if to harmonize with Wren's churches. They housed water tanks for hydraulic lifts. Between them soared until 1958 a segmental-arched iron train shed, at 108 feet (33 metres) taller even than that at St Pancras. In the brick substructure (converted to a sports club in 1980) the first cold store in Britain was made in 1875.

The rest has been rebuilt in two stages. To Cannon Street, a tall and dull curtain-walled office slab of 1961–6, by *J. G. L. Poulson* of scandalous memory. On the site of *E. M. Barry*'s bomb-damaged terminus hotel, built independently in 1867 after the railway ran out of funds. It was all-over Italianate of brick and *Blanchard*'s white-glazed terracotta, with funny symmetrical corner spirelets. Low range of shops added in front 1970–1, not improved by tawdry canopies of *c.* 1990 (a scheme by *Peter Foggo Associates* to replace the Cannon Street range was proposed in 1996). To the s, a giant 'air rights' block by the *BDP*, 1987–91, rests on piles driven through the platforms (engineers *Pell Frischmann*). Six storeys at the N are cut obliquely to two at the s, to preserve sight lines to St Paul's. Between the towers these two finish in a kind of prow. Offices are partly concealed to the sides by the rebuilt screen walls, but exposed across Upper Thames Street, where shallow projections and patterned cladding break up the visual mass. Inside, the giant trading floor of the London International Financial Futures Exchange (LIFFE), by the *Whinney Mackay-Lewis Partnership*.

CANNON STREET RAILWAY BRIDGE was built by *Hawkshaw*, 1863–6 (widened 1886–93). Five spans, up to 136 ft (40 metres), of quite shallow plate girders on ranks of six fluted cast-iron piers. Spoiled during strengthening work, 1979–81, when the Doric capitals were encased in concrete and modillion-like brackets removed from the spans.

The site of part of the station and viaduct is the STEELYARD of the Hanseatic Merchants. The port of Dowgate here (i.e. the mouth of the Walbrook) is mentioned in Edward the Confessor's time as belonging to men of Rouen. The predecessors of the Hanse merchants settled by the mid C12. Henry III gave the site to the Hanse merchants, whose legal successors kept it until 1853, despite the Hanseatic League's expulsion from England by Elizabeth I. Fragments of the C12 hall and other buildings were recorded in

1987. New buildings after 1666 were by *C. G. Cibber*, whose carved pediment survives in the Museum of London collection.

CENTRAL CRIMINAL COURT
Old Bailey

Of 1900–7 by *Mountford*, after a limited competition entered also by *Belcher* and *Florence*. One of the best examples in London of the Neo-English Baroque, in its favourite Portland stone. Forms are more disciplined and also more English than Mountford's work of the 1890s, and this too typifies 1900s fashions.

The dominant dome is derived from the Royal Naval Hospital, Greenwich, except for the scrolly brackets set over the paired columns of the diagonals. The famous gilt bronze statue of Justice on top is by *F. W. Pomeroy*. Main front, w, with two pairs of giant pilasters framing a recess with inset giant columns, also paired. Windows with Gibbs surrounds set against channelled stone. Rusticated ground floor, the stone finely pitted. Entrance with big segmental pediment with three powerful figures by *Pomeroy*: Truth, Fortitude, and the Recording Angel. Frieze within the recessed centre by *Alfred Turner*. Other work by such craftsmen as *Gilbert Seale* (plasterwork and sundry carving), *W. Aumonier* (stone carving), and *Bainbridge Reynolds* (ironwork). The gently convex Newgate Street front, n, has columns in the recessed centre, their clean lines marred by a mezzanine.

Stretching s down Old Bailey, an extension by *George Whitby* of *McMorran & Whitby*, 1966–72. In the firm's plain segment-arched style, with classical reminiscences of the Lutyens kind, more ghostly here than at their earlier Police Station in Wood Street (q.v.). The extension replaced part of Mountford's building, four columns from which stand in a garden off Warwick Square, behind (*see* Warwick Lane). Here the facing is of buff brick.

The usual entrance is in the extension, joining the Edwardian circulation spaces on the s. On the ground floor of the latter, a tripartite ENTRANCE HALL running N–S, with double-aisled side spaces and an Imperial staircase climbing from the middle. Much marble: green monolithic columns; walls faced in green, white and cream. First-floor GREAT HALL with domed centre, its architectural details much indebted to St Paul's interior. Pendentives carved with Virtues by *Pomeroy*. Crowded painted allegories in the lunettes of the apsed outer section, s, by *Gerald Moira*. Corresponding scenes on the N, by Moira's assistants, replace work by *Sir W. Blake Richmond*, destroyed by a bomb in 1941. By *Moira* also the central lunette showing the wartime emergency services and the replacement stained glass over the half-landing, all post-war. Dismal post-war painted figures in the main dome and spandrels. The original four courtrooms open off here. Fifteen more courtrooms are accommodated mostly in the extension, which opens off on the s on the ground and first floors. Its circulation spaces have plain, slender round- and segment-arched openings. Near the junction with the Edwardian work, they make an open cage within which the staircase climbs, with exhilarating interior views from the half-landing.

In the halls, several STATUES. On the first floor beneath the dome, three statues by *John Bushnell* from the tower of the second Royal Exchange, 1671 (q.v.): Charles I, Charles II, and Sir Thomas Gresham. They are the best intact examples of the Baroque manner Bushnell learned on his Continental travels, executed with the fervour of a convert (see Charles I's billowing draperies). Their companion is Elizabeth Fry, a stately figure by *Alfred Drury*, 1913. On the ground floor, mid-Victorian statues of monarchs, made for the Palace of Westminster. From N to S: William IV by *Theed*, 1867, William III by *Woolner*, 1868, George IV by *H. Weekes*, 1870, James I by *Thomas & Mary Thornycroft*, 1867, Mary II by *Alexander Munro*, 1863, Charles II (with spaniel) by *Weekes*, 1870, Charles I by the *Thornycrofts*, 1867.

A short stretch of Roman CITY WALL in the basement of the extension, E: foundations, first tile-course, and some 2 ft (60 cm) of squared masonry. An internal turret found immediately S in 1966, and not preserved, contained early C3 coin forger's moulds. Before the construction of the wall, a small cemetery was located here. This contained several fine funerary urns, one of carved porphyry, another a lead cinerary urn depicting a charioteer in relief.

Mountford's building stands on the site of NEWGATE GAOL, the masterpiece of *Dance the Younger*, 1769–78 (dem. 1902). There were three blind-walled courtyards, the central one set back to accommodate twin entrance pavilions and the Vanbrughian governor's house, rebuilt 1780–3 after damage in the Gordon Riots. Dance's terrifying rhetoric of incarceration still haunts the imagination. The stupendous rustication of every surface exercised great influence on the Edwardian Baroque revival. *Dance*'s SESSIONS HOUSE of 1769–74, forerunner of the present Court, lay immediately S. For the medieval Newgate, predecessor of Dance's prison, *see* Newgate Street.

CHARTERED INSURANCE INSTITUTE
Aldermanbury

By *M. E. & O. H. Collins*, 1932–4. Spare, quietly eccentric Tudorbethan, in smooth Portland stone. Big shaped gable; Romanesque touches in the columns at the entrance and on the uppermost floor. Large mullioned and transomed windows with heraldic glass to the hall, S. Top-lit open-well staircase, in free C17 style.

CITY OF LONDON SCHOOL FOR BOYS
Queen Victoria Street

By the *Corporation of London Architect's & Planning Department*, architect *Tom Meddings*, 1983–6. Part of the North Bank Development Scheme (*see* Upper Thames Street). It forms the W side of Peter's Hill, with a short front to Queen Victoria Street, N, and a longer entrance front facing the river, S. The falling ground means that this S part is much taller, though the whole is kept low to preserve views of St Paul's. Red-brown brick, the dominant motif plain upright windows mostly in groups of four. Entrance front with a recessed part-glazed centre flanked by stair-towers with glazed barrel-vaults: a loose, approximately symmetrical composition. Tightly planned within: lofty, largely windowless hall, w; glazed upper concourse opening on to a central rooftop playground; sports halls and swimming pool, N end, to shield the classrooms from traffic noise.

SCULPTURE. In the entrance, a figure of a boy by *Durham* called Waiting his Innings, 1866. On the concourse, John Carpenter by *Samuel Nixon*, 1845; also several good mid-Victorian busts. In the playground cloister, WAR MEMORIAL designed by *Sir Banister Fletcher*, 1919, with well-executed if sentimental figures by *C. L. Hartwell*. All from the previous school building on Victoria Embankment (q.v.).

The site is that of the second BAYNARD'S CASTLE, rebuilt here after 1275 (replacing the first castle by Black Friars Lane, q.v.), and again rebuilt on reclaimed land by Humphrey, Duke of Gloucester, some time after 1428. The C15 plan was trapezoidal, with four wings around a courtyard. Excavations in 1972–5 and 1984 exposed much of the foundations, showing that the N wall rested on the Roman riverside wall (*see* Introduction p. 41). In *c.* 1501 Henry VII added five projecting towers between two existing polygonal corner towers on the river front – a typical Tudor-Gothic multiplication of vertical accents. w extension of brick made *c.* 1550, stone-faced on the river front. One turret survived the Great Fire, lasting until 1720.

CITY OF LONDON SCHOOL FOR GIRLS
see BARBICAN

CITY THAMESLINK STATION
Ludgate Hill

The successor to the old Holborn Viaduct station. By *RHWL Partnership*, 1990–1, built underground around the former London, Chatham & Dover Railway route to Farringdon, as part of the Fleet Place development (q.v.). Above ground merely a row of three big glazed stone-framed boxes, surprisingly spacious inside. Designed to be incorporated into a new block on the whole site. A N entrance is accommodated in No. 1 Fleet Place, on the site of the old station platforms; the 1960s terminus building, N, survives for the time being (*see* Holborn Viaduct).

CLIFFORD'S INN
Fetter Lane

First mentioned in 1344, when Lord de Clifford's widow granted the property to apprentices of the Bench, who may already have been in residence. The last Inn of Chancery to be dissolved, in 1902. Of the legal buildings only the modest Neo-Gothic GATEHOUSE survives, at the end of Clifford's Inn Passage off Fleet Street, adjoining St Dunstan-in-the-West. Almost certainly by *Decimus Burton*, who was busy at the Inn 1830–4. Stock brick, crenellated, with crow-stepped doorcase gable. Perfunctory detail, typical of Burton's blind spot for Gothic. Demolished in 1935–6: the Gothick hall of 1767–8, incorporating C14 fabric, and chambers of 1663–9, 1782 and 1834. The Victoria and Albert Museum preserved a panelled interior of 1690 from the C17 chambers. Their replacements are bleak and charmless brick flats by *Daniel Watney & Sons*, overlooking the Public Record Office garden. Renovations of 1983 by *Boyd Auger* included refacing the entrance block on Fetter Lane, E. Here, super-imposed colonnades of GRC stand against bronzed-glass curtain-walling: amongst the first such revivals of classical forms for com-mercial buildings. They seem unsure whether to take themselves seriously.

COLLEGE OF ARMS
Queen Victoria Street

64 Built in 1671–3 (central block), 1682–8 (projecting wings). Three storeys of much-patched red brick. The centre was by *Maurice Emmett Jun.*, later Master Bricklayer to the Office of Works, and *Francis Sandford*, Lancaster Herald. The wings carry on Emmett's design (W wing built by the carpenter *John Hodge*, E wing by the mason *Ephraim Beauchamp*). The College originally had two short return wings on the S side, with a terrace between. These were lost when Queen Victoria Street was made, leaving the E wing one bay longer than the W. *George Plucknett* made good the exposed ends and lowered the courtyard (1867–8), and *H. A. Darbishire* added the stone steps and terrace (1870–71). The quadrangular plan reflected that of the late C15 mansion of the Earls of Derby, given to the College in 1555. Lady Margaret Beaufort, mother of Henry VII, lived there *c.* 1500. (A carved portcullis under the terrace, reset, may date from her occupancy.) Before 1555 the Heralds lived in a man-sion at Coldharbour, S of Upper Thames Street.

The main elevations are not entirely C17: a large eaves-cornice and pediments on the three frontispieces were replaced by simple parapets *c.* 1800. The scrawny giant Ionic pilasters remain, four on the centre and two on the wings. Jonesian garlanded capitals, but also diamond badges on the shafts: a typically impure artisan's combination. Impure too the pilasters' two-bay spacing on the wings, and the way they rest on narrow rusticated strips. Red tiled roof of C17 type, a happy restoration of 1954–6. The original entrance was from Godliman Street, W. High up on the wall there, a slim keystone and strip of cornice mark where its archway was. The walls have cores of reused rubble. Facing Peter's Hill, NE, the Record Room, a yellow brick addition with a canted end and Venetian window, by *Robert Abraham*, 1842–4. GATES across the forecourt, a splendid wrought-iron set from Goodrich Court, Herefordshire, presented in 1956. C18 style, said to have been made or remade by the *Bromsgrove Guild*, 1889; or else by *H. Prothero*.

Entrance is into the double-height COURT ROOM, wainscotted level with a balustraded E gallery. Against the N wall the imposing Earl Marshal's throne, somewhat reminiscent of a church reredos, with pilasters, garlands and a segmental pediment. Putti stand above the pilasters. Three carved armorials added *c.* 1707. Railed enclosure in front, with simple turned balusters. On the r., the wainscotted PUBLIC OFFICE, with excellent overmantel carved with thin looping garlands by *William Emmett*, Maurice's brother. (E of this a staircase with turned balusters; a second staircase, w, has heavily twisted balusters. The WAITING ROOM has bookcases concealed by C17 wainscotting. Other rooms are the Heralds' offices.)

CUSTOM HOUSE
Lower Thames Street

The first Custom House is known from the C14 on a site immediately E, and was extended 1381–2. Foundations of the extension were uncovered in 1973.[*] A turreted fortress-like building replaced it in 1559. *Wren* designed its successor, built with all haste after the Great Fire (completed 1671). Dutch in flavour, it had short projecting wings open to the ground floor, framing an eleven-bay block with a first-floor room for public business (called the Long Room). Burnt in 1718, and rebuilt to a design by *Thomas Ripley* (completed 1725, extended 1738–40), a storey higher, but otherwise similar. It burned down in 1814, before its replacement on its w side was complete.

The Present Custom House

1812–17 by *David Laing*, Surveyor to the Customs, the centre block towards the river rebuilt on concrete foundations by *Robert Smirke* in 1825–8 after Laing's work collapsed. It is suggested that he had unwisely hastened the work after the old House burnt. An immensely long building (488 ft or 149 metres). Front and sides are of Portland stone, the back of yellow brick. An un-nautical row of trees screens it from the river, towards which the centre projects slightly. Here Smirke repeated with greater projection the six-columned Ionic frontispiece of Laing's wings, on a continuation of Laing's rusticated basement with segment-headed windows (Smirke's carver *W. G. Nicholl*, masons *Thomas Piper & Son*). This centrepiece is stolid by comparison with Laing's less literally Grecian one, which had even, round-headed windows and a figure frieze, all with a strong flavour of contemporary Paris or St Petersburg. Simultaneously with Laing's work, the quay wall and river stairs were rebuilt to designs by *Rennie*. Laing's simple street front remains, with a pilastered centre flanked by projecting ends which originally housed the entrances.

Inside, Smirke made an austere new ENTRANCE HALL, N, with dog-leg staircases of stone at each end, screened on two sides by tall plain round-headed openings. They lead up to his fine, if frigid, LONG ROOM facing the river, occupying the whole central block above the ground floor. Here the public business was transacted. Its thirteen bays measure 190 ft (58 metres), with Tuscan pilasters to a coffered elliptical ceiling 54 ft ($16\frac{1}{2}$ metres) high. (Laing's room was less austere, with three shallow domes on Soanian pendentives.) Restoration by *SKF Architects*, 1992, re-created a long public

---

[*] On the Custom House generally, *see* the account published by RCHME (1993).

counter made in 1925. Smirke used iron construction here even more consistently than at his British Museum, begun slightly earlier (*see London 4: North*). Iron-framed curved lights pierce the ceiling above the cornice, and iron fireplates suspended from wooden trusses cover the rest of the ceiling. The cast-iron floor beams are of unique design, incorporating shoes for cross-timbers set immediately over iron joists that support cast arched ceiling plates. Ground floor ('King's Warehouse', now a canteen), and basement were both originally for storage of impounded cargoes etc. They have aisles with cast-iron columns: elongated Tuscan above, stocky Doric below (ironwork by *Foster, Rastrick & Co.* of Stourbridge).

Smirke's restored ROBING ROOM, beyond the Long Room, has wood-grained panelling and a gallery with an unusual panelled-in staircase, plain and spare. Some of *Laing*'s modest offices survive in the w wing, off a groin-vaulted corridor around a central light-well; not so his richer interiors in the bombed E wing, rebuilt externally in replica after war damage, 1962–6 (architects *F. L. Rothwell & H. G. Hexley* of the *Ministry of Public Building and Works*).

FENCHURCH STREET STATION

The terminus of the London and Blackwall Railway, the first incursion into the City by the railways (1841). Trains were worked by gravity and cable until 1849. Main façade of 1853–4, by *George Berkeley*. Eleven bays of gault brick with arched upper windows between pilasters. Across the whole front a clumsy big segmental pediment. Zigzag wooden canopy below. Offices by *A. Langley* facing Crosswall, added in 1881 when approach tracks were widened on the N side, were demolished *c.*1988. The terminus proper was remodelled behind this frontage by the *Fitzroy Robinson Partnership*, 1983–7 (engineers *Ove Arup & Partners*, creating the first fully butt-welded framed building). It is reticent by comparison with later 'air rights' schemes. Longitudinal concrete beams on piles support steel A-frame trusses over the platforms. Concourse and platforms are thus unobstructed, though uncomfortably low (glass entrance screen by *Ann Smythe*, 1987. cs). The frames make five office storeys, faced in anodized dark-brown panelling. At the w the upper storeys slope back to an open-framed ridge rising above the pediment. To the l. a green-glazed barrel-vaulted entrance lobby with rounded brick-clad access tower rising behind. A similar tower serves an entrance made further E, at No. 44 Crutched Friars (q.v.).

GENERAL POST OFFICE (FORMER)
St Martin's le Grand and King Edward Street

The G.P.O. moved here in 1829 from Lombard Street. Its grandly Greek Ionic premises by *Smirke* lay on the E side of St Martin's le Grand (enlarged *c.* 1845 and 1892, demolished 1912). Three large buildings followed to its w: the pedimented West Range of 1869–73 (demolished 1967), by *James Williams* of the *Office of Works*, where the present British Telecom Centre now stands (q.v.), then two large blocks surviving to N and w: the former North Range between St

Martin's le Grand and King Edward Street, 1889–95 by *Sir Henry Tanner* of the Office of Works, and the King Edward Buildings facing King Edward Street (w side), 1907–11, also by *Tanner* (principal assistant *R. J. Allison*). Their façades are ornate but unadventurous, in the way of most late C19 official architecture.

The NORTH RANGE presents heavy Italianate cliffs of Portland stone on all sides. Battered lower storeys with banded rustication. Pilasters above make an all-over effect. Keystones on the former E and W roadway entrances are carved with portraits of contemporary Postmasters-General. The G.P.O. left in 1984; in 1987–90 reconstructed on a steel frame as NOMURA HOUSE, by the *Fitzroy Robinson Partnership* (consultant architect *Ian Thomas*), behind, it is said, the largest retained façade in Europe. French-flavoured mansards were added above Tanner's low square turrets and attics. The aisled entrance hall from St Martin's le Grand replicates its predecessor. (MURAL by the Japanese artist *Nishida*, ninth floor.)

KING EDWARD BUILDINGS occupies most of the former Christ's Hospital site (*see* Newgate Street). It makes concessions to the Edwardian desire for stronger accents, but eschews the full Baroque artillery. Projecting penultimate bays with broken pediments. Some fashionable devices, e.g. the circular Hampton Court windows. Grand aisled interior with much green-marble facing, showy plasterwork, and bow-fronted Edwardian counter, in 1996 largely intact. First World War memorial with bronze figure by *Whitehead*. The NATIONAL POSTAL MUSEUM (established 1966) occupies an upper storey. Another public post office, also stone-faced and formally treated, occupies the site of the entrance to Christ's Hospital quadrangle on Newgate Street (q.v.). The Buildings of 1907–11 are of interest for their early reinforced-concrete construction, on the *Hennebique* system (British licensee *L. G. Mouchel & Partners*). The framing was frankly expressed at the rear, and also on the elevations of the large sorting-office block behind (scheduled for demolition in 1997). The use of *in situ* concrete, estimated here to have saved £60,000, became routine in Office of Works projects thereafter. Inside the sorting office, low arches span between piers on a 35 ft (10½ metre) grid: about twice the contemporary limit for iron or steel. The use of arches (quickly supplanted elsewhere by post-and-beam construction) marks it as an early, experimental structure (A. Saint). A new building by *Swanke Hayden Connell* is intended for the site.

In King Edward Street (called Stinking Lane in the Middle Ages, then Butcher's Hall Lane from the C17 until 1843), a STATUE of Rowland Hill, 1881, by *Onslow Ford*, his first major work. Until 1923 it stood E of the Royal Exchange.

ROMAN AND MEDIEVAL REMAINS. Preserved below ground in the G.P.O. yard, off Giltspur Street, are the medieval corner bastion of the CITY WALL, where it swung abruptly S, and a short stretch of the Roman wall itself, excavated in 1909. The bastion's hollow, horse-shoe-shaped walls are 7 ft (2 metres) thick. Its foundations at their deepest are 7 ft (2 metres) below those of the wall, beyond which it projects by 26 ft (8 metres). The internal face is rough, the external face carefully smoothed. The remains may be inspected by arrangement with the Post Office. Remains of two more bastions excavated in 1908–9 and of another uncovered in King Edward Street in 1887 were not preserved.

GUILDHALL
Guildhall Yard

The centre of the civic complex is still the great C15 Guildhall, with *George Dance the Younger*'s Hindoo-Gothic porch in front, and tantalizing remains of its predecessors beneath. Other early buildings have survived less well, and most of the offices etc. are post-war. The Guildhall has not stood alone since at least the late C13, when a chapel was built on the s side of the previous structure. By the late C15 a library stood s of this chapel, a gatehouse abutting the E wall of St Lawrence Jewry separated Guildhall Yard from the street, and a two-storey stone building (called the Mayor's Court) adjoined the Hall to the N. Chapel, Mayor's Court and Hall were all refitted after the Great Fire. Other offices grew up to the N, s and E, amongst them *Dance*'s celebrated Common Council Chamber (1777–8, dem. 1908), with its spare top-lit pendentive dome so influential on Soane. Victorian additions were grander, especially *Sir Horace Jones*'s Council Chamber (1883–4, destroyed 1940), a twelve-sided Gothic structure like a giant chapter house. The C19 is now represented only by Jones's Gothic former library and museum, E of the Hall (1870–2), and to the SE *Andrew Murray*'s Court House (1887–94) and the little Irish Chamber by *Joseph Walker* (1824–5).

Wholesale rebuilding, mooted since 1908, was about to begin to designs by *Sir Giles Gilbert Scott* when the Second World War broke out. Bombing raids burnt out the Hall and destroyed much else, including the lavishly appointed late C17 Aldermen's Court Room. Some of *Thornhill*'s paintings from the room survive at Plaisterers' Hall (q.v.). Restoration of the Hall fell to *Scott*, who also made a clean sweep of buildings on its N for his new office range (1955–8). Later work was by *Richard Gilbert Scott* of *Sir Giles Scott, Son & Partner* (chairman of Reconstruction Committee *Owen Campbell-Jones*). A raised forecourt was made in 1966–9 to the N, in connection with the system of elevated walkways s of London Wall (q.v.). Then Guildhall Yard was extended westwards to make a broad paved precinct, defined to N and W by a new L-shaped library and office wing (1969–75), abutting the 1950s offices W of the Hall. The visitor enters the Hall through this later wing. On the s side of the extended yard is St Lawrence Jewry (q.v.), restored to accommodate the Corporation's own ceremonies. A block by *Richard Gilbert Scott* (with *D. Y. Davies Associates*) for the Guildhall Art Gallery, approaching completion on the E side in 1997, will complete the civic sequence (*see* also Roman Remains, below).

THE GUILDHALL

Built by the master mason *John Croxton* or *Croxtone* from 1411 to c. 1429, when an agreement was made to glaze the E window.[*] It is

* *See* C. M. Barron, *The Medieval Guildhall of London* (1974), and C. Wilson, *Journal of the British Archaeological Association*, 1976.

known to have been at least the third Guildhall on the site, though for visible evidence of its predecessors one must go to the Undercroft (*see* p. 303 below). In spite of all that has happened to it in the Great Fire and the Blitz and all it has undergone at the hands of restorers and re-doers, the size and pride of the C15 work can still be appreciated. Perp, eight bays long, lying E–W with tall transomed two-light windows high up in the S and (concealed) N walls. In each end wall a splendid nine-light window, divided 2–5–2 by slender offset buttresses. Tracery of the central group with two-light sub-arches, flanking a panel-traceried central light. Similar two-light sub-arches to either side, with panelling, mouchettes and a quatrefoil above. The proportion from base to apex is that of an equilateral triangle. Massive octagonal corner turrets with buttresses, which continue along the sides. Everything to window-head level is to Croxton's design, though renewed. Some of the squared rubble masonry is also his, stripped of *Bernasconi*'s rendering (added 1805–7) by *Sydney Perks*, 1909.

Above the windows the restorers take over. To *Sir Horace Jones*'s medievalizing in 1864–8 are due the raised turrets and their pinnacles, the crocketted buttress-gables and the plain parapets (Croxton's hall was crenellated, with pinnacled buttresses). Jones also added a big single flèche with a spirelet, rather than re-create the two small louvres added in 1491 and destroyed in 1666. *Sir Giles Gilbert Scott* followed Jones in this when he reroofed the shell in handsome green Collyweston slates, 1953–4. The crenellated clerestory behind the parapet is also Scott's, where Jones had dormers (*see* Interior, below).

Competing for attention with the medieval and neo-medieval work is the deep Portland stone PORCH of 1788–9 by *Dance the Younger*, surprisingly daredevil in its mixing of Gothic, classical and Oriental motifs. Croxton's two-storey porch of c. 1425–30 survived the Great Fire, with incongruous additions of 1671 (by *Pierce*). Four accomplished C15 statues of Virtues from niches that flanked the original door were rediscovered in 1972 at Soughton Hall, Flintshire, and are now in the Museum of London. Remains of figures from the upper niches were identified in 1996. Dance incorporated the C15 lower storey into his new work, repeating the forms of the entrance in the shallow projecting doorway. Nine bays in all, divided into three by fluted buttresses continued up as big square pinnacles sporting hexagonal finials and Greek bits and pieces. Eccentric cresting on the parapet and doorcase. Bands of quatrefoil lozenges between the storeys. These lozenges and the cusped-headed pointed windows derive from William Hodges's *Select Views of India* (1786): the earliest example of Indian influence in English architecture, entirely characteristic of Dance's 'unshackled' eclecticism. One may speculate as to the choice of styles. Hodges thought the affinities between Moghul and Gothic architecture indicated a shared 'Saracenic' source, so Dance may have meant to evoke the much-debated origin of Gothic; but the City's Eastern trade may also be echoed. In contrast, the sword and mace in relief on the pinnacles resemble details on the façade of the church of the Knights of Malta in Rome (1764–7), by Dance's friend Piranesi. The E part of the porch, truncated by *Jones* c. 1865, was rebuilt 1909–10 by *Perks*, and the whole wing reconstructed in 1966–9 by *Richard*

THE SOVTH FRONT OF THE GVILDHALL AS RESTORED 1910

Guildhall. South front as restored 1910, drawn by T. Raffles Davison

Gilbert Scott, accommodating the cloister of the w extension (*see* below).

Interior

Only inside does the Hall's grand scale become fully apparent. It was the second largest structure in the medieval City after St Paul's, and at 151 ft (46 metres) by 48 ft (14½ metres) the largest civic hall in England, inferior only to the royal Westminster Hall (240 ft, 73 metres, by 67 ft, 20½ metres) as a single-span chamber. Interior

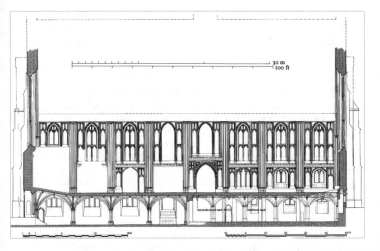

Guildhall. Section

details are much pulled about, but the original treatment of the walls is preserved. Splayed windows in two tiers, each with a single flanking panel. On the S side, second bay from the W, one of the lower windows – two lights under a four-centred arch – still exists, with window seats in the reveals. An embattled cornice ornamented with shields and fleurons divides the lower tier from the taller upper one. The various doorways fit into this all-over pattern. Between the windows substantial wall-shafts, of the typical C15 form of triple shaft and hollow moulding, with foliage capitals and octagonal caps. The dais is discreetly emphasized by statuary niches just inside the E window arch. Stone coving in little vaulted canopies (partly surviving behind the post-war panelling) topped the zone of blank walling below, where hangings were displayed. Traces of what is believed to have been C15 decoration, found in 1987 and 1994, indicated much use of green and gold, with red lining-out.

The present ROOF by *Scott* is of 1953–4, with pointed stone arches and a clerestory on concealed steel trusses. What Croxton's roof was like has been much debated. The wall-shafts and big external buttresses suggest something heavier than timber was intended, but there is no record of a stone vault. Traces of the original arrangement were erased in 1667–71 when the damaged shell was made good (probably by *Peter Mills*), raising the walls by a tall round-arched clerestory and coved ceiling that made no attempt to harmonize with the Gothic work below. But when this was taken down to make way for Jones's hammerbeam roof, a quantity of reused stones was found, corresponding to the curve of the relieving arches of the E and W windows but moulded on both sides: strong evidence that free-standing stone arches had supported the roof. This stone arch type of roof is known in England otherwise only at the early C14 Archbishop's Palace at Mayfield, Sussex. Hollar's sketch of the burnt ruins of London indeed shows something like such supports standing proud of the shell. But Scott's arches spring from several feet higher than these window arches, since the wall-shafts had themselves been raised in the C17 to make a continuous cornice. Both Jones and Scott mistook this for the original level, so while the present roof is of the C15 type, Croxton's arches sprang only from the level of the side-window imposts.

In other respects Croxton's Hall is less adventurous. The pattern of fenestration and panelling is transitional between the tall-windowed C13–C14 model and the clerestoried type with uninterrupted blank walling below, made fashionable again in the 1390s by Westminster Hall. Much is owed stylistically to the late C14 court style: the upper windows and transverse arch profiles resemble those at William Wynford's Winchester College and Cathedral nave, while the lower window tracery follows work by Henry Yevele. An indirect connection is the bequest to Croxton in 1418 of a pair of dividers by Yevele's former warden Walter Walton. But there is no cause to doubt that Croxton designed the Guildhall himself.

The C15 PORCH INTERIOR survives: it has boldly panelled walls and a two-bay tierceron vault. Another C15 survival is exposed inside Dance's part of the porch, r., set low down in the wall of the Hall proper: a doorway with square-headed surround, flanked by niches and with panelling and another niche over. This permitted direct access to the undercroft from outside. The stonework is largely of 1972, when it was restored as the main undercroft entrance, via a steep new staircase.

FURNISHINGS. All post-war apart from the restored monuments. CHANDELIERS, PANELLING and wooden GALLERIES in C15 Gothic style (made by the firm of *Maple-Martyn*) are to *Scott's* design. (C17 wainscot was removed and the Gothic stonework restored in Roman cement by *Dance c.* 1815–16. Gothic panelling on the blank E walls by *Mountague*, 1838, was replaced by *Jones* to his own design.) On the big W gallery (altered 1972) loom the sculpted GIANTS Gog and Magog, by *David Evans*, 1954. They replace figures of 1708 by *Richard Saunders*. – STAINED GLASS. Pallid sequence designed by *Scott*, with Lord Mayors' names and monograms. Made by *Powell*, 1954. Messy lower SW window by *Alfred Fisher*, 1989. – MONUMENTS. Five spectacular groups of statuary, with some C20 additions, conceal much of the lower walls. The earliest (Beckford and the elder Pitt) pay grateful homage to the City's allies in C18 controversies over trade and war. Their pyramidal compositions anticipate the monuments at St Paul's. – Lord Mayor Beckford, 1770–2 by *J. F. Moore*, stiff and uninspired. Beckford poses in mid-speech between reclining allegories of the City and Trade in mourning. – The elder Pitt by *Bacon Sen.*, 1782, the liveliest and most satisfying group. Pitt is in Roman dress, attended by Commerce, the City, and Britannia reclining on a lion to receive bounty from a cornucopia held by cherubs. – Nelson by *James Smith*, 1806–10, with Neptune, Britannia (with Nelson's portrait) and the City. Relief of Trafalgar on the plinth. Obscure by comparison with Flaxman's treatment of the subject (*see* St Paul's). – The younger Pitt by *Bubb*, 1806–13, a stilted group with Apollo, Mercury and Britannia on a sea-horse. – Wellington by *John Bell*, 1856, high on a pedestal between Peace and War, still in the St Paul's tradition. Strangely non-naturalistic relief of Waterloo below. – Royal Fusiliers' Memorial, 1907, with bronze figures by *Pomeroy*, inserted in the panelling of the walls. – Finally in 1955 the Valhalla or Pantheon of statues was increased by a seated bronze figure of Sir Winston Churchill, by *Oscar Nemon*.

Crypts

Below the Hall is an UNDERCROFT, divided half-way by a cross-wall. The E CRYPT is *Croxton*'s, an extremely impressive room of 19 nave and aisles four bays long. Too grand to have served merely for storage (see the big E doorway, to a long-lost Guildhall garden), its precise function is uncertain. Restored by *Bunning*, 1851, but largely original. Purbeck piers with four attached shafts and hollow chamfers, with matching responds. The tierceron vault has ribs with a characteristic long shallow hollowed chamfer. Three-light segment-headed windows, with STAINED GLASS by *Brian Thomas*, added during restoration in 1961.

Steps lead up to the older W CRYPT, restored in 1969–73 on the basis of remains discovered when brick barrel-vaults of *c.* 1667 were removed, and still looking very new. The former suggest a C13 or early C14 date; perhaps as late as the 1330s, when unspecified work on the Hall is recorded. Markedly plainer than its neighbour, aisled, with chamfered ribs springing from octagonal piers without capitals. Its incorporation into the C15 fabric left traces in the abrupt trun-cation of the vault by the cross-wall and – most tellingly – in the insertion of internal buttresses between the older responds, to the wider module of the new work (19 ft, 5¾ metres, instead of 16 ft, approx. 4¼ metres). The windows (restored, of C15 form) were fitted into this arrangement where possible (STAINED GLASS also by *Thomas*, 1973). It seems likely that the W crypt was originally of six bays rather than the present five, which would accord with ancient ward boundaries and with the old E alignment of Guildhall Yard. It would also match the dimensions of the 'Terra Gialle', recorded *c.* 1120 on an unspecified site and believed to have succeeded the previous town hall in Aldermanbury. A date in the 1330s would suit a section of ragstone- and flint-faced walling discovered in 1968 underneath the W porch wall. This suggests that the previous Guildhall was L-shaped, probably with the upper chamber and inner chamber mentioned in early C14 accounts in an E cross-wing. The wall rested on earlier walling, details of which suggested that the W crypt floor level was the ground floor of the C12 or C13 Guildhall. An older plastered recess discovered embedded in the N wall during the W crypt's restoration may have been from this building, indicating that some of its walls were reused.

OTHER BUILDINGS: S AND W

Important medieval buildings lay on the E side of Guildhall Yard, on the site of the new art gallery block. They may briefly be described. On the N lay a chapel, built *c.* 1285 and rebuilt or altered in the 1320s–30s by the King's craftsmen *Thomas of Canterbury* and *William Hurley*. A new aisled chapel by *Croxton* with a panelled front and rich seven-light window took its place *c.* 1430–55. An orna-mented screen wall was built *c.* 1450 between chapel and porch, across a vanished alley S of the Hall. S of the chapel was a two-storeyed library, built 1423–5 as a semi-public institution under the care of the chapel priests. This was lost at the Reformation, but the ensemble of porch, screen and chapel is recorded in c18 drawings: the effect was of richly decorated lower façades facing the yard in contrast to the rougher masonry of the Hall hemmed in behind. s of this group lay the building known as Blackwell Hall, bought by the Corporation in the late c14 and used as a cloth market until the 1790s, when the post-Fire structure (by *Peter Mills*) was adapted by *Dance* for use as law courts. In 1822 new law courts by *Mountague* replaced it, enlarged to incorporate fragments of the chapel in the N part. Blitzed remnants of this building on the chapel's reused foundations lasted until 1987. In the 1820s also a passage through to Basinghall Street called Guildhall Buildings was made to the s, and this remains.

The little IRISH CHAMBER on the SW corner, the only survivor of the late Georgian sequence, was designed in 1821 by *Joseph Walker* for the administration of the Corporation's Irish lands and built 1824–5. Two storeys, just above the domestic in ambition, with arched windows set in blind arcades on the stone-faced ground floor, brick above. False windows, N, conceal a vaulted strongroom. Further E, *Andrew Murray*'s former COURT HOUSE, 1887–94, uninspired rock-faced Gothic, with two non-matching court rooms (Mayor's Court and City of London Court) either side of a lower entrance section.

The seven-storey L-shaped EXTENSION to the N and W, by *Richard Gilbert Scott*, 1969–75, is on a much grander scale, requiring the demolition of Dance's plain office range (1787–91) on the W side of the old, narrow Guildhall Yard. Few will prefer the rather bleak open space resulting – made partly with the worthy intention of showing off the Hall – to the old narrow Guildhall Yard, called by Pevsner in 1957 'gratifyingly informal and intimate, in the best tradition of the City'. If the Gothic fountain formerly NE of the church (dismantled 1972) could be reinstated it might enliven things: it was by *John Robinson* with sculpture by *Durham*, 1866.

Scott's main N–S wing has closely spaced concrete verticals cantilevered out then set back in different planes. Bronzed window frames, recessed. The verticals repeat in various sizes the motif of a triangular-headed horseshoe opening, remotely evocative of Gothic, though not of the four-square Perp of the Hall. The effect is of a shallow *brise-soleil* on a very solid mass, straining too consciously for effect. Triangular heads also on the chunky chamfered polygon standing in front. It houses the ALDERMEN'S COURT ROOM, lit by slit windows and reached by a first-floor bridge. A lower N section, r., runs E–W to join the Hall. Towards the yard, a glazed cloister of inverted concrete pyramids on stalks links the old and new parts. Glazed strips separate the pyramids from each other and from the medieval walls. SCULPTURE in the cloister by *David Wynne*, Embracing Lovers, 1973. Translucent pyramids of Hayward Gallery type over the low angle of the wing light the reading room of the LIBRARY, entered from Aldermanbury and not otherwise expressed externally. Inside, a half-length bust of Chaucer by *Frampton*, 1901. The asymmetrical s end of the office wing has a tall arcade open to Aldermanbury, by a little pond and fountain W of

St Lawrence Jewry (q.v.). The Aldermanbury front repeats the handling of the courtyard front at excessive length.

OTHER BUILDINGS: N AND E

The former GUILDHALL LIBRARY and MUSEUM, 1870–2 by *Jones*, adjoins the Hall on the E, facing Basinghall Street. The library has served as a reception hall since 1975. Rock-faced Perp to match its neighbour, but gloomily done. Sculpted figures in niches by *Seale*. The steep-roofed forebuilding to the street houses the porch, a grand open-well staircase and an apsidal-ended committee room, with an enriched waggon-roof, Gothic bookcases and fireplace still *in situ*. Clerestoried first-floor principal room, long and tall and very church-like but for the square lanterns in the openwork timber roof. Galleries in the aisles housed the books. N window by *Ward & Hughes*, 1872. The more utilitarian ground floor (now a storeroom) housed the Guildhall Museum, merged with the former London Museum in 1975 as the Museum of London (q.v.). Architectural exhibits left behind include the plaster royal arms by *John Sherwood* from Wren's St Michael Bassishaw (*see* Basinghall Street).

Along the N of the Hall is the tall, broad brick block of municipal OFFICES by *Sir Giles Gilbert Scott*, 1955–7, painfully antiquated with its 1920s motifs along the ground floor and around the entrances and its equally 20s corrugated top frieze. The corrugations resemble details at the architect's slightly later Bankside Power Station (*see London 2: South*), but the whole ensemble has none of its stark grandeur. Also in an inter-war manner the ornamented corridor, adjoining the Hall within, and big panelled Livery Hall, with spectacularly ugly chandeliers. In building the offices remains of *Croxton*'s Mayor's Court block (begun 1425 and largely destroyed 1882) were exposed at the E end, but not preserved.

To the N of the offices is a raised precinct made over an underground car park, stepping down to Aldermanbury, w. Between the precinct and the blocks along London Wall are the small EDUCATION and PROBATION OFFICES (l. and r.), linked by steps under a canopy, built respectively as an exhibition hall and justice room by *Richard Gilbert Scott*, 1966–9. Over the Education Office and the steps, two fanciful concrete roofs of different heights, composed of a series of barrel-vaults resting on segmental arches and slender piers. At the ends each vault is broken off midway. The steps lead up to a passageway through the showy City Place House (*see* London Wall). In front, SCULPTURE of nude figures by *Karin Jonzen* called Towards Tomorrow, 1972.

ROMAN REMAINS

Excavations in Guildhall Yard in 1988–95 uncovered remains of London's ROMAN AMPHITHEATRE, 20 ft (6 metres) below street p. 36 level. They will be displayed in the basement of the new Art Gallery. The site is of great interest, and a successful display will be a welcome addition to the record of Roman London.

The chief interest of the remains is the E entrance to the gladiatorial arena. A curved stone-and-tile wall of *c*. A.D. 120, of which footings survive, retained an earth bank supporting the wooden tiers of seats. The wall is interrupted by an entrance passageway, flanked by two small square rooms originally concealed beneath the seating. Both had doorways leading directly on to the arena. The N room may have been a changing room or waiting room, perhaps housing a shrine to Nemesis similar to that known from the amphitheatre at Chester. Here the performers may have made their final preparations. The stone threshold of the S room had mouldings suggesting a sliding trap door: this implies that animals were caged here awaiting release into the arena. Bull and bear bones have also been found on site, as well as disarticulated human bones.

A series of large timber drains crossed the arena, and since these were unusually well preserved they should also form part of the display. They were repaired in the mid to late C3. This was the only large building known to have remained in use in the C4 in the W part of the Roman city: the latest arena floors include coins of 340–70.

The banks of the amphitheatre continued to influence medieval developments in the area. Although the site had unquestionably been long abandoned, it is notable that the Guildhall stands on the site of the tribunal, and that the alignment of St Lawrence Jewry appears to be influenced by the line of the S entrance and terrace of the amphitheatre.

GUILDHALL SCHOOL OF MUSIC AND DRAMA
see BARBICAN

INSTITUTE OF CHARTERED ACCOUNTANTS
Great Swan Alley, between Moorgate and Copthall Avenue

The building that made *John Belcher* famous, and a key monument of late Victorian taste. Extensions by Belcher's later partner *J. J. Joass*, 1930, and *William Whitfield*, 1964–70. The Institute, founded in 1880, held a competition in 1888. Belcher's winning design was a collaboration with his brilliant pupil *Beresford Pite*. It was built in 1890–3 and must have struck everyone then as eminently original and delightfully picturesque in its free Genoese Neo-Baroque and its successful integration of all manner of sculpture.

113 Belcher's part faces Moorgate Place. Not a large building. Crowded, thickly blocked Doric ground-floor columns in groups of three support a broad plain band that also reads as a tall entablature. Above the columns diminutive winged caryatid termini, breaching the cornice. Tall columns, also Doric, rise above the first-floor windows. Figure friezes between, below blocked round-arched windows, their surrounds variously treated. Deep, rich Corinthian cornice on top, the frieze omitted. Greater depth is established by the two-storey porch pedimented à la Michelangelo, and by a fanciful unglazed angle oriel with columns and a crowning figure of Justice. The return front to Great Swan Alley has three matching bays, then an open turret high up. There follow two two-storey bays and a second, recessed entrance within a Palladian doorway. Blind niche above with blocked columns, broken pediment and more terms.

The sculpture is by *Sir H. Thornycroft* (figure frieze and Justice) and *Harry Bates* (portals, termini, and atlantes to the corner oriel). In Bates's work the swirling forms and androgynous melancholy of the New Sculpture are already apparent. Both men were fellow-brothers of Belcher and Pite in the Art Workers' Guild. *John Tweed* and *C. J. Allen* assisted. *Joass's* extension carries on Belcher's design for six more bays along Great Swan Alley. The figure frieze here (by *J. A. Stevenson*) represents Building. The caryatids' hairstyles observe the fashions.

In 1959 *Sir William Whitfield* was commissioned to extend yet further and to provide a Great Hall to accommodate the newly merged Society of Incorporated Accountants. Final designs were accepted in 1964; the building was completed in 1970. The sensitive conjunction was most unusual at the time: Pevsner noted, 'here is proof, if proof is needed, that the uncompromisingly new can go with the old, if handled by an appreciative and imaginative architect'. The 1930 design was continued to the corner of Copthall Avenue, where a Neo-Belcher portal appears (carver *David McFall*); then the architect suddenly shows himself with a short, high, powerful stretch: concrete surfaces heavily reeded, and a windowless staircase expressed by its very steps showing. Such extreme articulation suggests Brutalist affiliations, although the other materials are markedly refined: crisp clear glazing, polished stone, and (high up) frosted glass. Whitfield's Great Hall cantilevers out into Laytham Court, N, the end wall with thin concrete mullions. 143

Inside, Belcher and Pite provided a tight sequence of spaces on an *ad hoc* plan, treated with a grandeur out of all proportion to their modest size. The result is disconcertingly playful – the last thing one expects from premises of such a subfusc profession. The arcaded and pilastered ENTRANCE HALL, little more than a corridor, has a coffered barrel-vault after Alessi's Palazzo Cambiaso, Genoa. One staircase climbs to the r., the MAIN STAIRCASE through an opening to the l. Its upper stages were rebuilt by *Whitfield*.* The MEMBERS' ROOM (former library) on the ground floor has Doric columns and a balustraded wooden gallery, leaping across the middle in a jaunty bridge (not in its original position). *Thornycroft's* bust of Belcher perches on a Baroque stone fireplace with lion's leg brackets. The most elaborate treatment is reserved for the former Council Chamber immediately above (now RECEPTION ROOM; restored 1988), reached from a cross-vaulted corridor with a weighty bust of Queen Victoria by *Onslow Ford*. It has a square, top-lit domed centre and two apsidal ends with Tuscan columns and balustraded galleries. Another gallery runs round the drum of the dome, with Ionic columns in groups of three. Two big wall-paintings by *George Murray*, 1913–14, fill the big blind arches of the other walls, above the panelling. Above the door, the Triumph of Law; opposite, Science bringing Order to Commerce. *Murray* also painted the delicate clock on the overdoor (made by *J. Walker*) and the zodiac around the dome. The SMALL RECEPTION ROOM, off the corridor, has a ceiling in the manner of Inigo Jones. Door-handles set very low trick the eye into thinking the whole room larger.

* Stained glass by *Henry Holiday*, removed in 1971, is now in a converted chapel at Henstridge, Somerset.

Whitfield's interiors lie to the E. His technical achievement was to support five office floors on exterior piers around the new GREAT HALL, allowing it to be column-free. A screen with Belcher detailing gives access from the staircase. A space of strong character. Great exposed concrete transverse beams with cantilevered ends rise up towards a wall with full-height glazing between the mullions. Pale wood panelling with thin raised strips. Decoration includes armorial engraved glass overdoors by *David Kindersley* (1980), a tapestry by *Eduardo Paolozzi*, and across the windows a perforated steel frieze by *Charles Normandale* (1985), with coloured glass behind: all good designs, but rather crowded in combination. A new COUNCIL CHAMBER was made from the lower part of Belcher's Great Hall, with lesser offices in a mezzanine. Circulation spaces have panelling or exposed concrete. A new entrance hall faces Copthall Avenue. Reeded concrete walls, brick floor radially set; wall hangings by *Penny Roberts* and *Julia Crallan*. Basement RESTAURANT designed by *Denise Lee*, with engraved glass by *Bill Moultrie* and a plaster relief by *Cathy Ward*, 1992.

LAW SOCIETY
Chancery Lane

The main part by *Lewis Vulliamy*: centre 1829–32, three-bay wings of 1848–50, N, and 1856–7, S; the latter by *P. C. Hardwick*, but matching exactly. The N part by *Charles Holden*, 1902–4, returning along Carey Street, keeps its own counsel. The growth reflects that of the solicitors' profession, loosely organized around the Inns of Chancery in the C16–C17, but largely unregulated before the Society's foundation in 1823.

92 *Vulliamy*'s front is cool and correct, its recessed Ionic portico (four unfluted columns) soundly Grecian, but without Attic pedantry. Of Portland stone, the basement Aberdeen granite. The order is apparently Vulliamy's invention, and not a souvenir of his Near-Eastern travels. Minimal carving, by *William Roseberry*. Wings with small thin pediments on the central first-floor windows. Muddled stuccoed Italianate elevation to Bell Yard, behind: a disappointing inconsistency. Of several phases, the section N of the entrance by *Hardwick* (1868–70). *Holden*'s part is a mighty square mass, with
116 identical façades to Chancery Lane, E, and Carey Street, N. Lower, plainer W continuation. The vocabulary is basically classical, but handled with a new sharp angularity. It was indeed Holden's first essay in this Neo-Mannerism, also pioneered by Beresford Pite and Belcher, but here of an elegance and independence all its own. Set-back upper corners keep it firmly distinct from Vulliamy's part. Above rises a smaller square mass (the former kitchens). Recessed ground-floor windows, the mullions with seated female figures by *Charles Pibworth*. Giant Venetian window with Doric columns over, managed with acute feeling for every block and moulding. On Holden's Chancery Lane railings, excellent gilded lion finials by *Alfred Stevens*, formerly at the British Museum (cf. Wellington Monument, St Paul's). Unspeakable post-war wall-fixed lamps.

The dining rooms and other reception rooms are much altered, the more formal library etc. much less so. An octagonal vestibule leads into a transverse HALL or broad corridor, lined with antae. On the far wall heraldic stained glass by *Benjamin Nelson*, *c.* 1904, removed from Holden's section. *Vulliamy*'s READING ROOM lies on the central axis. 30 ft (9 metres) high and somewhat bleak, it originally displayed newspapers and notices. Inset colonnades to each side (a smaller version of the portico order, of red scagliola by *Brown & Co.*). Galleries with cast-iron balconies behind. Coved ceiling with side-lit lantern. War Memorials by *Gilbert Bayes*: First World War with sentimental reliefs of children, side walls; Second World War with statue of Pallas Athene, far end.

The hall was extended at the S, 1856–7, for *Hardwick*'s STAIR-CASE. Two free-standing columns; apsed W end with sweeping iron-balustraded stairs: less elegant than it sounds. Big round-headed windows of 1926, with C17–C19 stained glass from the Chancery Lane Serjeants' Inn (q.v.); other panels in Holden's section. The first-floor LIBRARY occupies almost the whole C19 front. Central section 1830s; wider N and S parts in the 1848–57 wings carry on the original treatment. Giant Corinthian columns of green scagliola mark the extensions: two pairs to the S, one to the N, so the whole is not symmetrical. Delicate half-height iron balustrade. In the coffered ceiling an oblong lantern, with Grecian figure frieze. Round-headed marble fireplaces with fat wooden armorials over: most un-Greek, though Vulliamy's (*c.* 1848). (OLD COUNCIL ROOM of 1857, SW, with coffered ceiling and scroll frieze. By *Hardwick*, whose examination rooms etc. facing Bell Yard are much altered.)

Holden's interiors are less innovative than the exterior, but notable for their handling of space. The GRAND STAIRCASE, N of the hall, rises from a low ground floor under an arch, and returns in two flights to the lavish first-floor COMMON ROOM, on an elongated T-plan opening also on to the library. Pilasters of green cipollino marble with bronze and gilt trim. Much Arts-and-Crafts work: tiles by *de Morgan*; mahogany panelling carved by *Aumonier*, surmounted by *Conrad Dressler*'s Della Robbia-style plaques representing Human and Divine Justice, commissioned (to Holden's chagrin) in 1904.

LEADENHALL MARKET
Gracechurch Street

The Victorian Market

By *Sir Horace Jones*, 1880–1 (builder *B. E. Nightingale*). The tall 112 open-ended glass-roofed alleys show the influence of Mengoni's great Galleria in Milan (1865–77), both in general form and in the pragmatic accommodation of the cross-plan to the old street pattern. The E–W axis perpetuates the W approach from Gracechurch Street to the old market (see below), then skews S after the crossing to join the lane called Leadenhall Place. The shorter N–S avenue was given new approaches from Leadenhall Street (Whittington Avenue, N) and from Lime Street (Lime Street Passage, S). The main Grace-church Street front is nicely fancy, more so than Jones's earlier Smithfield and Billingsgate Markets (qq.v.), as if to tempt passing customers (though Leadenhall Market was originally mostly for wholesalers). Tall, narrow gabled houses of brick in C17 Dutch taste, with slim tourelles poking up in the returns, frame the frontispiece proper. This is of stone, raised high up on a girder visually supported at each end by iron columns and brackets: an improbable inhabited storey and mezzanine, then a broad curly gable and urns. Raised lettering in the lower panel, as gloriously commercial as a circus poster, spells out the name. Lesser versions of this frontispiece at the other entrances, omitting the offices.

Interiors are two-storeyed, iron-fronted, with offices above the shops. Arched timber trusses set close and high up support the glazing, arranged in a mansard with slats in the lower part – a version of the roof at Smithfield. The crossing is treated as an octagon with shorter diagonal sides and a square dome above. More columns here, with dragons cheekily squeezed in between capital and entablature. Everywhere else lots of stamped and cast detail, excellently picked out in rich colours in the restoration of 1990–1. Most shops no longer sell food, but some of those that do retain C19 shutters and spiked racks for hanging game (Nos. 1–5, N side). In the Lamb Tavern (No. 10, NE corner) a first-rate tile PICTURE entitled Building the Monument, 1671: Sir Christopher Wren explaining his plans. Signed *W. B. Simpson & Sons*, 1889.

The market was extended from 1885 into the SW quadrant, which has lesser glazed passages between a series of blocks, and into two-storey red brick ranges on both sides of Lime Street Passage and in Leadenhall Place. Their undemonstrative style is familiar from the W parts of Jones's Smithfield Market.

The Market before 1880

A market in Leadenhall Street, first recorded in 1321, was stipulated in 1345 as the place where 'foreigners' or non-Londoners might sell poultry (the market in the street called Poultry was for citizens only). It was held in the courtyard of *La Ledene Halle*, a lead-roofed mansion of the Nevilles of Essex, of early C13 construction. This stood roughly in the NW quadrant between the present market's W arm and Whittington Avenue. The property was conveyed to the Corporation in 1411. Then in 1439 the decision was made to rebuild it as a GARNER or grain store to reduce dependence on suppliers outside the City, with a central courtyard for the market. Simon Eyre, Lord Mayor in 1445–6, paid for much of the work, which was largely finished in 1447, completely by 1455. The partly burnt shell was reconstructed after the Great Fire. All but its W and S walls went between 1794 and 1812, for new market buildings by *Dance the Younger*. The rest mostly followed in 1880, but two fragments remained, of which that on the W side, 36 ft (11 metres) high, was recorded and demolished in 1985–6. Part of the S wall remains, invisible, behind Nos. 16–19 Leadenhall Market (W avenue, S side). The medieval design has since been recovered by the Museum of London.* Four three-storeyed crenellated ranges made an arcaded rectangular courtyard, skewed on the N side, with a chapel over a crypt projecting externally on the E. The show front lay to the N. It

---

* *See* Mark Samuel, 'The fifteenth-century garner at Leadenhall', *Antiquaries' Journal* 69 (1989).

was ashlared, of nine bays, with even two-light windows above a ground-floor arcade and two narrower turreted end bays housing spiral staircases. *John Croxton* and *John Hardy*, masons recorded as employed in 1442, are the best candidates for the ambitious design, which resembled Croxton's contemporary Guildhall work in some details.

Leadenhall Market stands over the E part of the great aisled BASILICA of the C2 Roman forum (*see* Introduction p. 32). A pier from its s arcade found in 1987, set over broader masonry foundations, survives in good condition in the basement of No. 90 Gracechurch Street (the l. part of the main entrance). As restored, it is tucked away behind a glass door within a hairdressing salon, incongruously surrounded by pebbles and plastic ferns.

LIVERPOOL STREET STATION

Opened in 1874–5; E extension in 1890–4; the Great Eastern Hotel 1880–4 and 1899–1901. The station splendidly refurbished and enlarged by *BR Architects' Department* (project architect *Nick Derbyshire*), in connection with the Broadgate redevelopment (q.v., Streets), 1985–91.

The Great Eastern Railway decided to extend here from Shoreditch in 1865, but shortage of funds delayed construction until 1873–5. A long-severed connection with the Metropolitan Railway, underground and immediately s, explains why the platforms lie so far below street level. Little money remained for the buildings, which were brick French Gothic, by the Company Engineer *Edward Wilson* (contractors *Lucas Bros.*). What they were like may be seen at the block facing Liverpool Street, w of the hotel: of 1985–91, but mostly copying the 1870s building (the rest, demolished, used to extend N and then w). Other parts of the reconstructed buildings either match the old work, or are unambiguously new. The exceptions are the tall, loosely Neo-Victorian twin brick towers with pyramidal roofs, which stand sentinel by the main entrances at the sw corner and on Bishopsgate. They mark where escalators descend to the remodelled concourse.

The glory of the station is its 1870s train shed (w half): one of the last to make a great show, before cheaper, visually duller late C19 systems took over; but all the s part is a matching extension of 1985–91, including the transept over the new concourse which links the whole width of the station. The 1870s roof has very broad twin naves and two narrow outer aisles, separated by a double row of columns. The surviving part begins at a second transept halfway up. This originally marked the concourse of the shorter, suburban platforms, w; the E nave continued s over the main-line platforms, with station buildings and approach ramp in the sw angle. Brunel's roof at Paddington also has transepts, though the main spans here are broader and higher (84 ft, or 25½ metres). The *Fairbairn Engineering Co.* of Manchester supplied the ironwork and may have assisted with Wilson's novel design, of cantilevered spandrel-bracket form, with light suspended trusses. Cast-iron pierced spandrels. The new parts may be distinguished by the four radial braces on their

N–S arches. Otherwise the match is meticulously correct. Though triplets of lancets in the w screen wall impart a Gothic flavour, the roof has round arches. The s part of this wall is also of 1985–91, as is the iron foliage of the capitals and the wooden valancing to the N openings, all to the 1870s design. Beyond the w platforms, the Broadgate's Exchange Square appears on its raft like a hallucination. The E platforms, added 1890–4, have been overbuilt by the Bishopsgate range of the Broadgate centre: a regrettable economy, though done more spaciously here than elsewhere. The demolished superstructure was by *W. N. Ashbee*: plainer train shed, with single colonnades, and buildings fronting Bishopsgate.

The new concourse is reached directly from the Underground, s, and seamlessly from the w via a shopping arcade that opens on to the s entrance to Broadgate Square. The lightness, clarity and ease of circulation will be particularly appreciated by any who knew the Stygian labyrinth that was old Liverpool Street. A new raised gallery runs round all four sides, in a contemporary idiom of white-coated steel and glass. It houses small shops. The E side also opens on to a bus station. Thus the difference of levels is nicely dramatized, and the concourse kept uncluttered. Trains mostly remain visible, tempering the post-steam-age tendency to treat them as a shameful secret to be hidden behind screens and shops. On the gallery's s wall, large FIRST WORLD WAR MEMORIAL from the former booking office, also with portrait reliefs by *Van Golberdinge* and *C. L. Hartwell*.

The GREAT EASTERN HOTEL faces on to the E concourse. It was built as an afterthought by *Charles & C. E. Barry*, 1880–4; extension by *Edis*, 1899–1901. Edis doubled the Bishopsgate range, NE, and added a low sw range facing Liverpool Street. He carried on the Barrys' Neo-Chambord style, in very red Essex brick, many-gabled, with mullioned and transomed windows. Papery detailing in Portland and Corsehill stone. Good interiors, mostly furnished by *Maples*. Of the 1880s the dining room, with square piers and a central dome of pretty coloured glass. In the extension, towards the station's Bishopsgate entrance, the Hamilton Hall (now a pub), a great saloon with nicely vulgar Rococo decoration after the Palais Soubise in Paris, several years before the Ritz in Piccadilly inaugurated the architectural *entente cordiale* for hotels. On the first floor a MASONIC TEMPLE by *Brown & Barrow*, made 1912. Admirably mysterious, glowing with mahogany and rich green marble, with much display of columns around the walls. Facing thrones in elaborate aedicules. Ceiling with a huge sunburst motif. Extensive refurbishment of the hotel is proposed (1996), by *Manser Associates*.

The old PRIORY OF ST MARY BETHLEHEM, founded 1247, stood on the station site. A hospital (Bedlam) was mentioned there in 1329, and by 1403 it specialized in the care of the insane. It survived the dissolution of the Priory, but moved to Moorfields in 1676 (*see* Finsbury Circus).

LLOYD'S OF LONDON
Leadenhall Street and Lime Street

By *Richard Rogers Partnership*, 1978–86 (engineers *Ove Arup & Partners*, team leader *Peter Rice*). The most consistently innovative building the City has seen since Soane's Bank of England, breaking absolutely with its usual preference for architectural safe investments.

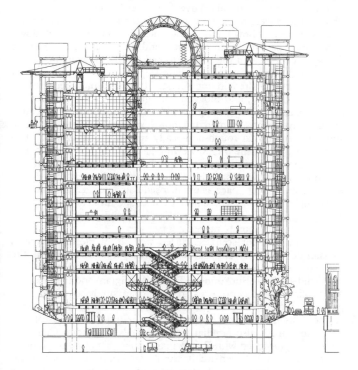

Lloyd's of London. Section

The heart is a rectangular block of offices measuring 220 ft (67 146 metres) by 150 ft (45½ metres), set back a little from the street, end-on but at a slight angle. This is half-hidden by six stacks of services, of varying heights, coming out at irregular points up to the street line. But one is so busy marvelling at the whole giant, stunningly articulated machine that this division between served spaces and servant structures hardly appears at first. For the services are not enclosed, but all piled up and clipped on, like the pipes and capsules of an oil-rig. The rationale, that services require replacement faster than the frame, is less convincing than the magnificent bravura with which the most unlikely units are marshalled into line: windowless round-ended staircases and stacks of portholed toilet pods all of stainless steel; ranks of external lifts like crystalline prisms; and six trim blue cranes on top. Pipes and ducts hurtle up the towers and snake out everywhere along the core. Here, the offices appear as panels of dull grey baffle-glass interrupted by clear lookout strips.

Between them, one notices that within all this steel the frame is of concrete. Its precise, beautifully finished cylindrical uprights appear more clearly on the other sides. The inventive use of engineering-derived detail is apparent down to the very smallest scale. The nocturnal view is no less extraordinary: the glass walls glimmer enigmatically, the outer parts glow with blue, amber and white light: a scheme devised by *Imagination*, 1988. The whole mass stands slightly off the ground, raised over a mysterious (but publicly accessible) cobbled well, bridged by walkways across from the pavement.

To see more of how the building functions, one must walk down Lime Street past the main entrance, and turn W along Lime Street Passage, for a view of the S face (to call it a façade would be most misleading). The upper storeys here step down to expose a glazed atrium, barrel-vaulted in the Crystal Palace fashion, covered in lattice-like framing, and plugged with giant pipes like motorcycle-engine exhausts. The glazing is triple-skinned. Inside, it descends some twelve floors, framed by more exposed concrete columns, appearing somewhat rough-and-ready against the glass walls. The closure in 1992 of the public viewing gallery here was a great pity. The bottom storey is an uninterrupted double-height trading floor, joined by paired elevators within the atrium to the next four floors, which face on to the space as unenclosed balconies. This whole area makes up 'the Room', where underwriters and brokers circulate and deals are struck face to face. Expansion is possible by adding further escalators to incorporate more floors.

One can hunt for sources: glazed walls from Pierre Chareau's Maison de Verre; servant and served spaces from Louis Kahn; the insistence on impermanence and technological contingency from such wild spirits as Buckminster Fuller, Archigram and the Japanese Metabolists; the technological romanticism surely as much from popular culture, films and science fiction as from the machine aesthetic as Corbusier's generation understood it. Much of this heady mixture is also familiar from Rogers's Pompidou Centre in Paris, 1971, designed with Renzo Piano. Like that building, Lloyd's bridged the gaps between architectural avant-garde, engineer, client, and public. In the process, Rogers gave the City its first C20 building that can truly be called famous, in the way that St Paul's or the Tower are famous.

This preoccupation with flexibility – the germ of the whole conception – is explained by Lloyd's history. Edward Lloyd's Coffee House began *c.* 1686 in Tower Street and moved to Lombard Street in 1691. From very early on, shipowners and merchants with interests in distant parts met and transacted business there. Out of this grew the famous insurance organization, which moved to Pope's Head Alley in 1769 and then to the Royal Exchange in 1774. Its space in the third, C19 Exchange was vacated in favour of purpose-built premises by *Sir Edwin Cooper* here, 1925–8. Cooper's aisled 'Room' was too small by the 1950s, when business moved to a new building across Lime Street (q.v.). When this, too, proved inadequate, the company resolved to rebuild the 1920s headquarters, making provision for further expansion. *Cooper*'s frontispiece to Leadenhall Street remains, treated frankly as a giant stone screen to the new building. Astylar, but no less imposing for that, with the doorway in a giant niche, and five upper square apertures beneath a broad top pediment (sculpted figures by *C. L. J. Doman*). It led originally via a long vaulted corridor to the main building, with a longer front to Lime Street. At the corner with Lime Street was Royal Mail House, also by *Cooper*, 1929–30.

Centrepiece of the new Room is the celebrated Lutine Bell, under a wooden tempietto by *Cooper*. (The ninth-floor Board Room comes from *Robert Adam*'s work at Bowood House, Wilts; salvaged in 1955 for the 1950s headquarters, and again reconstructed here, slightly enlarged, within a free-standing stone box. Ceiling with circular panels between delicate scroll-work; more such panels in the coving, with tall foliage panels on the walls: a delicate, feminine composition. The surrounding floor has classical decoration by *Jacques Granges*: an instance of the City's addiction to tradition for such inner sanctums, but in bizarre juxtaposition with Rogers's glass walls and tough concrete coffered ceilings. Otherwise several interiors by *Eva Jiricna*. Cooper's galleried library has been reconstructed within the basement.)

LLOYD'S REGISTER OF SHIPPING
Fenchurch Street

By *Collcutt*, 1899–1901, one of his best buildings; in 1997 in the throes of refurbishment and extension by *Richard Rogers Partnership* (*see* Fenchurch Street). Collcutt's building occupies the corner with Lloyd's Avenue (q.v.), and was built in connection with that street. Of Portland stone, not the brick and terracotta that one associates with the architect. Its Arts-and-Crafts Baroque is familiar from Belcher's Institute of Chartered Accountants (q.v.), with which it shares the motifs of intricate high relief and strong horizontals. The main part has blocked engaged Doric columns to the ground floor and tall Ionic columns framing big aedicules on the rusticated *piano nobile*. On the attic blocked compound piers and corner tourelles with figure friezes. Down Lloyd's Avenue it breaks up into discrete parts to disguise a shift in alignment. The loosening begins in the differently spaced columns in the third bay, where the front steps down. Then four bays treated as a miniature rusticated palazzo; a curved bay carried up as a sturdy domed tower with a loggia (formerly open); and a final section with playful fenestration reading as two bays below, three above. The decoration is integrated with complete success and repays close attention. By *Frampton* the Hopton Wood stone friezes with allegories of trade, ground floor, and the reliefs of maidens etc. on the tourelles; also two delicate bronze female personifications of Steam and Sail, at the corner. Other stone-carving by *J. E. Taylerson*. In the Fenchurch Street entrance wrought-iron gates by *Landsdowne* with repoussé enamel plaques. Stencilled marine decoration in the loggia by *Shrigley and Hunt*.

The INTERIORS could not be inspected, and the following description draws on Martin O'Rourke's account, published by Lloyd's Register, 1993. They are lavish and colourful, with marble lining, panelling and plasterwork (by *G. Jackson & Co.*), all to the highest standards of the time. Decorative painting by *Moira* (who also designed the stained glass) and *Brangwyn* (overmantels);

sculpture and carving in no less advanced taste, by *F. Lynn Jenkins* and by *Bertram* and *Henry Pegram* (chimneypieces). Tiles by *W. de Morgan*. The ENTRANCE HALL has a screen of columns to the STAIRCASE, l., and LANDING, making a single processional space to the first-floor apartments. On the staircase a bronze First World War memorial by *F. Arnold Wright*. On the landing, *Jenkins*'s ripe, exotic polychrome sculpture called The Spirit of British Maritime Commerce; also the bronze and ivory relief frieze. Grandest interior is the barrel-vaulted GENERAL COMMITTEE ROOM, behind the Fenchurch Street front. Paired Ionic columns of red marble with black and green trim. *Moira*'s Michelangelesque tempera ceiling shows the Four Elements, surrounded by the Zodiac and by other allegories. Ground-floor LIBRARY in the NE corner. L-shaped. Vaulting stencilled by *Shrigley & Hunt*. A second-floor room preserves remains of *Brangwyn*'s paintings of Dockside Labour, 1908–14.

LONDON BRIDGE

London's first bridge linking the City and Southwark was almost certainly ROMAN. The river crossing lay close to the line later adopted by the medieval structure, i.e. immediately downstream of the modern bridge. A ferry may initially have been preferred, but was apparently supplanted later by a timber construction (*see* Introduction p. 29). A timber structure found near Fish Street Hill in 1981 may have been a bridge pier base built *c.* A.D. 85–90, although this is uncertain. A shrine to Neptune, referred to on a lead curse recently found on the adjacent foreshore, may have been built on the bridge.

MEDIEVAL BRIDGES. A crossing was restored by *c.* 1000, and twice replaced in the C11–C12. It was aligned with Fish Street Hill. Timber gave way to stone in the next rebuilding, by the chaplain *Peter of Colechurch*, 1176–1209. It had nineteen arches, a drawbridge at the Surrey end, and a chapel built out over one of the central cut-waters. It was also, famously, lined with houses, first mentioned in 1201. Though much altered, Peter's bridge lasted until the 1820s. In 1282 five arches collapsed and were rebuilt. The chapel was enlarged in the late C14, and in 1426 a sturdy S gatehouse was built (see p. 55). In 1581 waterwheels were set up within two arches, to pump drinking water from the Thames. Many of the houses burnt in 1633 and 1666, but were rebuilt. Only in 1758–62 did *George Dance the Elder* and *Sir Robert Taylor* clear them away. They also replaced two central arches with a single span. So the bridge was latterly more curious than beautiful.

The C19 BRIDGE was built further W in 1823–31 to *John Rennie Sen.*'s design, by his son, also *John*. Five quite ambitious elliptical granite arches of up to 152 ft (46⅓ metres) span, on slightly troublesome timber-piled foundations. Widened in 1903–4, by cantilevering the footways. On demolition in 1968, the granite facework was sold and re-erected at Lake Havasu City, Arizona, USA. Remains of its screen walls may be seen by the Fishmongers' Hall (q.v.), and a land span in Southwark (*see London 2: South*). For the contemporary N approach *see* London Bridge Approach and King William Street.

The PRESENT BRIDGE is of 1967–72 by *Mott, Hay & Anderson*, with *Lord Holford* as architectural adviser. Prestressed-concrete cantilevers form three slender spans, founded on concrete piers dug deep into the clay. Short stone masts stand on the cutwaters. Though the spans are graceful, the effect is spoiled where the N span is infilled over the bank.

LONDON GUILDHALL UNIVERSITY
Minories

The former School of Navigation. By the *GLC Department of Architecture and Civic Design*, 1966–70 (architect *Sir Hubert Bennett*, education architect *Michael Powell*). L-shaped, four and five storeys. Simple aggregate-faced concrete bands and mullions, white and grey details. Large entrance to Crescent through the Minories range.

MANSION HOUSE*
Mansion House Street and Walbrook

Designed as a residence for the Lord Mayor by *George Dance the Elder*, Clerk of Works to the City of London. Begun in 1739, first occupied in 1752, and still in domestic use today amidst the banks, offices and shops of the centre of the City.

The idea of such a residence was first mooted after the Fire of 1666, but came to fruition only in the 1730s, when other cities, such as Dublin and York, were building or purchasing mansion houses for their mayors. It was conceived as a statement of civic power at a time when the City was asserting itself in financial and political

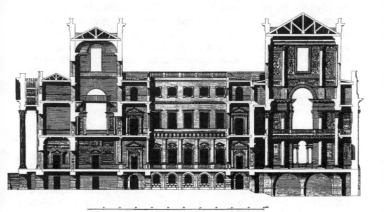

Mansion House. Section

* This entry was contributed by Sally Jeffery. Her *The Mansion House* (1994) is the essential work.

matters. The site, occupied before the Fire by St Mary Woolchurch Haw and its churchyard and afterwards by the Stocks Market, was finally chosen in 1736. Dance's Palladian design was preferred over others supplied by *Gibbs*, *John James*, *Isaac Ware*, *Giacomo Leoni*, *Batty Langley* and *Capt. de Berlain*.

Although reasonably regular in shape and conveniently central, the site was relatively small. On to it, Dance squeezed accommodation for the Lord Mayor and his household, rooms for large civic entertainments, and a Justice Room where the Lord Mayor presided as Chief Magistrate of the City. So the Mansion House was not quite a private palace like Burlington House. Nor was there room for the mews courts or service wings of such great West End houses, still less for the broad entrance courtyard introduced by Roger Pratt at his short-lived Clarendon House (1664). The constricted site instead suggested two exceptional features to the architect, neither of which remains intact. The first was the use of an internal courtyard at first-floor level, covered over in 1795 by *Dance the Younger* to provide more space and to safeguard the structure (a similar arrangement was followed at Spencer House some years later). The second was the two great transverse attics at front and back, crowning the Ballroom and Egyptian Hall respectively. They were removed in 1842 (front) and 1795 (rear). Other rooms were arranged on four floors, connected by four staircases. Of these, the Great Stair, SE, was removed in 1795, the SW stair replaced in 1931 and again in 1991–3. Principal state rooms are on the first floor, with the Ballroom and accommodation for the Lord Mayor and Lady Mayoress on the second. Both these floors were intended for use during grand entertainments. The ground floor was the domain of the servants and the kitchen, and the third floor contained bed-chambers.

A constantly increasing household demanded more accommodation and more office space, which C19 alterations had done little to supply. So in 1930–1 *Sydney Perks*, City Surveyor, with *Sydney Tatchell* as consultant, introduced a discreet upper attic. He also worked on the Egyptian Hall. The latest refurbishment was in 1991–3, under the direction of the Corporation of London, with *Donald W. Insall & Associates* as consultant architects for the historic areas. It saw the departure of the Court or Justice Room to No. 1 Queen Victoria Street next door (q.v.), the replacement of the Saloon roof, and improvements to circulation routes for visitors, as well as complete redecoration and air-conditioning.

Exterior

The building is faced with Portland stone, except for the S end where the brick is left exposed. The sides were closely bounded by other buildings, which deprived the lower floors of adequate daylight. It was for this reason, as much as for fashion, that Dance chose a courtyard plan, which allowed light to penetrate to the heart of the building.

The N entrance is distinguished by a giant hexastyle Corinthian portico on a rusticated base, probably inspired by Colen Campbell's Wanstead, Essex, though here set against a square-windowed attic. C18 illustrations show how powerfully it originally appeared amongst the older houses. The portico still holds its own as a visual hinge of the great crossing opened up in the C19 in front of the Bank and Royal Exchange. It was originally still more imposing, with twin double flights of steps flanking a small forecourt with obelisks and railings; but these were gradually reduced over the years, notably in connection with the new Queen Victoria Street, 1867. The pediment was carved by the young *Robert Taylor*, whose father, also *Robert*, was one of the mason-contractors. It shows the personified City of London, wearing a turreted crown and supporting the City's Coat of Arms, trampling Envy and receiving the benefits of Plenty brought to London by the River Thames. Good carving over the first-floor windows by another mason-contractor, *Christopher Horsnaile Jun.*

The side elevations are divided into three: six quietly Palladian bays in the centre; more powerful three-bay ends. These ends each have paired giant pilasters marking their centre and outer bays, but not the inner one, which is slightly recessed. Its details match those of the adjacent central section, thus easing the transition between centre and ends: an effect foreign to the high Palladianism of Burlington and his followers, with its insistence on the dry articulation of separate parts. The central bay at each end has on the first floor a very big Venetian window, and above it a giant round-headed window, rising through the cornice from the second floor to the third. These light the Ballroom and the Egyptian Hall. The imposing attics which originally surmounted these bays each had a large upright window and a pedimented gable. Dance's source for these was probably Campbell again, in his published design for the principal front of Houghton, derived in turn from the C17 angle towers of Wilton, Wilts. But in translation they acquired an almost Baroque air. Connoisseurs were not alone in their misgivings: teasing Londoners christened them the Mayor's Nest and Noah's Ark. Their removal has left the house with a much tamer appearance. The Doric w porch was added off-centre by *Bunning* in 1846 and is now the principal entrance.

Interior

The ground-floor rooms, considerably partitioned, now provide staff offices and dining rooms, gold and silver vaults, and entrance halls and cloakrooms for visitors, with the kitchen in its original position at the s end. The main entrance is through the WALBROOK HALL, intended for the stables but never so used, and adapted in 1846 as an entrance hall by *Bunning*, who designed the impurely elaborated ceiling. Inner porch and doorcase of 1991–3. The INNER HALL was once part of the vaulted area under the open central cortile. Modern rustication to the columns. It leads into the WAITING HALL, l. Here a good display of marble mayoral busts. Lavatories occupy the partitioned old SERVANTS' HALL, N. Doors from the waiting hall lead to two rectangular open-well staircases, placed behind the recessed linking bays of the N end. Both climb to the full height of the house. Their old-fashioned closed strings and generally modest details are explained when one remembers that they were secondary to the main staircase removed in 1795. The NORTH-EAST STAIRCASE retains its original form, and is unpainted, as originally, to display the carved oak. The NORTH-WEST STAIRCASE was extended to a curve on the first and second floors in 1860, so that the treads could be made shallower.

FIRST FLOOR. Dance's interiors are based on Palladian and Jonesian prototypes as illustrated by William Kent and Isaac Ware, with stately doorcases and marble chimneypieces (by *Christopher Horsnaile Jun.*) appropriate to such grand, semi-public spaces. But their special character derives from the distinctively lighter and more up-to-date Rococo details, notably the superb wood carving and moulded plaster trophies of the first floor, by *John Gilbert* and *George Fewkes* respectively. Comparison with Dance's drawings, made as late as 1748–9, suggests that these were last-minute additions in response to the Rococo fashion that found full expression shortly afterwards at Norfolk House and Chesterfield House. The whole interior was originally painted stone colour and white.

The original main axis formed a processional way from the portico across the courtyard and into the Egyptian Hall: the most inventive feature of Dance's design. The first interior thus encountered was the VESTIBULE just inside the portico. Here the grandeur of the interior is announced by the very richly ornamented coved ceiling, overdoors with plaster putti supporting the City Arms, and statuary niches alternating with six carved Rococo brackets by *Gilbert*. The rooms to l. and r., now used as offices, include the former Court Room (NE).

The PASSAGE ROOM leads from the vestibule through a screen of columns into the SALOON. This was formed when *Dance the Younger* covered over the courtyard in 1795. His roof was replaced in 1861–2 under *Bunning's* direction, and again in 1991–3. The new roof, loosely inspired by what is known of the design by the younger Dance, has over the central space a plain cove and octagonal toplight. The cross-passages at each end were always enclosed. They have especially extravagant plasterwork. The Doric columns across the short ends are original (fluted in the C19), but the colonnades along the sides are C19 introductions, renewed in 1991–3. They stand on the lines of C18 balustrades, which separated the central space from light-wells to the ground floor. In 1991–3 also one bay of the colonnades was infilled on each side, to accommodate lifts and other services. The three unblocked bays of the colonnade between now appear as screens to smaller rooms on either side. These were once lit by windows giving on to the courtyard, the stone aedicules of which survive beneath paint. The LONG PARLOUR, W side, was used for dining and receiving visitors, and is little altered since 1752. Deeply coffered ceiling, rich to the point of oppressiveness, with garlands and masks on the sides of the beams. Panelled walls, with aedicules around the windows. Grand chimneypiece with broken pediment and marble columns, S. The N chimneypiece is C19. On the E side lie two state DRAWING ROOMS, a matching pair created in 1822 using part of the space of the Great Stair, S (removed by *Dance the Younger* in 1795), and the old Common Parlour, N. The grisaille roundels (by *Edward Edwards*, 1774–5) and *Gilbert's* carved tabernacle frames from these spaces were rearranged, and the plasterwork of the old Common Parlour copied. A new chimneypiece was made for the S room, with overmantel by *William Daniels* (1822–3) to complement that by Edwards in the room to the N. Windows on to the courtyard were blocked, creating the only unornamented wall-space on the first floor. Mid-C19 inventory descriptions inspired the decorative schemes of 1991–3.

The EGYPTIAN HALL occupies the entire s part of the house above the ground floor. The inspiration was the reconstruction by Palladio of Vitruvius's Egyptian Hall, and Lord Burlington's fashionable version of it at the York Assembly Rooms. The difference here is that the end walls have applied half-columns instead of a full colonnade. The order is Corinthian, with round bases instead of the canonical square ones. The ancestry of the design was obscured in 1795, when the crazily tall clerestoried, flat-ceilinged third storey was replaced as unsafe by *Dance the Younger*'s coffered barrel-vault. The criss-cross bayleaf bands, of papier mâché, were added c. 1845. Grey and white decoration, with some gilding (the 1750s scheme was all white). In 1930 *Perks* and *Tatchell* opened the windows on the s and added the gallery, the latter reinstating a feature removed in 1795. C18 ladies had used it to view their menfolk dining. In the niches of the ambulatories stand magnificent marble statues, commissioned from eminent sculptors of the day in three lots in 1853, 1856 and 1861. Subjects are taken not from the ancients but from English literature, from Chaucer to Byron: a nice illustration of Victorian nationalistic enthusiasm. The artists of the 1853 batch are: *Baily* (Morning Star); *J.H. Foley* (Egeria); *Calder Marshall* (Griselda); *Lough* (the Elder Brother, from Comus); *MacDowell* (Leah); *F. Thrupp* (Timon of Athens). Those of the 1856 batch: *Wyon* (Britomart); *Durham* (Hermione); *Theed* (The Welsh Bard). The artists of the 1861 batch: *E. B. Stephens* (Alfred the Great); *J. S. Westmacott* (Alexander); *Durham* (Alastor); *John Hancock* (Il Penseroso); *Susan Durant* (The Faithful Shepherdess). Two more statues, both ordered in 1856, stand in the Saloon: *Foley*'s Caractacus and *Weekes*'s Sardanapalus. *Baily*'s figure of Genius, ordered 1856, was destroyed in 1941. Stained glass of 1868, by *Alexander Gibbs*: historical scenes in a well-understood early C16 manner. In 1991–3 a new fire-escape stair was constructed on the s, and the canopy of state from the old Justice Room (1879) installed.

After the creation of the first-floor drawing rooms, the second floor became more private, but its rooms were originally intended for show: hence their grand chimneypieces by *William Barlow*, and ornate plasterwork and carving. The largest interior is the long, narrow BALLROOM, where in the C18 guests of both sexes would mingle after dinner. In 1842 it was lowered by *William Mountague*, to complement the modified Egyptian Hall, and the present coved and coffered ceiling installed. The room retains Dance's hefty gallery and a magnificent set of plaster trophies celebrating music, dancing, drinking and love-making. Third-floor rooms are more utilitarian, with uncarved dados and plain walls, and simple chimneypieces.

MONUMENT

Fish Street Hill

Erected in 1671–6 to commemorate the Great Fire of London. 'A Colume or Pillar of Brase or Stone' was stipulated in the first Rebuilding Act of 1666. The design seems to have been a collaboration between *Wren* and *Hooke*, his friend and colleague in scholarship and architecture (though according to Aubrey by Hooke alone). It was raised on the site of the destroyed St Margaret Fish Street Hill, close to the house in Pudding Lane where the Fire began. Fish Street Hill then formed the approach to old London Bridge, so that the Monument greeted those crossing from the S; the present situation, off the main routes, dates from the 1830s and the new London Bridge alignment.

The Monument is of Portland stone and stands 202 ft (61½ metres) high, 70 ft (21⅓ metres) more than Trajan's column and enough even now to tower over its rebuilt surroundings. It is a fluted Roman Doric column on a tall pedestal, with a square balcony above the capital. On top is a drum and an elongated cupola (or as it was then called a cippus and a meta), with an urn of gilt copper by *Robert Bird*. The four sculpted dragons on the corners of the pedestal and the cartouches between them were carved by *Edward Pierce*. *Joshua Marshall* was master mason. The first design had flames of gilt brass coming out of loopholes all the way up and a phoenix at the top. Wren preferred a statue of Charles II or an allegorical female figure, but according to his letter of 1675 he was overruled by the King, who 'was pleased to thinke a large metal ball would be most agreeable, in regard it would give an ornament to the town, at a very great distance'. Kerry Downes points out that Wren probably wished to re-create literally the ancient formula of a statue on a column. The chief alteration since has been the addition of the iron cage to Wren's railings in 1842, following a spate of suicides.

66   On the W side of the pedestal is a large RELIEF by *Cibber*, who was paid for it in 1674. On the l. the City is represented despondent amongst burning ruins, upheld by Time. On the r. the King, in Roman attire, directs Architecture and Science to succour her as the rebuilt City rises behind. Peace and Plenty fly overhead. The figures are arranged in a plane and do not engage with the architectural perspective behind. The composition seems to derive from paintings of tapestries glorifying Louis XIV, but the conception reflects Cibber's Italian training. On the other three sides inscriptions in Latin giving particulars of the Fire. On the N side an inscription added in 1681 originally stated that the fire was caused 'by the treachery and malice of the popish faction ... to introduce popery and slavery'. This was effaced under James II, re-cut under William and Mary, and finally obliterated to antiquarian protests in 1830. Inside, the visitor ascends to the platform by 311 spiral steps of black marble. A further 34 steps continue into the urn itself, from which C18 visitors would chip pieces as souvenirs.

MUSEUM OF LONDON
London Wall

By *Powell & Moya*, 1968–76 (*Charles Weiss & Partners*, structural engineers), completing the London Wall scheme (q.v.). The Museum was conceived in 1961 as an amalgamation of the Corporation's collection with the London Museum. The former, founded in 1826, was housed from 1876 beneath the former Guildhall Library, then after the Second World War in the Royal Exchange. The latter was founded in 1912 and accommodated variously in Lancaster House and Kensington Palace. Powell and Moya were appointed in 1962 and drew up their first design in 1964-6. This was reworked as the present design, after the plan to build over the Ironmongers' Hall site, N (q.v.), was abandoned.

From pavement level the museum appears forbidding, not least because the entrance is not apparent. A broad, irregular white-tiled block extends along London Wall and up Aldersgate Street. Unity is given by a narrow ribbon of windows to the upper storey, just below the top. Facing Aldersgate Street the upper storey projects and the whole partly stands on piers, with a glazed corridor suspended below. At the corner, the museum spans between a high dark brick-clad plinth to an irregular, battered oval bastion, also of dark brick, that forms the roundabout where Aldersgate Street meets London Wall.

The entrance is at walkway level, facing a sunken garden made inside the roundabout. With its tall pilotis this part evokes Corbusier, though, as with the ribbon of windows, the manner is that of his Villa Savoye a generation before rather than the post-war work. But the juxtaposition of a hard-edged, white-tiled upper building floating above a rounded, black-brick-clad substructure also recalls Sir Denys Lasdun's Royal College of Physicians, Regent's Park, 1959–64 (*see London 3: North West*). Standing sentinel at the E, a tower of offices for rent (called Bastion House), on piers of fine biscuit-coloured concrete. Its sombre bronzed curtain-walling rebukes the undistinguished materials of the earlier London Wall towers, E.

The rationale of the museum's irregular, inward-turning design becomes clearer from the long entrance court, with its tall pitched and glazed roof. The decision to retain the Ironmongers' Hall led the architects to split the museum into two wings: offices and lecture hall in a W wing facing Aldersgate Street; galleries and library in a much larger E wing. Colossal STATUES of Isis and Osiris by *Gahagan*, more evocative than accurate, flank the public entrance (added 1994). They came from the front of *P. F. Robinson*'s Egyptian Hall, Piccadilly, 1812 (dem. 1905). Further E, in the little garden called Nettleton Court, MEMORIAL to John Wesley, 1981, a flame-like bronze scroll, cast by *Morris Singer*. The entrance court itself was partly glazed in by *Pentagram* in 1992, making a shop on the E. This makes it an excessively long walk to reach the galleries, which form two chronological circuits around a square courtyard. Their arrangement is apparent from a gallery by the ticket desks, which overlooks the lower floor and the glazed and barrel-vaulted ramp linking the levels along one side of the garden. The original layout (by *Higgins, Ney & Partners*, being revised from 1994), successfully integrated large- and small-scale exhibits in a varied sequence of exhibition rooms and reconstructed interiors. One master-stroke of the circuit is the piercing of the E gallery wall with two windows so that the visitor may scrutinize sections of the City wall as outdoor exhibits at appropriate points. In the courtyard a historical display of plants, designed by *John Harvey*, 1990.

While the contents of museums fall outside the scope of the

Buildings of England, many of the City's most significant archaeological finds mentioned on other pages may be found here. Other exhibits include part of a C14 statue of St Christopher, recovered from a wall of Tudor date in Newgate, a fine late C17 wrought-iron gate from Lovat Lane, and an excellent shopfront of *c.* 1770 from No. 15 Cornhill. One reconstructed interior stands out: Baring's bank office from No. 8 Bishopsgate, by *Lewis Cubitt*, 1853, altered by *Norman Shaw*, 1880–1.

PATENT OFFICE
Southampton Buildings

A confused, unimpressive complex, much larger than it appears from any one viewpoint. The story is of generally parsimonious expansion on a cramped site. Facing Southampton Buildings, first the symmetrical stone-faced Tudor LIBRARY BLOCK, r. By *Sir John Taylor*, executed by *Sir Henry Tanner*, 1899–1902. Incorporated, l., the surviving W part of STAPLE INN BUILDINGS, facing Staple Inn garden. By *Wigg & Pownall*, 1842–3, Jacobean, gault brick and stone. Built for the Taxing Masters in Chancery. Shaped gables damaged in 1941 were replaced by a crude parapet. Then a ruthlessly utilitarian section in nasty cheap cream brick, by the *Ministry of Works*, 1954–5 (replacing the bombed section and an extension of 1885–6). A giant, dispiriting Tudor wing eighteen bays long faces Furnival Street, E: 1906–8, by *H. N. Hawkes*. Other parts are dated by Michael Port to 1891–3 (s, facing Took's Court) and 1909–14.

Buried within, *Taylor*'s library, for public inspection of the patents. A harsh but spectacular space 140 ft (32½ metres) long, lit from skylights and a clerestory, with two tiers of steel-framed, fireproofed galleries (*Homan & Rogers*' system) on cast-iron Corinthian columns. Sparing decoration in the wrought-iron panels and cast-iron balusters to the gallery fronts. Original adjustable shelving by *W. Lucy & Co.* of Oxford. The design is an enlarged version of *Pennethorne*'s library (1866–7), which had replaced late C18 premises taken over in 1852. Bow-ended, barrel-vaulted Conference Room, reached by spiral staircase from the vestibule.

POLICE STATION
Bishopsgate

By *Vine & Vine*, 1935–8, replacing premises by *Jones*, 1865–6. Decidedly modern for the City then, though unexceptional by comparison with police stations elsewhere. Flat stone front with simple window bands. The only ornament vestigial horizontals and discreet motifs below the parapets. Granite-faced ground floor, the lintel a five-and-a-half-ton monolith, according to the *Architect's Journal* (1939) 'the largest piece of granite ever fixed in London'. Brick side elevations with streamlined Dudok-type doorcases. Much larger than the front suggests: seven-storey accommodation blocks extend back some 330 ft (over 100 metres).

POLICE STATION
Old Jewry

By *Sydney Perks*, 1929–31. Unusually discreet for a police station: two tall red brick four-storey ranges, domestic Neo-Early-Georgian, facing a narrow courtyard off the street. The arrangement follows that of an early C18 merchant's house and warehouse, bought in 1841 as the City Police headquarters, and the residence of its first Commissioner. Perks extended its site w on to Ironmonger Lane, adding there a stone front with acanthus bracket-cornice. He retained the fine wooden early C18 doorcase (N side), with fluted Doric columns, enriched frieze and big segmental pediment with foliage carving (copied on the s building). The C18 staircase of the N building was also kept. An excellent specimen of the open-well type: newels fashioned as Corinthian columns, slender balusters of fluted and barley-sugar pattern, three per tread. Full-height painted panelling. These forms, and the use of then newly fashionable mahogany, suggest a date *c.* 1730 (a C20 rainwater-head is dated 1726).

POLICE STATION
Snow Hill

Established *c.* 1875; rebuilt 1925–6 by *Sydney Perks*. A conservative but surprisingly fresh design. Narrow, of five storeys, the central faceted bow with bronze aprons. Ornate moulding above the ground floor; top cornice of untrammelled design.

POLICE STATION
Wood Street

By *McMorran & Whitby*, 1962–6. A singular essay in the classical 139 tradition for the 1960s, with distant echoes of Lutyens. McMorran had indeed worked with Lutyens's assistant, Horace Farquharson. The classical allusions seem now most solid and serious by comparison with the archness of 1980s Postmodernism. Four ranges around a courtyard, all faced in finest Portland ashlar. Lower floors with bands alternately smooth and rusticated in widely spaced blocks. The entrance façade on Wood Street is symmetrical, with big segment-headed windows to an upper lecture hall, hipped slated roof and giant rusticated stacks. To the l. a valiant attempt is made to assimilate the style to the elevated walkways of London Wall (q.v.). Rising behind – most unexpectedly – is a high tower (originally a residential 'section house'), also Portland-faced with segment-headed windows, topped by a pitched roof and gable proportioned like a pediment. The Love Lane front, s, is looser, with arched roadway entrances to one side of a pediment housing vents, etc. Stables are accommodated in the E range, in a traditionally proportioned lower block, merging oddly with plain repeated storeys of the tower.

PORT OF LONDON AUTHORITY (FORMER)
Trinity Square

121 By *Sir Edwin Cooper*, 1912–22: too late for the label Edwardian
Baroque, but still with the Edwardian optimism, like a super-palace
for an international exhibition. Established in 1908, in succession to
the Thames Conservancy on Victoria Embankment (q.v.). The contrast with that parsimonious building reflects both the Imperial
monumentalism of the new century and the greater powers of the
new Authority, which took over from the private dock companies.
Pepys Street (q.v.) and Muscovy Street were made on the N and S
sides. The Authority moved to Tilbury in 1970, and the building was
sold. Now WILLIS CORROON.

Cooper's competition-winning design has the Beaux-Arts virtues of
boldness and lucidity one expects from the period. The plan is
perfectly square, except where the SE corner is sliced off for the
entrance. Here a great Corinthian portico with six columns *in antis*
rises through three storeys. Set back above, a mighty square stepped
angle tower, with square columns to l. and r.: the dominant presence
on Trinity Square. Five-storey side ranges, with square end pavilions
also with giant Corinthian columns *in antis*. Those by the portico
contain the main staircases. Subsidiary entrances in the other
pavilions lead to lesser staircases in the inner angles. A uniform
entablature girdles the whole. The central court was occupied until
the Second World War by a domed rotonda of reinforced concrete,
110 ft (30½ metres) in diameter. The entrance vestibule flowed
directly into it, with subsidiary entrances through the outer ranges.
SCULPTURE. On the tower Father Thames, and (sides) allegories
of Exportation, l., in a galleon with sea horses, of Produce, r., in a
chariot with oxen; by *Albert Hodge*, executed by *C. L. J. Doman*. Near
the entrance, figures of Commerce and Navigation by *Doman*.
   The broad double-height entrance vestibule, worthy of a northern
City Hall, has giant pilasters and straw-coloured Subiaco marble
lining. Passages r. and l. to the main staircases, ahead to a straightforward curtain-walled block of 1975–6 (by *Mills Group Partnership*),
on the site of the rotonda. Long aisled halls around the outer ranges,
restored 1992–4. The grandest interiors form a second-floor suite.
They have heavy, rather coarse plaster ceilings and opulent oak and
walnut panelling, with limewood trophies etc. carved by *George
Haughton*. Largest is the vast former BOARD ROOM behind the
portico, with paired Corinthian pilasters. Along the S side four
COMMITTEE ROOMS, each in a different Order. Above, in a storey
formed within the mansard *c.* 1975, STAFF RESTAURANT by *Chris
Wilkinson*, 1993.

PUBLIC RECORD OFFICE
Chancery Lane

98 Built in stages 1851–96, largely to *Sir James Pennethorne*'s forbiddingly functional Gothic design of 1850.* Closed in 1997, its
records transferred to Kew and Islington.

* *See* Geoffrey Tyack, *Sir James Pennethorne and the Making of Victorian London* (1992).

The Office consolidated widely scattered papers on the site of the former Rolls Estate where government records were kept. It replaced the austerely Palladian Rolls House, 1717–24, *Colen Campbell*'s only building from his brief tenure as Deputy Surveyor of the Works. Construction was slow and intermittent: central block 1851–3; E wing, up to Fetter Lane, 1864–70; central tower, lower than first intended, 1865–7. The big Chancery Lane addition, W, through which visitors entered, is as late as 1891–6, by *Sir John Taylor*, but with only minor differences. This complex history, and the failure to complete the S range along the central roadway, gave the buildings a pleasantly varied plan: main, not very wide symmetrical Chancery Lane façade, long S front overlooking a lawn, visible from Fetter Lane, E, and an asymmetrical aspect in Fetter Lane proper. Towards Fetter Lane also a pretty hexagonal LODGE, dated 1901. The close called Rolls Place, off Fetter Lane, reveals yet another symmetrical group with two towers. The reason for such show here is that a major new road was planned to run immediately N when the building was begun.

The module throughout is a narrow upright storage bay, with boldly projecting sheer mullions and at the top a depressed triangular arch. Pennethorne inclined towards a classical treatment, but the buttresses and tall, narrow windows in tiers of three demanded by the iron framing led him to accept Gothic, 'if an ecclesiastical feeling can be at the same time avoided'. Thus it became the first major public building in the style after the Houses of Parliament, with which it shared the same builders and chief carver (respectively *J.&H. Lee* and *John Thomas*). The triangular arch motif recurs everywhere, and only the upper parts blossom out into Perp polygonal turrets, pierced parapets, and the like. The phases may best be distinguished by the differences at this upper level. On the central tower STATUES of four queens: Victoria, Elizabeth I, Anne, and Maud, all by *Durham*, 1866. Statues of kings on the 1890s section by *Farmer & Brindley*. Much of the rubble walling, in various stones, has had to be replaced (by *D. W. Insall & Associates*, c. 1990).

Lengthy, narrow corridors within underline the supremacy of function over show. Fireproof iron doors and brick arches throughout. Fireproof too the slate-shelved storage cells and cast-iron roof tiles. The double-height former ENTRANCE HALL, beneath the central tower, has scarcely enough Gothic trim to soften the square, bony fabric. The so-called ROUND ROOM for public searches (1864–6) is a minimally Gothic polygon with two galleries and a glazed iron roof.

In the former MUSEUM, near the W entrance, MONUMENTS from the Rolls Chapel. Dr Yonge, Master of the Rolls †1516, attributable to *Pietro Torrigiani*, is the earliest known English monument without Gothic reminiscences, and of a noble beauty and calm quite unheard of in the country at the time.* The formula is the Florentine one of a naturalistic effigy, recumbent on an arch-framed sarcophagus. Effigy of terracotta, setting of Caen stone. In the lunette a terracotta head of Christ flanked by two cherubs' heads. All with pure Early Renaissance detail and pure Roman lettering. The sarcophagus was raised within the arch before c. 1890, hence the

* *See* C. Gavin and P. Lindley, *Church Monuments* Vol. III (1988).

slightly squat proportions. The colouring (though not the gilding) perpetuates the C16 scheme. Fragments of carved angel frieze corresponding to that of Henry VII's Chapel, Westminster Abbey, were found when the monument was dismantled, strengthening the link with Torrigiani. – Richard Alington †.1561 and wife. Standing alabaster wall-monument, with the usual kneeling figures affronted across a prayer desk. Unusual composition: three kneeling daughters in relief against the front of the desk; main figures under coffered arches with finely carved garlands above; flanking columns of touch. Attributed to the *Cure* workshop (AW). – Lord Bruce of Kinloss †.1611, standing wall-monument of alabaster and touch with four kneeling figures in front of the plinth, semi-reclining effigy on it, lying on the side, cheek propped on hand. Black columns to l. and r. Attributed to *Maximilian Colt* (GF). – William Fortescue †.1749, framed inscription tablet, elegantly done. – STAINED GLASS. Heraldic, incorporating C17 and later panels from the chapel. – Of other furnishings, a statue of George I by *Laurent Delvaux*, from Rolls House, will remain at the building.

Against the SE end of the Chancery Lane range, facing E, the re-erected and incomplete early C13 chancel arch of the original ROLLS CHAPEL, which stood on the site of the 1890s extension. It has moulded capitals and a finely moulded arch. The much-altered chapel, founded by Henry III in 1232–3 for converted Jews, long served as the Rolls' own record office (not to be confused with the Neo-Norman church of St Thomas in the Liberty of the Rolls, by *C. Davy* and *J. Johnson*, 1842 (dem. 1886), which stood further N). The brick shed, E, incorporates plaster RELIEFS of the Continents designed by *Walter Crane*, from *W. S. Witherington*'s St Dunstan's House in Fetter Lane, 1886–7 (dem. 1976).

ROYAL EXCHANGE
Threadneedle Street and Cornhill

By *Sir William Tite*, 1841–4; the greatest of the City's C19 exchanges, and, discounting the bomb-damaged Baltic Exchange, now the only survivor. Its consequential architecture and decoration, superb site, and historical associations all suggest a public role, though general trading ceased as long ago as 1939, overtaken by specialist exchanges elsewhere.

The First and Second Royal Exchanges, 1566 and 1667

Sir Thomas Gresham formed the first Exchange in London on this site, 1566–70. Merchants previously met and did business walking in Lombard Street. Gresham brought over the Netherlandish architect *Hendryck van Paesschen*, and together they gave the City its first major Renaissance-style building. The model was the second *Beurs* (Bourse) at Antwerp, by Cornelis Floris (1531). Arcades of Doric columns around a quadrangle supported a pilastered upper storey with statues of kings in niches and shops behind. By the Cornhill entrance was a bell-tower. A lesser entrance faced Threadneedle Street. The detail was chaste by comparison with much later Netherlandish and English building, though less correct than the lavish triumphal arch raised by Antwerp's English Merchants for Charles V in 1550, probably under Gresham's direction.

The post-Fire replacement of 1667–71, following a similar plan and function, was the grandest monument of artisan classicism in the City. Begun to designs by *Jerman*, it was finished by the mason *Thomas Cartwright Sen.*, who may have designed the towered and arcaded Cornhill frontispiece. It is depicted on the cast-iron PUMP in Cornhill, near the SE corner: a chamfered and fluted obelisk signed by *Phillips & Hopwood*, Engine Makers, and dated 1799 (moved here 1848). Probably designed by *Nathaniel Wright* (Colvin). *George Smith* rebuilt the tower in 1819–24. The Royal Exchange Assurance took space in the upper offices in 1720, joined in 1774 by Lloyd's. The Exchange was still the unrivalled centre of the City's trade when it burned down in 1838.

The Third Royal Exchange, 1841

Sir William Tite came out on top from the scandalously mismanaged competition to replace the C17 Exchange. Amongst favoured entries was one 'ghosted' by *Cockerell*, who requested Tite's assistance with the estimates and ended up losing a limited competition against him the following year.* *Wren*'s St Benet Fink and St Bartholomew Exchange were casualties of the scheme. The contractor was *Thomas Jackson*. It is much larger than its predecessors – it was aligned E–W by taking in ground to the E and making a new open space towards the Mansion House – but perpetuates the arcaded central courtyard and (tucked away at the back) the tower.

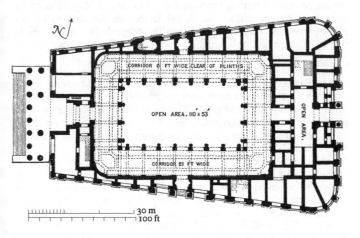

Royal Exchange. Ground-floor plan

Tite's building marks the disintegration of the classical revival in England. Purity is thrown to the winds for the sake of richness – a typical sign of the approaching Victorian Age. Only the W façade is

*The story is told in D. Watkin, *The Life and Work of C. R. Cockerell* (1974); *see* also R. Harper, 'A Sordid Inheritance', *R.I.B.A. Journal* 90 (1983).

still essentially classical, with its unfluted eight-column Corinthian portico and big pediment (sculpture in the pediment by *R. Westmacott Jun.*: Commerce holds the Exchange Charter, with merchants, stevedores etc.). But one notices the change in style in the shape and details of the porch, which has barrel-vaulting sugges-tive of the triumphal arch motif of Cockerell's design, echoed in the three big round-headed openings below. The parade of eclectic ornament intensifies along the sides, with repeated giant pilasters (omitted on the flanking sections of the N front), decorated arched windows, and thick garlands above the side entrances: motifs derived from the Baroque as well as the Dixhuitième. Florid big gates here and elsewhere by *Grissell*, of wrought iron with cast-iron ornament. The back has rounded corners and, in the middle, two attached and two detached giant columns marking the rear entrance. A slender tower rises above, with diagonally set columns in the Wren manner. On top, a weathervane in the shape of Sir Thomas Gresham's grasshopper device, said to be from the 1667 Exchange. The tapering site, 309 ft (94 metres) long, makes this front much wider than the W one – 175 ft (53 metres) as against 119 ft (33 metres). Around the sides, two-storey shops, each forming a fire-proof cell. They perpetuate the Elizabethan Exchange's dual func-tion of trading in luxuries as well as doing business face to face. On the N and NE Tite's design survives intact; the rest were built out between the pilasters in 1852. On the N frontispiece also statues of Whittington by *J. E. Carew* and Myddelton by *S. Joseph*, both 1844, and against the E tower one of Gresham in a niche (by *Behnes*, 1845). Around the whole runs a sympathetically detailed attic, added during reconstruction of 1986–91 for the Guardian Royal Exchange Assurance (successor to the Royal Exchange Assurance) by the *Fitzroy Robinson Partnership* (partner in charge *Colin Christmas*). At the W, it engulfs Tite's arcaded chimneys, originally open in the Vanbrugh manner.

The extent of the late C20 alterations becomes clear only in the COURTYARD, reached from the E via a barrel-vaulted passage with a top-lit lantern where a cross-passage intersects it. Tite's courtyard, open to the sky until 1883, has Tuscan columns set against narrow piers with rusticated arches. Since 1981–2 it has been occupied by a box-like steel-framed trading room made for the London International Financial Futures Exchange (architects *Whinney Mackay-Lewis Partnership*). Disused since 1991, it spoils the space entirely and hides the diapered C16 FLOOR reinstated by Tite; it should be removed. Tite's second, Ionic storey can presently only be viewed from the upper storeys. Above it a new Corinthian stage added by *Fitzroy*'s, accommodating two more storeys (see the piercing of the arches over its lower windows). The same architects also replaced *Charles Barry Jun.*'s glazed barrel-vaulted roof of 1883–4 with a shallower roof of elliptical profile and C19 detail, set on a balustraded parapet to Tite's original design but as it were moved one stage up.

Some interiors were preserved, including the Directors' Suite of the Royal Exchange Assurance, 1929 (SW), with a wainscotted Court Room in an unusually proficient late C17 idiom, and the Soane Room, 1922, based loosely on the Breakfast Room in Sir John Soane's house, a most unexpected choice for the date. In the new storey, an excellent display relating to the three Exchanges. (At the NE and SE corners, occupied until 1928 by Lloyd's, rooms of the 1840s survive.)

Around the outer walls of the ground-floor courtyard is an important series of PAINTINGS, installed 1895–1922 by individual and corporate donation after the courtyard was roofed over. Late Victorian and Edwardian Academic artists display their talents in twenty-three large historical scenes, which however fail to achieve convincing aesthetic unity despite their uniform format. Nine smaller full-length portraits of the 1920s punctuate the sequence. First of the large paintings was *Lord Leighton*'s The Phoenicians and the Early Britons (w wall). Of the remainder, the following deserve special notice: Burning of the Second Exchange, by *Stanhope Forbes*, 1920 (N wall); Modern Commerce, an allegory by *Brangwyn*, 1906, and Alfred the Great by *F. O. Salisbury*, 1912 (w wall); The Fire of London, another night-piece by *Forbes*, 1899 (s wall); Philip the Good by *E. A. Cox*, 1915 (E wall). More by *Salisbury* and such artists as *J. Seymour Lucas*, *E. A. Abbey* and *S. J. Solomon*. In the SE corner a dramatic STATUE of Charles II, a copy of 1792 by *John Spiller* after *Grinling Gibbons*'s statue in the centre of the C17 courtyard. The execution of the original must have been left to *Arnold Quellin*, who also worked on some of the kings for the niches around the courtyard (*see* Central Criminal Court for the survivors). In the NE corner, Queen Elizabeth I by *M. L. Watson*, 1844. In the NW corner a giant bust of Abraham Lincoln by *Andrew O'Connor*, 1930. Stored in 1996, statues of Queen Victoria by *H. Thornycroft*, 1896, formerly in the centre of the courtyard, and by *Lough* of Prince Albert, 1846.

ST BARTHOLOMEW'S HOSPITAL
West Smithfield

The site of St Bartholomew's Hospital has remained the same since it was established by Rahere in 1123. It survived the general wreck of hospitals at the Reformation only because the City prevailed upon Henry VIII to refound it in 1546. Part of the church of Rahere's Augustinian foundation survives in parochial use (*see* St Bartholomew-the-Great). Yet in early 1997 the future of his hospital is uncertain.

The heart of the hospital, and its chief architectural interest, is the main courtyard designed by *Gibbs* and built 1730–68, of which three ranges survive. Expansion thereafter was mostly at the expense of the houses ringing the site, so that later hospital buildings generally face outwards. Outside the central square, internal spaces are in consequence shapeless and unattractive. The C19 is remarkable for the chaste late classicism carried on by the hospital's surveyors *Philip Hardwick*, *P. C. Hardwick* and *Edward I'Anson*. Only under the latter's son *E. B. I'Anson* did the looser late Victorian manner show itself, and even then his vocabulary was Gibbsian. C20 additions by various architects are generally less interesting. Many occupy auxiliary sites in Little Britain, Cock Lane and Bartholomew Close (qq.v.), and N of the Charterhouse (*see London 4: North*).

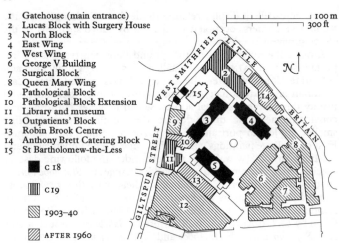

St Bartholomew's Hospital. Plan

BUILDINGS 1700–1870

Seen from West Smithfield, the hospital appears set back behind a long rusticated screen wall, between two Portland-faced entrance buildings. The GATEHOUSE, r., is a striking piece of design dated 1702. The building contract gives *Edward Strong Jun.* as the designer. Faithfully reconstructed and refaced in 1833–4 by *Philip Hardwick*, who added stubby windowless wings. The gatehouse proper might well form a feature of some up-to-date Oxford college of 1700. Certainly it is more emphatically Baroque than the Middle Temple gateway (1684). Narrow, of three bays in three diminishing storeys above the archway. Giant Ionic angle pilasters carry a pediment. In the centre a niche with stone STATUE of Henry VIII by *Francis Bird* (restored in 1988 by *John Sambrook*, for *D. W. Insall & Associates*). Framed by closely coupled Corinthian columns supporting a broken segmental pediment, with reclining figures representing Lameness and Disease (cf. Cibber's celebrated mad figures at Bethlehem Hospital, *c.* 1676). Carved decoration above the windows too, with crutches represented in the central second-floor window hood. The clock over it is an original feature.

The SCREEN WALL replaced tall tenement houses which screened the hospital from West Smithfield, and originally abutted both sides of the gatehouse. They were pulled down mostly in the early 1840s. *Philip Hardwick* provided the design of the wall. The recurring motifs of round-headed arches and broad flat piers do not add up to a coherent composition, due probably to the piecemeal progress of the work. On it a plain MONUMENT of granite and bronze to the Smithfield martyrs, by *Habershon & Pite*, 1870. On the corner with Little Britain, l., the LUCAS BLOCK, a much-altered amalgamation of several different structures. The disused entrance from West Smithfield was part of *P. C. Hardwick*'s Receiving Room (i.e. out-patients' department) of 1861. Its broad opening with columns and steps up led originally to a large hall, which incorporated earlier structures by *P. Hardwick* (1842). This was replaced in 1989–92 by *John Miller & Partners*, who added two plain upper storeys, crowned by an attractive broad-eaved Italianate loggia with seven little round columns. Projecting, r., a single-bay section, representing *P. Hardwick*'s former Surgery House (1842). This began as a single-storey rusticated structure, in 1889 heightened by two more storeys, astonishingly plain for that date. Earlier, more substantial late-lingering Palladianism in *P. Hardwick*'s section behind, again of 1842. It may be glimpsed through the screen wall, or (better) by passing through the gatehouse and turning l. past the little church of St Bartholomew-the-Less (q.v.), whose parish is coterminous with the hospital site. Seven bays, the ends very slightly projecting. The round-arched rusticated ground floor matches the screen wall. The whole might be a half-century earlier. Top storey of 1869, a regret-table addition. The low operating theatre, s, of 1842, was also heightened, in 1913.

Now back to the entrance axis by the gatehouse. Before Gibbs's rebuilding, the hospital buildings formed smallish quadrangles on either side of this line (called the Great Cloister), a plan clearly derived from the Augustinian foundation. By the early c18 this would have looked old-fashioned. The first London hospital to be rebuilt on a large scale to a set orderly pattern was Hooke's Bethlehem Hospital, 1675–6. St Thomas's followed in 1693–1709, the new foundation of Guy's in 1721–5. The decision to rebuild St Bartholomew's was taken in 1723, the year *Gibbs* joined the Board of Governors. In 1728 came the instruction to prepare a design. Work began in 1730, the architect giving his services gratis.

With its three remaining detached, solid, stately, stone-faced 76 blocks of eleven bays, Gibbs's court looks very much like the c18 *beau idéal* of a Cambridge college court. The detail is sparse and Palladian: quoins, a rusticated three-bay ground-floor frontispiece, with pediments to the first-floor windows above it and blocked surrounds to the windows on either side. Other windows have eared surrounds. The North Block through which one enters is pierced by a broad triple archway and distinguished also by projecting wings to the square. Low screen walls with archways originally linked the blocks.

The planning of the group is of some interest. Gibbs explained the use of separate ranges as a precaution against fire. It has also been suggested that the plague outbreak at Marseilles in 1719 gave a new impetus to the isolated block plan. Certainly the ward blocks (remaining on E and W) were planned to reduce cross-infection: the central entrance gave on to a passage serving the ground floor only, upper floors being reached from staircases attached at each end. Another advantage over the plan of spine block with spur wings, as used by Wren at the Royal Naval Hospital, Greenwich, was that construction in stages was easier. The dates are: North Block, 1730–2; West Wing, 1744–52; East Wing, 1757–68 (supervised by *William Robinson*). Craftsmen included *Robert Taylor* (to 1740) and *John Manning Jun.* (1752–8), masons, *James Horne* and *Tobias Priest*, joiners, *William Chapman* and *John Philips*, carpenters. The present Portland facing is however by *P. Hardwick*, 1850–2. It replaced Gibbs's Bath stone, used at the urging of the quarry-owner Ralph Allen: an early instance of its employment in London. Hardwick missed the opportunity to replace Gibbs's urns on the balustrade (removed 1810), and he may have altered slightly the dormered double mansard from the form shown on c18 views. Also by *Hardwick* the ornate FOUNTAIN with youthful atlantes in the centre (1859, restored 1988–90). LAMP-POSTS, SHELTERS etc. of the 1890s. Bath stone may still be seen in the passage through the North Block, the plaster vault of which was rebuilt in stone in 1926. c18 POOR BOXES here, of baluster form and rough workmanship.

Interiors

The interesting interiors are in the North Block. Gibbs designed this to house the Great Hall, approached by a grand staircase at the E end, and in the w part a Clerk's House. This w part burnt out in the Second World War, and the shell was reconstructed *c.* 1960 by *James M. Knowles*, who also made good damage to the block. The 75 STAIRCASE HALL is dark green and gold, with a cantilevered timber staircase climbing in three flights around a broad well. It is a sturdy, somewhat old-fashioned affair, with closed strings, simple balusters and a broad rail. The carved wooden chandelier was given in 1735. The staircase is best known for its two large canvases by *Hogarth*, representing The Pool of Bethesda and The Good Samaritan. He painted them in 1735–7, working without a fee. They represent an important episode in the c18 struggle to find a public for history painting apart from Court and Church. They are not without faults: the main figure-work is somewhat vapid, the landscape (by Hogarth's friend *George Lambert*, chief scene-painter at Covent Garden) un-inspired; but the attendant figures have Hogarth's usual spirited brushwork and characterization. In the principal characters some significant borrowings from the Raphael Cartoons and from Van Dyck. Lower scenes in grisaille, probably by a pupil, represent the founding of the hospital. One *Richards* did the heavy Rococo scroll-work frames and the paintings of medicinal plants just below the ceiling, which has a central oval with painted coffering. The wall below the landing has jarring painted shields and strapwork of 1867.

The GREAT HALL was fitted up by 1738. In proportion roughly a triple cube, 90 ft by 35 ft and 30 ft high (27 by 10½ by 9 metres). The first impression is of rich cream, gold, porphyry and dark brown. The ceiling here and in the stairhall is by the otherwise obscure *J.-B. Michele*, to Gibbs's design. Shallow guilloche bands make rectangu-lar panels filled with thin foliage scrolls. Highest relief is reserved for big central rosettes in the three main panels and the ten square lesser ones. Nine bays of windows, in two storeys: the result of the decision to preserve external uniformity around all four blocks. In the centre of the N wall, a Palladian fireplace with plain console-brackets and a pedimented overmantel. Opposite, a stained-glass WINDOW of Henry VIII giving the hospital its charter; made probably *c.* 1664, restored by *Price* in 1743. No dais, but at the w end a version of the Whitehall PORTRAIT of Henry VIII, in a pedimented surround with carved drops, designed by *Gibbs* with *Hogarth*'s advice. But these emphases count for less than the pattern of pedimented boards and painted panels lettered in gold with names of donors and officers. They extend over all the walls above the low dado and even on to the window embrasures. *Richards* did the earlier ones; the latest are of 1905. By the fireplace two carved and painted wooden STATUES of a wounded soldier and sailor (a half-figure), of mysterious origin, first recorded in the 1650s and probably not much older. Also displayed here are some of the hospital's BUSTS, by such artists as *Lough*, *Behnes* and *Sievier*. One other room of interest: the HENRY VIII ROOM (former Receiving Room), off the staircase hall on the ground floor. White-painted bolection-moulded panelling, dentil cornice, carved overmantel.

LATE C19 AND C20 ADDITIONS

C20 additions may briefly be dealt with. The fourth (SE) side of the square is the GEORGE V BUILDING (1934–7 by *W. T. A. Lodge* of *Lanchester, Lucas & Lodge*), a tall symmetrical stone-faced block, at once domineering and bland. Gibbs's block here (1736–40) had projecting wings to match the elevation facing it. Also by *Lodge* the red brick SURGICAL BLOCK behind, 1929–30, on part of the former Christ's Hospital site. Behind the NE block lies the ANTHONY BRETT CATERING BLOCK, 1988–90 by *Howell, Killick, Partridge & Amis*. The architects responded to the awkward site with a boldly modelled, near-windowless mass, best seen from Little Britain beyond the side gate. Stone-coloured stucco and ground-floor channelling evoke the older structures adjoining. Facing Little Britain further S, the tall QUEEN MARY WING, built 1921–9 as nurses' homes by *H. Edmund Mathews*. Two equal parts, set back at an obtuse angle. Without strong character. Behind the SW ward block, the ROBIN BROOK CENTRE by *Cusdin, Burden & Howitt*, 1979, feeble Neo-Georgian.

The best of the remainder face Giltspur Street, W of the gatehouse. First *E. B. I'Anson*'s PATHOLOGICAL BLOCK, 1907–9. Four storeys of even height. Seven bays, the ends and centre with paired lights. Devices derived from Gibbs (eared and blocked surrounds, key blocks) differentiate the windows of each storey; yet the result is generically Italianate rather than Neo-Gibbs or Neo-Palladian. Then a narrow stone-faced section from an extension by *Adams, Holden & Pearson*, 1963–70. Next, *Edward I'Anson*'s LIBRARY and MUSEUM, 1877–9, the hospital's first building to match Gibbs's work in scale and ambition. Exceptionally correct and disciplined for the date, resembling a giant club-house of the 1830s (compare his more licentious British & Foreign Bible Society, Queen Victoria Street, 1867–9). Battered granite plinth, flat-fronted Portland stone above, with square granite panels in a blank zone above tall pedimented first-floor windows. Gibbs is evoked in the ground-floor windows, and formerly also in a balustrade, above the generous cornice with its big lettering. The lower two floors house the library, which has a gallery with Gibbsian twisted balusters. Behind the blank upper walls, the museum is a well-preserved, utilitarian space with cast-iron gallery and skylights. Then *E. B. I'Anson*'s OUTPATIENTS' BLOCK, 1903–7 (assistant *Rowland Plumbe*). Larger and looser than its neighbours, with two pedimented sections broken forward asymmetrically. Rusticated entrance, broadly similar to those of the ward blocks, but with flanking bays copied from the mid-C18 Hartshorn Gate to the N (dem. 1877).

ROMAN REMAINS. This area, W of the town wall, was an intensively used Roman cemetery. Stone coffins discovered nearby in 1887, one of which contained a leaden coffin with cable-mouldings, are preserved in the library block.

ST BRIDE'S INSTITUTE
Bride Lane

By *Robert C. Murray*, 1893–4, after a competition assessed by Champneys. Established with funds from parochial charities to further technical education, particularly that connected with printing. A swimming pool and gymnasium were also included. Informal red brick, Queen Anne tinged with Wren. A gabled three-bay frontispiece faces N towards Fleet Street. Six large windows to a first-floor reading room, l. Steep roof with flèche. Entrance from St Bride's Passage, W, reached by steps up from Bride Lane. Well-preserved but unexceptional interiors. On the landing, *Frampton*'s BUST of Samuel Richardson, the C18 novelist.

ST PAUL'S CATHEDRAL CHOIR SCHOOL
New Change

1962–7, designed by *Leo de Syllas* of the *Architects' Co-Partnership* and carried out after his death by *Michael Powers*. Much appreciated by Pevsner (1973): 'The decision ... to have the choir school so close to the cathedral (and on such expensive ground) is much to be lauded. The way the architects have achieved a small scale close to the huge scale of the cathedral is equally to be lauded. What is more, their building is evocatively right. It conveys the concept of a children's building, with its projecting [leaded] roof looking like a funny hat reminiscent of the morel or some other edible fungus. The building is broken up into two parts by the low hall etc. between higher blocks. This reduces the scale yet more. The windows of the four-storey parts are placed in slits running from the ground level to the roof'. The low centre divides blocks for teaching and sleeping. It also allows views through to the cathedral whose materials the school echoes, although in rough roach instead of smooth Portland ashlar. The L-shaped S part has a matching smaller SE block, detached.

Incorporated at the SW corner, the restored tower of *Wren*'s ST AUGUSTINE WATLING STREET, or Old Change. The church was first mentioned *c.* 1148. Excavations in 1965 indicated a building 61 ft (18½ metres) long, with remains of a N aisle documented in the 1250s. As rebuilt in 1680–4 it was plain and modest, with a barrel-vault on Ionic columns and groin-vaulted aisles (mason *Edward Strong Sen.*). In 1695–6 the tower was completed and a graceful leaded steeple added. Its finial was altered to a heavier pointed spire in repairs of 1830 by *J. H. Taylor* and *Alfred Ainger*. Church body (restored by *Blomfield*, 1878) and spire were destroyed in 1941, but the latter was reconstructed according to its more slender original state by *Paul Paget* of *Seely & Paget*, 1966.

The tower is markedly oblong in plan and modest in scale,

perfectly proportioned in relation to both school and cathedral. Simple rectangular belfry apertures, then Baroque obelisk pinnacles and a lacy Baroque pierced parapet. Behind the parapet brackets rise from the corners to an open stage topped by urns, surmounted by a finial like an elongated onion. Surviving drawings in the hand of *Hawksmoor* suggest he was responsible for the design. They show the finial evolving from a giant pine cone like that of Wren's pre-Fire design for St Paul's.

For the old Choir School, *see* Carter Lane.

SERJEANTS' INN
Off Fleet Street to the s

The Inn was like an Inn of Chancery, but accommodated Serjeants-at-Law, who were barristers of superior rank. The Serjeants' Inns have a confusing history. Serjeants resided here 1424–42 and again from the c 16 to 1732. Another Inn, in Chancery Lane, was occupied 1442–59 and 1496–1877; its buildings, by *Sir Robert Smirke*, 1836–9, lasted until *c.* 1910. A third Serjeants' Inn, N of Holborn, was occupied 1459–96. Present offices by *Devereux & Davies*, 1951–8 (consultant *Sir Hubert Worthington*). Red brick, with a stone ground floor and stone dressings. Two long w wings make a court with a fountain. The lack of symmetry and of alignment between the E and s windows typifies the apologetic looseness of most post-war Neo-Georgian. The pedimented centrepiece recalls *Ezekiel Delight*'s Amicable Assurance offices here (1793, destroyed 1941).

At the w end, outside the Inn proper, is OLD MITRE COURT, before the Second World War a narrow, separate close. Mitre Court Buildings, s side, belong with the Inner Temple (*see* Temple p. 352). The w side is MITRE COURT CHAMBERS, a large and austere early c19 block of brick, five storeys by seven bays. Round-headed windows on the first floor, set in relieving arches in the projecting end bays. Mitre Court commemorates an Elizabethan inn, of which part of the cellar remains beneath Hoare's Bank, Fleet Street (q.v.).

SION COLLEGE
Victoria Embankment

Red brick Tudor Gothic with Ham Hill stone dressings, by *Sir Arthur Blomfield*, 1884–7 (first design 1880). It served as a social centre and library for the clergy of London. The college was established in 1631 under the will of Thomas White, rector of St Dunstan-in-the-West. Its first home was near St Alphege, London Wall. Blomfield's building is friendly, but like much of his work mechanically detailed and passionless. It suffers also from the demolition of its deep two-storeyed SE porch for the Blackfriars Underpass. The entrance was reconstructed by *Ronald Ward & Partners*, 1965–6, with a tactful new entrance on John Carpenter Street, E, and a less tactful low slit-windowed s extension, linking up with No. 9 Carmelite Street (*see* Victoria Embankment). Large s window above, flanked by asymmetrical turrets. It lights the galleried and clerestoried LIBRARY, which rises from the second floor. Open timber roof of pseudo-hammerbeam form. STAINED GLASS of historical figures by *Cox & Barnard*, 1951. On the ground floor a large dining room.

In 1996 the college was dissolved and its collections dispersed. The building is to be sold.

SIR JOHN CASS INSTITUTE
Jewry Street

Built 1898–1901 as a technical institute by *A. W. Cooksey*, with funds from Sir John Cass's bequest. Long astylar three-storey red brick front with Portland dressings in a cheerful free Wren manner. Central arched entrance, chamfered square stair-turret placed off-centre. On the r. it rises to four storeys, the top one reconstructed differently by *Werner Rees* after war damage, 1954. Also by *Rees* the sub-Georgian l. extension, 1931–4. (Inside, the boardroom of the Cass Foundation has a reset C18 fireplace. Two masonry fragments from the ROMAN CITY WALL are preserved in the basement.) In 1970 the institute became part of the City Polytechnic, since 1992 London Guildhall University. Redevelopment by *Chapman Taylor Partners* was proposed in 1996.

SIR JOHN CASS SCHOOL
Duke's Place and Mitre Street

By *A. W. Cooksey*, 1908, in cheerful Neo-Hampton Court Baroque. Brick and stone to Duke's Place, with a central cupola, on a rusticated plinth with pilasters above. Twin entrances with broken pediments and figures of CHARITY CHILDREN in niches, no doubt from the school in Houndsditch, rebuilt with Sir John's endowment in 1709–10. In 1869 it moved to Jewry Street (*see* Sir John Cass Institute). Now a primary school and the only state school in the City. The L-shaped plan has a five-bay stone frontispiece to Mitre Street, and playgrounds in the angle and on the roof. Demolition along Aldgate in 1979 exposed the utilitarian NE elevation.

INSIDE, the Governors' Board Room is made up of late C17 fabric saved from No. 32 Botolph Lane (dem. 1906). Fine fireplace; plaster ceiling dated 1670 with circular central panel, much enriched with fleshy foliage on the surround; formerly over the staircase of No. 32. The fielded panelling was altered slightly in arrangement and framing. On it, delightful PAINTINGS by *Robert Robinson* dated 72 1696, the earliest Chinoiserie wall paintings known. Over thirty in all, extending even to the door and to narrow strips on the chimney-breast sides. Subdued greenish colouring, not quite grisaille, with a riot of exotically imagined landscapes and people, Rococo rather than Baroque in spirit, but without the accurate delineation of costume etc. of the next century. Robinson also designed tapestries for the Soho manufactory that were sold to East India Company merchants, and his Botolph Lane patron was surely such a man. The school also has a fine lead STATUE of Sir John Cass in a walking attitude, by *Roubiliac*, 1751.

SMITHFIELD MARKET
West Smithfield

1866–7 by *Sir Horace Jones*, his first big scheme as City architect (contractors *Browne & Robinson*). He got the job in 1865, after a mismanaged competition failed to attract an adequate design. The site was enlarged from the N part of the old cattle market (*see* West Smithfield), which moved to Bunning's new Caledonian Market, Islington, in 1855 (*see London 4: North*). Meat was previously sold on a small scale in Newgate Street, but Smithfield became and remains the chief meat market for all London.

Jones's building is low and very long: 631 ft (192 metres) by 246 ft (75 metres). Of red Kentish brick with Portland stone decoration. The rather uncertain style Jones described as Italian, but 'more nearly allied to the Renaissance architecture of France, than the more severe Palladian school'. Blind arcading to the walls, with fluted Doric pilasters. Cast-iron louvres in the tympana. Urns on top. The central feature is the frontispiece to a covered N–S roadway called Grand Avenue. Broad, weak-looking elliptical cast-iron arches support a shallow stone pediment. Four marble female figures representing cities on each side, two by *C. S. Kelsey* (Gunnis). Dragons writhe in the spandrels. At the corners solid octagonal towers with copper-tiled domes, very prominent in long views. The stone-faced bays below them, with coupled pilasters and pediments, originally housed pubs. A similar arrangement of taverns marked Bunning's Caledonian Market. Jones's building also owes much to Bunning's plan for Smithfield (1860), made just before the coming of the railway complicated matters.

Inside, the Grand Avenue has cast-iron decorated spandrels and tie-beams, supporting a queenpost roof. Tall cast-iron railings with florid gates to each side. Also in the avenue a smattering of phone boxes of K2 and K6 type, and a WAR MEMORIAL with bronze figures signed *G. Hawkings & Son*. The gates guard the main E–W axis, called Buyers' Walk. Timber construction is used for the arch-braced trusses here. They rest on slender cast-iron arcades with foliate capitals. Lesser N–S passages intersect, three per side. Jones's original arrangement survived in the western part until late 1996. Nine parallel mansard roofs, with a mixture of glass louvres and slatted dormers, allow in light and air without overheating. The stalls, originally 162 in all, measure 36 ft (11 metres) by 15 ft (4½ metres). A mezzanine of timber-built offices is set back behind the arcades. The E half was reconstructed in 1992–5 by *HLM* to conform with burgeoning hygiene regulations. The new parts are clearly distinguished: a much larger office mezzanine, and glazed screens set in front of the arcades. A new glazed canopy runs round the outer walls, and on the N side are obtrusive rounded silvery pods with loading hatches. Such is the cost of keeping up to date. But need the C19 ironwork have been painted so gaudily?

Jones's superstructure is unexceptional in engineering terms, but more dramatic achievement lies invisibly below: a four-acre subterranean goods station made 1862–5, served from the Metropolitan Railway, joint undertakers of the line with the Great Western. The engineer was *John Fowler* of the Metropolitan. Twenty 240 ft

(73 metre) N–S girders rest on 180 stanchions. Their uneven spacing gave Jones much trouble with his plan. From their cross-girders brick arches are turned. Hydraulic lifts to the market were powered by accumulators in the towers. Spiral ramp for road access, in West Smithfield (q.v.).

Two big extensions line up to the W, linked by low covered avenues. First *T. P. Bennett & Son*'s POULTRY MARKET of 1962–3, replacing Jones's building of 1873–5, burnt 1958. Square in plan, the N and S walls with nine glazed bays between flat black brick piers. These have hexagonal glass bricks below, clear glazing above, carried up as a series of shallow gables: a handsome arrangement. Behind rises a shallow elliptical concrete dome, spanning the market space. At 225 ft (68½ metres) it is said to have been the largest such structure in Europe at the time. Light comes from glazed lunettes and from small circular piercings through the dome's surface.

Then the so-called GENERAL MARKET of 1879–83 by *Jones* (contractors *Mowlem & Co.*). It replaced the old Farringdon Market for fruit and vegetables, but was soon turned over to meat. Red Fareham brick and Portland stone, with octagonal terminal turrets: more explicitly French than the first market (see the little oval dormers), and plainer too. It meets Farringdon Street at an awkward angle. Here a line of shops with an office storey above, rising to two storeys in the middle. The NW part rebuilt in stone after a bomb fell in 1945. Market hall with arched wooden trusses on lattice girders, less lucid than the 1860s work. The main columns attracted contemporary interest: rolled channelled iron sections are riveted together above moulded bases. More railway sidings beneath, reached by a roadway on the S side. A covered canopy, S, spans an extension of West Smithfield to a similar, smaller market building, also by *Jones*, 1886–8. Wedge-shaped, the N frontispiece with carved boys riding dolphins (it was originally for fish). Long return wing to Snow Hill, S.

SOUTHWARK BRIDGE

By *Mott & Hay*, engineers, and *Sir Ernest George*, architect, 1912–21. Five steel arches, with granite cutwaters and fancy granite piers. Much less interesting and audacious than the elder *Rennie*'s predecessor of 1814–19 (Act of 1811), which had only three spans, of 210, 240, and 210 ft (64, 73 and 64 metres). This reduced the obstruction of a narrow part of the river. Piers of granite, on piled footings, supported cast-iron arches with solid ribs and triangulated open spandrels. The ironfounders, *Walkers* of Rotherham, were almost bankrupted by the work. The central span was the largest ever achieved in cast iron, four feet longer than Burdon's bridge at Sunderland of 1793–6. (*Telford* and *Douglass* proposed a 600 ft (183 metre) span for London Bridge in 1800 but this was unrealistically ambitious.)

STAPLE INN
Holborn

The largest of the former Inns of Chancery, transferred to the City from the Borough of Camden in 1994. A 'Stapled Hall' is recorded here possibly in 1283, definitely in 1333. The name probably comes from an aisled timber-built hall (Old English *stapel*, post), not from the wool-merchants of the Staple. Occupied by lawyers by 1415, until dissolution in 1884. Present buildings are late C16 and C18, with C20 restorations.

Facing Holborn, a long and high group of half-timbered Elizabethan houses, the most impressive surviving example in London. They were however extensively reconstructed in 1936–8 by *E. W. Spiller*, who inserted a steel frame to arrest the tottering timber one, and before that in 1887 by *Waterhouse*, after the Prudential Assurance intervened to save the Inn. The front is in two parts. The longer, l., was built in 1586 by the Inn's Principal, Vincent Engham. Symmetrical, with five gables and a central arched doorway into the courtyard. Two overhangs; oriel windows to each upper storey below the gable. Larger central oriels, in plan half-octagonal. Windows are Waterhouse's copies of surviving first-floor casements on the r. part. This slightly taller two-gable house is probably a little later. Also with two overhangs, also symmetrical, except for the coving below the r. first-floor oriel. Narrowly placed timber studs on both are mostly false, added in 1887 after C18 plaster was stripped off (only every fifth member is pegged to the horizontal); barge-boards also of 1887. Minimal decoration otherwise, e.g. the leaf-scroll corbel on the l. part, and on the stone gateway pilasters and a panelled soffit. No. 3 has a nice early C19 shopfront with Doric entablature, No. 4 (far l.) a late C18 cornice with C20 window. The plan of one-room shops and rear access to the upper chambers is probably original. Rear elevation faced with brick in 1826 (renewed 1936–8).

Other buildings lie around a square courtyard with trees, the s range facing a lower garden on the far side. Only Nos. 7–9 (E range), dated 1729, 1731 and 1734, survived a flying bomb in 1944. Red brick, red rubbed trim. The rest was patiently rebuilt in replica by *Maufe*, 1954–5. It comprises more C18 brick buildings (w range dated 1757 and 1759), and at the sw the HALL, originally built by the Principal Richard Champion, 1581. Four bays, with a plain E oriel. On top a square louvre of two stages. Pretty Gothick doorcases, dated 1753 on the garden side. The fanciful hammerbeam roof has not only the usual stalactite pendants but also extremely odd stalagmites standing on the hammers and collar beams (new panelling, late C16 in style, after the carving of the former w screen; over the fireplace a carved Elizabethan stone figure, found reused as rubble nearby; in the oriel heraldic glass of 1581–5). With the adjacent buildings, the home of the INSTITUTE OF ACTUARIES since 1887.

An archway by the hall leads to No. 10, dated 1747, but part of Maufe's work. It faces the garden on the w side; on the s side is the Patent Office (q.v.).

STOCK EXCHANGE
Threadneedle Street

An office tower between lower blocks, by *Llewelyn Davies, Weeks, Forestier-Walker & Bor* (executive architects *Fitzroy Robinson & Partners* and *Joseph, F. Milton Cashmore & Partners*), 1964–72. The tower, completed 1969, is a massive irregular heptagon 320 ft (97½ metres) high, constructed around two service cores, and faced with precast-concrete panels. These have heavy, close-set major and minor mullions, all chamfered, and small windows with large splayed heads and sills: an all-over, high-relief treatment. The major mullions continue down as piers, enclosing the recessed entrance. This is glazed on the E side, where it houses a staircase climbing slowly up around the core. A public, external staircase keeps pace with it outside the glass. Both rise up to the disused pedestrian deck, N. Within, rather Teutonic-looking bronze SCULPTURES of St George and St Michael, by *Sir Thomas Brock*, 1922. The former trading floor, 22,000 square ft (6,700 square metres), lies in the low W part, screened on the S by a long three-storey block. This has windows to match the tower, but rests on a polished Hantergantick granite plinth. The plan lost its *raison d'être* in the mid 1970s, when the ped-way scheme was abandoned, making nonsense of the elaborate podium; the trading floor in 1986, when face-to-face dealing ended. The latter has been converted to open-plan offices (1993).

The previous Stock Exchange was Victorian, an amalgam of work by *Thomas Allason Jun.* (1853–4) and *J. J. Cole* (1866 and 1882–7). Trading began in Threadneedle Street in 1774, at first in Government stock only; the first purpose-built premises, by *James Peacock*, 1801–2, were in Capel Court, off Bartholomew Lane, W (*see* Introduction p. 94).

TELEPHONE EXCHANGE
Farringdon Street

Called FLEET BUILDING. By the *Ministry of Works* (*W. S. Frost*), 1956–60. An impressively large stone-faced building extending back to Shoe Lane, with lower wings and an assertive twelve-storey slab rising above them at r. angles to Farringdon Street. On the front abstract ceramic MURALS by *D. Annam*, 1960.

TELEPHONE EXCHANGE
Fore Street

By *G. R. Yeats* (*Ministry of Works*), 1955–9. One of the lower blocks of the London Wall scheme (q.v.). Five-storey slab with offices behind, the detail comparable to its commercial counterparts. Post Office in front, in a slate-faced single-storeyed range with a roof of curved hoods.

TELEPHONE EXCHANGE
Houndsditch

1965–70 by the *Ministry of Public Building and Works* (*G. R. Yeats* and *P. W. Manning*). Four storeys to the street, the lower two somewhat fussy, with openwork concrete blocks and aggregate panels. Behind is a tall block with projecting fins.

TELEPHONE EXCHANGES
Queen Victoria Street

A complex of various dates, on both sides of the street. The N SIDE began with FARADAY HOUSE, by the *Office of Works* (principal architect *A. R. Myers*), 1932–3. Denounced immediately it went up for the damage its nine storeys and square-towered skyline inflicted on views of St Paul's; protective legislation swiftly followed. Classically detailed, attempting playfulness in the Lutyens way but spread too thinly. Lower extension of 1938–9, r., with quasi-Doric pilasters. Behind, a further extension, N of Knightrider Street (here now a private access road): a tall windowless concrete shelter of 1942, called The Citadel. Aggregate cladding of 1962–4, with upper office storeys, added by the *Ministry of Public Building and Works*. Round the corner, the former G.P.O. Central Savings Bank is also incorporated (*see* Carter Lane). The E part of the site accommodated the courts and chambers of DOCTORS' COMMONS, specialists in ecclesiastical and Admiralty law, from 1568 until dissolution in 1867. The last surviving parts, late C17–C18, were destroyed by a gas explosion in 1939. Redevelopment of the entire site is proposed (1996).

On the S SIDE, BAYNARD HOUSE, an acutely depressing L-shaped block built 1972–9, extending S over the road tunnels of the diverted Upper Thames Street. Consultant architects *Holford Associates*, structural engineers *Ove Arup & Partners*. Its massive projecting balconies might possibly approach monumentality, were they not clad in pre-cast aggregate panels. The W part houses a small museum. Recessed in the centre, a dingy raised garden. SCULPTURE here by *Richard Kindersley*, The Seven Ages of Man, 1980, a totem-pole of heads.

THE TEMPLE

No visible division exists between Middle and Inner Temple, and the two intermingled precincts are treated as one. The Temple Church and Master's House are held in common; otherwise each Inn has its own hall, library, chambers, and a gatehouse on Fleet Street. Badges of Pegasus (Inner Temple) and the Lamb and Flag (Middle Temple) help distinguish their ownership. To appreciate them, they must be wandered through at leisure, exactly like the Oxford and Cambridge colleges. The difference is that the Temple is larger and more complex than any college, and more complex and densely planned also than Lincoln's Inn and Gray's Inn, even after tidying-up in the C19 and after 1945. Lincoln's Inn in particular has more consistently impressive architecture, but lacks the extraordinary

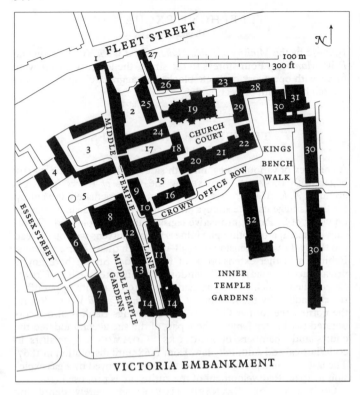

Temple. Plan

I	Middle Temple Gateway	17	Pump Court
2	Hare Court	18	Cloisters
3	Essex and Brick Courts	19	Temple Church
4	New Court	20	Inner Temple Hall
5	Fountain Court	21	Inner Temple Treasury
6	Garden Court	22	Inner Temple Library
7	Queen Elizabeth Building	23	Master's House
8	Middle Temple Hall	24	Farrar's Building
9	Lamb Building	25	Dr Johnson's Building
10	Carpmael Building	26	Goldsmith's Building
11	Harcourt Buildings	27	Inner Temple Gateway
12	Plowden Buildings	28	Mitre Court Buildings
13	Middle Temple Library	29	Francis Taylor Building
14	Temple Gardens	30	King's Bench Walk Buildings
15	Elm Court	31	Niblett Hall
16	Crown Office Row Buildings	32	Paper Buildings

variety of spaces made by the lanes and courts between the Temple's
buildings: here freely interpenetrating, there connected only by the
narrowest covered passages, and all gradually terraced down to the
generous tree-lined gardens along the river.

THE DEVELOPMENT OF THE TEMPLE

The religious order of the Knights Templar moved here from
Holborn, *c.*1160. One feature antedates their coming: Middle

Temple Lane, between Fleet Street and the river. The layout of the rest reflects the Temple's four-fold division around its knights, squires, armourers and other lay brothers, and priests and chaplains. The knights and squires almost certainly lived around a cloister s of the church, with a hall where the Inner Temple Hall now is, that is in the position of a monastic frater, and their own chapel by its entrance. The clergy lived e of the church where the Master's House now lies, according to a description of 1664. The lay brothers' hall, outside the consecrated precinct, was probably that mentioned in 1336–7 where Elm and Pump Courts now lie, superseded by the Middle Temple Hall c. 1570. The two gateways from Fleet Street are also known from 1336–7.

The Templars were suppressed in 1312, and in 1324 Parliament voted the property to the Order of St John. They took full possession in 1346, by which time parts were already leased to students of law. The peasants sacked the Temple in 1381. The administrative division into Inner and Middle Temple, recorded perhaps by 1404 and certainly by 1440–51, roughly follows that between the consecrated e part and the rest (part of the New or Outer Temple further w, never leased to the lawyers, was acquired in 1676). Apart from the church, the only medieval work remaining is two small C14 vaulted chambers by the Inner Temple Hall.

At the Dissolution the property went to the Crown, which granted the freehold to the Benchers of the Temple in 1608. After the Reformation the Inns of Court became fashionable as places of education for sons of the gentry. Admissions increased fivefold 1550–1650. From this golden age there remain the great Middle Temple Hall (1562–c. 1572) and the Inner Temple Gateway (1610–11). A C17 prospect view preserves the Temple's appearance just before the Great Fire (though dated 1671). C16–C17 chambers of up to five storeys predominate. Older ranges have straight or shaped gables, newer ones hipped roofs with dormers; at King's Bench Walk quoins and balustrades appear.

In 1666 the Great Fire destroyed the e part of the Inner Temple. Further fires in 1677, 1679 and 1683 swept away much of the rest. Rebuilding was managed by a committee, which mostly followed the system of making contracts with benchers prepared to raise new chambers in return for fees for admission to them. The highly standardized results adapted to the demands of the Rebuilding Acts 65 the Temple's preferred collegiate plan, established by c. 1630 at least, with uniform sets of rooms flanking a staircase. They have four even floors of brick. Ornament is restricted to sparse stone dressings, brick bands, wooden cornices (mostly replaced by brick parapets), and doorcases of stone or moulded brick on pilasters or brackets. Broad flush C18 sashes have replaced most of the original cross-windows. The oldest survivors are New Court, by the builder *Nicholas Barbon*, shortly before 1676. The Middle Temple's Parliament stipulated that other new chambers be modelled on Barbon's, which accounts for their general similarity. The grandest chambers, not by Barbon, are in King's Bench Walk, Inner Temple. The exception is Nos. 2–3 Middle Temple Lane, still in the timber-fronted pre-Fire tradition, though built as late as 1693–4.

It is not necessary to describe the C17 interiors one by one. Staircases have turned balusters and pendants on the newels.

Chambers have plain or bolection panelling, some round-arched doorways, and fireplaces with bolection surrounds, occasionally with garlands or panelled pilasters to the overmantels. Examples remain at Nos. 2–3 Middle Temple Lane, Nos. 2–3 Essex Court, New Court, Nos. 4–6 Pump Court, No. 1 Hare Court, and Nos. 2–5 King's Bench Walk.

Admissions declined in the C18, and non-legal trades moved in by the 1730s. Of the C18 only a few chambers remain (Essex Court, King's Bench Walk). The C19 saw much building in both parts of a reinvigorated Temple. At the Inner Temple first *Robert* and then *Sydney Smirke* built mostly sober classical ranges (King's Bench Walk); Sydney's Neo-Perp hall was a war casualty. At the Middle Temple *Henry Hakewill*, *James Savage* and *J. P. St Aubyn* employed collegiate Tudor Gothic, doubtless taking their cue from the Hall. The Inner Temple turned eclectic in the later C19, calling in *E. M. Barry* and *T. G. Jackson* for two typically flamboyant jobs at either end of Middle Temple Lane. Lesser work went to its surveyor *Arthur Cates*. The late C19 looked with sentimental affection on the late C17 brick chambers, and the process of replacement halted after the 1890s. The other important change was the making of Victoria Embankment (1864–70), which more than doubled the area of the gardens.

Deep wounds were inflicted in the Second World War, when the heart of the Inner Temple was torn out, and much damage done throughout. Replacements of the 1950s are mostly by *Sir Edward Maufe* (Middle Temple) and *Sir Hubert Worthington* (Inner Temple). Their reproductions of late C17–early C19 chambers blend in nicely, but the grander buildings, where a bolder hand was possible, are too often excessively timid and genteel. A programme of cleaning the older buildings is under way in 1996.

THE PRESENT BUILDINGS

The tour starts from the w end and from Fleet Street and progresses roughly eastwards. For the Temple Church, *see* Churches p. 266.

MIDDLE TEMPLE GATEWAY, 1683–4, was designed in his year as Treasurer by *Roger North*. It typifies the purer style introduced by such late C17 gentleman-amateur architects: handsome and straightforward, of brick and Portland stone, with four giant Ionic pilasters and a pediment above a rusticated basement. Mason *John Shorthose*, bricklayer *Joseph Lem*, carpenters *Thomas Woodstock* and *Robert Britton*. Good late C18 fanlights in the round-headed lesser openings. Balconies over them are an original feature. The previous gate was of 1520. Behind, in MIDDLE TEMPLE LANE on the l., Nos. 2–3 of 1693–4, exceptionally late timber-fronted London houses with oversailing upper floors. The violation of the Rebuilding Acts was doubtless prompted by the lane's intimate narrowness here. The fronts are plastered, with moulded floor-strings and a modillioned eaves cornice. Brick-faced ground floor, with the remains of an early C19 shop at No. 2. A few late C17 cross-windows remain on No. 3. Some weatherboarding high up on No. 2, which has five floors, one more than usual for the Temple after 1666. No. 4 (w side), a small C18 house, has a good late C18 shopfront with a flattened lunette in its straight-headed window. Crude contemporary Gothick tracery of timber in the house to the r. Then on the l. Nos. 2–3 HARE COURT, the only buildings in the Norman Shaw style in the Temple, 1893–4 by *Sir T. G. Jackson*. Dark-red brick, very tall, with bowed oriels on stone corbels and big dormers not aligned with the bays below. Good carved cherubs on the central corbel. The fine rubbed brick door-cases are copied from the late C17 No. 1 Hare Court (*see* p. 351 below).

The late C17 Pump Court, next door to Hare Court, will be explored later. Instead, turn r. into BRICK COURT. This was formerly divided from ESSEX COURT by a late C17 range destroyed in the war, since when they form one paved space with trees. N range of 1882–3 by *St Aubyn*, uninteresting Neo-Tudor, not helped by the storey added *c.* 1950 after bomb damage. At the SE No. 1 Brick Court, rebuilt 1909–10 in late C17 style by *Aston Webb*, incorporating a pedestrian route down Middle Temple Lane. The late C17 stone doorcase, reset, has a broken pediment with a ball in the centre. Then No. 1 Essex Court, of *c.* 1680, with moulded brick bands and pedimented doorcase on brackets. On the W side, *Barbon*'s Nos. 2–3 Essex Court, 1677, have more stone dressings than average (quoins, key blocks); yet the doorcases are modest, with straight heads. Wooden modillion cornice. No. 4, 1717, has tall segment-headed windows. To the N here, a top-glazed passage from No. 222 Strand (by *G. Cuthbert* & *W. Wimble*, 1883).

Now through the W archway to NEW COURT, a paved yard with a deep seven-bay W block, conveyed by its builder *Barbon* to the Temple in 1676. It cannot be as old as the date 1667 over the door, since he began developing the site of Essex House only in 1674. Rusticated quoins, astylar doorcase with round-arched doorway and segmental pediment. Rear staircase reached by a long passage. Next to it on the r., the LITTLE GATE, later C17 and doubtless also *Barbon*'s, with stone piers and fluted vases. The stuccoed N side, outside the Temple proper, is probably *Henry Mawley*'s chambers, called Devereux Court, exhibited in 1841. To the S the court is open. Steps lead down past early C19 Gothic iron LAMP-STANDARDS into the extensive L-shaped FOUNTAIN COURT, with large trees. Named from what is re-putedly the first permanent fountain in London, in a plain circular basin made in 1681. On the W side the back of Barbon's Essex Street, with one low rear extension, apparently early C18. The long arm of the L, with the Middle Temple Hall on the S side, will be taken in later. First down more steps on the S, into the Middle Temple Gardens with the view open to the river. On the r. GARDEN COURT, uninspired Neo-Jacobean of 1884–5 by *St Aubyn* in stone and raw red brick. The building beyond, best seen from the Embankment, is *Maufe*'s QUEEN ELIZABETH BUILDING, 1956, gently curved with pedimented ends slightly projecting. The steps and Bath stone Gothic parapets near here are all that the bombs left of *H. R. Abraham*'s Gothic Middle Temple Library (1858–61). Also C19 the two-storey S extension to the Hall (the former library), low enough not to block its windows: by *Henry Hakewill*, 1822–4. Stock brick and stone

Tudor Gothic, the details hopelessly unscholarly. They may be a hangover from Hakewill's first design (commissioned 1805). First-floor interiors: Parliament Chamber, E, with bow window added 1861 (good armorial stained glass of 1896), and Queen's Room, W, both with excellent fleshy plasterwork to *Maufe*'s designs (1947–9), exactly capturing the charm of provincial heraldic work of *c.* 1600. Buildings at r. angles to it belong with Middle Temple Lane (*see* below).

MIDDLE TEMPLE HALL (entrance from Fountain Court), the finest Elizabethan building in central London. Begun probably in 1562 by Edward Plowden, Treasurer, who summoned Sir John Thynne's chief carpenter *John Lewis* from Longleat, Wilts., in that year. By 1565 Lewis had returned to Longleat. A single hammer-beam roof there has similar detailing, suggesting that he designed both. Probably completed not long after 1570, the date in the W window glass. Though much altered and restored, the grand out-lines of the C16 building are immediately recognizable. Brick and stone, five bays, then a dais end distinguished by bay windows to the S as well as the N. Windows with mullions and transoms; each light with a depressed arch. On the N side the bay window is balanced by the porch to the screens passage. Six-light windows, not large, at E and W ends. Crenellated N parapet of 1745; funny Gothick buttresses of the W front, 1757–8, by the mason *Christopher Horsnaile Jun.* The Gothic louvre is *Maufe*'s renewal of one of *c.* 1826 by *Hakewill* (restoration completed 1950). Maufe re-created the square brick Neo-Tudor porch tower of 1830, by *Savage*, but omitted the lesser pinnacles, making it look somewhat bald. The lower stage had been reconstructed in 1930 by *Maurice Webb*, and this survives, with Gothic entrance vault and semi-circular steps (previous entrance towers of 1667 and 1745). Also by *Maufe* the E forebuilding, dated 1946–8, a storey higher than before the war.

25 The INTERIOR measures 101 ft by 40 ft by 59 ft high (30¾ by 12 by 18 metres), shorter but no less broad than the great halls of the 1520s–30s at Hampton Court and Christ Church, Oxford. Double hammerbeam roof in the Perp tradition, with such Elizabethan details as the pendants and the treatment of hammer-beams and collar-beams like classical entablatures. The members are handsomely proportioned, without either late Gothic en-crustations or the attenuated flatness of such roofs of the next generation as the hall of Trinity College, Cambridge. The stages are ceiled, masking the purlins. Curved braces link both stages of hammerbeams and march along between the kingposts high up. Posts above collar-beams and upper hammerbeams are fashioned as little columns. Urns perch on the lower hammerbeams. The spectacular Elizabethan SCREEN, of the early 1570s, has been much repaired especially after 1945. Roman Doric columns and metope frieze below. Round-headed doorways with well-carved winged figures in the spandrels. Figures of Hercules on the pedestal fronts. The doors with their openwork foliage carving are an addition of 1671, and it looks as if certain alterations were made to the arches and the frieze at that time. But the arches rest on obviously Elizabethan termini caryatids in the jambs. The upper storey has bigger caryatids above the columns and two-bay

openings made by uprights with lesser figures, each bay with two hanging sub-arches between. On the parapet, panels decorated by strapwork cartouches, and small statues in niches to match the two-bay division. Broad top cornice. The E side facing the passage has fluted Doric pilasters. The Hall is panelled to sill level, with an enriched Doric entablature. On the panels painted arms of Readers, dated 1597–1899, the earlier ones C18 renewals. Doric pilasters flank a buffet in the N oriel. Armorial STAINED GLASS of the 1570s onwards, with later, fancier glass in the S oriel (one piece signed by *James Pearson*, 1790). BUST of Edward Plowden by *Morton Edwards*, 1868.

The N side of Fountain Court is made by the tall back ranges of Brick Court and Essex Court, with a SUNDIAL dated 1685. The E side takes us back to MIDDLE TEMPLE LANE, where much war damage was replaced by Neo-Georgian ranges in red Dorking brick. On the E side they are, from N to S, LAMB BUILDING by *Maufe*, 1954, CARPMAEL BUILDING also by *Maufe*, 1955, incorporating a triumphal triple entrance to Crown Office Row, and the long HARCOURT BUILDINGS by *Worthington*, completed 1953, on the concrete foundations of a range of 1832–4 by *Smirke*. On the last a relief of Pegasus, salvaged from Smirke's building. The W side is PLOWDEN BUILDINGS, 1830–3 by *Savage* to *Hakewill*'s designs. Plain Tudor collegiate in gault brick with stone dressings. Stone-faced oriels on the projecting ends and centre. It suffers from the removal in the C20 of Hakewill's crow-stepped gables. Ornate S (Treasury) doorcase added 1896, probably by *H.J. Wadling*. More alterations in 1913 (N doorcase, by *Sir Aston Webb*) and 1905–6 (rear oriel, by *Sir Reginald Blomfield*). Smoking Room inside by *Sir Aston Webb & Son*, 1929, with Neo-Jacobean plasterwork by *Laurence Turner*. Then *Maufe*'s MIDDLE TEMPLE LIBRARY, Neo-Georgian, 1956–8, partly on the site of chambers of 1687. Pretty garden front with a pedimented centrepiece approached by a perron. Closing the end, further S than the old water gate, is TEMPLE GARDENS, a big Portland stone Victorian 100 block across an archway astride the lane, by *E.M. Barry*, 1878–9 (consultant *St Aubyn*). It must be seen from the S to be appreciated in all its Frenchified fat prosperity, like a block of expensive flats, with fully fashioned angle projections, figures, termini caryatids, and so on. Sculpted figures by *W. Calder Marshall* in niches by the gateway ('Learning' and 'Justice'), less convincing than the excellent carved atlantes, foliage etc. by Messrs *Mabey*. Waste-disposal shafts and coal lifts were provided. Oddly, the inner face of the Middle Temple's half is thriftily plain, the Inner Temple's part opposite as rich as the S front. Beyond, at the Victoria Embankment entrance, a dainty pedimented LODGE dated 1880.

East of Middle Temple Lane

We retrace our steps as far as the archway through Lamb Building into ELM COURT, which represents the amalgamation by *Maufe* of the old Elm Court and the little Fig Tree Court further E. Buildings are mostly his: the E range of Lamb Building (W), the S range of Pump Court (N, *see* below), and CROWN OFFICE ROW,

1953–5 (S). The latter is called from the Clerks of the Crown, who framed their indictments in the previous buildings from Tudor times to 1882. At the E end is an ugly two-storeyed rubble-faced attachment to the new Inner Temple Hall, which appears behind and above (for the Hall proper *see* below). It contains two probably C14 VAULTED ROOMS, one above the other. They come from the service end of the medieval hall, otherwise demolished in 1865, and may have formed the lower stages of a tower mentioned in some older accounts. The W wall aligns with that of the former W cloister range. Both have cross-vaults with hollow-chamfered ribs springing from floor level. In the lower room a large fireplace with a four-centred arch with foliated spandrels. Reset above it an angel of *c.* 1500 holding two shields. On the N wall, partly sunk below ground level, two blocked doorways: one with a two-centred, the other with a segmental arch. This hall was substantially of *c.* 1600 apart from its earlier open roof, which was similar to that at Lincoln's Inn Old Hall (1493). A round-headed doorway recorded in 1756 probably remained from the Templars' C12 hall. Much altered by *Robert Smirke*, 1816–17, and again in 1827 and 1837.

Back into Middle Temple Lane, where late C17 chambers a little further N announce PUMP COURT, a long and narrow paved space reached through a round-headed archway. N and W sides (except for part of Farrar's Building at the E end, for which *see* below) are of *c.* 1680, after the fire of 1679. They are modest enough, with unmoulded brick bands and uniform broken-pedimented doorcases on brackets. No. 5, NW corner, retains its eaves cornice. Sundial dated 1686 on a wooden panel (N side). The S side was rebuilt by *Maufe* in 1951–3, in a close approximation to the C17, but with a little pedimented frontispiece. Across the E side, *Maufe*'s CLOISTERS, 1949–52. Plain brick on an open arcaded ground floor with rows of Tuscan columns inside. He made them one bay shorter than before the war, in accordance with *Wren*'s drawings for the previous building of 1680–1. At the same time they were made deeper, hence two rows of columns to Wren's one. Arms to the court carved by *Barry Hart*. The medieval cloister here burnt in 1679; it had a brick storey of 1612 on top.

Standing under the cloister arcade one faces CHURCH COURT, a long, rather bleak paved space S of the Temple Church. It was divided until the Second World War by chambers of 1667. On the S side first the INNER TEMPLE HALL, 1952–5 by *Worthington* and *T. W. Sutcliffe* (consultant *Maufe*), of brick, Neo-Georgian, with large arched windows.[*] Inside, flat ceiling and restrained Neo-Georgian decoration. Heraldic stained glass by *Hugh Easton*, 1956. Further E and by the same architects the INNER TEMPLE TREASURY. Inside its N entrance, above the door, *Rysbrack*'s noble relief of Pegasus, made 1737–9 for the S entrance of the old hall. Then the INNER TEMPLE LIBRARY by *Sutcliffe*, completed 1958. The library is accommodated in double-height galleried rooms in the upper floors, facing a S terrace. Minimal late C17 style, with oak panelling. This range faces to the N the MASTER'S

---

[*] Destroyed in 1940–1: *Sydney Smirke*'s hall of 1866–70, late C14 Perp with a SE clocktower like Big Ben's; *Robert Smirke*'s library of 1819 (additions by *Edis*, 1881); and his Parliament Chambers of 1827–8.

HOUSE, set back behind an enviable garden NE of the church. It is a near-exact copy of *c.* 1955 by *Maufe* and *Worthington* of its predecessor, built in 1667 by the Master, Dr Ball: three storeys, seven bays, three-bay pediment. The E end of Church Court is closed by the Francis Taylor Building (*see* below).

Immediately W and N of the church, an interesting mid-Victorian group lines Inner Temple Lane. The corners with Hare Court on the W side are made by FARRAR'S BUILDING, l., 1875–6 by *Cates*, indecisive French-cum-Italianate, and DR JOHNSON'S BUILDING, r., 1857–8 by *Sydney Smirke*, an unshowy composition still just in the late classical style, of brick on a rusticated ground floor. Its rear façade to Hare Court is entirely Georgian in proportions, though with plate-glass sashes. Just W of Farrar's Building, No. 1 HARE COURT, *c.* 1680, with a central segmental-pedimented doorcase of rubbed brick. Some cross-windows remain. The S front faces Pump Court. The N side of Hare Court is made by No. 10 Fleet Street (q.v.). Further up the lane on the r., reached by a causeway across the churchyard, GOLDSMITH'S BUILDING, 1861 by *St Aubyn*. Red brick and stone, with carefully graduated horizontal rustication in the manner of Cockerell. The bulging plate-glazed corner oriel is more successful than the undersized entrance. Later, inferior top storey.

The INNER TEMPLE GATEWAY, 1610–11, stands at the N end, after the side ranges of buildings in Fleet Street. Much restored but still one of the best pieces of half-timbered work in London. As built by John Bennett, under licence from the Temple, it consisted of two blocks with a central staircase. The staircase and N block remain, restored in 1900–6 after a varied career which included a tenancy by Mrs Salmon's waxworks. The restorers were the *LCC Architects*, their first major restoration scheme (superintending architect *W. E. Riley*), in collaboration with the South Kensington Museum. They recessed the ground-floor front facing Fleet Street by 5 ft (1½ metres). It is of stone, with Elizabethan decorated end pilasters and round-arched doorway to the r. Can the mysterious date 1748 on the keystone refer to the heavy panelled doors? Two storeys above with two canted oriels, the second storey of which oversails again. Delicate balustrade with close-set uprights, with twin gables recessed behind. Reliable features are the posts between the oriels carved as pilasters, Doric above Ionic, and eight carved oak panels, formerly reset on an C18 false front but now incorporated in the upper oriels. Rear wing facing Inner Temple Lane, in the LCC's Free Style, with brown-glazed brick below, rough-cast above, and tile-hung gables. Lots of different window types, the narrow stone-framed lights, l., taken straight from Voysey. Inside, overlooking Fleet Street, PRINCE HENRY'S ROOM, with a heavy plastered ceiling. The name comes from the 26 badge of feathers and the initials P. H. in the plaster. Central star and the usual broad bands filled with scrolly foliage forming panels of complex shape. The badge suggests a connection with the Council of the Duchy of Cornwall, known to have been meeting somewhere in Fleet Street by 1618; but since the gatehouse served as a private inn called the Prince's Arms it was probably merely commemorative (compare the pargetted front of No. 78 High Street, Maidstone, Kent, also with the Prince of Wales's feathers and dated 1611). W wall with contemporary wood panelling divided by four Doric pilasters with strapwork decoration. Strapwork decoration in the frieze as well. Otherwise early C18 panelling and fireplace in the E wall. Excellent armorial STAINED GLASS in an early Stuart manner, *c.* 1906 by *Burlison & Grylls*. Late C17 newel staircase to the upper floors.

King's Bench Walk

Through the E end of Church Court begins the last part of the tour. This is the largest of the courts, of irregular oblong shape, and open to the S. That the court should be debased to use as a car park is a great pity. The E side has the character of one half of a fine avenue, its central part as close as we can now come to how the City's main thoroughfares must have looked in the late C17. The S part and the E and N sides are mostly early C19. Across the N end, MITRE COURT BUILDINGS by *Smirke*, 1830, stone-faced and symmetrical with discreet window mouldings. The gateway has granite imposts. *Worthington* rebuilt the bombed W part in 1951. To the SW of this the FRANCIS TAYLOR BUILDING, 1955–7 by *Maufe* in accordance with *Smirke*'s work of 1832–3. Stuccoed ground floor, yellow brick above.

Opposite this KING'S BENCH WALK proper begins. *Wren*'s name is connected with a range here undertaken by Francis Phelips in 1670, but he appears only to have surveyed the foundations; in the same year *Edward Tasker*, self-described as 'a skilful surveyor and contriver of buildings', claimed responsibility for Phelips's buildings at the Inn. But another fire in 1677 destroyed No. 4 and most of its neighbours, and it is unclear how much of 1670 remains. Nos. 1–2 were a pair, but No. 1 was rebuilt in 1949, keeping only the late C17 moulded brick doorcase. It has a semicircular head framed by panelled piers and a triangular pediment. No. 2 has five bays, the central one projecting, with a similar doorcase. Wooden cornice, hipped roof. Good wrought-iron LAMP-STANDARDS of *c.* 1800 here and further S: uprights fashioned as slender columns on pedestals, square lamps on the overthrows.

Nos. 3–6 lie further back. No. 3 has a return N wing refaced in 1797, of stock brick, with a broad flat doorcase with stone imposts and a stone attic block. A modern plaque dates it 1668, though it may be of 1677–8. Unusual plan, perhaps original: two rooms deep at the l., reached from the lobby via a corridor immediately behind the front of the adjoining bay. C17 staircase in the entrance lobby. The Alienation Office was here between 1577–1835. On the former Office garden behind, visible from Temple Lane, NIBLETT HALL, chambers of 1992–4 by *Rolfe Judd*, gabled red brick with windows in fancy stone panels. It replaced a building by *Sydney Tatchell* and *G. C. Wilson*, 1920–32. The main, E part of No. 3 is of four bays, dark-red brick, with a Doric doorcase with segmental pediment and main front staircase. Then Nos. 4–6, which differ in having seven bays, red brick confined to the dressings, and main staircases at the rear. Their moulded brick bands step down each party wall as the Walk slopes down to the river. No. 4 has a wooden cornice with paired modillions and a doorcase with foliage capitals and a triangular pediment. In the metopes the dates

1. The City, from Tower Bridge

2. Lothbury, from
the west, with
St Margaret by
Sir Christopher
Wren, 1683–92

3. St Paul's
Cathedral, from
the south-east
(photo 1950)

4. Bow Lane, from
the south

2 | 3
  | 4

5. Roman mosaic found in
   Leadenhall Street,
   engraving by J. Basire
6. Wall, *c.* 200, east of
   Cooper's Row
7. Sculpture of centurion
   from Camomile Street,
   c. late first century
8. Viking gravestone, C II,
   from near St Paul's
   Cathedral

9. Tower of London, White Tower, begun after 1077, from the south-east
10. Tower of London, White Tower, Chapel of St John, interior,
    c. 1080–1100
11. St Bartholomew-the-Great, founded 1123, choir, from the east

12. Temple Church, the round nave, consecrated 1185
13. Temple Church, chancel, consecrated 1240
14. Tower of London, Beauchamp Tower, 1280s, from the west
15. Tower of London, Bell Tower, 1190s, interior

12	14
13	15

16. St Helen Bishopsgate, thirteenth to fifteenth centuries, west front
17. St Giles Cripplegate, nave, c. 1545–50
18. Barnard's Inn, hall, early fifteenth century, from the south (photo c. 1927)
19. Guildhall, east crypt, by John Croxton, begun 1411

20 Temple Church, effigy of knight (Robert de Ros?), thirteenth century

21 Tower of London, St Peter ad Vincula, monument to John Holand, Duke of Exeter † 1447

22 St Helen Bishopsgate, monument to John de Oteswich and wife, late fourteenth century

23 Mercers' Hall, sculpture of the dead Christ, c. 1520–30

24. Tower of London, Queen's House, 1540 and later, from the north-east
25. Temple, Middle Temple Hall, c. 1562–70, interior
26. Temple, Inner Temple Gateway, 1610–11, detail of the ceiling
27. Cloth Fair, Nos. 41–42, seventeenth century

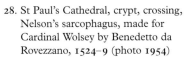

28. St Paul's Cathedral, crypt, crossing,
   Nelson's sarcophagus, made for
   Cardinal Wolsey by Benedetto da
   Rovezzano, 1524–9 (photo 1954)
29. Public Record Office Museum,
   monument to Dr Yonge † 1516, by
   Pietro Torrigiani
30. Tower of London, St Peter ad
   Vincula, detail of monument to Sir
   Richard and Sir Michael Blount,
   † 1564 and † 1592, attributed to the
   Cure workshop
31. St Helen Bishopsgate, monument to
   Sir Thomas Gresham † 1579
32. St Bartholomew-the-Great,
   monument to Sir Robert
   Chamberlayne † 1615, style of Colt

28	30
29	31
	32

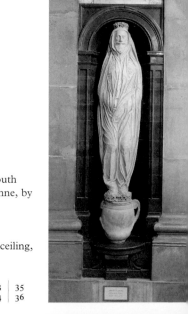

33	35
34	36

37. St Paul's Cathedral, Trophy Room, Great Model, designed by Sir
Christopher Wren, made by William Cleere, 1673–4

38. St. Paul's Cathedral, by Sir Christopher Wren, west towers, 1705–8

39. St Paul's Cathedral, by Sir Christopher Wren, 1675–1711, crossing
(photo 1971)

40. St Paul's Cathedral, detail of carving over the dean's door, by William
Kempster, c. 1705

41. St James
    Garlickhithe, by
    Sir Christopher
    Wren, detail of the
    tower, 1676–85,
    spire 1713–17
42. St Vedast alias
    Foster, by Sir
    Christopher Wren,
    1695–1701,
    spire 1709–12
43. St Martin
    Ludgate, by Sir
    Christopher Wren,
    1677–86, south
    elevation
44. St Dunstan-in-
    the-East, steeple,
    by Sir Christopher
    Wren, 1695–1701,
    from the south-
    east

45. St Benet Paul's Wharf, attributed to Robert Hooke, 1678–84
46. St Mary-le-Bow, by Sir Christopher Wren, 1670–80, west door to the tower
47. St Stephen Walbrook, by Sir Christopher Wren, 1672–80, interior
48. St Martin Ludgate, by Sir Christopher Wren, 1677–86, interior

45 | 47
46 | 48

49. St Mary Aldermary, by the Wren office, 1679–82, south aisle, ceiling
50. Spanish and Portuguese Synagogue, built by Joseph Avis, 1699–1701
51. St Paul's Cathedral, choir, wrought-iron screen, by Tijou, c. 1695–7
52. St Paul's Cathedral, choir stalls, carving by Grinling Gibbons,
   c. 1695–7 (photo 1954)

57. All Hallows Barking, font cover, by Grinling Gibbons, 1682
58. St Vedast alias Foster, font, by Thomas Hill, 1680s
59. St Margaret Pattens, royal arms, late seventeenth century
60. St Benet Paul's Wharf, communion table, *c.* 1686
61. St Magnus the Martyr, iron sword rest, 1708
62. All Hallows London Wall, monument to Joan Bence †1684,
    attributed to Jasper Latham

63. St Paul's
    Churchyard,
    Deanery, Dean's
    Court, after 1672
64. College of Arms, by
    Maurice Emmett
    Jun. and Francis
    Sandford, central
    block 1671–3, wings
    1682–8, from the
    south-east
65. Temple, Nos. 2–3
    Essex Court, by
    Nicholas Barbon,
    1677, elevation to
    New Court
66. Monument, by
    Sir Christopher Wren
    and Robert Hooke,
    1671–6, relief by
    Caius Gabriel Cibber

67. Apothecaries' Hall, screen,
    by Robert Burges and
    Roger Davies, *c.* 1673
68. Vintners' Hall, staircase,
    carved by Woodroffe,
    1671–5
69. Skinners' Hall, Court
    Room (Cedar Room),
    panelling probably by
    Sheffield, *c.* 1670
70. Fishmongers' Hall,
    sculpture of Sir William
    Walworth, by Edward
    Pierce, *c.* 1685

71. St Bartholomew's Hospital, gatehouse, 1702, by Edward Strong Jun., reconstructed by Philip Hardwick, 1833–4

72. Sir John Cass School, Mitre Street, Governors' Board Room, detail of painting by Robert Robinson, 1696

73. Laurence Pountney Hill, Nos. 1 and 2, built by Thomas Denning, 1703, doorcases

74. Mansell Street, No. 57, 1725, doorcase

75. St Bartholomew's Hospital, North Block, staircase hall, by James Gibbs
   paintings by William Hogarth, 1735–7
76. St Bartholomew's Hospital, by James Gibbs, central courtyard, 1730–6?
77. Mansion House, first-floor saloon, plasterwork, by George Fewkes,
   c. 1750

78. St Mary
    Woolnoth, by
    Nicholas
    Hawksmoor,
    1716–27, from
    the north-east
79. All Hallows
    London Wall, by
    George Dance
    the Younger,
    1765–7, interior
    (photo 1937)
80. St Michael
    Cornhill, wooden
    sculpture of
    pelican, by
    Joseph Glazeley,
    1775
81. St Botolph
    Aldgate, by
    George Dance
    the Elder, south
    aisle, detail of
    ceiling, 1741–4,
    with alterations
    by J.F. Bentley,
    1888–95

78 | 80
79 | 81

82. Bank of England, Court Room, by Sir Robert Taylor, 1767–8, altered (photo 1955)
83. Skinners' Hall, Dowgate Hill range, by William Jupp Sen., 1778–9
84. Watermen's Hall, by William Blackburn, 1778–80, Court Room
85. Stationers' Hall, refronted by Robert Mylne, 1800–1, east wing, r., by R.W. Mylne, 1885–7

| 82 | 84 |
| 83 | 85 |

ERECTED AT THE PUBLIC EXPENSE
TO THE MEMORY OF
VICE-ADMIRAL HORATIO, VISCOUNT NELSON, K.B.
TO RECORD HIS SPLENDID AND UNPARALLELED ACHIEVEMENTS,
DURING A LIFE SPENT IN THE SERVICE OF HIS COUNTRY
AND TERMINATED IN THE MOMENT OF VICTORY BY A GLORIOUS DEATH,
IN THE MEMORABLE ACTION OFF CAPE TRAFALGAR ON THE XXI OF OCTOBER MDCCCV.
LORD NELSON WAS BORN ON THE XXIX OF SEPTEMBER MDCCLVIII.
THE BATTLE OF THE NILE WAS FOUGHT ON THE I OF AUGUST MDCCXCVIII.
THE BATTLE OF COPENHAGEN ON THE II OF APRIL MDCCCI.

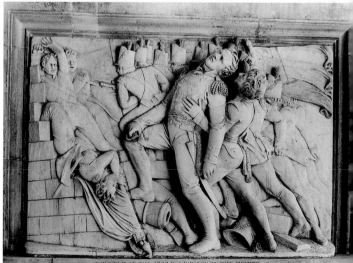

ERECTED AT THE PUBLIC EXPENSE TO THE MEMORY OF
MAJOR GENERAL BERNARD FOORD BOWES
WHO FELL GLORIOUSLY ON THE 27th JUNE 1812,
WHILE LEADING THE TROOPS TO THE ASSAULT OF THE FORTS OF SALAMANCA.

CHANTREY
SCULPTOR

86. St Paul's Cathedral, south transept, monument to Horatio Nelson, by John Flaxman, 1808–18
87. St Paul's Cathedral, north transept, monument to General Bowes †1812, by Sir Francis Chantrey
88. St Paul's Cathedral, crossing, monument to John Howard, relief by the elder Bacon, 1791–5
89. St Paul's Cathedral, south transept, monument to Lord Collingwood, by Sir Richard Westmacott, 1813–17

. Cutlers' Gardens, West Court, by Richard Jupp, 1792–4 and
  S.P. Cockerell, *c.* 1820, altered by R. Seifert & Partners, 1978–82,
  from the north-east
. Custom House, by Sir Robert Smirke, Long Room, 1825–8
. Law Society, by Lewis Vulliamy, 1829–57
. Fleet Street, Hoare's Bank, by Charles Parker, 1829–30, interior

94. St Dunstan-in-the-
    West, by John Shaw
    Sen., 1830–3, from
    the south-east
95. St Bartholomew-the-
    Less, by Thomas
    Hardwick, 1823–5,
    altered by
    P.C. Hardwick,
    1862–3, interior
96. Fishmongers' Hall,
    by Henry Roberts,
    1831–5, south front
97. Goldsmiths' Hall,
    by Philip Hardwick,
    1829–35, west front

| 94 | 96 |
| 95 | 97 |

98. Public Record Office, by Sir James Pennethorne, 1851–70, south
  front
99. Bishopsgate, National Westminster Bank, by John Gibson, 1864–5,
  Gibson Hall (former banking hall), engraving, c. 1866
100. Temple, Temple Gardens, by E.M. Barry, 1878–9, south elevation
101. Lombard Street, Nos. 39–40, by F. & F.J. Francis, 1866–8

106. St Michael
    Cornhill, east
    window, by
    Clayton & Bell,
    1858
107. St Paul's
    Cathedral, nave,
    Wellington
    monument, by
    Alfred Stevens,
    begun 1857,
    detail of Truth
    and Falsehood
108. Eastcheap,
    No. 43,
    shopfront
    c. 1835
109. Hart Street,
    The Ship, by
    M.E. Collins,
    1887

110. Drapers' Hall, Hall, by Herbert Williams, 1866–70, upper parts
     altered by T.G. Jackson and Charles Reilly Sen., 1899
111. Liverpool Street station, interor of train shed, designed by
     Edward Wilson, opened 1875, reconstructed by BR Architects'
     department, 1985–91, from the south-west
112. Leadenhall Market, by Sir Horace Jones, 1880–1, entrance from
     Whittington Avenue

113. Institute of
     Chartered
     Accountants,
     Great Swan
     Alley, by
     John Belcher,
     1888–93, from
     the south-west
114. Cornhill,
     Nos. 71–73,
     former Union
     Bank of
     Australia,
     by Goymour
     Cuthbert, 1896
115. Cullum Street,
     Nos. 14–16,
     Bolton House,
     by Aiselby,
     1907
116. Law Society,
     north extension,
     by Charles
     Holden, 1902–4

117. Bishopsgate Institute, by C. Harrison Townsend, 1892–4
118. Fetter Lane, No. 80, by Treadwell & Martin, 1902
119. St Paul's Cathedral, crypt, south aisle, monument to Randolph
    Caldecott, by Alfred Gilbert, 1887–95
120. Queen Victoria Street, Black Friar, saloon bar, by H. Fuller Clark,
    c. 1905, reliefs by Henry Poole

1. Port of London Authority (former), by Sir Edwin Cooper, 1912–22, from the east
2. Threadneedle Street, former Westminster Bank, by Mewès & Davies, 1922–31, and Old Broad Street, No. 1, by H. Chatfeild Clark, 1903, upper parts altered 1936 (photo 1960)
3. Finsbury Circus, Britannic House, by Sir Edwin Lutyens, 1921–5
4. Trinity Square, Mercantile Marine Memorial, by Sir Edwin Lutyens, 1926–8

125. Bury Street, Holland House, by H.P. Berlage, 1914–16
126. Cornhill, Lloyds Bank, by Sir John Burnet with Campbell-Jones & Smithers, 1927–30, banking hall
127. London Bridge Approach, Adelaide House, by Burnet & Tait, 1921–5 view from London Bridge
128. New Bridge Street, Unilever House, detail of sculpture over north entrance, by Sir William Reid Dick, 1930–2

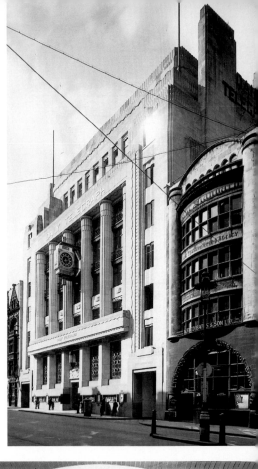

129. Fleet Street,
     Daily Telegraph
     building, by
     Elcock &
     Sutcliffe with
     Thomas Tait,
     1928–31
     (photo as new)
130. Fleet Street,
     Daily Express
     building, by Sir
     Owen Williams
     with Ellis &
     Clarke, 1930–3,
     entrance hall,
     by Robert
     Atkinson
131. Moorgate, Fox's
     umbrella shop,
     by Pollard, 1937
132. Minories, Ibex
     House, by
     Fuller, Hall &
     Foulsham,
     1935–7

137. London Wall, Austral House, by Gunton & Gunton, 1959–61, from the south-east
138. Golden Lane Estate, by Chamberlin, Powell & Bon, Goswell Road block, completed 1962
139. Police Station, Wood Street, by McMorran & Whitby, 1962–6, from the north-west
140. Barbican, view of the estate and arts centre, by Chamberlin, Powell & Bon, 1962–82, from the south-east

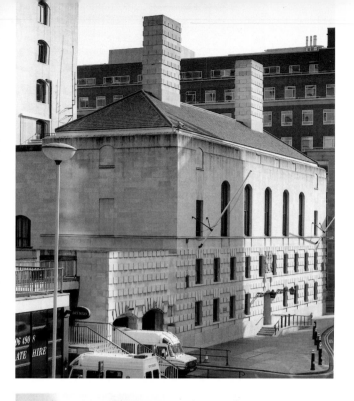

141. Throgmorton Avenue,
Drapers' Gardens,
tower, by R. Seifert
& Partners with
F. Norman James,
1962–7, seen from
Austin Friars

142. Leadenhall Street,
Commercial Union
Assurance and
Indosuez House
(former P & O), by
Gollins, Melvin, Ward
& Partners, 1963–9

143. Institute of Chartered
Accountants,
extension by William
Whitfield, 1964–70,
from Copthall Avenue

144. Queen Victoria Street,
Crédit Lyonnais, by
Whinney, Son &
Austen Hall, 1973–7

| 141 | 143 |
| 142 | 144 |

149. Queen Street, No. 36, by the Terry Farrell Partnership, 1982–6
150. Broadgate, Broadgate Arena, by Arup Associates, 1985–91, from the south-west
151. Mincing Lane, Minster Court, by GMW Partnership, 1987–91, detail of west elevation
152. Broadgate Centre, Exchange House, by Skidmore, Owings & Merrill, 1985–91, from the south-west

153. Cannon Street, Bracken House, by Sir Albert Richardson, 1955–9, and Michael Hopkins & Partners, 1988–91, from the north-east
154. Finsbury Circus, Britannic House, atrium, by Inskip & Jenkins, 1987–9
155. Fleet Place, No. 10, by Skidmore, Owings & Merrill, 1990–2

156. Chiswell Street, Milton Gate, by Denys Lasdun, Peter Softley &
Associates, 1987–91
157. Mansell Street, Insignia House, by Elana Keats & Associates
and John Winter & Associates with Jonathan Ellis-Miller,
1990–1

1677–8. Between Nos. 4 and 5 the best of the C18 railings, with decorative wrought-iron panels at intervals. The doorcase on No. 5 is especially rich, with unfluted brick Corinthian demi-columns against pilasters and a segmental pediment, the capitals and bases of stone. No. 6 has a doorcase similar to that of No. 3 (interior rebuilt c. 1948). Then a broad roadway to Tudor Street, faced by a GATEWAY of 1886–7 by *Cates*, a friendly asymmetrical design of banded stone with a two-storeyed octagonal lodge-cum-tower.

Back in the Walk, No. 7, c. 1685, has spreading stone stairs and a doorcase with a segment-headed pediment on piers with bracket-capitals repeated in profile to the sides: a device more common c. 1720. (Unusually rich interiors, with enriched doorcases and cornices.) The shell of No. 8, of five bays, may also be late C17, but it was reconstructed around a stone staircase by *John Gorham*, 1782, after a fire. His is the doorcase and probably also the second-floor stone dentil cornice. No. 9 by *Sir Robert Smirke*, 1836–7, severely plain grey brick. By Smirke also Nos. 10–11, 1814, seven bays, with round-headed doors and stone impost blocks, raised up on half-basements by the fall of the land, and the stone-faced Nos. 12–13 of 1829–30, with an unusual narrow canted bay in the centre and another in the return front to the river. They mark the limits of the shore before the Embankment was made.

On the W side of the Walk opposite, *Sir Robert Smirke*'s PAPER BUILDINGS, plain gault brick of 1838 in five storeys, with stone facing at the N end. Joining awkwardly on to its S end, a Neo-Tudor extension by *Sydney Smirke*, 1847–8, red brick with spidery black diapering (whence the nickname 'Blotting-Paper Buildings'). The inspiration seems to be Nonsuch, but it is a mechanical performance. Big octagonal corner bays with slender applied pinnacles on the first floor. Only at the top does the fenestration turn truly Tudor-Gothic, with three narrow pointed lights and blind tracery above. Pointed roofs and chimneys trimmed off after the war were restored in 1995–6.

The N end of Paper Buildings is overlooked by the Inner Temple Hall and Library (N). Beyond appears the pedimented E end of Maufe's Crown Office Row, loosely evoking the previous front here (by *Benjamin Timbrell*, 1737). Jolly plump Pegasus weather-vane on top. The S side is the INNER TEMPLE GARDEN. This was walled off from the river c. 1528, roughly on the line of the S end of Paper Buildings, and has been extended several times since. Wrought-iron GATES of 1730 by *Richard Ellis*, between stone piers with gadrooned urns, probably by the mason *Thomas Scott*, who did the semicircular steps beyond in 1729. On the gates a silvered Pegasus like a car badge, by *Harold J. Dow*, c. 1950. In the garden, two SUNDIALS: one of stone, made by *Edward Strong Sen.*, 1707; the other Italian lead work of c. 1700, fashioned as a crouching moor (moved from Clement's Inn, Strand, 1884). Nearer the river, two STATUES: a lead copy of the Roman Wrestlers, and a youth by *Margaret Wrightson*, 1971, of fibreglass. It replaced a stolen lead figure of 1775, given 1928 to commemorate Charles Lamb.

TOWER GATEWAY STATION
(DOCKLANDS LIGHT RAILWAY)
Minories

By *Arup Associates*, 1984–7, as the new railway's City terminus. Escalators rise to elevated platforms hard up against the s side of the railway viaduct to Fenchurch Street. Big glazed canopies over, domed or barrel-vaulted, already very grimy (1997). Blue brick lift shaft. Operation is automated, so no offices etc. on the platforms.

THE TOWER OF LONDON

The Tower, despite much restoration and alteration over the centuries, remains the most important work of military architecture in England. It is especially significant for the two great periods of improved defence, the reigns of William the Conqueror (1066–87) and of Henry III and Edward I (1216–72 and 1272–1307). In the Middle Ages the fortress doubled as a great royal palace, with apartments both in the towers and in lower buildings now lost. Later it served as state prison, arsenal and store. It is exceptionally well-documented, the detailed building accounts often supplemented by observations of medieval chroniclers.

The description follows the route for visitors in 1997: first the outer defences visible across the moat; then the sw entrance and s Outer Ward; then the Inner Ward, with the White Tower, mural towers, and later buildings. The Outer and Inner Line refer to the concentric curtain walls and their towers, the Outer Ward to the space between them. Within the Inner Ward are traces of a smaller enclosure, here called the Inmost Ward. The Inner Line has thirteen towers, the Outer Line five, plus the Middle Tower, sw, and two bastions at the N corners. The area within the outer walls is 12 acres (5 hectares), with moat and wharf 18 acres (7½ hectares).

The Tower presents four very different faces to the outside world. The E side can only be seen uncomfortably close to, from the elevated approach to Tower Bridge. Even so, the Outer and Inner Lines and the buildings of the Inner Ward appear stacked up to a great height. The N side has more of a castle air, though C19 ragstone rubble is much in evidence on the rebuilt Inner Line and the tall Waterloo Barracks in the Inner Ward. The w side is more convincingly ancient. More medieval fabric appears in the curtain walls, interrupted in the middle of the Inner Line by the (refaced) Beauchamp Tower, finest of the landward towers. They are offset by the backs of C16–C18 houses in mellow brick and tile, with chimneys sticking up anyhow. The s side, visible from Tower Wharf, has a different character, for several of the towers doubled as water gates. The best view of the proud White Tower from the City side is from here – from the s bank better still, rising above the trees on the wharf.

HISTORICAL DEVELOPMENT

The Tower 1066–1399

The Tower of London lies outside the City proper, in the former Liberty of the Tower, now part of the Borough of Tower Hamlets. But its area lies partly within the line of the Roman town wall, which ran slightly E of William's great White Tower, for William reused the old Roman fortifications as the E and S outer walls of his fortress (cf. Portchester, Hants). Within this angle, the defences to N and W apparently began as a ditch and palisaded rampart thrown up in haste after the Conquest. The S part of this first enclosure is perpetuated by the present Inmost Ward, S of the White Tower, from which fragmentary Roman and medieval remains survive. The White Tower itself was begun not long after 1077, and heightened or modified probably not long after completion. A wall was built around it in 1097, probably on the line of the first rampart.

In the 1190s the C11 area was roughly doubled, taking in much more land to the E. Chancellor Longchamp undertook the work, on behalf of the absent Richard I. The Bell Tower and the adjacent S wall of the Inner Ward remain from this campaign, though the N and E walls have been rebuilt or demolished. Longchamp also made a deep moat or ditch, which failed to fill.

The next great expansion was due to Henry III. He began by rebuilding the residential quarters of the Inmost Ward (1220–*c.* 1240), of which the Wakefield Tower remains to show their lavish quality. Then in 1238 he doubled the enclosed area again, building the present Inner Line on the N, E and W, and rebuilding much of the older S curtain. The work involved breaching the old Roman wall line on the E side. The new W and N defences were just as substantial as the rest, for Henry feared the Londoners within the City walls at least as greatly as any invaders outside them. Much of the work was completed in a later campaign, in 1258–61. The D-shaped towers of this C13 curtain wall have all been much rebuilt, though the Broad Arrow Tower (E side) is mostly intact. A moat was dug on the landward side, directed by a Fleming, *Master John le Fosser.*

The next transformation was effected by Henry's son Edward I, largely in 1275–85, with a speed and dispatch the politically troubled elder king never achieved. The master mason was *Robert of Beverley* (†1285), with *Brother John of Acre,* probably the overseer of the earth- and water-works. The accounts identify other masons, e.g. *Simon Pabenham II.* Edward completed Henry's curtain wall on the W side, and then raised an outer concentric curtain wall all round it. This required Henry's moat to be filled in, and land to be won from the river on the S side. A new moat was dug on the three landward sides. A formidable new landward entrance, SW (Lion Tower, Middle Tower and Byward Tower), replaced Henry's land-gate on the site of the present Beauchamp Tower. A new river entrance was also made at St Thomas's Tower, which doubled as royal apartments. Cross-walls within the Outer Ward, since removed, provided additional security. The work cost £21,000, twice Henry's expenditure: a sum equivalent to one of Edward's great Welsh castles. Many of these share the Tower's double-curtained plan, though their residential quarters were less lavish. Even so, it seems that Edward

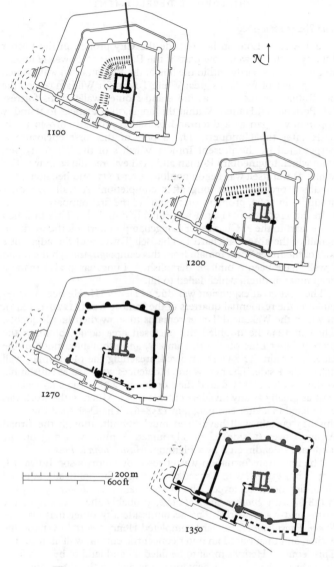

N

1100

1200

1270

200 m
600 ft

1350

■ BUILDING EXISTING BEFORE THIS PERIOD

■ NEW BUILDING IN THIS PERIOD

-- CONJECTURAL NEW BUILDING IN THIS PERIOD

— OUTLINE OF PRESENT TOWER DEFENCES

Tower of London
Plans showing progressive development

left his conception incomplete, for Edward II and III (1307–27 and 1327–77) raised and reinforced the Outer Line, and added some lesser towers where it faced the river. They also extended the wharf in front, a task completed under Richard II (1377–99). The outlines of the present Tower were thus effectively complete.

Developments from 1400

Later medieval work is minor, or has left no trace (e.g. Henry VII's improved lodgings). Henry VIII rebuilt the chapel of St Peter and modernized the royal apartments in the early 1530s, e.g. with a Renaissance 'Mantell of wainscot with antyke' in the long-vanished Dining Chamber. But thereafter the Tower became, in Holinshed's words, 'rather an armorie and house of munition, and thereunto a place for the safekeeping of offenders, than a palace roiall for a king or queen to sojourne in'. So there are no palatial interiors like those at Windsor. Relatively modest houses were built for the officers (Queen's House, etc.), and several towers adapted as prisons, where inscriptions bear poignant witness to their inmates' endurance. The defences were modestly updated, several walls and towers being adapted for ordnance after 1532 and in 1670–86. These and other alterations have left far fewer medieval features, at least externally, than at castles which fell into ruin. The White Tower served simultaneously as a magazine and as a repository for state papers. Late C18 plans show most of the Tower crowded with houses, stores and industrial buildings, many since removed. The Royal Mint, which operated within the West Outer Ward c.1300–1812, has left some C18 houses there. The Inner Ward has several larger buildings erected for the Board of Ordnance, grandest of which are the C17 New Armoury and C19 Waterloo Barracks.

After Waterloo the military functions dwindled, although the Chartist panic prompted the Constable, the Duke of Wellington, to overhaul the outer fortifications in 1845–52. Casemates of 1853 in the Outer Ward, N, are still purely functional, but the Waterloo Barracks of 1845 was Gothic. Antiquarian restoration began under *Salvin* (1852–69), and continued, less sensitively, under *John Taylor* of the Office of Works. So the Tower became primarily what it is today: a kind of monument to itself, and a showcase for the Crown Jewels and armour. But tourism here goes back at least to the Restoration, when visitors first paid to see the jewels and the displays of arms in the former Grand Storehouse. Much of the Tower remains garrisoned or residential, but since the 1970s public access has been extended to the East Inner Line and St Thomas's Tower. Since 1989 the Tower has been in the care of the Historic Royal Palaces Agency.

Further Reading

The best single account of the Tower's evolution is G. Parnell's *The Tower of London* (English Heritage, 1993). The RCHME volume (1930) gives a thorough description of the fabric up to the early C18. A more searching analysis of the medieval Tower is given by P.E. Curnow and R. Allen Brown, *The Tower of London* (DoE, 1984). J. Charlton (ed.) *The Tower of London: its buildings and institutions*

(1978) has much useful information especially on later periods. The best early accounts are J. Bayley's *History and Antiquities of the Tower of London* (1821) and John Britton and E. W. Brayley's *Memoirs of the Tower of London* (1830).

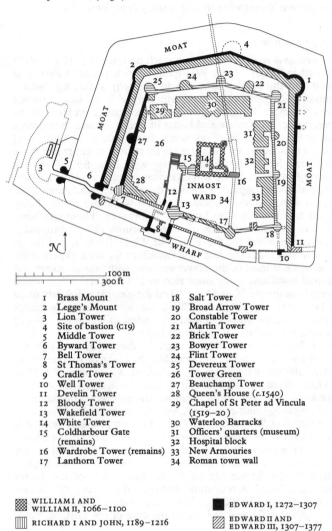

1	Brass Mount	18	Salt Tower
2	Legge's Mount	19	Broad Arrow Tower
3	Lion Tower	20	Constable Tower
4	Site of bastion (C19)	21	Martin Tower
5	Middle Tower	22	Brick Tower
6	Byward Tower	23	Bowyer Tower
7	Bell Tower	24	Flint Tower
8	St Thomas's Tower	25	Devereux Tower
9	Cradle Tower	26	Tower Green
10	Well Tower	27	Beauchamp Tower
11	Develin Tower	28	Queen's House (c.1540)
12	Bloody Tower	29	Chapel of St Peter ad Vincula
13	Wakefield Tower		(1519–20)
14	White Tower	30	Waterloo Barracks
15	Coldharbour Gate	31	Officers' quarters (museum)
	(remains)	32	Hospital block
16	Wardrobe Tower (remains)	33	New Armouries
17	Lanthorn Tower	34	Roman town wall

WILLIAM I AND WILLIAM II, 1066–1100

RICHARD I AND JOHN, 1189–1216

HENRY III, 1216–1272

EDWARD I, 1272–1307

EDWARD II AND EDWARD III, 1307–1377

C16 AND LATER

Tower of London. Plan

THE MOAT AND OUTER LINE

The MOAT is about 20 ft (6 metres) deep above the present infill level, and about 120 ft (36 metres) wide. The outer banks are brick revetments of 1670–86, before which the moat was wider still. The medieval limit was roughly on the line of the present counterscarp, made 1789–90 (railings on it of 1829). Only on the river side does the wharf make it much narrower. The moat was drained as late as the 1840s, and grassed over. The Tower Bridge Approach, made 1886–91, encroaches on the E part. Partial re-flooding is projected (1996), archaeological considerations permitting.

The WHARF along the S front was begun at the W in a modest way by Edward I, extended E to St Thomas's Tower and then rebuilt in stone by Edward III (c. 1338 and 1365–70), and further extended along the whole riverfront in the 1390s.

The walk around the outside of the moat allows the OUTER LINE to be inspected. The formula of a tall inner wall and low, largely towerless outer one is familiar from some of Edward I's Welsh castles (e.g. Beaumaris). It was long thought that the C13 outer wall was very low, as at Rhuddlan, but investigation in the 1980s suggested a respectable height of 17 ft (5 metres). It has been very much heightened over the years, and the moat-fill conceals the lower part of Edward I's work. The battlements are C19. On the E side, towards the N corner, a small square medieval projection: the survivor of three of uncertain date or purpose, perhaps for mounting stone-throwing machines.

The Brass Mount and Legge's Mount project from the NE and NW corners respectively. The larger BRASS MOUNT appears to be of Edward I's time, though later than his very first wall, foundations of which run through and behind (found 1913). On the stonework fragments of false ashlar carved with quoins have been identified. A brick-lined mural gallery may well belong with the works at the Tower for which Edward I ordered bricks from Flanders, an exceptionally early appearance of the material in England. Three original garderobe chutes on the E side. Originally open-backed, the mount was infilled and paved over by 1597 to make a solid artillery bastion, and hollowed out again in 1914. LEGGE'S MOUNT, projecting less pronouncedly, was conceived integrally with the curtain wall (cf. Caerphilly and Harlech). Traces of blocked crenellations at the S end indicate that there was further heightening early on. Then in 1682–6 the wall was raised some 20 ft (6 metres). Of this date the six gun-ports, now glazed. Parapet restored 1850. (In the basement an inserted skin and vault of early Tudor brick; traces of Tudor buildings from the Mint against the inner face.) A third bastion between the Mounts, built c. 1845, was bombed in 1940 and not rebuilt.

The most elaborate outworks, the remains of Edward I's landward approach, lie on the W side. The first defences encountered, on Tower Hill at the SW, are the remains of the causeway to the LION TOWER, which spanned an infilled W extension of the moat. No visible trace of the outermost medieval fortification here, a brick bastion of c. 1480.

The tower proper lay to the S, a large, low D-shaped bastion (dem. 1853). Part of the outline is marked out on the ground. Named from the lions of the royal menagerie, housed nearby until removal to Regent's Park in 1834. In 1341 there were a lion and lioness, four young lions, and a leopard.

The Middle Tower and Byward Tower, in line beyond, remain from the same campaign. The causeways between are partly C13, partly C18. Chases of a C13 drawbridge remain in front of the Middle Tower, visible through a fine double-chamfered arch, N. Both towers have big rounded towers to the outside and small square turrets sticking up behind. The MIDDLE TOWER was largely refaced in 1717–19 in Portland stone, in the round-arched Board of Ordnance manner: convincingly martial, though anachronistic and incorrect. The style has been associated with *Hawksmoor*, though there is no evidence he made designs for the Tower.* Simple windows with key blocks and plain imposts. Crenellations only on the square rear turrets (stonework between replaced medieval timber-framing). Carved armorial over the gateway by *Thomas Green*. Of the C13 the two-centred archway, with two chamfered orders and a double portcullis, and the elegantly elongated arrow-loops. No rear gate. Octagonal tower chambers, vaulted and lined with C13 brick. The loops have pointed embrasures.

With the BYWARD TOWER the SW angle of the Outer Line is reached. It preserves the motley appearance of most of the towers before C19 restoration: medieval Caen and Gatton stone, Portland stone patching, and plain brick parapet of *c.* 1800. The defensive features (arrow-loops, meurtrières and double portcullis) and octagonal chambers are better preserved than those of the Middle Tower. C16 two-storey timber-framed enclosure between the rear turrets (restored 1925–9). It perpetuates an original feature. The interiors, not open to the public, are exceptionally interesting. Vaulted N chamber with C13 fireplace, reached via a vaulted lobby with two-light C14 window. C13 fireplaces and pointed embrasures in the first-floor tower chambers, which are open behind to the central chamber. Here a portcullis with intact mechanism (front), separated by a substantial four-centred-arched timber screen from the rear chamber: fittings all apparently C16. Tiled floor, partly C14, laid diagonally. On the s wall, remains of a beautiful painted Crucifixion of *c.* 1400, its central figure destroyed by insertion of a C16 fireplace. To the r. St Michael and traces of St John, to the l. the Virgin. The gentle attitudes and such details as the coloured feathers of St Michael's wings recall the Wilton Diptych. Contemporary or near-contemporary decoration: on a green-painted chamfered beam above the screen, gold fleurs-de-lys, leopards and birds; red-and-white painted ashlar in the N tower chamber.

Passages lead from both floors of the rear s turret of the Byward Tower into a POSTERN, which appears externally as a lower, two-storeyed rough stone projection, with pointed s end. Mostly of 1350, replacing an entrance first made by Edward I. Two boxy C16 timber-framed storeys on top. Vaulted ground-floor passage with lion-mask boss. Traces of a drawbridge beyond, superseded when Henry VIII added a s brick-lined salient (the pointed section), with gunloops. A much-restored w doorway leads to a timber walkway on to the wharf.

---

*See Richard Hewlings, in J. Bold and E. Chaney (eds.), *English Architecture Public and Private: Essays for Kerry Downes* (1993).

OUTER WARD, SOUTH SIDE

Standing just within the Byward Tower, one would until the C18 have been enclosed by screen walls on the N and E. Now the magnificently massive BELL TOWER, which belonged to the W enlargement of the 1190s, appears unencumbered ahead. So far, the defences have been sophisticated but visually rather slight; here one first feels that the Tower is no mean fortress. Of polygonal shape on the first two stages (the only polygonal tower here), circular above. This suggests two phases of construction, probably close in date, as appears from the early form of the (blocked) upper two-light windows. The present windows are C18. It must be remembered also that until the 1280s the river lapped directly against the tower, which has a solid lower stage. A fenced-off well at the SE corner displays an excavated section of the Sussex marble plinth, with seven offsets, below the present, higher reclaimed ground. The tower originally rose some 80 ft (25 metres) above the water. Jutting from the parapet, a C17 timber bellcote, from which the twice-daily opening and closing of the Tower's gates was sounded. Two-storey interior above a solid base, reached from within the Queen's House (*see* below). (The lower floor has a garderobe lobby, then a steep and irregularly rib-vaulted chamber, the ribs of square section on foliate corbels. 15 Central foliate boss. Roughly circular upper chamber, unusually elaborate, with a continuous moulded stringcourse joining two-centred-arched apertures. C17 domed roof. In the 1970s remains were found of a stair-turret linking the floors; this may have fallen out of use in the C14, when lodgings were built on to the tower's inner face.)

The l. walk, inaccessible to the public, leads N towards Legge's Mount. Against the Outer Line the CASEMATES, a row of low late C18 brick houses and workshops for the Mint (indeed the Outer Ward is called Mint Street here). Proceeding E, the walling on the l. up to the Bloody Tower is also of the 1190s, though heightened in brick and much pierced with later windows. On the r. late C13 walling, heightened in the late 1330s (masons *Thomas de Dagworth* and *Simon of Dorset*), and again rebuilt 1679–80.

Opposite the Bloody Tower, r., ST THOMAS'S TOWER, built 1275–9 by Edward I. It held the main water gate (later called Traitors' Gate), accessible via a channel and bridge through the later wharf. On the inside a big depressed round arch. Towards the river a broad pointed arch and angle turrets. Lower stages ashlared. The form of a low turreted oblong tower projecting into the river may have been inspired by the barbican to the old Louvre in Paris, attributed to Philip Augustus, i.e. at least fifty years older. The storey above contained Edward's own lodgings, its royal status originally signalled by opening windows of coloured glass and stone statues facing the river. The timber-framed inner face was remodelled by *James Nedeham* in 1532–3, to form lodgings for the Earl of Oxford and Lord Sandys. Later the upper part served as a barracks and infirmary, the space below (basin re-flooded in the 1970s) as a tide-mill to pump in the Tower's water supply, later also as a gun-boring factory powered first by the tide, then by steam. Vibrations from this caused the collapse of the E end, whereupon *Salvin* restored it as the jewel-keeper's residence (1862–9). His are the windows, almost all the stonework, and the inner face's oriels and brick-nogging. A fragment of C13 ashlar remains on the W face of the SW turret. Salvin's covered bridge between the NE stair-turret and the Wakefield Tower, l., is a reminiscence of a medieval feature.

The interior is reached via the bridge from the Wakefield Tower (*see* below), which also formed part of the C13 royal apartments. There were two large apartments, plus rib-vaulted chambers in the turrets. The E turret has a piscina and aumbry, and has been identified as the oratory ('little chapel above the water') mentioned in the accounts. Restored as such by *RMJM* and *Caröe & Partners*, 1992–3, with the rest of the E apartment (the present partition is no earlier than the C16). Traces of a garderobe in the W wall indicate that Edward I's chamber (*camera*) lay on this side. In the C13 there was also an enclosure for the portcullis machinery. Chamber and hall (*aula*) had hooded stone fireplaces in the S wall (restored in the hall, E). The W apartment has been left as found. Below, much-altered mural galleries within all three walls.

Continuing E, more C14 walling, r. (rebuilt 'broader and higher' by *Master Walter of Canterbury*, 1325). The gateway and drawbridge across the moat here were first made probably in the later C17. The present gateway is C19. Then the CRADLE TOWER, which formed a secondary water gate. Begun in 1348 (mason *John of Leicester*), finished 1355. On an unusual, rather elegant T-shaped plan, the 'stem' projecting into the river, where it rests on two half-arches for the passage of water. Cut down in 1777 to make a gun platform; the upper part *Taylor*'s reconstruction, 1878–9, with three cusped lancets. The C14 gate passage and flanking chambers survive. River entrance under a segmental recess, with a concave outer and hollow inner order. Sophisticated two-bay vault of chalk, with diagonal and ridge-ribs of Reigate stone. Hollow circles instead of bosses. Grotesque carved corbels. In both chambers original cinquefoiled N lights. The former porter's lodge, E, has remains of a fireplace with bread oven. The W vestibule probably connected with the Lanthorn Tower, N, the King's residence from the earlier C14, via the W vice and a vanished bridge.

Next, E, late C19 offices against the curtain wall, then the little WELL TOWER, probably datable to 1275–85. Rectangular plan, E stair-turret, with remains of a cross-wall to the Salt Tower on the N face. Two quadripartite vaulted bays within, probably by *Simon Pabenham II*. In the S wall two chutes for drawing water from the river. Upper stages largely of 1879–80. Further E still, the DEVELIN TOWER, probably C14: see the characteristic squared rubble (N side), mixed with rebuilding of 1679–80. More such C14 masonry on the Outer Line wall adjoining. Originally a causeway led from the tower across the moat to the Iron Gate (dem. 1679), a small tower perhaps built in connection with the E extension of Tower Wharf in the 1390s. The causeway superseded a late C13 timber bridge here (remains excavated 1996).

INNER LINE: BLOODY TOWER AND
WAKEFIELD TOWER

Visitors enter the Inner Ward by the BLOODY TOWER. This began as a water gate contemporary with, and commanded by, the adjacent Wakefield Tower of *c.* 1225, but was deepened to the N by Edward I *c.* 1280, in connection with his St Thomas's Tower, though without any communication with it. Then in 1360–2 the upper storeys were entirely rebuilt (mason *Robert Yevele*), probably for the residence of the Constable of the Tower. Of the first phase the outer portal and barrel-vaulted porter's lodge, E, made partly within the thickness of the curtain wall. Of the second phase the side walls of the inner gateway (straight masonry break at the joint) and rear portal. Lierne vault of 1360–2, badly patched, with corbels and bosses carved with lions' heads. Sir Howard Colvin notes similarities with the contemporary vault of the Norman Gate at Windsor. Pronounced junction between C13 and C14 phases on the rear face. Uppermost stages by *Salvin*, 1868–9, perpetuate heightening of 1603, when the tower was converted as Sir Walter Ralegh's prison-house. External stairs, W, up to the first floor. The screened-off front chamber houses a portcullis and winch, probably C16. In the main, rear chamber, sections of a fine tiled 1360s floor, made at Penn, Bucks. Patterns include cinquefoils, lions, foliage and fleurs-de-lys. Of the 1360s the W window (mullion and transom of 1603), the (restored) fireplace, and a vaulted garderobe chamber at the SE; perhaps also the vice to the upper storey. Good inscriptions. Above, the wooden partitions of Ralegh's quarters were re-created from the evidence of joist holes in 1974. The long S room marks where the space of the wall-walk was taken into the interior in 1603.

The WAKEFIELD TOWER adjoins the Bloody Tower to the E. Circular, very massive, and second in size only to the White Tower. It belongs to Henry III's remodelling of the Inmost Ward, begun in the 1220s. Of this phase also the water gate later incorporated into the Bloody Tower, the walls running N to the Coldharbour Tower and E to the Lanthorn and Salt Towers, and the long-lost Great Hall against the Inner Line (*see* below). The interval between Wakefield and Lanthorn Towers is the usual distance between the Roman bastions on the town wall elsewhere, which may reflect the reuse of Roman foundations – a reminder that the Inner Line follows the Roman riverside wall. The Wakefield Tower commanded the water gate now incorporated in the Bloody Tower, and also a private royal postern to the E, stairs to which may be seen on the N side. The walls change from ashlar to rough masonry a third of the way up – much higher than if the ashlar had merely protected the walls from the river – which suggests two separate building campaigns. It seems that the tower is of two close phases between 1220 and *c.* 1240 (payments to fit up the chapel of the upper chamber, 1238). The big cylindrical form probably derives from the *donjons circulaires* of many of Philip Augustus's French castles. However, the tower was conceived as part of a sophisticated quasi-symmetrical plan, balanced by the Queen's lodgings in the former Lanthorn Tower, E. The Wakefield Tower may have been intended to rise higher, to match

its consort. Internal alterations made for Edward I included steps
to a passage and bridge s to his St Thomas's Tower. Simon
Thurley suggests that Edward may have used the tower as a
presence chamber and for formal state business, usefully placed as
it was between the King's Inner Hall (*Aula Regis*), against the
Inner Line sw of the Great Hall, and his more private apartments
in St Thomas's Tower (cf. Conway Castle).*

Abandoned as a royal residence in the early c14, the tower housed
first records, then the Crown Jewels (1870–1967), for which it was
adapted and Gothicized by *Salvin* (e.g. the transomed windows).
In 1992–3 the octagonal upper chamber was restored to a c13
appearance, inevitably partly speculative, by *RMJM* and *Caröe &
Partners*. Nonetheless it is the best-preserved of the major c13
residential apartments. Oratory in the se recess with contemporary aumbry, piscina and sedilia. The windowless recess opposite may have accommodated the king's chair, as in the restoration. c19 vault, on restored octagonal wall-shafts. Restored n
fireplace. The ground-floor chamber, also octagonal, is skewed to
the floor above. The window recesses are round-headed, not
pointed as above. Very tall s arrow-loops. Its c20 timber ceiling
re-creates a remarkable (c13?) structure destroyed in 1867, with
an additional central post. Originally the joists to the central ring-
beam were unsupported.

WHITE TOWER AND INMOST WARD

The n side of the Inmost Ward is formed by the WHITE TOWER,
begun some time after 1077 and by 1100 far advanced enough to
serve as the prison of Ranulf Flambard. According to the
Registrum Roffense, *Gundulf*, Bishop of Rochester, was in charge of

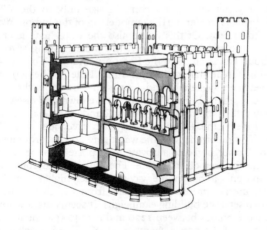

Tower of London, White Tower.
Cutaway from the south-east

* In *Architectural History*, 1995.

the work. It belongs to the small group of so-called hall keeps, a type confined to early Norman England, though possibly deriving from the lost C10 tower of the Norman Dukes at Rouen. At 107 ft (32½ metres) by 118 ft (36 metres), the White Tower is smaller only than the similarly planned keep at Colchester. Externally it is roughly square, strongly articulated by diminishing flat buttresses, with two W angle turrets, rounded NE turret, and apsidal E projection of the chapel, SE. There is archaeological evidence that this projection may have been an afterthought. The upper stage, too, shows evidence of second thoughts: investigations in 1996 found outlines of twin pitched roofs, rising from below the level of the present E and W mural galleries. Lead-lined drains from this first roof were located in the thickness of the W wall, below the gallery floors. This arrangement gave way to the present, higher shallow-pitched roofs, probably at an early date.

Walls are largely ragstone rubble, with some Quarr stone from the Isle of Wight. They were originally galletted and whitewashed, hence the name. At the foot they are some 12 ft (3½ metres) thick. Norman Caen stone dressings have gone, mostly replaced by Portland in the C17 and early C18. Windows chiefly remodelled early in the C18, in the round-arched Board of Ordnance style (cf. Middle Tower), but the blind arcading perpetuates the C11 arrangement (restoration by *Salvin*, 1861–2, spared this C18 work). The Norman window design survives high on the S elevation at the W: two pairs of two-light windows, each under a relieving arch. On the angle turrets (renewed) ogee caps probably of the mid 1530s, when the roof was strengthened to carry cannon. Proud weathervanes of 1668. The NE turret was refaced in 1914, removing a Victorian clock. The battlements received their present form in 1637–8 (mason *William Mills*).

This keep served as both stronghold and palace. Each floor is divided into three major apartments, a greater degree of sub-division than in the smaller C12 tower keeps. The White Tower remained free-standing for barely a century: the C12 added a low S entrance building (dem. 1674), the C14 a large E block (identified with the King's Wardrobe), demolished in the mid C19. The original S entrance, on the first floor, was reopened in 1973. The timber access stair probably follows the C11 arrangement. The main staircase is in the big NE turret; lesser stairs in the NW and SW turrets rise from the second floor to the roof. Once inside, the visitor ascends via a fourth stair, inserted in the C14 within the thickness of the S wall to give direct access to the chapel from the S forebuilding.

The interior has been given over to the display of arms and armour since the mid C19 (being reordered in 1996, after removal of many exhibits to the new museum in Leeds). The first (entrance) floor represents the lesser residential suite, with Great Hall, W, Great Chamber, NE, and vaulted chapel in the crypt below the Chapel of St John, SE. Traces of garderobes, N wall, and of fireplaces, the oldest known in England (W wall, and E wall of Great Chamber). Recesses in the N–E cross-wall, originally blind, have been cut through in modern times. Rows of timber posts supporting the ceilings are C18 insertions. The crypt chapel has a modern tunnel-vault and restored S windows in skewed embrasures. In the thickness of the N wall a windowless chamber. Above, the tall second floor (Banqueting Hall, Sword Room and Chapel of St John) was subdivided to make a third floor (Council Chamber and Tudor Room), perhaps in 1603–5. This runs across at the level of the springing of the original roof, identified in 1996. The present floor, probably of the 1690s, rests on rows of c18 timber posts. On this level again each chamber has a blocked fireplace. Three garderobes also, two in the N, one in the E wall. At third-floor level the walls carry a gallery, connecting with the gallery of the Chapel of St John. It is a barrel-vaulted passage about 4 ft (1 metre) wide inside the wall: a form clearly related to the charac-teristic hollow-wall technique of Norman church architecture in England (cf. also Rochester Castle and Castle Hedingham). It must originally have lain open to the air on the inward side. While it gave access to the chapel gallery, the chief function of the gallery stage must have been to bring the tower to a uniform height externally. The cross-wall may be of the first phase, or represent an addition made when the roof was raised. It has big round-headed openings. The present, well-preserved roof is of *c.* 1500.

The CHAPEL OF ST JOHN is the finest interior in the Tower of London, and one of the most impressive pieces of Early Norman architecture in England, very massive, and not relieved by ornamentation. Tunnel-vaulted nave – a great rarity in England – with groin-vaulted aisles and tunnel-vaulted gallery four bays long. Aisles and gallery continue round the apse as curved ambulatories. The vault ends in a semi-dome. Unmoulded arches on squat piers, round below and square in the gallery. Apse arches are markedly stilted. Primitive capitals, of the two-scallop type, or with a broad ribbed upright leaf at the angles and a broad T-cross in the middle. The last motif, of Anglo-German, not Norman derivation, suggests that the Confessor's masons were transferred here from Westminster Abbey. One quasi-Corinthian capital: elementary, stunted volutes, and necking of small stunted upright leaves. Used after the Reformation as a record repository, the chapel was restored by *Salvin*, 1864–6. Of this date the S windows and Bath stone patching of the Caen stone fabric. Salvin intro-duced C15–C18 STAINED GLASS, mostly enamelled or heraldic panels, some from Horace Walpole's collection at Strawberry Hill. The exit is via the basement, reconstructed in 1730–4 with brick vaults, except beneath the chapel.

To the S of the White Tower lay the INMOST WARD, a secure enclosure for the royal apartments within the Inner Ward. Its W and S boundaries were those of the C11 castle, its E boundary the former town wall. Remains are merely fragmentary. On the W side, traces of Henry III's rebuilding of the 1220s–30s. SW of the White Tower lie foundations of the COLDHARBOUR TOWER, a gatehouse with typically C13 circular towers on its N front. It prob-ably perpetuates a land-gate in the first, C11, enclosure. Running S from it, i.e. on the r. as one walks N from the Bloody Tower, a lofty but battered section of loopholed wall. The ditch in front is thought to be a relic of the first castle, thrown up probably in the winter of 1066–7, but filled in by the C13. Nothing remains of Henry III's Great Hall, some way E of the Wakefield Tower, built in the early 1230s, modernized by Edward III, and destroyed in the C17. It was about 70 ft (21⅓ metres) square, and presumably aisled, with a W chamber by the Wakefield Tower. Early illustrations show a substantial building with stately battlements to match the towers. A wall discovered at the E in 1975 may be evidence of an earlier, probably C12 Hall. On part of its site is now a low 1970s concrete shop, partly underground.

To the E of the White Tower, by the apse, the lower part of the WARDROBE TOWER survives (a C12 wall connecting the two was demolished in 1879). It dated probably from the 1190s. Its D-shaped plan follows that of a semicircular Roman bastion, for here we are back on the ancient line of the town wall. Part of its alignment is marked out on the ground nearby. The uncovered portion is 10 ft 6 in. (3¼ metres) long and 4 ft 9 in. (4½ metres) high. The sandstone plinth continues through the back of the bastion. The triple brick bonding course on its inner face corresponds to the level of the plinth. An internal turret was found in 1957 where the wall changed direction just N of the Wardrobe Tower; another section of Roman wall was uncovered within the Bowyer Tower in 1911 and again in 1993. Lesser Roman finds include masonry foundations and glass-furnace waste near the White Tower, and a stamped silver ingot with associated gold coins of after A.D. 395, found 1777 and now in the British Museum. Funerary inscriptions include the important tombstone found on Tower Hill (*see* Trinity Square) and a stone to Aulus Aufidius Olussa of the Pomptine tribe, born at Athens, found 1852.

THE INNER LINE: SOUTH EAST, EAST AND NORTH SIDES

The S part of the Inmost Ward is formed by the Inner Line, here much rebuilt by *Taylor*, c. 1885–8. His is the LANTHORN TOWER, E, on a slightly different site from the previous Lanthorn Tower, demolished 1777 after a fire. It was built 1220–6 for Henry III's Queen, as a counterpart to the Wakefield Tower (*see* above). W of the tower is Taylor's curtain wall, bald and straight, with blind arcading more like a railway retaining-wall than any work at the medieval Tower. Important remains of the ROMAN RIVERSIDE DEFENCES were excavated near here in 1976–7. The wall consisted of small, neatly-squared ragstone blocks with internal timber lacing, about 10 ft (3 metres) thick, with an angle at its E end. It was built up against the earlier riverside wall, which lay slightly S of the medieval curtain wall. Coin evidence indicates a date no later than the 390s, suggesting an association with the campaigns of Stilicho in the closing years of the C4. The narrow corridor between the two Roman walls, perhaps part of a river gate, was perpetuated by a kink in the previous curtain wall, swept away in Taylor's rebuilding.

Next the SALT TOWER, in the SE corner of the Inner Line. It projects externally as a three-quarter cylinder, with a rectangular stair-turret, N, and a W projection on to the wall-walk. Probably of c. 1238. On the S and E faces remains of Edward I's cross-walls to the Outer Line. Upper parts altered in the late C19. Entry is through the pentagonal basement chamber, up to a first-floor chamber, also pentagonal. Here an original hooded fireplace and a garderobe a few steps up the vice. Window of two trefoiled lights, from *Salvin*'s (faithful) restoration, 1856–7. On the wall the finest of all the carvings done by prisoners: an astronomical clock, carved by *Hugh Draper* and dated 1561.

The wall-walk continues N, behind later buildings on the E side of the Inner Ward (for which *see* below). The C13 wall was partly rebuilt in the C19, especially at the N. The mural towers are D-shaped. The BROAD ARROW TOWER has C19 windows, but is otherwise largely mid C13. Inner face flush with the curtain, with rectangular turrets to each side. Three floors, the topmost a late C19 insertion. The first floor, entered from the wall-walk, has a garderobe and a renewed fireplace. The staircase is dog-legged, not the customary spiral. S of the tower, visible externally, a blocked pointed postern arch, quite high up. The CONSTABLE TOWER, similar in plan but without the rear turrets, is late C19. The MARTIN TOWER, NE corner, is also D-shaped, but with rear projections along the angles of the curtain. Much altered *c.* 1669, when it became the Jewel Tower, and again in 1721, when external steps were made up to the first floor. Of 1721 probably also the pedimented S doorway on to the wall-walk. The upper parts are C18 brick repairs, with on the outer face one eruption of rubble stonework from an abandoned medievalizing scheme of 1905. Confusing interior: medieval wall-walk doorway, S, with hollow-moulded rear arch, and in the N turret two garderobes, one above the other; C18 mezzanine floor, partitions and panelling from the jewel-keeper's residence.

The sequence of D-shaped towers continues along the N inner line, behind the Waterloo Barracks. Much had to be rebuilt here after the fire that destroyed the Grand Storehouse in 1841 (*see* below). From E to W: BRICK TOWER, so called from an early C16 rebuilding, now all 1840s; BOWYER TOWER, externally similar but preserving the C13 ground-floor chamber, with single-chamfered rib-vault and one arrow-loop; FLINT TOWER, early C19, and DEVEREUX TOWER, NW corner, the largest of Henry III's angle towers to remain. D-shaped, but irregular, with SE and SW stair-turrets. Wholly refaced externally, with other alterations of 1683 and 1715. (Ground floor rib-vaulted in two irregular bays, with round-headed embrasures.) It is approached from the Inner Ward through a courtyard, made by a low, late medieval wall.

INNER LINE: WEST AND SOUTH-WEST SIDES,
AND TOWER GREEN

Proceeding S past the Chapel of St Peter ad Vincula, one reaches TOWER GREEN. Its trees and houses make it visually the most attractive part of the Tower. The curtain wall behind the whole W side was completed in 1281, incorporating Henry III's wall as its lower stage. Its special feature is the fearsome sequence of brick-lined arrow-loop chambers along the whole length, another reminder of the fraught relations between crown and citizenry; now blocked by a fine row of C16–C18 houses. These are interrupted by the BEAUCHAMP TOWER, Edward I's replacement of Henry III's main landward entrance, superseded in the 1280s. (Excavated in the moat in 1996, substantial ashlar footings with details resembling those of the late C12 Lion Tower, though with associated timbers dateable to 1240. They probably come from Henry III's 'noble gateway' which Matthew Paris describes as collapsing during construction in that year, although the timbers may represent an attempt to shore up an earlier structure.) The Beauchamp Tower is D-shaped, like Henry's towers, but is specially big and broad, to span the gatehouse foundations. There are also three storeys rather than two. The N turret is markedly larger than the S one. Refaced by *Salvin*, 1852–3, his first job of restoration at the Tower: see the big two-light window on the inner face. Each floor has five embrasures with pointed arches of C13 brick, most still with arrow-loops. Timber floors. First-floor chamber reached by a vice with more C13 brickwork. Notable inscriptions include a carving of c. 1553 by *John Dudley*, Earl of Warwick, with a floral border like embroidery, r. of the ground-floor fireplace.

Immediately N of the Beauchamp Tower, two pretty, wholly domestic-looking CHAPLAINS' HOUSES. The taller and narrower, S, is of 1735 (fine staircase), the other, N, of 1749. On the other, S side, twin early C17 brick HOUSES of three storeys plus attic and basement, with three straight gables and brick bands: a characteristic type, now extinct in the City proper. Built as a single house probably in the 1630s; subdivided in the early C18, with new staircases etc. Much the largest is the QUEEN'S HOUSE, SW angle, of 1540 and later. The name is misleading, for it housed the head officer of the Tower. Very manorial-looking: half-timbered with double-curved diagonal struts; carved bargeboards on the gables, four to each range. The far W bay, S side, housed a first-floor hall open to the roof, the far E the tall kitchen: both horizontally divided in 1607. The upper part of the hall became the Council Chamber. (Here a reset profile bust of James I and a pilastered tablet of 1608 commemorating the Gunpowder Plot.) Awkward C17 ground-floor brick extensions. Good staircase of 1687–8 in the S range. It replaced a C14 house (traces in the basement), probably built for the Constable in the 1360s in connection with work at the Bloody Tower; rooms within the C12 Bell Tower are incorporated (*see* above). Continuing clockwise, a diminutive two-bay C18 house, then an unappealing Neo-Tudor house by *Salvin*, after 1866.

FREE-STANDING BUILDINGS OF THE INNER WARD

The tour is clockwise from Tower Green.

CHAPEL OF ST PETER AD VINCULA. In the NW angle, N of the scaffold site. First mentioned c. 1130, it was not enclosed within the Tower walls until the 1230s. Rebuilt c. 1240, 1286–7, and finally in 1519–20. *Walter* and *Thomas Forster* did the work. John Harvey attributes the design however to *William Vertue*, then Master Mason at the Tower. A Chapel Royal since 1966. Plain, straightforward nave and N aisle, slightly shorter, but of equal width. Windows under depressed arches, of three lights, except for the broad five-light E nave window. Small quoined brick W tower with thin, pretty lantern. Originally of 1670–1; rebuilt apparently faithfully in *Taylor*'s restoration, 1876–7 (*Salvin* consultant). Of this date also the NE vestry and octofoil W window, a crass insertion. Taylor's flint and cement facing was partly removed by *H. G. Hexley*, 1971–3. A C16 S porch was demolished in 1862. Nave and aisle are divided by a four-bay arcade. Four-centred arches, slim piers of the usual four-shafts-four-hollows profile with capitals only to the shafts. A blocked window in the chancel N wall. C16 flat-pitched tie-beam roofs.

FITTINGS. FONT. Early C16, octagonal, with quatrefoils on panels: nothing remarkable in a village church, but rare for London. – ORGAN CASE. Made in 1699 by *Smith* for the Banqueting House, Whitehall, when that was converted into the Chapel Royal. Four slim towers, three flats. Modern instrument. – PISCINA in N aisle E wall; also a SQUINT, its exit blocked. – Excellent commemorative marble chancel PAVEMENT, 1870s. *Taylor's* Gothic reredos and pulpit went in the early 1970s. – MONUMENTS. An exceptional collection. John Holand, Duke of Exeter †1447. Transferred 1951 from St Katharine's Chapel, Regent's Park, to be near its original home at St Katharine's Hospital, E of the Tower (dem. 1825), where it stood screen-like between choir and N chapel. Tomb-chest with recumbent alabaster effigies of the Duke and two wives. Elaborate canopy with sharply angled four-centred arches. On the uprights figures in tiers, and beasts, little figures and grotesques. The arches cusped and sub-cusped with heads on the cusps. Angels in the spandrels, angels in the frieze. Above the outer frieze a blank upper zone with brackets for statuettes. – Alabaster tomb-chest to Sir Richard Cholmoundeley †1544 and wife, with indifferent recumbent effigies, all still Gothic. Chest with cusped lozenged panels. – Sir Richard and Sir Michael Blount, Lieutenants of the Tower, †1564 and †1592. Double standing wall-monument of alabaster and marble, the W part (Sir Michael) a later, matching addition. Double niches in each half, each with unusually fine effigies of kneelers gravely facing one another. The architectural frame is also distinguished: correct Corinthian columns, garlanded spandrels and mask keystones. Both parts attributed to the *Cure* workshop (AW). – Sir Allen Apsley †1630. Tablet with pediment and small relief of cherub. – Children of George Payler, *c.* 1650. Odd, gauche, but touching too, as so often in the mid C17. Erected at two dates, first the two children in an oval niche with two flanking putti, then the three plainer oval niches above, with busts of the parents and a third child. – Capt. Valentine Pyne †1677, muscular tablet flanked by cannon instead of columns; relief with a ship at the foot. – Sir John More †1679, convex, with graceful cherubs' heads below. – Gen. William Bridges †1716, pilastered tablet with bust. – Brick vaults to the N; a BUST of Sir Thomas More by *Raphael Maklouf*, 1970: one of many illustrious victims of C16 politics who were buried here. The vaults may be C15 or early C16 (first mentioned *c.* 1560).

WATERLOO BARRACKS. Of 1845, on the site of the Grand Store-house (1688–91, burnt 1841). Large and symmetrical, in grim and gaunt castellated medieval style. Designed, it seems, by *Major Lewis Alexander Hall* of the Ordnance Engineer's Department. The Crown Jewels are displayed on the ground floor (installation by *Sidell Gibson Partnership*, 1992–4). Of the same style and date the former OFFICERS' QUARTERS (now Royal Fusiliers' Museum), SE. S of the museum the former HOSPITAL BLOCK, originally two handsome brick houses of 1718–9, partly rebuilt after war damage, 1952. On the larger house, r., doorway with straight hood on scrolly corbels. The round-headed first-floor windows are unusual for the date.

NEW ARMOURIES, s of the Hospital Block. Built 1663–4, of rich red brick with orange brick dressings. Half-H-plan, two storeys, with tiled dormered attic and half-hipped gables, a transitional feature. The pilastered doorcase was added only in 1950, when the Armoury was converted into a museum. Proposed for conversion to a café, 1996. Within, original timber framing; also an excellent stone PEDIMENT from the Grand Storehouse, carved by *John Young Jun.* in 1691 (to be relocated). Arms of the Board of Ordnance with supporters, flanked by flags and a belligerent display of weaponry. Reset into the s exterior wall, two smaller armorials, one late C17, the other from the Ordnance Office of 1779, which stood on the South Inner Line.

For remains of the TOWER POSTERN, at the s end of the medieval City wall, *see* Trinity Square, p. 612.

TRINITY HOUSE
Trinity Square

The headquarters of the venerable Corporation of Trinity House, which looks after lighthouses, sea-marks etc. By *Samuel Wyatt*, 1793–6; rebuilt internally and extended by *Sir Albert Richardson*, 1952–3, after severe bomb damage, 1940. Before 1670 Trinity House was in Deptford (its home at Incorporation in 1514), then in Stepney. It probably antedates the C13, possibly even the Conquest. It later had headquarters off Lower Thames Street (rebuilt 1718). Wyatt's connection was apparently his lighthouse for Coke of Holkham at Dungeness, Kent, 1791.

Wyatt's façade is elegant yet serious, with none of the effeminacy of so many buildings of the Adam age. Stone-faced, of five bays, with a tall *piano nobile* on a rusticated basement. It is organized as a series of threefold divisions, each with a wider middle section. So the centre is recessed, and triply subdivided by unfluted Ionic columns (paired pilasters on the end bays). Straight-headed tripartite windows at the centre and ends, made by smaller Ionic columns. Reliefs over the windows: cherubs and lighthouses (ends); the Corporation's arms (centre). Medallions between of George III and Queen Charlotte, by the elder *Bacon*, of *Coade* stone. *Richardson*'s work appears, r., in a section set back for two bays, then coming forward as a big copper-topped canted bay, all of good stock brick over stone: a fluent, happy conjunction.

Richardson's interiors replicating Wyatt are remarkably convincing, though simplified. The ENTRANCE HALL is broad and plain, with straight-headed recesses and lesser round-topped niches. Inscribed stone here from the Trinity House, off Lower Thames Street, 1718. In the far wall, two Doric columns of *verde antico* scagliola frame an opening to the semicircular STAIRHALL. The staircase climbs in one flight and returns in twin curved arms to the landing. Simple outswept iron balustrade with anthemion panels. Light comes from a strikingly austere clerestory (compared by J. M.

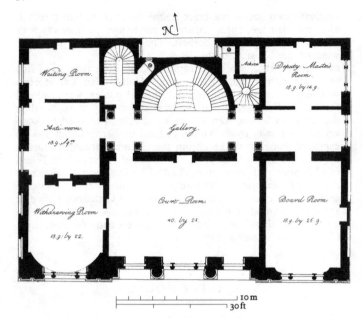

Waiting Room.

Anti-room.
18.9. 19"

Withdrawing Room.

13.3: by 22.

Archive

Gallery.

Court Room.
40. by 23.

Deputy Master's
Room.
18.9 by 14.9.

Board Room.

18.9 by 25.3.

10 m
30 ft

Trinity House. Plan in 1802

Robinson to half a lighthouse lantern). Grisaille coffering. Rooms to
l. and r. are also gained through paired columns, Doric below, and
Ionic on the first floor. Above the latter on each side a gallery open
to the second floor, with caryatids (carved by *Wheeler*) in line with
the columns: an excellently theatrical touch. Older furnishings came
from the Trinity Almshouses, Mile End Road (*see London 5: East
and Docklands*): four carved late C17 armorials in the lower corridor;
in the stairwell, two painted lead STATUES of Captains Richard
Maples and Robert Sandes. Respectively by *Jasper Latham*, 1683,
and *Scheemakers*, 1746, the latter in poor condition. The PAINTING
on the landing, a huge group portrait by *Gainsborough Dupont*, 1794,
includes Wyatt presenting his design. The lofty COURT ROOM
occupies the centre of the front. Foliage frieze; coving with nautical
allegories in grisaille; coloured central panel of cherubs manipulating
a giant orrery. Originally by *J. F. Rigaud*; as repainted by *Glyn Jones*,
it comes off remarkably well. Replica fireplace, white marble and
ormolu: Wyatt at his most French. Undemonstrative MASTER'S
ROOM, W, and LUNCHEON ROOM, E, with reset white marble fireplaces of *c.* 1800. Richardson's extension houses the elliptical-ended
LIBRARY, which doubles as a banqueting hall. Panelling conceals
the books. Armorial STAINED GLASS: in the E windows, late
C16–C18, from the first recorded Trinity House, at Deptford; other
windows by *Francis H. Spear*, 1953. Richardson's PEPYS ROOM,
immediately N, has the wide segment-headed openings favoured by
Wyatt and Soane; more in the restored ground-floor interiors.
Demolished *c.* 1990 Richardson's offices for rent at the rear, in
similar manner to the library, though much taller. New buildings by
Sheppard Robson are proposed, 1996.

LIVERY HALLS

In 1997 the City has thirty-four halls belonging to its Livery Companies, or Guilds. Their survival against the odds is a remarkable feature of the City's history. It is difficult to find exact parallels outside the capital. York has its Merchant Adventurers' Hall, the core of which is C14, and one might also mention such curiosities as the subdivision of the former Blackfriars at Newcastle upon Tyne as meeting rooms and almshouses for that city's guilds. But only the trades of such great Continental merchant cities as Antwerp or Brussels showed a comparably competitive spirit in their premises.

More than half of the halls remain on their medieval sites, though all have been wholly or partly rebuilt at least once. The catastrophes of 1666 and 1940–1 are largely to blame. So the periods now most widely represented are *c.* 1670–85 and (alas) *c.* 1950–65. The latter are generally traditional or Neo-Georgian in style, and in most cases the livery accommodation is combined with offices for rent. They are discussed more fully in the Introduction (*see* pp. 137–8). But the Livery Halls also contain impressive work of other periods, whether entire buildings, new wings or remodelled interiors: the results variously of changes of taste or site, of other fires and structural failures, and of attempts to maximize lettable income from what are often very valuable plots.

The Guilds originated as fraternities of tradesmen and craftsmen, incorporated mostly in the C14 or C15, though traceable in some cases to the C12, and in other cases established probably not much later. Their functions included regulation of trade, sociability, and mutual help, including funerals and masses for the dead. Other lay fraternities are known, some of which had halls: the best-known is the fine late C15 hall of the Brotherhood of the Holy Trinity (dem.), off Aldersgate Street. However, these took second place to the Livery Companies, whose liverymen to this day form the élite from which the Lord Mayor and Aldermen are chosen. Guilds ramified and specialized rapidly: the leather trade alone produced Cordwainers, Curriers, Glovers, Leathersellers and Saddlers. Corporate religious life ceased at the Reformation, and effective regulation of most trades lapsed in the C16–C17. The Guilds survived primarily as honorific, sociable and charitable bodies, although several retain close connections with their crafts. Their survival as sociable institutions helps explain the paucity in the City of gentlemen's clubs; less obviously, the Livery Halls also served many Nonconformist congregations in lieu of chapels when not otherwise required.

The minimum requirements of a Livery Hall are a court room for private business and modest entertainment, and a larger hall for greater social events, variously called the Banqueting Hall, Livery Hall, Great Hall, Dining Hall, or merely the Hall. These rooms correspond to, and derive from, the chamber and hall of the medieval town house. Early records indeed show Guilds acquiring such houses and putting them to use, minimally adapted. Only the Goldsmiths' and Merchant Taylors' Halls can demonstrate C14 origins, but most of the larger companies had acquired a hall by the end of the C15. The banqueting hall lay sometimes on the ground floor, sometimes on the first floor, the court room usually close by and on the same level. Grander Livery Halls might have many more rooms (the first Goldsmiths' Hall had several parlours, an armoury and a chapel), and most had houses or apartments for the beadle and other officers. Their usual arrangement was around a courtyard, reached through tenements along the street. This type of plan was mostly perpetuated when the Halls were rebuilt after the Great Fire: *see* Merchant Taylors' Hall, with its unique medieval survivals, and Tallow Chandlers' and Skinners' Halls, which are more consistently C17. Drapers' Hall, now mostly Victorian, retains a courtyard and also a small garden: the only survivor of a once-common amenity.

p. 398
p. 404

The present Livery Halls fall into several categories. Post-Fire work survives at nine of them, of which only six preserve convincing C17 interiors (Apothecaries, Innholders, Skinners, Stationers, Tallow Chandlers and Vintners). Skinners' Hall and Tallow Chandlers' Hall alone retain well-preserved C17 elevations, though there is also a remarkable little C17 warehouse attached to Stationers' Hall. The Apothecaries, Stationers, Tallow Chandlers and Vintners retain C17 woodwork in their banqueting halls, including fine enriched screens. With their tripartite compositions and superb carving, these rival or excel the great reredoses of the contemporary City churches. The best smaller interiors of the period are the Vintners' and Skinners' court rooms. Vintners' Hall has the finest remaining C17 staircase. C17 plasterwork has lasted much less well: only Innholders' and Drapers' Halls retain ceilings *in situ*, the latter altered. In addition, the Goldsmiths' C19 court room incorporates glorious plaster coving from its C17 predecessor. Painter-Stainers' Hall has panels from an interior decorated by members of the Livery in the early C18.

67, p. 407
69
68

Only one Georgian hall remains, and even this is strictly not a Livery Hall proper: *Blackburn*'s tiny and charmingly Adamesque Watermen's Hall, 1778–80. Good mid-C18 interiors survive at Skinners' Hall and Stationers' Hall. Of late Georgian work, Skinners' Hall has an elegant pedimented street range by *William Jupp*, 1778–9, Apothecaries' Hall two strange warehouse ranges of 1780–6, Stationers' Hall a front remodelled by *Robert Mylne*, 1800–1. Greater Georgian halls fell victim to Victorian rebuilding (Carpenters, Drapers, Grocers) or C20 bombing (Ironmongers, Salters). But four late classical halls remain from the 1830s: *Philip Hardwick*'s opulent Goldsmiths' Hall and *Henry Roberts*'s Grecian and gentlemanly Fishmongers' Hall, from the first half of the decade, and from its second half the more modest Armourers' and Braziers' Hall (by *J. H. Good*) and Dyers' Hall (by *Charles Dyer*). The best interiors of the first pair are all that one might wish. The latter are by less well-known architects, typical of those who served as the Livery Companies' surveyors well into the C20: a circumstance favouring safe rather than adventurous designs when rebuilding came around.

84
83
85
97
96

Victorian work now makes a modest show by comparison with Goldsmiths' and Fishmongers' Halls. Only Drapers' Hall (*Herbert*

Williams, 1866–70, altered 1898–9) preserves interiors evocative of High Victorian plutocracy. There is also the little Cutlers' Hall, in free Jacobean style (by *T. Tayler Smith*, 1886–7). Bombing accounted for the grand Clothworkers' and Leathersellers' Halls, and for the interiors of Carpenters' Hall. Grocers' Hall survived the raids but was burnt out in 1965, only a fragment of the front being retained in the rebuilding.

Of the C20 the earliest work of note is *Sydney Tatchell*'s Ironmongers' Hall (1922–5), a secluded Neo-Tudor building with extraordinarily elaborate plasterwork in the manner of *c.* 1600. The inter-war years were notable otherwise mostly for the removal of ill-advised Victorian additions and alterations to older, especially late C17 interiors. Post-war interventions in historic interiors have generally been more discreet, though one must question the tendency constantly to redecorate, polish and burnish every visible surface. No self-respecting Livery Company could relish picturesque decay, of course; but it is a relief to come on rooms which have been allowed to acquire some patina.

The following descriptions necessarily exclude the contents of the Livery Halls, highlights of the sculpture and significant relics of older premises excepted. Other treasures include fine paintings, furniture and chandeliers, and (as one would expect) a mass of superb plate (Goldsmiths pre-eminent, also Armourers, Clothworkers, Drapers, Fishmongers, Mercers, etc.). The Brewers, Fishmongers, Ironmongers, Merchant Taylors (2), Saddlers and Vintners preserve remarkable late medieval embroidered funeral palls. The Cloth-workers, Merchant Taylors and Vintners have other tapestries of note. Carvings include excellent C18 wooden figures of patron saints from the Companies' ceremonial barges, which were given up after 1856 (Fishmongers, Goldsmiths, Ironmongers), and processional shields of the C18 and later (Fishmongers, Stationers). Several Halls have specialist collections, e.g. of pewter at Pewterers' Hall. Interiors may usually be visited by appointment; some halls also hold exhibitions or concerts which are open to the public.

APOTHECARIES' HALL
Black Friars Lane

A courtyard building, of which the N and E ranges, by *Thomas Lock*, 1668–73, have some of the best-preserved C17 livery hall interiors. But its conspicuous peculiarity is the warehouse-like W and S ranges of 1780–6. They housed the Society's manufacturing operations: the Navy Stock, which supplied the Navy with drugs, and the Laboratory Stock, together with some houses for the officers. C20 alterations were by *Sir William Wells*, 1928–30, and *J. Sampson Lloyd*, 1983–7. The plan perpetuates part of the Dominican Friary (*see* Black Friars Lane), fragments of which are incorporated.

The Apothecaries, properly styled a Society, not a Company, seceded from the Grocers' Company in 1617. They bought the former Cobham House here in 1632. Lord Cobham had acquired the friary after the Dissolution and made his own house from its guest house, on the E side of the present courtyard. The N range consisted of a porter's lodge and gallery (*see* below), the S range of tenements; a screen wall lay on the W. Partial rebuilding in 1632–3 retained some old work, and sections of medieval masonry from the guest house survived even the Great Fire: a low patch of ragstone rubble in the outer E wall, and part of the (concealed) outer N wall, discovered in the 1980s to extend some 30 ft (9 metres) high, with unusual flint and ragstone decoration.

The WEST FRONT of the W range, facing Black Friars Lane, struggles hard to harmonize domestic, industrial and ceremonial features and functions. The architect for the work of 1780–6 was *Richard Norris*, one of three surveyors consulted in 1779, at first for a somewhat smaller rebuilding assignment. Eleven bays and three storeys of stock brick, the ground floor stuccoed. Centre and end bays slightly projecting, the latter carried up to four storeys. Each end bay has windows in a recessed central panel, marking where warehouse doors have been infilled. Sunken red-brick-trimmed roundels flank them (partly missing from the altered r. bay). Meagre Venetian window on the ground floor. Next to these end bays, two domestic-looking four-bay sections, with round-headed ground-floor windows. The two-bay segment-headed recess, l., was made in the early C19 for the Society's retail shop. In the r. part a coarse late C19 doorway. Central entrance with a reset C17 open-pedimented Doric doorcase, presumably from the previous courtyard entrance, for which *John Young*, mason, provided a 'draught' *c.* 1670. Is the whole narrow quoined central bay also a reminiscence of the C17? Armorial in the pediment, apparently of *c.* 1780.

The SOUTH FRONT, facing Playhouse Yard, preserves the warehouse character better, despite conversion to offices by *Lloyd* in the 1980s. Eight bays, the far r. one angled. Beyond appears the S end of the Hall, refaced after war damage. The bow-fronted No. 6, SE corner, is not what it seems. Its shell is the Society's late C18 magnesia warehouse, converted in 1983. Sashes were inserted, the walls heightened and extended N over a single-storey former counting-house (contemporary doorcase, facing E).

Entry to the COURTYARD is through an inner doorcase in the W range with Adamesque pilasters, dated 1786. The livery hall proper occupies three-storey N and E ranges. Built 1668–73, almost certainly to designs by the Society's Surveyor, the master carpenter *Thomas Lock*. *Edward Jerman*, *Capt. Richard Rider* and *Peter Mills* had all surveyed the burnt site earlier, apparently without providing designs, and in 1668 the Society had rejected designs by a Mr Kirbie, identified by Sir Howard Colvin with *Richard Kirby*. Craftsmen were *George Clisby*, carpenter, *Edward Salter*, bricklayer, and one *Blunt*, plasterer (the *Blount* who worked at St Sepulchre?).

The HALL lies along the E side, as did its predecessor, converted by Cobham from the friary guest house. It has four big upright first-floor windows, each with a circular window over it. Sashes and stucco facing (*Higgins*'s patent) of 1781–6, to match the inner faces of the W and S ranges.* The solid parapet and lean pediment replaced a C17 balustrade in 1793. Later arms within the pediment, probably of 1821, the date of the clock below. In that year also the window surrounds received their present shape. C17 brick walling

---

* Stucco on the W and S ranges carried out by *George Wyatt*, on the hall side by Messrs *Adam*, who may also have provided the W doorcase.

and brick bands remain on the opposite side, E, facing a small court-yard (also here, the small section of medieval walling mentioned above).

The plain NORTH RANGE rests on a widely spaced Tuscan colon-nade, its W part infilled and glazed in the late C18, its E part enclosed 1928–30 by *Sir William Wells*, with a rusticated stone doorcase. A steel frame was inserted into the C17 structure at the same time. The external staircase to the SOUTH RANGE, r., probably perpetu-ates that built by *John Young* in 1671, though early C19 views show it one bay further W. It originally led to a corridor into the screens pas-sage. On this side also an ornamental feature incorporating medieval carved stone fragments. In the middle of the courtyard an early C19 lamp, on the site of a well from the friary.

INTERIORS. The N doorcase leads into a STAIRHALL, enlarged on the ground floor in 1928–30 by taking in space from the colonnade. The C17 staircase climbs in three flights, exposed on the S by the removal of the former wall to the courtyard. Two columns mark where this formerly stood. Heavy balusters with short twisted shafts on urn-like bases. Heraldic stained glass of the 1670s, artificially back-lit. The LANDING with its pilastered panelling was also enlarged in 1928–30, taking part of the Library, W. The HALL, E, of five bays, retains C17 woodwork by *Robert Burges* and *Roger Davies* (paid 1673), now stained black: notably a magnificent reredos-like screen at the far (S) end, with coupled fluted Corinthian columns 67 and a wide broken pediment. Vigorously carved arms within, by one Philips, probably the King's Carver *Henry Philips*. Below, a half-length bust by *Nicholas Young*, 1671, of Gideon de Laune, Apothecary to Anne of Denmark and leader of the secession from the Grocers' Company. The screen was set back against the wall in 1793, the date also of the little musicians' gallery, N, with elegant wrought-iron balustrade, and probably of the ceiling too. This has a big fluted oval in the central panel and enriched modillion cornice. Painted a chaste cream, with discreet gilding. Plain fielded panelling around the walls: a good sober backdrop for the Society's excellent collection of full-length portraits. Stained glass: good roundel of an apothecary over the S screen by *Francis H. Spear*, dated 1931; late C16 panel with the Bristow arms, from Ayot St Lawrence, Herts. (given 1980), E wall; much C20 heraldry.

Immediately N, the COURT ROOM has still simpler panelling of 1673. Even the overmantel is barely ornamented. On the N wall an early C19 pedimented feature, formerly a setting for the Master's chair. Bold armorial stained glass of 1967, by *Carl Edwards*. The PARLOUR, NE angle, was in the C17 plainer still, with dado only. Now it has a Kentian mid-C18 fireplace from West Harling House, Norfolk (given 1939). Above the colonnade, i.e. off the landing to the W, the LIBRARY, with fireplace and panelling of 1682. The modest interior has a grand historical pedigree: it succeeds the gallery of the 1630s hall, heir in turn to that made 1522–3 between the guest house and Henry VIII's Bridewell Palace (*see* New Bridge Street), during the residence at the friary of the Emperor Charles V.

Ground-floor interiors are of little interest. The former KITCHEN, below the parlour, has a wide restored fireplace. The present kitchens lie further W. Other parts of the historic property are occupied by offices called Cobham House, N, built in connection with the most recent refurbishment (*see* Black Friars Lane); the land up to Church Entry, E, once the friary's Great Cloister, by a crude warehouse of 1927.

ARMOURERS' AND BRAZIERS' HALL
Coleman Street

A modest, masculine late classical building by *J. H. Good*, 1839–41. The Armourers' trades were first regulated in 1322 and chartered in 1453. The Company has held the site since 1428; the hall's much-repaired predecessor dated partly from the C15 (refronted 1795–6 by *William Cresswell*). Of stock brick, with dressings apparently of painted stone. Façade rather like a plain scaled-down Goldsmiths' Hall (q.v.): two tall storeys, seven bays, with in the centre four giant Roman Doric pilasters. Emblems of armour in the metopes. Low attic block with grand carved armorial over. Plain two-bay flanking sections. Fine LAMP over the door, on ornate cast-iron brackets. The return front to London Wall is also plain, of five bays, with a very top-heavy large-windowed upper storey. Heavy rusticated doorcase below. Between the fronts a deeply inset corner, meanly walled across below.

Good's interiors are of similarly unaffected sobriety. The top-lit STAIRCASE, approached through a screen made by two Ionic columns, is of Imperial type. Iron balusters with lotus motif. Square lantern from alterations by *Alexander Graham*, 1872–3. On the N wall a delicate plaster armorial, apparently C17; said to come from the Company's former almshouses in Old Jewry. A N–S landing gives access to the main rooms. The LIVERY HALL, S, lies E–W. Its appearance is mostly of 1872–3, notably the heavy timber coving and cumbersome oblong lantern, wagon-roofed, with Venetian windows in the short ends. No other windows: i.e. the S windows on the W front here are false. Doors with engraved glass by *Laurence Whistler*, 1959. Staircase and Livery Hall bristle with the Company's formidable collection of armour. Other interiors, largely unaltered, have coved or subdivided ceilings and good solid fireplaces and doorcases: COURT ROOM and LIBRARY, facing W, and spacious DRAWING ROOM, facing N.

BAKERS' HALL
Harp Lane, N of Lower Thames Street

By *Trehearne & Norman, Preston & Partners*, 1961–3, with *W. Newcombe-Wright* of the Bakers' Company. The first of the post-war livery halls in a Modernist idiom. The plan is a small square office tower for rent, set on a podium housing the Company. Reclad in brown brick by *Whinney, Mackay-Lewis & Partners*, with *John W. Tompkins*, 1984–6. At the same time separate entrances were made to the two parts. The livery suite is connected by a free-flowing STAIRCASE and VESTIBULES. By the entrance, stained glass with the Company's arms, given 1525, from the sequence in the aisles of St Andrew Undershaft (q.v.). On other walls, eight sophisticatedly bold lead-inlaid marble panels showing the history of the Company.

Designed by *Joseph Clarke* of *Clarke & Shoppee* (later Master of the Company) for the passage through that firm's street range of 1881–2 to the previous, C18 hall. COURT ROOM in the basement, panelled in ash and oak by *Tompkins*, 1989. Modest ground-floor LIVERY HALL with walnut and oak panelling of the 1960s. Three near-abstract stained-glass windows by *John Piper*, 1969, represent the fires which destroyed the previous halls (1666, 1715 and 1940). Carved arms of George II, from the hall built 1719–22. The first hall here was acquired in 1506; the Company is first recorded in the 1150s.

BARBER-SURGEONS' HALL
Monkwell Square, N of London Wall

By *Kenneth Cross*, 1966–9 (completed by *Laurence King & Partners*). A four-square yellow brick block, mildly Neo-Georgian, set in the gardens N of London Wall. E front of eleven bays, with small central pediment. Upper floors are offices for rent. Interiors are half-heartedly traditional. Large double-height BANQUETING HALL at the rear, with a giant rounded bow in the middle of the W side. The little COURT ROOM, N, has armorial stained glass dated 1660. The Barbers, first recorded in 1307, have been here since the early 1440s. The Surgeons, now dissolved, joined in 1540, but broke away in 1745. Their hall in Old Bailey, by *William Jones*, 1747–51, was demolished in 1803. The medieval hall was extended W *c.* 1605 on to a bastion of the wall, remains of which survive in the garden behind (*see* London Wall). In 1636–7 *Inigo Jones* added a remarkable anatomy theatre (dem. 1785), of oval plan, like that at Padua. The rest was rebuilt by *Edward Jerman*, completed by *Thomas Cartwright Sen.*, 1667–71. A large carved armorial in the present hall, dated 1671, appears to be that from its former Monkwell Street entrance. In 1863–4 *John Shoppee* demolished the S part; bombs destroyed the remodelled remnant in 1940.

BREWERS' HALL
Aldermanbury Square, S of London Wall

A subdued stone-clad block by *Sir Hubert Worthington*, 1958–60. The Company struggled with the Corporation to build such discrete headquarters, since the London Wall plan (q.v.) required a larger, more modern office building here. The result was described by Pevsner in 1962 as 'looking with its traditional forms rather like grey spats among blue jeans'. A long first-floor balcony marks the livery suite. Open-well timber staircase; Court Room and Hall in simpli-fied late C17 manner, oak- or pine-panelled. Fireplace in the former with tiny relief carved by *Wheeler*, who also did the entrance key-stone. Ground floor for rent.

The Brewers have been here probably since 1408; work on a hall by the Cambridge carpenter *John Pekker* is recorded in 1423. Excavations in 1958 revealed foundations possibly of the C15 domes-tic range, not aligned with the post-Fire hall. This was by the brick-layer *Caine*, 1670–3, to designs by the Company's surveyor *Thomas*

Whiting. Its vigorous courtyard frontage and near-intact interiors were destroyed in 1940.

BUTCHERS' HALL
Bartholomew Close

Stone-faced Neo-Georgian, by *Howard Kelly & Partners*, 1959–60. Tiers of windows placed asymmetrically on the tall front. Large round-headed windows to the second-floor Hall, their key blocks carved with animal heads. The previous building, by *Peebles*, 1884–5 (destroyed 1944), had a Hall in the same position. Earlier premises were in Pudding Lane (1677, rebuilt 1829), King Edward Street (to 1666) and Monkwell Street (*c*.1475 to before 1544). The guild is first mentioned as early as 1179. ENTRANCE HALL with engraved-glass screen by *John Hutton*, 1979: four voluptuous females, over-life-size. Panelled COURT SUITE, first floor, with a good white-marble chimneypiece by *Benin*, *Fils*, from James Wyatt's Henham Hall, Suffolk, 1793–7 (dem. 1953). Pilastered HALL with bad Adamesque plaster ceiling. Stained glass: pretty scenes by *T. & W. Ide*, 1993–4.

CARPENTERS' HALL
Throgmorton Avenue and London Wall

1876–80 by *W. W. Pocock*. Thickly and prosperously Cinquecento, richer than the contemporary offices lining Throgmorton Avenue (q.v.). Alternating pediments on columns, the aedicules separated by big detached Corinthian columns standing on projecting pedestals the whole height of the ground floor: an utterly incorrect but undeniably effective treatment. The w front is rudely disrupted by a great stone-faced bridge built out over the avenue, from *Whinney, Son & Austen Hall*'s reconstruction of the blitzed shell in 1956–60. It houses part of the new Banqueting Hall. They also made a ground-floor arcade along London Wall, within the C19 shell, and added several set-back office storeys.

First record of a Carpenters' Company proper is in 1333, though building regulations by the Master Carpenters are mentioned in 1271. They first leased property here in 1428, and bought the free-hold in 1520. The building demolished in 1873 was of many periods: hall of 1429, refronted and much altered by *William Pope* and *John Wildgos*, 1671; parlour of 1579; court room post-1664 (also by *Wildgos*); entrance hall, staircase and gateway by *William Jupp Sen.* and *William Newton* of London, *c*.1780.

The present hall lies further E, on the site of tenements called Carpenters' Buildings (by *John James*, 1735–6). The post-war interiors are mostly panelled in combinations of woods. In the ENTRANCE HALL, three C16 painted panels on lath and plaster, uncovered in the former banqueting hall in 1845. The artist, perhaps a Netherlands refugee, was probably following untraced engravings. They may date from redecoration in 1561 (a rare period for religious art), and are not without artistic merit, though little more than the under-drawing remains. The subjects are King Josiah rebuilding the

Temple, Christ in the Carpenter's Shop, and Christ teaching in the Synagogue (a fourth panel, Noah building the Ark, has disintegrated). Ground-floor COURT ROOM, panelled in burr oak and burr walnut. Here three Elizabethan oak panels, two dated 1579 (from the former parlour?), with scrawny strapwork framing arms and inscriptions. One is inscribed THOMAS HARPER MASTER, with his carpenter's mark. Best interior is the large BANQUETING HALL, with fluted elm and mahogany panelling, teak floor, and openwork cedar ceiling suspended below blue-painted plaster: a richly hued ensemble. The dais end altered 1966 to accommodate a bulbous carved allegory by *Wheeler*, called The Tree of Life. Big windows overlook the avenue. Incised figures by *James Woodford* in their reveals. Stained glass by *Alfred Fisher*, 1994: large but delicate armorials. More traditional first-floor RECEPTION ROOM (remodelled 1995), STAIRCASE etc., without merit.

CLOTHWORKERS' HALL
Dunster Court, off Mincing Lane

By *H. Austen Hall*, 1955–8, replacing the hall destroyed in 1941. Brick and stone Neo-Georgian, the livery hall lost in a big mass of offices for rent. The Guild was incorporated in 1528, amalgamating the Fullers and Shearmen. The present site is that of the Shearmen's Hall, acquired 1456 and rebuilt *c.* 1472. Later halls in 1549, 1633, 1668, and 1856–60 (by *Samuel Angell*). From the last the substantial iron gates at the present main entrance.

The parsimonious 1950s Neo-Georgian interiors were embellished in 1985–6 with new cornices, plasterwork etc. to designs by *D. W. Insall & Associates* (project architect *Nicholas Thompson*). The results work best in rooms of plausibly Georgian proportions, less well where the 50s bones show through. The big aisled ENTRANCE HALL has grisaille paintings of clothworking by *John O'Connor*. The DRAWING ROOM, COURT ROOM and COURT DINING ROOM, in manner mid C18 or early C19, lie to the r. Grander rooms, above, are reached by a Travertine-clad Imperial STAIRCASE with a glazed dome, at the opposite, l., end. On its half-landing a fixture incorporating carved ciphers of Charles I and James I, from a surround to their (destroyed) statues by *John Bumpstead*, made *c.* 1679. In a niche on the LANDING a jolly carved gilt-wood ram by *Jack Denny*, 1968. Barrel-vaulted RECEPTION ROOM, with carved wooden doorcases (by *Anthony Harrington*) and well-observed late C18 style plasterwork, both 1986. The LIVERY HALL is a large double cube with coved ceiling. Neo-Wren carving by *Harrington*; armorial stained glass by *Hugh Easton*, *c.* 1960–3.

For the Lambe's Chapel crypt in the little garden, SE, *see* All Hallows Staining.

COOPERS' HALL

For the Coopers' Hall, *see* Streets: No. 13 Devonshire Square.

CUTLERS' HALL
Warwick Lane

By *T. Tayler Smith*, 1886–7. Fine red brick and purplish sandstone, with a big Jacobean entrance frontispiece, l., balanced by a little ground-floor bow, r. Large unadorned upper windows, with mullions and transoms. Pretty terracotta frieze above the ground floor, by *Benjamin Creswick* of Sheffield, a discovery and protégé of Ruskin. It shows with serious-minded realism the contemporary manufacture of cutlery. Interiors are panelled Neo-Jacobean, less literal than the earlier C19 preferred: see the strange proscenium-like screen where the entrance hall turns r. into the rear stairhall, with columns resting on big carved elephants (the Company's badge). Good stained-glass window, l., showing historical and industrial scenes: by *Powell & Sons*, 1903. Facing the street, the COURT ROOM and COURT DINING ROOM, unequal spaces that can be thrown together by sliding doors. Overmantel in the former like a fancy dresser; its plain counterpart, opposite, a replacement after war damage (restoration by *Noel Clifton*). Excellent wrought-iron candelabra throughout. The little COMMITTEE ROOM, behind the entrance hall, has early C17 pilastered panelling, originally from a house near Great Yarmouth. The STAIRCASE rises around an elongated well. Armorial stained glass here, late C17 onwards; also a splendid carved panel of an elephant dated 1569: relics of the previous hall in Cloak Lane, established in the C15, but swept away by the present District Line. First-floor DINING HALL, not rich, but larger and taller than the façade suggests. Steep-pitched hammerbeam roof, ceiled and plastered between closely paired arched braces. The ends of the hammerposts erupt in elephant heads.

DRAPERS' HALL
Throgmorton Street

The finest surviving Victorian livery hall, with opulent interiors of 1866–70 by *Herbert Williams* to rival the richest Mayfair saloons. His street front (No. 27) was rebuilt again in 1898–9 by *T. G. Jackson* with *Charles Reilly Sen.*, to maximize the lettable frontage; some other alterations (Reilly was Williams's assistant in the earlier work).

The 1890s front is free commercial Northern Renaissance, stepping down from six to four storeys, E to W. Generally indecisive, the strongest accent a plain stone band below the first-floor cornice. Red brick and stone above, with good carved putti etc. Polished granite shopfronts below, brown stone with a black stone mezzanine. The Drapers' presence is signalled by Jackson's entrance, l., with big turbaned atlantes by *Henry Pegram*. Unusually deep basement for the date, reached by a circular stairwell, r. Its gold mosaic decoration of 1900 is a relic of Lyons' monster restaurant here, the largest in the City when new. At the far r. a wilfully non-matching three-bay stone section with giant Corinthian pilasters and big round-arched first-floor windows in aedicules. It screens the Hall, the apsed end of which appears high up. Beyond, twin three-bay stone fronts with

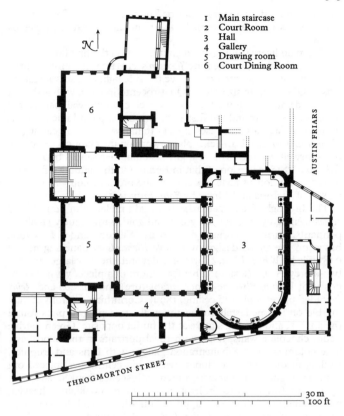

1   Main staircase
2   Court Room
3   Hall
4   Gallery
5   Drawing room
6   Court Dining Room

Drapers' Hall. First-floor plan

round-arched windows, of 1881–2. Built mostly for rent, they also contain some offices for the Hall.

The Drapers made woollen cloth. Their first hall was in St Swithin's Lane, acquired 1385 or 1408. In 1543 they bought the stone-built and turreted mansion of Thomas Cromwell here, by *James Nedeham* of the Royal Works (1532). The earliest surviving fabric is from its post-Fire replacement of 1668–71, by *Thomas Cartwright Sen.* to designs by *Edward Jerman* (bricklayer *Thomas Netheway*). A stuccoed, externally nondescript section survives, NW, visible from Throgmorton Avenue (reached by a passage through the l. end). The rest of this W front is of the 1890s, partly embellished in matching style by *Fitzroy Robinson Partnership*, 1989. The C17 part overlooks a little walled garden with mulberry trees (railings designed by *S.E. Dykes Bower*, 1972). The avenue itself replaced much larger gardens further N in 1875. Williams replaced not the C17 hall but its Adamesque successor by *John Gorham*, 1773–8.

The entrance passage runs along the W side of a modest COURT-YARD with a fountain, a legacy of the C16 plan. *Williams*'s High Renaissance inner ranges have rusticated arcading and a pilastered first floor, with giant plate-glass windows with garlands over. Best is the balustraded two-storey Court Room range, N. Top-heavy E and W sides of three storeys. In the tympana carved allegories by *Wyon*.

The main livery suite makes a circuit around the first floor. Access from the entrance passage is by *Jackson*'s STAIRCASE, lit from a first-floor triple window with oculi above the side lights (post-war stained glass). Of moderate size, richly Quattrocento in style, with alabaster balustrade and much marble work: Greek cipollino wall panels, red doorcases, and around the first-floor landing applied Ionic columns of breccia. Capitals and bases are C15 Italian work. Other carving by *Farmer & Brindley*. Low-relief plasterwork on the elliptical ceiling. In the stairwell, SCULPTURE of a girl fastening her sandal by *Rudolph Schadow*, 1818, a version of that in Berlin. On the landing a fireplace of 1825 with honeysuckle frieze, from the previous court room, and BUSTS of Victoria and Albert by *John Francis*, 1852.

The big, light COURT ROOM is an odd mélange of periods and styles: ceiling by *Williams*, all green and gold, with vaguely Jacobean pendants; enriched cornice devised by Williams and *J. D. Crace*, based on the 1770s design by *George Richardson*; panelling in late C18 style by *White Allom*, c. 1910–15. Beyond, the very large and rich two-storey HALL (E side). This feels more of a piece, yet is a composite of *Williams* (to the upper entablature) and *Jackson* and *Reilly* (arcaded upper walls and ceiling, 1899). Corinthian columns of dark marble on low pedestals round the walls, sweeping in pairs round the apse, S, and turning square at the buffet opposite. Green marble dado, chocolate walls, full-length royal portraits in the blind bays. The columns carry a balustraded gallery with urns and trophies. Ceiling in the manner of Jones, with a big central oval pieced out with rectangular end panels; painted with scenes from Shakespeare by *Herbert Draper*, 1910, in light, acid colours. (Williams's heavier, more elaborate ceiling was supported on atlantes and deep coving.) STATUES of Hypatia by *Richard Belt*, of Venus by *John Gibson*, c. 1850.

A narrow GALLERY across the S range opens off by the apse. Designed by *Jackson*, with carved wooden arabesques by *I. Carter* relating to the trade. The sumptuous DRAWING ROOM (W range) completes the circuit. The best preserved of Williams's interiors, though the light green and gold colour scheme is *White Allom*'s. Even Composite pilasters with painted panels in the shafts. Pier glasses corresponding to the windows between. Above the ornate pulvinated frieze, blind lunettes and brackets to a rich coffered stucco ceiling. White-marble chimneypiece, High Victorian Michelangelesque. SCULPTURE. Shepherd boy and dog by *Thorvaldsen*.

One older interior of note: the COURT DINING ROOM, off the landing on the N. The rectangular ceiling of c. 1670 survives, with central circle-in-square with semicircular projections. Garland and bayleaf mouldings in the Jones tradition. Altered in 1868: centre painted by *J. F. Barrias*; coving elaborated crashingly insensitively by *Williams*, in early C17 style. Creditable contemporary wainscot by *Crace*, mid-C18 style, with other furnishings.

DYERS' HALL
College Street and Dowgate Hill

By *Charles Dyer*, 1839–41; in 1856–7 extended E on to Dowgate Hill by *D.A. Cobbett*. This later part of red brick above stone, loosely Palladian, but with typically fiddly tripartite windows flanking the applied Ionic portico. Dyer's front faces College Street, S. It shows by contrast how readily the late classical idiom lent itself to memorable compositions. Stuccoed, with a channelled ground floor five windows wide, the central one the former main entrance. Above, four Doric pilasters frame three central round-headed windows, the middle one blind. Three square windows above the lower cornice, with tall urns in relief between them. Full modillion cornice above. This hall replaced a trim five-bay building by *Richard Jupp*, 1768–70, itself successor to a property of the 1730s; the first documented hall was in Thames Street, further W (*c.* 1545–1681). The Company is first recorded in the C14.

Dyer's ceremonial rooms are reached through Cobbett's wing via a groin-vaulted entrance, r., and a long glass-vaulted CORRIDOR, rather as in a Parisian house. Seven wall-paintings here of birds by *Sir Peter Scott*; bronze sculpture in the far niche by *M.J.A. Mercié*, *c.* 1910, an angel and fallen warrior. The 1840s interiors, all somewhat altered, are mostly oddly shaped to fit the slanted S wall. Ground-floor COMMITTEE ROOM with white-painted panelling in early C18 style, by *J. Hatchard-Smith & Son*, *c.* 1910. Engraved-glass armorial panel by *Laurence Whistler*, 1971. Central open-well STAIRCASE, late C17 style, probably also of *c.* 1910. The first-floor COURT ROOM lies N–S, along the E side. Large enough to double as a banqueting hall. At each end a screen of two Corinthian columns between pilasters, more widely spaced at the S. Here they frame a shallow outcurved bay with one window only, r.: an attempt to disguise the irregular angles. Rich rinceau frieze. Opulent ceiling of nine divisions, apparently C20, but a good match (a view of *c.* 1900 shows only three divisions). Late C17 armorial glass in the N window. Mahogany panelling of 1965. The chocolate-brown colour scheme by *H.T. Cadbury-Brown*, 1990, with clashing curtains designed by *Eduardo Paolozzi*, conceals Dyer's yellow scagliola columns and pilasters.

FARMERS' AND FLETCHERS' HALL
Cloth Street, S of Long Lane

An undemonstrative recent addition to the ranks of livery halls, by *Michael Twigg Brown & Partners*, 1986–7. The livery suite is on the lower ground floor. Above ground, patterned brick offices respect the modestly scaled surroundings.

For the previous Fletchers' Hall, *see* St Mary Axe.

FISHMONGERS' HALL
London Bridge Approach

The Fishmongers' Hall, by *Henry Roberts*, 1831–5, is one of only two City Companies' buildings designed in the grand manner. The other, exactly contemporary, is Goldsmiths' Hall. What makes Fishmongers' Hall unique amongst City livery halls is its conspicuous position, overlooking the Thames by London Bridge.

The Fishmongers trace their ancestry to the C14 Stockfishmongers and Saltfishmongers. The present site, one of several early premises, became their exclusive meeting place in the early C16. Excavations W of the hall in 1974 found the C2 Roman quay (*see* Introduction p. 34), C12–C14 revetments, and an overlying medieval house with a damaged C14 tile floor: the only such floor so far recorded *in situ* in London. The Company's C14 buildings lay further E. They were rebuilt during the C16 as a three-storey river range with the Livery Hall lying N, off Thames Street. The larger successor of 1667–9 had a Livery Hall facing the river and two-storey rear ranges making a courtyard. It was by *Edward Jerman* and *Thomas Lock*, assisted by *Edward Pierce*; further advice was given probably by *Hooke* or *Peter Mills*. It had an assured pedimented brick and stone front, comparable to contemporary astylar designs by Hugh May or Roger Pratt. Only such details as the aprons linking the windows vertically betrayed its City provenance.

The Hall was modernized by *John Gorham* in 1788–91, but in the 1820s the new London Bridge Approach required part of its site. Winner of the competition for its replacement, held in 1831, was the twenty-eight-year-old *Henry Roberts*. The Hall was built 1832–5, at a cost of £55,000. Chief assistant in Roberts's office at the time was *George Gilbert Scott*, but he seems not to have contributed to the design. The pervading influence is rather that of Sir Robert Smirke, whose pupil Roberts had been, and who had responsibility for the

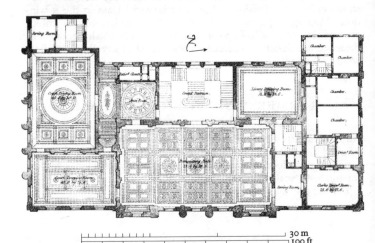

Fishmongers' Hall. First-floor plan, as built

other architecture of the bridge approaches. The Ionic order is of Smirke's favourite type, the concrete raft foundation followed Smirke's Custom House (q.v.), and the structural ironwork also recalls Smirke, though without his structural audacity (girders of 40 ft (12 metres), to Smirke's 56 ft (17 metres), at the British Museum).

The Present Building

The Hall faces the London Bridge Approach with a symmetrical 96 two-storey Portland front of eleven bays, and the river with a seven-bay front with six giant attached columns and a five-bay pediment. Giant antae at the angles. Windows of the upper storey are shorter than the lower by one subtle inch. Thanks to the situation level with the new high bridge, a terrace finds a place in front of the S façade, its arcaded granite plinth accommodating warehouses and open to the former wharf. The plinth was carefully calculated to harmonize with Rennie's London Bridge (q.v.). A pier with matching dentil-cornice, incorporated into the present bridge adjoining the riverside steps, formerly served as a screen wall between the Fishmongers' property and the bridge's previous, narrower alignment. Entrance from the Approach by a doorway in a three-bay loggia *in antis*. The central five bays above correspond to the Banqueting Hall inside. Crowning balustrade, interrupted over the entrance loggia by an attic with the Company arms, carved by masons of the contractors, *W. &L. Cubitt*. By the entrance the original GAS LAMPS survive.

To the W, disappointing offices of 1976–7 by *Holford Associates* facing Upper Thames Street and Swan Lane. An opening in the linking section supersedes the old lane down to the wharf. In Roberts's arrangement this ran through vaults under the Hall's projecting N and S wings. A little courtyard garden open to the river now occupies the enlarged space between these wings. Here a weathered stone STATUE of the Fishmongers' benefactor James Hulbert, by *Robert Easton*, 1728, brought from the Company's almshouses at Bray, Berks., in 1978. On the wall, carved stone ARMS by *Pierce*, from the Thames Street entrance of the C17 hall.

Interiors

Roberts's interior has been several times redecorated, first by *Owen Jones*, 1865, then by *J. D. Crace* to designs by *G. F. Bodley*, 1894. Toned down in 1926–7 by *H. Goodhart-Rendel*, and again redecorated in 1943–54 by *Austen Hall* after war damage. Restoration was conservative, and Roberts's Neo-Greek ensemble is largely intact. The rooms are softer and more eclectic than the exterior, but purer than the exactly contemporary interiors at Goldsmiths' Hall. The ENTRANCE HALL has delicate decoration and a cast-iron stove with gilt ornaments. Here a *Coade* stone statue of Charity with three children, 1791, by the elder *Bacon*, incongruously grouped with the Company's shield. A cross-wall separates this hall from the ample STAIRCASE HALL, disguising the lack of alignment. Towards the staircase a screen of four serene if heavy unfluted Doric columns of pink granite: an early use. The staircase itself is of the type then favoured for clubs and private palaces: one flight divides at r. angles

into two, which return at r. angles to the first-floor landing. Heavy iron balusters by *Dewers* of Old Street. Marble floor of 1926–7. In a niche on the half-landing, an uncommonly excellent over-life-size
70 statue of Sir William Walworth, Lord Mayor at the time of the Peasants' Revolt, carved from elmwood by *Pierce c.* 1685. He wears Tudor apparel and holds the dagger with which he will stab Wat Tyler. Displayed here also carved wooden panels of boys with dolphins, believed to be by *Peter Vangelder* from the work of 1788–91. Stained glass here and in the vestibule (see below) by *Hugh Easton*, 1951.

The large BANQUETING HALL opens off the landing. Strongly architectural, with a coffered elliptical vault on Corinthian pilasters of yellow scagliola. The profile of the vault matches the arches of Rennie's bridge. This ellipse and the way the pilasters overlap both depart from rigid Greek formulae, albeit that the pilasters copy those of Lysicrates's Monument. The gallery, large pier glasses and heraldic glass (by *Hancock & Rixon*) are original features. In the lunettes reliefs of sea gods by *Woodington*, 1840, in *Bielefeld*'s papier mâché. The court suite facing the river, S, suffered extensive bomb damage. The decoration of DRAWING ROOM and COURT DINING ROOM was renewed to the old design. The former has scagliola pilasters like the Banqueting Hall; the latter is severely masculine, with a subdivided ceiling. They are entered from an ingeniously contrived and detailed T-shaped VESTIBULE, partly domed and tunnel-vaulted, forms generally reminiscent of Soane. The ground-floor COURT ROOM was enlarged at the restoration (1951) by one bay. Fireplace with triton mask and seashell garlands under a broken pediment: the upper part of a piece by *Charles Easton*, installed 1741 in the previous Court Room. Another good C18 fireplace, not thought to be original to the building, in the little LIBRARY adjoining. It has portrait medallions, one of Inigo Jones.

The N part of the Hall is occupied by offices and residential accommodation (rebuilt 1961 by *Austen Hall*). They now connect with offices in the block of 1973–7. The basement warehouses were converted by *Holford Associates*, 1981, as offices for themselves. Inside the entrance from the wharf, vigorous sculptures of a fisherman and fisherwoman by *Alfred Turner*, 1901, originally in the staircase hall.

FOUNDERS' HALL
Cloth Fair

By *J. Sampson Lloyd* of *Green Lloyd*, 1984–6, on a new site. The Company was first recorded in 1365. The site of the first, C16 hall, rebuilt in 1669–72 and (by *J.B. Gardiner*) in 1844–5, is commemorated by Founders' Court, off Lothbury (q.v.). A later hall by *Aitchison*, 1877–8, survives in commercial use in St Swithin's Lane (q.v.).

147 The new Hall shows the cautious Neo-Vernacular contextualism of the 1970s moving towards Postmodern playfulness and colour. Long, narrow plan, aligned N–S. Five storeys. The main front faces St Bartholomew-the-Great, W, with pantiled gabled bays alternately receding and advancing. The latter have exaggerated jetties projecting in width as well as depth. Stock brick is the main material, varied

by other brick types and on the lower jetties by contrasting squared metal-framed glazing above cast aluminium spandrel panels. Simpler rear elevation to Kinghorn Street, E, with circular windows high up. Upper storeys house flats and offices. Near-matching S extension, completed 1990.

The LIVERY HALL lies in the basement, with natural light coming from porthole windows in a dark brick wall facing a sunken garden court. The rationale is that most Livery functions are artificially lit evening affairs (cf. Plaisterers' Hall). Hefty primitivist Doric columns make an entrance aisle. Full-height mirrors on the inner wall give illusory depth. Access is via a STAIRCASE at the N end, lit from a broad timber-framed bay at pavement level. PARLOUR on the ground floor. Some unexceptional C19 panelling and stained glass, transferred from the previous hall.

GIRDLERS' HALL
Basinghall Avenue

1960–1 by *C. Ripley* of *Waterhouse & Ripley*: Neo-Georgian. It thumbs its nose at the surrounding and exactly contemporary curtain-walled blocks of London Wall (q.v.). Fairly small, since without lettable space. Villa-like pedimented E front facing Coleman Street, the proportions not Palladian. Other elevations are more diffuse. Little garden at the rear. The hall of 1680–1 on the site, occupied by the Company since the 1430s, was destroyed in 1940.

GOLDSMITHS' HALL
Foster Lane

Built 1829–35, for one of the oldest and wealthiest Livery Companies, by its Surveyor *Philip Hardwick* (masons *Thomas Piper & Son*), with some fittings from its C17 predecessor. The Goldsmiths' Charter dates from 1327, when the trade was already concentrated in Cheapside. The first hall on the present site, acquired in 1339, is the earliest recorded of any Livery Company. Probably an unexceptional town house, it grew to encompass chapel, great hall, chamber, parlour, armoury and granary, besides an assay house for the Company's business in silver and gold, arranged on the usual court-yard plan. *Nicholas Stone* rebuilt all this, larger, in 1635–8. He insisted on absolute personal control: the first recorded instance outside the Royal Works of an architect 'practising' in the modern sense. *Inigo Jones* also took an interest, probably securing Stone's employment, and certainly helping with his design. How far the 1630s hall represented the advent of a purer Court style in the City is difficult to say, however, for it is known only from *Edward Jerman*'s reconstruction of its burnt-out shell in 1669. The Foster Lane front was of red brick with quoins, the projecting centre with a carved and pedimented two-storey frontispiece. Details were plausibly Jonesian, if without the purity of e.g. the Queen's House at Greenwich (*see London 2: South*). Jerman's bracketed eaves cornice may have followed Stone's design. The courtyard plan was perpetuated, with the great hall on the far (E) side.

97 *Hardwick*'s still larger replacement is a noble Portland stone palace on a plinth of Haytor granite. It occupies an entire block, a luxury denied the contemporary West End clubhouses with which it may be compared. The façade, too, is more grandiose than the clubs', more so even than Roberts's contemporary Fishmongers' Hall (q.v.), though less conspicuously placed. It is designed in a manner just changing from early C19 Neoclassical into a kind of Neo-English Baroque. The key motif is the giant order: columns by the entrance, giant pilasters on the sides and towards Gresham Street, N. They derive from such buildings as Webb's King Charles block at Greenwich. Baroque also is the way in which the relatively small façade is given six Corinthian columns and the windows between have thick balconies. Capitals after the Temple of Mars Ultor in Rome. Arms, emblems and trophies on the second floor carved by *Samuel Nixon*. Original cast-iron lamp-standards at the Foster Lane entrance. Towards Gutter Lane, behind, the arched windows of the Livery Hall appear, above an irregular single-storey extension. Added by *Hardwick* in 1847 to house furnaces, this now houses the Assay Office; altered *c.* 1970, with a new mansard roof.

Apart from Livery Hall and Court Room, the INTERIORS were altered after bomb damage to the SW corner in 1941. Restored from

1 Livery Hall
2 Anteroom
3 Court Room
4 Drawing room
5 South anteroom
6 Exhibition room
7 Luncheon room
8 Anteroom (was binding room)
9 Library

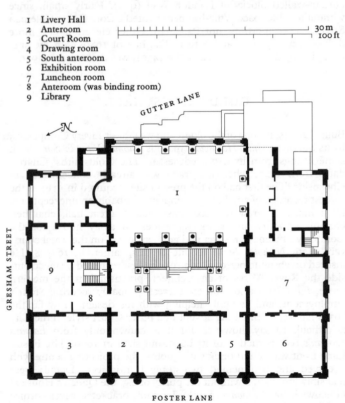

Goldsmiths' Hall. First-floor plan

1947 by *C. H. James*, succeeded in 1953 by *R. E. Enthoven*, with the Company's Surveyor *A. F. Westmore*; *F. Billerey* also contributed. Lost interiors were not re-created, and replacements vary from traditional to modern. More recent alterations by *D. W. Insall & Associates*, 1989–90. Hardwick's basic arrangement remains: a low entrance hall leads to a central stairhall, its gallery communicating between the main apartments facing Foster Lane, W, and the huge hall opposite.

The ENTRANCE HALL, restored by *Enthoven*, is reached through fine cast-iron openwork gates. The rear doorcase is *Insall*'s. Fielded oak panelling, partly from the Company's former property at East Acton Manor (dem. 1911). Steps climb gently through modern display screens by *Alan Irvine* (incorporating parts of Hardwick's openwork iron balusters), to the grandiose double-height STAIR-CASE HALL. Top-lit from lunettes between the pendentives of its shallow dome and skylights to the surrounding first-floor gallery. Painted coffering on the dome. The staircase starts in one flight and breaks by 90 degrees into two. Paired columns to the gallery, round the other three sides. The opulent coloured marble of staircase and balustrade dates from 1871, by *R. Hesketh* (restored 1954). It replaced Hardwick's wooden panelling, openwork balusters, and scagliola columns.

In the staircase hall, some notable SCULPTURE: beneath the gallery, r., a good mid-C19 marble group of Nestor, Telemachus and the Nymph; bust of William IV by *Chantrey* in a niche on the half-landing; four statues by *Nixon* of the Seasons (1844) on the staircase's lower pedestals, in character already thoroughly Victorian. On the upper landing, bronze head of Queen Elizabeth II by *David Wynne* (given 1973), and a strange bust of Edward III by *Armstead*. In 1989–90 a new LOWER STAIRCASE down to the groin-vaulted basement was contrived on the r. by *Insall*: it is barrel-vaulted with a single landing, a modest but pleasing variant of Bernini's Scala Regia.

The LIVERY HALL lies beyond the staircase hall, along the E side of the building. Redecoration by *Insall* added much gilding and lightened some surfaces of the scheme by *Aitchison*, 1892. Hardwick's fabric remains fundamentally unaltered, its scale and conception overpowering. An applied Corinthian order in yellow scagliola breaks on the long sides into ranges of four columns set in front of the pilasters, the high pedestal coming forward to support them. A lesser Doric order between the columns supports the arches of the round-headed windows and answering blind arcading opposite. The walls have large gilded swags and putti over giant pier glasses. Richly coffered ceiling. Top-lit apsed alcove, N wall, for ceremonial display of plate, of 1871 in its present form. Opposite, a gilded musicians' gallery, balustraded and breaking forward over fluted Ionic columns. This gallery was probably an afterthought, since details of the roof construction suggest the S wall was originally to have been in line with its front.* Six vast chandeliers, the main set of four by *Perry & Co.*, 1835. Armorial stained glass, the earlier shields (1833–50) by *Willement*. Busts of George III and IV, by *Chantrey*.

---

*I owe this information to Mr Donald Insall.

Across the landing, an ANTEROOM (restored by *Enthoven*) leads to the COURT ROOM, NW. *Hardwick* here attempted to reconstruct its predecessor of 1669, apparently as much from economy as sentiment. Enough survives to suggest its former sumptuousness. Bolection-moulded panelling; magnificent coving with rampaging scrolls, swags, herm-like figures and unicorns, now silvered and gilt: all from *Jerman*'s hall. The plaster ceiling is Hardwick's own, similar but not identical to the old, with an unusual pattern of big beams around a central quatrefoiled oval. Exceptionally deep-cut ornament: C17 work, refixed? Noble fireplace by *Cheere*, 1735, with big bearded draped terms. Much of the furniture was designed by *Hardwick* for the room. Kept here also an upright C2 Roman altar with a battered but graceful relief of a hunting deity (perhaps Diana or Atys) with quiver, bow and greyhound, found below the hall in 1830.

On the w side, s of the Court Room and enfiladed with it, lie the post-war interiors. *Billerey*'s DRAWING ROOM (1951) is restrained white-and-gold Louis XV, a world away from Hardwick's masculine solidity. *James*'s walnut-panelled SOUTH ANTEROOM and EXHIBITION ROOM, beyond, replace the destroyed Court Dining Room. The plain panelling of the exhibition room is in a modern style, subtly diapered with inlay, the display cases inset. In the centre of the s front, the panelled LUNCHEON ROOM, by *James* (the ceiling by *Insall*), apparently retaining the lower part of Hardwick's somewhat Baroque fireplace. A BINDING ROOM on the N side, between the court suite and Livery Hall, now serves as an anteroom to the library. It incorporates late C17 panelling, according to *The Builder* (1916), found in the cellars and reset by the Company's Surveyor *A. Burnett Brown* shortly before. It may therefore represent a further, modest survival from the 1669 hall. Fine swags and garlands over the fireplace; foliage cornice. The rest looks early C20. By *Enthoven* the restored ceiling with its little dome. The LIBRARY, fitted up in 1951, is in a plain, panelled late C17 idiom.

GROCERS' HALL
Grocers' Hall Court, off Prince's Street

By *Beard, Bennett & Wilkins*, completed 1970; incorporating part of the façade of the previous hall by the Company Surveyor *H. Cowell Boyes*, 1889–93, otherwise destroyed in a disastrous fire in 1965. Boyes's work, r., is of red brick with pedimented flat bays and ample stone dressings, in a Netherlandish style of *c.* 1600. The new part is of plain stone, with a big leaded mansard shared with the retained section: a nervous gesture towards continuity when a radically different treatment might have come off much better. By the entrance, a little statue of St Anthony of Vienne, from the demolished part. This was L-shaped and much larger than the present hall, with a projecting centre raised on a porte-cochère. Part of its site was taken for an extension to Lutyens's Midland Bank (*see* Poultry), also by *Beard, Bennett & Wilkins*.

The 1960s rebuilding represented the latest of several retrenchments on an ancient site. The Grocers ('Grossers', i.e. wholesalers) descend from the unlicensed guild of Pepperers, recorded in 1180. They bought Lord Fitzwalter's mansion here in 1427, when that property extended from Old Jewry, w, to the Walbrook, E, and built a fine new hall in 1428–33. Rebuilt (1668–9) within the C15 shell after the Great Fire, it was enlarged in 1680–2 (masons *Pierce* and *Richard Crooke*) and let to the Bank of England 1690–1734. In 1798–1802 a new hall by *Thomas Leverton* was built, and much of the garden, E, given up for Soane's Bank extension and the realignment of Prince's Street. Leverton's hall, nine severe bays with plain paired pilasters, was altered by *Joseph Gwilt*, 1838, and demolished in 1888. These halls all faced s towards Poultry; but Boyes's hall faced E, separated from Prince's Street by offices for rent, also by *Boyes* (Prince's Buildings, 1891, dem. 1967). The present sad triangular court, all that remains of the gardens, is reached through their replacement (*see* Prince's Street).

Reconstruction after the 1965 fire did not re-create Boyes's Jacobethan interiors. The new rooms are more modest (space was curtailed by the inclusion of a floor of offices for rent); nor is there any grand staircase to unify them. Decoration by *Colefax & Fowler*. Ground-floor RECEPTION ROOM behind the retained façade, dominated by three splendid Aubusson tapestries by *John Piper*, 1968, with semi-abstract designs recalling the fire. Busts on pedestals in the corners: notably Queen Elizabeth the Queen Mother, over-life-size bronze, by *Oscar Nemon*, c. 1986. The LIVERY HALL immediately above, smaller than its predecessor, is still a large room, discreetly modern in style. By the entrance, remains of the outstanding wrought-iron SCREEN by *Thomas Collins*, 1682–3, the only survival from the late C17 furnishings. Made up from the least damaged pieces, to about a third of its former size. It incorporates big foliage scrolls and shields. Other rooms are in a stripped early C19 manner. In the LIBRARY a fireplace of c. 1800 with the Company's arms, discovered in 1966 and believed to come from Leverton's hall. The COURT ROOM has a coloured marble fireplace from Princes' Buildings, but apparently also of c. 1800; also a bust of the younger Pitt by *Nollekens*. COURT DINING ROOM with segment-headed blind recesses.

HABERDASHERS' HALL (FORMER)
Staining Lane, N of Gresham Street

The first post-war livery hall to be completed (1954–6 by *A. S. Ash*), and the first to be demolished (1996). It formed the rear wing of Ash's Garrard House, Gresham Street (q.v.), and like that building was stone-faced, plain, and ineffectual. The Company plans to build a replacement in West Smithfield (q.v.). Fittings to be transferred include panelling of c. 1730 from Clifden House, Brentford, Hounslow, and a wrought-iron sword rest from St Michael Wood Street (dem.; *see* that street), made by *Robert Bird*, 1687.

The first hall here, begun in 1459, was worked on by the carpenters *Walter Tylney* and *Robert Wheatley*. After the Great Fire, a design supplied by *Jerman*, 1667, was executed under direction of the Livery (mason *Thomas Cartwright Sen.*). Its interiors, retained in *William Snooke*'s rebuilding of 1854–6, were destroyed by bombing in 1940.

INNHOLDERS' HALL
College Street

A nice coda to the sequence of livery halls along Dowgate Hill, N. The Company began as the Hostellers in the C13 or C14. A hall here is first mentioned in 1522. Modestly rebuilt after the Great Fire in 1667–71, for £1,211 (bricklayer *Lem*, carpenter *Darby*). The present hall retains some C17 fabric within C19 and C20 rebuildings, mostly by members of the *Mathews* family, who served as Company Surveyors. The C17 plan survives, with the Livery Hall separated from College Street by smaller rooms, i.e. without an intervening courtyard. Recent alterations in traditional style by *J. Sampson Lloyd* of *Green Lloyd Architects* (1988–90) incorporated No. 30, l., matching brick offices built 1958–9.

The present exterior is plain brick Neo-Georgian refacing by *E. D. Jefferis Mathews*, 1946–50, after war damage. Only the plinth remains from 1885–6, when the N part was rebuilt in Queen Anne style by *J. Douglass Mathews*. His replica of the C17 rubbed-brick doorcase and armorial survives. It frames the pretty carved DOOR (disused) of the C17 hall, with a swan-necked broken pediment and thick garlanded volutes up the sides. Around the corner, facing the public garden, W, appears the end wall of the Livery Hall, rebuilt after bombing in a more contemporary style.

A doorway in No. 30 leads to an ENTRANCE HALL, of 1988–90 in its present enlarged form. Tuscan columns mark the junction with the old vestibule space. Ahead, the OLD COURT ROOM occupies the NW corner. C17 ceiling (repaired by *E. D. Jefferis Mathews*, 1937), with a central oval frame of fruit and flowers. In the spandrels scrolled shields, one with the date 1670. The design is comparable with other post-Fire ceilings in the City (e.g. at the Sir John Cass School, 1669, q.v.), which unselfconsciously continue the Jones-Webb tradition. Also C17 the fireplace and most of the plain wainscoting. The LIVERY HALL, behind, also has C17 panelling, partly renewed. Post-war coffered ceiling, after that of 1784 (replaced 1885–6). In the new W wall a large square window. Opposite, a musicians' gallery of 1681, set centrally to a space created behind in 1988–90; previously placed across one angle, but not *in situ* there, its timber showing evidence of reuse from another context. Fireplace with simple marble surround of late C17 bolection type. A new STAIRCASE by *Lloyd* opens off the extended entrance hall. Stained glass here by *M. C. Farrar Bell*, 1977, showing inn signs. The COURT ROOM, of 1885–6, lies over the Old Court Room. Similar ceiling to its C17 predecessor, but with scrolly Rococo plasterwork in the central panel. The KITCHENS are said to have the oldest working gas ovens in London (1886).

IRONMONGERS' HALL
Shaftesbury Place, off Aldersgate Street

By *Sydney Tatchell*, 1922–5, a broad, low, spreading Neo-Tudor building hidden between the rear wings of the Museum of London (q.v.). Originally mostly hemmed in, except on the entrance side, W.

Red brick ground floor and half-timbered upper storey – a riskily suburban combination, redeemed by painstaking Arts-and-Crafts techniques and materials (though on a steel frame): hand-made bricks and ironwork; carving by *George Alexander*. Projecting, l., a pretty Tudor-Gothic stone porch; r., a bland brick office extension by *Fitzroy Robinson & Partners*, 1977–9.

Interiors are Neo-Jacobean and amazingly plausible. Their rich plaster ceilings and friezes are by *George Jackson & Sons*. Well-observed dowel-fixed oak panelling, overmantels etc. to match. Rough flagstones complete the illusion of secluded antiquity. Stained glass by *Reginald Bell* of *Clayton & Bell* (post-war additions by *M. C. Farrar Bell*). The plan is an elongated L-shape, with a little cloister and fountain at the outer angle. Plasterwork in the ENTRANCE HALL and CORRIDORS after ceilings at Haddon Hall, Derbyshire; in the LUNCHEON ROOM, after work at Audley End, Essex, and Loseley Park, Surrey; in the COURT ROOM, after Crewe Hall, Cheshire. Off the entrance hall a broad STAIRCASE and LANDING. On the latter, two statues: Alderman Beckford by *J. F. Moore*, c. 1767, the pose more twisted than the later version in the group at Guildhall (q.v.); Sappho, by *Tommaso Solari*, 1854. First-floor DRAWING ROOM lined with fine dusky blue tapestry by *Morris & Co.* BANQUETING HALL of double height, with elliptical ceiling. Tall oriel by the dais; deep gallery at the other end. The Waterford chandeliers (1803) come from the previous Ironmongers' Hall, Fenchurch Street: an imposing Gibbsian affair by *Thomas Holden*, 1748–50, demolished after air-raid damage sustained in 1917. It replaced a hall of 1578–87, by *Elias Jarman*. The Company, first recorded in 1328, acquired that site in 1457; a hall is recorded there by 1493.

LEATHERSELLERS' HALL
St Helen's Place, off Bishopsgate

Façade by *Henry Saul*, 1926, part of the formal close of early C20 offices lining St Helen's Place (*see* Bishopsgate). Saul's interiors, with those of the Victorian hall that lay further back (by *G. A. Wilson*, 1878), were destroyed in 1941. New, Neo-Georgian interiors by *Kenneth Peacock* of *Louis de Soissons & Partners*, 1949–c. 1959, with *F. R. Ragg*, Company Surveyor. The craftsmanship is above average throughout. Most interesting is Peacock's LIVERY HALL, a near-cube with a suave Soanian pendentive vault. Dark panelling of the lower walls, of walnut and rosewood. Balcony ironwork designed by *C. & R. Ironside*. RECEPTION ROOM with Doric pilasters. Other interiors (entrance hall, Assembly Hall, anteroom) are panelled in different woods, apart from the leather-hung FOYER. Here a fine, bold stained-glass window showing Henry VI, by *Leonard Walker*, 1937, from the previous Hall. Heavy leading; non-naturalistic colouring.

The Leathersellers are first recorded in 1372, and were chartered in 1444. They have changed or rebuilt their premises often. The first hall, on London Wall, is known by c. 1476. In 1544 the Company bought the convent attached to St Helen Bishopsgate here (q.v.). The nuns' dorter, suitably adapted, served as the hall until 1799. Then *William & Thomas Roper* built a new hall in the NE part of the site, and laid out St Helen's Place as a speculation (designs by *Nash* for a residential square, made 1800, were not used). This hall burnt down in 1819. Its Grecian replacement, by *W. F. Pocock*, lasted until 1929; after 1878 used as offices.

MERCERS' HALL
Cheapside

The Mercers, originally merchants of luxury cloths, rank first amongst the Livery Companies. So it is disappointing that their hall, by *Noel Clifton* of *Gunton & Gunton*, 1954–8, should be so characterless externally (called 'big, pretentious and wholly conventional' by Pevsner, 1962). Coupled pilasters emphasize the hall. Shops below; storeys of offices for rent above. Pedimented aedicules on top. Apologetic entrance in Ironmonger Lane, w. Further N here, sober pilastered offices by *Dendy Watney*, 1908–9: the only older part to survive the Second World War.

The site is of unusual interest and complexity. The Hospital of St Thomas of Acon or Acre was established here in 1227–8, to commemorate Becket's birthplace. The Mercers were using its hall by 1391, and by the early C15 had built a hall of their own immediately s of the Hospital church, standing over a chapel attached to it. Hall and chapel were rebuilt 1517–24. The Company took over the dissolved Hospital in 1542, whereupon the main church became their chapel: the only one attached to a livery hall to survive the Reformation. The Cheapside front was rebuilt in 1632–3, the whole in 1668–82, by *John Oliver*, to outlines suggested by *Edward Jerman* (masons *Thomas Cartwright Sen.*, to 1672, and *John* and *Nicholas Young*). Oliver's hall stood over an aisled ambulatory on the site of the church's nave, his chapel, E, on that of its chancel. In 1878–81 *George Barnes Williams* rebuilt the Cheapside front and *J. G. Crace* redecorated the interiors. The C17 frontispiece was re-erected at Swanage Town Hall, Dorset.

The present INTERIOR recapitulates the C17 plan (execution by *H. H. Martyn & Co.*), incorporating some older fittings. The Livery Hall stands on a broad aisled AMBULATORY with Doric columns, a regularized version of the C17 space. Here are two notable MONUMENTS from the former chapel and its predecessor. One is a unique
23 recumbent figure of the dead Christ on an Imperial robe, found during excavations here in 1954. Though in poor condition, it is both intensely moving and of high sculptural quality. The style suggests a Flemish artist and a date *c.* 1520–30. It probably formed the centrepiece of a sculpted mourning group, like that of about the same period at Mainz Cathedral.* The other monument is a restored recumbent effigy of Richard Fishborne †1625. Also a bust of John Colet, an early copy of a lost original by *Torrigiani*. The CHAPEL opens off the E end. Of double height and square plan: another echo of the C17 hall. Several late C17 FITTINGS, all of types familiar from contemporary City churches: sword rest of pole type;

---

* I am grateful to Dr Philip Lindley for these details. Dr Philip Ward-Jackson notes the similarity of the figure to that at Utrecht Cathedral, by Gerrit Splintersz, 1501–6.

royal and Company arms; carved cherubs' heads, lion and unicorn etc. The rest is loosely late C17 in style, except for the big cylindrical font, designed by *H. O. Corfiato* and *Sidney Loweth*, 1958.

The chapel is overlooked by a gallery off the reception landing, reached by a STAIRCASE off the SW corner of the ambulatory. Stained-glass window with two fine full-length figures of monarchs and the reset upper part of a figure of Becket, from the former Livery Hall windows by *Heaton, Butler & Bayne*, 1880 (new arrangement by *H. L. Pawle*, 1957). The RECEPTION LANDING is extremely odd: of double height on the l., with an upper gallery on superimposed colonnades, r. The l. part corresponds in height with the panelled LIVERY HALL, opening off on the N side. The ceiling is an unwieldy modified barrel-vault. On the S side, r., big mahogany-panelled and enfiladed COURT ROOM and DINING ROOM, over-looking Cheapside. Here ten excellent late C17 carved swags in the Gibbons manner, given 1817 and of unknown origin; also one near-matching piece by *Andrew Lonnie*, 1896–7 (another is in the ambulatory). The quality of carving in the late C17 hall may be seen on the half-landing of the staircase to the upper gallery. Here is a marquetry overmantel framed by a magnificent thickly carved frame, with garlands held in the beaks of twin eagles. In the centre a maid's head, the Mercers' badge. Carved by *John Baker*, 1682–3.

MERCHANT TAYLORS' HALL
Threadneedle Street

The only City livery hall with substantial medieval remains. Though indifferently preserved, they yet speak of the pride and wealth of medieval London. True to medieval tradition also is the hall's retire-ment from the highways: two narrow frontispieces on Threadneedle Street, N, and surreptitious S entrances from Sun Court and White Lion Court, off Cornhill, are all that betray its existence externally. The broad central courtyard, another ancient feature, is faced by late C17, Victorian and C20 ranges. The juxtaposition is intriguing, though hardly beautiful.

The Company were originally cutters and makers-up of cloth. The Guild is known from the early C14, although the present title dates only from incorporation in 1503. The site amalgamates two early medieval properties. The greater, N, formerly the house of the King's tent-maker John Yakeslee, passed in 1347 to trustees who held it for the Company. The present Livery Hall, N of the court-yard, was probably built or rebuilt by the Company later in the C14. A late C14 crypt, E, and the C15 Great Kitchen, SE, have also survived subsequent fires and rebuildings. Reconstruction after the Great Fire apparently followed designs by *Edward Jerman*, though C17 work now appears only in the slightly later W range (1681–3). *I'Anson*'s Gothic Court Room and Library ranges, E and S sides (1878–9), represent the C19. The main C20 episodes are *Sir Herbert Baker*'s cloister, 1927 (N side, S of the Livery Hall) and *Sir Albert Richardson*'s post-war restoration of the bombed Livery Hall and N wing.

The APPROACH to the medieval hall from Threadneedle Street is by two passages, both of them signalled by a broken-pedimented

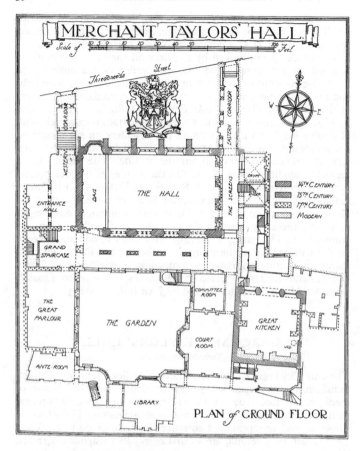

Merchant Taylors' Hall. Ground-floor plan in 1929

doorcase crowned by an armorial. The smaller w entrance, r., first made in 1844, appears as a Doric doorcase in the City Bank, Threadneedle Street (q.v.). Its details suggest the C20, i.e. later than its setting (1855–6). The main, E entrance is through a single bay by *Sir Reginald Blomfield*, 1925–6. Big round top window and other C18 French motifs, reminiscent of his contemporary Regent Street quadrants, Westminster. Reused broad stone doorcase below, with square and round Corinthian columns and a fine armorial in the pediment. Though plausibly late C17, it probably dates only from 1844, when a small courtyard behind was infilled and the street front rebuilt (earlier views show a much smaller doorcase).

A corridor continues from this E entrance into the screens passage of the LIVERY HALL. Nothing betrays its C14 origins, confirmed in early C20 investigations and again by exposure of the original ragstone walls after air-raid damage. But the very dimensions, 43 ft (13 metres) by 94 ft (28½ metres), show it was no mean structure. Otherwise all one sees is from *Richardson*'s restoration, completed

1959. His designs are unashamedly backward-looking, though re-deemed somewhat by impeccable craftsmanship: glowing mahogany panelling to the lower walls, with gilt acanthus scroll cornice; lean iron-balustraded gallery around all four sides; coffered ceiling of cedar and lime. Above the panelling appear refaced stone walls with tall square-headed windows. Good painted armorial stained glass by *Francis H. Spear*. The gallery opens at the W on to a top-lit upper parlour, over the W entrance corridor. At the E, the gallery supports the former organ from St Dionis Backchurch (*see* Fenchurch Street). By *Harris*, 1722–4; the festive pedimented case designed by *S.E. Dykes Bower*, 1966. Hidden behind panelling in the far W bay, N side, a remarkable niche or buffet of *c.* 1500, for the display of plate. Three-sided, tall, with blind elliptical-headed panelling below a fleuron frieze. In the head a diminutive fan-vault. Of the C14 fabric, slim buttresses (refaced and altered) and a broad four-centred arch on the far W bay, visible from the courtyard. Concealed features include rubble foundation-arches or culverts spanning between the buttresses (cf. St Margaret Lothbury), and a mysterious blocked N doorway. (A trap-door in the floor allows earlier, lower levels to be inspected: C14 beaten clay, tile overlay of 1646, and stone flags of 1675.)*

The medieval survivals extend to the CRYPT of *c.* 1375, E of the screens passage and parallel with it. It is associated not with the usual hall offices but with a late C14 chapel, part of which it under-lay. No religious function is known, and the crypt probably served rather as a shop or warehouse, entered directly from Threadneedle Street. Two vaulted bays survive; a third and remains of a fourth, N, were destroyed in 1853. Entrance at the S end, with two-centred head. The crypt is chalk-built, with Reigate stone dressings. Ribs and transverse arches are of one thickness and profile, elongated with a single hollow chamfer. They rise from semi-octagonal capitals resting on grotesque figure corbels.

Some way S of the crypt, unrelated to the Hall, stands the well-named GREAT KITCHEN, 37 ft 6 in. (11½ metres) square, built 1425–33. It replaced an earlier kitchen, perhaps that of Yakeslee's mansion. On the N side three very battered four-centred moulded arches on crudely renewed piers, opening on to an E–W passage. Do these, too, perpetuate a feature from Yakeslee's time? Above the arches three C17 windows. Blocked four-centred lights are said to remain in the S and W walls. The C15 roof was a steep octagonal pyramid (carpenter *John Goldyng*), probably based on the kitchen roof at the Black Prince's mid-C14 palace at Kennington, then in rural Surrey, which men from the Company went to inspect before completing the work. Moulded corbels within show where its principal timbers were. In the E and W walls great fireplaces, of C17 construction, but probably in the C15 positions. A chamfered plinth and traces of deep corner buttresses were found externally in 1878, when *Edward I'Anson* constructed two storeys of offices on top of the 3 ft thick medieval walls. From the same campaign his W (Court

---

* Other remodellings of the livery hall have left no trace. New roofs of 1583–8 (apparently hammerbeam) and after 1666 (probably coved) entailed rebuilding its upper walls. A fine W screen of 1674, designed by *Hooke*, lasted until the Second World War. Windows made Gothick 1793; altered again, 1828. New ceiling 1858; E wall pierced with windows 1872. Repanelled by *W.H. Nash*, 1892.

Room) and s (library) ranges, facing the courtyard. Of grey
Spinkwell stone, in a picturesque mixed Gothic evocative of France,
but with crow-stepped gables. Much movement in and out, with
steep and busy roof-lines. Windows mostly square-headed, with on
the ground floor pointed relieving arches. A band of blind panelling
divides the storeys. The COURT ROOM has panelling of 1923 by *Sir
Charles Nicholson*, in bland late C17 style; the Neo-Jacobean
LIBRARY is I'Anson's. In the corridor between them, a late C19
sculpture of a girl and dove, called Messagio d'Amore.

Along the N side of the courtyard, hard up against the Livery Hall,
runs a low arched-windowed CLOISTER by *Sir Herbert Baker*, 1927
(replacing *I'Anson*'s cloister). Double-aisled within, with groin-
vaults resting on elongated piers with Doric columns at the ends.
Here are displayed busts of the younger Pitt by *Nollekens* and of
Wellington by *E. Physick*. The cloister ends, w, in a spacious open-
well STAIRCASE by *Richardson*: a strange mixture of streamlined mid
C20 with Neo-C17 carving. Its predecessor, destroyed by bombing,
belonged with the w range of 1681–3 (bricklayer *Lem*, carpenter
Avis). Externally this is of red brick with quoins and tall renewed
windows. On the ground floor, immediately s of the staircase, the
panelled GREAT PARLOUR, late C17 in appearance with some
original panelling, though ceiling and fireplace are well-observed
restorations by *Sir R. Blomfield*, 1904. *Richardson*'s DRAWING
ROOM, above, is not strongly architectural in character. In the courtyard a paved garden with fountain and bronze statue by *Gilbert
Bayes*, 1914.

PAINTER-STAINERS' HALL
Little Trinity Lane, off Queen Victoria Street

Not much to look at externally: four bays, r. (No. 8) by *H. D. Searles-
Wood*, 1914–16; the hall proper of five bays, l. (No. 9), refronted in
post-war reconstruction by *D. E. Harrington*, 1959–61. The inner
shell of No. 9 is of 1668–70 (bricklayer *Luck*, carpenter *Bell*). The
Company has been here since 1532. The painters coloured solid
objects, the stainers woven fabrics: trades first mentioned in the C13
and fully incorporated 1581.

The reconstruction follows the C17 arrangement, as modified
1914–16. Loosely traditional interiors, of interest for C17 and early
C18 survivals. ENTRANCE HALL with dog-leg staircase. On the wall
facing the entrance, carved drops and garlanded capitals from the
former doorcase of 1675 by *Edward Pierce*, later Master of the
Company. COURT ROOM beyond, with excellent marble bust of
Thomas Evans in a niche, also by *Pierce*, 1688, with remains of its
former surround carved with palettes and brushes. Painted glass:
late C17 arms of Charles II; early C19 version of the Transfiguration
by Raphael. Shapeless first-floor LIVERY HALL, over the Court
Room. Adjacent, overlooking Little Trinity Lane, the PAINTED
CHAMBER, with painted panels from wainscotting installed 1703
(dismantled). The artists were mostly prominent liverymen of the
Company. Their work is somewhat disappointing, though characteristic of the English school of *c*. 1700. Miscellaneous subjects; panels

both above and below the chair-rail, like the C17 interior at the Sir
John Cass School (q.v.), whose artist *Robert Robinson* (†1706) is
represented by an outdoor still-life. Another still-life by *Marmaduke
Craddock*; other subjects are naval, mythological, *trompe l'œil*
(stamped gilt leather by *Edward Polehampton*, dated 1713), and
heraldic (by *Joseph Goodall*). On the landing a bronze sculpture of
St Luke and the Virgin by *Wheeler*, *c.* 1961.

PEWTERERS' HALL
Oat Lane

An endearingly domestic brick box by *D. E. Nye & Partners*,
1959–61. With the Girdlers' Hall, the only post-war livery hall to
eschew the inclusion of rented office space. The resulting modesty is
a relief after the faltering attempts at grandeur of some others. All
but Neo-Georgian, of two storeys, with sashes, rusticated ground-
floor brickwork, and a tiled hipped roof (heightened by *Lloyd Leroy*,
1996). Off-centre s entrance; main rooms behind the slightly convex
E front, overlooking the former churchyard of St Mary Staining (*see*
Oat Lane).

The Pewterers are first recorded in the mid C14 (chartered 1474).
The previous hall, in Lime Street, was rebuilt after 1496 by the
carpenter *Simon Birlyngham*. Post-Fire replacement by *John Wildgos*,
1668–70, dem. 1932. Some fittings survive in the present hall.
Ground-floor LIVERY HALL, unobtrusively modern, the ceiling
decorated in strong hot colours. LANDING with good armorial
stained glass by *Brian Thomas*, 1974. The large COURT ROOM
above the Livery Hall, explicitly Neo-C17, has panelling of 1672
from the Lime Street hall. Old-fashioned for that date: small plain
pilasters, shallow acanthus cornice interrupted by small rectangular
panels. Ceiling with a big oval central compartment, not well done
and harshly coloured. The C17 Master's Parlour was reconstructed
at the Geffrye Museum, Shoreditch.

PLAISTERERS' HALL
London Wall, s side

By *John Davies* of *Ronald Ward & Partners*, 1970–3. The most
bizarre case of the City's desire to combine a modern 'image' with
traditional ceremonial interiors, here Adamesque (to show off the
craft), but mostly well below ground level. The plan is a neat
solution to the combination of livery hall and lettable space. The former appears as a brick-faced front overlooking a garden made in the
excavations along Noble Street (q.v.). Entry is down steps housed in
a low polygonal structure on the corner, faced in red-brown
Whitwick brick. Further back rises an eleven-storey office tower
(No. 1 London Wall), aligned E–W. Gently canted sides with window
bands and aggregate-faced panels. Obsolescence has already overtaken the tower, proposed for replacement in 1994 (*see* London
Wall). The livery hall will be retained. Its GREAT HALL is the
largest of any City Livery Company. It has applied arcades on paired
pilasters. Coved ceiling. The standard of work is good, and sheer

nerve just about carries the whole mad enterprise through, though Adam never used such gentle motifs on this giant scale. Other interiors are awkwardly proportioned and less convincing. The Plaisterers were incorporated in 1501; the previous hall was in Addle Hill, off Carter Lane (1556, burnt in 1666 and rebuilt; burnt again 1882).

SADDLERS' HALL
Gutter Lane

By *L. Sylvester Sullivan*, 1955–8, stilted Neo-Georgian: a disappointment after his jazzy inter-war work in the City. The previous hall here, destroyed in 1940, was by *Jesse Gibson*, 1822–3 (refronted 1864–5). The first hall was built by 1427 (Company charter 1395), its post-Fire successor by 1672. The Company is housed in three stone-faced lower floors treated with pilasters, above a rusticated ground floor. At each end a matching porte-cochère with single-storey attic over. Set back, four red brick storeys of lettable offices, with pedimented aedicules at the ends. Tiled top storey added by *Denis Poulton*, 1970. Little entrance court behind (landscaped by *James Welch*, 1989). On its s wall a carved pediment dated 1877, from the former Foster Lane entrance. Here the offices rise directly from another pilastered façade. Five tall round-arched windows mark the Livery Hall, a pilastered double cube with a giant overblown Adamesque ceiling rose. Court Room, Livery Room etc. in enfilade along the E front. A barrel-vaulted s corridor with Tuscan columns completes the circuit.

SALTERS' HALL
Fore Street, N of London Wall

Designed in 1968 by *Sir Basil Spence*; built 1972–6, latterly under the successor practice the *John S. Bonnington Partnership* (engineers *Oscar Faber & Partners*). A much bolder solution to the combination of livery hall and office space than earlier post-war rebuildings. The hall is of strongly modelled concrete, set over a partly open ground floor and four smoked-glazed office storeys for rent. Firm concrete uprights at each end. The hall has a window band between concrete horizontals and a leaded top hamper (the Company's offices), both interrupted near the w end by a transverse concrete mass with canted ends (the Livery Hall). A cantilevered E projection houses the staircase. Surfaces are reeded and textured but also partly white-painted, suggesting faltering confidence in the aesthetic qualities of the material. At the Fore Street entrance, gorgeous wrought-iron gates dated 1887, alive with figures of birds: from the previous hall in St Swithin's Lane, by *Henry Carr*, 1823–7, bombed 1941 and later demolished. It had a consequential nine-bay front with an Ionic portico, of nervously vertical proportions. Four artificial stone panels from its anthemion frieze are fixed by the doorway. The Company, founded in 1394, had moved there to the former Oxford House in 1641 (rebuilt by *John Wildgos*, 1666–8); the first hall was in Bread Street (by *c.* 1475, rebuilt 1539 and partly in 1598). Of the interiors (consultant *David Hicks*), the ENTRANCE HALL is travertine-lined and plain. Here a bronze sculpture of a girl by *T. Woolner*, 1892. The livery suite, reached by lift, comprises chiefly a rosewood-panelled COURT ROOM, E, and double-height LIVERY HALL, W, with an anteroom between. The Livery Hall has fluted ash panelling, curved over at the top in line with the shallow elliptical ceiling. In each corner a tall window. Retractable screens allow the rooms to be thrown together.

SKINNERS' HALL
Dowgate Hill

The Skinners are furriers. Their first charter dates from 1327, their presence here from 1409. The property, first mentioned 1267, was known to Stow as Copped Hall. The Walbrook then formed its W boundary, but was covered over by the C17. The core of the present hall is post-Fire, probably on its medieval plan, with notable C18 and C20 additions and alterations.

The Dowgate Hill range, by *William Jupp Sen.*, is stately and prettily 83 detailed. Of five bays, painted stone, with rusticated basement, giant pilasters and a three-bay pediment. Frieze of lion-skins; pediment with lion and greyhound of *Coade* stone, modelled by the elder *Bacon* in 1770. The front is later, almost certainly of 1778–9, when rebuilding of the clerk's house here is recorded. 1779 is also the date on the rainwater-head of No. 9, l., a simple two-bay house, the rear wall of which appears of one build with the main front. The cross-vaulted entrance passage, l., has ribs of guilloche pattern. The E front of the hall faces a small courtyard. It was built to a 'moddle' by *John Oliver*, made 1668, and completed by *c.* 1670. Of fine red brick with blue headers, laid chequerwise in Flemish bond. The doorway is arched and flanked by pilasters. Carved spandrels, separate carved brackets above the pilasters. These carry (rather illogically) a big segmental pediment. Oddly detailed recessed double window to the gallery above, with carved brackets squeezed in at the sides. Segment-headed windows, partly blocked. Plain parapet of 1778. Other courtyard fronts, of C18 brick, appear over a graceful Ionic cloister added by *W. Campbell-Jones* between 1902 and 1916. The arches spring directly from the capitals. (Matching details on the screen wall facing College Street, SW, with semicircular openings high up; the C17 parts visible above and behind.)

INTERIORS. Entrance is from the courtyard, through the N cloister. Turning r., one enters *Jupp*'s FRONT HALL, with a high top-lit stairwell with plain balustrade and oval skylight. Turning l., the double-height OUTER HALL is reached. Made *c.* 1900 by *Campbell-Jones*, from the former kitchens. Good panelling in late C17 style. The circular gallery was introduced by *J. Sampson Lloyd*, 1984–6, with delicate iron balustrade (of the same date the parlour, converted from the former clerk's office in the N courtyard range). The dimly lit HALL proper is reached through a screen. Altered 1847–50 by *George Moore*, who blocked several windows, and again by *Campbell-Jones*, 1890–2, the date of the big skylight and the panelling. The latter, by *J. D. Crace*, was modelled on the late C17 work at Trinity College Chapel, Oxford. Lower stage with piers with carved brackets, upper stage with Corinthian columns at the far end,

Skinners' Hall. Ground-floor plan in 1916

Key to plan:
1 Front hall
2 Outer Hall
3 Hall
4 Charity Corridor
5 Old Court Room
6 Committee room

CLOAK LANE

DOWGATE HILL

30 m
100 ft

by a triple window. Between the upper piers, splendidly rich PAINT-
INGS by *Sir Frank Brangwyn*. The earliest are ten histories on the
long walls, 1902–9. They represent events from the Middle Ages to
the late C17, connected with the history of the Skinners and the fur
trade. In the far corners and over the gallery, three allegories added
by *Brangwyn* in the early 1920s, in a lighter palette. The CHARITY
CORRIDOR, along the far (W) side of the Hall, houses three
allegorical female figures in painted gesso by *Anning Bell*, 1903. The
corridor has austere unmoulded arched openings. It may be identi-
fiable with work by *William Jupp Jun.*, busy at the hall in 1801–3. It
leads to the handsome and generous open-well STAIRCASE of
c. 1670. Of three flights, with turned balusters decorated below with
little leaves, a deep string with acanthus carving, and massive square
newels. Plasterwork of 1737 by *Thomas Meakes* or *Meekes*, to designs
by *Dance the Elder*. There are similarities with the latter's work at the
Mansion House. The war-damaged wall by the bottom flight was
not reinstated (restorers Messrs *Campbell-Jones*), so the stairhall
flows into the OLD COURT ROOM, which suits the proportions of
neither space. The latter has restored panelling and pedimented
doorcases also by *Dance*, 1737. Two wall-mounted lanterns contain
diminutive painted statuettes of Sir Andrew Judd and Edward III,
late C17–C18; the latter, attributed by Lady Gibson to *Cibber*, the
model for one of the sculpted kings in the courtyard of the second
Royal Exchange (*see* Public Buildings). Also on the ground floor the
COMMITTEE ROOM, S of the stairhall: the lower room of a small
two-storey addition of 1678 (bricklayer *Lem*). Good late C17 fireplace with carved drops and the Company's arms, probably by one

Ffrench, 1679 (unless the room is the 'little parlour' fitted up by *Kedge*, 1685).

The staircase leads up to the COURT ROOM (Cedar Room), over the Old Court Room. Magnificent, very sophisticated cedar 69 panelling of *c.* 1670, probably by *Sheffield* (paid £85, apparently for carving alone). Forms are much more those of exterior architecture than is usual in the post-Fire livery halls: eared doorcases with pediments on brackets (those at the far end dummies), full-blooded modillion cornice, and enriched window surrounds. The wood is said to be Bermudian. About three-quarters of the C17 work survives. The simple ceiling replaces one of 1876, destroyed in the war. In the 1678 block the little LIBRARY, with limed oak fittings of 1964. A first-floor corridor leads back N to the Outer Hall gallery, from which a Venetian window of 1984–6 overlooks a flat roof garden, made by *Lloyd* over the kitchens, W. Access is through a W corridor, via a chamfered square brick pavilion with glazed octagonal lantern. The roofscape is further enlivened by the shaped rear gable of Lloyd's Pellipar House, r. (*see* Cloak Lane). In the cellars, the recent work exposed remains of massive revetment walls from the old Walbrook bank. Of brick above stone, apparently late medieval at the latest.

STATIONERS' AND NEWSPAPER MAKERS' HALL
Stationers' Hall Court, N of Ludgate Hill

A collage of work of every century since the Great Fire, much of it of high quality; the C19 work all by the *Mylne* family. The C14 Stationers' Company was reorganized in 1403 and chartered in 1557 (the Newspaper Makers joined in 1933). First recorded home thereafter was the former Peter's College, one of the colleges for chantry priests S of Old St Paul's Cathedral (q.v.). In 1606 the Company moved to Milk Street, but in 1611 bought the London house of Lord Abergavenny on the present site instead, 'converting the stone-work into a new faire frame of timber' (Stow). The property can be traced back to the Brittany Inn recorded under Edward I. Burnt in 1666, it was rebuilt in 1670–4 by the bricklayer *Robert Wapshott*, who may have provided the design. The C17 fixed the present plan: an elongated T-shape with the top aligned E–W and the Livery Hall N–S, making an inner and an outer courtyard. Much warehousing was provided to accommodate the Company's activities licensing publications. Some fabric from the former building may survive within the present walls (RCHME).*

The present E front of the Livery Hall, facing the OUTER COURT- 85 YARD, is by *Robert Mylne*, 1800–1. Part stone-faced, part rendered; astylar and flat, with slender round-headed windows and a fluted frieze. Decorative panels of putti in *Coade* stone above the cornice. Small medallion-like iron tie-plates securing the new front also form part of the composition. Fine iron lamp-standards flank the S door. A drawing of 1781 in the Company's possession shows the C17

---

* An early C19 watercolour at the hall puzzlingly shows the S wall of the hall as brick-built, with a two-light window of Tudor-Gothic type – though brick walls are unlikely to have survived the Great Fire.

façade, with square-headed cross-windows, each with an *œil-de-bœuf* light above; the entrances and main windows correspond to the present positions. The rendered w front preserves the C17 appearance. At r. angles to Mylne's front, a Portland stone wing by *R. W. Mylne*, 1885–7, heavy Northern Renaissance with a little off-centre canted bay with pointed roof-cum-spire. It replaced a three-storey C17 range. A new NE entrance passage was made from Amen Corner in connection, perpetuated in the 1960s Colonial Mutual House (*see* Ludgate Hill).

At the s end of the Livery Hall, a passage leads to the INNER COURTYARD, the site of Abergavenny House's garden, with a great plane tree in the centre (present layout 1930). The Court Room wing, N side, was rebuilt in red brick after war damage by *Dawson & Son*, 1957. It had last been rebuilt by *William Robinson* in 1757 in grey brick, above the arcaded basement-warehouse. Several architects of that name are known to have worked in mid-C18 London, the likeliest candidate being the East India Company's Surveyor (†1767). On the w side, an amazing survival: a late C17 storehouse, humble and single-storeyed, with wooden window frames of mullion-and-transom-cross type and prominent hipped and tiled roof. Not on Ogilby and Morgan's map (1676–9), but clearly not much later. The s side is made by St Martin Ludgate (q.v.).

The main entrance is in the 1887 wing. Here is the STOCK ROOM, where the public could consult the Company's registers. Fine carved panelling and overmantel from its predecessor of the 1670s; the latter with typical garlands etc. They may be by *Henry Foord*. The Victorian ceiling is a creditable Jonesian pastiche, given away by the thumping cornice. Photographs show that its predecessor was plainer, though this may not have been its original form. Stained glass: 1888 (Queen Victoria); 1983 (armorial). Steps lead down to the LIVERY HALL. *Robert Mylne*'s lucid ceiling of 1800 was re-created in 1952. Plain coving, big circular panels. Cornice and windows also as left by Mylne. Otherwise the room is still largely in its form of 1670–4. Panelling by *Stephen Colledge*, 1674; he was paid £300 and instructed to follow that at Grocers' Hall. Other woodwork is attributed to *Foord*, including the magnificent oak screen. It has a segmental pediment to the centre with seated figures in and on it, with a musicians' gallery above; the sections either side adapted to incorporate display cases. Arms on the rear wall (William III), formerly on top of the screen's pediment. Stained glass: w windows of *c.*1888, florid N window 1894, by *Mayer* of Munich, commemorating the early history of printing. Plainer armorial E windows, 1983–8.

Steps lead up to the COURT ROOM SUITE in the w wing. This was remodelled in 1825 by *W. Chadwell Mylne* within the shell of 1757, retaining some work from it, then in 1957 rebuilt in near-facsimile after bomb damage. First a little ANTEROOM, restored as an elongated octagon but previously a modified oval. Then the COURT ROOM, and in line with it and open to it at the far end the Card Room. The history of these rooms is complex. *Robinson*'s rebuilding of 1757 reused old panelling under a new dado cornice, as well as 'the old woodwork from the chimney', i.e. the present chimneypiece of *c.*1730, with big flanking scrolls in the William Kent style and luscious garlands above. The plaster ceiling is

Stationers' Hall.
Drawing of Livery Hall screen

Robinson's, restored using some original moulds. Large central rose; slender scrolls and garlands in the coving, with the Company's arms. Also Robinson's the modillion cornice and plaster overmantel, the latter in the richest and most free Rococo. Otherwise the lower walls were remodelled by *W. C. Mylne* in 1825, after consultation with *Robert Smirke*, but his panelled dado was not replaced after the war. So one now sees a mixture of *c.* 1730, 1757, 1825 and 1957. The CARD ROOM is *W. C. Mylne*'s, an irregular octagon top-lit by a rectangular lantern. The plasterwork has plain fielded panels. Two engaged columns of green scagliola, far wall, formerly ranged with similar columns which made a screen in the aperture between the rooms, regrettably not restored in 1957. On the far wall *Benjamin West*'s huge painting of King Alfred and the Pilgrim, given by Alderman Boydell in 1779.

TALLOW CHANDLERS' HALL
Dowgate Hill

Perhaps the best-preserved post-Fire livery hall, fitted into the N and W sides of a small courtyard off Dowgate Hill. The Apothecaries', Skinners' and Vintners' Halls have grander interiors, but have been more altered either inside or out. The plan probably reflects the arrangement of the pre-Fire hall, bought in 1476. The Company is first recorded in the C14.

The present hall is by the master bricklayer Capt. *John Caine*, 1671–3 (mason *Thomas Cartwright Sen.*, carpenter *Adam Taylor*, bricklayer *Jones*). *Jerman* was paid for a 'plot' in 1667, but Jones's contract specifies work to Caine's model. The courtyard is gained via a narrow passage with heavy iron gates through Nos. 3–7 Dowgate Hill, a four-storey former warehouse by *Joseph & Pearson*, 1883–4. Hard red brick free Gothic, with small-scale ornament in *Burmantofts'* terracotta (the N part matching work by *Damond Lock, Grabowski & Partners*, 1985–8). Ahead, w, the front of the hall. The elevation is really a version of the C17 Brewers' Hall, where Caine was already engaged on a design by *Thomas Whiting*, master joiner: a typical instance of the fluidity of roles in the rebuilding of Restoration London. The Hall stands over a rusticated ground-floor loggia, which screens the kitchens. This has square-headed openings, with attached Tuscan columns carrying segmental arches. Fleshy shields and foliage in the tympana. Pretty Renaissance glazed-tiled spandrels, from alterations by *E. N. Clifton*, 1871. Loggias to N and s have been infilled. Warm orange brick above, tuck-pointed. Five eared windows to the Hall, the middle one with a broken segmental pediment. Circular windows above. Deep eaves cornice. The parlour appears as three answering windows on the N front, the central one tripartite with a segmental pediment. Square-headed windows above. The two-bay s side was made good by *Sir Albert Richardson* and *H. Edmund Mathews* after war damage, 1947–55. A third bay, l., was apparently a casualty of the 1880s block, which here mostly matches the C17 fronts.

A carved wooden doorcase with flanking volutes in the NE corner leads to the STAIRCASE in the angle. Of square well type, rebuilt by *J. Douglass Mathews*, 1899–1901, with simple plain balusters. Some of the original, twisted, pattern remain on the top floor. Bolection-moulded panelling, C17 style, but of 1962. Inset on the first-floor landing, a mid-C18 leather screen with small painted scenes. The HALL, 56 ft (17 metres) long, has good wainscotting by *John Symes*, 1675. Foliage frieze around the whole. At the dais end, the Master's chair is emphasized by a broken pediment on brackets and half-pilasters. C17 royal arms in the pediment. Round-headed niche below, made only *c.* 1930. Extremely broad entrance doorcase, with Corinthian columns and broken pediment. There was originally a musicians' gallery over. The circular windows appear above the cornice. Near the dais, r., a small canted oriel: a very old-fashioned feature, though formerly paralleled at the Vintners' Hall. The ceiling, altered or wholly remade 1868, has hard, sharp lines (e.g. in the octagonal end panels); the C17-style foliage is more plausible. The C17 design was the plasterer's, not Caine's. Stained-glass windows of 1903, with full-length figures, l.; in the oriel, heraldic glass by *Carl Edwards*, 1969. The PARLOUR has wainscotting also of 1675, given by Sir Joseph Sheldon. His arms appear in festooned cartouches within the pediments of the doorcases (the far one false). Carved overmantel, off-centre to the ceiling, which has a big central oval between bands of three rectangular panels. The second-floor COURT ROOM, immediately above, uniquely retains its original fixed benches around the walls, returned as low screens two-thirds along: a plain, business-like ensemble. Panelled by *Symes*, including the cartouche over the Master's chair; he probably panelled the parlour also. Simple flat ceiling, of early C19 pattern.

The Cloak Lane front, N, is worth a glance for the narrow entrance bay by *J. Douglass Mathews*, 1905, on which is fixed a giant, excellently carved C17 shell hood. It came probably from the old Dowgate Hill front range, for which the carpenter *Charley Stanton* made designs *c.* 1670. The blind wall, l., was given pilasters by *J. Sampson Lloyd*, *c.* 1990, in conjunction with work at the Skinners' Hall (q.v.).

VINTNERS' HALL
Upper Thames Street

Though refaced and altered, the core of Vintners' Hall is still of the 1670s. The Vintners are first recorded here in the mid C14, but ownership was formalized only in 1446. Traces of what may have been the kitchens of this first hall were excavated to the S in 1989–91. Brick vaults beneath the present Court Room may be early C17.

The post-Fire hall, of 1671–5, can no longer be appreciated externally. It had a U-shaped plan open to Upper Thames Street, N, with the Hall in the centre, Court Room to the W, and lesser offices to the E: an advance on the old-fashioned courtyard plan, though not yet symmetrical in detail. The designer may have been *Edward Jerman*, whose brother *Roger* was master carpenter. Other craftsmen were *Lem*, bricklayer, *William Hammond*, mason, *Symes*, joiner, and *Withers*, plasterer; seven carvers are also recorded (*see* below). Its subsequent history is bound up with street widening and with development of the Company's adjacent property. In 1821–2 the wings were truncated to widen Upper Thames Street, and the E wing wholly rebuilt in connection with the new Southwark Bridge. Then in 1908–10 *A. H. Kersey* built a new E wing on a site slightly further W, in connection with Thames House (*see* Queen Street), refaced the W wing, and took what remained of the courtyard to make a new entrance corridor. Recent redevelopment of Company land to the S and W prompted the most recent work, by *Biscoe & Stanton*, 1989–92. They created new interiors mostly within the Edwardian parts, and added others on the S, between the hall and the new offices called Vintners' Place (*see* Upper Thames Street). A passage was also made into the N part of Thames House.

Kersey's Upper Thames Street front has two non-matching gabled parts in rich, delightfully informal French Renaissance. Intricately channelled stone, with on the first floor small Ionic columns and pilasters, continued as a screen over the central entrance corridor. The space above this corridor was partly overbuilt by *Biscoe & Stanton*. The windowless W part is the C17 court room wing refaced. C17 fabric appears beyond the refaced part, facing the alley called Vintners' Court, W: rough brick walling with a blocked round-headed two-light window to the Hall high up at the far end. The ENTRANCE VESTIBULE and CORRIDOR display *Coade* stone figures of two swans (1800) and a charity boy in a tail-coat (1840), the latter

from the former Ward School in the vanished Brickhill Lane, further
E. The corridor is something of a makeshift: the r. wall (W) the
former external wall of the Court Room, the l. wall (E) with broad
openings to the much-remodelled Edwardian wing. A short passage
leads off l. to an elliptical staircase down to basement cloakrooms,
made 1972–3 by *Saunders Boston*. In its niches busts of C. Tawke by
Baily, 1845, and Henry White by *Durham*, 1861. At the end of the
main corridor a small LOBBY. Here a naïve wooden group of St
Martin and the beggar, probably that observed by Hatton on the
Hall screen in 1708, and a war memorial carved by *Esmond Burton*,
1920.

From the lobby, a door leads off l. to the C17 STAIRHALL within
the w wing, through what was previously a separate office, knocked
through in 1883. A broad archway shows where the dividing wall
stood. In the S wall a C17 fireplace with enriched overmantel. The
68 C17 staircase climbs in four flights around a square well. It has
stocky newels and rails and fabulously elaborate balusters, each
quite thin but with a fat band carved with leaves and flowers. £39
was paid for carving it to *Woodroffe*, doubtless the *William Woodroffe*
who worked at old Brewers' Hall. The other carvers were *Colledge*,
almost certainly the Stephen Colledge employed at Stationers' Hall;
Miller, Young, Stacy, Philip Milner, and *Thomas Gowin*. On the lower
newels a carved lion and unicorn, probably C19. Other newels
support C17 carved baskets of fruit, repeated in relief against the
dado. At half-height a stained-glass window showing five kings feast-
ing at the hall, probably salvaged from work by *Campbell, Smith &
Campbell* in a courtyard cross-passage built 1883 (dem.). The upper
stairwell, rebuilt 1896–7, has pilastered walls and a side-lit lantern.

The COURT ROOM opens off the stairhall, r. A broad, dimly lit
apartment with fine enriched full-height panelling by the joiner
Symes. Slender drops frame the windows, which are blocked on the
w side. Fuller swags over the fireplace and below the shallow
acanthus cornice, which has late C17–early C18 carved shields.
Cross-beamed ceiling of 1908–9; did it replace plasterwork of
comparable richness?

Another doorway leads l. from the stairhall into the HALL, also
with woodwork designed by *Symes*. w wall with two blind doorcases
and between them a noble broken-pedimented aedicule framed by
coupled Corinthian pilasters. Royal arms over of *Coade* stone, 1802.
Opposite, the screen proper, since 1822 set back against the wall.
The centre has single fluted Corinthian columns and a round-
headed relieving arch. Flanking, round-headed niches with segmental pediments. The rich wrought-iron minstrels' gallery was
probably made as part of *Crace*'s work in 1876. Where the cornice
returns against the long sides stand two carved urns, reputedly
salvaged from Wren's St Benet Gracechurch (*see* Gracechurch
Street). Until 1876 the panelling was carried up to a matching height
between the round-headed windows. Crace's stone window
surrounds were removed in restoration by *Alexander Gale* and
Esmond Burton, 1948–9. Enriched C17 panels with carved heads
below the sills. Did the windows originally have round-headed
tracery, like the blocked w window? Removed in the mid C19, a
canted oriel by the former dais, SW: an archaizing feature shared
with Tallow Chandlers' Hall (q.v.), where Symes also worked,

though there is no evidence that he provided plans for either. Ceiling with plaster shields, by *Gale*, 1933, after the C17 example at Winchester College, but bittily coloured. Carved wooden sword rest of 1705.

Other interiors are late C19 or late C20. S of the Hall, the GASSIOT ROOM, a windowless smoking room formed 1989–92. It reuses Neo-Early Georgian woodwork of 1899, from a demolished predecessor, SW. In the overmantels paintings of the riverside, of the later C19 (by *John Cleghorn*) and 1977 (by *David Cobb*). Also of 1989–92 the SWAN ROOM, W (blind windows with *trompe l'œil* river views by *Colin Failes*, 1996). The chief first-floor interior is the DRAWING ROOM over the Court Room, with delicate, feminine Neo-Jacobean decoration of 1899 by *Conrad Schmidt*. The E side opens on to space formed over the entrance corridor in 1989–92. Other interiors were formed within the Edwardian E wing (the Neo-Regency LIBRARY and the SITTING ROOM), with a glazed CONSERVATORY made over a single-storey section between the upper storeys of the E wing and the Hall proper.

WATERMEN'S HALL
St Mary-at-Hill

The City's only C18 livery hall. The Company was founded in 1555; earlier halls lay S of Lower Thames Street (rebuilt 1670, moved 1720). The present hall, built in 1778–80 on a new site, was *William Blackburn*'s first design (presented 1776). The builder was *Thomas Barnes*. No larger than a medium-sized house, but treated with some consequence: of stone, with rusticated basement, giant coupled Ionic pilasters and pediment, tripartite upper window with Doric columns for mullions. Lunette like an enormous domestic fanlight. The awkwardly multiplied horizontals of the ground floor betray Blackburn's inexperience. Other detail similar to the style of Samuel Wyatt: festoon frieze, plaques of tritons and oars, all of *Coade* stone; tiny dolphins carved in the capitals. Incorporated in 1981–3, No. 17 (r.), dated 1786, formerly the Fellowship Porters' Hall (dissolved 1894). Of similar size, but much simpler. Stock brick. First floor with elliptical-headed triple window; lunette over. Ground floor with triple blind arcading to the C18 design, of 1981–3 by *Cluttons' Staff Architects*. By them also No. 16 for the Company, likewise Neo-Georgian.

Blackburn's interiors are reached through No. 17, via a WAITING ROOM panelled in 1983 with timber salvaged from C19 riverside warehouses. The ground-floor PARLOUR has a graceful low-relief plaster ceiling with big central oval. Groin-vaulted entrance passage alongside. Rear STAIRCASE of stone, compactly cantilevered around a semicircular-ended well, and top-lit from an oval skylight. Simple iron balustrade, garlanded first-floor frieze, lower band of Vitruvian scroll. The finest interior is the delightful COURT ROOM, all pale 84 blue and pink, across the whole of Blackburn's first floor. Oval ceiling on pendentives, with delicate festoons and scalloped fluting arranged concentrically. In the lunettes and pendentives circular reliefs and scrolls. Festoon frieze, stepped down where it crosses the window. Pilasters with lotus capitals here. Fireplace with fine relief of a river god, and a fat, solid armorial overmantel of painted wood or plaster, most unexpected amidst such refinement. The first floor of Nos. 16–17 is the large FREEMEN'S ROOM (1983), with a perfunctory Neo-Georgian ceiling.

WAX CHANDLERS' HALL
Gresham Street

A composite: tough rusticated granite ground floor from *Charles Fowler*'s Italianate hall, 1852–4 (his last building), otherwise destroyed 1940; superstructure by *Lord Mottistone* of *Seely & Paget*, 1954–8. Mottistone's curiously attenuated replacement storeys are of brick, like their predecessors. Tall windows to the second-floor Livery Hall. Copper-clad mansard. Inside, a reset limewood OVERMANTEL of *c.* 1700, opulently carved with game birds and flowers in the Gibbons manner, from a former Company property in Aldersgate Street. Mottistone's interiors are traditional in style, without strong character.

The Company, first recorded in 1330, had a hall here by 1525, converted from a brewhouse. The post-Fire hall by *Edward Jerman*, 1668–70, was replaced in 1792–3 by *Richard Wooding*, and demolished in turn for the new Gresham Street, 1849.

STREETS

ABCHURCH LANE

Runs N from Cannon Street to Lombard Street, across King William Street (cf. Clement's Lane and Nicholas Lane, equally narrow). The name, recorded from *c.* 1240–50, derives from St Mary's church (q.v.), whose paved churchyard makes a breathing-space on the w side at the S.

In this S part, facing the church, No. 20 (NEDBANK), a surviving façade from *George Sherrin*'s former Cannon Street Buildings, 1884–5. Conventional large-windowed ground floor mostly of polished purple granite, then three diminishing red brick storeys with plain Doric columns on pedestals, and three attic sections each of three bays. The upper windows have a different rhythm, as if two distinct buildings had been spliced together. The Cannon Street front, demolished in redevelopment by *Haslemere Estates* (1979–81), had more ornate gables.

Immediately N of the church (w side), No. 15, the former Gresham Club, by *W. Campbell-Jones*, 1914–15. Restored in 1994 as the LONDON CAPITAL CLUB, with new storeys added. Big windows, lots of carving on keystones, aprons etc. The entrance bay projects l. of a three-bay dining room. At the rear, a parish room adjoining St Mary Abchurch (accessible from Sherborne Lane): hence the carving in the Wren style on the main façade, more rounded and fleshy than the blockish style that comes in *c.* 1905. Interiors also evoke the late C17, but with much use of mahogany.

ALDERMANBURY

First recorded in the early C12. The name refers to the burgh or house of the aldermen, that is probably the early medieval 'town hall'. One theory is that it derives from the appropriation by the City's Ealdormen in the C11 of a royal palace based on the E gate of the ROMAN FORT. The fort's E ditch and robbed wall were located on the E side, opposite Love Lane, in 1965–6. Truncated at the N by the post-war London Wall scheme (q.v.), Aldermanbury is itself now almost entirely post-war. The chief loss, at the SE, was the Bradbury Greatorex warehouse (1845, dem. *c.* 1965), a London precursor to 'Greek' Thompson at Glasgow.

From the S, Barrington House (w side; *see* Gresham Street) faces the 1970s Guildhall extension (*see* Public Buildings). On the corner with Love Lane (w side), an excellently varied formal garden marks the site of *Wren*'s church of ST MARY ALDERMANBURY

(1671–5) and its churchyard. First mentioned in 1181 but likely to have been a late Saxon foundation. Excavations revealed that it began as a simple two-celled structure, with side chapels added to the chancel in the C13. A later aisled five-bay plan probably dated from rebuilding in 1438, paid for by the Lord Mayor Sir William Estfield. The C15 foundations, reused by Wren, are laid out for inspection. Fragments of late medieval ledger-slabs are incorporated. The blitzed remains of Wren's church were re-erected in 1965–9 at Westminster College, Fulton, Missouri. Its peculiarity was the singling-out of the middle bay by an oblong groined vault, continued N and S as a kind of transept, as at St James Garlickhithe (q.v.). In the former churchyard to the S, a MONUMENT to John Heminge and Henry Condell, compilers of Shakespeare's First Folio: a granite pedestal with the bard's stodgy bust (by *Charles J. Allen*). Designed and presented by *C. C. Walker*, 1896.

Overlooking the churchyard on the N, No. 1 LOVE LANE, 1989–91 by *Rolfe Judd*, a pretty stone-faced building with small windows, with the practice's favourite metal balconies and some Secessionist touches like the banded piers. Lead-clad undulating upper storeys, glass-brick-walled ground floor. Love Lane, first recorded in 1336, runs S of the churchyard through to Wood Street.

On the other side (E) of Aldermanbury is the raised precinct N of Guildhall, announced by an abstract glass FOUNTAIN by *Allen David*, 1963–4, given 1969. The street then narrows, before widening out into Aldermanbury Square. On this side just before the square, the Chartered Insurance Institute (*see* Public Buildings), then facing the square, No. 21, plain stone-faced with stainless-steel ground floor by *T. P. Bennett & Son*, 1964. No. 1 Aldermanbury Square (STANDARD CHARTERED), opposite, by *Amos Broome Associates*, 1987–9, clad in yellow cast stone with strong verticals rising up into pointed dormers. The jazzy, brashly coloured details evoke a Great West Road factory of the 1930s rather than the solidity of the City.

ALDERMANBURY SQUARE was made in 1962 as part of the London Wall scheme. It occupies part of the site of the old Addle Street, which ran W to Wood Street. In the centre an apologetic ornamental feature with a little fountain. The disparate sizes and styles of the buildings prevent it feeling either like a proper square or a proper precinct. On the N side is the Brewers' Hall (q.v). For the other buildings here, *see* London Wall.

ALDERSGATE STREET

A long street, straggling N into Clerkenwell from the former gate, which stood at the N end of St Martin's le Grand. Just beyond here, the Museum of London's roundabout marks the junction with London Wall; further N, the Barbican development (*see* Public Buildings) and Golden Lane Estate occupy the E side (q.v.).

ALDERSGATE itself stood S of St Botolph. The Roman origin of the gate was proved in 1939, when a mass of Roman masonry was found beneath the roadway. This suggested a bastion-like projection on the gate's W side. The two central piers underlay the street's E side. The northern pier cut through the footings of the City wall, to which the gate was slightly askew: strong evidence that it was a later insertion. Called Ealdredsgate in the C11 Laws of Ethelred; C11 occupation was excavated immediately NW in 1984. The medieval gate, rebuilt in 1617, was repaired and beautified after the Fire in 1670; dem. 1761. The fine late C15 fraternity hall of the Holy Trinity at St Botolph just beyond lasted into the early C19.

In the C16–C17 the aristocracy favoured the vicinity: Howell's *Londinopolis* (1657) said Aldersgate Street 'resembleth an Italian street more than any other in London, by reason of the spaciousness and uniformity of the buildings ... on both sides where of there are divers fair ones'. Best known is Thanet (later Shaftesbury) House, on the courtyard plan, refronted *c.* 1641 perhaps by *Inigo Jones*. It had a giant Ionic pilaster order supporting an entablature interrupted by windows. This façade lasted, much mutilated, until 1882; the Ironmongers' Hall (q.v.) now occupies the rear of the site. By that date the area's status had long been in decline. Air raids made nearly a clean sweep, though C19 and early C20 buildings survive at the NW and SE. ^{p. 65}

On the E side, No. 1 ALDER HOUSE faces St Botolph. By *George & T. S. Vickery*, 1922–5, big stone-faced offices with windows grouped vertically in elliptical-headed recesses. Original ground-floor display windows and steep roof, intact in 1997. No. 10, free Postmodern offices by *B. L. Adams* of *Green Lloyd & Adams*, 1984–6: channelled stone verticals, round-topped leaded dormers. A plaque records the former Cooks' Hall (1500–1771). The roundabout by London Wall is closed on the W side by *Fitzroy Robinson Partnership*'s tall, boldly patterned and stagey development (No. 200, CLIFFORD CHANCE), proposed in 1983 and built in modified form 1991–2. Two stepped blocks at r. angles, the N block rising taller behind. An atrium floor joins the blocks, with glazing stepping down ziggurat-wise from on high. It bridges over the new MONTAGUE STREET, which runs through to Little Britain. The brown stone facing ends short of the top in a pattern of stepped gables. Black-clad recessed verticals crowned by white globular lights at intervals, and black-clad upper parts restlessly broken in outline, to reduce the visual bulk. No. 200 steps down messily to Little Britain, where a lower extension is of patterned red brick (No. 20). The scheme erased a warren of small courts and side-streets.

Further up on the W side, the dreadful MITRE HOUSE by *Seifert Ltd*, 1986–90. Confused polished stone-clad front, interrupted high up by three apparently purposeless openwork projections. Six underground storeys supply parking space lost by the demolition of *Oscar Garry & Partners*' colourful, Brutalist-tinged multi-storey car park here (1961). No. 150 by *John Gill Associates*, 1987–90, polished brown stone with partially exposed frame; then *Howell & Brooks*'s slab for the former London Salvage Corps, 1958–60, making the S corner with Long Lane (demolition proposed). No. 137, brick offices with shallow round-headed glazed bays and brightly coloured detail, is by *Rolfe Judd Group Practice*, 1987–9. It incorporates a footbridge from the Barbican estate and Barbican Underground station's entrance hall, without making much of either. No. 133 (NatWest), dated 1874, is the former London & County Bank by *C. J. Parnell*. Closely and delicately detailed mid-C16 Italian: engaged Doric columns to the ground floor, then aedicules with Ionic columns on the first floor, Corinthian pilasters and segmental pediments on the second. No. 131, a Portland stone warehouse of 1937 by *G. E. & K. G. Withers*, has some spiky Expressionist motifs.

The w side of Aldersgate Street beyond Carthusian Street belongs in the borough of Islington (*see London 4: North*). Buildings are a mixture: modest, anonymous late C18 and C19 brick; office blocks of *c.* 1980; and speculative flats (e.g. Cathedral Lodge, Nos. 110–115, 1995). On the s corner with Fann Street (E side), a reset carved stone RELIEF of 1908 by *Horace Grundy*, of figures in C16 dress refining gold. From the premises of W. Bryer & Son, gold refiners, at old Nos. 53–54 Barbican (dem. 1962). Opposite the Golden Lane Estate, the ORION APARTMENT HOTEL at No. 7 GOSWELL ROAD, by *Boisot Waters Cohen Partnership*, 1993. Hard red brick with upright windows, softened by vertical balcony framing which descends somewhat arbitrarily bay by bay from the l. It introduced a new form of business hotel, with provision for self-catering in its 120 rooms. No. 23 (ITALIA CONTI HOUSE), typical offices of the date (1962), but with colour nicely used: black brick, green mullions, and mauve mosaic below.

ALDGATE

The w part of Aldgate High Street, within the old City wall (marked by Jewry Street, s, and Duke's Place, NW). A GATE into the Roman city stood at Aldgate, and a cross-section through the city wall and rampart, recorded here in 1977, is represented in modern tiling in the pedestrian subway under Duke's Place. In 1052 called Æst Geat, in 1108 Alegate (Old Gate). Rebuilt in the early C12, it served as Chaucer's house in 1374–85. Again rebuilt in 1607–9, and demolished in 1761. C13–C14 undercrofts recorded within the gate, long demolished, are evidence for distinguished stone buildings here.

ALDGATE PUMP stands at the junction of Fenchurch and Leadenhall Streets. A 'well' here is mentioned in the early C13. The present tapering stone pier with vermiculated blocks looks mid C18, but with a Victorian pedimented top and brass dog's-head spout. Until the 1860s it stood slightly further E.

Then No. 1 (s side), GUARDIAN ROYAL EXCHANGE, 1987–90 by *Keith Dalton & Associates*. A big corner block of polished brown stone, still with vertical emphasis in the early 1980s way, but with historicizing touches creeping in around the glazed entrance (r.). Opposite, only the flank of the Sir John Cass School (*see* Public Buildings), exposed by road-widening.

ALDGATE HIGH STREET

It leads NW from the old Aldgate (*see* above), continuing beyond the City boundary as Whitechapel High Street. The first written record is *c.* 1095. Never a wealthy or fashionable district; excavations nearby in 1974 found remains of C16–C17 industry and rubbish-tipping. Contemporary narrow-fronted timber-framed houses survived in numbers into the 1900s.

Two mid-C17 houses remain at the SE corner: Nos. 46 and 47 (the HOOP AND GRAPES), possibly post-Fire, but unmistakably of an older type. Similar but piquantly non-matching rendered fronts, each with a square timber-framed bay. Modillion eaves-cornices, lesser cornices at half-height on the bays. No. 47 retains a horizontal sash where the bay rises through the cornice. Tiled hipped roofs on both bays. No. 47's projecting sashed front and pentice roof look C18. Plan with three separately framed sections arranged in depth, the middle one containing closed-string stair-case, a small lightwell, and a corridor linking the front and smaller rear sections. (Upper rooms with later C17 panelling and box cornices.) In front, two posts carved with vines, apparently C17. The neat mid-C18-type shopfront of No. 46 is a restoration by *Rolfe Judd* for Haslemere Estates, 1983; less well-managed front to Mansell Street, with close-set bays of C17 type above a banal subway entrance. No. 48 is a battered two-bay Georgian house, perhaps of 1803 (boundary plaque).

Opposite (N), ALDGATE HOUSE (SEDGWICK GROUP), a giant-four-square block by *Fitzroy Robinson & Partners*, 1971–6. The City's first big deep-plan office, reflecting advances in air-con-ditioning etc. and the interest in more flexible and informal 'land-scaped' offices (following the *Bürolandschaften* of 1960s Germany). It also continued the movement outward to such cheaper, less restricted sites. Eight storeys. The even, somewhat heavy eleva-tions are raised high on pilotis over a driveway. Chamfered uprights of light-pink Sardinian granite. The much greater height required to service the deep floors is very apparent.

The rest of the N side is Aldgate station, E, and St Botolph, W (*see* Public Buildings; Churches). Between, the former Eagle Star by *C. W. Kempton & Partners*, 1972–7, awaits demolition in 1997. Narrow slab set end-on, with unfriendly slit windows.

On the S side again, undistinguished Victorian (E) and C20 (W) buildings frame the forecourt of Aldgate Bus station. SCULPTURE here by *Keith McCarter*, Ridirich, 1980, abstract bronze. For the W corner with Minories, q.v. Curving to Jewry Street, Nos. 87–89, handsome stucco, the detail still undilutedly Italianate. Probably by *D. A. Cobbett*, 1860 (tender in *The Builder* for that year, for Moses & Son, clothiers). The S bay, in Jewry Street, a matching extension of 1996.

AMEN COURT

A U-shaped court with two rows of canons' houses, of the 1670s and 1870s, separated by a garden. Named probably from the proces-sional route of the clergy around St Paul's precincts (cf. Ave Maria Lane, adjacent, and Paternoster Row). The S part was originally a close called Amen Corner; the present name dates from 1877, when the N extension replaced the ancient Oxford Arms Tavern.

The s entrance retains brick gatepiers with ball-finials, plausibly contemporary with Nos. 1–3 beyond. These were built in 1671–3 by *Edward Woodroffe*, for the three Canons Residentiary of St Paul's. The accounts have him 'contriving and drawing a design' in 1670: enough to dismiss the legend that they were by Wren. Red brick, each of five bays and two storeys on a half-basement, with attics. No doorcases, just C18 doors with fanlights over, on the outer houses placed asymmetrically. C18 sashes. Late C18 torch extinguishers by the doors. Inside, the typical post-Fire plan: a central staircase with a room either side and another in the rear projection. (No. 1 has good C17 panelling, staircases, fireplaces and windows; more modest survivals at No. 3.) The GARDEN beyond has an atmosphere comparable to the drowsiest cathedral close. The s boundary is Stationers' Hall (q.v.), the w a mysterious wall of some antiquity. Medieval lower stages of ragstone and flint, C18 and C19 brickwork above. Said to come from Dance's Newgate Gaol, but it was his Sessions House that adjoined this site. It cannot be the City wall proper, which lay 7 ft (2 metres) further w.

On the n side, Nos. 4–9, a pretty, freely designed range of red brick houses of Norman Shaw character, built for the minor canons in 1878–80 by – curiously enough – *Ewan Christian*, who is usually a Goth. Christian's output of clergy houses for the Ecclesiastical Commissioners was prodigious, but here he plainly took great pains. The houses, restored in 1990, have broken outlines, big chimneys and shell-headed doorcases. A recurrent motif is the raised grid of brickwork on the gables. No. 9 (w, now the Deanery) lies s, linked to the others by a gatehouse in the collegiate tradition, with a pedimented oriel facing Warwick Lane. An inscribed Latin tablet attests to the architect's piety.

AMERICA SQUARE
with CROSSWALL

Both laid out 1768–74 as part of *Dance the Younger*'s development for Sir Benjamin Hammett, just E of the City wall line. Crosswall (until 1939 John Street) connects the Square to Crutched Friars, within the walls. The rest lies s of the viaduct to Fenchurch Street station (*see* Crescent). Widening of this approach in the 1880s truncated the square at the s.

The notable buildings are all 1980s designs. Predominant is No. 1 (s and w sides), bulky and assertive offices by *RHWL Partnership*, 1988–91 (engineers *Ove Arup & Partners*), built up and over the platforms of Fenchurch Street station on the 'air rights' principle. Patterned polished stone cladding to the open-framed rusticated base. Upper windows in big vertical curtain-walled panels. Intersecting with it, a tall slab set end-on to Crosswall and extending across the railway. Lower and upper zones are integrated by treating the Crosswall end with strenuous verticalism: unbroken window panels flank a glazed triangular projection which shoots up beyond the parapet. In each long side of the slab, visible at a distance, a giant segmental glazed gable lights an upper atrium.

On the lower corners square towers with glazed drum-like turrets. Other details are a somewhat arch reprise of the jazzier end of Art Deco: sunburst glazing to the main entrance, chromed finials like radio masts, etc. Stained glass by *Brian Clarke* in the entrance (CS).

Part of the Roman CITY WALL found during construction, standing about 6 ft (just under 2 metres) high, is preserved within the basement offices, just visible from the street. Part of a later bastion was also found, as well as an intramural road used during construction of the wall.

On the E side, No. 2, AMERICA HOUSE, by *Sir John Burnet, Tait & Partners*, 1987–9, a shockingly tawdry exercise in Postmodern pattern-making. Smaller buildings on the N side are numbered with Crosswall. No. 13, 1984–5 by *Greenaway & Partners*, has deep-set windows, sleek silver floor bands and a curved corner. No. 10, by *Joseph & Partners*, 1980–2, is an outlier of their Emperor House in Jewry Street (q.v.), with purple brick instead of brown.

ARTHUR STREET

Built *c.* 1830 on a steep curve to join Upper Thames Street with the new King William Street. The name probably commemorates the Prime Minister, Arthur, Duke of Wellington. On the W corner with Upper Thames Street, *Trehearne & Norman, Preston & Partners'* MINSTER HOUSE, 1954–7, is a good example of their light, friendly style. Convex-fronted, with incised diapered spandrels, the top two storeys (of eight) recessed. No. 10, on the E corner with Martin Lane, is a hybrid. To the r., a glazed-brick and stone frontage by *Brown & Barrow*, illustrated 1905, of the type with oriels inset in round-arched recesses, a device in England more often used singly. Rebuilt by *Covell Matthews Wheatley*, 1985–6, with three new l. bays, reminiscent of the older part, but done without finesse. The high-relief granite front at No. 6 is by *Fitzroy Robinson Partnership* and *William F. Newman & Associates*, 1981–3, in connection with retained façades in Martin Lane (q.v.).

ARTILLERY LANE

Made *c.* 1682, running E from Bishopsgate across the Old Artillery Ground: land formerly owned by St Mary Spital and used by the Tower Ordnance and Honourable Artillery Company earlier in the C17. The lane's Georgian marvels lie outside the City, in the meandering E part (*see London 5: East and Docklands*); the narrow W part is mostly Victorian warehouses and houses, in character already of the East End. Most imposing is Nos. 26–30 (S side), by *Hammack & Lambert*, 1883–4, with colonnettes and incised decoration on the lintels. Nos. 15–19 facing, 1865, have polychrome brick bands and cogged cornice strips. Nos. 4–10 (S side, by Bishopsgate) imitate the warehouse manner: by *Graham Sea Brook Partnership*, 1989–91. Further E, BUNGE HOUSE, 1985–8 by *Heery Architects*, Postmodern offices with a glazed corner to Fort Street.

AUSTIN FRIARS

So called from the church of Austin Friars, which later became the Dutch Church (q.v.). The rest of the friary was parcelled up by William Paulet, Marquess of Winchester, who built himself a new house on the N part (*see* Great Winchester Street). To the s, the close called Austin Friars winds around the church. In the later C17 and C18 it was lined with grand houses. Late Victorian office 141 chambers now predominate, a handsome and varied group built mostly to accommodate small stockbroking firms. Many were undertaken by the Drapers' Company, whose hall adjoins (sw, q.v.). It will be noticed how briskly the Drapers' architect *Charles Reilly Sen.* kept up with architectural fashions.

The street begins inconspicuously through a covered passage in No. 123 Old Broad Street (q.v.). Nos. 2–6 facing, AUSTIN FRIARS HOUSE, 1911–12, is by *Reilly*. Festively classical, with giant pilasters on pedestals, round-arched ground-floor windows, and much rustication. Refurbished 1987–90 by *Fookes, Ness & Gough*, with a startling life-size STATUE of a friar by *T. Metcalfe*, l. Other buildings are closer in size to the houses they replaced. Opposite Austin Friars House, rear ranges of buildings facing Throgmorton Street. Then No. 29 in the corner, which belongs with the E part of the Drapers' Hall front. Continuing on the w (l.) side, No. 28 by *Reilly*, 1894, Free Style this time, in red brick and terracotta. Ground floor with big segmental arches of grey stone resting on thin supports without capitals. Mullioned and transomed first-floor windows, separated by polygonal shafts rising from corbels. The second floor is recessed. No. 27, Neo-Georgian in stone, by *A. C. Blomfield & C. H. Driver*, 1929–31. No. 26, red brick above purple granite, a bit stodgy, dated 1899 in the big triangular gable and 1901 in the doorcase. Signed by *R. Langton Cole*, architect to the C19 Stock Exchange.

No. 25, red brick infill with discreet free detail by *Rolfe Judd*, 1988–91, is part of a development behind the retained façades of Nos. 22–24 beyond. These are all of 1888, forming the s side of the entry made in that year through to Throgmorton Avenue (q.v.). No. 24, by *Ebenezer Gregg*, and No. 22, by *Reilly*, solid eclectic Renaissance in stone, make the corners.

Between them, No. 23, by *Aston Webb & Ingress Bell*, an exceedingly naughty piece of round-arched design, evocative at several removes of late Flamboyant Gothic. Three bays, with two staircase windows above the central doorway half a storey higher up, which gives a disquieting effect. The top storey with two-light square-headed windows cutting into a blank trellis of tiny rod-like colonnettes. Teasingly odd lettering over the door and on the rainwater heads. It gives entry to COMMERZBANK. *Rolfe Judd*'s new interior is intelligent and enjoyable. A small lobby houses a spiral stair, the well with reset ROMAN TESSERAE discovered on site. They came from two substantial buildings on the banks of the

Walbrook, probably houses of the later C1, abandoned in the mid C2. Cool six-storey atrium beyond the lobby, faced in a grid of raised ribs with tall terracotta pilaster-piers. No. 21 (N side), also by *Reilly*, c. 1888, is similar to Nos. 22 and 24, with a handsome big chimneystack. The façade is incorporated into the Morgan Grenfell development in Great Winchester Street (q.v.). No. 15 next door, by *Frank Hay Roberts*, 1890–2, forms the N corner with the older part of Austin Friars. The design resembles Reilly's, with a rounded corner and a long return façade to a small raised alley. Top storey of 1913.

Then on the N side Nos. 12–14, a nicely domestic group behind balustraded forecourts. Nos. 12 and 14 both by *E. A. Gruning*, of 1881–2 and 1883, red brick in the Shaw tradition. No. 14, l., has a pilastered ground floor and a rich terracotta frieze above. No. 12, r., formerly the merchant bankers Frühling & Goschen, has a deep square-headed door canopy in the manner of c. 1700 and very tall windows, with a terracotta frieze repeated from Gruning's No. 11 Tokenhouse Yard (q.v.). Between them, No. 13, eclectic stone-faced Renaissance dated 1875. The poky Austin Friars Passage runs through to Great Winchester Street beyond No. 12. Nos. 10–11 are bulky free Jacobean in stone, of 1896–8, with a projecting porch. Beyond, the street ends in AUSTIN FRIARS SQUARE, made up of the rear ranges of 1990s offices on Old Broad Street. At the SW corner of the square, No. 6a, AUGUSTINE HOUSE, completed 1957, plain stone offices by *Arthur Bailey* on the E part of the old church site and forming a group with its replacement. Carved figure by *John Skeaping*.

BARBICAN ESTATE *see* PUBLIC BUILDINGS

BARTHOLOMEW CLOSE

A straggling backwater E of Little Britain. It begins there as an irregular square, rambles narrowly NE then NW, and turns back on itself to another little square S of St Bartholomew the Great's Lady Chapel. The route reflects the haphazard development of St Bartholomew's precinct after the Reformation. Timber-framed buildings of this period lingered into the C20, but its present, somewhat shabby buildings are mostly late C19 to early C20 warehouses, interspersed with utilitarian post-war blocks for St Bartholomew's Hospital. Big 1980s commercial ranges on Aldersgate Street make a backdrop.

Entering the close from Little Britain at the S, the r. and l. sides are formed by the hospital's Gloucester House and Queen Elizabeth II Wing (*see* Little Britain). The Butchers' Hall (q.v.) occupies the NW side. Diagonally opposite, Nos. 61–61a by *William Hudson*, 1871–2: the former City of London Union offices, which administered the workhouse. No. 61, tall and sober Italianate of four bays; No. 61a lower, with an almost unmoulded Venetian window and a little pediment.

Leaving the square on the E, DOMINION HOUSE at No. 59 (N side)

preserves part of Evans, Lescher & Webb's pharmaceutical ware-house, an early job by *Aston Webb*, 1879 (two bays, l.). Not strongly personal: red brick, with gable and large segment-headed windows in Board School Queen Anne manner. Webb added the three r. bays in 1892 and a rear extension (as No. 47) in 1910.*
Nos. 54–58, up to the corner, C18 houses adapted as warehouses in the C19, with extra storeys on top. At Nos. 28–29 opposite (s side), flats by *GMA Architecture* are under construction (1997). Next to them, facing back down towards the square, brown brick flats by *Seifert Ltd*, *c.* 1990 (No. 30), part of their development in Aldersgate Street behind.

HALF MOON COURT, beyond on the r., is named from a vanished tavern in Aldersgate Street. Unpretending early C20 commercial buildings on its N side (e.g. No. 12, 1908 by *H. E. Knight*). Next a sleepy little yard called BARTHOLOMEW PLACE, first developed in the late C17. No. 38a, an asymmetrical former pub of 1897 by *Dear & Winder*. Flats by *J. Sampson Lloyd*, part of the Founders' Hall development (q.v.), stand E of St Bartholomew's Lady Chapel, facing Kinghorn Street. s of St Bartholomew's choir, on the site of Prior Bolton's lodging of *c.* 1517, rises the Close's grandest warehouse: the former Israel & Oppenheimer, six storeys of civilized brick Neo-Wren by *Walter Pamphilon*, 1912. The narrow MIDDLESEX PASSAGE on its l., on the line of an ancient route through the Priory's dormitory, runs back to No. 61a on the first square.

BARTHOLOMEW LANE

First recorded 1308; named from the former St Bartholomew Exchange at the SE corner, known from the early C12. *Wren*'s aisled replacement of 1675–83 went in 1840–1, when Threadneedle Street was widened for the new Royal Exchange. *Cockerell*'s Sun Life Assurance (1842) stood on the site until 1970: it was perhaps his best exercise in the grand style at the very moment when the restraint of the Grecian and Roman taste was finally given up. Pleas to save it failed because of the storey inserted in 1895 (architect *F. W. Porter*); yet this work was done with exemplary tact. *Fitzroy Robinson & Partners*' ROYAL BANK OF SCOTLAND makes an unexciting replacement. Seven storeys of polished stone and blue-tinted window bands, the entrance in the canted corner. It forms part of the Stock Exchange redevelopment (q.v.). To the N, the poky CAPEL COURT, the Exchange's main entrance before the rebuilding. The Capels, an important C16 City family, had their house here. Nos. 1–4 beyond, the former Allied Assurance, 1932–3 by Messrs *Joseph* and *Mewès & Davis*, echoes with diminished urbanity the latter architects' composition for the London, County & Westminster Bank, facing down the Lane from Lothbury (q.v.), N. The Bank of England makes up the W side.

*Ian Dungavell kindly supplied these details.

BASINGHALL STREET

Called not from a hall but from 'haw' or yard. The older form survived to 1900 in the form of St Michael Bassishaw (w side), modestly rebuilt by *Wren* in 1676–9 (steeple 1712–14). Excavation in 1965 showed that the early two-celled church (first recorded in the C12) had been rebuilt in the C15, like so many City churches. There is still a Bassishaw ward. There is no certain connection with the Basings, one of the great City families of the C13. A site so close to Guildhall proved attractive to the Livery Companies: the Coopers, Weavers, Masons and Girdlers all had halls here from the C15–C16. But the first three were given up in the 1850s–60s, and the last was destroyed in 1940. Truncated at the N by the post-war London Wall alignment, the street now finishes at Basinghall Avenue (made 1893). The W side is taken up by the Guildhall complex (q.v.); the E side still has a typical mixture of offices.

From the s, Nos. 6–8 are part of Nos. 93–95 Gresham Street (q.v.). Then Nos. 9–12, routine stripped classical with metal panels between stone piers, by *Delissa Joseph*, 1922–5. Nos. 13–14, LIBRARY CHAMBERS, are by *Ford & Hesketh*, 1877–8. Tall red brick Gothic, the storeys with big windows and mullions; on the top floor connection is made between them by Gothic arches on stocky columns; crowned by a central gable with a round window. Then *Henry Tanner*'s red brick façade for the Selection Trust (Nos. 15–16), 1935, modern-minded for the City at that date, but not otherwise remarkable. It hardly prepares one for MASON'S AVENUE behind, where it joins *T. Schaerer*'s adjacent Neo-Tudor effort of 1928: stone-faced ground floor, four storeys of flimsy applied half-timbering. The avenue is first recorded as Tristram's Alley (1548); the present title commemorates the Masons' Hall, established on the s side by the 1520s and dem. 1864. On its site, Nos. 12–14 by *Parfitt & Craig Hall*, 1978–80, in dark polished stone with closely spaced flat bays above a recessed ground floor, like their earlier Nos. 30–32 Coleman Street (q.v.), then No. 15, the OLD DR BUTLER'S HEAD, two early C19 stock-brick properties combined, each with windows in segment-headed reveals. Storeys were added in connection with Nos. 12–14. The ground floor, altered and set forward, has carved drops attached: could they be late C17?

Back in Basinghall Street, WOOLGATE HOUSE (CHASE MANHATTAN) by *C. Lovett Gill & Partners*, 1963–8, under demolition in 1997. It was a large complex, well and simply detailed with plain horizontal bands faced with white mosaic, partly offset by narrow grey concrete verticals. Generous passages led between polished black granite pilotis through to Coleman Street via a large entrance courtyard, laid out by the *Design Research Unit* with *Gordon Bowyer* as a garden with low semicircular walls and a fountain; interiors by the same. On the site of the Wool Exchange, by *J. Gordon* of Glasgow, Venetian, 1873–4; itself on the site of the old Weavers' Hall. Towards the street, a hieratic abstract stainless steel SCULPTURE, Ritual, by *Antanas Brazdys*, 1969.

To the N, Nos. 35–36, by Messrs *Joseph*, 1958–61, a slab running along Basinghall Avenue intersecting with a taller slab to

Basinghall Street. Façades similar to contemporary buildings on London Wall immediately N (e.g. Austral House, *see* p. 543) but still with apologetic little decorative details in the manner of Bucklersbury House (Queen Victoria Street, q.v.). The Girdlers' Hall (q.v.) is on the N side of Basinghall Avenue. For the City Tower (No. 40) and Nos. 55–60, *see* London Wall.

BEVIS MARKS

It runs NW–SE, just inside the line of the City wall; fragments of Roman wall have been found on the N side. By 1405 called Bevesmarkes, from Buries Marks, the town house of the Abbot of Bury St Edmunds (s side). Widened 1979. With Camomile Street, NW, and Duke's Place, SE (qq.v.), it makes one long main thoroughfare, without strong character.

The w corners with St Mary Axe belong with that street. Then mostly post-war buildings of medium height. On the s side, two long office blocks by *Lister, Drew & Associates*, 1980–4, both extending over the pavement. No. 6 is all glossy mirror-glass, corners and profiles remorselessly rounded. Glazed barrel-vaulted canopy over the walkway. Modest central atrium, with upper storeys cantilevered inwards as it rises. BIIBA HOUSE, E of Bury Street, of orangey brick, has a reset late C19 pediment marking the entry to the Spanish and Portuguese Synagogue (q.v.), via a matching doorcase and wrought-iron gates.

Opposite (N side), No. 24, BEVIS MARKS HOUSE, by *Ivan Starkin*, 1983–4. The previous façade of *c.* 1925 is retained facing Bevis Marks, with a reconstructed corner turret. Heavy granite-clad framing to Houndsditch. An extremely ugly combination. Further on, Nos. 17–18, CREECHURCH HOUSE: smart warehouse facing Creechurch Lane, E, by *Lewis Solomon & Son*, 1935, with metal-faced floors between stone mullions; w extension by *Theo H. Birks*, 1962–6, H-plan, with blue curtain-walling and projecting floor strings between blue brick sections.

Back on the s side, ARTHUR CASTLE HOUSE, by *Architects' Comprehensive Design Group*, 1978–81, not high, the main front on Creechurch Lane. Polished brown-pink Sardinian granite, uniform flush windows, bronzed panelling.

BILLITER STREET

Recorded as *Belyetereslane* in 1298, from the 'belleyesterers' or bell-founders who lived here. The building worth a look is *Edward Ellis*'s Nos. 19–21 (E side), dated 1865, florid, coarse, but very lively Renaissance-eclectic. Nine bays, large for City offices of its date, curving gently to the street. Rusticated end bays in red-and-white stone, with big segmental ground-floor pediments carved with lumpen cherubs and emblems suggestive of the trading companies originally based here. Ground floor between with large segment-headed windows, first floor with rounded double lights separated by granite columns. Two plainer upper storeys, but not enough to prevent the effect of all-over ornament. Refurbished *c.* 1930, with a new central doorcase to a columned hall. Otherwise, mostly side and rear elevations, notably the 1950s Lloyd's building (*see* Lime Street). On the W side near the N end, the little No. 5, ABSALON HOUSE, infill of the smoked-glass curtain-walling type, by *C. A. Cornish & Associates*, 1975–8.

BIRCHIN LANE

Called in 1260 *Bercherverelane*, i.e. lane of the beard-cutters. This was a prosperous area at the heart of the Roman town, just W of the basilica of the forum. Remnants of over half a dozen elaborate late ROMAN MOSAIC PAVEMENTS have been found here. Part of a Roman bakehouse furnished with bread ovens was discovered at Nos. 22–23 in 1987.

No. 18 (E side) is *W. W. Gwyther*'s former Commercial Bank of Sydney, 1885, not large, with giant pilasters of polished red Peterhead granite and a small pediment (façade incorporated by the *Thomas Saunders Partnership* into Nos. 60–62 Lombard Street adjoining, 1983–5). No. 20, red brick with pilasters above fat columns at the entrance, is by *R. Seifert & Partners*, 1986–9. Also incorporated, retained façades, l.: Nos. 22–23, with bowed leaded aprons in a big stone surround, coarse but up to date (1916 by *E. Greenop*); No. 25 by *William Wallace*, 1914, with brown granite ground floor, Portland stone above, the end bays fashioned as giant aedicules.

More early C20 buildings on the W side. Nos. 2–4, by *Dunn & Watson*, 1910, were for the Edinburgh Life Assurance Co. Five bays, fashionably Neo-Palladian, with three big first-floor pediments on consoles. Nos. 5–7 (formerly Norwich Union), 1935–7 by *Gunton & Gunton*, has vaguely Egyptian motifs.

BISHOPSGATE

A long street, beginning in the City's heart and running N to the boundary with Shoreditch. Named from the medieval GATE (*Portam Episcopi* in Domesday), by tradition restored by St Erkenwald, C7 Bishop of London. Repaired in 1648; replaced as late as 1733–4, by *George Smith* and *John James*. Unlike other London gates, theirs lacked upper chambers, giving it more the appearance of a Roman triumphal arch. Demolished 1761. Houses within and without the gate are mentioned as early as the C13.

Of famous later mansions, that of Sir John Crosby †1476 (which incorporated Crosby Hall, now in Chelsea) stood near Great St Helen's, Sir Paul Pindar's (†1650) on the W side N of Liverpool Street station (façade now in the Victoria and Albert Museum), and Sir Thomas Gresham's (†1579) further S on the E side, where Gresham College operated until 1710. Bishopsgate was the first City street to be gas-lit (*c.* 1810). The division into Bishopsgate Within and Without ended in 1911, but the smaller scale N of the old gate is still marked, excepting Liverpool Street station and the Broadgate Centre on the E side.

ROMAN REMAINS. The street roughly follows the course of the ROMAN ROAD which led on to Ermine Street. Excavations on the E side in 1980, by Crosby Square, found part of this road, 24 ft (over 7 metres) wide. It followed a line of slightly higher ground which had attracted sporadic prehistoric settlement. Remains of a Roman timber structure here, clearly associated with the road, may have been part of an early town gate, from before the northward extension of the city boundary in c. 200. This extension necessitated a new mural gate, of which fragmentary traces of masonry were excavated in 1905 and 1921 on the site of the medieval gate. Numerous C1–C2 burials lay around the gate (*see* also Camomile Street). Roman houses formerly lining the road have yielded a number of mosaic pavements.

South part, to Wormwood Street and Camomile Street

We begin at the crossroads with Cornhill and Leadenhall Street. The E SIDE was widened in the late 1970s, though the roadway remains narrow, and the new buildings stand back behind trees.* The first two are by *GMW Partnership*, 1974–81: No. 4, TOKYO MARINE (formerly Banque Belge), a seven-storey corner slab, and No. 8 (formerly Baring Bros.), a twenty-storey tower. They invite comparison with GMW's earlier pair of towers in Leadenhall Street around the corner. The minimal Miesian envelope of the 1960s is updated by means of reflective smoked glass – a common enough development in the 70s, but done here with extreme precision and refinement, in flush bands between bronzed panelling. No. 8, less extensively glazed, has recessed lower storeys to accommodate a staircase and part of the pedway, leading nowhere useful.

Opposite (W side), a good, grand Victorian group begins with Nos. 3–5, the former Royal Bank of Scotland, by *T. Chatfeild Clarke*, 1877. Of Bath stone, the four storeys unusually composed, with two-storey applied Ionic arcading below, giant Corinthian pilasters above. Enriched frieze. Putti in the spandrels carved by *Anstey*, not at his best. Rebuilt behind the façade, 1983–5, by *Covell Matthews Wheatley Partnership*. Nos. 7–9, office chambers of 1892 by *H. Alexander Pelly*, with pilasters of polished purple granite (being rebuilt behind by *Rolfe Judd*, 1997). No. 11, plainer chambers of 1903 by *G. H. Hunt*, still with the old number 118. LLOYDS BANK stands on the Threadneedle Street corner. By *T. Knolles Green*, 1874–6 (originally the Hampshire Banking Co., later Capital & Counties Bank). Rusticated ground floor, cabled pilasters over, turning to full columns at the corner: a prosperous, if unimaginative, treatment. The nice low glazed lantern was added probably in 1882; then in 1893 *Kidner & Berry* raised a near-matching four-bay extension along Threadneedle Street.

* Amongst buildings lost: Nos. 2a–6, *Cooper*'s Banque Belge, 1923–4, deliberately French; No. 8, *Norman Shaw*'s Baring Bros., 1881, very domestic red brick, on a site occupied by Baring since 1806 (*see* also Museum of London, Public Buildings); extended in 1913 by his pupil *Horsley* (Nos. 10–12); Nos. 30–32, Bank of Scotland, 1896, by *Gwyther*.

The corner was the site of St Martin Outwich, recorded *c.* 1196 and rebuilt by *S. P. Cockerell* in 1796–8. On demolition, its mostly C15 predecessor had a nave, S aisle and SW tower.

The NATIONAL WESTMINSTER BANK (No. 15) by *John Gibson*, 1864–5, forms the N corner with Threadneedle Street. Designed as the head office of the National Provincial Bank; now part of a complex by *R. Seifert & Partners*, 1970–81, including the NatWest Tower (*see* Old Broad Street). It is the best bank in the Victorian City, inside and out on a par with the palatial banks of contemporary Scotland. Proudly one-storeyed to the street, as if in riposte to the Bank of England (long in dispute with the National Provincial over the issue of notes). But, in accordance with the general development of style in the sixty years between Soane and Gibson, all is done with much more swagger. Large arched windows with enriched frames. Fluted Composite columns between, coupled to frame the entrance, which was placed at the rounded S corner to qualify for a more prestigious Threadneedle Street address. Broad cornice. Much SCULPTURE: above the windows, Pre-Raphaelite allegorical reliefs by *John Hancock*, each with an angel presiding over scenes of human endeavour; statues over the columns by Messrs *Colley*, representing England and Wales (over the doorway), Manchester and London (far l. and r.), and lesser cities (five single figures). Gibson added the two matching N bays in 1878–9; higher relief sculpture here.

Within, a grand, formal banking hall, 118 ft (36 metres) by 50 ft (15 metres), set end-on to the street. Counters etc. were removed 1980–2, when it was converted into an assembly room for the bank (called the Gibson Hall), with an anteroom to the N. Three big glass saucer-domes provide the lighting. Big chandeliers of 1980. Around the walls thickly crowded Corinthian columns of red-streaked Devonshire marble. At the short ends they support triple arcades. Frieze of reliefs of putti busy banking and coining at the N end. Gibson's roof used boxed plate-iron, conservative for the 1860s. The present banking hall is in *Seifert*'s Nos. 21–23, a bland grey-granite-clad forebuilding to the NatWest tower behind. Marble lining, a coffered ceiling and chandeliers palely attempt to supply some sense of occasion. Gibson's bank replaced a fine Palladian mansion by *Sir Robert Taylor*, *c.* 1750, adapted for the National Provincial *c.* 1840 by *J. B. Watson*.

Back to the E side for Nos. 22–24 (formerly Crédit Suisse), by *Sidney Kaye, Firmin & Partners*, 1974–8. Solid and wealthy-looking, as befits a bank. Big squarish windows with rounded corners and stainless-steel mullions, polished Baltic Brown granite cladding. Stainless-steel doors with curved gilded strips, by *Algernon Asprey* and *Jeremy Mackay-Lewis*.

Nos. 26–40, the former STANDARD CHARTERED BANK, is by *Fitzroy Robinson Partnership*, 1980–5 (senior partner *Leonard Bitcheno*, job architect *Robin Booth*, structural engineers *Pell Frischmann*). It signalled the eclipse of the office tower as the preferred form for a major bank, in favour of the American atrium fashion, here adopted on a scale unprecedented in London. The atrium appears as a five-storey glazed centre in the long, straight front, framed by mighty chamfered piers and strong upper horizontals faced in red Brazilian granite. Across the front a section of ped-way, doubling as an entrance canopy and joined by a bridge to the NatWest complex opposite. The N section spans the entry to Great St Helen's. The rear walls of the atrium recede on an irregular diagonal plan towards a glazed central section, allowing views into Crosby Square (the route through remains a public right of way). The huge internal volume was alas altered in 1990, after the bank sold up: the narrower upper atrium was roofed over, and the jungle of tall trees removed. Some of the long spanning footbridges remain, but the apologetic present furnishings hardly do justice to the space, which originally recalled Kevin Roche's influential indoor garden at the Ford Foundation Building, New York (1967).

The rest of the w side up to Wormwood Street is just two big blocks, both reconstructed after bomb damage in 1993. No. 55, also by *Fitzroy*'s, was originally built in 1988–91. Very long, gently curved stone-faced front, horizontally divided into a dark stone podium, four upper storeys of square recessed windows in two sizes, then set-backs. Big inset entrance bow, set off-centre. The paraphrased classical detail, above average, echoes Otto Wagner here and there. Then No. 99, a twenty-six-storey tower of elongated hexagonal plan (by *Ley, Colbeck & Partners* and *R. Seifert & Partners*, 1970–6), stripped to the frame by *GMW Partnership*, 1994–6. Their new cladding has pale blue and white panels between flush aluminium mullions, less emphatically vertical than the original stainless-steel fins and green glazing, and much less attractive. Podium heightened from two to four storeys.

Lower, mostly smaller buildings on the E side, facing: Nos. 42–44 by *Scott, Brownrigg & Turner*, 1982–3, mainly curtain-walled; No. 46, a mid-C18 house, refronted in the early C19 and again after 1993; No. 48 by *H.H. & M.E. Collins*, 1896, tall, showy Second Empire, with pilasters and balconies piled up beneath a heavy bracket-cornice. The massive block at Nos. 52–68 is the former Hudson's Bay House, 1926–8 by *Mewès & Davis* (consultant *Sir Charles Allom*). Slowly curved fourteen-bay Palladian front, with rusticated strips marking the divisions. Octagonal cupola. Doric pilasters to the ground floor, and Canadian frontier motifs in the metopes. In the middle, columns and fine iron gates give entry to ST HELEN'S PLACE. This formal close of tall C20 offices ends in a decidedly French façade of 1929, again by *Mewès & Davis*. The rest, alternately pilastered and plain, is mostly by *Henry Saul*, 1921–6; the S side, just within the entrance, mirrors the older No. 17 opposite, by *H. Chatfeild Clarke*, 1912. By *Saul* also the Leathersellers' Hall at No. 15 (q.v. for the history of St Helen's Place).

Next, the shattered St Ethelburga (q.v.), then No. 80, a reconstruction by *Fitzroy Robinson Partnership*, 1993–5, of their bomb-damaged Kansallis House, 1982–5. Nine storeys, the exposed smooth concrete frame with superimposed rounded verticals. Set-back top storey with diagonally angled windows. CLARK'S PLACE housed the Marine Society *c.* 1775–1979, and the Parish Clerks' Hall from the late C15 to 1547; nothing to see now. The Camomile Street corner is No. 90, *Fitzroy*'s again (1971–5), with big canted smoked-glass bays (replaced 1993–6) in thin stone framing.

North part, as far as Norton Folgate

The old Bishopsgate stood just N of the crossroads here. One relic: a big gilded mitre, crudely carved, reset on BISHOPSGATE HOUSE (Nos. 106–126, E), a concrete slab by *Ley, Colbeck & Partners*, 1971–5. Paired windows set near-flush; reeded stair-tower, s.

On the w side, a modest brick-faced building by *Fitzroy*'s (1995–7, on a re-used 1950s frame), echoes the silhouette of the 1920s Stone House (*see* below). Then St Botolph and its churchyard. No. 117, much-mauled C18 with a Neo-Georgian shopfront of 1936. Nos. 119–121, the stuccoed WHITE HART INN, rebuilt *c.* 1829 when Liverpool Street was formed. The courtyard entrance remains from the previous, mid-C16 building here; the first inn was older still. The Great Eastern Hotel beyond belongs with Liverpool Street station (*see* Public Buildings).

The E side continues with a group by *Richardson & Gill*, interesting in its varied responses to the approaching Modern style. On the N corner with Houndsditch, No. 136, STONE HOUSE, 1926–8, with a vestigial giant order interlocking with a grid of floor bands, minimally ornamented. Down Houndsditch, the slightly smaller STAPLE HALL (completed 1931), more explicitly simplified, with streamlined corners and superimposed flat piers and cornices. Both have Richardson's characteristic squared-off attic. In STONE HOUSE COURT between, the little No. 1, a white-faience-clad house of *c.* 1931, turns puckishly Neo-Regency, with sashes and a projecting Gothick shopfront. Similar shopfronts inserted in the older Nos. 3–5, r.

Then, back in Bishopsgate, a random, rather scruffy sequence of smaller, mostly older buildings, in utmost contrast with Liverpool Street station and the Broadgate Centre opposite: Nos. 142–146 (DEVONSHIRE CHAMBERS), 1878–9, of painted stone, with sturdy superimposed columns and a slim semicircular central bow; Nos. 152–154 by *W. H. Duffield*, 1889, gabled red brick, which goes Dutch to match the Great Eastern Hotel; No. 158 by *Wadmore & Baker*, 1885–6, red brick late Gothic. Set back, Nos. 162–164, a pretty Tudor Gothic former fire station of 1884–5 by *George Vulliamy*, being converted to offices in 1997. Nos. 166–170 of 1988–91 by the *Thomas Saunders Partnership*, red brick and stone with a central flat bow, all looking inflated beyond its natural size.

After New Street, a ramshackle run at Nos. 172–180, then the Police Station (q.v.). Glum treeless court beyond, renamed VICTORIA AVENUE in misguided homage in 1901. Nos. 186–188, by *de Metz & Birks*, have fairly early curtain-walling (completed 1957). Nos. 194–200, a six-storey stationers' warehouse of 1887, the lower part all glazed between giant pilasters. CATHERINE WHEEL ALLEY recalls the last of the City's galleried coaching inns, demolished *c.* 1911. DIRTY DICK'S pub (Nos. 202–204), 1870, perhaps by *D. R. Dale*, has twin Gothic arches under one relieving arch. In the tympanum a circular relief of the old Bishopsgate. The N corner of Middlesex Street is No. 212, WOODIN'S SHADES, a pub of 1893, probably by *Eedle & Myers*. Nos. 214–216, a bank of 1906 by *W. Campbell-Jones*, discreet Free Style with pilasters. After the Bishopsgate Institute (*see* Public Buildings), Nos. 232–238

(BARCLAYS BANK), 1894, on the corner with Brushfield Street, in a sober unenriched style recalling Philip Webb. Beyond, a large new building for ABN AMRO by *EPR Partnership*, under construction 1997, on land transferred to Tower Hamlets in 1994.

BLACK FRIARS LANE

Called Water Lane until 1940. The present name commemorates the London HOUSE OF THE DOMINICANS, or BLACK FRIARS, formerly on the site. They moved here from Shoe Lane in 1276, when Robert Fitzwalter granted them as a site for a larger foundation two Norman fortresses: the moated C12 Montfitchet Tower, and to its s the first Baynard's Castle (for the second Baynard's Castle *see* City of London School for Boys, Public Buildings). They were commemorated in the medieval name of Castle Street (1352–3). To make further space, the City wall was rebuilt further w, up to the line of the Fleet; parts of this wall were recorded beneath Pilgrim Street, further N, in 1989. The friary buildings were terraced down the hill: the church on the highest ground to the N, other rooms mostly arranged around the great s cloister. They had semi-official status as the meeting place of the King's Council and of other convocations. At the Dissolution most of the site passed to Lord Cobham, whose house became the Apothecaries' Hall in 1632 (q.v.). In its later C17 and C18 incarnation, this is now the chief architectural interest of the lane.

The FRIARY has left the following traces. Parts of the N and E walls of the Guest House survive inside the Apothecaries' Hall. Further w, C13 rubble masonry from the s wall of the Principal's Hall is visible in a little paved courtyard off IRELAND YARD, reached via Playhouse Yard s of the Hall. Part of its N wall, with a blocked C14 window 10 ft (3 metres) high, was discovered in 1988 and is preserved within No. 69 Carter Lane (q.v.). Further w, CHURCH ENTRY runs up to Carter Lane on the alignment of the cross-passage between nave and choir usual in English mendicant churches. Part of the nave's site remains on the w side, as the former burial ground of St Ann Blackfriars. This parish, established at the Reformation in part of the friary, built a new church on the site of the choir in 1598, but was joined with St Andrew-by-the-Wardrobe after the Great Fire. Other bits of Blackfriars have turned up over the years: in 1925 a chunk of choir walling and a Purbeck shaft and capital were moved to St Dominic, Southampton Road, Camden; in 1989 fragments of tracery and C15 Venetian stained glass were found, reused to line a well s of Apothecary Street, w of Black Friars Lane.

In Church Entry, ST ANN'S VESTRY HALL (ANCIENT MONUMENTS SOCIETY), 1905 by *Banister Fletcher & Sons*, E side, occupies part of the former choir. Unusually well-treated Edwardian Baroque, but on the smallest scale. Inside, a single barrel-vaulted panelled chamber with a delicate little w gallery. Also a reset pedimented tablet dated 1671, from a demolished house nearby. Signed by John Young, churchwarden: the master mason (resident close by?) PLAYHOUSE YARD is named from the theatre established by James and Richard Burbage within the friary buildings (1596). The C18 buildings on the N side belong with Apothecaries' Hall.

The S part of the W side of Black Friars Lane was lost to the London, Chatham & Dover Railway's viaduct in the 1860s; the rest has mostly lain waste since the Second World War. One building of interest: Nos. 15–17, by *Edward Power*, 1870, polychrome brick Gothic with striped voussoirs over a stone-faced ground floor. Built for the great railway caterers Spiers & Pond, whose large establishment here has otherwise gone. By it, steps up over the railway made in 1990 preserve the route of Apothecary Street, which passed underneath the line's previous viaduct. The site to the N lies largely vacant in 1997. Facing (E side), COBHAM HOUSE (No. 20), by *J. Sampson Lloyd* of *Green Lloyd & Adams* for the Apothecaries, 1981–3. Reminiscent of 1930s civic Neo-Georgian. First a part curving to the street, then a square pedimented entrance tower containing air-conditioning louvres, then a five-storey range with first-floor arcading. No. 7, by *T. P. Bennett & Son*, 1984–6, has an archly Second Empire flavour.

The street continues N of Carter Lane as LUDGATE BROADWAY. Nos. 10–13 here are by *Sheppard Robson*, 1982–5. S section with Gibbs surrounds, the main part of brown brick with a rounded corner, the top with a pretty flush pattern suggesting triangular gables.

BLOMFIELD STREET

The E boundary of the old Lower Moorfields (*see* Finsbury Circus). Called Broker Row until *c.* 1860; renamed after the Bishop of London, father of the architect Sir Arthur Blomfield.

The W SIDE is dominated by the giant Edwardian offices of Finsbury Circus. One older building: FINSBURY HOUSE (Nos. 22–23), with polished grey stone columns in two orders and an acute NE corner. By *Gordon, Lowther & Gunton*, 1893–4; harbinger of much work by that firm in the Circus proper. On the E SIDE, No. 14, stone-faced offices of 1928 by *M. E. & O. H. Collins*, with elaborate set-backs along New Broad Street; No. 12, BELL COURT HOUSE, 1887, with close-set pedimented windows, style of *T. H. Smith*; Nos. 4–10 by the *Fitzroy Robinson Partnership*, of brick, broken up in self-effacing mid-1970s manner, but later: 1985–7. Long front along Liverpool Street.

BOTOLPH LANE

One of the steep lanes running S from Eastcheap, known from *c.* 1300. Named from the church of St Botolph Billingsgate in Lower Thames Street (q.v.), from which the lane was cut off in the early 1980s when Peninsular House was built (*see* Monument Street). In Monument Street also *Seifert*'s Faryners House, which makes up most of the W side. Its rear part is on the site of St

George Botolph Lane, rebuilt by *Wren* 1671–6 and demolished in 1904: hence St George's Lane, N.

On the E side, Nos. 36–38, attractive infill by *Rolfe Judd Group Practice*, 1986–8, red brick and stone with a bow and blocked columns at the entrance. Otherwise mostly workmanlike late C19, some refurbished in the 1980s for the City Village scheme (*see* Lovat Lane). They continue along the little paved BOTOLPH ALLEY, reached through Nos. 40–41. On its N side, No. 7, a small late C17 or early C18 house with flush sash-boxes. The alley is known from the 1270s, as Cate Lane.

BOUVERIE STREET

Laid out *c.* 1799 through the sloping site of the old Whitefriars (*see* Whitefriars Street) by the Pleydell-Bouverie family (hence also the little Pleydell Street, W).

On the W SIDE, No. 62 Fleet Street, Jacobean of *c.* 1888, with original shopfront. Further down, Nos. 6–8 by *Seifert Ltd*, 1988–90, clumsy red brick, the upper floors corbelled out. The rest is all former newspaper buildings. No. 10, formerly *Punch*, 1929–30 by *Thompson & Walford*, wholly domestic Neo-Georgian. Across Temple Lane, a gritty concrete extension to Harmsworth House (*see* Tudor Street): by *Royce, Hurley & Stewart*, 1974–8. On the E SIDE, the long range of Freshfields (*see* Fleet Street), then the utilitarian former *Evening News* extension by *Ellis, Clarke & Gallanaugh*, 1956, with a covered bridge across the street high up. MAGPIE LANE, redolent of industrial decay, runs through to Whitefriars Street, via Ashentree Court.

BOW LANE

4 A narrow pedestrianized shopping street, mostly modest C19 (though much reconstructed or refurbished), with still narrower courts and alleys opening off it. Of late C9 origin (probably part of Alfred's new *burh*), when it led straight down to the waterfront. The continuation S of Cannon Street is now called Garlick Hill (q.v.). Until the C16, the section N of Watling Street was called Hosier Lane, the part to the S Cordwainer Street.

The interesting buildings are in the N part. Nos. 41–43 (E side), 1870s offices with wide tripartite windows and fluted piers. Nos. 6–8 opposite, 1871 by *T. K. Green*, for the stationer John Nichols. Endearingly naïve Italian Gothic in red brick with polychrome bands and encaustic tiles. In the tympana carved medallions of youthful heads with emblems of the trade. Gothic shopfronts with iron structure honestly expressed. That on the l. is a replica made 1977–9, when Nos. 3–9 and the buildings behind were refurbished by *Elsom Pack & Roberts Partnership*.

In GROVELAND COURT, through Nos. 4–5, a much-remade wrought-iron gateway, apparently early C18, said to date from a visit by William and Mary to WILLIAMSON'S TAVERN on the S side (rebuilt by *Gunton & Gunton*, Neo-Georgian, 1932). Opposite, a much-reconstructed late C17 house. Its N front, altered in the C18, faces the narrow parallel alley of BOW CHURCHYARD, where another C18 front adjoins it at r. angles.

Back in Bow Lane, No. 2, a good three-bay late C18 house. On the E again, the late C19 Nos. 44–47 were rebuilt behind by *Fitzroy Robinson & Partners*, 1978–83, extending along the narrow WELL COURT which runs through to Queen Street. Nos. 48–51 by *Haslemere Estates*, 1970–2, do their best to fit in. Then No. 52, a brick warehouse by *J. Young & Son*, 1873, with narrow keystones and spindly iron colonnettes, and No. 54, a substantial five-bay late C18 house with late C19 shopfront.

BREAM'S BUILDINGS

In origin a little C18 close off Chancery Lane, widened and cut through to Fetter Lane in 1882. Some interesting late Victorian buildings, and one outstanding C20 one.

First the late C19. At the NW, No. 5, 1888–90, by *Christopher Shiner*, wild and colourful, with stock Queen Anne devices (corbelled-out oriels, pargetted coving) inserted between plain piers banded with green and white glazed brick. Nos. 7–9, dated 1896, hard red brick, only just still Gothic. More decidedly Gothic Nos. 11–13, the former Athenaeum, also of red brick. By *William C. Street*; called 'lately erected' in 1892. Four bays, four storeys, twin gables, with an arcade to the street (originally also lighting a basement printing hall), and continuous labels linking the windows: old-fashioned, but thoughtful.

Then the flat and feeble 1970s FIELD HOUSE. Buildings facing it on the S side include No. 6, before 1893, with storeys differentiated by arcading, plain mullions etc. and No. 8, 1899, Neo-Tudor office chambers, with storeys by contrast in a uniform grid. Next to No. 8, the rear of ROLLS HOUSE, a curtain-walled early 1960s slab. The main front faces S on to Rolls Buildings, off Fetter Lane.

On the N side again, a fragment of the burial ground of St Dunstan-in-the-West, with mature trees. Overlooking it, the former OFFICES of *Yorke, Rosenberg & Mardall*, 1960–1, designed when *F. R. S. Yorke* was still alive. Few English architects had designed their own offices at that time. The small, compact six-storey building had drawing offices in a semi-basement, with three upper storeys set back and a penthouse set back again. Three bays, the upper part on the r. broken abruptly round the corner. It was amongst the earliest examples of the firm's hallmark, white glazed brick-sized tiles laid without visible bonding. They sheathe the concrete frame exactly. The window frames, of timber, also used materials unconventionally. Entrance up steps from GREYSTOKE PLACE, a pedestrian alley on the N side.

BRIDE LANE

A quiet L-shaped back-street, first recorded as *vico Sancte Brigide*, 1205. It runs between Fleet Street and New Bridge Street, behind

Ludgate Circus. St Bride's church appears high up above the retaining wall on the W side, St Bride's Institute on the S side (qq.v.), where the Abbot of Faversham's Inn stood *c.* 1150–1521. The Abbot of Winchcombe and Bishop of St David's also had houses here.

The other worthwhile building is the former ST BRIDE AND BRIDEWELL SCHOOLS, 1840, at Nos. 16–17. A composition reminiscent of a contemporary Nonconformist chapel. Two storeys, three bays wide, in stock brick with round-headed openings. Small one-bay pediment resting on console corbels, but no other entablature. (Two Charity Children probably dating from its foundation in 1711 are in St Bride.) Refurbished *c.* 1984–5 by *Elsom Pack & Roberts Partnership*, joining their Nos. 7–8 New Bridge Street (q.v.). BRIDE COURT, an alley through to New Bridge Street, was made into a covered shopping passage in 1925, without architectural ambition.

BRIDEWELL PLACE

Laid out in 1872–3 in an L-shape across the site of the Bridewell Hospital (*see* New Bridge Street), by *Frederick Marrable*, succeeded by *T. H. Wyatt* and then by *Richard Roberts*. One building of note: No. 2, the former St Bride's Vicarage. By *Champneys*, 1885. Nice five-bay, three-storey red brick front in the later C17 English style, facing down Tudor Street. Triangular- and segmental-pedimented dormers, big chimneystacks. At r. angles to it, the former St Bridget's House (*see* Tudor Street). Opposite, a building by the *Rolfe Judd Group Practice* with *North & Partners*, 1978–80. Brown brick over an open stone-faced colonnade. Proposed for rebuilding by *Arup Associates* (1996). Early C19 brick ranges on New Bridge Street appear behind.

BRIDGEWATER SQUARE

Developed from 1688 after an early C16 mansion owned by the Earl of Bridgewater burned down. *Wren* was a partner in the development, and many of his colleagues and craftsmen (*Hawksmoor, W. Emmett, E. Strong Sen., H. Doogood*) took building leases. A public appeal saved the square in 1925. Its garden remains, merged on the N side with a larger garden facing Fann Street. In 1997, the square is returning to residential use: flats by *Hunter & Partners*, 1995–7, stand on the N and E sides, the design disappointingly heavy; on the S side, flats are to be made within Nos. 6–9, offices of 1926, their tall round-headed window recesses spiced up with coloured brickwork by *Prudential Architects*, *c.* 1985.

BROADGATE
and FINSBURY AVENUE

The largest and most impressive private post-war development in the City. It proves that the voracious demands of commerce

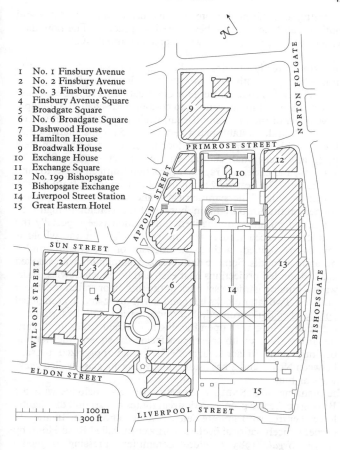

1   No. 1 Finsbury Avenue
2   No. 2 Finsbury Avenue
3   No. 3 Finsbury Avenue
4   Finsbury Avenue Square
5   Broadgate Square
6   No. 6 Broadgate Square
7   Dashwood House
8   Hamilton House
9   Broadwalk House
10 Exchange House
11 Exchange Square
12 No. 199 Bishopsgate
13 Bishopsgate Exchange
14 Liverpool Street Station
15 Great Eastern Hotel

Broadgate Development. Plan

and technology can work in harness with generous and humane principles of planning. What made it possible was the demolition of old Broad Street station in 1985, and British Rail's simultaneous desire to exploit the 'air rights' of Liverpool Street station, immediately E. Broad Street station was the terminus of the North London Railway, French Renaissance, by its engineer *W. Baker*, 1864–5 (altered 1913). There was no medieval Broad Gate. The architects, *Arup Associates* (S and W parts) and *Skidmore, Owings & Merrill*, senior partner *Bruce Graham* (N and E parts), worked closely with British Rail throughout (1985–91). Big atrium blocks are arranged on 29 acres (11¼ hectares) around three new pedestrian squares, two at the S and one at the NE. Their planning was determined by estimates of the natural routes pedestrians would follow. Grand axes are renounced in favour of the admirable English tradition of informal addition and opening-up of part from part. Construction made maximum use of prefabrication, including entire lavatory pods and pre-assembled cladding. Special pleasures include the large-scale sculpture, commissioned with commendable disregard for the tame and the pretty, and the no less imaginative use of water features and planting – all following the best American practice. The boundary revisions of 1994 brought the whole precinct into the City.

The story really begins earlier, in FINSBURY AVENUE, immediately w, with SBC WARBURG (No. 1), by *Peter Foggo* of *Arup Associates*, 1982–4. Built for Greycoat City Properties, whose director Stuart Lipton went on to co-found Rosehaugh Stanhope, developers of the main site. Begun while plans for the entire site were still fluid, it established a new standard for speculative office blocks, with its deep, flexible floor plans within a uniform steel grid, airy octagonal central atrium (upper parts infilled in 1996–7), and extremely rapid construction (thirteen weeks to raise the frame). The best view is not from the avenue but from Wilson Street (W side). The symmetrical E and W fronts are externally framed, in the Arup tradition, but detailed according to high-tech axioms of minimal, dramatized construction (see especially the taut cross-braced framing to the walkways). Yet the whole is immensely refined, without mannerism or extravagant multi-plication of motifs. Sombre dark-bronzed aluminium, with smoked glass. Rounded projections near each end house windowless stair-ways. Hanging gardens set back at the fifth floor soften the upper outlines. Two later blocks lie N and NW (Nos. 2 and 3, completed 1988), also dark-bronzed, but more varied and less rigorous externally: No. 2 with open framing to different scales on its vari-ous fronts, No. 3 with sheer glass facing the square, the framing behind visible in some lights. The broad top-glazed passage between Nos. 1 and 2 has astonishingly delicate glass-walled walk-ways high up.

The planning of FINSBURY AVENUE SQUARE belongs with the Broadgate Centre proper. Pedestrian routes run around the slightly lower centre, with granite setts, benches and trees. In the SW corner a nicely satirical bronze SCULPTURE called Rush Hour, by *George Segal*, 1983–7: glum commuters pressing doggedly forward; by the entrance from Eldon Street, S, a fountain with a falling sheet of water. The E side gives access to BROADGATE SQUARE, past an enigmatic glazed circular tower housing con-ference rooms. All the buildings are by *Arup Associates*. They make a more picturesque, less austere composition than the Finsbury Avenue ranges, with projecting towers and bays here and there, and non-matching corner turrets where the E block faces Liverpool Street. Lower floors have external *brise-soleil* screens of pink Swedish granite, in line with the revived fashion for polished stone; upper floors have aluminium-clad set-backs, the slightly messy roof-lines partly disguised by more hanging gardens. Green-tinted glazing. The stone screens vary in size from a square grid to close rectilinear patterns like Moorish lattices. Open colonnades below, extending along Liverpool Street and Eldon Street to the S. All the blocks have well-designed atria just within the façades, mostly opening on to or just within the inner corners of the square. All are worth a look, especially the circular one at No. 6 (NE corner).

The BROADGATE ARENA, centrepiece of the square, is a circular amphitheatre missing its SE quadrant, and rising up on the other

p. 143

150

sides in open, Travertine-faced tiers. Echoes of a Roman ruin are accentuated by hanging and climbing plants rambling over it. In summer the arena is used for displays and performances, and between times the steps and terraces attract people in the easy, unforced way of the best Italian cities; in winter it serves as a skating rink (the debt to the Rockefeller Center, New York, is clear). The tiers also house shops and restaurants. A lower level connects with the walkways and passages that enter from the S. Where a shop-lined passage from Liverpool Street station intersects from the E here, a SCULPTURE by *Richard Serra*, called Fulcrum, 1987. Five giant rusting iron slabs, upended and in equipoise. Of immense, tragic power. Other sculptures: SE corner, Leaping Hare on Crescent and Bell by *Barry Flanagan*, a visual pun; NW corner, Bellerophon taming Pegasus, by *Jacques Lipchitz*, 1966 (in the foyer of Union Bank of Switzerland, reached off Liverpool Street, a bronze horse, also by *Flanagan*). Where one leaves the square on the N side, steel GATES and SCREENS by *Alan Evans*; beyond, by Appold Street, Ganapathi and Devi by *Stephen Cox*, 1988, two oiled granite torsos, in a small garden ringed with trees.

All the rest is by *SOM*, of similar height and mostly also with atria inset at the entrances, but more varied and eclectic in style. Monotony is thus avoided, but with an inevitable loss of coherence, not helped by some awkward sites. First three blocks of diminishing size along Appold Street, built on the former railway approaches to Broad Street station. From S to N: No. 1 (DASHWOOD HOUSE), roughly cube-shaped, rather coarse, with chamfered corners and a big frontispiece with stair-towers flanking a round-arched rusticated entrance. Light brown stone facing; windows in a rhythm of two narrow and one broad. Wall drawings in the atrium by *Sol LeWitt*, 1988 (in the Broadgate Club, basement, a giant MOSAIC of a wave, designed by *Howard Hodgkin*). Then HAMILTON HOUSE, plainer, with narrow windows, and a forebuilding to Exchange House (*see* below), with a very Mediterranean glazed-tile FOUNTAIN by *Joan Artigas*, NW corner. N of Primrose Street, the much larger BROADWALK HOUSE, the only concrete-framed building here. Warm orange concrete cladding, a good approximation to terracotta (for the buildings opposite (W side), *see London 4: North*).

EXCHANGE SQUARE forms the centrepiece of the N section. It rests on a raft made high over the approach tracks to Liverpool Street. It is reached up steps between No. 1 Appold Street and Hamilton House. The dominant presence is EXCHANGE HOUSE (N side), the only block to show SOM's continuing development of the 152 steel-framed Miesian tradition. A simpler and more workmanlike handling than Arups' Finsbury Avenue: an even eleven-storey cage, the offices recessed a few feet within the dull blue framing. A parabolic arch spans the whole breadth, reaching near the top. Close inspection reveals its composition from a number of straight members, to regrettably jerky effect. With other arches concealed within, it carries the weight on to giant battered stone-faced pedestals at the corners. Bony, angled escape staircases on the return fronts. The ground floor is void, apart from a glazed box for escalators and lifts, and a spiral staircase down to offices in the plinth. The slot of sky thus exposed frames a fine distant view of

St Leonard, Shoreditch: the accidental result of the failure, so far, to complete the NE part, intended to bridge the tracks N of Primrose Street.

The other blocks, facing outwards to the streets around, relate much less well to the square, which does not really make a satisfactory whole. But there is plenty going on. The S side overlooks the restored train shed of Liverpool Street station, with dizzying views of departing trains. Little cafés and kiosks on the brink. Broad steps to the N face a central performance space. They curve out from a stone pier with ropes to support an awning. At the E end a huge shallow cascade; above and behind it a vast SCULPTURE by *Fernando Botero*, The Broadgate Venus, appears as if frolicking in the waters. SCULPTURE at the W end, The Broad Family, by *Xavier Corbero*, a very disturbing little gathering.

The final stretch faces Bishopsgate, built on a raft constructed over the E platforms of the station. Bishopsgate is reached from the NE corner via rather disappointing steps down to an alley. At the corner with Primrose Street, No. 199, a tall grey-stone-faced slab with a curved curtain-walled corner. SCULPTURE in front by *Bruce McLean*, called Eye-I, *c.* 1992: brightly painted open metal in the shape of a face. To the S, BISHOPSGATE EXCHANGE, the monster of the group: a vast, tyrannical, near-symmetrical office slab some 800 ft (244 metres) long, strenuously detailed in a Chicago Neo-Beaux-Arts way, faced in grey and red granite with sections of bronzed panelling. The grey granite runs up around the giant segmental projection in the centre and the flat bays just short of each end. Glazed gables here, versions of the over-familiar Crystal Palace type. Small turrets on the corners. Despite the expensive finishes (see the lamps, parapets and bus shelters in front), the whole savours strangely of the film-lot. The recessed ground floor gives access to the offices, via large lobbies interspersed with shops. More works of art in these lobbies. From N to S, No. 175 (EUROPEAN BANK OF RECONSTRUCTION AND DEVELOPMENT) has a giant, embarrassing fresco after Raphael, facing the escalator; No. 155 has twin bronze female torsos by *Jim Dine*, excessively large. Another walkway at the back of the block connects Exchange Square with the station's E entrance.

BRUSHFIELD STREET

Made in 1784–5. With Sun Street (partly erased by Liverpool Street station, opposite), it joined Spitalfields with Smithfield Market, via Chiswell Street. Called Union Street until 1870; Mr Brushfield was the local representative on the Metropolitan Board of Works. Only the SW section is in the City.

On the S side, Nos. 8 and 10, replicas of two-bay houses of the mid-1780s illegally demolished in 1983, then No. 14, the genuine article, in 1994 incorporated into the Bishopsgate Institute behind (q.v.). Christ Church Spitalfields unforgettably terminates the vista to the E.

BURY STREET

An L-shaped street, formerly the boundary between the Abbot of Bury St Edmunds' house (w side; cf. Bevis Marks) and Holy Trinity Priory.

One outstanding building: No. 32 (HOLLAND HOUSE), 1914–16 by 125 *Berlage*, the leading Dutch architect of his generation. For the Kroller-Mullers, Dutch shipping magnates and enlightened patrons of the arts. It is a remarkable design, very idiosyncratic, and very alien to the London of its date. Built after Berlage's visit to America in 1911, and showing the influence of Sullivan's great office buildings. Narrow four-storey SE front, separate W front a storey higher, both with intense vertical stress: a convention much exploited in Germany shortly afterwards. The steel frame is clad in wide-jointed faience coloured a nacreous grey-green. Its chamfered uprights merge into one windowless faceted mass in oblique views. Recessed floor panels with sunk bosses for ornament. Top storey set back, with openwork balcony also of faience. Plinth and angle strips of black granite, carried up around the entrances. The corner by the SE entrance is fashioned as an odd stylized ship's prow, alarmingly large (carver *J. Mendes da Costa*). Undistinguished W extension by *Gotch & Partners*, 1967: Portland stone uprights carrying on Berlage's, then smoked-glass bays further E.
  Interior decoration of 1916 by *Bart van der Leck*, its completion overseen by *Henri van der Velde* after Berlage fell out with the family. Strongly coloured, radically simple mosaic ceilings, octagonal light fittings etc., best seen in the entrance lobby of the W front. They have no contemporary parallel in English commercial interiors. Narrow iron staircase at the SE.
  The division into two fronts is to accommodate Nos. 33–34, SW. By *Delissa Joseph*, 1912, for Messrs Budge, grain dealers. Its French-influenced Portland stone forms appear embarrassingly staid in this context. Further N, E side: No. 12, a solid five-bay early C19 house with rusticated ground floor, perhaps built after most of Bury Street burnt out in 1811; Nos. 5–10, by *Hildebrandt & Glicker*, designed 1977, a long polished red Texan granite front with recessed splayed windows.
The W side belongs with the Baltic Exchange site (*see* St Mary Axe).

BYWARD STREET

Cut through from Great Tower Street to the SW corner of Trinity Square, 1882–4, in connection with the Metropolitan Railway line beneath. Very busy since the 1960s, when it was incorporated into the main E–W route along the river via an extension made from Lower Thames Street. All Hallows Barking lies on the S side.

On the N side at the W, KNOLLYS HOUSE, a slab by *Howard, Souster & Fairbairn*, completed 1962, refurbished *c.* 1985 with bronzed floor bands and narrow dark fins. Decorative ground-floor panels to a bank at the l. Then a block of typically solid early C20 Portland stone offices, of which only the hybrid No. 16 belongs in Byward Street (for the rest, *see* Trinity Square). Arcaded ground floor by *George Sherrin*, 1909, housing the former Mark Lane station (remodelled by *Haslemere Estates*, 1978, after the new station opened on Tower Hill). The upper storeys were offices for Messrs van den Bergh, margarine manufacturers, added by *Delissa Joseph*, 1911. Some French touches, such as Joseph's favourite piers with cartouche-capitals. A rear extension by *Joseph*, c. 1922, faces Muscovy Street.

CAMOMILE STREET

It follows the inner line of the City wall between Bishopsgate and St Mary Axe. The name records the abundance of this medicinal plant on the 16 ft (5 metres) of ground kept clear within the wall in the Middle Ages (cf. Wormwood Street).

Remains of a fine late C4 semicircular ROMAN BASTION, solid to its surviving height of 10 ft (3 metres), were revealed on the N side in 1876. Its builders had reused shattered remnants of sculptured monuments, including fragments of fluted pilasters, column shafts, canopies and cornices. Most had come from the cemetery at Bishopsgate (q.v.). Three particularly striking pieces are now in the Museum of London: a small lion, a colossal bearded head, and an uninscribed effigy of a legionary soldier or junior officer, dressed in late C1 style and holding a stylus and writing tablets.

The Fraternity of the Papey, a hospital for poor priests founded in 1442 in the former parish church of St Augustine Papey, stood at the NE corner with St Mary Axe until the Reformation.

On the S side, the former Ellerman Lines, 1955–7 by *Fitzroy Robinson & Hubert H. Bull*. Projecting lower storeys with narrow uprights, tall neutral stone-faced slab above, heightened since. Opposite towards the W end, KEMPSON HOUSE, by *C. Lovett Gill & Partners*, 1959–61, amongst the first free-standing polygonal office towers in London. The plan is an elongated hexagon of moderate size and height (fourteen storeys), stone-faced to Camomile Street, curtain-walled on the other sides. Pilotis carry a low W wing across a driveway. Silly porch added c. 1988. OUTWICH STREET, immediately E, was cut through to Houndsditch across the old line of the wall as late as 1963. Facing it, MEES PIERSON (No. 23), by *Holford Associates*, 1988–90, a routine atrium block with curved corners and shallow bows above darker rusticated stone. Recessed in its Camomile Street front, a little planted court: the former burial ground of St Martin Outwich (*see* Bishopsgate, S end).

CANNON STREET

The E part of Cannon Street follows the line of a Roman street, part of which was found beneath St Swithin in 1960–1. On its S side, beneath Cannon Street station, stood the monumental Roman building complex known as the Governor's Palace (*see* Introduction p. 34). Further W, Cannon Street crosses what was a prosperous quarter within the early Roman town, and several fine town houses have been excavated hereabouts (*see* Watling Court, below). The houses were associated with the road to Ludgate, which was deflected N from the present direct alignment by the need to cross the Walbrook (*see* Watling Street). Sunken timber cellars of the C10–C11 have been discovered in the W part: beneath Bracken House (S side) in 1955, and on the site of Watling Court (N side) in 1978. The latter included the largest so far found, later used as the foundation for a square C12 masonry structure, possibly the tower of a great house. These cellars indicate that an important market was then being carried on in the area between Queenhithe and Cheapside. The medieval Cannon Street – once Candlewick or Candlewright (i.e. candle-maker) Street – was extended W of Walbrook in 1847–54, to plans drawn up by *J. B. Bunning* in 1846. It superseded the ancient line of Watling Street and Budge Row as the main route E out of St Paul's Churchyard. The S side of the medieval part was widened too.

The significant architectural division is not now that between original part and extension, but results from heavy air-raid damage at the W end, so that everything from St Paul's to Queen Victoria Street dates from the 1950s or after. To the E, some classical 1850s warehouses survive; then further E a mixed C19–C20 bag in the oldest part of the street. The slope down into the valley of the Walbrook halfway along is still marked.

North side, from the West

First, GATEWAY HOUSE (formerly Wiggins Teape), by *Trehearne & Norman, Preston & Partners*, 1953–6. A big block still in the cornice-line tradition, but with the pretty abstract decoration of the time. Gently curved front, set back, with a projecting wing on the r. In the angle a green forecourt, continuing the bits of gardening SE of St Paul's. Brown or yellow brick used in bold blocks (ground floor altered 1979); abstract Venetian glass mosaic panels (first floor) and tiles (cornice) designed by *M. S. Rice*. Glazed and rounded attic storey, set back. Central pedestrian passage on the line of the former Friday Street. Set up in 1968 against the E wall, BUST of Admiral Arthur Philip, founder and first Governor of Australia, a copy of that by *C. L. Hartwell* at St Mary-le-Bow (q.v.). Flanking reliefs by *W. Hamilton Buchan* and *Sharon Keenan* (a replacement of 1976). The originals came from a towering monument of 1932, designed by *D. Hope-Johnston* and *J. Reeve Young*, formerly attached to the destroyed St Mildred Bread Street. At Nos. 31–37, a new building by *Arup Associates* is intended (1996).

WATLING COURT at Nos. 41–53 beyond (MIDLAND BANK) is by *Fitzroy Robinson & Partners*, 1977–81. Strongly articulated, with exposed bronzed polygonal bays between paired stone-clad verticals. Too heavy altogether. Behind, it accommodates itself to Bow Lane and Watling Street with a polite mixture of small-scale vertical sections and retained and pastiche façades, arranged around an enlarged SALTERS' COURT. Inside the main entrance is a small display summarizing the excavations here in 1978. Next to it, fragments of two ROMAN MOSAIC PAVEMENTS from a well-appointed town house of *c.* A.D. 80–90. Although poorly preserved,

they are notable as some of the earliest such pavements known
from Britain. The small black-and-white tesserae are typical of
the period. The larger formed the border to a substantial pavement, and incorporates a register of leaves and tendrils. The other
is a quartered circle, one of nine such inset within a red tile and
concrete (*opus signinum*) pavement, unfortunately displayed without any indication of its original setting.

Beyond Queen Victoria Street, Nos. 61–63, *c.*1855, of the lofty
Italianate type. No. 65 is an older survivor: the former Sugar Loaf,
an interesting pub of *c.*1820–30 with the familiar curved corner
and shallow round-headed recesses, but around the windows
unusual Grecian aedicules, blockish and flat. On the other corner
with Queen Street, Nos. 69–73, the former London Chamber of
Commerce by *Gunton & Gunton*, 1933–57, built in three stages
but one style. Tepidly Deco with plain stone mullions. Open
bronze panels by the main entrance, in the oldest part. Refurbishment in 1974–80 by *Farrington Dennis Fisher* added storeys on the
r. and a lumpy copper-clad roof extension.

The little passage called TOWER ROYAL, beyond, preserves the
name of the medieval mansion also commemorated in St Michael
Paternoster Royal. After this come the long rear ranges of Temple
Court and Bucklersbury House (*see* Queen Victoria Street).
WALBROOK HOUSE on the corner with Walbrook, plain, stone-
faced and dull, by *Henry Tanner*, 1957. Nos. 97–101, HABIB
BANK, a refacing of 1976–8 by *Whinney, Son & Austen Hall* of
an inter-war building. Flat front, brown granite clad, punctuated
by six repetitious storeys of close-set projecting windows; excessively tall sloping attic above with windows recessed between big
stone fins. At No. 103 are *Fred Jameson*'s polychromatic stone
offices for the Registered Land Company, 1866. A remarkable
mid-Victorian Veneto-Byzantine effort: ground floor and first
floor of four bays with large arched openings, second floor with
windows no less wide but of two lights, top floor with eight
instead of four windows – a flush, even, carefully planned façade,
and an early example of the doubling of the windows as the
storeys rise. *Seale* did the carving. Nos. 105–109, 1974–8 by

Cannon Street.
Elevations between Dowgate Hill and Queen Street *c.* 1856

Richard Sheppard, Robson & Partners, tall and narrow to the street with a splayed and cantilevered corner, and on the r. a windowless polygonal stair-tower: a strongly modelled composition, sleekly clad in polished red Dakota granite with big bronzed mirrored windows.

This brings us to SALTERS' HALL COURT, named from the Salters' Company, whose three successive halls of 1641–1941 lay to the N (*see* Salters' Hall). On its N side, the CHURCHYARD of *Wren*'s St Swithin of 1677–86, burnt out in the Second World War and later demolished. Its square interior was spanned by a unique octagonal dome, echoed in the octagon made by the scooped-out upper corners of the NW tower and the octagonal leaded spire above. Excavations in 1960–1 revealed reuse of foundations of an aisled church of *c.* 1420. It had three-bay arcades, with traces of a possible NW tower. Fragmentary chalk foundations of its predecessor suggested a slight building with a s aisle, of uncertain date (first records are late C12). An inscribed late C13 heart-burial slab with engraved figure found here is in the Museum of London. The churchyard survives as a raised garden in the court.

No. 111, the OCB CORPORATION, occupies the site of the church. By *Biscoe & Stanton,* 1961–2, tall and rather narrow, with neat curtain-walling on piers of serpentine marble. In its s front the mysterious *Saxum Londiniense* or LONDON STONE, placed behind an iron grille, just as it formerly appeared in the s wall of the church. It previously stood on the s side, near the middle of the present widened Cannon Street. Known to have been a London landmark by *c.* 1100, its purpose and significance are unknown, though it appears to have stood on the site of the entrance to the great Roman building known as the Governor's Palace. It has been speculated that it formed part of a column from the entrance façade, or that it was the milestone from which distances were measured in Roman Britain. Only a rounded apex of Clipsham limestone remains, with grooves worn in the top.

Beyond St Swithin's Lane, Nos. 113–121 were refurbished or rebuilt by *William Nimmo & Partners* for the Drapers' Company, 1981–4.

No. 113 on the corner is by *E. A. Gruning*, 1869–70. Still Italianate, orthodox by comparison with his contemporary work in Tokenhouse Yard (q.v.). Paired columns of pink Peterhead granite to the ground floor, and columns to the first-floor tripartite windows; bracket cornice with rounded dormers above. Much exposed structural ironwork within and below the ground-floor windows. Nos. 115–117, 1875 by *J. L. Holmes*, have very large windows divided by tiers of tall polished columns of Tuscan derivation. The SHOP on the l. (No. 115) is of special interest as a work by *Walter Gropius* and *Maxwell Fry*, 1936. It has the black Vitrolite glass facing of many luxury shops of the day (it was originally the Mortimer Gall electrical goods showroom), but there is a whiff of Dessau in the free-standing cylindrical stanchion by the curved corner and the glass bricks of the stall-riser. No. 119 (SHERBORNE HOUSE), infill of 1981–4, stone-faced and flat in a simplified version of the 1850s warehouses on the S side. To SHERBORNE LANE, behind, it is of red brick, with entrance through No. 14, a retained stone façade of 1892, nicely licentious Renaissance. The lane's name euphemistically contracts the *Shittebowrelane* recorded in 1276.

In Cannon Street again, No. 121, tall and narrow free classical of 1904–5, perhaps by *Davis & Emmanuel*. Nos. 123–127 are by *Huntly Gordon*, 1894–5. Very red brick and terracotta. Big, asymmetrical relieving arches to the shop windows. Asymmetrical top to match, and on the l. a frieze with putti doing divers kinds of jobs. There are some Art Nouveau touches. No. 129, dated 1899, shows a rather mechanical use of Arts-and-Crafts motifs. Nos. 131–133 by *Campbell-Jones, Son & Smithers*, dated 1921, conventional plain classical. Across Abchurch Lane, Nos. 135–141 by *Haslemere Estates*, 1979–81, partly a recladding of a building of 1957, l., and partly a replacement for a building of 1884–5 by *Sherrin*, r. (for its retained side façade, *see* Abchurch Lane). Then Nos. 143–149, the former Phoenix Assurance, a curtain-walled slab by *Lewis Solomon, Kaye & Partners*, 1962–3. For the corner building, *see* King William Street.

South side, from the West

The first building is the L-shaped former Old Change House at Nos. 2–6, by *Theo H. Birks*, 1958–9, with a long side elevation towards DISTAFF LANE. Windows and infill panels were replaced by *Lister, Drew & Associates*, 1982. The present Distaff Lane forms a slip-road down to Queen Victoria Street. Up to the 1850s this route was called Little Distaff Lane, while Distaff Lane proper became part of the Cannon Street extension. Distaffs were made and sold there from at least the C12.

To its E, BRACKEN HOUSE, built in 1955–9 for the *Financial Times* by *Sir Albert Richardson*, the central part rebuilt to great effect for the Obayashi Corporation by *Michael Hopkins & Partners*, 1988–91. Pevsner described it in 1962 as 'puzzling . . . not of the Classical Re-Revival or Neo-Georgian which one otherwise connects with Sir Albert; rather as if it were a self-conscious revival of a forty-year-old "Modern"'. But in fact Bracken House has strong affinities with Richardson's other post-war buildings,

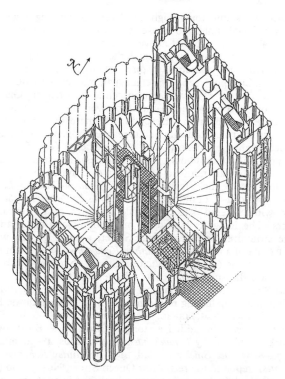

Cannon Street, Bracken House. Axonometric view

e.g. the demolished rear ranges at Trinity House (*see* Public Buildings). Moreover, if classicism depends on the implied presence of a controlling order, Bracken House is classical indeed; that is, in the classical manner of Gunnar Asplund or – still more – of Schinkel. The façades of its two office blocks survive, facing N and S. Their Hollington sandstone plinths and rosy brick piers evoke the pink of the *F. T.*'s pages. The copper cornice has weathered to a harmonious green. Chamfered corners. Newspaper offices lay in the N block, the entrance marked by an elaborate astrological CLOCK. Its central sun has the features of Churchill (the chairman Sir Brendan Bracken's former boss), modelled by *Frank Dobson*. The S block, on a skewed axis, housed offices for rent. It is similar but for the rounded stair-turrets at the corners.

Richardson's octagonal printing house between them has been replaced by *Hopkins'* new office core, designed after Bracken House the first post-war building to be Listed in 1987. The result is a compromise, but a brilliant one. The older architect claimed inspiration from the plan of Guarini's Palazzo Carignano, Turin, where flat wings flank an elliptical entrance block. Hopkins' curved fronts achieve a closer correspondence to this model, making greater use of the site. Indeed, they bulge out as if squashed in the vice of Richardson's blocks. Close-set projecting bays four storeys high cantilever out from big brackets. Dull gun-metal finish to these and to the elegantly bony cylindrical framing exposed above. The bays have on each side single green-tinted panes which catch the light as the front curves. Iron-framed C19 buildings inspired their forms (e.g. Oriel Chambers, Liverpool, 1864 by Peter Ellis), but here structure and ornament fuse in a way that transcends historicism. Glazed canopy on a spindly metal skeleton over the Friday Street entrance. Attic and plinth correspond to Richardson's. An atrium lies N–S around a central core of lifts reached by glazed walkways. The details are more delicate than on the exterior (e.g. the metal grids and glass-brick floors of the balconies), but machine-like enough to evoke an industrial rather than electronic age.

Next, No. 20, a slick recladding by *Whinney Mackay-Lewis Partnership*, 1982–3, of offices by *Stone, Toms & Partners*, 1960–1. Black with silvered sills-cum-balconies projecting; rounded corners. The image is high-tech, but without any articulation of the structure. Towards Friday Street, a small garden with SCULPTURE of a leopard by *Jonathan Kenworthy*, 1985. Then the Crédit Lyonnais (*see* Queen Victoria Street). Nos. 40–46, built 1853–5, are the surviving W part of a terrace that extended to Queen Street. Brick, still classical as much as Italianate, with a running moulding linking round-headed first-floor windows. Big bracket cornice. Nos. 44–46, l., were rebuilt 1981–4 by *T. P. Bennett & Son*, who added a storey. (CORNEY & BARROW'S restaurant at No. 44 by *Tchaik Chassay*, 1985.) Nos. 48–50, offices of 1974–8 by *Alec Shickle* (reclad 1996 by *Hurley Robertson & Associates*), replaced the rest. After Queen Street, Nos. 52–60 (by *Cotton, Ballard & Blow*, 1971) were demolished in 1996 for a new building by *Seifert Ltd*. Nos. 62–74 are mostly survivors of 1850s warehouses. They may be by such architects as *T. Hague*, *J. T. Knowles Sen.*, *Elkington* or *Griffiths*, all of whom were busy in the street. Painted brick above stone or stucco, with channelled end piers of quoins and big cornices above. No. 64 is more consequential, with an arcaded ground floor with mask key-blocks. (Storeys added to Nos. 62–64 by *GMW Partnership*, 1980–2.) Nos. 66–68, a replacement of *c.* 1910. Nos. 70–74, originally only two storeys high and one room deep, once made a symmetrical composition with the demolished No. 76. Tripartite windows to the first floor, further up the scale of Italianate enrichment than its neighbours. Raised by two storeys apparently in the later C19; then given a mansard in 1982–4 by *Ley, Colbeck & Partners*, who extended it on to the former churchyard of St John the Baptist, facing Cloak Lane behind. The present No. 76 is of 1985–8 by *The Halpern Partnership*, red brick and stone in an inter-war manner, with a big curved bow and dominant rounded attic storeys.

After Cannon Street station (*see* Public Buildings), No. 80 on the corner with Bush Lane, a startling tower by *Arup Associates*, 1972–6, stocky with chamfered corners, prominent in views from the W. London Transport's proposed Fleet Line ran under the site, requiring that the tower be raised high on four giant steel legs. The space beneath, to have housed a new station, has instead a garden with on the r. a patent-glazed entrance lobby (rebuilt 1994–5). But the feature one remembers is the stainless steel diagonal lattice across the dark reflective glass cladding. It realizes in steel the 'exoskeleton' principle used earlier by the practice (e.g. at the Vaughan Building, Somerville College, Oxford), but with more than a nod to Buckminster Fuller. The framing takes the full weight of the floors, which can thus be column-free within. Fire regulations required that the frame be filled with water. The juxtaposition with the verticals carried up from the legs is awkward, and the diagonal lattice is hard to reconcile with one's expectations of load-bearing structure; but as an engineering solution it is pleasingly ingenious.

Less excitement thereafter. Nos. 86–88, warehouses of 1851, match those further w. Nos. 90–96, the BANK OF CHINA by the *GMW Partnership*, 1989–91, a routine Postmodern job, symmetrical in polished granite with a glazed centrepiece and the usual set-backs and simplified cornice. It extends w to a brick-clad elevation facing BUSH LANE. The lane, named from a tavern known in 1445, runs s down towards Upper Thames Street, but is blocked there by Princess House (q.v.). No. 28, on its corner with Gophir Lane (E), pastiche early C19, belongs with the Bank of China scheme, but THE BELL pub at No. 29 (l.) is the authentic early Victorian article.

Back in Cannon Street Nos. 98–106, BANCO BILBAO VIZCAYA, a stone-faced building by *Gervase Bailey* of 1936–7 (refurbished 1980). No. 108, RABOBANK NEDERLAND, 1986–90 by *Seifert Ltd*, stone-faced with windows alternately wide and narrow. Small sculpture at the E corner, Break the Wall of Distrust, by *Zurab Tsereteli*, 1990. Nos. 110–114, between Laurence Pountney Lane and Martin Lane, by *Elsom, Pack & Roberts*, 1972–7, make a small precinct with a lower block behind. Cladding of red Swedish granite, absolutely flush in the YRM manner. Nos. 116–126 are the featureless Candlewick House, 1935 by *Val Myer & Watson Hart*. Towering copper-clad mansard added *c.* 1979 by *Peter Black & Partners*. The curved E corner towards King William Street marks the alignment of the former Crooked Lane.

CARMELITE STREET

First listed in 1893; still with much red brick architecture of that decade. The alignment roughly follows the old Whitefriars Dock, infilled when the Victoria Embankment was made (q.v.).

On the w SIDE near the N end, No. 4, WHEATSHEAF HOUSE, a stately warehouse of 1891 by *Wylson & Long*. Lower two storeys recessed within applied round-arched arcading, plain pilasters to the upper storeys. The square N tower looks like an afterthought. No. 6, the former National Press Agency, mostly faces s on to Tallis Street. By *E. T. Hall*, 1896. The applied arcading is here of full height, with terracotta bays protruding on the first floor. Two-storey oriel over the corner entrance. Then CARMELITE HOUSE, oldest survivor of the great newspaper factories in the Fleet Street quarter. By *H. O. Ellis*, 1897–9, for Lord Northcliffe's Associated Newspapers. Neo-Tudor red brick and stone, the storeys vertically diminishing, with flat bays between half-octagonal buttresses carried up as pinnacles. Big square corner tower with a leaded ogee lantern. The restored stairhall below has delicate, incongruous Pompeian decoration and a central lift-shaft with decorative iron guards; no grand reception space otherwise. Lord Northcliffe's Empire-style boardroom (*c.* 1900), later moved to Northcliffe House in Tudor Street, is now at the new Associated Newspapers headquarters in Kensington High Street (*see London 3: North West*). The façades have been incorporated into New Carmelite House (Victoria Embankment, q.v.), which also replaced *Ellis & Clarke*'s carefully proportioned extension of 1936.

On the E SIDE, the block N of Tallis Street retains façades from the Guildhall School of Music (*see* John Carpenter Street). In the centre of the S part, No. 7, formerly the chief fire station of the City division. By the *LCC Architects' Department* (Fire Department architect *Robert Pearsall*), 1896–7. Excessively tall and plain Neo-Tudor Gothic, drily detailed. Rebuilt behind by *Halpern & Partners*, 1978–82.

CARTER LANE

Called *Carterestrate* in 1295, when it ran E from the Blackfriars precincts to the line of Old Change. The E part, called Little Carter Lane until 1866, now lies open to St Paul's (*see* St Paul's Churchyard (s side)). Further w, pre-c20 buildings survive thanks to decades of planning blight caused by an abortive plan to divert E–W traffic s of St Paul's. Rebuilding in and around the lane since *c.* 1985 has diluted but not erased the area's nicely half-forgotten air, with courts and still narrower lanes between mostly Victorian warehouses.

On the S side at the W end Nos. 79 and 81, two modest c18 houses (dated *c.* 1720 by Dan Cruickshank), with early c19 stucco fronts. Both have little low attics with horizontally-sliding sashes. The tiny CARTER COURT, entered through No. 81, is an atmospheric survival of the kind of close that, crowded with poor tenants, made up the foulest London slums. On the N side, Nos. 68–74, a warehouse dated 1880. Of brick, with big iron columns and polished granite door jambs. To its E, Nos. 56–66, part of the Cobb's Court development (*see* Ludgate Hill), here with a replica front of 1860s Lombardic character, l., and a plainer, looser section beyond; then Nos. 52–54 by the *John Brunton Partnership*, 1986–7. A filled ditch found beneath the site in 1986 may have been that of the c12 Montfitchet Tower, which stood near here until 1276.

Opposite (s side again), warehouses of *c.* 1890–1930, then No. 69 by *Michael Squire Associates*, 1988–91, offices in patterned brick and with a chamfered corner, tactful without dullness; a fragment of the Blackfriars is preserved within (*see* Black Friars Lane). Honest, robust warehouse of 1864 at Nos. 63–67 (contractors *Newman & Mann*), then the RISING SUN pub at No. 61, *c.* 1840, with fine Ionic columns to the ground floor. Facing (N side) are modest warehouses of 1877–80 (Nos. 42–50), part of the Ludgate Square development off Creed Lane to the N (*see* Ludgate Hill). Between Burgon Street and St Andrew's Hill (s side), No. 59a, *c.* 1900, reverts to the early C19 device of windows in round-arched recesses. Beyond, the entrance to Wardrobe Place (q.v.) is made under No. 58, which looks C18 under its stucco (rebuilt behind, 1990). Next, offices of 1883–4 by *George Edwards* in white brick, extending down ADDLE HILL. At the bottom, the former Bell pub, 1879–81 by *C. H. Cooke*. The lowering building opposite, built 1890–4 by *Sir Henry Tanner* of the *Office of Works* for the Post Office Central Savings Bank, has been adapted as part of the adjacent telephone exchange called Faraday House (*see* Public Buildings). It has superimposed Doric orders set against white-glazed brick. The old name *Athelingestrate* implies the residence of a Saxon prince, but Addle Hill was truncated by Queen Victoria Street in 1867 and hardly looks regal today.

Back in Carter Lane, the N side up to Dean's Court is the former ST PAUL'S CHOIR SCHOOL, 1874–5 by *Penrose* in what might be called the South Kensington style, that is with rich Renaissance sgraffito decoration along the first floor, Venetian windows, and a general air of Bergamo or Brescia. These parts are more attractive than the other finishes, of pale stone, terracotta and brick. Used as a youth hostel since 1975 (restored by *Niall Phillips Associates*, 1991–2). The little red brick front dated 1890, l., probably also by *Penrose*, was the entry to the former Deanery stables.

For the buildings further E, *see* St Paul's Churchyard.

CARTHUSIAN STREET

Named of course from the Charterhouse to the N (*see* Charterhouse Square). Excavations on the S side in 1986 indicated settlement in the C13, before the monks came (1371). The area was then on the City's outermost fringes. The present street dates from at least the C17. The N side was widened in 1819, when James Humphreys, victualler, undertook to build six houses. Nos. 6–7 are probably of that date. The SUTTON ARMS next door, a good Neo-Jacobean pub of 1898, preserves its entrance front.

One building on the S side: the CHAMBER OF SHIPPING, in a block of 1985–9 by *Ronald Ward & Partners*, including ten flats. Red brick, laid herringbone-fashion beneath the windows, reminiscent of late C19 commercial Gothic. Entrance under a rounded gable, l. On the front a cast-iron SIGN from the previous Chamber in Bury Court. Shallow barrel-vaulted lobby.

CHANCERY LANE

The backbone of the legal quarter, a slow curve and a slow climb from Fleet Street and the Temple to Holborn and Gray's Inn. Made *c.* 1160 through the Templars' farmland; in 1278 called *Converslane*, after the house for converted Jews on the E side, founded *c.* 1231. Edward III gave this to the Keeper of the Rolls of Chancery in 1377; the Public Record Office (q.v.) stands on the site. Gardens lined the lane in the early C16: Lincoln's Inn on the W side, those of the Bishops of Chichester and of Lincoln opposite. Lincoln's Inn still dominates the NE part, built right up to the street with no gardens or tenements between. Otherwise much rewarding C19–C20 architecture, plenty of ripe High Victorian commercial fronts amongst them. Since 1994 the E side is wholly in the City, the w side in the Borough of Camden (Holborn to Lincoln's Inn) and City of Westminster (Bishop's Court to Fleet Street).

Both sides are taken together. We begin at the Fleet Street end. One big building on the E side, some way up: DENTON HALL, Beaux-Arts Baroque by *A. C. Blomfield* for the Law Union and Rock Insurance, 1911. Angled square entrance tower, squared-off details after Joass or Holden. Reconstructed around an atrium by *Knapton, Deane & Thompson*, 1984–8 (banking hall by *T. B. Whinney* retained). It replaced buildings of Serjeants' Inn (q.v.).

The w side facing was mostly widened after 1855. The tall fronts, in various styles and materials, nicely demonstrate the mid-Victorian progress from enriched historicism into unbridled eclecticism. First No. 126, the former Law Union Insurance, 1857 by *J. Warnham Penfold*, Neo-Jacobean in yellow-brown stone, with bitty badges on the pilasters and a fancy parapet. No. 125 is *George Legg*'s former Mitre Tavern, 1855–6. Italianate stucco, round-arched windows, round-arched shopfront with Corinthian columns and dosserets supporting vases and little caryatids. Nos. 123–124, by *F. H. Fowler*, 1858–9, for Button's the confectioner, polychromatic brick and stone, round-arched with some Lombardic cast-iron tracery, but still with a Renaissance cornice. No. 122, by *Michael Squire Associates*, 1989–91, part of rebuilding behind Nos. 123–126: thoughtfully detailed stone-faced infill, with an entrance to the yard called Andrews Crosse. Nos. 119–120, 1860, ripest Italianate stucco with a big console-cornice. Nos. 116–118, two early C19 brick houses. No. 116 has shallow round-arched window surrounds; perhaps rebuilt after a fire in 1824. No. 115, the former Hodgson's the auctioneers, 1863 by *G. Pownall*, set off-centre to a little linking r. bay. Round-arched windows, very plain brick above, smothered in carved masks, bats, and columns with foliage capitals below.

No. 114, the former Law Fire Office by *Thomas Bellamy*, 1857–9, taller and infinitely more refined. Professor Donaldson in his obituary for Bellamy said that in this front he 'rose to the level of Palladio'. Be that as it may, it is an imposing and restrained piece of Italianate design. Three bays, with steps up to the columned central doorcase. The three storeys diminish in scale and in degrees of rustication. Delicately carved Cinquecento details by *C. S. Kelsey* (see the arabesques of firemen's helmets etc. on the doorcase). Similar details on Bellamy's rear extension facing Bell Yard, 1874–6. Inside, a lavish open-well staircase behind a screen made by tall Ionic columns, leading to a first-floor boardroom: an ensemble worthy of a medium-sized West End club and unusual in the Victorian City, where display rooms generally kept to the ground floor. Fine iron balustrade with little Ionic colonnettes. No. 114 was converted in 1996 by *Blee Ettwein Bridges*, for the Law Society next door (q.v.).

Facing the Law Society, the gaunt Public Record Office (q.v.). Further N (E side), No. 22, WEATHERALL, GREEN & SMITH, a solid six-storey block with narrow upright window slots in

Portland roach, by the *Kenzie Lovell Partnership*, 1975, and No. 27,
LONSDALE CHAMBERS, 1876, long, formal and uninspired.

Back on the w side, No. 95, the stately former Union Bank of
London, 1865 by *F. W. Porter*. Three superimposed pilaster orders
face Carey Street. Screens of columns stand in front on the
Chancery Lane front: an unusually profligate display for a branch
bank (it cost £29,100). Canted corner entrances, lively skyline
of chimneys and dormers. Banking hall with slender iron
columns. Nos. 93–94, EDE & RAVENSCROFT, *c.*1890 by
Knightley, sophisticatedly plain, the red bricks variously laid and
carved, showing the influence of advanced Gothic Revival work.
Fine contemporary interior with display cases, restored *c.*1992.
No. 92 looks Georgian, with a mid-C19 stucco front. Nos. 88–90,
DENNING HOUSE, broad stone Neo-Jacobean with a little
oriel, by *Waterman & Lewis*, 1900. The very narrow No. 87,
Butterfieldian Gothic chambers of bright red and yellow brick, by
the young *Arthur Blomfield*, 1863. The original ground-floor
design, a big two-centred arch, was re-created *c.*1993. Then at
Nos. 80–86 a development of 1990, stitching together three unremarkable Queen Anne façades (No. 80 dated 1891), with a
crude new section bridging a shopping arcade made in
CHICHESTER RENTS. With BISHOP'S COURT to the N, the
name commemorates the Bishop of Chichester's property here,
mostly rented from the early C15 by Lincoln's Inn. Chambers for
the Inn above the stone-faced POST OFFICE beyond, 1966–9 by
K. A. Williams, quite elegant, with a hipped slated roof (called
Hale Court). For the rest of Lincoln's Inn, *see London 4: North*.

On the E SIDE, No. 33, red brick early French Gothic with black
bands, probably by *Giles & Gough*, 1873–4 (but given to *A.
Bridgman* in *Building News* 31, 1875). The C19 design was repeated
facing Rolls Passage in reconstruction by *EPR*, 1988. HALSBURY
HOUSE, 1989–91 by *BDP*, grey granite-clad, has detail indebted
to Terry Farrell. Recessed segmental bays to Cursitor Street. On
its N corner, SUN ALLIANCE HOUSE (Nos. 40–43), five-storey
chambers probably of the later 1830s, much extended, spoiled by
horrible brown rendering. Nos. 44–45, by *Howard V. Lobb &
Partners*, a clean curtain-walled job of 1964–5, the design repeated
at Nos. 48–49, 1973. OLDEBOURNE HOUSE between (Nos.
46–47), severe brick chambers of 1892 with mullioned window
bands, survives from a pair by *Somers Clarke Jun.* and *J. T.
Micklethwaite*. It gives access to the little QUALITY COURT,
where QUALITY HOUSE (s side) is by *Gervase Bailey*, 1928,
somewhat after designs by *Oliver Hill*, 1924. Still in the Lutyens-
Wrenaissance manner, well-detailed and in good materials: grey
brick with red lacing, above a stone-faced basement. Strype
derived the court's name from newly-built houses there (1720).

Continuing on the E side, Nos. 50–52, LAW SOCIETY HOUSE,
again by *H. V. Lobb & Partners*, 1973–7, brown brick with groups
of slit windows. Then *Richardson & Houfe*'s inflated CHANCERY
HOUSE, 1947–53. Brick and stone, dogmatically composed in the
manner of a Parisian hôtel, that is with a tall rear range and l. and
r. wings joined by a low entrance range (since heightened).
Elevations with stripped brick pilasters, without the clarity of
Richardson's best pre-war work. Beneath lie the London Silver

Vaults, successors to the safe deposit vaults in NEW STONE
COURT here, undertaken by *Thomas Clarke* to his own designs,
1880–90. Part of its immensely monotonous stone front remains
at Nos. 67–72, following an ugly gap left by bombing. Small
pilaster-piers to the storeys, each with different windows, still in
the manner of *c.* 1870. Facing, after Lincoln's Inn, fussy buildings
of 1876: No. 76, red brick Gothic by *Alfred M. Ridge*, with a giant
pointed arch and balcony in the gable; Nos. 74–75 by *Lewis Isaacs*,
French Renaissance, formerly continuing w along High Holborn.

CHARTERHOUSE SQUARE

Charterhouse Square perpetuates the site of the cemetery of the
Carthusian monastery which Sir Walter Manny founded in 1371. He
had previously given land here to the City to bury victims of the
Black Death (1348–9). The surviving monastery buildings lie on the
N. Since the Dissolution, they have served successively as house,
school, and almshouses (*see London 4: North*).

The leafy square (called Charterhouse Yard in the C17) is actually
an irregular pentagon in shape. It retains cobbled roadways and
gates. Described in 1708 as 'a pleasant place of good, and many new
buildings'; but successive waves of commercial and industrial building have left it with somewhat motley architecture.

Of the early period only Nos. 4–5 (E side), four-storey houses of
c. 1700, refronted in yellow brick with red trim in the late C19.
Three bays each, with another half-bay on No. 5. Flush windows.
Doorcases of *c.* 1840 perpetuate the original paired arrangement.
Nos. 2–3, r., a lodging-house with clumsy late C19 Jacobean
stucco ornament towards Carthusian Street. To the l. of Nos. 4–5,
FLORIN COURT is a towering ten-storey block of businessmen's
flats of 1936 by *Guy Morgan*. Buff brick variously patterned, modishly streamlined around the recessed entrance. Inside were
squash courts, a dining room and cocktail bar. Then Nos. 10–11,
Neo-Georgian, with twin canted bays uneasily cantilevered out,
by *H. C. Wilkerson & Partners*, 1957–9. At r. angles to them and
backing on to the Charterhouse proper, a group of four nicely varied early C19 houses: No. 12a, 1825–6, narrow, with brick frieze
and two-storey rounded bow; Nos. 12–13, with sunk panels above
the second-floor windows; No. 14, with round-arched first-floor
windows and an extra storey. Next to it, the railings, wall and
gatehouse of the Charterhouse precinct, with other buildings
rising behind in fairy-tale isolation.

Beyond the gatehouse, a hefty block of red brick chambers (Nos.
18–21): the former Charterhouse Hotel, by the Charterhouse's
Surveyor *E. B. I'Anson*, 1902. Symmetrical with three gables and
three bays. No. 22, l., is a survivor of five houses built 1786–8 by
John Wilkinson Long, carpenter of Christ's Hospital. Doorway of
the Bedford Square pattern with vermiculated rustication and
Coade stone mask. A covered passage with another mask and
swags over gives access to a mews. (A first-floor ceiling has C19
painted roundels of Architecture, Music, Painting and Sculpture,
by sometime resident *Thomas Stowers*, landscape and topo-

graphical painter.) Substantial iron GATES in front, probably of 1791, mark the site of the Charterhouse's gatehouse. Hollow uprights with urn-finials divide the central roadway from pedestrian gates on each side.

The w side is the former Collett's hat factory, c. 1956–60 by *Lewis Solomon, Son & Joseph*. In 1988 converted to a bank: the square would benefit from its replacement. The s side became part of the City in 1994. It is all utilitarian brick warehouses of the large-windowed showroom type, built 1876–8 after the Metropolitan Railway cutting was made behind (1861–5) and an extension of Charterhouse Street was cut into the square's sw corner (1869–75). *Coutts Stone* designed the central group (Nos. 37–40). Most now serve as offices and studios. *CZWG*'s conversion of No. 41 (1980) was amongst the first. *Harper Mackay* adapted No. 33 for themselves in 1994, opening up the acute s corner's stairwell but keeping its C19 wooden staircase.

CHARTERHOUSE STREET

A long straight street made 1869–75 between the newly formed Holborn Circus and Smithfield Market. The older and narrower Charterhouse Lane was incorporated at the E end, where it turns N into Charterhouse Square. Since 1994 Charterhouse Street has marked the City's northern boundary, superseding a line wavering along the course of the long-vanished Fagswell Brook. Later C19 and C20 buildings for the meat industry dominate the long central section, facing the market. The railway cutting behind kept them relatively low, but also allowed their basements to be rail-served. Most striking are the broad, flat-fronted cold stores, c. 1900 and after, superseding stores improvised in the market's basements in the 1880s. Plenty of buildings of the 1870s remain between.

w to E: No. 1 (N side), 1950s Neo-Georgian with a curved front, harmonizes with the houses of Ely Place behind (*see London 4: North*). Nos. 11–15 are by *Chapman Taylor*, 1976–9, part of a large development extending some way N. Restless front with projecting flat green-glazed bays of different heights. Two lower storeys clad in Portland roach, with slit windows. A covered bridge crosses to Atlantic House (*see* Holborn Viaduct). Through the block, a passage on the line of the old Saffron Hill steps down, then up to a series of small gardens on different levels along the rear wing (r.). Along the w side, ST ANDREW'S HOUSE, four-storey working-class flats in brick by *Sir Horace Jones* for the City, 1874. Centre and ends project. Delicate elliptical iron arcades between, with pierced balustrades. The design resembles Jones's Corporation Buildings, Farringdon Road (1865, dem.), London's first municipal working-class flats.

Back in Charterhouse Street, *Livings Leslie Webber*'s No. 19 (1992) curves to the w corner with Farringdon Road. White and polished pink stone piers, segmental arches and bronze cladding. Across Farringdon Road, Nos. 47–49 are *T. H. Smith*'s cold store for the Port of London Authority, 1914. Portland stone above arcaded granite, with rusticated end bays: all safely and solidly classical.

Blind central panel with giant inscription in mosaic. Empty in 1996. Then *C. S. Peach*'s Central Cold Storage (1899), for the margarine manufacturers van den Bergh. Refurbished as a power-generating plant 1990. Colourful glazed-brick and stone front. Festive stocky copper-clad pavilion roofs high up. Blind upper wall, with under the central gable a curious faience Rococo cartouche. On the ground floor, Ionic half-columns fade into pilasters and then corbel-capitals in the outer bays. Big square chimney behind.

Warehouses of the 1870s follow: Nos. 55–57, 1873, a handsome gault brick palazzo with square-headed windows, taller than it is wide; No. 61, dated 1878, broader and coarser; No. 63, wedge-shaped to fit the railway cutting; Nos. 67–77 (1872), polychrome brick and stone Venetian Gothico-Renaissance, with a naïve but vigorous façade, worth rescuing from its present decay (1997). Shops below round-arched Palladian windows with columns. Circular apertures in the relieving arches. No. 77a, the Metropolitan Cold Store by *Samuel Yeo*, 1923, is dull. The stone-fronted Meat Inspection Offices at Nos. 79–83, by the *Corporation of London Engineer's Department*, 1930, have a shallow-carved frieze of animal heads, designed by *H. H. Martyn & Co*. Then No. 87, a warehouse of 1870 with round- and segment-headed windows, eminently typical of the well-preserved City fringe of Clerkenwell: by *Lewis Isaacs*, District Surveyor to Holborn. This begins at the corner with Cowcross Street (*see London 4: North*). The other ancient route here is St John Street, which led N past St John's Priory. Set back between them, a former sausage-maker's premises, a memorable Free Style building with a carved relief of a boar, dated 1897. It makes an excellent visual stop in line with the market's Grand Avenue. BARCLAYS BANK on the E corner (No. 89), dated 1871, was the London Joint Stock Bank, again by *Isaacs*. Portland stone and stock brick, handsomely Italianate, with a canted corner entrance below a big rounded oriel. The late date comes out in the busy roofline.

Then the street turns N away from the City boundary, which continues along the S side of Charterhouse Square. This N part represents the ancient approach to the Charterhouse from the road N to Clerkenwell.

The S side of this section is made by a wedge-shaped building of *c*. 1875, red brick with a stone-faced corner and granite columns. No. 105 (N side), utilitarian brick, is signed by *J. H. Schrader*, 1871. Nos. 109–113, a cold store of 1900 by *A. H. Mackmurdo*, has a sensitive red brick façade, orthodox Neo-Wren but for the narrow tall windows between the pilasters. It was amongst this fastidious designer's last works before premature retirement to Essex and dreams of rural utopia. As redeveloped for offices (1988–9), the ground floor is recessed behind arcading: a more honest way to handle a façade-job, but rather awkward visually. Next to it the FOX AND ANCHOR INN, 1898, tall and narrow, with a joyful front of *Doulton*'s coloured tiles, by *W. J. Neatby* of the firm. A picture of the fox fills a shaped gable ballooning upwards. The flattest of flat bays below, flanked by grinning gargoyles. Touches of Art Nouveau whiplash forms here and there. Recessed entrance to the long and dark interior, which has a top-lit labyrinth of little snugs at the back. No. 117, a plain warehouse of 1874 by *Isaacs*, preserves a small rear vestry room for St Sepulchre's parish. No. 119 is late C18. Finally Nos. 121–123 (1907), a decent red brick warehouse built as stock rooms for commercial travellers using the Charterhouse Hotel in the square next door (q.v.). Probably by the hotel's architect *E. B. I'Anson* (the same builders were employed).

CHEAPSIDE

The widest street of the medieval City, recorded as early as 1104, possibly by *c*. 1067. The w part diagonally crosses the line of a main Roman road between the Walbrook crossing at Bucklersbury and the w gate at Newgate, which was one of the earliest features of Roman London. A short E continuation colonized a triangular space formed between Bucklersbury and Poultry in the C10–C12.

'Cheap' means market, and Cheapside was often called Westcheap to distinguish it from the market at Eastcheap. Cheapside's mercantile heyday was in the C12, before rival sites at the Stocks and on the quays grew up, and in that century the picturesque names of the side streets derived from the goods sold there are first recorded: Wood Street, Milk Street, Bread Street, Honey Lane, and Friday Street where fish was sold. In the C12–C14 the street also housed 'selds', specialized enclosed markets like bazaars. The marketing of necessities gave way in the later Middle Ages to luxury goods, and even now Cheapside remains the City's principal shopping street. It was adorned by conduits in the middle and at each end, and, until its destruction in 1643, by one of Edward I's Eleanor Crosses. Fragments of the Cross, with shields in trefoilheaded panels, are in the Museum of London. The pointed tunnelvaulted cistern of the East or Great Conduit, built *c*. 1245, was discovered beneath the roadway in 1995. The breadth of Cheapside lent it to tournaments and parades, one of which is recorded in an engraving of 1638. This shows substantial half-timbered gabled houses of three to five storeys, like those at Staple Inn (*see* Public Buildings). Of four medieval churches in the street, only St Mary-le-Bow was rebuilt after 1666: St Michael-le-Querne at the w end, St Peter Cheap or Wood Street on the N side (*see* below) and St Mary Colechurch by Old Jewry all disappeared.

The C19 saw Cheapside largely rebuilt as warehousing and office chambers, with a few grandiose headquarters buildings. War damage was severe and when rebuilt the street was widened along much of the N side. The post-war buildings, mostly stone-clad, are disappointingly bland, punctuated mercifully by the steeple of Wren's St Mary-le-Bow on the s side and the projecting former Atlas Assurance on the N.

From St Paul's Churchyard east to King Street and Queen Street

At the w end, at the end of the N precinct of St Paul's, is a sevenstorey octagonal building cantilevered out from a concrete core, by *Gotch & Partners*, completed 1971. Portland roach panelling, with bands of dark-framed windows. Services in a leaded top

floor. It makes an adequate if rather obvious visual stop to the end
of the street and to St Martin's le Grand to the N. Cheapside
begins on this curved N corner at Nos. 161–162, built in 1924–6 as
the Westminster Bank by *Gunton & Gunton*, more conservative
than their contemporary Empire House on the N (*see* St Martin's
le Grand), with Doric half-columns below. Then No. 150, ST
VEDAST HOUSE, also by *Gunton & Gunton*, completed 1964:
stone-clad, the centre projecting.

At the SW corner with New Change, overlooking with its concave W
front the E end of St Paul's, the vast NEW CHANGE BUILDINGS
by *Victor Heal* for the Bank of England, 1953–60. Pevsner found it
reactionary 'almost beyond comprehension'; but in fact it typifies
the backward-looking 'cornice line' type favoured in early post-
war reconstruction. The ground floor stone-clad with rounded
windows, red brick above, all heavy and generally just utilitarian,
but dressed up with occasional columns at the top, silly little semi-
period balconies and other small motifs, and sculpture (by
Wheeler, Esmond Burton and others) in what might be called the
George VI style. The general stuffiness is redeemed a little by the
way it responds to the surrounding streets: to New Change, W, a
long convex monotonous front (entrance hall with MOSAIC by
Boris Anrep); at the NW corner a symmetrical frontispiece facing
Newgate Street; to Cheapside a set-back arcaded section. It leads
to a shapeless public courtyard, disastrously bleak despite the
plain fountain and lead cisterns, in C18 style but dated 1960,
scattered about. Here the disparate heights of the ranges become
obvious. The N–S pedestrian route follows the line of Friday
Street, where St Matthew, smallest of Wren's City churches (built
1682–5), stood until 1886. Facing Bread Street, E, a turfed sunken
courtyard crossed by a causeway, with a FOUNTAIN by *Ernest
Gillick*, with a female figure, 1959.

On the N SIDE again, CHEAPSIDE HOUSE (Nos. 134–147), between
Foster Lane and Gutter Lane, 1958–9 by *Theo Birks*: better than
average, with a curved flush stone-clad front and a shallow
projecting section towards New Change, l. Upright windows,
enlivened above by aprons of rough stone and by a stack of
mosaic-panelled balconies. Then No. 130, THREE KEYS HOUSE,
offices of 1978–82 by *T. P. Bennett & Son*. Antiquated for the date,
with close-set bevelled verticals in Portland roach. The NE part
faces Wood Street, N of the churchyard (*see* below).

Older buildings follow: Nos. 128–129, by *Ford & Hesketh*, 1884, with
twin shallow canted bays and a coved cornice with incised ornament; No. 127, modest free classical of 1909 by *T. H. Smith*; then
low shops at Nos. 124–126, much altered, but still recognizable as
of C17 origin. They are almost the last survivors of the 'least sort
of building' defined in the Rebuilding Act of 1667. The simplest
possible plan, each shop with one room below and one above.
Frontages are C19 and later, notably that of WOODERSON'S the
shirtmakers on the corner, with curved plate glass and fittings of
c. 1902, when the range was truncated to widen Wood Street. The
shops are so narrow because of the position of ST PETER'S
CHURCHYARD facing Wood Street behind, made after the Great
Fire on the site of St Peter Cheap (the first shops here were
licensed in 1401). The rear wall to the churchyard has apparently

been refaced since the RCHME examined it in the 1920s and is no longer of C17 brickwork, but a stone tablet dated 1687 survives. The unusually elaborate churchyard railings are dated 1712, on the reverse of a little plaque of St Peter with his keys.

The great and ancient plane tree leaning over the shops from the churchyard is also an effective foil to the excellent Nos. 117–122, MITRE HOUSE, by *R. N. Wakelin* of *Campbell-Jones & Sons*, completed 1965, on the E corner with Wood Street. Ground floor mostly Spanish travertine-faced, with a small projecting jeweller's shop, JOHN DONALD, by *Stefan Buzas & Alan Irvine*, r. This has a window with splayed corners, a motif repeated in the shop's interior. Above, dark glass with girders showing behind, relics of an unbuilt section of ped-way. Then seven storeys of well-detailed curtain walling with polished grey granite floor strings, broken in two by a narrow recess. It rises higher along Milk Street behind (now partly pedestrian), pierced by a roadway N of which it forms three brick-faced sides to MITRE COURT, with a ground-floor cloister of shallowest segment-headed arches.

Back on the S SIDE, BOW BELLS HOUSE by *Cotton, Ballard & Blow*, 1958–9. Elevations are stone-clad grids with green mosaic spandrels, the areas of stone large and plain. To Cheapside a projecting ground floor and first floor. It forms the W and N part of BOW CHURCHYARD, with a passage through from Bread Street. The paved churchyard was extended W and S after the Second World War. In the small central garden a bronze STATUE of Capt. John Smith by *Charles Rennick*, 1960, after one by *William Couper* in Jamestown, Virginia. On the S side a building by *Hamilton Associates* is under construction (1997). Back in the street, hard against the tower of St Mary-le-Bow, YORKSHIRE BANK (Nos. 56–58), 1958–9 by *Trehearne & Norman, Preston & Partners*. An early use of polished stone as a way of distinguishing bank fronts from other offices, after the Portland-and-columns convention fizzled out.

Opposite, No. 107, the SUN LIFE ASSURANCE SOCIETY, by *Antony Lloyd* of *Curtis Green, Son & Lloyd*, 1955–8. Large, stone-faced, and featureless but for the stainless-steel-clad entrance within a kind of giant Gibbs surround carved with signs of the zodiac. A passageway named Honey Lane pierces the block, some 50 ft (15 metres) E of the pre-war street of that name. Rear projections house pubs, facing Russia Row and Trump Street. Foundations and floors of a C2 bath-building were found on the site in 1955. E extension, 1964, with grooved uprights and polished steel sills facing King Street.

After Bow Lane on the S side, Nos. 60 and 61, plain stone-faced buildings on narrow pre-war plots, respectively by *C. J. April*, 1956, and *R. Seifert*, 1954. Then some inter-war survivors. Nos. 62–63, CHEYNE HOUSE, 1924–5, red brick Neo-Early-Georgian with a nice acanthus cornice, by *G. A. Crawley* and *Gervase Bailey*. Nos. 64–66, the former British General Insurance, 1930–3 by *M. E. & O. H. Collins*. A tall façade, playfully handled. Four giant tapering pilasters rise from bases of acanthus scroll. They lack capitals but are overtopped with big urns on the parapet. The inner pair merge into a big central window frame. Maurice Webb's Commercial Union Insurance, Cornhill (1929) is similar:

is this a coincidence, as that firm took over the British General in 1927? Rebuilt behind the façade by *Sheppard Robson Architects*, 1989–92, with an entrance made in new stone- and brick-clad ranges facing the little Crown Court. Nos. 67–68, on the corner with Queen Street, offices of 1938 by *Robert Angell & Curtis*, refurbished 1984 by *Janusz S. Kent*. Stripped classical with a chamfered corner and vestigial grooved piers.

From King Street and Queen Street east to Poultry

The E corner of King Street, N side, is BARCLAYS BANK, the former Atlas Assurance, by that accomplished eclectic *Thomas Hopper*, 1834–6. An all-over, high relief composition in the grandest Italian manner. Arcaded and rusticated ground floor, two upper floors of equal height with paired superimposed pilasters at each end, windows with pediments variously triangular and segmental. The first-floor windows have in addition half-columns and little balconies. The ground floor is an early appearance in the City of grey Cornish granite (cf. Fishmongers' Hall). It has been much altered and extended. The pedestrian arcade along Cheapside was made through the bomb-damaged shell in reconstruction by *Waterhouse & Ripley*, 1952. The original entrance was in the three-bay Cheapside front, and the rest had only four bays on either side. The present six-bay form dates probably from *E. N. Clifton*'s extension, 1857. The next bay N is of 1893–4, by *Waterhouse*, with paired pilasters by the present main entrance. Baroque sculpted Atlas and globe over, by *Farmer & Brindley*. The doorcase below Atlas was altered in 1927–9, when yet another N extension was built by *Michael Waterhouse* (Nos. 3–7 King Street). Rusticated ground floor to match Hopper's. Otherwise big flat classical aedicules with columns and balconies, and a steep slated mansard. It runs N to Prudent Passage, which was remade on a new alignment. The circular entrance lobby with staircase rising at the far end also looks 1920s. The plainer Ironmonger Lane front has, S, an aedicule on the fourth bay, marking the limit of Hopper's work. On the second and third bays here blind panels above the first-floor windows, replacing Hopper's former mezzanine windows. The narrow rusticated section, r., belongs with Waterhouse's work.

The rest of the N side of Cheapside as far as Poultry is formed by the lifeless Portland block by *Gunton & Gunton* of 1954–60 housing the MERCERS' HALL (q.v.). On the S side, Nos. 73–75 by *Fitzroy Robinson Partnership*, 1990–6, stretches down Queen Street. It revives the astylar commercial classicism of *c.* 1925, with details culled from surrounding buildings. No. 80, 1994–6, is also *Fitzroy*'s. Stone-faced grid with tall central glazed section. On top a loggia with paired cylindrical columns. It replaced the tall Bolsa House, by *Kenneth Lindy & Partners*, with a lower block by *B. & N. Westwood, Piet & Partners*, 1964. The street continues as POULTRY.

CHISWELL STREET

Called *Chyselstrate* in 1217, perhaps from an old word for pebble, or from one of the wells N of London mentioned by Fitzstephen, *c.* 1174. The S side, E of Moor Lane, was transferred to the City in 1994; the N side remains in the Borough of Islington.

WHITBREAD'S BREWERY site straddles the W end of the street. Samuel Whitbread moved here in 1749, taking over a handsome dwelling house for his own use (now the Partners' House). The brewery which he developed had by the later C18 become one of the sights of London. *John Smeaton* helped design the underground cisterns for holding the beer; a James Watt steam engine was introduced in 1785; the Royal family visited in 1787, when there were 200 men and 80 horses. By the end of the C19 the brewery had grown to six acres, extending N–S from Errol Street to Silk Street. Only the historic core of the site remains, converted as Company Headquarters, and conference and banqueting suites after the brewery closed in 1976; the rest has been rebuilt as flats and offices.

The PARTNERS' HOUSE is on the S side of Chiswell Street, a red brick house right on the street, dating from *c.* 1700, tactfully extended, and now of nine bays and four storeys. The centre five bays are the original house. Central doorway with carved brackets and an iron overthrow with lamp. Low ground floor with altered windows, but the three upper floors all with very narrow blind recesses between the windows, characteristic of *c.* 1700. Moulded floor bands, the lower one rising around the blind arched tympanum of the central first-floor window. The extension on the l. (E) side has a single large window on the first floor, for a reception room, now Board Room, created in 1756. Big coved cornice over all except the two l. bays. Inside a central passage leads to the stairs, back l. Lower flights with angular Chinese Chippendale balustrade staircase, continued in the same mode by an extra half flight to the Board Room, a fine room extending the whole depth of the house. Four symmetrically arranged doorcases with octagonal panels; fine Rococo fireplace with scrolled broken pediment and panel with musical instruments. The upper flights of the main stair still of *c.* 1700: closed string with spiral balusters. C18 fielded panelling in some other rooms, but the rest of the house much altered.

To the W of the Partners' House, r., the KING'S HEAD pub, *c.* 1860; adjoining, down Whitecross Street, a Neo-Wren front with oversized Doric pilasters, dated 1904. E of the Partners' House is a carriageway through a range of 1891, with top floor of the 1950s. A row of C19 offices to its l., opening on to quite an elaborate top-lit stair. Then Nos. 53–55, late C18 three-bay houses, and ST PAUL'S TAVERN, on the corner with Milton Street, from its proportions also late C18, but with stuccoed surrounds added *c.* 1840. (Milton Street is the old Grub Street, renamed in 1830 to escape its notorious connotations of literary hackwork.) On the S part of the former brewery site, along Silk Street, two irregularly composed office blocks by the *Fitzroy Robinson Partnership*, 1976–81. The corners rise up as stocky angled towers.

Pastel-coloured cladding by *Sheppard Robson*, 1994–6, replaces the original mirror-glass.

The YARD behind Chiswell Street can also be entered by a tall narrow archway from Milton Street dating from 1979, cut through the stable range. The L-shaped stables, rebuilt in the 1860s onwards, were on three floors, with iron columns and brick vaults; they continue along the rear of the buildings along Chiswell Street, where a fragment of a ramp to the upper floors remains.

On the s side of the yard is the SUGAR ROOM of 1792, with two rows of arched windows. The low building housing the Speaker's Coach (drawn by Whitbread's horses from the 1840s) was added in 1986; the polygonal entrance lobby with tall brick arches dates from 1977–9, by *Wolff Olins* in association with *Roderick Gradidge*, when the buildings were converted to conference suites, and the whole given a somewhat spurious 'heritage' flavour. A slate stair made from old fermenting vessels leads to the one survival from the early brewing buildings, the PORTER TUN ROOM, a storehouse where the beer barrels were kept to mature. Begun in 1774, now divided horizontally into two banqueting rooms. It is 160 ft (49 metres) long and has a 60 ft (18 metres) span. The important survival is the spectacular open timber kingpost roof of 12 bays, 160 ft (49 metres) by 65 ft (20 metres). Brick vaults below.

On the N side of Chiswell Street there remains the brewery depot, where the beer was casked, a long thin courtyard with gates to the road and buildings on three sides. These are of 1867, replacing buildings of 1771 (as is recorded on the sundial at the end). W and N wings with continuous bands of windows. Converted in 1995 as student accommodation for the Guildhall School of Music, by *D. Y. Davies Associates*. Further W, a good late C18 terrace (Nos. 43–46). A modern plaque dates it 1774, which seems too early for the round-headed doorways and unaligned lower and upper windows. Perhaps by *Dance the Younger*, who designed houses for Whitbread in the street.

Continuing E, MICHAEL HOUSE (No. 35) by *Architech*, 1989–90, stone-faced with bitty blocks for ornament, and DIANA HOUSE (No. 33), by *Hans Biel*, 1954–5, six stone-clad storeys, which made innovative use of aluminium-framed windows. In the forecourt a cast stone STATUE of Diana by *Arthur Fleischman*. For the rest of the N side, *see London 4: North*.

On the s side, one last building within the City: MILTON GATE, an island block by *Denys Lasdun, Peter Softley & Associates* for Land Securities (1987–91). A thoughtful and generally successful development of the atrium type. Its powerful chamfered mass is clad in a triple-skinned envelope of sea-green glass, bolted on in even, precise, upright panes – a material worlds away from the massive *in situ* concrete of Lasdun's best-known buildings. It has a mysterious translucence quite different from the usual mirror-glazing. Steel frame within the wide cavity, which accommodates balconies for window-cleaning, and serves also as a warm-air vent, reducing the cost of air-conditioning. Seven main storeys, carried up in sundry towers and angles, and breaking out to N and S in triplets of flat bays, derived rather arbitrarily from Mackintosh's School of Art in Glasgow. Pitched aluminium roofing, with in the centre a white-clad concrete cylinder housing services (echoes of

Louis Kahn?). Atrium planned on diagonals, the entrances marked by round black brick piers at the E corners. Walkways bridge it high up from lifts in the service core, intriguingly isolated by a tiny moat.

CLEMENT'S LANE

A *vicus sancti Clementis* is recorded in 1241. The oldest building is Nos. 27–28 St Clement's House, by the brothers *Francis* (E side). Built for the City Offices Company in 1864, as little bosses on the front record. Gault brick. Shouldered-arched windows above a serpentine-faced ground floor ornamented with masks. Pedimented doorcases at each end. Details, e.g. the Gothic-derived foliage carving, are more eclectic than their pile of 1868 for the Company at Nos. 39–40 Lombard Street (q.v.). Through Nos. 27–28 runs a passage called LOMBARD COURT, crossed at the far end by a bridge with elaborate polychrome Gothic details, apparently a later addition. Perhaps by *J. E. Saunders*, busy in the Court in 1872. Nos. 3 and 4 Lombard Court to its E (dem.), 1866–7 by *Francis*, had windows matching the Clement's Lane front. On the N side here a pastiche Georgian pub, part of a scheme by the *Fitzroy Robinson Partnership*, 1981–5, with a sombre black marble grid with recessed splayed windows on Clement's Lane (Nos. 29–31). Similar façade to PLOUGH COURT, off Lombard Court to the N, reached through a kind of roofed-in atrium. Beneath it, the court is carried on a bridge across a sunken basement in which a garden has been made. The E side of Plough Court (No. 37 Lombard Street), 1983–5, also *Fitzroy*'s, has historicizing round arches and contrasting black marble columns. Back in Clement's Lane, Nos. 6–8 (W side), the former Agra Bank Chambers, 1883. Renaissance, with giant pilasters.

CLOAK LANE

Probably called from its *cloaca* or open sewer formerly running E into the Walbrook, but also known into Stow's time as Horseshoe Bridge Street.

On the S side, No. 9 PELLIPAR HOUSE, by *J. Sampson Lloyd* of *Green Lloyd Adams* for the Skinners' Company, 1987–91, the façade an inventive fantasia on C19 commercial motifs. Superimposed Doric columns, in the manner of e.g. Sherrin, separated by chamfered blocks instead of an entablature. A more orthodox arcade and entablature to the ground floor. Flat, shallow bays framed by twisted metal colonnettes fill this giant grid, recalling mid-C19 experiments in iron-framed construction. On their leaded floor-panels a circular motif of sixes and sevens, a reference to the ancient precedence dispute between Skinners and Merchant Taylors. Flaming urn-finials add to the fun. The gabled rear elevation facing the Skinners' Hall goes Neo-Georgian. Part of the same job are the pilasters added to the blind N wall of the Tallow Chandlers' Hall, l., and most of the former College Hill

Chambers, 1887–9, r., retained as SCANDIA HOUSE. This is of red brick with flat bays of cross-windows and Romanesque touches to the doorcases. A nicely irregular new entrance façade faces the little courtyard off College Hill. The Cutlers' Hall occupied the w part of the site from the mid C15 until the Metropolitan and District Railway was built beneath the lane in 1884.

Set into the rear of Nos. 70–74 Cannon Street, on the N side at the E, is a little stone monument to another railway casualty, the former burial ground of the church of St John the Baptist. The church was not rebuilt after 1666; bits of churchyard lasted into the mid 1980s.

CLOTH FAIR

Formed *c.* 1590 across the land of St Bartholomew's Priory by its new owner Lord Rich (cf. Middle Street). The name is from the cloth traded at Bartholomew Fair. The original layout is still discernible on the N side: plots are shallower than the medieval burgage type, and frequently punctuated by narrow alleys (Barley Mow Passage, Cloth Court, etc.). This tight planning and the street's narrowness reflect how crowded London was then becoming: a density more palpable before the mid C20, when the last houses lining the s side were removed to expose St Bartholomew's churchyard; early C17 houses lasted here until 1917.

N SIDE, from w: Nos. 43–45, a solid late C18 terrace, has good brickwork with red rubbed-brick window heads. Good shopfronts of *c.* 1800 to Nos. 43 and 51, facing Barley Mow Passage behind (l.), discreetly restored in work for the Landmark Trust (1975–6 and 1986–7). Nos. 41–42 is an exceedingly fine C17 merchant's
27   house, perhaps as early as the first leases in 1614, but of a type current into the later C17 despite proscription in the 1667 Rebuilding Act (cf. Nos. 46–47 Aldgate High Street). Four storeys, red brick, with a pair of two-storeyed rectangular wooden bay windows crowned by pediments to each front. Narrow single lights between them on the main front. Deep modillion cornice below the roof. The paired half-hipped gables with weatherboarding above have a look of rural Kent or Essex; yet such gables appear in innumerable old views of London. Restored in 1930 by *Lord Mottistone* of *Seely & Paget* as an office and residence. The firm remained here until 1976. Mottistone introduced the ground-floor elliptical-headed apertures and the leaded casements, and rebuilt the C17 staircase at the rear. The present *trompe-l'œil* painting of the bay panels is probably also his. (C17 interior features include a moulded fireplace surround on the ground floor, a first-floor panelled anteroom, and second-floor panelled gallery.)

At Nos. 39–40 a pair of mid-C18 houses, refronted in stucco *c.* 1830, with quoins and broad tripartite windows. The shopfronts look of the same date. As late as 1976 they housed the last of the street's cloth merchants. The decline of the area in the later C19 appears from the RISING SUN's modest scale and materials. By *W. M. Brutton*, 1896. Then Nos. 26–37, two blocks of houses flanking an entrance court to offices facing Long Lane, all by *Renton Howard Wood Levin*, 1981–5. The three- or four-storey brick or stucco ranges are treated asymmetrically, with recessed entrances and square bays like those on Nos. 41–42: on the whole an accomplished exercise in picturesque contextualism, though let down by the messy roofline. The Founders' Hall on the S side (q.v.) marks the end of the street.

COCK LANE

Quiet, dark and steep, still paved with granite setts, and not immune to the decay and demolitions afflicting the W part of Smithfield. First recorded *c.* 1200, as *Cockeslane*; probably named from the breeding here of fighting cocks. The Abbots of Leicester and Glastonbury had Inns here.

Near the bottom on the N side, SARACEN'S HEAD CHAMBERS (Nos. 36–37), an early C19 warehouse with broad segment-headed windows and a plain cornice. The jolly Jacobean-Renaissance ground-floor office front dates from *c.* 1880. Nos. 31–32 further up, a boxy refurbished mid-C19 brick warehouse, with windows recessed in vertical panels at the ends. No. 12 (S side), offices by *James M. Knowles* for St Bartholomew's Hospital, 1974–8, has near-flush window bands between red brick.

COLEMAN STREET

Probably named from charcoal burners living here by the C11. After the City wall was abandoned, the street was pushed N to join Fore Street, but this section disappeared under the London Wall development. In the 1830s Coleman Street was bypassed as a main N–S route by the new Moorgate Street (the S part of the present Moorgate). Larger and more recent buildings on the E side run through to Moorgate and have their main façade there, so Coleman Street comes off second-best architecturally.

The S corners belong with Gresham Street (W) and Lothbury (E). Nos. 36–40 (W side), *David du R. Aberdeen*'s former Swiss Bank extension, 1961–4, was demolished in 1996. Its lively undulating upper storeys set it above other curtain-walled offices of the date. A new building by *Sidell Gibson* is proposed (*see* also Nos. 97–99 Gresham Street). On the site was the bombed St Stephen Coleman, a modest single-chambered church by *Wren*, 1674–7, with a steeple like the lower stage of St Lawrence Jewry's; the church began as a chapel of St Olave Jewry, made parochial as late as 1456. Then Nos. 30–32, with windows in closely spaced flat projecting bays, by *Parfitt & Craig Hall*, 1972–5. The attractive facing is Norwegian silver-grey schist. It spans the entrance to Mason's Avenue (*see* Basinghall Street).

Opposite (E side), Nos. 51–52 and 54–55, near-matching offices of 1889–90 by *Gordon & Lowther*, rich and solid, with plain ground floors and applied superimposed Corinthian columns all of polished red-brown granite. Nos. 51–52 (l.), narrower, has a slender iron column to the ground floor. No. 53 between, by *J. Collier*, 1865, French-accented Italianate, has tripartite windows changing with typical looseness to double ones beneath the cornice. All are façades only, having been twice rebuilt behind by the firm of *Fitzroy Robinson* in connection with the former Metropolitan Life Assurance (*see* Moorgate). The second time, a pilastered third floor was tactfully added to the outer pair, matching the height of No. 53.

Buildings flanking Great Bell Alley – named after a long-lost Coleman Street tavern – face Moorgate. Then No. 58, a tall late c18 three-bay house front retained as part of No. 23 Moorgate (by *Rolfe Judd*, 1979–81). The Travertine-faced Nos. 64–66 are by *Seifert*, completed 1955, as determinedly symmetrical as his contemporary Woolworth's, Marylebone Road (*see London 3: North West*).

Opposite (w side), the extensive site of the former Woolgate House (*see* Basinghall Street). To its N, No. 4 by *T. P. Bennett Partnership*, 1993–6, a reversion to Portland stone, with bows and bays of different sizes. Facing White Horse Yard behind, No. 16, a tall block of 1985–8 by *EPR Partnership*, with narrow windows recessed in a polished stone-clad frame. A shallow bay projects clumsily to the N. For Austral House N of Basinghall Avenue, *see* London Wall. Back on the E side, after more rear façades, No. 74: stone-faced offices of 1916 by *W. A. Lewis*, turning playful at the top. Further N a substantial mid-c18 four-bay house (No. 80), altered *c.* 1800, when a storey was added above the stone modillion cornice. Doric doorcase and Georgian ground floor from refurbishment by *De Brandt, Joyce & Partners*, 1989. (Inside, open-well staircase with turned balusters and ramped and panelled dado with fluted pilasters.) Adjoining, the ARMOURERS' AND BRAZIERS' HALL (q.v.) makes the corner with London Wall.

COLLEGE HILL

A wonderfully unpredictable assortment of pre-c20 buildings lines the central part between Cloak Lane and College Street. College Hill is so called from the college founded under Dick Whittington's will in 1424–5, in his house N of the church of St Michael Paternoster Royal at the SE corner. Before that the street was called Royal Street or Tower Royal.

Nos. 19–20 next to the church is the former MERCERS' SCHOOL, built 1829–32 by *George Smith* (Whittington's trustees were the Mercers' Company). Two storeys and five bays of Italianate stucco, with quoins and alternating window pediments like a miniature West End club. A high clerestoried classroom survives on the first floor at the r. Part of the former college next door at No. 22: towards the street two spectacular late c17 stone portals with big open segmental pediments on volute corbels and thick fruit and flower carving below. Above each round-headed gateway circular windows with garlands. The entablature is lost. They rival the richer of the Livery Halls' contemporary street frontispieces.

The work must be from before 1676, the date of Ogilby and Morgan's map on which it appears. The designer may have been *John Oliver*, who did the Mercers' Hall, or possibly his masons *John* and *Nicholas Young*. Similar round windows appear on the Hall's frontispiece (now part of Swanage town hall), which Oliver designed and the Youngs carved; but that composition is fussy by comparison. The plan suggests that the narrow recessed centre, with its round-headed window of typically early C18 type, represents the later infilling of a courtyard entrance.

From the gateway of No. 22 a courtyard is reached in which stands a four-bay, three-storey brick house (No. 21), the survivor of a pair undertaken here by *Nicholas Barbon*, described as newly built in 1688. The first occupant was Sir Alexander Rigby, merchant. The front wall looks like C20 rebuilding. Nice mid-C18 doorcase on Ionic columns; substantial eared and pedimented doorcases of similar date within. (Two panelled staircases with twisted balusters; one, rising to the first floor, is dated 1724 by Dan Cruickshank, the other, at the rear and of full height, is probably original; in other rear rooms are box cornices and corner chimneypieces, not necessarily *in situ*.) Restored by *Haslemere Estates*, 1986–7. The N part of the courtyard was rebuilt 1987–91 on different levels by *J. Sampson Lloyd* of *Green Lloyd Adams*, including the redevelopment of College Hill Chambers on the s side of Cloak Lane (q.v.).

The w side begins at the s with big mid-C19 warehouses, running back from Queen Street. No. 10, s, has unusual badges to the first-floor piers. Then No. 4, a solid three-bay red brick house of *c.* 1730–40. Later stucco to the ground floor. The nicely moulded cornice is repeated facing the dour Newcastle Court behind. Open-pedimented carved doorcase with an emperor's head, flanked by cherubs' heads curiously like those on church monuments. Well-preserved panelled interior. The staircase climbs from the rear. Its barley-sugar balusters, enriched tread ends etc. continue up to the second floor. This suggests the ground floor served in the City fashion as a counting-house, with living accommodation above. The stolid No. 1 on the corner with Cloak Lane is a former police station of 1885–6, the last survivor of several by *Sir Horace Jones*. Channelled stone below, stock brick above, with decorative iron grilles.

COOPER'S ROW

So called from the coopers who stored their casks in recesses against the City wall; but called Woderouelane in 1260 and Woodroffe Lane at least until *c.* 1700. In 1862 *Norman Shaw*'s first British building, an obscure warehouse, went up here: 'Gothic of a kind, but very likely hulking and incoherent' (A. Saint).

On the E SIDE, the former Midland House by *R. Seifert & Partners*, 1961–3: a tall slab at r. angles to the street, interlocking with a lower, curtain-walled street range with a passage through to a courtyard behind. On the slab end a mediocre coloured abstract relief. In the courtyard is a large section of CITY WALL, 35 ft (10½ metres) high and 100 ft (30½ metres) long, which was formerly incorporated in a warehouse. The Roman wall can be seen rising 6 from the basement car park, near the original ground level, to just above the present-day level of the courtyard. The triple course of tiles near the bottom is not a bonding course, but a facing course only. At a corresponding level on the outer face, which can be inspected by passing through the modern archway in it, is a sandstone plinth. Above is a fine portion of the medieval wall, probably representing almost its full height. The parapet walk survives at the s end, and an indication of the stairway leading to it can be seen in the masonry. In the upper part a window and four loopholes with round-headed embrasures. Putlog holes for a timber gallery below. The wall has been dated to the C12, perhaps as late as c. 1200, by the round-headed apertures; deposits of this period were excavated in 1985 from the outer ditch here.

The Neo-Georgian range rising up beyond the wall belongs with the Crescent (q.v.). For buildings on the E side further s, see Trinity Square.

COPTHALL AVENUE

An L-shaped street made 1889–90. The main part runs s from London Wall, mostly on the line of the old Little Bell Alley. Several archaeological excavations have explored this area of the upper Walbrook valley. Early in the C2, the tributaries of the Walbrook were channelled into timber drains, allowing the development of an industrial quarter here. Ground plates and floors of several timber buildings were unusually well preserved by the later reversion of the area to marshland.

At the N end, two giant 1980s blocks on London Wall (q.v.). Then on the E SIDE buildings of moderate size and height, facing the Institute of Chartered Accountants (see Public Buildings). Nos. 20–22, by *R. B. Marsh*, 1900, is retained as part of No. 60 London Wall. Red granite ground floor, giant doorcase, off-centre gable, vaguely late Gothic diagonal shafts between. Nos. 14–16 next door, the former Mathiesons the printers, is by *T. Barnes-Williams*, 1892. Classical, with two storeys with enormous windows between giant piers: an extreme case of this common late C19 device for maximizing daylight. Cross-windows on the top floors. Nos. 10–12 by *Rolfe Judd*, 1986–9, symmetrical and strongly articulated in Portland stone and pink Ross o' Mull granite, with much advancing and receding of the planes. Historicizing motifs follow on from the firm's earlier No. 68 Cornhill (q.v.), but lack its freshness. Then a gap for an unbuilt ped-way bridge from the Drapers' Gardens complex, whose tower rises behind (see Throgmorton Avenue). Nos. 4–6, by the *Fitzroy Robinson Partnership*, 1985–6, has polished red stone mullions above a rusticated ground floor; much squared-off detail.

Opposite, W SIDE, No. 7 (PIERCY HOUSE) is by *Trehearne & Norman, Preston & Partners*, 1962. Six storeys, mostly curtain-walled, with green-glass panels and aluminium fins, spoiled by painting. Further s, No. 3, office chambers of 1875, part of the

Clothworkers' Company development in Telegraph Street (*see* Moorgate). Yellow stone, fancy and eclectic: Renaissance details, Gothic chamfering. Glazed top storey by the *Swinhoe Measures Partnership*, 1991. The avenue continues E from here into Throgmorton Avenue, through part of the Angel Court development (*see* Throgmorton Street).

CORNHILL

Cornhill is the highest point in the City. The height is immediately appreciable when one looks s down Gracechurch Street at the E end. The street was probably formed by the C11, extending the line of Cheapside into Leadenhall Street and clipping the NW corner of the then ruinous Roman Basilica (*see* Introduction p. 32). The name, known from *c.* 1100, comes from the former corn market held here. In the C18 it was dominated by linen drapers and luxury shops. Today, there is no better place to observe the burgeoning ambition and stylistic variety of the City's grander banks and offices between the 1850s and 1930s. Indeed there is so much going on that Cornhill seems much longer than it really is, especially E of the Royal Exchange. Nor is it an architectural monoculture: the commercial palaces are nicely punctuated by two Wren churches and an C18 house on the s side, and the pre-Victorian scale survives close at hand in intricate little courts and alleys (for those on the s side, *see* Cornhill and Lombard Street, Alleys between). Recent additions are admirably sympathetic to the context.

North side, west to east

The street starts at the W at the ROYAL EXCHANGE (q.v.). In front of this, *Chantrey*'s equestrian STATUE of Wellington, 1844, faces the hub of the City with calm assurance. Posthumous execution from Chantrey's model was by *Henry Weekes*. The plinth has been raised to incorporate a ventilation shaft, spoiling its proportions. A kind of low-walled precinct around it, added 1985 with benches and cast-iron lamps, carries the wedge of land up to the road crossing. Further E a WAR MEMORIAL of 1919–20 by *Sir Aston Webb*, with bronze sculpture by *Alfred Drury*. A third STATUE on an oval plinth-cum-ventilation shaft in the middle of Cornhill is of the engineer J.H. Greathead (of the Greathead Shield), 1993, by *James Butler*.

More for the lover of sculpture in ROYAL EXCHANGE BUILDINGS, a small, exclusively pedestrian square behind the Exchange. At the s end a FOUNTAIN: under a Grecian red granite canopy a bronze maiden called Serenity, a copy of 1993 (by *S.R. Melton*) of *J. Whitehead*'s stolen original placed here in 1911. It commemorates the Jubilee of the Metropolitan Drinking Fountain and Cattle Trough Association. It originally stood W of the Exchange where the war memorial now is, but took the place of Rowland Hill's statue after that was removed to St Martin's le Grand, *c.* 1920 (*see* General Post Office). Another fountain at the N end with a charming seated figure of a nursing mother in the French heroic peasant manner, by *Dalou*, signed 1879. Its plinth (by

J. Edmeston) once supported columns and a square dome. Nearby, seated also and steadily looking N, the bronze STATUE of the American philanthropist George Peabody, who established the Peabody Trust, by *W. W. Story*, 1868. A granite portrait herm of Julius Reuter, by *Michael Black*, 1976, faces the Exchange entrance.

The Buildings themselves, on the E side of the square, are by *Sir Ernest George & Yeates*, 1906–10 (carving by *Albert Hodge*). Giant Doric aedicules over the entrances. The cornice is unbroken, as if the Baroque were being reined in. Curved corners echo those of the Exchange opposite. The banded bulgy rustication is a memorable device. Cornice and corners owe something to *I'Anson*'s pioneering red brick offices of 1842–4 previously on the site, a later extension of which survives in Finch Lane behind (q.v.). On Finch Lane's E corner, Nos. 78–80, CO-OP BANK, the former Union Building by *Gunton & Gunton*, 1922, has tall fluted Doric columns on a two-storey granite podium. At Nos. 75–77 the chaste retained façade of the former District Bank, by *Francis Jones & H. A. Dalrymple*, 1924–5. Plain storeys are sandwiched between a round-arched, channelled ground floor and an enriched cornice. No. 74, 1874 by *T. T. Smith*, uncouth free Renaissance in red brick with stone bands. In 1995 converted into flats, a use unthinkable in the old financial heartland ten years before.

114 Nos. 71–73, BANCO AMBROSIANO VENETO, the former Union Bank of Australia by *Goymour Cuthbert*, 1896, a memorable granite front with incised Grecian ornament and pilasters, then termini caryatids by *Herbert Pegram* on the top floor. The deployment of high sculptural relief on the flat wall is very satisfying. Only the admixture of Renaissance details betrays the date as late C19 and not C20. Plainer extension to the l., with similar detail. The aisled banking hall with its tall Ionic columns was retained in refurbishment by *Rolfe Judd Group Practice*, 1981–4, in connection

148 with the new No. 68, by *Richard Dickinson* of the practice. Its symmetrical façade echoes Hawksmoor, Mackintosh, and the Secession, an early and still fresh example of such Postmodern allusiveness. The low ratio of glazing to solid wall and the revival of close-set glazing bars were also innovative. Cornice levels are carefully aligned with their neighbours'. Remains of a wall of the C2 basilica of the Roman forum are preserved in the basement of No. 73, but cannot be viewed. Nos. 66–67, the former London & Lancashire Life Assurance, 1880–1 by *T. Chatfeild Clarke*, is 'in the style of François I', as he described it. Coupled columns between large tripartite windows. Much carving, putti and portrait medallions. An extension of 1885 faces the little Sun Court behind, adjoining part of the Merchant Taylors' Hall (q.v.).

No. 65, SHANGHAI COMMERCIAL BANK, was built by *E. I'Anson*, 1870, for the trading house of Messrs King, but with much space for rent. Plain Italian Neo-Gothic in grey brick, only three bays wide. The arches are round under slightly pointed voussoirs emphasized by a thin extrados moulding. The top floor is more ornate, with six narrow arches. Decorated terracotta strings by *Cubitt*. A C19 appearance was restored to the ground floor in

1984–6, and little steel inserts of lions added to the bosses. From a previous building, Smith, Elder & Co. had published Thackeray, the Brontës and the *Cornhill Magazine*.

A long passage leads to WHITE LION COURT behind, with its big C18 house, said to date from 1767. Four storeys, five bays wide, the entrance off-centre. The storeys are curiously proportioned, with the largest windows to a second-floor saloon. Rusticated stucco etc. on the ground floor, added in 1849 for Lloyd's Register of Shipping (here *c.* 1834–1901). Refurbished 1987–90, adding new offices behind. (Good open-well staircase of full height with slender balusters and column-newels; second-floor saloon with grand doorcases with bayleaf friezes and rich modillion cornice, with painted cartouches of the Lloyd's Lady, *c.* 1835.) Nos. 62–64 on the corner with Bishopsgate, the Halifax Building Society, 1987–9 by *Rolfe Judd Group Practice*. Stone-clad with all-over channelling on a battered plinth, nicely done, but without the resonance of No. 68. On the cornice to the chamfered corner stands an undersized SCULPTURE of Demeter by *Terry Powell*.

South side, west to east

Tall and grandiose early to mid-C20 buildings face the Royal Exchange. No. 1, the ROYAL INSURANCE, was built for the Liverpool & London and Globe Insurance by *J. Macvicar Anderson*, 1905. The little dome at the W corner makes the principal accent of the principal crossing of the City. Free Ionic order above two storeys of banded rustication. Sculpted maidens and a globe on the N front. A fine oval banking hall at the corner was retained in refurbishment by *Howard Lobb, Ratcliffe, Leather & Partners*, 1978–9. They also extended the Cornhill front E by two bays in a similar style. Plainer stone-faced extension to Lombard Street, tactfully matching the proportions. Then Nos. 13–14, the former Scottish Equitable Assurance Society, 1910 by *J. S. Gibson*. Seven narrow storeys, variously treated and sculpturally embellished. Square open turret on top, uncannily like a favourite Lutyens device of the 1920s.

LLOYDS BANK at Nos. 15–22 was designed by *Sir John J. Burnet* with *Campbell-Jones & Smithers* as executive architects, 1927–30, as befitted the bank's headquarters and main City office. In the grand manner of American Beaux-Arts Classicism, with none of the tendencies to abstraction of Burnet and Tait's earlier Adelaide House, nor the Neo-Mannerist individualism of Lutyens's Midland Bank headquarters in Poultry a few hundred yards away. An upright giant Corinthian order on a peristyle rises through three storeys. Broad plain attic. To Lombard Street there are pilasters. The lucid plan is symmetrical either side of a line bisecting the wedge-shaped site, with a high top-lit banking hall in the centre which has aisles of sober marble Ionic columns. The counters fit in between. Carving and plasterwork by *Joseph Armitage*, floor mosaic by *Gilbert Bayes*. (Fifth-floor boardrooms etc., in late C17 style.) There follow three palatial insurance offices of the same period, all tall and symmetrical but with interesting differences of detail. No. 24, the former Commercial Union Assurance by *Maurice Webb*, 1929, was built in a rush when work on Lloyds caused the previous building (by *J. Macvicar Anderson*, 1895) to collapse. Graeco-Egyptian detail and a pediment, but large horizontal windows as a concession to fashionable plainness. Below the pediment, the window surrounds project to merge with the outer mouldings of the fluted piers, a quirky detail of the kind Webb Senior favoured in the 1920s. Carved paired brackets at the top in the form of seated lions, carried around in relief at the sides (carving and other sculpture by *Laurence Turner*). The set-backs here allow natural light to both sides of the boardroom. Wide, galleried entrance hall, unusually generous for an insurance office of the date. Nos. 28–30, SCOTTISH WIDOWS, 1934–5 by *W. Curtis Green & Partners*.* Plain stone with no controlling order, the windows alternately single and tripartite. Pedimented set-back attic with sculpted figures. Some jazzy touches to the ironwork at the entrance and on the white-glazed-brick rear elevations. The spacious office hall was converted to a restaurant in 1997. Then No. 32, the former Cornhill Insurance by *Gunton & Gunton*, 1935, with plain piers and a flat Ionic aedicule above. Wooden doors with period scenes designed by *B.P. Arnold* and carved by *W. Gilbert*, 1939. Rear upper extension by *Clarke Penner Architects*, 1990.

Nos. 33–35 were built as the National Discount Offices by the brothers *Francis*, 1857–8 and tall for the date. They are in the richest palazzo style with lots of Cinquecento motifs in the manner of e.g. Peruzzi, but also with French-derived dormers. Joint-stock discount companies were a new phenomenon of the mid 1850s, and the desire to show they had arrived is very evident in all this plutocratic display. A plainer brick extension faces Birchin Lane.

By now we are past the Royal Exchange, and the scale diminishes somewhat. Nos. 36–38, routine stripped classical by *Campbell-Jones & Smithers*, 1923, for the Merchants Marine Insurance Co. Nos. 39–42, two Victorian properties housing UNION PLC, refurbished with great finesse by the *Fitzroy Robinson Partnership*, 1975–9. Nos. 39–41 were built for the company's predecessor, the Union Discount Co., by *J. Macvicar Anderson*, 1889–90. Rich and heavy, with the architect's favourite superimposed orders across five bays and two high storeys. Arcaded below, aedicules above. Pilastered attic and then dormers. Fitzroy's painting of the front a deep crimson is entirely successful. (On it a medallion of the poet Thomas Gray by *F. W. Pomeroy*, 1917; surround designed by *Perks*.) The retained banking hall has a high, gleaming majolica ceiling of *Doulton*'s tiles and a counter and gallery with dark reused woodwork. No. 42, a former hat warehouse, now serves as the entrance. By *Tabberer*, 1876–7, tall and narrow with polished purple granite piers in five storeys, the top one arched. The upper storeys now house the lavatories, masked by glass lacily engraved with the company's crest. A purple granite extension down St Michael's Alley beyond replaces work by *Anderson*, 1899.

The porch of St Michael Cornhill follows with the steeple zooming up above. Against the church, Nos. 45–47, the dull former Sun Insurance Co. by *Campbell-Jones, Son & Smithers*, 1924–5. The

---

* Mr J. Sampson Lloyd says that the designer was *Antony Lloyd*, who had just been made a partner in the practice.

late C18 house at No. 48 demonstrates the tendency to extreme tallness in the City's street architecture of that date. No. 50 was Prescott, Dimsdale, Tugwell & Cave's Bank, by *H. Cowell Boyes*, 1891–2. Friendly red brick, loosely late C17 with a tall arcade of grey granite Tuscan columns and four close-set balustraded balconies to the second-floor windows. These mark the CITY UNIVERSITY CLUB, which preserves modest interiors of 1906. (The banking hall, under a glazed dome at the rear, has alabaster and mahogany panelling. Disused but intact in 1997.) Nos. 52–53 by *Stanley Hall, Easton & Robertson*, 1931, for Harris, Forbes & Co. Plainer and taller than its neighbours and coarser too, with repeated plain storeys of brick. Its steel frame and hollow-pot floors allowed exceptionally fast construction. Nos. 54–55 by *Runtz*, 1893, red *Doulton* terracotta in an asymmetrical Loire Château style more familiar in Mayfair. Angle turret, mullioned and transomed windows, gable with squatting demon.

St Peter's church peeps over modest two-storey late C19 shops at Nos. 56–57. These are the last survivors of the low structures once common against City church walls. Nos. 58–60, a tall eclectic Renaissance commercial block by *Tabberer*, 1877, makes the corner with Gracechurch Street.

CORNHILL and LOMBARD STREET,
alleys between

Just enough survives of the intricate series of passages and of their C18 and C19 buildings to give an idea of the density of the old City, and of the taverns and chop-houses around which so much business revolved here in its commercial heart. A great fire here in 1748 gives a *terminus post quem*; a lesser fire followed in 1765.

By No. 39 Cornhill is the entrance to BALL COURT. Here is SIMPSON'S, in two houses apparently of *c.* 1700, with brick bands, though they must date from after 1748. Lower r. extension, late C18 or early C19. The main shopfront has pilasters framing a bow. The shopfront, looking late C18, is actually of *c.* 1900, when such traditional taverns that survived were getting self-conscious. Tactfully restored by *Michell & Partners*, 1980.

A covered passage leads from Ball Court to CASTLE COURT. On its s side, the stuccoed GEORGE AND VULTURE, made up of three altered properties rebuilt after 1748. Four storeys, the ground floor extended towards the court in the early C19. The friendly panelled interior is mostly late C19 (on the first-floor staircase a reset carved C18 aedicule with ribbon and floral enrichment; upper flights have closed-string stairs of earlier C18 type). A passage leads through to a tiny back corner facing GEORGE YARD, where until 1855 stood another George and Vulture, featured in the *Pickwick Papers*. George Yard has been greatly enlarged from a narrow alley in successive C20 rebuildings of Barclays Bank on the e side (*see* Lombard Street). Its N side is made by *GMW Partnership*'s tall red brick ST MICHAEL'S HOUSE, 1993–5, with repeated shallow bows nicely reminiscent of the Free Style of *c.* 1900.

A cramped passage leads w beneath the George and Vulture to
BENGAL COURT, which has tall houses of *c.* 1800 on the N side
(restored 1989–90). Back to Castle Court for the Victorian buildings of ST MICHAEL'S ALLEY, which leads N back up to
Cornhill. The JAMAICA WINE HOUSE by St Michael's churchyard is by *Banister Fletcher*, 1885. Red brick and red Mansfield
stone, loose in the 1880s way, with big iron-mullioned bays; the
N part built over the C19 cloister of St Michael. Well-preserved
interior. It is the successor to a celebrated coffee house of that
name, established in the alley probably *c.* 1675 and known on this
site by 1748. Facing, No. 4 by *William Lee*, 1864, tall and slim,
with a giant, cheerfully illiterate relieving arch; No. 3, sedate late
classical, *c.* 1840.

No comparable pleasures in the alleys to the E (ST PETER'S COURT,
BELL INN YARD) and W (CHANGE ALLEY, COWPER'S
COURT), which are little more than white-glazed canyons
between big C20 buildings facing the main thoroughfares, not
always on their ancient alignments (e.g. Change Alley).

CREECHURCH LANE

A narrow street, of composite origin. The S part, off Leadenhall
Street, formed part of Bury Street, the ancient W boundary of Holy
Trinity Priory (*see* also Duke's Place and Leadenhall Street). The
main gate of the priory, rebuilt in the C14 and dem. in 1822, crossed
the lane just N of the junction with Bury Street. The first Synagogue
of the Resettlement lay near here (1656). After 1884 the lane was
extended N, incorporating the former King Street, a late C16–C17
formation across the priory site, and Duke Street, cut across the line
of the City wall to Houndsditch *c.* 1779.

On the E side after St Katharine Cree, an interesting group of late
C19 warehouses. Nos. 2–16, CREECHURCH BUILDINGS, well-
preserved tea warehouses of 1886–7 (contractor *Franklin S. King*).
Of brick, each three-light bay with a segmental rusticated relieving
arch of stucco. The treatment continues around an internal courtyard. Conversion to flats is proposed (1997). Then the more
ambitious CREE HOUSE (Nos. 18–20), by *M. E. Collins*, 1891–2,
for Phillips & Co., fruiterers, free red brick and terracotta, with
good fruity carved panels etc. The arcaded ground floor with
banded voussoirs accommodated fruit stalls. Other floors had
small windows high up (since enlarged) so coconuts could be
stacked; behind the parapet was apparatus 'for carrying on the
bleaching of nuts' (*Building News* 61, 1891). After Mitre Street,
Nos. 22 and 24: four-storeyed tea warehouses of 1895, yellow
brick dressed with red, above stone-faced ground floors. The little
SUGAR BAKERS' COURT between them was first laid out *c.* 1586
by *William Kerwin*. The E side of Creechurch Lane here is the
extension to Berlage's offices in Bury Street (q.v.).

More warehouses down MITRE STREET, an early C19 formation
cut through courts and yards formed within the priory church
after the Dissolution. On the S side, Nos. 27–28, 1891 by *F. Adams
Smith*, with elliptical windows and chamfered verticals finishing as

big mitres; Nos. 29–31, 1888, more utilitarian. Nos. 12–14 facing, by *Weightman & Bullen*, 1983–5, reproduce the late C19 warehouse type. Further E, Nos. 32–40, flat-fronted in stone, with the over-familiar device of an inset convex entrance bay; by *Ley, Colbeck & Partners*, 1989–91, part of their No. 78 Leadenhall Street (q.v.).

Buildings W and NW belong with Bevis Marks (q.v.). For International House, opposite them, *see* Duke's Place.

CRESCENT

Part of *Dance the Younger*'s planned development for Sir Benjamin Hammett of Taunton, built 1767–70 (*see* also America Square). Its importance is that it introduced to London the devices of residential crescent and circus. The source was probably the Woods' much grander layouts in Bath (Royal Circus laid out 1754, Royal Crescent 1766).

Only CRESCENT preserves any Georgian fabric, with much recent restoration. Entry from Minories is via Hammett Street, now merely a passage through the London Guildhall University building (*see* Public Buildings) – an unsympathetic neighbour, though better than the unsightly 1930s electricity substation, SW corner. There were eleven houses (compare the younger Wood's thirty), of stock brick with rubbed dressings, each of three bays and four storeys. Original doorcases remain on Nos. 6 and 7, with unusually detailed Doric columns and triglyph friezes. These façades were restored by *Lyons, Sleeman & Hoare*, 1985–6 (with Nos. 41–43 Trinity Square), who also built careful replicas at Nos. 8–11, 1986–91. Looser Neo-Georgian behind, with picturesque pedimented gables (visible from the pedestrian passage through the Roman wall into Cooper's Row, N).

Through the S range of the university building one reaches the site of the CIRCUS. This was heavily bombed, though one house (of twelve) lasted until Tower Hill was widened in the late 1970s. The miniature scale is apparent from the surviving part of its granite-paved roadway on the grass verge here (though the houses did stand back from the kerb).

CROSBY SQUARE *see* GREAT ST HELEN'S

CROSSWALL *see* AMERICA SQUARE

CRUTCHED FRIARS

A street of some striking juxtapositions. The name comes from the house of the Friars of the Holy Cross (Crutch coming from *crux*), founded *c.* 1298 on the S side (church rebuilt *c.* 1520). The W part of the street keeps its alternative name of Hart Street (q.v.). The friary site is roughly bisected by the present Savage Gardens. By the early

C19 Crutched Friars was mostly given over to warehouses; then in 1839 the railway to Fenchurch Street bisected it. Some older buildings survive against the odds, amidst much post-war rebuilding.

The street begins at the w by St Olave. On the s side, Walsingham House (*see* Seething Lane) and Mariner House (*see* Pepys Street). On the N SIDE, after New London House (*see* London Street), No. 41, a wine warehouse of 1869–70 by an unknown architect, a creditable and very early essay in the style of *c.* 1700, in red brick with segment-headed windows and key blocks (converted to a pub in 1996). It takes its cue from No. 42, an excellent red brick house of *c.* 1725. Three bays, with two further bays over an archway, r. Both sections are framed with rusticated piers. Doorcase with fluted Corinthian pilasters, carrying the typical early Georgian frieze rising to a point in the middle. Nice area railings of later C18 type. The ground-floor window with iron colonnettes dates from a warehouse conversion of 1872. Some plain panelled interiors remain. The archway leads into FRENCH ORDINARY COURT, which straggles up towards Fenchurch Street in a cavernous passage below the station. The name probably comes from a C17 tavern selling 'ordinaries', meals served at a fixed time and price, although its alignment is C15 or older. Then at No. 44 the retained façade of the former GREAT NORTHERN AND GREAT WESTERN RAILWAYS DEPOT, built in 1855–6 on a wedge-shaped site left by the railway, and reconstructed 1983–7 as part of the Fenchurch Street station redevelopment (q.v.). Very plain brick, but well-proportioned: segment-headed ground-floor windows between round windows like big portholes, segment-headed windows above, minimal pilasters on the second floor.

On the s side just before the railway, SAVAGE GARDENS, named from the garden of Sir Thomas Savage, whose house stood on the site of the present Trinity House (*see* Public Buildings) in the early C17. No buildings of interest. The station platforms swerve across the street on an impressive skewed brick arch dating from 1839, and, N, on girders from the widening of 1881. Skulking under the latter on the w, the CHESHIRE CHEESE pub, *c.* 1881, called after its predecessor, a gabled and jettied house of *c.* 1600.

Beyond the railway, the street curves gently NE. Buildings are mostly big offices of after *c.* 1970, which fill most of their street blocks. On the s SIDE, JARDINE HOUSE (No. 6), on the acute corner with Crosswall, by *Scott Brownrigg & Turner*, 1986–8. Curtain-walled, with bands of pink granite alternately polished and unpolished, the windows diminishing in size as the building rises. At the corner entrance the upper storeys break forward on either side of recessed curved glazing, which penetrates a rounded and canti-levered upper storey to emerge as a little domed turret above. Modified inside by *Michael Hopkins* and *Eva Jiricna*, 1989, with one of the latter's trademark spidery staircases in a circular atrium snaking down to basement level. (Top-lit boardroom reworked by the two with a delicate 'umbrella' below the glazing.) Then Nos. 3–5, LUTIDINE HOUSE, an older building refronted with pilaster-piers *c.* 1990. Nos. 1–2, ROMAN WALL HOUSE, offices of 1905 with tall pilasters at irregular intervals.

On the N side after Lloyd's Avenue, FRIARY COURT (TOUCHE

Ross), a big, irregular and fairly low building by *Chapman Taylor Partners* (1981–5). Pink-granite-clad, polished or left rough, with slit windows to the ground floor and mullioned ones above; little glazed and rounded corner oriels; the detail free of historicism. Main entrance on the corner with Northumberland Alley, w, named from the Inn of the Earl of Northumberland, of which C15 remains were found during construction. To its N, it is set back behind a large and wholly unexpected sunken water garden, with a covered walkway round at street level. The central feature here is a big rounded glazed bay, variously treated as it rises through the floors. Upper storeys on pairs of slender close-set piers, rising to full height; similar piers on the other fronts end weakly over the ground floor. Inset at the SE corner, an eerily static SCULPTURE of two friars by *Michael Black*.

The truncated remains of RANGOON STREET extend N. Made in the mid 1890s on the site of the East India Company's tea warehouses. None of *Delissa Joseph*'s original buildings remains.

The street continues as JEWRY STREET.

CULLUM STREET

Built after the Great Fire and named after the landowner Sir Thomas Cullum, whose mansion previously stood here. It runs irregularly down from Lime Street to Fenchurch Street.

Of interest only Nos. 14–16 on the s side, BOLTON HOUSE, dated 1907 and signed *Aiselby Archt.*: a gay front with plenty of peacock green and pale blue majolica offset against white and grey, with a big foliage frieze; the style licentious, with touches of Art Nouveau and even of Moorish (the trefoiled first-floor windows). Façade incorporated with the new Nos. 154–156 Fenchurch Street behind (*GMW Partnership*, 1981–5), with storeys crudely added in a slated hamper.

CURSITOR STREET

Named after the Cursitors, who issued writs for the Court of Chancery until 1835. Their office was on the corner with Chancery Lane. The street was divided amongst the Borough of Camden and the Cities of London and Westminster until 1994.

On the s SIDE, Nos. 27–29, an interesting brick Free Style factory of *c.*1908, with elongated gables over the end bays. Then SPECTRUM HOUSE (Nos. 20–26), by *Thomas Saunders & Associates*, 1971–5, long, low, and unusually strongly modelled. Two storeys cantilever out over a recessed ground floor and half-basement. Segmental arches between the support beams, broad segment-headed windows in red aggregate-faced panels over. Upper storeys slope back.

No buildings of note on the N side.

CUTLER STREET and CUTLERS' GARDENS

An L-shaped street on the N side of Houndsditch. Named from the Cutlers' Company, who owned the land. The S part is the old Woolpack or Woolsack Alley, widened and renamed *c.* 1734, the E part the former White Street, widened when the Metropolitan Railway tunnelled through in the mid 1870s. N of this E part, CUTLERS' GARDENS: a modern office development on the site of the great late Georgian EAST INDIA COMPANY WAREHOUSES, parts of which are incorporated. The company was chartered in 1600, and enjoyed a monopoly of trade with the East Indies until 1813. Tea was the major commodity handled here. The location so far from the river needs some explanation. In the C18 London's trade was restricted to the 'Legal Quays' along the City foreshore, and warehoused within the City. Only in the 1800s was this monopoly broken, and new enclosed docks and warehouses established downstream.

The earliest section is the Old Bengal Warehouse, 1769–71, on the S side of New Street, to the NW. Major construction took place to its E in 1792–1800, and a SW extension was added *c.* 1820 adjoining Devonshire Square. At five acres it was the largest of several such complexes built for the company in the C18. The others mostly lay nearer the river, e.g. in Seething Lane and Crutched Friars (dem.). The company's surveyors designed the buildings: first *Richard Jupp* (executor *George Wyatt*), 1769–71, then Jupp alone, joined and then succeeded by *Henry Holland* (1792–1800), and finally *S. P. Cockerell* (*c.* 1820). Both Holland and Cockerell carried on Jupp's style. The long inward-facing blocks made interpenetrating courtyards on an irregular layout, defined by New Street (W), Middlesex Street (N), Harrow Place (E), and Cutler Street (S): quite different from the spacious quadrangles or detached rows of the late Georgian docklands. In 1854 *George Aitchison Sen.* added a sixth storey to most of the warehouses, for the St Katherine's Dock Co., which had bought them in 1836. The Port of London Authority used them until 1976. Then in 1978–82 the site was redeveloped for Greycoat Estates and Standard Life by *R. Seifert & Partners*. That they were saved was due to the steady attrition of dockside warehouses in the 1970s, and the consequent resistance to wholesale clearance. The result was a compromise: E and NE parts were entirely rebuilt, S and W parts mostly reconstructed within the Georgian walls. There are 600,000 square ft of offices, with shops and a few flats. Part of the remainder was more gently converted, by *Quinlan Terry*, 1984–5.

The view from Cutler Street announces the mixture of old and new. Retained warehouse fronts form a broad forecourt. Of yellow brick, with segment-headed windows. The l. block by *Jupp*, 1796–7, the r. by *Holland*, 1800. Their arcaded ground floors are from Seifert's reconstruction, as is the whole matching S wall of *Cockerell*'s range by Devonshire Square (far l.). Glazed lobbies within the arcades give access to the offices. Just within the gates, HOUSES of *c.* 1800 for the East India Company's officers, two on the l., one on the r., with stone dressings and rusticated round-arched doorways. GATES of iron between rusticated stone gateways with ornamental ball-finials, by *Quinlan Terry*. The gateways replaced simpler Georgian piers.

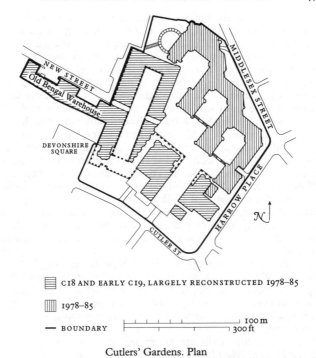

CI8 AND EARLY CI9, LARGELY RECONSTRUCTED 1978–85

1978–85

— BOUNDARY

100 m
300 ft

Cutlers' Gardens. Plan

A wholly new front by *Seifert*'s closes the vista. Its arcaded and rusticated ground floor echoes the front of 1799 it replaced (whence the square clock over). The most serious loss was not these inner parts but the mighty Middlesex Street warehouse front, NE (1799), which had staggered windowless ranges rising above a tall screen wall. The new façade forms the s front of the central spur of the new buildings, seven- to ten-storeyed, with matching dark flush window bands and rich golden-brown Brazilian granite cladding. Big chamfered corner piers. The plan is roughly the CI8 one regularized, with N spur blocks making three narrow courtyards, diminishing in depth W to E. The result has a certain sober dignity. The spaces between are also generally attractive, with trees and fountains (landscaping by *Russell Page*). A shopping arcade runs s from the SE angle, back down towards Cutler Street. In the CENTRAL COURT (l.), SCULPTURE by *Denys Mitchell*, The Cnihtengild, 1990. Giant knight in armour on a caparisoned horse, patinated bronze, with fanciful Celtic surface decoration. The plinth makes one slow revolution annually. The Cnihtengild were late CIO knights to whom King Edgar granted the Ward of Portsoken, beyond the City wall.

The w wall of the Central Court is again CI8, with a rusticated archway to a passage into the restored WEST COURT. A pitilessly 90 plain close measuring some 250 ft (76 metres) by 50 ft (15 metres). Six storeys of diminishing segment-headed windows. The N part, beginning just s of the cross-passage, is by *Jupp*, 1792–4 (bricklayer *Thomas Poynder*); the s part the matching extension by

Cockerell, c. 1820. All but the w side of the s part were reconstructed by *Seifert's*. They filled in the loading bays, and, most
regrettably, replaced the sashes with mute tinted plate glass. The
former appearance is preserved on Cockerell's extension, s of the
entrance alignment. This section was sensitively converted to
offices by *Terry*, 1984–5, with part of the Old Bengal Warehouse
immediately behind. Entry from the West Court via a corridor
and steps up to a new stone doorcase after Bramante. Off to the l.,
the double-apsed c18 stairhall, cleaned down to the brick.
Cantilevered staircase with rough-hewn stone treads; Chinese
Chippendale balustrade by Terry. (Original timber floors with
wooden piers, plain or fashioned as Doric columns; other columns,
of cast iron, recased 1984–5. The later phases used fireproof
hollow-pot construction instead, not preserved internally: probably
reflecting the influence of Holland.) The conventions of polite
architecture reassert themselves on the symmetrical outer front of
the West Court, facing New Street: twelve bays, the ground floor
with round-arched windows and at each end a flat rusticated
stone archway.

At r. angles here, along the s side of New Street, *Jupp's* OLD
BENGAL WAREHOUSE now shows the c18 character best. Five
original storeys, rusticated stone below bare yellow brick. Simple
stone cornice. Its projecting two-bay ends and three-bay centre,
with shallow walled courts between, were not repeated on the
later blocks. The w part still empty in 1997.

Back in Cutler Street, in the SE angle, CUTLERS' COURT, by
Renton Howard Wood Levin Partnership, 1981–4, also for Greycoat
Estates. Polished brown granite facing, small windows, bays
variously angled. It was the first British essay in American 'fast-
track' construction, facilitated especially by steel floor decking (*see*
Introduction p. 142). NE extension, 1990–2, more explicitly
Postmodern. It extends s on to Houndsditch (as No. 123), around
a courtyard called Clothier Street.

Cutler Street continues E as WHITE KENNETT STREET (Back
Gravel Lane until *c.* 1955). Here a white-faience-clad warehouse
erected over the Underground railway cutting, by *Lewis Solomon
& Son*, 1936.

DEVONSHIRE ROW

It leads from Bishopsgate into Devonshire Square. Entirely rebuilt
after the Metropolitan Railway tunnelled along it in the mid 1870s.

Unpretentious warehouses on the s SIDE. Nos. 3–11, 1879, has shallow-arched three- and five-light windows. By contrast with such
industrial vernacular, the N SIDE shows commercial architects
adopting Queen Anne fashions. The BULL pub is by *W. S. R.
Payne*, 1876. Anglo-Dutch; red Fareham brick with carved aprons
and panels. Inset third-floor balcony to the publican's quarters.
Next door, Nos. 8–18, uniform three-storey warehouses over
shops, 1878–9 by *W. W. Neve*, a pupil of Shaw. One of those c19
buildings that foreshadowed c20 structural grids. Sunflower
panels ornament the upper piers. The rear wall incorporates a

freakish late C16 survival: low red brick walling some 115 ft (35 metres) long, with a few simple stone-mullioned windows. It formed part of the N front of 'Fisher's Folly', a huge house built between 1567 and 1579 by Jasper Fisher, Clerk in Chancery, later a property of the Earl of Devonshire (*see* Devonshire Square below).

DEVONSHIRE SQUARE

The site of the garden of the Earl of Devonshire's house (*see* Devonshire Row above), sold in 1675 to *Nicholas Barbon*, who built up the square between 1678 and 1708. The atmosphere of a true square has gone; the East India Company's warehouse barged into the NE corner *c.* 1820 (for which *see* Cutler Street), and E and s sides lie partly open between mostly C20 buildings, the most obtrusive the Houndsditch Telephone Exchange, s side (q.v.).

The earliest survivors are the fine mid-Georgian pair, Nos. 12 and 13 (N). Their rusticated stone doorcases with Ionic columns and pediments on pulvinated friezes look *c.* 1740 (a print of 1728 shows the C17 sequence intact). Four bays, four storeys plus half-basement. Of the two, No. 12 is better preserved internally, though restored by *Robert C. Murray*, 1886, to 'as far as possible, its original condition' (*Building News*): an interesting minor landmark of early Neo-Georgian taste. Generous central open-well staircase set back from the front, with Ionic pilasters at the entrance. Two-flight staircase with typical ramped handrails, enriched tread ends, and column-newels; more individual balusters (two per tread), with twisted shafts on candlestick-like bases. Enriched first-floor doorcases and panelled doors. In the front room, E, a remarkable fireplace of *c.* 1820, with pivoting back-to-back double grate. Otherwise much good panelling, mid-C18 style, but doubtless partly of 1886. No. 13 became the COOPERS' HALL in 1958. The plan differs slightly, e.g. in the arrangement of the staircase. Interiors adapted by *E. W. Palmer*, with some Neo-Georgian embellishment. Their previous halls had stood since 1490 in Basinghall Street; the fourth incarnation there (by *George Barnes Williams*, 1865) was destroyed in the Blitz.

Proceeding anticlockwise from No. 13: No. 14, plain late C19 commercial; No. 15 by *H. Chatfeild Clarke*, 1898, nicely dressed-up red brick and stone, with bulgy second-floor pilasters on brackets; Nos. 16–17 and No. 1, flanking the entrance to Devonshire Row, decent red brick commercial of *c.* 1900, with white-rendered upper storeys in the manner of early LCC work; No. 2 by *W. L. Lucas*, 1926, the former Imperial Continental Gas Co., grey brick Neo-Georgian with a four-column porch.

DOWGATE HILL

Built over the mouth of the Walbrook. The early Roman canalization of this river appears to have taken watercourses either side of an island structure where a mill may have been located. Slightly upstream of this were massive and well-decorated buildings. Explorations within the basements of Nos. 3–7 have found Roman marble-clad walls surviving to a height of 8 ft (2½ metres). The present name is from a watergate, known from the early C12, in the long-vanished riverside wall S of Upper Thames Street. A narrow inlet called Dowgate Dock survived here until the mid C20.

83 On the W side Cannon Street station, on the E three happily surviving Livery Companies' halls. They form the grandest sequence of all the rich and varied pre-C20 buildings in the block defined by Cannon Street and Upper Thames Street, N and S, Queen Street and King William Street, E and W. In each case the hall proper lies some way further back. At the N end, facing a courtyard made through Nos. 3–7, the Tallow Chandlers' Hall (q.v.). After the Skinners' Hall (q.v.), No. 9, a narrow two-bay house, dated 1779 on the rainwater-head. Dyers' Hall (q.v.) completes the sequence.

DUKE'S PLACE

The SE continuation of Bevis Marks, along the inside of the City wall. Until 1939 called Duke Street; named from Thomas Howard, Duke of Norfolk (†1572), who inherited the house built by Thomas Audley on the site of Holy Trinity Priory after 1531 (*see* also Creechurch Lane and Leadenhall Street).

On the S SIDE, INTERNATIONAL HOUSE, by *Joseph, F. Milton Cashmore & Partners*, 1969–75. Nine-storey stone-faced N–S slab, unequal three-storey wings along the street. Fin-like mullions and rounded window-heads and sills make a (somewhat arbitrary) decorative pattern. Main entrance from Creechurch Lane, via CREECHURCH PLACE, the site of HOLY TRINITY PRIORY's outer court. Matching S extension to Mitre Street, 1978–81. MITRE SQUARE, in the SE angle here, marks the site of the priory cloister. Excavations in 1979 found remains of its C12 W range, doubled to the W in the C13–C14, the C13 W end of the church (beneath Mitre Street), and a C13 belfry. Remains of the N choir aisle were exposed further E in 1908, during the construction of the Sir John Cass School, and fragments of the S choir remain within the foyer of No. 76 Leadenhall Street (qq.v.). Two C17 religious buildings were founded in the vicinity: St James (1622, E side: hence St James's Passage), rebuilt 1727 and demolished 1874; and the Great Synagogue on the N (destroyed 1941), of 1690, but frequently rebuilt: in 1722, 1765–6 (*Dance Sen. & Jun.*), 1788–90 (*James Spiller*), and 1852 (*John Wallen*).

On the N SIDE, run-of-the-mill post-war offices, typical of their three consecutive decades: from W to E, GREENLY HOUSE, by *Lewis Solomon, Son & Joseph*, completed 1950, still in the stripped pre-war manner; DUKE'S HOUSE, 1962 by *R. Seifert & Partners*, stone-faced, with simple polished mullions; IRONGATE HOUSE, 1973–8 by *Fitzroy Robinson Partnership*, seven even storeys on pilotis, with upright windows deeply recessed in polished red Transvaal granite framing. The E front overlooks a garden made when the road was widened; completed 1979.

EASTCHEAP

Recorded by *c.* 1100, and called after the medieval market (cheap, chepe) held here. East is, in contrast to Westcheap or Cheapside, the principal London market. The medieval W limit was some way beyond the E end of the present Cannon Street, its E end on the line of Rood Lane. The W and E sections were called Great and Little Eastcheap respectively. The present width dates from 1882–4, when the S side was rebuilt to accommodate the Metropolitan Line. At the same time it was extended E by the incorporation of Little Tower Street, where the present street bends S. On the N side, small to medium-sized Victorian buildings survive in unbroken sequence, amongst them some tall and extraordinary 1860s warehouses. Several 1880s blocks remain opposite.

North side, west to east

The corner building is the National Provident Institution (*see* Gracechurch Street). Then Nos. 5–7, *A. H. Kersey*'s former National Provincial Bank, 1920–2, with ornamented metal floor panels. First Victorian building is No. 11, 1884, one of several C19 buildings here with ornate lower office floors and plainly treated warehousing above. Shouldered Gothic arches to the first floor. Nos. 13 and 15, both narrow, loosely Italianate: No. 13 with a pedimented gable and semicircular balcony; No. 15 by *R. Fabian Russell,* 1885. Nos. 19–21, EASTCHEAP BUILDINGS, speculative offices of 1881 for the Drapers' Company, by its surveyor *Charles Reilly Sen.* Large, of stone, with pilasters, big pedimented doorcase and much small-scale detailing.

On the E corner with Philpot Lane, No. 23, 1861–2 by *John Young & Son,* offices and warehousing for Messrs Hunt & Crombie, spice merchants. Vigorous Lombardic Gothic, polychrome brick, its five diminishing storeys topped by an enriched terracotta cornice (by *Blanchard,* an early use for a commercial building). The offices are distinguished by stone facing on the first two floors, now painted. Above, light buff brick with dark mortared joints. Near-flush walls; deep-set round-arched windows of various sizes, their squat colonnettes banded or blocked. Brick voussoirs in sunburst patterns. Shell-shaped medallions on the Philpot Lane front identify client, architect and builder (*Piper & Wheeler*). Where the building sets back here, a tiny carving of mice eating cheese appears just below the cornice.* Reconstructed by *YRM Architects,* 1984–7, with Nos. 25–35 beyond.

First, No. 25, a gabled and substantial former pub by *Bird & Walters,* 1892–3. Polished black columns below and on the recessed first floor, where romping putti are carved in the spandrels. No. 31, 1860, again by *Young & Son,* narrow, like No. 11 with Gothic first-floor windows below plainer buff brick, here within a relieving arch like a giant Gibbs surround. Altered parapet. Nos. 33–35, the masterpiece of *R. L. Roumieu,* was built in 1868 as the London depot of Hill & Evans, vinegar-makers of Worcester. One of the maddest displays in London of gabled

104

---

*I owe this to the observation of Mr Laurie Kinney.

Gothic; called by Ian Nairn 'the scream that you wake on at the end of a nightmare'. Red brick with blue brick bands and diapering, dressed in Tisbury stone with Devonshire marble columns, all organized into a frenzy of sharp gables, a shaft resting on top of a gable, others starting on corbels. Strictly symmetrical withal: twin three-bay outer sections narrow as they rise, exposing a recessed centre with a dormer in the steep roof. Spiky foliage-finials and roof-cresting on top (ironwork by *Peard & Jackson* of Holborn). Contractors *Browne & Robinson*, carving by *Frampton & Williamson*. The cost was £8,170. In 1987 the arcaded ground-floor design and iron gates were re-created.

Much quieter after that, with large-windowed late C19 blocks with banded piers (No. 37, and No. 39, dated 1893), or pilasters (the big No. 41, Rood Street corner). No. 43 forms a handsome group with the entrance to St Margaret Pattens. Early C18, stuc-coed and given an excellently architectural shopfront shortly after 1833. This has a big flattened bow between matching double doors with Grecian ornament. Each door is framed by Corinthian columns supporting a full, correct cornice (No. 45 adjoining, by *Kenneth Lindy & Partners*, 1966, replicates another early C18 house formerly here). The shop faces ROOD LANE, named from a crucifix in St Margaret's churchyard destroyed in 1538 (Stow). Finally, No. 51, offices by *R. Seifert & Partners*, 1986–7. Strong chamfered forms; storeys variously distinguished, corbelled out near the top as if inspired by Roumieu and then set back in two storeys of round-arched windows. Polished Brazilian granite facing. It replaced part of Plantation House (*see* Fenchurch Street), to which it is linked via an internal courtyard with a fountain.

South side, from east to west

Between Idol Lane and St Mary-at-Hill, a single development, Nos. 30–40, 1988–92 by *T. P. Bennett Partnership*, based loosely on the late Victorian buildings it replaced. They were: No. 40, 1890 by Messrs *Shoppee*; No. 38 by *George Sherrin*, 1905, with a rear range of 1888 to St Mary-at-Hill; and Nos. 30–36 by *T. R. Richards*, c. 1885. Nos. 22–24 by *George Edwards*, 1884–5, eclectic, with gar-landed frieze; rebuilt by *Sheppard Robson*, 1984–7, reinstating a Victorian pattern of shopfronts. Then No. 20, PEEK HOUSE, by *Peebles*, 1883–5, for Peek Bros., tea and coffee dealers. Bulgy corner tower, with singular Graeco-Egyptian details. Over the door an amusing relief of camels and a driver, by *Theed*. Earlier buildings for Peek's adjoin, in Lovat Lane and St Mary-at-Hill (qq. v.). Between Lovat Lane and Botolph Lane, Nos. 14–16, dated 1890. Lively Northern Renaissance, with pediments and flat bays, below shaped gables. Ground floor of polished purple stone. Rebuilt inside by *T. P. Bennett Partnership*, 1988–90. On the site of St Andrew Hubbard, not rebuilt after the Great Fire, and later of the King's Weigh House, a plain brick mid-C18 building with ground-floor Doric colonnade. Then No. 10, 1985–6 by the *Whinney Mackay-Lewis Partnership*, of unpolished stone, with a pedimented bay, turret and oriel in the manner of c. 1890. Nos. 6–8, LLOYDS BANK, stone-clad offices by *Damond Lock*,

Grabowski & Partners, 1987–80, rummages in Terry Farrell's box of tricks. Nos. 2–4, NATWEST BANK, by *Campbell-Jones & Sons*, completed 1959, boring channelled stone.

The bank faces PUDDING LANE, famous as the starting-point of the Great Fire. The name, recorded 1360, derives not from baking but from 'puddings' or entrails of slaughtered beasts which were carried down from Eastcheap to the river. The block beyond, up to Fish Street Hill, is by *Frank Sherrin*, 1910–11, friendly free Jacobean, with shallow stone bows and a polygonal corner turret. Boyish atlantes to the corner entrance. One of several buildings by the architect for sites over the Metropolitan Railway, after electrification in 1905 removed the need for open cuttings. Refurbished 1985–6 by *DEGW* with an indifferent extension down Pudding Lane. St Leonard Eastcheap stood on the site until 1666; its churchyard fell victim to the railway in 1882. For the w corners, *see* Gracechurch Street.

ELDON STREET and SOUTH PLACE

Part of *Dance the Younger*'s redevelopment of Lower Moorfields (*see* Moorgate). His plan for South Street (the present Dominion Street, running N from South Place) was submitted in 1793, the streets around built up in the early C19 when Eldon was Lord Chancellor, together with Finsbury Circus on the s (q.v.). The original houses were replaced from *c.* 1885.

From the E end, the N side belongs to the Broadgate complex (q.v.). Facing, NEW LIVERPOOL HOUSE (Nos. 15–17), 1988–91, unnervingly accurate pastiche of the red brick Flemish taste of a century before, by *T. P. Bennett Partnership*. Nos. 18–19 next door are the real thing: by *Delissa Joseph*, illustrated 1893. Five storeys plus triangular gables, with piers and floor-strings in a mechanical grid; painted a nasty grey. Nos. 20–26, red brick of 1885–9, hardly taller than the houses they replaced. Surprisingly crude for the architects: *Davis & Emmanuel*. Then much taller C20 rear ranges to Finsbury Circus.

The N side was transferred to the City from Finsbury in 1994. Dull mid-C20 offices at the E end, then much activity by *George Sherrin*: St Mary Moorfields Catholic Church (q.v.), and the stone-faced ELDON HOUSE next door (1907), free Tudor, with flat bays and twin shaped gables, the ground floor with garlands and pilasters carved by *Daymond & Son*. It housed the offices of Messrs Sadgrove, furniture makers. Showrooms were provided facing w on to Wilson Street, beyond the little RED LION pub on the corner. This is solid, decent brick of *c.* 1860, with fat quoins and heavy cornice.

The street continues as the wider SOUTH PLACE, still the boundary between the City and the old borough of Finsbury. SPENCER HOUSE (N side) is not the Edwardian structure it seems, but a conversion of Sadgrove's warehouse into office chambers by *Sherrin*, 1907. He applied quoins, aprons and a top storey to the stock-brick carcase, probably of the original development (boundary plaque of 1818). COVENTRY HOUSE next door, red brick free classical, with a little copper-roofed corner dome, *c.* 1910. Beyond, a big block of offices over shops was completed in 1996 by *Sheppard Robson* (project architect *Graham Anthony*, engineers *Ove Arup & Partners*). The minimal vocabulary and sleek finishes show the influence of Norman Foster: a change from the firm's Postmodern City jobs of a few years before. A giant curved glazed screen on a silvery lattice faces the N end of Moorgate. Here a department store is accommodated. Silver-clad stair-towers break up the bulk facing Finsbury Pavement. An atrium rises from the third floor inside.

One building of note on the S side: the tall façade of the RIVER PLATE HOUSE extension, 1927–9 by Messrs *Joseph*. Ground-floor columns, shallow triple round-arched recesses in the centre of the upper floors. An inscription commemorates *William Brooks*'s Unitarian Chapel here (1824). Storeys were added and a new W section built, 1986–90: *see* Finsbury Circus.

FARRINGDON STREET

A broad and straight thoroughfare, continuing the line of New Bridge Street N into the Farringdon Road. First made in 1734–7, over the bed of the silted-up Fleet River or Holbourne. Excavations in 1990 at the S end, E side, revealed an eyot close to the E bank on which was built a water-mill, warehouse and jetty, all of timber construction. Tree-ring dating indicated erection shortly after A.D. 116. In medieval times the river banks were revetted, and noxious trades such as tanning and butchery were carried on. A series of bridges spanned its still-busy channel; the name of Old Seacoal Lane (E side) recalls the barges that came along here. Unnavigable by the 1650s, the Fleet revived after the Great Fire, when *Wren* supervised the reconstruction of its banks as 30 ft (9 metre) wharves, as far as the line of Holborn Hill (executed 1670–4 by *John Ball* and *Sir Thomas Fitch*).

After 1737, Farringdon Street provided a new home for the former Stocks Market, first in the roadway in single-storey arcaded ranges by *Dance the Elder*, then from 1828–9 to 1874 in buildings by *Mountague* half-way up the W side. The busy bridge of Holborn Viaduct (q.v.) makes an animated visual stop towards the N end. The street continues N out of the City as Farringdon Road, made 1845–63. Buildings are a mixture, with large, medium-height post-war structures predominant. Many formerly housed firms connected with the newspaper industry.

For buildings N of Holborn Viaduct, *see* that street and also Smithfield Market (Public Buildings). S of the viaduct, PLUMTREE COURT (Coopers & Lybrand), W side, is the former Standard House by *Ellis, Clarke & Gallanaugh*, completed 1965, where the *Evening Standard* was published. Softened in refurbishment by *Dennis Lennon & Partners*, 1981–3, it now has thin polished metal verticals and an arcaded loggia reminiscent of De Chirico at street level, repeated at the top. (Also arcaded the internal courtyard, under a pitched pantiled roof.) The great complex next door is the Telephone Exchange called Fleet Building (*see* Public Buildings).

Opposite (E SIDE), a murky alley called Turnagain Lane (in 1293 *Wendagayneslane*), named because it lacked a bridge across the river; but now Holborn Viaduct makes the other end impassable. Then Nos. 32–35, two matching Portland stone ranges flanking Newcastle Court, formerly the offices of the engineers Babcock & Wilcox, by *Victor Wilkins*, 1921–2. Five r. bays, three l. bays, with typical flat, blockish classical stone forms. At the entrance, reliefs of putti busily engaged in industrial design, signed *G. Alexander*. Nos. 27a–31, 1954–7 by *Ellis, Clarke & Gallanaugh*, straightforward, with long horizontal window-bands in a big seven-storey stone frame. Two further storeys set back above. Then *T. K. Green & Son*'s Nos. 26–27, dated 1886, lively Jacobean-cum-Dutch with shaped gables and a second-floor tourelle. The materials are brick and high-relief terracotta (by *Gibbs & Canning*), now painted. The two lower storeys, made on *Homan & Rogers*' fireproof system, housed Messrs Harrild, printing-machine manufacturers. No. 25 (FLEETWAY HOUSE) is by *R. Seifert & Partners*, 1979–82, flush-fronted in polished brown Sardinian granite with square smoked-glass windows. *T. P. Bennett & Son*'s No. 20, 1984–7, has grey-granite-clad floor strips and windows tinted a soapy turquoise. 1930s-style rounded corner to OLD FLEET LANE. Until 1990 this was the W part of Fleet Lane, a route recorded from the mid C13, which survived as a passage beneath Holborn Viaduct station until its redevelopment in 1990–2 as Fleet Place (q.v.).

Back on the W side, Nos. 75–79 are a big office development by *RHWL Partnership*, 1990–4. Stone-clad, strenuously articulated in the big-business way, with giant round-headed windows and bits of cornice jutting out high up. It runs back to face St Bride Street, to which it has big curved corners, and returns past a courtyard garden along Harp Alley as Nos. 81–82 Farringdon Street. This is smaller, of banded red brick, with big oriels. Sandwiched between, No. 80, the former Hoop and Grapes, the only survivor from before the Fleet Canal was covered over. Built in 1721, converted to a pub *c.* 1830, and partly refronted after war damage. The red brick pier, l., perpetuates a typically early C18 red brick pilaster strip. (Staircase of *c.* 1830 to the first floor, *c.* 1720 beyond, with column-newels; some modest mouldings and cornices. Brick-vaulted cellars beneath date possibly from quayside warehousing made 1670–4.) After Harp Alley, Nos. 83–86 by *Eric H. David*, 1949–51 (formerly Associated Press), stone-faced, tall staircase window to the l. For the rest of the W side, *see* St Bride Street.

No. 14, facing on the E side, is CAROONE HOUSE, by *Murray, Ward & Partners*, 1970–1. Six storeys, curved corner, with continuous windows between variously patterned slate bands, since painted in light colours to shoddy effect. A Congregational Memorial Hall is incorporated behind, successor to the blackened High Victorian monster by *Tarring*, 1872–5. This was rock-faced E. E. with Italian touches, with a great square tower and spiky pavilion roof. The site is that of the Fleet Prison, known by 1130, rebuilt *c.* 1335 and thrice more after burning in the Peasants' Revolt (1381), Great Fire and Gordon Riots (1780). Substantial medieval remains were recorded in excavations off Fleet Place in 1988–90. In its latter days (it closed only in 1842), the prison was a byword for venality and neglect. Finally GATE HOUSE, routine commercial façades of 1873 (rebuilt behind by *Chapman Taylor Partners*, 1981–5).

FENCHURCH STREET

Called perhaps from *faenum* or hay, referring to an ancient hay-market (cf. Gracechurch Street), perhaps from fenny ground on the banks of the long-lost Langbourn nearby. The long street curves slowly NE, generally but imprecisely following the line of a Roman road which led diagonally into town from the Colchester road (through Aldgate), to meet a main E–W street passing in front of the forum between Gracechurch Street and Rood Lane. The main Roman public buildings at the W end of Fenchurch Street also included the C1 forum's military storehouses (destroyed in the revolt of A.D. 60) and its massive C2 successor. Excavations in the SE part of Fenchurch Street in 1983, at Nos. 5–12, found early Roman work-shops replaced *c.* A.D. 75 by an unusual aisled hall (on all these *see* Introduction p. 30). The W end with its post-war bank buildings is effectively part of the financial district. Further E, early to mid-C20 offices for shipping and trading concerns survive in some numbers. Outstanding is Lloyd's Register of Shipping (q.v.), built at the turn of the century, when the East India Company's bonded warehouses which had dominated the E end of the street since the late C18 were being replaced.

From Gracechurch Street east to Mincing Lane

From the W, the S corner with Gracechurch Street (q.v.) is under redevelopment in 1997. Then No. 10, KLEINWORT BENSON, 1981–5 by *Denys Lasdun, Redhouse & Softley* for Land Securities. A taut, slick-skinned design, but without the sense of occasion of the practice's better-known works. Eight slick-skinned storeys in silvery aluminium, with narrow mullions and exposed framing above. The first floor is open as a shallow balcony to the street. The main KLEINWORT BENSON building is next door, between Philpot Lane and Rood Lane. By *CLRP Architects*, with *Wallace F. Smith* as consultant, 1963–8. From a two-storey podium, with shops set back beneath a cantilevered storey with slit windows, rises an overpowering but undeniably impressive twenty-storey slab of sheer curtain-walling, finished by a dark band projecting over a recessed roof-storey. Main entrance on Rood Lane. After three decades its materials have worn well – much better than the contemporary concrete Barclays' tower at the N corner with Gracechurch Street (q.v.), under demolition in 1997. Its low E wing, up to Lime Street, occupied the site of *Wren*'s St Dionis Backchurch, 1670–86 (dem. 1878), a modest aisled church with SW tower. Wren apparently reused the medieval foundations, giving it a plan remarkable for lacking a single r. angle.

Still on the N side, a disparate block between Lime Street and Cullum Street. First Nos. 157–159, 1910, an early work by *L. Sylvester Sullivan* for the City of London Real Property Co. Triple windows with narrow sidelights (the influence of Chicago?); carved garlands on the floor panels. The unbroken upper cornice swings nicely around the turreted corner. Nos. 154–156, by *GMW Partnership*, 1981–5, an enjoyably extreme example of the fashion for broken outlines: superimposed canted bays of dark-tinted glass, three times cantilevered out to the old street line, then stepping back so that it is both laterally and vertically symmetrical. The glazing of the upper bays slopes inwards at the bottom, as if corbelled. The whole evokes such multi-faceted Tudor-Gothic set-pieces as that at Thornbury Castle, blown up larger. No. 153, Dutch red brick by *Osborn & Russell*, 1880, has a diminutive relief of two men in a boat beneath a doublet (the Peterboat and Doublet), once advertising Tull & Co., rope and twine makers. Nos. 150–152 are a quirky hybrid by *Sheppard Robson & Partners*, completed 1976. Two narrow fronts: the l. new, with a bronzed-glass screen in front of a rendered façade based on the late Georgian house previously here; the r. of *c.* 1865, refined round-arched Italian Gothic office chambers in stone, one bay wide with two- and three-light windows, incorporated in the rebuilt front as a kind of giant flat panel. Nos. 143–149, SACKVILLE HOUSE, has tall pilaster-piers and a vaguely Spanish Baroque portal, by *Gervase Bailey*, 1931–2. Nos. 141–142, 1974–5 by *A.F. Westmore*, tall, of the flush smoked-glass type. Nos. 136–40 by *Stroud & Nullis*, 1966–9. The upper four storeys have horizontal Portland roach bands, now very grubby; the lower two have more pronounced vertical supports and splayed corners.

On the s SIDE, CHESTERFIELD HOUSE on the corner of Rood Lane is by *Howard, Souster & Fairbairn*, completed 1957, stone-faced and lacklustre. Then that remarkable, incoherent building PLANTATION HOUSE, begun in 1935 to designs by *A.W. Moore*. It served the commodities markets (rubber and tea especially), housed in numerous offices and sale-rooms around light-wells with broad, hotel-like semi-public passages between. By 1939 it covered most of the block bounded by Mincing Lane, Rood Lane and Eastcheap, but its size is not immediately apparent. The most powerful section faces Fenchurch Street. Five bays wide, the lower two storeys with an engaged Doric order and a balcony on top, then giant Corinthian columns set back over a mezzanine, with bronze floor bands between. More storeys set back above. On the floor bands are painted bosses. To Mincing Lane it is roughly symmetrical, twenty-three bays long with five storeys arranged as three above two. Two main entrances, marked by giant inset columns above. Another section faces Rood Lane. An extension made 1951–4 faces Great Tower Street (q.v.). The NE part of the street block is formed by earlier buildings: GUILD HOUSE (Nos. 36–38), by *Campbell-Jones & Smithers*, 1928, of stone, with Doric columns below and cartouches between the fourth-floor windows à la Cooper; and the plainer No. 40, also 1928, on the corner with Mincing Lane. Plans by *Arup Associates* to rebuild all but the sw corner of this island block were published in 1996.

On the n side again, FOUNTAIN HOUSE, by *W.H. Rogers* (*Sir Howard Robertson* consultant), 1954–8, another undertaking by the CLRP Co. The first office tower in London to repeat the motif of Gordon Bunshaft's Lever House, New York (1952), that is a low horizontal block with a tall tower above, here set end-on to the street. The tower's curtain-walling has been renewed, but the details were always disappointing. With its podium curving to the street and lower return wing along Cullum Street, the composition is tentative compared with later versions of the formula (cf. Castrol House, Marylebone Road, *London 3: North West*). The little FEN COURT, set back on the E side, preserves part of the churchyard of St Gabriel or St Mary Fenchurch Street, first mentioned in 1108, which stood in the roadway until the Great Fire. Three C18 table tombs survive amidst benches and trees.

From Mincing Lane east to Aldgate

On the S side, after Mincing Lane, first the rear of the CLOTHWORKERS' HALL block (q.v.), then GERLING GLOBAL (No. 50), 1979–81 by *P. E. Williams*, in dark polished stone. Rather an irresolute design: horizontal first-floor windows, upright windows above. Nos. 51–54, NORWICH UNION, stone-faced and reactionary with rusticated lower floors set forward, by *Lewis Solomon, Son & Joseph*, 1951–6. Opposite (N side), No. 120, AIG EUROPE BANK, 1972–6 by *T. P. Bennett & Son*, large, with shallow projecting floor strips coated in grooved black plastic, an example of the indefatigable exploration of unconventional cladding in the 1970s. Then CORY BUILDINGS (No. 117), by *E. Stones*, 1921, completed by *W. Gilbee Scott* (1923). Rusticated arcade to the first two floors, a big round-arched entrance with carved trophies etc., then two plainer storeys under a big cornice with foliage frieze. The intrusive mansard replaced Stones's dormers and big panelled chimneystacks in 1976.

The S side opens up by Mark Lane as a kind of forecourt to Fenchurch Street station. First the free-standing MARINE ENGINEERS' MEMORIAL BUILDING by *Ronald Ward & Partners*, 1954–7 (consultant architect *Victor Wilkins*). A satisfactory design in the form of intersecting blocks. The lower block, stone-clad, contains the entrance to the Marine Engineers' Institute; at the S a fourteen-storey tower with red brick panels in a stone frame, aligned E–W. No. 60 across London Street, by *James S. Gibson*, 1906, free commercial classical, has a corner oriel supported by carved mermen. Apple-green glazed brick behind. No. 63 is a prosperous stuccoed survivor of *c.*1850, with channelled piers and bracket-cornice. No. 65, BLACK SEA AND BALTIC HOUSE, does its best to be modern: curved corners, peculiar canted metal-framed bay windows. By *F. Taperell & Haase*, 1927; the outlines taken from unused designs by *Richardson & Gill*, 1924. Then No. 67, the little EAST INDIA ARMS, illustrated by Tallis in 1838 and not much older. Red brick, curved corner. Next to it, *Paul Hoffman*'s Nos. 68–70, 1910, an odd composition with three-storey round-topped bays and a central staircase marked by a few small windows: a consequence of the shallow plan enforced by the CHURCHYARD of St Katharine Coleman behind. This retains its railings to ST KATHARINE'S ROW. The gates look C18. *James Horne*'s plain brick church of 1739–40 went in 1925; its replacement (by *E. G. W. Souster* and *Stanley Hamp*) in 1996, for a new building for Lloyd's

Register of Shipping (*see* Public Buildings) by *Richard Rogers Partnership*. *Rogers*'s plan, as revised in 1997, includes a new entrance block (by *Rolfe Judd*) on the site of Nos. 68–70, with a further block to the sw, facing Fenchurch Place.

Back on the N side, No. 110, a dreary grey-granite-clad block by *Fitzroy Robinson & Partners*, 1972–5; No. 108, red brick office chambers by *W. M. Yetts*, 1886; then the entrance to FENCHURCH BUILDINGS, a narrow alley of C16 origin, running up to Leadenhall Street. Notable amongst its early C20 white-faience-clad offices is *Richardson & Gill*'s Nos. 9–13 (w side), 1924–7, carefully calculated to minimize cornices or other projections likely to block the light. The other side with its pretty curved bows is by *M. E. & O. H. Collins*, 1923, part of FURNESS HOUSE. The main entrance is from Leadenhall Street (q.v.); a subsidiary front faces Fenchurch Street, beyond the *Thomas Saunders Partnership*'s unconvincing neo-1920s No. 107, 1988–90. This front is grandiose and rather busy, with Tuscan aedicules on the first floor, giant Ionic pilasters above, and then a huge central slated mansard with copper embellishments against which a stone-faced gable rises.

On the S side, two buildings from the late C19 development called Lloyd's Avenue. The prize building is Lloyd's Register of Shipping (No. 71, *see* Public Buildings). On the opposite corner (still on the S side), LLOYDS BANK (Nos. 72–75), dated 1900, offices by *Davis & Emmanuel*. Free Northern Renaissance, with engaged blocked columns akin to Lloyd's Register. Symmetrical Fenchurch Street front, finished with an impressive three-storey pyramid of aedicules and gables. Rebuilt behind in plain brick by *Fitzroy Robinson Partnership*, c. 1979. After some modest properties, Nos. 82–84, by the *Fitzroy Robinson Partnership*, 1980–2, has shallow smoked-glass bays and grey granite cladding. No. 90, ZURICH BUILDING, by *EPR Partnership*, 1988–90, a bold symmetrical stone front with the familiar recessed segmental bay beneath a big gable. The rear ranges face Saracen's Head Yard, off Jewry Street.

On the N side, No. 100, a stone-faced grid, the lower two storeys of green-veined marble; by *Cluttons' Staff Architects*, 1969–71. Then a clumsy flat stone-clad façade by *The Halpern Partnership*, 1987–90, with big simplified window surrounds and other Postmodern details. Part of the job was the reconstruction of HARTSHORN ALLEY, mentioned by Stow, with rough aggregate walls and a coved ceiling. Subdued lighting and the lack of a clear line of sight lend mystery to the passage through to Leadenhall Street, where the retained façade of Nos. 62–65 is incorporated. Then *Terry Farrell Partnership*'s No. 69, 1986–7, for Central & City Properties. Farrell's chunky stone-clad style takes the Leadenhall Street corner well, with an open engaged drum serving as an entrance to the MIDLAND BANK. The cylindrical motif re-emerges above in a little round turret, designed as a boardroom, with curved glazing exposed by lower openings to suggest that it forms a continuous vertical volume: a much-imitated device. The side elevations have the architect's favourite tripartite division. On the lower floors window surrounds in coloured granite detailed to suggest bolting-on, plainer upper storeys, then a plain raked cornice and set-backs.

The Leadenhall Street entrance is announced by polished steel columns under a big triangular opening.

The street continues E as Aldgate (q.v.).

FETTER LANE

A 'New Street' was made c. 1245 between Fleet Street and Holborn. Called *Faytureslane* in 1292, perhaps from the Old French *faitor* or lawyer. The alignment follows the E edge of the Saxon settlement of Lundenwic (*see* Introduction p. 43); an ornate C9 sword pommel was found here in the C19. The E side was widened after 1841, but interesting early Victorian buildings at the S end, including *John Shaw Jun.*'s Neo-Jacobean Infants' School, 1849 (Nos. 3–4), and the remarkably dignified and Schinkelesque Nos. 7–9 by *T.L. Donaldson*, c. 1857, were demolished c. 1975 to widen it further. The N part was heavily bombed, so that Fetter Lane is now largely post-war.

From the S, after the corners to Fleet Street, CITADEL HOUSE (E side), by *Julian Keyes Partnership*, 1972–6, dour grey concrete with a close vertical rhythm on the convex front. The middle storeys project. On the W side here, Clifford's Inn (*see* Public Buildings), then the fortress-like ST DUNSTAN'S HOUSE, by *George Trew Dunn Beckles Willson Bowes* for the Lord Chancellor's Office, completed 1980. Tall, faced in aggregate panels, broken up into narrow canted bays and small windows. To its N and W the Public Record Office and its garden (*see* Public Buildings), in which are displayed parts of the previous St Dunstan's House. Back on the E side, WINCHESTER HOUSE, 1977–82 by *Michael Lyell Associates*. Similar composition to Citadel House, but clad in blue mirror-glass, with a projecting stair-tower faced in blue Larvikite stone by a new entrance to Crane Court behind.

Then much rebuilding of the bombed area, beginning on the E side with the Goldsmiths' Company's precinct by *C. Edmund Wilford & Son*, 1959–63. At the S end a curtain-walled tower on a broad plinth, aligned with two lower blocks facing New Fetter Lane which branches off to the NE (LINTAS HOUSE and No. 11). A passage through Lintas House leads to the forecourt of Newspaper House (*see* New Street Square). The line of Fetter Lane proper runs further W. *James Butler*'s naturalistic statue of John Wilkes (1988) marks the junction. By it, at the corner of Bream's Buildings (W side), the former Du Pont House, seven straightforward curtain-walled storeys by *R. Seifert & Partners*, completed 1963. Then No. 100 (OYEZ HOUSE), 1949–58 by *T. P. Bennett & Son*, a restless composition of various blocks and heights in stone-dressed brown brick, less marked by traditional reminiscences than most such immediately post-war offices. Refurbished 1983 by the *Mills Group Partnership*, with new windows and service hamper. At its NE corner, No. 95, 1972–5 by *Douglas Marriott, Worby & Robinson*. Window bands, polished blue-grey stone floor strips. Opposite on the E side, MONOTYPE HOUSE by *Hannen & Markham*, 1953–5, dull. Then a huddle of small mid-1950s offices

(Nos. 44–53), all due for replacement; the rear wing of the former W.H. Smith building in New Fetter Lane (q.v.); and the old *Daily Mirror* site up to Holborn.

The w side livens up with *Green Lloyd Architects*' development of the former Mercers' School site, 1988–92. At the corner, a bulky stone and brick section with semicircular oriels, diminishing in relief along Norwich Street. Beyond, a handsome screen façade of superimposed orange-red terracotta Doric columns and segmental red brick arches, reminiscent of early C19 industrial buildings (though here adorning a steel frame). The arches run back into the ground-floor lobby, visible through patent glazing. Below the windows dark panels with a circular decorative motif. The courtyard behind is less successful, polychromatic, and crowded with columns supporting repeated set-backs on the r. In the NE corner a passage into Barnard's Inn (*see* Public Buildings). Little circular lobbies manage the shift in alignment. Facing the Inn, a tall stone-faced frontispiece or gate-tower with a giant Dutch gable, in sympathy with retained sections of the 1890s school buildings.

Back in Fetter Lane, plain brick mid-C19 houses at Nos. 82–84, then No. 80, dated 1902, by *Treadwell & Martin*: an outlying 118 survivor of their Buchanan's Distillery, which lay to the N. Stone-faced, symmetrical, with characteristic attenuated buttresses and a big gable in a kind of Art Nouveau Dutch. At the top two well-carved youthful caryatids crouch beneath a shell-headed niche (carver *Daymond & Son*).

FINCH LANE

Named from a C13 resident (called *Finkeslane c*. 1240). No. 22 (w SIDE), by *E. I'Anson*, 1845–6, is an outlying survivor of his important block of Italianate offices facing the Royal Exchange (*see* Cornhill).* The narrow lane occasioned very extensive glazing, though still subject to Italianate discipline. Two lower storeys with five recessed giant windows, apparently iron-framed, divided by a thin floor-string (altered). Scarcely smaller windows in two red brick and stone upper storeys. Later extension along ROYAL EXCHANGE AVENUE, r., with shouldered Gothic-derived arches. It looks later than 1854, the date in the gable facing Threadneedle Street. The pilastered doorcase here is plainly a late C19 addition. On the E SIDE, Nos. 1–3 by *Saville & Martin*, 1891–2. Red brick and stone, the ground floor (a former restaurant) with elaborate foliage frieze and good big herm-mullions. Plainer chambers over. Nos. 6 and 7, modest mid-Victorian. *See* Threadneedle Street for the rest.

FINSBURY AVENUE *see* BROADGATE

---

* I am grateful to Peter Jefferson-Smith for this discovery.

FINSBURY CIRCUS

The City's only counterpart to the great green islands of Mayfair and
Marylebone. Laid out from 1815 by the City Surveyor, *William
Mountague*, on the old Lower Moorfields, on the generous oval plan
made by his predecessor *Dance the Younger* in 1802. This plan, a
splendid coda to Dance's play with rounded spaces at the Minories
in 1767 (*see* Crescent), was several years late because Bethlehem
Hospital had first to be relocated from *Hooke*'s palatial pavilioned
building on the s side (1675–6). The garden has tall plane trees and
serpentine paths from the C19 layout, with a bowling green made in
1909 in the centre. Notable the pretty circular pavilion for a drinking
fountain, by *John Whitehead & Son*, 1902 (N side), with tiled conical
roof and Gothic woodwork, after Philip Webb's well-head at the Red
House, Bexleyheath, Kent.

Nothing remains of the early C19 houses, which in character
looked back to the plainer of Dance's houses in Finsbury Square to
the N, begun 1777 (*see London 4: North*). Their leases fell in from
1899. Last to go, in 1936, was *William Brooks*'s London Institution,
1815–19 (*Thomas Cubitt*'s first major undertaking), the stately
Grecian portico of which was the central feature of the N side. The
replacements were grandiose classical office chambers, larger than
anything seen before in the City; with well-judged 1980s insertions
these still dominate the Circus. They are mostly of Portland stone
with a giant order high up, the earlier blocks with pavilions emphasizing their several entrances. First SALISBURY HOUSE, by *Davis &
Emmanuel*, 1899–1901, making the whole sw quadrant. A fancy
French palace of Bath stone, the cornice in straight sections against
the concave front. Lower façade to London Wall, with groups of
three bays alternately ornamented. The 800 office rooms inside
required light-wells of unprecedented size. Then the little street
called Circus Place, unusually wide because Dance projected a new
road s to Lothbury from here.

Continuing anticlockwise, the SE quadrant is LONDON WALL
BUILDINGS, 1901–2 by *Gordon & Gunton*, more Baroque, with
massive pedimented pavilions. The central pavilion roof went in
the Blitz. On the first floor alternating pediments on little
columns. Towards London Wall smaller-scale motifs: blocked
columns, Gibbs surrounds. At the NE corner offices by *G. D.
Martin*, begun in 1903, extending E to Blomfield Street and N to
Eldon Street. A relentless display of giant columns, the third-floor
windows with aedicules on columns resting on the bays below.
Attic blocks with Michelangelesque broken pediments. Rebuilt
behind by *T. P. Bennett Partnership*, 1983–9, retaining inset doorcases of coloured marble. Then Nos. 16–18, by *Gordon & Gunton*,
designed 1915 and begun 1921, more consciously monumental
and symmetrical. In No. 16 a brown-marble-lined entrance hall,
with a screen of columns and an Imperial staircase (restored
1988).

Centrepiece of the N side, visible from London Wall across the
garden, is *GMW Partnership*'s BANK OF TOKYO, 1987–92, stone-
faced, with an assertive giant pediment and interpenetrating
lunette over rusticated lower floors. Inside, a light-well-cum-

atrium with diminishing circular openings from fourth floor to basement. Smaller-scale detail on Nos. 7–11, RIVER PLATE HOUSE, 1986–90 by *Kenzie Lovell Partnership*. A composition reminiscent of *c.* 1900, rendered in chunky simplified forms: coupled giant columns above, colonnettes to the first- and second-floor windows. (Retained façade of 1927–9 to South Place: *see* Eldon Street.)

Finally, at the NW corner leading on into Moorgate, the Circus's one masterpiece: *Lutyens*'s BRITANNIC HOUSE, for the Anglo- 123 Persian Oil Company (later B.P.), 1921–5. Done with care and lavish expense, comparable with his near-contemporary Midland Bank, Poultry. Here also the style owes much to North Italian Mannerism, interpreted freely but with great discipline, without shocks or discords. The low ratio of void to solid is particularly striking, with mostly small windows deeply set. Six storeys below the top cornice, divided horizontally into two stages of three. The lower stage projects slightly towards Finsbury Circus as a seven-bay entrance frontispiece that would make a perfectly proportioned façade in its own right. Rusticated ground floor, the few accentuated first-floor windows flanked by recessed columns in a very Lutyensesque way. Above, a storey behind a balustrade makes a plinth to a giant Corinthian order, with the cornice broken forward above each column and frothy garlands between the capitals. Triumphal arch rhythm at each end, broken slightly forward in counterpoint to the frontispiece below. Seven bays between, alternately wide and narrow, marking the chairman's office suite. Plain attic, plainest hipped Coniston-slated roof, with none of Lutyens's favourite stacks or aedicules. Carved figures by *Derwent Wood*, distributed about the various corner set-backs, not grouped as the Edwardians would have done them; excellent lesser carving by *Broadbent & Son*. Plainer S front, without the giant order. The Moorgate front (W) is a straight, slightly over-extended version of that to Finsbury Circus.

The INTERIOR was rebuilt with tact and imagination by *Inskip* 154 *& Jenkins* in 1987–9 (executive architects *W. Nimmo & Partners*, engineers *Ove Arup & Partners*), who retained Lutyens's grand circulation spaces, a novelty in a 1920s commercial building. From the broad, columned entrance hall a pilastered corridor on the Circus axis leads to an apsed chamber, which originally met corridors on the other axes. Here a magnificent inlaid marble floor in C17 Italian fashion. A staircase of grey Brescia marble (slightly altered) opens l. off the corridor. It climbs slowly through four floors in complex barrel-vaulted flights and landings, crossing and re-crossing the central axis in a graduated, varied progress familiar from Lutyens's country houses. It leads now to a broad platform made within a semicircular atrium, a reticent, cool space with walls clad in a well-proportioned grid of plain Portland stone. This replaced Lutyens's twin light-wells and straightforward pilastered boardroom (a replica of which has been made in the basement). Also kept, the fourth-floor chairman's office, a vaulted space with columns, and two first-floor offices. Externally all that is visibly new is a sheer white- and grey-clad front, tucked away N in South Place Mews. In 1991 B.P. returned to the refurbished building.

FINSBURY PAVEMENT *see* MOORGATE

FISH STREET HILL

The ancient route down to Old London Bridge, formerly also called Bridge Street; not to be confused with Old Fish Street Hill, by St Nicholas Cole Abbey. It closely follows the line of a Roman road leading down from the forum to the crossing of the Thames. For remains associated with the Roman waterfront and bridge in the lower part of Fish Street Hill, *see* London Bridge (Public Buildings) and Upper Thames Street. The MONUMENT is the chief interest (*see* Public Buildings); other buildings face Monument Street (q.v.).

FLEET PLACE

Constructed 1990–2 for Rosehaugh Stanhope and the British Rail Property Board, on the site of Holborn Viaduct station (masterplan by *Renton Howard Wood Levin*, 1987). The whole owes much to the same developers' earlier Broadgate scheme (q.v.). Trains are diverted underground to the new City Thameslink station (q.v.). Four large deep-plan office blocks, in a line N–S, use the land thus released. No. 100 New Bridge Street and No. 100 Ludgate Hill are described under those streets.

The other two are Nos. 1 and 10 Fleet Place, reached from LIMEBURNER LANE (called Seacoal Lane until 1990). By *Skidmore, Owings & Merrill*, both of ten storeys, facing a new L-shaped pedestrian court called Fleet Place made at the level of the old station platforms. Each block inventively displays its external steel framing: a theme common to much of the practice's recent American work, but less apparent at Broadgate.

First No. 10, strongly vertical, with a sheer concave E front to the lane. Slim uprights of flat black-coated fire-engineered steel, with dark stone slabs attached by glittering stainless-steel bolts. They make pairs of bays each of two lesser bays. Green glazing between. Open framing above and at the rounded NE corner, wherein are balconies. Recessed ground floor. The whole is extremely impressive – much in debt to the machine aesthetic, but glamorous and faintly sinister at the same time.

No. 1 overlooks Fleet Place from the N side. Its lean cream-enamelled steel frame defines repeated horizontal panels of grey infill and glass. The two projecting central bays have framing haphazardly left void on some floors, like twin filing cabinets with some drawers missing. On the E and W sides, the four middle floors project diagonally on a sawtooth plan. The N part houses an entrance to City Thameslink station.

On the W side of Fleet Place, *SOM*'s CORNEY & BARROW's restaurant, a low, skeletal timber box glazed in below and open above, embracing at the l. a grey drum for the kitchen and services. On the E side, an arcaded screen wall from Holborn Viaduct station, *c.* 1874. SCULPTURE: Man with Pipe, by *Bruce McLean*, open painted metal (SE); Echo, by *Stephen Cox*, 1993, two large androgynous stone torsos, by the entrance of No. 1. A disappointingly cramped staircase leads from the sw corner to Farringdon Street, via Old Seacoal Lane.

FLEET STREET

The ancient route between the City and Westminster, recorded from 1002. Called after the River Fleet or Holbourn, which formed the valley which is now Farringdon Street and New Bridge Street (E end). Many medieval ecclesiastical palaces stood just off the street, while Inns of Court and Chancery were set up in the C14 at the W end, where the legal connection still dominates. Medieval development did not extend far N, and this is why so few streets open off it. Instead there are mostly narrow courts and closes, many named after inns and hostelries (for those on the N side, *see* p. 502). Lesser buildings mostly occupy deep, narrow plots: another legacy of the Middle Ages.

But to the C20, Fleet Street means publishing, and newspaper publishing in particular. First to set up shop was Wynkyn de Worde, near Shoe Lane (*c.* 1500). The *Daily Courant*, the first regular daily (1702), was published near the E end, but only in the later C19 did the newspaper industry crowd into a street previously better known for banks, insurance offices and hotels. One magnet was the Press Association, Wine Office Court (*see* p. 502), another the land made available by the Victoria Embankment after *c.* 1880. The *Daily Telegraph* was first to build on Fleet Street proper (1881–2); its building of 1929 and that of the *Daily Express* of 1930 remain. These were effectively self-contained factories, with imposing front offices and printing works below or behind. Smaller and more common were the London offices of provincial papers, printed elsewhere: early C20 views show giant, visually chaotic lettering all over their façades. Around this time the S side was much rebuilt for road widening. Bomb damage was relatively slight, and the whole street was designated a conservation area, 1971–81. The newspapers moved out to less restricted sites mostly in the late 1980s. Since then some premises have been redeveloped for legal and financial tenants, although the 1980s boom is less evident here than elsewhere in the City.

Fleet Street offers no continuous parade of commercial palaces like those of Cornhill or Lombard Street. Indeed, after the fine C19 group at the W end, much of it is unremarkable or even rather shoddy. But the quiet parts nicely set off the great C20 newspaper premises, and amongst the small properties some good late C17 houses remain in use as pubs. The walk E is also tremendously exciting, as the slow curve that hinges visually on St Dunstan-in-the-West's delicate spire gradually brings St Paul's into view across the valley of the Fleet.

Temple Bar and south side, west to east

Until 1878, the City was entered through TEMPLE BAR, a gateway of 1670–2 ascribed by venerable tradition to *Wren*, though probably not designed by him. It replaced a gate known by *c.* 1350. The C17 structure was re-erected at Theobalds Park, Herts, and replaced in 1880 by *Sir Horace Jones*'s slim MEMORIAL in the roadway. Tall pilastered pedestal of granite and coloured stone, crowded with carved trophies and much bronze sculpture: statues of Queen Victoria and Prince Edward by *Boehm*; charming crammed bronze reliefs of Victoria's visits to the City by *C.S. Kelsey* (N) and *C.H. Mabey* (S); other reliefs by *Mabey* (W and E, the latter representing old Temple Bar). On top a spiky griffin rampant, by *C.B. Birch*.

No. 1, CHILD'S BANK, by *Gibson*, 1878–80, is quiet and stately High Renaissance, like a club. Tall ground floor with vermiculated rustication and projecting end bays, two storeys of channelled masonry with engaged Corinthian columns above. No. 3, the wine merchants WEINGOTT'S, a much-altered C18 house with shopfront and panelled interior of *c*. 1900. After the Middle Temple Gateway (*see* Public Buildings: The Temple), the former Legal and General Assurance (No. 10), by *Edis*, 1885, red brick and *Burmantofts'* terracotta, with a big gable, cross-windows and rich Flemish detail. One broader bay, r., throws the symmetry; this is of 1904, replacing the first premises (by *Hopper*, 1838). No. 14, *George Aitchison Sen.*'s former Union Bank of London, 1856–7, tall, sober Italianate, with structural ironwork exposed in the window frames. Of the same date *J.H. Stevens*'s No. 16 (SIMMONDS' BOOKSHOP), narrow, fancy and tasteless, with the original shopfront echoed in a triple-arched third-floor window. Facing Inner Temple Lane, reached through the Inner Temple Gateway next door (*see* The Temple), No. 15, the former Rainbow Coffee House, by *Rawlinson Parkinson*, 1859–60. Four storeys, stuccoed above, like a bank below, with Tuscan pilasters and large windows. The second coffee house in England was established here *c*. 1656 (John Aubrey). (Coffee Room ceiling by *H. Parsons*, with enriched coffering and swags, originally decorated by *Sang*.)

Back in Fleet Street, No. 19, BARCLAYS BANK, rebuilt in 1898–9 by Barclays' favourite architect *A.C. Blomfield*, when it took over Gosling's Bank here. Restrained composition with shallow wings and giant order, resembling Child's Bank. The later date shows e.g. in elaborated aprons between the windows. No. 21, the former London and Provincial Law Life Assurance, 1853–5, by *John Shaw Jun*. Slender Purbeck stone Renaissance front of one broad and two narrow flanking bays, licentious but delicate, with superimposed pilasters and some French details, e.g. the garlanded oval lights on the second floor (formerly the manager's drawing room). Venetian motif on the ground floor, echoed in its iron-traceried arched central light. Before street widening, it had a forecourt with matching blind screen walls against the (demolished) buildings adjacent.

No. 22 is THE COCK, by *Gilbert & Constanduros*, 1912, unconvincing half-timbered roughcast, fronting a building of *c*. 1888 (by *T. Verity*) cut back for street widening. Inside, a timber C17 overmantel from the old Cock Inn, formerly opposite: simple strapwork panel between male and female herms. Nos. 23–28, TEMPLE BAR HOUSE, broad, tall free classical-cum-Baroque of 1902, with flat oriels at each end and lots of blocked window surrounds. By the same hand as Nos. 231–232 Strand, Westminster. No. 29, *W.G. Bartleet*'s former Promoter Insurance, 1860, 'a Parisian absurdity in variegated materials, stuck with texts and symbols' (Summerson). The main hall is now a shop. Nos. 30–32, a towering Portland stone composition by *Knightley*, 1883, French-accented Queen Anne, with shallow canted bays. Formerly Messrs Philip, map and chart printers, whose drawing offices were behind the pointed fourth-floor dormers. FALCON COURT, reached through it, is mostly Neo-Georgian barristers' chambers by *Ansell & Bailey*, 1958. No. 33, a tall two-bay late C18 house, was Murray's the publishers, 1768–93.

HOARE'S BANK is the finest early C19 bank in London. By *Charles Parker*, 1829–30, when most private banks still favoured adapted houses. Of Bath stone, five bays plus slightly projecting one-bay wings, three-storeyed with arched ground floor and low central attic block. The very restrained late classical manner is unexpected from the author of the Italianizing *Villa Rustica* (1832–41). Iron first-floor balconies of *c.* 1935 do no harm. The bank was also (and nominally remains) the Hoares' private residence; their bank has been here since 1690. Both house and bank are entered from the l. bay. Here, a staircase with elongated iron Doric column-balusters. (Living accommodation on upper floors has simple Grecian detail; *Wyatville* advised on the plan.) Parker's plain, masculine, discreet banking hall is a world away from the competitive display of Victorian joint-stock banks. Flush-panelled, with antae-flanked doorcases and semicircular recesses above. Counter on the two sides best favoured for daylight. In the centre a fine Grecian bronze columnar stove, made by Parker's brother *Samuel*. A pierced screen wall separates this 'shop' from the counting house behind: a plan common to most early banks. Rear extensions by *Sir Herbert Baker* (partners' room, 1929, E side), and *Devereux & Davies* (1958, W side), face inward to an attractive courtyard garden.

A long early C20 sequence follows. Nos. 40–43, free classical with pilasters and little balconies, by *Oswald C. Wylson*, exhibited 1913; Nos. 44–45, MITRE HOUSE, by *M.K. Matthews*, 1929, with an entry to Mitre Court (*see* Serjeants' Inn); No. 47, EL VINO'S, plain red brick of *c.* 1910, with a good Edwardian front and cavernous interior. Grandeur returns with Nos. 49–50, NORWICH UNION INSURANCE, by *Jack McMullen Brooks*, 1911. An attractive Baroque composition, the central arched niche with allegorical sculpted group by *A. Stanley Young*. Above, a screen of columns between projecting wings. To the r. an archway into Serjeants' Inn, to the l. the main entrance, cleverly accommodated. Steps up to a pretty oval entrance vestibule with marble pilasters. In the main hall, painted frieze of classical figures by *George Murray*, illustrated 1916. Narrow fronts follow. No. 53, *c.* 1905, a bizarre Flamboyant Gothic confection with diapered scarlet and green glazed brick. No. 54, by *Trehearne & Norman*, 1927, of the type with chamfered uprights. Nos. 56–57, almost half as high again and indeed too tall, is *Percy Tubbs, Son & Duncan*'s former *Glasgow Herald*, 1927. A shallow bronze bow rises from first to third floors. Stone uprights above. Lots of Neo-Grèc decoration reminiscent of the 1925 Paris exhibition. No. 61, on the Bouverie Street corner, of white faience with a big lunette, was a J. Lyons café (1910).

The wedge-shaped site between Bouverie Street and Whitefriars Street, formerly the *News of the World*, was redeveloped by *YRM Partnership*, 1988–9. The main new block lies back, announced by a rather awkward forebuilding of grey and black granite. In its l. part a Postmodern classical triumphal arch with cylindrical columns. Windows have close-set glazing bars after Mackintosh. The entrance arch leads to a formal courtyard, with a sunk circular light-well and passages open to the streets on either side. The s side is FRESHFIELDS, in a much larger block with a deep convex entrance clad in white stone, and less small-scale detail than on the forebuilding. Long flat fronts to Bouverie Street and Whitefriars Street revert to sombre grey and black, impressively forbidding and solid, of eight storeys, set back above to preserve classical proportions. Light metal balconies and narrow recessed bays at intervals. Inside, a long, cool full-height atrium, tapering outwards in line with the walls. Cantilevered upper floors narrow the aperture. Flanking the entrance block, older buildings and retained façades: No. 63 (r.), the former *Scotsman*, routine French classical of 1921–2 by *Frank Matcham & Co.*; No. 66 (l.), THE TIPPERARY, a stuccoed two-bay post-Fire house for which Peter Mills is recorded setting out foundations in 1667–8, with a good pub interior of 1895 (original top-lit central staircase with turned balusters above first-floor level); then No. 67, urbane stone offices with a curved corner by *A.A.H. Scott*, 1926, an outlying harbinger of his demolished *News of the World* premises. Built 1930–2, this had grid-like façades of rusticated stone to Bouverie Street and Whitefriars Street, sterner than No. 67.

After Whitefriars Street, No. 70, by the *Thomas Saunders Partnership*, 1983–6, an early example of Postmodern fun and games, with tall skinny pilasters with cartoon-like Ionic capitals, already looking very dated. Nos. 72–78, CHRONICLE HOUSE by *Ellis & Clarke*, 1923–4, flat-fronted with pilasters, nothing special. Bust of the journalist T.P. O'Connor, by *F. Doyle Jones*, 1934. Nos. 80–81, BARCLAYS BANK, 1921–4 by *C.J. Dawson, Son, & Allardyce*, pilastered Greek Ionic with two little oriels poking out.

Beyond Salisbury Court, the great stone bulk of REUTERS and the PRESS ASSOCIATION, 1934–8 by *Lutyens* (associate architects *Smee & Houchin*). Lutyens is recognizable by the wide, deep entrance niche on the narrower Fleet Street front, the doorway flanked by tapering pilasters and surmounted by a circular window with a bronze figure of Fame (originally on the parapet); also by rustication into which Doric pilasters disappear on the corner (formerly a bank). The rest seems straightforward, until one looks steeply up and discovers the fun the architect has had at the top: a recessed structure with concave front and pedimented extremities, crowned by a broad circular drum without a dome. This tripartite division into ornamented base, plain middle and eyecatching top suggests a skyscraper *in parvo* rather than Lutyens's commercial palaces of the 1920s, with their lovingly differentiated storeys. Upper storeys not as simple as they first appear: walls are subtly battered like shallow buttresses, and windows diminish in width as they rise. The main entrance is a tight succession of Travertine-clad spaces: a lobby apsed to l. and r. leads to a small hall with semicircular arches reminiscent of Soane; on its l. side a staircase climbs around a square stairwell. In the hall a jolly wooden post-box-cum-clock. Reuters' executive suites were in the set-back seventh floor, with a separate entrance from Salisbury Square. By this, a former pub, marked by strange big discs between key blocks: patterns that later excited the pioneer American Postmodernists. Also here an arched passage to St Bride's church, calculated perfectly to open up a vertical view of the steeple as one advances.

Then ST BRIDE'S AVENUE, cut through after 1824, also to show off St Bride's steeple. Buildings beyond are all of *c.* 1900. On the avenue's E corner, No. 88, the former *Birmingham Post*, 1900–2 by *Belcher & Joass*, forward-looking in its astylar stripped classicism but oddly lacklustre otherwise. Further on, Nos. 90–94, ST BARTHOLOMEW'S HOUSE, by *H. Huntly Gordon*, 1900, red brick offices with stone-fronted shops below, free Tudor with a big gable. Stubby Ionic columns on a continuous fourth-floor string. Doorcase with cherubs by *Gilbert Seale*. No. 96 (THE OLD BELL), one of two funny low fronts built shortly after 1897, joins on to a three-storeyed late C17 house facing St Bride's churchyard, probably that for which foundations were set out here in 1669. Its central staircase is unusually well-preserved from first floor upwards. Facing it across Bride Lane, Nos. 98–100, the big Neo-Jacobean PUNCH TAVERN, 1894–7 by *Saville & Martin*. Excellent tiled entrance from Fleet Street, with big paintings of Mr and Mrs Punch. Inside, a curious hammerbeamed miniature skylight.

The north side, east to west

The N side has fewer grand C19 buildings and more narrow frontages and big post-war blocks. After the Ludgate Circus block (q.v.), POPPINS COURT, named from the popinjay or parrot device of the Abbot of Cirencester, whose house was here by 1416; no buildings of interest. On the corner with Shoe Lane, Nos. 120–129, the former DAILY EXPRESS, the first true curtain-walled building in London, substantially by *Sir Owen Williams*, 1930–3. The associate architects *Ellis & Clarke* proposed a conventionally steel-framed, stone-faced building, but Williams took over the job late in 1929 because his bold concrete frame doubled the unobstructed width of the basement printing hall. Elevations are sheathed in black Victrolite or transparent glass, the panels set in chromium strips, absolutely smooth except for the recessed upper storeys. Rounded corner to Shoe Lane, then a cantilevered loading bay. Printing works behind (1926–7, by Ellis & Clarke) were demolished *c.* 1990. A matching curved corner at the far Fleet Street end was demolished for an extension of 1972–4 (by *Ellis, Clarke & Gallanaugh*), also black-glazed, but too large for comfort.

Williams wanted completely clear glazing to expose the frame (cf. his contemporary Boots factory, Beeston, Notts, with its tough machine aesthetic), but was overruled, by Lord Beaverbrook, it is said. Its columns, tapered downwards to maximize floor space, support main beams of 3 ft (nearly 1 metre) section. Lesser beams were cast integrally with the floors. Visible through a big glazed panel, the luxurious and sensational ENTRANCE HALL, 130 large enough to accommodate advertisers delivering copy. Designed by *Robert Atkinson* in the full flight of Deco fantasy: archaizing plaster reliefs representing Industry (by *Eric Aumonier*), silvered and gilt, a giant Expressionistic silvered pendant in a ceiling with frilly coving, and other shimmering motifs. Full-height oval stairwell beyond. The building awaits a new use in 1996. It swept away RACQUET COURT, once the best-preserved of the late C17 courts off Fleet Street, though of this period only two five-bay houses remained.

The w corner of Shoe Lane is No. 130, stone-clad offices by *Richard M. Roe*, 1907, with panelled pilasters and weird mix-and-match Gothic details.

GOLDMAN SACHS, by the American firm *Kohn Pederson Fox Associates*, 1988–91 (executive architects *EPR Partnership*) occupies the buildings between No. 131 and Nos. 135–141. The plan resembles Freshfields: mostly retained façades to Fleet Street, a big new block facing a courtyard behind. The new work appears discreetly at the narrow No. 131. No. 133, the former MERSEY HOUSE, 1904–6, is an original and successful design, owing something to Harrison Townsend's Horniman Museum (*see London 2: South*). Stone-faced front with a big arched ground floor of granite, below a shallow convex bay flanked by rounded buttresses or turrets. Above the bay a little close-set arcade and plain curved gable. Who was the architect? As restored, it gives entry to a high glazed cloister around the courtyard (of which more later). Then the former DAILY TELEGRAPH (Nos. 135–141), by *Elcock & Sutcliffe*, with *Thomas Tait*, 1928–31 (*Sir Owen Williams* was consulting engineer, but the extent of his involvement is uncertain). The *Telegraph* moved here in 1863. This building replaced premises by *Arding, Bond & Buzzard* (1881–2). Tait and Elcock were old colleagues from Burnet's Glasgow offices, but the simplifying tendencies of much of Burnet's and Tait's other work were abandoned here in favour of a noisy Neo-Graeco-Egyptian – an adequate advertisement for the paper when new, no doubt, though immediately trumped by the *Daily Express*. Big columns high up between end bays with roadway entrances, which rise up as flanking pavilions. Giant projecting Deco clock (by the *Birmingham Guild*); modernistic touches in the ironwork and fluting (carver *S. Rabinovitch*). Egyptian display cases and ground-floor lobby, restored in 1988–91 (also preserved, the *Telegraph*'s fifth-floor office suite, in the early C18 style preferred for such inner sanctums). A new rear façade faces PETERBOROUGH COURT (named from the Bishop of Peterborough's Inn here, after *c.* 1420): tall windows with a close grid of glazing bars after Mackintosh. Goldman Sachs' main building is on the N side of the court (the former printing works site): a sleek, complex pile, not the usual atrium block, but a deep, stocky tower 190 ft (58 metres) high (permitting more open-plan dealing rooms), broken up by set-backs on differing alignments determined by surrounding streets. Tall glazed cloister around the courtyard's N and E sides, in a grey-stone-clad frame. Its N axis is not quite that of the main block, which appears above as a broad five-storey section, with recessed convex curtain-walling between stone-faced, square-windowed corner towers. Set back on top, but visible through a slot in the curtain-walling, a giant flattened segmental gable, housing double-height dining rooms. The N side opens into a part-circular reception lobby, given a sombre, masculine glamour by a suspended beaten metal ceiling and much plain polished stone. Escalators beyond ascend to a corridor to the central elevator core.

Back to Fleet Street, for the narrow, gabled No. 142, *Hooker & Hemmings*'s former King & Keys pub, 1884. Carving by *Frampton*, spoiled in 1995, when the front was painted a queasy green. Nos. 143–144, QUEEN OF SCOTS HOUSE, 1905 by *R.M. Roe*, mercilessly Gothic of Flemish Flamboyant character. Two barge-boarded gables. The statue of Mary Stuart was the romantic idea of the developer, Sir John Tollemache Sinclair M.P. Nos. 145 and 146 are late C17 houses, crudely refronted (typical post-Fire plans with staircase compartment and unlit closet between front and rear rooms; staircases with ball-finials and turned balusters). No. 145 forms part of the CHESHIRE CHEESE, with a good later C18 shopfront on the main rear part, facing Wine Office Court. Flush sash-boxes above. It originated as a pair of small late C17 houses, amalgamated and heightened probably in 1755. Each had one room per floor, with a staircase compartment boxed out of one corner: an arrangement still discernible in the entrance passage in the S part. Screened off on the r. here, the bar famous for associations with Dr Johnson's circle: most atmospheric, but with largely early to mid-C19 fittings. E extension by *Waterhouse & Ripley*, c. 1991, who gave No. 145 a Neo-Georgian shopfront to Fleet Street.

Narrow, mostly mean buildings follow; then a sequence of big, neutral stone-faced C20 offices. Nos. 154–160, by *Campbell-Jones, Sons & Smithers*, 1924–6, have twin banks at each end marked by giant pilasters. Close-set chamfered uprights between. Plain lumbering upper storeys added 1960. Then Nos. 161–166, HULTON HOUSE, by *A.S. Ash*, 1955–7, and Nos. 167–170 by *R. Seifert & Partners*, 1961–2. The fancy façade of No. 172, by *George Pidding*, 1881, is incorporated with Nos. 174–176 by *R.F. White & Associates*, 1986–9, on the corner with Fetter Lane. Its novelty is the prefabricated yellow brick panels on its terracotta-dressed front.

On the opposite corner, No. 180, clumsy offices by the *Thomas Saunders Partnership*, 1982–4. Banded red brick, broken up into shallow gables against curtain-walling to disguise the mass above: an advance towards full-blown Postmodern pattern-making. Down HEN AND CHICKENS COURT the rudimentary Gothic VESTRY to St Dunstan-in-the-West, 1839. Nos. 184 (by *Farebrother, Ellis & Clarke*) and 185, narrow red brick fronts of 1892–3, of the type with an oriel inserted within a big relieving arch, replaced the last early C17 timber-framed group in Fleet Street. No. 186, probably by *Meakin, Archer & Stoneham*, c. 1913, has naïve mosaic bands naming the newspapers formerly here.

On the far side of St Dunstan, No. 187 (T.S.B.), built as the Law Life Assurance in 1834 by *Shaw Jun.*, on land left over from his father's rebuilding of the church. A very early example both of the purpose-built insurance office and of the Jacobean Revival, quite well done in gault brick and stone, with a semicircular bay window. Matching r. extension of 1900, a storey lower, by *W.E. Clifton*, who made the present entrance and who may have reused Shaw's oriel from the former E front. Shaw's first-floor Jacobean ceiling survives. Nos. 188–190, COUTTS & CO., by *Anderson*,

Forster & Wilcox, 1963–7, has giant circular windows on the ground floor, faced in the black stone called gabbro. Upper storeys Portland-faced with window bands. Behind, it incorporates a cross-wall from *Soane*'s Praed's Bank, 1801 (dem. 1923), with one broad round arch joining the flues (visible from Clifford's Inn Passage, r.).

The corner with Chancery Lane is HAMMICKS BOOKSHOP (Nos. 191–192), 1962, remodelled in 1985–6 by *YRM Partnership*. Flush pink granite, upright windows, undulating canted bows with metal railings at the corner. Opposite, No. 193, ATTENBOROUGH'S, fussy free Renaissance in red sandstone by *Archer & Green*, 1883, curved to the corner with Chancery Lane. The little terracotta figure towards Fleet Street is Kaled (from Byron's *Lara*), after *Giuseppe Grandi*'s original of 1872. Then a former branch of the Bank of England by *Sir Arthur Blomfield*, 1886–8. High Victorian Renaissance, far more opulent than most private or joint-stock banks. Projecting three-storeyed wings carried up as towers, the rest two-and-a-half storeys, on a heavily rusticated half-basement of Aberdeen granite. Dark red marble columns in two orders; much Shap and Peterhead granite too. Venetian ground-floor windows. The capacious banking hall is now a pub. (Transferred to the City of Westminster in 1994, together with No. 193.)

FLEET STREET, ALLEYS NORTH of

Between Shoe Lane, E, and Fetter Lane, W, are a number of courts which in their seclusion and intricacy are a welcome relief from the noise of Fleet Street. Not enough old buildings survive to preserve a pre-C20 atmosphere. One must explore off Carter Lane or Cornhill for that. But there is still a good scattering of late C17 houses, amidst C19–C20 relics of the printing industry and much rebuilding of the late 1970s onwards.

WINE OFFICE COURT begins the sequence. The licensing office for selling wine stood here until 1666. On the W side, just off Fleet Street, Nos. 1–3, a neat early C19 brick terrace with elliptical-headed windows and steps up to the doors. It would not look out of place in Clapham or Richmond. Opposite, the Cheshire Cheese, and further N the mighty mass of Goldman Sachs (for both *see* Fleet Street). Facing the latter, No. 7 (DEAN WACE HOUSE), 1868–70 by *John S. Lee*, the first home of the Press Association. Stone-dressed brick with little barley-sugar iron columns to broad tripartite windows. Wine Office Court turns E into Shoe Lane. To the N here, a paved open space called GUNPOWDER SQUARE, laid out 1989. On the S side, No. 1, by *Simpson Gray Associates*, 1987–90, a rather top-heavy front of stone-dressed red brick, making play with quotations from Norman Shaw's Swan House, Chelsea (q.v. *London 3: North West*).

HIND COURT next, opened up into the S part of Wine Office Court in connection with No. 10 Gough Square (N), by *Phippen Randall & Parkes*, 1980–1, red-brown brick with an assertive leaded attic. 1950s blocks in late C17 manner here and in the L-shaped BOLT COURT further W, named from a C15 inn. Of these, No. 10 Bolt

Court (NE corner) has curiosity value as an early work by *Richard Seifert*, 1953. No. 11, S, is two small late C17 houses combined, with early C19 stucco below. The N side here is the former School of Illustrated Printing by the *LCC Architects*, 1912, severely plain but for a shell-headed doorcase.

GOUGH SQUARE, further N, is really a long L-shaped space, paved with granite setts, gas-lit, and with multifarious C19–C20 cast-iron bollards. The Gough family built it up in the latest C17. The chief original survivor is No. 17, DR JOHNSON'S HOUSE, which makes the W end of the N part. Johnson lived here 1748–59; his famous *Dictionary* was compiled in the attic. Red brick with bands and rubbed trim. Doorcase with reeded capitals and cornice of *c.* 1775. Flush sash-boxes from the restoration by *Alfred Burr*, 1911, when the house became a museum (the final bay on the N is blocked by No. 1, five bays wide, also of *c.* 1700 but heightened and rebuilt behind). No. 17 is one room deep, with a central open-well staircase with turned balusters, and windows also in the N and S walls. The back wall is windowless. Much simple pine panelling, some with cupboards behind. A hinged first-floor partition folds back to throw two rooms together. To the S, the diminutive Curator's House (doubtless by *Burr*) plays Boswell to Johnson across a tiny garden. Red brick, with enjoyably oversized English Baroque details and twin doorcases copied from the main house.

The square's N and E sides were rebuilt in the 1950s and refurbished in the 1990s, taking their cue from the remaining late C17 houses. The effect is like the rebuilt parts of the Temple. In the SW angle, a large building by *The Halpern Partnership*, 1987–92, brown and red brick with stone dressings, in a kind of Neo-Wrenaissance but for a large penthouse with flat eaves cornice and gaudy gilded colonnettes.

JOHNSON'S COURT and ST DUNSTAN'S COURT, next in sequence along Fleet Street, contain nothing of interest. Instead, leave Gough Square by the covered carriageway in the NW corner, into PEMBERTON ROW. The name commemorates an early C17 benefactor of the Goldsmiths' Company, before which it was Three Leg Alley. At the NE corner stood *John Shaw Jun.*'s Neo-Romanesque Holy Trinity Gough Square (1837; dem. 1913). On the S side, No. 5, a much-altered house of *c.* 1700. Its two-and-a-half bays are repeated on No. 4, 1907, yellow and red brick with a stone cornice. No. 1, by the *GMW Partnership*, 1989–91, is a hulking coloured brick affair with canted bays and low matching projections.

RED LION COURT is the turning l. from Pemberton Row. The S part is simple early C20 warehouses (e.g. Nos. 4–7 by *Griffin & Woollard*, 1907, refurbished with peculiar tile cladding in 1979), or infill of the 1970s and later (e.g. No. 1 by *RHWL Partnership*, 1984–7, Italianate pastiche). Older buildings at the N end, where one comes in. No. 8 (E side) is early C19 of irregular plan. Opposite, a little walled courtyard, and on its N side the red brick former premises of Messrs TAYLOR & FRANCIS, built probably after a fire in 1808. Typical of the unassuming premises of C18–C19 printers. Brick dentil-cornice, carried along the E gable like a pediment (restored). Little lunettes to the court below. On the front the handsome sign of the printer Abraham Valpy, 1820s: a hand pouring oil into a Greek lamp and the motto 'alere flammam'. Adjoining at r. angles, the rear walls of Nos. 5 and 6 Crane Court.

CRANE COURT proper is reached by returning to Fleet Street and continuing w. Nos. 5 and 6, E side, date from c. 1670, and are the earliest known buildings by *Nicholas Barbon* to survive. Burnt out in 1971, they were carefully reconstructed by *Ramsay, Coombes & Cooper* for *Haslemere Estates* (1975). No. 5, wholly refronted, of red brick, has five bays with a central entrance in the manner of the Temple chambers. No. 6 has three bays, with a nice early C18 pilastered doorcase with alternating rustication. (Inside both, sections of two original staircases, bolection-moulded panelling, and several handsome first-floor plaster ceilings with big foliage wreaths: the best, reconstructed in No. 5, comparable with those e.g. at Innholders' Hall or the Sir John Cass School.) Of interest otherwise only No. 2, a gawky warehouse front by *J.H. Stevens*, 1863, with four-light sashed windows behind round-arched screens of iron colonnettes. The integrity of Crane Court was lost by rebuilding of the E side in the 1970s. Its history is illustrious: the Royal Society met until 1780 in premises by *Wren* (1711), and in the 1840s *Punch* and the *Illustrated London News* began their existence here. Demolished c. 1975, *T.L. Donaldson*'s Royal Scottish Corporation, Scottish Baronial red brick of 1877–80, across the N end.

FOSTER LANE

The name garbles that of St Vedast's church, whose steeple stands at the E corner with Cheapside (S end). St Leonard Foster Lane, a church built or rebuilt c. 1236 on the w side just N of St Vedast, was not rebuilt after the Great Fire. A Roman road linking the main w road beneath Cheapside with the gate to the Wood Street Roman fort has been found behind the E side of the lane. Massive masonry footings seen in 1830 beneath the Goldsmiths' Hall may have been part of the podium for a Roman temple or shrine; a C2 altar from the site is preserved at the hall (q.v.).

The whole w side was formerly occupied by mid-1920s buildings facing St Martin's le Grand (q.v.); redevelopment of the N part was in progress in 1996. On the E, N of St Vedast's rectory (*see* St Vedast) and Priest's Court, a huddle of modest buildings. No. 5 is a late C17 house crudely refaced after war damage. Flush sashboxes perpetuate the original arrangement. N of No. 6, ROSE AND CROWN COURT joins PRIEST'S COURT behind: both extremely narrow alleys even by City standards. They were extended through to Gutter Lane in post-war rebuilding there. From Priest's Court, Saddlers' Hall (q.v.) may be overlooked through an iron screen in the wall. No. 10, by *John Gill Associates* for the Goldsmiths' Company, 1981–4, copies part of the adjoining Nos. 11–12, Elyot House. These offices of 1896 make derivative use of fashionable free classical detail. The great mass of Goldsmiths' Hall rises immediately beyond (q.v.). In CAREY LANE between (the medieval Kiron Lane), only a utilitarian warehouse of 1904 (s side). This and Nos. 11–12 Foster Lane are proposed for replacement.

FREDERICK'S PLACE

A close off Old Jewry, an oasis of domesticity with Georgian houses on both sides. They would be nothing special in the West End, but are memorable for being one of the speculations of the *Adam* brothers. As C18 houses they also have great rarity value in the City.

In 1772 the Adams took a lease on a late C17 house built by Sir John Frederick, Lord Mayor, set back from Old Jewry behind a court-yard (the present close). As at their Adelphi, begun the same year, the designs were undertaken by *Robert* and *James Adam*; drawings at the Soane Museum are signed by *James*, who may have done most of the work. Work began in 1775, houses going up piecemeal after the manner of ordinary builders, with no single controlling elevation. But in 1776 the brothers lost interest and sold the lease on the N side to *Samuel Dowbiggin*, who built the houses there in 1776–8.

The Adams' work begins at No. 35 Old Jewry, a plain three-bay house with bracket-cornice. Pilastered ground-floor shopfront of 1866. On the S corner with Frederick's Place, No. 8 has Victorian-looking alterations to ground-floor windows, although the N door-case looks original. Interior much altered in 1915. No. 7, set back and also with an altered ground floor, originally ran through to No. 35. Largest and least altered is No. 6, of six bays, with round-headed ground-floor windows and a square-headed doorcase with Adamesque pilasters. (First-floor front drawing room with Adam ceiling: oval panel with central concave-sided diamond and relief medallions after the Antique.) No. 5, a small stuccoed Victorian warehouse, replaced that built for the merchant who lived at No. 6. The messy W end is formed by the rear of the Mercers' Hall (q.v.) and Dauntsey House (*see* Ironmonger Lane).

On the N side, *Dowbiggin*'s three-bay No. 4 takes up the Adams' motif of round-headed ground-floor windows. The interior was re-modelled by *Soane*, 1806–9: the last survivor of his domestic work in the City. His is the simple, compact staircase, r., to the first-floor landing. Ahead here, on the opposite side of the house, *Dowbiggin*'s elegant oval staircase swings up to the third floor: an unusual shift of axis. Circular skylight by Soane, the thick plasterwork probably a C20 addition. First-floor rooms with swagged frieze with oval plaques and bucrania, perhaps Soane's; good fireplaces probably of the 1770s.* Adjoining, the present No. 1 is a composite of Dowbiggin's work and rebuilding of 1915–16 by *Allan F. Vigers* after a fire: the new work in the centre with plain brick pilasters and stone doorcase, the retained façade of old No. 2 on the r. The N corner with Old Jewry was rebuilt by *Vigers & Co.*, 1955–8, after bomb damage; it is higher, but otherwise passably close to the old manner. C18 RAILINGS, with overthrows, torch extinguishers and little urns to some uprights.

---

* I am grateful to Ptolemy Dean for his help with No. 4.

FURNIVAL STREET

The w boundary of the City until 1994. The land hereabouts belonged to Malmesbury Abbey until the Reformation, after which the Willoughby family filled it with tenements. Called Castle Street until the 1880s; the new name commemorates Furnival's Inn, an Inn of Chancery formerly on the N side of Holborn. This was established by 1408, rebuilt by *Daniel Thomas* in 1640, and demolished in 1818.

Medium-sized buildings mostly of 1980 onwards line the E side. First at the N end, *Architech's* Nos. 40–41, 1988–90, a good full-blooded bowed front of damson brick, with a giant lunette set back above. External framing makes a screen to the bow window. No. 39 is a curious relic: the entrance to deep AIR-RAID SHELTERS, 1942–3 (engineers *Mott, Hay & Anderson*). Heavy steel crane on the brick front. Nos. 36–37, simple brick, by *Rolfe Judd Group Practice*, 1981–2, before the advent of Postmodern detailing. Nos. 34–35, flats by *Goddard Manton Partnership*, 1994–5, like a late Victorian fancy warehouse. Nos. 32–33 are two late C17 houses, probably of 1690. Three stuccoed bays each, No. 32 of four storeys, No. 33 with a tile-hung attic. Simple early C19 doorcases. (Original panelling in both houses; closed-string staircase in No. 32.) Nos. 30–31, 1982–5 by *Prudential Assurance Architects Department*, purple brick, much broken backward and forward. Nos. 27–29, red brick, the factory of Messrs Hadley, stationers (1900 by *S. Knight*), drastically reconstructed as offices *c.* 1975. On the s corner of Norwich Street, the simple CASTLE pub (*Gardiner & Theobald*, 1901), then the JEWISH CHRONICLE, refronted *c.* 1960 by *Vivien Pelley* in concrete and brick with one storey of round-headed windows.
Facing, BEACHCROFT STANLEYS, 1987–9 by *Covell Matthews Wheatley*, a banded buff brick slab offset at each end by a recessed dark-green-glazed bay. Further N, the looming Neo-Elizabethan Patent Office extension (*see* Public Buildings).

GARLICK HILL

Continues the line of Bow Lane down to the old Garlick Hithe, where that herb was landed. Characteristic early C20 warehouses on the E side. In their midst, No. 21, 1987–9 by the *Fitzroy Robinson Partnership*, counterfeits the odd stone pilasters of the more demonstrative warehouse of *c.* 1892 it supplanted.

GILTSPUR STREET

Said to be named from gilded spurs, perhaps a medieval shop sign to tempt knights attending tournaments in Smithfield, N. Widened and straightened in connection with *Dance the Younger's* prison called the Giltspur Street Compter (1787–91, dem. 1855), an exercise in the rusticated manner of Newgate Gaol. The Post Office's yard opposite St Sepulchre, E side, marks the approximate site.*

* On the Compter *see* Dorothy Stroud, *Architectural History*, 1984.

To its N, the great parade of late C19 to early C20 Portland stone
blocks for St Bartholomew's Hospital (see Public Buildings).
Typical C20 commercial architecture faces them. Nos. 8–9 by the
church, offices dated 1907, red brick above stone, neatly handled
on the narrow S part with pilasters and broken pediments. In the
Neo-Wren manner popularized e.g. by Blomfield, perhaps by *Daw,
Wills & Church* (cf. their No. 2 St Andrew's Hill). The slated roof,
glazing etc. are perfectly preserved: a sight now almost as scarce as
a mid-Victorian shopfront, though much less appreciated. Over
the entrance a bronze stag's head: has it strayed from the WHITE
HART next door (by *S. Yeo*, 1930–2)? No. 6, 1910, a free classical
warehouse by *E. Greenop* with thin second-floor pilasters. Across
Cock Lane, No. 1 (CITY & GUILDS), friendly big red brick with
stone bands and cast detail, by *GMW Partnership*, 1988–91. On the
S corner, a little gilt figure in late C17 style, inscribed 'Puckeridge
fecit Hosier Lane'. The carved inscription (formerly painted on his
chest) proclaims 'This Boy is in Memmory put up for the late FIRE
of LONDON occasioned by the sin of Gluttony 1666'. It was here,
then called Pie Corner, that the Fire is supposed to have ended its
course from the famous Pudding Lane bakery. The name Pie
Corner may come from a trade sign, or from the cooked food trade
(Ralph Tresswell's survey drawings of *c.* 1612 show large ovens in
properties nearby).

GODLIMAN STREET

Said to be named from 'godelmynges', skins used by shoemakers,
though also called Paul's Wharf Hill in the C13–C14. In 1369 the Dean
and Chapter of St Paul's contracted a range of twenty shops here.
Substantial ROMAN WALLS retaining a raised terrace, found running
from Addle Hill to Peter's Hill, may have been part of a large public
construction: perhaps a temple precinct with an altar or temple
structure awaiting identification somewhere S of St Paul's Cathedral.

Nos. 17 and 21, uninspired brown brick offices by *R. Seifert &
Partners*, 1973–85, span KNIGHTRIDER STREET, E side. Here,
No. 17 incorporates façades replicating the modest early C19
HORN TAVERN. The W part of Knightrider Street, opposite, is
now an access road within Faraday House (see Telephone
Exchanges, Queen Victoria Street, Public Buildings), but until the
mid C19 it formed part of the now-fragmented E–W route through
the City that also encompassed Great St Thomas Apostle, etc.

GOLDEN LANE

Named probably from Richard son of Golda, who owned land here
in 1245 (in 1274 called *Goldeslane*). It runs N from Beech Street,
which lies under the Barbican development, into Old Street outside the City. On the W side is the Golden Lane Estate (see next
entry). On the E side, No. 1, remains of the former Cripplegate
Institute, founded from parochial charities in 1891, and built
1893–6, by *Sidney R.J. Smith* with *Frederick Hammond*, St Giles's

parish surveyor. Red brick and stone, free Jacobean. Sculpture at
the portal proclaims its educational mission. *Ergon Design Group*
reconstructed the building for offices, 1987–92, after the Institute
moved to Worship Street. The entrance hall was preserved and the
inserted storeys match (more storeys in the usual mansard, behind
a reused pediment), but the proportions have been spoiled. Big red
brick W extension, strenuously ornamented with giant open pediments and oriels. Across Brackley Street, BERNARD MORGAN
HOUSE, a Section House by the *Metropolitan Police Architects'
Department*, completed 1960. Long slab, well-detailed, with infill
of the concrete frame in dark brick and knapped flint. Low rear
service wing. It now accommodates City Police staff.

GOLDEN LANE ESTATE

Built for the City Corporation by *Chamberlin, Powell & Bon*, who won
a competition in 1952; the first parts were completed in 1957. It was
the first phase of the replanned London Wall and Barbican area to
be completed. 1,400 flats were provided, intended mostly for single

1   Great Arthur House
2   Swimming pool
3   Tennis court
4   Nursery school
5   Community centre

100 m
300 ft

Golden Lane Estate. Plan

people and couples working in the City, in ten well-proportioned
blocks on a free grid around four traffic-free courts of differing
sizes. Rigorous 'hard' landscaping rather than grass or trees: tougher
and more self-consciously urban than such pioneering late 1940s
London schemes as Powell & Moya's Churchill Gardens or Tecton's
Hallfield Estate, Paddington (the architects said they had 'no desire
to make the project look like a garden suburb'). At the same time the
blocks are well-detailed and carefully distinguished from one another,
with none of the mass-produced air of much later local authority
housing. Boundary changes in 1994 transferred the whole estate to
the City from Islington.

Centrepiece and focus is GREAT ARTHUR HOUSE, a sixteen-storey tower aligned N–S, with golden-yellow glass curtain-walling and two stacks of concrete balconies. So much colour still seems daring, and must have been stunning at the time, when it was for a while London's tallest block of flats. Perched on its roof is a butterfly-winged concrete structure masking the water-tanks: an early and much-remarked expression of discontent with pre-war Modernism's limited vocabulary of forms. The lower blocks are aligned mostly E–W. They have load-bearing brick-faced cross-walls, framing opaque glass cladding coloured red and blue. Some have perforated concrete balconies, and here the motifs are multiplied to excess. Some glazing-in of staircases etc. was carried out in 1987. Between the blocks, a swimming pool, bowling green (now a tennis court), nursery school and community centre, exploiting the different levels left by the deep basements of bombed properties. In the NE court a curious walled circular enclosure, like a sheep fold.

The later phase along Goswell Road, completed 1962, has shops 138 below flats expressed as metal-framed projections with mosaic panels, intriguingly angled to the gently convex front, all under a segmental-curved canopy of concrete. In the canopy's unmodulated mass, the late-Corbusian language of the architects' adjacent Barbican Estate is anticipated.

For the W side of Goswell Road here, *see* Aldersgate Street.

GOODMAN'S YARD

The name records a C16 farmer of fields formerly owned by the nuns of the Minories. Stow recalled being sent to him for milk as a child. One building, by *Fitzroy Robinson Partnership*, 1979–83, on the S side. A long slab with close-set concrete fins, and twin round glazed stair-towers. The effect is as of a multi-storey car park converted to offices. In the little garden by the entrance, large abstract polished metal SCULPTURE, Judex, by *Keith McCarter*, 1983.

GRACECHURCH STREET

Gracechurch has nothing to do with 'grace'; the name, known from 1276, derives from grass and an ancient hay-market. It was formed by the late C10 to connect with the new London Bridge known by *c.* 1000, bisecting the site of London's ROMAN FORUM. A mid-C1 p. gravelled piazza here was replaced *c.* A.D. 70–85 by a large building, 33 about 330 ft (100 metres) N–S by 165 ft (50 metres) E–W, comprising four wings around a split-level central courtyard with a basilica to the N (*see* Introduction p. 32 and Leadenhall Market). The present S entry from King William Street, on the C19 bridge alignment, follows a wide curve across the Eastcheap–Cannon Street route. The rest runs straight up to Bishopsgate. Its architecture is mostly tall C20 offices with no style or period predominant, enlivened by a few C19 survivals.

North Part: Cornhill to Lombard Street

For the NE corner, *see* Leadenhall Street. The W SIDE begins at the
N with the E front of St Peter Cornhill. Then Nos. 1–2, classical
offices by *H.S. Saunders*, c. 1908, with enriched window surrounds.
The plain eight-storeyed elevation of No. 3, the former Guinness
Mahon by *R. Seifert & Partners*, 1964–8, shows the practice at its
best. Flush window bands are set in front of angled inner windows
of saw-tooth plan. On the top floor the outer glazing is dispensed
with, and the rhythm of the angled windows is only half as fast. By
night the front is transformed, as the inner glazing catches the light.
Less interesting towards St Peter's churchyard, N, with plain
concrete bands and thick mullions. Good entrance hall, with free-
standing staircase and mezzanine gallery. In the porch, a rustic
demi-figure of the 'Mercers' Maid', in a square panel dated 1669,
formerly in CORBET COURT behind. A C12 stone house was
recorded here in 1872. No. 9 is the former Hongkong & Shanghai
Bank, by *W. Campbell-Jones*, 1912–13. Symmetrical French-
flavoured façade, with giant pilasters and keystones. Big volutes
continue the lines of the pilasters into the attic. Floor-panels on
the second floor were originally inscribed in Chinese. Carving by
Messrs *Aumonier*. Attractive banking hall, with coloured marble
columns and marble and mosaic lining (threatened with redevelopment in 1996). For the huge new premises of Barclays
Bank, *see* Lombard Street. The crossing with Lombard Street and
Fenchurch Street here was known in the Middle Ages as Carfax
(quatre vois), where bankers would meet each other.

On the E SIDE, first the nicely blowsy entrance pavilions to
Leadenhall Market (*see* Public Buildings). No. 85 next door, offices
of 1934–5 by *E. Howard & Partners*. Tall frontispiece with enriched
uprights and cornice strip, the details Deco-cum-Egyptian. Nos.
81–83, a satisfying stone palazzo front of 1874 with round-headed
windows to the main floors and paired straight-headed windows
with colonnettes on the third floor. The architect was *Henry S.
Legg*. It houses the entrance to BULL'S HEAD PASSAGE, which
runs back into Lime Street Passage and the outlying buildings of
Leadenhall Market. On the N side of the passage, Nos. 2–4, plain
brick with tripartite windows under shallow relieving arches, were
built for the Skinners' Company in 1840–1. Back on Gracechurch
Street, No. 77 is a clumsy stone-faced Postmodern exercise by the
Kenzie Lovell Partnership, 1983–6, with rounded half-piers and a
square bay projecting on the corner with SHIP TAVERN PASSAGE.
The little SWAN TAVERN dated 1898, by *E.B. I'Anson*, spans the
passage. On the corner with Fenchurch Street was the uninspired
Barclays Bank complex, 1968–72 by *CLRP Architects* (under
demolition 1997). A chamfered square tower of some thirty storeys,
small upright windows each in a projecting pre-cast frame: a consistent and remorseless display of concrete. A lower wing E extends
up to Lime Street. Offices by *John Simpson & Partners* are proposed
for the site (1997).

South Part: Lombard Street to Eastcheap

For the offices of 1868 on the w side, *see* Lombard Street. Plain and rather nerveless extension at Nos. 26–32, built in 1977–82 by *Wilson Mason & Partners*. Arcaded black granite to the banking hall, plain stone above.

On the E side, a new building by the *Halpern Partnership* is under construction at the S corner with Fenchurch Street in 1997.* Nos. 55–58, GRACECHURCH HOUSE, by *Sheppard Robson Architects*, 1990–2, is stone-faced with paraphrased classical detail and iron balcony rails. On the rear wall of Gracechurch House is a reset carved late C19 armorial of the Clothworkers' Company. Nos. 51–54, ABBEY NATIONAL, built as speculative offices by *L. Sylvester Sullivan*, 1928–30. In the vertical variety of the C20 commercial style, with many narrowly set uprights. Slightly pointed lower parapet like a giant shallow pediment. Rear elevations to Talbot Court repeat the uprights in white faience. The corner with Eastcheap is made by the NATIONAL PROVIDENT INSTITUTION at No. 48, by *Antony Lloyd* of *Green, Lloyd & Son*, 1957–9. Stripped classical, old-fashioned for the date, but thoughtfully and gracefully done. An eight-storey block with minimal applied pilasters on the upper storeys faces Gracechurch Street. A lower wing follows the curve of Eastcheap. *R. Kerr*'s previous premises here, of 1863, were an early exercise in the mansarded French manner.

Back on the W side, Nos. 33–36, the former British Overseas Bank by *Campbell-Jones, Son & Smithers*, 1920–3, with shallow canted end bays. Then the long slow curve of Nos. 37–41, built for the Commercial Bank by *F.R. Gould Wills*, 1914–20. Giant pilasters with much shallow detail between. Broken segmental pediments crown the end sections.

The line of Gracechurch Street continues as Fish Street Hill, the approach to old London Bridge.

GREAT ST HELEN'S and CROSBY SQUARE

Great St Helen's could still be described in 1957 as 'a maze of alleyways between Bishopsgate and St Mary Axe'; but rebuilding since (notably the Commercial Union and P & O group, Leadenhall Street) has made it a shapeless and unsatisfactory leftover, merging with the similar Undershaft at the SE.

St Helen's church with its brick offices lies on the N side. N of the church, ungainly offices at Nos. 34–35 by *Stevens Hayes Dunne*, 1996–7. By the entrance from Bishopsgate, W, No. 36, *c*. 1892, domestic in scale and Queen Anne manner, spoiled by metal windows of 1929. The Skinners' almshouses, a mid-C16 foundation of Sir Andrew Judd, previously stood here. Other turn-of-the-century casualties were a fine pilastered mid-C17 house at Nos. 8–9, and Crosby Hall, Sir John Crosby's celebrated mid-C15 mansion, whose hall was taken down and re-erected in Chelsea in 1908–9 (*see London 3: North West*). Crosby's monument is in St Helen,

---

* Two predecessors of unusual interest. *Wren*'s St Benet Gracechurch (1681–7) fell victim to street widening in 1867–8. Its steeple had an obelisk on a dome (cf. St Peter Cornhill). The church is first recorded *c*. 1181; St Benet's Place, S, preserves its name. *Whinney, Son & Austen Hall*'s Midland Bank, 1958–61 (altered 1985), with curtain-walling of varying heights, was one of the City's first unabashedly Modern buildings outside the areas of wholesale rebuilding.

as is that of a later (C16 and early C17) resident, Sir John Spencer.

CROSBY SQUARE, to its s, now makes a forecourt to the former Standard Chartered Bank, with a view through its tall glazed lobby to Bishopsgate (q.v.). On the N side, a good new building by *Hurley Robertson & Associates*, 1994–7, with convex green curtain walling between sandstone-faced uprights. One older building facing: MOCATTA HOUSE, 1908 by *Henry Saul*, white artificial stone.

GREAT ST THOMAS APOSTLE

Part of the long-fragmented E–W route that included Knightrider Street and Fish Street (*see* Godliman Street). Named from the former church, rebuilt *c.* 1371 and destroyed in 1666. Typical modest warehouses of 1876–85 on the s side (e.g. Nos. 5–7 by *Hammack & Lambert*, 1877) are proposed for replacement by the *T.P. Bennett Partnership* (1996). No. 15 opposite, similar, of the type with colonnettes to the windows. By *W. Hancock*, 1887. MARC HOUSE (Nos. 13–14), by *C.A. Cornish & Associates*, 1989–91, makes patterns in stone and brick.

GREAT TOWER STREET

Called *la Tourstrate* in 1287. Widened on the N side in 1882–4, when the street was dug up to accommodate the Metropolitan Railway. With Byward Street, cut through from near its E end into Trinity Square at the same time, it now functions as the E continuation of Eastcheap.

N SIDE. At the w end, MILLOCRAT HOUSE, 1951–4 by *A.W. Moore*, an extension to Plantation House (*see* Fenchurch Street). The 1930s design is varied slightly, e.g. by channelling the lower piers. Then the phantasmagoric Minster Court (*see* Mincing Lane).

s SIDE. Nos. 1–4, HARRISON & CROSFIELD, dated 1911. Free Style, classically inflected, but with shallow curved bays alternating with flat sections instead of any great show of orders. Over the entrance a broad balcony with columns. By *Edgar Stones*; rebuilt for the company in 1988–91 by *T.P. Bennett Partnership*, who repeated a plainer version of the front towards Idol Lane. Then a sequence mostly in red brick: Nos. 5–10 by *Gunton & Gunton*, 1949–51, tepid Neo-Georgian; beyond St Dunstan's Hill, a TELEPHONE EXCHANGE, 1920–3, with squared-off classical motifs; grim late 1960s concrete extension, l. Further on two confident exercises in the mid-C17 manner. Nos. 24–25 (Ocean House), by *Charles Watkins*, 1908, has quoins, eared surrounds, and a big pedimented doorcase of polished stone. No. 27 is the former CHRIST'S HOSPITAL OFFICES, 1913–15 by *A.C. Blomfield*. Built after the school moved to Sussex, to administer its London estates and as a club and examination hall. A very nice symmetrical façade with giant pilasters and an upswept gable over the middle bay, carried out in exceptionally good brickwork. Stone cornice and doorcase.

The main front office was sensitively converted to a pub in 1995. In 1927 a new entrance was made in the long E front. This then faced a twisting alley called Water Lane, which explains the plainness of the façade here. The Venetian window high up lights the former Council Chamber. (Panelling in a rich Neo-Wren manner.)*

Water Lane was swept away in the later 1960s, when the line of Lower Thames Street was extended N to join Byward Street. Further down here, BOWRING HOUSE (No. 28), a stocky ten-storey tower by *Raymond J. Cecil & Partners*, 1970–2. The cladding is silvery stainless steel in well-proportioned floor bands, main and lesser mullions and transoms. Indented corner to the street. Uniform white tiling behind. The free-standing block beyond houses the Bakers' Hall (q.v.).

The E part of Great Tower Street remains as a paved passage between All Hallows Barking and the Tower Place precinct (*see* Tower Hill).

GREAT WINCHESTER STREET

William Paulet, Marquess of Winchester, acquired the Austin Friars' land here at the Dissolution. The present L-shaped street was made by the early C18 over the garden of his Winchester House, formerly on the S side. A part of the house, of brick with cross-windows, remained until 1839. Two successive office buildings called Winchester House stood on the N side: the first by *F.T. Pilkington*, 1885–7, gargantuan Continental Baroque, extended to London Wall 1901–5 by *Belcher & Joass* with novel Viennese-flavoured details; the second by *Gunton & Gunton*, 1962–8, with a tall W slab.

The whole N side up to London Wall was in 1997 being redeveloped by *Swanke Hayden Connell* for DEUTSCHE MORGAN GRENFELL. Older premises of Morgan Grenfell occupy the SW corner. By *Mewès & Davis*, 1925–6, in their chaste Frenchified Palladian manner. Above the entrance a concave section with giant Ionic pilasters, off-centre, to make a frontispiece to the vista from Old Broad Street. Rebuilt behind around an atrium by *Rolfe Judd*, 1986–90, with retained C19 façades to Austin Friars and a new section in Throgmorton Avenue (qq.v.). On the S side, Nos. 21–22, a flat stone front by *Paul Hoffman*, 1915, still with Free Style touches, with bulgy pilasters like cut-outs and a running moulding linking the attic pediments. UNITED OVERSEAS BANK at No. 19, by *R. Seifert & Partners*, 1973–6, is a dark polished stone grid with windows recessed.

GRESHAM STREET

The name dates from 1845, when the street was pieced together from widened older lanes not quite in alignment with one another. From E to W, they were St Anne's Lane (St Martin's le Grand to Noble Street), Maiden Lane (to Wood Street), Lad Lane (to Aldermanbury) and Cateaton Street (to Lothbury). This explains its uneven course

---

* I owe these details to the hospital's archivist David Young.

and the way the older Goldsmiths' Hall faces w, not N on to the street. The new name honoured the City's C16 benefactor, whose foundation, Gresham College, had just moved to the N side. It falls into two parts, either side of the shift in alignment by Guildhall and St Lawrence Jewry, which punctuates the view from the w. The heavily bombed w part was rebuilt *c.* 1955–60 as a series of large office blocks in the friendly Modernism of the day, several let down by huge drab rear ranges. The E part is mostly mid C19 to early C20. Two Livery Halls and two churches, small open spaces on the N side and the central drama of Guildhall all make the progress a lively one. Both sides are taken together.

From w to E, No. 7 (N side), modest later C19 commercial, makes a good foil to *Wren*'s St Anne and St Agnes (q.v.). Then the GOLDSMITHS' GARDEN on the site of the church of St John Zachary, not rebuilt after the Great Fire. First made by firewatchers in 1941, it was redesigned after the war by *Peter Shepheard*, *c.* 1962 (modified 1995 by *Anne Jennings*). The raised w section with two large trees was the old churchyard, the sunken E part with its brick retaining walls the site of the church itself (recorded from *c.* 1181). Above looms No. 29, a large L-shaped block by *Ellis, Clarke & Gallanaugh*, completed 1957. To Gresham Street it is concave, with slender stone verticals.

Facing it (s side), the great early C19 block of Goldsmiths' Hall contrasts poignantly with the little reconstructed Wax Chandlers' Hall; then Nos. 2–12 (the former Post Office Engineering Department), 1957–8 by *Easton & Robertson*, a nine-storey slab with lower wings projecting irresolutely to the street and a long return wing to Wood Street. Opposite, N, *A.S. Ash*'s Garrard House (1954–6) was demolished in 1996. It was a dull, stone-faced pile, incorporating the Haberdashers' Hall (q.v.) facing Staining Lane behind.

After Wood Street, an atrium block by *GMW Partnership*, 1987–91 (N side) replaces *Richardson & Gill*'s sound and serious stone-faced Leith House (1925). It has routine oversized Postmodern motifs (broken pediment, red windows) in grey granite cladding. Curved corner, lower floors recessed behind a shallow colonnade. It faces Nos. 14–18, CLEMENTS HOUSE, one of the best office buildings in the City of its date (1954–7). By *Trehearne & Norman, Preston & Partners*, especially handsome in the abstract mosaic panels between the windows, some with a W-pattern and some with a kind of crazy-paving motif. It retains its glazed, airy double-height entrance lobby with asymmetrical flights of stairs to a first-floor balcony. A roof terrace is emphasized by a delicate pergola.

On the N side again, Nos. 59–67, BARRINGTON HOUSE by *Sir John Burnet, Tait & Partners*, 1954–6: restless in materials – stone, brick, coloured spandrels – and restless in shapes, including the management of a diversity of heights. Sadly dull behind, facing Love Lane and Wood Street.

This brings us to Guildhall and St Lawrence Jewry; facing them (s side), No. 30, 1958–61 by *Ellis, Clarke & Gallanaugh*, a long slab with a central entrance, last in the sequence of post-war blocks. Harmonious grey and mauve mosaic panels provide the individual touch of luxury then favoured.

After King Street and the Guildhall Yard entrance, the street narrows; stone-faced C19 commercial buildings dominate much of the s side, later buildings the N. On the N side, BANCA DI ROMA (Nos. 81–87) by the *Thomas Saunders Partnership*, 1983–8, a pastiche of the stuccoed style of *c*. 1830 as seen in 'improved' streets like Moorgate, too flat in detail and too heavy in its double mansard to be convincing. At the back it goes feebly Gothic as a gesture to Guildhall. Just round the corner in Guildhall Yard, No. 23 King Street, an attractive free Northern Renaissance neighbour in honey-coloured stone, 1905. The NATIONAL BANK OF AUSTRALIA, on the corner of Gresham Street and Basinghall Street, is the former Gresham College, 1911–13, by the Mercers' Company Surveyor *Dendy Watney* and the City Surveyor *Sydney Perks*. Neo-Palladian, with a giant order, and balconies projecting between. Channelled basement. Proportions are modified by the lecture theatre being on the tall ground floor, like a banking hall. Carving inside and out by *Seale*, well above average. The theatre survives, lavishly panelled in oak. It has blind aedicules with coupled columns between tall pilasters. Partly rebuilt within the shell by *Waterhouse & Ripley c.* 1982. Gresham College is now based at Barnard's Inn (*see* Public Buildings).

On the opposite corner of Basinghall Street, Nos. 93–95, by *Robert Angell & Curtis*, 1927, with plainer sections between channelled stone bays slightly projecting. Small dome on the corner. Nos. 97–99 beyond, by *Sidell Gibson*, proposed 1997, will re-create the giant pilasters and the corner turret of the former Swiss Bank, by *Meakin, Archer & Co.*, 1923–25.

On the s side, the E corner with King Street is Nos. 42–44 (BANCA COMMERCIALE ITALIANA), the former Queen's Assurance Company, by *Sancton Wood*, 1850–2. The better quality than the run-of-the-mill mid-C19 commercial architecture will immediately be noticed, and the loss of most grand mid-C19 City offices makes it a still more valuable survival. Stone-faced, with quite refined Italian detail. The chamfered entrance corner with its little ornamented bow breaks away from the simple palazzo formula, and windows are more closely spaced than in e.g. the Italianate clubs of Smirke, of whom Wood was a pupil. Ground-floor arcade with shouldered segmental arches on Tuscan columns: another innovation characteristic of the 1850s, possibly appearing for the first time here. Refurbishment *c.* 1978 by *Whinney, Son & Austen Hall* (bronze doors by *John McCarthy*) alas added a storey: originally a pitched roof and big chimneystacks rose immediately above the upper cornice.

Smaller fronts beyond: No. 46, *c.* 1865, tall, with shouldered arches; No. 48, *c.* 1860, busy mid-C16 Italianate with close-set windows; No. 50, attractive free classical of 1908, with a shallow canted corner bay. Probably by *George Vickery*, whose office was here. Across Ironmonger Lane, No. 52, stone-clad Postmodern of 1987–91 by *Stanley Peach & Partners*, with a round corner turret (replacing a much-restored three-bay late C17 brick house); No. 54, low-relief Italianate, 1878. Then late 1930s buildings, set back for an uncompleted street widening scheme: Nos. 56–60 by *G. Thrale Jell*, 1936, sullenly plain but for an upper Doric aedicule; Nos. 62–66, the former Westralia House, stone-faced with Deco touches, by *Bernard Evans*, 1938.

GUTTER LANE

Derived from one Goudren or Godrune (*Godrun lane* in the late C12). Bomb damage was heavy, and all is post-war but for Goldsmiths' Hall (q.v.), the back of which appears at the N end. Opposite, running s to Goldsmith Street, an unsightly car park behind Nos. 2–12 Gresham Street. On the w side, spanning the access road to the Saddlers' Hall on the s (q.v.), No. 33 (SCHRODERS' INVESTMENT MANAGEMENT), faced in unpolished stone with aggressive vertical mullions. By *R. Seifert & Partners*, 1986–90. A ROMAN BUILDING containing an unusually early apsed reception room, probably a dining room, was found beneath (1988). It had a late C1 or early C2 black-and-white mosaic pavement with red border. Here also stood the Broderers' (Embroiderers') Hall, from *c.* 1520. Its final incarnation (by *Huntly Gordon*, 1892, destroyed 1940) was no more than a tall ornamented warehouse with a modest livery suite incorporated.

HART STREET

The continuation of Crutched Friars w up to Mark Lane. In the C14 recorded as both *Olafstrete* (after St Olave's church, q.v.) and *Herthstrete*; it is thought that hearthstones were made here. One building of interest: No. 3, THE SHIP pub by *M.E. Collins* (s side), a single-bay Neo-Jacobean front dated to 'Jubilee Year 1887'. Spirited and riotously ornamental, with canted bow window and lots of vinous and nautical ornament, now painted.

HAYNE STREET *see* LONG LANE

HENEAGE LANE

A narrow turning off Creechurch Lane, running up to Bevis Marks. Worth the detour to see the plain E front of the Bevis Marks Synagogue (q.v.). To its l., VALIANT HOUSE by *Peter Black & Partners*, 1978–81, seven storeys of glazed bands and dark brown panelling. Pilotis carry it over Heneage Place. The streets were C16 developments by Sir Thomas Heneage, on land formerly owned by Bury St Edmund's Abbey.

HIGH HOLBORN

The w part of the Roman highway out of the City at Newgate; so called from the slope from here E down into the Fleet River valley, before Holborn Viaduct was made (q.v.). The SE part up to Chancery Lane was transferred to the City in 1994; the w part and the N side are in the Borough of Camden (*see London 4: North*).

We begin at Chancery Lane (S SIDE). For the w corner, *see* that street. The E corner is No. 312, 1851, classical stucco with a

Doric cornice; squeezed in beneath, giant Greek Doric pilasters and a Neo-Grèc corner porch, added in 1921 by *Bourchier, Tatchell & Galsworthy*. Then Nos. 313 (by *Lewis Isaacs*, 1873) and 314 (by *Johnstone & Paine*, 1878), stuccoed or painted commercial Victorian; Nos. 315–318, hefty gabled Neo-Tudor offices in red brick, dated 1907.

The rest of the S side is HERON HOUSE, by *E.S. Boyer & Partners*, 1967–9, and the very similar No. 333, formerly National Westminster House (now BRITISH GAS), by *Gordon Charratou* of the *J. Seymour Harris Partnership*, 1965–8. They make one long façade, several times slightly broken, taking its cue from Staple Inn beyond (q.v.). Eight storeys, the ground floor partly recessed behind piers. Long window bands above, the floors marked by continuous concrete projections sloping on their lower surfaces, which are pleasingly lightened by gold mosaic. On Heron House what might be described as the semblance of balconies, three times repeated on each floor from the second to the top. The main (SW) entrance faces Southampton Buildings (so called from the Earls of Southampton's house, here by 1544, redeveloped 1652). Inside, three gryphon-shaped enamelled brackets, from the banking hall gallery of *Knightley*'s phantasmagoric Birkbeck Bank (1895–6), formerly on the site. It was the first major building faced in *Doulton*'s Carraraware: colourful externally, with historical portrait medallions sculpted by *John Broad*; the circular top-lit banking hall no less garish. For Staple Inn Buildings, *see* Holborn.

NORTH SIDE. Opposite the mouth of Chancery Lane, BRACTON HOUSE, a brash front designed by *D.Y. Davies*, 1987, with flat Postmodern patterning in brown, white and pink, and a forbidding bronze SCULPTURE in a niche at street level: The Artist as Hephaestos, a self-portrait by *Eduardo Paolozzi* (commissioned by the developers, London & Bristol). Nos. 31–33 by *Delissa Joseph*, 1900, gabled red brick with a long first-floor terracotta balcony: one of several blocks by Joseph for the Central London Railway (it housed Chancery Lane station until 1934). Nos. 29–30, narrow, decent enough, with polished black marble uprights, 1964–5 by *Jackson & Greenen*. The CITTIE OF YORKE (formerly Henekey's Tavern), is a narrow stone-faced pub, rebuilt in 1923–4 (possibly by *Ernest R. Barrow*), still with the pretty Tudor detail of the type favoured by Treadwell & Martin in the late C19. Memorable interior: long, narrow and very high, with giant vats on a balcony over the bar, facing a clerestory and little cubicles for the customers. Some retained C19 features. Next the completely rebuilt C17 GATE-WAY to Gray's Inn (*see London 4: North*), by *Fitzroy Robinson & Partners*, 1964–5, with Nos. 19–20 adjacent, a good, simple elevation in purple brick with marble-faced floor bands. The corner of Gray's Inn Road is No. 7, by *Trehearne & Norman, Preston & Partners*, 1955–7, an up-to-date façade (thin verticals, green spandrel panels), but with a two-storeyed entrance feature conventionally placed in the centre. Glazed-in top storey, formerly an open-trellis canopy.

HOLBORN

The short central section of the Roman N highway into the City from the W, between High Holborn and Holborn Viaduct. The name is from the Holebourne ('old bourn' or stream), a tributary of the River Fleet. The Templars' first London estate was on the S side, before they moved to the present Temple (*c.* 1128–*c.* 1162). Wealthy houses were built here in the C17. The later C19 saw department stores established, notably Gamage's (N side), *c.* 1895–1905 by *J. Sawyer*, demolished 1974. The exceptional width is partly due to demolition in 1867 of Middle Row, an island block at the W end. Early C19 granite obelisks here mark Holborn Bars, barriers first erected in the C12 to levy duties on traffic into the City. In the roadway further E, the Royal Fusiliers' WAR MEMORIAL, with figure of a soldier by *Albert Toft*, 1922.

The N SIDE, transferred to the Borough of Camden in 1994, is dominated by *Waterhouse*'s PRUDENTIAL ASSURANCE. One of London's Victorian Gothic showpieces, an overwhelming mass of red brick and terracotta with tall ranges around an internal courtyard. The dates are various but the style remained consistent, established by the first portion, at the corner of Brooke Street (l.), in 1879. The rest of the front followed in 1899–1906. The 1879 parts were then rebuilt in 1932 by Messrs *Joseph*.

Pevsner's description of 1957 displayed respect rather than enthusiasm. 'The Prudential is an earnest, thoughtful design even if without warmth. Long symmetrical façade of fiery red brick and red terracotta, amply gabled, and with a big central tower crowned by a pyramid roof with spike. The windows all lancets except that on the second floor simple plate tracery is introduced. It seems in the details all done from the best models. Yet the sheer multiplication of the motifs deprives them of their efficacy.'

But the street front is only part of the story. The approach to the heart of the complex is contrived with drama: first a deep rib-vaulted archway, then a small courtyard which opens on the N side by a very wide arch into the generous main court, now called Waterhouse Square. Here the N and E ranges have arched ground-floor windows, some of them opened up in the 1990 restoration (by *EPR Partnership*) to form a kind of cloister walk. Bronze WAR MEMORIAL by *F. V. Blundestone*, 1922. Two angels support a dying soldier. Standing women with wreaths below. In the front range, l., is the main hall and staircase. These and other circulation areas are all lavishly faced in glazed terracotta, the material Waterhouse used to good effect in the Natural History Museum, but here more brightly coloured. Restored in 1990; new work of this time added a deep back range extending N to Greville Street. Along Brooke Street, its sleek purple granite cladding and elementary mouldings butt up awkwardly against the old parts.

Between Brooke Street and Gray's Inn Road (w), offices by *Gordon Collis* for the Prudential, 1986; seven storeys, plain brown brick. Further E, the excessively large block between Leather Lane and Hatton Garden is by *R. Seifert & Partners*, 1974–81. Plum-tinted glazing between pale stone floor bands. Clumsy ground-floor shopping arcade.

The s SIDE begins at the w end with the rambling half-timbered front
of Staple Inn (q.v.). At its w end, numbered with High Holborn
(as No. 335), STAPLE INN BUILDINGS, 1901, by *Waterhouse*. As
red and gabled as the Prudential (and developed by them), though
more free Tudor than Gothic. Waterhouse wanted buff terracotta,
not red, but the latter was thought to preserve the Prudential
'image'. Lower central section to the alley called Staple Inn
Buildings.

At the E end of Staple Inn, No. 9, stone-faced, the ground-floor
windows with shallow pointed heads; by *Prudential Architects*,
1972–5. After Furnival Street, Nos. 14–18, PRESTIGE HOUSE,
stripped classical of 1923 by *Gilbert & Constanduros*. No. 19
announces DYERS' BUILDINGS, a claustrophobic paved close of
offices by *John Wimble*, 1871–8. Bleak and forbidding (over-
developed, the C20 would say), in stock brick with terracotta
guilloche bands. Big windows like shopfronts set slightly forward
below. One older building breaks the sequence: No. 2 (NW), a
five-bay, three-storey house of *c.*1840, stuccoed below, with a
pilastered doorcase with lions' heads. The site of the Dyers'
Company's almshouses, founded 1551, moved to the City Road in
1771.

Back in Holborn Nos. 20–23, HALTON HOUSE, neutral brick and
stone by *H. Chatfeild Clarke*, 1907, with an entrance to Barnard's
Inn (q.v.); reconstructed and heightened by *Green Lloyd Architects*,
1987–92. Nos. 24–31 by *Yates, Cook & Darbyshire*, 1955–7. Still
classical, with giant pilasters and cornice, visually unsupported by
the lower storeys. Turret on the Fetter Lane corner with an undersized copper-clad lantern. The DAILY MIRROR BUILDING
beyond, 1957–60 by *Sir Owen Williams & Partners* and *Anderson,
Forster & Wilcox*, was due for demolition in 1997 for a new development by *Norman Foster & Partners*. It was the last of the great newspaper headquarters of the Fleet Street precinct to be built.
Williams's concealed concrete frame provided a spreading podium
and deep basement for printing, from which rose a tall slab of
scarlet curtain-walled offices, aligned N–S.

HOLBORN CIRCUS

The northern *rond-point* of the Holborn Viaduct scheme (1863–9).
Of the C19 buildings only No. 1 Hatton Garden remains (N side),
dated 1870, with concave front. C20 rebuilding of the rest has made
a broad, windswept intersection without strong architectural
character: *see* Holborn Viaduct (E), Holborn (W), and New Fetter
Lane (S). In the centre, an equestrian STATUE of Prince Albert
by *Charles Bacon*, given by Charles Oppenheim, unveiled 1874.
He raises his hat as a salute, a singular gesture for an officer –
doubly singular when perpetuated in bronze – but in the polite
tradition of royal respect for the City. On the plinth, reliefs
commemorating the Great Exhibition and third Royal Exchange,
also by *Bacon*.

HOLBORN VIADUCT

Built 1863–9 by *William Haywood*, Surveyor to the City, as a much-needed improvement in the connection of the City with the West End (contractors *Hill & Keddell*). Until then all traffic had to dip down into the valley of the Fleet and climb up again. Schemes for a raised crossing had been put forward before, but progress was confined to the making of a new street called Skinner Street by *Dance the Younger*, 1802–3, running E out of Farringdon Street to supersede the twisting line of Snow Hill. The E part of the viaduct stands on Skinner Street, the w on the old street called Holborn Hill. The whole development cost £2,100,000, including the associated St Andrew Street and St Bride Street (down to Ludgate Circus) and Charterhouse Street (up to Smithfield Market; qq.v.). The viaduct itself is a lengthy vaulted causeway, 1400 ft (427 metres) long and 80 ft (24 metres) wide. The main vault supports the roadway, lesser vaults the pavements. Each of the latter houses water, gas and telegraph pipes in a top chamber, ground-level vaults accessible from adjacent buildings below, and a subterranean sewer. Below the central vault ran a pneumatic dispatch tube.

The cast-iron BRIDGE skewed over Farringdon Street is the most conspicuous feature. On its open cast-iron parapet stand four bronze statues provided by *Farmer & Brindley* (Science and Fine Art, N) and *H. Bursill* (Commerce and Agriculture, s). Four bronze winged lions keep them company. Below, hexagonal granite piers support ornate and massive cast-iron work (made by *John Cochrane*). The girders are painted warm red and gold, with a recurring griffin motif in the openwork spandrels of their segmental arches.

The ensemble is best seen from Farringdon Street, reached by staircases within the corner buildings. Of these, Nos. 25 and 26 (s side) remain from four stone-faced offices conceived integrally with the bridge's design. Haywood was assisted in the architectural detailing by *Thomas Blashill*. Their style is Italian Gothic, of the Florentine, not the Ruskinian Venetian, brand. In niches on the façades, statues of Sir Henry Fitzaylwin, first Lord Mayor of London, and Sir Thomas Gresham.* Scrolly carved stone balconies rest on brackets carved as atlantes below.

From the bridge one can walk w to Holborn Circus or E to Newgate Street. Little of the 1860s–70s remains in either direction, and the big office blocks are mostly of 1950–70. Heading w, the N corner of the bridge is ATLANTIC HOUSE, by *T.P. Bennett & Son*, completed 1951. Brick above stone, rather broken up in its various elements, with a streamlined s end and a mercilessly long side to Farringdon Street. It was amongst the largest of the Lessor Scheme blocks (*see* Introduction p. 127). Facing, MORLEY HOUSE, 1985–8, by the same firm. Stone-clad, with chamfered uprights and a tall mansard, but without explicit historicizing. Then the City Temple with its corner spire (q.v.). A little bridge carries the viaduct over Shoe Lane. Opposite St Andrew's church, No. 40, 1950–6 (formerly Chartered Consolidated), again by *Bennett &*

*The other houses had statues of Sir Hugh Myddelton, promoter of the New River scheme, and Sir William Walworth, Lord Mayor in Chaucer's time.

Son. Of stone, with a broad, convex w front facing a little garden by Holborn Circus. It has shallow reliefs on African themes. N extension to Charterhouse Street (1959).

Proceeding E beyond the main bridge, twin grim grey concrete slabs by *T.P. Bennett & Son* face each other: BATH HOUSE (N side), under construction 1970, mostly set back, with a windowless stair-tower to Farringdon Street; facing, No. 21 (1972–6), equally dispiriting, with a large section of ped-way at the E end. Then on the N side No. 65, REMINGTON RAND, 1956–60, by *J. Seymour Harris & Partners*, of two different heights. Refurbished 1980–1 by the same firm, with horrible mottled tile cladding: an early instance of such updating of a post-war building. WILLIAMS NATIONAL HOUSE opposite, by *Ronald Ward & Partners*, 1961–3, replaced the old Holborn Viaduct station building, itself closed 1990 (*see* City Thameslink station). Ten well-proportioned storeys of curtain walling, set back above, with a large cantilever cornice. A canopy of shallow curves marks the former station concourse entrance. Proposed for replacement by *SOM*, 1996.

Next door, Nos. 1–10, the former Spiers and Pond's Hotel by *Evans Cronk*, 1874, a seven-storey cliff in hotelier's French Renaissance. The style, popularized by Knowles's Grosvenor Hotel, Victoria (1860–2), here has more of the low-relief, all-over ornament the 1870s preferred (*Lewis Isaacs*'s Holborn Viaduct Station Hotel next door, 1874–6, bombed 1941, was similar). Big steep central pavilion, smaller pavilion at the E end. Two-light windows to the rooms. Attic dormers with red stone columns. By *c.* 1900 it had become offices. The 1870s roof-line and shopfronts were re-created in 1984 by *Rolfe Judd Group Practice*, for Friends Provident Life.

HOUNDSDITCH

The street records the ditch outside the City wall from Aldgate to Bishopsgate, known from 1275. Stow derived the name from the dead dogs dumped in it. The address has certainly never been in high favour. From the C16 to C19 second-hand clothes were sold here. Present buildings are C20 and nothing special.

From the w end, the s side belongs with Camomile Street, the N side with Bishopsgate. Then on the N a little garden and an ELECTRICITY SUBSTATION, dressed in flat Neoclassical stone and brick patterns. By *LEB Architects Dept.*, 1985–8. Next to it the Telephone Exchange (q.v.). At the SE corner with St Mary Axe, CHATSWORTH HOUSE, 1972–80 by *North & Partners*, with close-set smoked-glass bays. The s side beyond belongs with Bevis Marks and Duke's Place (qq.v.), which follow the old City wall's inner line. The E part replaced three late C18 houses facing GORING STREET, laid out (as Castle Street) by *Dance the Younger* in the early 1770s, across the line of the City wall.

On the N side, Nos. 115–123 (Cutlers' Court) belong with Cutler Street (q.v.). Then No. 133, a large, deep block by *Carl Fisher & Partners*, 1986–91. Its heart is an elaborate atrium, of full height in front, overlooked by bridges and by floors stepping back behind, to where another atrium rises from the third floor. But the pedestrian is offered only unfriendly grey stone-clad elevations, with minimal fenestration busily patterned, two vague oriels and a concavity high up. The NE corner is ST BOTOLPH'S HOUSE, by *R. Seifert & Partners*, completed 1966. A large, flashy, ceramic-clad block with their usual tapering shaped piers. Shops projecting below, corner with jazzy abstract relief. It incorporates a second TELEPHONE EXCHANGE, and a CAR PARK behind (altered 1986).

HUGGIN HILL and LITTLE TRINITY LANE

Huggin Hill is known from the C14 as *Hoggenelane*, i.e. a place where hogs were kept; in 1269 called *Sporuneslane*. The attractively complex CLEARY GARDENS (remodelled 1985–8) step down the w side, exploiting the basements of demolished buildings. At the foot may be seen part of the great retaining wall of the ROMAN BATHS. These were extended at least twice in the late C1 and early C2 but demolished in the mid C2. The wall is of ragstone with a double course of bonding tiles near the top, and is faced on the s side with *opus signinum* (concrete with broken tile). Other remains investigated in 1969 and 1988–9 are preserved, buried respectively beneath Fur Trade House (s, *see* Upper Thames Street) and Senator House (w, *see* Queen Victoria Street). The area has been identified with the late C9 tenement called *Hwaetmundes Stan* (*see* Introduction p. 44), though this apparently did not incorporate standing Roman remains.

On the E side, the mean rear wall of the Painter-Stainers' Hall (q.v.), reached via the covered HUGGIN COURT into LITTLE TRINITY LANE. Here stood the German Lutheran Church, built probably by *Caius Gabriel Cibber*, 1672, in succession to the burnt Holy Trinity the Less, and demolished 1875. Its reredos, in the Gibbons manner, is in the Victoria and Albert Museum.

IDOL LANE

In 1677 spelt Idle Lane, supposedly because no craftsmen or traders worked there; before that called St Dunstan's Lane (recorded 1265), after St Dunstan-in-the-East on the E side. This name now applies to the church's approach from the w. One interesting building: No. 9, on the corner facing the church tower, originally two early C18 houses, made into one *c.* 1770. The stucco arcading of the ground floor seems to be early C19, i.e. later than the date 1793 in the suspiciously recent-looking iron fanlight of the doorway. Inside, a broad staircase and panelling, apparently early C18, but with plausible 1920s alterations. First-floor rooms with enriched pedimented doorcases of *c.* 1770, and one fireplace with relief panel of a Roman sacrifice. To the N, the arcaded motif is taken up by the rear of the Guinness Mahon building (*see* St Mary-at-Hill). Then Nos. 2–4, 1915 by *T.H. Smith*, of white faience, with fully-fledged giant pilasters.

IRONMONGER LANE

A very narrow street which widens unexpectedly on the E side into a garden, presided over by the tower of *Wren*'s St Olave Jewry (q.v.). Excavations at Nos. 24–25 in 1980 suggested the lane was formed in the early C11. The name is recorded in 1190. The ironmongers' unsociably smoky trade had moved mostly to Fenchurch Street by the mid C15.

From the S end, the E SIDE makes a forecourt to the Mercers' Hall and its offices (q.v.). Then Nos. 7–8 (DAUNTSEY HOUSE), by *R.L. Hesketh*, 1909. Neo-Wren, red brick with quoins, the lower floor recessed to light the basement. ST OLAVE'S COURT, next, is a paved alley running through to Old Jewry, s of the former churchyard. Further N, No. 9, built as the rectory of St Margaret Lothbury: bleak red brick Neo-Jacobean by *E. Christian*, dated 1892. Beyond, No. 11, built in 1768 for the linen draper Thomas Fletcher. Three-bay front, originally with a counting-house facing the street, living accommodation on top and warehouses behind. Original pedimented doorcase with Ionic columns; the rest of the ground floor late C19. Top storey of the 1840s, when it became Mullen's Hotel. Also of that date the recessed l. bay, on the site of the old warehouse yard. The frontage lines respect pre-Fire property boundaries. (Preserved *in situ* beneath, a small C3 mosaic pavement from a Roman house, discovered in 1949 during reconstruction by *Campbell-Jones & Sons* after bombing.) Then the rear elevation of the Old Jewry Police Station (*see* Public Buildings).

The W SIDE is a study in C20 Neo-Georgian: after the Atlas Assurance extension, s (*see* Cheapside), Nos. 24–25 by *Douglas Marriott, Worby & Robinson*, 1979–83, late C17 pastiche with a huge mansard, part of a development facing King Street and there given a modern handling; Nos. 21–23, 1904, in an attractive post-Fire idiom in red brick, with twin broken-pedimented doorcases (the l. one a copy of *c.* 1975); finally Nos. 17–20, stock brick, 1957–61 by *John V. Hamilton*.

JEWRY STREET and VINE STREET

A gloomy street, gently curving N from the end of Crutched Friars into Aldgate. Known by 1349 as Poor Jewry. The E side backed against the City wall. A substantial section of the Roman wall, discovered in 1905 and further excavated in 1979–80, is preserved in the basement of EMPEROR HOUSE, a large brown brick development at the s end by *Joseph & Partners*, 1981. It may be viewed through a glazed canopy from a yard off VINE STREET behind, accessible via India Street (formerly George Street). India Street was cut across the wall's line *c.* 1770 in connection with *Dance the Younger*'s development of America Square, Crescent, etc. (qq.v.). Vine Street is older, being named from the vineyard of the Minoresses outside the wall. The wall measures 30 ft (9 metres) by 9 ft (nearly 3 metres) high, the bonding courses and sandstone plinth at the original ground level strongly marked. Also visible is the chalk foundation of a semicircular bastion added in the C4, in this instance demolished by the C13. More fragments of wall remain in the basement of the Sir John Cass Institute (q.v.), further N on the E side of Jewry Street.

On Jewry Street's W side, BOUNDARY HOUSE (Nos. 7–17) has a curtain-walled slab to the street and a taller tower behind. By *Sydney Clough & Partners*, 1954–8. No. 5, DAWSON'S HOUSE, by *Biscoe & Stanton*, 1979–82, brown brick, with upright windows in a busy array of bays. Carlisle Avenue between, made in 1894 in connection with redevelopment of the East India Company's land here, has no buildings of note.

JOHN CARPENTER STREET

First listed in 1888; part of the grid of streets laid out by the Corporation after the completion of the Victoria Embankment. It bisected the former City Gas Works' site (founded 1814). John Carpenter was a C15 benefactor whose legacy was later allotted to the City of London School for Boys, formerly on the E side.

Premises for J.P. MORGAN, by *BDP*, 1987–91, stand on most of the former school site. The development was symptomatic of the flight to less restricted sites on the City's fringes in the wake of financial deregulation. A very long unbroken grey granite block, reminiscent of early C20 American simplified classicism. Two-storey rusticated base and cornice, upper storeys with plain piers and a much deeper cornice. On the corner parapet a fiddly Soanian colonnade to screen the services. Horizontals follow through from the former school hall, incorporated at the S end (*see* Victoria Embankment). Entrance through a lower, part-glazed linking section.

On the W side at the N, a smaller, near-matching lettable block, re-placing the old City of London School for Girls (1894). At the S, it incorporates on three sides the façades of the former Guildhall School of Music. The main part, by *Sir Horace Jones*, 1885–7, faces S to Tallis Street. Three-storeyed, with superimposed pilasters and a French-flavoured attic-cum-pavilion. Terracotta panels of musical instruments; other carving on musical themes. On John Carpenter Street, a N extension of 1897–8 by *Andrew Murray*, taller and more mannered: festooned oculi in a mezzanine, upper storeys with paired pilasters.

Further S, TALLIS HOUSE, amiable Postmodern Queen Anne by *Royce, Hurley & Stewart*, 1985–7, and JOHN CARPENTER HOUSE (1978–82), rendered with tall windows, part of *Halpern & Partners'* redevelopment of the Fire Station in Carmelite Street (q.v.).

KINGHORN STREET *see* MIDDLE STREET

KING'S ARMS YARD *see* TOKENHOUSE YARD

KING STREET

One of the few improvements undertaken after the Fire of 1666 was to open up a route in a straight line from the river to Guildhall. King Street is the part of this route N of Cheapside, the longer Queen Street that to the S. Buildings are typically mixed office frontages.

The S corners and the Atlas Assurance extension, E side, belong with Cheapside (q.v.). On the w side, Nos. 36–37 KING'S HOUSE, 1905–6, by *H.H. & M.E. Collins*. Colourful in its use of stone: grey granite plinth, Portland piers and ground-floor cornice, warm yellow stone upper floors, with tall Borrominesque piers. Heightening during reconstruction by the *Rolfe Judd Group Practice*, 1984–8, has spoilt the proportions. N of Trump Street, No. 34 (BANCO DO BRASIL) by *Alan W. Pipe & Sons*, completed 1957, stone-faced and anodyne; enlivened in 1991 by *Lister Drew Haines Barrow*'s patent-glazed entrance lobby projecting between keeled piers.

Opposite, Nos. 9–12, 1979–83 by *Douglas Marriott, Worby & Robinson*, with shimmering stainless-steel verticals and repeated narrow projecting bays between. A pastiche late C17 front faces Ironmonger Lane behind. Then some narrower frontages: No. 14, of stone, by *C.E. Parker & J.S. Cohen*, old-fashioned for the date: 1951–8; No. 15, dated 1912, classical, with iron balconies and delicate ornament, by *A.C. Blomfield*. More early C20 buildings opposite, on the w side, best of which is *George Vernon*'s Nos. 31–32, 1923, with a cornice-cum-balcony with big blockish urns. Further N, No. 28, dated 1868 and signed T. C. C., suggesting *T. Chatfeild Clarke*. An original treatment of a narrow frontage: ground-floor granite columns, tall channelled pilaster-piers of a contrasting stone rising the full height of the building. Diminishing floors with stone panels with foliage carving between. Facing, Nos. 16–17, stock-brick offices by *R.P. Browne* of 1867, Lombardic, with round-arched windows on alternating piers and columns. Well-meaning but obtrusive plain white marble arcaded ground floor, by *Thomas Saunders & Associates*, 1973–4.

The street continues N of Gresham Street. For the former Queen's Assurance Company on the SE corner and for No. 23 King Street by Guildhall Yard, *see* Gresham Street.

KING WILLIAM STREET

Built in connection with the new London Bridge between 1829 and 1835. It runs SW from where St Mary Woolnoth faces the hub of streets by Bank and Mansion House, then turns S at the line of Eastcheap and Cannon Street, approaching the bridge on a viaduct across Upper and Lower Thames Street. A giant granite statue of the King by *Nixon*, 1844, which stood opposite the bridge, was moved to Greenwich Park in 1935. Nothing remains of the original stuccoed street frontages designed by *Sir Robert Smirke*. They were long and largely symmetrical, some with pilastered frontispieces, but without the high relief and picturesque incidents of Nash's earlier Regent Street (a more modest version survives in the form of Smirke's range of *c.* 1840 in Moorgate; some of his contemporary buildings on the S bridge approach may be seen in Southwark). Their successors, mostly grand banks and offices of the early C20, have themselves largely been replaced or drastically refurbished since the 1970s. In this work the firm of *Fitzroy Robinson* has been particularly busy.

Lombard Street to Cannon Street

The best buildings are in this NW part. They have irregular sites made by the street's intersections with the grid of older lanes. First No. 1, on the S side opposite St Mary Woolnoth, by *Campbell-Jones & Smithers*, 1921–2, for the London Assurance Corporation. Lively and compressed but not entirely successful in composition: the l. corner with a domed turret, the r. corner canted; astylar stripped classical between them, with tall window surrounds linking first and second floor. Redevelopment by *GMW Partnership*, begun 1996, will incorporate the façades into a new building stretching down St Swithin's Lane. Next to it, Nos. 3–7, DAIWA BANK, the former Phoenix Fire Assurance by *J. Macvicar Anderson & H.L. Anderson*, begun 1915. Arcaded ground floor with rustic bands, then a mezzanine; the upper two storeys with fluted Corinthian pilasters, turning to columns in the round in the recessed centre. The forms are close to the measured Italianate of the 1850s, though on a grandiose scale. Bronze phoenix over the door and carving by *C.H. Mabey*. Refurbished by *Fitzroy Robinson Partnership*, 1983–7: to Abchurch Lane the façade of an addition of 1931–2 by *Campbell-Jones & Sons* was reconstructed, while to Sherborne Lane (r.) a new stone façade takes up motifs from the main front, then goes plainer round the back. The marvellously spacious entrance hall retains the Andersons' octagon of tall green marble columns supporting an arcaded gallery. Separate fire and life insurance departments originally opened off to either side.

For the building by the church on the N side opposite, *see* Lombard Street. Then Nos. 81–82, MOSCOW NARODNY BANK, built as the London Life Association by *W. Curtis Green*, 1925–7. A monumental front with recessed giant Corinthian columns in the centre between broken-pedimented bays, nothing in the least original, but distinguished in the serene handling of the material. Rewarding sculpture: over-life-size Michelangelesque allegories in the pediments by *H.W. Palliser*, smooth and simplified; more traditional putti etc. at the portal by *C.L. Hartwell*. Reconstruction in 1982–5 by *Fitzroy Robinson Partnership* made an unsympathetic new front to Nicholas Lane, with big glazed sections and a rounded glazed stair-tower.

145 Back on the S side, Nos. 8–13 BANQUE NATIONALE DE PARIS, by *Fitzroy Robinson & Partners*, 1974–8. Grand and imposing, with rounded corners and a big solid cornice matching the height of its neighbours. The cladding is orange-buff Sardinian granite. Large tall rounded piers at ends and centre make a kind of giant order, with a lesser order of lower piers between; but the proportions are not those of an orthodox classical building. The presiding influence is the American architect Kevin Roche (cf. the practice's Nos. 7–8 Prince's Street, where the order is less explicit). Opposite is No. 75, WESTPAC BANKING CORPORATION. On the r., the retained façade of the former Standard Bank by *Meakin, Archer &*

Co., 1924, whose office was here. The orders are used with unusual licence: paired Tuscan columns on the ground floor, much smaller Tuscan columns inset on the mezzanine, then giant Ionic half-columns to the upper storeys. Matching l. extension up to Nicholas Lane by *Fitzroy Robinson Partnership*, 1986–9 (fitted out by *YRM Engineers* and *Thomas Saunders Partnership*). New entrance in a giant niche, off-centre to the whole. Side elevations in a variant of the style of the Banque Nationale de Paris.

On the N corner with Cannon Street (W side) is No. 18, PHOENIX HOUSE, by *GMW Partnership*, 1980–3. Stone fronts with projecting upper storeys between rounded corners with floor bands in a darker polished stone. Nos. 70–72 on the NE side opposite, the oldest building in the street, curves up the corner of Clement's Lane. By *Frederic Chancellor*, 1879–80, for the Reliance Life Assurance, in a remarkably restrained and rather elegant classical idiom. Giant pilaster order to the upper storeys. Refurbished by *Holford Associates*, 1986–9, with a big mansard swinging round against St Clement's church tower. Next to it, No. 69, the former Bank of Victoria by *Oswald P. Milne*, 1914, has a tall, narrow three-bay front with pilasters below.

Then the giant No. 68, the GUARDIAN ROYAL EXCHANGE ASSURANCE by *H.L. Anderson*, 1920–2, facing S towards London Bridge and the bridge approach and extending E to Gracechurch Street. Tall paired columns to the ground floor and mezzanine. One of the twin entrances served a branch of Lloyds Bank (bank architects *Campbell-Jones, Son & Smithers*). Windows in vertical tiers on the plainer upper storeys, then a square central attic with dome and cupola, for which special permission was needed to exceed the usual height limits. But a cupola alone does not make a big building monumental and worthy of an outstanding site.

Cannon Street to London Bridge Approach

After Cannon Street the buildings are mostly late C20. No. 24 BKB HOUSE on the W side, by *Ronald Ward & Partners*, 1986–9, has rounded corners and simplified piers and cornice. A tall abstract stained-glass window by *Goddard & Gibbs Studios* faces Arthur Street. Opposite, Nos. 52–55 SVENSKA HOUSE, by *Sheppard Robson*, 1989–91, in a simplified version of 1920s stripped classical, curved to follow the street line. Polished granite bow over the main entrance on Eastcheap. The copper-clad roof with boxy plant housing was designed to protect sight-lines to the Monument. In the basement a generously proportioned new ticket hall to Monument Underground station (consultant engineers *YRM*). Adjoining, Nos. 47–51 by *R. Angell*, 1913, plain squared-off classical with a curved corner (in 1997 due for demolition). Nos. 39–45, by *GMW Partnership*, 1994–7, echoes the mass and motifs of Adelaide House, adjacent (*see* London Bridge Approach).

No. 33 opposite, of 1974–84 by the same practice for CLRP, occupies the quadrant made with Arthur Street and Upper Thames Street. A bold composition, as the site demanded, but rather coarsely detailed, and markedly unlike the practice's earlier Miesian idiom. A heavy octagonal bastion rises from the lower street level. On it eleven stone-clad storeys of offices on a cross plan, with canted angles between equal arms. The lower floors are linked by projecting curtain-walling, making another octagon. It erased the last part of the old Miles Lane, named after St Michael's church which stood in Crooked Lane nearby. It was of 1684–98, probably by *Hooke* rather than Wren (AG), with a gloriously baroque leaded steeple of 1709–14. It was destroyed in 1831 for the new bridge approaches.

LAURENCE POUNTNEY HILL

Called after St Laurence's church, lost in 1666, and after Sir John de Pulteney, builder of Penshurst in Kent and four times Lord Mayor in the 1330s, who endowed it with a college. The old church lay on the E side, its site divided by a sunken path from the churchyard on the S. They have railings of *c.* 1780 and several trees. To the W lay Pulteney's house (licence to crenellate 1341).

On the W side now are Nos. 1 and 2, the finest early C18 houses remaining in the City, if not in London. Built in 1703 by *Thomas Denning*, citizen and salter, who sold them for £3,190 the following year. A Thomas Denning was carpenter to St Michael Paternoster Royal, and if this is the same man their design may well be his. Only Queen Anne's Gate can be compared with them. The carving round the doors is indeed very similar. Of the two groups, Laurence Pountney is the richer. Foliage friezes round the door frames and in the cornice above. The segmental shell-hoods are also sumptuously carved, one with a charming relief of cherubs at bowls. The houses make a mirrored pair of red brick, four-storeyed, with brick bands. Each of four bays, the inner two recessed. Brackets in the top cornice are also thickly set and carved, broken forward in threes between the windows. The group goes round into Suffolk Lane, where the reconstruction of No. 2 during *Haslemere Estates'* restoration of the pair in 1973–4 is apparent; but No. 2's largely new main front is excellently done. (The house had been hacked about by *Woodthorpe* in 1855.) No. 1 has an original open-well staircase in the angle. It has open strings and spiral newels as well as balusters: both advances on the usual post-Fire type. Elliptical archways to the passages off the landings, N. (Some original panelling and fireplaces remain.)

Not much thereafter. No. 3 by *CLRP Architects*, *c.* 1970, purple brick, with boxed-out windows facing a road cut through from Suffolk Lane in 1968–9. On the E side, No. 8, by *Richard M. Roe*, 1905. Red brick with pilasters, Free Style, the S front pleasingly treated with arcaded windows and a big lunette in the gable. At r. angles to this front, Nos. 6 and 7, both 1900–1, red brick with stone trim, with pretty Arts-and-Crafts Renaissance details. No. 6 has angel terms on the ground-floor piers. No. 7 (a retained façade) is by *E.B. I'Anson*, who moved his office here from No. 7a Laurence Pountney Lane (q.v.).

LAURENCE POUNTNEY LANE

A lane here is first recorded in 1248. As at the neighbouring Laurence Pountney Hill and Suffolk Lane, the best remaining buildings are wholly domestic: Nos. 7a and 9, two nice stately late C17 brick houses with rubbed brick trim to the narrow windows, form a single block at the S. No. 7a, facing the former churchyard of St Laurence Pountney, was built *c.* 1670 and partly reconstructed in the early C18. The I'Ansons practised from here from 1851. *Edward I'Anson* made the doorway into the churchyard in 1860. In the 1870s a triple-arched Veneto-Byzantine window was also knocked through, with extraordinary indifference to context. Good, typical staircase of *c.* 1730, but in a central open well that must perpetuate the C17 plan. No. 9 has an interesting late C18 shopfront to the E and a restored bracket-cornice.

Facing the N part of the churchyard is the new No. 6, 1987–8 by *Thomas Saunders Partnership*, uninspired brown brick with stone dressings. To the W it incorporates the façade of No. 7 Laurence Pountney Hill (q.v.). Set back behind a small courtyard on its N side is No. 5, a much-restored plain late C18 house, L-shaped, with the return bay facing the entrance. For the big post-war buildings on the E side, *see* Arthur Street and Cannon Street.

LAWRENCE LANE

First recorded *c.* 1200. It once connected St Lawrence Jewry with Cheapside, but post-war rebuilding blocked its N and S exits. It now forms a quiet back street, reached from Trump Street, S, and from Milk Street via the widened Mumford Court (in origin a close of post-Fire houses), NE.

Its buildings are on the E side (all proposed for redevelopment in 1996). At the N end, STREETS HOUSE is a good, lean four-storey block with big display windows on the ground floor, completed 1966 by *Knapton, Deane & Partners*. To its S, a modern reincarnation of BLOSSOM'S INN, which is recorded on the site from the later C14: two older office buildings refaced by *Campbell-Jones & Sons*, 1969, with a startling new façade of white mosaic below shiny projecting fins. Another inn, the former Trumpeter, is thought to be commemorated in the post-Fire TRUMP STREET; no buildings of note.

LEADENHALL STREET

The name recalls the lead roof of a C13 manor house, the ancestor of Leadenhall Market (*see* Public Buildings). In the Middle Ages the street was not so named, but treated as an extension of Cornhill (W) and Aldgate (E). Leadenhall Market stands over the E part of the great aisled BASILICA of the C2 Roman forum (*see* Introduction p. 32). Mosaics from several ROMAN TOWN HOUSES have also been found hereabouts. The most famous, unearthed W of St Mary Axe in 1803, is now in the British Museum. It is 11 ft (nearly $3\frac{1}{2}$ metres) square, 5 colourful and intricate, with Bacchus riding the traditional tiger in a central roundel.

EAST INDIA HOUSE stood on the E part of the Lloyd's site until 1861. By *Theodore Jacobsen*, 1726–9; enlarged 1796–9 by *Richard Jupp*, who used a design by *Henry Holland* for the porticoed Leadenhall Street front (ex inf. Nicholas Brawer). Its presence made the street a favourite address for shipping and insurance companies. No. 34, bombed 1941, was NEW ZEALAND CHAMBERS, by *Norman Shaw*, 1871–3: the enormously influential pioneer of a domestic, intimate and human style of commercial architecture, that found a readier reception in the West End than the City. By the mid C 20 grand stone-faced offices lined the W part, with a diminuendo E to small-scale Victorian and Georgian remnants.* Two tremendous gestures have since transformed the W end: on the N side, the 1960s Commercial Union plaza; opposite it, the Lloyd's Building (*see* Public Buildings), barely fifteen years later, but in the greatest possible contrast. Further E, much work of the 1970s–80s, following the old street line.

Gracechurch Street east to St Mary Axe

The walk is from W to E. At the corner with Gracechurch Street, S, No. 1 (SUN ALLIANCE), a large red-granite-clad block of offices over shops, 1983–9 by *Whinney Mackay-Lewis Partnership*. An early attempt to humanize a big block by evoking pre-war traditions: clear horizontal divisions between arcaded lower floors (the mezzanine tucked within the arches) and plainer upper storeys, turning round-arched on top. Canted corner with squat turret. Then Nos. 7–10, RAFIDAIN BANK, 1924–7 (formerly Friends Provident), Doric below, with a big angled oriel and neat concave cornice at the Whittington Avenue corner, and No. 11, NATWEST, the mild three-bay former Bank of Adelaide, dated 1912. Then the reset front of the 1920s Lloyd's is reached (*see* Lloyd's); but first the tall stone fronts opposite (N side) demand attention. No. 147 was Grace & Co., a private New York bank, by *J. W. O'Connor* of that city, 1926–7. Solid McKim-style Renaissance, the entrance a pilastered Venetian motif, with domestic Adamish detail (banking hall with screen of Ionic columns and Adamish cornice; Adamish first-floor boardroom; both long disused in 1997). Nos. 145–146 by *William Nimmo & Partners*, 1989–92, takes motifs from Lutyens next door, the first-floor detailing lapsing into tentative invention.

The MIDLAND BANK (Nos. 139–144), 1929–31, has an elevation by *Lutyens* on a building by *Whinney, Son & Austen Hall*. An ingeniously calculated drawing-board design, treated with much self-possession, despite the unspectacular size and position. Typical of Lutyens the ground-floor windows tucked under big arches. Arched mezzanine windows, with sills coming down segmentally. Narrow windows in the upper storeys. Attic recessed between broken-pedimented aedicules, above which rise matching square open turrets, visible at a distance. Saucer domes in the ground-

---

* More recent late Victorian losses, typically showy: Nos. 1–6 by *Edmeston*, 1882, dem. 1983; Nos. 99–103 by *J.L. Holmes*, 1879, dem. *c.* 1973. CUNARD HOUSE (No. 88), by *Mewès & Davis*, 1929–30, elegantly plain, was dem. 1995.

floor loggia, but no Lutyens alchemy within (WAR MEMORIAL with figures by *Albert Toft*, 1921).

Then two major buildings by *Gollins, Melvin, Ward & Partners*, 1963–9, INDOSUEZ HOUSE (formerly Peninsular & Oriental Line), l., and the COMMERCIAL UNION ASSURANCE, ahead and at r. angles. They face a spacious piazza, paved and part-sunken, with six trees. The P&O is a square ten-storey tower, set on a two-and-a-half storey podium which comes up to the street. The Commercial Union, almost exactly twice as tall at 387 ft (118 metres), has twenty-eight storeys. Before bomb damage in 1992, its cladding proclaimed the Miesian manner with which the practice made its name; indeed, its bronzed finish got closer to Mies van der Rohe's immaculate purity than any contemporary London building (cf. Seagram Building, New York, 1958). *RHWL*'s replacement cladding recapitulates the original effect, with a slight loss of patina. RHWL also closed in the first-floor ped-way. Below, a recessed glazed entrance storey, visually weak, though spectacular within, with giant escalators; SCULPTURE here by *Max Bill*, 1966–7, a sectioned granite sphere. The floors are suspended from beams cantilevered from the concrete core on top and at half-height. The mullions also double as hangers, so the cladding is strictly not true curtain-walling. The half-height plant storeys serve the P&O too. Both towers have solid top hampers. The P&O's less lofty proportions are tellingly emphasized: floor-levels are stressed by projecting strings, later converted into balconies with thin rails and vertical upright struts (1987–8, modified after 1993); square windows between, instead of the Commercial Union's upright double-squares. The previous P&O complex was of great interest: a Greek Doric courtyard house of 1846–8 behind an ornate street front by *Currey*, 1858, extended by *Collcutt*, 1893, w, and *Collcutt & Hamp*, 1922–5, E. A relic of the last faces an access road w of the P&O, visible from stairs up to the ped-way off Leadenhall Street: *P.G. Bentham*'s SCULPTURE of Navigation, a burly figure in a niche.

St Mary Axe east to Aldgate

If the rest seems tame after this, there is yet much worth seeking out. On the s side, Nos. 21–26, 1953–6 by the *Prudential Assurance*'s architects, and No. 27, refronted by *Ley, Colbeck & Partners*, 1948–50, insipid plain stone; the latter vamped up with a new entrance by *Rolfe Judd Group Practice*, 1984–6. Nos. 34–35, WINTERTHUR HOUSE, by *GMW Partnership*, 1987–92, stone-clad and symmetrical, enlivened by a complex glazed entrance with views down into the basement and into the lobby, reached by cylindrical automatic doors like an airlock. Nos. 36–38, the former Scandinavian Bank by *Yorke, Rosenberg & Mardall*, 1970–3, introduced their Chicago-derived flush-fronted style to the City: uniform floors and piers of polished yellow-brown stone, absolutely flush smoked-glass bands, with razor-sharp mitred glass joints on the Billiter Street corner.

On the N side, the block between St Mary Axe and Creechurch Lane begins beyond St Andrew Undershaft with Nos. 114–116, LLOYDS BANK, by *E.B. Ellis*, 1891, the street's only Victorian survivor,

stone-faced, with a little corner tourelle. Then earlier C20 buildings, including Nos. 107–112, BANKSIDE HOUSE, a lumpen affair
of 1931, and Nos. 104–106 by *Joseph's*, 1924, quite pleasing, with
three giant bronze-spandrelled window panels defined by bay-leaf
cabling. No. 100, by *Fitzroy Robinson & Partners*, 1971–5, a dark,
gaunt, merciless grid. Another building by *Fitzroy's*, designed 1994,
is intended at No. 88.

Back on the s side, the very large INSTITUTE OF LONDON
UNDERWRITERS (Nos. 42–49), also by *Fitzroy Robinson &
Partners*, 1972–8. Bronzed window-bands between narrow floor-
bands of polished purple stone, reminiscent of Nos. 36–38, but less
suavely done. The flush Leadenhall Street front has shallow
recessed windows near each end and a discreet central entrance.
Concealed within is the first large atrium in a new building in
London, a long, plain space, originally with plants climbing on free-
standing timber frames. Beyond, Nos. 52–56, FURNESS HOUSE,
by *M.E. Collins*, with *L. Sylvester Sullivan* of the City of London
Real Property Co., 1919–21 (reconstructed internally by *DEGW*,
1989). An overpowering but weakly organized Beaux-Arts
classical front: Ionic columns below, with bronze panels between;
astylar above, with plenty of balconies, blockish swags, fasces etc.
In two parts, each with an attic block set over the entrance; the
more important, l. (now LONDON METALS EXCHANGE), with
bronze-capitalled Corinthian columns to the doorcase. Lesser front
to Fenchurch Street (q.v.). Nos. 62–65, by *A.H. Kersey* and
Richardson & Gill, 1922, of yellow sandstone, arcaded below, with
more of Kersey's prettiness than of Richardson's austerity. Rebuilt
behind by *The Halpern Partnership*, 1987–90, with a new front to
Fenchurch Street (q.v., as also for No. 69, the acute corner block).

Back on the n side, after St Katharine Cree, a late 1980s stretch, all
Postmodern, with big simplified details and patterns: Nos. 80–84,
1988–90 by *Hamilton Associates*; No. 78, by *Ley, Colbeck & Partners*,
1989–91; No. 76, SWISS RE HOUSE, 1986–7 by the *GMW
Partnership*, making an acute corner with Mitre Street. Inside the
lobby of the last, an extraordinary fragment of the Augustinian
HOLY TRINITY PRIORY, disencumbered in 1984 of later walling
which had ensured its survival. It is a tall late C14 or C15 pointed
arch from the choir's s aisle wall, which formerly led to a s chapel.
Of greensand, with plain hollow double chamfers dying into
the jambs without capitals. This was inserted into an earlier arch,
probably C12, the core of which partially remains. Traces of
diagonal vault ribs on the inner face. Also uncovered were
foundations of the C12 s wall and s transept, with, in the angle, a
chapel with an apsed E end, squared-off externally (preserved in a
chamber to the rear of the foyer, roughly on its original site). This
older work was of ragstone, flint and Roman tile, with a chamfered
external plinth of Caen stone. It is more likely to date from rebuilding documented after a fire between 1147 and 1167 than from the
first church of Queen Matilda's foundation, 1108. The central
vessel of the church is represented by the line of Mitre Street (*see*
Creechurch Lane), some 35 degrees off true E–W orientation: an
aberration enforced by the City wall alignment. The priory buildings have left further traces in the street plan s of Duke's Place
(q.v.).

LIME STREET

Known by the late C12, as *Lymstrate*. The name is not from fruit but from the lime-burners and sellers formerly there. It runs S from Leadenhall Street between present and former Lloyd's buildings, then snakes down to Fenchurch Street in a reverse curve, tight enough for sudden unexpected views. The dominant presence here is Leadenhall Market (W side), reached by two lanes, LEADENHALL PLACE and LIME STREET PASSAGE, the latter made *c.* 1885. They have red brick shop blocks of the 1880s, similar but plainer to the market proper. In 1932 remains of the N–S ROMAN ROAD skirting the E side of the forum were found E of Lime Street Passage.

Other buildings, from the N end: first the former LLOYD'S, by *Terence Heysham*, 1950–7 (E side; *see* also Lloyd's of London, Public Buildings). Portland stone, very large, much broken-up in composition. Though unashamedly backward-looking, it is amongst the City's more individual buildings of that decade, and responds interestingly to its site. A convex bow with five giant round-headed windows faces Lime Street. Curved set-back above, from which a bridge formerly joined Lloyd's demolished 1920s premises opposite. Little Neo-Georgian portal, r., large arched roadway frontispiece, l. Long, convex S front to Fenchurch Avenue, treated symmetrically, with matching giant windows to the street and set-backs above, between taller sections carried straight up for eight storeys. They have allegorical figures carved in relief by *James Woodford* high up, as if on a super-cinema. A further tall block, set back, pokes up in the middle. Another big bow faces Billiter Street, E. All these lower windows light 'the Room', a gently-curving two-storeyed hall with square marble piers (altered by *DEGW*, *c.* 1990).

The rest is mostly C19–C20 offices for insurance and shipping concerns, who sought proximity to Lloyd's. No period, style or material dominates. The City of London Real Property Co. raised the first three on the E side. No. 40, stone-faced offices of 1939–40 by *Henry Tanner*, has a pilastered frontispiece facing FENCHURCH AVENUE, where it is No. 4. Repeated set-backs above; almost a stepped section. Carved arms of the Carpenters' Company, which laid out the avenue in the 1870s, with the Fishmongers' Company and the Bridewell and Bethlehem Hospitals. In the avenue otherwise only characterless twin stone-faced blocks by *Howard, Souster & Fairbairn*, 1956.

Back in Lime Street, Nos. 37–39 are by *L. Sylvester Sullivan*, 1929. A familiar type with bronze floor-panels between close-set verticals, but individually done, with an eye on American fashions. The verticals step back above the fourth floor, to end a storey higher not in capitals or a cornice but anthemion finials. More Neo-Grèc details below (carver *Henry Poole*). Two bronze-faced top storeys are an original feature. Nos. 34–36 (ROYAL INSURANCE), 1970–4 by *Sheppard, Robson & Partners* (partner in charge *John Heywood*). Sharply angled ends, the storeys between bridging a passage with shops through to Cullum Street. The cladding is bronzed aluminium with upright windows, each with a shallow aproned frame: richer materials than the brown brick idiom familiar from the firm's previous educational buildings and housing.

The same architects' Nos. 12–13 opposite, 1973–5, deploys the same motifs on a smaller scale. BEEHIVE PASSAGE leads through it to the market. Next door on the N, *Burnet, Tait & Partners*' CIGNA HOUSE, 1972–5, ugly pre-cast concrete; on the S, the little BUNCH OF GRAPES pub (No. 14), 1893 by *William Wimble*, enriched free Renaissance in stone. FORUM HOUSE (Nos. 15–18), offices by *Gervase Bailey & G. Thrale Jell*, 1932–5, shows the influence of Richardson & Gill's sober stripped classicism. It replaced the fire-damaged Pewterers' Hall (q.v.).

ASIA HOUSE opposite, 1912–13 by *Fair & Myer*, has four storeys of all-over white faience with wide dark joints. Ground-floor columns, channelled verticals. Exotic oriental figures in niches by the door and high up. Nos. 28–30, the former Waterlow Bros., commercial Gothic of 1876–9, has two-light windows and a machicolated cornice, with plenty of polished stone piers etc. Façade restored and rebuilt behind in 1984–5 by *Burnet, Tait & Partners*, with No. 27 (SHIP TAVERN). This curving brick pub front of 1837 was probably by *Robert Davidson*, surveyor to Truman's brewery. Stucco surrounds, already turning impure. No. 21 facing, after Lime Street Passage, is office chambers by *D.A. Cobbett*, 1866–7. Red brick and stone, tall, with tripartite windows to the lower floors. The Italianate detailing is old-fashioned for the date. Big carved armorial of the Skinners' Company over the entrance to Ship Tavern Passage. Replacement proposed by *John Simpson & Partners*. No. 26 (E side), by *Richard Ellis*, 1982–5, only just Neo-Deco. Excavations here in 1982–3 revealed a well-preserved Roman cellar which had been reused down to the Great Fire. *Tabberer*'s No. 24, dated 1900, has superimposed pilastered storeys in coloured stone, untouched by late Victorian fashions.

LITTLE BRITAIN

Called *Brettonestrete* in 1329, from Robert de Bretoune who inherited property here in 1274: evidence that suburban development was already under way just N of the City wall. The prefix, current by the C17, comes from the fallacy that a Breton enclave lay here (cf. Petty France). The NW part, between the corner with Bartholomew Close and West Smithfield, was known first as Duck Lane (recorded 1316), then until 1885 as Duke Lane. Booksellers dominated the street from the mid C16, followed by goldsmiths and clothing trades from the mid C18 to C20.

The modest C19 and C20 warehouses at the S end, where the street turns sharply E, were mostly demolished *c.* 1985, for the new Montague Street and No. 200 Aldersgate Street (q.v.). The late C20 has turned it back into a residential enclave, for the retained façades of Nos. 6–19 now front a development of flats by *GMA Architecture*, 1995–6, facing St Botolph's churchyard. From the W, they include: No. 6, a plain stone-faced warehouse by *Tabberer*, 1877, for Messrs Stillwell, gold-lace manufacturers; No. 7, tall, residually Gothic, *c.* 1880; No. 8, a former pub by *Edgar A. Hawkins*, dated 1892, Dutch and asymmetrical; Nos. 9–10, loosely Tudor with stone bands, 1897; and No. 12, a tall brick

Lombard-Gothic warehouse by *J. Young & Son* for the Manchester draper Wellington Williams, 1858–9, which has five storeys of superimposed even arcading on slender detached columns: still a novel formula at the time, though here without the refinement of Aitchison's No. 61 Mark Lane (1864). Carving of capitals etc. by *Seale*. Last in the sequence is Nos. 16–17, offices in cast stone by *G. & T.S. Vickery*, 1924. By *GMA Architecture* also the seven-storey flats on the corner with King Edward Street opposite (1994–6). Nothing risky: red brick, rusticated basement, rounded corner.

Then N towards Smithfield. ST BARTHOLOMEW'S HOSPITAL looms large on the W side (*see* Public Buildings). Its GLOUCESTER HOUSE, on the NE corner with Montague Street, by *Adams, Holden & Pearson*, 1958–61, houses twelve storeys of nurses' rooms in a straightforward tall brick slab. Stone-faced entrance block in front. A no less tall extension by the same for the College of Nursing makes the SE corner of Bartholomew Close behind. The wilfully narrow windows with tiny chunky sills betray the later date: 1976. Routine early to mid-C20 offices and warehouses beyond, then the hospital's brown brick QUEEN ELIZABETH II WING by the same architects, 1955–61. The street emerges into West Smithfield beyond (q.v.).

LITTLE TRINITY LANE *see* HUGGIN HILL

LIVERPOOL STREET

Made in 1825–9 by widening Old Bethlem Lane; renamed after Lord Liverpool, not the city. Railway buildings dominate. On the N SIDE, the Broadgate Centre, W, and Liverpool Street station, E (*see* Public Buildings). The S SIDE is mostly of the late 1870s, when the Metropolitan Railway arrived.

S SIDE from W to E: No. 1 belongs with Blomfield Street; the RAILWAY TAVERN (No. 15) by *G. Low*, 1877, has a curved corner and big square channelled piers; Nos. 17–33, the former Metropolitan Railway station, 1876, by its engineer *Edward Wilson*. Really just a long shallow range of shops with rooms above, given consequence by French pavilion roofs. Gault brick. Within, the METROPOLITAN ARCADE, by *Frank Sherrin*, 1911–12, made after electrification permitted building over the tracks; reconstructed 1994–5 in discreetly traditional manner. Nos. 34–37, ALDERMAN'S HOUSE, 1982–4 by *Fitzroy Robinson Partnership*, an orange brick box raised on piers over White Horse Yard.

LLOYD'S AVENUE

Laid out in 1899 across the site of former East India Company warehouses. The developer James Dixon collaborated with Lloyd's Register of Shipping (*see* Public Buildings), whose new headquarters were built at the NW corner with Fenchurch Street. Its architect *T. E. Collcutt* supervised the remainder, together with *B. Emmanuel*.

On the W SIDE next to Lloyd's, No. 4, CORONATION HOUSE, 1902, by *Emmanuel* with *Collcutt* as consultant. Symmetrical nine-bay Ham stone front with plenty of blocked columns. Of the same type and date No. 6, and No. 3 (E side). No. 8 is *Norman Shaw*'s last building, built 1907–8 as the Associated Portland Cement Manufacturers' headquarters. The restrained front is based on his Parr's Bank, Liverpool, 1899: Doric columns of polished granite below, channelling on the first floor, then two plainer floors, the windows doubled on the topmost. The early concrete frame (*Kahn* system) was destroyed in rebuilding behind, 1971–2.

On the E SIDE, No. 1 MARLOW HOUSE, by *G. Bailey*, 1929, stands out from its *fin-de-siècle* neighbours. Three shallow symmetrical bays of glass and metal panels, topped by a surprisingly old-fashioned Tudor-Gothic vine-scroll frieze. Rebuilt behind by the *Fitzroy Robinson Partnership*, 1980–2, with extension facing the narrow Northumberland Alley (a ROMAN PAVEMENT discovered here in 1787 is now at the Society of Antiquaries).

At the Crutched Friars end, both buildings were rebuilt in 1972–5: No. 5 (E side) by *Gollins Melvin Ward & Partners*, with bronzed floor-panels between concrete mullions of U-section; the more appealing No. 10 opposite by *Lister, Drew & Associates*, with broad windows in a grid of polished dark brown stone, given crinkly undulations towards Crutched Friars.

LOMBARD STREET

For the Victorians this gently winding street was synonymous with financial might. Sir John Summerson quotes Walter Bagehot's *Lombard Street* (1873): 'by far the greatest combination of economical power and economical delicacy that the world has ever seen'. The banking connection is ancient. The early C14 name commemorates the Italian financiers who were of such great importance in Europe in the earlier Middle Ages. One such house, the Bardi of Florence, tenanted the former Inn of the late C13 Mayor Rokesley from 1318–38. This stone building, which survived into Stow's time, is commemorated under a later name in Pope's Head Alley (N side, not on its original alignment). The E end of the street, near the junction with Gracechurch Street, is older still, since it overlies a Roman E–W street that is one of the earliest features of London (*see* Fenchurch Street).

The City's first purpose-built private bank, Asgill's by *Taylor* (1757, dem. 1915), was at No. 70. Others followed intermittently over the next century, but most banking was still carried on from modified town houses until their grand rebuilding initiated by *C. O. Parnell*'s London and County Bank at No. 21 (1861–2, dem. *c.* 1965). The seal was set on Lombard Street as the heart of the banking world when the hanging bank signs banned by Charles II were revived for Edward VII's coronation. Signs apart, however, it must be admitted that Lombard Street today is disappointing: the liveliest

C19 buildings have gone, and those built after *c.* 1920 are not amongst the best of the period.

Lombard Street starts at the Mansion House and at once reaches an open triangle with the church of St Mary Woolnoth facing w. The triangle is formed by the meeting of Lombard Street and King William Street and thus did not exist in its present form until the 1830s. The s side of the triangle is the former SCOTTISH PROVIDENT INSTITUTION, Nos. 1–6 by *Dunn & Watson*, 1905–8 and 1915, assisted by *W. Curtis Green*. A long curving front with a giant order above. A pair of columns *in antis* sets forward at each end. The unusual Byzantinizing enrichments to doorcases, lesser columns etc. were carved by *Laurence Turner* (A. S. Gray notes that *A. C. Dickie* of the partnership had just returned with a full sketchbook from Near Eastern travels). Rebuilt by *JLW Building Surveying Services*, 1985–7, retaining the modest entrance hall and one other interior.

For the buildings on the N side up to Lloyds Bank, *see* Cornhill. Lloyds faces St Mary Woolnoth. Rising up behind it, E, Nos. 10–15, a big Portland complex designed in 1938 by *Whinney, Son & Austen Hall*, begun shortly after, but finished only in 1961. All-over rustication, shown in a drawing of 1940, was abandoned in execution, and the building is weak and denatured. On Lombard Street it accommodates first a POST OFFICE (No. 10), with an alley called Post Office Court through to King William Street and a recessed tripartite entrance dated 1951. The Post Office headquarters, transferred here from Threadneedle Street *c.* 1678, moved to St Martin's le Grand in 1829. Then COUTTS & CO. (No. 15), with an imaginative banking hall by *Lionel Brett, Boyd & Bosanquet*, 1961, sadly deprived *c.* 1990 of its subtly lit approach through inner lobbies, but still with its domes with gold mosaic within, a touch of Yamasaki or Philip Johnson. At the far end a cast of *Chantrey*'s seated figure of Mr Coutts of 1824. (Boardroom with murals by *Jean Clark*, 1956.) To King William Street little turrets high up. The E part here was originally the Bankers' Clearing House, completed 1955. A classical design by the *Whinney Mackay-Lewis Partnership* (1992) is intended to replace the whole.

Nos. 67–70 opposite (N side), another over-large complex, by *Sir Herbert Baker & A. T. Scott*, 1930–2. BANQUE PARIBAS (formerly Martin's Bank) at Nos. 68–70 spans Change Alley to No. 67, ROYAL BANK OF SCOTLAND (formerly Glyn, Mills & Co.). Both of red brick above stone, flat-fronted, with Baker's favourite round- and segment-headed windows and spindly Cinquecento balustrade (carver *Joseph Armitage*). Characteristic of Baker too the over-inflation of the essentially domestic Bankers' Georgian brick idiom. Baker's banking halls are lost, but No. 68 acquired a new internal courtyard in a refurbishment of 1984–6 by *Whinney Mackay-Lewis Partnership*.

On the s side, No. 21, the NATIONAL WESTMINSTER BANK by *Mewès & Davis*, 1963–9, shows what the traffic-obsessed 1960s had in mind for the future of Lombard Street: plain and rectilinear in stone, seven storeys high, set far back for street widening. The long porte-cochère was to facilitate drive-in banking. After

Nicholas Lane, Nos. 24–28 (s side), aggressively Imperial. Built as Royal Insurance Buildings by *Gordon & Gunton*, 1910. Motifs are multiplied without reserve: flat-fronted bays with sides both concave and convex, giant half-columns, and a domed oriel, l. Neat domed entrance lobby, retained in reconstruction by *Waterhouse & Ripley*, 1980–2. The early concrete frame (*Considéré* system) was destroyed. Nos. 33–34 Nicholas Lane were also incorporated (q.v.).

On the N side, Nos. 60–62, built as the Commercial Bank of Scotland by *J. Macvicar Anderson*, 1889–90. Of the type with superimposed columns, here of different Scottish granites. Round-headed windows. Narrow extension of 1922 by *H. L. Anderson*, r.; storeys added by the *Thomas Saunders Partnership*, 1983–5. Then St Edmund's church, and next to it George Yard. This serves as the approach to the vast and boastful new BARCLAYS BANK at No. 54, 1986–94 by *GMW Partnership*, what is called in America a skyline signature building. Three bulgy grey-clad towers of varying heights face Gracechurch Street. They have rounded and glazed tops, each like the Chrysler building in New York without its finial. The tallest, in the centre, is of seventeen storeys. Barrel-glazed features step up from the lower towers against its sides. The lower floors, treated as a podium block, are more conventionally handled, with polished grey granite cladding and rounded piers with transoms inset. Intermittent big coved cornice with gilt metal decoration stuck on. Curved front to Lombard Street, where there is a public bank. The main entrance faces George Yard, dramatically recessed under an excessively shallow barrel-vault. By it five reliefs by *Sir Charles Wheeler* from Barclays' previous premises here, commissioned from *Sir Herbert Baker* in 1946 and posthumously executed by *A. T. Scott & V. Helbing*, 1959–64 (extended up to George Yard 1969–71). Barclays has had a bank on the site since 1728. On part of its site stood *Wren*'s big, plain All Hallows Lombard Street, 1686–94; in 1938–9 the last City church to be demolished for its site value. The pre-Fire church, existing by 1052–70, had a C13 N aisle, widened *c.* 1400 and again in rebuilding of 1494–1544, when a S aisle and W tower were added. The latter incorporated a stone porch salvaged at the Dissolution from St John's Priory, Clerkenwell. Wren's tower was reused with other fittings at the new All Hallows, Twickenham (*see London 2: South*).

Back on the S side, No. 32, CLYDESDALE BANK, by *Maurice H. Bebb* and *Notman & Lodge*, 1963–4, an early and ugly use of the sheer marble facing and flush windows that became so popular in the following decade. Set on the wall by the entrance are some grotesque carved bosses, the hoodmould stops of *Waterhouse*'s Clydesdale Bank of 1864–6 which it replaced. This was round-arched Gothic-cum-Romanesque, Italian in derivation but already strongly personal in style. No. 38 by *Robert Walker*, 1873–5, the former Union Discount Corporation, vaguely French, with pilasters to each storey. Reconstructed in an early façade-job by *Fitzroy Robinson & Partners*, 1969.

101 The giant and showy commercial palace at Nos. 39–40 is by the brothers *Francis*, 1866–8, for the City Offices Company (builder *Myers*). Italianate all-over decoration was here carried to new

extremes (carver *F. G. Anstey*). Each storey has an order and entablature. Aedicules to the first-floor windows. Third-floor windows of two lights. Thickly enriched top cornice. Iron railings between the piers of the ground floor have Gothic-derived foliage, as if the architectural riches of c16 Italy were not enough.

LONDON BRIDGE APPROACH

Built in the 1830s as a wider s continuation of King William Street, carrying the traffic on a bridge across Upper and Lower Thames Street. c20 widening of this bridge and of King William Street beyond has eroded the once-dramatic contrast between narrow Street and spacious Approach. Two buildings form its sides: the Fishmongers' Hall, w (q.v.), and Adelaide House, E. They make an impressive contrast, the one of moderate height, reticent in its Neo-Greek forms, the other spectacular in its very forbiddingness.

ADELAIDE HOUSE was built as offices and warehousing by *Sir John Burnet & Tait*, 1921–5 (engineers *Sir Douglas Fox & Partners*). One of the first commercial buildings in London to break away from classical precedent, though preliminary drawings of 1920 in the City of London Record Office show Burnet still wrestling to reconcile classical conventions with so many superimposed storeys. At the same time Adelaide House is more rhetorical than Burnet's earlier Kodak House in Kingsway, Westminster. A big tall block with a slightly taller angle tower, at 148 ft (45 metres) London's highest commercial building when new. Narrowly set uniform mullions on three sides, between small upright windows with star motifs sunk into their aprons, all framed between sheer end piers. Egyptianizing top cornice applied in strips stopping short of the corners, pierced with more windows. The whole building has indeed, if any period flavour, something faintly Egyptian; but owes obvious debts also to the Chicago School (the even façades) and to Frank Lloyd Wright (the cornice). Very low entrance from the bridge, with squat unfluted Greek Doric columns of black Belgian marble. Carved figure over by *Reid Dick*. Lesser entrance from Lower Thames Street. The E front, facing St Magnus's church, is crudely treated in white glazed brick. A new quay made in front had rubber flooring to reduce noise. Also innovative for London were Adelaide House's central ventilation, internal mail system, and miniature golf on the roof.

LONDON STREET

A grand title for a minor street. Named after John London, Warden of the Ironmongers' Company in 1724. It forms a kind of forecourt to Fenchurch Street station. At the s end, NEW LONDON HOUSE, a smallish office tower with rebated corners by *Elsom, Pack & Roberts*, 1972–7, reclad in 1990–2 by *Allies & Morrison*. By the latter the green glass curtain-walling and Miesian I-beam mullions. A two-storey podium clad in polished brown stone extends down to Crutched Friars, where it was to have housed a station on the abortive Fleet Line extension.

LONDON WALL

London Wall has two parts: the medieval street at the E, which ran just inside the City wall between Old Broad Street and Coleman Street, and its w continuation, realigned and extended up to Aldersgate Street in the 1950s, through the most heavily bombed area of the City. The medieval street is much older than its first mention in 1388 (first called London Wall in 1547). The remaining part was widened on the N side c. 1900, in connection with the rebuilding of Finsbury Circus; post-war rebuilding has also seen much widening on the s side. The pre-war street continued w of Moorgate as a narrower route lined with warehouses; the main traffic thoroughfare was Fore Street, to the N. The new, wider alignment lies s of both, and only traces survive of the former street plan hereabouts. Many of the integrated office towers, slabs and walkways of the post-war plan have themselves been replaced since the late 1980s.

Old Broad Street west to Coleman Street

All Hallows' church is nicely placed on the N SIDE, overlooked by 1980s brick elevations behind retained fronts on New Broad Street (qq.v.). The section of ROMAN WALL on which the church rests continues in its medieval form as the N boundary of the churchyard. Traces of what may have been another late C4 bastion, the westernmost in the series, were found further w in 1988. The outer ditch here also contained coin moulds and counterfeiting debris, from an illegal mid-C3 mint. A small Roman memorial stone to Grata, daughter of Dagobitus, was found nearby in 1837. The corner with Blomfield Street is No. 85, by the *Casson Conder Partnership*, 1987–9. This has deeply modelled polygonal bays and projecting mullions clad in coarsely jointed white and orange-brown stone, with a corner turret.

On the s side, a large building by *Swanke Hayden Connell* for Deutsche Morgan Grenfell is under construction (1997). W of this, on the N side, the bulky backs of the big buildings of Finsbury Circus (q.v.), for which London Wall was widened some 10 ft (3 metres) c. 1900. On the s side, the Carpenters' Hall and No. 2 Throgmorton Avenue (qq.v.), then a few late C19 survivors. Next No. 60, amongst the more characterful large Postmodern blocks; by *Fitzroy Robinson Partnership*, 1990–2. Five storeys rise to eight behind, around two white-clad atria. A dominant off-centre frontispiece, aligned with Circus Place opposite, is faced in bulging channelled limestone with thin dark bands, continuing in coffered pattern into the arched entrance recess. Twin attics and a little loggia above. The rest is plainer, with a covered walkway for shops, and recessed broad curved bays. The façade of Nos. 20–22 Copthall Avenue is incorporated (q.v.). Also by *Fitzroy*'s No. 45, 1984–6 (with *Steven Scrivens*), similarly bulky, its motifs at once plainer and multiplied with less control. Grey-granite-faced below, with more shops; reconstituted Portland stone above; red granite towards Copthall Avenue. Upper storeys of black glass step back, with an openwork corner turret. On the avenue front the entrance to ROBERT FLEMING, with a glimpse of a dramatic atrium with trees and a central core of glazed lifts; here many of the company's paintings are displayed.

After Moorgate, No. 34 (s side), a big late C18 house of four bays and storeys. It looks across a little garden with a SCULPTURE of a gardener by *Karin Jonzen*, 1971, to a little row of early C19 houses (*see* Moorgate). The E corner with Coleman Street is the Armourers' and Braziers' Hall (q.v.).

The replanned London Wall: Coleman Street west to Aldersgate

The whole area ahead, together with the Barbican area to the N, is the product of compulsory purchase and post-war replanning. In 1954–5 several rebuilding plans were drawn up for the City and LCC, both individually and in collaboration, as well as a bold but unrealistic speculative scheme for the entire area (designed by *Serge*

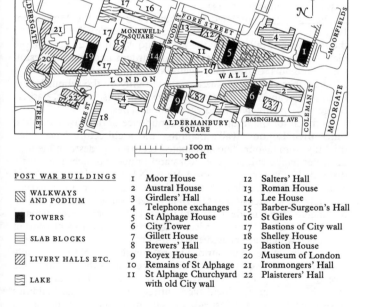

London Wall.
Plan of completed scheme, 1976

Kadleigh, William Whitfield and *Patrick Horsbrugh*). The present layout follows the LCC–City scheme announced in September 1955. The LCC planned the alignment of the new main road (then called Route XI) and introduced the concept of an integrated sequence of office towers. Detailed development was planned jointly by *H. A.*

Mealand, City Planning Officer, and the LCC's *Sir Leslie Martin* (and later *Sir Hubert Bennett*). Bulk, heights, and module of the new buildings were determined, though the final designs were by private architects. The scheme was particularly important as the first in England to provide a pedestrian upper walkway throughout, with plenty of access stairs, a broad but intermittent pedestrian deck, and bridges across the street and to the Barbican Estate, N.

The plan had six curtain-walled tower blocks (five of which remain), mostly of eighteen to twenty storeys and almost but not quite identical, spaced equidistantly at an oblique angle to the street, four on the N and two on the S. Eight-storey buildings were freely but not casually grouped around them and in axis with them. These mostly have stone-faced framing grids with coloured spandrels for decoration. The tallest tower, Britannic Tower, stands further N (*see* Ropemaker Street). Numerous little kiosks for shops were provided on the deck, from which the buildings were originally entered, with the ground reserved for traffic and deliveries. The street itself is a dual carriageway, with pavements, but almost exclusively used by vehicles. Beneath it lies a long underground car park. The ultimate inspiration is clearly the vertically separated circulation systems of Corbusier's Ville Radieuse. The fateful decision that these walkways ('ped-ways') should be extended throughout the City was taken in 1959: *see* Introduction p. 131.

The plan was completed in the mid 1970s with the Museum of London with its tower and roundabout and the smaller tower over the Plaisterers' Hall, both at the W end (qq.v.). In the 28 acres of the plan generous provision was made for gardens and open spaces, in which remains of the City walls are displayed. Otherwise the Modernist environment was interrupted only by the rebuilt Livery Halls dotted about on their ancient sites (Girdlers, Brewers, Barber-Surgeons), mostly in doggedly traditional styles.

So much for the unquestioning confidence of the 1950s and 60s. Since then London Wall's planning and architecture have fallen mightily from favour. The anticipated rebirth of pedestrian life high up never happened, and the kiosks and upper entrances are mostly disused. While the extension of Route XI E to Aldgate produced some widening (*see* also Wormwood Street and Camomile Street), the planned W extension to Old Bailey fizzles out in a little cut called Montague Street, made in the late 1980s. In that decade the demand for offices with elaborate services and deep plans led to a blizzard of proposals which anticipated the near-complete replacement of the 1960s architecture, in favour of a more intensive use of the site. Only two schemes were carried out (Alban Gate, across the middle of the street, and City Place House, both *see* below), but these were enough to disrupt the lucid plan entirely. Some original buildings have been refurbished instead. In 1997 more replacements are in progress on the S side. These will not add up to a coherent whole; it remains to be seen whether they will relate satisfactorily to their neighbours.

The first building, and the first tall block to be completed (1960), is MOOR HOUSE, on the N side at the corner of Moorfields, blocking the E end of Fore Street. By *Lewis Solomon, Kaye & Partners*. Shops both to the deck and at ground level. Its 225 ft (68½ metres) of curtain-walling looks shabby in 1997. New street entrance by *Simon Sturgis*, 1992, with an oversailing canopy. SCULPTURE by the door, one of *Barry Flanagan*'s leaping hares, 1994. Lower office blocks extend N from here along Moorfields (q.v.). First on the S side is AUSTRAL HOUSE, a low block by *Gunton & Gunton*, 1959–61, particularly attractive seen from the S, where the dark green curtain-walling is offset by serpentine marble on the lower mullions and yellow-tinted glazing above the street entrance. 137

Other buildings are best seen from the N deck, attainable by steps S of Moor House; the dedicated will need to cross to the S side here and there. W of Moor House, the deck widens along FORE STREET, NW. The name (recorded in 1330) refers to its route, just outside the old City wall. On its N side, one of the low blocks accommodates a Telephone Exchange (*see* Public Buildings). On the deck some lightweight polygonal shopping pavilions of 1966 remain; the rest were demolished in 1995 for a garden. The second tower on London Wall, beyond, is ST ALPHAEGE HOUSE, by *Maurice Sanders Associates*, 1960–2, very similar to Moor House, but with stilts around a recessed lower floor.

The first tower on the S side is CITY TOWER, by *Sir John Burnet, Tait & Partners*, 1962–4, reclad in 1985 by *GMW Partnership* with sleek blue reflective glazing and a grand street entrance from Basinghall Avenue. On its E side a section of pedestrian deck called Bassishaw Highwalk, linked by a bridge to the N side, with a split-pyramid roof light to the offices below. W of this space stands the big brash CITY PLACE HOUSE (Nos. 55–60), 1988–92 by *Swanke Hayden Connell*. It replaced Gillett House, by *Ralph Tubbs*, 1963–5, distinguished from the other low buildings by its brick cladding. Art Deco reminiscences in the metal-faced floors, red and white stone cladding and the upper set-backs. A pyramidal turret marks where it bridges over Bassishaw Highwalk on its course down to the rear of Guildhall. To London Wall the mass is repeatedly broken back. Street entrance from Basinghall Avenue with a deep, intimidatingly grand marble-lined lobby. Still on the S side, the walkway is interrupted for the Brewers' Hall (q.v.). Beyond, the second tower: ROYEX HOUSE, by *R. Seifert & Partners*, 1961–3. Its special feature, concealed by the uniform envelope, was its pre-cast H-frame construction.

Back to the N side, where the remains of St Alphage's church (q.v.) stand by the roadside. In the garden to the NW, visible from the deck, a fine stretch of the CITY WALL remains where it made the N churchyard wall. The Roman portion at the base is a double wall (seen in the E section). The outer wall is the refaced remnant of the N wall of the early C2 Roman fort; the inner is the thickening added during incorporation into the later Roman City wall. Above, medieval rebuildings, including a portion of small ashlar with courses of knapped flints, attributed to the mid C14. On top of the E part, brickwork battlements with a diaper pattern of dark brick, ascribed to Mayor Joceline's rebuilding in 1476–7. On the N face a section of chequerwork masonry, probably C14, from the first St Alphage, abandoned at the Reformation; older masonry below, of uncertain date.

On the N side of the churchyard is the Salters' Hall (q.v.); to the W, the stone-faced ROMAN HOUSE, the first block to be completed

(1957), by *R. N. Wakelin* of *Campbell-Jones & Sons*. Main part to Wood Street, low return wing along Fore Street, where an inscription records the first bomb to fall on the City in the Second World War, 25 August 1940.

The old CRIPPLEGATE lay just to the w. No Roman gateway has been found, but the N gate of the Roman fort must have been here; it presumably became a City gate when the fort's N wall was incorporated into the City wall. The first documentary mention is *c.* 1000. It was rebuilt in 1491, repaired in 1663, and pulled down in 1760–1. The name may come from the cripples who begged there in the Middle Ages, or from the medieval *cripule* or tunnel. It led only to a short entry into Fore Street, where it turned NW into Redcross Street – now buried beneath the Barbican development to the N and W (q.v.). Further remains of the Roman fortifications are preserved within the underground car park, entered by several ramps on both sides of the street: at the E end, a substantial free-standing piece of city wall, with courses of bonding tiles; at the W end, by the entrance just E of the Museum of London, the base of the N part of the Roman fort's W gate (not always on public view): two central piers, rectangular guard-room tower to the N.

Now for the cuckoo in the nest: the enormous ALBAN GATE, two contiguous towers by *Terry Farrell Partnership* (engineer *Ove Arup & Partners*), built for MEPC 1988–92. The inspiration for its set-backs and broken profiles, no less than for the striped pink and grey stone cladding, is the Postmodern reinterpretation of the American interwar skyscraper by Michael Graves (the architect insists that it also derives from the idea of a giant gatehouse). The concept was to replace one tower block (Lee House, by *Bernard Gold & Partners*, 1961–2, consultant *A. J. Shickle*), and to extend its envelope SW, bridging the crossroads of Wood Street and London Wall. The awkward conjunction between the two alignments is the weakest feature. The best is the selectively drama-tized structure: huge segmental arches bridge London Wall, their tympana filled by a glazed-in pedestrian court suspended on raking steel rods. The framing also appears high up on the S front facing Wood Street, through a big patent-glazed oriel. To E and W, the stone facing frames a glazed upper section like a giant seg-mental pediment, lighting a central atrium. The main office entrance is at deck level, where restaurants and shops are also provided. Here also a baffling bronze SCULPTURE of a nude couple by *Ivan Klapez*, 1992, called Unity. Part of the develop-ment is a low residential W block, with playful, rather over-articulated fronts of pleasant orange-red brick patterned with stone dressings. The struts descending diagonally where the walk-way continues W teasingly suggest a giant drawbridge, as if the flats were a barbican to the main 'keep' behind.

The flats form the E and S sides of MONKWELL SQUARE, formed after the war on the site of Monkwell Street, named probably from the C12 Muchewella family. Here Farrell has made a formal garden with raised circular centre, balustrades and obelisks of various sizes. On its E side the Barber-Surgeons' Hall (q.v.), and further E a grassy garden, overlooked by the Museum of London (q.v.), whose offices complete the sequence of towers on the N side.

The most impressive remains of the CITY WALL may be seen in and around the garden. A great hollow corner bastion stands SW of St Giles's church, facing a moat-like extension of the Barbican's lake. It marks where the wall turned through 90 degrees at the NW corner of the Roman fort. The fabric is clearly medieval in origin, almost certainly of the same build as the bastion remaining to foundation level to the E, S of the church and W of a further section of wall. This bastion must be late medieval (C13 pottery was found beneath in 1966). (To see these remains properly, make a detour to the churchyard within the Barbican Estate.) More traces S of the corner bastion, followed by the lower stages of a third bastion, excavated to form a setting for the Barber-Surgeons' herb garden. Another 50 yds (45 metres) S, a fourth medieval bastion, found in 1865, with what are probably medieval arrow slits, filled with later brickwork.

On the S side after Alban Gate, new headquarters for DAIWA SECURITIES by *Richard Rogers Partnership* are under construction (1997), partly on the site of another 1960s telephone exchange; the 1960s block in Noble Street, E, was demolished in 1996 for a new building by *Sheppard Robson*. At its N end, facing London Wall, the churchyard of the former St Olave Silver Street is laid out as a garden. A late C17 or C18 tablet commemorates the church, first recorded *c.* 1200 and destroyed in 1666. The low polygonal structure and office tower W of Noble Street (No. 1 London Wall) belong with the Plaisterers' Hall (q.v.); the tower, completed only in 1973, was in 1994 proposed for replacement by *Norman Foster Architects*.

LONG LANE with HAYNE STREET

First recorded in 1440. It runs NE from Smithfield to Aldersgate Street, marking the old N boundary of St Bartholomew's Priory. The 'Agas' map shows the priory wall still intact in the 1560s, but it was built up by Stow's time (1598). The narrow, shallow individual plots resemble those of contemporary developments in Cloth Fair and Middle Street behind (qq.v.). In 1869–85 the N side was widened in connection with the new Smithfield Market and Metropolitan Railway. The best buildings are on the S side, including two notable houses of *c.* 1700. Otherwise it is largely C19, with much tactful but uninspired late C20 infill.

S SIDE. From the W, the BARLEY MOW (No. 50), brick and stucco of *c.* 1850, the name in good black capitals above. Nos. 51–52, commercial mid C20, in noisy black and white tiles. Between Nos. 56 and 58, RISING SUN COURT perpetuates the ancient alignment of a gate to the old Liberty of St Bartholomew. Nos. 60–61, of brick, 1862, has the rounded upper corners to the windows typical of that date. Nos. 62–67, brown brick offices by *Renton Howard Wood Levin*, 1981–5, part of a mixed-use development also facing Cloth Fair. Neo-Victorian, but with a mannered treatment of the first-floor windows. Nos. 69–70 are a broad five-bay house of *c.* 1720, much altered, but recognizably of the kind with windows half as wide as the rest at each end (now blocked).

Typically early C18 also the segmental window heads and the
moulded cornice. The top storey looks C19. Nos. 71–72, YE OLD
RED COW, a plain thick-set pub of 1877, still wholly Gothic in
detail. No. 74 is a rare survival: a late C17 timber-framed house,
just one bay wide. Four storeys, with a first-floor jetty and broad
C18 sashes. Boxy tile-hung top storey. Under the paint it is
apparent that the front is not of brick but mathematical tile, never
common in London. Late C17 fabric behind C19 brick fronts at
Nos. 75–76. Nos. 77–79, by *Francis Bennett Associates*, 1984–5,
with a broken pediment from the Postmodern dressing-up
chest.

The N SIDE, shorter because of the market building at the W, is
mostly undistinguished medium-sized post-war offices. Nos.
18–19 are by *Morrison, Rose & Partners*, 1972–4, brick with
smoked glass window bands. The upper storeys step back down
HAYNE STREET, named after its developer in the early 1870s. Of
this date the unpretentious brick warehouse at Nos. 8–10 (W side),
and No. 3 opposite, a little house perched on the brink of the railway cutting. Back in Long Lane, Nos. 9–12, by *Ley, Colbeck &
Partners*, 1956–9, of the first wave of curtain-walled speculative
offices. Further E, Nos. 1–5, brown-tile-faced with an ugly hipped
superstructure, by *Hugh V. Sprince & Partners*, 1971–5.

LOTHBURY

A short street connecting Gresham Street and Throgmorton Street,
passing the Bank of England on the N. The likeliest derivation of the
name is from the fortified 'bury' of a family called Lotha (cf.
Bucklersbury, Poultry). The word occurs by 1180–92, as a suffix to
2 St Margaret's church (N side). On either side of the church stand
commercial buildings of unusual interest.

Starting at the W end, on the N side between Coleman Street and
Moorgate, Nos. 3–4, built for the Northern Assurance by
Mountford & Gruning, 1907–9. The Assurance was founded in
Aberdeen, whence came the grey granite for its plain, massive
forms. All small-scale detail is tellingly renounced. Ground floor
with bold banded rustication and round-headed windows. Giant
order above, recessed between rounded corners. Strongly horizontal cornice, omitting an architrave. Extra storeys were contrived between the big top aedicules by *Peter Ednie & Partners*,
1982–5, faced in stone cut from the old fabric. Facing it across
Moorgate, No. 5 BANK SADERAT IRAN, dated 1886, in stone
of contrasting colours with good sharp eclectic detail. At the end
of the close called FOUNDERS' COURT, the retained one-bay
fancy Italianate front of Messrs BROWN, SHIPLEY & CO.'s
offices, originally the Central Electric Telegraph Station; 1847 by
J. A. Hunt. The rest was rebuilt in the 1970s (*see* Moorgate).
The Founders' Hall stood here between the 1530s and the
mid C19.

The former Royal Bank of Canada at No. 6, completed 1932 by
Stanley Hall and *Easton & Robertson* with *S. G. Davenport* of
Montreal, rises against the tower of the church. Slim front with

refined all-over Adamesque detail in low relief, let down by an unfinished top storey of brick.

The OVERSEAS BANKERS' CLUB at No. 7, E of St Margaret, is an amazing building for its date: 1866. Built for the General Credit Company, one of the limited liability discount houses set up after 1858, by the elder *Somers Clarke* (builder *Lucas Bros.*, carving by *Carter*). Portland-faced Venetian Gothic, when context and convention still favoured the classical; sumptuously handled, yet so crisp it looks like a C20 revival. One-bay façade to Lothbury, flanked by slim twisted shafts all the way up. The brown sandstone plinth is interrupted by a big round-arched portal with red and white stone surround and three orders of black marble columns, moved here from the Tokenhouse Yard front between 1892 and 1919. Over it, a big traceried window and openwork balcony on corbels carved as sphinxes. Square-headed second- and third-floor windows are combined in a single panel by thin cable-mouldings, a device without Venetian precedent; indeed, the whole is stiffer and more rectilinear than anything the Venetian Quattrocento produced. Between these windows a finely carved medievalizing relief by *Redfern*. Elaborate rounded chimneys with cornices; a few alterations to the roof. On the long Tokenhouse Yard front, the grid is softened: round- and ogee-headed windows are grouped in giant panels two and three bays wide, between end bays with paired windows. Square panels inlaid with coloured marble discs, sexfoil reliefs and bosses provide ornament. The front to the church has rings of inlaid discs straight out of Ruskin's *Stones of Venice*. The Venetian theme extends inside to a convincing bottle-glass screen, apparently original, reset on the staircase.

Then the gently curving front of the NATIONAL WESTMINSTER BANK, by *Mewès & Davis*, 1921–32, on a scale befitting its original function as the London, County & Westminster Bank's headquarters. Pilastered ground floor and mezzanine, plainer storeys above. Taller entrance section with paired columns, placed asymmetrically to face down Bartholomew Lane. Small-scale ornament in sundry styles, used in proportion to this frontispiece rather than the whole façade. The splendid banking hall has ranges of stretched Ionic columns around a large square skylight. Doric columns support a gallery around the sides. In 1996 converted to an exhibition space, by *DEGW*. Branch bank on the r., facing Angel Court. (Well-preserved offices on upper floors, in Adam, Louis XIV and late C17 styles.) The grandly rusticated front of its predecessor here, *Cockerell* and *Tite*'s London & Westminster Bank (1837–9), proclaimed the arrival of the joint-stock bank in the capital.

LOVAT LANE

A narrow winding lane between Eastcheap and Lower Thames Street, still with C19 granite setts and a central gutter. The Abbot of Waltham's Inn lay to the E *c.* 1200–1540. The medieval name Love Lane was changed in 1939 to avoid confusion with the Love Lane off Aldermanbury.

At the N end, No. 31 (E side), Peek's former warehouse, now a rare survival in the City. Of 1852 (contractor *H. Burton*), solid and sturdy, too early for the movement away from plain load-bearing walls towards frame-and-infill construction. Six storeys, not high, with windows doubled at the top. Eloquently massive granite doorcase, perhaps from 1884, when Peek's No. 20 Eastcheap was built (q.v.). Then the brick tower of St Mary-at-Hill. Opposite, No. 4, a humble stuccoed early C19 house with a convex front. Further S a few C19 survivals, e.g. No. 28 (E side), with a massive blocked doorcase. Then on both sides CITY VILLAGE, a development of small brick and stucco offices, 1981–4, replacing warehouses redundant after Billingsgate Market closed. It is really a giant infill scheme, with new parts outnumbering the old. The City planners requested 'extrovert' architecture, a challenge answered by the *Thomas Saunders Partnership* with a vengeance. Some motifs are plundered from the textbooks: Nos. 8–9 (W side) has curved oriels and a shaped gable recalling *fin-de-siècle* Budapest; Nos. 25–26 opposite has Regency balconies. Others are entirely novel, such as the giant keyhole-dormer on Nos. 8–9, or No. 14's porthole windows linked by stone curlicues. Interrupting the W side, a retained red brick warehouse façade of *c.* 1912, a rough simulacrum of a mansion of 1669 (called No. 32 Botolph Lane) which it replaced. Parts of the interiors were reconstructed at the Sir John Cass School (q.v.). As a picturesque composition the group works well, but the wilful eccentricity soon jars. Outlying parts to St Mary-at-Hill and Botolph Lane are less demonstrative. A later phase at the S end faces Monument Street (q.v.).

LOWER THAMES STREET

The continuation of Upper Thames Street downstream of London Bridge, now part of the busy main E–W artery along the river. For the Roman and medieval periods, *see* Upper Thames Street. The highlights are on the S side: Adelaide House (*see* London Bridge Approach), St Magnus's church, the former Billingsgate Market, and the Custom House (qq.v.). The riverside warehouses have gone, replaced by big office blocks largely of the 1970s–80s.

The first blocks on the N side are described under Monument Street. On the S side beyond the church, MAGNUS HOUSE, 1973–81 by *R. Seifert & Partners*. Main block aligned N–S, lower wing intersecting at r. angles. Recessed window bands, sharp-edged aggregate-faced sills. The concrete frame is exposed high up. In the angle a heavy podium faced in polished stone supports part of the ped-way, favoured this late here because of the busy road. In front, a broad riverside walkway extends up to the old Billingsgate Market, past SAMUEL MONTAGU (No. 10), by *Covell Matthews Wheatley Partnership*, 1983–5. A large example of the broken-up, all-over mirror-glass fashion, which the City never really took to heart. A squared petrol-blue grid steps up to fourteen storeys from E to W, with irregular boxing-out on the N and S. Atrium in the centre with wall-climber lifts. The church of St Botolph Billingsgate stood on part of the site until 1666. First mentioned in the mid C12, though excavations in 1982–3 found nothing earlier than a C14 S wall and chapel and a C15 undercroft. The church was rebuilt in the later C16. Its churchyard may be seen in Monument Street (q.v.).

Now back to Lower Thames Street. Opposite the market, at the W corner with St Mary-at-Hill, the former Billingsgate Christian Mission, by *G. Baines*, 1889. Red brick with a corner oriel and very tall first-floor windows, in no particular style, but pleasant enough. Then No. 100, ST MARY'S COURT, a long slab by *Fitzroy Robinson & Partners*, 1973–7. Polished grey stone bands, flush uprights and mullions. Matching W and N ranges around a courtyard. Entrance recessed beneath an abutment for an unbuilt pedestrian bridge, r., planned when complete demolition of the market was mooted.

No. 100 occupies the site of the COAL EXCHANGE of 1847–9, the masterpiece of *J. B. Bunning*. It was demolished for road-widening in 1962, to universal dismay. Within its spirited but conventionally Italianate exterior lay a daring iron-framed glass-roofed rotonda with three galleries, their cast-iron rope ornament 'immensely elaborate and crushingly tasteless' (Pevsner). In the painted decorations of mining scenes, tree ferns etc. (by *Sang* and *Melhado*), the mid-Victorian concern for earnest encyclopedic documentation was already manifest. Hitchcock's *Early Victorian Architecture* (1954) gave it three pages of detailed exposition. The first Coal Exchange here was of 1770: a reminder that Billingsgate was for centuries the main wharf for coal as well as fish.

A late ROMAN TOWN HOUSE and PRIVATE BATHS are preserved in the basement of No. 100. One of the most complete relics of Roman architecture in London, first discovered in 1848

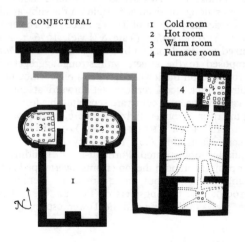

CONJECTURAL

1 Cold room
2 Hot room
3 Warm room
4 Furnace room

30 m
100 ft

Lower Thames Street.
Plans of late Roman town house and private baths

during excavations for the Coal Exchange. Further investigations followed in 1968–70. The Corporation of London hopes one day to open them to public display. The first ruins encountered, to the w, are of the bath house, which stood on a terrace overlooking the river. Its walls differ from the other structures in being constructed entirely of red tile. A large unheated room to the s, with a red mosaic floor, is likely to have been the cold room (*frigidarium*). To the N, two small apsed chambers – probably the hot and warm rooms (*caldarium* and *tepidarium*) – were heated by pillared hypocausts. The furnace heating the E room is well preserved, as are the flues within the walls which carried the heated air out of the building. A buttressed terrace wall N of the baths, set over timber piles, supported the s façade of a C3 building. Remains of a domestic reception wing E of the baths probably belonged with the same structure. Walls were of the usual tile-coursed ragstone. The reception rooms contain good channelled hypocausts. Its relationship with the bath block is unclear. The present display follows the reconstruction preferred by Peter Marsden, who was responsible for the excavations of 1968–9, which suggests that the baths were entered from the N, and that a corridor had been built alongside the terrace wall there; but a direct entry into the hot rooms would be most unusual.

The E part of the island block is Nos. 4–9 St Dunstan's Hill, offices of 1981–3 by the *Fitzroy Robinson Partnership*. Dark curtain-walling with tentative angled-out lights at intervals. Pleasing view up the hill of St Dunstan-in-the-East's steeple and garden. Opposite the Custom House, NORSKE BANK, a large white stone-clad slab of 1974–81, also *Fitzroy*'s. The ends are fashioned as big turrets, aspiring to picturesqueness. Slit windows in splayed surrounds.

The main road climbs NE, as Byward Street. Lower Thames Street proper continues along the river, accessible via the subway higher up. On the N side the podium of Tower Place (*see* Tower Hill). Opposite, first SUGAR QUAY (Tate & Lyle), 1976–7, a well-managed mixed-use development by *Fitzroy Robinson & Partners*. Tightly composed to the street, with strong aggregate-faced horizontals rounded on the lower edge and a big cornice-like top balcony. Paired brick-faced verticals set forward at each end. Greenish glazing between. A courtyard separates this from a lower wing facing the river. Stronger horizontals here, serving on top as balconies for flats. Then THREE QUAYS HOUSE, the former General Steam Navigation Co., 1956–9 by *Brian O'Rorke*, a pleasant, quietly sophisticated Portland-faced building. The ground floor projects on both the long fronts, overtopped at the w where a stubby wing juts out on square piers. Demolition is proposed (1996). The floating piers of TOWER QUAY beyond give excellent views of the City and the Tower, especially at high tide.

LUDGATE CIRCUS

Made in 1864–9 in connection with the Holborn Viaduct scheme. Three of the quadrants remain, by different architects, all typical of the showy eclecticism of *c.* 1870. The sw quadrant, 1874–6 by *John Wimble*, has French oval dormers. The NW quadrant is LUDGATE HOUSE (originally Thomas Cook's), 1872–3, by *Horace Gundry*. Taller and more Palladian, with fancy ironwork balconies. Broad flat leaded dome on top, added perhaps in 1906, when a matching extension was built in Fleet Street by *Arnold Mitchell* and *Smee & Houchin*. On both parts lots of cherubs and exotic masks. Facing the circus, a BAS-RELIEF of Edgar Wallace by *F. Doyle Jones*, 1934. Loosest of the quadrants is the OLD KING LUD (NE), by *Lewis Isaacs*, 1870–1. Crowded windows, crowded round-headed dormers with thorny iron finials. Rebuilt behind in 1991–2 (*see* No. 100 Ludgate Hill). The SE quadrant, destroyed by bombing, awaits re-creation in 1997.

LUDGATE HILL

Called Ludgate Street until 1865. The best approach to St Paul's. The W front steadily reveals itself as one climbs the hill, set off perfectly by the steeple of St Martin's church (N side). Wren cannot have calculated on this view, for the old Ludgate blocked the street just W of the church until 1760–1. Then from 1866 the view from the bottom of the hill was interrupted again, by the heavy cast-iron bridge to the former Holborn Viaduct station, removed in 1990.

The route originated as a ROMAN ROAD through the Roman W cemetery, crossing the Fleet by a timber bridge near Ludgate Circus. A tombstone found at St Martin in 1669 shows a life-size Roman soldier in tunic and cloak; dedicated to Vivius Marcianus of the Second Augustan Legion, and set up by Januaria Martina, his most devoted wife. A hexagonal column was found nearby in 1806, erected by the slave Anencletus to his eighteen-year-old wife Claudia Martina. Both are exhibited at the Museum of London. The existence of a Roman LUDGATE can safely be presumed. The first mention is probably in a charter of 857, as *Westgetum*. The current name is from the Old English *ludgeat*, back gate or postern. A substantial CII–CI2 timber abutment for a bridge across the Fleet was excavated at the bottom of the hill in 1988–90. The gate was rebuilt *c.* 1215 and again in 1586 by *William Kerwin*, with a thin pilastered frontispiece. Statues from Kerwin's gate are preserved at St Dunstan-in-the-West (q.v.). Apart from St Martin, buildings are Victorian (S side widened 1863–91) and post-war, built after heavy bomb damage to the W end.

The N side, from the W: No. 100, by *Skidmore, Owings & Merrill*, 1989–92, on land released when Holborn Viaduct station closed (*see* also Fleet Place). Large and heavy, though anxious not to offend. Lower range to Ludgate Hill with cornices and rusticated basement. Taller, symmetrical front to Limeburner Lane, with fewer classical trimmings. Then HILLGATE HOUSE, a large complex of slabs by *Theo Birks*, completed 1961, reclad in bronzed facing by *Kenzie Lovell Partnership*, 1982. Eight-storey block to Ludgate Hill, set back, with shops beneath a canopy added in 1982; side ranges to Limeburner Lane (W) and Old Bailey (E); at the N end a curtain-walled twelve-storey slab. The E corner with Old Bailey is a mild stone-faced building of 1980–5 by *T. P. Bennett*

& Son, with balconies on the curved corner. Part of the scheme, YE OLDE LONDON pub by the church, loose Renaissance-Victorian pastiche.

On the s side, first City Thameslink station (q.v.), surrounded by long-vacant land up to Pageantmaster Court, then Nos. 45–47, the former City Bank, 1890–1. *Collcutt* at his most playful; buff terracotta and red brick, with turrets and big gables. Giant round arches to the good lofty banking hall. Reconstructed 1989–90 by *Archer, Boxer & Partners*, who heightened it behind in a matching style. Remains of the late C13 CITY WALL extension were discovered here in 1988 (*see* Introduction p. 44). The architects also replicated the front of old No. 43, by *Lewis Solomon*, 1878, with a decorative cast-iron second-floor balcony. Similar balconies are the distinguishing feature of other buildings on the s side, all run-of-the-mill enriched classical. Nos. 39 and 37, *c.* 1890, of three bays, rather French; No. 35, 1881. Nos. 25–33, three replicated Victorian façades by *Elsworth Sykes Partnership*, 1990–1, the showy centre (No. 29) originally by *Joseph & Smithem*, 1885–7, with third-floor herms. New brick fronts to Pilgrim Street (w) and around a pleasant new courtyard (called Priory Court); COBB'S COURT leads thence to the s part, facing Carter Lane (q.v.).

Back on the n side of Ludgate Hill, Nos. 34–40 by *T. Dudley*, 1874–5, a gross five-storey pile of painted stone, as tall as St Martin's tower alongside. Nine bays of round-arched windows, giant superimposed Corinthian half-columns and pilasters, lesser applied columns scattered about anyhow. Big shell-headed entrance niche. Nos. 30–32 by *Charles Reilly Sen.*, 1900, Free Style, with twin flat bows and broad bands of terracotta and red glazed brick. On the s side, Nos. 19–23 by *Joseph & Pearson*, 1878–9, with a balcony like those further w.

An archway leads into LUDGATE SQUARE, a curving close of warehouses laid out in the late 1870s. *Charles Bell*'s Nos. 1–3 (r.), towering Gothic of 1877, was demolished *c.* 1990 but for the iron-framed ground floor, derelict in 1997. Nos. 6–7, 1885, with stone trim and very large windows but no obvious iron framing; Nos. 8–9, dated 1881, probably by *George Edwards*, with the familiar iron colonnettes. The n side is late C19 plain pastiche, continued NE along Creed Lane: by *Fitzroy Robinson Partnership*, 1986–90, behind the retained façade of Nos. 11–17 Ludgate Hill, 1885. Through it passes the glazed-in CREED COURT, called after a previous, smaller close.

Last on the n side, COLONIAL MUTUAL HOUSE, by *Trehearne & Norman, Preston & Partners*, 1960–3, with a curved seven-storey front with shallow abstract patterning. It really forms the beginning of the n precinct of St Paul's (q.v.).

MANSELL STREET

Laid out between 1682 and 1700, probably by Sir William Leman, and named after a member of his family (the n part called Somerset Street until *c.* 1860). A main traffic artery from the late 1890s, when a s extension joined it with the new Tower Bridge Approach. Before 1994, the City boundary wavered E to take in part of the N end; now the W side lies in the City, the E side in Tower Hamlets. Large 1980s offices dominate, the majority in rudimentary developers' Postmodern, coarser than most contemporary work within the City. Otherwise some flats, and an important pair of early Georgian houses.

The walk is from N to S. First on the E side, two blocks by *Fitzroy Robinson Partnership*. The SEDGWICK CENTRE, 1986–8, a long block end-on to Mansell Street, has a chunky stone-faced grid and heavy top cornice, familiar from their 1970s work in Aldgate High Street. A concealed atrium descends into a basement shopping centre. STANDON HOUSE, 1980–3, is smaller but otherwise similar. Next, MANSELL COURT, 1987–9 by *EPR Partnership*, polished red granite, routine, with a big barrel-vault over the entrance.

Opposite (W side), Nos. 18–32 by *Sidney Kaye, Firmin & Partners*, 1979–82, offices on a T-plan, the rear wing lower. Bronzed frame, brown brick infill. Then the GUINNESS TRUST ESTATE, 1977–81 by *Trehearne & Norman, Preston & Partners*, on the site of a railway goods depot (part of the scheme for the offices further W: *see* Minories). Deck-access slabs of six to eight storeys, along the street and at r. angles to the S, sunken garden in the angle: an old-fashioned layout when most public housing had abandoned large-scale clearance and monumental compositions. Unattractive brown brick finishes, with clumsy, apologetic leaded mansards. More flats in MARLYN LODGE, S: near-windowless forebuilding to the street, bronzed canted bays above.

Back on the E side, No. 49 is by the same firm, with *Ian Mistry*, 1988. Brown stone with scarlet trim, symmetrical about an ungainly glazed corner with external lifts. Weedy false gables high up. Then Nos. 57 and 59, two splendid houses dated 1725, restored in 1988 by *Trehearne & Norman* after long neglect. Five bays and three storeys each, the wider central bays broken forward. No. 57, richer and better preserved, is of red brick and Portland stone. Frontispiece with wide round-headed double 74 doorway and wide broken pediment on full fluted Doric columns; the rest of the ground floor all restoration. The stone apron of the window above fills the centre of the pediment. Channelled stone piers at each end, stone strings, stone key-blocks to the segment-headed windows. The attic has blind sunk panels. This self-assured, somewhat retardataire Baroque speaks of a mercantile prosperity at a comfortable pyschological distance from the fashionably Palladian West End. No. 59, of stock brick with red trim, is dressed in poorer stone, with a simple round-headed doorway: did it lose a full doorcase in 1880, the date on its rainwater-head?

More stone-faced Postmodern offices at Nos. 69–77; then INSIGNIA 157 HOUSE, by *Elana Keats & Associates* and *John Winter & Associates* with *Jonathan Ellis-Miller*, 1990–1 (engineers *Ove Arup*). An early manifestation of the spare, cool minimalism that returned to favour in the 1990s, coming here like a draught of pure water after too many coloured sweets. White-panelled upright front, shallow central projecting glass box with internal tubular steel framing, jointed and braced in the high-tech manner. It functions both as an entrance lobby and a sort of applied atrium overlooked by the six glazed-in office floors. LLOYDS CHAMBERS opposite, by the *Fitzroy Robinson Partnership*, 1980–3, is entered from the narrow Portsoken Street, N, through a giant polygonal glass-walled atrium – an early example. It punctuates the mass of a building longer than it is tall, with big rounded piers and windows cantilevered out in flat bays to Mansell Street and Goodman's Yard (S). At the W end a public garden. Portsoken Street (Swan Street until *c.* 1930) is named from Portsoken Ward, for which *see* Cutler Street.

For buildings S of the railway bridge *see* Minories.

MARK LANE

Recorded from *c.* 1200, as *Marthe-lane*, probably after a woman called Martha. The Corn Exchange operated on the E side, S end, until 1987. The first ('Old') exchange, 1747–50 by the elder *Dance* around an open court, was partly rebuilt in 1827–8 by *George Smith* with *A. B. Clayton*, who added a second ('New') exchange in the Greek taste. *George Legg* roofed in the old court in 1852. Rebuilt by *E. & E. B. I'Anson* after 1881, and again rebuilt on a reduced site by *Terence Heysham* after war damage.

At the N end, W side, the little tower of All Hallows Staining (q.v.). To its S ST OLAVE'S CHURCH HALL, by *Halliday & Greenwood*, 1954–7, a harmless low brick building. Beyond Dunster Court, the vast and bewildering E front of the *GMW Partnership*'s Minster Court (*see* Mincing Lane).

The E SIDE begins at the London Street corner with *Richardson & Gill*'s MARLON HOUSE, Nos. 71–74, 1933–4, an unfussy streamlined job in cast stone. Nos. 69–70, a neat little curtain-walled front coloured dark blue, is part of a T-shaped block with the main front to New London Street behind; by *CLRP Architects*, 1962–5. Nos. 64–66 by *Dennis Crump & Partners*, 1971–5: bronzed glazing bands, soapy off-white marble-faced floors. The S corner with Hart Street is No. 63, mid 1950s, flashily refronted in 1984–5 by *Trehearne & Norman, Preston & Partners*.

103 Mark Lane's outstanding building is Nos. 59–61, by *Aitchison*, 1864, an arcaded flush stone front on concealed iron framing, exquisitely dressed in the Veneto-Byzantine manner. A relatively early example of speculative offices, built for the Innes Brothers, whose City of London Real Property Company was founded that year. Six bays, with the shallowest decorated stringcourses marking four storeys. Upper floors have stocky columns with foliage capitals, the altered ground floor segmental arches. Cleaning in 1981, during renovation by the *Ronald Fielding Partnership*, revealed the quality of Aitchison's inlays and incised mastic-filled decoration. The free and eclectic motifs suggest Owen Jones's influence; but, as Hitchcock noted in 1949, the presiding spirit is Ruskin's *Stones of Venice*. An ornate iron staircase noted by Hitchcock has been destroyed, apparently in previous refurbishment (1958). Nos. 52–58 are a large atrium block by the *Fitzroy Robinson Partnership*, 1990–6. Eight storeys, grey and white

stone, treated as six three-bay sections each with a flat bay high up. No. 50, by *Trehearne & Norman, Preston & Partners*, 1988–91. Symmetrical, not wide, with pediment and big glazed bow over rusticated red granite. A mid-C13 rib-vaulted undercroft found beneath in 1957 was not preserved.

MARTIN LANE

The Italianate former RECTORY on the E side was built by *John Davies* for St Clement Eastcheap in 1851–3 (adapted for offices by the *Rolfe Judd Group Practice*, 1978–80). Three bays of brick with stone dressings, then a slender campanile on the corner. Its crude square top stage replaced an ornate cupola some time before 1935. Big clock attached, late C17 style, but dated 1853. Shallow bow facing the churchyard, the site of the old St Martin Orgar, given to St Paul's in the C12 by Orgar the deacon. Excavations in 1987 revealed foundations of a Saxo-Norman E apse, made square-ended in the C13; a S chapel with vaulted crypt was a later addition. The church went in 1666, but its tower survived until the widening of Cannon Street in 1847. From 1697 to *c.* 1825 it formed part of a Huguenot chapel.

No. 27 on the same side, stone-faced offices of 1864 by *T. E. Knightley*. The rounded glazed corner is the memorable feature. Otherwise large windows with colonnettes, between repeated pilasters. Heightened by one matching storey by *Fitzroy Robinson Partnership* with *William F. Newman & Associates*, 1981–3; included in the scheme were the refurbishment of No. 28, red brick offices of *c.* 1875 facing the courtyard behind, and chunky new granite-faced fronts to the S and on Arthur Street. The stuccoed OLDE WINE SHADES at No. 6, diagonally opposite, has very large close-set windows, betraying it as one of the houses built shortly after 1666. Alterations include the shopfront, apparently *c.* 1800, and an open-well staircase with the column-newels and slender turned balusters typical of *c.* 1720. (Good mid-C18 marble chimneypieces and doorcase on the first floor.)

MASON'S AVENUE *see* BASINGHALL STREET

MIDDLESEX STREET

Home of the teeming Petticoat Lane market, until *c.* 1830 the street's name also. For most of its length Middlesex Street forms the boundary between the City and the East End. The buildings do not let you forget this.

On the W (City) SIDE, monumental 1970s–80s offices turn their backs on the street. From the S, they are Aldgate House, Beaufort House (*see* Aldgate High Street and St Botolph Street respectively), and, further up, Cutlers' Gardens (*see* Cutler Street). Just before the last is the MIDDLESEX STREET ESTATE, by the *Corporation of London Architect's Department*, 1965–75. Very hard and very urban, even by the standards of the time. Aggressive six-storey outer ranges of partially stepped section in black engineering brick, their dominant motif fiddly slotted concrete balconies. Alarmingly steep steps up to a raised internal courtyard (intended to join up with the ped-way). From the back rises a slender square tower. Deck access to the blocks around the courtyard. Shops here, converted to flats 1996–7. More shops in the outer ranges.

Run-down warehouses of *c.* 1900 line most of the E SIDE, with post-war buildings further s. None is worth singling out. More interesting buildings lie in the NW part. This dates from 1892–6, when the LCC extended Middlesex Street into Bishopsgate, along parts of the course of Sandy's Row and Widegate Street (qq.v.). In the s angle, EAST INDIA HOUSE (No. 109), an eight-storey slab by *Harrison & West*, 1989–91, in pleasing banded yellow brick and Portland roach, with a giant broken pediment. Rounded corner turrets; on the l. one prances a bronze horse by *Judy Boyt*. Lower section down Catherine Wheel Alley, r. Opposite, Nos. 110–116, a low, disappointingly weak block of 1987–9 by *YRM Architects*, in brown brick and pink stone. Then on the s side some late C19 survivors: No. 119, a red brick warehouse with rather Baroque gable-end; Nos. 125–129, L-shaped, unpretentious red brick, formerly the Jewish Board of Guardians – a reminder of the former ethnic composition of the area. By *Davis & Emmanuel*, 1895–6. – SCULPTURE at the SE end, a bronze cone with figures in relief by *Richard Perry*, 1995.

MIDDLE STREET
with NEWBURY STREET and KINGHORN STREET

Middle Street continues the line of Cloth Fair to the E. With Newbury Street on the s, it represents the latter phase of Lord Rich's redevelopment of St Bartholomew's Priory (leases issued *c.* 1590–1614). Shallow plots were laid out in parallel E–W rows, bounded by Cloth Street (E) and Kinghorn Street (W). His plan largely survives: see the narrow paved alley called East Passage between Middle Street and Long Lane. A still narrower alley between Middle Street and Newbury Street disappeared in the later C19.

The best buildings face Kinghorn Street. No. 1, the HAND AND SHEARS (s side), was built probably in 1830 and has windows set in recessed segment-headed panels typical of that date. Excellent original pub front, with spindly Ionic half-columns at the entrances between piers with incised Soanian detail. The name comes from the opening ceremony of Bartholomew Fair, latterly staged here, when the Lord Mayor cut the first cloth. Adjoining it to the s, No. 31 NEWBURY STREET, is a house of 1795, restored in 1977 by *John Anstey*. Opposite No. 1, No. 25 (N side), a neat, spiky little building by *Hodges & Haxworth*, 1981–2, for themselves. Curtain-walled, with a pattern of clear and opaque blue panels within a strong glazing grid. A balcony above, then a pitched roof of broken outline. Entered from No. 24, C19 brick with fabric of *c.* 1700 behind (ex inf. Martin Haxworth).

A little further on, Nos. 4–5 (Middle Street, s side), a quirky early C19 pair of houses. Brick, four storeys, with segment-headed tripartite windows and a narrow round-headed panel recessed in the centre: a motif popular *c.* 1820. The rest is largely still unassuming later C19 and early C20 warehouses, some converted into offices from *c.* 1980. The best is No. 23, OSCAR FABER (N side), with segment-headed windows and red brick trim, restored by *Goddard Manton Partnership*, 1985–6. Recent construction here plays with the vocabulary of these buildings: Nos. 6–9 Middle Street (s side), 1987–9 by *Whinney Mackay-Lewis Partnership*, and the boldly patterned Nos. 10–14 beyond, by *Michael Twigg Brown & Partners*, 1986–7, which houses the Farmers' and Fletchers' Hall (q.v.).

MILK STREET

First recorded *c.* 1140 and named from the extension of the Cheapside market here. Remains of substantial C12 stone houses were found on the E side in 1972 and 1977, set over Roman remains which included a C2 town house with a fine mosaic pavement (now in the Museum of London). Two churches were not rebuilt after the Great Fire: St Mary Magdalen Milk Street, on the w side near Cheapside, and All Hallows Honey Lane to the E. The latter's site became a market, for which the younger *Dance* built premises in 1787–93; in 1835 *Bunning*'s Gothic City of London School replaced it (dem. *c.* 1882). The former course of Milk Street into Cheapside, s, was pedestrianized in the 1960s, and the road diverted into Wood Street, passing under Mitre House (*see* Cheapside).

On the E SIDE two office blocks of 1970s design show that decade's interest in synthetic cladding materials. To the N, with a curved corner to Mumford Court, No. 10 (GIROBANK) is a weird affair by *E. G. Chandler* of the *Corporation of London Architect's Department*, 1972–5. Chocolate-brown tiles on the lower and upper storeys, big GRP panels on the two storeys between, with a shallow diamond-embossed pattern below the windows. The upper storeys set back behind odd pierced parapets. Nos. 1–6 to the s, a large block of varying height by *Sidney Kaye, Firmin & Partners*, 1978–82, with mirrored windows and cheap-looking buff corrugated cladding. The s part extends into Russia Row (the name first appears as late as 1810 and may commemorate the Napoleonic Wars).

On the w SIDE of Milk Street, N of Mitre House, Nos. 18–28, lumbering convex-fronted red brick and stone by *S. Peach & Partners*, completed 1959.

MINCING LANE

The name, first recorded in 1189, comes from *mynechene*, the Anglo-Saxon word for nuns. The Abbot of Colchester's Inn lay on the E side from the late C14. On the w side is Plantation House (*see* Fenchurch Street). Before Plantation House, the tea and rubber trades were carried on variously from *Joseph Woods*'s Sale Rooms (E side), 1811–12: a landmark in the shift of business away from the traditional coffee houses. Its replacement, *Lewis Glinton*'s Commercial Sale Rooms, 1859–60, had (as latterly extended) more than 200 offices and sample rooms.

On the E side, N end, the Clothworkers' Hall (q.v.), then beyond Dunster Court the giant MINSTER COURT, three outrageously arch office blocks by *GMW Partnership*, 1987–91, grouped into one jagged pile. It replaced a sequence of mostly 1950s blocks bounded by Mark Lane, Great Tower Street and Dunster Court. The architects have rejected both the slick envelopes of the City's 1970s office towers and the rigorous glamour of the Lloyd's Building (the latest previous addition to the City skyline), in favour of the shock tactics of instant recognizability. All three blocks have rosy polished granite cladding in a bewildering variety of fins and angles, like Hanseatic Gothic done in stiff folded paper. From a distance the dominant feature is the great steep gables with upswept ends, housing the services. An elliptical arcade runs around the ground floor. Main entrance up steps to a court open towards Mincing Lane, with greenish-glazed canopies sloping down from a great height. Facing the street, three naturalistic bronze SCULPTURES of horses by *Althea Wynne*, 1989–90. The plan becomes apparent beyond. Two taller blocks at N (the thirteen-storey No. 1) and NE (the slightly lower No. 2, with STAINED GLASS by *Graham Jones* in the lobby) are separated by a narrow top-glazed passage. Shops and restaurants line a rather constricted lower passage between them, overlooked by the court's upper part. The larger, lower No. 3 on the S, also separated by a top-glazed passage, houses the LONDON UNDERWRITING CENTRE. Interiors by *YRM* (structural engineering *YRM Anthony Hunt Associates*) are arranged on nine floors open to a giant circular atrium. In its centre, a stack of paired escalators (the tallest in the world on completion in 1993), dizzyingly suspended on four clusters of rods. These fan out above to separate suspension points from a giant ring-beam, its centre glazed to the sky. The inspiration is clearly the organization of the Lloyd's Building, where face-to-face business is likewise carried over several floors.

MINORIES

The long straight street runs N–S just outside the former City ditch. So called from the Franciscan convent of Holy Trinity of the Minoresses or Poor Clares, founded by the Earl of Lancaster in 1293, formerly on the E side. Excavations in Haydon Street, 1983, suggested the church's E end was semi-octagonal; other minor remains survive *in situ* (*see* Haydon Street below). Associated postwar finds include the lead coffin of Lady Mowbray and a fine but mutilated carved female figure of *c.* 1335, probably of the 'Old Law'. The convent precinct became the parish of Holy Trinity in 1566, with a church converted from a lesser chapel off St Clare Street. Modestly rebuilt in 1706, destroyed in 1940. Minories also crosses the site of the extensive E ROMAN CEMETERY (*see* Introduction p. 40). Best of the many finds was a stone sarcophagus found off Haydon Street in 1853, with the bust of a young man in a gadrooned medallion, and, inside, a decorated lead coffin.

The walk is from s to N. Minories begins at the busy NE corner of Tower Hill. On the E side, SCEPTRE COURT, a triangular seven-storey island block by *R. Seifert & Partners*, 1986–90. Motifs the shallowest triangular bows, close-set, and glazed corners. Then HAMBROS BANK, a clumsy thick-set block of polished grey-green stone, broken up into upright flat bays of varying height and width. By *R. Seifert & Partners*, 1985–8. It replaced part of a multi-storey CAR AND LORRY PARK, by the *Corporation of London Architect's Department* (*E. G. Chandler*), 1968–70; the E part remains, its concrete finishes unusually good, reeded or aggregate-faced. Student halls of residence, intended to stand on top, remained unbuilt. For the W side opposite, *see* London Guildhall University, Public Buildings. Then the railway bridge to Fenchurch Street, with Tower Gateway station (E side; q.v.).

The rest is a rather down-at-heel mixture of warehouses (mostly of before 1914) and post-war offices, plainer than most City archi-tecture. From s to N: Nos. 52–56, PWS GROUP (E side). By *Halpern & Partners*, 1971–5, job architect *Michael Cousins*. An early appearance of (bright orange) mirrored glass. Curved corner, curved upper storeys stepping back. Long front to Goodman's Yard. Polygonal stair-tower on Minories of exposed board-marked concrete – an incongruous hangover from 1960s fashions. Still on the E side, IBEX HOUSE, offices of 1935–7 by *Fuller, Hall & Foulsham*, streamlined indeed and faced with imperishable slabs of buff and black faience (faithfully restored by *Rolfe Judd*, 1994–5). Long bands of glass (London's longest when new), whizzing round curved corners, most spectacularly on the long side elevations. These have central glazed stairwells, exposed where the floors set back high up. The rigidly symmetrical composition and Deco detailing over the entrances are more conservative.

Off the E side in HAYDON STREET, a sturdy 1860s brick warehouse (N side), sensitively converted to offices in 1988. The basement incorporates the SW corner walls of the Minoresses' cloister. The NE corner is ST CLARE HOUSE, by *Howard, Fairbairn & Partners*, 1956–7. Quite boldly composed for the date: towards Minories a five-storey light-brown-brick block, behind it at r. angles a thirteen-storey slab with blue curtain-walling, surmounted by a slightly higher stair-tower. Then the tall THREE LORDS pub, dated 1890 but a replica of 1985. Opposite (W side), run-of-the-mill commercial: No. 135, a broad-fronted warehouse with segmental pediment, by *R. George Bare*, 1910; modest post-war offices at Nos. 139–141 (*Hammett & Norton*, 1964–5), Nos. 142–144 (*W. Holford & Partners*, 1971–3), Nos. 146–154 (two 1950s blocks refronted *c.* 1978 by *Tanner & Partners*). Back on the E side, set back overlooking Aldgate Bus Station, a giant develop-ment by *Trehearne & Norman, Preston & Partners*, 1977–81, on former railway land. Central thirteen-storey slab (LATHAM HOUSE), flanked by convex six-storey wings, the N one rather longer. The central block is also curved at the s end. All have close-set fins faced in rust-red aggregate chips, bronzed floor panels and tinted windows. The scheme includes a garden and housing estate behind (*see* Mansell Street).

The rest of the E side has the modest Nos. 6–12, 1891–3, with second-floor balconies corbelled out, and Nos. 2–5 by *Keith Dalton & Associates*, 1986–8, with rounded verticals and green cladding. On the w corner, the former Portsoken House, by *G. Val Myer*, 1927–8. Tall stone-faced c20 commercial, emphatically earlier in style than Ibex House; without the simplicity of the architect's Broadcasting House, Westminster (1931). French classical ornament in scattered patches.

MITRE STREET *see* CREECHURCH LANE

MONUMENT STREET

The original setting of the Monument was a modest space called Monument Yard, on the E side of Fish Street Hill. When London Bridge was rebuilt further w after 1829, a new street (called Arthur Street East) was cut through to it from King William Street. Then in 1884–7 an extension was made from the E end into Lower Thames Street, easing traffic from Billingsgate, and the present name bestowed.

Starting at the Monument, the sw and nw corners belong with King William Street. At the NE, nicely stepped back, No. 45 Fish Street Hill, offices for Lloyds Bank completed 1967 by *David Landaw*. Eight storeys, stone-faced, with a glazed-in section of ped-way, l. Opposite (s side), GARTMORE HOUSE (No. 18), stone-faced, with weedy columns to each floor and a turret echoing St Magnus's lantern, s. By *Colhern & Phillips*, 1985–7. A ped-way route along its w side turns E into CENTURION HOUSE, by *GMW Partnership*, 1980–4. This is grey stone-clad, strongly vertical, much broken up with narrow windows boxed out at the top, shallow set-backs along Lower Thames Street, and steps down to preserve views of the Monument, w.

Beyond Pudding Lane, FARYNERS HOUSE (N side), by *R. Seifert & Partners*, 1969–71. Sharp-edged window bands, aggregate-faced floors. Massive Y-shaped piers, which the practice then favoured almost regardless of context, are used to dramatic effect along the Botolph Lane roadway. By the same practice PENINSULAR HOUSE opposite, 1979–83. Eight-storey slab to Lower Thames Street, raised on a podium for the ped-way, with a bridge across to the s. The slab's two lower storeys extend up to the line of Monument Street. Polished red Finnish granite facing, smoked-glass windows, divided by narrow slots into shallow bays. It replaced *inter alia Peebles*'s Billingsgate Buildings, 1888–90, for the dried fish trade.

Beyond Botolph Lane (N side), a scrubby open court, the former CHURCHYARD of St Botolph Billingsgate. Could the iron GATES be c18, reset? The church, destroyed in 1666, stood s of Lower

Thames Street (q.v.). E of the churchyard, Nos. 33–37, replicated late C19 red brick and terracotta, and Nos. 41–43, brown brick and stone, eccentrically detailed, with an onion dome like the turret of S.P. Cockerell's St Anne Soho, Westminster, and a ship for a weathervane; both of 1982–5, part of the *Thomas Saunders Partnership*'s City Village scheme (*see* Lovat Lane). On the E corner with Lovat Lane, No. 47, the WALRUS AND CARPENTER, a Dutch-flavoured pub dated 1889 in yellow glazed brick, by *J.A. Ashton*.

MOORFIELDS

Known as Little Moorfields until 1878. Hollar's map (1666) shows the W side built up, facing a tree-lined strip separated by houses along Moorgate Street from the open space of Moorfields proper (see Moorgate).

The present E side belongs with Moorgate; the W side with the Barbican–London Wall redevelopment. At its S end, a large complex by *Leo Hannen Associates*, completed 1973. Seven-storey slab to the street, its grey floor panels with jagged relief pattern. On the ground floor shops and the new Moorgate station entrance. Balcony-like abutment, l., for an unbuilt extension of the ped-way. Escalators lead to a paved upper court made over the station platforms, connecting with the walkway along London Wall, S. Slightly lower W slab, with a gloomy passage to a narrower court and a matching parallel slab to Moor Lane. N side lower still, partly brick-faced, with an irritating parapet with flimsy concrete segmental arches. In Moor Lane was the last new Anglican church built in the City: *Cockerell*'s short-lived St Bartholomew (1847–1902), the nominal successor to Wren's St Bartholomew Exchange.

Further N, two more grey-clad slabs, the nearer and better *Cotton, Ballard & Blow*'s TENTER HOUSE of 1962–4, aligned E–W. Uprights recessed between floor bands, windows further recessed. Named from the vanished Tenter Street, so called from the tenter-grounds for drying cloth in the old Moorfields. MOORFIELDS HOUSE, by *Alan W. Pipe & Partners*, 1962–5, raised on pilotis, forms the E side of the forecourt of Britannic Tower (*see* Ropemaker Street).

MOORGATE

Moorgate runs N from Lothbury for almost a third of a mile, to the City's N boundary. It was laid out in two stages. Much the most recent is the S part (called Moorgate Street until 1921), cut through in the 1830s in connection with the rebuilding of London Bridge. It bisected several little alleys from Coleman Street to the W, as may still be seen (King's Arms Yard, Great Swan Alley, etc.). It provided an approach from the S to where the old MOORGATE stood in London Wall (demolished 1760). The main gate dated only from 1415, when a small medieval postern was replaced by a major structure at the cost of Thomas Falconer, Mercer (there may have been a

Roman postern here, although this is not established). Rebuilt in 1472, then in 1672 (by *Thomas Cartwright Sen.*) as a three-storey pedimented structure rather like old Temple Bar.

The street's N part originated in 1415, when a causeway was made from the new gate along the W side of the marshy open space called Moorfields (hence its older names Moorfields Pavement or Finsbury Pavement: the latter still current for the part outside the City). There was a fairly large cemetery here in Roman times. The name Moorfields is recorded by 1068. For centuries the City could find little use for it but the winter skating on bones described by Fitzstephen, *c.* 1174, or quarrying brick-earth for the City wall repairs of 1477. Drainage was achieved thereafter by dumping rubbish to raise the ground. Part was set aside for archery in 1498, and when Stow wrote (1598) Moorfields was 'a garden to the city . . . for citizens to walk and take the air and for merchants' maids to dry clothes in'. In 1605–13 it was laid out as a park, with formal avenues and trees. *Hooke*'s Bethlehem Hospital rose on its S side in 1675–6, but wholesale development began only in 1778 (Act obtained 1768), when Finsbury Square was laid out on the N part, to *Dance the Younger*'s plan (*see London 4: North*). In the 1790s Dance planned the present Finsbury Circus and Eldon Street within the City (qq.v.). Dance's houses on the E side here fell to street widening, *c.* 1900.

From Lothbury north to London Wall

This S part was originally lined with even stuccoed ranges of 1835–9. *Smirke* designed their façades as more modest versions of his King William Street fronts, unpedimented and mostly astylar (*see* also Nash's contemporary West Strand Improvements, Westminster). Architects such as *E. I'Anson* seem to have been responsible for the mixture of offices and domestic accommodation behind, again on the model of Nash's developments. Stone-faced offices began to replace them *c.* 1885, and in 1927 it was estimated that half had already gone. A single terrace survives on the W side, by London Wall. Otherwise, banks and insurance offices predominate, the best dating from 1890–1930. There has been much rebuilding since *c.* 1985.

Beginning at the S, the corner buildings belong with Lothbury (q.v.). Then on the E side BROWN, SHIPLEY & CO. (No. 2), 1970–5 by *Fitzroy Robinson & Partners*. A striking, high-relief design in dark-brown stone (Blaubrun granodiorite). Four bays of large windows in splayed moulded frames. The upper storeys have lesser mullions, making two lights. Bronze DOORS by *John Poole*, with sculpted bosses. Matching façade to St Margaret's churchyard. The trading house of Brown, Shipley moved here from Liverpool in 1863, originally to the old Central Electric Telegraph building (*see* Founders' Court, Lothbury). No. 4 is the former British Bank of South America, by *Dunn & Watson*, 1913–15. Neo-Palladian, with an applied order on a rustic base. Byzantinizing capitals like those on the practice's earlier Scottish Provident Institution in Lombard Street. Two pilastered upper stories are an unfortunate addition by *Fitzroy Robinson & Partners*, *c.* 1976.

Opposite (W side), two nicely contrasting blocks of the 1890s. BASILDON HOUSE (Nos. 7–11), office chambers by *Gordon, Lowther & Gunton*, 1897–9, is opulent and rather vulgar, in a free Renaissance turning Baroque style. Giant order of polished Peterhead and Rubislaw granite on the upper floors, made square at the corners. Large central segmental bow over the entrance, big urns above. The N front to King's Arms Yard hardly less grandiose. Sympathetically detailed attic and mansard of 1988–92, by the *Whinney Mackay-Lewis Partnership*. They retained the fine wrought-iron entrance gates and some ground-floor halls, which have octagonal-coffered ceilings. Its companion is Nos. 13–15 (ARAB BANK), designed as the Metropolitan Life Assurance Society headquarters by *Aston Webb & Ingress Bell*, 1890–3. Here is a richness of craftsmanship, as against Basildon House's richness of materials. The idiom is Franco-Flemish, as popularized by Sir Ernest George, but carried out in Portland stone, not brick. Windows are arranged in rigid horizontal panels defined by sheer stone bands. A flamboyant polygonal angle tower with spiky spirelet, richly ornamented, contrasts arrestingly with these smooth bands. On the oriel and elsewhere, sculpted Virtues in niches by *Frith*. The top windows are smaller and twice as narrowly set. Steep slated roof, with dormers and chimneystacks. No interiors survive. The façades have been rebuilt behind twice: first in 1966, a pioneering scheme that achieved a 25 per cent increase in office space, then in 1986–9, with Nos. 51–55 Coleman Street (q.v.). *Fitzroy Robinson & Partners* did both jobs.

Back on the E side, Nos. 8–10, the former National Bank of New Zealand, 1921–2, one of several blocks for the Clothworkers' Company here by their surveyor *Henry Tanner*. Much Grecian ornament, squared off. At Nos. 12–18 a new building by *Frederick Gibberd, Coombes & Partners* is in progress (1997).

Between the two, TELEGRAPH STREET was developed by the Clothworkers' Company in the 1870s from the E part of Great Bell Alley. Telegraph companies and stockbrokers occupied such buildings as No. 8 (S side), 1874 by *Edward Browning* of Stamford, of stone, with free Gothic detail intelligently done. The little red brick No. 1, *c.* 1905 with blocked columns, constricts the E exit to Copthall Avenue.

Back in Moorgate, No. 17, CREDITO ITALIANO (W side), 1969–72 by *Fitzroy Robinson & Partners*, has projecting floor bands of rough Portland stone and a long front to Great Bell Alley. Nos. 19–21, 1919–21, anonymous, by Messrs *Joseph*. The characterful No. 23, 1979–81 by the *Rolfe Judd Group Practice*, has visually unsupported leaded projections marking the narrow storeys. Little medallion-like bosses ornament them. Then the PROVIDENT MUTUAL LIFE ASSURANCE (Nos. 25–31), by *Campbell-Jones, Son, & Smithers*, 1920–2. The broad façade is treated in relief, with giant pilasters and flat half-urns. Channelled piers emphasize the off-centre entrance bay. Nos. 33–39, of 1966, was refaced in 1984 in white stone by *Cecil Denny Highton & Partners*, with partly projecting floors and a huge sloping mansard. NORTHGATE HOUSE opposite (E side) has canted metal-panelled bays connecting the windows vertically between channelled masonry piers: an appealing composition. N part by *Fred. W. Marks*, 1920–2, S extension by *Tanner*, 1937, with bays more widely spaced. Demolition is proposed (1996).

Still on the E side, LLOYDS BANK (Nos. 30–34), by *Whinney Mackay-Lewis Partnership*, 1986–9. Dense, chunky stone forms corbel out slightly from the ground floor. Narrower windows above, double-spaced; corner turret. The effect is like a paraphrase of some office chambers of the 1880s. Facing Great Swan Alley, a bronze sculpture of a swan in flight. No. 36, the former Ocean Accident, by *Sir Aston Webb & Son*, dated 1928. The Commercial Union, Webb's patron, had taken over the company in 1910. Webb's new building is subtle and inventive. Five strongly rectilinear bays with paired giant pilasters at the ends. Mullioned triple windows between, with simplest recessed mouldings. Above, an attic with mullions treated as shaped piers, a larger top cornice, then storeys set back. Much playful nautical detailing: seahorses, ship's-prow capitals, and in a corner niche a charming sculpted lighthouse (with working light) and a galleon in relief. To MOORGATE PLACE behind, reached through a passage to the r., is a tall pedimented front, its five upper storeys diminishing within a single giant panel. Small upright windows, grouped 2–3–2. Big square chimneystacks above. The rear of the passage preserves a section of Ocean Buildings, 1900–3 by *W.H. Atkin-Berry* of *Kidner & Berry*. Free Tudor red brick and stone, to match Ocean's previous (demolished) headquarters by *Huntly Gordon*, 1894, on the N side of Moorgate Place. The Institute of Chartered Accountants lies on the E side (q.v.).

Back to Moorgate for No. 41 (w side), 1977–8 by *Sidney Kaye, Firmin & Partners*: window bands between polished stone, conventionally done. No. 51, by *Fitzroy Robinson Partnership*, 1985–7, symmetrical, in brown granite with shallow all-over rustication. Deeply-recessed first- and fourth-floor balconies, contrasting upright windows set flush between. A mysteriously lit groin-vaulted passage leads to Coleman Street. No. 55, by the *T.P. Bennett Partnership*, 1986–90, in polished grey stone. A domineering composition rather like a 1920s office block, except that the windows in their narrow bays project rather than recede. Atrium at fourth-floor level. Nos. 63–73 survive from *Smirke*'s stucco fronts. The symmetrical four-storeyed terrace has round-headed first-floor windows and intermittent balustrade. Rounded corner to a return façade to London Wall. They were amongst the last to go up (occupied 1841). Good shopfronts of *c.* 1900 to Nos. 67–69, of the recessed entrance type.

On the E side, No. 46, by *T.P. Bennett & J.D. Hossack*, 1925, tall and narrow, with large windows grouped in a single big panel. Nos. 48–54 by *Alan W. Pipe & Sons*, 1955–7, stodgy. Nos. 56–60 by *Richardson & Gill*, 1922, a discreet palazzo composition, but with ground-floor columns and segment-headed mezzanine windows. *T.P. Bennett & Son*'s HALIFAX (Nos. 62–64), 1932, Deco, has a rounded corner turret to London Wall.

From London Wall north to the City Boundary

The oldest part of the street. London Wall dramatically opens up on the w side (q.v.). At the NW, Moor House, the first of London

Wall's office towers, overlooks a little garden. On its N side, a group of older houses, originally part of Fore Street (*see* London Wall). No. 83 (E corner) and No. 118 adjacent, are late Georgian under fancy French stucco of *c.* 1875. No. 118 (FOX's umbrellas) has an excellent Modern front of 1937 made by *Pollard*, in black 131 Vitrolite, stainless steel and neon; contemporary interior. Unaltered late Georgian survivors at No. 118a (W corner), and at No. 87 in Moorgate, one of several houses built by *Henry & John Lee*, 1833–4. Its red brick is unusual for that date. No. 8 Moorfields, behind, is of the same build.

Opposite (E side), Electra House (now part of LONDON GUILDHALL UNIVERSITY), still dominates the street. 1900–3 by *Belcher & Joass*, for the Eastern Telegraph Company, with much lettable space. It should be compared with the less emphatic monster office blocks of the period in Finsbury Circus behind. Six storeys, with a giant order high up. Octagonal central dome set over a concave section above the main cornice. The relief diminishes from bulgy bands on the ground floor to degrees of channelling above, but the effect is not subtle. Much sculpture dotted about, its impact slight on such a scale. Indeed the decline is palpable from the finely calculated games of Belcher's nearby Institute of Chartered Accountants twelve years before (Pevsner in 1957 found Electra House 'bragging and unoriginal'). Sculptors include *Frampton* (spandrels by the entrance, of figures receiving and transmitting messages), *Goscombe John* (allegorical reliefs of India, China etc., third floor, centre), and *F. W. Pomeroy* (reliefs in the entrance, cherubs supporting the openwork bronze globe on the dome). Other carving by *C. J. Allen* and *Herbert Hampton*. Free Ionic columns to the portal, with droll little dolphins in the bronze capitals. More columns to the double-height barrel-vaulted entrance hall. The end wall has a first-floor balcony. Coarse stained glass in the lunette designed by *Powell*; painted decoration by *George Murray* does not survive. An intended S extension was not built. The present well-composed and attractive corner block is by *R. E. Enthoven* and *R. J. Mock*, 1959. The Moorgate front matches Electra House in height, the London Wall front rises taller behind.

For Britannic House N of Electra House *see* Finsbury Circus.

On the W side, the former AMRO bank, 1975–81 by *Trehearne & Norman, Preston & Partners*: a long mute slab in warm-coloured Sardinian beige granite, with windows recessed in an even chamfered grid. The entrance has a modest atrium, amongst the first in the City. The big hole in the front was for an unrealized section of ped-way, from which views into the atrium were intended.

No. 141 (MOORGATE STATION), by *T. Phillips Figgis*, 1900, was the head office of the City and South London Railway Company, which started the first tube line. Red brick with stone bands à la Scotland Yard, big triangular gable, and a round corner turret with columns round the top. The delightful coat of arms above the Moorgate entrance shows tube trains passing under the Thames. Ground floor altered *c.* 1976, the rest reconstructed 1984–7, reversing post-war alterations to the bomb-damaged Moorfields front. Then a long block by *Chapman Taylor & Partners* for Land Securities, 1988–90 (replacing *Richardson &*

Gill's pioneering stripped-classical Moorgate Hall, 1915–16). Six strongly articulated storeys in polished grey and pink granite. Shallow off-centre entrance bay, with shops beyond. Porthole windows on the first floor. FINSBURY PAVEMENT HOUSE on the E corner, by *R. Seifert & Partners*, 1971–2, has aggregate-faced floors and the trademark Y-shaped pier. For the block across South Place, N, *see* Eldon Street. In the distance appears the extra-ordinary rocket-shaped stone tower of *Joass*'s Royal London House, on the N side of Finsbury Square (1928).

NEW BRIDGE STREET

A broad and busy street, made *c.* 1764 as an approach to the new Blackfriars Bridge. It follows the line of the Fleet River, previously canalized between new quays under *Wren*'s supervision, 1670–4 (*see* Farringdon Street). The 1860s brought upheavals: Ludgate Circus cut into the N end, the railway pushed through behind the E side, and the Victoria Embankment and Queen Victoria Street barged across just N of the bridge. The S section was again reconstructed after 1963 for the Blackfriars Underpass.

On the W side, the section up to Tudor Street was the site of the former BRIDEWELL HOSPITAL, originally Henry VIII's Bridewell Palace (1515–23), two irregular brick-built courtyards, very plain by comparison with Nonsuch or Hampton Court. Excavations in 1978 found the E range of the main courtyard, with fragments of a gallery which ran S at r. angles from the hall to a Thames-side gate (*see* also Tudor Street). In 1553 Edward VI gave the palace to the City, who used it until 1855 as a school, workhouse and prison. Then in 1872–3 Bridewell Place was laid out across its site (q.v.).

The remains of a ROMAN SHIPWRECK, found in 1962 during preliminary work on the embankment, are displayed at the Tower Hill Pageant, Tower Hill (q.v.). A flat-bottomed sailing ship some 52 ft (16 metres) long, built *c.* A.D. 140 for coastal and inland waters, had sunk later in the C2 with a cargo of Kentish ragstone, thought to have been for the town wall.

The best buildings are on the W side. From the N: No. 2, THE ALBION, 1862, typically fancy. Then Nos. 7–8, red brick with lighter trim, 1983–5 by *Elsom Pack & Roberts Partnership*. An applied arcade embracing the lower floors hints at the historicist revival. After Bride Lane, Nos. 10–12, FLEET HOUSE, by *Shingler & Risdon*, 1957–61, with cylindrical piers supporting the upper floors. The bulky building facing is No. 100, part of *RHWL Partnership*'s redevelopment of Holborn Viaduct station and its approaches, 1990–2 (*see* also Fleet Place). Near-symmetrical to the street, the upper parts broken up. Dull pink Sardinian granite cladding, cut back at the ends, as if to expose the grey-glass panelling. Also of grey glass two broad three-storey bows, the N one a storey higher, as if forced up by the entrance. Bright mosaic-faced canopy by *Brian Clarke*, with matching abstract stained glass at the entrance.

The S corner with Bridewell Place is No. 13, by *Richard Roberts*, 1873–4, eclectic gault brick in the Holborn Viaduct manner, once one of a pair. No. 14 is the former BRIDEWELL GATEHOUSE, from the rebuilding of the E range of Bridewell Hospital by *James Lewis*, 1802–8. A graceful stone-faced three-bay front with giant Tuscan pilasters and pediment, with none of the rusticated terrorism of Dance's Newgate. Pretty keystone head of Edward VI; good railings and lamps (surviving interiors: the barrel-vaulted entrance, cantilevered stone staircase off to its r., and good rooms of domestic character, one with a rear bow). The rear (board-room) range of 1865–70, demolished 1978, incorporated four prison cells from the hospital's former E range in its basement. No. 15 has a sophisticated channelled stone front probably of 1908–9, with delicate motifs of late C18 derivation; early C19 fabric may survive behind. The corner with Tudor Street is Nos. 16–18, built in 1903–5 for the London Missionary Society by *Spalding & Spalding* and *H. Cheston*: a beetling free Baroque mass in the Belcher manner, the separate parts not well integrated.

On the E side, Nos. 35–38 by *Stone Toms Stephenson*, 1983–6, stone-clad, coarse, with canted bays. Part of the realigned CITY WALL of 1283–1320, found here in 1984, is preserved beneath. It was some six feet across, widening at the N, perhaps to buttress a bridge across the Fleet known to have continued on the line of Apothecary Street. Construction was of good ashlar mixed with rag and flint rubble, with brick repairs probably of the 1670s. Then Nos. 30–34, NEW BRIDGE STREET HOUSE, 1913–14 by *Robert Angell*, with an applied Ionic order and dormered mansard. Its unsightly party wall spoils the view from the S.

On the W side again, the contemporary BLACKFRIARS HOUSE, built by *F. W. Troup*, 1913–17 as Spicer Brothers' warehouse and office. A much more radical and honest treatment of a steel frame – more logical indeed than all but a handful of English pre-First-World-War commercial designs. The structure of the eight-storey block is expressed as a functional grid, its white facing (*Doulton*'s Carraraware) given simplified classical piers. The top two storeys read as a kind of giant cornice. Windows here originally had paired lights in the Victorian office tradition, destroyed by crude uniform refenestration in 1976. Troup's Arts-and-Crafts loyalties emerge in the fine iron railings (first floor), and in the obelisk entrance piers.

Then UNILEVER HOUSE, by Lever Bros.' architect *J. Lomax Simpson*, with *Burnet, Tait & Partners*, 1930–2.* Largest of the City's interwar prestige headquarters, less austere than Burnet's Lloyds Bank, Cornhill, but simpler than Lutyens's 1920s palaces. It replaced the vast De Keyser's Royal Hotel (1874), taken over by Lever Bros. in 1921. The composition can be taken in at a glance in long views. A giant stone quadrant curves down to the Victoria Embankment, with a projecting heavily rusticated ground floor (windowless to reduce traffic noise, and top-lit from behind the parapet), diminishing rustication with round-headed windows above, then giant Ionic columns between the fourth and sixth floors. At each end stone entrance projections surmounted by

---

* A note by Simpson in the RIBA Library (1973) claims exclusive credit, demoting Burnet and Tait to rubber-stamping the final design; but they exhibited it as a joint work with Simpson at the Royal Academy, and the City of London Record Office has drawings signed by them alone.

28 strenuous giant figures restraining horses (Controlled Energy), by
    Sir William Reid Dick; below, mermaid and merman by *Gilbert
    Ledward*. Excessively naturalistic parapet figures by *Nicholas
    Munro*, added during a generally sensitive refurbishment in
    1977–83 (consultant *Theo Crosby*). Windows were pierced through
    the attic to make a new storey, and a new N entrance lobby made,
    with eclectic Neo-Art Deco lights, columns and other fittings. The
    space flows into a new N extension up to Tudor Street, giving it a
    rather confusing shape. Stained glass at the N entrance by *Amber
    Hiscott*. Further in, a giant hardwood screen from Nigeria and
    other imported works of various dates referring to the company's
    activities. (In the lifts, panels designed by *Eric Gill*, 1930–2.)

Back on the E side, the Black Friar pub and the offices W of
    Blackfriars station belong with Queen Victoria Street. Nearer the
    bridge, the line of the waterfront before the Underpass came is
    marked by a red brick warehouse of *c.* 1885 (No. 181 Queen
    Victoria Street), with rounded corners and dominant horizontals.
    In front, a granite DRINKING FOUNTAIN of 1861, with a bronze
    Woman of Samaria by *Wills Bros*. Further S, *C. B. Birch*'s STATUE
    of Queen Victoria (1896) stands sentinel in the roadway.

NEW BROAD STREET

A short semi-pedestrianized street of offices between Old Broad
Street, E, and Blomfield Street, W. In origin a C17 close called Petty
Wales; renamed when Old Broad Street was extended past the E
end *c.* 1737. The present curious numbering remains from when this
N extension was also called New Broad Street.

Buildings on the N SIDE, all of 1907–8, still have early Edwardian
    exuberance. From W to E, No. 42 (SWEDBANK) by *Ernest Flint*,
    with blocked Ionic columns by the outswept central oriel and
    lunettes above; Nos. 39–41, FRIARS HOUSE, plainer, by *A. C.
    Blomfield*; No. 35, the former Egypt House, by *F. W. Marks*, with
    carved sphinxes etc. by *Daymond & Son*. All three rebuilt behind
    by *T. P. Bennett Partnership*, 1989–90, destroying early concrete
    framing at Friars House (*Kahn* system, its first English use).

The S SIDE begins at No. 53 (W), 1885, built for the CLRP Co.,
    probably by its architect *Edwin Crockett*, according to Robert
    Thorne. Superimposed pilaster-piers, a familiar treatment. Rebuilt
    behind by *Casson Conder Partnership*, *c.* 1988.

Then CABLE HOUSE, a long front by *Paul Hoffman*, 1905–6, red
    brick above stone. Symmetrical but loose, like a mansion block
    (Hoffman's speciality). It is specially interesting for what remains
    of *Voysey*'s only surviving commercial interiors, 1906–10, designed
    for the Essex & Suffolk Equitable Insurance, whose Secretary
    S. C. Turner commissioned a Voysey house at Frinton, Essex, in
    1905. They have been partly re-created by *William Nimmo &
    Partners* (for Haslemere Estates), who rebuilt Cable House behind
    the façade in 1986–9. Voysey is announced in the hanging oak
    sign by the E entrance and in the r. windows, with even glazing
    bars and heraldic glass panels. In the area below, more windows
    and a simple oak door with tapering ironwork, all reset. Though

his furniture has gone, Voysey's unique blend of friendliness and fastidiousness can still be enjoyed. Tall black-marble lobby fireplace, with shaped gabled overmantel and gilt crosses for ornament. Simple stripy tiled hearth. Stairhall behind with characteristic close-set oak balustrade screen (originally unvarnished), square newels and arched iron overthrows. Reconstructed to lead down to the basement, where two former ground-floor rooms are reassembled in their old relationship. Their semi-open layout was more spacious than the Edwardian commercial norm. The Clerks' Office has simple glazed semicircular openings to the corridor. Inside, a shallow colonnade of square black-marble-faced piers. Two more fireplaces here, with semicircular gables. The l. one has the company's arms, the r. an octagonal-faced clock. Two more in the Manager's Office. A glazed opening overlooked the clerks at work. Panelled dado with built-in cupboards, their hinges and locks with Voysey's trademark heart-shaped piercings.

NEWBURY STREET see MIDDLE STREET

NEW FETTER LANE

Created after the war in the badly destroyed area between Fetter Lane and Farringdon Street, supplanting the N part of Fetter Lane as a main N–S route.

At the NE corner, the confused red brick minimum-Georgian complex of THAVIES INN HOUSE by *Lewis Solomon, Son & Joseph*, with a bank of 1939 to Holborn Circus and a taller, plainer slab to New Fetter Lane behind, 1955–60. On the same side, the curtain-walled ORBIT HOUSE by *Anderson, Forster & Wilcox*, 1958–60 (demolition proposed). (Bartlett Court, into New Street Square to the S, preserves the name of Bartlett's Buildings, a vanished court of late C17 houses of which fifteen survived as late as 1929.)

On the W side, after the *Daily Mirror* site (*see* Holborn), the former W. H. SMITH, by *Casson, Conder & Partners*, 1972–6. An irregularly polygonal tower, friendly despite its eleven storeys, with oriels corbelled out on the lead-clad uppermost storeys. Oriels, upright fenestration and modelling owe much to the practice's slightly earlier NatWest building, Manchester. A long W wing accommodates BARTLETT'S PASSAGE, an alley connecting with Fetter Lane, to which it has a flush brick front with alternate bays recessed above.

NEWGATE STREET

A busy main road that merges with Holborn Viaduct at the W end. The plan of a Roman-type GATE was established by excavations in 1875, 1903, and 1909. It had a double roadway flanked by guard-room towers projecting beyond the City wall, 18 ft (5½ metres) to the N and 8 ft (2½ metres) to the S. Before the wall was built, this area was suburban: excavations for the British Telecom building (N side)

in 1978–9 revealed much about late C1 and early C2 roadside buildings here (*see* Introduction p. 31). Cremation burials and pottery
kilns have also been found, and the Museum of London contains an
amusing graffito scratched by a disgruntled workman on a tile:
'Austalis has been going off on his own every day for thirteen days'.

The medieval Newgate was rebuilt at least three times: possibly in
the C12; in 1423–32 (by Whittington's executors); and in 1672. It
was the last City gate to be demolished, in 1776–7, fifteen years after
the others. The prisoners it housed were removed to Dance's new
gaol to the S (*see* Central Criminal Court, Public Buildings). A meat
market was held in the street between at least the C12 and the 1860s.
Remains of St Nicholas Shambles, closed 1551, were found at the
British Telecom site: they suggested an C11 foundation, with extensions up to the C16. On the N side was the Franciscan or Grey
Friars' House, founded in 1225. CHRIST'S HOSPITAL took over its
buildings in 1552. The school's post-Fire premises were variously by
Peter Mills, *Hooke*, and *Oliver* (1667–83), with *Wren* and *Hawksmoor*
(Sir John Moore's Writing School, 1692–5); notable later work by
James Lewis (1793) and *John Shaw Sen.* (1820–32, including the
Gothic Great Hall). These were demolished after Christ's Hospital
moved to Horsham in 1902, and the site divided between the
G.P.O., S and W, and St Bartholomew's Hospital, NE (*see* Public
Buildings).* All that remains is the carcase of Wren's Christ Church
(q.v.), corresponding to the chancel of the friars' church.

The interest of the N SIDE is the run of 1870s commercial buildings
W of Christ Church. First Nos. 102–103, then *T. Chamberlain*'s
grander Nos. 104–105, 1876–7, a brick warehouse with pedimented doorcases and windows variously shaped. After the
former G.P.O., No. 114 by *Alfred M. Ridge*, 1876–7, also in a
businesslike Italo-French style. By contrast, Nos. 115–117, by *Ford
& Hesketh*, 1879, are Queen Anne of the gabled Ernest George
type. Nos. 118–126 again by *Ridge*, 1874–5. Nos. 118–125 make
one long symmetrical composition: outer parts with round-headed
windows, more ornate centre with second-floor aedicules.
No. 126, the VIADUCT TAVERN, curves to the corner with
Giltspur Street. Fine interior of 1899 by *Arthur Dixon*, with the
usual carved panelling, cut glass etc.; also three large PAINTINGS
of women in publican's Burne-Jones manner, signed *Hal*.
The E part of the S SIDE belongs with St Paul's Churchyard (q.v.).
Then Nos. 6–9 by *Ronald Ward & Partners*, 1964–6, dull (for the
C17 relief on the front *see* Warwick Lane). Nos. 4–5, SVENSKA
HOUSE, 1971–3 by *R. Seifert & Partners*: sharp and clean-lined,
with five close-set bays defined by narrow slits in the polished
black granite cladding.

NEW STREET

An L-shaped street, once Hand Alley, renamed and partly rebuilt in
1782. Excavation here in 1978 found extensive remains of C17
houses and gardens and associated cottage industries of the nascent

_____

* Two of *Shaw*'s gatehouses were re-erected at Horsham. Parts of the Great Hall survive at Christ's Hospital School for Girls, Hertford.

East End. Late Georgian warehouses built for the East India Company tower over the s and e sides (*see* Cutler Street). Lesser, Victorian warehouses on the n side, with a few older domestic survivors.

Starting at the entrance from Bishopsgate, Nos. 1–2 (altered) and 3–4, not large, are both by *Charles Bell*, 1882–4, with typical slim iron colonnettes. Nos. 3–4, of white Suffolk brick, had early gas-fired air-conditioning by the *Aeolus Ventilating Co.* of Holborn, for H. W. Eaton & Sons, silk brokers. Then Nos. 5–7, late c18 brick houses with pedimented doorcases on unfluted columns with Adam-style capitals. Nos. 10–11, a tough brick warehouse of 1870, round-arched at the top. Probably by *N. S. Joseph*.

At the corner, the MAGPIE pub, *c.* 1830, with tripartite windows and what looks like the original pilastered front. Where New Street turns n, the vista is closed by a rusticated pilastered archway surmounted by a free-standing ram. It leads to the courtyard of No. 21 (formerly Cooper's wool warehouse), a large bare brick mass with a few remaining segment-headed windows. All by *Herbert Williams*, 1863–4 (top storey 1868). Converted to offices 1981–2, with ground-floor alterations. The courtyard's e side, along the alley called Cock Hill, is a diminutive mid-c19 brick warehouse (restored 1996, adding a matching third storey).

NEW STREET SQUARE

The centrepiece of the area between New Fetter Lane and Farringdon Street, redeveloped after severe war damage as a sequence of forbidding big blocks. The streets here were laid out in the 1650s by the Goldsmiths' Company, who named East and West Harding Streets to the s after the donor of the land in 1513.

The square has always had buildings rather than a garden in the middle (cf. old Paternoster Square, St Paul's Churchyard). Currently it is *R. Seifert & Partners*' No. 25, 1967–8, a seven-storey block with chamfered corners, its precast members and splayed stilts typical of the firm's later 1960s work. At the ne corner a twelve-storey automatic CAR PARK by *H. V. Lobb & Partners*, 1962–3, concrete and dark brick. Along the s side, bisecting the pre-war line of Great New Street, NEWSPAPER HOUSE, by *R. Seifert & Partners*, 1957–9. Brown brick with window bands, the ground floor open to a forecourt on the s. By the entrance in the e return wing, a streamlined SCULPTURE of three printers by *Dudeney*. Attached at the s, *T. P. Bennett & Son*'s CEDRIC HOUSE, 1983–5, smoked glass above reeded concrete, entered from EAST HARDING STREET. On the s side here, *Seifert*'s PEMBERTON HOUSE, 1954, with another carved figure outside (also by *Dudeney*?).

NICHOLAS LANE

First mentioned 1244. It runs n–s between Lombard Street and Cannon Street, across the line of King William Street. Named from the former church of St Nicholas Acon, which stood until 1666 in the N part, W side, beneath the National Westminster Bank (*see* Lombard Street). Extant in 1084, and no older than the second quarter of the C11, the date of a coin discovered beneath the foundations during excavation in 1963–4. Later S aisle and W extension.

Opposite, No. 33 is an early building by *Collcutt*, 1875. Narrow with a bargeboarded dormer. One window of six lights on each floor with a transom. Coving below the dormer, a motif favoured e.g. by Philip Webb. It has incised decoration. Adjoining, l., Nos. 34–37, the solidly old-fashioned retained façade of *J. Macvicar Anderson*'s National Bank of Scotland, 1907. Eight bays, rusticated with large masks below, two-light windows with granite colonnettes above. Top storey added by *Waterhouse & Ripley*, 1976–82, when the front was incorporated into Nos. 24–28 Lombard Street.

In the S part, Nos. 12–13 by *Thomas Saunders & Associates*, 1979–82, curtain-walled with a slightly bowed front, and No. 14, refronted *c.* 1974 by *Sidney Kaye, Firmin & Partners* in brown polished granite.

NOBLE STREET

Interesting for the vantage point it gives of remains of the Roman wall. It continues the line of Foster Lane N of Gresham Street to London Wall. Thomas le Noble held property here *c.* 1322, though the Middle Ages also called it Foster Lane indiscriminately. Every building was destroyed in the Blitz. Chief loss was the Coachmakers' Hall at the NE (rebuilt by *William Young* for the Scriveners' Company, 1671–5, and rebuilt for the Coachmakers in 1870 by *F. Chancellor* retaining post-Fire woodwork). On the site stood *Gunton & Gunton*'s Shelley House (1958–60, dem. 1996), one of the more attractive low blocks of the London Wall scheme (q.v.).

After the war the W side was cleared and not rebuilt. At the S end St Anne and St Agnes (q.v.) faces the street across a garden. N of here, overlooked by ruinous walls redolent of the Blitz, the remains of the ROMAN WALL are laid out in a wide trench along the street. Excavations of 1950–1 showed that it consisted in fact of two constructions, one against the other, making a whole of normal width. The earlier was that of the fort of *c.* A.D. 100 (*see* Introduction p. 35), antedating the town wall of *c.* A.D. 200 and subsequently incorporated into it. The S end of this surviving stretch marks the rounded SW corner of the fort, in the angle of which are traces of a small square turret. The foundations of another, intermediate, turret can be seen further N, near where the trench broadens into the sunken garden of the adjacent Plaisterers' Hall (q.v.).

NORWICH STREET

In origin Magpie Yard, off Furnival Street; renamed Norwich Court *c.* 1770; widened and opened into Fetter Lane in 1897. The NE part is the Barnard's Inn development (*see* Fetter Lane). Then Nos. 3–5, by *Terry Farrell Partnership*, 1986–9, with a central three-storey section like a portico in relief and lots of banded stone cladding, much too muscular for the narrow street. Facing, Nos. 6–10, 1981–3 by *Comprehensive Design Group*. Chunky brick with window bands, upper storeys slightly projecting. To Greycourt Place behind, the storeys step down past a smoothly rounded central stair-tower.

OAT LANE

Called probably from an oat market held here by *c.* 1500. The Pewterers' Hall lies on the N side (q.v.). The garden to its E, with large trees and a few battered tombstones, was the site of St Mary Staining and its churchyard, from at least the late C12 until 1666. The name Staining, probably pre-Conquest, is thought to refer to property owners here from Staines in Middlesex; also commemorated in STAINING LANE, known from *c.* 1180, which runs S from the E end.

OLD BAILEY

A bailey or rampart was thrown up just outside the City wall as an extra line of defence, perhaps at the Conquest, certainly by *c.* 1166. Old Bailey (in 1287 *La Ballie*) follows its line. There were formerly two streets: Great Old Bailey, running straight from N to S, and Little Old Bailey, which cut through from near its N end to a point further W on Newgate Street. The ground between them, cleared in the 1770s to make space in front of Dance's Newgate Prison, now sets off the Central Criminal Court on the prison's site (*see* Public Buildings). A section of Roman town wall is preserved within.

Excavations at No. 20 in 1988 revealed three successive levels of ROMAN BUILDING. C1 and C2 pottery kilns had been replaced by a late C2 octagonal building, probably a Romano-Celtic temple, set on a hilltop overlooking the Fleet valley and commanding the main road into London along Newgate (*see* Newgate Street). This building was in turn replaced by an early C4 masonry structure with heated rooms.

Facing the Court, Nos. 16–17 (BRITANNIA HOUSE), 1912–20 by *Arthur Usher* for the London, Chatham & Dover Railway, whose Holborn Viaduct terminus lay behind. French-flavoured Edwardian Baroque in Portland stone, with plenty of garlands and cartouches. Michelangelesque figures over the door symbolize travel by rail and sea. No. 20 to its S is a nine-storey building by *RHWL Partnership*, 1988–9, backing on to the Fleet Place development (q.v.), but not part of it. Stone-clad and self-aggrandizing, with blockish forms on a rusticated base of dark-grey granite. E and W elevations have a giant glazed concave niche breaking into a central pediment. The model is inter-war America (compare that import, Bush House, Westminster).

The rest of the w side is occupied by the Hillgate House complex (*see* Ludgate Hill). Facing it, further s, two former warehouses of some pretension: Nos. 7–10 (READER'S DIGEST), 1908–10 by *Paul Hoffman* for Photocrom Ltd., Portland stone, free classical, with elliptical-headed upper windows with wiry hoodmoulds and other discreet Art Nouveau touches; No. 6, the former Linoleum Manufacturing Co. warehouse by *Searle & Hayes*, 1895, warmly coloured in the Collcutt manner with bands of terracotta, brick and granite.

OLD BROAD STREET

It runs NE from Threadneedle Street to Liverpool Street. Called *Bradestrete c.* 1200, but its name has often changed: Threadneedle Street was commonly included with it in the Middle Ages, while the whole extension N of London Wall, made *c.* 1737, was called New Broad Street until the 1930s.

The street alternates dramatically between sequences of mostly C19–earlier C20 offices and big 1960s–70s groups with towers and low forebuildings. These juxtapositions begin at the s end, where the Stock Exchange (*see* Public Buildings) faces a fine run of older offices on the E side. For No. 1 *see* Threadneedle Street. Nos. 2–3, the former Marine House, by *Thompson & Walford*, 1915–16, was amongst the tallest offices in the City when new. An early, if derivative, example of the stripped-classical idiom, with giant stone pilasters. Discontinuous numbering thereafter. No. 9, the rear façade of *Mewès & Davis*'s Westminster Bank, 1923–32, more like their usual Franco-American idiom (after McKim of New York) than the main front on Threadneedle Street. Nos. 10–11, formerly Lazard Bros., 1925. Tall, brick and stone, in the Neo-Early Georgian manner then favoured for merchant banks. Façades and interiors by *Victor Heal*, structure by *Gunton & Gunton*. Banking hall facing ADAM'S COURT, r. Ahead here, good Neo-Rococo wrought-iron gates to the raised court behind the NatWest Tower (*see* below). They look some twenty years later than the date 1833 in the head.

Continuing along Old Broad Street, Nos. 13–17, the former National Bank, 1861 by *E. N. Clifton*. A typically dignified and solid High Victorian front, with four diminishing storeys of windows in aedicules. No. 18 by *Nelson & Innes*, 1865, four bays wide, rusticated in the French way. Nos. 1–18 are proposed for conversion into a hotel (1997), with Nos. 40–53 Threadneedle Street.

The w side begins at the corner with Throgmorton Street with No. 123, the former Hambros, 1864–6 by *Edward Ellis*. Brick and stone, in a rather poor, mild, debased Gothic. No. 120 by the *Fitzroy Robinson Partnership*, 1989–93, a reprise of the 1920s classicism of (especially) Mewès & Davis, only slightly simplified.

On the E side again, No. 19 is the CITY OF LONDON CLUB, by *Philip Hardwick*, 1833–4. A nicely reticent painted stone front of seven bays and two storeys with high attic. Doric pilasters to the upper storey in the Palladian manner, i.e. not the early

Cinquecento of Barry's contemporary West End clubs. First-floor windows with thin alternating pediments and sections of balustrade, the latter neatly echoed in the front screen wall. Thick console-cornice, thick doorway hood. Above the cornice an excessively heavy blind attic, which drawings at the club suggest was a late revision to the design. Inside, vestibule with triple-arched screen to a typically early C19 staircase, starting in one flight and breaking round into two, each returning in two arms. Simple cast-iron balustrade. The ground-floor Dining Room lies behind the staircase. A double cube, with three arched, tripartite windows with Ionic columns and glazed lunettes. Around the walls antae, not pilasters: a Grecian touch. Facing the front on the first floor, two sober smoking rooms in enfilade. The Guest Dining Room, l. of the entrance, has accomplished Adamesque plasterwork by *Waring & Gillow*, c. 1900, added between Hardwick's heavy crossbeams. Sensitively refurbished by *Max Gordon* of the *Louis de Soissons Partnership*, 1979, with a new roof garden and remodelled top storey.

Then the NATWEST TOWER complex, 1970–81 by *R. Seifert & Partners* (engineers *Pell Frischmann*). Fifty-two storeys high, and at 600 ft (183 metres) Britain's tallest building for ten years, until Pelli's tower at Canary Wharf went up. The tower stands back, flanked by low grey-granite-faced wings extending up to the street (another wing faces Bishopsgate next to Gibson's former bank of 1864–5, q.v.). It is modelled as three overlapping half-hexagons with rounded corners, rather like the bank's emblem in section. They cantilever out from the concrete service core, each stepping up progressively by two storeys. Shimmering close-set stainless-steel fins emphasize the vertical. Black glass between. Though construction was much delayed, the tower epitomized up-to-date London when new. Yet its slow construction with *in situ* concrete service core, its relatively shallow office floors, the inclusion of ped-ways, and the need for widespread clearance to build it all followed 1960s methods that were already obsolescent by completion (a great conservation struggle saved the City of London Club: *see* above). The bank indeed moved elsewhere after the terrorist bomb attack in 1993 (refurbishment by *GMW*, in progress 1997, will preserve the elevations, with a new glazed forebuilding and giant upswept canopy in front). Only in long views does the Tower have enduring success, as a bold focus and centre-piece for the City's lesser towers.*

Back to the W side, where in 1997 a new building by *Peter Foggo Associates* is under way at Nos. 109–118. The S part occupies the site of St Peter-le-Poer, first mentioned 1181, rebuilt 1788–90 by *Jesse Gibson* with an unusual top-lit circular nave, and dem. 1908. Then PINNERS' HALL (Nos. 105–108), offices by *Fitzroy Robinson Partnership*, 1992–3, fairly literally classical, with rusticated lower floors and columns and piers over. Inside, an elaborate atrium garden with waterfall, the storeys facing it stepped down, except for one oversailing at the top. The plain C19 hall of

---

*Previously on the site the Excise Office, by *William Robinson*, 1769–75, Palladian, with four-storey stone ranges around two courtyards; replaced by giant offices by *Tite* and *E. N. Clifton* 1854–6; again rebuilt 1921.

the Pinners' Company here was dem. *c.* 1925. Opposite, a building by *EPR*, under construction in 1997, replaces Goodenough House (1955–60 by *Ley, Colbeck & Partners*, slab and podium formula, but still stone-faced). For the NW corner with London Wall, *see* Great Winchester Street.

Then a short, straight run N beyond London Wall, up to Liverpool Street. The NE part was wholly rebuilt in 1972–7. The L-shaped perimeter range is BROAD STREET HOUSE, by *Ley, Colbeck & Partners*. Polished brown-granite-faced podium for the elevated walkway; tall shallow slab along Wormwood Street, with smoked-glass curtain-walling in a white-stone-faced frame; lower block along Old Broad Street, alienating at street level. Within the angle DASHWOOD HOUSE, a crisp free-standing square tower of some eighteen storeys overlooking St Botolph's churchyard. By *Yorke Rosenberg Mardall*, 1972–6. Polished brown-red granite facing, flush windows twice divided by mullions as wide as the floor bands. At the corners more mullions, not the practice's usual, angled windows. S of the tower a curious Moorish KIOSK, a former Turkish bath, by *S. Harold Elphick*, 1894–5 (modelled on the C19 shrine at the Church of the Holy Sepulchre, Jerusalem). Blue faience, brick, intricate raised terracotta all in Islamic patterns. Dainty onion-dome (for the water-tanks), with painted glass bulb and crescent finial. A staircase in the E apse descends to surprisingly spacious lower rooms (restored as a restaurant *c.* 1980), with coloured moulded tiles to Elphick's designs.

Opposite, the E side is all Victorian. No. 94 and Nos. 90–92, 1884–5, similar in attractive orange-red brick and stone, the rubbed and carved brick ornament especially good on No. 94. *Edwin T. Hall* did Nos. 90–92. After New Broad Street, Nos. 81–89, a long Northern Renaissance stone façade by *F. Adams Smith*, 1886. It avoids the cliché of superimposed pilasters in favour of such devices as tapering piers, console-brackets and small paired columns. Little open corner turret. Rebuilt behind by *T. P. Bennett Partnership*, 1989–90 (with Nos. 35–42 New Broad Street), who added a sympathetically detailed mansard. Nos. 76–80 by *E. H. Burnell & Henry S. Legg*, 1877. All manner of windows; detail infused with unusually licentious Italian Gothic and Grecian motifs. Lightweight iron-framed construction enables it to span the Underground railway route.

Corner buildings on both sides belong with Liverpool Street (q.v.).

OLD JEWRY

Until King Street was made after the Great Fire, Old Jewry was the chief route N from Cheapside to Guildhall. The area was set aside for the Jews of London from at least the C12, and the street is probably the *vicus judeorum* mentioned *c.* 1130. Their synagogue stood at the NW corner. Increasing extortion and maltreatment by the Crown culminated in their expulsion in 1290. The property that had housed the synagogue served from C14 to mid C16 as a royal wardrobe.

On the W side, the closes of the Police Station (No. 26, reached through Nos. 27–32) and of Frederick's Place (qq.v.) survive from the grand merchant houses built after the Great Fire. They demonstrate the persistence of the medieval tendency to set back such houses behind lesser frontages on the thoroughfares. The street's most remarkable building, *Soane*'s National Debt Redemption Office of 1818–19, stood at the NE corner until *c.* 1900. For the 1950s Bank Buildings on the site, *see* Prince's Street.

To the S of these, the stone-faced No. 11 (AIB BANK), 1932 by *Robert Angell & Curtis*, in that firm's straightforward commercial stripped-classical manner. It faces on the W Nos. 27–32 (KOREA EXCHANGE BANK). At first glance of *c.* 1925, with the metal panels between stone verticals typical of the date; but in fact as late as 1950–8, by *Waterhouse & Ripley*. The S part is on the site of the former church of St Olave Jewry (q.v.). S of this, buildings belong with Frederick's Place, and the Mercers' Hall (qq.v.). Opposite (E side), No. 8, the former Commonwealth Bank of Australia, by *Vickery & Joass*, 1930–1. Smooth classical forms of American Beaux-Arts derivation, the composition still genuinely imposing for the late date. Plain below with big apertures, paired giant columns higher up with bronze-faced floor panels between, large mansard squeezing in three extra storeys on top.

PATERNOSTER SQUARE
see ST PAUL'S CHURCHYARD

PEPYS STREET

Made *c.* 1912 in connection with the new Port of London Authority building on the S. On the N side, first Walsingham House (*see* Seething Lane). Then the MIDLAND BANK OFFICES, the former Mariner House, by *Carl Fisher & Associates*, 1961–4: big and straightforward on a broad H-plan, with narrow white-tiled floor strips and dark blue spandrels. Facing Cooper's Row, No. 1, a seven-storey block by *Thomas Saunders & Partners*, 1972–4, with aggregate-faced precast-concrete panels incorporating sunken rounded windows. Both are proposed for demolition (1996). For the SE part, vacant in 1997, *see* Trinity House, Public Buildings.

PHILPOT LANE

Named after Sir John Philpot, Lord Mayor 1378–9, who owned property hereabouts. Before that called after St Andrew Hubbard, burnt in 1666 and not rebuilt: it stood opposite the S junction with Eastcheap.

Well-documented C17–C18 houses (w side) nicely demonstrate the tendency of greater dwellings of that time to lurk off the highways. Nos. 2–3 (N end) face a little court, reached through an archway from a demolished mid-C19 building. Three stuccoed bays, part of the house of Nathaniel Letten, merchant, *c.* 1670, later divided and heightened by one storey. Handsome flat door-hood on big brackets. Refurbished by *David Landaw & Partners*, 1987–9, with rear extension. No. 5, red brick and stone with gaunt plate-glazed windows, 1978–83 by *McMorrow, Gough & Chung*, who also reconstructed Nos. 7–8, replicating their mostly early C19 three-bay fronts (1985–6). The shell is post-Fire, made into two dwellings in the 1720s by John Letten, Nathaniel's son. Of the latter date probably the staircase, fielded panelling, and other preserved fittings. (A tunnel-vaulted UNDERCROFT was discovered in 1979. Of brick with chamfered stone cross-ribs and traces of external windows, much altered but probably C15–C16.)

A stone-dressed carriageway through No. 7 leads to BRABANT COURT. This is probably post-Fire, named from a C17 proprietor called Braborne. No. 4 (s side) was newly built by Letten in the 1720s. Red brick, four bays and four storeys, the top one apparently later. Segment-headed windows with flush sash-boxes (restored 1985–6). Good doorcase, of wood, with entablature and segmental pediment broken forward over Doric pilasters. Panelled interiors. C19 iron gates beyond, reset. Back in the lane, Nos. 9–10, 1983–5 by *Sheppard Robson*, treated as a sequence of three narrow brick fronts.

On the E side, the big Kleinwort Benson tower (*see* Fenchurch Street). To its s, Nos. 14–15, FENGATE HOUSE, 1983–90 by *Yorke Rosenberg Mardall*, has a short façade to Philpot Lane with a longer range facing the yard behind the tower. The plain grey cladding changes to grey granite facing, r., the junction marked by an exposed cylindrical pier. The development includes rebuilding behind the C19 Nos. 23–35 Eastcheap (q.v.).

POULTRY

The continuation of Cheapside E of Old Jewry. The E part is properly called Mansion House Street. First recorded in 1301 as *Poletria*, after the poulterers who traded here.

This was a very busy part of the Roman town. Excavations in 1996 on the s side revealed a complex early Roman street junction where roads converged on the crossing of the Walbrook, slightly further E. Part of what was probably a temple precinct lay s of this junction. Bucklersbury, a little street on the s side erased in 1994, was named from the Bukerels, a powerful City family recorded first in 1104 and established here *c.* 1240 in a 'bury' or fortified mansion on the banks of the Walbrook, across Queen Victoria Street. Stow described the remaining parts of this 'great stone building', which were then 'of long time … divided and letten out into many tenements'.

Until 1994, the s side was lined with buildings almost entirely of *c.* 1870, most notably *J. & J. Belcher*'s much-loved Mappin & Webb, 1870–1. Gothic with a circular Franco-Flemish angle tower at the corner with Queen Victoria Street, facing what was for long years the busiest crossing in England. Buildings of the same vintage lined Bucklersbury and faced Queen Victoria Street, s. Indeed, they constituted the best group of High Victorian commercial architecture then remaining in the City's centre, products of the concurrence of

the making of Queen Victoria Street and the boom years 1868–73.*
They were razed only after a protracted and bitterly fought
campaign for their retention, prompted originally by a scheme for
Lord Palumbo by *Mies van der Rohe* (designed 1962–8, but delayed
by lease acquisitions), with an eighteen-storey tower at the w end of
a new square planned to extend across Queen Victoria Street up to
the Mansion House. Its rejection in 1985, after a celebrated public
enquiry, marked a high point of opposition to wholesale redevelopment of what remained of the Victorian street-scape. The wedge-
shaped site is instead being filled with Lord Palumbo's development
by *James Stirling, Michael Wilford & Associates* (*see* below), finally
approved only after the result of a further public enquiry was unsuccessfully challenged in the Lords.

NORTH SIDE. By Old Jewry, SCOTTISH LIFE HOUSE, 1968–70 by
Joseph, F. Milton Cashmore & Partners. All stone-faced, with quite
an elaborate elevation echoing the proportions of the Midland
Bank next door. Top windows recessed below segmental arches,
carried on mullions running down through five floors, like a
rudimentary giant order. At first-floor level four RELIEFS by *Mitzi
Cunliffe*.

Next the MIDLAND BANK HEADQUARTERS, 1924–39 by *Lutyens*
(executive architects *Gotch & Saunders*). Lutyens owed the job to
his friendship with the bank's chairman Reginald Mackenna, for
whom he had designed the gem-like little Midland Bank in
Piccadilly (1922). Despite its giant scale, the same loving attention
to detail is here everywhere apparent. The vocabulary comes from
Italian Mannerism, first deployed by Lutyens at Heathcote,
Yorkshire (1906), but here it clothes a lofty steel-framed mass
without the control of an implicit order. Large arched ground
floor with recessed entrance and the architect's favourite dis-
appearing Doric pilasters. Big keystones with carved heads to the
windows. Mezzanine above with scallop-shaped keystones, then
three storeys made into one by tall unadorned arches with banded
rustication, the height of both stone blocks and storeys gradually
and very subtly diminishing. Smoother bands interrupting the
channelled stone mark where the façade sets back, an inch at a
time. Each end is rebated above the mezzanine, to accommodate
the figure of a fat boy with a goose, designed by *Lutyens* and
carved by *Sir William Reid Dick*. Two further storeys above the
rustication, coming forward in the middle in Lutyens's typical

---

* Also demolished in 1994: POULTRY. Nos. 14–15, 1872, Italianate, probably by *A.
Bridgman*. Nos. 12–13 by *F. Chancellor*, 1875. One bay only, remarkably original, with
Elizabethan windows much wider than high and pretty terracotta friezes of royal
progresses by *Joseph Kremer*. Nos. 9–11 by *F. J. Ward*, 1875, Venetian Gothic, with a
façade to Queen Victoria Street. Nos. 4–5 by *R. H. Moore*, 1869–70, for the restaurant
pioneer Frederick Sawyer, with eclectic Gothic arcading typical of the sixties. No. 3, a
five-storeyed late Georgian house. Nos. 1–2 by *John Belcher Jun.*, 1875, in the Norman
Shaw taste. BUCKLERSBURY. No. 7 (1872) and 8, the GREEN MAN (1877) by
Woodthorpe. No. 38, a tall, narrow Gothic front of the 1860s. QUEEN VICTORIA
STREET. Nos 12–22, 1872, loosely Renaissance; Nos. 26–38 by *F. J. Ward*, a triangular
island block of 1871–3, richest debased Italian.

Also swept away, the former CHURCHYARD OF ST BENET SHEREHOG, at the N
end of Sise Lane off Queen Victoria Street. Excavated foundations of the church
destroyed in 1666 indicated a small aisleless structure of reused Roman ragstone with
Saxon long-and-short quoins. Pottery finds indicate a date 1050–80.

aedicule erection, crowned in this case by a low lead-panelled dome which is only visible from a distance. Last to be completed was the Prince's Street front, shorter but otherwise almost identical.

Immensely impressive interior: very tall, and broader than anything previously seen in a City bank, with a forest of square Corinthian columns in green African verdite, off-set against white marble walls. Their arrangement is determined by the intersection of axes from the Poultry and the Prince's Street entrances. At their meeting-point stands a circular marble basin like a well-head, now used as a reception desk but originally a light-well for the safe deposit hall below. This is reached by a staircase of Imperial plan on the l. The lower level has a Tuscan pilaster order and on the stairs two of Lutyens's exclamation-mark terms. Here also a bronze version of the Boy with Goose, signed *Ceccioni*. A high proportion of Lutyens's wooden fittings survive: note especially the inner doorcases with clocks on top, the kind of unexpected combination he loved. (Off a fifth-floor corridor with apsed ends and paired Corinthian columns, the original boardroom and directors' dining room, both with enriched friezes and panelling; also a smoking room with an octagonal lobby made by paired black-marble columns. Other fifth- and fourth-floor offices retain panelling, fireplaces and doorcases by Lutyens.)

To the r., the little St Mildred's Court commemorates *Wren's* St Mildred Poultry (1671–4, dem. 1872).* On the corner site to Prince's Street the NATIONAL WESTMINSTER BANK. It was built for the National Provincial Bank in 1929–32 by *Sir Edwin Cooper*, a late work. The bank's headquarters remained in Bishopsgate, but the big new branch provided much office space conveniently near the Bank of England. Quite an effective composition, with a gently convex corner with a pair of giant columns inset above facing the Mansion House; but next to Lutyens's, Cooper's bank appears tame. Gone are the high jinks of his Port of London Authority, though there is still plenty of Neo-Baroque sculpture (allegorical group on the parapet by *Ernest Gillick*, 'Britannia seated between the figures of "Higher Mathematics" and "Lower Mathematics", supported by "Mercury" and "Truth", with the "Owl of Wisdom" in one corner': A. S. Gray). The detail too is more fiddly than Lutyens's, with all the stonework channelled to various degrees: a subtlety that works better close to than at a distance. Rebuilding behind the façade by the *T. P. Bennett Partnership*, 1994–7, retained Cooper's D-shaped banking hall with its columns and bronze figures by *C. L. J. Doman*; three panelled rooms reconstructed on the first floor.

SOUTH SIDE. *Stirling's* hard-edged and strongly articulated design, commissioned instead of Mies's tower in 1986 (revised 1988), is due for completion in 1997 (execution by *Michael Wilford Associates*). Despite Stirling's almost infallible power to shock, it has already been so quarried for motifs by other practices (e.g. the shallow curtain-walled bays of curved and triangular plan) that it will surely appear a decade out of time on completion. But its intelligent expression of interior volumes undoubtedly elevates the

* Stonework survives in the grounds of Thorpe Hall, Louth, Lincs.

design above the commercial horde (a covered pedestrian route will approximate to the line of Bucklersbury, and a new entrance to the Underground will be incorporated). Whether the little corner turret with its nautical wing-like balconies can hold its own facing the crossing remains to be seen.

PRINCE'S STREET

Laid out after the Great Fire, though its present straight course is due to westward expansion by the Bank of England, 1798–1805 (E side). Only in the 1830s did it become part of a major route, by the construction of King William Street and Moorgate Street.

On the w side first *Cooper*'s National Westminster Bank and *Lutyens*'s Midland Bank (*see* Poultry). Then Nos. 7–8, the former Manufacturers Hanover Trust, by *Fitzroy Robinson & Partners*, 1970–2. The composition owes something to Kevin Roche's Ford Foundation Building, New York, 1967. Tall, with recessed ground floor and nine bays of windows grouped in threes. Paired verticals, faintly evocative of a giant order. They have dark Blaubrun granite cladding, used here for the first time in Britain. Grocers' Hall Court lies behind (*see* Grocers' Hall). On the corner with Gresham Street, the Portland stone BANK BUILDINGS by *Victor Heal*, 1949–62, keep the classical flag fluttering. Decidedly symmetrical, with a curved front. Attenuated Doric columns to the projecting banking hall. Urns and aedicules on top pick up motifs from Soane's and Baker's Bank opposite. Previous buildings of this name on the site were by *Soane*, 1801–10, and *A.C. Blomfield*, 1900, ornately Neo-Palladian. A characteristic gable end of Soane's building survives, trapped between later party walls.

QUEEN STREET

With King Street, the only noteworthy new street laid out after the Fire. The direct route it made between Guildhall Yard and the river (at first to river stairs, then from 1819 to Southwark Bridge) was blocked in 1993, when the junction with Upper Thames Street was closed to road traffic. Excavations at No. 61 in 1986 found C3 remains of a large arcaded building overlooking the Roman waterfront.

From N to S: Nos. 6–7, w side, stone-faced by *Detmar Blow*, 1907. Remarkably restrained, perhaps reflecting the influence of *Fernand Billerey*, then newly recruited to the practice. The four-storeyed FLEECE TAVERN, 1878 (No. 8) is grand and ornate for a pub. Bath stone, with cast-iron balconies to the large-windowed first floor, formerly a restaurant. Across Well Court, ALDERMARY HOUSE, an early City scheme by *Fitzroy Robinson & Partners*, 1959–63. Splayed corners, stone-faced, with a roof terrace and rounded penthouse on top. The tall entrance lobby has a glazed overdoor engraved by *Helen Monro*. Down PANCRAS LANE opposite, between buildings facing Cheapside and Queen Victoria Street, may be seen the burial ground of the former St Pancras

Soper Lane, destroyed in 1666. Excavation in 1963 revealed a nave 19 ft 4 in. (nearly 6 metres) wide, and an apsidal chancel, of C12 date.

After Queen Victoria Street and Cannon Street, the little forecourt in front of Nos. 27 and 28 (w side) partly preserves the site of another burial ground, of St Thomas Apostle. The pair are two of the finest remaining C18 private houses in the City, No. 27 of three bays, No. 28 of five bays. Each has a doorway up about ten steps. The symmetrically placed doorcases have unfluted Ionic columns, bulgy friezes, and pediments. The segment-headed windows, doorcases and general proportions suggest a date *c.* 1730. No. 28 has original panelling on the ground floor; one delicate first-floor ceiling of *c.* 1770. Older buildings continue on the E side, with big warehouses of the 1850s, continuing the sequence from Bunning's Cannon Street extension. Nos. 65–66, 1852, with stuccoed ground floor, brick above, with latish-classical stucco surrounds and channelled piers; No. 64 with segment-headed windows and a more utilitarian handling of the first floor; Nos. 62–63 of 1851 (perhaps by *Griffiths*), altered in refurbishment of *c.* 1980.

Two 1980s blocks face this group, s of late C19 warehouses on the corner of Great St Thomas Apostle. The new LONDON CHAMBER OF COMMERCE at No. 33 is by *EPR Partnership*, 1986–90, symmetrically composed about a big entrance and patterned in a grid of pink and brown granite. The similar No. 36 alongside was the first building by the *Terry Farrell Partnership* to be completed in the City (1982–6). Much of its Secessionist-derived detail has become over-familiar by imitation elsewhere, but this does not diminish the panache with which it is used here to order an assertive but intelligently composed façade. Symmetrical, flush-windowed and vertically tripartite. Five-storey projections respect the prevailing street height, above a steeply battered plinth clad in black stone with rusticated bands. The bolted-on stonework is frankly expressed. Recessed entrance under a glazed canopy between the projections, presenting a steel wall to the street so that entry is through doors half-hidden on either side. High up, a curved glazed attic between the projections lights a boardroom, suggesting the full height of the building behind. The Skinners Lane front is partly brick-faced.

Two more 1980s blocks on the corners with Upper Thames Street. No. 40, w side, by *Fitzroy Robinson Partnership*, 1989–91, illustrates the tendency in the late 1980s towards more literal pastiche – here of the C19 buildings opposite – spoilt by a polygonal front pretending to be curved. The Postmodern pattern-making on *Renton Howard Wood Levin*'s No. 61 of 1985–7 opposite is no match for that on No. 36.

The street continues up to Southwark Bridge as QUEEN STREET PLACE. On the E side, No. 10, a giant development of 1986–91 by *Fitzroy Robinson Partnership*, replaces a complex of separate buildings by *C. Edmund Wilford & Son*, 1960–3. Here, the practice's granite-clad manner of e.g. the mid-1970s Banque Nationale de Paris in King William Street is repeated on an excessively large scale, modified by the stratified projecting horizontals generally favoured for riverside sites. Large atrium entrance on the w.

Symmetrical to the river, with a big grid motif to the lower floors. The LITTLE SHIPS CLUB is accommodated here.

On the other corner, THAMES HOUSE of 1911–12, by *Stanley Hamp* of *Collcutt & Hamp* for the Liebig Extract of Meat Company. A big and jolly front, approximately symmetrical, with blocked columns, oriels with concave sides sticking out between, and plenty of big figures sculpted in stone and bronze (by *W. Bainbridge Reynolds*, *Richard Garbe*, and – over the central entrance – *F. Lynn Jenkins*). Both the sculpture and the horizontal contrast between plain and enriched storeys are still in the decorative tradition of Lloyd's Register of Shipping of a decade before, but the details mix sinuous Art Nouveau with newly fashionable rectilinear classical forms. The unusually lavish boardrooms etc. were partly retained in reconstruction by *Biscoe & Stanton*, c. 1990–1, in connection with the Vintners' Place scheme (*see* Upper Thames Street). This also required the demolition beyond of all but the retained portal of *Kersey, Gale & Spooner*'s Vintry House, 1927. *H. W. Palliser* carved the tympanum, a female figure showing the influence of archaic Greece, but unabashedly nude rather in the way of Eric Gill. Vintry House had sheer mullions between glass and metal panels in ten storeys: enough to infringe distant views of St Paul's, sealing its fate when redevelopment came up.

QUEEN VICTORIA STREET

Cut through in 1867–71 at a net cost of £1,076,000, joining Victoria Embankment and Blackfriars Bridge with the heart of the City by the Mansion House (engineer *Edward Power*). Such a connection had long been sought, and the section SW of Cannon Street was able to use the route of New Earl Street, part of an uncompleted scheme of the 1850s. Space beneath was exploited for new sewerage, water and gas mains, and – under the W part – the new District Railway. The route curves slowly NE half-way along, but the pedestrian notices this less than its long, steady slope down to the river. The ancient (mostly Alfredian) streets bisected by the broad new road have rather dwindled away since, and only Queen Street survives as a major N–S cross-route.

The most interesting buildings are survivors of the 1870s. In the E part they have characteristic elongated triangular sites, the product of the new oblique alignment. The *Companion to the Almanac* for 1877 found '... many of them in very questionable taste, the ornaments tawdry, overcrowded, misplaced, and obtrusive, but the *ensemble* is not ineffective'. This ensemble cannot now be easily envisaged, especially after the demolitions for No. 1 Poultry at the NE (q.v.). But the survivors, mostly at the E, were amongst the grandest and most elaborate: further W, plainer warehousing was more common. Big blocks fill the gaps between, mostly post-war and low enough to preserve the view of St Paul's.

East part, from Mansion House to Cannon Street

The sandstone CITY MAGISTRATES' COURT at No. 1 was built in 1873–5 as the National Safe Deposit by *Whichcord*. In the palazzo style, somewhat debased as the late date would make one expect, but restrained by comparison with the showier efforts of the 1860s. Superimposed orders on the rounded corners, arcaded rusticated ground floor with masks alternately male and female, and windows in alternating aedicules on the first floor. A 1920s mansard has unfortunately replaced Whichcord's ornamented attics and tall stacks. Four storeys of armour-plated safe deposit vaults survive beneath, the first in Britain, partly converted to cells etc. for the new courtrooms above by the *Culpin Partnership*, 1988–91.

BUCKLERSBURY HOUSE is by *O. Campbell-Jones & Sons*, 1953–8. Probably the largest, or at any rate the bulkiest, of London's 1950s office buildings. It was also the first City design to abandon the street line in favour of the free plot-ratio formula (*see* Introduction pp. 127–9). A fourteen-storey slab 204 ft (62 metres) high runs N–S from Queen Victoria Street to Cannon Street, with three six-storey spurs linked by lower sections symmetrically projecting towards Walbrook. The elevations play safe: much shallow panelled stone-facing, with stone mullions between sections of olive-green curtain walling. The fine engraved glass of classical gods by *John Hutton* above the main entrance commemorates the Mithraeum found on the site (*see* below). The long-necked Romano-British figures suggest the influence of David Jones. More glass by Hutton at the Cannon Street entrance.

Immediately SW of Bucklersbury House, at r. angles and forming one group with it, is TEMPLE COURT, by *O. Campbell-Jones* and *Ronald Fielding*, completed 1962 for the Legal and General Assurance. A tall similarly handled slab, slightly lower, with alternating spandrel bands of stone and blue-grey tile. To Cannon Street a three-storeyed forebuilding and an unlovely courtyard. A shop-lined alley off Cannon Street between the groups (continued along the N of Temple Court below the entrance podium) is called BUDGE ROW, after the old continuation of Watling Street, which lay S and W.

A TEMPLE OF MITHRAS was uncovered by Professor Grimes on the site of Bucklersbury House in 1954. The discovery of the temple and its treasures caused considerable public stir, in response to which it was decided to raise the remains for reconstruction on a terrace N of Temple Court, some way W of its original site adjacent to Walbrook. The alignment was also changed, from N–S to E–W. The effort is not wholly successful, but it typifies the approach to archaeological reconstruction favoured at the time, and the display has an important place in the recent history of archaeology.

Mithraic belief originated in Persia, and was particularly popular amongst military and commercial communities of the kind found in Roman London. Its central mystery concerned the god's slaying of a bull in a cave. This represented the triumph of light and life over darkness and death, and the temple was built to provide a dark, subterranean cavern for mystic worship and ritual. London's small basilican temple was first built *c.* A.D. 245, and the remains displayed illustrate its original form. The timber-floored central nave was reached down two steps, offering a symbolic descent from the double doorway which opened on to the room

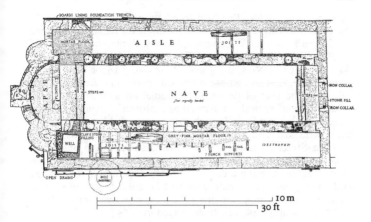

Queen Victoria Street, Temple of Mithras.
Plan as revealed by excavation

from the main antechamber or narthex (not excavated). The nave
had narrow aisles for the worshippers, formed by arcades of seven
columns carried on sleeper walls. At the far end two steps led up
to the sanctuary, where an altar was placed within a curved apse
reinforced by external buttresses. At the apse end of the S aisle was
a shallow timber-framed well, which provided the fresh water
needed for ritual ablutions. In the present reconstruction all the
timber elements are unconvincingly replaced in stone.

In the early C4 the superstructure was largely rebuilt, and the
columns removed. The nave floor was also raised at this juncture,
as it was in many other phases of rebuilding, and several of the
most important temple sculptures were laid to rest in a pit,
perhaps suggesting that the cultic practice here had changed.
Several of these sculptures were C2 pieces in Italian (Carrara)
marble. They included a head of Mithras which had been deliberately struck off, and fine heads of Minerva and the Graeco-
Egyptian god Serapis. Later contexts from the temple produced
a marble group of Bacchus and his attendants, and a richly
decorated silver strainer or infuser that had been concealed in a
wall. Some other sculptures of equivalent quality, found in 1889,
may have been thrown into the Walbrook as ritual deposits, and
are likely to have derived from the temple. They included a bull-
slaying group in relief, dedicated in fulfilment of a vow by Ulpius
Silvanus, a veteran of the Second Augustan Legion; the head and
part of a torso of a river god; and the headless figure of a Genius
by a ship's prow. All these finds are now on display at the
Museum of London, where they form the most important group
of classical sculpture known from Roman Britain.

Also at the Museum of London is an outstanding C2 MOSAIC
PAVEMENT from a heated apsidal room, found near the corner of
Bucklersbury opposite in 1869. It has floral motifs surrounded by
geometric patterns.

At the corner of Queen Street opposite, the wedge-shaped former
BANK OF LONDON AND SOUTH AMERICA by *Victor Heal*,

1950–7 (Nos. 40–66). Portland-faced, with weak classical details: the tired offspring of the interwar tradition for banks represented by Cooper's National Westminster, Poultry. Replacement proposed by *Peter Foggo Associates*, 1995. Diagonally opposite, Nos. 39–53, 105 ALBERT BUILDINGS, the grandest surviving 1870s block (built 1871). By *F. J. Ward*, whose office was here. The *Building News* called it 'the sort of pretentious Mediaeval against which the "Queen Anne" revival is intended as a protest'. Arcaded Gothic, mixed English and Early French, with a remarkable assortment of window heads. The whole centre – eight bays – towards Queen Victoria Street is raised. Thickly bracketed cornices or corbel-tables, mostly uninterrupted. The individual shopfronts survive. Opposite, flanking the E end of St Mary Aldermary, Nos. 68–72 and 74–82, modest French classical triangular blocks of *c.* 1873. (Beneath the former, remains of a long cross-vaulted UNDER-CROFT, probably C15, largely destroyed in 1825.)

West part, from Cannon Street to New Bridge Street

144 Nos. 84–94, CREDIT LYONNAIS, reinterprets the 1870s rounded triangular formula in the innovative materials and prefabricated forms of a century later. It is by *Whinney, Son & Austen Hall* (structural engineers *Ove Arup & Partners*), 1973–7, the first building anywhere to be wholly clad in glass-fibre-reinforced cement. Separately expressed storeys marked by narrow black bands slope gently out at an angle of five degrees, with bands of splayed windows set in shaped and rounded light-coloured reveals. Larger windows and slight projections to the floor bands mark the entrances. More conventional to Bread Street, W, with flush windows. On the site was *Wren*'s domed St Mildred Bread Street (1681–7), which had the most intact furnishings of any such church until destruction in 1940.

For the post-war sequence on the N side as far as Peter's Hill, *see* Cannon Street and St Paul's Churchyard. Wren's St Nicholas Cole Abbey (q.v.) stands high up, punctuating the group. Opposite, a sequence of 1980s office blocks. No. 63, 1989–91 by *Thomas Saunders Partnership*, anthologizes the worst clichés of stone-clad Postmodern offices. It incorporates the entrance to Mansion House Underground station, replacing a characteristic Portland-faced entrance by *Holden* of 1926–9 (altered 1961). No. 63 partly conceals the very large ROYAL BANK OF CANADA HOUSE by *Sidney Kaye Firmin Partnership*, with the Canadian architects *Crang & Boake*, 1983–8, its splayed corner entrance set back behind a little forecourt. Irregularly broken and recessed façades clad in flush dark-brown granite, with thin mullions. (The smaller No. 71a, r., differently clad, houses the branch bank, linked by a covered bridge.) A glazed gable marks the main entrance. From here a grandiose atrium passes right through to an Upper Thames Street entrance. Where the atrium steps down is a water-feature in which is set the Doric PORTICO of the Neo-Georgian Beaver Hall, by *Williams & Cox*, 1927–8, formerly on the site.

Beyond No. 71a, after Cleary Gardens (*see* Huggin Hill for Roman remains here), SENATOR HOUSE, by *Chapman Taylor Partners*,

1986–91. Symmetrical in patterned polished stone, set back behind lawns as if on a bypass. A small atrium descends three storeys, due to the falling ground. Then two 1960s blocks: WALKER HOUSE, Nos. 87–95, by *Ronald Ward & Partners*, 1964–7, curtain-walled between dark brick ends; and the large SALVATION ARMY HEADQUARTERS by *H.M. Lidbetter*, 1960–3, still decorative in the 1950s manner with its ornamental stone panels and little balconies. Remains were found beneath and to the w of a large ROMAN PUBLIC BUILDING, raised on previously open land by the usurper Allectus in 293–4 (*see* Introduction p. 41).

From here the steps of Peter's Hill link St Paul's with the river. Along the w side on the s are the City of London School with St Benet's church in its angle, facing the College of Arms on the N side (*see* Churches, Public Buildings). Then on both sides the vast complex of Telephone Exchanges (*see* Public Buildings), stretching between Carter Lane and the Thames: the towering Faraday House and extensions, N, the dismal Baynard House, s. Next to Faraday House, No. 146, the former BRITISH AND FOREIGN BIBLE SOCIETY, by *E. I'Anson*, 1867–9. Above its battered granite plinth, a good, quiet Italianate palazzo seven bays wide; only such Gothic-derived details as the incised flower vases tell of its real date. Earnest carving of an open Bible in the tympanum. The high entrance hall with steps up to a balustraded first-floor gallery was restored during refurbishment by *T.P. Bennett & Son*, 1987–9, and a plausibly Victorian roofline reinstated.

After St Andrew-by-the-Wardrobe high on its hill, the BAYNARD CASTLE pub (No. 148), cheery Queen Anne with rounded gables. Simpler than the rampaging terracotta-encrusted design by *Major Wieland* illustrated in *The Builder*, 1876: was this design toned down in execution? Then PRINTING HOUSE SQUARE, the former premises of *The Times* by *Llewelyn Davies, Weeks & Partners* (executive architects *Ellis, Clarke & Gallanaugh*), 1960–5. The old square, not open to the street, housed the various premises of the King's Printing House (1740), bought by John Walter of *The Times* in 1784. New front buildings of 1868–74, elaborately understated in red and yellow brick with weakly segment-headed windows, were largely the work of the great *John Walter II*, working without architect or contractor. Their 1960s replacements lie open to Queen Victoria Street on the s. T-shaped block of offices on the l., smaller range on the r. Continuous window bands between green slate strips, the blank end walls grey-mosaic-faced. Each block consists of two halves (planned separately), divided by a spinal corridor. This is expressed externally by split-pitched roofs: a motif of Scandinavian derivation, first used by the designers at their planned village at Rushbrooke, Suffolk (1955–63). Between them lies the printing house by *Ellis, Clarke & Gallanaugh*, 1935–7, behind a matching curtain wall. The earlier date is given away by its Adamesque brick E front to St Andrew's Hill. *The Times* moved to Gray's Inn Road in 1974, and *Yorke Rosenberg Mardall* refitted the building. Complete replacement is proposed by *SOM* (1996).

Facing on the s, the dull elevated slab of *R. Seifert & Partners*' MERMAID HOUSE, 1977–81 (formerly Touche Remnant).

Strongly horizontal to match the practice's offices over BLACKFRIARS STATION on the E (*see* Public Buildings), with heavy stairways in front to the elevated walkway. A brown brick rear wing along the roadway beneath (called after Puddle Dock, infilled in the mid C20) contains the MERMAID THEATRE, conceived by the late Lord Miles and established by public subscription. It was initially converted by *Devereux & Davies* in 1957–9 from the bombed lower floors of the extraordinary City Mills building, a towering pedimented warehouse of 1850 on a long and narrow plan. Its contractor, *James Ponsford*, employed no architect. C19 brick is exposed inside, under a shallow concrete tunnel-vault of 1957–9. But during Seifert's refacing and extension, the Doric-columned entrance retained in the 1950s was swept away, and there is now no external sign either of its C19 origins or of the 1950s auditorium, which formerly rose above in the manner of the Royal Festival Hall. Extensive rebuilding of the complex was proposed in 1996 (*Sir Norman Foster & Partners*, master planners).

Beyond the railway bridge on the S side, the street turns into New Bridge Street (q.v.). Stranded on the N side, the last of the 1870s buildings: the celebrated BLACK FRIAR (No. 174), as remodelled the best pub in the Arts-and-Crafts fashion in London. In origin a commonplace wedge-shaped pub of 1873 (probably by one *Merrick*). The ground floor was rebuilt by *H. Fuller Clark c.* 1905, i.e. some time after the 1890s pub boom. The artists, none of them pub specialists, went to work with a vengeance. Outside, bits of metalwork, mosaic, and enamel, with alarming reliefs in the frieze carved by *Henry Poole*. Inside, the saloon bar (restored in 1983 by *Jamie Troughton* with *Larkin, May & Co.*) has pink-and-white veined marble slabs, and arch monkish narratives told in three friezes of copper figures, by *Poole*. Inglenook in the grand manner. The small barrel-vaulted extension under the adjoining railway arch was added as a snack bar by *Clark* in 1917–21. Yet more ornate: inlay in mother-of-pearl etc.; sculpture by *Poole* and *F. Callcott* in bronze and alabaster mixing monkery with Aesop and nursery rhymes. Lots of mirrors further dizzy the drinker, who may muse on Andrew Saint's suggestion that the space slyly parodies Westminster Cathedral's vaulted marble-lined interior.

120

ROPEMAKER STREET

On the City's N boundary, so named by the C18 from its rope-walk. The S side formed part of the Barbican–London Wall plan, after the street was laid waste in the Second World War. Here a broad forecourt and on its W side BRITANNIC TOWER, former headquarters of B.P. At thirty-five storeys and 395 ft (120 metres) it was the tallest office building of the scheme and for some years the tallest building in the City. *F. Milton Cashmore* and *Niall D. Nelson* began the design in 1958, with *Lord Holford* as consultant on layout; construction was in 1964–7. Plain rectangular envelope, corresponding to London Wall's anonymous towers, but with tall stainless-steel-clad concrete ribs of two sizes, sloping almost imperceptibly inwards two-thirds of the way up. Greenish glazing between (sealed for air-conditioning, an early occurrence in

London), twice punctuated by windowless red-brown-clad
service floors. Elain Harwood suggests the influence of SOM's
similarly-framed Union Carbide building, New York, completed
1960. Cashmore's earlier B.P. House opposite (1956–60, dem.)
was by contrast a heavy stone-faced affair, with no hint of this
coming embrace of the corporate idiom of 1950s America. Low
glazed podium (N end altered *c.* 1978), containing a high marble-
lined entrance hall (interiors by *Design Research Unit*). Low SW
satellite block with uniform mullions by Moor Lane. Of the works
of art originally commissioned for it, only a Portland stone RELIEF
by *Gwythyr Irwin* by the main entrance remains in 1997.* Part of
Holford's layout the broad pool with abstract fountain to the SE,
crossed by a leisurely looping ramp up to the podium: an arrangement at once visually enjoyable and extremely inconvenient. Sold
by B.P. in 1996; remodelling to a height of 660 ft (201 metres) was
proposed in 1997, by *Santiago Calatrava*.

Further W, sections of ELEVATED WALKWAY hint at the visual chaos
the completed ped-way scheme would have produced: N–S walk,
part of Britannic Tower, with elegant fluted supports of oval cross-
section; E–W walk to its N heavy and obtrusive, with lime-green-
clad glazed canopy. The Barbican Estate's massively solid forms
begin opposite.

The N side is all recent buildings, notably MERRILL LYNCH (No.
25), a whole block by *Covell Matthews Wheatley*, completed 1987.
Ten storeys wrap a rather over-modelled glazed atrium, exposed
at the SE corner entrance. The fronts have a high-tech image, with
lightweight metal balconies supported free of the dark glass and
silvered framing.

ST ANDREW'S HILL

Named from the church of St Andrew-by-the-Wardrobe at the
bottom of the hill, by Queen Victoria Street. W of the church,
Nos. 31–32, a well-preserved plain warehouse of 1875 with segmental window heads and a nicely rounded N corner. Further N,
two stock-brick C18 houses, reminiscent of a self-respecting
domestic past in the City: No. 35 of *c.* 1766 (the RECTORY), three
bays wide with a good Doric doorcase and an odd little wooden
oriel overlooking the church, added *c.* 1914 by *F. R. Gould Wills*;
No. 36, similar but of five bays, plus another bay, r., with a
curiously tall narrow doorway. Crude C19 top storey, suggestive of
use as a warehouse. Nos. 40–41, also C18, were heavily restored in
1985.

Two interesting buildings opposite, N of the former *The Times* printing house (*see* Queen Victoria Street): No. 7, the COCKPIT pub of
c. 1865, with a rounded corner with stucco machicolations and a
tiny mezzanine to an internal gallery; then, after utilitarian warehouses of the 1890s, No. 2 near the top of the hill, by *Daw, Wills
& Church*, 1912, a jauntily asymmetrical Neo-Wren warehouse in
red brick and stone.

---

*Removed from the hall a steel sculpture by *Robert Adams*, from the canteen a mural
by *Edward Bawden*.

More plain late C19 warehouses off Ireland Yard on the W, up two steep paved lanes called BURGON STREET and FRIAR STREET (e.g. No. 5 Burgon Street, 1881, in 1979 one of the area's first conversions of warehouses into offices, by *Chapman Taylor Architects*). For the remains of the Blackfriars in Ireland Yard, *see* Black Friars Lane.

ST ANDREW STREET

Made in the mid 1860s across Thavies' Inn and St Andrew's burial ground, as the N part of the route between Holborn Circus and Ludgate Circus (cf. Shoe Lane, St Bride Street). The only C19 survivors are *Teulon*'s group at the NE (*see* St Andrew Holborn). On the W side they face first Thavies Inn House (*see* New Fetter Lane), then Nos. 6–16, a big curtain-walled job by *Hannen & Markham*, 1955–9. To the S ST ANDREW'S HOUSE (No. 18), 1986–9 by *Covell Matthews Wheatley Partnership*. Big, self-consciously symmetrical front of polished stone, with the centre section boxed out and glazed in bands. On the corner with Shoe Lane opposite (E), Nos. 9–13, offices of 1971–5 by *Raymond Cecil & Partners*, with pre-cast grooved concrete panels coloured a dour brown.

ST BOTOLPH STREET

Part of the 1970s road system remodelled NE of Aldgate. The N side is one huge, transatlantic-flavoured detached block: BEAUFORT HOUSE, by *Renton Howard Wood Levin Partnership*, 1987–9. Thirteen storeys, with dealing floors in the giant grey-stone-clad plinth. Speculative offices above, their first storey with ridiculous stuck-on aedicules. Entrance in the near-symmetrical SW front, facing a forecourt made over the Underground railway cutting. Here a vast, showy broken pediment high up, in rusticated red stone, the opening below entirely glazed. Higher wings with flat glazed bows. The main interior is (as often) more successful: lofty barrel-vaulted lobby, marble-lined, overlooked by galleries at the far end. Glazing above these admits light from an elevated open central court.

ST BRIDE STREET

Opened in 1871 between Shoe Lane and the new Ludgate Circus. The only street of the Holborn Viaduct improvements where the original architecture survives on both sides.

From the N, the W side up to Poppins Court stood vacant in 1997, following partial demolition of the *Daily Express* extension (*see* Fleet Street). Opposite, a consequential block by *RHWL Partnership* extending E to Farringdon Street (q.v.). To its S, Nos. 8–18, by *D. R. Stewart*, 1964–6. Eight-storey block set back, three-storey wing projecting, r. Windows in bands, walls clad in grey and white mosaic and tile. A narrow stone-faced front faces Farringdon Street.

Then the 1870s take over. On the w side, Nos. 5–13, a long brick block of 1872–4 by *Albert Bridgman*. Close-set windows with shouldered arches, becoming round-arched at the third floor. Some terracotta detail. No. 3 was the warehouse of the fashionable interior decorators Collinson & Lock, by the young *Collcutt*, 1872–3. Red brick, tall and symmetrical, with a big central gable broken by a pointed arch. It has the big-boned strength one associates with Collcutt's former master Street, but Collcutt avoids explicit Gothicizing in favour of simple stone dressings and plain pattern-making in brick. Two carved gargoyle-like figures project, saving it from starkness. The premises originally ran through to old No. 109 Fleet Street (dem. 1907), modishly refaced by Collcutt in plaster scattered with incised Japanese foliate circles. He also designed ebonized 'aesthetic' furniture for the firm.

On the corner with Farringdon Street opposite (E), the wedge-shaped No. 2, formerly MARTIN'S BANK CHAMBERS, 1872. By *Henry Currey*, for the British Mutual Investment Co. (refurbished 1980–1 by *Austin-Smith:Lord*). Minimal round-arched classical façades with key blocks. On the top storey, smaller windows closely spaced within a fast rhythm of continuous arcading: a treatment more common in America. Three N bays on each front are a later extension.

ST DUNSTAN'S HILL

A steep descent from Eastcheap, past the ruin of St Dunstan-in-the-East in its garden (q.v.). Facing it (E side), PINNACLE HOUSE, red brick, by the *Elsworth Sykes Partnership*, 1988–91. Familiar motifs: big rounded glazed corner with turret, rudimentary cornices.

Buildings w of the church belong in Idol Lane, those further s in Lower Thames Street and St Mary-at-Hill (qq.v.).

ST MARTIN'S LE GRAND

A broad straight street connecting Aldersgate with Newgate Street and Cheapside. Nothing remains of the religious house from which it is named, founded *c.* 1056 on the E side by two brothers called Ingelric and Girard as a secular college or royal free chapel and dissolved in 1542. It had been rebuilt or repaired in the mid C12, in 1258–61, and most tantalizingly in 1360–72 by its Dean, William of Wykeham, who rebuilt the chapter house. In the C19 the street became the preserve of the Post Office: first *Smirke*'s G.P.O. of 1824–9 on the former college site, then larger buildings on the w side after 1869–74 (*see* General Post Office, Public Buildings). Mid-1920s commercial buildings of Portland stone succeeded Smirke's G.P.O., when the street was widened in anticipation of joining up with a proposed new bridge s of St Paul's.

From the s, Nos. 2–14 (EMPIRE HOUSE), on the e side, built as a
warehouse by *Gunton & Gunton*, 1925–6, below average for the
date especially in the clumsily contrived second floor above the
mezzanine. Then No. 16, the much more adventurous former
Courtaulds' warehouse by *L. Sylvester Sullivan*, 1924–5. Sheer flat
upright pilasters set very narrowly, with decorated metal floor
panels recessed between. An attic storey is inserted between the
order and the big cyma recta cornice with palm-leaf motif (carver
Henry Poole). Low Greek Doric columns to the entrance; other
mouldings also according to the Neo-Grèc fashion, but the close-
set stone verticals owe much to such Chicago firms as Holabird
and Roche. The top-floor showroom has a saw-tooth-glazed factory
roof (under alteration 1996). To Foster Lane an audacious wide-
span loading bay. Beyond, *Gunton & Gunton*'s buildings of
1924–8 (Armour House and Union House), similar to Empire
House, were demolished in 1995, for a new building by the
American firm *Genzler & Associates*.

NORTH of Gresham Street, ST MARTIN'S HOUSE, a spirited
Northern Renaissance pile dated 1891, with corner tourelle and
on the s front a steep attic-cum-gable. Above-average carved
panels. Behind a routine Italianate stucco front of 1856, the LORD
RAGLAN at No. 61 is perhaps early c18. The shallow cornice
survives from a previous refacing by *Cottingham* in 1830, but his
Soanian blind attic has gone. The cellars are said to be pre-Fire
and to incorporate remains of the City wall where it adjoined
Aldersgate. The kink in the alignment n of the pub marks the
position of the old gate, where Aldersgate Street begins (q.v.).

ST MARY AXE

First recorded 1260. Named from St Mary Axe church, recorded by
the late c12. It stood on the w side, but closed *c.* 1565. Scanty
remains were discovered in 1951 and 1989. Its 'axe' was a relic of
the martyrdom of St Ursula and her 11,000 virgins. Traces of a
V-shaped ditch of military pattern, at least 7 ft (2 metres) deep and
over 13 ft (4 metres) wide were exposed in 1995 at the Baltic
Exchange (e side). Until infilling between A.D. 130 and A.D. 150, this
may have bounded the c1 Roman settlement. The street was
extended n of Bevis Marks in 1773–6, across the line of the later City
wall. Its old near-slums mostly went in a fire in 1893. Then the early
c20 Baltic Exchange brought big commercial buildings in its wake.
These have mostly been rebuilt at least once since. The s end of the
street is dwarfed by the Commercial Union tower (*see* Leadenhall
Street). The whole area was badly damaged by a terrorist bomb in
1992.

On the e side, after St Andrew Undershaft, FITZWILLIAM HOUSE
(No. 10), by *Hamilton Associates*, 1988–91. Of the high-relief, Neo-
Beaux-Arts brand of Postmodern: symmetrical, with a big gable,
lesser shallow oriels, and smoothed-off columns and cornices.
Then the former BALTIC EXCHANGE, its future still unresolved
after severe bomb damage. Designed by *T. H. Smith* and *W.
Wimble*, 1900–3, when the Exchange moved from the former

South Sea House, Threadneedle Street. Like much grand City architecture of that time, it was still entirely Victorian, untouched by Webb, Shaw, the Arts and Crafts, or any other such influences. Lower floors faced in pink-granite arcading, upper floors with detached giant pink-granite columns, pediment with figures carved by *Seale*. Weaker front to Bury Street, brick above stone, the triple-arched entrance with funny blocked Doric columns. The exchange hall was aisled and marble-lined, with big exedrae, first-floor galleries and a large glazed dome on Roman Doric columns: not inventive, but a very attractive, spacious ensemble, of great interest as the last survivor of the type in the City. Demolished in 1992–5: pretty s extension by *Kenneth Lindy & Partners*, 1955–6; also the Chamber of Shipping, Bury Court (N), 1939 by *Burnet, Tait & Lorne*, progressive-minded, but without the Modern Dutch affiliations of their best 1930s work. A vast skyscraper 1,076 ft (328 metres) high, proposed for the site by *Norman Foster & Partners* in 1996, looks unlikely to proceed.

Opposite (w side), EXCHEQUER COURT, large seven-storey offices by *Fitzroy Robinson Partnership*, 1992–5 (replacing a bomb-damaged building designed 1988). Dark rustication below, banded stone above, the detailing mostly familiar from e.g. their earlier No. 55 Bishopsgate. Centre and projecting ends empha-sized respectively by a convex section with giant curtain-walled panel and by pavilions. The façade of No. 8 St Helen's Place is incorporated behind (*see* Bishopsgate). Next door, Nos. 55–59, BANGKOK BANK, 1970–80 by the same firm. Smoked glass above marble, all rather off-the-peg.

Older buildings survive on the E side, N of Bury Court. No. 40, formerly Spillers, is by *Sir Edwin Cooper*, 1922–4. An urbane design. Plain walling reading as flat piers, some with Cooper's favourite oval reliefs where one expects capitals. The ground floor has its own channelled piers with Doric cornice. Steep pantiled roof; pleasing central double-height lobby (restored by *Feilden & Mawson, c.* 1989), with staircase (l.) to a circular gallery. No. 46, a brick warehouse façade by *J. E. Saunders*, 1894. Shouldered segment-headed arches on square piers, in a rhythm 1–3–1: an old-fashioned formula. The armorial commemorates the Fletchers' Company, who acquired a hall here by the C16, but leased it from the mid C18.

The SE corner with Bevis Marks is the NATIONAL BANK OF GREECE, polished golden-brown granite with window bands. 1977–81 by *A. Arvanitakis*. On the NE corner opposite, EAGLE STAR (No. 60), 1986–8 by *Elsworth Sykes Partnership*. Open arcaded ground floor, big round-headed openings and dormers of various sizes. By the entrance a bronze-gilt eagle made by *H. H. Martyn & Co.*, from the former headquarters in Threadneedle Street (by *Gunton & Gunton*, 1924); sculpted slab in the lobby by *Mark Frith*, 1989. The NW corner, with Camomile Street, w side (Nos. 63–71), is by *BDP*, 1989–92. A reworking of the 1920s commercial idiom: rusticated granite-faced lower floors, Portland pilaster strips and bronzed infill above. Short square entrance tower in Camomile Street, with a clear-glazed staircase bay to the l. Chatsworth House, NE, belongs with Houndsditch.

ST MARY-AT-HILL

Recorded in 1275 and named after the church, whose E front and rectory make an attractive group on the W side (q.v.). Immediately N, Nos. 6–7, an early work by *Ernest George & Thomas Vaughan*, 1873: the house of Sir Henry Peek, whose office and tea warehouse adjoined (*see* No. 20 Eastcheap, which also forms No. 4 here, and No. 31 Lovat Lane). The architects were simultaneously busy at his estate at Rousdon, Devon. Of polychrome brick, still Gothic in detail, with terracotta-trimmed windows set deep in the flush façade. A true High Victorian toughness in the blank l. part, where the windows face the churchyard. Overdoor facing the churchyard passage inscribed 'LE MAITRE VIENT'.

The whole E side was widened in the later C19 and again opposite the church as a forecourt to GUINNESS MAHON, 1970–5 by *Howell, Brooks, Tucker & Partners*. Stone-faced frame, with floors combined in one giant white-tiled panel: a displeasing combination. Lower S return wing. Contextual brick front to Idol Lane behind. Displayed against a wall, N, a reset rusticated brick arch from its grim Victorian predecessor.

To the S of the church, Nos. 9–10 (W side), eclectic commercial dated 1895, incorporated with Nos. 11–15, part of the *Thomas Saunders Partnership*'s City Village scheme (*see* Lovat Lane). For Nos. 16–18, *see* Watermen's Hall; for buildings further S, *see* Lower Thames Street.

ST PAUL'S CHURCHYARD

The setting of St Paul's Cathedral, largely replanned after the ravages of the Second World War, is in the late 1990s once more under discussion. How the medieval cathedral close was laid out is described under St Paul's Cathedral, pp. 157–8. Wren's speculative Baroque plan of 1666 (*see* Introduction p. 67) set the cathedral at the acute corner of a major road junction; but what setting he may have preferred for his finished building is unknown. All we have is a drawing of *c.* 1710 by *Hawksmoor*, showing a broad arcaded piazza tapering from E to W, set back slightly from just E of the transepts to just W of the portico. At the W, a semicircular exedra frames a large domed baptistery. Surrounding streets open off at irregular intervals. Was Hawksmoor fired by the Fifty Churches Act (1710) to hope that the government would underwrite a worthy setting for the new cathedral? Nothing was done, however, and the old street pattern was kept; the Deanery was rebuilt on its ancient site, while the new Chapter House was placed baldly N of the cathedral (*see* below).

The outlines of the old street plan remain. Immediately W of the cathedral, the road from Ludgate Hill splits into a broad route along the S side and a lesser N route leading towards Cheapside (a N–S route joining the two formerly scraped past the E apse). Victorian London instinctively made a good job of this inheritance, widening Ludgate Hill into an opening sufficient to take in the façade, and making space at the SE corner during the Cannon Street extension, 1847–54 (q.v.). About this time large textile warehouses rose around the churchyard, in height almost a match to the walls of the cathedral (e.g. Messrs Cook's by *Knowles Sen.*, 1852–4, dem. 1960, facing the s transept). A few survive at the sw, of *c.* 1900. War damage to the rest of the area encompassed near-complete destruction to the se, e and n. In Paternoster Row, a workmanlike street n of the cathedral, hardly one building survived the night of 29 December 1940, which wiped out 6,000,000 books and with them a large portion of the English book trade.

After the War a thoroughgoing replanning of the cathedral's setting was inevitable. The City's planner *F. J. Forty* proposed a grand formal setting as early as 1944. This had brick and stone office blocks of uniform height facing an elongated square, with a n entrance, in line with the transept, made by an extended King Edward Street, and a corresponding pedestrian approach extending s to the river. The general effect may be seen immediately e of St Paul's, where New Change Buildings (for which *see* Cheapside) 133 follows the curve of the broad post-war street called New Change, e of the post-war extension of the churchyard. But such conservatism was execrated by progressive-minded critics, and in 1955 *Lord Holford* was consulted by the housing minister, Duncan Sandys. Holford's report of 1956 was adopted in 1958, slightly revised, and the plan given its final form in 1962. The area n of the cathedral was completed in 1967.

North side

The n side retained the street in the cathedral's shadow as a pedestrian route, bounded by office blocks of varying heights in a Modernist idiom, by *Trehearne & Norman, Preston & Partners,* set around a traffic-free precinct elevated over a basement car park. Their picturesque asymmetry was anticipated in sketches for the site by Hugh Casson published in the *Architectural Review,* 1945. The PLAN may briefly be described. Three equidistant ten-storey slabs are aligned n–s along the tapering triangle bounded also by Newgate Street and Warwick Lane, the central one with a pedestrian passage beneath. Lower blocks around and between are planned mostly on a rectilinear grid. The sw block (JUXON HOUSE) forms the n side of the Ludgate Hill approach, stepping back by St Paul's w front.

On the n side here, a broad flight of steps leads up to an open space called PATERNOSTER SQUARE, between the first and second medium-sized blocks (the old square, where the Newgate meat market was once held, occupied roughly the same area). A slim sixteen-storey curtain-walled tower, nw, is placed to minimize disruption to distant views of St Paul's. The e part is more densely planned, with shops facing a square made between the blocks.

Described as 'outstandingly well conceived' by Pevsner in 1973, the precinct has been much criticized in recent years, and awaits demolition in 1997 in favour of more intensive development (compare its generous plot ratio of 2.2:1 to the pre-war figure of 3.1:1, or the 3.5:1 of the replanned London Wall (q.v.)). In defence of the old plan, its better buildings are mutedly character-ful without undue self-assertiveness: particularly Juxon House and the little BANCROFT HOUSE, just e of the steps, with their grooved stone verticals with recessed dark slate panels. The ground-level pedestrian plaza by the churchyard with its trees must also be accounted a success. But Paternoster Square is draughty and harsh, the one SCULPTURE (by *Elizabeth Frink*, 1975, called Paternoster – Shepherd and Sheep) an inadequate palliative. The open space here seems profligate by contrast with the claustrophobic E end. Views of the cathedral are not always well-managed, especially the frustrating snapshot of the N transept door down a long passage through the buildings. Furthermore, the raised level diminishes the cathedral's presence and obstructs much pedestrian circulation (elevated walkways which were to have linked it with the system along London Wall, q.v., remained unbuilt). The Cheapside approach up covered steps is particularly forbidding. (Here a carved TABLET dated 1668. A boy sits on a pannier, with the legend 'When ye have sought the Citty round/ Yet still this is the high'st ground'; but Cornhill is higher by one foot. The old Panyer Alley here was named probably from the panniers made there for the Bread Street market.)

Redevelopment proposals and counter-proposals since the mid 1980s have mirrored the convulsions of architectural fashion and public opinion. Rebuilding was first proposed in 1985. A competition two years later was won by *Arup Associates*, who designed stripped classical ranges planned at the old ground level, on a series of curves and crescents facing the cathedral. A rival mixed-use plan by *John Simpson*, traditional in materials and Neoclassical or Neo-Georgian in dress, attracted enough support to be adopted in modified form by a new consortium of developers in 1989, with *Terry Farrell & Co.* as master planners. It was notable for its repudiation of the legacy of post-war architecture and planning: much of the old street pattern was to be revived, around which were designs for large office buildings by different architects in a mix-and-match historicism, including Neo-Gothic. Approved in 1993, this has itself been superseded, and *Sir William Whitfield* was appointed consultant to the latest developers in 1996. In late 1996, proposals are to re-establish the former ground level, with a central colonnaded square by *Whitfield*. Architects of the other blocks, capable of separate development, will be *Allies & Morrison, John Simpson & Partners, Michael Hopkins & Partners*, and *MacCormac Jamieson Prichard*.

Wren's CHAPTER HOUSE of 1712–14 remains on the N side, W of the transept. Red brick with rubbed dressings and stone trim (bricklayer *R. Billinghurst*, mason *Edward Strong Jun.*). Three storeys on a basement, seven bays wide, the central three projecting. Matching pedimented entrances at each end. Even quoins. Plain aprons below the windows, which are largest on the first floor. Quoins and aprons closely resemble those of Marlborough House (1709–11). *Vitruvius Britannicus* credits this to Christopher Wren Jun. alone, though he may only have been assisting his father. Could Wren Jun. have had a hand in the Chapter House design too? Surfaces are much renewed and unattractive. Restoration of the war-damaged shell by *Godfrey Allen*, 1957, recreated the W entrance hall. This has a screen of Doric columns and an open-well stone staircase rising against the N wall. W of the Chapter House, a tiny square PUMP of cast iron, dated 1819, set up by St Faith's parish and formerly against the churchyard railings. Opposite, an underground chamber was made by the cathedral in 1970 for the CATHEDRAL WORKS DEPARTMENT (architects *Seely & Paget*).

South side

The S side was also to have been rebuilt and its traffic diverted away from the cathedral along the line of Carter Lane (report by *Holford* commissioned 1964, submitted 1968): plans abandoned in the 1970s. Holford's biographers describe the resulting mixture as 'inaction formalised and incorporated in a local plan'. At the W end, Portland stone warehouses apparently in continuous late Victorian sequence. But No. 1 is a replica of *Herbert Ford*'s predecessor of *c.* 1896, by *John Gill Associates*, 1985–7. The shallow window reveals of the long, bland front give the game away. The unlikely result is to make one grateful for the relative honesty of façade-jobs. Pastiche C19 fronts to Creed Lane, smaller in scale. No. 4, 1903, has a profusion of columns and pilasters, corresponding both to single storeys and to the grouping of the storeys in pairs. On the corner a turret with copper-clad dome.

Then down DEAN'S COURT for the former DEANERY, the City's 63 best surviving C17 mansion. It is set back in seclusion behind a massive brick wall with twin carriageways and carved pineapples on the parapet. No documentation supports the traditional attribution to *Wren*; *Edward Woodroffe* and *John Oliver* reported on the cost of a new deanery in 1669, and the former signed the building contract (1672). But Wren may well have been consulted: the Dean, William Sancroft, was a close associate, and the façade is more sophisticated than Woodroffe's workmanlike house-fronts in Amen Court (q.v.). Of two storeys, seven bays wide, in red brick with rubbed trim. The broad windows form a much higher proportion of the front than at the Chapter House, in which matter both buildings reflect the contemporary fashion. Eared surrounds. Dormers in a hipped roof above a wooden modillion cornice. Neat double stair on a shallow stone arch. Ornament is reserved for the doorcase: pilasters with carved drops, straight hood on lion-mask brackets. The plan is loose and empirical, the staircase opening asymmetrically off the hall, r. Heavily twisted balusters. Answering, lesser staircase, l. Plain C17 panelling in other rooms. Restored as offices by *Haslemere Estates*, 1981–2, after the Dean moved to Amen Court, with a new SW wing replacing a previous extension; in 1996 converted as the Bishop of London's palace. The first deanery here was as early as 1145.

Back in the churchyard, Nos. 5–13, 1895–8 by *Ford* for Messrs Pawson & Leaf: the largest of the warehouses, occupying a whole island site. Grandly treated with a giant order between first and third floors, two further floors, and an attic with dormers and a little pediment. Rear ranges of brick. The style 'may be described as a City type of free Renaissance' (*Building News*). *Gilbert Seale* did the carving. The first four floors were offices and warehouses, the floors above housed dormitories, dining rooms etc. for the staff, reached by nine lifts, then still a relative novelty.

Beyond Godliman Street all was demolished by 1960, and a

wedge-shaped garden occupies the site. In its NW corner by the
road, a circular INFORMATION PAVILION by the *Corporation of
London Architect's Department*, built in 1951 as part of the Festival
of Britain and moved here in 1955 from E of the Festival Garden
(*see* below). The lightweight paired supports, continuous glazing
and cross-braced lantern still proclaim the Festival style, but brick
has replaced the red, white and grey panelling. In the garden the
FIRE BRIGADE WAR MEMORIAL, with sculpted figures by *John
W. Mills*, 1991. Overlooking it from the S side, WREN HOUSE
(No. 15 Carter Lane), built 1933–5 by *Searle & Searle* as a warehouse for Messrs Cook, rebuilt and enlarged by *Swanke Hayden
Connell*, 1990–1. Bloodlessly Neo-Wren, like a St John's Wood
mansion block.

SERMON LANE, along its E side, is named either from coin-clippers
(Sheremoiners) or from a C13 landowner called Adam Sermoni-
cinarius. It merges at the S into PETER'S HILL, a pedestrian
passage made through the middle of the garden on the S transept
axis. Further down, this crosses Queen Victoria Street to connect
with the riverside walk. The N part dates from *c.* 1962, the S part
from twenty years later, after the Upper Thames Street tunnel
was completed (*see* that street for the former St Peter's church).
The way the cathedral emerges as one climbs the steps is wholly
successful. In the other direction the route gives a grand vista of
Bankside Power Station, in 1997 under conversion for the Tate
Gallery. A footbridge across the Thames is intended here.

Beyond the steps to the E, a promising new development for
NISSHO IWAI is in progress in 1997, by *Rolfe Judd* (landscape
consultants *Charles Funke Associates*): office ranges on the S and W
of OLD CHANGE SQUARE, the latter also extending most of the
way along the N side. A restaurant pavilion is intended for the
centre. The view of the steeple of St Nicholas Cole Abbey (SE
corner) will be preserved. The original offices (by *Alec J. Shickle* of
Campbell-Jones & Sons, 1961–5), of smaller bulk, faced a concrete
precinct 150 ft (45¾ metres) square. The whole shared the characteristic failings of Paternoster Square: generous but bleak public
space, awkward and unwelcoming lesser pedestrian approaches
(especially from Queen Victoria Street, S, from which a car park
beneath the square was entered). Further E, in the nook of Old
Change House (*see* Cannon Street, S side), a small SCULPTURE of
Icarus by *Michael Ayrton*, 1973. Near here stood *Wren*'s St Mary
Magdalen Old Fish Street, 1683–7; dem. 1893 after a fire. Its
peculiarity was a stone lantern on a stepped pyramid.

On the N side of Cannon Street, SE of the cathedral, a GARDEN laid
out in 1951 by *Sir Albert Richardson* as part of the City's contribution to the Festival of Britain. Its formal plan, classical stone
parapets and fountain are hardly what one associates with the
event. At the W end, a SCULPTURE called The Young Lovers, by
Georg Ehrlich, 1973. The garden's rounded W perimeter follows
that made *c.* 1850 on the corner of the new Cannon Street and the
former road immediately E of the cathedral; the paved section just
W of the fountain represents the line of another street, the former
Old Change, on to which faced St Augustine's tower, N (*see* St
Paul's Cathedral Choir School). Until 1884, ST PAUL'S SCHOOL
stood immediately E of the cathedral. Its post-Fire premises by

Jerman were replaced by *George Smith*'s consequential Grecian school in 1823–4; the monster warehouse by *Delissa Joseph* and *F. Hemmings* that succeeded it was destroyed by bombing. Another casualty was CORDWAINERS' HALL, by *H. Chatfeild Clarke*, 1909–10, last of five successive halls here from 1440.

ST SWITHIN'S LANE

Called *vicus Sancti Swithuni* in 1270. It is a narrow street, still largely to pre-C20 scale, though the N part is all post-war.

First No. 1 (W side), with shallow classical detail knowingly used, by *T. Heysham*, 1954 (altered 1973). NEW COURT is the headquarters of Rothschild & Sons, by *Fitzroy Robinson & Partners*, 1963–5, opulently faced with darkest polished granite, and white polished marble surrounds for accentuated windows. The great Nathan Rothschild had made his home here in the mid 1800s. Later bank buildings had a range to the street (by *John Davies*, 1836) and a rear range facing a courtyard (by *Nelson & Innes*, 1857–60). This courtyard motif is preserved, and the street is open to it below. The higher W part looks into the churchyard of St Stephen Walbrook at the back. At No. 10 (l.) an extension of 1976–7, by *Richard Ellis*, flush-windowed in light grey Italian granite with stone fins, the upper storeys sloping back. ST SWITHIN'S HOUSE behind a larger courtyard, is of 1949–53 by *Gunton & Gunton* (elevation by *R. W. Symonds*). Tall, heavy and inert, in Portland stone. Its return wings give it the symmetrical staggered profile of such pre-war buildings as Senate House (University of London). Principal front to Walbrook, with statuary by *Charoux*: four standing workers, and higher up a group of five. To the lane, it is on the site of the house of FitzAilwyn, first mayor of London; the Salters' Hall (q.v.) occupied the site from 1641 until the Blitz. Replacement proposed by *Sidell Gibson* (1997). On the E side, a new development by *GMW Partnership* is in progress in 1997 (designed 1993), behind retained façades in King William Street.

Several C19 buildings lie to the S. W side: No. 13, the modest former Founders' Hall by *Aitchison*, 1877–8, has shops below and Corinthian pilasters on the upper floors. The last survivor of several C19 Livery Halls with minimum Livery accommodation (here, merely a third-floor Court Room), in an outwardly orthodox commercial building. No. 15, glazed-brick warehouse of 1888 with big bracketed and pedimented doorcase of polished granite; No. 17, slim-fronted with big windows and spindly iron colonnettes, 1866.

On the E side, Nos. 18–23 were reconstructed *c.* 1987 by *William Nimmo & Partners*, for the Drapers' Company (*see* also Cannon Street). Storeys were added to Nos. 21–23, offices of 1880 by the Drapers' surveyor *Charles Reilly Sen.*, who had his office here. Stone, with incised foliate decoration and channelled piers. Two-light windows with colonnettes. Facing a little cobbled yard behind, No. 20 is an eight-bay house of *c.* 1800, possibly incorporating earlier fabric. A shed-like wooden crane house of the same period survives to the r. Its intact 'Capital Patent Crane' was already present in 1805, when the wine merchant George Sandeman took over No. 20. No. 19 back in the lane, infill by *Nimmo & Partners*, with a frieze of sheep skulls reset on its plain stone front from a large, altered late C18 house previously on the site, and reset granite doorcases of *c.* 1900. Also preserved was a mysterious barrel-vaulted UNDERGROUND PASSAGE some 100 ft (30 metres) long, running parallel to the street. It is probably C14, of squared chalk with flint and tile wall-courses. Below No. 20, under cellars of *c.* 1800, is another C14 vaulted cellar. Then No. 18, white brick offices with a Doric entablature, 1889 by *Delissa Joseph.*

SALISBURY COURT

The entry from Fleet Street to the former Bishop of Salisbury's Inn (*see* Salisbury Square below). On the w side, GREENWOOD HOUSE, dated 1878, by *Alexander Peebles* for the Vintners' Company. Queen Anne, much indebted to Shaw for its generally domestic air. Red brick and terracotta, shaped gables, the decoration oversized. A larger section facing Fleet Street was demolished *c.* 1920. No. 8 (l.), a narrow warehouse by *Sextus Dyball*, 1874, the front almost entirely glazed.

SALISBURY SQUARE

The little enclosure off Fleet Street, never a planned square, marks the forecourt of the once extensive house of the Bishops of Salisbury (site acquired *c.* 1200). Excavations to the s in 1986–7 revealed a mid-C14 riverside wall with dumping behind it to reclaim land. In 1564 the property was bought by the Sackville family, later Earls of Dorset, commemorated by Dorset Rise at the se corner. Wholesale redevelopment from the 1960s on has left the square a hodge-podge.

Two big office complexes dominate. On the w side, the dreary FLEETBANK HOUSE, 1971–5, by *C. Edmund Wilford & Sons*, grey-granite-clad and strongly horizontal. Lower wings extend into the square. Shapeless passages through them to Hood Court (N) and, down cavernous stairs, to Primrose Hill (s). No. 8 on the s side (KPMG), a big block by *EPR Partnership*, 1987–90. Tall, square, blockishly symmetrical front in banded brown stone, variously recessed. Silly corner clock turret by Dorset Rise, facing which is a lean-to atrium high up. On the e side, No. 10, ST BRIDE'S HOUSE, vaguely traditional brick by *T. P. Bennett & Son*, 1982–5. The undistinguished twin gables were retained from Bell's Buildings, 1908 by *F. W. Foster*. St Bride's Passage between them, open to St Bride's church on the N side, leads through to Bride Lane. No. 12 is just recognizable as a mid- to late C18 house, much altered for use as a warehouse. Then *Lutyens*'s Reuters building (*see* Fleet Street). No. 1 on the N side, an early C18 five-bay brick house with giant angle pilasters, is largely a post-war reconstruction.

In the middle of the square, a modest plain OBELISK of grey granite commemorating Lord Mayor Waithman (†1833), by *James Elmes*. It came here from Bartholomew Close, *c.* 1975. Until *c.* 1951 it stood at the S end of Farringdon Street, facing an obelisk of 1775 once at the N end of New Bridge Street.

SANDY'S ROW

The boundary of the City S of Artillery Lane, until the late C17 the boundary also of the Old Artillery Ground (*see* Artillery Lane). Called from its C18 builder; the S part, with the former Sandy's Street, SW, merged with Middlesex Street in 1892–6. The N part retains the close, murky atmosphere of the old inner East End. The corner with Widegate Street is the KING'S STORES pub, by *W. M. Brutton*, 1902. Otherwise mostly later C19, notably the stark front of the Sandy's Row Synagogue (*see London 5: East and Docklands*).

SEETHING LANE

The strange name is thought to be from the Old English *sifethen*, 'full of chaff', a reference to the Corn Market in Fenchurch Street. Several Romano-British pavements have been recorded here. On one lay a poorly executed and mutilated sculptured group, now in the Museum of London, representing the three mother goddesses seated side by side.

CORN EXCHANGE CHAMBERS at No. 2 (E side) has a nicely Italian front. Arcaded stone-faced ground floor, red brick with arched windows to the speculative offices above. Naturalistic carving of the window spandrels, relatively early for a secular building. The date is 1859, the architect *E. I'Anson* (rebuilt behind the façade by *Fitzroy Robinson Partnership*, 1990). The main Corn Exchange lay behind, in Mark Lane (q.v.).

On the E side is a railed strip of garden and across it the side elevation of the Port of London Authority building (*see* Public Buildings). This replaced *c.* 1910 the warehouses of the East and West India Docks Co. here, which had superseded in turn *Wren*'s Navy Office of 1682–3 (dem. *c.* 1788). Here and in its predecessor (founded 1656) worked Samuel Pepys, who is commemorated by a BUST by *Karin Jonzen*, 1983, in the garden, and in Pepys Street at the N (q.v.). WALSINGHAM HOUSE to the N, by *E. G. W. Souster*, 1929, combines bronze floor bands and blockish detail in low-relief pilastered façades on three sides.

SHERBORNE LANE *see* CANNON STREET

SHOE LANE

It runs between Holborn and Fleet Street. Known c. 1200, as 'Sholond', or land shaped like a shoe. The buildings, all post-war, are in the central section, which was incorporated into the new route made in the mid 1860s between Holborn Viaduct and Ludgate Circus. For those on the E side, see Farringdon Street.

On the W SIDE, by the fork with St Bride Street, HILL HOUSE, large eight-storey offices by the *Ronald Fielding Partnership*, 1975–9. Polygonal, with fluted pre-cast concrete panels and big projecting floor bands with splayed sills. Upper storeys set back. A perpendicular stair-tower maintains the vertical on Shoe Lane. The public library in the basement uses foundations of c. 1960, laid for the *Daily Telegraph*'s printing works, but never so used.

To the N is Shoe Lane's dominant building: the INTERNATIONAL PRESS CENTRE in its little precinct, by *R. Seifert & Partners*, 1968–75. Not one of their most impressive or memorable towers. Eighteen storeys on big piers above a recessed lobby (altered 1991). Near-square on plan, each side sloping back from a windowless central recess, as if four slender identical towers were bundled together. Clad in brown pre-cast panels with rounded corners, finished off weakly without crowning emphasis. Low rear wing to New Street Square. No. 75, N, repeats the motifs of the tower, at one-third of the height. Nos. 66–73, by *H. V. Lobb & Partners*, 1959–62, are merely dreary.

SMITHFIELD STREET see WEST SMITHFIELD

SNOW HILL

The name is older than the present alignment, made c. 1870 to connect the new Holborn Viaduct with Farringdon Street below. The first Snow Hill (in the C13 *Snore Hylle*) lay further S. Notoriously steep and twisting, it was superseded in 1802–3 by the new Skinner Street (see Holborn Viaduct, the E part of which follows the same alignment).

On the S side only bleak rear ranges of 1960s blocks on Holborn Viaduct. On the N side, after Smithfield Market, some 1870s survivors, amidst later rebuilding. On the corner of Smithfield Street facing up the hill, No. 10, ungainly red brick with cast stone frontispiece and other decoration, by *Holford Associates*, 1988–9. After Cock Lane, Nos. 6–9 by *Fitzroy Robinson & Partners*, 1974–6, more discreet, in plain brown brick with a curved corner and square windows in splayed reveals. After the Police Station at No. 5 (see Public Buildings), No. 4, by *T. Chatfeild Clarke*, dated 1875, a former furniture warehouse. Steeply gabled, assimilating devices filched from Nesfield and Philip Webb; red brick with rubbed trim, sunflower panels, and nice iron railings in front. Nos. 1–3 revert to the Italianate manner of most of the Holborn Viaduct scheme, here with uncouth masks at the top of the piers.

Built 1873; reconstructed behind 1986–7 by *Green Lloyd Adams*. St Sepulchre's church (q.v.) ends the street.

SOUTH PLACE *see* ELDON STREET

SUFFOLK LANE

Called after the C15 seat of the de la Poles, Earls of Suffolk, established in the mansion built by Sir John de Pulteney a century before (*see* also Laurence Pountney Hill). The Merchant Taylors' School stood on part of its site from 1561 to 1875, latterly in a building of the 1670s by *Hooke* (E side).

The handsome big house at No. 2 (w side) is still recognizable, despite alterations, as of Hooke's time. One John Taylor, merchant, was living there by 1674. L-shaped, with the entrance and open-well staircase in the angle of the stuccoed N wing, which is set back behind a little court. The date of 1788 suits the style of the nice reeded frieze at first-floor level here. (Inside, good, strongly Rococo plasterwork of *c.* 1740.) A wing of exposed brick faces Gophir Lane on the S, raised on brick-vaulted cellars. Two bays to the l. have bold quoins and squarer windows, suggesting alterations of *c.* 1700 (cf. the contemporary houses in Laurence Pountney Hill, whose backs are opposite).

Suffolk Lane crosses the site of one of the more enigmatic public buildings of Roman London, often referred to as the Governor's Palace (*see* Introduction p. 34).

TEMPLE AVENUE

Part of the late C19 street grid laid out N of the Victoria Embankment. On the w side, against the Temple boundary, TEMPLE CHAMBERS, by *Whichcord*, completed posthumously in 1887. Near-symmetrical stone offices 350 ft (107 metres) long, reminiscent of contemporary mansion blocks in Marylebone or Victoria. Vaguely Jacobean, without decisive accents but with pilasters, balconies and canted bays giving undulating oblique views. On the E side, TEMPLE HOUSE, by *Frederick Boreham*, 1892–4, with close-set oriels and an undernourished clock turret on the angled corner to Tallis Street. Built as premises for Horace Marshall & Co., newsagents and printers.

For buildings further S, *see* Victoria Embankment.

THREADNEEDLE STREET

Formerly Three Needle Street, probably called after a street sign. In the Middle Ages it was usually treated as part of (Old) Broad Street. Traces of several well-appointed late ROMAN TOWN HOUSES have been recorded in the area. Two coloured mosaic pavements featuring geometric and floral patterns are now in the British Museum.

The Hospital of St Anthony of Vienne was established 1243, in a former synagogue on the N side. Huguenots took it over in 1550. Their chapel, rebuilt after 1666, was replaced 1842–4 by the Hall of Commerce, to its developer *Edward Moxhay*'s surprisingly accomplished French-influenced designs. Intended to rival the Royal Exchange, it was instead converted to a bank in 1855 (by *Woodthorpe*). Its former frieze, by *Musgrave Watson*, is in a garden in Napier Street, Islington (*see London 4: North*).

The street first runs between the Bank of England, N, and Royal Exchange, S (*see* Public Buildings). We begin further E, where Old Broad Street forks NE by the Stock Exchange. On the S side, No. 1, an eight-storey wedge with curved ends, by the *Fitzroy Robinson Partnership*, 1987–91. A good, humane design, historically resonant, but without direct quotation. Double-height ground floor, mezzanine, then three-storey bays of faintly Elizabethan flavour, but with superimposed plain cylindrical columns. Floor-strings with dark stone bands follow their undulations. Close-meshed glazing bars. The site of *Wren*'s St Benet Fink, a quirky elongated decagon (1670–5, dem. 1842). A C10 wheel-headed cross was found in its former churchyard.

Then on both sides a splendid unbroken progression of stone-faced banks and offices, of every generation between 1850s and 1920s. In 1997 many await new uses. The N corner (No. 1 Old Broad Street), by *H. Chatfeild Clarke*, 1903, for the Indemnity Mutual Marine Insurance. Acute end like a liner's prow. First-floor Gibbs surrounds, concave window reveals below. Clarke's corner stacks and reliefs were trimmed off in 1936, when *Mewès & Davis* rebuilt the upper parts as an extension of their WESTMINSTER BANK (Nos. 51–53, 1922–31). This evokes a grand High Renaissance Roman palace: its convex front, gentle all-over rustication and third-floor window frames from Peruzzi's Palazzo Massimi; its central first-floor feature from Michelangelo's parts of the Palazzo Farnese (carvers Messrs *Aumonier*). Tuscan columns below. The bank was Davis's favourite work. Rear front to Old Broad Street (No. 9). (Banking hall with coupled columns and coffered ceiling, altered.)

Opposite (S side), the former CITY BANK, on the E corner with Finch Lane. By Messrs *Moseley*, 1855–6, the City's oldest surviving premises for a joint-stock bank. In the heavy palazzo style, with a rounded corner. Here, especially by the entrance, the detail turns Mannerist: blocked columns, pilasters vanishing into channelled rustication. Ground-floor windows have gloriously rich iron screens. To Threadneedle Street a lower, simplified cornice, apparently because this section was originally separately owned. Remodelled internally in 1889 and in 1909, when *T. B. Whinney* added six closer-spaced bays along Finch Lane. Of the latter date the two fine circular banking halls with columns, in 1997 long disused.

On the N side again, Nos. 43–47, by *T. H. Smith*, 1890. Tuscan granite columns and granite frieze to a ground-floor banking hall, giant pilasters to chambers above. Both orders rest on pedestals – a typical late C19 refusal of the grand gesture. Roof altered. No. 42, a tactful extension of 1957 (by *Waterhouse & Ripley*) to

J. Macvicar Anderson's former Eagle Insurance, 1902 (No. 41), a narrow, chaste palazzo, with channelled ground floor and first-floor aedicules. No. 40, latest C19, sets back behind a little gated courtyard. Of Bath stone. Tall coupled columns frame a Venetian window. Spandrel figures with camels. The archway below leads via Adam's Court into Old Broad Street. Nos. 40–51 are proposed for conversion into a hotel (1997), with Nos. 1–18 Old Broad Street.

The S side facing has a long run of offices screening Merchant Taylors' Hall (q.v.). All are channelled below, with two upper storeys and mansard: Nos. 28–29 of 1910 by *H. Alexander Pelly* with *J. J. Burnet*, the former Bank of New South Wales, with unadorned window openings; No. 32 by *T. B. Whinney & Austen Hall*, 1919–20, more ornate, incorporating an entrance bay to the hall (consultant here *Sir Reginald Blomfield*); No. 34 by *Campbell-Jones, Son & Smithers*, 1929–30. For No. 39 (Lloyds Bank), *see* Bishopsgate.

Last on the N side is the BANK OF SCOTLAND (Nos. 37–38). Built as the British Linen Bank, 1902–3 by *Macvicar Anderson*. Heavy Palladian, rusticated and arched below, columns above, with pilastered end bays. Attic blocks with square chimneys, rather mid C19 in manner. Colourful banking hall: bright faience ceiling (*Burmantofts*), red and green marble; somewhat altered when the rear parts were rebuilt by *Dennis Lennon & Partners*, 1980–1. Of this date the simplified classical colonnade facing the raised court by the NatWest Tower (*see* Old Broad Street). It is on the site of the South Sea Company's headquarters (South Sea House), a workmanlike stone-dressed pile probably by *James Gould*, 1724–5 (Colvin); latterly home to the Baltic Exchange, 1857–1900. Over the r. doorway a RELIEF of two seated figures against ships' rigging. Anderson retrieved this from the younger *Bacon*'s former studio, where (he claimed) it had been since South Sea House refused to pay the sculptor's fee; but it has clearly been re-worked.

THROGMORTON AVENUE

Begun in 1875–6 by the Drapers' and Carpenters' Companies, and extended S in the 1880s. Planned by *Charles Reilly Sen.* for the Drapers and *W. W. Pocock* for the Carpenters. The N part by London Wall replaced both the Drapers' ancient garden, which had stopped the Great Fire's progress N, and the previous Carpenters' Hall; Pocock's new hall lies further E, at the NE corner (q.v.). Pocock and Reilly supervised the new office chambers, Portland-stone-clad like the hall, but less demonstrative, with façades in lower relief. This homogeneous private, gated development contrasts remarkably with the stylistic anarchy of contemporary new public streets.

Grandest of the chambers is No. 2 by *John Norton*, 1879–81 (NW corner), partly hidden by the post-war Carpenters' Hall extension over the avenue. French Renaissance, with carved medallions (by *Daymond*, disappointing) between five diminishing floors of close-set windows for the many little rooms needed by the Submarine Telegraph Company. Pneumatic tubes originally linked it to the

G.P.O., Stock Exchange, and Threadneedle Street. Buildings beyond have similar shallow horizontals, big windows and flat mostly Northern Renaissance detail. Giant pilasters on Nos. 4–6 (by *F. Chancellor*) and No. 10, both 1881, on the w side. Nos. 5 and 7 (E side) have superimposed pilasters. Odd one out is No. 8 (w side), the former Provincial Bank of Ireland, 1879–81 by *Edward Salter*, still in the plain palazzo manner. Later buildings further s are connected with the new entrance made in 1888 from Austin Friars (q.v.). No. 17 (E side), a rather mechanical stone-clad Postmodern job by *Rolfe Judd Group Practice*, 1986–8, is an extension of Morgan Grenfell's premises in Great Winchester Street behind. Incorporated (r.), part of the façade of No. 19, GARDEN HOUSE, by *Davis & Emmanuel*, 1889–90, at the corner with the Austin Friars entry, similar in style to Reilly's buildings there.

The w side was swept away for DRAPERS' GARDENS (NATIONAL WESTMINSTER BANK), by *R. Seifert & Partners* in collaboration with *F. Norman James*, 1962–7, for the developer Harry Hyams. The main building is a plainly detailed 326 ft (99⅓ metres) tower, more clean-lined than the same team's contemporary Centre Point, but similarly distinctive in shape: here, a convex back and front and indented sides. Massive tapering supports cantilever dramatically from the reinforced concrete core. Floor sills clad in grey mosaic project emphatically between green glazing. On top a deep dark balcony slot, then a solid storey added late during building. Entrance up steps through a low L-shaped range extending also along Copthall Avenue, where it stands on cylindrical steel-clad columns. By the entrance a fountain, and more steps up, r., to a deserted raised inner courtyard, a relic of the elevated walkway scheme.

Beyond Copthall Avenue on the w side, WARNFORD COURT, dated 1884, by *Reilly*. Long, uninspired symmetrical front with lots of small-scale Northern Renaissance motifs and a tiny central pediment. Opposite, the Drapers' Hall (q.v.), with its little garden and its offices bridging the passage into Throgmorton Street.

THROGMORTON STREET

Named after Sir Nicholas Throckmorton, the Elizabethan courtier. A narrow street in which the character of the Victorian City could until the mid 1960s be experienced without much C20 interference. The s side has since been wholly rebuilt for the Stock Exchange (*see* Public Buildings).

The N side begins at the w with the ANGEL COURT development (Nos. 30–35). By *Fitzroy Robinson & Partners*, 1974–80, for the Clothworkers' Company. The street front announces the motif of flat chamfered bays in all-over polished purple Dakota marble. This material and its then-innovative application in pre-fabricated panels reflect American practice. Large tinted flush windows, thin black surrounds. The range runs N along ANGEL COURT behind, closing it to E and w. A twenty-storey tower of irregular octagonal section shoots up within the NE angle. On its far (E) side are murky ramps to an elevated walkway – amongst its last large-scale uses after the early 1970s (*see* Introduction p. 131). At the outer NW corner a bridge crosses Copthall Avenue to an outlying block; by which stage one is rather surfeited with purple marble. Otherwise the group relates to the old street pattern surprisingly well.

On the w side of Angel Court, two late C19 fronts: Nos. 9–10, with granite ground-floor columns and aedicules over; No. 11 with central giant pilasters. Both rebuilt behind by *YRM*, 1987–90. For the National Westminster Bank to their s, *see* Lothbury.

Back to Throgmorton Street. Warnford Court belongs with Throgmorton Avenue; then the long front of the Drapers' Hall (qq.v.). No. XXVI (thus) is the former Imperial Ottoman Bank. By *William Burnet*, 1871. Round-arched, with just a touch of the Orient, though the detail is mostly Venetian early Renaissance. Portland stone (painted), with Mansfield detailing and inserts of red granite and serpentine. Venetian of a different kind at No. 25, five-bay polychromatic Gothic offices, with all windows pointed and on the top floor twice as many as below. 1869–70 by *T. Chatfeild Clarke*. Some nice carving (by *Anstey*), but not a strongly personal design.

TOKENHOUSE YARD and KING'S ARMS YARD

Developed in the early C17 on the Earl of Arundel's Lothbury property. An office dispensing trade tokens, used in lieu of scarce current coin, stood here 1634–72 (*see* Introduction p. 66). On the w side, a way through was made in 1882 into King's Arms Yard (known from 1393, as King's Alley). Both escaped the usual decline of such back-streets into linear light-wells between large offices, and still offer a rewarding selection of late C19 and C20 commercial buildings.

On the w, No. 19 is the BANK OF ENGLAND DINING CLUB, 1924–5 by *F. W. Troup*. Foundations and some ashlar were reused from *G. Somers Clarke*'s Italianate Auction Mart Building, 1867, which adjoined his surviving General Credit Company building (*see* Lothbury). Troup's lightweight steel framing allowed five storeys to Clarke's three, hence the unusually tall and narrow shape. Somewhat harsh grid-like façades, reflecting Troup's unused designs for rebuilding the Bank proper. Tall pilasters up to the penultimate storey dominate. Triplets of windows and small-scale decoration between. Closer-set windows at the top (cf. his earlier Spicer Bros., New Bridge Street). Around the corner in KING'S ARMS YARD, an extension of 1958–62 by *Peter S. Ednie*. A well-proportioned Modern front, curiously at odds with the stuffiness of the Bank's 1950s offices in Cheapside and Prince's Street. Strong colours, opulent materials: five types of stone, including serpentine alternating with projecting Portland blocks along the floor bands. Yellow-tiled reveals; plain stone surround to the whole, below a roof canopy. The N side of King's Arms Yard is TOKENHOUSE BUILDINGS by *E. Bassett Keeling*, dated 1882, i.e. when the entrance to Tokenhouse Yard was made. Remarkably plain and undemonstrative for Keeling, in white cold-cast terra-cotta (probably *Lascelles*), with square panels of ornament.

Back in Tokenhouse Yard, Nos. 6–8, E side, are the former Bank of London & South America, by Messrs *Joseph*, 1925–6. Solidly Greek Doric with widely spaced columns, and a tall block of offices behind (rather perfunctorily detailed), set back to allow top-lighting of the former banking hall. No. 9, compact red brick and (painted) sandstone offices by *R. E. Tyler*, 1882, with festive relief decoration of loosely Renaissance type, the ground floor recessed to make the most of the light. Facing, No. 17, *c.* 1880, four enjoyably tasteless dark brick storeys with dogtooth bands and ornate stone windows linked vertically. No. 16, adjoining, is again by *Keeling*, 1880. The red brick and painted sandstone façade was originally wildly eclectic, its bloody-minded decoration remotely of Renaissance derivation but without any obvious precedent; but tame classical stone refacing of the 1950s has spoilt the lower floors. (The less ornate N front to Telegraph Street survives intact, *see* Moorgate.)

The N side of the yard extends E, making an L-shape. Along most of it lies the remarkable No. 11, by *E. A. Gruning*, 1869–71, for the merchant bank Frederick Huth & Co. The date is close to Norman Shaw's revolutionary New Zealand Chambers, Leadenhall Street, and if No. 11 is less radical in composition, its decoration is no less impatient with High Victorian formulae. Long unbroken front of red gauged brick, warm and sensuously precise. Bracketed stone sills to the large first-floor windows, which are crowned not by pediments or aedicules but by upswept gables with circular plaques. Further plaques between the windows, linked by beautifully delicate garlands, all in fine terracotta. Top storey of inferior brickwork, though apparently original (illustrated 1880). The richly carved stone doorcase has a deep broken-pedimented hood on alarming lion-head brackets. Inside, a columned hall and an open-well staircase in later C17 style, with twisted balusters and enriched tread ends; the main first-floor room has an ornate ceiling also in late C17 style. Can they be as early as 1871? The narrowest passageway through No. 11 allows its N front to Telegraph Street to be inspected: radically plain, flush even to the extent of recessed downpipes, with rising triplets of round-headed lights marking the staircase, r., and a large window with exposed structural ironwork, l. This plainness (in contrast to the N front of No. 16, r.) is because it originally faced the narrow Great Bell Alley, widened and renamed Telegraph Street only in 1874 (*see* Moorgate).

Back in Tokenhouse Yard, *Gruning*'s more modest No. 12 is four-storeyed, also red brick. Entry is via a low return wing, apparently altered, with a doorcase dated 1872, with bearded heads in lieu of lions. The covered bridge joining No. 12 with No. 10, plain red brick late C19 offices, is a regrettable addition of 1963 by *Fitzroy Robinson & Partners* for CAZENOVE'S, who moved into No. 11 in 1937 and have since expanded into adjacent properties.

TOOK'S COURT

A sleepy L-shaped lane off Cursitor Street, until 1994 mostly in the Borough of Camden. Called Tucker's or Duck Court in the late CI7; described by Strype (1720) as 'large and well-built'. Of that period Nos. 14–15, in the S part: houses framed by giant Baroque Ionic pilasters of rubbed brick. Three storeys and three bays, narrow windows with segmental heads also of rubbed brick. The frieze and generous dentil cornice survive in full only on No. 15 (Dickens's house, with a good original staircase). Grand rusticated doorcases to both houses. No. 16, also early CI8, was refronted in the early CI9. Otherwise all utilitarian CI9. The Patent Office overlooks the N and NE parts (*see* Public Buildings).

TOWER HILL

The area W, N, and NE of the Tower, and affording good views of it. The scaffold on Tower Hill lay NE of All Hallows' church, within the gardens of Trinity Square (q.v.). The Tower and its surroundings belong not in the City but in the old Liberties of the Tower, self-governing until 1855 (now incorporated with the Borough of Tower Hamlets). This allowed the Governor of the Tower to keep the precincts free of encroachments. In 1887 a new road was driven across just N of the moat, in connection with tunnelling for the District Railway (cf. Eastcheap and Byward Street). Mass tourism is now the dominant presence, and the open space W of the Tower suffers in 1997 from an excess of bollards and a squalid litter of kiosks and poor signage; improvements are proposed, under a master plan by *BDP*.

Approaching the Tower from the NW, one first encounters TOWER HILL TERRACE, a viewing platform made in 1951 (by *Hannen & Markham*) on the basement of a bombed warehouse of 1864, built by *George Myers*, apparently without an architect. The cyclopean battered granite plinth is exposed by falling ground, S; eight upper storeys were destroyed in 1940. Inside, cast-iron columns, cross-girders, and shallow brick arches (of air bricks, an early use), extending into three lower vaulted levels. These were converted for the TOWER HILL PAGEANT by the *Terry Farrell Partnership*, 1987–91. The new entrance is down steps under a glazed pitched roof with the ghost of a pediment. Standing guard, six virile wooden SCULPTURES of bell-jacks in CI6 costume, from the campanile of *H.A. Darbishire*'s Columbia Market, Bethnal Green, 1864–9 (dem. 1958).

To the S lies TOWER PLACE, planned jointly by the City Corporation, LCC, and the former Borough of Stepney, 1962–6; *Sir Basil Spence* acted as consultant. Highly praised by Pevsner on completion, it has not aged well: the raised pedestrian podium is under-used and unhelpfully inaccessible from E and S, and the aggregate-faced buildings (by *Anthony Beckles Willson* of *George: Trew: Dunn*, in association with *CLRP Architects*) are remarkably grubby in 1997. The plan is an S-shaped five-storey block arranged round two informal courtyards, one flanked by All

Hallows, the other open towards the river. At the W end a sixteen-storey tower. Vertical accents, strongly emphasized by thin irregularly placed mullions on the lower blocks, and by the varied modelling of the tower. The podium houses a pub and a coach and car park, entered through battered rusticated walls of granite to Lower Thames Street. In the W courtyard, SCULPTURE of a hammer-thrower by *John Robinson*, 1973.

In front of the E range, a little circular turret of 1926, by the *Office of Works*. It gives entry to the former TOWER SUBWAY, the prototype of the London Tubes (though conceived forty years later than the Brunels' Thames Tunnel further E). Built in 1869–70 by *P. W. Barlow*, the engineer, on a patent taken in 1864; *J. H. Greathead*'s tunnelling shield was employed. Pedestrians soon replaced the original cable-driven cars, but since 1896 it has carried only hydraulic mains.

Further S, within the outer gates of the Tower and facing its main entrance, the former TOWER ENGINE HOUSE of 1863 (now the souvenir shop). By *Salvin*, then much employed at the Tower proper. A sophisticated essay in stripped Gothic. Stock brick, the ground-floor arcade with six unmoulded pointed arches. Small segment-headed windows above, in gables with pointed-arched bargeboards. They rest on muscular chamfered brackets corbelled out. To the l. a square tower with sashes in lancet-headed recesses. A free-standing chimney has disappeared. Immediately S, the little WHARFINGER COTTAGE, preposterously domesticated for its riverside situation. Its half-timbered gables, Gothic bargeboards, and fishscale-tiled roof all evoke the work of e.g. George Devey. Probably also by *Salvin*, who in 1863 designed his own house at Fernhurst, Sussex, in a similar style.

TRINITY SQUARE

The name for the oddly-shaped NW extension of Tower Hill. The central space and the buildings towards the E belong not in the City but in the Liberties of the Tower (*see* Tower Hill). The oval garden, W, was laid out by *Samuel Wyatt*, 1797, as a setting for his Trinity House, N side (*see* Public Buildings), and reduced in area in 1883–7. The dominant building is not Trinity House but the former Port of
121 London Authority, NW corner (*see* Public Buildings). Apart from this maritime pair, the monuments and remains of the former City defences command more attention than the buildings proper. The replanning of Tower Hill, being formulated in 1996 by *BDP*, is likely to transform the SE part, where visitors approach the Tower from the Underground.

124 MERCANTILE MARINE MEMORIAL. At the S end of the gardens, overlooking the Tower and the Thames. By *Lutyens*, 1926–8. An open tunnel-vaulted three-bay structure 64 ft (19½ metres) long, in a dignified classical style. Unfluted Doric columns. The vault and stepped attic block recall the architect's Great War memorials on the Continent. The names of the dead are recorded on bronze plaques treated like rusticated walling. The traffic thundering along Tower Hill a few feet away robs it of little of its power to

move. Immediately N, the less assertive 1939–45 memorial takes the form of a sunken garden, by *Maufe*, 1952–5. The plan suggests a cathedral chevet crossed by a hollow boat-shape. The conception of a memorial to the missing itself in the form of a void is intelligent, but let down by indifferent lettering and by *Wheeler's* strangely jaunty reliefs.

On the W side, two typical early C20 stone-faced offices: No. 14, r., the former Swedish Chamber of Commerce, 1920–2 by *Niven & Wigglesworth*; No. 15, l., formerly the General Steam Navigation Co., by *E. B. I'Anson*, 1908–9, heightened 1931 by *Alfred Roberts*. He added a Palladian extension facing N to Muscovy Street, made in 1912 across the old Muscovy Court (named after the C16 Russian colony here).

Then to the NE corner, where Cooper's Row enters the square. On the E side here, from the N, Nos. 42–43, a late C18 house with central top-lit staircase, and No. 41, the former Navy Sick and Hurt Board offices, 1772, a three-bay house on a somewhat larger scale, with an aedicule to the central first-floor window. Both refurbished by *Lyons, Sleeman & Hoare*, 1985–6, with a tall rear extension topped by a cupola and weathervane. On No. 41 a bronze medallion of Lord Wakefield of Hythe, by *Cecil Thomas*, 1937. No. 40, red brick offices by *C. Watkins*, 1901, altered. Then a good, plain five-storey block by *CLRP Architects*, 1961, adapted for TOWER HILL UNDERGROUND STATION in 1967. Flush-glazed between narrow mullions. In front lies a raised E extension of the main gardens (called Wakefield Gardens). Here a giant SUNDIAL designed by *John Chitty*, with historical reliefs by *Edwin Russell*, 1992.

CITY WALL. Further E, a fine section of the wall stands in a sunken garden, approximate to Roman ground level. The N end retains the Roman inner facing, with regularly coursed square ragstone blocks, a triple facing-course of tiles at the base, and three courses of bonding tiles at intervals above it. These run through the thickness of the wall, as can be seen further S, where the facing has gone, revealing the inner core of ragstone rubble and concrete. The Roman wall survives to a height of just over 10 ft (3 metres); above this, medieval rebuilding makes a total of over 25 ft (7½ metres). In the rebuilt part tiles and stone are randomly mixed up. At the S end of the wall, adjacent to Tower Hill, two walls forming half of the foundation of a Roman internal turret. (Further traces of the Roman wall high in the wall S of platform 1, Tower Hill station – a small piece in section with a course of bonding tiles – and at No. 41, where the basement preserves a fine piece showing the external face with sandstone plinth.)

In front of the wall in Wakefield Gardens, a modern cast of the inscription from the TOMBSTONE of the Procurator Classicianus. Six fragmentary lines of well-cut letters, interpreted thus: 'To the memory of Gaius Julius Alpinus Classicianus, of the Fabian tribe, son of Gaius ... Procurator of Britain. [This tablet was erected by] his wife Julia Pacata Indiana, daughter of [Julius] Indus.' The story of its discovery is unusually interesting. The three top lines and the fine 'bolster' with corner scrolls were found in 1852 during excavation of a Roman bastion in the former Trinity Place, immediately N. They were incorporated in a mass of other monumental material, including cornices and column-drums, reused as building material when bastions were added to the existing wall. The next part, containing the last three lines, came to light placed upside-down in the base of the same bastion during construction of the electricity substation in the Crescent, 1935. The pieces have been reassembled in the British Museum, a gap being left for the middle lines which described the Procurator's career before his arrival in Britain. The STATUE in the gardens has nothing to do with Classicianus or with Roman London, but was introduced between the wars by the indefatigable Rev. Clayton of All Hallows. The C19 composite derives from two ancient originals, having the head of Trajan combined with the body of Augustus.

Facing the wall is a second station entrance, with sunken concrete-lined passages to funnel visitors s underneath Tower Hill. By the Tower moat here, remains of the medieval TOWER POSTERN, laid out as excavated in 1978: the lower parts of the s side of the gate passage, apparently of unusual dog-leg plan, and a s tower which originally overlooked the moat. Traces of a portcullis rebate within the stop-chamfered gate jamb; loops in the E wall and splayed NE corner of the tower, and in the return facing the main gateway. Staircase in a polygonal NW turret. Precise dating is difficult: remains of vaulting found in the infilled basement were of C14 type, but the typically C13 chamfering of the openings suggests the vault was inserted later. Though the postern cannot be older than the late C13 moat, it may perpetuate an exit called *Cungate* near here, mentioned in 1108. Stow records its partial abandonment after subsidence in 1440.

TUDOR STREET

A late C19 name (1891) for a composite street: the mid-C16 Tudor Street or King Tudor Street was extended w in 1849 up to Whitefriars Street, and further w again along the old Temple Lane in the 1880s, when the s side was laid out in a grid bounded by the Victoria Embankment (q.v.). C19–C20 buildings connected with the newspaper industry still predominate.

At the E end, Nos. 2–4, on the corner of Bridewell Place (N side), the former Institute of Journalists, by *H. L. Florence*, 1902–4 (converted to chambers 1997). A pretty essay in the tradition of Norman Shaw's Scotland Yard. On the s side, facing Bridewell Place, *Fitzroy Robinson Partnership*'s Unilever House extension, 1974–81. Stone-clad, with an elegant bronzed screen with paired vertical fins incorporating narrow balconies. Gilt SCULPTURE of a girl by *Bernard Sindall* over the Watergate entrance, visible down Kingscote Street. An apsidal projection at the NW corner repeats the outlines of a stair-tower on the former gallery of Henry VIII's Bridewell Palace, from brick foundations found in 1978 (*see* also New Bridge Street). Continuing w along Tudor Street, the two big near-matching blocks of J. P. Morgan (*see* John Carpenter Street).

The other side of Bridewell Place is KPMG, housed in a complex of three office buildings by *Trehearne & Norman, Preston & Partners*,

1950–7, refaced in colourful granite by *Renton Howard Wood Levin Partnership*, 1984–6. Of the 1980s the Egyptianizing top cornices and new main entrance from the courtyard facing Dorset Rise, off Tudor Street further W. The clean 1950s lines are still apparent, e.g. in the concave-ended former Kildare House (N), and in the former St Bridget's House (E), with its rounded bay housing a free-wheeling spiral staircase. These previously had more varied, small-scale diapered and tiled ornament. In the courtyard, a FOUNTAIN with a large equestrian St George and the Dragon, by *Michael Sandle*, 1988.

Further on, No. 22, GOULDEN'S, a painfully dull red brick slab by the *Fitzroy Robinson Partnership*, 1983–8, and No. 24, a solid stuccoed block of *c.*1830, with a battered Doric doorcase to Whitefriars Street. Then on the S side, a wholly late C19 block of warehouses, more reminiscent of Manchester than London: CLAN HOUSE (Nos. 19–21), plain red brick with pilaster-piers and segment-headed windows, built for Sir George Newnes's *Westminster Gazette*, 1893; a narrow section of Temple House (*see* Temple Avenue); and the tough-minded Nos. 23–27, the former Argus Printing Co. works by *C.V. Hunter*, 1896–7. Rusticated stone ground floor with grotesque heads and a corner relief of Argus, red brick and red Ruabon terracotta over, with plain cross-windows on two diminishing top storeys.

The block opposite, N, begins with NORTHCLIFFE HOUSE, by *Ellis & Clarke*, 1925–7, overspill from Carmelite House (*see* Carmelite Street); the home of the *Daily Mail* until 1989. Unremarkable stripped-classical façades of reconstituted stone, with bronze floor strips and Egyptian touches on the cornice. Over the corner entrance a low polygonal tower, added 1929. High proportion of glass to wall, set near-flush. Ground-floor loading bays. The printing basement, in 1997 still intact, was the first in Britain with reel feed from beneath presses in horizonal lines, a system emulated at the much grander *Telegraph* and *Express* on Fleet Street. It stands on the site of the celebrated Whitefriars Glass Works, commemorated in GLASSHOUSE ALLEY, l.; its closure in 1923 marked the end of glassmaking in the City. Nos. 28–30, the WHITE SWAN TAVERN, pilastered brick of 1882, by *F. Adams Smith*. Then the printing works of the former *Evening News*, 1926–30 by *M.E. & O.H. Collins*, extending up Bouverie Street. It faces HARMSWORTH HOUSE, the former *News Chronicle*, 1937–9 by *Tubbs, Duncan & Osburn*, streamlined red brick (for the extension in Bouverie Street, q.v.). No. 36, a concrete-panelled pub by *Royce, Hurley & Stewart*, 1972–3, in grating juxtaposition with the Inner Temple gateway. For Temple Chambers opposite (S side), *see* Temple Avenue.

UPPER THAMES STREET

Outside the bombed area to the N, no area of the City has changed as much in recent years as Upper and Lower Thames Street. Until the later C20, the route primarily served the innumerable wharves and riverside warehouses of the port of London. The little lanes on the S side that led down to these survive here and there between big post-war blocks, but in nothing like their old density. Their intricacy and the former maze-like property boundaries reflected piecemeal land reclamation in Saxon and medieval times. The street proper is also built over land won from the Thames, most of it during various operations of the C1–C3. Much detail of all these processes has been revealed by recent archaeology (*see* Roman and Medieval Riverside below).

The oldest witnesses to this mercantile past are the substantial merchants' houses built after the Great Fire, e.g. in Laurence Pountney Lane and Suffolk Lane, to the N (qq.v.). But from the early C19 growing trade drove out the residential population in favour of increasingly large warehouses. High land values and constricted sites precluded the rectilinear gigantism of those at the artificial docks downstream, and the City's warehouses were typically tall rather than broad, as may be seen from the surviving example on Brook's Wharf.

Air raids destroyed much property, especially on the N side of the street. Many of the replacements, mostly detached offices of the 1950s–60s, have been rebuilt from *c.* 1985. These post-war buildings are low, even somewhat squat, to preserve the view of St Paul's. The less damaged part W of Queen Street remained devoted to ware-housing, and new warehouses were still being built into the 1960s. By the end of that decade, however, riverside trade was in acute decline, and further rebuilding has swept away any vestige of Upper Thames Street's pre-war atmosphere of 'warehouses, horse-lorries and smells' (Pevsner).[*]

More drastically, the Blackfriars Underpass (begun 1963) and North Bank Development Scheme (1972–80) transformed the street from a relatively narrow road used primarily for access into an E–W trunk route. This required the diversion of the W part through a tunnel further S, continuing on reclaimed land beneath the Blackfriars Bridge approach to join the Victoria Embankment. Two slip-roads from Queen Victoria Street on the N join the new section at Puddle Dock and at White Lion Hill, which passes over Upper Thames Street's tunnel. Large, low buildings of the 1970s–80s further E exploit the space over the tunnel. None of this is friendly to pedestrians, who may want to follow the riverside walkway where this has been completed. The dedicated traffic-hater may prefer to view the buildings of the S side from the Surrey bank.

The Roman and Medieval Riverside

Post-war upheavals have allowed the pre-C17 history of the riverside to be reconstructed in unprecedented detail, aided by the excellent preservation of timber structures in the moist, dense riverside ground. From E to W, the chief excavations were: in Lower Thames Street, at the Custom House (1973), W of Billingsgate Market (1982), Magnus House (1974–8), and Pudding Lane (1981); in

---

[*]Demolished since 1970: No. 46 by *Burges*, 1866, the two-bay warehouse that intro-duced to London the motif of a big Gothic arch within a gable framing the upper win-dows; Messrs Waterlow's warehouse on Broken Wharf, 1881–2; Nos. 20–21 Queenhithe, Neo-Wren by *F. E. Williams*, 1902. Earlier demolitions: No. 15, the Carron Company warehouse, *c.* 1840, probably by *Henry Garling*; No. 22 by *Edis*, 1872, a warehouse with low, prettified Gothic offices in front.

Upper Thames Street, at Seal House (1974), Ebbgate House (1981), Public Cleansing Department (1959), Queen Street Place (1988), Vintners' Place (1989–91), Bull Wharf (1990–4), Swiss Bank House (1974–6) and Baynard's Castle (1972–5).

The pre-Roman foreshore and the main C1 timber quays lay N of Thames Street, from which a short length of one quay (from Lower Thames Street) has been restored and is on display at the Tower Hill Pageant (*see* Tower Hill). Further w, timber quays were located to either side of the mouth of the Walbrook in early phases. An early pottery kiln operated near to the site of St James's church, apparently run by an immigrant potter whose business failed to survive the Boudiccan revolt. On the terraced hillside overlooking the river stood some of Roman London's principal public buildings: the so-called Governor's Palace, the great Flavian baths, etc. (*see* Introduction p. 34 and Huggin Hill). Later extensions mean that the early C3 waterfront lies s of the road (Queen Street Place), over which was built the late Roman RIVERSIDE WALL (*see* Introduction p. 41). Later Roman town houses were subsequently built on the N side of Lower Thames Street, of which substantial remains are preserved at No. 100 there (q.v.).

The C3 Roman quays fell into decay in Saxon times, hastened by erosion from rising river levels. Further reclamation was typically much smaller in scale, along individual wharves and hithes. It probably spread outwards from three Saxon centres: the landing-points at Queenhithe (*see* below) and Billingsgate (*see* Billingsgate Market, Public Buildings), and the foreign settlement at Dowgate, later the Steelyard (*see* Cannon Street Station, also Public Buildings). The presence of four churches s of the street (All Hallows the Great and Less, St Botolph, St Magnus) suggests that by the C12, when the parishes were formed, these points represented substantial areas of reclamation and occupation.

A variety of methods was used to win land from the water. Saxon post-and-plank revetments, staves, and clay banks consolidated with timbers and wattle fencing have all been found (Queen Street Place). By the C12, larger, more complex prefabricated post-and-plank revetments were used, braced at front and back (Queen Street Place). Up to seven consecutive riverfronts were made in one place (Vintners' Place, C10–C16). The process came to an end largely in the C15, as stone walls replaced timber, though reclamation continued here and there as docks were infilled, e.g. at Billingsgate.

Early medieval riverside structures had foundations of split beech and oak (C12 warehouse, Queen Street Place), later replaced by medieval chalk and ragstone. Industrial and commercial structures included a C13 dyehouse (Ebbgate House) and a C14 stone arcaded structure associated with the dock basin called the East Watergate, infilled later in that century, the site later used for Baynard's Castle. On the Cleansing Department's site was the remarkable Whittington's Longhouse, one of the public improvements made by his executors after 1423. It was a tide-flushed public lavatory with sixty-four places in two facing rows. Almshouses on top were abandoned in the earlier C17, the public convenience only in the later C19. Other medieval structures of interest included such fine houses as those of the Abbots of St Mary, York, the King's Carpenter Hugh Herland, and the great medieval architect Henry Yevele. In the

C14–C15, different sections of Upper Thames Street were known variously as Roper Street, Stockfishmonger Row and The Vintry, of Lower Thames Street as Billingsgate Street (centre) and Petty Wales (E). Of the churches, several were not rebuilt after the Great Fire (All Hallows the Less, St Botolph Billingsgate, St Martin Vintry, St Mary Mounthaw, St Nicholas Olave, St Peter Paul's Wharf).

London Bridge west to Cannon Street Railway Bridge

The narrowest part of the street, lined with tall and heavy buildings, somewhat softened by small trees. For King William Street House and Minster House on the N side, *see* King William Street and Arthur Street respectively. On the S side, Nos. 104–108 SEAL HOUSE, *Holford Associates*' dull, grey offices of 1973–7, adjoins the Fishmongers' Hall on the W (q.v.). Shallow floor bands and vertical piers, stone-faced below and concrete above. Across Swan Lane, the practice's similar EBBGATE HOUSE, 1980–4, with a multi-storey car park in the part towards Upper Thames Street. Then the huge MONDIAL HOUSE, 1969–76 by *Hubbard Ford & Partners*, for the International Telephone Service. Big projecting floors in irregularly stepped sections on three sides. White glass-fibre panelling on the upper floors, bush-hammered aggregate-faced concrete below, where part of the ped-way is incorporated. The massive sills and narrow recessed window bands combat solar gain. The lowest two floors extend towards the river as a podium on which stand large cooling vents. The result looks variously like a ship, a ziggurat, or, from across the river, like a giant typewriter. Seen close to, it is merely intimidating. Rounded apertures on the r. mark a fire station, with its yard down ALL HALLOWS LANE.

The lane commemorates All Hallows the Great, recorded (as *Semannescyrce*) as early as 1100–7. A fine NE Perp tower appears in pre-Fire views. Rebuilt by *Wren* in 1677–84, its end was pro-tracted: the NE tower went in 1876, the rest in 1894, apart from a replacement S tower (by *E. I'Anson*), destroyed in the Blitz. Nearer the river lay the C14 mansion called Coldharbour, its site later occupied by the City of London Brewery, 1862–1941. Its chimney and symmetrical river front of 1885 (architects *Scammell & Colyer*) were notable landmarks of the old City.

On the N side, a new building by *Sidell Gibson Partnership* is taking shape in 1997. Part of a C1 masonry wall, found in 1995, will be displayed within. Against the Cannon Street railway bridge, with its bulky 'air rights' superstructure (*see* Cannon Street Station, Public Buildings) rises No. 152, PRINCESS HOUSE (formerly Barclays Bank), by *Campbell-Jones & Sons (Alec J. Shickle)*, 1965–7, an impressive, well-detailed slab with continuous polished stainless-steel mullions and black spandrel panels. A lower block at r. angles at the corner of Suffolk Lane neatly forms a bridge above an entrance into Bush Lane.

Cannon Street Railway Bridge west to the road tunnel

Facing the river beyond the railway bridge is the PUBLIC CLEANSING DEPARTMENT, by the City Architect, *E. G.*

Chandler (consultants *Sir Hugh Casson & Neville Conder*), 1958–62. Tough-looking flat façades with complex fenestration in black engineering brick, with exposed framing making an open-work parapet. Alongside the flanking wall of the railway, COUSIN LANE leads down to its riverside loading dock (filled in 1995–6). The lane is known from 1280, when a Cousin family held property here. Two modest brick buildings face the dock: by *Diamond Redfern Wilkins*, 1982–3, and *Amos Broome Associates*, 1989–91 (SPENTHORN HOUSE). They make an excellent foil to the towers of Cannon Street. Back on the N side of Upper Thames Street, the ungainly DOWGATE HILL HOUSE stands on the corner of Dowgate Hill. By *Hamilton Associates*, 1986–8, in Portland stone with a few traditional details on top. It faces WHITTINGTON GARDEN, made in 1960: on its N side St Michael Paternoster Royal is pleasantly exposed. Then Queen Street crosses Upper Thames Street, with buildings on all four corners (q.v.).

Thereafter the street becomes less friendly to pedestrians, as the N pavement disappears near where St James Garlickhithe stands. Opposite St James is the Vintners' Hall (q.v.). Projecting beyond, the inflated tetrastyle portico of that high point of naïve revivalism VINTNERS' PLACE, 1990–3 by the *Whinney Mackay-Lewis Partnership* for the Vintners' Company. A similarly showy but much less useful portico some 50 ft (15 metres) high faces the river, in the centre of a broader symmetrical front built out over the foreshore: compensation for volume lost when its taller 1920s predecessor Vintry House was demolished under the St Paul's sightlines rule (for its preserved portal, *see* Queen Street). But more dismaying than the facile appropriation of classical pomp is the indifference to its disciplines: the dark stone plinths of the riverside portico do not match that of the main block, and a big raw hole is made in the N façade over Kennet Wharf Lane. The display does not let up inside. From Upper Thames Street, an apsed lobby leads to an aisled barrel-vaulted stairway veering down to a long and excessively narrow atrium. This has stocky Doric arcades, stone-faced floors above, then clear glazing which continues across the opening. Much lavish Italianate decoration, of questionable propriety: lobby ceiling painted with Leda and the Swan by *Ricardo Cinalli*, marble after St Peter's Basilica, etc.

Beyond Kennet Wharf Lane, a big new office building by *Kohn Pederson Fox Associates*, begun in 1996, has erased the old Bull Wharf Lane (first recorded as Dibles Lane, *c.* 1300). The site extends W up to the dock called QUEENHITHE. The name has been connected with four different queens, but its first recorded name (899) is *Aetheredeshyth*. The dock was created fortuitously by later land reclamation on either side (cf. Billingsgate Market). The atmosphere of a working river lingered around the muddy inlet until 1996, when the last warehouse was demolished. A big brick-clad development by *Hubbard Ford & Partners*, 1972–5, makes the dock's N and W sides. Flats in a riverside block called Queen's Quay (built as a hotel but never so used), offices with narrower slit windows in a clumsy slab called Queensbridge House, which spans Upper Thames Street like a motorway bridge. Along the W side runs part of the ped-way.

Opposite Queenhithe (N side), the s front of the Royal Bank of Canada sets back (*see* Queen Victoria Street). Then the assertive No. 25 Little Trinity Lane (Fur Trade House), a fur warehouse built as late as 1968–72 by the *Corporation of London Architect's Department* (City architect *E. G. Chandler*). Uprights lifting it over the lane continue across the top as exposed trusses. s elevation with concrete beam-ends projecting between white mosaic panels. *Wren*'s St Michael Queenhithe (1676–86) stood here until 1876.

Beyond Queensbridge House, Upper Thames Street bends s away from its old route (marked on the N side by the tower of St Mary Somerset, q.v.) to descend towards the tunnel. Stew Lane leads down to the river and to BROOK'S WHARF, where No. 48 is the City's last surviving true riverfront warehouse. 1874 and typical of the date: seven storeys of painted brick with flat pilaster-piers and cogged cornice. Its double-height roadway, open to the river, was exploited when a pub was made in the lower storeys in 1966–8 (architect *H. G. Clinch*). But in 1997 the warehouse stands derelict at the riverside end of a vacant site. Brook's Wharf is first recorded as Broke Wharf in 1531; Stew Lane is named for the stews or baths for women mentioned here in 1427.

The riverside walk from the tunnel to Blackfriars Railway Bridge

BROKEN WHARF beyond leads the grateful pedestrian back to the riverside walkway. SIR JOHN LYON HOUSE along the E side was built for the tea trade by *Kersey, Gale & Spooner*, 1963–9. Bright-red brick, L-shaped plan. Arcaded ground floor faced in red sandstone to the wharf (w), with three big polygonal projections. Flat river front with a simple loggia in knapped flint and jaunty white-painted wooden oriel on the corner. The wharf's name is ancient: in the early C13, rival abbots quarrelled as to liability for its repair, and for forty years it was left to rot.

Further along the broad riverside walkway, SWISS BANK HOUSE, a large, low block clad in beige stone, 1987–8 by *R. Seifert & Partners*. Plain but for crude decorative motifs in a child's building brick manner, altogether unworthy of its site. Part of the same development the marble-faced NORFOLK HOUSE, a smallish block of private flats in the quiet triangular precinct in front. At the w, Swiss Bank House faces the steps called PETER'S HILL on the axis of St Paul's dome, which looms thrillingly near. The first Peter's Hill, a narrow lane extending N to the old Knightrider Street, dwindled in importance after it was bisected by Queen Victoria Street. The name is from St Peter Paul's Wharf, first recorded *c.* 1170 and not rebuilt after the Great Fire, walls from which were located in 1961 and 1981–4. The City of London School for Boys lies beyond (*see* Public Buildings), on the site of the second Baynard's Castle.

The walkway continues to Blackfriars Bridge, made noisome by the re-emergence of Upper Thames Street from its tunnel. Buildings further w are better seen from Queen Victoria Street.

VICTORIA EMBANKMENT

The E part of *Sir Joseph Bazalgette*'s great Embankment of 1864–70 lies in the City. Its 100 ft (30½ metres) roadway was far wider than anything the City had yet seen. An Embankment between Westminster Bridge and Blackfriars Bridge was recommended by a Royal Commission as early as 1844, but the starting-point was the Metropolitan Board of Works' scheme of 1860 for a main sewer to collect outfalls which previously discharged into the river. The Metropolitan District Railway (the present District Line) also runs within the Embankment.

The City's part begins at TEMPLE GARDENS. Good views W from here, as the river curves round. The iron lamp-standards with dolphins twined round the foot (by *C. H. Mabey*) and the benches with cast-iron camel supporters are part of Bazalgette's conception. Along the Temple waterfront, a sequence of architectural MEMORIALS or features. Outside the City proper is *Bazalgette*'s broad rusticated arch at Temple Stairs (1868), impressive in its simplicity. Within the arch, a little block records the naming of this section 'King's Reach' in 1934. On it bronzes of boys riding ships or dolphins, by *C. L. J. Doman*. Marking the City's boundary, two GRIFFINS, signed by *Dewer*, 1849, brought in 1963 from the demolished Coal Exchange, Lower Thames Street (q.v.). On the garden railings a weathered portrait plaque by *Mabey*, 1902, commemorates Queen Victoria's last visit to the City. By the river further E, the SUBMARINE WAR MEMORIAL, a large granite slab designed by *A. H. Ryan Tenison* (1922), with relief figures by *F. Brook Hitch* and tiny bronze anchors like coat-hooks all over.

Buildings face the river E of the Temple. The group of ornate, relatively narrow riverside façades has no parallel in central London. They are separated from the street by forecourts or gardens made over the Underground route. Many have long return fronts to the contemporary streets that make a grid on the partly reclaimed land up to Tudor Street. Dates are somewhat later than the Embankment because the grand public or semi-public premises the City preferred were slow to come.

First HAMILTON HOUSE, 1898–1901, by *Sir William Emerson*, formerly the Employers' Liability Corporation. Free Renaissance with pilasters and oriels. Thin baluster-piers (an Aston Webb motif) frame the elliptical-headed windows. A richly carved sand-stone band near the top interrupts the Portland stone. Hefty dormered roof with big stacks. Then TELEPHONE HOUSE, by *A. N. Bromley*, 1898–1902, confidently Shavian free Baroque, in much higher relief than Hamilton House. The return front to Temple Avenue, twenty-one bays long, has a pedimented centre between gabled pavilions and lots going on high up. Cherubs sit on the first-floor pediments.

Then the EMPLOYMENT APPEAL TRIBUNAL (built as the Exchequer & Audit Department). Sober Neo-Wren in red brick and stone, with pilastered end bays; *c.* 1903. According to Michael Port, probably by *Sir Henry Tanner* or *H. N. Hawkes*. NEW CARMELITE HOUSE, by *Trehearne & Norman*, 1989–93, stone-faced, with simplified forms derived from its neighbours: bulgy flattened oriels, half-cylindrical columns, and gables and turrets breaking up the skyline. Narrow atrium inside, with open W galleries; the façades of old Carmelite House are incorporated behind (*see* Carmelite Street). No. 9 Carmelite Street is the former Thames Conservancy Offices, 1893–4, by *Hunt & Steward*. Red brick Gothic to match Sion College next door (*see* Public Buildings), as the City Lands Committee insisted, but more eclectic and less eventful. Boxy two-storey stone oriel facing the river. Commercial offices from 1909, when the Port of London Authority was founded.

After Sion College, the former City of London School for Boys, now part of J.P. MORGAN. The oldest and grandest of the late Victorian sequence; by *Davis & Emmanuel*, 1880–2. An amazingly unscholastic Portland façade, rather like a permanent exhibition palace, as if in deliberate contradistinction to the brick Board Schools of the time. Mainly French Neo-Renaissance, two-storeyed, with windows recessed within five big arches (marking the first-floor hall), carried on two superimposed orders of coupled columns. In the spandrels, statues of luminaries by *J. Daymond & Son* (other carving by *Seale*). Steep hipped roof of green Westmorland slate, with a central slim lantern balanced by angle turrets. These have Wren-like octagonal concave-sided lower parts with columns. The school moved to new premises in 1986 (*see* Public Buildings), and the block was restored in 1991 as part of *BDP*'s new premises for J.P. Morgan (*see* John Carpenter Street). The hall is used for conferences. Generous open roof: tie-beams above the coving support clusters of columns from which longitudinal and transverse arches spring. Some of *Heaton, Butler & Bayne*'s stained glass remains (illustrated 1886). Crusty plaster-work by *E.T. Taylor*; more in the marble-lined Imperial staircase and colonnaded landing, N.

For Unilever House beyond, *see* New Bridge Street. To its S and E, the Embankment was extended and reconstructed after 1963 for the BLACKFRIARS UNDERPASS (City Engineer *F.J. Forty*), merging with the realigned Upper Thames Street E of Blackfriars station.

VINE STREET *see* JEWRY STREET

WALBROOK

A Saxon name, meaning the brook of the Britons (Wal as in Cornwall or Wales, from *wealh* meaning foreigner or slave). The ancient stream bed, with banks revetted in timber in the earlier Roman period, lay about twenty-five yards W of the street. For the Mithraeum on its E bank, *see* Introduction p. 40 and Queen Victoria Street. By Stow's time the brook had silted up and was covered over, and the street had become a favourite place for rich merchants' houses.

Against the W front of St Stephen Walbrook, No. 38, a stark stone

box of *c.* 1960 by *D. Armstrong Smith*. Its gargantuan neighbours
are Bucklersbury House (W side, *see* Queen Victoria Street) and
St Swithin's House (E side, *see* St Swithin's Lane). The court S of
St Stephen preserved until *c.* 1875 the mansion and warehouses of
John Polexfen, merchant, built 1668.

WARDROBE PLACE

A delightful close off Carter Lane, remote and intimate, with four
shady trees. Named from the Great Wardrobe, removed from the
Tower to Lombard Street in 1311 and transferred hither in the
1360s to the former house of Sir John Beauchamp, which the king
had bought for the purpose. It stood here till 1666. Though
altered and later in date, the houses on the W side are typical of
the many larger courts and closes of the post-Fire City. No. 2 is
set back, of five bays, early C18, with stucco window surrounds
and round-headed doorcase of *c.* 1860. Shallow plan, with one
room either side of a central dog-leg staircase. (Two early C18
painted overmantels with skating scenes etc. in the Dutch manner
were revealed in late 1970s restoration.) Nos. 3–5 beyond are
dated *c.* 1714 by Dan Cruickshank. Three bays each, with segment-
headed windows and straight-headed flush sash-boxes of the
type proscribed in 1709. Late C18 doorcases to Nos. 4 and 5.
WARDROBE HOUSE on the S, dated 1881, Ernest George-derived
in red brick with rubbed trim, in 1997 very woebegone. On the E
side, utilitarian late C19 rear ranges to Addle Hill (*see* Carter
Lane).

WARWICK LANE and WARWICK SQUARE

Warwick Lane is recorded in the mid C13 as *Eldedeneslane*; the
present name comes from the Beauchamp Earls of Warwick, who
had a house here from 1351. They are commemorated also by a
crude stone RELIEF dated 1668, now on Nos. 6–9 Newgate Street
(NW corner), showing the earl in his armour; inscribed as restored by
J. Deykes, architect, 1817.

The E SIDE of Warwick Lane belongs with the N precinct of St Paul's
(*see* St Paul's Churchyard). On the W SIDE, first Cutlers' Hall at
the N (q.v.). The College of Physicians, rebuilt in 1672–8 by
Hooke, stood here until demolition 1866–79. Then the extensions
to the Central Criminal Court (*see* Public Buildings), forming the
N and E sides of WARWICK SQUARE; on the S corner is ST
PAUL'S HOUSE, by *Victor Heal & Partners*, 1961–5, large and
plain, clad in rough red brick.

After Amen Court, AMEN LODGE, an aggressive red- and brown-
brick-clad block of flats by *Norman Bailey & Partners*, 1959–61,
with Brutalist affiliations in its asymmetrical balconies, recessed
first floor, and cantilevered upper storeys. The street continues as
AVE MARIA LANE, which was part of the cathedral precinct
before the Reformation. For Colonial Mutual House here, *see*
Ludgate Hill.

WATLING STREET

Known by *c.* 1213, and called *Aethelingstrate* in the C13. The present name is a corruption of this, and has nothing to do with the Roman highway called Watling Street. The alignment follows the Roman road W to Ludgate. It remained the chief route between St Paul's Churchyard and Cannon Street, via an E continuation called Budge Row, until the Cannon Street extension was made in the 1850s. The truncated remains now form a quiet back street.

A measure of its former importance is that five churches stood here before the Great Fire, of which only St Mary Aldermary and the tower of St Augustine incorporated in the new Choir School survive (*see* Churches, Public Buildings). *Wren*'s lamented St Antholin (1678–88) stood until 1875 in the now erased part E of Queen Victoria Street. It was domed, with a unique elongated octagonal plan, and a tall stone spire (partly preserved at Round Hill, Forest Hill: *see London 2: South*). Wren's All Hallows Bread Street (1681–4), S side, an unaisled church with an arcaded top to the tower added 1697–8, succumbed in 1877. St John Friday Street, not rebuilt after 1666, was on the site of Gateway House (*see* Cannon Street). Excavations in 1954 recorded C11 foundations giving internal dimensions about 27 ft (8 metres) square. The chancel was slightly widened in complete rebuilding of the C13–C14.

The W part is sandwiched between tall 1950s blocks facing Cheapside and Cannon Street (q.v.). The narrow vista between them towards St Paul's is splendid. The Choir School with St Augustine's tower appears at the end, low in the shadow of St Paul's, and the cathedral is seen at a happy angle, with the dome completing the picture. Just enough older buildings survive further E to preserve the character of a typical lesser City street before the Second World War. The commercial fronts of the 1870s make an interesting study.

On the N side, No. 77, 1878, a narrow stone front with eclectic classical forms employed with unusual restraint. No. 76, a spare white-faience-clad affair of 1923, was clearly designed so as not to trap dirt. Display windows on two lower storeys, then a shallow segmental bow with cross-windows. Little coloured discs and diamonds for ornament. No. 73, beyond, a stone-faced warehouse of 1872, has Gothic-derived shouldered-arched windows and chamfered reveals. Iron colonnettes divide the central double bay. No. 72, red brick of 1889, has pilasters and eared aedicules: an early instance of such literal evocation of post-Fire architecture. Then No. 9 Bow Lane on the corner, probably of 1793 when the corner was widened.

Buildings opposite (S side) were reconstructed as part of the large WATLING COURT development of 1977–81 by *Fitzroy Robinson & Partners*, which faces Cannon Street (q.v.). Nos. 19–21 is a brick warehouse of 1876 designed by the owner *D. King*. Segment-headed windows with iron colonnettes, two plainer storeys above: a less ambitious design than its contemporaries opposite. Fitzroy's plain infill separates it from Nos. 24–26, a trimmings and braid warehouse by *Herbert Ford*, 1871. Large tall windows between alternating iron colonnettes and piers in diminishing storeys. The very tall ground floor (rebuilt as a pub) formerly housed a factory, top-lit via open galleries within. Across Bow Lane, the OLDE WATLING pub at No. 29, apparently post-Fire or early C18, but refaced in 1947. The flank of St Mary Aldermary appears a little beyond.

Opposite, the E corner with Bow Lane is Nos. 70–71, a modest brick Italianate warehouse, by *Tillott & Chamberlain*, 1862. Nos. 67–69, of faience, 1908 by *Hesketh & Stokes*. Shallow polygonal bow flanked by higher bays against set-back upper storeys. Pretty turquoise brick infill.

WEST SMITHFIELD with SMITHFIELD STREET

Smithfield is from 'smooth field', the open ground outside the City walls. Its counterpart East Smithfield lies outside the City, E of the Tower. A livestock market is known to have been held at West Smithfield from the C10. The C14 and C15 saw tournaments held here. Executions made a more sinister spectacle, most infamously Queen Mary's burning of Protestants in the 1550s. The open market-place kept its importance as London spread around it in the C16 and C17, and a N extension was made in the early C19. Only in 1855 did the livestock and slaughtering business move to Islington, after long complaints at 'the shameful place … all asmear with filth and fat and blood and foam' (Dickens). The raucous and chaotic Bartholomew Fair, seven centuries old, was wound up in the same year.

The present form of West Smithfield is essentially of the 1860s. In that decade, the N part of the irregular, six-acre market-place was taken for Jones's meat market (*see* Public Buildings), constructed over the new Metropolitan Railway. The S part of the market-place remains, four-sided and of indeterminate shape, tailing off into Giltspur Street, S. Smithfield Market and St Bartholomew's Hospital form the NW and SE sides, neither of them too high to destroy the feeling of spaciousness. Railed off in the middle is a mysterious broad spiral ramp which originally served underground railway sidings beneath the market buildings. The circular central garden with its tall trees was laid out in 1872. Here a FOUNTAIN, with a draped classical bronze figure of Peace by *J. Birnie Philip*, 1873. The broad pedestal alone survives of its fearsome octagonal-domed Romanesque stone canopy (by *Francis Butler*).

On the NE and SW sides a congeries of mostly C19 and early C20 buildings, many connected with the meat trade (cf. Charterhouse Street). LLOYDS BANK (Nos. 64–66), on the Long Lane corner, was formerly Hill & Sons Bank, by *Scott & Cawthorn* of Brighton, 1885. Still in the Italianate tradition, but infused with more fanciful detail (see the squat piers to the ground-floor windows). Two storeys were added *c.* 1905, the uppermost with applied loggias with slender Doric columns. Nos. 58–59, 1906, were by *George Vickery* for W. & J. Biggerstaff, bankers and cattle market agents (converted to flats by *KSS Architects*, 1996). Tall stone Free Style front, with big curved armorial pediment-gable. Little domed turret on the canted r. corner. Over the entrances and on the fourth floor stylized Art Nouveau trees, a stock motif by that date, but nicely carved. (Ground floor and basement retain the standard marble-panelled walling and mirrored ceiling from an early C20 Lyons' Tea Room.) Then the entrance to Little Britain, by the gatehouse to St Bartholomew-the-Great (q.v.).

On the w side, Nos. 24–30, on the s corner with Hosier Lane, an early case of the turn away from the hard forms of the 1960s (1971–4, by *Fitzroy Robinson & Partners*). Red brick with narrow segment-headed windows close-set in threes, linked by flush stone bands. Slated hipped roof. Monster of the group is WEDDEL HOUSE, a hulking mass of offices built in 1907 for the meat trade. Red brick with stone trimmings spread thinly; on the l. a lower gabled section. The Haberdashers' Company intends to build a new Livery Hall on the site (1997). No. 12, by *Rawlinson Parkinson*, 1869, has a good pub front with thin cast-iron columns. Kings'-head capitals betray the old name. Round-arched medieval above. No. 11, *c.* 1900, with Shavian influence in its banded gable and bow. *Eedle & Myers* refronted the BISHOP'S FINGER pub (Nos. 9–10) in 1890, with a flying-arched gable linking two dormers.

West Smithfield continues round the corner, made by No. 8, red brick of 1892 with coarse Gothico-Moorish trimmings (the numbering is a relic of the NW part of the old market-place). Nos. 6–7, commercial classical of 1889 by *A. Howard*, has the cast stone lion sign of Herbert & Sons, scalemakers, promising 'Justice and Strength'. SMITHFIELD CHAMBERS (Nos. 2–5), 1883, is an extension of No. 12, similarly handled.

The street continues as SMITHFIELD STREET, curving s to Snow Hill. The former main w approach to the market, before Charterhouse Street was made in the 1870s; until the early C19 called Cow Lane. The decline of the meat trade is indicated in the half-century-old bomb site, s, and the long-derelict red brick cold store at No. 1a beyond, N, by *Reeves & Styche*, 1899. Applied stone arcading relieves its windowless walls. HOSIER LANE off to the E, still more blighted, has in 1997 no buildings worth attention. Yet it is ancient: hosiers were first recorded here in 1338.

WHITEFRIARS STREET

Called Water Lane until 1844. It formerly ran down to a narrow dock on the line of the present Carmelite Street. The new name commemorates the CARMELITE FRIARY founded by Richard of Cornwall in the mid C13 for fugitive monks from Mount Carmel, Syria. It lay between the w side and the Temple. The friary church was built *c.* 1253, enlarged in the early C14, and wholly rebuilt 1348–1420. After the Dissolution, the Great Hall became the Whitefriars Playhouse (1576). The rest, exempt from the City's jurisdiction until 1697, degenerated into slums (called 'Alsatia'), teeming with felons and debtors. One monastic remnant: a simple vaulted UNDERCROFT, preserved beneath the Freshfields building, w side (*see* Fleet Street): probably C14, with entry via a later curved stone stair.

For Northcliffe House further s, *see* Tudor Street. On the E side near Fleet Street, No. 35, the COACH AND HORSES, by *B. Wilkinson*, 1897–8, enfeebled Queen Anne, then the forecourt of the domineering Fleetbank House (*see* Salisbury Square). At its s end, THE HARROW (No. 22), two early C18 red brick properties with segment-headed windows and rubbed dressings, with another front to Primrose Hill behind. No. 21, offices by *Trehearne & Norman*, 1989–91, yellow brick above purple granite, with an oversized shallow bow.

WHITTINGTON AVENUE

Made *c.* 1880 as an approach to the new Leadenhall Market from Leadenhall Street. Richard Whittington had owned property nearby. The W SIDE is the rear of No. 1 Leadenhall Street (q.v.). On the E SIDE, No. 1, offices with shops below by *Holford Associates*, 1988–91, replaced a late C19 block from when the street was made. Large, confused stone-faced façade, with fluted columns after those on the market. A canted bay, l., marks the entrance.

WIDEGATE STREET

A narrow street on the City's eastern fringe, named probably from the White Gate that led into the old Artillery Ground at the E end. The W part, up to Bishopsgate, was absorbed into Middlesex Street in 1892–6. On the N side, Nos. 24 and 25, modest houses of the late 1720s. Their little set-back tiled attics with weaver's windows suggest a connection with the nearby Spitalfields silk trade. No. 25 retains flush sash-boxes (near-intact interior, part-panelled, with closed-string staircase). Opposite, Nos. 12–13, with ceramic reliefs of bakers by *P. Lindsey Clark*, 1926.

WOOD STREET

So named by the C12, from the department of the Cheapside market held in the s part. It runs N up to Fore Street, hard up against the Barbican Estate. Up to the old line of the City wall, the N part perpetuates the N–S route through the ROMAN FORT. Remains of two C2 buildings, probably from its barracks, were found on the site of St Alban's church in 1962. The N continuation is disguised where the mighty office block called Alban Gate straddles its junction with the present London Wall (q.v.). Until the Second World War, consequential Victorian textile warehouses-cum-showrooms dominated the street and the neighbouring Gresham Street; but they have gone without trace.

For buildings at the s end, including the churchyard of St Peter Cheap, *see* Cheapside. Then on the w side, No. 125, DRESDNER BANK HOUSE, 1985–8 by *Lister, Drew & Associates*, a late use of rough red brick facing rather than polished stone, with strong verticals and dark windows. Splayed corner entrance. Opposite, the former COMPTER HOUSE, Nos. 4–9, by *Ronald Ward & Partners*, 1953–6, a predominantly horizontal façade, i.e. harking back to Mendelsohn and specifically to his great convex-fronted Schocken department store, Chemnitz (1928). The green slate floor bands have weathered much better than many contemporary materials. MITRE COURT, behind, preserves the C19 cover of OLD COMPTER CELLARS, formerly the dungeons of the Wood Street Compter (1555–1792). The other sides of the court are made by Mitre House (*see* Cheapside).

Then on both sides long return wings of buildings on Gresham Street (q.v.). The SW corner was the site until 1897 of *Wren*'s St Michael Wood Street, a modest single-chambered church of 1670–5 reusing much recased C13 work, with a pilastered and pedimented E frontispiece. A crude pointed steeple was added *c.* 1804. N of Gresham Street on the W side, Nos. 92–100 (HILL, SAMUEL & CO.), designed for the Nestlé Company by *T. P. Bennett & Son*, 1957–8. Straightforward, clean and without mannerisms, stone-faced, the windows facing E and S in big panels of even bands. Nos. 90–91 by *Gunton & Gunton*, 1957, refaced. Demolition of the pair is proposed. Immediately N, a pilastered Telephone Exchange by *Office of Works Architects*, 1928–9, was demolished in 1991 despite spot-listing; on its site a new building by *Richard Rogers Partnership* is under construction in 1997 (*see* London Wall). Facing, the street splits in two either side of the tower of St Alban Wood Street, by Wood Street Police Station (qq.v.).

WORMWOOD STREET

A bleak traffic artery between Old Broad Street and Bishopsgate, continuing the line of London Wall and forming part of the main E–W traffic route after widening on the S side in the 1970s. In the Middle Ages the medicinal herb wormwood was grown here, on the open land within the city wall (cf. Camomile Street). The S side is occupied by the podium building of No. 99 Bishopsgate (q.v.), the N side by the tall slab of Broad Street House (*see* Old Broad Street). Two older survivors to its E: No. 25, a modest two-bay C18 house, one of a terrace of six built up to the old wall line in 1771–2; No. 26, by *Joseph & Smithem*, 1889, in Bath stone with shallow carved panels.

GLOSSARY

Numbers and letters refer to the illustrations (by John Sambrook)
on pp. 636–43.

ABACUS: flat slab forming the top of a capital (3a).

ACANTHUS: classical formalized leaf ornament (4b).

ACCUMULATOR TOWER: *see* Hydraulic power.

ACHIEVEMENT: a complete display of armorial bearings.

ACROTERION: plinth for a statue or ornament on the apex or ends of a pediment; more usually, both the plinth and what stands on it (4a).

AEDICULE (*lit.* little building): architectural surround, consisting usually of two columns or pilasters supporting a pediment.

AGGREGATE: *see* Concrete.

AISLE: subsidiary space alongside the body of a building, separated from it by columns, piers, or posts.

AMBULATORY (*lit.* walkway): aisle around the sanctuary (q.v.).

ANGLE ROLL: roll moulding in the angle between two planes (1a).

ANSE DE PANIER: *see* Arch.

ANTAE: simplified pilasters (4a), usually applied to the ends of the enclosing walls of a portico *in antis* (q.v.).

ANTEFIXAE: ornaments projecting at regular intervals above a Greek cornice, originally to conceal the ends of roof tiles (4a).

ANTHEMION: classical ornament like a honeysuckle flower (4b).

APRON: raised panel below a window or wall monument or tablet.

APSE: semicircular or polygonal end of an apartment, especially of a chancel or chapel. In classical architecture sometimes called an *exedra*.

ARABESQUE: non-figurative surface decoration consisting of flowing lines, foliage scrolls etc., based on geometrical patterns. Cf. Grotesque.

ARCADE: series of arches supported by piers or columns. *Blind arcade* or *arcading*: the same applied to the wall surface. *Wall arcade*: in medieval churches, a blind arcade forming a dado below windows. Also a covered shopping street.

ARCH: Shapes *see* 5c. *Basket arch* or *anse de panier* (basket handle): three-centred and depressed, or with a flat centre. *Nodding*: ogee arch curving forward from the wall face. *Parabolic*: shaped like a chain suspended from two level points, but inverted. Special purposes. *Chancel*: dividing chancel from nave or crossing. *Crossing*: spanning piers at a crossing (q.v.). *Relieving or discharging*: incorporated in a wall to relieve superimposed weight (5c). *Skew*: spanning responds not diametrically opposed. *Strainer*: inserted in an opening to resist inward pressure. *Transverse*: spanning a main axis (e.g. of a vaulted space). *See also* Jack arch, Triumphal arch.

ARCHITRAVE: formalized lintel, the lowest member of the classical entablature (3a). Also the moulded frame of a door or window (often borrowing the profile of a classical architrave). For *lugged* and *shouldered* architraves *see* 4b.

ARCUATED: dependent structurally on the arch principle. Cf. Trabeated.

ARK: chest or cupboard housing the

tables of Jewish law in a synagogue.

ARRIS: sharp edge where two surfaces meet at an angle (3a).

ASHLAR: masonry of large blocks wrought to even faces and square edges (6d).

ASTRAGAL: classical moulding of semicircular section (3f).

ASTYLAR: with no columns or similar vertical features.

ATLANTES: *see* Caryatids.

ATRIUM (plural: atria): inner court of a Roman or C20 house; in a multi-storey building, a toplit covered court rising through all storeys. Also an open court in front of a church.

ATTACHED COLUMN: *see* Engaged column.

ATTIC: small top storey within a roof. Also the storey above the main entablature of a classical façade.

AUMBRY: recess or cupboard to hold sacred vessels for the Mass.

BAILEY: *see* Motte-and-bailey.

BALANCE BEAM: *see* Canals.

BALDACCHINO: free-standing canopy, originally fabric, over an altar. Cf. Ciborium.

BALLFLOWER: globular flower of three petals enclosing a ball (1a). Typical of the Decorated style.

BALUSTER: pillar or pedestal of bellied form. *Balusters*: vertical supports of this or any other form, for a handrail or coping, the whole being called a *balustrade* (6c). *Blind balustrade*: the same applied to the wall surface.

BARBICAN: outwork defending the entrance to a castle.

BARGEBOARDS (corruption of 'vergeboards'): boards, often carved or fretted, fixed beneath the eaves of a gable to cover and protect the rafters.

BAROQUE: style originating in Rome *c*.1600 and current in England *c*.1680–1720, characterized by dramatic massing and silhouette and the use of the giant order.

BARROW: burial mound.

BARTIZAN: corbelled turret, square or round, frequently at an angle.

BASCULE: hinged part of a lifting (or bascule) bridge.

BASE: moulded foot of a column or pilaster. For *Attic* base *see* 3b.

BASEMENT: lowest, subordinate storey; hence the lowest part of a classical elevation, below the piano nobile (q.v.).

BASILICA: a Roman public hall; hence an aisled building with a clerestory.

BASTION: one of a series of defensive semicircular or polygonal projections from the main wall of a fortress or city.

BATTER: intentional inward inclination of a wall face.

BATTLEMENT: defensive parapet, composed of *merlons* (solid) and *crenels* (embrasures) through which archers could shoot; sometimes called *crenellation*. Also used decoratively.

BAY: division of an elevation or interior space as defined by regular vertical features such as arches, columns, windows etc.

BAY LEAF: classical ornament of overlapping bay leaves (3f).

BAY WINDOW: window of one or more storeys projecting from the face of a building. *Canted*: with a straight front and angled sides. *Bow window*: curved. *Oriel*: rests on corbels or brackets and starts above ground level; also the bay window at the dais end of a medieval great hall.

BEAD-AND-REEL: *see* Enrichments.

BEAKHEAD: Norman ornament with a row of beaked bird or beast heads usually biting into a roll moulding (1a).

BELFRY: chamber or stage in a tower where bells are hung.

BELL CAPITAL: *see* 1b.

BELLCOTE: small gabled or roofed housing for the bell(s).

BERM: level area separating a ditch from a bank on a hill-fort or barrow.

BILLET: Norman ornament of small half-cyclindrical or rectangular blocks (1a).

BLIND: *see* Arcade, Baluster, Portico.

BLOCK CAPITAL: *see* 1a.

BLOCKED: columns, etc. interrupted by regular projecting blocks (*blocking*), as on a Gibbs surround (4b).

BLOCKING COURSE: course of stones, or equivalent, on top of a cornice and crowning the wall.

BOLECTION MOULDING: covering the joint between two different planes (6b).

BOND: the pattern of long sides (*stretchers*) and short ends (*headers*) produced on the face of a wall by laying bricks in a particular way (6e).

BOSS: knob or projection, e.g. at the intersection of ribs in a vault (2c).

BOW WINDOW: see Bay window.

BOX FRAME: timber-framed construction in which vertical and horizontal wall members support the roof (7). Also concrete construction where the loads are taken on cross walls; also called *cross-wall construction*.

BRACE: subsidiary member of a structural frame, curved or straight. *Bracing* is often arranged decoratively e.g. quatrefoil, herringbone (7). See also Roofs.

BRATTISHING: ornamental crest, usually formed of leaves, Tudor flowers or miniature battlements.

BRESSUMER (*lit.* breast-beam): big horizontal beam supporting the wall above, especially in a jettied building (7).

BRICK: see Bond, Cogging, Engineering, Gauged, Tumbling.

BRIDGE: *Bowstring*: with arches rising above the roadway which is suspended from them. *Clapper*: one long stone forms the roadway. *Roving*: see Canal. *Suspension*: roadway suspended from cables or chains slung between towers or pylons. *Stay-suspension* or *stay-cantilever*: supported by diagonal stays from towers or pylons. See also Bascule.

BRISES-SOLEIL: projecting fins or canopies which deflect direct sunlight from windows.

BROACH: see Spire and 1c.

BUCRANIUM: ox skull used decoratively in classical friezes.

BULLSEYE WINDOW: small oval window, set horizontally (cf. Oculus). Also called *oeil de boeuf*.

BUTTRESS: vertical member projecting from a wall to stabilize it or to resist the lateral thrust of an arch, roof, or vault (1c, 2c). A *flying buttress* transmits the thrust to a heavy abutment by means of an arch or half-arch (1c).

CABLE OR ROPE MOULDING: originally Norman, like twisted strands of a rope.

CAMES: see Quarries.

CAMPANILE: free-standing bell tower.

CANALS: *Flash lock*: removable weir or similar device through which boats pass on a flush of water. Predecessor of the *pound lock*: chamber with gates at each end allowing boats to float from one level to another. *Tidal gates*: single pair of lock gates allowing vessels to pass when the tide makes a level. *Balance beam*: beam projecting horizontally for opening and closing lock gates. *Roving bridge*: carrying a towing path from one bank to the other.

CANTILEVER: horizontal projection (e.g. step, canopy) supported by a downward force behind the fulcrum.

CAPITAL: head or crowning feature of a column or pilaster; for classical types see 3; for medieval types see 1b.

CARREL: compartment designed for individual work or study.

CARTOUCHE: classical tablet with ornate frame (4b).

CARYATIDS: female figures supporting an entablature; their male counterparts are *Atlantes* (*lit.* Atlas figures).

CASEMATE: vaulted chamber, with embrasures for defence, within a castle wall or projecting from it.

CASEMENT: side-hinged window.

CASTELLATED: with battlements (q.v.).

CAST IRON: hard and brittle, cast in a mould to the required shape. *Wrought iron* is ductile, strong in tension, forged into decorative patterns or forged and rolled into e.g. bars, joists, boiler plates; *mild steel* is its modern equivalent, similar but stronger.

CATSLIDE: *See* 8a.

CAVETTO: concave classical moulding of quarter-round section (3f).

CELURE OR CEILURE: enriched area of roof above rood or altar.

CEMENT: *see* Concrete.

CENOTAPH (*lit.* empty tomb): funerary monument which is not a burying place.

CENTRING: wooden support for the building of an arch or vault, removed after completion.

CHAMFER (*lit.* corner-break): surface formed by cutting off a square edge or corner. For types of chamfers and *chamfer stops see* 6a. *See also* Double chamfer.

CHANCEL: part of the E end of a church set apart for the use of the officiating clergy.

CHANTRY CHAPEL: often attached to or within a church, endowed for the celebration of Masses principally for the soul of the founder.

CHEVET (*lit.* head): French term for chancel with ambulatory and radiating chapels.

CHEVRON: V-shape used in series or double series (later) on a Norman moulding (1a). Also (especially when on a single plane) called *zigzag*.

CHOIR: the part of a cathedral, monastic or collegiate church where services are sung.

CIBORIUM: a fixed canopy over an altar, usually vaulted and supported on four columns; cf. Baldacchino. Also a canopied shrine for the reserved sacrament.

CINQUEFOIL: *see* Foil.

CIST: stone-lined or slab-built grave.

CLADDING: external covering or skin applied to a structure, especially a framed one.

CLERESTORY: uppermost storey of the nave of a church, pierced by windows. Also high-level windows in secular buildings.

CLOSER: a brick cut to complete a bond (6e).

CLUSTER BLOCK: *see* Multi-storey.

COADE STONE: ceramic artificial stone made in Lambeth 1769–c.1840 by Eleanor Coade (†1821) and her associates.

COB: walling material of clay mixed with straw. Also called *pisé*.

COFFERING: arrangement of sunken panels (coffers), square or polygonal, decorating a ceiling, vault, or arch.

COGGING: a decorative course of bricks laid diagonally (6e). Cf. Dentilation.

COLLAR: *see* Roofs and 7.

COLLEGIATE CHURCH: endowed for the support of a college of priests.

COLONNADE: range of columns supporting an entablature. Cf. Arcade.

COLONNETTE: small medieval column or shaft.

COLOSSAL ORDER: *see* Giant order.

COLUMBARIUM: shelved, niched structure to house multiple burials.

COLUMN: a classical, upright structural member of round section with a shaft, a capital, and usually a base (3a, 4a).

COLUMN FIGURE: carved figure attached to a medieval column or shaft, usually flanking a doorway.

COMMUNION TABLE: unconsecrated table used in Protestant churches for the celebration of Holy Communion.

COMPOSITE: *see* Orders.

COMPOUND PIER: grouped shafts (q.v.), or a solid core surrounded by shafts.

CONCRETE: composition of *cement* (calcined lime and clay), *aggregate* (small stones or rock chippings), sand and water. It can be poured into *formwork* or *shuttering* (temporary frame of timber or metal) on site (*in-situ* concrete), or *pre-cast* as components before construction. *Reinforced*: incorporating steel rods to take the tensile force. *Pre-stressed*: with tensioned steel rods. Finishes include the impression of boards left by formwork (*board-marked* or *shuttered*), and texturing with steel brushes (*brushed*) or hammers (*hammer-dressed*). *See also* Shell.

CONSOLE: bracket of curved outline (4b).

COPING: protective course of masonry or brickwork capping a wall (6d).

CORBEL: projecting block supporting something above. *Corbel course*: continuous course of projecting stones or bricks fulfilling the same function. *Corbel table*: series of corbels to carry a parapet or a wall-plate or wall-post (7). *Corbelling*: brick or masonry courses built out beyond one another to support a chimneystack, window, etc.

CORINTHIAN: *see* Orders and 3d.

CORNICE: flat-topped ledge with moulded underside, projecting along the top of a building or feature, especially as the highest member of the classical entablature (3a). Also the decorative moulding in the angle between wall and ceiling.

CORPS-DE-LOGIS: the main building(s) as distinct from the wings or pavilions.

COTTAGE ORNÉ: an artfully rustic small house associated with the Picturesque movement.

COUNTERCHANGING: of joists on a ceiling divided by beams into compartments, when placed in opposite directions in alternate squares.

COUR D'HONNEUR: formal entrance court before a house in the French manner, usually with flanking wings and a screen wall or gates.

COURSE: continuous layer of stones, etc. in a wall (6e).

COVE: a broad concave moulding, e.g. to mask the eaves of a roof. *Coved ceiling*: with a pronounced cove joining the walls to a flat central panel smaller than the whole area of the ceiling.

CRADLE ROOF: *see* Wagon roof.

CREDENCE: a shelf within or beside a piscina (q.v.), or a table for the sacramental elements and vessels.

CRENELLATION: parapet with crenels (*see* Battlement).

CRINKLE-CRANKLE WALL: garden wall undulating in a series of serpentine curves.

CROCKETS: leafy hooks. *Crocketing* decorates the edges of Gothic features, such as pinnacles, canopies, etc. *Crocket capital*: *see* 1b.

CROSSING: central space at the junction of the nave, chancel, and transepts. *Crossing tower*: above a crossing.

CROSS-WINDOW: with one mullion and one transom (qq.v.).

CROWN-POST: *see* Roofs and 7.

CROWSTEPS: squared stones set like steps, e.g. on a gable (8a).

CRUCKS (*lit.* crooked): pairs of inclined timbers (*blades*), usually curved, set at bay-lengths; they support the roof timbers and, in timber buildings, also support the walls (8b). *Base*: blades rise from ground level to a tie- or collarbeam which supports the roof timbers. *Full*: blades rise from ground level to the apex of the roof, serving as the main members of a roof truss. *Jointed*: blades formed from more than one timber; the lower member may act as a wall-post; it is usually elbowed at wall-plate level and jointed just above. *Middle*: blades rise from halfway up the walls to a tie- or collar-beam. *Raised*: blades rise from halfway up the walls to the apex. *Upper*: blades supported on a tie-beam and rising to the apex.

CRYPT: underground or half-underground area, usually below the E end of a church. *Ring crypt*: corridor crypt surrounding the apse of an early medieval church, often associated with chambers for relics. Cf. Undercroft.

CUPOLA (*lit.* dome): especially a small dome on a circular or polygonal base crowning a larger dome, roof, or turret.

CURSUS: a long avenue defined by two parallel earthen banks with ditches outside.

CURTAIN WALL: a connecting wall between the towers of a castle. Also a non-load-bearing external wall applied to a C20 framed structure.

CUSP: *see* Tracery and 2b.

CYCLOPEAN MASONRY: large irregular polygonal stones, smooth and finely jointed.

CYMA RECTA and CYMA REVERSA: classical mouldings with double curves (3f). Cf. Ogee.

DADO: the finishing (often with panelling) of the lower part of a wall in a classical interior; in origin a formalized continuous pedestal. *Dado rail*: the moulding along the top of the dado.

DAGGER: *see* Tracery and 2b.

DEC (DECORATED): English Gothic architecture *c.* 1290 to *c.* 1350. The name is derived from the type of window tracery (q.v.) used during the period.

DEMI- or HALF-COLUMNS: engaged columns (q.v.) half of whose circumference projects from the wall.

DENTIL: small square block used in series in classical cornices (3c). *Dentilation* is produced by the projection of alternating headers along cornices or stringcourses.

DIAPER: repetitive surface decoration of lozenges or squares flat or in relief. Achieved in brickwork with bricks of two colours.

DIOCLETIAN OR THERMAL WINDOW: semicircular with two mullions, as used in the Baths of Diocletian, Rome (4b).

DISTYLE: having two columns (4a).

DOGTOOTH: E.E. ornament, consisting of a series of small pyramids formed by four stylized canine teeth meeting at a point (1a).

DORIC: *see* Orders and 3a, 3b.

DORMER: window projecting from the slope of a roof (8a).

DOUBLE CHAMFER: a chamfer applied to each of two recessed arches (1a).

DOUBLE PILE: *see* Pile.

DRAGON BEAM: *see* Jetty.

DRESSINGS: the stone or brickwork worked to a finished face about an angle, opening, or other feature.

DRIPSTONE: moulded stone projecting from a wall to protect the lower parts from water. Cf. Hoodmould, Weathering.

DRUM: circular or polygonal stage supporting a dome or cupola. Also one of the stones forming the shaft of a column (3a).

DUTCH or FLEMISH GABLE: *see* 8a.

EASTER SEPULCHRE: tomb-chest used for Easter ceremonial, within or against the N wall of a chancel.

EAVES: overhanging edge of a roof; hence *eaves cornice* in this position.

ECHINUS: ovolo moulding (q.v.) below the abacus of a Greek Doric capital (3a).

EDGE RAIL: *see* Railways.

E.E. (EARLY ENGLISH): English Gothic architecture *c.* 1190–1250.

EGG-AND-DART: *see* Enrichments and 3f.

ELEVATION: any face of a building or side of a room. In a drawing, the same or any part of it, represented in two dimensions.

EMBATTLED: with battlements.

EMBRASURE: small splayed opening in a wall or battlement (q.v.).

ENCAUSTIC TILES: earthenware tiles fired with a pattern and glaze.

EN DELIT: stone cut against the bed.

ENFILADE: reception rooms in a formal series, usually with all doorways on axis.

ENGAGED or ATTACHED COLUMN: one that partly merges into a wall or pier.

ENGINEERING BRICKS: dense bricks, originally used mostly for railway viaducts etc.

ENRICHMENTS: the carved decoration of certain classical mouldings, e.g. the ovolo (qq.v.) with *egg-and-dart*, the cyma reversa with *waterleaf*, the astragal with *bead-and-reel* (3f).

ENTABLATURE: in classical architecture, collective name for the three horizontal members (architrave, frieze, and cornice) carried by a wall or a column (3a).

ENTASIS: very slight convex deviation from a straight line, used to prevent an optical illusion of concavity.

EPITAPH: inscription on a tomb.

EXEDRA: *see* Apse.

EXTRADOS: outer curved face of an arch or vault.

EYECATCHER: decorative building terminating a vista.

FASCIA: plain horizontal band, e.g. in an architrave (3c, 3d) or on a shop front.

FENESTRATION: the arrangement of windows in a façade.

FERETORY: site of the chief shrine of a church, behind the high altar.

FESTOON: ornamental garland, suspended from both ends. Cf. Swag.

FIBREGLASS, or glass-reinforced polyester (GRP): synthetic resin reinforced with glass fibre. GRC: glass-reinforced concrete.

FIELD: see Panelling and 6b.

FILLET: a narrow flat band running down a medieval shaft or along a roll moulding (1a). It separates larger curved mouldings in classical cornices, fluting or bases (3c).

FLAMBOYANT: the latest phase of French Gothic architecture, with flowing tracery.

FLASH LOCK: see Canals.

FLÈCHE or SPIRELET (lit. arrow): slender spire on the centre of a roof.

FLEURON: medieval carved flower or leaf, often rectilinear (1a).

FLUSHWORK: knapped flint used with dressed stone to form patterns.

FLUTING: series of concave grooves (flutes), their common edges sharp (arris) or blunt (fillet) (3).

FOIL (lit. leaf): lobe formed by the cusping of a circular or other shape in tracery (2b). Trefoil (three), quatrefoil (four), cinquefoil (five), and multifoil express the number of lobes in a shape.

FOLIATE: decorated with leaves.

FORMWORK: see Concrete.

FRAMED BUILDING: where the structure is carried by a framework – e.g. of steel, reinforced concrete, timber – instead of by load-bearing walls.

FREESTONE: stone that is cut, or can be cut, in all directions.

FRESCO: al fresco: painting on wet plaster. Fresco secco: painting on dry plaster.

FRIEZE: the middle member of the classical entablature, sometimes ornamented (3a). Pulvinated frieze (lit. cushioned): of bold convex profile (3c). Also a horizontal band of ornament.

FRONTISPIECE: in C16 and C17 buildings the central feature of doorway and windows above linked in one composition.

GABLE: For types see 8a. Gablet: small gable. Pedimental gable: treated like a pediment.

GADROONING: classical ribbed ornament like inverted fluting that flows into a lobed edge.

GALILEE: chapel or vestibule usually at the w end of a church enclosing the main portal(s).

GALLERY: a long room or passage; an upper storey above the aisle of a church, looking through arches to the nave; a balcony or mezzanine overlooking the main interior space of a building; or an external walkway.

GALLETING: small stones set in a mortar course.

GAMBREL ROOF: see 8a.

GARDEROBE: medieval privy.

GARGOYLE: projecting water spout often carved into human or animal shape.

GAUGED or RUBBED BRICKWORK: soft brick sawn roughly, then rubbed to a precise (gauged) surface. Mostly used for door or window openings (5c).

GAZEBO (jocular Latin, 'I shall gaze'): ornamental lookout tower or raised summer house.

GEOMETRIC: English Gothic architecture c. 1250–1310. See also Tracery. For another meaning, see Stairs.

GIANT or COLOSSAL ORDER: classical order (q.v.) whose height is that of two or more storeys of the building to which it is applied.

GIBBS SURROUND: C18 treatment of an opening (4b), seen particularly in the work of James Gibbs (1682–1754).

GIRDER: a large beam. Box: of hollow-box section. Bowed: with its top rising in a curve. Plate: of I-section, made from iron or steel plates. Lattice: with braced framework.

GLAZING BARS: wooden or sometimes metal bars separating and supporting window panes.

GRAFFITI: *see* Sgraffito.

GRANGE: farm owned and run by a religious order.

GRC: *see* Fibreglass.

GRISAILLE: monochrome painting on walls or glass.

GROIN: sharp edge at the meeting of two cells of a cross-vault; *see* Vault and 2c.

GROTESQUE (*lit.* grotto-esque): wall decoration adopted from Roman examples in the Renaissance. Its foliage scrolls incorporate figurative elements. Cf. Arabesque.

GROTTO: artificial cavern.

GRP: *see* Fibreglass.

GUILLOCHE: classical ornament of interlaced bands (4b).

GUNLOOP: opening for a firearm.

GUTTAE: stylized drops (3b).

HALF-TIMBERING: archaic term for timber-framing (q.v.). Sometimes used for non-structural decorative timberwork.

HALL CHURCH: medieval church with nave and aisles of approximately equal height.

HAMMERBEAM: *see* Roofs and 7.

HAMPER: in C20 architecture, a visually distinct topmost storey or storeys.

HEADER: *see* Bond and 6e.

HEADSTOP: stop (q.v.) carved with a head (5b).

HELM ROOF: *see* IC.

HENGE: ritual earthwork.

HERM (*lit.* the god Hermes): male head or bust on a pedestal.

HERRINGBONE WORK: *see* 7ii. Cf. Pitched masonry.

HEXASTYLE: *see* Portico.

HILL-FORT: Iron Age earthwork enclosed by a ditch and bank system.

HIPPED ROOF: *see* 8a.

HOODMOULD: projecting moulding above an arch or lintel to throw off water (2b, 5b). When horizontal often called a *label*. For label stop *see* Stop.

HUSK GARLAND: festoon of stylized nutshells (4b).

HYDRAULIC POWER: use of water under high pressure to work machinery. *Accumulator tower*: houses a hydraulic accumulator which accommodates fluctuations in the flow through hydraulic mains.

HYPOCAUST (*lit.* underburning): Roman underfloor heating system.

IMPOST: horizontal moulding at the springing of an arch (5c).

IMPOST BLOCK: block between abacus and capital (1b).

IN ANTIS: *see* Antae, Portico and 4a.

INDENT: shape chiselled out of a stone to receive a brass.

INDUSTRIALIZED or SYSTEM BUILDING: system of manufactured units assembled on site.

INGLENOOK (*lit.* fire-corner): recess for a hearth with provision for seating.

INTERCOLUMNATION: interval between columns.

INTERLACE: decoration in relief simulating woven or entwined stems or bands.

INTRADOS: *see* Soffit.

IONIC: *see* Orders and 3c.

JACK ARCH: shallow segmental vault springing from beams, used for fireproof floors, bridge decks, etc.

JAMB (*lit.* leg): one of the vertical sides of an opening.

JETTY: in a timber-framed building, the projection of an upper storey beyond the storey below, made by the beams and joists of the lower storey oversailing the wall; on their outer ends is placed the sill of the walling for the storey above (7). Buildings can be jettied on several sides, in which case a *dragon beam* is set diagonally at the corner to carry the joists to either side.

JOGGLE: the joining of two stones to prevent them slipping by a notch in one and a projection in the other.

KEEL MOULDING: moulding used from the late C12, in section like the keel of a ship (1a).

KEEP: principal tower of a castle.

KENTISH CUSP: *see* Tracery and 2b.

KEY PATTERN: *see* 4b.

KEYSTONE: central stone in an arch or vault (4b, 5c).

KINGPOST: *see* Roofs and 7.

KNEELER: horizontal projecting stone at the base of each side of a gable to support the inclined coping stones (8a).

LABEL: *see* Hoodmould and 5b.

LABEL STOP: *see* Stop and 5b.

LACED BRICKWORK: vertical strips of brickwork, often in a contrasting colour, linking openings on different floors.

LACING COURSE: horizontal reinforcement in timber or brick to walls of flint, cobble, etc.

LADY CHAPEL: dedicated to the Virgin Mary (Our Lady).

LANCET: slender single-light, pointed-arched window (2a).

LANTERN: circular or polygonal windowed turret crowning a roof or a dome. Also the windowed stage of a crossing tower lighting the church interior.

LANTERN CROSS: churchyard cross with lantern-shaped top.

LAVATORIUM: in a religious house, a washing place adjacent to the refectory.

LEAN-TO: *see* Roofs.

LESENE (*lit.* a mean thing): pilaster without base or capital. Also called *pilaster strip*.

LIERNE: *see* Vault and 2c.

LIGHT: compartment of a window defined by the mullions.

LINENFOLD: Tudor panelling carved with simulations of folded linen. *See also* Parchemin.

LINTEL: horizontal beam or stone bridging an opening.

LOGGIA: gallery, usually arcaded or colonnaded; sometimes free-standing.

LONG-AND-SHORT WORK: quoins consisting of stones placed with the long side alternately upright and horizontal, especially in Saxon building.

LONGHOUSE: house and byre in the same range with internal access between them.

LOUVRE: roof opening, often protected by a raised timber structure, to allow the smoke from a central hearth to escape.

LOWSIDE WINDOW: set lower than the others in a chancel side wall, usually towards its w end.

LUCAM: projecting housing for hoist pulley on upper storey of warehouses, mills, etc., for raising goods to loading doors.

LUCARNE (*lit.* dormer): small gabled opening in a roof or spire.

LUGGED ARCHITRAVE: *see* 4b.

LUNETTE: semicircular window or blind panel.

LYCHGATE (*lit.* corpse-gate): roofed gateway entrance to a churchyard for the reception of a coffin.

LYNCHET: long terraced strip of soil on the downward side of prehistoric and medieval fields, accumulated because of continual ploughing along the contours.

MACHICOLATIONS (*lit.* mashing devices): series of openings between the corbels that support a projecting parapet through which missiles can be dropped. Used decoratively in post-medieval buildings.

MANOMETER or STANDPIPE TOWER: containing a column of water to regulate pressure in water mains.

MANSARD: *see* 8a.

MATHEMATICAL TILES: facing tiles with the appearance of brick, most often applied to timber-framed walls.

MAUSOLEUM: monumental building or chamber usually intended for the burial of members of one family.

MEGALITHIC TOMB: massive stone-built Neolithic burial chamber covered by an earth or stone mound.

MERLON: *see* Battlement.

METOPES: spaces between the triglyphs in a Doric frieze (3b).

MEZZANINE: low storey between two higher ones.

MILD STEEL: *see* Cast iron.

MISERICORD (*lit.* mercy): shelf on a carved bracket placed on the underside of a hinged choir stall seat to support an occupant when standing.

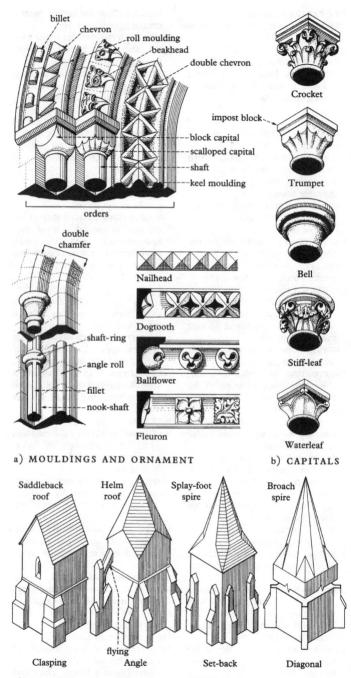

a) MOULDINGS AND ORNAMENT

b) CAPITALS

c) BUTTRESSES, ROOFS AND SPIRES

FIGURE I: MEDIEVAL

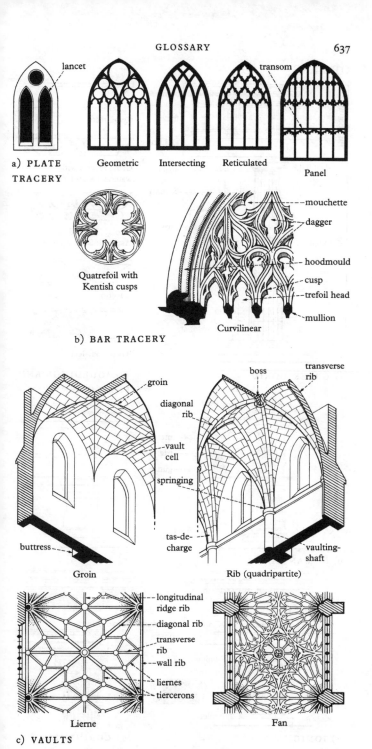

a) PLATE TRACERY

Geometric   Intersecting   Reticulated   Panel

lancet · transom

Quatrefoil with Kentish cusps

Curvilinear — mouchette, dagger, hoodmould, cusp, trefoil head, mullion

b) BAR TRACERY

Groin — groin, vault cell, buttress

Rib (quadripartite) — boss, transverse rib, diagonal rib, springing, tas-de-charge, vaulting-shaft

Lierne — longitudinal ridge rib, diagonal rib, transverse rib, wall rib, liernes, tiercerons

Fan

c) VAULTS

FIGURE 2: MEDIEVAL

ORDERS

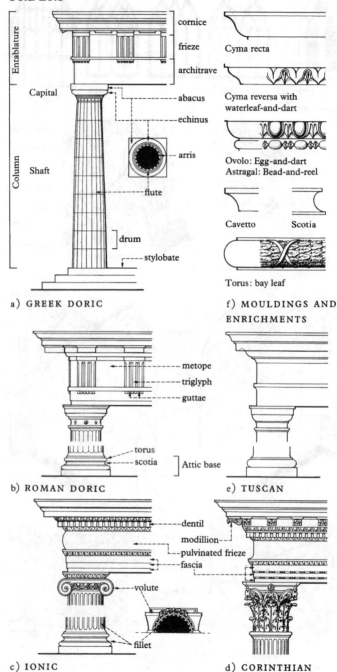

a) GREEK DORIC

- Entablature
  - cornice
  - frieze
  - architrave
- Capital
  - abacus
  - echinus
- Column
  - Shaft
    - arris
    - flute
  - drum
  - stylobate

f) MOULDINGS AND ENRICHMENTS

Cyma recta

Cyma reversa with waterleaf-and-dart

Ovolo: Egg-and-dart
Astragal: Bead-and-reel

Cavetto   Scotia

Torus: bay leaf

b) ROMAN DORIC

- metope
- triglyph
- guttae
- torus
- scotia
- Attic base

e) TUSCAN

c) IONIC

- dentil
- modillion
- pulvinated frieze
- fascia
- volute
- fillet

d) CORINTHIAN

FIGURE 3: CLASSICAL

a) PORTICO

acroterion — tympanum — antefixa — column — anta — pronaos — naos — naos

Distyle in antis Prostyle

Anthemion & Palmette Guilloche Key pattern

Rinceau Husk garland Vitruvian scroll

Console Diocletian window Acanthus

Broken pediment Lugged architrave

Segmental pediment Shouldered architrave

Venetian window

Open pediment — console — cartouche

keystone blocking

Swan-neck pediment Gibbs surround

b) ORNAMENTS AND FEATURES

FIGURE 4: CLASSICAL

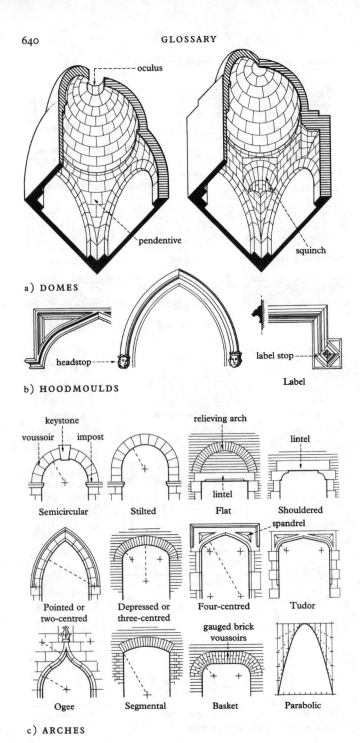

a) DOMES

b) HOODMOULDS

c) ARCHES

FIGURE 5: CONSTRUCTION

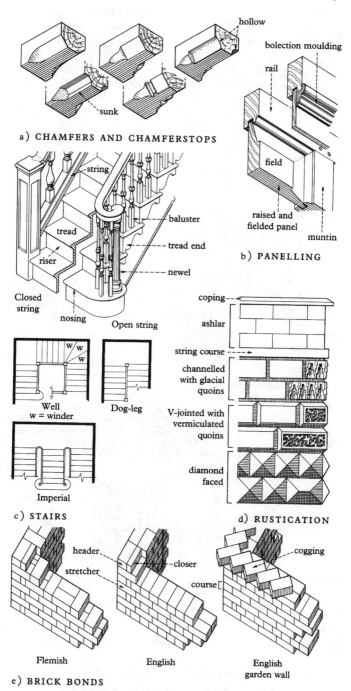

hollow

bolection moulding

rail

a) CHAMFERS AND CHAMFERSTOPS

field

string

baluster

tread

tread end

riser

newel

raised and
fielded panel

muntin

Closed
string

nosing

Open string

b) PANELLING

w / w
w

Well
w = winder

Dog-leg

coping

ashlar

string course

channelled
with glacial
quoins

V-jointed with
vermiculated
quoins

Imperial

diamond
faced

c) STAIRS

d) RUSTICATION

header

closer

stretcher

cogging

course

Flemish

English

English
garden wall

e) BRICK BONDS

FIGURE 6: CONSTRUCTION

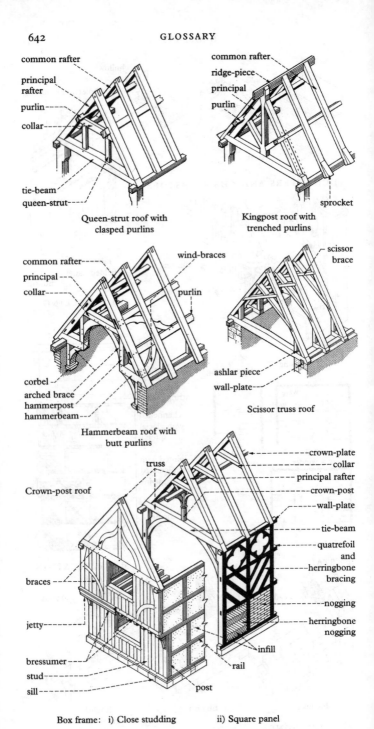

Queen-strut roof with clasped purlins

Kingpost roof with trenched purlins

Hammerbeam roof with butt purlins

Scissor truss roof

Crown-post roof

Box frame: i) Close studding   ii) Square panel

FIGURE 7: ROOFS AND TIMBER-FRAMING

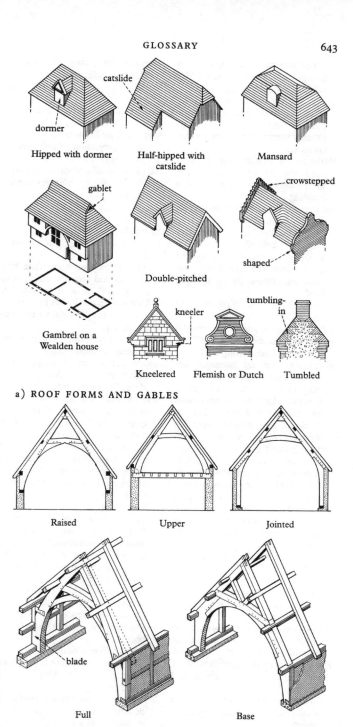

Hipped with dormer

Half-hipped with catslide

Mansard

Gambrel on a Wealden house

Double-pitched

Kneelered

Flemish or Dutch

Tumbled

a) ROOF FORMS AND GABLES

Raised

Upper

Jointed

Full

Base

b) CRUCK FRAMES

FIGURE 8: ROOFS AND TIMBER-FRAMING

MIXER-COURTS: forecourts to groups of houses shared by vehicles and pedestrians.

MODILLIONS: small consoles (q.v.) along the underside of a Corinthian or Composite cornice (3d). Often used along an eaves cornice.

MODULE: a predetermined standard size for co-ordinating the dimensions of components of a building.

MOTTE-AND-BAILEY: post-Roman and Norman defence consisting of an earthen mound (motte) topped by a wooden tower within a bailey, an enclosure defended by a ditch and palisade, and also, sometimes, by an internal bank.

MOUCHETTE: see Tracery and 2b.

MOULDING: shaped ornamental strip of continuous section; see e.g. Cavetto, Cyma, Ovolo, Roll.

MULLION: vertical member between window lights (2b).

MULTI-STOREY: five or more storeys. Multi-storey flats may form a *cluster block*, with individual blocks of flats grouped round a service core; a *point block*: with flats fanning out from a service core; or a *slab block*, with flats approached by corridors or galleries from service cores at intervals or towers at the ends (plan also used for offices, hotels etc.). *Tower block* is a generic term for any very high multi-storey building.

MUNTIN: see Panelling and 6b.

NAILHEAD: E.E. ornament consisting of small pyramids regularly repeated (1a).

NARTHEX: enclosed vestibule or covered porch at the main entrance to a church.

NAVE: the body of a church w of the crossing or chancel often flanked by aisles (q.v.).

NEWEL: central or corner post of a staircase (6c). Newel stair: see Stairs.

NIGHT STAIR: stair by which religious entered the transept of their church from their dormitory to celebrate night services.

NOGGING: see Timber-framing (7).

NOOK-SHAFT: shaft set in the angle of a wall or opening (1a).

NORMAN: see Romanesque.

NOSING: projection of the tread of a step (6c).

NUTMEG: medieval ornament with a chain of tiny triangles placed obliquely.

OCULUS: circular opening.

OEIL DE BOEUF: see Bullseye window.

OGEE: double curve, bending first one way and then the other, as in an *ogee* or *ogival* arch (5c). Cf. Cyma recta and Cyma reversa.

OPUS SECTILE: decorative mosaic-like facing.

OPUS SIGNINUM: composition flooring of Roman origin.

ORATORY: a private chapel in a church or a house. Also a church of the Oratorian Order.

ORDER: one of a series of recessed arches and jambs forming a splayed medieval opening, e.g. a doorway or arcade arch (1a).

ORDERS: the formalized versions of the post-and-lintel system in classical architecture. The main orders are *Doric, Ionic,* and *Corinthian.* They are Greek in origin but occur in Roman versions. Tuscan is a simple version of Roman Doric. Though each order has its own conventions (3), there are many minor variations. The *Composite* capital combines Ionic volutes with Corinthian foliage. *Superimposed orders*: orders on successive levels, usually in the upward sequence of Tuscan, Doric, Ionic, Corinthian, Composite.

ORIEL: see Bay window.

OVERDOOR: painting or relief above an internal door. Also called a *sopraporta.*

OVERTHROW: decorative fixed arch between two gatepiers or above a wrought-iron gate.

OVOLO: wide convex moulding (3f).

PALIMPSEST: of a brass: where a metal plate has been reused by turning over the engraving on the back; of a wall-painting: where one overlaps and partly obscures an earlier one.

PALLADIAN: following the examples and principles of Andrea Palladio (1508–80).

PALMETTE: classical ornament like a palm shoot (4b).

PANELLING: wooden lining to interior walls, made up of vertical members (*muntins*) and horizontals (*rails*) framing panels: also called *wainscot*. *Raised and fielded*: with the central area of the panel (*field*) raised up (6b).

PANTILE: roof tile of S section.

PARAPET: wall for protection at any sudden drop, e.g. at the wall-head of a castle where it protects the *parapet walk* or wall-walk. Also used to conceal a roof.

PARCLOSE: see Screen.

PARGETTING (*lit.* plastering): exterior plaster decoration, either in relief or incised.

PARLOUR: in a religious house, a room where the religious could talk to visitors; in a medieval house, the semi-private living room below the solar (q.v.).

PARTERRE: level space in a garden laid out with low, formal beds.

PATERA (*lit.* plate): round or oval ornament in shallow relief.

PAVILION: ornamental building for occasional use; or projecting subdivision of a larger building, often at an angle or terminating a wing.

PEBBLEDASHING: see Rendering.

PEDESTAL: a tall block carrying a classical order, statue, vase, etc.

PEDIMENT: a formalized gable derived from that of a classical temple; also used over doors, windows, etc. For variations see 4b.

PENDENTIVE: spandrel between adjacent arches, supporting a drum, dome or vault and consequently formed as part of a hemisphere (5a).

PENTHOUSE: subsidiary structure with a lean-to roof. Also a

separately roofed structure on top of a C20 multi-storey block.

PERIPTERAL: see Peristyle.

PERISTYLE: a colonnade all round the exterior of a classical building, as in a temple which is then said to be *peripteral*.

PERP (PERPENDICULAR): English Gothic architecture c. 1335–50 to c. 1530. The name is derived from the upright tracery panels then used (see Tracery and 2a).

PERRON: external stair to a doorway, usually of double-curved plan.

PEW: loosely, seating for the laity outside the chancel; strictly, an enclosed seat. *Box pew*: with equal high sides and a door.

PIANO NOBILE: principal floor of a classical building above a ground floor or basement and with a lesser storey overhead.

PIAZZA: formal urban open space surrounded by buildings.

PIER: large masonry or brick support, often for an arch. See also Compound pier.

PILASTER: flat representation of a classical column in shallow relief. *Pilaster strip*: see Lesene.

PILE: row of rooms. *Double pile*: two rows thick.

PILLAR: free-standing upright member of any section, not conforming to one of the orders (q.v.).

PILLAR PISCINA: see Piscina.

PILOTIS: C20 French term for pillars or stilts that support a building above an open ground floor.

PISCINA: basin for washing Mass vessels, provided with a drain; set in or against the wall to the S of an altar or free-standing (*pillar piscina*).

PISÉ: see Cob.

PITCHED MASONRY: laid on the diagonal, often alternately with opposing courses (*pitched and counterpitched* or *herringbone*).

PLATBAND: flat horizontal moulding between storeys. Cf. stringcourse.

PLATE RAIL: see Railways.

PLATEWAY: see Railways.

PLINTH: projecting courses at the

foot of a wall or column, generally chamfered or moulded at the top.

PODIUM: a continuous raised platform supporting a building; or a large block of two or three storeys beneath a multi-storey block of smaller area.

POINT BLOCK: see Multi-storey.

POINTING: exposed mortar jointing of masonry or brickwork. Types include *flush*, *recessed* and *tuck* (with a narrow channel filled with finer, whiter mortar).

POPPYHEAD: carved ornament of leaves and flowers as a finial for a bench end or stall.

PORTAL FRAME: C20 frame comprising two uprights rigidly connected to a beam or pair of rafters.

PORTCULLIS: gate constructed to rise and fall in vertical grooves at the entry to a castle.

PORTICO: a porch with the roof and frequently a pediment supported by a row of columns (4a). A portico *in antis* has columns on the same plane as the front of the building. A *prostyle* porch has columns standing free. Porticoes are described by the number of front columns, e.g. tetrastyle (four), hexastyle (six). The space within the temple is the *naos*, that within the portico the *pronaos*. *Blind portico*: the front features of a portico applied to a wall.

PORTICUS (plural: porticūs): subsidiary cell opening from the main body of a pre-Conquest church.

POST: upright support in a structure (7).

POSTERN: small gateway at the back of a building or to the side of a larger entrance door or gate.

POUND LOCK: see Canals.

PRESBYTERY: the part of a church lying E of the choir where the main altar is placed; or a priest's residence.

PRINCIPAL: see Roofs and 7.

PRONAOS: see Portico and 4a.

PROSTYLE: see Portico and 4a.

PULPIT: raised and enclosed platform for the preaching of sermons. *Three-decker*: with reading desk below and clerk's desk below that.

Two-decker: as above, minus the clerk's desk.

PULPITUM: stone screen in a major church dividing choir from nave.

PULVINATED: see Frieze and 3c.

PURLIN: see Roofs and 7.

PUTHOLES or PUTLOG HOLES: in the wall to receive putlogs, the horizontal timbers which support scaffolding boards; sometimes not filled after construction is complete.

PUTTO (plural: putti): small naked boy.

QUARRIES: square (or diamond) panes of glass supported by lead strips (*cames*); square floor-slabs or tiles.

QUATREFOIL: see Foil and 2b.

QUEEN-STRUT: see Roofs and 7.

QUIRK: sharp groove to one side of a convex medieval moulding.

QUOINS: dressed stones at the angles of a building (6d).

RADBURN SYSTEM: vehicle and pedestrian segregation in residential developments, based on that used at Radburn, New Jersey, U.S.A., by Wright and Stein, 1928–30.

RADIATING CHAPELS: projecting radially from an ambulatory or an apse (see Chevet).

RAFTER: see Roofs and 7.

RAGGLE: groove cut in masonry, especially to receive the edge of a roof-covering.

RAGULY: ragged (in heraldry). Also applied to funerary sculpture, e.g. *cross raguly*: with a notched outline.

RAIL: see Panelling and 6b; also 7.

RAILWAYS: *Edge rail*: on which flanged wheels can run. *Plate rail*: L-section rail for plain unflanged wheels. *Plateway*: early railway using plate rails.

RAISED AND FIELDED: see Panelling and 6b.

RAKE: slope or pitch.

RAMPART: defensive outer wall of stone or earth. *Rampart walk*: path along the inner face.

REBATE: rectangular section cut out of a masonry edge to receive a shutter, door, window, etc.

REBUS: a heraldic pun, e.g. a fiery cock for Cockburn.

REEDING: series of convex mouldings, the reverse of fluting (q.v.). Cf. Gadrooning.

RENDERING: the covering of outside walls with a uniform surface or skin for protection from the weather. *Lime-washing*: thin layer of lime plaster. *Pebble-dashing*: where aggregate is thrown at the wet plastered wall for a textured effect. *Roughcast*: plaster mixed with a coarse aggregate such as gravel. *Stucco*: fine lime plaster worked to a smooth surface. *Cement rendering*: a cheaper substitute for stucco, usually with a grainy texture.

REPOUSSÉ: relief designs in metalwork, formed by beating it from the back.

REREDORTER (*lit.* behind the dormitory): latrines in a medieval religious house.

REREDOS: painted and/or sculptured screen behind and above an altar. Cf. Retable.

RESPOND: half-pier or half-column bonded into a wall and carrying one end of an arch. It usually terminates an arcade.

RETABLE: painted or carved panel standing on or at the back of an altar, usually attached to it.

RETROCHOIR: in a major church, the area between the high altar and E chapel.

REVEAL: the plane of a jamb, between the wall and the frame of a door or window.

RIB-VAULT: see Vault and 2C.

RINCEAU: classical ornament of leafy scrolls (4b).

RISER: vertical face of a step (6c).

ROACH: a rough-textured form of Portland stone, with small cavities and fossil shells.

ROCK-FACED: masonry cleft to produce a rugged appearance.

ROCOCO: style current *c.* 1720 and *c.* 1760, characterized by a serpentine line and playful, scrolled decoration.

ROLL MOULDING: medieval moulding of part-circular section (1a).

ROMANESQUE: style current in the CII and CI2. In England often called Norman. *See also* Saxo-Norman.

ROOD: crucifix flanked by the Virgin and St John, usually over the entry into the chancel, on a beam (*rood beam*) or painted on the wall. The *rood screen* below often had a walkway (*rood loft*) along the top, reached by a *rood stair* in the side wall.

ROOFS: Shape. For the main external shapes (hipped, mansard etc.) see 8a. *Helm* and *Saddleback: see* IC. *Lean-to*: single sloping roof built against a vertical wall; lean-to is also applied to the part of the building beneath.
Construction. *See* 7.
Single-framed roof: with no main trusses. The rafters may be fixed to the wall-plate or ridge, or longitudinal timber may be absent altogether.
Double-framed roof: with longitudinal members, such as purlins, and usually divided into bays by principals and principal rafters. Other types are named after their main structural components, e.g. *hammerbeam*, *crown-post* (see Elements below and 7).
Elements. *See* 7.
Ashlar piece: a short vertical timber connecting inner wall-plate or timber pad to a rafter.
Braces: subsidiary timbers set diagonally to strengthen the frame. *Arched braces*: curved pair forming an arch, connecting wall or post below with tie- or collarbeam above. *Passing braces*: long straight braces passing across other members of the truss. *Scissor braces*: pair crossing diagonally between pairs of rafters or principals. *Wind-braces*: short, usually curved braces connecting side purlins with principals; sometimes decorated with cusping.
Collar or *collar-beam*: horizontal transverse timber connecting a pair of rafter or cruck blades (q.v.), set between apex and the wall-plate.
Crown-post: a vertical timber set centrally on a tie-beam and supporting a collar purlin braced to it longitudinally. In an open truss

lateral braces may rise to the collar-beam; in a closed truss they may descend to the tie-beam.

Hammerbeams: horizontal brackets projecting at wall-plate level like an interrupted tie-beam; the inner ends carry *hammerposts*, vertical timbers which support a purlin and are braced to a collar-beam above.

Kingpost: vertical timber set centrally on a tie- or collar-beam, rising to the apex of the roof to support a ridge-piece (cf. Strut).

Plate: longitudinal timber set square to the ground. *Wall-plate*: plate along the top of a wall which receives the ends of the rafters; cf. Purlin.

Principals: pair of inclined lateral timbers of a truss. Usually they support side purlins and mark the main bay divisions.

Purlin: horizontal longitudinal timber. *Collar purlin* or *crown plate*: central timber which carries collar-beams and is supported by crown-posts. *Side purlins*: pairs of timbers placed some way up the slope of the roof, which carry common rafters. *Butt* or *tenoned purlins* are tenoned into either side of the principals. *Through purlins* pass through or past the principal; they include *clasped purlins*, which rest on queenposts or are carried in the angle between principals and collar, and *trenched purlins* trenched into the backs of principals.

Queen-strut: paired vertical, or near-vertical, timbers placed symmetrically on a tie-beam to support side purlins.

Rafters: inclined lateral timbers supporting the roof covering. *Common rafters*: regularly spaced uniform rafters placed along the length of a roof or between principals. *Principal rafters*: rafters which also act as principals.

Ridge, ridge-piece: horizontal longitudinal timber at the apex supporting the ends of the rafters.

Sprocket: short timber placed on the back and at the foot of a rafter to form projecting eaves.

Strut: vertical or oblique timber between two members of a truss, not directly supporting longitudinal timbers.

Tie-beam: main horizontal transverse timber which carries the feet of the principals at wall level.

Truss: rigid framework of timbers at bay intervals, carrying the longitudinal roof timbers which support the common rafters.

Closed truss: with the spaces between the timbers filled, to form an internal partition.

See also Cruck, Wagon roof.

ROPE MOULDING: *see* Cable moulding.

ROSE WINDOW: circular window with tracery radiating from the centre. Cf. Wheel window.

ROTUNDA: building or room circular in plan.

ROUGHCAST: *see* Rendering.

ROVING BRIDGE: *see* Canals.

RUBBED BRICKWORK: *see* Gauged brickwork.

RUBBLE: masonry whose stones are wholly or partly in a rough state. *Coursed*: coursed stones with rough faces. *Random*: uncoursed stones in a random pattern. *Snecked*: with courses broken by smaller stones (snecks).

RUSTICATION: *see* 6d. Exaggerated treatment of masonry to give an effect of strength. The joints are usually recessed by V-section chamfering or square-section channelling (*channelled rustication*). *Banded rustication* has only the horizontal joints emphasized. The faces may be flat, but can be *diamond-faced*, like shallow pyramids, *vermiculated*, with a stylized texture like worm-casts, and *glacial* (frost-work), like icicles or stalactites.

SACRISTY: room in a church for sacred vessels and vestments.

SADDLEBACK ROOF: *see* 1c.

SALTIRE CROSS: with diagonal limbs.

SANCTUARY: area around the main altar of a church. Cf. Presbytery.

SANGHA: residence of Buddhist monks or nuns.

SARCOPHAGUS: coffin of stone or other durable material.

SAXO-NORMAN: transitional Romanesque style combining Anglo-Saxon and Norman features, current *c.* 1060–1100.

SCAGLIOLA: composition imitating marble.

SCALLOPED CAPITAL: *see* 1a.

SCOTIA: a hollow classical moulding, especially between tori (q.v.) on a column base (3b, 3f).

SCREEN: in a medieval church, usually at the entry to the chancel; *see* Rood (screen) and Pulpitum. A *parclose screen* separates a chapel from the rest of the church.

SCREENS or SCREENS PASSAGE: screened-off entrance passage between great hall and service rooms.

SECTION: two-dimensional representation of a building, moulding, etc., revealed by cutting across it.

SEDILIA (singular: sedile): seats for the priests (usually three) on the s side of the chancel.

SET-OFF: *see* Weathering.

SETTS: squared stones, usually of granite, used for paving or flooring.

SGRAFFITO: decoration scratched, often in plaster, to reveal a pattern in another colour beneath. *Graffiti*: scratched drawing or writing.

SHAFT: vertical member of round or polygonal section (1a, 3a). *Shaft-ring*: at the junction of shafts set *en delit* (q.v.) or attached to a pier or wall (1a).

SHEILA-NA-GIG: female fertility figure, usually with legs apart.

SHELL: thin, self-supporting roofing membrane of timber or concrete.

SHOULDERED ARCHITRAVE: *see* 4b.

SHUTTERING: *see* Concrete.

SILL: horizontal member at the bottom of a window or door frame; or at the base of a timber-framed wall into which posts and studs are tenoned (7).

SLAB BLOCK: *see* Multi-storey.

SLATE-HANGING: covering of overlapping slates on a wall. *Tile-hanging* is similar.

SLYPE: covered way or passage leading E from the cloisters between transept and chapter house.

SNECKED: *see* Rubble.

SOFFIT (*lit.* ceiling): underside of an arch (also called *intrados*), lintel, etc. *Soffit roll*: medieval roll moulding on a soffit.

SOLAR: private upper chamber in a medieval house, accessible from the high end of the great hall.

SOPRAPORTA: *see* Overdoor.

SOUNDING-BOARD: *see* Tester.

SPANDRELS: roughly triangular spaces between an arch and its containing rectangle, or between adjacent arches (5c). Also non-structural panels under the windows in a curtain-walled building.

SPERE: a fixed structure screening the lower end of the great hall from the screens passage. *Spere-truss*: roof truss incorporated in the spere.

SPIRE: tall pyramidal or conical feature crowning a tower or turret. *Broach*: starting from a square base, then carried into an octagonal section by means of triangular faces; and *splayed-foot*: variation of the broach form, found principally in the south-east, in which the four cardinal faces are splayed out near their base, to cover the corners, while oblique (or intermediate) faces taper away to a point (1c). *Needle spire*: thin spire rising from the centre of a tower roof, well inside the parapet: when of timber and lead often called a *spike*.

SPIRELET: *see* Flèche.

SPLAY: of an opening when it is wider on one face of a wall than the other.

SPRING or SPRINGING: level at which an arch or vault rises from its supports. *Springers*: the first stones of an arch or vaulting rib above the spring (2c).

SQUINCH: arch or series of arches thrown across an interior angle of a square or rectangular structure to support a circular or polygonal superstructure, especially a dome or spire (5a).

SQUINT: an aperture in a wall or through a pier usually to allow a view of an altar.

STAIRS: *see* 6c. *Dog-leg stair*: parallel flights rising alternately in opposite directions, without an open well. *Flying stair*: cantilevered from the walls of a stairwell, without newels; sometimes called a *Geometric* stair when the inner edge describes a curve. *Newel stair*: ascending round a central supporting newel (q.v.); called a *spiral stair* or *vice* when in a circular shaft, a *winder* when in a rectangular compartment. (Winder also applies to the steps on the turn). *Well stair*: with flights round a square open well framed by newel posts. *See also* Perron.

STALL: fixed seat in the choir or chancel for the clergy or choir (cf. Pew). Usually with arm rests, and often framed together.

STANCHION: upright structural member, of iron, steel or reinforced concrete.

STANDPIPE TOWER: *see* Manometer.

STEAM ENGINES: *Atmospheric*: worked by the vacuum created when low-pressure steam is condensed in the cylinder, as developed by Thomas Newcomen. *Beam engine*: with a large pivoted beam moved in an oscillating fashion by the piston. It may drive a flywheel or be *non-rotative*. *Watt* and *Cornish*: single-cylinder; *compound*: two cylinders; *triple expansion*: three cylinders.

STEEPLE: tower together with a spire, lantern, or belfry.

STIFF-LEAF: type of E.E. foliage decoration. *Stiff-leaf capital see* 1b.

STOP: plain or decorated terminal to mouldings or chamfers, or at the end of hoodmoulds and labels (*label stop*), or string courses (5b, 6a); *see also* headstop.

STOUP: vessel for holy water, usually near a door.

STRAINER: *see* Arch.

STRAPWORK: late C16 and C17 decoration, like interlaced leather straps.

STRETCHER: *see* Bond and 6e.

STRING: *see* 6c. Sloping member holding the ends of the treads and risers of a staircase. *Closed string*: a broad string covering the ends of the treads and risers. *Open string*: cut into the shape of the treads and risers.

STRINGCOURSE: horizontal course or moulding projecting from the surface of a wall (6d).

STUCCO: *see* Rendering.

STUDS: subsidiary vertical timbers of a timber-framed wall or partition (7).

STUPA: Buddhist shrine, circular in plan.

STYLOBATE: top of the solid platform on which a colonnade stands (3a).

SUSPENSION BRIDGE: *see* Bridge.

SWAG: like a festoon (q.v.), but representing cloth.

SYSTEM BUILDING: *see* Industrialized building.

TABERNACLE: canopied structure to contain the reserved sacrament or a relic; or architectural frame for an image or statue.

TABLE TOMB: memorial slab raised on free-standing legs.

TAS-DE-CHARGE: the lower courses of a vault or arch which are laid horizontally (2c).

TERM: pedestal or pilaster tapering downward, usually with the upper part of a human figure growing out of it.

TERRACOTTA: moulded and fired clay ornament or cladding.

TESSELLATED PAVEMENT: mosaic flooring, particularly Roman, made of *tesserae*, i.e. cubes of glass, stone, or brick.

TESTER: flat canopy over a tomb or pulpit, where it is also called a *sounding-board*.

TESTER TOMB: tomb-chest with effigies beneath a tester, either free-standing (tester with four or more columns), or attached to a wall (*half-tester*) with columns on one side only.

TETRASTYLE: *see* Portico.

THERMAL WINDOW: *see* Diocletian window.

THREE-DECKER PULPIT: *see* Pulpit.

TIDAL GATES: *see* Canals.

TIE-BEAM: *see* Roofs and 7.

TIERCERON: *see* Vault and 2c.

TILE-HANGING: *see* Slate-hanging.

TIMBER-FRAMING: *see* 7. Method of construction where the structural frame is built of interlocking timbers. The spaces are filled with non-structural material, e.g. *infill* of wattle and daub, lath and plaster, brickwork (known as *nogging*), etc. and may be covered by plaster, weatherboarding (q.v.), or tiles.

TOMB-CHEST: chest-shaped tomb, usually of stone. Cf. Table tomb, Tester tomb.

TORUS (plural: tori): large convex moulding usually used on a column base (3b, 3f).

TOUCH: soft black marble quarried near Tournai.

TOURELLE: turret corbelled out from the wall.

TOWER BLOCK: *see* Multi-storey.

TRABEATED: depends structurally on the use of the post and lintel. Cf. Arcuated.

TRACERY: openwork pattern of masonry or timber in the upper part of an opening. *Blind tracery* is tracery applied to a solid wall.
Plate tracery, introduced *c.* 1200, is the earliest form, in which shapes are cut through solid masonry (2a).
Bar tracery was introduced into England *c.* 1250. The pattern is formed by intersecting moulded ribwork continued from the mullions. It was especially elaborate during the Decorated period (q.v.). Tracery shapes can include circles, *daggers* (elongated ogee-ended lozenges), *mouchettes* (like daggers but with curved sides) and upright rectangular *panels*. They often have *cusps*, projecting points defining lobes or *foils* (q.v.) within the main shape: *Kentish* or *split-cusps* are forked (2b).
Types of bar tracery (*see* 2b) include *geometric(al)*: *c.* 1250–1310, chiefly circles, often foiled; *Y-tracery*: *c.* 1300, with mullions branching into a Y-shape; *intersecting*: *c.* 1300, formed by interlocking mullions; *reticulated*: early C14, net-like pattern of ogee-ended lozenges; *curvilinear*: C14, with uninterrupted flowing curves; *panel*: Perp, with straight-sided panels, often cusped at the top and bottom.

TRANSEPT: transverse portion of a church.

TRANSITIONAL: generally used for the phase between Romanesque and Early English (*c.* 1175–*c.* 1200).

TRANSOM: horizontal member separating window lights (2b).

TREAD: horizontal part of a step. The *tread end* may be carved on a staircase (6c).

TREFOIL: *see* Foil.

TRIFORIUM: middle storey of a church treated as an arcaded wall passage or blind arcade, its height corresponding to that of the aisle roof.

TRIGLYPHS (*lit.* three-grooved tablets): stylized beam-ends in the Doric frieze, with metopes between (3b).

TRIUMPHAL ARCH: influential type of Imperial Roman monument.

TROPHY: sculptured or painted group of arms or armour.

TRUMEAU: central stone mullion supporting the tympanum of a wide doorway. *Trumeau figure*: carved figure attached to it (cf. Column figure).

TRUMPET CAPITAL: *see* 1b.

TRUSS: braced framework, spanning between supports. See also Roofs and 7.

TUMBLING or TUMBLING-IN: courses of brickwork laid at right-angles to a slope, e.g. of a gable, forming triangles by tapering into horizontal courses (8a).

TUSCAN: *see* Orders and 3e.

TWO-DECKER PULPIT: *see* Pulpit.

TYMPANUM: the surface between a lintel and the arch above it or within a pediment (4a).

UNDERCROFT: usually describes the vaulted room(s), beneath the main room(s) of a medieval house. Cf. Crypt.

VAULT: arched stone roof (sometimes imitated in timber or plaster). For types see 2c.
Tunnel or *barrel vault*: continuous semicircular or pointed arch, often of rubble masonry.

Groin-vault: tunnel · vaults intersecting at right angles. *Groins* are the curved lines of the intersections.

Rib-vault: masonry framework of intersecting arches (ribs) supporting *vault cells*, used in Gothic architecture. *Wall rib* or *wall arch*: between wall and vault cell. *Transverse rib*: spans between two walls to divide a vault into bays. *Quadripartite* rib-vault: each bay has two pairs of diagonal ribs dividing the vault into four triangular cells. *Sexpartite* rib-vault: most often used over paired bays, has an extra pair of ribs springing from between the bays. More elaborate vaults may include *ridge ribs* along the crown of a vault or bisecting the bays; *tiercerons*: extra decorative ribs springing from the corners of a bay; and *liernes*: short decorative ribs in the crown of a vault, not linked to any springing point. A *stellar* or *star* vault has liernes in star formation.

Fan-vault: form of barrel vault used in the Perp period, made up of halved concave masonry cones decorated with blind tracery.

VAULTING SHAFT: shaft leading up to the spring or springing (q.v.) of a vault (2c).

VENETIAN or SERLIAN WINDOW: derived from Serlio (4b). The motif is used for other openings.

VERMICULATION: *see* Rustication and 6d.

VESICA: oval with pointed ends.

VICE: *see* Stair.

VILLA: originally a Roman country house or farm. The term was revived in England in the C18 under the influence of Palladio and used especially for smaller, compact country houses. In the later C19 it was debased to describe any suburban house.

VITRIFIED: bricks or tiles fired to a darkened glassy surface.

VITRUVIAN SCROLL: classical running ornament of curly waves (4b).

VOLUTES: spiral scrolls. They occur on Ionic capitals (3c). *Angle volute*: pair of volutes, turned outwards to meet at the corner of a capital.

VOUSSOIRS: wedge-shaped stones forming an arch (5c).

WAGON ROOF: with the appearance of the inside of a wagon tilt; often ceiled. Also called *cradle roof*.

WAINSCOT: *see* Panelling.

WALL MONUMENT: attached to the wall and often standing on the floor. *Wall tablets* are smaller with the inscription as the major element.

WALL-PLATE: *see* Roofs and 7.

WALL-WALK: *see* Parapet.

WARMING ROOM: room in a religious house where a fire burned for comfort.

WATERHOLDING BASE: early Gothic base with upper and lower mouldings separated by a deep hollow.

WATERLEAF: *see* Enrichments and 3f.

WATERLEAF CAPITAL: Late Romanesque and Transitional type of capital (1b).

WATER WHEELS: described by the way water is fed on to the wheel. *Breastshot*: mid-height, falling and passing beneath. *Overshot*: over the top. *Pitchback*: on the top but falling backwards. *Undershot*: turned by the momentum of the water passing beneath. In a *water turbine*, water is fed under pressure through a vaned wheel within a casing.

WEALDEN HOUSE: type of medieval timber-framed house with a central open hall flanked by bays of two storeys, roofed in line; the end bays are jettied to the front, but the eaves are continuous (8a).

WEATHERBOARDING: wall cladding of overlapping horizontal boards.

WEATHERING or SET-OFF: inclined, projecting surface to keep water away from the wall below.

WEEPERS: figures in niches along the sides of some medieval tombs. Also called mourners.

WHEEL WINDOW: circular, with radiating shafts like spokes. Cf. Rose window.

WROUGHT IRON: *see* Cast iron.

INDEX OF ARTISTS

Entries for partnerships and group practices are listed after entries for a single surname.

INDEX OF STREETS AND BUILDINGS

Principal references are in **bold** type. References in *italic* are to buildings which no longer stand, and to defunct streets or street names. References in roman type within an italic entry are to remaining parts or furnishings of a vanished building. Roman remains are listed under 'Roman'.